Fourth Edition

Managerial
ACCOUNTING

STACEY WHITECOTTON
Arizona State University

ROBERT LIBBY
Cornell University

FRED PHILLIPS
University of Saskatchewan

McGraw Hill Education

MANAGERIAL ACCOUNTING, FOURTH EDITION

Published by McGraw-Hill Education, 2 Penn Plaza, New York, NY 10121. Copyright © 2020 by McGraw-Hill Education. All rights reserved. Printed in the United States of America. Previous editions © 2017, 2013, and 2011. No part of this publication may be reproduced or distributed in any form or by any means, or stored in a database or retrieval system, without the prior written consent of McGraw-Hill Education, including, but not limited to, in any network or other electronic storage or transmission, or broadcast for distance learning.

Some ancillaries, including electronic and print components, may not be available to customers outside the United States.

This book is printed on acid-free paper.

1 2 3 4 5 6 7 8 9 LWI 21 20 19 18

ISBN 978-1-259-96495-4 (bound edition)
MHID 1-259-96495-7 (bound edition)
ISBN 978-1-260-41398-4 (loose-leaf edition)
MHID 1-260-41398-5 (loose-leaf edition)

Portfolio Manager: *Tim Vertovec*
Product Developers: *Michele Janicek/Kristina Dehlin*
Marketing Manager: *Katherine Wheeler*
Content Project Managers: *Pat Frederickson/Brian Nacik*
Buyer: *Sandy Ludovissy*
Design: *Matt Diamond*
Content Licensing Specialist: *Beth Cray*
Cover Images: *(Frappuccino) ©M. Unal Ozmen/Shutterstock, (Watch) ©blackzheep/Shutterstock, (Meeting Room) ©ImageFlow/Shutterstock, (Living Room) ©AlexRoz/Shutterstock, (Car) ©Caracarafoto/Shutterstock*
Compositor: *SPi Global*

All credits appearing on page or at the end of the book are considered to be an extension of the copyright page.

Library of Congress Cataloging-in-Publication Data

Names: Whitecotton, Stacey, author. | Libby, Robert, author. | Phillips, Fred, author.
Title: Managerial accounting / Stacey Whitecotton, Arizona State University, Robert Libby, Cornell University, Fred Phillips, University of Saskatchewan.
Description: Fourth Edition. | Dubuque : McGraw-Hill Education, [2019] | Revised edition of the authors' Managerial accounting, [2017]
Identifiers: LCCN 2018047557 | ISBN 9781259964954 (alk. paper)
Subjects: LCSH: Managerial accounting.
Classification: LCC HF5657.4 .W495 2019 | DDC 658.15/11—dc23
LC record available at https://lccn.loc.gov/2018047557

mheducation.com/highered

Dedication

To Mark, Riley, and Carley! Thanks for your love, patience, and inspiration.
STACEY WHITECOTTON

Laura Libby and Brian Plummer, Oscar and Selma Libby.
ROBERT LIBBY

I dedicate this book to the best teachers I've ever had: my Mom and Dad, Barb, Harrison, and Daniel.
FRED PHILLIPS

Meet the Authors

Stacey Whitecotton

Stacey Whitecotton is an associate professor of accounting in the W. P. Carey School of Business at Arizona State University. She received her PhD and Masters of Accounting from The University of Oklahoma and her Bachelors in Business Administration from Texas Tech University. Stacey teaches managerial accounting and has received numerous awards for outstanding teaching at the undergraduate and graduate level.

Stacey's research interests center around the use of decision aids to improve the decision-making behavior of financial analysts, managers, and auditors. Her research has been published in *The Accounting Review, Organizational Behavior and Human Decision Processes, Behavioral Research in Accounting, Auditing: A Journal of Practice and Theory,* and *The Journal of Behavioral Decision Making.*

Stacey and her husband Mark enjoy traveling and the many outdoor activities Arizona has to offer with their two children, Riley and Carley.

Robert Libby

Robert Libby is the David A. Thomas Professor of Accounting and Accounting Area Coordinator at Cornell University, where he teaches the introductory financial accounting course. He previously taught at the University of Illinois, Pennsylvania State University, the University of Texas at Austin, the University of Chicago, and the University of Michigan. He received his BS from Pennsylvania State University, where he was selected as the 2018 Outstanding Accounting Alumnus, and his MAS and PhD from the University of Illinois; he also completed the CPA exam (Illinois).

Bob was selected as the AAA Outstanding Educator in 2000 and received the AAA Outstanding Service Award in 2006 and the AAA Notable Contributions to the Literature Award in 1985 and 1996. He has received the Core Faculty Teaching Award multiple times at Cornell. Bob is a widely published author

and researcher specializing in behavioral accounting. He has published numerous articles in *The Accounting Review; Journal of Accounting Research; Accounting, Organizations, and Society;* and other accounting journals. He has held a variety of offices, including vice president, in the American Accounting Association, and he is a member of the American Institute of CPAs.

Fred Phillips

Fred Phillips is a professor at the University of Saskatchewan, where he has taught introductory financial accounting for more than 20 years. He also has taught introductory accounting at the University of Texas at Austin and the University of Manitoba. He previously worked as an audit manager at KPMG. Fred holds an undergraduate business degree in accounting, and earned a PhD in accounting from the University of Texas at Austin. He is a non-practicing CPA, CA (in Canada).

Fred's main career interest is accounting education. He has been recognized with more than 30 awards, as chosen by his students and peers. His peer-reviewed publications include education-focused research and instructional cases in *Issues in Accounting Education,* as well as professional judgment studies in the *Journal of Accounting Research* and *Organizational Behavior and Human Decision Processes,* among others. He is a current member of the Teaching, Curriculum, & Learning and Two-Year College sections of the American Accounting Association. In his spare time, Fred is a Tennis Canada official, calling lines at ATP, WTA, and ITF matches.

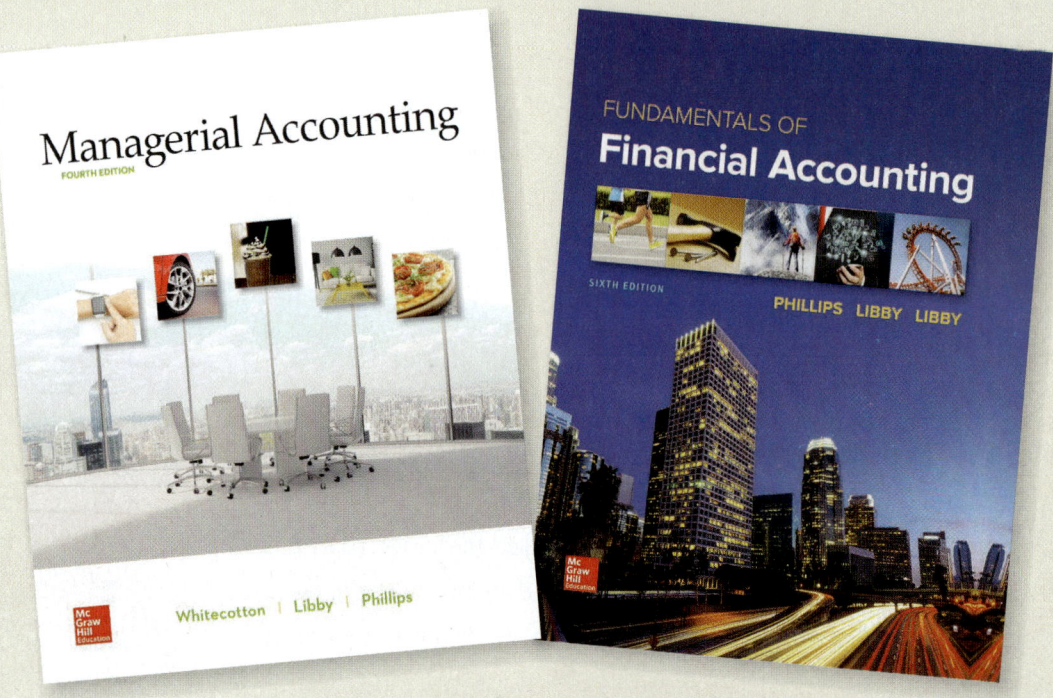

From the award-winning, market-leading Libby/Phillips author team comes a modern, relevant, and engaging textbook for today's managerial accounting student. Whitecotton/Libby/Phillips *Managerial Accounting* brings lively and engaging coverage of managerial accounting topics and decision-making focus to the managerial accounting course. Pair *Managerial Accounting* with Phillips/Libby/Libby *Fundamentals of Financial Accounting*, 6e, to provide a truly comprehensive solution to your students.

McGraw-Hill Education/Jill
Braaten, photographer

Chapters 5 & 6 Focus Company:
Starbucks Coffee

©Jeff Pachoud/AFP/Getty Images

Chapters 7 Focus Company: IKEA

©GaudiLab/Shutterstock

Chapters 10 & 11 Focus Company: Apple

Managerial Accounting
by Whitecotton/Libby/Phillips

This text prepares students for success in business by incorporating four key components that will motivate and guide them through managerial accounting and beyond:

 Managerial accounting builds student interest

Managerial accounting instructors face significant challenges; how to engage students in the managerial accounting course, how to keep them motivated throughout the course, and how to teach them accounting in a way that connects conceptual understanding to the real world. *Managerial Accounting* **engages and motivates students by presenting accounting in the context of recognizable companies such as Starbucks, Toyota, Levi Strauss & Company, and Apple,** and then integrates those companies throughout the chapter discussions.

② **Managerial accounting fosters decision making and analytical skills**

Most students taking managerial accounting will not become accounting majors and accountants; instead, they will use accounting information in their professional lives to make business decisions. *Managerial Accounting* **shows students how managers use accounting information to make business decisions in companies they know from their everyday lives.** This approach helps students develop the analytical and critical thinking skills they will need to succeed in their future careers.

③ **Managerial accounting helps students become better problem solvers**

Students' problem solving skills are put to the test through robust end of chapter content. Additionally, Demonstration Cases and Skills Development Cases provide students with an opportunity to practice their comprehension and understanding of the material.

④ **Managerial accounting uses technology to enhance student learning**

Today's students have diverse learning styles and numerous commitments. They want technology supplements that will help them study more efficiently and effectively. **McGraw-Hill Connect, which includes adaptive and interactive study features such as SmartBook, Concept Overview Videos, Auto-Graded Excel Simulations, and Guided Examples, as well as a repository of additional resources tied directly to** *Managerial Accounting,* will improve students' engagement in and out of class, help them maximize their study time, and make their learning experience more enjoyable.

> " I would describe Whitecotton as the *best introductory managerial textbook that I have used,* because of its writing style, its inclusion of only relevant material, its choice of focus companies that students easily relate to, and the common sense manner in which the material is explained "
>
> —Laura Ilcisin, University of Nebraska at Omaha

> " This is one of the *best textbooks for the introductory managerial accounting course.* The book covers all of the relevant topics for this course and is extremely well organized. Each chapter begins with solid learning objectives linked to the text and uses a focus company, which relates to the students, to illustrate the concepts of the chapter. "
>
> —Ronald O. Reed, University of Northern Colorado

> One of the **greatest strengths** of Whitecotton is the **focus companies.** The utilization of these companies allows students to connect managerial accounting concepts to real-world enterprises.
>
> —Tal Kroll, Ozarks Technical Community College

> This is a freshly written managerial accounting textbook. It addresses a complete range of managerial accounting topics critical to today's business environment. The language is as easy to understand as the discussion is in depth. **I would definitely recommend [this book] to my colleagues** as a good choice for the course.
>
> —Ronald Zhao, Monmouth University

Managerial Accounting has a variety of features that complement the way you teach and the way today's students learn. From study tips and advice to guide students through difficult topics to clear and relevant examples, each chapter offers students the tools they need to succeed.

© Mark Dierker/McGraw-Hill Education

Chapter 4 Focus Company: Toyota

©SumanBhaumik/Shutterstock

Chapters 8 & 9 Focus Company: Levi Strauss & Co.

Chapter Openers—Focus Companies

Each chapter of *Managerial Accounting* opens with an engaging scenario or story using a familiar company. The same focus company is used throughout the entire chapter so that students can see how the concepts and calculations apply to a real-world company they are already familiar with.

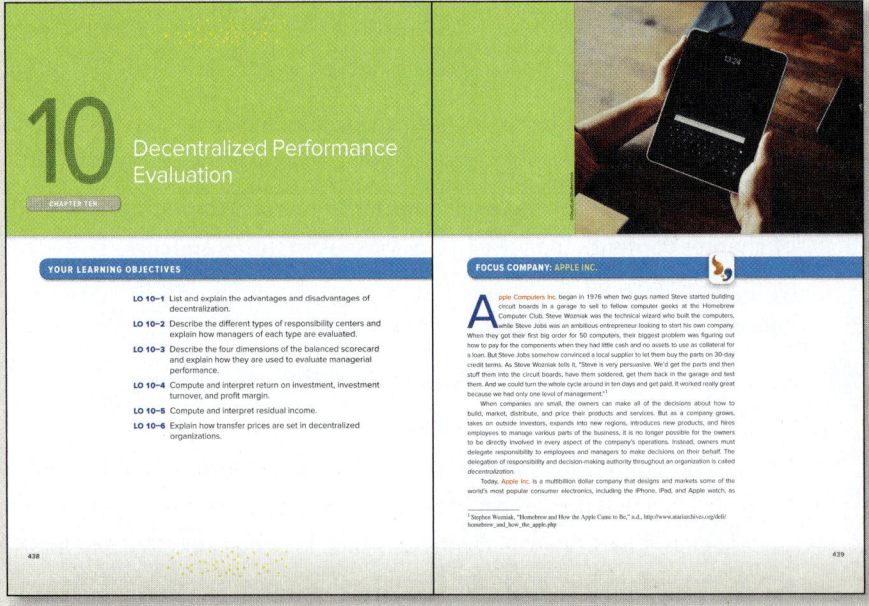

Bring Managerial Accounting Content to Life

How's It Going?
Self-Study Practice

Research shows that students learn best when they actively engage in the learning process. Self-Study Practice quizzes ask students to pause at critical points throughout each chapter to ensure they understand the material presented before moving ahead.

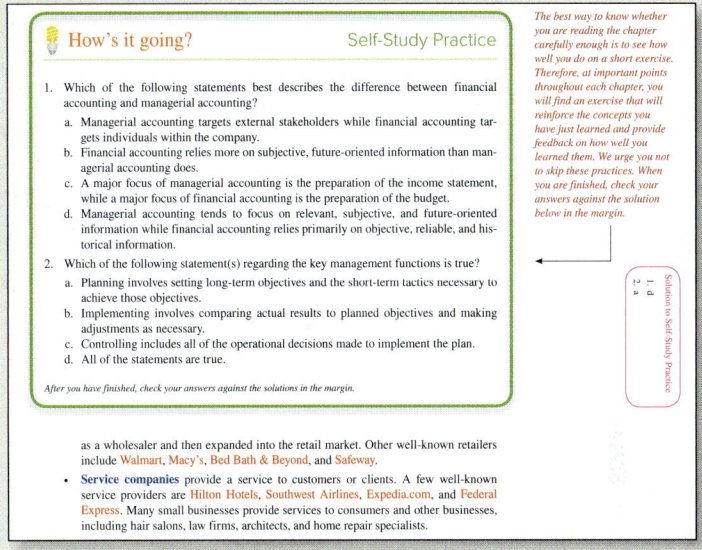

Coach's Tips

Every student needs encouragement and Coach's Tips are just one of the ways *Managerial Accounting* fulfills that need. Coach's Tips appear throughout the text offering tips, advice, and suggestions about how to learn the key concepts.

Spotlight Features

Each chapter includes Spotlight features focusing on important concepts, such as decision making or ethics. These features are designed to further engage students and provide instructors with material for in-class discussion. **New** to this edition are **Big Data and Analytics** features that highlight how big data and analytics can affect how managers make decisions.

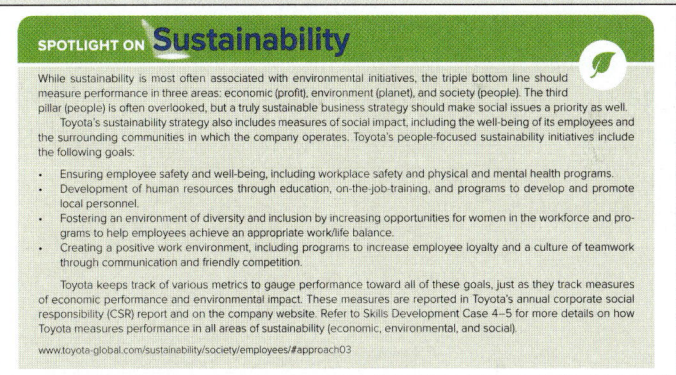

- **Spotlight on Decision Making**—Good decision making is essential in business, whether you are preparing, using, or analyzing accounting information. Spotlight on Decision Making features use real-world examples to illustrate the relevance of accounting to decision making.

- **Spotlight on Ethics**—Making ethical business decisions is more crucial than ever. Spotlight on Ethics features convey the importance of acting responsibly in business.

- **Spotlight on Service**—The majority of today's students will graduate prepared to take a job in the country's ever-growing service sector. Spotlight on Service features describe how key managerial accounting topics are applied in service settings.

- **Spotlight on Sustainability**—Sustainability is a growing area of concern for businesses. Spotlight on Sustainability features describe how and why managers in modern organizations make decisions based on more than economic results, including measures of environmental performance and societal impact.

- **Spotlight on Big Data Analytics**—A topic that is becoming increasingly important to managers and accountants is the use of big data and analytics to help managers make more informed business decisions. At opportune places throughout this text we will highlight how managers in our focus company or other real-world organizations use big data and analytics to make managerial decisions.

Review and Practice Material Build a

Each chapter of *Managerial Accounting* is followed by an extensive variety of end-of-chapter material that examines and integrates concepts presented in the chapter.

> **" The text is very well written and makes many of the difficult concepts accessible to students. . . . The *end of chapter material* is also written at several levels and *allows the instructor* to mix and match learning objectives and difficulty levels *to create challenging but informative assignments.***
>
> —Kristian Mortenson, Oregon State University

Demonstration Case

End-of-chapter review material begins with a demonstration case that provides another self-study opportunity for students. The demonstration case is practice material that mimics what students will see in the homework. The accompanying solution allows students to check their understanding of the material before completing and submitting homework for a grade. It can also serve as a study tool for exams.

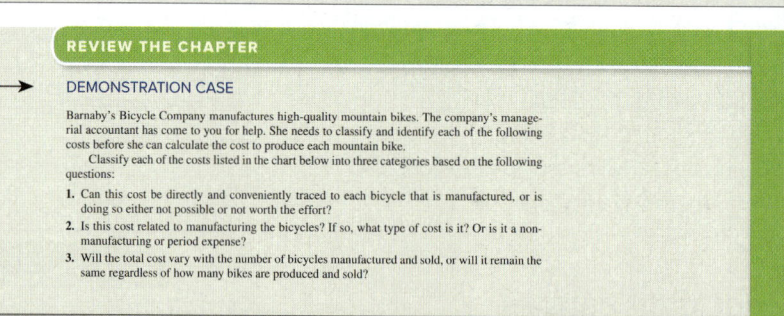

REVIEW THE CHAPTER

DEMONSTRATION CASE

Barnaby's Bicycle Company manufactures high-quality mountain bikes. The company's managerial accountant has come to you for help. She needs to classify and identify each of the following costs before she can calculate the cost to produce each mountain bike.

Classify each of the costs listed in the chart below into three categories based on the following questions:

1. Can this cost be directly and conveniently traced to each bicycle that is manufactured, or is doing so either not possible or not worth the effort?
2. Is this cost related to manufacturing the bicycles? If so, what type of cost is it? Or is it a non-manufacturing or period expense?
3. Will the total cost vary with the number of bicycles manufactured and sold, or will it remain the same regardless of how many bikes are produced and sold?

---

184 CHAPTER 4 Activity-Based Costing and Cost Management

CHAPTER SUMMARY

LO 4–1 **Assign indirect costs to products or services using a single volume-based cost driver.**

- A traditional cost system assigns indirect (overhead) costs to products or services using a volume-based measure, such as the number of direct labor hours, machine hours, or units produced. This system, while simple, assumes that all indirect costs are driven by volume and ignores other factors, such as the complexity of the production process and other non-volume drivers of cost.
- Unlike traditional cost systems that rely strictly on volume-based allocation measures, activity-based costing (ABC) systems include measures that capture something other than the sheer volume of units produced or customers served.

Chapter Summary by Learning Objectives

Each chapter concludes with an end-of-chapter summary that revisits the learning objectives from the beginning of the chapter.

Key Terms

Each chapter includes a list of the key terms introduced in the chapter and page references for those terms. Full definitions for all key terms are found in the back of the text.

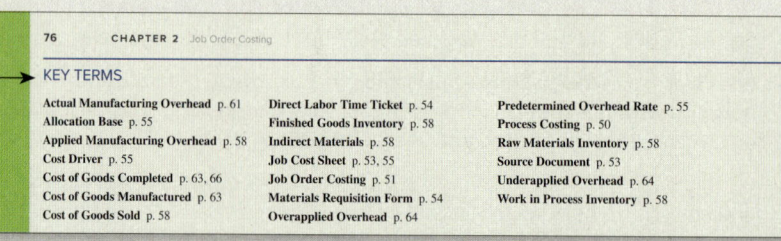

76 CHAPTER 2 Job Order Costing

KEY TERMS

Actual Manufacturing Overhead p. 61	Direct Labor Time Ticket p. 54	Predetermined Overhead Rate p. 55
Allocation Base p. 55	Finished Goods Inventory p. 58	Process Costing p. 50
Applied Manufacturing Overhead p. 58	Indirect Materials p. 58	Raw Materials Inventory p. 58
Cost Driver p. 55	Job Cost Sheet p. 53, 55	Source Document p. 53
Cost of Goods Completed p. 63, 66	Job Order Costing p. 51	Underapplied Overhead p. 64
Cost of Goods Manufactured p. 63	Materials Requisition Form p. 54	Work in Process Inventory p. 58
Cost of Goods Sold p. 58	Overapplied Overhead p. 64	

Strong Foundation for Future Success

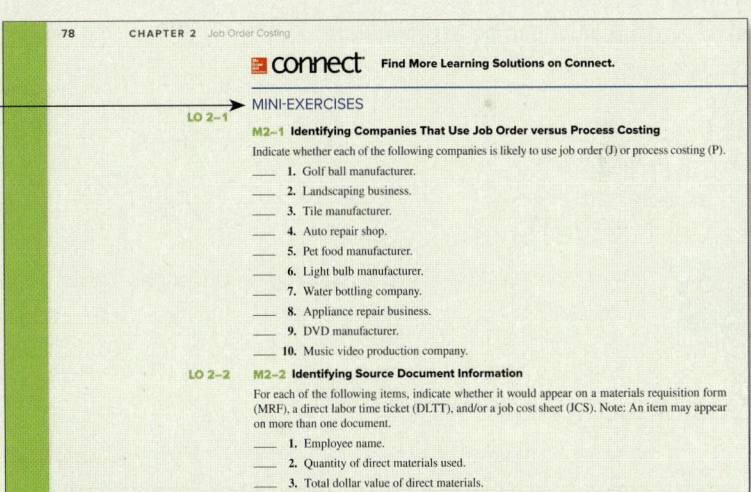

Questions

Each chapter includes 10—20 questions that ask students to explain and discuss terms and concepts from the chapter. These open-ended questions provide a great jumping off point for class discussion.

Multiple-Choice Questions

Each chapter includes 10 multiple-choice questions that let students practice basic concepts. Solutions for all questions are provided in the back of the text.

Mini-Exercises

Mini-exercises in each chapter illustrate and ask students to apply learning objectives from the chapter to a simple scenario.

Exercises

Exercises illustrate and ask students to apply single and multiple learning objectives from the chapter. Animated, narrated Guided Examples that walk through a similar exercise in a step-by-step fashion are available for select exercises when enabled by instructors in Connect.

> *The Whitecotton/Libby/Phillips text is a well-written book . . . The text uses companies that students are familiar with to illustrate managerial accounting concepts. It provides a variety of end-of-chapter questions as well as check-points throughout the chapters for students to use to gauge their level of understanding.*
>
> —Holly Sudano, Florida State University

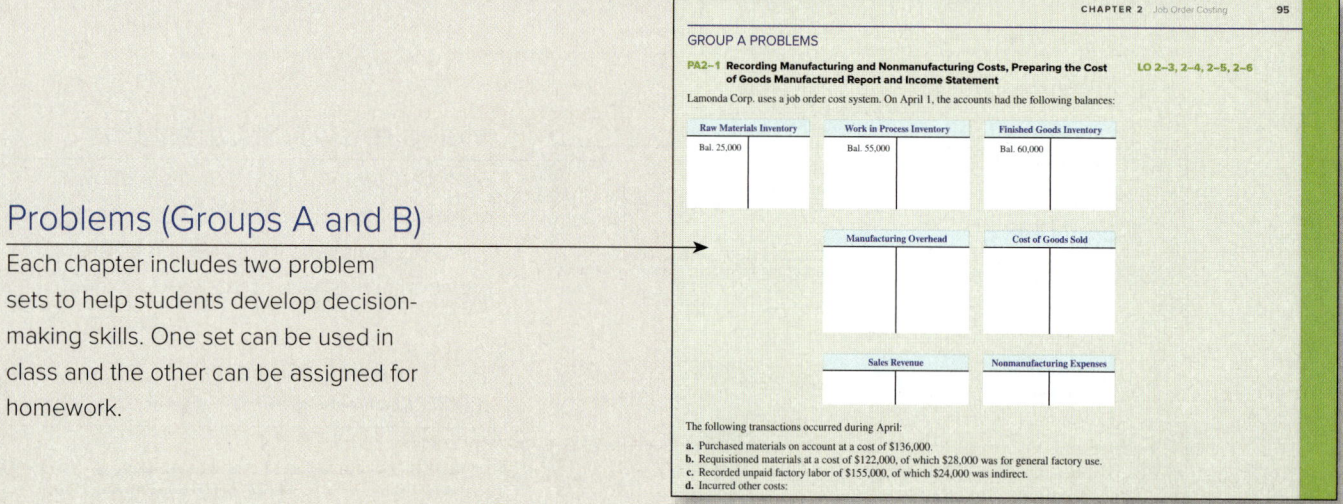

Problems (Groups A and B)

Each chapter includes two problem sets to help students develop decision-making skills. One set can be used in class and the other can be assigned for homework.

Level-Up Questions

 In each chapter, particularly challenging questions, designated by the level-up icon, require students to combine multiple concepts to advance to the next level of accounting knowledge.

Sustainability Questions

 In select chapters, questions, designated by the sustainability leaf icon, require students to apply the chapter concepts in a sustainability-related context so that they will understand how the managerial accounting system can be expanded to focus managers' attention on more than economic results, including the impact of their decisions on the environment and society.

Skills Development Cases

Select chapters offer a case that direct students to a web-based video about a real product or service. Students use the concepts they learned throughout the chapter to answer questions about the video, bringing the concepts to live. These cases help students develop critical thinking and communication skills, and allow for group discussions and projects.

What's New in the Fourth Edition?

In response to feedback and guidance from numerous managerial accounting faculty, the authors have made many important changes to the third edition of *Managerial Accounting,* including the following:

- Integrated new focus companies, including a house-flipping example (HGTV) and Levi Strauss & Co.
- Increased coverage of sustainability accounting and how the importance of three factors (people, profit, and planet) affect the triple bottom line, including adding a new Spotlight on Sustainability feature in select chapters.
- New Spotlight on Big Data and Analytics highlights topics relating to big data, data visualization, and data and business analytics.
- Edited each chapter to improve exposition and to clarify problem areas based on reviewer and student feedback.
- Added new mini-exercises and exercises to each chapter, including matching problems that cover key terms and

definitions. This was based on instructor feedback that they want simple and short exercises to assign to students before they cover the material in class.

- New to Connect in the 4th edition, Concept Overview Videos teach each chapter's core learning objectives and concepts through an engaging multimedia presentation. These learning tools bring the text content to life through video, audio, and checkpoint questions that are graded for accuracy – ensuring students complete and fully comprehend the material. Concept Overview Videos harness the full power of technology to truly engage and appeal to all learning styles. COVs are ideal in all class formats—online, face-to-face or hybrid.

CHAPTER 1: INTRODUCTION TO MANAGERIAL ACCOUNTING

Focus Company: California Pizza Kitchen

- Updated statistics on the role of service and merchandising jobs, including a new exhibit which shows the dramatic trend in employment over the past 40 years. Added a section explaining why students need to know about manufacturing firms even if they are much more likely to go to work in a service or merchandising setting.
- Added a discussion of big data analytics, including definitions and examples of "big data" and the three different types of analytics.
- Added four **new** mini-exercises and three **new** exercises covering basic concepts in managerial accounting.
- Added a **new** skills development case describing how managers at California Pizza Kitchen used analytical techniques to better understand their consumption of energy expenses so that they could reduce spending and enhance their sustainability goals.
- Edited chapter to improve exposition and to clarify problem areas based on reviewer and student feedback.
- Reviewed and updated end-of-chapter material and solutions.

CHAPTER 2: JOB ORDER COSTING

New Focus Company: HGTV

- Updated the chapter focus company to be a house-flipping business, similar to the many TV shows students may be familiar with from HGTV.

- Simplified the exhibits showing the flow of manufacturing costs in job order costing to enhance students learning.
- Added five **new** mini-exercises and three **new** exercises covering basic concepts in job order costing.
- Edited chapter to improve exposition and to clarify problem areas based on reviewer and student feedback.
- Reviewed and updated end-of-chapter material and solutions.

CHAPTER 3: PROCESS COSTING

Focus Company: Fetzer Vinyards

- **New** Spotlight on Sustainability describing how Fetzer recently used **big data analytics** to track one of their key sustainability metrics and achieve an aggressive goal to reduce water consumption by 15 percent from 2015 to 2020.
- Added a numerical example to illustrate how subsequent departments would account for transferred-in costs in process costing.
- Added four **new** mini-exercises and three **new** exercises covering basic concepts in process costing.
- Edited chapter to improve exposition and to clarify problem areas based on reviewer and student feedback.
- Reviewed and updated end-of-chapter material and solutions.

CHAPTER 4: ACTIVITY-BASED COSTING AND COST MANAGEMENT

Focus Company: Toyota Motor Company

- Added six **new** mini-exercises and two new exercises, including four that apply activity based costing concepts to a **service setting.**

- Edited chapter to improve exposition and to clarify problem areas based on reviewer and student feedback.
- Reviewed and updated end-of-chapter material and solutions.
- Updated the skills development case describing Toyota's key sustainability metrics.

CHAPTER 5: COST BEHAVIOR

Focus Company: Starbucks

- Added definition and examples of discretionary and committed fixed costs.
- Simplified the supplement on variable versus absorption costing to enhance student understanding and learning of this challeingng topic.
- Added three **new** mini-exercises and three **new** exercises covering basic concepts in cost behavior.
- Edited chapter to improve exposition and to clarify problem areas based on reviewer and student feedback.
- Reviewed and updated end-of-chapter material and solutions.

CHAPTER 6: COST-VOLUME-PROFIT ANALYSIS

Focus Company: Starbucks

- **New** Spotlight on Big Data Analytics describing how managers at Starbucks use big data analytics to improve the customer experience.
- Added three **new** mini-exercises and two **new** exercises covering basic concepts in cost-volume-profit anlaysis.
- Edited chapter to improve exposition and to clarify problem areas based on reviewer and student feedback.
- Reviewed and updated end-of-chapter material and solutions.

CHAPTER 7: INCREMENTAL ANALYSIS FOR SHORT-TERM DECISION MAKING

Focus Company: IKEA

- **New** Spotlight on Decision Making illustrating how incremental analysis relates to the current debate about whether the U.S. Postal Service is making or losing money by delivering products for Amazon and other high-volume sellers.
- Added two **new** mini-exercises, six **new** exercises, and two **new** problems covering incremental analysis.
- Edited chapter to improve exposition and to clarify problem areas based on reviewer and student feedback.
- Reviewed and updated end-of-chapter material and solutions.

CHAPTER 8: BUDGETARY PLANNING

New Focus Company: Levi Strauss & Co.

- Updated all chapter examples and exhibits illustrating how to prepare the master budget for a hypothetical division of Levi Strauss & Co.
- **New** Spotlight on Big Data Analytics describing how managers at Levi Strauss used technology and analytics to improve the customer experience, manage inventory, and improve operating efficiency.
- Added six **new** mini-exercises and three **new** exercises covering basic concepts in budgeting.
- Edited chapter to improve exposition and to clarify problem areas based on reviewer and student feedback.
- Reviewed and updated end-of-chapter material and solutions.

CHAPTER 9: STANDARD COSTING AND VARIANCES

New Focus Company: Levi Strauss & Co.

- Updated all chapter examples and exhibits illustrating how to compute variances for a hypothetical division of Levi Strauss & Co.
- Added discussion of the differences between actual, normal and standard cost systems.
- Simplified the chapter supplement by covering journal entries for direct materials and direct labor variances only.
- Added two **new** mini-exercises and two **new** exercises covering basic concepts in variance analysis.
- Edited chapter to improve exposition and to clarify problem areas based on reviewer and student feedback.
- Reviewed and updated end-of-chapter material and solutions.

CHAPTER 10: DECENTRALIZED PERFORMANCE EVALUATION

Focus Company: Apple

- Updated Apple data, including operating information, business strategy and financial results.
- Updated transfer pricing example to reflect the estimated contribution margin and incremental profit earned on the transfer and sale of an Apple watch.
- Added one **new** mini-exercise and one **new** exercise covering basic concepts in performance evaluation.
- Edited chapter to improve exposition and to clarify problem areas based on reviewer and student feedback.
- Reviewed and updated end-of-chapter material and solutions.

CHAPTER 11: CAPITAL BUDGETING

Focus Company: Apple

- **New** introductory example describing how Edmunds.com uses the payback method to analyze the economic benefits of investing in a hybrid vehicle.
- Added one **new** mini-exercise and two **new** exercises covering basic concepts in capital budgeting.
- Edited chapter to improve exposition and to clarify problem areas based on reviewer and student feedback.
- Reviewed and updated end-of-chapter material and solutions.

CHAPTER 12: STATEMENT OF CASH FLOWS

Focus Company: Under Armour Inc.

- Updated focus company illustrations.
- Reviewed and updated end-of-chapter material and solutions.

CHAPTER 13: MEASURING AND EVALUATING FINANCIAL PERFORMANCE

Focus Company: Lowe's

- Updated focus company analyses.
- Revised Exhibit 13.5 and related discussion to reflect changes made to all other chapters.
- Updated discussion to reflect FASB's going concern standards update.
- Reviewed and updated end-of-chapter material and solutions.

Students—study more efficiently, retain more and achieve better outcomes. Instructors—focus on what you love—teaching.

SUCCESSFUL SEMESTERS INCLUDE CONNECT

FOR INSTRUCTORS

You're in the driver's seat.

Want to build your own course? No problem. Prefer to use our turnkey, prebuilt course? Easy. Want to make changes throughout the semester? Sure. And you'll save time with Connect's auto-grading too.

65%
Less Time Grading

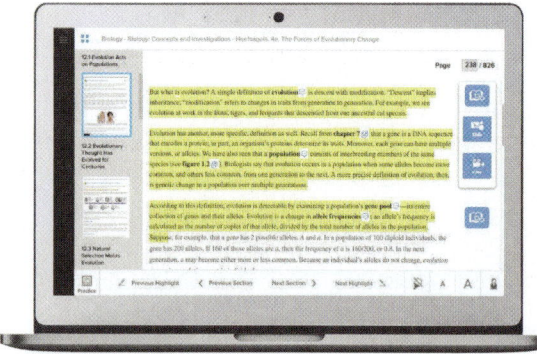

They'll thank you for it.

Adaptive study resources like SmartBook® help your students be better prepared in less time. You can transform your class time from dull definitions to dynamic debates. Hear from your peers about the benefits of Connect at **www.mheducation.com/highered/connect**.

Make it simple, make it affordable.

Connect makes it easy with seamless integration with any of the major Learning Management Systems—Blackboard®, Canvas, and D2L, among others—to let you organize your course in one convenient location. Give your students access to digital materials at a discount with our inclusive access program. Ask your McGraw-Hill representative for more information.

©Hill Street Studios/Tobin Rogers/Blend Images LLC

Solutions for your challenges.

A product isn't a solution. Real solutions are affordable, reliable, and come with training and ongoing support when you need it and how you want it. Our Customer Experience Group can also help you troubleshoot tech problems—although Connect's 99% uptime means you might not need to call them. See for yourself at **status.mheducation.com**

©Shutterstock/wavebreakmedia

FOR STUDENTS

Effective, efficient studying.

Connect helps you be more productive with your study time and get better grades using tools like SmartBook, which highlights key concepts and creates a personalized study plan. Connect sets you up for success, so you walk into class with confidence and walk out with better grades.

"I really liked this app—it made it easy to study when you don't have your text-book in front of you."

—Jordan Cunningham,
Eastern Washington University

Study anytime, anywhere.

Download the free ReadAnywhere app and access your online eBook when it's convenient, even if you're offline. And since the app automatically syncs with your eBook in Connect, all of your notes are available every time you open it. Find out more at **www.mheducation.com/readanywhere**

No surprises.

The Connect Calendar and Reports tools keep you on track with the work you need to get done and your assignment scores. Life gets busy; Connect tools help you keep learning through it all.

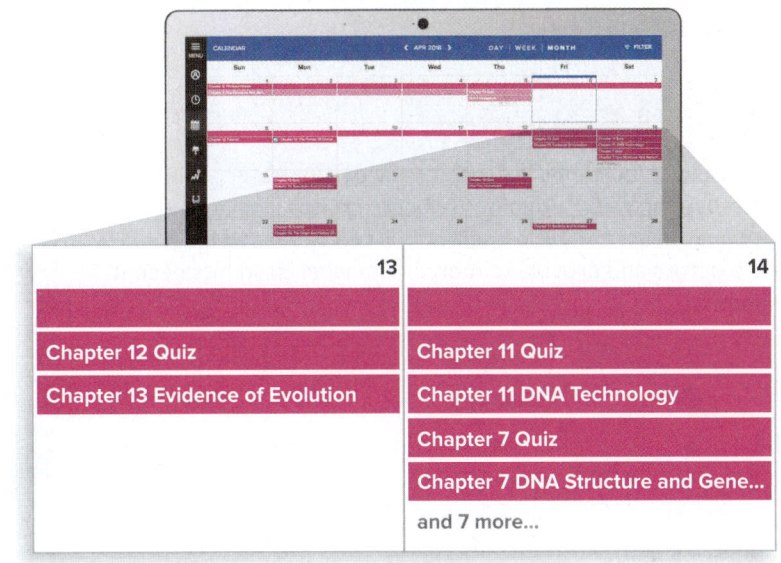

	13		14
Chapter 12 Quiz		Chapter 11 Quiz	
Chapter 13 Evidence of Evolution		Chapter 11 DNA Technology	
		Chapter 7 Quiz	
		Chapter 7 DNA Structure and Gene...	
		and 7 more...	

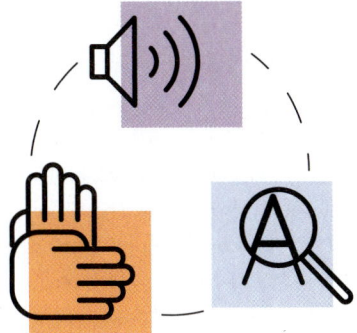

Learning for everyone.

McGraw-Hill works directly with Accessibility Services Departments and faculty to meet the learning needs of all students. Please contact your Accessibility Services office and ask them to email accessibility@mheducation.com, or visit **www.mheducation.com/accessibility** for more information.

Connect Accounting

Connect helps students learn more efficiently by providing feedback and practice material when they need it, where they need it. Connect grades homework automatically and gives immediate feedback on any questions students may have missed.

End-of-chapter questions in Connect include:

- Mini-Exercises
- Exercises
- Group A Problems

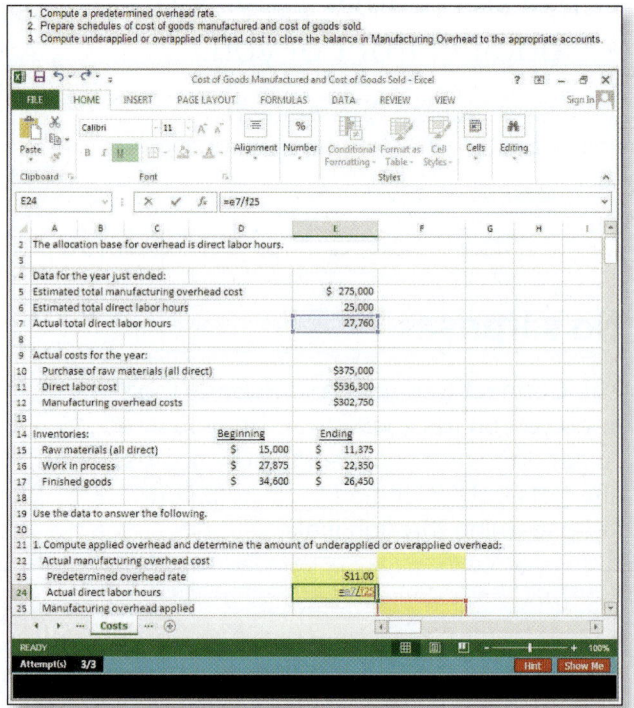

Concept Overview Videos

New for this edition, the Concept Overview Videos cover each learning objective through narrated, animated presentations. Formerly Interactive Presentation, each Concept Overview Video has been enhanced for improved accessibility, and includes both the visual animations and transcript to accommodate all types of learners. The Concept Overview Videos also pause frequently to check for comprehension with assignable, auto-graded Knowledge Check questions.

Excel Simulations

Simulated Excel questions, assignable within Connect, allow students to practice their Excel skills—such as basic formulas and formatting—within the content of financial accounting. These questions feature animated, narrated Help and Show Me tutorials (when enabled), as well as automatic feedback and grading for both students and professors.

Guided Examples

The Guided Examples in *Connect* provide a narrated, animated, step-by-step walkthrough of select exercises similar to those assigned. These short presentations can be turned on or off by instructors and provide reinforcement when students need it most.

©Microsoft

☑ **MCGRAW-HILL CUSTOMER EXPERIENCE GROUP CONTACT INFORMATION**

At McGraw-Hill Education, we understand that getting the most from new technology can be challenging. That's why our services don't stop after you purchase our products. You can contact our Product Specialists 24 hours a day to get product training online. Or you can search the knowledge bank of Frequently Asked Questions on our support website. For Customer Support, call **800-331-5094** or visit **www.mhhe.com/support**. One of our Technical Support Analysts will be able to assist you in a timely fashion.

Acknowledgments

Many dedicated instructors have devoted their time and effort to help us develop this text. We would like to acknowledge and thank all of our colleagues who helped guide our decisions. This text would not be what it is without the help of our contributors:

Editorial Review Panel

Dawn Addington, *Central New Mexico Community College*

Gilda Agacer, *Monmouth University*

Markus Ahrens, *Saint Louis Community College*

Thomas Arcuri, *Florida State College*

Kwadwo Asare, *Bryant University*

Jane Austin, *Oklahoma City University*

Vidya Awasthi, *Seattle University*

Jon Backman, *Spartanburg Community College*

Bala Balachandran, *New York University*

Scott Bartley, *Trident Technical College*

William Belski, *Samford University*

Amy Bentley, *Tallahassee Community College*

Phillip Blanchard, *University of Arizona*

Patrick Borja, *Citrus College*

Benoit Boyer, *Sacred Heart University*

Jeff Brennan, *Austin Community College*

Ann Brooks, *University of New Mexico*

Gay Lynn Brown, *Northwest Florida State College*

Amy Browning, *Ivy Tech Community College*

Myra Bruegger, *Southeastern Community College*

Esther Bunn, *Stephen F. Austin State University*

Laurie Burney, *Mississippi State University*

Kevin Cabe, *Indiana Wesleyan University*

Charlie Caliendo, *University of Minnesota-Minneapolis*

Dana Carpenter, *Madison Area Technical College*

Karin Caruso, *Southern New Hampshire University*

Nancy Cassidy, *University of Nebraska-Lincoln*

Chiaho Chang, *Montclair State University*

Chak-Tong Chau, *University of Houston-Downtown*

Darlene Coarts, *University of Northern Iowa*

Debora Constable, *Georgia Perimeter College—Dunwoody*

Susan Convery, *Michigan State University*

Robert Conway, *University of Wisconsin at Platteville*

Debra Cosgrove, *University of Nebraska*

Nancy Coulmas, *Bloomsburg University of Pennsylvania*

Cheryl Crespi, *Central Connecticut State University*

Kathy Crusto-Way, *Tarrant County College*

David Deeds, *University of Northern Iowa*

Elizabeth Devos, *University of Texas at El Paso*

Edward Douthett, *George Mason University*

Jan Duffy, *Iowa State University*

Dennis Elam, *Texas A&M—San Antonio*

Robert Ellison, *Texas State University-San Marcos*

Gene Elrod, *University of North Texas*

Emmanuel Emenyonu, *Southern Connecticut State University*

Diane Eure, *Texas State University—San Marcos*

Amanda Farmer, *University of Georgia*

Xiujun (Sue June) Farrier, *Tarrant County College*

Christos Fatouros, *Curry College*

Patti Fedje, *Minot State University*

Jerry Ferry, *University of Northern Alabama*

John Gabelman, *Columbus State Community College*

Mohamed Gaber, *State University of New York at Plattsburgh*

MaryElla Gainor, *Bryant University*

Deborah Garvin, *University of Florida at Gainesville*

Karen Geiger, *Arizona State University*

June F. Panter Geppert, *Austin Community College*

Thomas Grant, *Kutztown University of Pennsylvania*

Olen Greer, *Missouri State University*

Andrew Griffith, *Iona College*

Cindy Gruber, *Marquette University*

Meng Guo, *University of Texas-San Antonio*

Theresa Hammond, *San Francisco State University*

Heidi Hansel, *Kirkwood Community College*

Judith Harris, *Nova Southeastern University*

Candy Heino, *Anoka-Ramsey Community College*

David Henderson, *College of Charleston*

Donna Hetzel, *Western Michigan University*

Margaret Hicks, *Howard University*

Rob Hochschild, *Ivy Tech Community College*

Mahmud Hossain, *University of Memphis*

Maggie Houston, *Wright State University*

Peggy Hughes, *Montclair State University*

Susan Hughes, *University of Vermont*

Audrey Hunter, *Broward College*

Kathy Hurley, *Boise State University*

Laura Ilcisin, *University of Nebraska-Omaha*

John Illig, *State College of Florida*

Pamela Jackson, *Augusta State University*

Robyn Jarnagin, *Montana State University-Bozeman*

Iris Jenkel, *Saint Norbert College*

Carolyn Johnson, *Northern Oklahoma College*

Shondra Johnson, *Bradley University*

Jeffery Jones, *College of Southern Nevada*

Sandra Jordan, *Florida State College*

Celina Jozsi, *University of South Florida*

Jai Kang, *San Francisco State University*

Ed Kaplan, *University of West Florida*

Cindi Khanlarian, *University of North Carolina at Greensboro*

Stacy Kline, *Drexel University*

Mehmet Kocakulah, *University of Southern Indiana*

William Koprowski, *College of Charleston*

Tal Kroll, *Ozarks Technical Community College*

Cynthia Krom, *Marist College*

Wikil Kwak, *University of Nebraska-Omaha*

Scott Lane, *Quinnipiac University*

Luke Lammer, *Loras College*

David E. Laurel, *South Texas College*

Ron Lazer, *University of Houston*

Chuo-Hsuan (Jason) Lee, *State University of New York at Plattsburgh*

Christy LeFevers, *Catawba Valley Community College*

Catherine Lubaski, *Southern Illinois University*

Joan Luft, *Michigan State University*

Catherine Lumbattis, *Southern Illinois University at Carbondale*

Jeanette Maier-Lytle, *University of Southern Indiana*

Diane Marker, *University of Toledo*

Linda Marquis, *Northern Kentucky University*

Scott Martens, *University of Minnesota*

Angie Martin, *Tarrant County College*

Josephine Mathias, *Mercer County Community College*

Suzanne McCaffrey, *University of Mississippi*

Florence McGovern, *Bergen Community College*

Brian McGuire, *University of Southern Indiana*

Shaen McMutrie, *Northern Oklahoma College*

Pam Meyer, *University of Louisiana at Lafayette*

Earl Mitchell, *Santa Ana College*

Cathileen Montesarchio, *Broward Community College*

Arabian Morgan, *Orange Coast College*

Kristian Mortenson, *Oregon State University*

Matt Muller, *Adirondack Community College*

Gerald Myers, *Pacific Lutheran University*

Penelope Nall, *Limestone College*

Michael Newman, *University of Houston*

Chris O'Byrne, *Cuyamaca College*

Emeka Ofobike, *University of Akron*

Angela Pannell, *Mississippi State University*

Susanna Pendergast, *Western Illinois University*

Jo Ann Pinto, *Montclair State University*

Ronald Premuroso, *University of Montana*

Jessica Rakow, *Louisiana State University*

Vasant Raval, *Creighton University*

Ronald Reed, *University Northern Colorado*

Gayle Richardson, *Bakersfield College*

Patti Roshto, *University of Louisiana at Monroe*

Luther Ross, *Central Piedmont Community College*

Martin Rudnick, *William Paterson University*

Angela Sandberg, *Jacksonville State University*

Michael Schusler, *Portland State University*

Randall Serrett, *University of Houston*

Christine Solomon, *Trident Technical College*

Charlene Spiceland, *University of Memphis*

Patrick Stegman, *College of Lake County*

Dean Steria, *State University of New York at Pittsburgh*

Jane Stoneback, *Central Connecticut State University*

Arlene Strawn, *Tallahassee Community College*

Scott Stroher, *Glendale Community College*

Karen Sturm, *Loras College*

Holly Sudano, *Florida State University*

James Sugden, *Orange Coast College*

Barbara Sumi, *Northwood University*

Ellen Sweatt, *Georgia Perimeter College*

Pavani Tallapally, *Slippery Rock University of Pennsylvania*

Diane Tanner, *University of North Florida*

Michael Tydlaska, *Mountain View College*

Linda Vaello, *University of Texas—San Antonio*

Joan Van Hise, *Fairfield University*

Jeff Varblow, *College of Lake County*

Kiran Verma, *University Massachusetts—Boston*

Sharon Walters, *Morehead State University*

Mary Ann Welden, *Wayne State University*

Anne Wessely, *Saint Louis Community College*

Jane Wiese, *Valencia Community College*

Blair A. William, *Slippery Rock University*

George Williams, *Bergen Community College*

Neil Wilner, *University of North Texas*

Joseph Winter, *Niagara University*

Jeffrey Wong, *University of Nevada at Reno*

Pete Woodlock, *Youngstown State University*

Jan Woods, *Appalachian State University*

Janet Woods, *Macon State College*

John Woodward, *Polk State College*

Christian Wurst, *Temple University*

Myung Yoon, *Northeastern Illinois University*

Jeffrey Yost, *College of Charleston*

Ronald Zhao, *Monmouth University*

We are grateful to the following individuals who helped develop, critique, and shape the extensive ancillary package: Ann Brooks, *University of New Mexico;* Tony Cardinalli; Donna Hetzel, *Western Michigan University;* Patti Lopez, *Valencia College;* Barbara Muller, *Arizona State University;* Helen Roybark, *Radford University;* and Beth Woods.

Last, we thank the extraordinary efforts of a talented group of individuals at McGraw-Hill Education who made all of this come together. We would especially like to thank our managing director, Tim Vertovec; Pat Plumb, our portfolio manager; Kevin Moran, our director of digital content; Xin Lin, our digital product analyst; Katherine Wheeler, our marketing manager; Pat Frederickson and Brian Nacik, our lead content project managers; Matt Diamond, our senior designer; and Lori Hancock, our content licensing specialist.

Stacey Whitecotton
Robert Libby
Fred Phillips

BRIEF CONTENTS

CONTENTS

Fourth Edition

Managerial
ACCOUNTING

Introduction to Managerial Accounting

CHAPTER ONE

At the beginning of each chapter, you'll see a list of learning objectives that identify the key topics you need to master. You can also use the list as an outline for taking notes as you read through the chapter.

YOUR LEARNING OBJECTIVES

LO 1–1 Describe the key differences between financial accounting and managerial accounting.

LO 1–2 Describe how managerial accounting is used in different types of organizations to support the key functions of management.

LO 1–3 Describe the importance of ethics, sustainability, and decision analytics in managerial accounting.

LO 1–4 Define and give examples of different types of costs:

Out-of-pocket or opportunity costs

Direct or indirect costs

Variable or fixed costs

Manufacturing or nonmanufacturing costs

Product or period costs

Relevant or irrelevant costs

©Frazer Harrison/Getty Images for Los Angeles Magazine

FOCUS COMPANY: CALIFORNIA PIZZA KITCHEN

As you start what is probably your second accounting course, you may be wondering why you need to take yet another accounting class. Wasn't one course enough? Which of the following best describes your motivation for learning about managerial accounting?

Top 10 Reasons to Take a Managerial Accounting Course

10. Accounting is truly interesting and exciting.
9. I always wanted to be an accountant when I grow up.
8. My advisor said I had to take it.
7. Accountants get good-paying jobs, even in the worst economy.
6. The accountant is always the hero in action movies.
5. I want to get rich and stay that way.
4. The rich guy always gets the girl in romance movies.
3. I want to start my own business and need to create a business plan.
2. Accounting will fulfill my foreign language requirement. (It's Greek to me.)
1. I'm enrolled in an accounting course???

Whatever your reason for taking this course, it will come in handy at some point in your future. This is true regardless of your intended career path, whether it is to start your own business, work for a large corporation, go into politics, work in health care, become a fashion designer, teach high school, work on a farm, or start a charitable foundation. Accounting is the language of business, and understanding it will help you make better business and personal decisions.

Throughout this book, you will see how managerial accounting is used by managers in real-world companies. Most of these companies sell a product or service that you encounter everyday, like a cup of Starbucks coffee, your iPhone, or the pizza you may have for lunch. Let's begin with a company that put a new spin on pizza with innovative flavors like BBQ chicken and Thai peanut sauce.

California Pizza Kitchen (CPK) was started in 1985 when two disillusioned attorneys, Larry Flax and Rick Rosenfield, decided to ditch their legal pads and open a restaurant in Beverly Hills, California. Their hearth-baked pizzas were an instant hit with an LA crowd seeking delicious and innovative food served in a casual but upscale setting. Since then, CPK has broadened its menu selection and expanded to more than 200 cities and 15 countries around the world. Today, you can enjoy one of CPK's delicious menu items in over 250 full-service restaurants; at CPK/ASAP "quick serve" stations in airports, universities, and sports arenas; or by purchasing a CPK pizza from the freezer of your local supermarket to bake at home.

As you read this chapter, try putting yourself in the shoes of one of the following managers:

- General manager responsible for the day-to-day operations of a CPK restaurant, including staffing, customer service, cost management, and compliance with Food and Drug Administration (FDA) regulations.
- Kitchen manager responsible for preparing delicious food while controlling the cost of ingredients and training the kitchen staff.
- Purchasing manager responsible for buying the freshest ingredients at the lowest possible cost, from both local and national suppliers.
- Regional manager responsible for the overall success of 25 CPK restaurants throughout the Pacific Northwest. Your annual performance evaluation is based on sales growth, profitability, and customer satisfaction.
- Senior executive responsible for expanding the CPK brand into new domestic and global markets.

Think about the types of decisions you would have to make in your chosen role and, most of all, the information you would need to make those decisions. Chances are that much of that information would come from the company's managerial accounting system.

ORGANIZATION OF THE CHAPTER

Role of managerial accounting in organizations

- Comparison of financial and managerial accounting
- Functions of management
- Ethics, sustainability, and decision analytics

Role of cost in managerial accounting

- Cost terminology
- Direct versus indirect costs
- Variable versus fixed costs
- Manufacturing versus nonmanufacturing costs
- Product versus period costs
- Relevant versus irrelevant costs

At the start of each chapter, you'll find an organizational graphic that provides a visual framework to show how the chapter concepts fit together.

Role of Managerial Accounting in Organizations

COMPARISON OF FINANCIAL AND MANAGERIAL ACCOUNTING

The primary goal of any accounting system is to capture, summarize, and report useful information to users so that they can make informed decisions. The key difference between financial accounting and managerial accounting is the intended user of the information. **Financial accounting** information is aimed at **external users**, or those outside the organization such as investors, creditors, and regulators. **Managerial accounting** information is aimed at **internal users**, or those working inside the organization, such as business owners, managers, and employees.

Because the intended users of the information are different, there are several other differences between financial and managerial accounting. Accountants prepare external financial statements according to generally accepted accounting principles (GAAP), which provide external users certain advantages in terms of their comparability and objectivity. However, internal managers often need more detailed information than those financial reports can capture. Managers need information that is timely and relevant to the specific decision at hand. Rather than knowing what happened last year or last quarter, managers need to know what is happening today and be able to predict what will happen tomorrow. See Exhibit 1–1 for a summary of the key differences between financial accounting and managerial accounting.

Throughout this text, we will provide you with tips to highlight explanations of selected topics. Please read them carefully.

> **Learning Objective 1–1**
> Describe the key differences between financial accounting and managerial accounting.

>  **COACH'S TIP**
> Financial accounting is sometimes referred to as **external** reporting while managerial accounting is referred to as **internal** reporting. The difference is whether the intended users are inside or outside the company.

EXHIBIT 1–1   Differences between Financial and Managerial Accounting

	Financial Accounting	**Managerial Accounting**
User perspective	Used by external parties, such as investors, creditors, and regulators	Used by internal parties, such as managers and employees
Types of reports	Classified financial statements prepared according to GAAP	Various internal reports, such as budgets, performance evaluations, and cost reports
Nature of information	Objective, reliable, historical	Subjective, relevant, future oriented
Frequency of reporting	Prepared periodically (monthly, quarterly, annually)	Prepared as needed, perhaps day-to-day or even in real time
Level of detail	Information reported for the company as a whole	Information reported at the decision-making level (by product, region, customer, or other business segment)

Left: ©Andersen Ross/Brand X/Corbis; Right: ©Robert Nicholas/Getty Images

To illustrate these differences, let's return to California Pizza Kitchen (CPK). Until 2011, CPK was a publicly traded company whose stock was traded on the NASDAQ stock exchange. The Securities and Exchange Commission (SEC) requires all publicly traded companies to file quarterly and annual reports that include an income statement, balance sheet, statement of cash flows, and disclosures about the accounting methods used to prepare the financial statements. These reports are publicly available to anyone with an interest in the company, including government regulators, financial analysts, and investors who are considering buying or selling stock in the company. The year-end financial statements of publicly traded companies must be audited by an independent accounting firm, such as Ernst and Young or KPMG, to determine whether the reports were prepared according to GAAP.

In 2011, CPK was acquired for $470 million by Golden Gate Capital, a private-equity firm that owns other well-known restaurant chains, such as On the Border. Because it is now privately owned, CPK is no longer required to report its financial results to the SEC and the public at large. The last time that CPK released financial results to the public was in April of 2011, shortly before being bought by Golden Gate Capital. Although the external financial statements provide a glimpse into the company's financial performance, they are probably not that relevant to most of CPK's managers and employees who are more concerned about the day-to-day operations of the business than the corporate financial statements. The results reported in the external financial statements are generally most relevant to the C-suite executives (CEO, CFO, etc.) who are directly responsible for the financial performance of the company and who must answer to the firm's shareholders and board of directors.

The managerial accounting system, in contrast, provides the more detailed information that managers "behind the scenes" need to do their jobs. This internally oriented information is not publicly available and is often proprietary in nature. Even so, we can gain some insight into the internal accounting system by considering statements made by managers in the press releases that often accompany the external financial statements. For example, in their final press release before the buyout, co-CEOs Rick Rosenfield and Larry Flax stated that they would improve future shareholder value by focusing on "menu-optimization," "cost management at both the restaurant and corporate level," "shifting the sales mix to higher margin items," "expanding international locations," and introducing new menu offerings that are "in line with health and wellness trends."[1] If you think about the vast array of information that managers would need to achieve these broad objectives, you can get a sense for the types of information the managerial accounting system must provide.

To better understand how managerial accounting is used, we must consider the various functions that managers perform and what types of information they need to do their jobs.

FUNCTIONS OF MANAGEMENT

Learning Objective 1–2
Describe how managerial accounting is used in different types of organizations to support the key functions of management.

Regardless of the type and size of the organization they manage, all managers perform the same basic functions: Planning, Implementing, and Controlling. These functions are part of a continuous or ongoing cycle, called the Plan-Implement-Control cycle, as illustrated in Exhibit 1–2. Throughout this cycle, managers must make a variety of decisions, and the managerial accounting system must provide information to help them make those decisions.

- **Planning** is the future-oriented part of the management cycle. The first step in planning is to establish goals or objectives, along with the tactics that will be used to achieve those goals. Managers have to make a variety of "who, what, when, where, and how" decisions as they plan. For example: Who is my target customer? What product or service do they need and how much will they pay for it? Where and when will I provide the product and service? What resources will I need? Once managers know the answers to these questions, the next step is to create a **budget** that lays out the plan in monetary or financial terms. The budget helps managers organize their plan and ensure that they have the necessary resources to carry it out.

- **Implementing** means putting the plan into action. During the implementation phase, managers must lead, direct, and motivate others to achieve the objectives set in the

---

[1]Press Release May 5, 2011: "California Pizza Kitchen Announces Financial Results for the First Quarter of 2011."

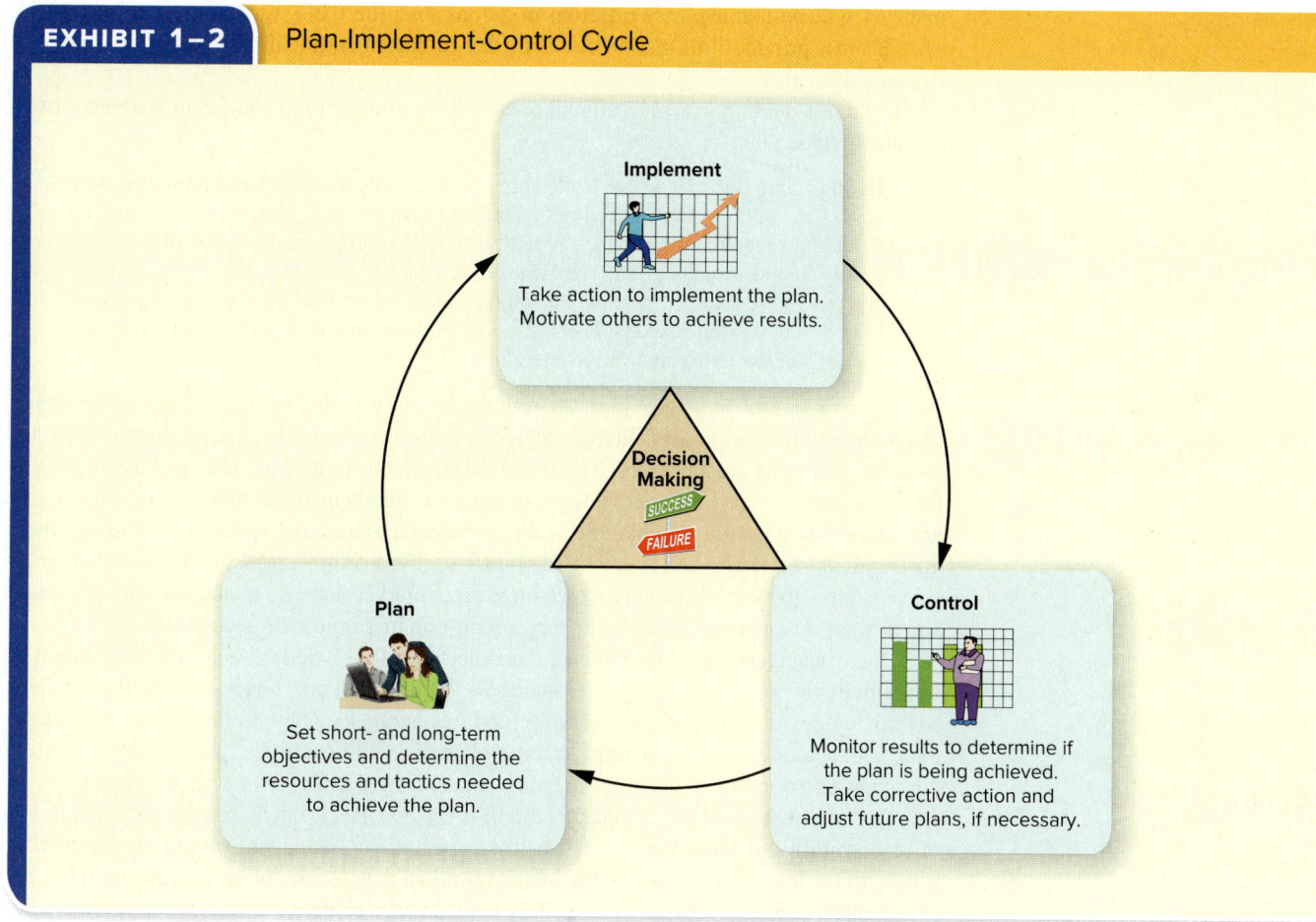

EXHIBIT 1–2 Plan-Implement-Control Cycle

Implement
Take action to implement the plan.
Motivate others to achieve results.

Decision Making
SUCCESS
FAILURE

Plan
Set short- and long-term objectives and determine the resources and tactics needed to achieve the plan.

Control
Monitor results to determine if the plan is being achieved. Take corrective action and adjust future plans, if necessary.

planning stage. The decisions made during the implementation phase are sometimes called operational decisions. For example: Who should I purchase supplies from? When do I need them? How many employees should I hire? How much should I pay them? How do I train them? Again, the managerial accounting system should provide useful information to help managers answer these and other questions.

- **Controlling** is the final step in the management process. During the control phase, managers keep track of how they are doing and whether any actions must be taken to adjust the plan. The managerial accounting system plays a key role in helping managers measure and monitor the company's performance to see whether the planned objectives are being met. If not, managers may need to take corrective action to get back on track.

An easy way to think about the Plan-Implement-Control cycle is in terms of an air traffic control system. Before the flight, the pilot must file a flight **plan** that details when and where the plane will be flying. **Implementing** includes all of the actions the pilot takes to fly the plane. The pilot may fly the plane himself, or delegate it to a copilot. The **control** system includes the cockpit instruments the pilot uses to guide the plane, as well as the monitoring systems used by air traffic control. The goal of these control mechanisms is to make sure the plane does not deviate too far from the flight plan. When that happens, the system should provide a signal that the pilot needs to take corrective action.

To extend this analogy to the business world, managers are like pilots flying a plane and the managerial accounting system is the set of tools that help the pilot get the plane to its destination. The tools can be as simple as a report on a piece of paper, or as sophisticated as an information system that provides real-time data to managers on their handheld devices. These tools must provide timely, relevant, and accurate information to help managers do their jobs.

At California Pizza Kitchen, everyone from the kitchen manager to the CEO needs information to plan, implement, and control within their area of responsibility. Because the kitchen manager will be making very different decisions than the CEO, the managerial accounting system must provide information for both day-to-day operational decisions and long-term strategic decisions.

In its last publicly released annual report, CPK provided the following statement of its overall strategic plan:

> Our objective is to extend our leadership position in the restaurant and premium pizza market by selling innovative, high-quality pizzas . . . and related products and by providing exceptional customer service, thereby building a high degree of customer loyalty, brand awareness and superior returns for our stockholders. To reach these objectives, we plan to increase our market share by expanding our restaurant base in new and existing markets, leveraging our partnerships in nontraditional and retail channels and offering innovative menu items.[2]

As you can see, this high-level **plan** lays out the key factors that managers believe are important to the company's success—a high degree of customer loyalty, increased market share, and superior returns for stockholders. It also includes the tactics that managers will use to achieve these objectives—serve innovative food, provide excellent customer service, and expand into new and existing territories. One role of the managerial accounting system is to translate these goals into more specific and measurable objectives. For example, how will the company measure customer loyalty? What percentage increase in market share do managers want to achieve and in what time period? What is the target return on investment for shareholders?

Once managers have determined the objectives they want to achieve, they begin to **implement** the plan by buying raw materials, hiring workers, negotiating with suppliers, advertising new menu items, and serving food to customers. They might also provide incentives to motivate workers to achieve specific objectives. For example, they might give restaurant managers bonuses or perks for meeting targeted sales goals for new menu items.

To **control** the business, managers monitor various metrics that are relevant to their area of responsibility. If these metrics fall below expectations, managers should take corrective action. In the last annual report, CPK managers noted that "we regularly review the sales mix of our menu items and replace lower selling items in each category with new menu items once or twice per year. Because of our ability to quickly adapt our menu, we believe that we are able to meet our customers' changing tastes and expectations."[3]

As you can see, the managerial functions of planning, implementing, and controlling are interconnected. One function leads to another, and managers use feedback from the process to improve future decision making. Throughout, managers must make a variety of decisions and they need relevant, up-to-date information, including cost estimates, competitor pricing, market demand, and consumer preferences. Much of this information comes from the managerial accounting system.

Before we move on, try the Self-Study Practice to make sure you understand the major differences between financial and managerial accounting and the key functions of management.

Types of Organizations

Managerial accounting information is used by managers in all types of organizations: large and small, public and private, profit and nonprofit. Traditionally, businesses are classified into one of three categories:

- **Manufacturing firms** purchase raw materials from suppliers and convert them into finished products, such as Apple iPods, Harley-Davidson motorcycles, Levi Strauss jeans, and Ford cars and trucks.

- **Merchandising companies** sell the goods that manufacturers produce. Merchandisers that sell exclusively to other businesses are called **wholesalers.** Merchandisers that sell to the general public are called **retailers.** For example, Sam's Club started out

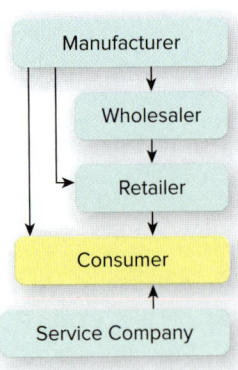

Selling Goods and Services to Customers

Manufacturer → Wholesaler → Retailer → Consumer ← Service Company

---

[2]California Pizza Kitchen, Inc., Annual Report for the fiscal year ended January 2, 2011, Form 10-K, United States Securities and Exchange Commission, filed March 17, 2011.

[3]Ibid.

How's it going?   *Self-Study Practice*

1. Which of the following statements best describes the difference between financial accounting and managerial accounting?

   a. Managerial accounting targets external stakeholders while financial accounting targets individuals within the company.
   b. Financial accounting relies more on subjective, future-oriented information than managerial accounting does.
   c. A major focus of managerial accounting is the preparation of the income statement, while a major focus of financial accounting is the preparation of the budget.
   d. Managerial accounting tends to focus on relevant, subjective, and future-oriented information while financial accounting relies primarily on objective, reliable, and historical information.

2. Which of the following statement(s) regarding the key management functions is true?

   a. Planning involves setting long-term objectives and the short-term tactics necessary to achieve those objectives.
   b. Implementing involves comparing actual results to planned objectives and making adjustments as necessary.
   c. Controlling includes all of the operational decisions made to implement the plan.
   d. All of the statements are true.

After you have finished, check your answers against the solutions in the margin.

The best way to know whether you are reading the chapter carefully enough is to see how well you do on a short exercise. Therefore, at important points throughout each chapter, you will find an exercise that will reinforce the concepts you have just learned and provide feedback on how well you learned them. We urge you not to skip these practices. When you are finished, check your answers against the solution below in the margin.

Solution to Self-Study Practice
1. d
2. a

as a wholesaler and then expanded into the retail market. Other well-known retailers include Walmart, Macy's, Bed Bath & Beyond, and Safeway.

- **Service companies** provide a service to customers or clients. A few well-known service providers are Hilton Hotels, Southwest Airlines, Expedia.com, and Federal Express. Many small businesses provide services to consumers and other businesses, including hair salons, law firms, architects, and home repair specialists.

Increasingly, the lines between manufacturing, merchandising, and service companies are becoming less clear. Many businesses, including California Pizza Kitchen, do not fall neatly into a single category. Some would consider CPK to be a service firm because it serves food to customers. Others would consider it a manufacturing company because it purchases raw materials (ingredients) and converts them into a finished product (a meal). And what about the frozen CPK pizzas that you can buy in your local supermarket? Those products are manufactured by Nestlé, which pays CPK a royalty fee (percentage of sales revenue) to use its recipes and brand.

As we will see in later chapters, the focus of managerial accounting is somewhat different in manufacturing firms than in merchandising and service firms. In the past, managerial accountants focused much of their efforts on preparing reports to keep track of the costs of raw materials, labor, and other costs incurred to produce a physical product. Today, nonmanufacturing firms make up an increasingly large proportion of the marketplace. In 2017, the U.S. government estimated that 80.2 percent of the nation's gross domestic product (GDP) stemmed from service activities.[4] The following chart shows the trend in employment in goods-producing and service-providing industries over the past 40 years. As you can see, the number of employees working in service sector jobs has increased dramatically over the past 40 years, while the number of employees working in manufacturing jobs has remained relatively constant. Today, about 85 percent of the people employed in America work in nonmanufacturing fields such as health care, education, and retail, and the trend toward service industries is expected to continue.

---

[4]CIA, *The World Factbook,* https://www.cia.gov/library/publications/resources/the-world-factbook/geos/us.html.

🏈 **COACH'S TIP**

When you graduate, you are about four times more likely to go to work in a service or merchandising setting than a manufacturing company. Even so, you need to have a basic understanding of how managerial accounting works in manufacturing firms because you will most likely still work with manufacturing firms, perhaps as a buyer or other business partner. To make the manufacturing process more tangible, we will use examples of products that you encounter every day, so that you can more easily visualize how the products are made.

Growth in Services and Merchandising Jobs

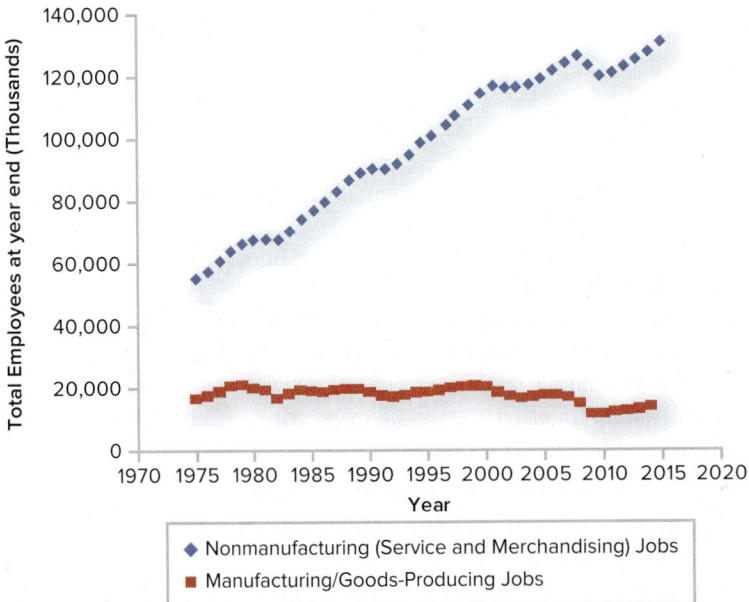

Data from U.S. Department of Labor, Bureau of Labor Statistics, Employment Database. http://www.bls.gov/data/#employment , accessed April 21, 2015.

Although nonmanufacturing firms make up an increasingly large percentage of our economy and workforce, many of our examples will be applied to companies that make a physical product, such as pizza, an automobile, or an Apple Watch. There are a few reasons why managerial accounting is often applied in a manufacturing setting:

1. It is easier for students to visualize a physical product and think about the various costs and activities that are required to make it. We intentionally chose products and companies that most students are familiar with so that you can immediately apply the concepts to something you understand and encounter on a daily basis.

2. Accounting in manufacturing firms is more complex than nonmanufacturing firms because the product goes through several stages of completion (raw materials, work-in-process, and finished goods) before it is finally sold. Some of the terminology that you will learn in the first few chapters of this book, such as the difference between manufacturing and nonmanufacturing costs, is only relevant to manufacturing firms.

While we start out discussing managerial accounting in manufacturing settings, virtually all of the concepts and tools can be applied in nonmanufacturing settings as well. Once you've mastered the manufacturing example, extending it to a service or merchandising setting should be relatively simple. Throughout the book, we will provide examples of how the concepts and techniques could be applied in service settings as well.

Finally, it is important to note that managerial accounting information is vital to nonprofit organizations, including hospitals, universities, and charitable organizations. Although these organizations do not exist strictly to earn profit for shareholders, their managers still need timely and relevant information to prepare budgets, manage resources, and make strategic and operational decisions.

ETHICS, SUSTAINABILITY, AND DECISION ANALYTICS

Ethics and the Sarbanes Oxley Act

Learning Objective 1–3
Describe the importance of ethics, sustainability, and decision analytics in managerial accounting.

All managers, regardless of the type of organization they work for, are responsible for creating and maintaining an ethical work environment, including the reporting of accounting information. **Ethics** refers to the standards of conduct for judging right from wrong, honest from dishonest, and fair from unfair. Although some accounting and business problems have clear right or wrong answers, many situations require accountants and managers to weigh the pros and cons of alternatives before making final decisions.

Often, there is no one right answer to ethical dilemmas and hard choices will need to be made. Do not tolerate acts of fraud, such as employees making up false expenses for reimbursement, punching in a time card belonging to a fellow employee who will be late for work, or copying someone's ideas and claiming them as your own. Also be aware that not all ethical dilemmas are clear-cut. Some situations will require you to weigh one moral principle (e.g., honesty) against another (e.g., loyalty).

When faced with an ethical dilemma, you should apply the following three-step process:

1. Identify who will be affected by the situation—both those who will appear to benefit (often the manager or employee) and those who will be harmed (other employees, the company's reputation, owners, creditors, and the public in general).

2. Identify and evaluate the alternative courses of action.

3. Choose the alternative that is the most ethical—and that you would be proud to have reported in the news.

Unfortunately, not everyone abides by these general guidelines. For example, the reputation of business managers and accountants was tarnished in the late 1990s and early 2000s due to high-profile scandals at companies like at Enron and WorldCom. In response to these scandals, Congress enacted the **Sarbanes-Oxley (SOX) Act of 2002**. Although SOX was primarily aimed at renewing investor confidence in the external financial reporting system, it has many implications for managers as well.

The Sarbanes-Oxley Act focuses on three factors that affect the accounting reporting environment: opportunity, incentives, and character.

Opportunities for Error and Fraud SOX attempts to reduce the **opportunity** for error and fraud. A requirement under SOX is that management must conduct a review of the company's internal control system and issue a report that indicates whether the controls are effective at preventing errors and fraud. This requirement places more responsibility on all managers (not just accountants) for the accuracy of the reporting system. For example, marketing managers are now responsible for making sure their staff members submit accurate sales and expense reports. SOX also places additional responsibilities on the boards of directors and external auditors to reduce the opportunity for errors and fraud.

Incentives for Committing Fraud SOX attempts to counteract the **incentive** to commit fraud by providing stiff penalties, such as monetary fines and jail time. For example, violators must repay any money obtained via fraud and can be assessed additional fines of up to $5 million. Executives cannot avoid these penalties by declaring personal bankruptcy, which explains why a former sales director at Computer Associates will be giving 15 percent of every paycheck he earns for the rest of his life to a fraud restitution fund. SOX also increased the maximum jail sentence for fraudulent reporting to 20 years. Total jail time can add up to

Most chapters include Spotlight features focusing on decision making, ethics, and sustainability. These features are designed to illustrate the relevance of accounting in real-world decision making.

SPOTLIGHT ON Ethics

Accounting Scandals

Typically, fear of personal failure and greed drives accounting scandals. Initially, some people may appear to benefit from fraudulent reporting. In the long run, however, fraud harms most individuals and organizations. When it is uncovered, the corporation's stock price drops dramatically. In the case involving MicroStrategy, the stock price dropped 65 percent from $243 to $86 per share in a single day of trading. Creditors are also harmed by fraud. WorldCom's creditors recovered only 42 percent of what they were owed. They lost $36 billion. Innocent employees also are harmed by fraud. At Enron, 5,600 employees lost their jobs, and many lost all of their retirement savings. The auditing firm Arthur Andersen, which once employed 28,000 people, went out of business after becoming entangled in the WorldCom and Enron frauds.

even more than that because federal sentencing guidelines allow judges to declare consecutive jail terms for each violation.

Character of Managers and Employees   Finally, SOX emphasizes the importance of the **character** of managers and employees. Admittedly, it is difficult for a law to make people act appropriately, but SOX introduces new rules that should help employees of good character make the right decision when confronted with ethical dilemmas. For example, audit committees are now required to create anonymous hotlines that allow employees to submit concerns they may have about suspicious accounting or auditing practices. SOX also gives federal employees whistle-blower protection to prevent retaliation by those charged with fraud.

Finally, to reinforce good character, public companies must adopt a code of ethics for senior financial officers. Unfortunately, simply adopting a code of ethics does not ensure that managers will act ethically. Most experts agree that ethics must be embedded in the organizational culture and that top managers who lead by example will drive ethical behavior in the organization.

According to a recent Statement on Management Accounting (SMA) released by the Institute of Management Accountants (IMA), companies with strong ethical cultures are rewarded with higher productivity, improved team dynamics, lower risks of fraud, streamlined processes, improved product quality, and higher customer satisfaction. But to achieve these rewards, companies must move beyond simply complying with laws such as SOX and create a culture that embeds ethics throughout the organization.

Before we move on, take a moment to complete the following Self-Study Practice to make sure you can identify factors that influence ethical behavior.

Solution to Self-Study Practice

1. +/I (increased pressure to report stronger financial results)
2. –/C (less likelihood that unethical behavior will go unreported)
3. –/O (strong oversight by directors)

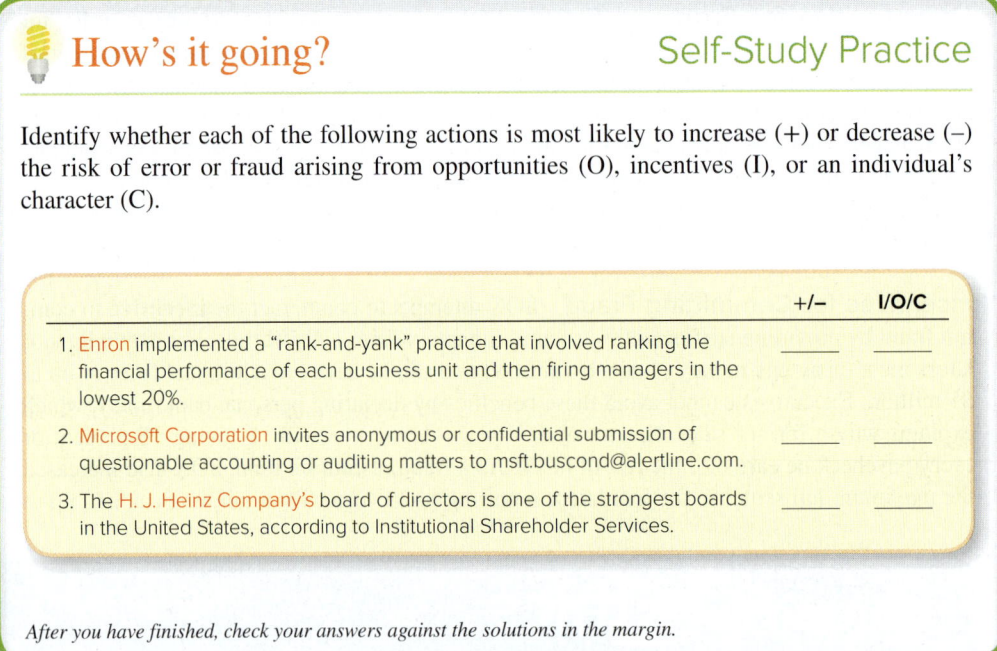

How's it going?   Self-Study Practice

Identify whether each of the following actions is most likely to increase (+) or decrease (–) the risk of error or fraud arising from opportunities (O), incentives (I), or an individual's character (C).

	+/−	I/O/C
1. Enron implemented a "rank-and-yank" practice that involved ranking the financial performance of each business unit and then firing managers in the lowest 20%.	_____	_____
2. Microsoft Corporation invites anonymous or confidential submission of questionable accounting or auditing matters to msft.buscond@alertline.com.	_____	_____
3. The H. J. Heinz Company's board of directors is one of the strongest boards in the United States, according to Institutional Shareholder Services.	_____	_____

After you have finished, check your answers against the solutions in the margin.

Sustainability Accounting

Managerial accounting has traditionally focused on providing managers with the information they need to make decisions that create economic value or profit for shareholders. In today's changing world, managers are responsible for more than achieving financial results, and are accountable to many groups other than shareholders. Modern managers must balance the priorities and needs of many stakeholders, including employees, customers, suppliers, regulators, and society. **Sustainability accounting** is an emerging area of accounting that is aimed at providing managers with a broader set of information to meet the needs of multiple stakeholders, with the goal of ensuring the company's long-term survival in an uncertain and resource-constrained world.

The simplest definition of sustainability is the ability to last or survive for a long time. When applied to business, **sustainability** is the ability to meet the needs of today without sacrificing the ability of future generations to meet their own needs. To accomplish this goal, managers must consider three factors when making decisions: society, economy, and the environment. These three pillars of sustainability are called the **triple bottom line** and are often represented by **3 Ps: People, Profit, and Planet**.

Accountants can play a key role in helping organizations achieve their sustainability goals by measuring and managing triple bottom line performance. While traditional accounting systems focused almost exclusively on economic results (e.g., profit), sustainability accounting expands the focus to measure the impact of business decisions on social issues (people) and the environment (planet). Just as accountants have always measured and managed a firm's economic performance, today's accountants often measure and manage a firm's social impact and environmental performance as well.

The following diagram provides a historical perspective on the relative importance of the three factors that make up the triple bottom line.

COACH'S TIP

Although some people equate sustainability with being environmentally friendly or "green," it is a much broader concept than that. A truly sustainable business strategy is one that simultaneously achieves economic results while creating benefits for society (e.g., reduce poverty, respect human rights, prevent disease) and the environment (e.g., limit climate change, reduce greenhouse gas emissions).

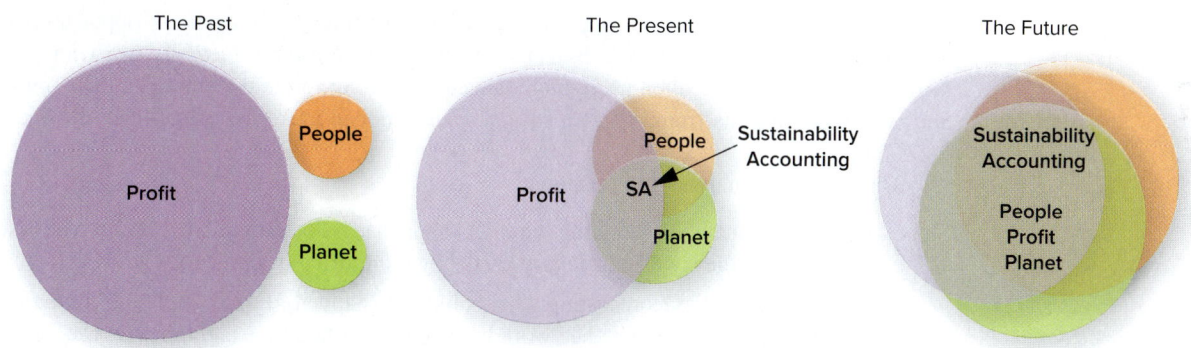

In the past, accounting focused primarily on profitability measures such as net income (revenue – expenses), return on equity, and other measures of economic success. Social and environmental factors were not usually at the forefront of managers' decision making, and in many cases financial results were achieved at the expense of society (people) and the environment (planet).

Today, managers are beginning to recognize that a business strategy focused solely on achieving economic or financial results is not sustainable. In the long-run, a business cannot survive without people (e.g., customers, employees, and suppliers) and natural resources (e.g., water, clean air, and fuel). As a result, modern organizations are building sustainable business practices into their business strategies and including sustainability accounting methods such as the triple bottom line into their performance management systems. For example, most public companies now issue **corporate social responsibility (CSR)** reports that provide sustainability-related information, including measures of social and environmental impact.

While sustainability accounting is an emerging and critically important area in accounting, the reality is that most of today's businesses and managers are still driven *primarily* by economic results. For sustainability initiatives to really take shape and change the way a company does business, it must be linked to the company's overall corporate strategy and embedded in the day-to-day operations and culture of the company. As that happens, sustainability can become a more integrated part of the business model, and sustainability accounting measures such as the triple bottom line are likely to emerge as a more mainstream part of the reporting process.

Throughout this textbook, we will highlight some of the sustainability initiatives and reporting issues faced by managers in real-world companies and relate these initiatives to other topics in managerial accounting.

Decision Analytics

A topic that is becoming increasingly important to managers and accountants is the use of big data and analytics to help managers make more informed business decisions. **Big data analytics** involves the use of analytical techniques to gain valuable insights from data that is so large or complex that it cannot be analyzed using traditional data bases and spreadsheets. So what makes data "BIG"?

- *Volume:* The sheer amount or volume of data can be overwhelming and exceed the capacity of many company's servers. For example, it is estimated that Walmart collects more than 2.5 petabytes (2.5 quadrillion bytes) of customer data per hour.[5]

- *Velocity:* The data arrives with great velocity or speed, including not just data on past events but also that which is created in real time, as events are occurring.

- *Variety:* The data comes in a variety of formats (e.g. text, numerics, images, audio, and video), and is generated from a variety of sources, devices, and sensors, including geographic, financial, and social media data.

If "BIG" data relates to the volume, velocity, and variety of data, what is analytics? **Analytics** is the process of discovering and communicating meaningful patterns and insights from data to find more intelligent ways of operating a business, managing resources, enhancing customer service, reducing operating costs, or pursuing other business opportunities. Although differences exist at a technical level, the terms *big data, business analytics,* and *business intelligence* are often used interchangeably to refer to the extraction of meaningful and actionable insights from big data so that managers can make more intelligent business decisions.

Three types of analytics are common:

- Descriptive analytics (showing what has happened). For example, UPS *describes* the operating efficiency of its delivery trucks by monitoring gas mileage.

- Predictive analytics (forecasting what is likely to happen). For example, UPS *predicts* future repairs and maintenance work by analyzing idling time and miles driven.

- Prescriptive analytics (recommending a course of action). For example, UPS uses customer location and real-time GPS data to *prescribe* the most efficient routes for delivering its packages.

Amazon.com is now experimenting with something it calls "anticipatory shipping" where it uses past purchases, website traffic, and geographic data to ship a product to a region before a customer even places the order. By shipping in advance, and later specifying the exact delivery location when an actual purchase occurs, Amazon hopes to be able to reduce both shipping time and shipping costs.

In addition to these business examples, big data analytics is proving useful in other fields such as health care and law enforcement. For example, by tracking search terms entered into Google by people in various regions of the United States, analysts can predict flu outbreaks faster than by monitoring hospital admission records. As another example, big data analysts cross-referenced public crime records with data from ride-sharing apps to discover that DUI arrests fell by 10 percent after Uber entered a major metropolitan market.

At opportune places throughout this book we will highlight how managers in our focus company or other real-world organizations use big data and analytics to make managerial decisions. Refer to Skills Development Case S1-5 at the end of this chapter for a real-world case study describing how managers at California Pizza Kitchen used analytical techniques to better understand their consumption of energy expenses so that they could reduce spending and enhance their sustainability goals.

---

[5]Andrew McAfee and Erik Brynjolfsson, "Big Data: The Management Revolution," *Harvard Business Review,* October 2012.

Role of Cost in Managerial Accounting

As described earlier in this chapter, the goal of managerial accounting is to provide managers with the information they need to plan, implement, and control within their area of responsibility. Much of the information that managers need to make decisions is based on cost data. For example, a restaurant manager at CPK might need to know how much it costs to prepare a new menu item to decide how much to charge for it. A kitchen manager might need to know the cost of a specific pizza component such as dough or sauce to decide whether to make it in-house or buy it from a supplier. Managers also need cost information to prepare daily, weekly, and monthly operating budgets. These budgets help managers ensure that they have the necessary resources to run the business and to control spending.

Cost information is important for accountants too. They use it to value inventory and determine the profitability of various products, regions, divisions, or other segments of the business. Although accountants and managers should consider things other than cost when making decisions, cost control remains a critical concern for most organizations, particularly in a tough economy or when profit margins are declining due to increased competition. In the next section, we describe alternative ways to categorize costs based on different criteria.

COST TERMINOLOGY

Throughout this textbook, we will use a lot of different labels to describe cost. It can be confusing at times because there are many different types of cost systems and ways to categorize cost. The most important thing to remember is that we will treat costs differently depending on how the information will be used. Will the cost information be used for financial reporting purposes? If so, we have to follow the rules of GAAP. Will it be used to determine the profitability of a product or service? If so, we need to understand the nature of the product or service to decide what costing method is appropriate. Will the cost data be used for decision making? If so, we need to consider how costs will behave or change depending on what decision alternatives the manager is considering. Will it be used to evaluate the performance of a manager? If so, we need to think about what costs are under the manager's direct control.

In this chapter, we introduce the terminology you will use to categorize or sort cost into different "buckets," including

- Direct or Indirect
- Variable or Fixed
- Manufacturing or Nonmanufacturing
- Product or Period
- Relevant or Irrelevant

Each of these classifications will be based on different criteria depending on how the information will be used. In later chapters, you will learn more about how to use this cost information for different managerial purposes, including product costing, cost management, decision making, planning and control, and performance evaluation. For now, you just need to recognize and define the terms.

To make these classifications more concrete, we will use California Pizza Kitchen's actual operating costs as an example. Exhibit 1–3 shows the breakdown of CPK's total operating costs as reported in their last publicly issued financial report. As you can see, CPK's operating costs are made up of wages and salaries (37 percent); food, beverages, and supplies (23 percent); occupancy costs such as rent, utilities, and property taxes (22 percent); general and administrative expenses (8 percent); and other miscellaneous expenses (10 percent). The "other" category includes the costs to open a new restaurant, such as rent during the construction period, hiring and training the initial workforce, buying the food used in training, and marketing costs.

Learning Objective 1–4
Define and give examples of different types of costs.

 **COACH'S TIP**

The key thing to remember is that **different costs terms are used for different purposes.** Thus, a single cost can be classified in more than one way, depending on how the information will be used.

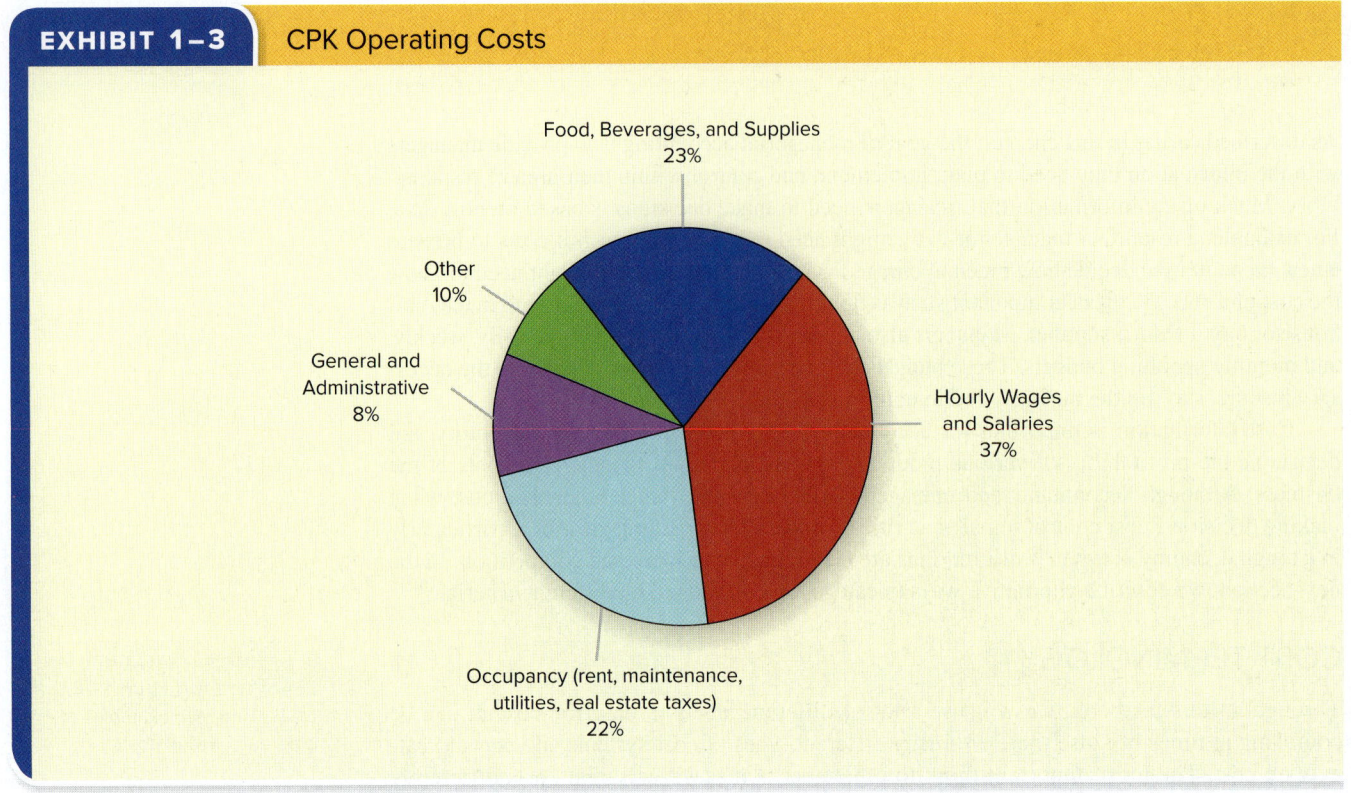

EXHIBIT 1–3   CPK Operating Costs

DIRECT VERSUS INDIRECT COSTS

When managers use cost information, they typically want to know the cost of something specific. It could be a menu item (e.g., a 16-inch BBQ pizza), a particular ingredient (e.g., pizza dough), an activity (e.g., serving a customer), or a specific part of the business (e.g., a restaurant). We call these specific things *cost objects*. A **cost object** is any item we want to know the cost of. In your own personal life, you might want to know the cost of attending school for a semester, the cost to buy and operate a car, or the cost of a vacation you would like to take over spring break. Each of these items would be considered a cost object.

As an example, assume you want to know how much it is costing you to take this accounting course. In that case, the course (managerial accounting) is the cost object. How would you go about determining the cost of this course? You would probably start with the costs that are easily attributed to a specific course, such as the cost of tuition and books. Costs that **can be directly and easily traced** to the cost object are called **direct costs**. But there are other costs associated with your education that aren't directly related to one course. Examples include the cost of driving to and from campus, the cost of your computer, and the cost of the supplies you use in class. These costs are difficult to trace to a specific class if you are taking more than one class at a time. Even if you could keep track of the cost of the pencils and paper you use in a specific class, it probably isn't worth the effort to do so. Costs that **cannot be traced** to the cost object, or that are **not worth the effort** of tracing, are called **indirect costs**. When classifying a cost as direct or indirect, the question to ask is whether the cost can be directly and conveniently traced to the cost object. If the answer is yes, it is a direct cost. If it is no, it is an indirect cost.

At California Pizza Kitchen, costs can also be classified as direct or indirect. Recall that 23 percent of CPK's operating cost is for food, beverages, and supplies. Can all of these costs be traced to a specific cost object, such as a new menu item that managers are trying to price? The cost of ingredients used to make the menu item would generally be classified as a direct cost, so long as it is worth the effort to trace the cost. However, it may not be worth the effort to try to figure out the exact cost of every ingredient that goes into the menu item. If CPK doesn't see value in tracing these costs to the cost object, they would be classified as indirect costs instead.

COACH'S TIP

Whether a cost is direct or indirect depends on whether it is both **possible** and **convenient** to trace the cost to a cost object. Costs that *could* be traced but are not worth the effort to trace are also classified as **indirect costs.**

Labor costs, which make up 37 percent of CPK's annual operating costs, can also be categorized as either direct or indirect depending on whether they can be directly and conveniently traced to the product or service the company is delivering. Direct labor would include the cost of employees who are involved in preparing meals or serving customers, such as line cooks, bartenders, waiters, and waitresses. Indirect labor would include the kitchen manager and general restaurant manager because these individuals are generally responsible for supervising other employees rather than preparing and serving meals directly to customers.

What about the 22 percent that CPK spends on occupancy costs such as rent, maintenance, utilities, and property taxes? If we are trying to determine the cost of serving a specific customer (the cost object), costs such as rent and supervision would be considered indirect costs. However, if the manager is trying to determine the cost of operating a specific restaurant (the cost object), occupancy costs such as rent and utilities would be direct costs. CPK calls these costs "direct operating and occupancy costs" because they are associated with a specific restaurant. Costs incurred outside of the restaurant, such as general and administrative expenses and national advertising, would be considered indirect. Remember, whether a cost is considered direct or indirect depends on the cost object we are trying to trace it to.

VARIABLE VERSUS FIXED COSTS

For internal decision making, managers often want to know how costs will change if something else changes, such as the number of units produced or the number of customers served. **Variable costs** are those that change, in total, in direct proportion to changes in activity levels. In describing its major operating costs, CPK's annual report states that "food, beverage, and paper supplies are variable and increase with sales volume."[6] In other words, as CPK prepares more meals and serves more customers, the total cost of food, beverages, and supplies will also increase.

As you can see from the following graph, although **total** variable costs vary with the number of customers served, the **per-unit** or **average** cost of food, beverages, and supplies will remain the same, regardless of the number of customers served. For example, if the number of customers served doubles, CPK will need to purchase more ingredients, such as pizza dough. But the amount of dough used to make each pizza doesn't change. (Note: for simplicity, this scenario ignores other factors that drive down unit variable costs, such as discounts for buying ingredients in bulk.)

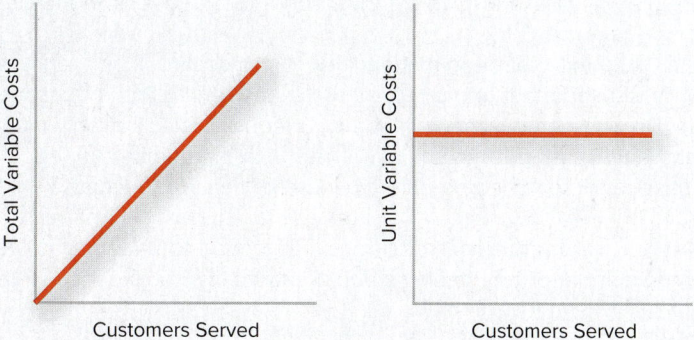

> **COACH'S TIP**
>
> In deciding whether a cost is variable or fixed, be sure to think about whether the **total cost** will change. Looking at average or unit cost will reveal an entirely different pattern, which we examine more closely in Chapter 5.

Fixed costs are those that stay the same, in total, regardless of activity level. Examples of fixed costs for CPK include rent, manager salaries, depreciation, and property taxes. When we say that a cost is fixed, that doesn't mean it will never change; it simply means that the total cost won't change because we produce more units or serve more customers.

Although **total** fixed costs are constant, **average** or **per-unit** fixed costs vary inversely with the number of units produced or the number of customers served. That is because

---

[6]California Pizza Kitchen, Inc., Annual Report for the fiscal year ended January 2, 2011, Form 10-K, United States Securities and Exchange Commission, filed March 17, 2011.

spreading a constant amount over more units or customers drives down the average cost. For example, if the number of customers served doubles, total rent cost remains the same, but the average cost of rent **per customer** will decrease because we divide the total rent cost by a larger number of customers.

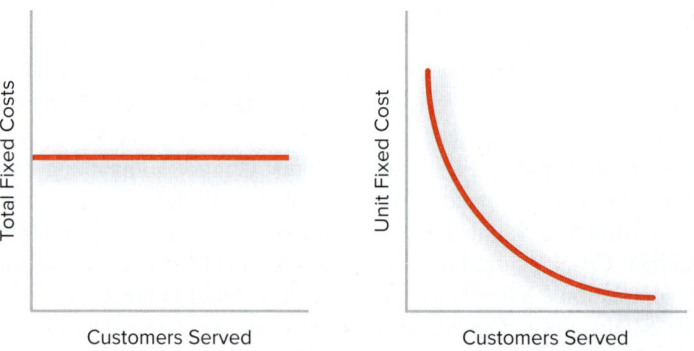

In most real-world businesses, costs do not behave in the perfectly predictable patterns described. For example, CPK's annual report states that "direct operating and occupancy costs generally increase with sales volume, but decline as a percentage of restaurant sales."[7] This tells us that direct operating and occupancy costs are not strictly variable or strictly fixed. Some costs, such as server wages and utilities, will increase with higher levels of sales, while other costs, such as management salaries and property taxes, will be incurred regardless of sales. These so-called *mixed costs* are discussed in more detail in Chapter 5.

SPOTLIGHT ON Decision Making

Predicting Fixed and Variable Costs

Assume you are the treasurer of a student club at your university and you are on the planning committee for the end-of-year social event. The committee is in charge of finding a location; renting tables and chairs; and hiring a DJ, photographer, and caterer for the event. Your responsibility as treasurer is to set the budget for the event and make sure the committee stays within that budget.

Which costs would you expect to vary with the number of people attending? Which costs will be the same regardless of how many people attend the event? Why is it important for you to know the answers to these questions? When planning a social event, the cost of the venue, DJ, and photographer will be incurred regardless of how many people attend the event. The cost of catering (food and drinks), tables, and chairs will vary with the number of people who are expected to attend. You need to understand these relationships to prepare a budget for the event because the total cost will depend on the number of guests.

Managers must answer similar questions when making business decisions. They need to understand which costs will vary with the number of units produced or the number of customers served and which will be incurred regardless of these factors.

MANUFACTURING VERSUS NONMANUFACTURING COSTS

For financial reporting purposes, costs must also be classified based on whether they relate to manufacturing or nonmanufacturing activities. This distinction applies only to companies that make a physical product, such as Dell (computers), Honda (cars and trucks), Harley-Davidson

---

[7]California Pizza Kitchen, Inc., Annual Report for the fiscal year ended January 2, 2011, Form 10-K, United States Securities and Exchange Commission, filed March 17, 2011.

(motorcycles), and Maytag (appliances). It does not apply to merchandisers or service companies that do not make a physical product.

Because CPK is not a traditional manufacturing company, let's consider the costs incurred by Nestlé to manufacture, distribute, and sell frozen pizzas under the CPK brand. To differentiate between manufacturing and nonmanufacturing costs, we need to consider whether the cost relates to manufacturing or **making** the frozen pizzas, as opposed to marketing, delivering, and selling them.

Manufacturing costs represent all of the costs associated with producing or manufacturing a physical product. They are generally classified into one of three categories:

- **Direct materials** include the major material inputs that can be directly and conveniently traced to each unit of product (the cost object). For a frozen pizza manufacturer, direct materials include the major ingredients (e.g., dough, sauce, cheese, and meat), as well as packaging materials (e.g., plastic and cardboard). Miscellaneous ingredients and materials (e.g., seasonings and glue for the cardboard box) that are not worth tracing to each individual unit would be considered indirect materials and included in manufacturing overhead.

- **Direct labor** refers to the "hands on" labor that can be directly and conveniently traced to the product, such as the wages of employees on the pizza production line and in the packaging department. It does not include employees who rarely touch the product as it is being produced, such as supervisors, maintenance workers, and factory engineers. The costs associated with those employees are considered indirect labor and counted as part of manufacturing overhead.

- **Manufacturing overhead** includes all manufacturing costs **other than direct materials and direct labor** incurred to produce a physical product. It includes all of the costs associated with *making* the product that cannot be traced to a specific unit, such as indirect materials, indirect labor, factory rent, factory insurance, and factory utilities. Manufacturing overhead does *not* include costs that happen outside of the factory walls (e.g., marketing, distribution, or sales), only those indirect costs that are related to manufacturing the product.

When added together, direct materials and direct labor are referred to as **prime costs**. For manual production processes, the direct materials and direct labor often represent the *primary* costs incurred to make the product. As manufacturing has become more automated and labor has shifted from direct labor (i.e., line-worker wages) to indirect labor (i.e., engineers and supervisors), manufacturing overhead has become a much larger percentage of total manufacturing cost.

Direct labor and manufacturing overhead are referred to collectively as **conversion costs**. These are the costs needed to *convert* direct materials into a finished product. For Nestlé, conversion costs include all costs incurred to convert raw ingredients into a finished product (pizza).

Notice that direct labor is included in both prime costs (direct materials + direct labor) and in conversion costs (direct labor + manufacturing overhead). As such, you cannot add prime costs to conversion costs to determine the total manufacturing cost, because direct labor is included in both components. The sum of the three manufacturing costs (direct materials + direct labor + manufacturing overhead) gives us the total manufacturing cost. Alternatively, you could add prime cost to conversion costs and then subtract the direct labor to prevent it from being counted twice.

Nonmanufacturing costs are the costs associated with running the business and selling the product as opposed to manufacturing the product. They are generally classified into one of two groups:

- **Marketing or selling expenses** are incurred to get the final product to the customer. For Nestlé, they would include advertising, sales personnel, and the cost of distributing the frozen pizzas to grocery stores.

Prime Cost =

Direct Materials
+
Direct Labor

Conversion Cost =

Direct Labor
+
Manufacturing Overhead

- **General and administrative expenses** are associated with running the overall business. They include general management salaries, rent and utilities for corporate headquarters, and corporate service functions such as the accounting, payroll, and legal departments. Nestlé would also place the salaries of those who manage the company's relationship with CPK under this category.

PRODUCT VERSUS PERIOD COSTS

COACH'S TIP

The distinction between period and product costs is a matter of **when** the cost is matched against revenue on the income statement. Period costs are expensed as soon as they are incurred. Product costs are recorded initially as inventory and do not appear on the income statement until the product is sold.

The difference between product costs and period costs determines **how and when** the cost will be matched up against revenue on the income statement. This distinction really has more to do with financial accounting (external reporting) than managerial accounting. However, it is important for manufacturing firms that hold significant amounts of inventory because it determines whether a cost is counted as inventory (an asset on the balance sheet) or as an expense on the income statement. Classifying a cost as product or period can affect the reported profitability of the company's products, customers, and divisions.

For external reporting purposes, GAAP requires that all manufacturing costs be treated as **product costs**, or costs that are assigned to the product as it is being manufactured. Product costs are also called **inventoriable costs** because they are counted as inventory (an asset) until the product is sold. Remember that manufacturing costs include direct materials (e.g., major ingredients and packaging materials), direct labor (e.g., wages of employees who make the pizzas), and manufacturing overhead (e.g., supervisor salaries, miscellaneous ingredients, factory rent, and utilities, etc.). These costs must follow the flow of the product as it is being produced and are initially recorded in one of the following inventory accounts: Raw Materials Inventory, Work in Process Inventory, or Finished Goods Inventory. Once the product is finally sold, product costs are reported as Cost of Goods Sold and matched up against sales revenue on the income statement.

Nonmanufacturing costs are called **period costs** or period expenses because they are expensed during the period incurred. Unlike product costs that flow through several inventory accounts before being reported as Cost of Goods Sold, nonmanufacturing costs are expensed as soon as they are incurred. Examples of nonmanufacturing or period expenses include advertising, sales commissions, distribution expenses, and general and administrative salaries. Refer to Exhibit 1–4 for an illustration of the different treatment of product and period costs under GAAP.

Later chapters demonstrate how to account for the flow of manufacturing costs through the various inventory accounts before being reported as Cost of Goods Sold. For now, you simply need to recognize that manufacturing costs (product costs) will be treated differently than nonmanufacturing costs (period costs) for financial reporting purposes.

RELEVANT VERSUS IRRELEVANT COSTS

For managerial accounting information to be useful for decision making, it must be **relevant** to the specific decision that managers are trying to make. In today's information age, managers have access to a tremendous amount of data, much of which is irrelevant to the decision at hand. In addition, managers sometimes fail to incorporate relevant information into their decisions because it is not easily captured by the accounting system. Determining what information is relevant to managerial decisions is one of the most important skills that you will learn in this course. A **relevant cost** has the potential to influence a decision; an **irrelevant cost** will not influence a decision. For a cost to be relevant, it must occur **in the future** and **differ** between the various alternatives the manager is considering. Costs that differ between decision alternatives are sometimes called incremental or **differential costs**. For example, a manager at CPK might be trying to decide whether to make or buy pizza dough, lease or purchase restaurant equipment, or keep or drop an unprofitable menu item. Different costs are relevant and irrelevant for each of these scenarios. For example, the cost of wheat or flour used to make pizza dough is relevant to the decision about whether to make or buy the dough,

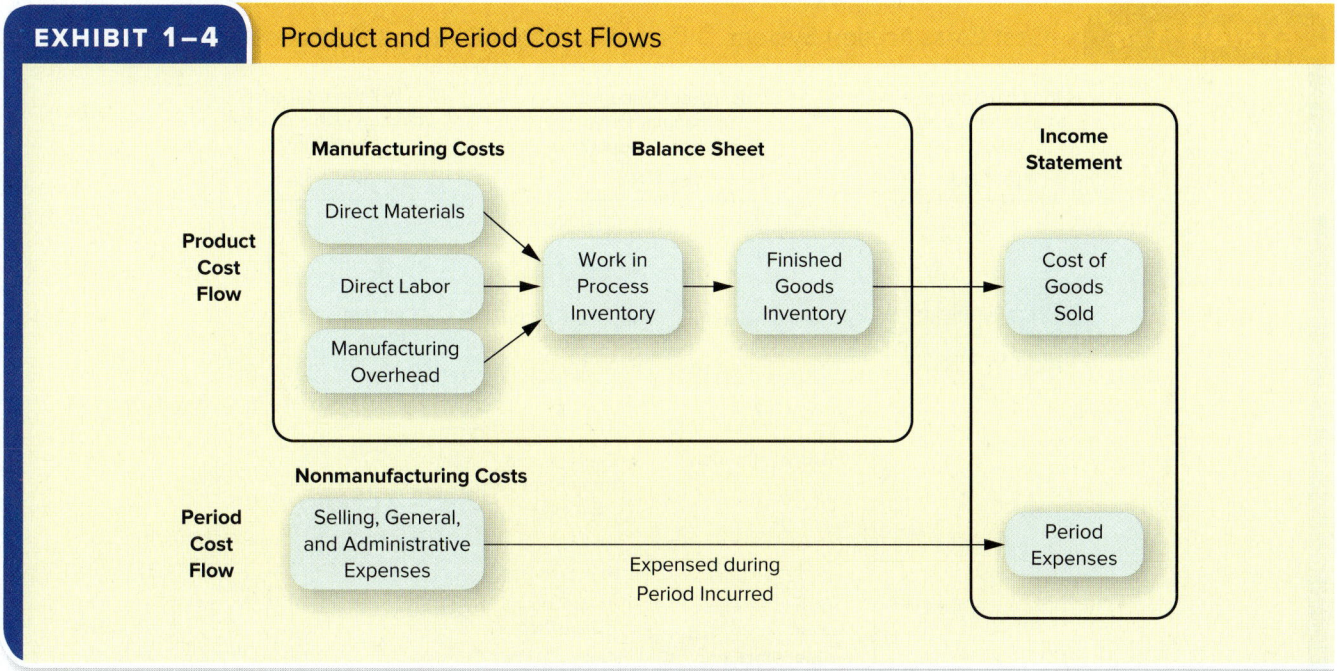

EXHIBIT 1–4   Product and Period Cost Flows

but is not relevant to the decision about whether to lease or purchase equipment. In addition, if a cost has already been incurred, the amount spent in the past is not relevant to what a manager decides to do in the future. So, if CPK has already purchased enough dough to last the rest of the month, the amount of money spent on the dough is irrelevant to the decision about whether to continue to buy pizza dough or to begin making it. The money has already been spent. Costs that have already been incurred are called **sunk costs**. Although **sunk costs are irrelevant** for decision making, it is often very difficult for managers to ignore what happened in the past and focus only on the future.

Another important distinction is the difference between an out-of-pocket costs and an opportunity cost. **Out-of-pocket costs** involve an actual cash payment. In your personal life, these are costs you pay "out of your pocket" for things such as food, clothing, and entertainment.

Unlike an out-of-pocket cost that involves an outlay of cash, an **opportunity cost** is the cost of **not** doing something. In other words, it is the forgone benefit (or lost opportunity) of the path not taken. Anytime you choose to do one thing instead of another because of limited time or money, you incur an opportunity cost. For example, if you are going to school full-time, you are giving up the opportunity to earn money by working full-time. The potential salary you could be making if you were not in school is an opportunity cost of pursuing your education.

Opportunity costs occur in business any time resources are constrained and managers must choose to do one thing at the expense of another. For example, a manager at CPK might be asked to close the restaurant to host a private event such as a corporate holiday party. By doing so, the company loses the opportunity to sell food and drinks to other customers. The managerial accounting system can help managers identify the opportunity cost based on the amount of profit that would normally be generated on a given night. If that opportunity cost is too high, managers might decide that they will only host private events on certain days or times of the week when business is slow.

Exhibit 1–5 provides a summary of the various ways to categorize or classify costs. Each classification requires you to ask a different question to determine how the information will be used in managerial accounting. We will reference this terminology throughout the book as we consider how managers use cost and other managerial accounting information to make decisions for their organization.

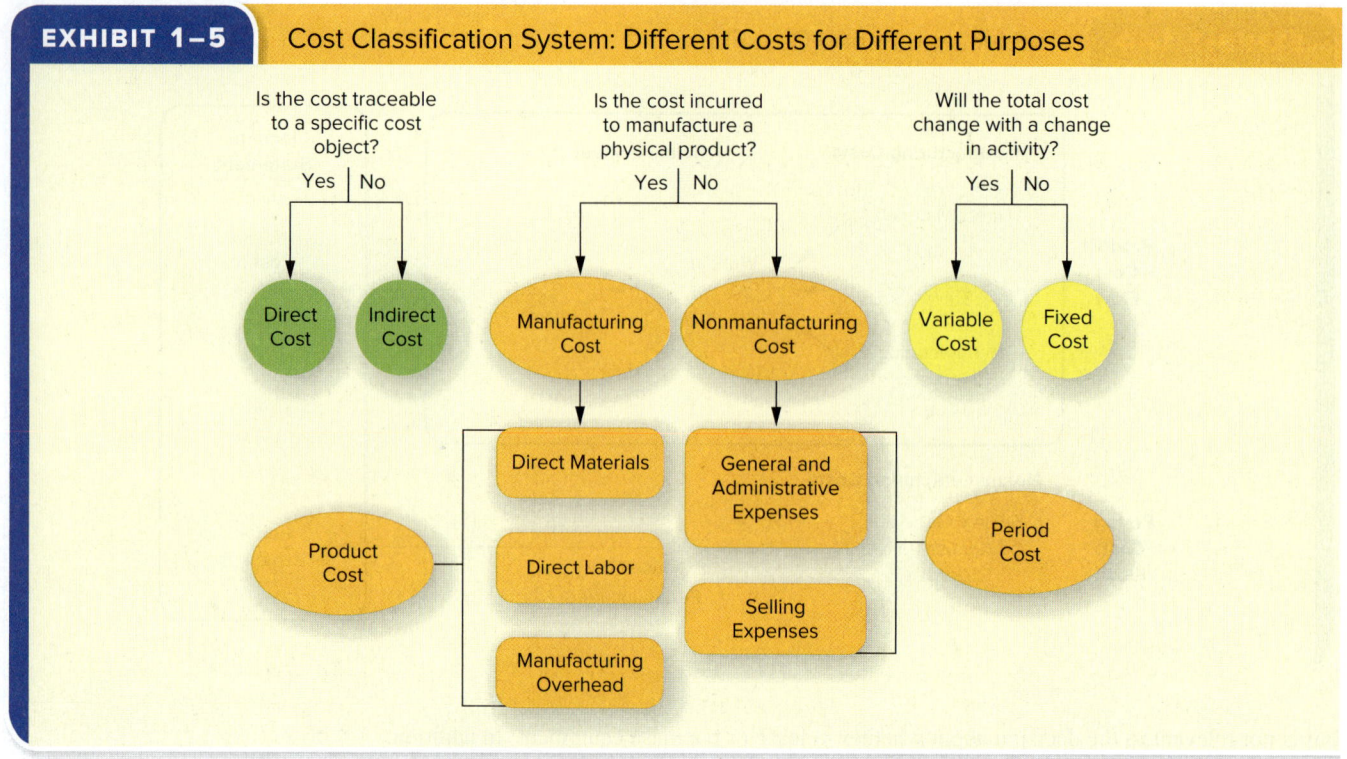

EXHIBIT 1–5   Cost Classification System: Different Costs for Different Purposes

Before continuing, complete the following Self-Study Practice to see how well you understand the cost terminology.

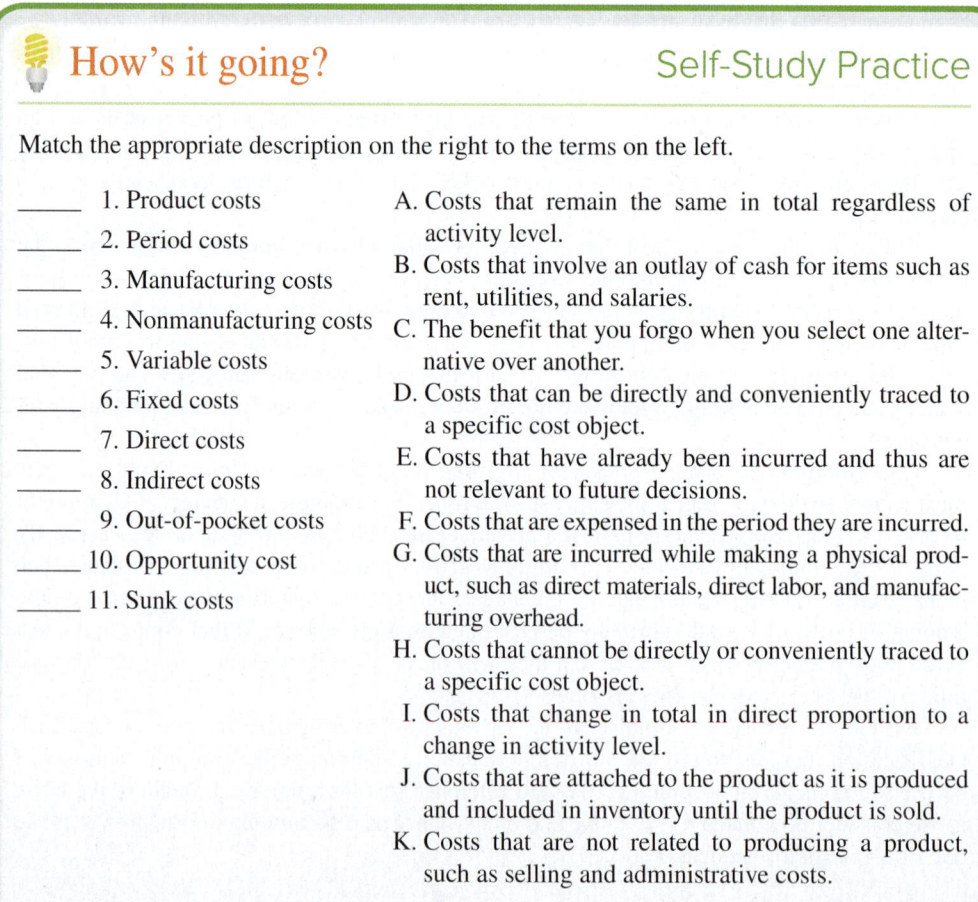

How's it going?   Self-Study Practice

Match the appropriate description on the right to the terms on the left.

_____ 1. Product costs
_____ 2. Period costs
_____ 3. Manufacturing costs
_____ 4. Nonmanufacturing costs
_____ 5. Variable costs
_____ 6. Fixed costs
_____ 7. Direct costs
_____ 8. Indirect costs
_____ 9. Out-of-pocket costs
_____ 10. Opportunity cost
_____ 11. Sunk costs

A. Costs that remain the same in total regardless of activity level.
B. Costs that involve an outlay of cash for items such as rent, utilities, and salaries.
C. The benefit that you forgo when you select one alternative over another.
D. Costs that can be directly and conveniently traced to a specific cost object.
E. Costs that have already been incurred and thus are not relevant to future decisions.
F. Costs that are expensed in the period they are incurred.
G. Costs that are incurred while making a physical product, such as direct materials, direct labor, and manufacturing overhead.
H. Costs that cannot be directly or conveniently traced to a specific cost object.
I. Costs that change in total in direct proportion to a change in activity level.
J. Costs that are attached to the product as it is produced and included in inventory until the product is sold.
K. Costs that are not related to producing a product, such as selling and administrative costs.

After you have finished, check your answers against the solutions in the margin.

Solution to Self-Study Practice

1. J
2. F
3. G
4. K
5. I
6. A
7. D
8. H
9. B
10. C
11. E

SUPPLEMENT 1A CAREERS THAT DEPEND ON ACCOUNTING KNOWLEDGE

Accounting knowledge can make the difference in your ability to land a dream job, whether you hope to work in production and operations management, human resources, finance, marketing, or another field. Exhibit 1S–1 displays nonaccounting jobs that could be available to you at the world's leading companies and explains how accounting knowledge can be vital to these positions.

EXHIBIT 1S–1	Accounting Knowledge Can Benefit All Majors

Production and Operations Management

Production Manager, Nintendo: Figure out how to make a $250 3DS for $100.71.

Outsourcing Specialist, Apple: Coordinate more than 20 suppliers of parts for the next iPad, at the same total cost as legacy iPads.

Human Resources

Compensation Analyst, Google: Develop affordable, attractive global pay programs.

Labor Relations Manager, NBA Players' Union: Assist in salary renegotiations involving the $58 million salary cap and 57% revenue sharing guarantee.

Accounting

Finance

Investment Analyst, Goldman Sachs: Assess value of investing $50 million in Facebook.

Financial Analyst, Target Corporation: Help credit card segment reduce the number of days awaiting collections from customers.

Marketing

Brand Manager, H. J. Heinz Company: Set prices to achieve 5% annual sales growth.

Customer Business Developer, Procter & Gamble: Collaborate with accounting to enhance customer profits and cash flows.

Sources: http://techland.time.com/2011/03/29/the-incredibly-cheap-100-nintendo-3ds; http://blogs.forbes.com/johnray/2011/03/11/isuppli-teardown-of-the-ipad-2-investor-edition/; http://www.isuppli.com/Teardowns/News/Pages/iPad-2-Carries-Bill-of-Materials-of-$326-60-IHS-iSuppli-Teardown-Analysis-Shows.aspx; http://www.nytimes.com/2011/05/25/sports/basketball/players-accuse-nba-of-failing-to-bargain-in-good-faith.html?_r=1&ref=nationallaborrelationsboard.
Photo: ©Rubberball/Getty images

REVIEW THE CHAPTER

DEMONSTRATION CASE

Barnaby's Bicycle Company manufactures high-quality mountain bikes. The company's managerial accountant has come to you for help. She needs to classify and identify each of the following costs before she can calculate the cost to produce each mountain bike.

Classify each of the costs listed in the chart below into three categories based on the following questions:

1. Can this cost be directly and conveniently traced to each bicycle that is manufactured, or is doing so either not possible or not worth the effort?

2. Is this cost related to manufacturing the bicycles? If so, what type of cost is it? Or is it a nonmanufacturing or period expense?

3. Will the total cost vary with the number of bicycles manufactured and sold, or will it remain the same regardless of how many bikes are produced and sold?

The first item in the chart is completed as an example.

| | QUESTION 1 | | QUESTION 2 | | | | QUESTION 3 | |
| | | | PRODUCT COSTS | | | PERIOD COSTS | COST BEHAVIOR | |
	Direct Cost	Indirect Cost	Direct Materials	Direct Labor	Mfg. Overhead	Nonmfg. Expenses	Variable Cost	Fixed Cost
Alloy tubing used to make the bicycle frames	X		X				X	
Hourly wages paid to employees who cut and weld the alloy tubing								
Factory rent								
Bicycle wheels and tires								
Miscellaneous bicycle components								
Insurance on the factory								
Insurance on the president's company car								

Suggested Solution

| | QUESTION 1 | | QUESTION 2 | | | | QUESTION 3 | |
| | | | PRODUCT COSTS | | | PERIOD COSTS | COST BEHAVIOR | |
	Direct Cost	Indirect Cost	Direct Materials	Direct Labor	Mfg. Overhead	Nonmfg. Expenses	Variable Cost	Fixed Cost
Alloy tubing used to make the bicycle frames	X		X				X	
Hourly wages paid to employees who cut and weld the alloy tubing	X			X			X	
Factory rent		X			X			X
Bicycle wheels and tires	X		X				X	
Miscellaneous bicycle components		X			X		X	
Insurance on the factory		X			X			X
Insurance on the president's company car		X				X		X

CHAPTER SUMMARY

LO 1–1   **Describe the key differences between financial accounting and managerial accounting. p. 5**

- Financial accounting information is used by external stakeholders, such as investors, creditors, and bankers.
- Managerial accounting information is used by managers inside the organization.

- Financial accounting information tends to be reliable, objective, and historical in nature.
- Managerial accounting information tends to be relevant, timely, and future oriented.
- Financial accounting is reported through the income statement, balance sheet, and cash flow statement.
- Managerial accounting relies on a variety of reports targeted at specific decisions, including budgets, cost reports, and performance evaluations.
- Financial accounting reports are prepared on a monthly, quarterly, or annual basis.
- Managerial accounting reports are prepared as needed.
- Financial accounting reports are prepared at the company level.
- Managerial accounting reports are prepared at the divisional or departmental level appropriate to the decision being made.

Describe how managerial accounting is used in different types of organizations to support the key functions of management. p. 6   LO 1–2

- Managerial accounting is used in all types of organizations, including manufacturing, merchandising, and service firms.

- Although managerial accounting often focuses on manufacturing firms, it is becoming increasingly important for service companies and merchandisers, which are gaining importance in today's economy. It is also useful for nonprofit organizations such as universities, charities, and hospitals.

- Regardless of the type of organization, all managers perform the same basic functions:
  - Planning, or setting long-term objectives along with the short-term tactics needed to achieve them.
  - Implementing, or putting the plan into action.
  - Controlling, or monitoring actual results against the plan and making any necessary adjustments.

Describe the importance of ethics, sustainability, and decision analytics in managerial accounting. p. 10   LO 1–3

- Ethics refers to the standards for judging right from wrong, honest from dishonest, and fair from unfair. Managers confront ethical dilemmas that do not have clear-cut answers. They must apply their own personal judgment and values to weigh the pros and cons of alternative courses of action.

- The Sarbanes-Oxley (SOX) Act of 2002 increases managers' responsibility for creating and maintaining an ethical business and reporting environment. It attempts to reduce fraudulent reporting in three key ways:
  - **Opportunity.** SOX requires managers to issue a report that indicates whether the company's internal controls are effective in preventing fraud and inaccurate reporting. The act also places increased responsibility on the board of directors, audit committee, and external auditor.
  - **Incentives.** SOX imposes stiffer penalties, including jail time and monetary fines, for those who commit fraud.
  - **Character.** SOX emphasizes the importance of individual character in preventing fraudulent reporting and requires public companies to implement anonymous tip lines, whistle-blower protection, and codes of ethics.

- Sustainability is an emerging field that allows organizations to achieve economic results while fulfilling their obligations to society and protecting the environment for future generations. The triple bottom line measures a company's performance toward its sustainability goals by including measures of economic success (profit), social impact (people), and environmental impact (planet).

- Decision analytics involves the use of analytical tools and techniques to provide valuable and actionable insights from data so that managers can make more intelligent business decisions. It is referred to as "big data" when the data is so large or complex that it cannot be analyzed using traditional spreadsheets and data bases. Managers can use decision analytics for descriptive, predictive, or prescriptive purposes.

LO 1–4 **Define and give examples of different types of costs. p. 15**

- Costs can be classified in a variety of ways, depending on how the information will be used:
  - Direct costs can be directly and conveniently traced to a specific cost object.
  - Indirect costs either cannot be traced to a specific cost object or are not worth the effort of tracing.
  - Variable costs change, in total, in direct proportion to changes in activity.
  - Fixed costs remain the same, in total, regardless of activity.
  - Manufacturing costs are associated with making a physical product. They can be classified as direct materials, direct labor, or manufacturing overhead.
  - Nonmanufacturing costs are associated with selling a product or service or running the overall business.
  - GAAP requires manufacturing costs to be treated as product costs and nonmanufacturing costs to be treated as period costs.
  - Product costs are assigned to a product as it is being produced; they accumulate in inventory accounts until the product is sold.
  - Period costs are reported as expenses as they are incurred.
  - Relevant costs are future-oriented costs that differ between decision alternatives.
  - Irrelevant costs are those that remain the same regardless of the alternatives and thus will not affect the decision.

KEY TERMS

Budget p. 6
Controlling p. 7
Conversion Costs p. 19
Corporate Social Responsibility (CSR) p. 13
Cost Object p. 16
Differential Costs p. 20
Direct Costs p. 16
Direct Labor p. 19
Direct Materials p. 19
Ethics p. 10
Financial Accounting p. 5
Fixed Costs p. 17
General and Administrative Expenses p. 20

Implementing p. 6
Indirect Costs p. 16
Inventoriable Costs p. 20
Irrelevant Cost p. 20
Managerial Accounting p. 5
Manufacturing Costs p. 19
Manufacturing Firms p. 8
Manufacturing Overhead p. 19
Marketing or Selling Expenses p. 19
Merchandising Companies p. 8
Nonmanufacturing Costs p. 19
Opportunity Cost p. 21
Out-of-Pocket Cost p. 21
3 Ps: People, Profit, and Planet p. 13

Period Costs p. 20
Planning p. 6
Prime Costs p. 19
Product Costs p. 20
Relevant Cost p. 20
Sarbanes-Oxley (SOX) Act of 2002 p. 11
Service Companies p. 9
Sunk Costs p. 21
Sustainability p. 13
Sustainability Accounting p. 12
Triple Bottom Line p. 13
Variable Costs p. 17

PRACTICE MATERIAL

QUESTIONS

1. What is the primary difference between financial accounting and managerial accounting?

2. Explain how the primary difference between financial and managerial accounting results in other differences between the two.

3. Why are traditional, GAAP-based financial statements not necessarily useful to managers and other internal parties?

4. Explain the difference between service companies, merchandising companies, and manufacturing companies.

5. Consider the area within a 3-mile radius of your campus. What service companies, merchandising companies, and manufacturing firms are located within that area?

6. What are the three basic functions of management?

7. How are the three basic management functions interrelated?

8. What are ethics and why is ethical behavior important to managers?

9. What events or factors led to the creation and enactment of the Sarbanes-Oxley Act of 2002?

10. How did the Sarbanes-Oxley Act affect managers' responsibility for creating and maintaining an ethical business and reporting environment?

11. How did the Sarbanes-Oxley Act attempt to reduce fraudulent reporting by addressing opportunity, incentives, and character?

12. According to a recent Statement on Management Accounting (SMA), what are some of the potential benefits of a strong ethical business climate?

13. Why are businesses starting to incorporate sustainability into their business model?

14. What factors does sustainability accounting include that traditional accounting systems do not?

15. What three factors make "big data" difficult to analyze using traditional tools such as spreadsheets and databases.

16. Describe the three types of analytics. Give an example of how a manager at California Pizza Kitchen might use each type of analytics.

17. Think about all of the choices you make on a day-to-day basis: everything from driving versus riding a bike to school or deciding where to have lunch. Pick three decisions you have made today. Identify an out-of-pocket and opportunity cost for each decision.

18. Why is it important for managers to be able to determine the cost of a particular item? Name one decision that a company might make using cost information.

19. Explain the difference between a direct cost and an indirect cost. Take a look at your purse or wallet. Name two direct costs of making your purse or wallet. Name two indirect costs of making it.

20. Explain the difference between fixed and variable costs. Give an example of a cost that varies with the number of

miles you drive your car each week and an example of a cost that is fixed regardless of how many miles you drive your car each week.

21. Explain the difference between relevant and irrelevant costs. What are the two criteria used to determine whether a cost is relevant?

22. Suppose you and your friends are planning a trip for spring break. You have narrowed the destination choices to Panama City, Florida, and Galveston Bay, Texas. List two costs that are relevant to this decision and two costs that are irrelevant to this decision.

23. What are prime costs? Why have they decreased in importance over time?

24. What types of costs are included in manufacturing overhead? Other than direct materials and direct labor, what costs would *not* be included in manufacturing overhead?

25. Why can't prime cost and conversion cost be added together to arrive at total manufacturing cost?

26. What is the difference between product and period costs in terms of how and when they are treated in the financial statements (balance sheet and income statement)?

27. Explain why product costs are also called *inventoriable costs* and how those costs move through a company's financial statements.

28. What triggers the movement of product costs from an asset on the balance sheet to an expense on the income statement?

29. If you wanted to know the total amount of period costs for a company, which financial statement(s) would you consult?

30. Suppose a company accountant incorrectly classified advertising costs as a product cost. What impact would this have on the company's financial statements?

MULTIPLE CHOICE

1. The **primary** difference between financial accounting and managerial accounting is that
   a. Financial accounting is used by internal parties while managerial accounting is used by external parties.
   b. Financial accounting is future oriented while managerial accounting is historical in nature.
   c. Financial accounting is used by external parties while managerial accounting is used by internal parties.
   d. Financial accounting is prepared as needed (perhaps even daily), but managerial accounting is prepared periodically (monthly, quarterly, annually).

2. Which of the following companies is most likely to be considered a manufacturing company?
   a. Burger King.
   b. Abercrombie and Fitch.
   c. Supercuts.
   d. Maytag.

3. Which of the functions of management involves monitoring actual results to see whether the objectives set in the

planning stage are being met and, if necessary, taking corrective action to adjust the objectives or implementation of the plan?
   a. Implementing.
   b. Controlling.
   c. Planning.
   d. Selling.

4. Suppose you have decided that you would like to purchase a new home in five years. To do this, you will need a down payment of approximately $20,000, which means that you need to save $350 each month for the next five years. This is an example of
   a. Directing/Leading.
   b. Controlling.
   c. Planning/Organizing.
   d. Selling.

5. If the number of units produced increases, then
   a. Unit variable costs will increase.
   b. Unit fixed costs will decrease.

c. Total variable costs will remain the same.

d. Total fixed costs will increase.

Use the following information regarding Garcia Company for questions 6–8.

Factory rent	$5,000
Direct labor	8,000
Indirect materials	1,000
Direct materials used	3,500
Sales commissions	2,500
Factory manager's salary	4,000
Advertising	1,500

6. What is Garcia's total manufacturing cost?

   a. $25,500.

   b. $24,000.

   c. $21,500.

   d. $10,000.

7. What is Garcia's prime cost?

   a. $11,500.

   b. $12,500.

   c. $15,500.

   d. $21,000.

8. What is Garcia's manufacturing overhead?

   a. $24,000.

   b. $12,500.

   c. $14,000.

   d. $10,000.

9. Suppose you are trying to decide whether to sell your accounting book at the end of the semester or keep it as a reference book for future courses. If you decide to keep the book, the money you would have received from selling it is a(n)

   a. Sunk cost.

   b. Opportunity cost.

   c. Out-of-pocket cost.

   d. Indirect cost.

10. Which of the following would *not* be treated as a product cost under GAAP?

   a. Direct materials.

   b. Manufacturing supervisor's salary.

   c. Sales commissions.

   d. All of the above are product costs.

 **Find More Learning Solutions on Connect.**

MINI-EXERCISES

LO 1–1   **M1–1 Comparing Financial and Managerial Accounting**

Match each of the following characteristics that describe **financial** accounting, **managerial** accounting, **both** financial and managerial accounting, or **neither** financial nor managerial accounting.

____ **1.** Is future oriented.	**A.** Financial accounting
____ **2.** Is used primarily by external parties.	**B.** Managerial accounting
____ **3.** Is relied on for making decisions.	**C.** Both financial and managerial accounting
____ **4.** Is historical in nature.	**D.** Neither financial nor managerial accounting
____ **5.** Has reports that can be obtained through the company website or requested from the company CFO for publicly traded companies.	

____ **6.** Is reported in aggregate for the company as a whole.

____ **7.** Has reports that may be created daily or even in real time.

____ **8.** Is used mostly by managers within the company.

____ **9.** Must be accurate to help decision makers.

____ **10.** Is always available on the Internet to any interested party.

LO 1–1, 1–2, 1–4   **M1–2 Matching Terminology**

Match each of the terms on the left with the appropriate definition on the right. Not all definitions will be used.

Term	Definition
_____ **1.** Budget	**A.** Accounting information that is aimed at external users
_____ **2.** Controlling	
_____ **3.** Direct Costs	**B.** Accounting information that is aimed at those working inside the organization
_____ **4.** Financial Accounting	
_____ **5.** Fixed Costs	**C.** The establishment of goals and objectives along with the tactics that will be used to achieve them
_____ **6.** General and Administrative Expenses	**D.** The process of putting a plan into action
_____ **7.** Merchandising Companies	**E.** The measurement and monitoring of a company's performance to see if planned objectives are being met
_____ **8.** Product Cost	
_____ **9.** Sunk Costs	**F.** A company that purchases raw materials and converts them into finished products
_____ **10.** Sustainability	**G.** A company that sells manufactured products
	H. The cost of not doing something
	I. Costs that can be reasonably traced to a cost object
	J. Costs that cannot be reasonably traced or are not worth the effort to trace to a cost object
	K. Costs that change in direct proportion to changes in activity level
	L. Costs that remain the same per unit of activity
	M. Costs that vary inversely per unit of activity
	N. Direct materials plus direct labor
	O. Money that has already been spent
	P. Costs that differ between alternatives
	Q. A plan in monetary or financial terms
	R. Inventoriable costs
	S. The ability to meet today's needs without sacrificing the ability of future generations to meet their own needs
	T. Period costs

M1–3 Matching Terminology   LO 1–1, 1–2, 1–4

Match each of the terms on the left with the appropriate definition on the right. Not all definitions will be used.

Term	Definition
_____ **1.** Conversion Costs	**A.** A company that purchases raw materials and converts them into finished products.
_____ **2.** Differential Costs	
_____ **3.** Indirect Costs	**B.** A company that sells manufactured products
_____ **4.** Manufacturing Costs	**C.** Provides information about a company's social and environmental impact
_____ **5.** Manufacturing Firms	
_____ **6.** Nonmanufacturing Costs	**D.** The cost of **not** doing something
_____ **7.** Opportunity Costs	**E.** Costs that can be reasonably traced to a cost object
_____ **8.** Relevant Cost	
_____ **9.** People, Profit, and Planet	**F.** Costs that cannot be reasonably traced or are not worth the effort to trace to a cost object
_____ **10.** Variable Costs	**G.** Costs that remain the same, regardless of the level of activity

H. Costs that remain the same per unit of activity

I. Costs that vary inversely per unit of activity

J. Items that can conveniently be traced to each unit of product

K. Direct materials plus direct labor

L. Direct labor plus manufacturing overhead

M. Direct materials plus direct labor plus manufacturing overhead

N. Costs associated with the running of the business and the selling of the product

O. A plan in monetary or financial terms

P. Information that is useful for decision making

Q. Information that will not make a difference to a decision

R. Money that has already been spent

S. Costs that change between alternatives

T. Triple bottom line

LO 1–2   M1–4 Identifying Management Functions

You were recently hired as a production manager for Medallion Company. You just received a memo regarding a company meeting being held this week. The memo stated that one topic of discussion will be the basic management functions as they relate to the production department. You are expected to lead this discussion. To prepare for the discussion, briefly list the three basic functions of management and how those functions might relate to your position as production manager.

LO 1–3   M1–5 Classifying Sarbanes-Oxley (SOX) Objectives and Requirements

Match each of the following SOX requirements to the corresponding objective by entering the appropriate letter in the space provided.

_____ 1. Establish a hotline for employees to report questionable acts.

_____ 2. Increase maximum fines to $5 million.

_____ 3. Require management to report on effectiveness of internal controls.

_____ 4. Legislate whistle-blower protections.

_____ 5. Require external auditors' report on effectiveness of internal controls.

A. Counteract incentives for fraud.

B. Reduce opportunities for error and fraud.

C. Encourage good character.

LO 1–3   M1–6 Identifying Ethical Dilemmas

The following is a short list of scenarios. Write a brief statement about whether you believe the scenario is an ethical dilemma and, if so, who will be harmed by the unethical behavior.

1. You are a tax accounting professional and a client informs you that some of the receipts used in preparing the tax return have been falsified.
2. A friend gives you his accounting homework assignment. You change his name to yours on the top of the paper and turn in the assignment as your work.
3. You are an employee at a local clothing store. Your manager asks you to sell her a few expensive items priced at $1,200 but charge her only $100.

LO 1–4   M1–7 Classifying Costs

Jackson Lamps manufactures and sells table lamps. Determine whether each of the following is fixed (F) or variable (V).

---- **1.** Lamp shades.

---- **2.** Glue and screws.

---- **3.** CEO's salary.

---- **4.** Assembler's wages.

---- **5.** Rent for the factory.

---- **6.** Plant supervisor's salary.

---- **7.** Depreciation on delivery truck.

---- **8.** Power used for welding equipment.

---- **9.** Sales commissions.

M1–8 Classifying Costs   LO 1–4

Top Shelf Company builds oak bookcases. Determine whether each of the following is a direct material (DM), direct labor (DL), manufacturing overhead (MOH), or a period (P) cost for Top Shelf.

---- **1.** Depreciation on factory equipment.

---- **2.** Depreciation on delivery trucks.

---- **3.** Wood used to build a bookcase.

---- **4.** Production supervisor's salary.

---- **5.** Glue and screws used in the bookcases.

---- **6.** Wages of persons who assemble the bookcases.

---- **7.** Cost to run an ad on local radio stations.

---- **8.** Rent for the factory.

---- **9.** CEO's salary.

---- **10.** Wages of person who sands the wood after it is cut.

M1–9 Classifying and Calculating Cost   LO 1–4

Refer to M1-8. Assume that you have the following information about Top Shelf's costs for the most recent month:

Depreciation on factory equipment	$1,800
Depreciation on delivery trucks	800
Wood used to build bookcases	1,500
Production supervisor's salary	2,800
Glue and screws used in the bookcases	250
Wages of persons who assemble the bookcases	2,500
Cost to run an ad on local radio stations	600
Rent for the factory	3,500
CEO's salary	3,000
Wages of person who sands the wood after it is cut	1,600

Determine each of the following costs for Top Shelf.

1. Direct materials used.

2. Direct labor.

3. Manufacturing overhead.

4. Prime cost.

5. Conversion cost.

6. Total manufacturing cost.

7. Total nonmanufacturing (period) cost.

LO 1–4   **M1–10 Calculating Costs**

Randy Inc. produces and sells tablets. The company incurred the following costs for the May:

Advertising cost for monthly television ads	$ 4,000
Attachable keyboard	18,000
Insurance for delivery truck	400
Factory supervisor's salary	3,100
Marketing manager's salary	2,800
Assembly worker wages	15,000
Miscellaneous soldering material used to seal case	600
Hourly wages for factory security guard	1,750
CEO's salary	6,500
Speakers	4,750

Determine each of the following:

1. Direct material.
2. Direct labor.
3. Manufacturing overhead.
4. Total manufacturing cost.
5. Total period cost.
6. Total variable cost.
7. Total fixed cost.

LO 1–4   **M1–11 Classifying Costs**

You are considering the possibility of pursuing a master's degree after completing your undergraduate degree.

1. List three costs (or benefits) that would be relevant to this decision, including at least one opportunity cost.
2. List two costs that would be irrelevant to this decision.

LO 1–4   **M1–12 Classifying Costs**

Lighten Up Lamps, Inc., manufactures table lamps and other lighting products. For each of the following costs, use an X to indicate the category of product cost and whether it is a prime cost, conversion cost, or both.

	PRODUCT COSTS			Prime Cost	Conversion Cost
	Direct Materials	Direct Labor	Mfg. Overhead		
Production supervisor salary					
Cost of lamp shades					
Wages of person who assembles lamps					
Factory rent					
Wages of person who paints lamps					
Factory utilities					
Screws used to assemble lamps					

LO 1–4   **M1–13 Calculating Missing Amounts**

For each of the following independent cases A through D, compute the missing values in the table below.

Case	Direct Materials	Direct Labor	Manufacturing Overhead	Prime Cost	Conversion Cost
A	$900	$1,300	$2,000	$?	$?
B	400	?	1,325	2,650	?
C	?	700	1,500	2,880	?
D	?	750	?	1,600	2,000

M1–14 Classifying Type of Company   LO 1–2

Indicate whether each of the following businesses would most likely be classified as a service company (S), merchandising company (Mer), or manufacturing company (Man).

_____ **1.** Merry Maids.
_____ **2.** Dell Computer.
_____ **3.** Brinks Security.
_____ **4.** Kmart.
_____ **5.** PetSmart.
_____ **6.** Ford Motor Company.
_____ **7.** Bank One.
_____ **8.** Ralph Lauren.
_____ **9.** Dillard's.
_____ **10.** Sam's Club.

M1–15 Identifying Direct and Indirect Costs for a Service Company   LO 1–4

Refer to M1-14. Choose one of the companies you classified as a service company. For that company, identify two direct costs and two indirect costs. What is the cost object?

M1–16 Identifying Direct and Indirect Costs for a Merchandising Company   LO 1–4

Refer to M1-14. Choose one of the companies you classified as a merchandising company. For that company, identify two direct costs and two indirect costs. What is the cost object?

EXERCISES

E1–1 Making Decisions Using Managerial Accounting   LO 1–1

Suppose you are a sales manager for Books on Wheels, Inc., which makes rolling book carts often used by libraries. The company is considering adding a new product aimed at university students. The new product will be a small, collapsible, wheeled tote designed specifically to aid students in transporting textbooks across campus.

Required:

1. List five questions you and the company would need to answer before proceeding with the development and marketing of this new product.
2. For each question identified in requirement 1, identify the information you would need to answer the question as well as the expected source of that information.
3. Identify three serious consequences of either not obtaining the information you need or obtaining inaccurate information.

E1–2 Identifying Management Functions   LO 1–2

Refer to E1-1. Suppose that, after a thorough investigation, Books on Wheels decided to go forward with the new product aimed at university students. The product, The Campus Cart, has gone into production, and the first units have already been delivered to campuses across the country.

Required:

Match each of the following steps that took place as Books on Wheels moved through the decision making, production, marketing, and sale of The Campus Cart with the correct phase of the management process.

_____	**1.** Identifying five college campuses to serve as test markets.	**A.**	Planning
_____	**2.** Setting the goal of $1 million in annual sales by the year 2018.	**B.**	Implementing
_____	**3.** Hiring workers for the manufacturing facility.	**C.**	Controlling
_____	**4.** Overseeing the production and shipment of The Campus Cart.		

_____ **5.** Preparing one-, three-, and five-year budgets that detail the necessary resources and costs that will be incurred to meet the projected sales forecasts.

_____ **6.** Deciding which new markets to expand into based on the first year's sales results.

_____ **7.** Implementing a bonus system to reward employees for meeting sales and production goals.

_____ **8.** Deciding to spend more advertising dollars in regions where sales were slower than expected.

LO 1–3   **E1–3 Identify sustainability issues affecting the triple bottom line.**

For each of the following sustainability initiatives, indicate whether it will impact social (S), environmental (En), or economic (Ec) factors in the triple bottom line. Include more than one factor as appropriate.

_____ **1.** Implementing a health and wellness program to improve employees' health, reduce stress, improve productivity, and reduce employee turnover.

_____ **2.** Ensuring that all future construction projects are LEED certified.

_____ **3.** Implementing a just-in-time inventory system to reduce inventory costs and improve product quality.

_____ **4.** Providing all employees with glass water bottles to reduce the use of plastic water bottles and the cost of company-sponsored lunches.

_____ **5.** Purchasing web conferencing software to give employees the flexibility to work remotely, reduce the number of miles they must commute to work, and save on travel costs for off-site meetings.

_____ **6.** Creating a code of conduct for suppliers to establish guidelines on labor wages, working conditions, health and safety.

_____ **7.** Expanding into international markets to increase market share.

LO 1–4   **E1–4 Classifying Costs**

Suppose you have just finished your third year of college and expect to graduate with a bachelor's degree in accounting after completing two more semesters of coursework. The salary for entry-level positions with an accounting degree is approximately $48,000 in your area. Shelton Industries has just offered you a position in its northwest regional office. The position has an annual salary of $40,000 and would not require you to complete your undergraduate degree. If you accept the position, you would have to move to Seattle.

Required:

Identify with an X whether each of the following costs/benefits would be relevant to the decision to accept the offer from Shelton or stay in school. You may have more than one X for each item.

	Relevant Cost or Benefit	Irrelevant Cost or Benefit	Sunk Cost	Opportunity Cost
$40,000 salary from Shelton				
Anticipated $48,000 salary with an accounting degree				
Tuition and books for years 1–3 of college				
Cost to relocate to Seattle				
Tuition and books for remaining two semesters				
$19,000 from your part-time job, which you plan to keep until you graduate				
Cost to rent an apartment in Seattle (assume you are currently living at home with your parents)				
Food and entertainment expenses, which are expected to be the same in Seattle as where you currently live				
Increased promotional opportunities that will come from having a college degree				

E1–5 Classifying Costs   LO 1–4

Wilson's Furniture Company incurs the costs listed in the following table.

Required:

Use an X to categorize each of the following costs. You may have more than one X for each item.

	PRODUCT COSTS				
	Direct Materials	Direct Labor	Mfg. Overhead	Variable Cost	Fixed Cost
Factory equipment depreciation					
Factory supervisor salary					
Factory utilities					
Factory insurance					
Furniture assembler wages					
Furniture lumber					
Glue and screws					
Factory property taxes					

E1–6 Classifying Costs   LO 1–4

Dirk Inc. produces and sells model cars. It incurs the costs listed in the following table.

Required:

Use an X to categorize each of the following costs. You may have more than one X for each item.

	PRODUCT COSTS			Period Cost	Variable Cost	Fixed Cost
	Direct Materials	Direct Labor	Mfg. Overhead			
CFO salary						
Factory utilities						
Factory supervisor salary						
Store equipment depreciation						
Factory equipment depreciation						
Advertising (monthly)						
Model car tires						
Store property taxes						
Factory insurance						
Factory worker wages						
Marketing manager salary						
Glue and screws						
Machine maintenance costs						

LO 1–4   **E1–7 Classifying Costs**

Seth's Skateboard Company incurs the costs listed in the following table.

Required:

Use an X to categorize each of the following costs. You may have more than one X for each item.

	PRODUCT COSTS			Period Cost	Prime Cost	Conversion Cost
	Direct Materials	Direct Labor	Mfg. Overhead			
Production supervisor salary						
Cost of fiberglass						
Wages of assembly person						
Sales commission						
Cost of high-grade wheels						
Screws						
Factory rent						
Wages of skateboard painter						
Factory utilities						
Utilities for corporate office						

E1–8 Calculating Costs

LO 1–4

Cotton White, Inc., makes specialty clothing for chefs. The company reported the following costs for 2018:

Factory rent	$42,000
Company advertising	18,000
Wages paid to seamstresses	75,000
Depreciation on salespersons' vehicles	25,000
Thread	1,000
Utilities for factory	22,000
Cutting room supervisor's salary	30,000
President's salary	75,000
Premium quality cotton material	42,000
Buttons	750
Factory insurance	15,000
Depreciation on sewing machines	6,000
Wages paid to cutters	50,000

Required:

Compute the following for Cotton White:

1. Direct materials.
2. Direct labor.
3. Manufacturing overhead.
4. Total manufacturing cost.
5. Prime cost.
6. Conversion cost.
7. Total period cost.

E1–9 Calculating Costs

LO 1–4

Cartwell Inc. makes picture frames which are sold in a local retail store and through various websites.

Wood for frames	$10,000
Rent for retail store	3,000
Depreciation on office equipment	400
Assembly worker wages	2,000
CEO's salary	3,500
Glue and nails	200
Online sales commissions	1,450
Glass for frames	4,000
Depreciation on factory equipment	600
Factory utilities	375
Stain for frames	425

Required:

Determine each of the following:

1. Direct material.
2. Direct labor.
3. Manufacturing overhead.

4. Total manufacturing cost.
5. Total period cost.
6. Total variable cost.
7. Total fixed cost.
8. Total prime cost.
9. Total conversion cost.

LO 1–4   **E1–10 Calculating Missing Amounts**

For each of the following independent cases (A through E), compute the missing values in the table:

Case	Prime Cost	Conversion Cost	Direct Materials	Direct Labor	Manufacturing Overhead	Total Manufacturing Cost
A	$?	$?	$2,000	$1,500	$3,500	$?
B	6,600	11,500	2,300	?	7,200	?
C	?	8,000	1,400	3,250	?	9,400
D	?	?	?	2,100	3,100	6,200
E	11,500	20,500	3,800	?	?	?

LO 1–4   **E1–11 Classifying and Calculating Costs**

The following information is available for Wonderway, Inc., for 2018:

Factory rent	$40,000
Company advertising	20,000
Wages paid to laborers	82,000
Depreciation for president's vehicle	8,000
Indirect production labor	1,800
Utilities for factory	36,000
Production supervisor's salary	30,000
President's salary	60,000
Direct materials used	34,500
Sales commissions	7,500
Factory insurance	12,000
Depreciation on factory equipment	26,000

Required:

Calculate each of the following costs for Wonderway:

1. Direct labor.
2. Manufacturing overhead.
3. Prime cost.
4. Conversion cost.
5. Total manufacturing cost.
6. Period expenses.

LO 1–4   **E1–12 Classifying Costs**

Blockett Company makes automobile sunshades and incurs the costs listed in the table below.

Required:

Use an X to categorize each of the following costs. You may have more than one X for each item.

| | Period Cost | PRODUCT COSTS | | | Prime Cost | Conversion Cost |
		Direct Materials	Direct Labor	Mfg. Overhead		
Company president's salary						
Factory rent						
Cost of reflective material						
Wages of material cutter						
Wages of office receptionist						
Thread and glue						
Depreciation for salesperson's car						
Factory supervisor's salary						
Factory utilities						
Factory insurance						

E1–13 Classifying and Calculating Costs   LO 1–4

Noteworthy, Inc., produces and sells small electronic keyboards. Assume that you have the following information about Noteworthy's costs for the most recent month.

Depreciation on factory equipment	$ 800
Depreciation on CEO's company car	100
Speakers used in the keyboard	1,100
Production supervisor's salary	2,800
Glue and screws used in the keyboards	370
Wages of persons who install the speakers	3,000
Cost to run an ad on local radio stations	600
Utilities for the factory	1,200
Personnel manager's salary	2,500
Wages of person who attaches legs to keyboards	1,950

Required:

Determine each of the following for Noteworthy:

1. Total product cost.
2. Prime cost.
3. Manufacturing overhead.
4. Direct labor.
5. Conversion cost.
6. Total variable cost (with number of units produced as the activity).
7. Total fixed cost (with number of units produced as the activity).

E1–14 Identifying Relevant and Irrelevant Costs   LO 1–4

Suppose that your brother, Raymond, recently bought a new laptop computer for $800 to use in his land surveying business. After purchasing several add-on components for $400, he realized that they are not compatible with the laptop and, therefore, he cannot use the computer for its intended purpose of mapping land coordinates using GPS satellites. He has also purchased a one-year service agreement and warranty for the add-on components for $75. The computer cannot be returned, but Raymond has found a new laptop costing $1,200 that will work with his GPS mapping components. Raymond is trying to decide what to do now and has asked your advice.

Required:

1. Identify the costs that are relevant to Raymond's decision.
2. Are there any costs that are irrelevant?
3. Suppose that Raymond made the following statement: "I can't get a new computer now. I have to get my money's worth from the old one." Is Raymond's logic correct?

LO 1–4   **E1–15 Calculating Missing Amounts**

For each of the following independent cases (A–E), compute the missing values in the table:

Case	Prime Cost	Conversion Cost	Direct Materials	Direct Labor	Manufacturing Overhead	Total Manufacturing Cost
A	$ 9,400	$ 16,100	$ 4,300	$?	$11,000	$?
B	?	?	12,000	7,300	24,500	43,800
C	55,300	107,500	43,200	?	?	?
D	?	47,350	21,400	13,250	?	68,750
E	?	?	?	15,100	22,900	55,700

LO 1–4   **E1–16 Explaining Manufacturing Cost Categories**

Manufacturing costs can be classified into three categories—direct materials, direct labor, and manufacturing overhead. Over the years, manufacturing companies have changed significantly with advances in technology and the automation of many manufacturing processes.

Required:

Explain how the relative proportion of materials, labor, and overhead is likely to have changed over the last 100 years. Be specific in your discussion of which types of costs have increased and which have decreased.

LO 1–4   **E1–17 Explaining Effects of Cost Misclassification**

Donna is a cost accountant for Northwind Corp. She is very efficient and hard-working; however, she occasionally transposes numbers when recording transactions. While working late recently, Donna accidentally recorded $19,000 of advertising cost instead of the correct $91,000. The transaction was correctly recorded in all other respects.

Required:

Explain how Donna's error will affect the following:

1. Manufacturing Costs.
2. Inventory.
3. Cost of Goods Sold.
4. Period Expenses.
5. Net Income.

GROUP A PROBLEMS

LO 1–1   **PA1–1 Comparing Financial and Managerial Accounting**

You have been asked to take part in an upcoming Young Professionals meeting in your area. The program planned for the evening will cover many aspects of today's business world. Specifically, you have been asked to explain why there are two types of accounting—financial and managerial—and why they are both relevant to a company's employees. The program director would like for you to cover differences between the two types of accounting as well as how each type plays a role within today's competitive environment.

You will have 15 minutes for your presentation plus a 15-minute question-and-answer period at the end. Your audience is composed primarily of entry-level managers from all fields (marketing, human resources, production, etc.). Assume that they all have some familiarity with accounting, but few are practicing accountants.

Required:

1. Prepare a detailed outline identifying your topic of discussion.
2. List at least five questions you may be asked during the question-and-answer period. Briefly discuss your answers to these questions.

PA1–2 Identifying Management Functions   LO 1–2

Your friend, Suzie Whitson, has designed a new type of outdoor toy that helps children learn basic concepts such as colors, numbers, and shapes. Suzie's product will target two groups: day care centers in warm climates and home school programs. Suzie has come to you for help in getting her idea off the ground. She has never managed a business before and is not sure what functions she will need to perform to make her venture successful.

Required:

Briefly explain to Suzie the three major functions of management. For each function, give three examples of questions that Suzie will need to answer to make her business venture a success.

PA1–3 Identifying and Resolving Ethical Dilemmas   LO 1–3

You are one of three partners who own and operate Mary's Maid Service. The company has been operating for seven years. One of the other partners has always prepared the company's annual financial statements. Recently, you proposed that the statements be audited each year because it would benefit the partners and prevent possible disagreements about the division of profits. The partner who prepares the statements proposed that his Uncle Ray, who has a lot of financial experience, do the job for a low cost. Your other partner remained silent.

Required:

1. What position would you take on the proposal? Justify your response.
2. What would you recommend? Give the basis for your recommendation.

PA1–4 Classifying Costs; Calculating Total Costs; Identifying Impact of   LO 1–4
**   Misclassification**

Assume that Suzie Whitson (PA1-2) has decided to begin production of her outdoor children's toy. Her company is Jiffy Jet and costs for last month follow.

Factory rent	$ 3,200
Company advertising	1,000
Wages paid to assembly workers	30,000
Depreciation for salespersons' vehicles	2,000
Screws	500
Utilities for factory	900
Assembly supervisor's salary	3,500
Sandpaper	150
President's salary	6,000
Plastic tubing	4,200
Paint	250
Sales commissions	1,200
Factory insurance	1,000
Depreciation on cutting machines	2,000
Wages paid to painters	7,500

Required:

1. Identify each of the preceding costs as either a product or a period cost. If the cost is a product cost, decide whether it is for direct materials (DM), direct labor (DL), or manufacturing overhead (MOH).
2. Identify each of the preceding costs as variable or fixed cost.

3. Determine the total cost for each of the following:
   a. Direct materials.
   b. Direct labor.
   c. Manufacturing overhead.
   d. Prime cost.
   e. Conversion cost.
   f. Total product cost.
   g. Total period cost.
   h. Total variable cost.
   i. Total fixed cost.

4. Suppose all period costs were incorrectly identified as product costs. What impact could that have on Jiffy Jet's financial statements? Be specific.

GROUP B PROBLEMS

LO 1–4   **PB1–1 Comparing Product and Period Costs**

You have been asked to take part in an upcoming Young Professionals meeting in your area. The program planned for the evening focuses on today's manufacturing environment. Specifically, you have been asked to explain how manufacturing firms determine how much it costs to make their product and why some costs are initially recorded as inventory while other costs are expensed immediately. The program director would like for you to (1) discuss the rules for determining whether a cost should be treated as a product cost or period cost and (2) explain the types of costs that would be included in each category, how each flows through the accounting system, and the implications of the distinction between product costs and period costs for financial reporting (income statement versus balance sheet).

You will have 15 minutes for your presentation plus a 15-minute question-and-answer period at the end. Your audience is composed primarily of entry-level production personnel although people from other fields (marketing, human resources, production, etc.) will be attending. Assume that they all have some familiarity with accounting but few are practicing accountants.

Required:

1. Prepare a detailed outline identifying your topic of discussion.
2. List at least five questions you may be asked during the question-and-answer period. Briefly discuss your answers to these questions.

LO 1–2   **PB1–2 Identifying Management Functions**

Your friend, Maria Cottonwood, has designed a new type of fire extinguisher that is very small and easy to use. It will target two groups of people: people who have trouble operating heavy, traditional extinguishers (e.g., the elderly or people with disabilities) and people who need to store extinguishers in small spaces such as a vehicle. Maria has come to you for help in getting her idea off the ground. She has never managed a business before and she is not sure what functions she will need to perform to make her venture successful.

Required:

Briefly explain to Maria the three major functions of management. For each function, give three examples of questions that Maria will need to answer to make her business venture a success.

LO 1–3   **PB1–3 Identifying and Resolving Ethical Dilemmas**

When some people think about inventory theft, they imagine a shoplifter running out of a store with goods stuffed inside a jacket or bag. But that's not what the managers at the Famous Footwear store on Chicago's Madison Street were dealing with. Their own employees were the ones stealing the inventory. One scam involved dishonest cashiers who would let their friends take a pair of Skechers without paying for them. To make it look like the shoes had been bought, cashiers would ring up a sale, but instead of charging $50 for shoes, they would charge only $2 for a bottle of shoe polish. When the company's managers saw a drop in gross profit, they decided to put the accounting system to work. In just two years, the company cut its Madison Street inventory losses in half. Here's how a newspaper described the store's improvements:

> ### Retailers Crack Down on Employee Theft
> *SouthCoast Today,* September 10, 2000, Chicago
> By Calmetta Coleman, *Wall Street Journal* Staff Writer
>
> . . . Famous Footwear installed a chainwide register-monitoring system to
> sniff out suspicious transactions, such as unusually large numbers of
> refunds or voids, or repeated sales of cheap goods.
>
> . . . [B]efore an employee can issue a cash refund, a second worker must
> be present to see the customer and inspect the merchandise.
>
> . . . [T]he chain has set up a toll-free hotline for employees to use to
> report suspicions about co-workers.

These improvements in inventory control came as welcome news for investors and creditors of Brown Shoe Company, the company that owns Famous Footwear.

Required:

1. Explain how the register-monitoring system would allow Famous Footwear to cut down on employee theft.
2. Think of and describe at least four different parties that are harmed by the type of inventory theft described in this case.

PB1–4 Classifying Costs, Calculating Total Costs, and Identifying Impact of Classifications   LO 1–4

Assume that Maria Cottonwood (PB1-2) has decided to begin production of her fire extinguisher. Her company is Blaze Be Gone, whose costs for last month follow.

Factory rent	$ 2,000
Company advertising	500
Wages paid to assembly workers	25,000
Depreciation for salespersons' vehicles	1,000
Screws	250
Utilities for factory	800
Production supervisor's salary	4,000
Sandpaper	150
President's salary	6,000
Sheet metal	7,500
Paint	750
Sales commissions	1,700
Factory insurance	2,000
Depreciation on factory machinery	5,000
Wages paid to painters	5,500

Required:

1. Identify each of the preceding costs as either a product or a period cost. If the cost is a product cost, decide whether it is for direct materials (DM), direct labor (DL), or manufacturing overhead (MOH).
2. Identify each of the preceding costs as variable or fixed cost.
3. Determine the total amount for each of the following:
   a. Direct materials.
   b. Direct labor.
   c. Manufacturing overhead.
   d. Prime cost.

  e. Conversion cost.
  f. Total product cost.
  g. Total period cost.
  h. Total variable cost.
  i. Total fixed cost.

4. Explain why the depreciation on the salespersons' vehicles is treated differently than the depreciation on the factory machines. How might this difference impact Maria's financial statements in terms of the balance sheet and income statement?

SKILLS DEVELOPMENT CASES

LO 1–4   **S1–1** **Video Case Assignment: Identifying Manufacturing Costs**

©McGraw-Hill Education

Go to www.YouTube.com and search for **How It's Made,** a television show produced by the Discovery Channel that shows how thousands of products and services are created. Find a product that interests you by browsing through the episode list or using search terms such as *baseball bats* or *stackable potato chips.*

Watch the video and answer the following questions:
- What product did you choose? Briefly describe how the product is made.
- What are the major material inputs into the product? Pick one type of material used to make this product and find out how much it costs. List one decision that managers might make based on the cost of materials.
- Did you observe any direct labor in the video? Did you observe any indirect labor? What is the difference?
- List three examples of manufacturing overhead that you observed in the video. How does manufacturing overhead differ from direct materials and direct labor?
- How much do you think it costs to make a single unit of this product? List two decisions that managers would make based on the cost of the product.
- List two costs the company incurs that are not related to **making** the product. How and why are these costs treated differently than the manufacturing costs identified previously?

LO 1–4   **S1–2** **Identifying Changes in Manufacturing Process and Costs Due to Automation**

In recent years, many companies have invested in equipment to automate processes that were once performed manually. A simple example is a drive-through car wash, where robots wash and dry the cars rather than people.

Required:

Think of another company that might upgrade to an automated system and answer the following questions.

1. What physical changes would the conversion to automation cause in the way the company does business?

2. What impact, both positive and negative, might automation have on employee morale?

3. What impact might automation have on the skill level of the company's workforce?

4. How might automation affect the quality of the product and the efficiency of the company's processes?

5. How would you expect automation to affect direct materials, direct labor, and overhead costs? Would you expect any of these costs to increase or decrease?

6. How would you expect automation to affect variable costs and fixed costs? Would you expect either of these costs to increase or decrease?

7. How might automation affect the price consumers pay for the product?

8. How might automation affect the company's bottom line, both immediately and several years in the future?

LO 1–2   **S1–3** **Identifying Service, Merchandising, and Manufacturing Firms: Internet Research**

As discussed in the chapter, companies are often classified into one of three categories: service, merchandising, and manufacturing.

Required:

1. Choose one well-known company from each category and explore that company's website. On the website, find a brief company description as well as the most recent published financial statements. Based on the company description, support your categorization of the company as service, merchandising, or manufacturing. If the company falls into more than one of these categories, describe how.

2. Look at the income statement and balance sheet for the company and list any factors that would support your categorization of the company as a service, merchandising, or manufacturing organization.

S1–4 Interviewing Local Manager to Identify Sustainability Initiatives

LO 1–3

Required:

Arrange a visit with a local business and interview the manager about the firm's sustainability goals and initiatives. The objective of the interview is to gain an understanding of what the company is currently doing in the area of sustainability and to make recommendations for actions the company could take to improve its triple bottom line. Some potential interview questions are listed below:

1. What does sustainability mean to you and to your business?

2. Have you implemented any sustainability initiatives over the past five years.

3. Have you heard of the triple bottom line? If so, what are you doing to enhance performance in the three key areas? If not, describe the triple bottom line for them and ask what they are doing to to enhance performance in the three key areas.

4. What does your company do to enhance or serve the community in which you operate?

5. Describe how you and your employees are rewarded. Is it through annual raises, bonuses, perks, or promotions? Are these rewards linked to performance? How do you measure performance?

6. Do you think implementing sustainable business practices can help attract and retain better employees or more loyal customers?

S1–5 Using decision analytics to reduce energy consumption and enhance sustainability at California Pizza Kitchen

LO 1–3

The following example is adapted from a real-life case study developed by ENGIE Insight, a technology-enabled energy consulting company that helps companies identify opportunities to reduce energy consumption/spending and manage its energy resources.

When the recession hit in 2009, restaurants like California Pizza Kitchen that rely heavily on consumer discretionary spending were among the first to take a hit. As consumers tightened their wallets and stopped eating out as often, CPK saw its sales drop and growth rate come to a halt. When company expenses didn't drop at the same rate, managers at CPK were forced to look closely at their expenses to identify opportunities for savings. One big ticket item that stuck out like a sore thumb was a $21 million dollar line item for energy expense. Restaurants are a big consumers of energy due to the demand for heating, cooling, and lighting, as well as utilities to run cooking equipment and sanitation devices.

According to a CPK Senior Vice President: "Once we realized how much we were spending on that one operating expense, it was clear that this was where we had the opportunity to make the biggest impact in terms of cost-cutting."

To achieve this goal, CPK engaged ENGIE Insight to analyze its energy consumption data and identify opportunities to reduce consumption/spending and manage its energy resources. ENGIE Insight was already processing and auditing the company's energy expenses and had developed a vast database of energy consumption and trends for more than 250 CPK locations.

Consultants at ENGIE developed integrated performance reports that allowed CPK managers to compare energy consumption across locations that were similar in terms of climate, size, and hours of operation, as well as benchmark against industry averages provided by the Department of Energy. This allowed CPK managers to identify the restaurant chain's worst performing locations, analyze what made them outliers in terms of energy use, and put solutions in place that would get them in line with the portfolio average.

"These reports made it possible for our company to understand where we are and navigate where we can go," said a CPK executive. "We were able to establish a performance benchmark, set goals, and report very specifically on our progress."

Armed with this data, CPK managers were able to quickly identify and prioritize areas for improvement, such as

- Requesting that all HVAC service providers conduct free HVAC inspections and tune-ups.
- Switching to compact fluorescent light bulbs.
- Adjusting temperature set points to maintain consistent results.
- Closing window shades.
- Running dishwashers only when dish trays are full, which reduces water, chemical, and energy usage.
- Installing low-flow aerators on hand sinks.
- Performing monthly reviews of restaurant results to identify the worst performers.

These relatively small changes had an immediate impact on the company's energy consumption and spending, with electricity usage decreasing by 4.3 percent and natural gas usage decreasing by 2.82 percent in the first year alone.

According to ENGIE's experts, California Pizza Kitchen's energy problems were not uncommon. While CPK managers were experts in managing the basic costs associated with running their business, they lacked a fundamental understanding of energy's impact on the bottom line and were unaware of the best actions to take to reduce energy costs. Once equipped with the right data, they were able to translate what was once a big unknown into big savings.

Required:

1. Explain whether utility expenses are considered a variable, fixed, or mixed cost.
2. Describe how managers at CPK used the energy performance reports for the functions of planning, implementing, and controlling.
3. Describe how the energy initiative at CPK impacted its sustainability goals. What elements of the triple bottom line were affected and how?
4. Explain how CPK's energy initiative relied on descriptive analytics, predictive analytics, and prescriptive analytics. What type of analytic expertise do consultant firms such as ENGIE provide?

2

Job Order Costing

CHAPTER TWO

YOUR LEARNING OBJECTIVES

LO 2–1 Describe the key differences between job order costing and process costing.

LO 2–2 Describe the source documents used to track direct materials and direct labor costs to the job cost sheet.

LO 2–3 Calculate a predetermined overhead rate and use it to apply manufacturing overhead cost to jobs.

LO 2–4 Describe how costs flow through the accounting system in job order costing.

LO 2–5 Calculate and dispose of overapplied or underapplied manufacturing overhead.

LO 2–6 Calculate the cost of goods manufactured and cost of goods sold.

LO 2–7 Apply job order costing to a service setting.

LO 2–S1 Prepare journal entries to record manufacturing and nonmanufacturing costs in a job order cost system.

FOCUS COMPANY: HGTV

Have you ever watched one of the those house-flipping shows on HGTV, such as Fixer Upper, Flip or Flop, or Property Brothers? While the characters on these shows are "reality TV" celebrities, most of them started out as entrepreneurs who used their creative talents to transform outdated homes into something buyers would be willing to pay money for.

In this chapter, we use a fictitious house-flipping example to illustrate how you would keep track of the costs of remodeling a home and thus the profit you would earn if you sold it for more than its cost. Because each project is unique and requires different amounts of materials, labor, and overhead, we will track the cost of each job or project using job order costing.

In the next few chapters, you will learn about several different cost systems. The characteristics of the cost systems will vary depending on the type of product or service the company sells and the method used to assign costs to those products or services. But the ultimate objective of all cost systems is the same: to determine the cost of something specific, such as a product, a service, a department, a process, or an activity. Later chapters will then explore how managers can use cost and other types of information to make decisions, plan for the future, control spending, and improve performance. Let's start by comparing two types of cost systems: job order costing and process costing.

Job order versus process costing	Assign manufacturing costs to jobs	Record the flow of costs in job order costing	Overapplied or underapplied manufacturing overhead	Prepare the cost of goods manufactured report	Job order costing in a service firm
• Process costing • Job order costing	• Manufacturing cost categories • Materials requisition form • Direct labor time tickets • Job cost sheet • Predetermined overhead rates	• Record the purchase and issue of materials • Record labor costs • Record applied manufacturing overhead • Record actual manufacturing overhead • Transfer costs to finished goods inventory and cost of goods sold • Record non-manufacturing costs	• Calculate overapplied or underapplied manufacturing overhead		

Job Order versus Process Costing

Learning Objective 2–1
Describe the key differences between job order costing and process costing.

Imagine that you go out to dinner with a friend. You are on a limited budget, so you order the cheapest thing on the menu and a glass of ice water. Meanwhile, your friend orders two drinks, an appetizer, entrée, and dessert. When it is time to pay the bill, would it make more sense to split the check equally or get a separate bill for each person at the table?

This simple scenario highlights the basic difference between job order and process costing. Process costing is similar to splitting the check, where the total cost is spread equally over the number of units (or in the case of a meal, the number of people at the table). This simple method works well as long as the cost of each unit (or meal) is about the same.

With job order costing, a separate cost record is kept for each unique product or customer, similar to getting separate checks at a restaurant. This method makes sense when some products or customers are more costly to produce or serve than others. Job order costing is used by companies that provide customized products or services, such as a house flipping business, a custom cabinet manufacturer, or interior design firm.

The key difference between job order and process costing is whether the company's products or services are heterogeneous (different) or homogeneous (similar). See Exhibit 2–1 for a summary of other differences between job order and process costing.

PROCESS COSTING

Process costing is used by companies that make **standardized** or **homogeneous** products or services, such as:

- Coca-Cola beverages.
- Kraft macaroni and cheese.
- Charmin toilet tissue.
- Exxon petroleum products.

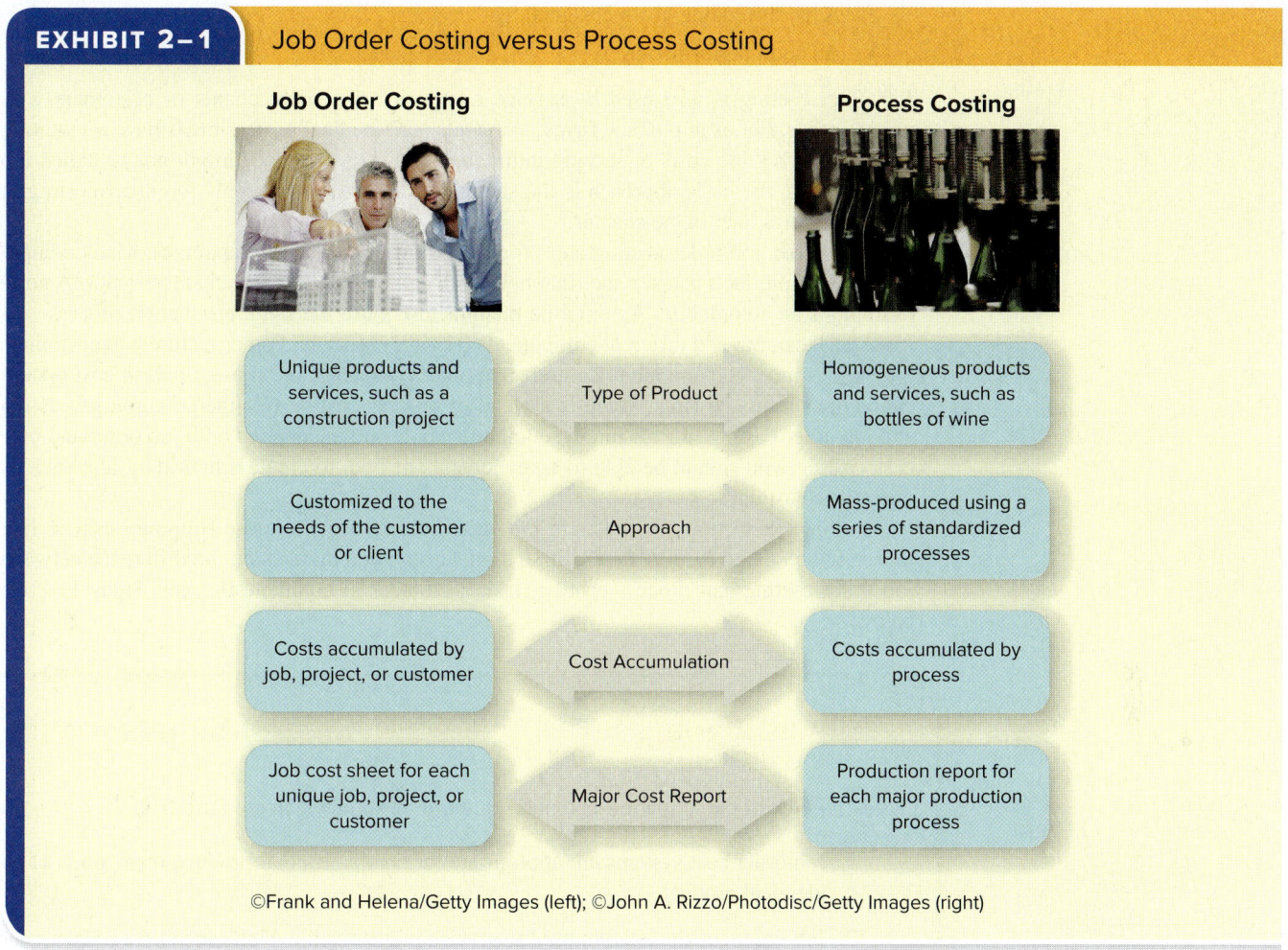

EXHIBIT 2–1 Job Order Costing versus Process Costing

Job Order Costing | | **Process Costing**

Job Order Costing		Process Costing
Unique products and services, such as a construction project	Type of Product	Homogeneous products and services, such as bottles of wine
Customized to the needs of the customer or client	Approach	Mass-produced using a series of standardized processes
Costs accumulated by job, project, or customer	Cost Accumulation	Costs accumulated by process
Job cost sheet for each unique job, project, or customer	Major Cost Report	Production report for each major production process

©Frank and Helena/Getty Images (left); ©John A. Rizzo/Photodisc/Getty Images (right)

These, and many other common products, are produced using a standardized production process so that each unit of the product is identical to the next. Because each unit is the same, companies that make these products do not need to track the cost of each unit individually. Instead, process costing breaks the production process down into its basic steps, or processes, and then averages the total cost of each process over the number of units produced. The basic process costing formula is

$$\text{Average Unit Cost} = \frac{\text{Total Cost}}{\text{Total Units Produced}}$$

Although this formula makes process costing sound simple, a few questions complicate its use in the real world. For example, how much cost should a wine producer such as Fetzer Vineyards assign to a barrel of wine that is still in process—when all of the ingredients (harvested grapes) have been added but the aging process is not yet complete? These issues will be discussed in the next chapter, which focuses specifically on process costing.

JOB ORDER COSTING

Job order costing is used in companies that offer **customized** or **unique** products or services. Unlike process costing, in which each unit is identical to the next, companies use job order costing when each unit or customer differs from the next. Examples include

- A custom home built by Toll Brothers.
- A 747 aircraft built by Boeing.

- A royal wedding gown designed by Alexander McQueen.
- An audit performed by PricewaterhouseCoopers.

Job order costing is also used by service companies that serve clients or customers with unique needs. For example, law firms, architects, and medical professionals have accounting systems to track the costs of serving individual clients. Although it might not be called job order costing, the basic approach is the same. We discuss how to apply job order costing in serving settings later in the chapter.

Of course, job order costing and process costing represent two extremes. Many companies provide products and services that have both common and unique characteristics. A good example is an automobile. Automobile manufacturers use the same production processes to make each car, but add different components (engines, seats, and other features) to customize the various models. Auto manufacturers and other companies often use a hybrid cost system called **operations costing**, which is a blend of process costing (for the common processes) and job order costing (for the unique components). If you understand both job order and process costing, you should be able to take elements of both to create a hybrid system such as operations costing.

In the next section, we illustrate job order costing using a house flipping business like those seen on many HGTV shows. First, to make sure you understand the difference between job order costing and process costing, take a moment to complete the Self-Study Practice below.

 How's it going?   Self-Study Practice

Indicate which of the following statements are true (T) and which are false (F).

_____ 1. Job order cost systems are appropriate for companies that produce many units of an identical product.

_____ 2. Job order costing is often used in service industries in which each client or customer has unique requirements.

_____ 3. A builder of custom swimming pools is more likely to use process costing than job order costing.

_____ 4. A company such as Coca-Cola is more likely to use a process costing system than a job order cost system.

_____ 5. In process costing, costs are averaged to determine the unit cost of homogeneous goods and services.

After you have finished, check your answers against the solutions in the margin.

Solution to Self-Study Practice

1. F
2. T
3. F
4. T
5. T

Assign Manufacturing Costs to Jobs

MANUFACTURING COST CATEGORIES

As you learned in Chapter 1, manufacturing costs are divided into three categories:

- **Direct materials** are the major material inputs that can be directly and conveniently traced to each project or job. Examples of direct materials used in flipping a home include cabinets, flooring, fixtures, paint, and appliances. Incidental materials or supplies that are not worth the effort of tracing to specific jobs would be counted as indirect materials and included in manufacturing overhead.

- **Direct labor** is the hands-on labor that can be directly and conveniently traced to each job. Examples of direct labor would include workers who demolish and rebuild walls; install cabinets, fixtures, and flooring; and paint. Labor supervision or project management would be considered an indirect cost and included in manufacturing overhead.

- **Manufacturing overhead** includes all other **indirect** manufacturing costs, or those that cannot be directly or conveniently traced to a specific project or job. Examples of the manufacturing overhead required to renovate a house include indirect materials, indirect labor, project supervision, depreciation on construction equipment, and utilities and insurance incurred during the renovation process.

The goal of a job order costing system is to track or accumulate the costs of a each unique product, project, or service. These costs are recorded on a document called the **job cost sheet**, which provides a detailed record of the total cost of each job. For direct materials and direct labor, all we need is a good record-keeping system that uses **source documents** to trace these direct costs to specific jobs. But manufacturing overhead, by definition, is not traceable to specific products or jobs. Instead, we need a systematic way of **assigning** the indirect manufacturing overhead cost to jobs.

Refer to Exhibit 2–2 for an illustration of how the three types of manufacturing costs are assigned to jobs in a job order cost system.

The most important thing to notice in Exhibit 2–2 is that direct materials and direct labor costs are assigned to jobs differently than manufacturing overhead costs. Direct materials are traced to jobs using a source document called a materials requisition form. Direct labor is traced to jobs using labor time tickets. Manufacturing overhead is assigned to jobs using a predetermined overhead rate, which will be discussed in the next section of this chapter.

Let's start by assigning direct costs to specific jobs using materials requisition forms and direct labor time tickets. For our example, assume you have started a house flipping business with one of your college classmates. He/she provided the start-up capital to buy several "fixer

COACH'S TIP

In a manual (paper-based) accounting system, a source document is a hard copy document similar to the receipt you get when you buy something at a store. As companies move to electronic systems that record and store information digitally, they use technology such as bar codes, computer scanning devices, and other tools to track costs. For simplicity, we illustrate the "old-fashioned" method using paper documents to trace direct materials and direct labor costs to specific jobs.

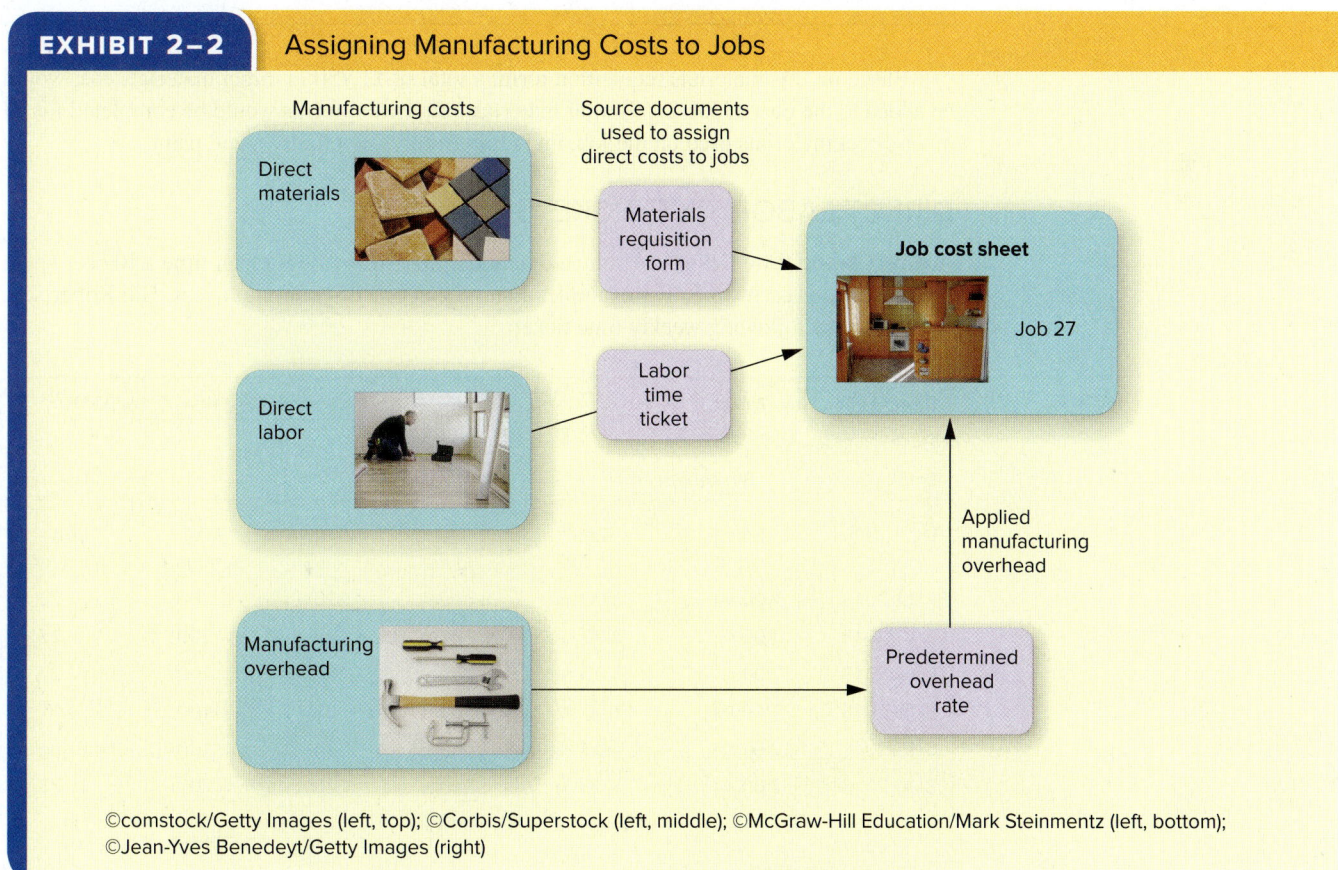

EXHIBIT 2–2 Assigning Manufacturing Costs to Jobs

©comstock/Getty Images (left, top); ©Corbis/Superstock (left, middle); ©McGraw-Hill Education/Mark Steinmentz (left, bottom); ©Jean-Yves Benedeyt/Getty Images (right)

uppers" in your college town. You are responsible for managing the business and have hired a general contractor to oversee the day-to-day operations. You like to review weekly status reports showing the costs incurred on each project. One of the flips currently in process is a 3-bedroom "fixer upper" located at 2719 N. Willow Drive. This project is referred to as Job 27 in the accounting system. You are also about to start work on a new project that is labelled Job 28.

MATERIALS REQUISITION FORM

Learning Objective 2–2

Describe the source documents used to track direct materials and direct labor costs to the job cost sheet.

Before materials can be used on a job, a **materials requisition form**—a form that lists the quantity and cost of the direct materials used—must be filled out. This form is used to control the physical flow of materials out of inventory and into production. It also provides all of the detail needed to assign direct material cost to specific jobs.

As an example, assume that you have contracted with a local wholesaler to purchase various types of flooring material for your renovation jobs. Before any material can be delivered to the job site, a materials requisition form like the one that follows must be completed.

COACH'S TIP

Source documents always include identification numbers that can be used to cross-reference the documents in the accounting system. This document ties material requisition form #523 to Job #27, the project at 2719 N. Willow Dr.

Materials Requisition Number:	MR 523		Date: 8/12/2018

Job Number: 27

Description: 2719 N. Willow Drive

Material Description	Quantity	Unit Cost	Total Cost
18 × 18 inch travertine	300 sq. ft.	$ 2.50	$ 750
4 × 6 decorative border	40 sq. ft.	$15.00	600
3 bags of grout	40 lb.	$10.00	400
Total cost			$1,750

Authorized Signature _____

Based on this materials requisition form, a total of $1,750 in direct materials cost would be added to the cost of Job 27. Similar materials requisition forms would be completed for all other direct materials used on the job, including fixtures, appliances, and paint.

DIRECT LABOR TIME TICKETS

A **direct labor time ticket** is a source document that shows how much time a worker spent on various jobs each week. For example, assume that one of your employees, Bill Robertson, completed the following weekly time ticket:

Direct Labor Time Ticket			Dates:		Monday 8/12—Friday 8/16, 2018	

Ticket Number: TT 335

Employee: Bill Robertson

Date	Time Started	Time Ended	Total Hours	Hourly Rate	Total Amount	Job Number
8/12/2018	7:00 AM	3:00 PM	8 hours	$25	$ 200	27
8/13/2018	7:00 AM	3:00 PM	8 hours	25	200	27
8/14/2018	7:00 AM	3:00 PM	8 hours	25	200	27
8/15/2018	7:00 AM	11:00 AM	4 hours	25	100	27
8/15/2018	12:00 AM	4:00 PM	4 hours	25	100	Training
8/16/2018	7:00 AM	3:00 PM	8 hours	25	200	28
		Weekly totals	40 hours		$1,000	

Authorized Signature _____

This time ticket shows that Bill Robertson spent 28 hours on Job 27. Because Bill makes $25 per hour, a total of $700 (28 × $25) would be charged to Job 27. Bill also spent 4 hours in company training. Since this cost is not directly traceable to a specific job, it would be considered indirect labor and included as part of manufacturing overhead. The other 8 hours of Bill's time (8 × $25 = $200) would be charged to Job 28.

JOB COST SHEET

The **job cost sheet** is the most important document in a job order costing system as it is used to accumulate all of the costs incurred on a specific job. For example, the costs from the preceding materials requisition form and labor time ticket would be posted to the job cost sheet for the Job 27 as follows:

Job Cost Sheet

Job Number: 27

Date Started: 7/09/2018

Date Completed:

Description: 2719 N. Willow Drive, Job #27

Actual Direct Materials		Actual Direct Labor			Applied Manufacturing Overhead
Req. No	Amount	Ticket	Hours	Amount	
MR 523	$1,750	TT 335	28	$700	?

Notice that this job cost sheet shows the actual amount of direct materials and direct labor incurred on Job 27 based on the material requisitions form (MR 523) and direct labor time ticket (TT 335). But we have not yet recorded the manufacturing overhead costs. The method for assigning manufacturing overhead to jobs is described next.

PREDETERMINED OVERHEAD RATES

The third type of cost that must be assigned to jobs is **manufacturing overhead**. Unlike direct materials and direct labor costs, manufacturing overhead costs are those that cannot be directly traced to specific jobs. The general contractor, for example, and equipment used during the renovation process, are used on multiple jobs.

Because they cannot be directly traced to a specific job, manufacturing overhead costs must be *assigned* or *applied* using a **predetermined overhead rate**. There are three steps to assigning manufacturing overhead costs using a predetermined overhead rate, as follows:

1. Determine the allocation base (cost driver).
2. Calculate the predetermined overhead rate.
3. Apply manufacturing overhead to jobs by multiplying the predetermined overhead rate by the actual value of the allocation base (cost driver).

The first step is to select the **allocation base** that will be used to assign the indirect or manufacturing overhead cost to jobs. Because manufacturing overhead costs are not traceable to specific jobs, accountants must use some other observable measure, called an *allocation base*, to assign these indirect costs to products or services. Ideally, the allocation base should be a **cost driver**, or a measure that causes or influences the amount of manufacturing overhead cost incurred.

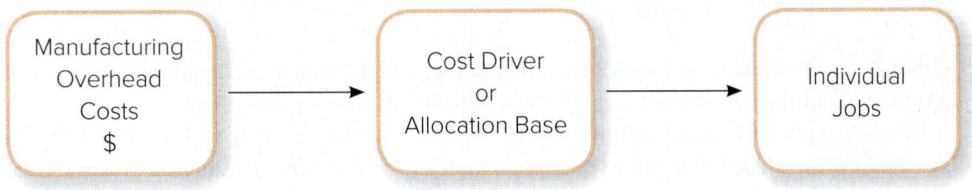

Learning Objective 2–3
Calculate a predetermined overhead rate and use it to apply manufacturing overhead cost to jobs.

🔨 COACH'S TIP

The following terms are used somewhat interchangeably:

Indirect Cost → Overhead
Assign → Allocate → Apply
Allocation Base → Cost Driver

While these terms have the same basic meaning, they may have a slightly different connotation depending on the context in which they are used. For example, an indirect cost might be called *manufacturing overhead* in a production setting, but *administrative or corporate overhead* in a service setting. In this chapter, we *apply* manufacturing overhead to specific jobs. In later chapters, we will *allocate* indirect costs to products and services. The language is different, but the process is the same.

Because home remodeling is a labor-intensive business, direct labor hours or direct labor cost is the most appropriate cost driver. Industries that are highly automated, such as automobile or semiconductor manufacturers, might use machine time as a cost driver. Other companies might use an industry-specific cost driver such as passenger miles for an airline or patient days for a hospital.

In our example, we will use a single cost driver, direct labor hours, to assign manufacturing overhead costs to jobs, though real-world companies often use more than one. In Chapter 4, we illustrate how to use activity-based costing to assign indirect costs to products and services using multiple activity cost drivers.

Now that we've selected direct labor hours as the cost driver, the second step is to compute a predetermined overhead rate that we will use to assign manufacturing overhead costs to jobs. We calculate the predetermined overhead rate as follows:

$$\text{Predetermined Overhead Rate} = \frac{\text{Estimated Total Manufacturing Overhead Cost}}{\text{Estimated Total Cost Driver}}$$

This overhead rate is usually calculated for an entire year to avoid the fluctuations in costs and activity that result from seasonal variation and peaks in demand. The rate is predetermined because it is estimated **in advance** based on **estimated** rather than actual values. We often do not know the actual manufacturing overhead cost until after the month, quarter, or year has ended, too late for managers who need the information to make decisions. Thus, accountants must use their best estimate of the coming year's manufacturing overhead based on past experience and any expectations they have about how the costs might change in the future.

For our house-flipping example, assume that you have estimated annual manufacturing overhead costs to be $150,000 and total direct labor hours to be 10,000. Based on these estimates, we calculate the predetermined overhead rate as follows:

COACH'S TIP

When you are asked to calculate a **predetermined overhead rate,** remember that it should be based on **estimated** rather than actual numbers. This rate is set in **advance** before the actual numbers are known.

$$\text{Predetermined Overhead Rate} = \frac{\$150,000}{10,000} = \$15 \text{ per direct labor hour}$$

What does a predetermined overhead rate of $15 mean? This is the amount of manufacturing overhead cost that we should apply for every hour of direct labor in order to cover all of the indirect costs of the job. Note that this is not the direct labor rate that we pay employees, but rather the extra amount that we need to add to cover the **indirect costs** of flipping a home, such as indirect materials, indirect labor, depreciation on equipment, and supervisors' salaries.

Once the predetermined overhead rate is established, the third step is to apply manufacturing overhead costs to specific jobs. We do this by multiplying the predetermined overhead rate by the actual direct labor hours for each job, as follows:

$$\frac{\text{Predetermined}}{\text{Overhead Rate}} \times \frac{\text{Actual}}{\text{Cost Driver}} = \frac{\text{Applied}}{\text{Manufacturing Overhead}}$$

Although we used estimated values to compute the predetermined overhead rate, we use the **actual** value of the cost driver to apply manufacturing overhead costs to jobs.

For example, how much manufacturing overhead should we apply to Job 27 and Job 28 based on the time ticket that Bill Robertson completed for the week of August 12? Recall that

Bill worked 28 hours on Job 27 and 8 hours on Job 28. He also spent 4 hours in employees training. The manufacturing overhead applied to each job would be computed as follows:

Predetermined Overhead Rate $15	×	Actual Direct Labor Hours for Job 27 28	=	Overhead Applied to Job 27 $420
Predetermined Overhead Rate $15	×	Actual Direct Labor Hours for Job 28 8	=	Overhead Applied to Job 28 $120

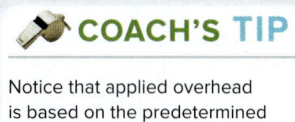

COACH'S TIP

Notice that applied overhead is based on the predetermined (**estimated**) overhead rate multiplied by the **actual** number of direct labor hours worked on each job.

Based on Bill Robertson's direct labor time ticket, we would apply $420 (28 hours × $15) in manufacturing overhead to Job 27 and $120 (8 hours × $15) to Job 28. The 4 hours he spent in training would not be applied to specific jobs because it is indirect labor. We would make similar calculations for all other employees based on their direct labor time tickets.

Accountants can apply manufacturing overhead costs every time they record direct labor (e.g., as part of weekly or biweekly payroll), or they can wait until the job is completed and apply all of the manufacturing overhead at once (based on the total direct labor hours worked on the job). If some jobs are still in process at the end of an accounting period, however, accountants must make sure that all cost records are up-to-date by applying overhead to all jobs in process at the end of the period.

Because the predetermined overhead rate was based on estimated data, **applied** manufacturing overhead is unlikely to be the same as the **actual** manufacturing overhead cost incurred. You will see how to record actual manufacturing overhead costs and how to account for any difference between actual and applied manufacturing overhead later in this chapter. First, complete the following Self-Study Practice to make sure you know how to calculate the predetermined overhead rate and assign manufacturing overhead costs to jobs.

💡 How's it going? — Self-Study Practice

Carlton Brothers Construction Company applies manufacturing overhead to jobs on the basis of direct labor hours. At the start of the year, the company estimated total manufacturing overhead to be $96,000 and total direct labor hours to be 12,000. Actual manufacturing overhead and direct labor hours were $100,000 and 10,000, respectively.

The direct materials and direct labor costs assigned to two jobs is summarized below:

	Job A	Job B
Direct materials	$10,000	$8,000
Direct labor	$5,000	$4,000
	(250 hours)	(200 hours)

1. Compute the predetermined overhead rate.
2. Determine the total manufacturing cost of Jobs A and B.

After you have finished, check your answers against the solutions in the margin.

Solution to Self-Study Practice

1.

$96,000 ÷ 12,000 = $8.00 per Direct Labor Hour

	Job A	Job B
Direct materials	$10,000	$8,000
Direct labor	$5,000	$4,000
Applied manufacturing overhead	250 hours × $8 = $2,000	200 hours × $8 = $1,600
Total Manufacturing Cost	$17,000	$13,600

2.

Record the Flow of Costs in Job Order Costing

This section describes how manufacturing costs are recorded in a job order cost system. We use T-accounts to illustrate how the costs flow through the various inventory accounts and eventually into Cost of Goods Sold. The detailed journal entries for these transactions are covered in the supplement to this chapter. Although you don't have to remember too much about debits and credits, you should recall from your financial accounting class that all asset (inventory) and expense (cost) accounts increase with a debit to the left side of the account and decrease with a credit to the right side of the account.

The three inventory accounts used to record manufacturing costs follow:

- **Raw Materials Inventory** represents the cost of materials purchased from suppliers but not yet used in production. This account includes both direct materials that can be traced to specific jobs (flooring, cabinets, etc.) and the **indirect materials** that cannot be traced to specific jobs (screws, nails, and so on).

- **Work in Process Inventory** represents the total cost of jobs that are in process at any point in time. Any cost that is added to the Work in Process Inventory account must also be recorded on the job cost sheet. **The job cost sheet serves as a subsidiary ledger to the Work in Process Inventory account**. Thus, the total cost of all jobs in process should equal the balance in Work in Process Inventory.

- **Finished Goods Inventory** represents the cost of jobs that have been completed but not yet sold. The cost of a completed job remains in Finished Goods Inventory until it is sold.

All manufacturing costs are included in one of these three inventory accounts and reported as an asset on the balance sheet until the job is sold. When a job is sold, its total manufacturing cost is transferred out of Finished Goods Inventory and into **Cost of Goods Sold**, where it will be matched up against sales revenue on the income statement. See Exhibit 2–3 for an illustration of how manufacturing costs flow through these inventory accounts before being recognized as Cost of Goods Sold.

When materials are purchased, the cost is initially recorded in Raw Materials Inventory. As materials are used, the cost is transferred to either Work in Process Inventory (for direct materials) or to Manufacturing Overhead (for indirect materials).

All costs added to the Work in Process Inventory account must be assigned to a specific job and recorded on the individual job cost sheet. Notice that only direct materials and direct labor costs are added directly to the Work in Process Inventory account. All indirect or manufacturing overhead costs flow through the Manufacturing Overhead account because these costs (by definition) are not directly traceable to specific jobs. Instead the indirect manufacturing overhead costs must be **applied** to Work in Process Inventory (and the job cost sheet) using a predetermined overhead rate and actual cost driver as described in the previous section.

The Manufacturing Overhead account is a temporary or clearing account that is used to accumulate actual and applied manufacturing overhead costs. Actual manufacturing overhead costs are recorded on the debit (left-hand) side of the Manufacturing Overhead account. The corresponding credit would be to another balance sheet account such as cash, accounts payable, or accumulated depreciation. **Applied manufacturing overhead** represents the indirect manufacturing costs that are assigned to specific jobs by multiplying the predetermined overhead rate by the actual value of the cost driver. Applied manufacturing overhead is added to Work in Process Inventory with a debit, with a corresponding credit to the Manufacturing Overhead account. Again, any costs added to Work in Process Inventory must also be added to the job cost sheet.

As jobs are in process, the Work in Process Inventory account and job cost sheet accumulates the **actual** direct materials, **actual** direct labor, and **applied** manufacturing overhead cost of each job. When a job is completed, its total manufacturing cost is transferred out of Work in Process Inventory and into the Finished Goods Inventory account. When the job is sold, the cost is transferred to the Cost of Goods Sold account where it will be matched against Sales Revenue on the income statement.

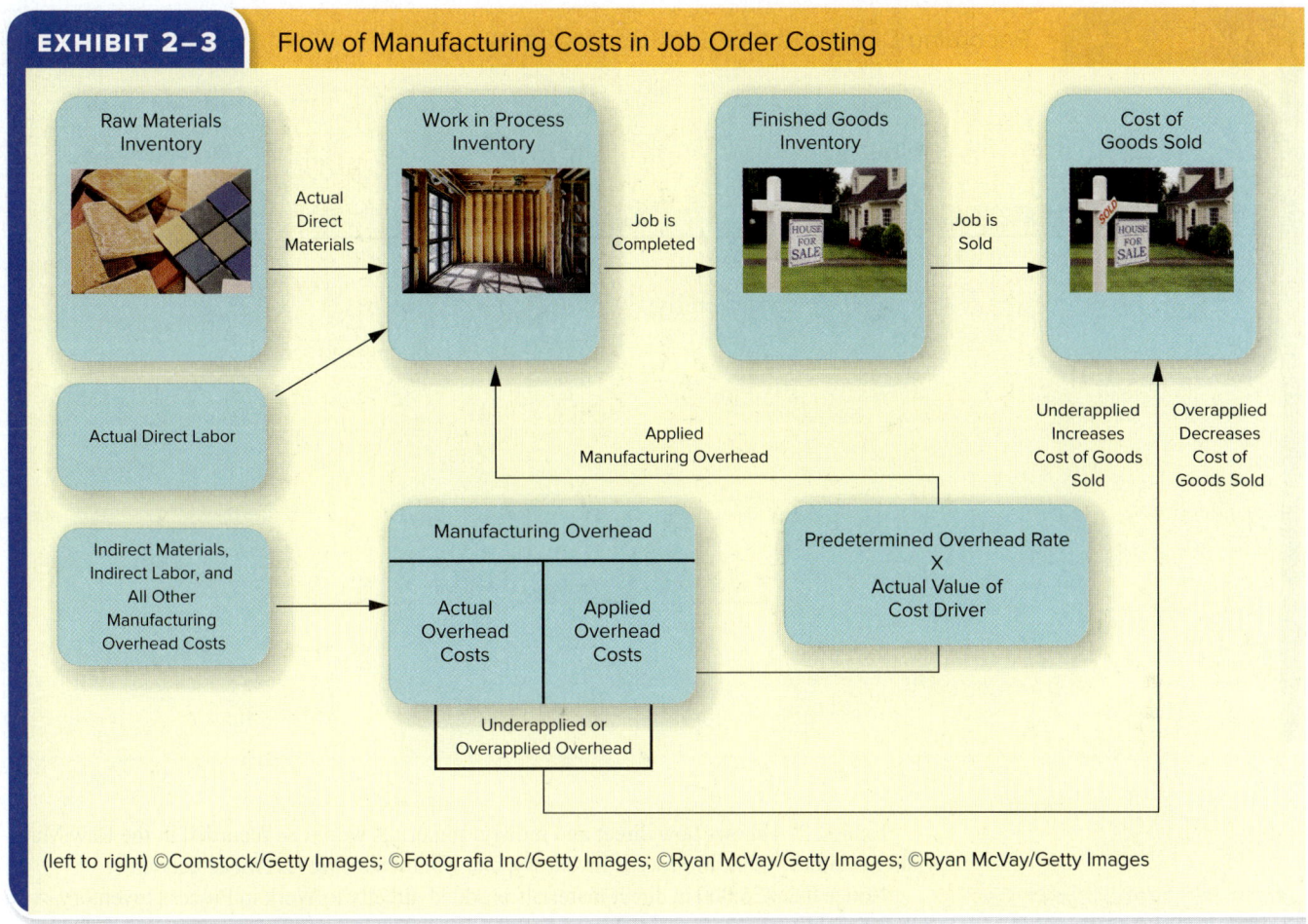

EXHIBIT 2–3   Flow of Manufacturing Costs in Job Order Costing

(left to right) ©Comstock/Getty Images; ©Fotografia Inc/Getty Images; ©Ryan McVay/Getty Images; ©Ryan McVay/Getty Images

At the end of the reporting period, any difference between actual and applied manufacturing overhead (represented by the balance in the Manufacturing Overhead account) must be accounted for. Companies can either adjust Cost of Goods Sold directly, as shown in Exhibit 2–3, or adjust Work in Process Inventory, Finished Goods Inventory, and Cost of Goods Sold. Later in the chapter, we illustrate the first of these two methods.

The next section provides an example to illustrate the flow of manufacturing costs in job order costing. For this example, assume that you are currently working on two house-flipping projects, Job 27 and Job 28. The purchase price of each property ($250,000 and $200,000, respectively) is included in the Beginning Balance of Work in Process Inventory. The company also started the period with $10,000 in Raw Materials Inventory and has two completed (but not sold) projects in Finished Goods Inventory at a total cost of $600,000.

RECORD THE PURCHASE AND ISSUE OF MATERIALS

When materials are purchased, they are initially recorded in Raw Materials Inventory. This account includes the cost of all materials (direct and indirect) that have been purchased but not yet used in production. As materials are issued to production, the costs are taken out of Raw Materials Inventory (with a credit) and debited to either Work in Process Inventory (for direct materials) or Manufacturing Overhead (for indirect materials). Any cost that is debited to Work in Process Inventory must also be added to the individual job cost sheet.

As an example, assume that you purchased $25,000 worth of direct materials (flooring, appliances, and paint), $15,000 of which was used for Job 27 and $10,000 for Job 28. You also issued $500 in painting supplies, tiling compound, and other minor materials for use on both jobs.

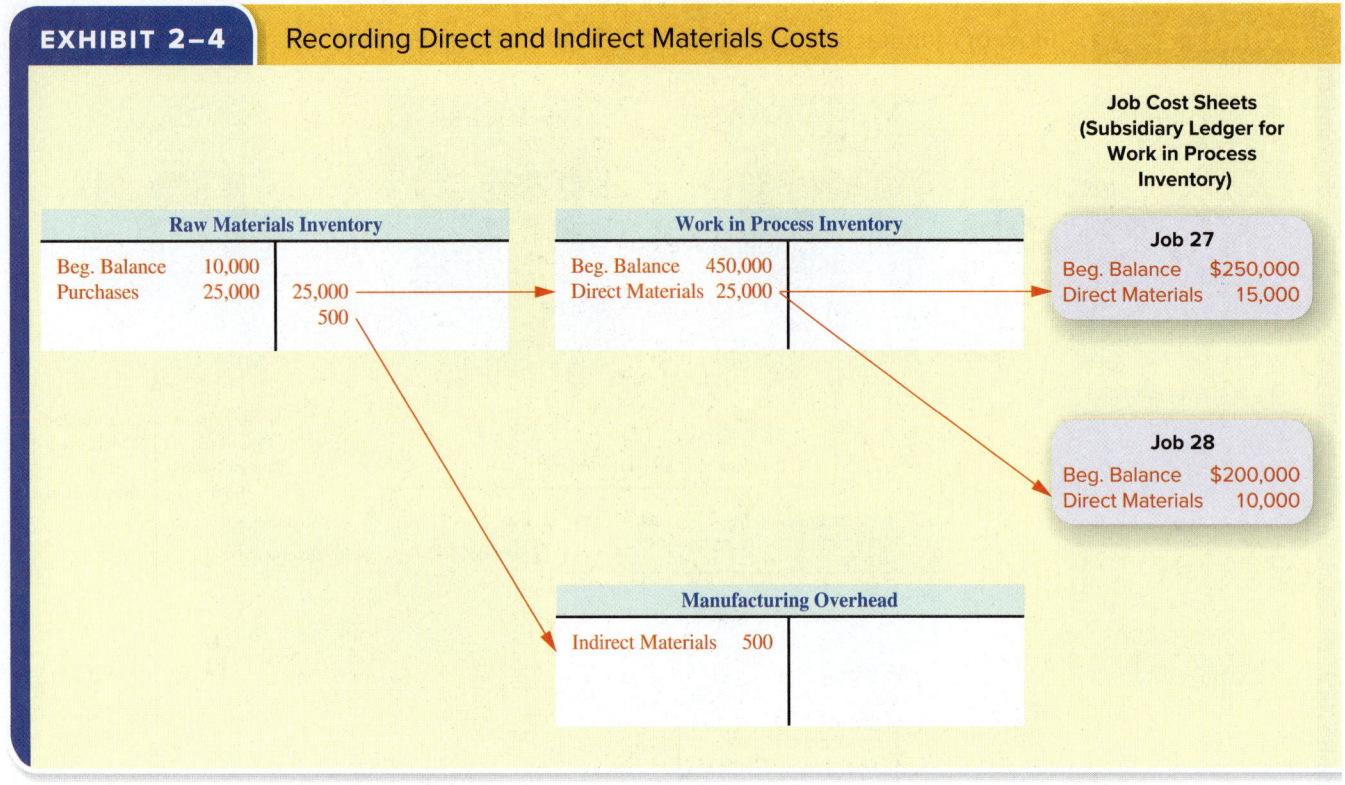

| EXHIBIT 2–4 | Recording Direct and Indirect Materials Costs |

Exhibit 2–4 shows how direct and indirect materials would be recorded in the Raw Materials Inventory, Work in Process Inventory, and Manufacturing Overhead accounts.

Notice that $25,000 in direct materials is added directly to Work in Process Inventory, with $15,000 being recorded on Job 27 and $10,000 recorded on Job 28. These job cost sheets serve as a **subsidiary ledger** to the overall Work in Process Inventory account. Thus, the total cost of all jobs in process should equal the balance in the Work in Process Inventory account.

The $500 of indirect materials is recorded as actual manufacturing overhead on the debit (left) side of the Manufacturing Overhead account.

RECORD LABOR COSTS

Labor costs are recorded based on the information captured on the direct labor time tickets. If the labor can be traced to a specific job, the cost is debited to Work in Process Inventory and added to the individual job cost sheet. Indirect labor is recorded on the actual (debit) side of the Manufacturing Overhead account.

Assume you paid $7,500 for labor, $4,000 of which was for Job 28 and $2,000 for Job 29. You also paid the general contractor who manages both projects $1,500.

See Exhibit 2–5 for a summary of how labor costs would be recorded in Manufacturing Overhead, Work in Process Inventory, and the job cost sheets.

RECORD APPLIED MANUFACTURING OVERHEAD

Unlike direct materials and direct labor costs, which can be directly traced to specific jobs, manufacturing overhead costs must be **applied** to jobs based on the predetermined overhead rate that was estimated at the beginning of the accounting period.

Recall that we computed a predetermined overhead rate as follows:

$$\text{Predetermined Overhead Rate} = \frac{\$150,000}{10,000} = \$15 \text{ per direct labor hour}$$

COACH'S TIP

Remember that only **direct** materials are added to Work in Process Inventory. **Indirect** materials are added to Manufacturing Overhead because they cannot be traced to specific jobs.

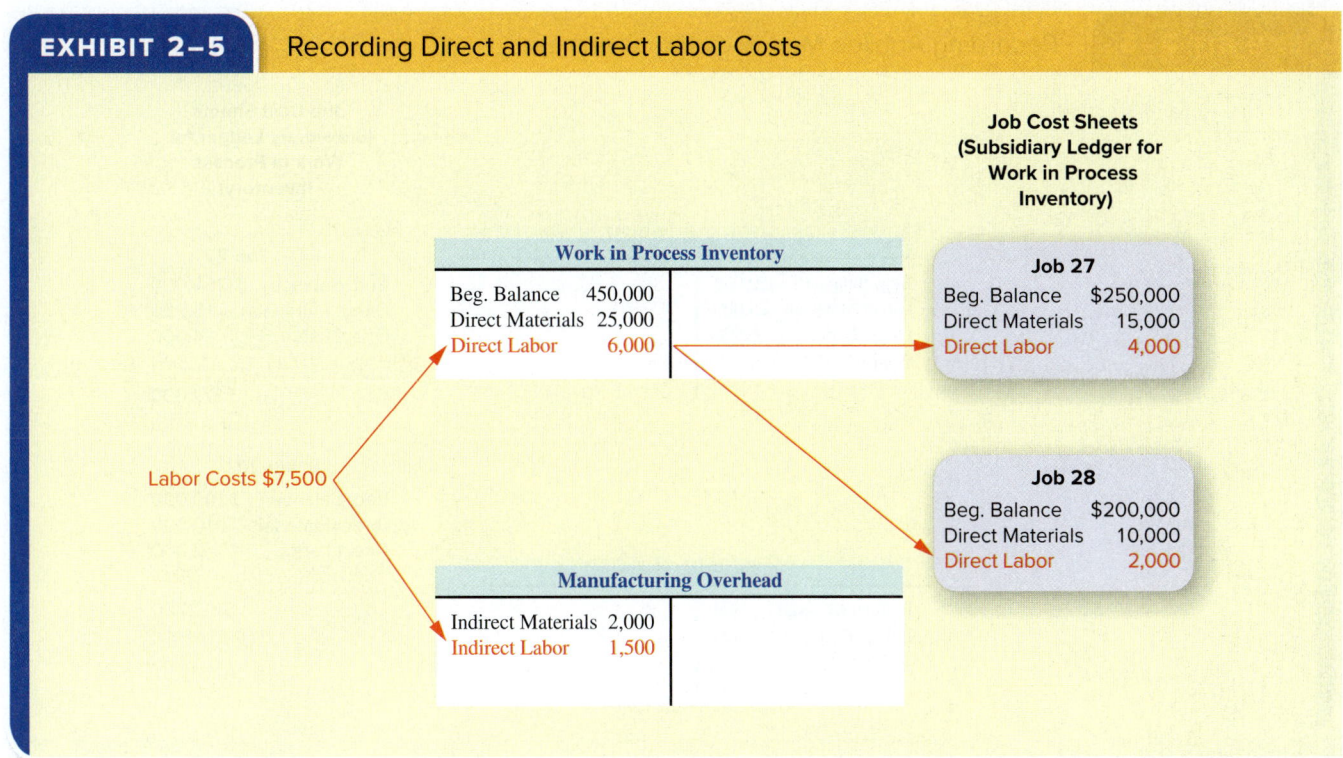

EXHIBIT 2–5   Recording Direct and Indirect Labor Costs

To apply manufacturing overhead to Work in Process Inventory and the individual job sheets, we need to multiply the $15 overhead rate by the actual number of labor hours worked on each job. Assume that the time tickets reported 200 direct labor hours for Job 27 and 100 direct labor hours for Job 28. Applied manufacturing overhead for each job would be computed as follows:

Applied Manufacturing Overhead (Job 27): 200 hours × $15 = $3,000

Applied Manufacturing Overhead (Job 28): 100 hours × $15 = $1,500

 **COACH'S TIP**

Manufacturing overhead rates can be based on direct labor time (hours) or direct labor cost (dollars). As long as the hourly labor rate is the same for each job, the result will be the same. However, that is not always the case. Read the problem carefully to determine whether you should use direct labor hours or direct labor cost (or some other cost driver) to compute the predetermined overhead rate and apply manufacturing overhead.

Applied manufacturing overhead is recorded on the debit (left) side of the Work in Process Account (and the individual job cost sheet), with a corresponding credit to the right side of the Manufacturing Overhead Account as shown in Exhibit 2–6.

RECORD ACTUAL MANUFACTURING OVERHEAD

While we use a predetermined overhead rate to **apply** manufacturing overhead to Work in Process Inventory and the job cost sheets, we still need to record all of the actual manufacturing overhead costs incurred. **Actual manufacturing overhead** includes all manufacturing-related expenses that cannot be traced to specific jobs, including indirect materials used at the job site, indirect labor, depreciation on tools or equipment, and insurance and property taxes incurred during the renovation process. These costs would be added to the debit (left-hand) side of the Manufacturing Overhead account, as shown in Exhibit 2–7. The corresponding credit would be to a balance sheet account, such as Cash, Accumulated Depreciation, or Accounts Payable.

EXHIBIT 2–6   Recording Applied Manufacturing Overhead

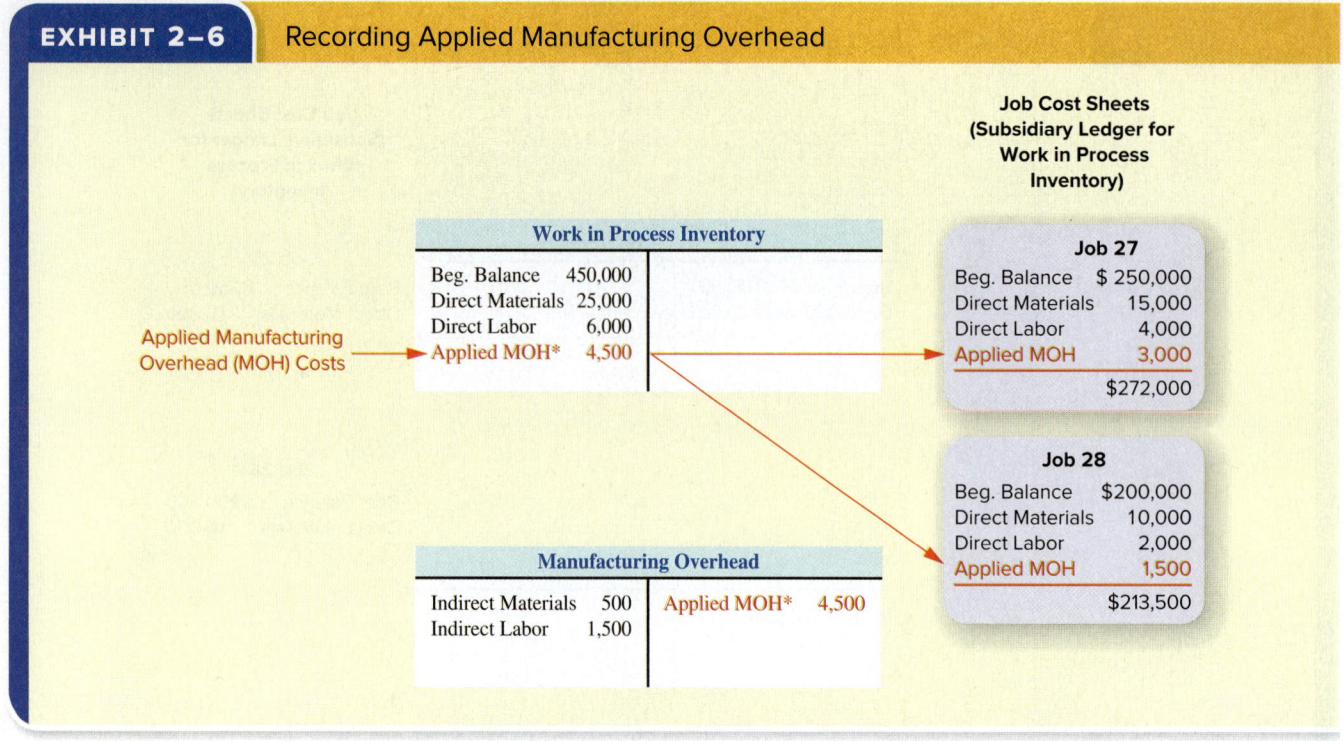

Exhibit 2–7 shows that we have recorded a total of $5,500 in **actual** manufacturing overhead costs on the debit side of the account. The $4,500 on the credit side of the Manufacturing Overhead account represents the amount of overhead that was **applied** to Work in Process using the predetermined overhead rate. We discuss how to handle the $1,000 balance, which represents the difference in actual and applied manufacturing overhead, in the next section.

EXHIBIT 2–7   Recording Actual Manufacturing Overhead Costs

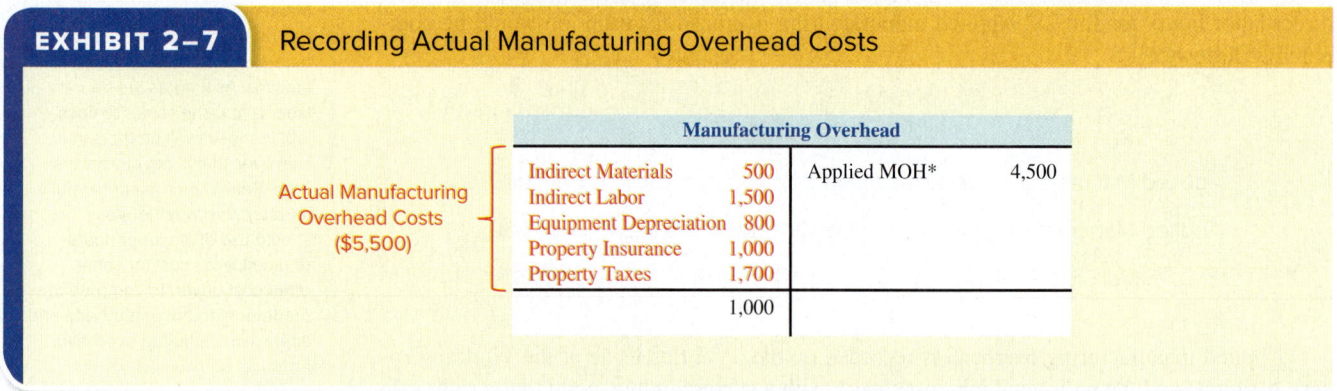

TRANSFER COSTS TO FINISHED GOODS INVENTORY AND COST OF GOODS SOLD

Once a job is complete, its total manufacturing cost is transferred out of Work in Process Inventory and into Finished Goods Inventory. Remember that the job cost sheet provides a summary of the actual direct materials, actual direct labor, and applied manufacturing overhead for each job. In our example, the total cost recorded for Job 27 includes the beginning balance of $250,000, plus $15,000 in direct materials, $4,000 in direct labor, and $3,000 in applied manufacturing overhead. Thus, the total cost of Job 27 after the renovation is complete is $272,000.

When Job 27 is complete, the total manufacturing cost of $272,000 will be transferred out of Work in Process Inventory and into Finished Goods Inventory, as shown in Exhibit 2–8.

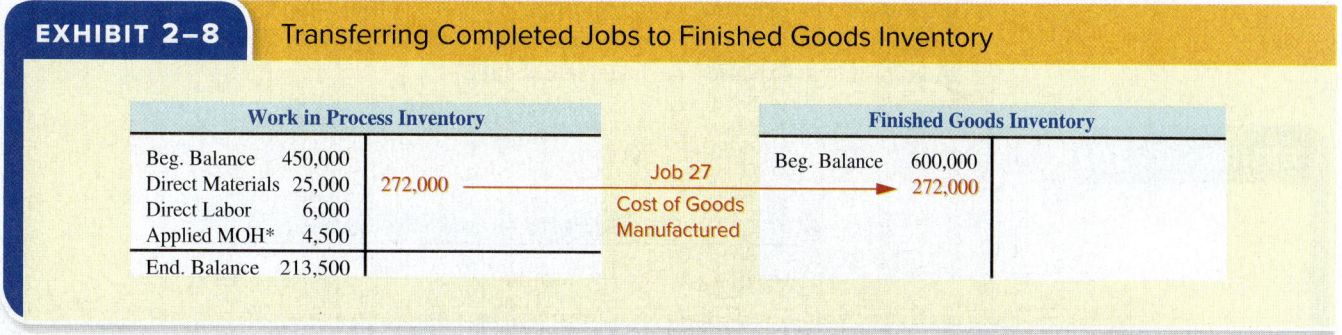

EXHIBIT 2–8 | Transferring Completed Jobs to Finished Goods Inventory

The total manufacturing cost that is transferred out of Work in Process Inventory and into Finished Goods Inventory is referred to as **cost of goods manufactured** or **cost of goods completed**. The remaining balance of Work in Process Inventory represents the cost of jobs still in process. In this example, the $213,500 ending balance in Work in Process Inventory represents the manufacturing cost for Job 28, which is not yet complete.

When the home is sold, its total manufacturing cost will be transferred out of Finished Goods Inventory and into Cost of Goods Sold. For example, assume that we sold Job 27 for $350,000. Its total manufacturing cost of $272,000 would be transferred out of Finished Goods Inventory and into Cost of Goods Sold. We also need to record the $350,000 sales price with a debit to cash (or accounts receivable) and credit to Sales Revenue, as shown in Exhibit 2–9.

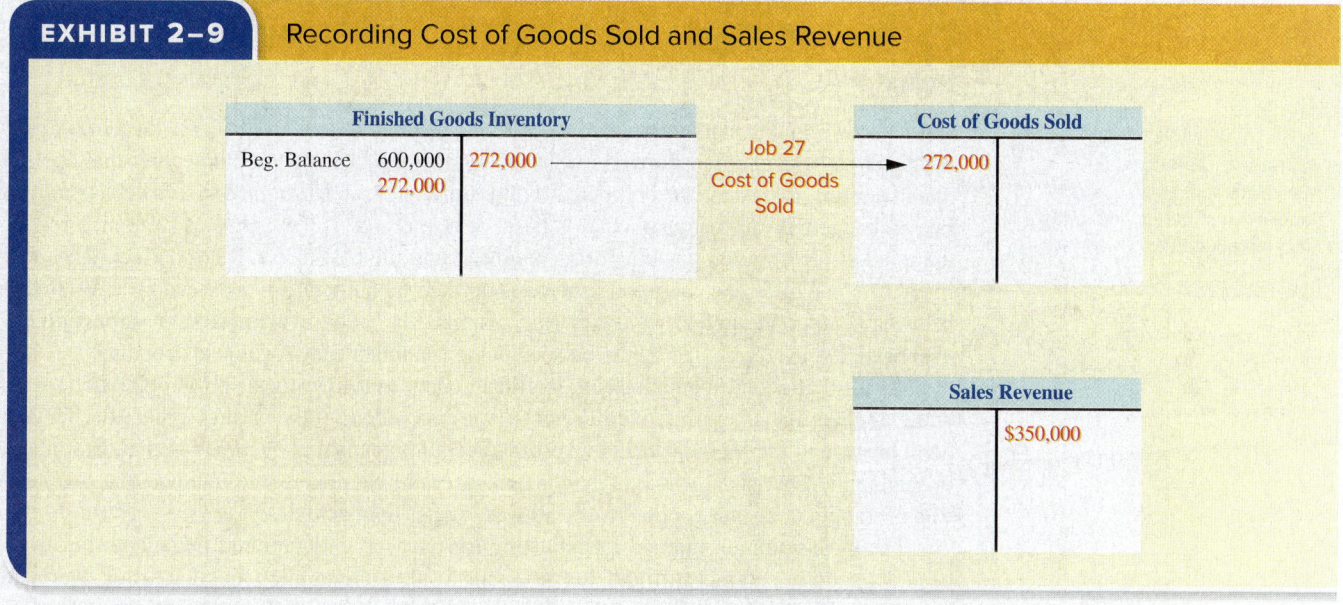

EXHIBIT 2–9 | Recording Cost of Goods Sold and Sales Revenue

The preliminary gross profit earned on the sale of Job 27 is $78,000, or the difference between the sales price of $350,000 and cost of goods sold of $272,000. However, we still need to account for two factors. First, we need to record the nonmanufacturing costs associated with selling the home and running the overall business. Second, we need to adjust for any difference in over- or underapplied manufacturing overhead.

RECORD NONMANUFACTURING COSTS

In addition to the manufacturing costs that flow through Work in Process Inventory, Finished Goods, and Cost of Goods Sold, companies incur other nonmanufacturing costs that relate to selling the product, as well as running the business. Recall that nonmanufacturing costs are referred to as period costs because they are expensed during the period incurred.

In our home-flipping example, selling expenses would include the cost of staging the home, advertising expenses, real-estate commissions, and other closing costs. Administrative expenses include general and administrative salaries, office supplies, and property taxes and depreciation on office buildings. These nonmanufacturing costs are reported as Selling and Administrative Expenses, as shown in Exhibit 2–10.

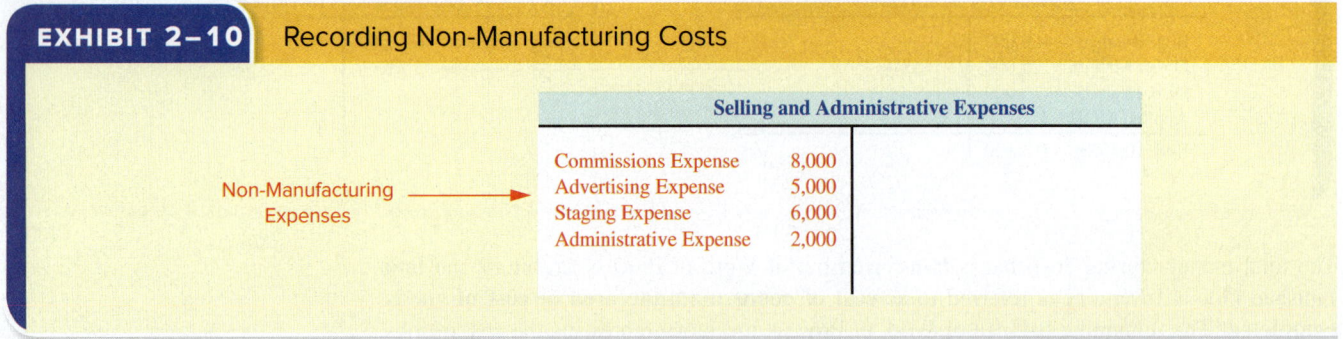

EXHIBIT 2–10 Recording Non-Manufacturing Costs

Selling and Administrative Expenses	
Commissions Expense	8,000
Advertising Expense	5,000
Staging Expense	6,000
Administrative Expense	2,000

Non-Manufacturing Expenses →

In the next section, we show how to adjust for the difference in actual and applied manufacturing overhead.

Overapplied or Underapplied Manufacturing Overhead

CALCULATE OVERAPPLIED OR UNDERAPPLIED MANUFACTURING OVERHEAD

In an ideal world, the manufacturing overhead cost **applied** to jobs would equal the **actual** manufacturing overhead cost incurred. But in reality, this rarely happens. Remember that applied manufacturing overhead was computed by multiplying a predetermined (estimated) overhead rate by the actual value of an allocation base, or cost driver. If the estimates were incorrect or the relationship between manufacturing overhead and the cost driver is not perfect, there will likely be some difference between actual and applied manufacturing overhead. The difference between actual and applied manufacturing overhead is called **overapplied** or **underapplied overhead** and is represented by the balance in the Manufacturing Overhead account.

Recall that actual manufacturing overhead costs were recorded on the debit (left) side, while applied manufacturing overhead costs were recorded on the credit (right) side. Thus, a debit balance in the Manufacturing Overhead account means that overhead was underapplied, or that applied overhead was less than actual. A credit balance would indicate that overhead was overapplied, or that applied overhead was greater than actual.

The most common method for adjusting for over- or underapplied manufacturing overhead is to add or subtract it from Cost of Goods Sold. Underapplied manufacturing overhead would be added to Cost of Goods Sold (to increase it from applied to actual), while overapplied manufacturing overhead would be subtracted from Cost of Goods sold (to decrease it from applied to actual), as follows:

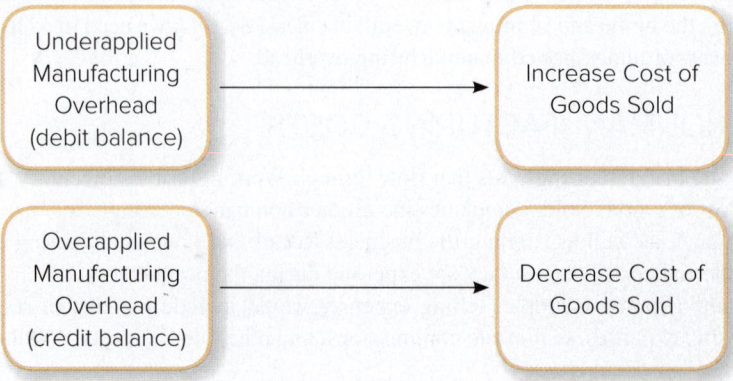

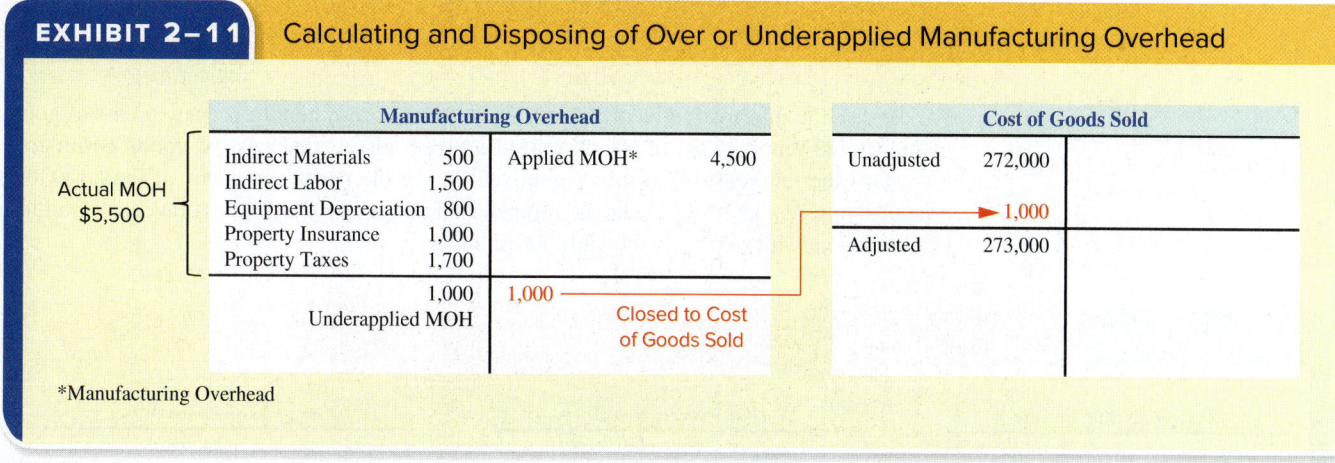

EXHIBIT 2–11	Calculating and Disposing of Over or Underapplied Manufacturing Overhead

Manufacturing Overhead				Cost of Goods Sold		
Indirect Materials	500	Applied MOH*	4,500	Unadjusted	272,000	
Indirect Labor	1,500					
Equipment Depreciation	800				1,000	
Property Insurance	1,000			Adjusted	273,000	
Property Taxes	1,700					
	1,000	1,000				
Underapplied MOH			Closed to Cost of Goods Sold			

Actual MOH $5,500

*Manufacturing Overhead

The manufacturing overhead costs recorded for our house-flipping example are summarized in Exhibit 2–11. Recall that we recorded $5,500 in actual manufacturing overhead costs (debits) and $4,500 in applied manufacturing overhead (credits), leaving a debit balance of $1,000. In this case, manufacturing overhead is underapplied, because actual was more than applied.

To eliminate the $1,000 underapplied manufacturing overhead balance, we need to increase Cost of Goods Sold (with a debit) and eliminate the balance in the Manufacturing Overhead account (with a credit). This increases Cost of Goods Sold from $272,000 to $273,000. It will also reduce the gross profit reported on Job 27 by $1,000 since it was the only job sold during the period.

In most real-world situations, the total cost of jobs sold during the period will be much greater than the cost of jobs still in process or in finished goods inventory at the end of the period. If a company has a significant amount of work in process or finished goods inventory, accountants may need to distribute the underapplied or overapplied overhead between Cost of Goods Sold (the income statement) and the inventory accounts (the balance sheet). This more complicated approach of adjusting multiple accounts is covered in advanced cost accounting textbooks.

Take a moment to make sure you understand how to calculate over- and underapplied manufacturing overhead by completing the following Self-Study Practice.

>  **COACH'S TIP**
>
> The debit balance in Manufacturing Overhead means that actual overhead cost was $1,000 more than the applied overhead cost. That is, overhead was underapplied. A credit balance will appear when actual overhead is less than applied overhead—that is, when overhead is overapplied.

 How's it going?   *Self-Study Practice*

Carlton Brothers Construction Company applies manufacturing overhead to jobs at a rate of $8.00 per direct labor hour. The following estimated and actual information is available.

	Estimated	Actual
Total manufacturing overhead	$96,000	$90,000
Total direct labor hours	12,000	11,000

1. Calculate the over- or underapplied overhead.
2. Will the adjustment for over- or underapplied overhead increase or decrease Cost of Goods Sold?

After you have finished, check your answers against the solutions in the margin.

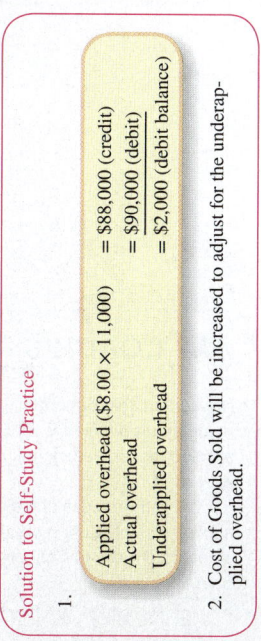

Solution to Self-Study Practice

1.
Applied overhead ($8.00 × 11,000) = $88,000 (credit)
Actual overhead = $90,000 (debit)
Underapplied overhead = $2,000 (debit balance)

2. Cost of Goods Sold will be increased to adjust for the underapplied overhead.

Prepare the Cost of Goods Manufactured Report

We can use the information recorded in the job order cost system to prepare a cost of goods manufactured report. **Cost of goods manufactured**, also called **cost of goods completed**, represents the total cost of all jobs completed during the period. In terms of the cost flows previously presented, it is the total cost transferred out of Work in Process Inventory and into Finished Goods Inventory, as shown in Exhibit 2–12.

EXHIBIT 2–12	Summary of Cost Flows

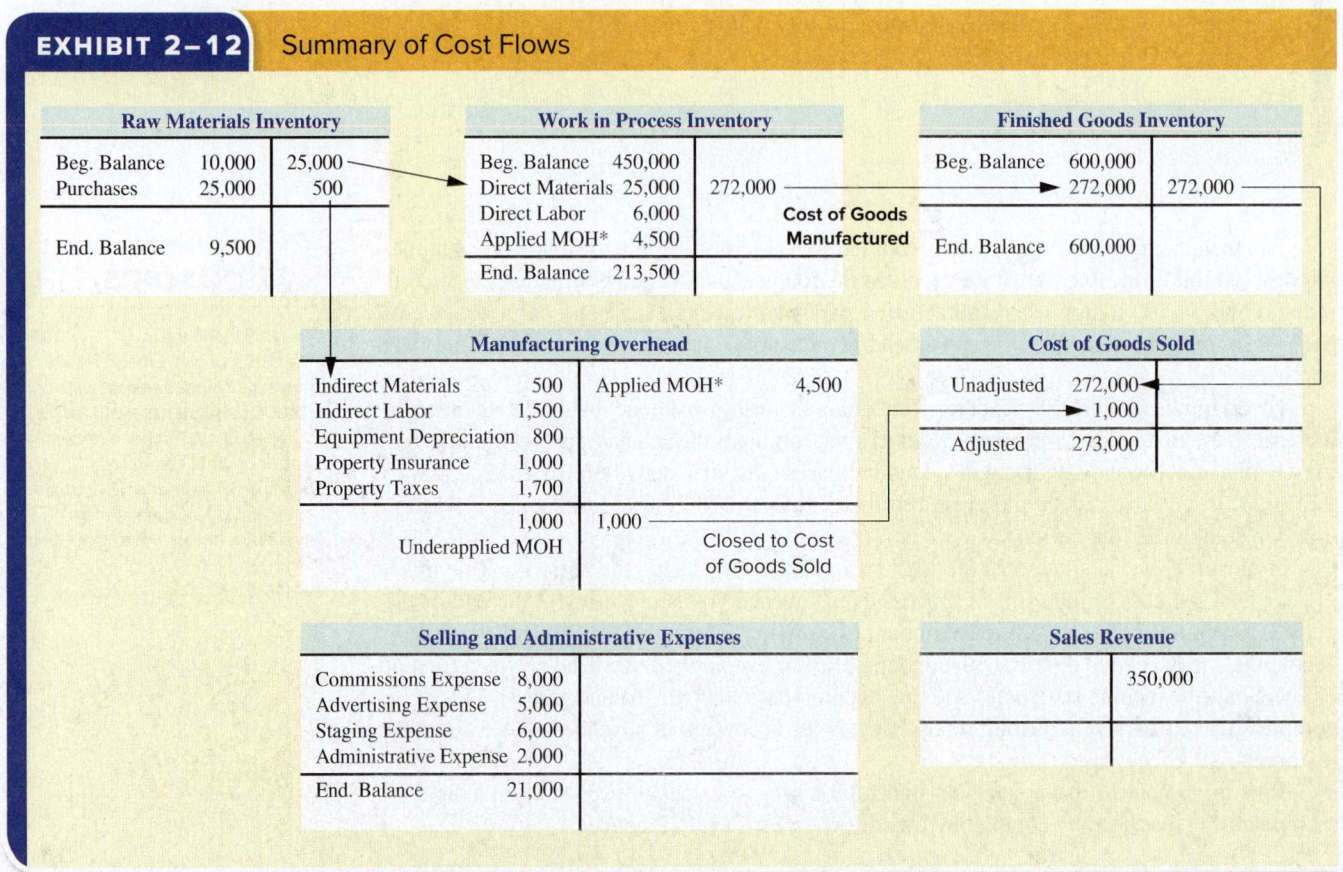

Using the T-accounts shown in Exhibit 2–12, we can prepare a cost of goods manufactured report for our house-flipping business, as follows:

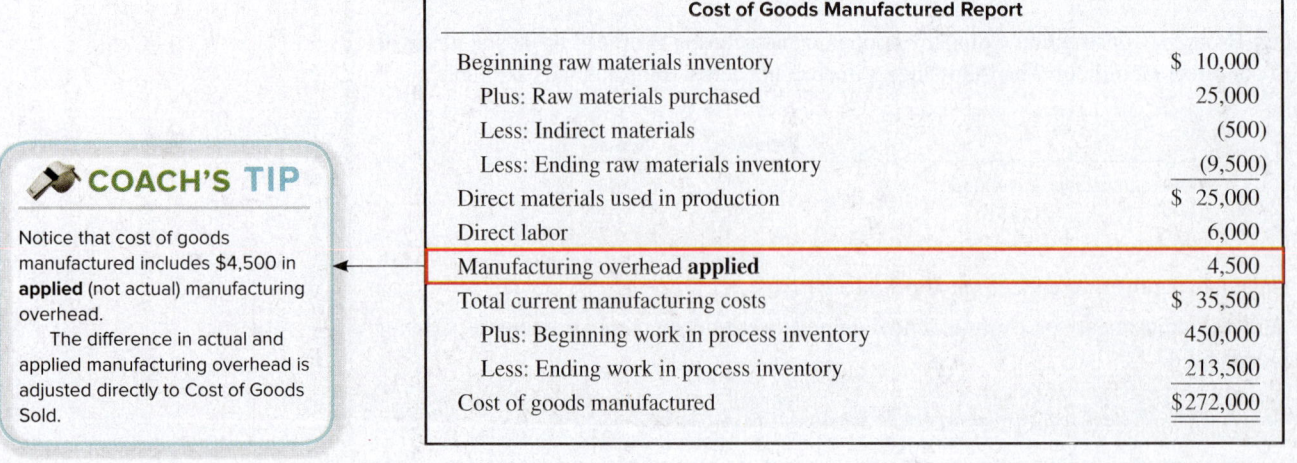

Cost of Goods Manufactured Report	
Beginning raw materials inventory	$ 10,000
Plus: Raw materials purchased	25,000
Less: Indirect materials	(500)
Less: Ending raw materials inventory	(9,500)
Direct materials used in production	$ 25,000
Direct labor	6,000
Manufacturing overhead **applied**	4,500
Total current manufacturing costs	$ 35,500
Plus: Beginning work in process inventory	450,000
Less: Ending work in process inventory	213,500
Cost of goods manufactured	$272,000

The **cost of goods manufactured report** summarizes the flow of manufacturing costs through Raw Materials Inventory, Work in Process Inventory, and into Finished Goods Inventory. In addition to tracking the costs added to these accounts during the period, we must use the beginning and ending inventory values to determine how much cost flowed out of each account during the period.

The cost of goods manufactured report begins with Raw Materials Inventory. We started the period with $10,000 in raw materials inventory, then purchased an additional $25,000 in raw materials. If we subtract the amount of indirect materials issued to production and the amount of material on hand at the end of the period, we can determined how much direct material was used in production. In this case, direct materials used is the $25,000 that was transferred from Raw Materials Inventory into Work in Process Inventory. Next, we add the direct labor ($6,000) and applied manufacturing overhead ($4,500) to determine the total manufacturing cost added to the Work in Process Inventory account during the period. In this case, we added $25,000 in direct materials, $6,000 in direct labor, and $4,500 in applied manufacturing overhead, for total current period manufacturing cost of $35,500 ($25,000 + $6,000 + $4,500). We must also take into account the cost of any jobs that were in process at the beginning of the period or that are still in process at the end of the period. To determine the cost of jobs completed and transferred out of Work in Process Inventory, we add the cost of any jobs in process at the beginning of the period ($450,000) and subtract the cost of jobs still in process at the end of the period ($213,500) to determine the cost of all jobs completed during the period.

The $272,000 transferred out of Work in Process Inventory and into Finished Goods is called **cost of goods manufactured** or **cost of goods completed**.

Next, we can create an income statement. We start with sales revenue and then subtract the cost of all jobs sold during the period. Because we had some completed but unsold homes in Finished Goods at the beginning and end of the period, we need to adjust for the beginning and ending value of Finished Goods Inventory.

When we add the beginning value of Finished Goods Inventory ($600,000) to the cost of goods completed ($272,000), and then subtract the ending value of Finished Goods Inventory ($600,000), we see that unadjusted Cost of Goods Sold is $272,000. It is unadjusted because it is based on the **actual** direct materials, **actual** direct labor, and **applied** manufacturing overhead for all jobs completed and sold during the period. When we adjust for the fact that actual manufacturing overhead was $1,000 higher than the amount applied, we arrive at an adjusted Cost of Goods Sold of $273,000.

Income Statement		
Sales revenue		$350,000
Less: Cost of goods sold		
Beginning finished goods inventory	600,000	
Plus: Cost of goods manufactured	272,000	
Less: Ending finished goods inventory	(600,000)	
Unadjusted cost of goods sold	272,000	
Plus: Underapplied manufacturing overhead	1,000	273,000
Gross profit		$ 77,000
Less: Selling and administrative expenses		21,000
Net operating income		$ 56,000

To find gross profit, or profit before nonmanufacturing expenses, we subtract adjusted Cost of Goods Sold of $273,000 from sales revenue of $350,000 to get $77,000 in gross profit. We then subtract selling and administrative expenses of $21,000 from gross profit, resulting in $56,000 in net operating income.

This example was designed to illustrate how job order costing works in a very simple manufacturing setting in which only two jobs were worked on during the period. The next section describes how job order costing can be applied to a service firm.

SPOTLIGHT ON sustainability

Sustainability is very important in the construction industry. According to the Environmental Protection Agency (EPA), residential buildings account for 20 percent of the nation's total energy consumption and greenhouse gas emissions. By changing the way that homes are designed and the materials used to build them, home builders can create economic benefits for both the firm (new products and markets, premium prices) and the homeowner (reduced operating costs), while lessening the impact on the environment (planet) and creating healthy living environments for homeowners (people).

Green or sustainable building is an emerging market that will continue to grow as more and more consumers become attuned to and committed to achieving a sustainable lifestyle. Some sustainable building initiatives include energy-saving features such as high-efficiency heating and cooling systems; renewable energy sources such as solar; and environmentally friendly building materials such as manufactured wood and recycled materials. The most ambitious sustainable building initiative is the goal of a "net zero" building, or one that generates as much energy as it uses. While very few builders are currently achieving that goal, there is little doubt that the trend toward sustainable building will continue and become more achievable as technology advances.

Companies that compete in the green building arena need a managerial accounting system that includes sustainability-related metrics in addition to the traditional economic data that is captured by the accounting system. For example, the job order cost system should not only include information about the cost and quantity of materials used on the job, but also whether the materials meet the company's sustainability standards in terms of how and where they were sourced and whether they are "environmentally friendly." Defining these standards and definitions is the challenging part, but the EPA and other industry sources provide a number of tools and guidelines that can help companies define their sustainability goals. Refer to Exercise 2-27 for a simple example of how the job order cost system can be adapted to include sustainability-related information.

Sources:
http://www.epa.gov/greenbuilding/index.htm
http://www.wbdg.org/resources/greenproducts.php

Job Order Costing in a Service Firm

Learning Objective 2–7
Apply job order costing to a service setting.

Job order costing is used in many professional service firms, including accounting firms, law firms, advertising and public relations firms, architectural and engineering firms, and health care providers. All of these businesses offer specialized services to clients that have unique needs or demands. For example, an accounting firm such as Ernst and Young provides auditing, consulting, and tax planning services to clients of varying sizes and from different industries. In service firms, each client or account is equivalent to a job in a manufacturing setting. Instead of tracking the cost of unique jobs, the accounting system will track the time and resources spent serving a specific client or account. As in manufacturing firms, managers of service firms need cost information to price their services, to budget and control costs, and to determine the profitability of different types of clients.

Because service firms tend to be labor-intensive, the primary driver used to assign cost is *billable hours*. A billable hour is time that can be traced to a specific client, similar to direct labor hours in a manufacturing setting. In professional service firms, each employee keeps track of the time spent on each client's account so that the client can be charged or billed for that cost. As you would expect, an hour of a senior partner's time at Ernst and Young will be charged at a much higher rate than a billable hour for a staff accountant.

In addition to the direct cost of the employee's time, the accounting system will record any other costs that can be directly attributed to a specific client's account. This might include the cost of travel to the client's site or "wining and dining" a major client. Unlike a manufacturing firm, most service providers don't use a lot of direct materials. One exception would be health care providers who use specialized devices (e.g., hip implants) or expensive drugs (e.g., anesthesia) to treat patients. In the medical field, the accounting system will charge these high-cost items to the patient's account. More generic supplies such as gauze and bandages would be treated as indirect costs and assigned using an allocation base, or cost driver, such as the number of days a patient is hospitalized, or *patient days.*

Service firms incur many other indirect costs that cannot be traced to specific clients or accounts. Examples include the time that employees spend on training, paperwork, and supervision; the salaries of administrative personnel; rent and utilities; and infrastructure costs such as computers and networks. These indirect costs are treated just like manufacturing overhead in a factory. They are assigned to individual clients or accounts based on an allocation base such as billable hours (for an accounting firm) or the number of patient days (for a hospital). In other words, there will be an additional charge applied to each client's account to cover the indirect costs of providing the service. In Chapter 4, we illustrate how to use activity-based costing to assign indirect costs to different types of customers or clients. This method can be used in conjunction with job order costing to determine the cost of providing services to different types of clients.

As you can see, job order costing works almost the same in a service setting as it does in a manufacturing setting. The main difference is the language that is used in different industries to describe the various costs, customers, and accounts.

SUPPLEMENT 2A JOURNAL ENTRIES FOR JOB ORDER COSTING

Learning Objective 2–S1
Prepare journal entries to record manufacturing and non-manufacturing costs in a job order cost system.

This supplement illustrates the journal entries used to record the flow of costs in job order costing. We will use the same transactions from the house-flipping example covered in the chapter, which are summarized in T-account form in Exhibit 2–12.

RECORDING THE PURCHASE AND ISSUE OF MATERIALS

When materials are purchased, the total cost is debited to the Raw Materials Inventory account. The credit should be to Cash or Accounts Payable, depending on the form of payment. The journal entry to record the purchase of $25,000 in raw materials is shown below:

	Debit	Credit
Raw Materials Inventory	25,000	
Accounts Payable		25,000

When materials are placed into production, the cost is debited to either Work in Process Inventory (for direct materials) or Manufacturing Overhead (for indirect materials). The credit entry should be to Raw Materials Inventory.

The journal entry to issue $25,000 of direct materials and $500 of indirect materials is shown below:

	Debit	Credit
Work in Process Inventory	25,000	
Manufacturing Overhead	500	
Raw Materials Inventory		25,500

COACH'S TIP

Notice that only **direct** materials are added (debited) to Work in Process Inventory. **Indirect** materials are debited to Manufacturing Overhead because they cannot be traced to specific jobs.

RECORDING LABOR COSTS

Direct labor costs are debited to Work in Process Inventory. Indirect labor costs are debited to Manufacturing Overhead. The corresponding credit should be to Wages Payable. The journal entry to record the direct and indirect labor for our house flipping example is shown below:

	Debit	Credit
Work in Process Inventory	6,000	
Manufacturing Overhead	1,500	
Wages Payable		7,500

RECORDING APPLIED MANUFACTURING OVERHEAD

Manufacturing overhead costs are **applied** to jobs by debiting the Work in Process Inventory account and crediting the Manufacturing Overhead account. In our house-flipping example, we applied $4,500 in manufacturing overhead, as follows:

	Debit	Credit
Work in Process Inventory	4,500	
Manufacturing Overhead		4,500

TRANSFERRING COSTS TO FINISHED GOODS INVENTORY AND COST OF GOODS SOLD

When a job is completed, the total cost of the job must be transferred from the Work in Process Inventory account to the Finished Goods Inventory account. The journal entry to transfer Job 27 from Work in Process Inventory to Finished Goods is shown below:

	Debit	Credit
Finished Goods Inventory	272,000	
Work in Process Inventory		272,000

When the job is sold, the total cost is transferred from Finished Goods Inventory to Cost of Goods Sold. A journal entry is also made to record sales revenue. For example, the journal entries to record the sale of Job 27 for a sales price of $350,000 would be as follows:

	Debit	Credit
Cash or Accounts Receivable	350,000	
Sales Revenue		350,000
Cost of Goods Sold	272,000	
Finished Goods Inventory		272,000

RECORDING ACTUAL MANUFACTURING OVERHEAD

Actual manufacturing overhead costs are recorded on the debit side of the Manufacturing Overhead account. The credit is to Cash, Accounts Payable, Prepaid Assets, Accumulated

Depreciation, or other balance sheet account, depending on the nature of the transaction. The journal entry to record property taxes, insurance, and depreciation on construction equipment is shown below:

	Debit	Credit
Manufacturing Overhead	3,500	
Property Taxes Payable		1,700
Prepaid Insurance		1,000
Accumulated Depreciation		800

RECORDING NONMANUFACTURING COSTS

Unlike manufacturing costs, which are recorded in inventory until the product is sold, non-manufacturing costs are expensed during the period in which they are incurred. The journal entries to record selling and administrative expenses for our example are as follows:

	Debit	Credit
Commissions Expense	8,000	
Cash or Accounts Payable		8,000
Advertising Expense	5,000	
Cash, Prepaid Expense, or Accounts Payable		5,000
Home Staging Expense	6,000	
Cash or Accounts Payable		6,000
Selling, General, and Administrative Expenses	2,000	
Cash, Prepaid Expense or Accounts Payable		2,000

RECORDING OVERAPPLIED OR UNDERAPPLIED MANUFACTURING OVERHEAD

After recording the actual and applied manufacturing overhead in our house-flipping example, the Manufacturing Overhead account had a debit balance of $1,000. This means that actual manufacturing overhead costs (debits) were more than applied manufacturing overhead (credit) costs, or that overhead was underapplied.

The journal entry to eliminate the $1,000 debit balance in the manufacturing overhead account and increase Cost of Goods Sold is shown below:

	Debit	Credit
Cost of Goods Sold	1,000	
Manufacturing Overhead		1,000

The effect of this entry is to increase the Cost of Goods Sold account by $1,000. If Manufacturing Overhead had been overapplied (with a credit balance), we would have debited the Manufacturing Overhead account to eliminate the balance and credited (decreased) Cost of Goods Sold.

These journal entries are summarized in the T-accounts in Exhibit 2–12 and form the basis for the Cost of Goods Manufactured report and Income Statement described in the previous section.

REVIEW THE CHAPTER

DEMONSTRATION CASE

Pacific Pool Company (PPC) builds custom swimming pools for homeowners in California, Arizona, and Nevada. PPC uses material requisition forms and direct labor time tickets to trace direct materials and direct labor costs to specific jobs. Manufacturing overhead is applied to jobs at a rate of $100 per direct labor hour. During the first month of operations, the company recorded the following transactions:

a. Purchased $200,000 in raw materials.
b. Issued the following materials to production:
   - $130,000 was directly traceable to specific jobs.
   - $20,000 was not directly traceable to specific jobs.
c. Recorded the following labor costs (paid in cash):
   - Direct labor $50,000
   - Construction supervision   30,000
d. Recorded the following actual manufacturing overhead costs:
   - Construction insurance $ 5,000
   - Construction equipment depreciation   25,000
   - Pool permits and inspections   5,000
e. Recorded the following nonmanufacturing costs:
   - Office equipment depreciation $ 3,000
   - Rent and insurance on owner's company car 2,000
   - Advertising costs   10,000
f. Applied manufacturing overhead to jobs in process based on 900 actual direct labor hours.
g. Completed 15 pools at a total cost of $195,000.
h. Finalized the sale of 13 pools that cost a total of $176,000. The other 2 pools are completed and awaiting inspection by the customer before the sale is finalized.
i. Recorded sales revenue of $325,000 on the 13 pools that were sold.
j. Closed the Manufacturing Overhead account balance to Cost of Goods Sold.

Required:

1. Show how all of these costs would flow through the following accounts:

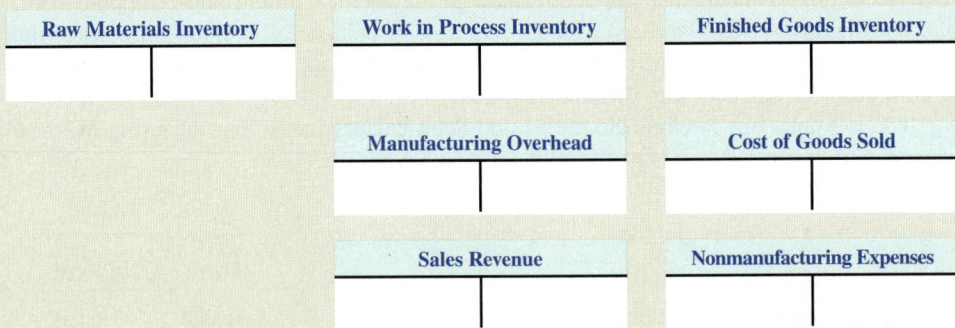

2. Assuming there were no beginning balances in any of the accounts, calculate the ending balance in the following accounts:
   a. Work in Process Inventory.
   b. Finished Goods Inventory.
   c. Manufacturing Overhead (over/underapplied).
   d. Cost of Goods Sold (after the overhead adjustment).

3. Prepare a cost of goods manufactured report for PPC.

4. Prepare an income statement showing the adjustment to Cost of Goods Sold.

Suggested Solution

1. and 2.

Raw Materials Inventory				Work in Process Inventory				Finished Goods Inventory	
(a) 200,000	(b) 150,000			(b) 130,000	(g) 195,000			(g) 195,000	(h) 176,000
				(c) 50,000					
				(f) 90,000					
Bal. 50,000				Bal. 75,000				Bal. 19,000	

Manufacturing Overhead			Cost of Goods Sold	
(b) 20,000	(f) 900 × $100 = $90,000		(h) 176,000	(j) 5,000
(c) 30,000				
(d) 35,000				
Bal. 85,000	(j) 5,000 Overapplied		Bal. 171,000	

Sales Revenue		Nonmanufacturing Expenses	
	(i) 325,000	(e) 15,000	

3.

PACIFIC POOL COMPANY
Cost of Goods Manufactured Report

Beginning raw materials inventory	—
Plus: Raw materials purchases	$200,000
Less: Indirect materials	(20,000)
Less: Ending raw materials inventory	(50,000)
Direct materials used	$130,000
Direct labor	50,000
Manufacturing overhead applied	90,000
Total current manufacturing costs	$270,000
Plus: Beginning work in process inventory	—
Less: Ending work in process inventory	(75,000)
Cost of goods manufactured	$195,000

4.

PACIFIC POOL COMPANY
Income Statement

Sales revenue		$325,000
Less: Cost of goods sold		
Beginning finished goods inventory	—	
Plus: Cost of goods manufactured	195,000	
Less: Ending finished goods inventory	19,000	
Unadjusted cost of goods sold	176,000	
Less: Overapplied manufacturing overhead	5,000	171,000
Gross profit		$154,000
Less: Selling, general, and administrative expenses		15,000
Net operating income		$139,000

CHAPTER SUMMARY

LO 2–1   Describe the key differences between job order costing and process costing. p. 50

- Process costing is used in companies that make homogeneous products using a continuous production process.
- Job order costing is used in companies that make unique products or provide specialized services.

LO 2–2   Describe the source documents used to track direct materials and direct labor costs to the job cost sheet. p. 54

- Direct materials are issued to production using a materials requisition form that shows the costs and quantities of all materials requested and the job they were used for.
- Direct labor costs are recorded using labor time tickets showing the amount of time workers spent on each specific job.
- The direct costs incurred for each job are recorded on separate job cost sheets.

LO 2–3   Calculate a predetermined overhead rate and use it to apply manufacturing overhead cost to jobs. p. 55

- Because manufacturing overhead costs cannot be traced directly to individual jobs, we use an allocation base, or cost driver, to calculate a predetermined overhead rate so that we can apply manufacturing overhead costs to each specific job.
- We call the overhead rate *predetermined* because it is calculated before actual costs are incurred, allowing managers to project the cost of a job before it begins.
- The predetermined overhead rate is calculated by dividing the estimated total manufacturing overhead cost by the estimated value of the cost driver.
- Manufacturing overhead is applied to specific jobs by multiplying the predetermined overhead rate by the actual amount of the cost driver used on the job.

LO 2–4   Describe how costs flow through the accounting system in job order costing. p. 58

- Initially, raw materials purchases are recorded in the Raw Materials Inventory account.
- When materials are placed into production, direct materials are recorded in the Work in Process Inventory account; indirect materials are recorded in the Manufacturing Overhead account.
- When labor costs are incurred, direct labor is recorded in the Work in Process Inventory account; indirect labor is recorded in the Manufacturing Overhead account.
- Applied manufacturing overhead costs are recorded on the debit (left) side of the Work in Process Inventory account and the credit (right) side of the Manufacturing Overhead account.
- Actual manufacturing overhead costs are recorded on the debit (left) side of the Manufacturing Overhead account.
- When a job is completed, the total cost of goods completed is transferred out of Work in Process Inventory (with a credit) and into Finished Goods Inventory (with a debit).
- When the job is delivered to the customer, the total cost is transferred out of Finished Goods Inventory (with a credit) to the Cost of Goods Sold account (with a debit).
- Nonmanufacturing costs are recorded as selling and administrative expenses and are expensed during the period incurred.

LO 2–5   Calculate and dispose of overapplied or underapplied manufacturing overhead. p. 64

- Actual overhead costs are recorded on the debit (left) side of the Manufacturing Overhead account; applied manufacturing overhead costs are recorded on the credit (right) side. Any balance in the Manufacturing Overhead account represents the amount of overapplied or underapplied overhead.
- If the overhead account has a debit (left) balance, actual overhead costs were higher than applied overhead costs; that is, overhead was underapplied.
- If the overhead account has a credit (right) balance, applied overhead costs were higher than actual overhead costs; that is, overhead was overapplied.
- At the end of the year, the balance in the Manufacturing Overhead account is transferred to Cost of Goods Sold account. Overapplied overhead decreases (credits) the Cost of Goods Sold account; underapplied overhead increases (debits) the Cost of Goods Sold account.

Calculate the cost of goods manufactured and cost of goods sold. p. 66   **LO 2–6**

- The total manufacturing cost that flows out of Work in Process Inventory and into Finished Goods Inventory is called *cost of good manufactured.* When the product is sold, the total cost is called *cost of goods sold* and is transferred to the Cost of Goods Sold account.

- Initially, the cost of goods manufactured and the cost of goods sold are based on actual direct materials, actual direct labor, and applied manufacturing overhead costs.

- The Cost of Goods Sold account is updated to reflect actual manufacturing overhead costs through an adjustment for overapplied or underapplied manufacturing overhead.

Apply job order costing to a service setting. p. 68   **LO 2–7**

- Job order costing is often used by professional service firms that provide unique services to clients with different needs. Examples include accounting firms, law firms, architectural firms, and health care providers.

- Just like manufacturing firms, service firms will charge direct costs of labor and materials to specific client accounts. Indirect costs must be assigned to clients using an allocation base, or cost driver, such as billable hours (for an accounting firm) or patient days (for a hospital).

- Although job costing works essentially the same in a service setting as it does in a manufacturing setting, language and terminology differs, as do the types of allocation bases used to assign indirect costs to customers.

Prepare journal entries to record manufacturing and nonmanufacturing costs in a job order cost system. p. 69   **LO 2–S1**

- Journal entries can be used to record the flow of manufacturing costs through the Raw Materials Inventory, Work in Process Inventory, Finished Goods Inventory, and Cost of Goods Sold accounts.

- Actual direct materials and actual direct labor are recorded as debits to the Work in Process Inventory account, with a credit to Raw Materials Inventory or Cash/Wages Payable.

- Applied manufacturing overhead costs are recorded with a debit to the Work in Process Inventory account and a credit to the Manufacturing Overhead account.

- Actual manufacturing overhead costs are recorded with a debit to the Manufacturing Overhead account and a credit to the appropriate balance sheet account.

- The balance in the Manufacturing Overhead account represents overapplied or underapplied overhead. A debit balance means that actual overhead costs were greater than applied, or that overhead was underapplied. A credit balance means that applied overhead was greater than actual, or that overhead was overapplied.

- When jobs are completed, Finished Goods Inventory is debited, with a credit to Work in Process Inventory. When a job is sold, Cost of Goods Sold is debited and Finished Goods Inventory is credited.

- Nonmanufacturing costs, or period costs, are recorded in expense accounts during the period incurred.

Key Formulas	
To Calculate	**Formula**
Predetermined overhead rate	$\dfrac{\text{Estimated Total Manufacturing Overhead Cost}}{\text{Estimated Cost Driver}}$
Applied overhead	Predetermined Overhead Rate × Actual Units of the Cost Driver
Overapplied or underapplied overhead	Actual Overhead – Applied Overhead
	A positive value indicates that overhead cost was underapplied. A negative value indicates that overhead cost was overapplied.

KEY TERMS

Actual Manufacturing Overhead p. 61
Allocation Base p. 55
Applied Manufacturing Overhead p. 58
Cost Driver p. 55
Cost of Goods Completed p. 63, 66
Cost of Goods Manufactured p. 63
Cost of Goods Sold p. 58

Direct Labor Time Ticket p. 54
Finished Goods Inventory p. 58
Indirect Materials p. 58
Job Cost Sheet p. 53, 55
Job Order Costing p. 51
Materials Requisition Form p. 54
Overapplied Overhead p. 64

Predetermined Overhead Rate p. 55
Process Costing p. 50
Raw Materials Inventory p. 58
Source Document p. 53
Underapplied Overhead p. 64
Work in Process Inventory p. 58

PRACTICE MATERIAL

QUESTIONS

1. What is the difference between job order and process costing?

2. What types of companies are likely to use job order costing? Give three examples.

3. What types of companies are likely to use process costing? Give three examples.

4. Many service industries use job order costing to keep track of the cost of serving clients. Can you think of a service industry that provides fairly homogeneous services? Describe the industry and explain why it might use process costing rather than job order costing.

5. Give two examples of an itemized cost sheet that you have received recently (e.g., a medical bill or a tuition statement would qualify as an itemized cost record).

6. Many companies use a modified costing system that blends certain elements of process costing and job order costing. Can you think of a company that makes products or provides services that have certain similarities (similar to process costing) but also allows a certain degree of customization (similar to job order costing)? Give an example.

7. What are the three major types of manufacturing costs that are accounted for in a job order cost system? Describe and give an example of each type of cost for an auto repair shop that uses job order costing.

8. What is the purpose of a job cost sheet? What information should it contain?

9. The job cost sheet serves as a subsidiary ledger to the Work in Process Inventory account. Explain what this means and how you would verify this.

10. What is the purpose of a materials requisition form? What information should it contain?

11. Explain how the cost of direct and indirect materials flows through the Raw Materials, Work in Process, and Manufacturing Overhead accounts.

12. What is the primary source document used to trace the cost of direct labor to specific jobs? What information should it contain?

13. Some would argue that costs would be more accurate if overhead costs were assigned to jobs using an overhead rate based on actual overhead costs and the actual value of the allocation base, rather than estimated amounts. Do you agree or disagree with this view? Explain.

14. Why is manufacturing overhead assigned to Work in Process Inventory in a different manner than direct materials and direct labor? Explain how it is different.

15. Explain how and why depreciation on office equipment is treated differently than depreciation on manufacturing equipment.

16. How is a predetermined overhead rate calculated? How does a company decide which allocation base to use to calculate the rate?

17. How do you apply manufacturing overhead to the Work in Process Inventory account? Is it based on estimated or actual data?

18. Will the amount of manufacturing overhead that is applied to Work in Process Inventory be equal to the actual amount of manufacturing overhead costs incurred? Why or why not?

19. How do you know when manufacturing overhead is overapplied? What type of balance would you expect to see in the Manufacturing Overhead account?

20. How do you know when manufacturing overhead is underapplied? What type of balance would you expect to see in the Manufacturing Overhead account?

21. Explain the most common method of eliminating any balance in the Manufacturing Overhead account at year-end. What account(s) is (are) adjusted? What happens to the account(s) when manufacturing overhead is overapplied? Underapplied?

MULTIPLE CHOICE

1. Why would a company use process costing rather than job order costing to compute product cost?

   a. The company produces units to customer specifications.
   b. The company manufactures a product using a series of continuous processes that results in units that are virtually identical from one to the next.
   c. The company wants to track the cost of materials, labor, and overhead to specific customers.
   d. The company wants to assign manufacturing overhead using an overhead rate based on direct labor hours.
   e. All of the above.

2. The source document used to specify the quantity and unit costs of raw materials issued into production is called a

   a. Production order form.
   b. Materials requisition form.
   c. Direct labor time ticket.
   d. Predetermined overhead rate.
   e. Job cost sheet.

3. Which of the following source documents serves as a subsidiary ledger for the Work in Process Inventory account?

   a. Production order form.
   b. Materials requisition form.
   c. Direct labor time ticket.
   d. Predetermined overhead rate.
   e. Job cost sheet.

4. Comstock Company uses a predetermined overhead rate based on machine hours to apply manufacturing overhead to jobs. Estimated and actual total manufacturing overhead costs and machine hours follow:

	Estimated	Actual
Total overhead cost	$100,000	$110,250
Machine hours	20,000	21,000

   What is the predetermined overhead rate per machine hour?
   a. $4.76.
   b. $5.00.
   c. $5.25.
   d. $5.51.

5. Refer to the information in question 4. How much is over- or underapplied overhead?

   a. $10,250 overapplied.
   b. $10,250 underapplied.
   c. $5,250 overapplied.
   d. $5,250 underapplied.
   e. None of the above.

6. Which of the following cost(s) is (are) recorded directly into the Work in Process Inventory account?

   a. Direct materials.
   b. Indirect materials.

   c. Direct labor.
   d. Both a and c.
   e. All of the above.

7. Actual manufacturing overhead costs are recorded

   a. On the left (debit) side of the Work in Process Inventory account.
   b. On the right (credit) side of the Work in Process Inventory account.
   c. On the left (debit) side of the Manufacturing Overhead account.
   d. On the right (credit) side of the Manufacturing Overhead account.
   e. Both b and c.

8. Applied manufacturing overhead costs are recorded

   a. On the left (debit) side of the Work in Process Inventory account.
   b. On the right (credit) side of the Work in Process Inventory account.
   c. On the left (debit) side of the Manufacturing Overhead account.
   d. On the right (credit) side of the Manufacturing Overhead account.
   e. Both a and d.

9. The Manufacturing Overhead account has a $10,000 debit balance that is closed directly to Cost of Goods Sold. Which of the following statements is true?

   a. Actual manufacturing overhead was less than applied manufacturing overhead.
   b. Actual manufacturing overhead was more than applied manufacturing overhead.
   c. The entry to eliminate the balance in Manufacturing Overhead will decrease Cost of Goods Sold.
   d. The entry to eliminate the balance in Manufacturing Overhead will increase Cost of Goods Sold.
   e. Both a and c.
   f. Both b and d.

10. Before disposing of its year-end manufacturing overhead balance, Delphi Corporation had the following amounts in Manufacturing Overhead and Cost of Goods Sold:

Applied manufacturing overhead	$100,000
Actual manufacturing overhead	90,000
Unadjusted cost of goods sold	800,000

    If Delphi closes the balance of its Manufacturing Overhead account directly to Cost of Goods Sold, how much is adjusted cost of goods sold?

    a. $790,000.
    b. $810,000.
    c. $890,000.
    d. $900,000.
    e. None of the above.

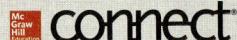 **Find More Learning Solutions on Connect.**

MINI-EXERCISES

LO 2–1

M2–1 Identifying Companies That Use Job Order versus Process Costing

Indicate whether each of the following companies is likely to use job order (J) or process costing (P).

_____ 1. Golf ball manufacturer.

_____ 2. Landscaping business.

_____ 3. Tile manufacturer.

_____ 4. Auto repair shop.

_____ 5. Pet food manufacturer.

_____ 6. Light bulb manufacturer.

_____ 7. Water bottling company.

_____ 8. Appliance repair business.

_____ 9. DVD manufacturer.

_____ 10. Music video production company.

LO 2–2

M2–2 Identifying Source Document Information

For each of the following items, indicate whether it would appear on a materials requisition form (MRF), a direct labor time ticket (DLTT), and/or a job cost sheet (JCS). Note: An item may appear on more than one document.

_____ 1. Employee name.

_____ 2. Quantity of direct materials used.

_____ 3. Total dollar value of direct materials.

_____ 4. Applied manufacturing overhead.

_____ 5. Hours worked by an employee.

_____ 6. Hours a specific employee worked on a particular job.

_____ 7. Job start date.

_____ 8. Time an employee clocked in or out.

_____ 9. Different jobs that a specific employee worked on.

LO 2–1, 2–2, 2–3, 2–4, 2–5

M2–3 Matching Terms in Job Order Costing

_____ 1. Allocation Base

_____ 2. Direct Labor Time Ticket

_____ 3. Indirect Costs

_____ 4. Job Cost Sheet

_____ 5. Job Order Costing

_____ 6. Materials Requisition Form

_____ 7. Overapplied Overhead

_____ 8. Underapplied Overhead

_____ 9. Predetermined Overhead Rate

_____ 10. Process Costing

A. A detailed record of costs incurred to complete a specific job.

B. A source document that shows how a worker spent time each week.

C. An accounting system used by companies to make standardized or homogeneous products or services.

D. An accounting system used by companies that offer customized or unique products or services.

E. Major inputs that can be directly and easily traced to a product, job or service.

F. Hands-on work that goes into producing a product, job or service.

G. Costs not easily traceable to producing a product, job or service.

H. The amount of actual overhead is greater than the applied overhead.

I. A form that lists the quantity of direct materials to be used in a job.

J. Indirect costs that are allocated to each job.

K. Estimated manufacturing overhead divided by estimated cost driver.

L. A measure that causes or influences the incurrence of a cost.

M. Total cost divided by units produced.

N. The amount of actual overhead is less than the applied overhead.

O. Actual direct materials plus actual direct labor plus applied manufacturing overhead.

Match each term on the left with the best definition on the right. Note: Not all definitions will be used.

M2–4 Matching Terms in Job Order Costing   LO 2–4, 2–6

_____ **1.** Actual Manufacturing Overhead

_____ **2.** Applied Manufacturing Overhead

_____ **3.** Cost of Goods Manufactured

_____ **4.** Cost of Goods Sold

_____ **5.** Direct Materials

_____ **6.** Finished Goods

_____ **7.** Indirect Materials

_____ **8.** Raw Materials Inventory

_____ **9.** Work in Process Inventory

A. Materials that cannot be directly or conveniently traced to a specific unit or job.

B. Total production cost assigned to goods that were produced during the period.

C. Cost of materials purchased from suppliers that have not yet been used in production.

D. Actual amount of indirect manufacturing costs incurred during the period.

E. Materials that can be directly and conveniently traced to a specific unit or job.

F. Indirect manufacturing costs that have been assigned to a specific unit or job using a predetermined overhead rate.

G. Cost of units or jobs that are incomplete at any given point in time.

H. Total manufacturing cost of jobs or units sold during the period.

I. Costs of all units completed and ready for sale at any given point in time.

Match each term on the left with the best definition on the right. Note: Not all definitions will be used.

M2–5 Computing Applied Manufacturing Overhead and Conversion Cost   LO 2–3

Job 31 has a direct materials cost of $300 and a total manufacturing cost of $900. Overhead is applied to jobs at a rate of 200 percent of direct labor cost.

Use the relationships among total manufacturing costs, conversion cost, and prime cost to determine the following costs for Job 31:

a. Conversion cost.
b. Direct labor cost.
c. Manufacturing overhead cost.
d. Prime cost.

M2–6 Calculating Predetermined Overhead Rates   LO 2–3

Carey Company applies manufacturing overhead costs to products as a percentage of direct labor dollars. Estimated and actual values of manufacturing overhead and direct labor costs are summarized here:

	Estimated	Actual
Direct labor cost	$600,000	$550,000
Manufacturing overhead	900,000	850,000

1. Compute the predetermined overhead rate.
2. Interpret this rate and explain how it will be used to apply manufacturing overhead to jobs.
3. Explain whether you used estimated or actual values to compute the rate, and why.

LO 2–3   **M2–7 Calculating Applied Manufacturing Overhead**

Refer to M2–6 for Carey Company.

1. Determine how much overhead to apply to production.
2. Explain whether applied overhead was based on actual values, estimated values, or both.

LO 2–5   **M2–8 Calculating Over- or Underapplied Manufacturing Overhead**

Refer to M2–6 for Carey Company.

1. Compute over- or underapplied overhead.
2. Explain how you would handle the over- or underapplied overhead at the end of the accounting period. Which accounts will be affected? Will the accounts be increased or decreased?

LO 2–3   **M2–9 Calculating Predetermined Overhead Rate**

Hamilton Company applies manufacturing overhead costs to products based on direct labor hours. The company estimates manufacturing overhead cost for the year to be $250,000 and direct labor hours to be 20,000. Actual overhead for the year was $260,000.

1. Compute the predetermined overhead rate
2. If the company actually used 22,000 direct labor hours, how much manufacturing overhead is applied to their job?

LO 2–5   **M2–10 Calculating Over- or Underapplied Manufacturing Overhead**

Refer to M2–9 for Hamilton Company.

1. Compute over- or underapplied overhead.
2. Which accounts will be affected by the over- or underapplied manufacturing overhead? Will the accounts be increased or decreased to adjust for the over- or underapplied manufacturing overhead?

LO 2–4   **M2–11 Identifying Inventory Accounts**

Cooper Billiards manufactures pool tables. Complete the following table to indicate which account increases or decreases as a result of each action. Note: An action may affect **more than one account**.

Action	Raw Materials Inventory	Work in Process Inventory	Finished Goods Inventory	Cost of Goods Sold
a. Table frames, legs, felt, and pockets are delivered to the inventory storeroom.				
b. Factory manager requisitions table frames, legs, felt, and pockets to build 30 pool tables.				
c. Factory workers assemble the pool tables.				
d. 18 pool tables are completed and moved to the showroom.				
e. Customers purchase 10 tables.				

LO 2–5   **M2–12 Determining Missing Amounts**

Determine missing amounts to complete the following table:

Case	Actual MOH	Applied MOH	Over/Underapplied	Amount
A	$100,000	$105,000	$?	$?
B	79,000	?	Underapplied	1,000
C	?	261,300	Overapplied	14,000
D	141,000	135,000	?	?

M2–13 Recording the Purchase and Issue of Raw Materials   LO 2–2, 2–4

Fairfield Company's raw materials inventory transactions for the most recent month are summarized here:

Beginning raw materials	$20,000	
Purchases of raw materials	90,000	
Raw materials issued		
Materials requisition 1445	25,000	For Job 101
Materials requisition 1446	35,000	For Job 102
Materials requisition 1447	30,000	Used on multiple jobs

1. How much of the raw materials cost would be added to the Work in Process Inventory account during the period?
2. How much of the raw materials costs would be added to the Manufacturing Overhead account?
3. Compute the ending balance in the Raw Materials Inventory account.

M2–14 Preparing Journal Entries   LO 2–S1

Refer to the information in M2–13.

1. Prepare the journal entry to record the purchase of raw materials.
2. Prepare the journal entry to record the issuance of raw materials to production.

M2–15 Recording Direct and Indirect Labor Costs   LO 2–2, 2–4

Fairfield Company's payroll costs for the most recent month are summarized here:

Item	Description		Total Cost
Hourly labor wages	750 hours @ $30 per hour		
	200 hours for Job 101 =	$6,000	
	300 hours for Job 102 =	9,000	
	250 hours for Job 103 =	7,500	$22,500
Factory supervision			4,000
Production engineer			8,000
Factory janitorial work			2,500
Selling, general, and administrative salaries			9,000
Total payroll costs			$46,000

1. Calculate how much of the labor costs would be added to the following accounts:
   a. Work in Process Inventory.
   b. Manufacturing Overhead.
   c. Selling, General, and Administrative Expenses.
2. Explain why some labor costs are recorded as work in process, some as manufacturing overhead, and some as period costs.

M2–16 Preparing Journal Entries   LO 2–S1

Refer to M2–15.

1. Prepare the journal entry to record Fairfield Company's payroll costs.
2. The company applies manufacturing overhead to products at a predetermined rate of $50 per direct labor hour. Prepare the journal entry to apply manufacturing overhead to production.

LO 2–3, 2–4, 2–5   **M2–17 Calculating Over- or Underapplied Overhead Costs**

Refer to M2–16 for Fairfield Company. Its actual manufacturing costs for the most recent period are summarized here:

Item	Description		Total Cost
Direct materials	Used on Jobs 101 and 102		$60,000
Indirect materials	Used on multiple jobs		30,000
Hourly labor wages	750 hours @ $30 per hour		
	200 hours for Job 101 =	$6,000	
	300 hours for Job 102 =	9,000	
	250 hours for Job 103 =	7,500	22,500
Factory supervision			4,000
Production engineer			8,000
Factory janitorial work			2,500
Selling, general, and administrative salaries			9,000
Other manufacturing overhead costs (factory rent, insurance, depreciation, etc.)			7,500
Other selling, general, and administrative costs (office rent, insurance, depreciation, etc.)			6,000

1. Post the preceding information to Fairfield Company's Manufacturing Overhead T-account.
2. Compute over- or underapplied manufacturing overhead.

LO 2–S1   **M2–18 Preparing Journal Entries**

Refer to M2–17 for Fairfield Company.

1. Prepare the journal entry to close the Manufacturing Overhead account balance to Cost of Goods Sold.
2. Explain whether the entry in requirement 1 will increase or decrease Cost of Goods Sold and why.

LO 2–6   **M2–19 Calculating Total Current Manufacturing Cost**

The following information is available for Walker Industries:

Beginning work in process inventory	$ 30,000
Ending work in process inventory	25,000
Cost of goods manufactured	180,000

Compute total current manufacturing costs.

LO 2–6   **M2–20 Calculating Cost of Goods Sold**

The following information is available for Baker Industries:

Cost of goods manufactured	$320,000
Beginning finished goods inventory	45,000
Ending finished goods inventory	35,000

Compute the cost of goods sold.

LO 2–3, 2–6   **M2–21 Calculating Direct Materials Used in Production**

The following information is available for Rodriguez Industries:

Direct labor	$ 60,000
Total current manufacturing costs	300,000

Manufacturing overhead is applied to production at 200 percent of direct labor cost. Determine the amount of direct materials used in production.

M2–22 Interpreting the Job Cost Sheet   LO 2–2

You recently had your car repaired and received the following bill:

Parts	$560
Labor (8 hours × $30 per hour)	240
Miscellaneous costs (20% of direct labor)	48
Total repair cost	$848

List three costs that likely would be included in the miscellaneous category.

M2–23 Calculating Missing Amounts and Cost of Goods Manufactured   LO 2–6

For each of the following independent cases A through D, compute the missing values:

Case	Total Current Manufacturing Costs	Beginning Work in Process Inventory	Ending Work in Process Inventory	Cost of Goods Manufactured
A	$7,200	$2,100	$1,650	$?
B	3,960	?	2,385	4,590
C	?	1,350	3,000	7,000
D	4,740	750	?	4,125

M2–24 Calculating Missing Amounts and Cost of Goods Sold   LO 2–6

For each of the following independent cases A through D, compute the missing values:

Case	Cost of Goods Manufactured	Beginning Finished Goods Inventory	Ending Finished Goods Inventory	Cost of Goods Sold
A	$5,270	$760	$850	$?
B	6,750	?	325	6,900
C	?	750	895	4,375
D	1,900	250	?	1,750

EXERCISES

E2–1 Posting Direct Materials, Direct Labor, and Applied Overhead to T-Accounts,   LO 2–2, 2–3, 2–4
Calculating Ending Balances

Oak Creek Furniture Factory (OCFF), a custom furniture manufacturer, uses job order costing to track the cost of each customer order. On March 1, OCFF had two jobs in process with the following costs:

Work in Process	Balance on 3/1
Job 33	$ 7,500
Job 34	6,000
	$13,500

Source documents revealed the following during March:

	Materials Requisitions Forms	Labor Time Tickets	Status of Job at Month-End
Job 33	$ 3,500	$ 6,500	Completed and sold
Job 34	6,000	7,800	Completed, but not sold
Job 35	4,200	3,250	In process
Indirect	1,300	2,140	
	$15,000	$19,690	

The company applies overhead to products at a rate of 150 percent of direct labor cost.

Required:

1. Compute the cost of Jobs 33, 34, and 35 at the end of the month.
2. Calculate the balance in the Work in Process Inventory, Finished Goods Inventory, and Cost of Goods Sold accounts at month-end.

LO 2–S1   **E2–2 Preparing Journal Entries**

Refer to the information in E2–1 for Oak Creek Furniture Factory.

Required:

Prepare journal entries to record the materials requisitions, labor costs, and applied overhead.

LO 2–2, 2–4   **E2–3 Analyzing Labor Time Tickets and Recording Labor Costs**

A weekly time ticket for Joyce Caldwell follows:

Direct Labor Time Ticket		Dates:	Monday 8/13 — Friday 8/17, 2018	
Ticket Number:	TT 338			
Employee:	Joyce Caldwell			
Date	Time Started	Time Ended	Total Hours	Job Number
8/12/2018	7:00 AM	3:00 PM	8 hours	Job 271
8/13/2018	7:00 AM	3:00 PM	8 hours	Job 271
8/14/2018	7:00 AM	3:00 PM	8 hours	Job 272
8/15/2018	7:00 AM	11:00 AM	4 hours	Job 272
8/15/2018	12:00 AM	4:00 PM	4 hours	Maintenance
8/16/2018	7:00 AM	3:00 PM	8 hours	Job 273
		Weekly totals	40 hours	
		Hourly Labor Rate	× $ 30	
		Total Wages Earned	$1,200	

Required:

1. Determine how much of the $1,200 that Joyce earned during this week would be charged to Job 271, Job 272, and Job 273.
2. Explain how the time spent doing maintenance work would be recorded.

LO 2–S1   **E2–4 Preparing Journal Entries**

Refer to the information presented in E2–3 for Joyce Caldwell.

Required:

Prepare a journal entry to record Joyce's wages.

E2–5 Calculating Predetermined Overhead Rate and Applied Overhead

LO 2–3

Wheeler's Bike Company manufactures custom racing bicycles. The company uses a job order cost system to determine the cost of each bike. Estimated costs and expenses for the coming year follow:

Bike parts	$ 350,000
Factory machinery depreciation	55,000
Factory supervisor salaries	140,000
Factory direct labor	300,000
Factory supplies	7,500
Factory property tax	37,500
Advertising cost	14,500
Administrative salaries	80,000
Administrative-related depreciation	16,000
Total expected costs	$1,000,500

Required:

1. Calculate the predetermined overhead rate per direct labor hour if the average direct labor rate is $15 per hour.

2. Determine the amount of applied overhead if 18,500 actual hours are worked in the upcoming year.

E2–6 Finding Unknown Values in the Cost of Goods Manufactured Report

LO 2–3, 2–6

Mulligan Manufacturing Company uses a job order cost system with overhead applied to products at a rate of 150 percent of direct labor cost. Selected manufacturing data follow:

	Case 1	Case 2	Case 3*
Direct materials used	$12,000	f.	$15,000
Direct labor	25,000	e.	i.
Manufacturing overhead applied	a.	18,000	j.
Total current manufacturing costs	b.	45,000	35,000
Beginning work in process inventory	10,000	g.	9,000
Ending work in process inventory	12,000	7,000	k.
Cost of goods manufactured	c.	46,000	32,000
Beginning finished goods inventory	15,000	10,000	l.
Ending finished goods inventory	12,000	h.	6,000
Cost of goods sold	d.	48,000	34,000

*Hint: For Case 3 (parts i. and j.), first solve for conversion costs and then determine how much of that is direct labor and how much is manufacturing overhead.

Required:

Treating each case independently, find the missing amounts for letters *a to l*. You should do them in the order listed.

E2–7 Calculating Overhead Rates, Actual and Applied Manufacturing Overhead, and Analyzing Over- or Underapplied Manufacturing Overhead

LO 2–3, 2–5

Cambridge Manufacturing Company applies manufacturing overhead on the basis of machine hours. At the beginning of the year, the company estimated its total overhead cost to be $325,000 and machine hours to be 25,000. Actual manufacturing overhead and machine hours were $372,000 and 26,000, respectively.

Required:

1. Compute the predetermined overhead rate.

2. Compute applied manufacturing overhead.

3. Compute over- or underapplied manufacturing overhead.

LO 2–S1

E2–8 Preparing Journal Entries

Refer to the information presented in E2–7 for Cambridge Manufacturing Company.

Required:

1. Prepare the journal entries to record actual and applied manufacturing overhead.
2. Prepare the journal entry to transfer the overhead balance to Cost of Goods Sold.

LO 2–4, 2–6

E2–9 Calculating Cost of Jobs

Manufacturing costs for Davenport Company during 2018 were as follows:

Beginning Finished Goods, 1/1/18	$24,100
Beginning Raw Materials, 1/1/18	35,500
Beginning Work in Process, 1/1/18	110,300
Direct Labor for 2018	$275,300
Ending Finished Goods, 12/31/18	22,400
Ending Raw Materials, 12/31/18	40,250
Ending Work in Process, 12/31/18	120,600
Material Purchases for 2018 (including $15,000 of indirect material)	304,200

Required:

1. Compute direct material used.
2. Compute applied overhead if the company applies overhead at a rate of 0.75 (75 percent) of direct labor cost.
3. Compute total manufacturing cost.
4. Compute cost of goods manufactured.
5. Compute cost of goods sold.

LO 2–6

E2–10 Preparing Cost of Goods Manufactured and Income Statement

Refer to the information presented in E2–9.

Required:

1. Prepare a Cost of Goods Manufactured report.
2. Prepare a Partial Income Statement if sales revenue was $1,250,000 and operating expenses were $210,000 for 2018.

LO 2–4

E2–11 Calculating Cost of Jobs in Work in Process, Finished Goods, and Cost of Goods Sold

Jenkins Company uses a job order cost system with overhead applied to jobs on the basis of direct labor hours. The direct labor rate is $20 per hour, and the predetermined overhead rate is $15 per direct labor hour. The company worked on three jobs during April. Jobs A and B were in process at the beginning of April. Job A was completed and delivered to the customer. Job B was completed during April, but not sold. Job C was started during April, but not completed. The job cost sheets revealed the following costs for April:

	Job A	Job B	Job C
Cost of Jobs in Process, 4/1/2018	$12,000	$1,000	$ -
Direct Materials Used	2,000	8,000	9,000
Direct Labor	10,000	8,000	3,000
Applied Manufacturing Overhead	?	?	?

Required:

If no other jobs were started, completed, or sold, determine the balance in each of the following accounts at the end of April:

a. Work in Process
b. Finished Goods
c. Cost of Goods Sold

E2–12 Applying Job Order Costing in a Service Setting

Optimum Health Inc. provides diet, fitness, and nutrition services to clients who want a healthier lifestyle. The company customizes a program for each client based on their individual goals that includes diet recommendations (prepackaged food and supplements), nutrition counseling, and guided fitness (personal training). The company uses a modified job order cost system that keeps track of the cost of the food, vitamins, and nutritional supplements the company provides to each client, as well as the amount of time nutrition and fitness consultants spend with each client. Optimum applies all indirect operating costs (e.g., rent, utilities, and management salaries) as a percentage of the consultant's labor cost.

During the most recent year, the firm estimated that it would pay $200,000 to its consultants and incur indirect operating costs of $300,000. Actual consultant labor costs were $215,000 and actual indirect operating costs were $290,000. The cost records for three of Optimum's clients are summarized below:

	Judy	Tom	Elizabeth
Food and nutritional supplements	$500	$1,000	$300
Nutritional counseling ($15 per hour)	150	300	180
Personal fitness training ($20 per hour)	400	600	800
Indirect operating costs	?	?	?

Required:

1. Compute the predetermined overhead rate.
2. Determine the total cost of serving each client.
3. Assume the company charges clients an up-front fee of $400. Food and nutritional supplements are priced at 30 percent above cost. Clients are charged $40 per hour for consulting services (both nutrition counseling and personal training). Determine the profitability of each client.

E2–13 Calculating the Cost of Finished and Unfinished Jobs

Following is partial information for Delamunte Industries for the month of August:

Work In Process	
Balance, August 1	$ 41,000
Direct materials used	75,000
Direct labor	120,000
Manufacturing overhead applied (based on direct labor cost)	90,000

Jobs finished during August are summarized here:

Job #	Cost of Jobs Completed
234	$58,000
237	65,000
231	74,500
246	67,500

Required:

At the end of August, only one job, Job 248, was still in process. The direct labor cost incurred on Job 248 as of August 31 was $24,000.

1. Calculate the predetermined overhead rate that was used to apply manufacturing overhead to jobs during August.
2. Determine the balance in Work in Process at the end of August.
3. Determine how much of the direct materials cost and applied overhead would be recorded for Job 248 as of August 31.

LO 2–3, 2–7 **E2–14 Computing Overhead Rate and Billing Rate for Service Firm**

McBride and Associates employs two professional appraisers, each having a different specialty. Debbie specializes in commercial appraisals and Tara specializes in residential appraisals. The company expects to incur total overhead costs of $346,500 during the year and applies overhead based on annual salary costs. The salaries and billable hours of the two appraisers are estimated to be as follows:

	Debbie	Tara
Annual Salary	$150,000	$81,000
Billable Hours	2,000	1,800

The accountant for McBride and Associates is computing the hourly rate that should be used to charge clients for Debbie and Tara's services. The hourly billing rate should be set to cover the total cost of services (salary plus overhead) plus a 20 percent markup.

Required:

1. Compute the predetermined overhead rate.
2. Compute the hourly billing rate for Debbie and Tara.

LO 2–3, 2–4, 2–6 **E2–15 Calculating and Posting Sales Revenue and the Total Cost to Complete a Job to T-Accounts**

Aquazona Pool Company is a custom pool builder. The company recently completed a pool for the Drayna family (Job 1324) as summarized on the incomplete job cost sheet below.

Job Cost Sheet

Job Number: 1324

Date Started: 7/8/2018

Date Completed: 8/30/2018

Description: Drayna Pool

Direct Materials		Direct Labor			Applied Manufacturing Overhead		
Req. No	Amount	Ticket	Hours	Amount	Hours	Rate	Amount
MR 3345	$1,500	TT 335	31	$ 600			
MR 3372	1,000	TT 340	39	800			
MR 4251	1,250	TT 385	31	600			
MR 4263	1,750	TT 425	34	700			
MR 5236	2,000	TT 445	23	500			
	$7,500		158	$3,200	?	?	?

Cost Summary

Direct Materials Cost	$7,500
Direct Labor Cost	3,200
Applied Manufacturing Overhead	?
Total Cost	

The company applies overhead to jobs at a rate of $15 per direct labor hour.

Required:

1. Calculate how much overhead would be applied to Job 1324.
2. Compute the total cost of Job 1324.
3. Assume the company bids its pools at total manufacturing cost plus an additional 30 percent. If actual costs were the same as estimated, determine how much revenue the company would report on the sale of Job 1324.
4. Calculate how much gross profit Aquazona made on the sale of the Drayna pool, before any adjustment for over- or underapplied manufacturing overhead.

LO 2–S1 **E2–16 Preparing Journal Entries**

Refer to the information presented in E2–15 for Aquazona Pool Company.

Required:

Prepare journal entries to record cost of goods sold and sales revenue for Job 1324. Assume the total cost of Job 1324 is currently in the Finished Goods Inventory account and that the Draynas paid for the pool with cash.

E2–17 Identifying Manufacturing Cost Flow through T-Accounts LO 2–4

Letters (*a*) through (*g*) represent several recent transactions that were posted to some of Johnson Company's T-accounts.

Raw Materials Inventory		Manufacturing Overhead	
(*a*)	(*b*)	(*c*)	(*e*)

Work in Process Inventory		Finished Goods Inventory	
(*b*)	(*f*)	(*f*)	(*g*)
(*d*)			
(*e*)			

Cost of Goods Sold	
(*g*)	

Required:

Assign letters (*a*) through (*g*) to the following descriptions to indicate how the transactions would be recorded in the T-accounts. The purchase of raw materials is provided as an example, where the letter (*a*) represents a debit to Raw Materials Inventory.

Description	Transaction
Applied manufacturing overhead	
Recorded direct labor	
Recorded the cost of jobs completed	
Purchased raw materials	(*a*)
Recorded actual manufacturing overhead	
Recorded the cost of jobs sold	
Issued raw materials to production	

E2–18 Calculating Actual and Applied Manufacturing Overhead Costs and Over- or Underapplied Overhead Costs LO 2–3, 2–4, 2–5, 2–6

Verizox Company uses a job order cost system with manufacturing overhead applied to products based on direct labor hours. At the beginning of the most recent year, the company estimated its manufacturing overhead cost at $300,000. Estimated direct labor cost was $400,000 for 20,000 hours. Actual costs for the most recent month are summarized here:

Item Description	Total Cost
Direct labor (1,500 hours)	$33,000
Indirect costs	
Indirect labor	4,500
Indirect materials	2,500
Factory rent	4,200
Factory supervision	4,700
Factory depreciation	5,600
Factory janitorial work	1,200
Factory insurance	2,600
General and administrative salaries	3,100
Selling expenses	2,300

Required:

1. Calculate the predetermined overhead rate.
2. Calculate the amount of applied manufacturing overhead.
3. Calculate actual manufacturing overhead costs.
4. Compute over- or underapplied overhead.

LO 2–S1   **E2–19 Preparing Journal Entries**

Refer to the information presented in E2–18 for Verizox Company.

Required:

1. Prepare the journal entry to apply manufacturing overhead to Work in Process Inventory.
2. Prepare the journal entry to record actual manufacturing overhead costs. The credit can be to a generic account titled Cash, Payables, and so on.
3. Prepare the journal entry to transfer the Manufacturing Overhead account balance to Cost of Goods Sold. Does this increase or decrease Cost of Goods Sold? Why?

LO 2–3, 2–4, 2–5   **E2–20 Recording Manufacturing Costs**

Reyes Manufacturing Company uses a job order cost system. At the beginning of January, the company had one job in process (Job 201) and one job completed but not yet sold (Job 200). Job 202 was started during January. Other select account balances follow (ignore any accounts that are not listed).

Raw Materials Inventory	Work in Process Inventory	Finished Goods Inventory
1/1 32,000	1/1 15,500	1/1 20,000

Cost of Goods Sold	Manufacturing Overhead	Sales Revenue

During January, the company had the following transactions:

a. Purchased $20,000 worth of materials on account.
b. Recorded materials issued to production as follows:

Job Number	Total Cost
201	$12,000
202	21,000
Indirect materials	3,200
	$36,200

c. Recorded factory payroll costs from direct labor time tickets that revealed the following:

Job Number	Hours	Total Cost
201	100	$ 2,150
202	500	10,750
Factory supervision		5,000
		$17,900

d. Applied overhead to production at a rate of $25 per direct labor hour for 600 actual direct labor hours.

e. Recorded the following actual manufacturing overhead costs:

Item	Total Cost	Description
Factory rent	$ 3,100	Paid in cash
Depreciation	2,500	Factory equipment
Factory utilities	1,750	Incurred but not paid
Factory insurance	1,250	Prepaid policy
	$ 8,600	

f. Completed Job 201 and transferred it to Finished Goods Inventory.
g. Sold Job 200 for $31,000.

Job 202 was still in process at the end of January.

Required:

1. Post the preceding transactions to T-accounts. Create an additional account called Miscellaneous Accounts to capture the offsetting of debits and credits to other accounts such as Cash, Payables, Accumulated Depreciation, and so on.

2. Compute the ending balance in the following accounts:
   a. Raw Materials Inventory.
   b. Work in Process Inventory.
   c. Finished Goods Inventory.
   d. Cost of Goods Sold (unadjusted).
   e. Manufacturing Overhead.

3. Compute the total cost of Jobs 201 and 202 at the end of January. Where does this cost appear in the T-accounts?

E2–21 Calculating Missing Amounts and Cost of Goods Manufactured and Sold   LO 2–3, 2–4, 2–5, 2–6

For each of the following independent cases (1 to 4), compute the missing values. Note: Complete the missing items in alphabetical order.

	Case 1	Case 2	Case 3	Case 4
Beginning raw material	$ 7,000	e.	$16,000	$ 55,000
Raw material purchases	63,000	24,500	33,312	o.
Indirect materials issued	1,400	2,000	1,200	1,000
Ending raw materials	2,800	4,500	i.	46,750
Direct materials used	a.	27,000	26,976	n.
Direct labor	40,600	f.	j.	61,625
Manufacturing overhead applied	72,800	80,700	24,864	270,865
Total current manufacturing costs	b.	151,200	74,320	m.
Beginning work in process	57,400	65,200	k.	51,260
Ending work in process	c.	g.	33,000	118,050
Cost of goods manufactured	194,600	159,600	71,380	412,950
Beginning finished goods	100,800	h.	41,520	p.
Ending finished goods	112,000	60,200	l.	198,600
Cost of goods sold	d.	142,000	90,700	419,700

LO 2–6   **E2–22 Calculating Cost of Goods Manufactured and Sold and Preparing an Income Statement**

StorSmart Company makes plastic organizing bins. The company has the following inventory balances at the beginning and end of March:

	Beginning Inventory	Ending Inventory
Raw materials	$33,000	$22,000
Work in process	25,000	44,000
Finished goods	60,000	58,000

Additional information for the month of March follows:

Raw materials purchases	$ 84,000
Indirect materials used	10,000
Direct labor	55,000
Manufacturing overhead applied	85,000
Selling, general, and administrative expenses	58,000
Sales revenue	450,000

Required:

Based on this information, prepare the following for StorSmart:

1. A cost of goods manufactured report.
2. An income statement for the month of March.

LO 2–S1   **E2–23 Preparing Journal Entries**

Pental Manufacturing Company incurred the following transactions during the year:

a. Purchased raw materials on account, $50,500.
b. Requisitioned raw materials of $32,000 to the factory, which included $8,300 of indirect materials.
c. Accrued factory labor costs of $81,400, which included $17,000 of indirect labor. The workers have not yet been paid.
d. Incurred actual manufacturing overhead costs (on account) of $90,000.
e. Recorded depreciation for office equipment of $7,000.
f. Manufacturing overhead was applied at the rate of 150 percent of direct labor cost.
g. Completed jobs costing $102,000.
h. Sold jobs costing $70,000 for $87,500 on account.

Required:

1. Journalize transactions a–h.
2. Compute the over- or underapplied overhead
3. Prepare the journal entry to transfer the over- or underapplied balance to Cost of Goods Sold.
4. Compute adjusted cost of goods sold.

LO 2–S1   **E2–24 Preparing Journal Entries**

A recent materials requisition form for Christopher Creek Furniture Manufacturers follows:

Requisition Number	Job Number	Item Description	Total Cost
MR 234	25	¼" maple planks	$450
MR 235	26	¼" cherry planks	320
MR 236	27	½" birch planks	280
MR 237	Indirect	Wood screws, etc.	200

Required:

Prepare the journal entry to record the issuance of materials.

E2–25 Preparing Journal Entries

LO 2–S1

Floyd's Auto Repair Shop uses a job order cost system to track the cost of each repair. Floyd's applies its garage or shop overhead at a rate of $20 per direct labor hour spent on each repair. Floyd's uses the following accounts to track the cost of all repairs:

Raw Materials (parts and supplies)		Repair Jobs in Process		Cost of Repairs Completed and Sold		Garage/Shop* Overhead Costs	

* Because an auto shop does not manufacture a product, the overhead cost would include all of the indirect costs that are incurred in the garage or shop that cannot be traced to a specific repair job.

The following transactions occurred during the most recent month:

(a) Purchased raw materials (parts and supplies) on account $16,000.

(b) Used $14,000 in raw materials (parts and supplies). Of this, $10,000 was for major parts that were traceable to individual repair jobs, and the remainder was for incidental supplies such as lubricants, rags, fuel, and so on.

(c) Recorded a total of $12,000 in direct labor cost (for 500 hours) that are owed but not yet paid.

(d) Applied overhead to repair jobs at a rate of $20 per direct labor hour.

(e) Recorded the following actual overhead costs:

Rent on garage (prepaid in the prior month)	$8,000
Depreciation on repair equipment	2,500
Garage supervisor's salary (owed but not yet paid)	4,000

(f) Completed repair jobs costing $40,000 and charged customers at cost plus an additional 30 percent. (**Note:** You can bypass the Finished Goods Inventory account, which is not appropriate in this context.)

Required:

Prepare journal entries for transactions (*a*) through (*f*) using the account names shown and other appropriate accounts such as Cash, Payables, Accumulated Depreciation, Prepaids, and Sales Revenue.

E2–26 Applying Job Order Costing in a Service Setting

LO 2–3, 2–4, 2–7

Marsha Design is an interior design and consulting firm. The firm uses a job order cost system in which each client represents an individual job. Marsha Design traces direct labor and travel costs to each job (client). It assigns indirect costs to clients at a predetermined overhead rate based on direct labor hours.

At the beginning of the year, the managing partner, Marsha Cain, prepared the following budget:

Direct labor hours (professional)	5,000
Direct labor costs (professional)	$500,000
Indirect costs:	
Support staff salaries	$ 50,000
Office rent	55,000
Office supplies	20,000
Total expected indirect costs	$125,000

Later that same year, in March, Marsha Design served several clients. Records for two clients appear below:

	Oliverio	McComb
Direct labor cost (professional)	$4,000	$3,000
Travel costs	500	100
Direct labor hours	40 hours	30 hours

Required:

1. Compute Marsha Design's predetermined overhead rate for the current year.
2. Compute the total cost of serving the clients listed.
3. Assume that Marsha charges clients $250 per hour for interior design services. How much gross profit would she earn on each of the clients above, ignoring any difference between actual and applied overhead?

LO 2–2   **E2–27 Sustainability and Job Order Costing**

Panderia Homes builds single-family homes near Santa Fe, New Mexico. The company prides itself on designing beautiful homes that are built in ways that reduce environmental impact and provide energy savings, long-lasting value and comfort, at a price that middle-income families can afford.

Panderia's sustainability standards include the following requirements:

• At least 80 percent of total raw material costs will be sourced from local suppliers (within a 100 mile radius) to reduce transportation costs and to boost the local economy.

• At least 60 percent of lumber will come from recycled sources rather than virgin wood.

• All appliances will be ENERGY STAR® rated to reduce energy consumption by an average of 50 percent.

• All paints, woodwork, and carpet materials will emit low or zero volatile organized compounds (VOCs) for improved air quality.

Panderia's job order cost system is designed to capture data to determine whether the company is meeting these standards. The job cost sheet for a job that is in process is summarized below:

Material Type	Quantity	Unit Cost	Total Cost	Supplier Location	% from Recycled Materials	Meets Energy and Conservation Standards?
Lumber	1,000	$20.00	$20,000	Albuquerque, New Mexico	80%	Yes
Appliances	8	$2,000	$16,000	Los Angeles, California	10%	Energy Star Rated
Cabinets	40	500	$20,000	Santa Fe, New Mexico	30%	Low-VOC
Windows	50	200	$10,000	Taos, New Mexico	20%	Low-E

Required:

1. Is Panderia meeting each of its sustainability standards? Why or why not?
2. How could managers use the information to make sustainability improvements?

GROUP A PROBLEMS

**PA2–1 Recording Manufacturing and Nonmanufacturing Costs, Preparing the Cost   LO 2–3, 2–4, 2–5, 2–6
of Goods Manufactured Report and Income Statement**

Lamonda Corp. uses a job order cost system. On April 1, the accounts had the following balances:

Raw Materials Inventory	Work in Process Inventory	Finished Goods Inventory
Bal. 25,000	Bal. 55,000	Bal. 60,000

Manufacturing Overhead	Cost of Goods Sold

Sales Revenue	Nonmanufacturing Expenses

The following transactions occurred during April:

a. Purchased materials on account at a cost of $136,000.
b. Requisitioned materials at a cost of $122,000, of which $28,000 was for general factory use.
c. Recorded unpaid factory labor of $155,000, of which $24,000 was indirect.
d. Incurred other costs:

Selling expense	$44,000
Factory utilities	26,000
Administrative expenses	15,000
Factory rent	30,000
Factory depreciation	24,000

e. Applied overhead at a rate equal to 135 percent of direct labor cost.
f. Completed jobs costing $375,000.
g. Sold jobs costing $402,000.
h. Recorded sales revenue (on account) of $500,000.

Required:

1. Post the April transactions to the T-accounts. (**Note:** Some transactions will affect other accounts not shown; e.g., Cash, Accounts Payable, Accumulated Depreciation. You do not need to show the offsetting debit or credit to those accounts.)

2. Compute the balance in the accounts at the end of April.

3. Compute over- or underapplied manufacturing overhead. If the balance in the Manufacturing Overhead account is closed directly to Cost of Goods Sold, will Cost of Goods Sold increase or decrease?

4. Prepare Lamonda's cost of goods manufactured report for April.

5. Prepare Lamonda's April income statement. Include any adjustment to Cost of Goods Sold needed to dispose of over- or underapplied manufacturing overhead.

PA2–2 Preparing Journal Entries

Refer to the information presented in PA2–1 for Lamonda Corp.

Required:

Prepare all of Lamonda's necessary journal entries for the month of April.

PA2–3 Calculating Predetermined Overhead Rates, Recording Manufacturing Costs, and Analyzing Overhead

Tyler Tooling Company uses a job order cost system with overhead applied to products on the basis of machine hours. For the upcoming year, the company estimated its total manufacturing overhead cost at $420,000 and total machine hours at 60,000. During the first month of operations, the company worked on three jobs and recorded the following actual direct materials cost, direct labor cost, and machine hours for each job:

	Job 101	Job 102	Job 103	Total
Direct materials used	$19,200	$14,400	$9,600	$43,200
Direct labor	$28,800	$11,200	$9,600	$49,600
Machine hours	1,000 hours	4,000 hours	2,000 hours	7,000 hours

Job 101 was completed and sold for $60,000.

Job 102 was completed but not sold.

Job 103 is still in process.

Actual overhead costs recorded during the first month of operations totaled $45,000.

Required:

1. Calculate the predetermined overhead rate.
2. Compute the total manufacturing overhead applied to the Work in Process Inventory account during the first month of operations.
3. Compute the balance in the Work in Process Inventory account at the end of the first month.
4. How much gross profit would the company report during the first month of operations before making an adjustment for over- or underapplied manufacturing overhead?
5. Determine the balance in the Manufacturing Overhead account at the end of the first month. Is it over- or underapplied?

PA2–4 Preparing Journal Entries

Refer to the information in PA2–3 for Tyler Tooling Company.

Required:

1. Prepare a journal entry showing the transfer of Job 102 into Finished Goods Inventory upon its completion.
2. Prepare the journal entries to recognize the sales revenue and cost of goods sold for Job 101.
3. Prepare the journal entry to transfer the balance of the Manufacturing Overhead account to Cost of Goods Sold.

PA2–5 Recording Manufacturing Costs and Analyzing Manufacturing Overhead

Christopher's Custom Cabinet Company uses a job order cost system with overhead applied as a percentage of direct labor costs. Inventory balances at the beginning of 2018 follow:

Raw materials inventory	$20,000
Work in process inventory	15,000
Finished goods inventory	32,000

The following transactions occurred during January:

a. Purchased materials on account for $26,000.
b. Issued materials to production totaling $40,000, 80 percent of which was traced to specific jobs and the remainder of which was treated as indirect materials.
c. Payroll costs totaling $69,700 were recorded as follows:

$18,000 for assembly workers

5,200 for factory supervision

31,000 for administrative personnel
15,500 for sales commissions

d. Recorded depreciation: $8,500 for factory machines, $2,400 for the copier used in the administrative office.

e. Recorded $4,000 of expired insurance. Forty percent was insurance on the manufacturing facility, with the remainder classified as an administrative expense.

f. Paid $7,800 in other factory costs in cash.

g. Applied manufacturing overhead at a rate of 300 percent of direct labor cost.

h. Completed all jobs but one; the job cost sheet for the uncompleted job shows $10,000 for direct materials, $3,000 for direct labor, and $9,000 for applied overhead.

i. Sold jobs costing $70,000. The revenue earned on these jobs was $91,000.

Required:

1. Set up T-accounts, record the beginning balances, post the January transactions, and compute the final balance for the following accounts:

   a. Raw Materials Inventory.
   b. Work in Process Inventory.
   c. Finished Goods Inventory.
   d. Cost of Goods Sold.
   e. Manufacturing Overhead.
   f. Selling, General, and Administrative Expenses.
   g. Sales Revenue.

2. Determine how much gross profit the company would report during the month of January **before** any adjustment is made for the overhead balance.

3. Determine the amount of over- or underapplied overhead.

4. Compute adjusted gross profit assuming that any over- or underapplied overhead balance is adjusted directly to Cost of Goods Sold.

PA2-6 Finding Unknowns in the Cost of Goods Manufactured Report and Analyzing Manufacturing Overhead   LO 2-3, 2-4, 2-5, 2-6

The following information was obtained from the records of Appleton Corporation during 2018.
• Manufacturing Overhead was applied at a rate of 125 percent of direct labor dollars.

• Beginning value of inventory follows:
  • Beginning Work in Process Inventory, $12,000.
  • Beginning Finished Goods Inventory, $25,000.

• During the period, Work in Process Inventory decreased by 20 percent, and Finished Goods Inventory increased by 25 percent.

• Actual manufacturing overhead costs were $135,000.

• Sales were $450,000.

• Adjusted Cost of Goods Sold was $325,000.

Required:

Use the preceding information to find the missing values in the following table:

Item	Amount
Direct materials used	$?
Direct labor	?
Manufacturing overhead applied	125,000
Total current manufacturing costs	?
Plus: Beginning work in process inventory	12,000
Less: Ending work in process inventory	?
Cost of goods manufactured	?
Plus: Beginning finished goods inventory	25,000
Less: Ending finished goods inventory	?
Unadjusted cost of goods sold	?
Over/Underapplied overhead	?
Adjusted cost of goods sold	325,000

LO 2–3, 2–5

PA2–7 Selecting an Allocation Base and Analyzing Manufacturing Overhead

Amberjack Company is trying to decide on an allocation base to use to assign manufacturing over-head to jobs. The company has always used direct labor hours to assign manufacturing overhead to products, but it is trying to decide whether it should use a different allocation base such as direct labor dollars or machine hours.

Actual and estimated data for manufacturing overhead, direct labor cost, direct labor hours, and machine hours for the most recent fiscal year are summarized here:

	Estimated Value	Actual Value
Manufacturing overhead cost	$594,000	$655,000
Direct labor cost	$396,000	$450,000
Direct labor hours	16,500 hours	18,000 hours
Machine hours	7,500 hours	8,500 hours

Required:

1. Based on the company's current allocation base (direct labor hours), compute the following:
   a. Predetermined overhead rate.
   b. Applied manufacturing overhead.
   c. Over- or underapplied manufacturing overhead.

2. If the company had used direct labor dollars (instead of direct labor hours) as its allocation base, compute the following:
   a. Predetermined overhead rate.
   b. Applied manufacturing overhead.
   c. Over- or underapplied manufacturing overhead.

3. If the company had used machine hours (instead of direct labor hours) as its allocation base, compute the following:
   a. Predetermined overhead rate.
   b. Applied manufacturing overhead.
   c. Over- or underapplied manufacturing overhead.

4. Based on last year's data alone, which allocation base would have provided the most accurate measure for applying manufacturing overhead costs to production?

5. How does a company decide on an allocation base to use in applying manufacturing overhead? What factors should be considered?

LO 2–3, 2–4, 2–5, 2–6

PA2–8 Recording Manufacturing Costs, Preparing a Cost of Goods Manufactured Report, and Calculating Income from Operations

Dobson Manufacturing Company uses a job order cost system with manufacturing overhead applied to products on the basis of direct labor dollars. At the beginning of the most recent period, the company estimated its total direct labor cost to be $65,000 and its total manufacturing overhead cost to be $91,000.

Several incomplete general ledger accounts showing the transactions that occurred during the most recent accounting period follow:

Raw Materials Inventory		
Beginning Balance	15,000	?
Purchases	95,000	
Ending Balance	30,000	

Work in Process Inventory		
Beginning Balance	30,000	?
Direct Materials	70,000	
Direct Labor	$50,000	
Applied Overhead	?	
Ending Balance	20,000	

Finished Goods Inventory		
Beginning Balance	40,000	?
Cost of Goods Completed	?	
Ending Balance	50,000	

Cost of Goods Sold		
Unadjusted Cost of Goods Sold	?	
Adjusted Cost of Goods Sold	?	

Manufacturing Overhead				
Indirect Materials	10,000	?	Applied Overhead	
Indirect Labor	15,000			
Factory Depreciation	13,000			
Factory Rent	7,000			
Factory Utilities	3,000			
Other Factory Costs	10,000			
Actual Overhead	58,000			

Sales Revenue	
	300,000

Selling, General, and Administrative Expenses		
Adm. Salaries	28,000	
Office Depreciation	20,000	
Advertising	15,000	
Ending Balance	63,000	

Required:

1. Calculate the predetermined overhead rate.
2. Fill in the missing values in the T-accounts.
3. Compute over- or underapplied overhead.
4. Prepare a statement of cost of goods manufactured.
5. Prepare an income statement, including an adjustment to cost of goods sold for the over/underapplied manufacturing overhead.

GROUP B PROBLEMS

PB2–1 Recording Manufacturing and Nonmanufacturing Costs, Preparing Cost of Goods Manufactured Report and Income Statement   LO 2–3, 2–4, 2–5, 2–6

Coda Industries uses a job order cost system. On November 1, the company had the following balance in the accounts:

Raw Materials Inventory	
Bal. 62,000	

Work in Process Inventory	
Bal. 22,900	

Finished Goods Inventory	
Bal. 130,000	

Manufacturing Overhead	

Cost of Goods Sold	

Sales Revenue	

Nonmanufacturing Expenses	

The following transactions occurred during November:

a. Purchased materials on account at a cost of $270,500.
b. Requisitioned materials at a cost of $195,500, only $180,000 of which was traceable to specific jobs.
c. Recorded unpaid factory labor of $267,000, 80 percent of which was direct.

d. Incurred other costs:

Selling expenses	$ 65,300
Factory utilities	68,300
Administrative expenses	92,500
Factory rent	125,000
Factory depreciation	64,800

e. Applied overhead during the month totaling $290,000.
f. Completed jobs costing $607,250.
g. Sold jobs costing $557,700.
h. Recorded sales revenue (on account) of $850,000.

Required:

1. Post the November transactions to the T-accounts. (**Note:** Some transactions will affect other accounts not shown; e.g., Cash, Accounts Payable, Accumulated Depreciation. You do not need to show the offsetting debit or credit to those accounts.)
2. Compute the balance in the accounts at the end of November.
3. Compute over- or underapplied manufacturing overhead. If the balance in the Manufacturing Overhead account is closed directly to Cost of Goods Sold, will Cost of Goods Sold increase or decrease?
4. Prepare Coda's cost of goods manufactured report for November.
5. Prepare Coda's November income statement. Include any adjustment to Cost of Goods Sold needed to dispose of over- or underapplied manufacturing overhead.

LO 2–S1   **PB2–2 Preparing Journal Entries**

Refer to the information presented in PB2–1 for Coda Industries.

Required:

Prepare all of Coda's necessary journal entries for the month of November.

LO 2–3, 2–4, 2–5   **PB2–3 Calculating Predetermined Overhead Rates, Recording Manufacturing Costs, and Analyzing Overhead**

Knight Company uses a job order cost system with overhead applied to products on the basis of machine hours. For the upcoming year, Knight estimated its total manufacturing overhead cost at $450,000 and its total machine hours at 150,000. During the first month of operation, the company worked on three jobs and recorded the following actual direct materials cost, direct labor cost, and machine hours for each job:

	Job 101	Job 102	Job 103	Total
Direct materials cost	$25,500	$17,000	$ 8,500	$51,000
Direct labor cost	$11,900	$ 8,500	$13,600	$34,000
Machine hours	8,000 hours	4,000 hours	5,000 hours	17,000 hours

Job 101 was completed and sold for $75,000.

Job 102 was completed but not sold.

Job 103 is still in process.

Actual overhead costs recorded during the first month of operations were $56,000.

Required:

1. Calculate the predetermined overhead rate.
2. Compute the total overhead applied to the Work in Process Inventory account during the first month of operations.
3. Compute the balance in the Work in Process Inventory account at the end of the first month.

4. How much gross profit would the company report during the first month of operations before making an adjustment for over- or underapplied manufacturing overhead?

5. Determine the balance in the Manufacturing Overhead account at the end of the first month. Is it over- or underapplied?

PB2–4 Preparing Journal Entries   LO 2–S1

Refer to the information in PB2–3 for Knight Company.

Required:

1. Prepare a journal entry showing the transfer of Job 102 into Finished Goods Inventory upon its completion.

2. Prepare the journal entries to recognize the sales revenue and cost of goods sold for Job 101.

3. Prepare the journal entry to transfer the balance of the Manufacturing Overhead account to Cost of Goods Sold.

PB2–5 Recording Manufacturing Costs and Analyzing Manufacturing Overhead   LO 2–3, 2–4, 2–5

Hamilton Custom Cabinet Company uses a job order cost system with overhead applied based on direct labor cost. Inventory balances at the beginning of 2018 follow:

Raw materials inventory	$15,600
Work in process inventory	33,500
Finished goods inventory	42,300

The following transactions occurred during January:

a. Purchased materials on account for $42,000.

b. Issued materials to production totaling $45,000, 85 percent of which was traced to specific jobs and the remainder of which was treated as indirect materials.

c. Payroll costs totaling $30,000 were recorded as follows:

> $17,300 for assembly workers
>
> 8,400 for factory supervision
>
> 2,500 for administrative personnel
>
> 1,800 for sales commissions

d. Recorded depreciation: $9,000 for factory machines and $25,000 for the copier used in the administrative office.

e. Recorded $9,000 of expired insurance. Sixty percent was insurance on the manufacturing facility, with the remainder classified as an administrative expense.

f. Paid $7,900 in other factory costs in cash.

g. Applied manufacturing overhead at a rate of 200 percent of direct labor cost.

h. Completed all jobs but one; the job cost sheet for the uncompleted job shows $18,000 for direct materials, $7,000 for direct labor, and $14,000 for applied overhead.

i. Sold jobs costing $40,000 during the period; the company adds a 25 percent markup on cost to determine the sales price.

Required:

1. Set up T-accounts, record the beginning balances, post the January transactions, and compute the final balance for the following accounts:

   a. Raw Materials Inventory.

   b. Work in Process Inventory.

   c. Finished Goods Inventory.

   d. Cost of Goods Sold.

   e. Manufacturing Overhead.

   f. Selling, General, and Administrative Expenses.

   g. Sales Revenue.

2. Determine how much gross profit the company would report during the month of January **before** any adjustment is made for the overhead balance.

3. Determine the amount of over- or underapplied overhead.

4. Compute adjusted gross profit assuming that any over- or underapplied overhead is adjusted directly to Cost of Goods Sold.

LO 2–3, 2–4, 2–5, 2–6   **PB2–6 Finding Unknowns in the Cost of Goods Manufactured Report and Analyzing Manufacturing Overhead**

The following information was obtained from the records of Martinez Corporation during 2018.

1. Manufacturing overhead was applied at a rate of 175 percent of direct labor dollars.

2. Beginning value of inventory follows:
   a. Beginning Work in Process Inventory, $32,000.
   b. Beginning Finished Goods Inventory, $15,000.

3. During the period, Work in Process Inventory decreased by 25 percent and Finished Goods Inventory increased by 30 percent.

4. Actual manufacturing overhead costs were $105,000.

5. Sales were $750,000.

6. Adjusted Cost of Goods Sold was $325,000.

Required:

Use the preceding information to find the missing values in the following table:

Item	Amount
Direct materials used	$?
Direct labor	?
Manufacturing overhead applied	122,500
Current manufacturing costs	?
Plus: Beginning work in process inventory	32,000
Less: Ending work in process inventory	?
Cost of goods manufactured	?
Plus: Beginning finished goods inventory	15,000
Less: Ending finished goods inventory	?
Unadjusted cost of goods sold	?
Overhead adjustment	?
Adjusted cost of goods sold	325,000

LO 2–3, 2–5   **PB2–7 Selecting an Allocation Base and Analyzing Manufacturing Overhead**

Timberland Company is trying to decide on an allocation base to use to assign manufacturing overhead to jobs. The company has always used direct labor hours to assign manufacturing overhead to products, but it is trying to decide whether it should use a different allocation base such as direct labor dollars or machine hours.

   Actual and estimated results for manufacturing overhead, direct labor cost, direct labor hours, and machine hours for the most recent fiscal year are summarized here:

	Estimated Value	Actual Value
Manufacturing overhead cost	$700,000	$750,000
Direct labor cost	$437,500	$464,000
Direct labor hours	25,000 hours	27,000 hours
Machine hours	12,500 hours	13,000 hours

Required:

1. Based on the company's current allocation base (direct labor hours), compute the following:
   a. Predetermined overhead rate.
   b. Applied manufacturing overhead.
   c. Over- or underapplied manufacturing overhead.

2. If the company had used direct labor dollars (instead of direct labor hours) as its allocation base, compute the following:

    a. Predetermined overhead rate.
    b. Applied manufacturing overhead.
    c. Over- or underapplied manufacturing overhead.

3. If the company had used machine hours (instead of direct labor hours) as its allocation base, compute the following:

    a. Predetermined overhead rate.
    b. Applied manufacturing overhead.
    c. Over- or underapplied manufacturing overhead

4. Based on last year's data alone, which allocation base would have provided the most accurate measure for applying manufacturing overhead costs to production?

5. How does a company decide on an allocation base to use in applying manufacturing overhead? What factors should be considered?

PB2–8 Recording Manufacturing Costs, Preparing a Cost of Goods Manufactured Report, and Calculating Income from Operations

LO 2–3, 2–4, 2–5, 2–6

Carlton Manufacturing Company uses a job order cost system with manufacturing overhead applied to products on the basis of direct labor dollars. At the beginning of the most recent period, the company estimated its total direct labor cost to be $42,000 and its total manufacturing overhead cost to be $75,600.

    Several incomplete general ledger accounts showing the transactions that occurred during the most recent accounting period follow:

Raw Materials Inventory

Beginning Balance	10,000	?
Purchases	85,000	
Ending Balance	$18,500	

Work in Process Inventory

Beginning Balance	30,000	?
Direct Materials	?	
Direct Labor	35,000	
Applied Overhead	?	
Ending Balance	20,000	

Finished Goods Inventory

Beginning Balance	60,000	?
Cost of Goods Completed	?	
Ending Balance	40,000	

Cost of Goods Sold

Unadjusted Cost of Goods Sold	?
Adjusted Cost of Goods Sold	?

Manufacturing Overhead

Indirect Materials	10,000	? Applied Overhead
Indirect Labor	20,000	
Factory Depreciation	13,000	
Factory Rent	12,000	
Factory Utilities	5,000	
Other Factory Costs	14,000	
Actual Overhead	74,000	

Sales Revenue

	280,000

Selling, General, and Administrative Expenses

Adm. Salaries	30,000	
Office Depreciation	20,000	
Advertising	19,000	
Ending Balance	69,000	

Required:

1. Calculate the predetermined overhead rate.
2. Fill in the missing values in the T-accounts.
3. Compute over- or underapplied overhead.
4. Prepare a statement of cost of goods manufactured.
5. Prepare an income statement, including an adjustment to cost of goods sold for the over/underapplied manufacturing overhead.

SKILLS DEVELOPMENT CASES

LO 2–1

©McGraw-Hill Education

S2–1 Video Case Assignment: Identifying Characteristics of Job Order Costing

Go to www.YouTube.com and search for **How It's Made,** a television show produced by the Discovery Channel that shows how thousands of products and services are created. Find a product or service for which job order costing would be appropriate, such as animated films, special effects make-up, luxury sports cars, artificial limbs, or other specialized products or services.

Watch the video and answer the following questions:

- What product or service did you choose? Why is job order costing appropriate for this setting?
- Why does the company that makes the product or service need a cost system? Describe two decisions a manager would make based on cost information.
- List two direct costs of making the product or service. Describe how the company would track these costs to specific jobs, projects, or customers.
- List three indirect costs of making the product or service. Describe how the company would assign these costs to specific jobs, projects, or customers. What allocation base (cost driver) would be appropriate for this setting?

LO 2–1, 2–2, 2–3

S2–2 Applying Job Order Costing to an Entrepreneurial Business

Assume you are going to become an entrepreneur and start your own business. Think about your talents and interests and come up with an idea for a small business venture that provides a unique product or service to local customers. You can select any business venture you want, but if you are struggling to come up with an idea, here are some examples:

Catering
Wedding-planning consulting
Video production company
Pool building company
Personal shopping service
Interior design business
Flower shop
Rock-climbing guide service
River-rafting company
Web design company

Required:

For whatever business venture you select, answer the following questions:

1. What would the major costs of your business be? Try to classify the costs into the areas of direct materials; direct labor; manufacturing overhead; and selling, general, and administrative expenses. (**Hint:** Not all businesses will have all of these cost classifications.)
2. Why would you need to determine the cost of providing your product or service to individual customers? In other words, what types of decisions would you expect to make based on job order cost information?
3. In general, would you expect your company's indirect (overhead) costs to be less or more than the direct costs (direct labor and materials)? What allocation base do you think you would use to charge overhead costs to individual customers? How much do you think the overhead rate would need to be?
4. Create a job cost sheet for a hypothetical "average" customer that includes estimates of the major costs of serving that customer. How much do you think you would need to charge to cover all of the costs plus provide a reasonable profit for yourself?

LO 2–3, 2–4, 2–5, 2–6, 2–S1

S2–3 Comprehensive Job Order Costing Case

Sampson Company uses a job order cost system with overhead applied to products based on direct labor hours. Based on previous history, the company estimated its total overhead for the coming year (2018) to be $720,000 and its total direct labor hours to be 24,000.

On January 1, 2018, the general ledger of Sampson Company revealed that it had one job in process (Job 102) for which it had incurred a total cost of $15,000. Job 101 had been finished the previous month for a total cost of $30,000 but was not yet sold. The company had a contract for Job 103 but had not started working on it yet. Other balances in Raw Materials Inventory and other assets, liabilities, and stockholders' equity accounts are summarized below.

SAMPSON COMPANY
General Ledger Accounts

Raw Materials Inventory

1/1 Balance	10,000

Manufacturing Overhead

Work in Process Inventory (WIP)

1/1 Balance	15,000

Finished Goods Inventory

1/1 Balance	30,000

Individual Job Cost Sheets (subsidiary ledgers to WIP)

	Job 102	Job 103
Beg. Balance	15,000	—
+ Direct Materials		
+ Direct Labor		
+ Applied OH		
Total Mfg. Cost		

Cost of Goods Sold

Sales Revenue

Selling, General, and Administrative Expenses

Cash and Other Assets

1/1 Balance	100,000

Payables and Other Liabilities

85,000	1/1 Balance

Stockholders' Equity

70,000	1/1 Balance

During January, the company had the following transactions:

a. Purchased $10,000 worth of raw materials on account.
b. Issued the following materials into production:

Item	Cost	Explanation
Direct materials	$7,000	Job 102, $2,000; Job 103, $5,000
Indirect materials	2,000	Used on both jobs
Total materials issued	$9,000	

c. Recorded salaries and wages payable as follows:

Item	Cost	Explanation
Direct labor	$10,000	Job 102, $6,000; Job 103, $4,000
Indirect labor	4,000	For factory supervision
Salaries	5,000	For administrative staff
Total payroll cost	$19,000	

d. Applied overhead to jobs based on the number of direct labor hours required:

Job Number	Direct Labor Hours
Job 102	300 hours
Job 103	200 hours
Total	500 hours

e. Recorded the following actual manufacturing costs:

Item	Cost	Explanation
Rent	$ 6,000	Paid factory rent in cash
Depreciation	5,000	Factory equipment
Insurance	3,000	Had one month of factory insurance policy expire
Utilities	2,000	Received factory utility bill but did not pay it
Total cost	$16,000	

f. Recorded the following general and administrative costs:

Item	Cost	Explanation
Advertising	$2,000	Advertising paid in cash
Depreciation	3,000	Office equipment
Other expenses	1,000	Micellaneous expenses incurred but not paid
Total cost	$6,000	

g. Sold Job 101, which is recorded in Finished Goods Inventory at a cost of $30,000, for $55,000.
h. Completed Job 102 but did not sell it; Job 103 is still in process at year-end.

Required:

1. Compute and interpret the predetermined overhead rate.
2. Prepare journal entries to record the January transactions and post the entries to the general ledger T-accounts given earlier in the problem.
3. How much overhead would be applied to jobs during the period?
4. Compute the total cost of Jobs 102 and 103 at the end of the period. Where would the cost of each of these jobs appear on the year-end balance sheet?
5. Calculate the amount of over- or underapplied overhead.
6. Prepare the journal entry to dispose of the overhead balance assuming that it had been a year-end balance instead of a month-end balance. Post the effect to the general ledger T-accounts.
7. Prepare a statement of cost of goods manufactured report.
8. Prepare a brief income statement for Sampson Company including the adjustment for over- or underapplied overhead.

3

Process Costing

CHAPTER THREE

YOUR LEARNING OBJECTIVES

LO 3–1 Describe the key features of a process costing system.

LO 3–2 Reconcile the number of physical units using the weighted-average method.

LO 3–3 Calculate the number of equivalent units using the weighted-average method.

LO 3–4 Prepare a process costing production report using the weighted-average method.

LO 3–S1 Prepare a process costing production report using the first-in, first-out (FIFO) method.

LO 3–S2 Prepare journal entries to record manufacturing costs in a process cost system.

©Hill Street Studios/Blend Images LLC

FOCUS COMPANY: FETZER VINEYARDS

State agencies often allocate funding to public universities based on the number of full-time equivalent students. A full-time equivalent (FTE) is a standardized measure of workload. For example, if a full course load is defined as 12 credit hours per semester, a student enrolled in 12 credit hours would be counted as 1 FTE, while a student enrolled in 6 credit hours would be counted as 0.5 FTE. If your university has 10,000 full-time students and 8,000 part-time students enrolled in an average of 6 credit hours, what is the total number of full-time equivalent students?

If you answered 14,000, (10,000 full-time) + (50% × 8,000 part-time), you have already mastered one of the most important topics in this chapter, the calculation of an equivalent unit. An equivalent unit is the mechanism that we use to convert partially completed units (similar to part-time students) into the equivalent of a full unit. In this example, a part-time student enrolled in 6 credit hours was equivalent to half of a full-time student.

In process costing, we must make a similar calculation for units that are partially complete at the end of an accounting period. Doing so provides information to managers about the cost of units still in process and meets GAAP's requirement that all manufacturing costs be assigned to the product and counted as inventory until it is sold.

To illustrate how process costing works, we visit Fetzer Vineyards, one of the most innovative companies in the California wine industry and a leader in sustainable winemaking. Barney Fetzer began producing wine in Northern California in 1968, long before terms like "sustainability," "green," and "eco-friendly" became so trendy. But he was open to new ways of doing things and knew that good earth was the key to growing good grapes, which in turn make great wine. Over the past few decades, Fetzer has developed an innovative approach to winemaking that has allowed the company to grow and prosper (profit), while protecting the environment (planet) and contributing to society (people). These sustainable business practices are a core part of Fetzer's business model and employee culture and are ingrained into everything they do.

Throughout this chapter, we use a winemaking example to illustrate how process costing works. Although we simplify things and the numbers we use in our examples are fictional, the accounting methods we show are actually used by wineries and other process-oriented industries to determine the cost of making wine and other standardized products. Later in the chapter, we highlight some of the sustainable business practices that Fetzer uses to produce great wine in an environmentally friendly, socially responsible, and economically viable way.

ORGANIZATION OF THE CHAPTER

Basic concepts in process costing	Prepare the production report (weighted-average method)
• Flow of costs in process costing • Process costing production report	• Step 1: Reconcile the number of physical units • Step 2: Convert physical units into equivalent units • Step 3: Calculate cost per equivalent unit • Step 4: Reconcile the total cost of work in process inventory • Step 5: Prepare a production report • Accounting for subsequent production departments

Basic Concepts in Process Costing

Learning Objective 3–1
Describe the key features of a process costing system.

In the last chapter, you learned about job order costing systems. This chapter describes another type of costing system, process costing. Remember that job order costing is used by companies that offer **customized** products or services, such as a custom-built home, highway construction project, or legal defense. Because each individual product or customer is unique, companies use a job cost sheet to keep track of the cost of each individual unit, or job.

Process costing is used by companies that produce **homogeneous** products or services, or those that are produced through a series of standardized processes. Canned and bottled goods, frozen foods, paper products, and petroleum products are examples of homogeneous products that result from a standardized process. Although process costing is most often identified with manufacturing companies, it can also be used by service firms that perform routine processes, such as an insurance company that has a claims processing department or a financial institution that processes home refinance loans.

See Exhibit 3–1 for a comparison of the flow of costs in process costing versus job order costing.

As you can see, there are many similarities between job order and process costing. They both use the same three categories of manufacturing costs: direct materials, direct labor, and

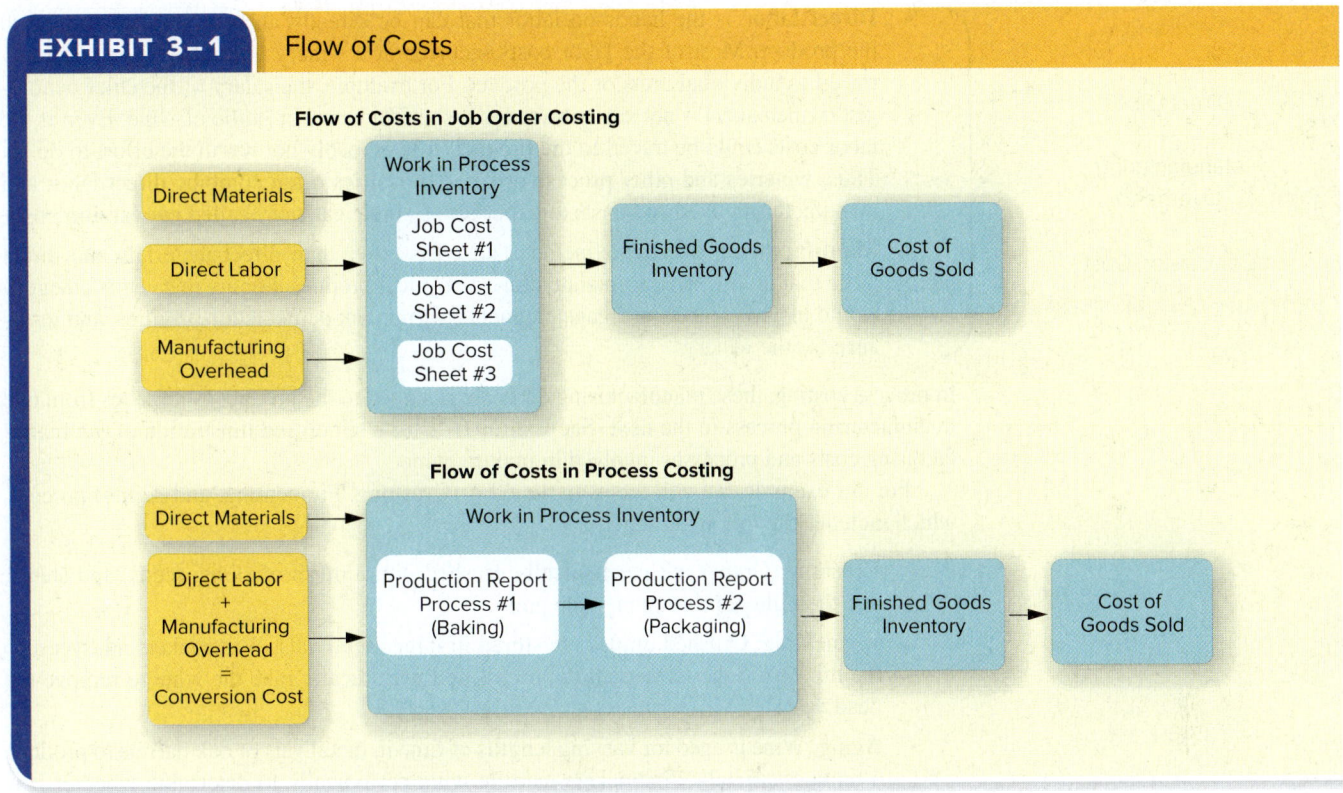

EXHIBIT 3-1 Flow of Costs

manufacturing overhead. However, process costing often combines direct labor and manufacturing overhead into a single category called conversion cost.

In process costing, each unit is similar to the next, so we don't need to keep a separate cost record for each unit produced or customer served. Instead, firms that use process costing break the production process down into its various stages or processes and keep track of the cost of each process using a document called a production report. The production report summarizes the total manufacturing cost incurred in each process and then spreads or averages it across the total number of units produced or customers served. As the product moves from one process to another, the manufacturing costs continue to accumulate until the product is completed, at which point the costs are transferred to Finished Goods Inventory and ultimately Cost of Goods Sold.

Although this description makes process costing sound simple, a few questions complicate its use in the real world. For example, how much cost should Fetzer assign to wine that is still in process at the end of an accounting period—that is, when all of the ingredients (grapes) have been added, but the fermenting and aging process is not yet complete? Determining how much cost to assign to partially complete units is the focus of much of this chapter.

As you can see, the basic flow of costs is the same in process costing as it was in job order costing. The key difference is that manufacturing costs are accumulated by **process** rather than by job. Next, let's look in a bit more detail to see how manufacturing costs will flow through the accounts in our winery example.

FLOW OF COSTS IN PROCESS COSTING

As a review, recall the three types of manufacturing costs that must be assigned to the product and recorded as inventory until the product is sold:

- **Direct materials** are the major material inputs that can be directly and conveniently traced to the product. For a winemaker, this category would include the cost of grapes and any other major material inputs such as the bottles and corks used in the bottling process.

> Direct Labor
> +
> Manufacturing
> Overhead
> =
> Conversion Cost

- **Direct labor** is the hands-on labor that can be directly and conveniently traced to the product. Most of the labor costs incurred at a winery are indirect, or not easily traced to individual units of the product. For example, the salary of the chief oenologist (winemaker) is not easily traced to a specific barrel or bottle of wine. Even if the labor costs could be traced to the product, it is probably not worth the effort to do so. Thus, wineries and other process-oriented industries often combine direct labor and manufacturing overhead costs together into a single category called **conversion cost**.

- **Manufacturing overhead** includes all costs other than direct materials and direct labor that are incurred to manufacture a physical product. For a winery, this category would include rent or mortgage payments, equipment depreciation, utilities, and insurance for the winery.

In process costing, these manufacturing costs are assigned to the product as it moves from one manufacturing process to the next. See Exhibit 3–2 for a simplified illustration of the manufacturing costs and processes involved in making wine.

For our example, we will focus on the CFA (Crushing, Fermenting, and Aging) process, which includes the following steps:

- Crushing: Grapes are mechanically crushed into a mush of skins, seeds, and stems, and then filtered through a wine press.

- Fermenting: Crushed grapes are stored in large metal vats. Winemakers add yeast to the mix to aid the fermentation process and periodically rake the wine to remove the dead yeast.

- Aging: Wine is aged for varying lengths of time in metal vats or oak barrels to produce a unique varietal. Winemakers test the wine periodically to determine whether it is appropriately aged.

In our example, the cost of direct materials (harvested grapes) would be added at the start of the CFA process and accumulated in a Work in Process Inventory account. Additional manufacturing costs would be incurred during the CFA process. In most modern manufacturing environments, direct labor is a relatively small portion of the total manufacturing cost and is often combined with manufacturing overhead into a single category called conversion cost. For simplicity, we assume that conversion costs are incurred uniformly throughout the CFA process. These costs are accumulated in the Work in Process Inventory account as the product is being manufactured. After the wine is fully aged, which can take months or even years, its total manufacturing cost (direct materials + conversion cost) is transferred out of the CFA Work in Process Inventory account and into the Bottling Department, which would have its own Work in Process Inventory account. Additional materials such as bottles and corks and additional conversion costs (direct labor and overhead) will be added during the bottling process. When the bottling process is complete, the total manufacturing costs will be transferred to Finished Goods Inventory.

When the product is sold, the manufacturing costs are transferred to **Cost of Goods Sold** where they are matched against sales revenue on the income statement. As you learned in previous chapters, **nonmanufacturing costs** are expensed during the period incurred rather than being counted as part of the cost of the product.

The next section describes the production report that is used to determine the cost of each production process.

PROCESS COSTING PRODUCTION REPORT

The foundation of a process costing system is the **production report**. This report provides information about the number of units and manufacturing costs that flow through a production process during an accounting period. It is used to determine how much manufacturing cost to transfer out of Work in Process Inventory and into the next processing department (or Finished Goods Inventory if it is the last production process) and to value any units that are in process at the end of the accounting period. A separate production report is prepared for each major production process on either a monthly or a quarterly basis.

| EXHIBIT 3–2 | Process Costing Flow for a Winery |

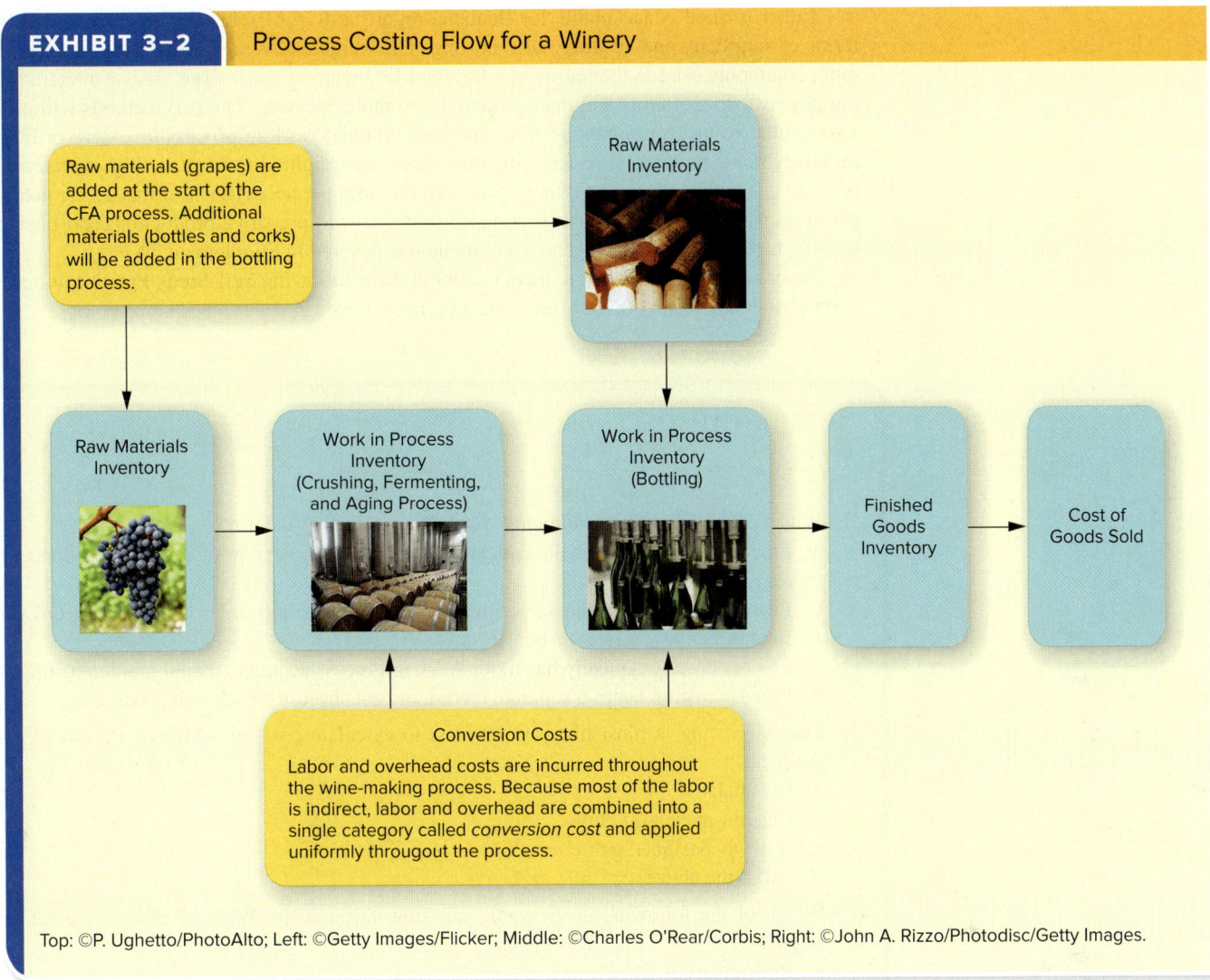

Top: ©P. Ughetto/PhotoAlto; Left: ©Getty Images/Flicker; Middle: ©Charles O'Rear/Corbis; Right: ©John A. Rizzo/Photodisc/Getty Images.

The production report serves two purposes. First, it is a tool that managers can use to monitor and control production costs. It tells managers how many units were completed during the period, how many are still in process, and how much it costs to produce each unit. This information is useful for many managerial decisions, including product pricing and cost control.

Second, the production report provides accountants the information needed to record manufacturing costs in the accounting system. Because this book focuses on the use of accounting information by managers rather than accountants, we do not show all of the journal entries needed to record manufacturing costs in process costing. These journal entries are illustrated in Supplement 3B.

Throughout the remainder of this chapter, we illustrate how to prepare and interpret a production report for the CFA process. For this process, we define a *unit* as one barrel of wine. About 740 pounds of crushed grapes are required to fill a standard barrel of wine. After the wine has been fermented and aged for an appropriate amount of time, the barrels are transferred to the Bottling Department, where each barrel will yield about 300 bottles (25 cases) of wine.

Before we prepare the production report, we must make an assumption about how the units and costs flow through the CFA process. We can use one of two methods to prepare a process costing production report: the **weighted-average method** or the **first-in, first-out (FIFO) method**. The key difference between the two methods is how they deal with any units and costs that are in beginning Work in Process Inventory.

Either method is acceptable for financial reporting (GAAP), but there are trade-offs in terms of simplicity and accuracy of reporting. The weighted-average method is simpler and more commonly used in the real world, but the FIFO method gives more precise attention to the physical flow of units and may sometimes be more accurate. The two methods will provide similar results for companies that maintain minimal work in process inventory or have relatively stable production patterns. In most cases, the weighted-average method is preferred because it is simpler, less costly to prepare, and provides the necessary information for managerial decision making. The next section illustrates how to prepare a production report using the weighted-average method. The FIFO method is covered in Supplement 3A.

Before continuing, take a moment to complete the following Self-Study Practice to make certain you understand the basic concepts in process costing.

 How's it going?   Self-Study Practice

1. Which of the following statements about process costing is false?
   a. Process costing is used in companies that produce very homogeneous products or services.
   b. Process costing uses the same inventory accounts as job order costing to record the flow of manufacturing costs.
   c. Process costing typically has more Work in Process accounts than job order costing.
   d. Process costing keeps a separate record, or cost sheet, for each unit produced.

2. Process costing is most likely to be used to calculate cost for which of the following products?
   a. Golf balls
   b. Custom-made golf clubs
   c. A newly designed golf course
   d. All of the above

3. Which of the following costs would not flow through the Work in Process Inventory account?
   a. Raw materials
   b. Direct labor
   c. Conversion costs
   d. Sales commissions

After you have finished, check your answers against the solutions in the margin.

Prepare the Production Report (Weighted-Average Method)

Five steps are involved in preparing a production report:

1. Reconcile the number of physical units.
2. Convert physical units into equivalent units.
3. Calculate cost per equivalent unit.
4. Reconcile the total cost of Work in Process Inventory.
5. Prepare a production report.

Each of these steps is described in the following sections.

STEP 1: RECONCILE THE NUMBER OF PHYSICAL UNITS

The first step in preparing a production report is to determine how many physical units the company worked on during the period. To do so, we first add the number of units that were on hand at the beginning of the period to the units that were started during the current period. Then we determine whether those units were completed during the period or were still in process at the end of the period. The formula to reconcile the number of physical units is shown.

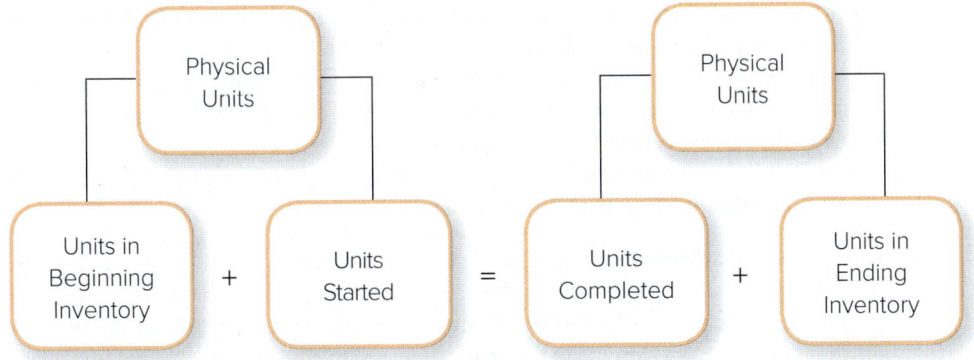

As an example, assume Fetzer had 200 barrels of wine in the CFA process at the start of a new accounting period. During the period, workers started another 1,800 barrels into the CFA process. At the end of the period, 400 barrels of wine were still in the CFA process. Based on this information, how many barrels of wine were completed and transferred out of the CFA process during the current period?

To answer this question, we reconcile the physical units as follows:

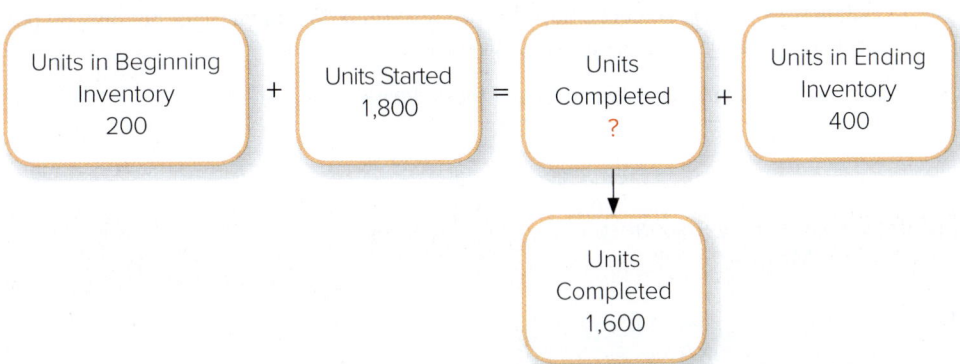

We must account for a total of 2,000 units, 200 that were on hand at the beginning of the period plus 1,800 that were started this period. If we still have 400 units on hand at the end of the period, we must have completed 1,600 units. You can use this basic formula to find any unknown value, so long as you know the other three. Sometimes you will solve for the number of units completed, sometimes for the number of units started, and sometimes for the number of units remaining in beginning or ending inventory.

STEP 2: CONVERT PHYSICAL UNITS INTO EQUIVALENT UNITS

The next step in preparing the production report is to calculate the number of equivalent units. An **equivalent unit** is a measure used to convert partially completed units into the equivalent of a full unit. We need to compute equivalent units so that we can determine the cost of partially complete units, similar to the way a university would determine the cost of a part-time student. Even though the units are incomplete, there are still costs associated with those units, and the accounting system needs a way to track those costs.

Computing equivalent units is particularly important for products that take a long time to manufacture, such as wine that must be aged for months or even years before it is ready for sale. For example, a manager at a winery may want to know the cost of wine that is in process to predict how much profit the company would make if the wine were sold at today's market price. Accountants also need to know the cost of units that are in process in order to prepare financial statements. Remember that GAAP requires all manufacturing costs to be counted as part of the cost of the product and reported as inventory (an asset) until the product is sold. By converting partially completed units into equivalent units, we can assign an appropriate value to those units for financial statement reporting.

Under the weighted-average method, the only partially completed units we need to deal with are the units in ending inventory. The weighted-average method combines or averages the cost of units that were in process at the beginning of the period with the cost of units that were started during the current period. Essentially, it assumes that all of the work (and cost) occurred during the current period.

To illustrate the calculation of equivalent units using weighted-average, we assume the following additional details about the CFA process:

- Direct materials (harvested grapes) are added at the beginning of the process. Thus, once the grapes are added to the CFA process, the product is 100 percent complete with respect to direct materials. Any indirect materials that are added during the CFA process (such as yeast) are treated as manufacturing overhead and included in conversion cost.

- Conversion costs (direct labor and manufacturing overhead) are incurred uniformly throughout the CFA process.

- As established in Step 1, 1,600 barrels were completed and transferred to the Bottling Department.

- The remaining 400 barrels in ending inventory were 60 percent through the CFA process. Because direct materials (grapes) are added at the start of the process, these 400 barrels are 100 percent complete with respect to direct materials, but only 60 percent complete with respect to conversion costs.

See Exhibit 3–3 for a visual representation of these details.

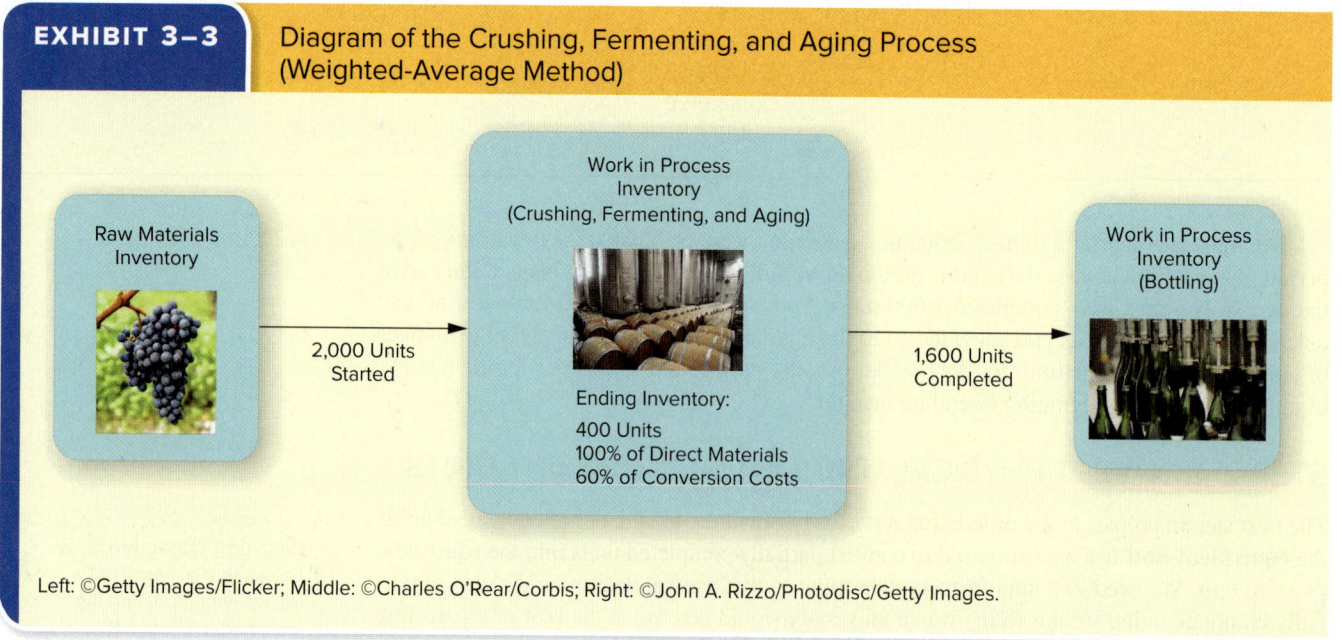

EXHIBIT 3–3   Diagram of the Crushing, Fermenting, and Aging Process (Weighted-Average Method)

Raw Materials Inventory

2,000 Units Started

Work in Process Inventory (Crushing, Fermenting, and Aging)

Ending Inventory:
400 Units
100% of Direct Materials
60% of Conversion Costs

1,600 Units Completed

Work in Process Inventory (Bottling)

Left: ©Getty Images/Flicker; Middle: ©Charles O'Rear/Corbis; Right: ©John A. Rizzo/Photodisc/Getty Images.

For the 1,600 units that were completed and transferred to the Bottling Department, equivalent units are the same as physical units, because these units are 100 percent complete. However, we must convert the 400 partially complete units in ending inventory into the equivalent of a full unit. This is analogous to the way we converted a part-time student into the equivalent of a full-time student in the introduction to this chapter. To calculate equivalent units, we multiply the number of physical units in ending inventory by their percentage of completion as follows:

$$\text{Units in Ending Inventory} \times \text{Percentage of Completion} = \text{Equivalent Units}$$

Based on the data for this example, the units in ending inventory are 100 percent complete with respect to direct materials, but only 60 percent complete with respect to conversion cost, so we have to complete two separate calculations to determine the equivalent units for each, as follows:

$$\underset{400}{\text{Units in Ending Inventory}} \times \underset{100\%}{\text{Percentage of Completion}} = \underset{400}{\text{Equivalent Units for Direct Materials}}$$

$$\underset{400}{\text{Units in Ending Inventory}} \times \underset{60\%}{\text{Percentage of Completion}} = \underset{240}{\text{Equivalent Units for Conversion Cost}}$$

For the units in ending inventory, the equivalent units for direct materials equal 400 (same as physical units) because the units in ending inventory are 100 percent complete with respect to direct materials. But the units in ending inventory are only 60 percent complete with respect to conversion cost. Therefore, the number of equivalent units for conversion cost is 60 percent of 400 units, or 240 **equivalent** units.

When we add the number of units completed to the number of equivalent units in ending inventory, we get total equivalent units of 2,000 for direct materials and 1,840 for conversion cost, as shown in the following table:

| | Physical Units | EQUIVALENT UNITS | |
		Direct Materials	Conversion Cost
Completed and transferred	1,600	1,600	1,600
Ending inventory	400	400 (100% × 400)	240 (60% × 400)
Total	2,000	2,000	1,840

In the next step, we use these numbers to determine how much it costs to produce each equivalent unit. Before moving to Step 3, complete the following Self-Study Practice to reconcile physical units and calculate equivalent units using the weighted-average method.

 How's it going?   **Self-Study Practice**

Aqua-Fit manufactures and sells fitness drinks to fitness clubs across the country. The company uses weighted-average process costing to determine the cost of the drinks. All materials (water, juice, vitamins, and bottles) are added at the beginning of the process, and conversion costs are incurred uniformly throughout the process.

At the start of the most recent period, the company had 1,000 bottles in process. These units had 100 percent of the direct materials but only 40 percent of the conversion cost. During the period, an additional 9,000 bottles were started. The period ended with 3,000 bottles in inventory. These units were 100 percent complete with respect to direct materials and 20 percent complete with respect to conversion cost.

1. How many units were **completed** during the period?
    a. 6,000   b. 7,000   c. 8,000   d. 9,000

2. For the ending inventory, the number of equivalent units for direct materials and conversion would be as follows:

	Direct Materials Equivalent Units	Conversion Cost Equivalent Units
a.	3,000	2,400
b.	3,000	600
c.	600	2,400
d.	600	600

After you have finished, check your answers against the solutions in the margin.

STEP 3: CALCULATE COST PER EQUIVALENT UNIT

Now that we know how many equivalent units to account for, the third step is to determine the cost per equivalent unit for each type of cost (direct materials and conversion cost). To calculate cost per equivalent unit, we divide the total manufacturing cost by the total number of equivalent units that we calculated in Step 2. The total manufacturing cost includes the cost of the units in beginning inventory plus the costs that were incurred during the current period.

$$\frac{\text{Beginning inventory} + \text{Current Costs}}{\text{Equivalent Units}} = \frac{\text{Cost per}}{\text{Equivalent Unit}}$$

As this formula shows, the weighted-average method combines the beginning inventory costs with the costs that were incurred during the current period and averages that cost across the number of equivalent units. Because the number of equivalent units is different for direct materials and conversion costs, we must make a separate calculation for each category.

Assume the total manufacturing costs for the CFA process are as follows:

	Direct Materials	Conversion Cost
Beginning inventory costs	$ 84,000	$ 81,120
Current manufacturing costs	810,000	918,000
Total manufacturing costs	$894,000	$999,120

If we plug these costs into the formula, we get a cost per equivalent unit of $447 for direct materials and $543 for conversion costs, as follows:

$$\frac{\underset{\$84,000}{\text{Beginning inventory}} + \underset{\$810,000}{\text{Current Costs}}}{\underset{2,000}{\text{Equivalent Units}}} = \begin{array}{c}\text{Direct Materials Cost} \\ \text{per Equivalent Unit} \\ \$447\end{array}$$

$$\frac{\underset{\$81,120}{\text{Beginning inventory}} + \underset{\$918,000}{\text{Current Costs}}}{\underset{1,840}{\text{Equivalent Units}}} = \begin{array}{c}\text{Conversion Cost} \\ \text{per Equivalent Unit} \\ \$543\end{array}$$

What do these numbers mean? Recall that a unit was defined as a barrel of wine. Thus, the total cost to process a barrel of wine through the CFA process is $447 for direct materials (grapes) plus $543 for the direct labor and overhead cost (conversion costs) incurred to convert the grapes into wine. Each barrel that is transferred out of the CFA process will be transferred at a cost of $990 ($447 + $543). Additional manufacturing costs would be incurred in the next step of the production process to bottle, cork, and package the wine. The Bottling Department would prepare its own process costing production report and would treat the $990 transferred-in cost the same way we treated the costs of the raw materials (grapes) that were added at the start of the CFA process.

But remember that not all of the wine is ready to be transferred to bottling. Some of it is still aging. The next step is to reconcile the total manufacturing cost to determine how much cost to transfer out of the CFA process (and into Bottling) and how much to attach to the units that remain in the CFA Work in Process Inventory account as ending inventory.

STEP 4: RECONCILE THE TOTAL COST OF WORK IN PROCESS INVENTORY

The fourth step is to reconcile the total cost of Work in Process Inventory. We must account for any costs that were in Work in Process Inventory at the beginning of the period plus any costs that were added during the current period. The costs to be accounted for in our winery example are shown next:

	Direct Materials	Conversion Cost	Total Cost
Beginning work in process	$ 84,000	$ 81,120	$ 165,120
Current period costs	810,000	918,000	1,728,000
Total costs	$894,000	$999,120	$1,893,120

We need to account for a total of $1,893,120 in manufacturing costs in the CFA Work in Process Inventory account. Most of this cost will be transferred out with the 1,600 units completed and transferred to Bottling. The remainder will stay in the CFA Work in Process Inventory account with the units in ending inventory.

To determine the cost of the units completed and the cost of the units in ending inventory, we simply multiply the number of equivalent units (from Step 2) by the cost per equivalent unit (Step 3) for both direct materials and conversion cost, as shown next:

COST ASSIGNED TO UNITS COMPLETED AND ENDING INVENTORY			
	Direct Materials	**Conversion Cost**	**Total Cost**
Units completed	1,600 × $447 = $715,200	1,600 × $543 = $868,800	$1,584,000
Ending inventory	400 × $447 = $178,800	240 × $543 = $130,320	309,120
Total cost			$1,893,120

Of the $1,893,120 total manufacturing cost in the CFA Work in Process Inventory account, $1,584,000 will be transferred out with the 1,600 units completed and transferred to Bottling. The other $309,120 will remain in the CFA account as ending inventory, as shown in the following T-accounts.

Work in Process Inventory (CFA)			
Beginning costs	165,120	1,584,000 Completed and transferred	→
Current period costs	1,728,000		
Balance	309,120		

Work in Process Inventory (Bottling)		
Transferred-in costs	1,584,000	

STEP 5: PREPARE A PRODUCTION REPORT

The final step in process costing is to summarize the results of Steps 1 through 4 into a **production report**. This report provides a summary of what occurred in the production process during the accounting period. It includes information about the number of physical units (Step 1), number of equivalent units (Step 2), cost per equivalent unit (Step 3), and a reconciliation of the cost of Work in Process Inventory (Step 4). See Exhibit 3–4 for an example of a production report for the CFA process.

ACCOUNTING FOR SUBSEQUENT PRODUCTION DEPARTMENTS

In a process costing system, the product continues to accumulate manufacturing costs as it passes from one production process to the next. The production report in Exhibit 3–4 shows that the cost of a barrel of wine coming out of the CFA process is $990 per barrel. This represents the cost of the harvested grapes, as well as the costs incurred to crush, ferment, and age the wine. Additional costs will be incurred during the bottling process for materials, labor, machinery, utilities, and other manufacturing costs. Accountants would follow the same five steps used in our CFA example to prepare a separate production report for the Bottling Department to determine the cost of the bottling process.

Recall that each barrel contains enough wine to fill about 300 standard (0.75 liter) bottles. Thus, the 1,600 barrels transferred into the bottling process will yield enough wine to fill 480,000 bottles (1,600 × 300 = 480,000). The $990 cost per barrel coming out of the CFA process and going into the bottling process translates to $3.30 per bottle ($990 ÷ 300 bottles = $3.30). This cost is called a **transferred-in cost** because it represents the manufacturing cost that is transferred from one production process to another (from the CFA process into the Bottling process). In the Bottling Department, the transferred-in cost would be treated just like the cost of the harvested grapes that were added at the start of the CFA process.

As a simplified example, assume that additional materials costs of $0.20 per unit and additional conversion costs of $0.25 per unit are added during the bottling process. In this

EXHIBIT 3–4   Production Report (Weighted-Average Method)

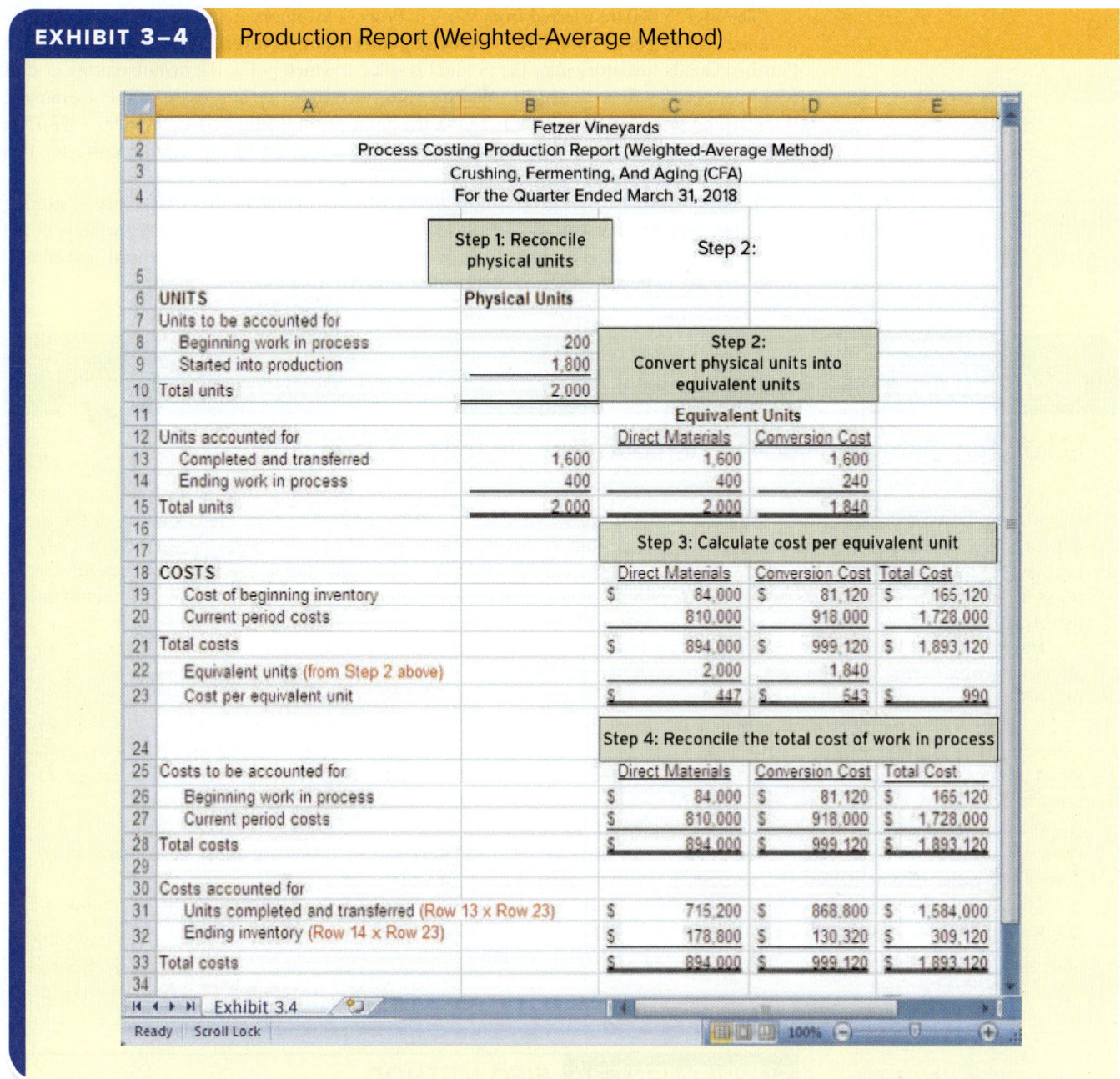

	A	B	C	D	E
1			Fetzer Vineyards		
2			Process Costing Production Report (Weighted-Average Method)		
3			Crushing, Fermenting, And Aging (CFA)		
4			For the Quarter Ended March 31, 2018		
5			**Step 1: Reconcile physical units**	**Step 2:**	
6	UNITS	Physical Units			
7	Units to be accounted for				
8	Beginning work in process	200	**Step 2:**		
9	Started into production	1,800	Convert physical units into		
10	Total units	2,000	equivalent units		
11			Equivalent Units		
12	Units accounted for		Direct Materials	Conversion Cost	
13	Completed and transferred	1,600	1,600	1,600	
14	Ending work in process	400	400	240	
15	Total units	2,000	2,000	1,840	
16					
17			**Step 3: Calculate cost per equivalent unit**		
18	COSTS		Direct Materials	Conversion Cost	Total Cost
19	Cost of beginning inventory		$ 84,000	$ 81,120	$ 165,120
20	Current period costs		810,000	918,000	1,728,000
21	Total costs		$ 894,000	$ 999,120	$ 1,893,120
22	Equivalent units (from Step 2 above)		2,000	1,840	
23	Cost per equivalent unit		$ 447	$ 543	$ 990
24			**Step 4: Reconcile the total cost of work in process**		
25	Costs to be accounted for		Direct Materials	Conversion Cost	Total Cost
26	Beginning work in process		$ 84,000	$ 81,120	$ 165,120
27	Current period costs		$ 810,000	$ 918,000	$ 1,728,000
28	Total costs		$ 894,000	$ 999,120	$ 1,893,120
29					
30	Costs accounted for				
31	Units completed and transferred (Row 13 x Row 23)		$ 715,200	$ 868,800	$ 1,584,000
32	Ending inventory (Row 14 x Row 23)		$ 178,800	$ 130,320	$ 309,120
33	Total costs		$ 894,000	$ 999,120	$ 1,893,120
34					

Exhibit 3.4

Ready   Scroll Lock   100%

case, the cost of wine transferred out of the bottling process would be $3.75 per unit (bottle), which includes the $3.30 transferred-in cost from the CFA process, $0.20 for materials used in the bottling process, and $0.25 for conversion cost incurred in the bottling process. If 460,000 bottles were completed during the period, the total manufacturing cost of $1,725,000 ($3.75 × 460,000 = $1,725,000) would be transferred out of Work in Process Inventory (Bottling) and into Finished Goods Inventory, as shown below:

Work in Process Inventory (CFA)				**Work in Process Inventory (Bottling)**				**Finished Goods Inventory**
Beginning costs	165,120	1,584,000	→	Transferred-in costs	1,584,000	1,725,000	→	1,725,000
Current period costs	1,728,000	Completed and		Direct materials	96,000	Completed and		
		transferred		Conversion cost	120,000	transferred		
Balance	309,120			Balance	75,000			

The $1,725,000 transferred from Work in Process Inventory to Finished Goods Inventory is called **cost of goods completed** or **cost of goods manufactured.** This cost will remain in Finished Goods Inventory until the product is sold, at which point, the manufacturing cost of $3.75 per bottle will be deducted from the sales price to arrive at gross profit. For example, if the selling price for each bottle is $8.00, the gross profit would be $4.25 ($8.00 − $3.75 = $4.25) per bottle. The detailed journal entries to record the manufacturing costs for this example are illustrated in Supplement 3B.

Keep in mind that cost of goods sold represents the cost of making the product (manufacturing costs), but not other costs such as advertising, the cost of the tasting room at the winery, or the cost to distribute it to retailers such as BevMo or Total Wine. These selling, general, and administrative costs are treated as period costs and expensed during the period incurred.

SPOTLIGHT ON sustainability

Using Big Data Analytics to Achieve Sustainability Goals

Fetzer Vineyards is a pioneer when it comes to sustainable winemaking. The company doesn't just claim to be sustainable, but can actually demonstrate it through the various sustainability metrics the company has been tracking for decades. Managerial accountants play a key role in the *measurement of sustainability* (called sustainability accounting) by capturing and reporting information to managers to help them achieve the organization's sustainability goals. Sustainability accounting must extend beyond traditional economic data to include measures of environmental performance and/or social impact.

Managers at Fetzer recently used **big data analytics** to track one of their key sustainability metrics and achieve an aggressive goal to reduce water consumption by 15 percent from 2015 to 2020. In 2015, the company used an average of 3.65 gallons of water per gallon of wine produced. By 2016, it had reduced it by 12 percent to 3.24 gallons.

In 2017, Fetzer announced it was installing technology-enabled water meters throughout its Hopland California campus to collect and analyze water usage data in real time so that managers could quickly pinpoint leaks and avoid unnecessary water waste. This technology should allow Fetzer to meet its 2020 water efficiency goal two years early, in 2018.

According to Fetzer's CFO Cindy DeVries "Integrating data analytics and cloud computing technologies with our winery operations allows us to leverage crucial environmental data to achieve our sustainability goals . . . at a time when conserving water is more important than ever."

This is one of many sustainability initiatives at Fetzer Vineyards. Refer to Exercise 3-3 to see how the company changed its bottling process to reduce direct materials usage (glass) and greenhouse gas emissions.

Sources: www.fetzer.com/sustainability; www.sustainablewinegrowing.org/certifiedparticipant/5/Fetzer_Vineyards_Bonterra_Vineyards.html.

SUPPLEMENT 3A   FIFO METHOD

Learning Objective 3–S1
Prepare a process costing production report using the first-in, first-out (FIFO) method.

The example presented throughout this chapter showed how to prepare a production report using weighted-average process costing. This supplement uses the same example to show how to prepare a production report using the first-in, first-out (FIFO) method. The primary difference between weighted average and FIFO is the treatment of beginning inventory. The weighted-average method averages the cost of the units in beginning inventory with the cost of the units that were started during the current period. FIFO assumes that the units in beginning inventory were completed first, before any new units were started during the current period. Exhibit 3–5 summarizes the differences between these two methods.

The same five steps are required to prepare a production report using the FIFO method as the weighted-average method:

1. Reconcile the number of physical units.
2. Convert physical units into equivalent units.

EXHIBIT 3–5	Comparison of Weighted-Average and FIFO Process Costing	
	Weighted Average	**FIFO**
Cost flow assumption	Averages the cost of units in beginning inventory with the cost of units that were started during the period	Assumes that the units in beginning inventory were completed before any new units were started
Units	Combines the units in beginning inventory with the units that were started during the period	Separates the units in beginning inventory from those that were started during the current period
Cost	Combines the cost of beginning inventory with the costs that were incurred during the current period	Separates the costs of beginning inventory from the costs that were incurred during the current period
Advantages	Is simpler than FIFO and more frequently used in the real world	More closely matches the actual flow of costs in many process industries and therefore may be more accurate than weighted average
Disadvantages	May not be as accurate as FIFO for companies that hold significant inventories	More complicated than weighted average and rarely used in the real world

3. Calculate cost per equivalent unit.
4. Reconcile the total cost of Work in Process Inventory.
5. Prepare a production report.

Step 1: Reconcile the Number of Physical Units

The first step in preparing a production report is to determine how many physical units were worked on during the period. To do so, we first add the number of units that were on hand at the beginning of the period to the number of units that were started during the current period. Then we determine whether those units were completed during the period or are still being worked on at the end of the period. The formula to reconcile the number of physical units is as follows:

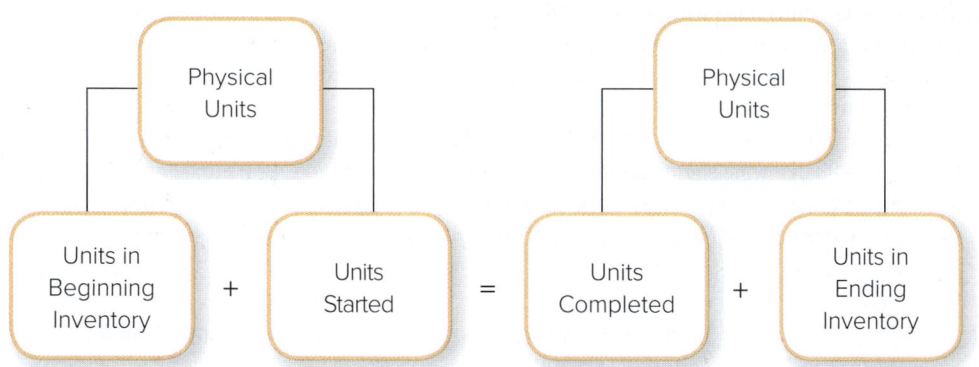

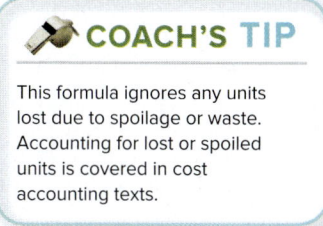

COACH'S TIP

This formula ignores any units lost due to spoilage or waste. Accounting for lost or spoiled units is covered in cost accounting texts.

As an example, assume Fetzer had 200 barrels of wine in the CFA process at the start of a new accounting period. During the period, workers started another 1,800 barrels into the CFA process. At the end of the period, 400 barrels of wine were still in the CFA process. Based on this information, how many barrels of wine were transferred out of the CFA process during the current period?

To answer this question, we reconcile the number of physical units as follows:

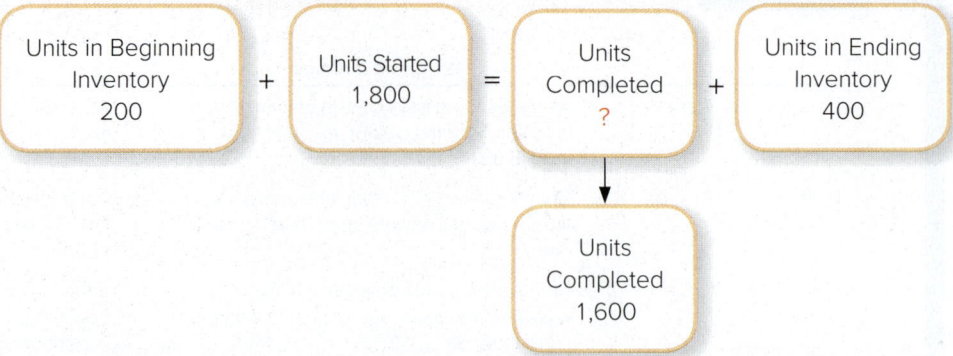

We must account for a total of 2,000 units, 200 that were on hand at the beginning of the period plus 1,800 that were started this period. If we have only 400 on hand at the end of the period, we must have completed 1,600 units. You can use this basic formula to find any unknown value, so long as you know the other three. Sometimes you will solve for the number of units completed, sometimes for the number of units started, and sometimes for the units in beginning or ending inventory.

Under the FIFO method, we must also determine how many units were *both* started *and* completed during the current period. Those units would have made it all the way through the CFA process during the current period, so they would not be part of either beginning or ending inventory.

The number of units that were both started **and** completed during the current period can be computed in one of two ways, as shown in the following formulas:

> Units Completed − Units in Beginning Inventory = Units Started **and** Completed

or

> Units Started − Units in Ending Inventory = Units Started **and** Completed

Remember that FIFO assumes that the units in beginning inventory were completed first. Thus, not all units that were completed during the current period were started during the current period; the units that were in beginning inventory were started during the last period. Likewise, some of the units that were started during the current period were not completed; they remain in ending inventory.

In our example, we had a total of 2,000 physical units to account for: 200 from beginning inventory plus 1,800 that were started during the period. During the period, 1,600 units were completed; 400 were still in process at the end of the period. How many units were both started **and** completed during the current period? The answer is 1,400 units, as shown in the following formulas:

> Units Completed − Units in Beginning Inventory = Units Started **and** Completed
> 1,600   200   1,400

or

> Units Started − Units in Ending Inventory = Units Started **and** Completed
> 1,800   400   1,400

To summarize Step 1, the number of physical units worked on during the period can be reconciled as follows:

	Physical Units
Beginning inventory	200
Started and completed	1,400
Ending inventory	400
Total units	2,000

Step 2: Convert Physical Units into Equivalent Units

The next step in preparing the production report is to calculate the number of equivalent units. An **equivalent unit** is a measure used to convert partially completed units into the equivalent of a full unit.

Why must we calculate equivalent units? Companies often have units in process at the beginning and end of an accounting period. This is particularly true for products that take a long time to manufacture, such as wine that must be aged for months or even years before it is ready for sale. Even though the units are incomplete, their cost must be recorded on the balance sheet as Work in Process Inventory. Remember that GAAP requires all manufacturing costs to be counted as part of the cost of the product and reported as inventory (an asset) until the product is sold. By converting partially completed units into equivalent units, we can assign an appropriate value to those units for financial statement reporting.

To illustrate the calculation of equivalent units using FIFO, we assume the following additional details about the CFA process:

- Direct materials (grapes) are added at the beginning of the process. Thus, once a barrel of wine has been started in the CFA process, it will have 100 percent of the required direct materials.

- Conversion costs (direct labor and manufacturing overhead) are incurred uniformly throughout the process.

- The 200 barrels in beginning inventory were 70 percent through the CFA process. The first-in, first-out method assumes that these units were completed first, before any new units were started during the current period.

- Of the 1,800 units started during the current period, only 1,400 were completed this period. These units made it all the way through the CFA process without getting "stuck" in beginning or ending inventory.

- The 400 barrels in ending inventory were 60 percent through the CFA process. Because direct materials (grapes) are added at the start of the CFA process, these 400 barrels are 100 percent complete with respect to direct materials, but only 60 percent complete with respect to conversion cost.

These details are presented in the form of a diagram of the production process in Exhibit 3A.1.

To calculate equivalent units, we need to consider how much work was done during the **current** period to complete the 200 units in beginning inventory, to produce 1,400 units from start to finish, and to get the 400 units in ending inventory 60 percent complete with respect to conversion cost. This calculation must be made separately for direct materials and conversion costs because those costs are added at different points in the production process.

Because direct materials are added at the start of the process, we did not need to incur any additional direct materials costs to complete the units in beginning inventory. Thus, beginning inventory required zero equivalent units of direct materials during the current period. Because the units in beginning inventory were already 70 percent complete with respect to conversion

| EXHIBIT 3A–1 | Diagram of the Crushing, Fermenting, and Aging Process (FIFO Method) |

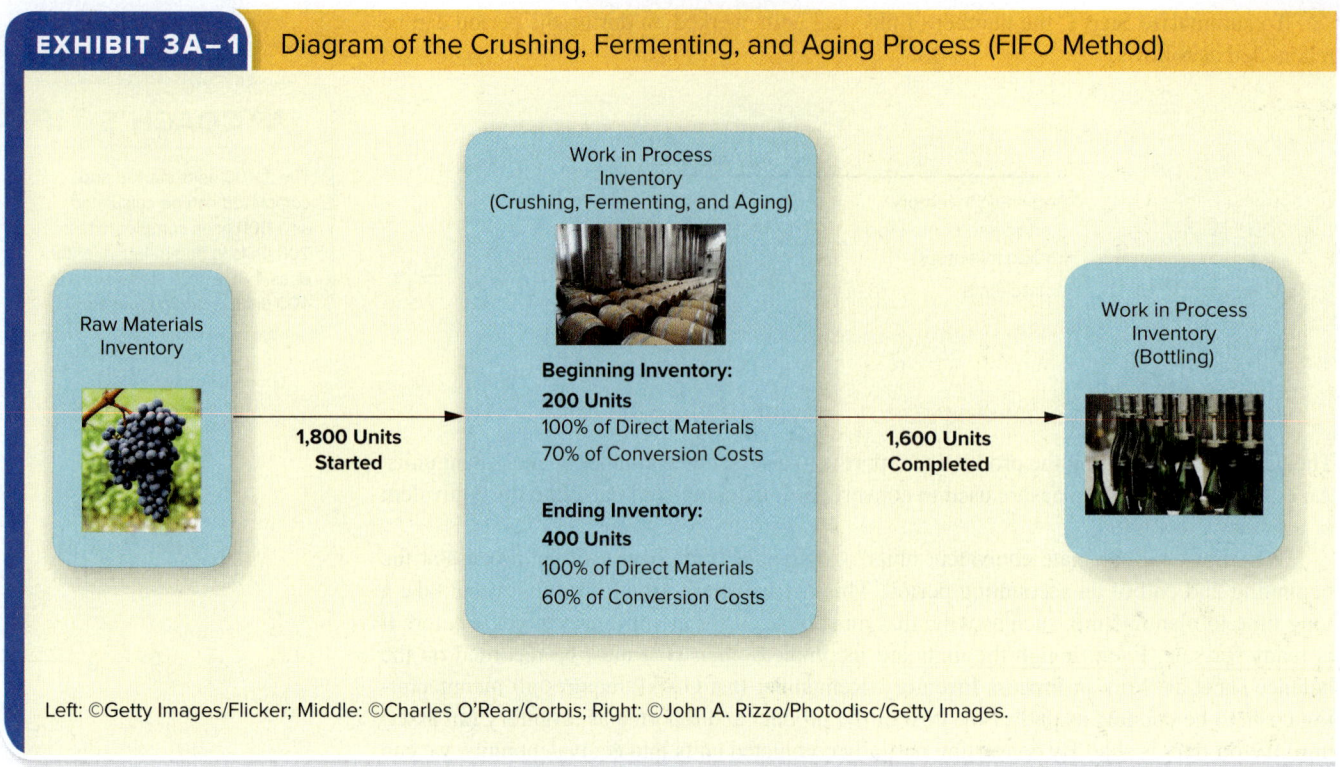

Left: ©Getty Images/Flicker; Middle: ©Charles O'Rear/Corbis; Right: ©John A. Rizzo/Photodisc/Getty Images.

cost, they required only 30 percent conversion effort during the current period. So, we multiply the 200 physical units by 30 percent to arrive at 60 equivalent units of conversion cost for the beginning inventory units.

The 1,400 units that were started **and** completed went all the way through the CFA process during the current period. Because all work on those units happened during the current period, the number of equivalent units is the same as the number of physical units.

The 400 units in ending inventory were started during the current period and received the entire amount of direct materials at the beginning of the process. Thus, the number of equivalent units for direct materials is the same as the 400 physical units in ending inventory. Those units went only 60 percent of the way through the conversion process during the current period, however. Therefore, the number of equivalent units for conversion would be 60 percent of the 400 units in ending inventory, or 240.

Finally, we calculate total equivalent units by adding the number of equivalent units for beginning inventory, units started **and** completed, and ending inventory. This calculation gives us 1,800 equivalent units of direct materials and 1,700 equivalent units of conversion cost as shown in the following table. In the next step, we use these numbers to calculate cost per equivalent unit.

		EQUIVALENT UNITS	
	Physical Units	**Direct Materials**	**Conversion Cost**
Beginning inventory	200	0	60 (200 × 30%)
Started and completed	1,400	1,400	1,400
Ending inventory	400	400	240 (400 × 60%)
Total	2,000	1,800	1,700

Before moving to Step 3, complete the following Self-Study Practice to reconcile physical units and calculate equivalent units using the FIFO method.

How's it going?   Self-Study Practice

Aqua-Fit manufactures and sells fitness drinks (with added vitamins and minerals) to fitness clubs across the country. The company uses a FIFO process costing system to determine the cost of the drinks. All materials (water, juice, vitamins, and bottles) are added at the beginning of the process, and conversion costs are added uniformly.

At the start of the most recent period, the company had 1,000 bottles in process. These units were 100 percent complete with respect to direct materials but only 40 percent complete with respect to conversion cost. During the period, an additional 9,000 bottles were started in the process. The period ended with 3,000 bottles that were 100 percent complete with respect to direct materials and 20 percent complete with respect to conversion cost.

1. How many units were **completed** during the period?

2. How many units were **started and completed** during the period?

3. How many equivalent units of conversion would be required to **complete** the beginning inventory?

4. Calculate the number of equivalent units of direct materials and conversion for the units in ending inventory.

After you have finished, check your answers against the solutions in the margin.

Step 3: Calculate Cost per Equivalent Unit

The third step is to calculate cost per equivalent unit for each type of cost (direct materials and conversion cost). To calculate cost per equivalent unit under FIFO, we divide the current period's costs by the total number of equivalent units calculated in Step 2, as follows:

$$\frac{\text{Current Costs}}{\text{Equivalent Units}} = \text{Cost per Equivalent Unit}$$

We do not include beginning inventory costs in the cost per equivalent unit calculation under the FIFO method because we are only concerned with the cost of work performed during the current period. The cost of beginning inventory was incurred in a prior period and would have been accounted for in that period's production report.

The cost per equivalent unit calculations for our winery example are shown as follows. Because the number of equivalent units differs for direct materials and conversion cost, we must calculate each category separately.

$$\frac{\substack{\text{Current Costs} \\ \$810,000} }{\substack{\text{Equivalent Units} \\ 1,800}} = \substack{\text{Direct Materials Cost} \\ \text{per Equivalent Unit} \\ \$450}$$

$$\frac{\substack{\text{Current Costs} \\ \$918,000} }{\substack{\text{Equivalent Units} \\ 1,700}} = \substack{\text{Conversion Cost per} \\ \text{Equivalent Unit} \\ \$540}$$

The cost per equivalent unit is $450 for direct materials and $540 for conversion cost. Thus, the total cost to process a barrel of wine through the CFA process is $990 ($450 + $540). In the next step, we use these numbers to determine the cost of the units completed and transferred to Bottling, as well as the cost of the units that are still in process at the end the period.

Step 4: Reconcile the Total Cost of Work in Process Inventory

The fourth step in preparing the production report is to reconcile the total cost recorded in the Work in Process Inventory account. The total cost includes the cost that was already in the account at the beginning of the period plus the direct materials and conversion costs that were added to the process during the period.

The costs to be accounted for in our winery example are summarized as follows:

	Direct Materials	Conversion Cost	Total Cost
Beginning work in process	$ 84,000	$ 81,120	$ 165,120
Current period costs	810,000	918,000	1,728,000
Total costs	$894,000	$999,120	$1,893,120

As you can see, we need to account for a total cost of $1,893,120 for the CFA process. Notice that part of this cost ($84,000 + $81,120) relates to the units that were already in process at the beginning of the period. Because FIFO assumes that these units are completed first, the cost of beginning inventory is automatically transferred out of the Work in Process Inventory account with the units that were completed and transferred.

The current period costs of $810,000 and $918,000 were included in the calculation of cost per equivalent unit in Step 3. To determine how much of this cost should be transferred out and how much should remain in the Work in Process Inventory (CFA) account with the units in ending inventory, we multiply the cost per equivalent unit by the number of equivalent units, as follows:

COST ASSIGNED TO COST OF GOODS COMPLETED AND ENDING INVENTORY, FIFO			
	Direct Materials	Conversion Cost	Total Cost
Beginning inventory costs	$ 84,000	$ 81,120	$ 165,120
Cost to complete beginning inventory	—	60 × $540 = $ 32,400	32,400
Units started and completed	1,400 × $450 = $630,000	1,400 × $540 = $756,000	1,386,000
Ending inventory	400 × $450 = $180,000	240 × $540 = $129,600	309,600
Total cost			$1,893,120

- The 200 units in beginning inventory carried a cost of $165,120 ($84,000 + $81,120) from the prior period. During the current period, the company incurred additional conversion costs for 60 equivalent units to complete the beginning inventory at a total cost of $32,400 (60 × $540). Thus, the total cost of the units in beginning inventory is $197,520 ($165,120 + $32,400). Because FIFO assumes that the units in beginning inventory are completed first, this cost will be transferred out of the CFA Work in Process account and into the Bottling Department.

- The 1,400 units that were started **and** completed during the current period made it all the way through the CFA process during the current period. These units cost $450 for direct materials and $540 for conversion, for a total cost of $1,386,000 [1,400 × ($450 + $540)]. This cost will be transferred out of the CFA Work in Process account and into the Bottling Department.

- The 400 units that remain in ending inventory are valued at $450 per equivalent unit for direct materials or $180,000 (400 × $450). The conversion cost attached to these units would be $129,600 (240 equivalent units × $540 per equivalent unit), for a total ending inventory cost of $309,600 ($180,000 + $129,600).

The following T-accounts show how these costs would appear in the Work in Process Inventory (CFA) account at the end of the accounting period:

Work in Process Inventory (CFA)				Work in Process Inventory (Bottling)	
Beginning costs	165,120	1,583,520	→	Transferred-in costs 1,583,520	
Current period costs	1,728,000	Completed and transferred			
Balance	309,600				

The total cost of goods completed is $1,583,520. This cost is transferred out of the CFA Work in Process Inventory account and into the Work in Process Inventory account for the Bottling Department. The $309,600 that remains in the CFA Work in Process account represents the cost of the units that are still in process at the end of the accounting period. This will become the beginning balance of the Work in Process Inventory (CFA) account in the next accounting period.

Step 5: Prepare a Production Report

The final step in process costing is to summarize the results of Steps 1 through 4 into a production report. This report provides a summary of what occurred in the production process during the accounting period. It includes information about the number of physical units (Step 1), equivalent units (Step 2), cost per equivalent unit (Step 3), and a reconciliation of the cost of work in process (Step 4). See Exhibit 3A–2 for a production report for the CFA process based on the FIFO method.

If you compare this FIFO process costing report to the weighted-average report from Exhibit 3–4, you will see that the reports are structured very similarly. The FIFO report is

---

EXHIBIT 3A–2   Production Report (FIFO Method)

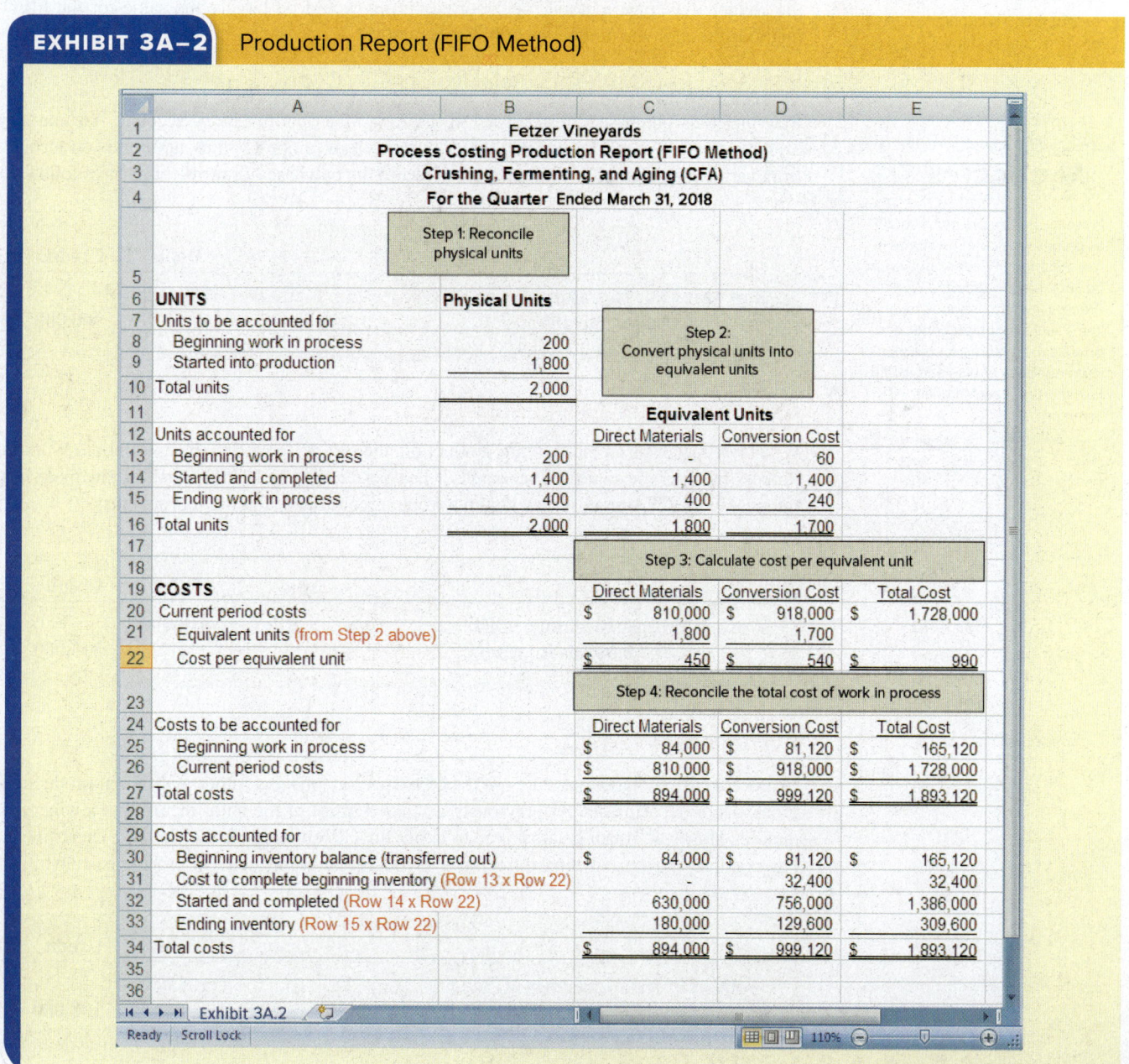

Fetzer Vineyards
Process Costing Production Report (FIFO Method)
Crushing, Fermenting, and Aging (CFA)
For the Quarter Ended March 31, 2018

Step 1: Reconcile physical units

UNITS	Physical Units				
Units to be accounted for					
Beginning work in process	200				
Started into production	1,800				
Total units	2,000				

Step 2: Convert physical units into equivalent units

Units accounted for		**Equivalent Units**		
		Direct Materials	Conversion Cost	
Beginning work in process	200	-	60	
Started and completed	1,400	1,400	1,400	
Ending work in process	400	400	240	
Total units	2,000	1,800	1,700	

Step 3: Calculate cost per equivalent unit

COSTS		Direct Materials	Conversion Cost	Total Cost
Current period costs		$ 810,000	$ 918,000	$ 1,728,000
Equivalent units (from Step 2 above)		1,800	1,700	
Cost per equivalent unit		$ 450	$ 540	$ 990

Step 4: Reconcile the total cost of work in process

Costs to be accounted for		Direct Materials	Conversion Cost	Total Cost
Beginning work in process		$ 84,000	$ 81,120	$ 165,120
Current period costs		$ 810,000	$ 918,000	$ 1,728,000
Total costs		$ 894,000	$ 999,120	$ 1,893,120

Costs accounted for		Direct Materials	Conversion Cost	Total Cost
Beginning inventory balance (transferred out)		$ 84,000	$ 81,120	$ 165,120
Cost to complete beginning inventory (Row 13 x Row 22)		-	32,400	32,400
Started and completed (Row 14 x Row 22)		630,000	756,000	1,386,000
Ending inventory (Row 15 x Row 22)		180,000	129,600	309,600
Total costs		$ 894,000	$ 999,120	$ 1,893,120

Exhibit 3A.2

Ready   Scroll Lock   110%

slightly more detailed and gives more attention to the units that were on hand at the beginning of the period. In this particular example, the end result is very similar. The cost of units completed during the period was $1,584,000 for the weighted-average method compared to $1,583,520 for the FIFO method, a difference of only $480. You get the same $480 difference if you compare the value of ending Work in Process Inventory of $309,120 under weighted-average to $309,600 for FIFO. The two methods may not always provide such similar results, particularly if production or manufacturing costs fluctuate from period to period and the company maintains significant levels of Work in Process Inventory. As a manager you need to understand when the methods will produce different results and whether the extra calculations required by FIFO are worth the effort.

SUPPLEMENT 3B JOURNAL ENTRIES FOR PROCESS COSTING

Learning Objective 3–S2
Prepare journal entries to record manufacturing costs in a process cost system.

This supplement describes journal entries recording the flow of manufacturing costs in a process costing system. We use journal entries that reflect the numbers from our example using the weighted-average method. The journal entries would be largely the same for the FIFO method, although the numbers would vary slightly.

Purchase Raw Materials

Raw materials purchased are recorded in the Raw Materials Inventory account. Assume, for example, that Fetzer purchased $900,000 of raw materials (grapes, bottles, and corks) on account from various suppliers. The journal entry to record the purchase of raw materials is as follows:

> **COACH'S TIP**
>
> In reality, perishable items such as grapes would not be stored in raw materials inventory, but would be immediately added to Work in Process Inventory. Nonperishable items such as bottles, corks, and boxes can be stored for much longer periods of time and would flow through Raw Materials Inventory.

	Debit	Credit
Raw Materials Inventory	900,000	
Accounts Payable		900,000

Issue Raw Materials into Production

When raw materials are placed into production, the cost is debited to the appropriate Work in Process Inventory account. For example, when Fetzer adds $810,000 worth of raw materials (grapes) to the CFA process, accountants would record the following journal entry.

	Debit	Credit
Work in Process Inventory (CFA)	810,000	
Raw Materials Inventory		810,000

Record Labor Costs

In process costing, labor costs are not traced to specific jobs, but rather to different production processes or departments. As previously discussed, most of the labor incurred at a winery is indirect. However, it can be attributed to either the CFA process or the Bottling Department. For example, the journal entry to record $108,000 in labor for the CFA process is shown:

	Debit	Credit
Work in Process Inventory (CFA)	108,000	
Salary or Wages Payable		108,000

A similar journal entry would be made for labor incurred in the bottling process.

Record Manufacturing Overhead Costs

As you learned in a prior chapter, manufacturing overhead costs are applied to Work in Process Inventory using a predetermined overhead rate that is based on some secondary allocation measure. For example, a winery might apply overhead costs based on the number of barrels processed or the amount of time the wine is fermented and aged. The bottling process might apply overhead based on direct labor hours or the number of bottles processed

Assume Fetzer applies $450 in manufacturing overhead to each barrel started in the CFA process. During the most recent period 1,800 barrels were started, resulting in $810,000 in applied overhead (1,800 barrels × $450 = $810,000). The journal entry to apply overhead to the CFA process is shown next:

	Debit	Credit
Work in Process Inventory (CFA)	810,000	
Manufacturing Overhead		810,000

In addition to applied overhead, we also need to record the actual manufacturing overhead cost incurred. For example, if Fetzer incurred $800,000 in actual manufacturing overhead costs during the period, accountants would make the following journal entry:

	Debit	Credit
Manufacturing Overhead	800,000	
Cash, Accounts Payable, etc.		800,000

Recall that Manufacturing Overhead is a temporary account that is used to keep track of actual and applied manufacturing overhead. Actual overhead costs are debited to the account, while the applied amount appears on the credit side. The difference in actual and applied manufacturing overhead is adjusted directly to Cost of Goods Sold at the end of the year. Refer to Chapter 2 on job order costing for more details on how to account for overapplied or underapplied overhead.

Transfer Cost from One Production Process to the Next

When a unit is transferred from one production department to the next, the manufacturing cost must be transferred to the next Work in Process Inventory account. For example, when 1,600 barrels of wine are through the CFA process at a cost of $990 per barrel, accountants would transfer $1,584,000 (1,600 × $990) from the Work in Process Inventory (CFA) account to the Work in Process Inventory (Bottling) account, as follows:

	Debit	Credit
Work in Process Inventory (Bottling)	1,584,000	
Work in Process Inventory (CFA)		1,584,000

Record Manufacturing Cost in Subsequent Department

Additional materials, labor, and applied overhead would be added to Work in Process Inventory (Bottling) using journal entries similar to those described for the CFA process.

For example, the journal entries to record $96,000 in direct materials, $80,000 in direct labor, and $40,000 in applied manufacturing overhead in the bottling department would be as follows:

	Debit	Credit
Work in Process Inventory (Bottling)................................	96,000	
Raw Materials Inventory...		96,000
Work in Process Inventory (Bottling)................................	80,000	
Wages Payable		80,000
Work in Process Inventory (Bottling)................................	40,000	
Manufacturing Overhead..		40,000

Record Cost of Goods Completed

When the product is through the last production process, the total manufacturing cost is transferred out of the last Work in Process Inventory account and into Finished Goods Inventory. In our winery example, each bottle of wine accumulates $3.75 in total manufacturing cost. When 460,000 bottles are completed, a total of $1,725,000 (460,000 × $3.75) is transferred to Finished Goods Inventory, as follows:

	Debit	Credit
Finished Goods Inventory	1,725,000	
Work in Process Inventory (Bottling)		1,725,000

The cost transferred from Work in Process Inventory into Finished Goods Inventory is called **cost of goods manufactured** or **cost of goods completed**.

Record Cost of Goods Sold and Sales Revenue

When the product is sold, its total manufacturing cost is reported as cost of goods sold. If Fetzer sells 400,000 bottles, the total manufacturing cost of $1,500,000 (400,000 × $3.75) would be transferred from Finished Goods Inventory to Cost of Goods Sold. If the average sales price was $8.00 per bottle, the company would report $3,200,000 (400,000 × $8.00) in sales revenue. These journal entries are shown next:

	Debit	Credit
Cost of Goods Sold	1,500,000	
Finished Goods Inventory		1,500,000
Cash or Accounts Receivable	3,200,000	
Sales Revenue		3,200,000

The difference between sales revenue ($3,200,000) and cost of goods sold ($1,500,000) is unadjusted gross profit of $1,700,000. It is *unadjusted* because it is based on *applied* manufacturing overhead. If actual overhead is different than the amount applied, adjusted gross profit could be more (if overapplied) or less (if underapplied) than $1,700,000. Remember that gross profit is calculated before nonmanufacturing costs such as distribution fees, advertising, and other selling, general, and administrative expenses are accounted for. These costs are expensed during the period incurred as described in previous chapters.

REVIEW THE CHAPTER

DEMONSTRATION CASE A: WEIGHTED-AVERAGE METHOD

Bellagio Olive Oil Company manufactures extra virgin olive oil using a series of processes to convert olives into olive oil. These steps include cleaning the olives, grinding them into a paste, mixing to increase olive oil yield, separating the olive oil from the fruit, extracting the olive oil, storing, and bottling.

In the Mixing Department, direct materials (olives) are added at the beginning of the process, and conversion costs are incurred uniformly throughout the process. At the beginning of the most recent accounting period, Bellagio had 20,000 units in the mixing process that were 30 percent complete. It started an additional 150,000 units into the process and ended the period with 40,000 units in process, 40 percent complete with respect to conversion cost. The Mixing Department's partially completed production report follows.

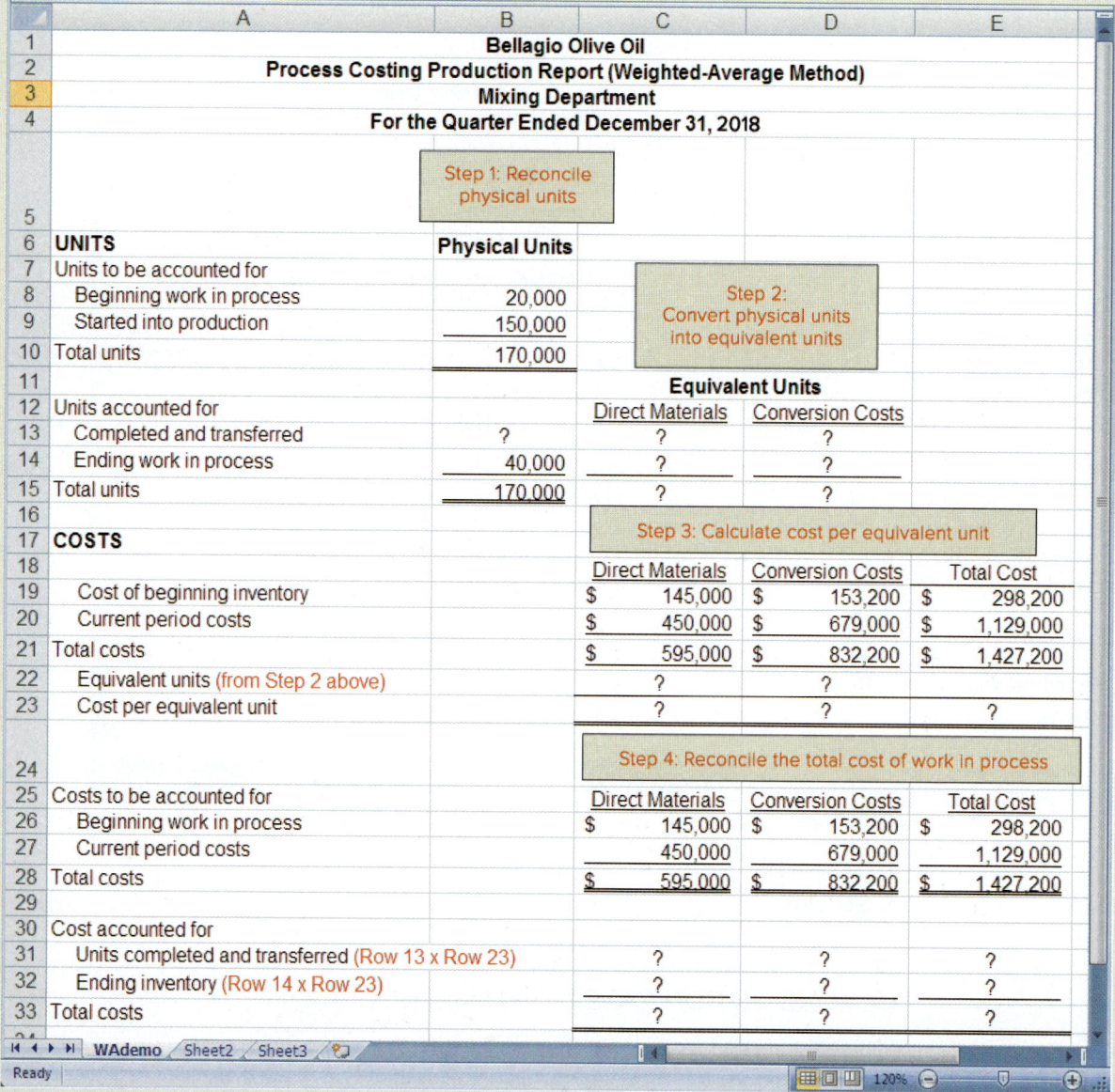

Required:

1. Complete steps 1 through 4 by filling in the question marks in Bellagio's production report.

2. What is the total cost of the units completed and transferred during the quarter?

3. What is the balance in Work in Process Inventory (Mixing) at the end of the quarter?

Suggested Solution

1.

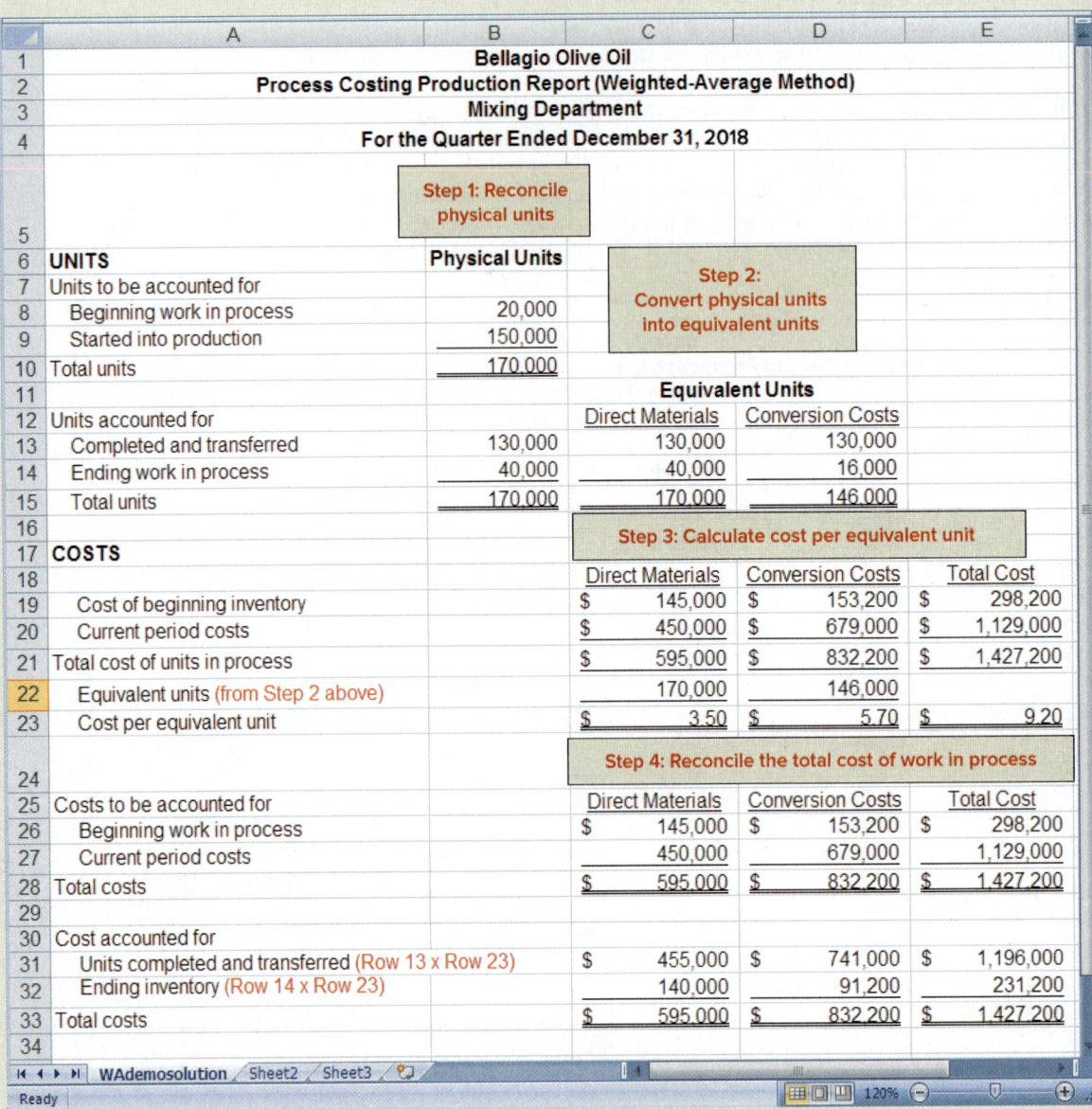

2. $1,196,000

3. $231,200

DEMONSTRATION CASE B: FIFO METHOD

Bellagio Olive Oil Company manufactures extra virgin olive oil using a series of processes to convert olives into olive oil. These steps include cleaning the olives, grinding them into a paste, mixing to increase olive oil yield, separating the olive oil from the fruit, extracting the olive oil, storing, and bottling.

In the Mixing Department, direct materials (olives) are added at the beginning of the process, and conversion costs are incurred uniformly throughout the process. At the beginning of the most recent accounting period, Bellagio had 20,000 units in the mixing process that were 30 percent complete. It started an additional 150,000 units into the process and ended the period with 40,000 units in process, 40 percent complete with respect to conversion cost. The Mixing Department's partially completed production report follows.

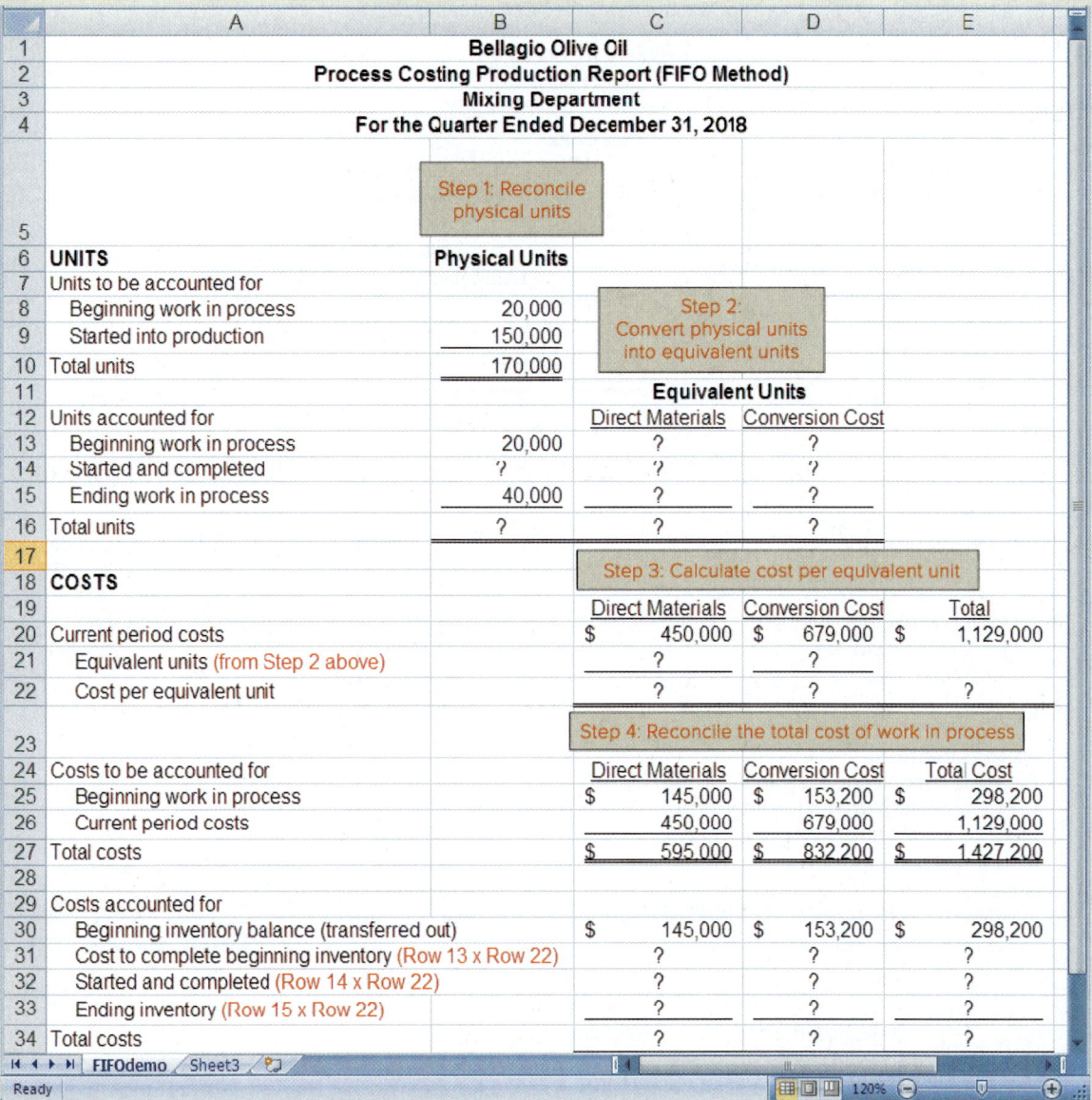

	A	B	C	D	E
1		Bellagio Olive Oil			
2		Process Costing Production Report (FIFO Method)			
3		Mixing Department			
4		For the Quarter Ended December 31, 2018			
5		Step 1: Reconcile physical units			
6	UNITS	Physical Units			
7	Units to be accounted for				
8	Beginning work in process	20,000	Step 2: Convert physical units into equivalent units		
9	Started into production	150,000			
10	Total units	170,000			
11			Equivalent Units		
12	Units accounted for		Direct Materials	Conversion Cost	
13	Beginning work in process	20,000	?	?	
14	Started and completed	?	?	?	
15	Ending work in process	40,000	?	?	
16	Total units	?	?	?	
17					
18	COSTS		Step 3: Calculate cost per equivalent unit		
19			Direct Materials	Conversion Cost	Total
20	Current period costs		$ 450,000	$ 679,000	$ 1,129,000
21	Equivalent units (from Step 2 above)		?	?	
22	Cost per equivalent unit		?	?	?
23			Step 4: Reconcile the total cost of work in process		
24	Costs to be accounted for		Direct Materials	Conversion Cost	Total Cost
25	Beginning work in process		$ 145,000	$ 153,200	$ 298,200
26	Current period costs		450,000	679,000	1,129,000
27	Total costs		$ 595,000	$ 832,200	$ 1,427,200
28					
29	Costs accounted for				
30	Beginning inventory balance (transferred out)		$ 145,000	$ 153,200	$ 298,200
31	Cost to complete beginning inventory (Row 13 x Row 22)		?	?	?
32	Started and completed (Row 14 x Row 22)		?	?	?
33	Ending inventory (Row 15 x Row 22)		?	?	?
34	Total costs		?	?	?

FIFOdemo / Sheet3

Ready   120%

Required:

1. Complete Steps 1 through 4 by filling in the question marks in Bellagio's production report.
2. What is the total cost of the units completed and transferred during the quarter?
3. What is the balance in Work in Process Inventory (Mixing) at the end of the quarter?

Suggested Solution

1.

	A	B	C	D	E
1		Bellagio Olive Oil			
2		Process Costing Production Report (FIFO Method)			
3		Mixing Department			
4		For the Quarter Ended December 31, 2018			
5		**Step 1: Reconcile physical units**			
6	**UNITS**				
7	Units to be accounted for	**Physical Units**		**Step 2: Convert physical units into equivalent units**	
8	Beginning work in process	20,000			
9	Started into production	150,000			
10	Total units	170,000			
11			**Equivalent Units**		
12	Units accounted for		Direct Materials	Conversion Cost	
13	Beginning work in process	20,000	-	14,000	
14	Started and completed	110,000	110,000	110,000	
15	Ending work in process	40,000	40,000	16,000	
16	Total units	170,000	150,000	140,000	
17					
18	**COSTS**		**Step 3: Calculate cost per equivalent unit**		
19			Direct Materials	Conversion Cost	Total Cost
20	Current period costs		$ 450,000	$ 679,000	$ 1,129,000
21	Equivalent units (from Step 2 above)		150,000	140,000	
22	Cost per equivalent unit		$ 3.00	$ 4.85	$ 7.85
23			**Step 4: Reconcile the total cost of work in process**		
24	Costs to be accounted for		Direct Materials	Conversion Cost	Total Cost
25	Beginning work in process		$ 145,000	$ 153,200	$ 298,200
26	Current period costs		450,000	679,000	1,129,000
27	Total costs		$ 595,000	$ 832,200	$ 1,427,200
28					
29	Costs accounted for				
30	Beginning inventory balance (transferred out)		$ 145,000	$ 153,200	$ 298,200
31	Cost to complete beginning inventory (Row 13 x Row 22)	$	-	$ 67,900	67,900
32	Started and completed (Row 14 x Row 22)		330,000	533,500	863,500
33	Ending inventory (Row 15 x Row 22)		120,000	77,600	197,600
34	Total costs		$ 595,000	$ 832,200	$ 1,427,200

FIFOdemosolution

Ready   120%

2. $298,200 + $67,900 + $863,500 = $1,229,600

3. $197,600

CHAPTER SUMMARY

LO 3–1   **Describe the key features of a process costing system.**

- Process costing is used by companies that produce homogeneous (similar) goods or services in a series of standardized processes.

- Manufacturing costs are recorded in the Raw Materials Inventory, Work in Process Inventory, and Finished Goods Inventory accounts until the product is sold, at which point they become part of Cost of Goods Sold.

- Process costing systems maintain a separate Work in Process Inventory account for each major production process. A production report is prepared for each production department to summarize the flow of units and costs through the process during an accounting period.
- Two methods can be used to prepare a process costing production report: the weighted-average method and the FIFO method. The primary difference between the two methods is the treatment of the units and costs in beginning inventory.

Reconcile the number of physical units using the weighted-average method. LO 3–2

- The total number of units that were worked on during the period can be reconciled using the following formula:

    Beginning Units in Process + Units Started = Ending Units in Process + Units Completed

Calculate the number of equivalent units using the weighted-average method. LO 3–3

- An equivalent unit is an adjustment that is made to convert partially complete units into the equivalent of a full unit.
- The weighted-average method calculates equivalent units for ending inventory only.
- Equivalent Units = Physical Units × % of Completion

Prepare a process costing production report using the weighted-average method. LO 3–4

- The production report summarizes the costs and units that flow into and out of the production process during a given period. It summarizes the following steps:

    Step 1: Reconcile the number of physical units.
    Step 2: Convert physical units into equivalent units.
    Step 3: Calculate cost per equivalent unit.
    Step 4: Reconcile the total cost of Work in Process Inventory.
    Step 5: Prepare the production report.

Prepare a process costing production report using the first-in, first-out (FIFO) method. LO 3–S1

- The key difference between FIFO and the weighted-average method is the treatment of the units in beginning inventory. FIFO separates the units in beginning inventory from the units that were started and completed during the period; the weighted-average method does not.
- The steps for preparing a production report using FIFO are the same as for the weighted-average method.

    Step 1: Reconcile the number of physical units.
    Step 2: Convert physical units into equivalent units.
    Step 3: Calculate cost per equivalent unit.
    Step 4: Reconcile the total cost of Work in Process Inventory.
    Step 5: Prepare the production report.

Prepare journal entries to record manufacturing costs in a process cost system. LO 3–S2

- The journal entries used to record manufacturing costs in process costing are similar to those used in job order costing.
- Direct materials and direct labor costs are debited to the Work in Process Inventory account of each production process as incurred. The credit is to a balance sheet account such as Raw Materials Inventory, Cash, or Wages Payable.
- Applied manufacturing overhead costs are debited to the Work in Process Inventory account and credited to the Manufacturing Overhead account.
- Actual manufacturing overhead costs are debited to the Manufacturing Overhead account and credited to the appropriate balance sheet account. Any difference in actual (debit) and applied (credit) manufacturing overhead is closed to Cost of Goods Sold at the end of the period.
- As the product moves from one production process to the next, its total manufacturing cost is transferred from one Work in Process Inventory account to the next.
- When the product is finished, its total manufacturing cost is debited to Finished Goods Inventory and, once it is sold, the total manufacturing cost is debited to Cost of Goods Sold.

KEY TERMS

Conversion Cost p. 112   First-In, First-Out (FIFO) Method p. 113   Transferred-In Cost p. 120
Equivalent Unit p. 115   Production Report p. 112   Weighted-Average Method p. 113

PRACTICE MATERIAL

QUESTIONS

1. Briefly describe the differences between job order and process costing. Give an example of a type of company that would use each one.

2. Briefly explain the underlying logic of a process costing system and its assignment of costs to products.

3. Explain the differences between Raw Materials Inventory, Work in Process Inventory, and Finished Goods Inventory accounts.

4. Explain the flow of costs in a process costing system, including the type of accounts used and the respective financial statement on which the cost appears.

5. What are the five steps in preparing a weighted-average production report?

6. Why is a production report important to a company?

7. What is the difference between conversion cost and manufacturing overhead?

8. What two methods can be used to prepare a process costing production report? What is the key difference between them?

9. How is the number of physical units reconciled to prepare a production report?

10. Why must a company calculate equivalent units when using process costing?

11. How can a unit be 100 percent complete with respect to materials but only partially complete in terms of conversion effort?

12. How do the weighted-average and the FIFO methods treat beginning inventory?

13. Is the weighted-average method or FIFO method usually more accurate? Why?

14. What are the steps in preparing a FIFO production report? Are they different from the steps to prepare a weighted-average production report?

15. When are the weighted-average and FIFO methods likely to arrive at different estimates of product cost?

16. What does a credit to the Work in Process Inventory account represent?

17. What triggers the cost of manufacturing to be transferred from the balance sheet to the income statement?

MULTIPLE CHOICE

1. Which of the following is most likely to use a process costing system?
   a. A company that builds and installs custom cabinetry.
   b. A company that makes one style of office chair.
   c. A janitorial service.
   d. A paving company.

2. Work in process includes
   a. Direct materials.
   b. Direct labor.
   c. Manufacturing overhead.
   d. All of the above.

3. Suppose Shadow Company has 250 units in beginning inventory, 400 units started in production, and 175 units in ending inventory. How many units did Shadow complete?
   a. 25.
   b. 325.
   c. 475.
   d. Number cannot be determined.

4. If Wilson Corp. has 450 units that are estimated to be 60 percent complete, how many equivalent units are there?
   a. 270.   c. 210.
   b. 100.   d. 450.

5. Masterson Company has calculated a cost per unit of $4.00 for materials and $8.50 for conversion to manufacture a specific product. Ending work in process has 1,000 units that are fully complete for materials and 70 percent complete for conversion. How much will Masterson have in its ending Work in Process Inventory?
   a. $12,500.   c. $8,750.
   b. $5,950.   d. $9,950.

6. Testa Company has no beginning work in process; 12,000 units were transferred out and 6,000 units in ending work in process are 100 percent complete for materials and 40 percent complete for conversion. If total materials cost is $90,000, the direct materials cost per unit is
   a. $4.   c. $6.
   b. $5.   d. None of the above.

7. Anderson, Inc., has 1,000 units of ending work in process that are 100 percent complete for materials and 60 percent complete for conversion. If the cost per equivalent unit is $3 for materials and $6 for conversion, what is the total value of Work in Process Inventory?

   a. $6,000.   **c.** $9,000.
   b. $8,000.   **d.** $6,600.

8. The primary difference between FIFO and weighted-average methods of process costing has to do with the treatment of

   a. Beginning inventory.
   b. Ending inventory.
   c. Number of units started.
   d. Direct materials.

9. When calculating equivalent unit cost using the weighted-average method, which of the following amounts are combined?

   a. Ending finished goods and cost of goods sold.
   b. Beginning finished goods and cost of goods sold.
   c. Beginning work in process and beginning finished goods.
   d. Beginning work in process and current period costs.

10. The journal entry to record the issuance of direct materials into production includes

   a. A credit to cash.
   b. A debit to work in process.
   c. A credit to finished goods.
   d. A debit to cost of goods sold.

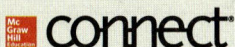 **Find More Learning Solutions on Connect.**

MINI-EXERCISES

M3–1 Matching Terminology

LO 3–1, 3–2, 3–3

Match each of the terms on the left with the appropriate definition on the right. Not all definitions will be used.

Term	Definition
____ **1.** Conversion Costs	**A.** Provides information about the number of units and manufacturing costs during an accounting period.
____ **2** Equivalent Unit	**B.** A measure used to convert partially complete units into a full unit.
____ **3.** First-in, First-Out	**C.** The reconciliation of the number of physical units worked on during the period.
____ **4.** Production Report	**D.** Direct materials plus direct labor.
____ **5.** Weighted-Average Method	**E.** Direct labor plus manufacturing overhead.
	F. Direct materials plus direct labor plus manufacturing overhead.
	G. Combines the cost of units in process at the beginning of the period with the cost of units that were started during the current period.
	H. Assumes that the units in process at the beginning of the period are completed before any new units are started in the current period.
	I. A detailed record of the costs incurred to complete a specific job.

M3–2 Identifying Companies That Use Process Costing

LO 3–1

Identify three manufacturing and one nonmanufacturing firms in which process costing is likely used. For each, explain the characteristics of that company that make it appropriate to use a process costing system.

M3–3 Compute Costs for Manufacturing Company

LO 3–1

San Tan Company manufactures light bulbs. Once produced, the bulbs are packaged and sold to wholesalers for distribution to grocery stores and large retailers like Walmart. The following costs were incurred by San Tan Company during April:

Electricity for factory	$15,400
Labor	30,600
Rent on factory	22,600
Insurance on factory	1,300
Glass for bulbs	54,800
Cardboard for packaging	6,600

For the month of April, compute the following costs for San Tan Company:

Manufacturing overhead

Direct materials

Conversion cost

LO 3–2   **M3–4 Calculating Physical Units**

Eagle Company had 1,150 units in work in process on January 1. During the month, Eagle completed 4,800 units and had 2,000 units in process on January 31. Determine how many units Eagle started during January.

LO 3–2   **M3–5 Calculating Physical Units**

For each of the following independent cases (A to D), compute the missing value in the table.

Case	Beginning Units	Units Started	Units Completed	Ending Units
A	800	4,600	3,300	?
B	2,400	1,600	?	3,200
C	?	1,500	2,460	5,120
D	690	?	1,800	1,360

LO 3–2, 3–3   **M3–6 Calculating Physical Units and Equivalent Units (Weighted-Average Method)**

Stone Company produces carrying cases for CDs. It has compiled the following information for the month of June:

	Physical Units	Percent Complete for Conversion
Beginning work in process	70,000	55%
Ending work in process	92,000	70

Stone adds all materials at the beginning of its manufacturing process. During the month, it started 180,000 units.

Using the weighted-average method, reconcile the number of physical units and calculate the number of equivalent units.

LO 3–S1   **M3–7 Calculating Physical Units and Equivalent Units (FIFO)**

Refer to M3-6 for information regarding Stone Company. Using the FIFO method, reconcile the number of physical units and calculate the number of equivalent units.

LO 3–2, 3–3   **M3–8 Calculating Physical Units and Equivalent Units (Weighted-Average Method)**

Laser Resources produces and sells laser components and accessories. All materials are added at the beginning of the process. It has compiled the following information regarding its physical units for the month of November:

	Physical Units
Beginning work in process, 65% complete for conversion	15,000
Units started	55,000
Units transferred out	48,000
Ending work in process, 15% complete for conversion	

Using the weighted-average method, reconcile the number of physical units and calculate equivalent units for materials and conversion cost.

LO 3–2, 3–3   **M3–9 Calculating Physical Units and Equivalent Units (Weighted-Average Method)**

Laser Resources produces and sells laser components and accessories. All materials are added at the beginning of the process. It has compiled the following information regarding its physical units for the month of November:

	Physical Units
Beginning work in process, 30% complete for conversion	
Units started	46,000
Units transferred out	62,000
Ending work in process, 45% complete for conversion	12,000

Using the weighted-average method, reconcile the number of physical units and calculate equivalent units for materials and conversion cost.

M3–10 Calculating Cost per Equivalent Unit (Weighted-Average Method)

LO 3–2, 3–3

Cliff Company manufactures file cabinets. The following cost information is available for the month of December:

Beginning work in process	
Direct materials	$ 68,000
Conversion cost	124,000
December costs	
Direct materials	136,000
Conversion cost	210,000

Cliff had 17,000 equivalent units of direct materials and 12,000 equivalent units of conversion cost. Using the weighted-average method, calculate Cliff's cost per equivalent unit for materials and conversion during December.

M3–11 Calculating Cost per Equivalent Unit (FIFO)

LO 3–S1

Refer to M3-10 for information regarding Cliff Company. Using the FIFO method, calculate Cliff's cost per equivalent unit for materials and conversion during December.

M3–12 Assigning Costs to Units

LO 3–3, 3–4

Pearl Company has the following production information for October: 60,000 units transferred out and 20,000 units in ending work in process that are 100 percent complete for materials and 60 percent complete for conversion costs. Materials cost is $12 per equivalent unit and conversion cost is $16 per equivalent unit. Determine the cost assigned to the units transferred out and the units in ending work in process using the weighted-average method.

M3–13 Assigning Costs to Units

LO 3–3

Roland Corp. had the following production information for August:

Beginning work in process	0
Units started and completed	40,000
Ending work in process	8,000

Roland's ending work in process is 100 percent complete for materials and 30 percent complete for conversion. Roland uses the weighted-average costing method and has computed direct materials cost per equivalent unit of $10 and conversion cost per equivalent unit of $24. Determine the cost assigned to units transferred out and to ending work in process.

M3–14 Preparing Journal Entries

LO 3–S2

Refer to the information for Roland Corp. in M3-13. Prepare the journal entry to transfer the cost of completed units to Finished Goods Inventory.

M3–15 Calculating Equivalent Units (Weighted-Average Method)

LO 3–3

The Cutting Department of Sonora's Textiles has the following information about production and costs for the month of July:

- Beginning work in process, 9,200 units that are 100 percent complete as to materials and 35 percent complete as to conversion costs.
- 15,000 units transferred out.
- Ending work in process, 6,200 units 100 percent complete as to materials and 65 percent complete for conversion.

Using the weighted-average method, compute the number of equivalent units of production for materials and conversion for the month of July.

LO 3–S1   **M3–16 Calculating Equivalent Units (FIFO)**

The Cutting Department of Sonora's Textiles has the following information about production and costs for the month of July:

- Beginning work in process, 9,200 units that are 100 percent complete as to materials and 35 percent complete as to conversion costs.
- 15,000 units transferred out.
- Ending work in process, 6,200 units 100 percent complete as to materials and 65 percent complete for conversion.

Using the FIFO method, compute the equivalent units of production for materials and conversion for the month of July.

LO 3–S1   **M3–17 Compare Weighted-Average and FIFO Process Costing**

Determine whether each the following statements describes the weighted-average method (*WA*), the FIFO method (*FIFO*), or both methods (*Both*).

_____ Is simpler and more frequently used in the real world.

_____ Assumes the units in beginning inventory were completed before any new units were started.

_____ Acceptable for external reporting (GAAP).

_____ More closely matches the actual flow of costs in many process industries and therefore may be more accurate.

_____ Assumes that all of the work and all of the cost associated with beginning inventory occurred during the current period.

LO 3–4   **M3–18 Calculating Physical Units and Equivalent Units (Weighted-Average Method) for a Subsequent Department**

Crayons Forever uses a three department production process to produce its crayons. The Molding Department, Labeling Department and Packaging Department. During the month of May, the Molding Department completed and transferred 4,800,000 molded crayons, with a cost of $240,000, to the Labeling Department. The labeling materials are added at the beginning of the process. At the beginning of May, the Labeling Department had 200,000 molded crayons in beginning work in process, 25 percent through the labeling process. At the end of May, 360,000 molded crayons were on hand, 65 percent of the way through the labeling process.

Using the weighted-average method, reconcile the number of physical units and calculate the number of equivalent units for the Labeling Department for the month of May. Transferred-in costs are treated as materials added at the start of the labeling process.

LO 3–S2   **M3–19 Preparing Journal Entries for Process Costing System**

During its first month of operation, Portia Company purchased $90,000 of materials on account and requisitioned $64,000 of materials for use in production. The company recorded $30,000 of unpaid direct labor cost and applied $20,000 of manufacturing overhead. Prepare Portia's journal entries to record these events.

EXERCISES

LO 3–1   **E3–1 Understanding Process Costing**

Suppose your sister Becky and her three best friends start a small business making beaded bracelets. They plan to purchase the materials, assemble the jewelry themselves, and sell the finished pieces to friends at school. Other than minor color and design differences, the bracelets will be virtually alike. Your sister realizes that they must cover their costs before they can expect any profit and is trying to determine the cost per bracelet. Becky thinks that she should include the cost of each individual bead used in a bracelet and is becoming frustrated with the process of tracing each bead.

Required:

Explain to Becky why she should be using a process costing system to determine the cost of the bracelets. Include a description of process costing as well as reasons that it is appropriate for her business.

E3–2 Computing Manufacturing Costs for Process Costing

LO 3–1

All of the following companies manufacture toasters. The following costs were incurred by each company during September:

	Warner Co.	Painted Trails Co.	Catalina Inc.	Sunrise Co.
Direct labor	$12,600	$ 9,750	$ 72,800	$36,200
Rent	68,000	4,250	97,400	55,000
Utilities	3,300	2,000	16,900	8,500
Heating elements	87,500	42,600	101,500	65,400
Depreciation	6,500	10,300	28,600	38,400

Required:

1. What is the total conversion cost for Warner Co.?
2. What is the total manufacturing overhead for Painted Trails Co.?
3. What is the total conversion cost for Catalina Inc.?
4. What is the total manufacturing overhead for Sunrise Co.?

E3–3 Changing Direct Material Inputs to Reduce Costs and Energy Consumption

LO 3–1

In 2008, Fetzer Vineyards redesigned its bottling process to use a more lightweight bottle by reducing the thickness of the glass and removing the "punt" or indentation at the base of the bottle. The result was to reduce the weight of each wine bottle from a little over 20 ounces to 17 ounces, for a 16 percent reduction in the amount of glass used per bottle. This reduced the overall glass usage by 2,173 tons in a year in which the company produced about 23 million bottles of wine.

Reducing the weight of each bottle also reduced the amount of energy needed to produce it, the amount of fuel required to transport it throughout the supply chain, and the energy needed to landfill or recycle the bottle after consumption. The result was a 14 percent reduction in annual greenhouse gas emissions, or 2,985 tons of CO_2 equivalents in the supply chain.

Dr. Ann Thrupp, Fetzer's sustainability manager at the time, was quoted as saying:

"Lightweighting our bottle is a double-bottom line innovation good for the environment and for efficient operations that supports our goal of being a sustainable business." (www.sustainable-brands.com/news_and_views/articles/fetzer-bottles-wine-lighter-weight-glass)

Required:

1. Compute the annual savings in direct materials costs (glass) assuming a price of $50 per ton of glass.
2. In addition to the direct materials cost savings, would Fetzer realize any other economic benefits from this initiative? Explain.
3. What did Dr. Ann Thrupp mean by "double bottom line"? What would make it a "triple bottom line"?

E3–4 Computing Unknown Manufacturing Costs for Process Costing

LO 3–1

The following four companies use a process cost system:

	Solana Co.	Vista Co.	Ray Inc.	Lindsay Company
Conversion cost	a.	$235,600	$56,750	h.
Direct labor	$43,200	c.	$25,500	$13,500
Depreciation	$ 2,500	$ 17,600	f.	$ 1,600
Manufacturing overhead	$25,700	$143,800	e.	g.
Rent	$16,200	d.	$10,300	$ 850
Direct materials	$89,300	$362,250	$39,800	$17,250
Supervisor's salary	$ 5,400	$ 19,650	$ 2,900	$ 2,100
Utilities	b.	$ 24,400	$ 9,050	$ 650

Required:

Treating each case independently, find the missing amounts for letters a through h. You should do them in the order listed.

LO 3–2, 3–3

E3–5 Calculating Physical Units and Equivalent Units (Weighted-Average Method)

Oasis Company adds all materials at the beginning of its manufacturing process. Production information for selected months of the year follows:

	Beginning Work in Process				Ending Work in Process	
Month	Units	Conversion Complete (percent)	Units Started	Units Transferred Out	Units	Conversion Complete (percent)
February	3,000	50	?	38,000	13,000	30
June	8,400	75	46,600	?	8,000	45
September	?	20	52,800	50,000	4,600	60
December	5,800	30	44,000	42,800	?	70

Required:

1. Reconcile the number of physical units to find the missing amounts.
2. Calculate the number of equivalent units for both materials and conversion for each month.

LO 3–S1

E3–6 Calculating Physical Units and Equivalent Units (FIFO Method)

Refer to the information for Oasis Company in E3-5.

Required:

1. Reconcile the number of physical units to find the missing amounts. Determine the number of units started and completed each month.
2. Calculate the number of equivalent units for both materials and conversion for each month using the FIFO method.

LO 3–2, 3–3

E3–7 Calculating Equivalent Units, Cost per Equivalent Unit, Reconciling the Cost of Work in Process (Weighted-Average Method)

Silver Company manufactures kites and has the following information available for the month of April:

Work in process, April 1	
(100% complete for materials, 40% for conversion)	52,000 units
Direct materials	$ 80,000
Conversion cost	$110,000
Number of units started	158,000 units
April costs	
Direct materials	$226,000
Conversion cost	$336,000
Work in process, April 30	
(100% complete for materials, 20% for conversion)	80,000 units

Required:

Using the weighted-average method, complete each of the following steps:

1. Reconcile the number of physical units worked on during the period.
2. Calculate the number of equivalent units.
3. Calculate the cost per equivalent unit rounded to five decimal places.
4. Reconcile the total cost of work in process.

LO 3–S1

E3–8 Calculating Equivalent Units, Cost per Equivalent Unit, Reconciling the Cost of Work in Process (FIFO)

Refer to E3-7 for information regarding Silver Company.

Required:

Complete all requirements for E3-7 using the FIFO method.

E3–9 Calculating Equivalent Units, Cost per Equivalent Unit, Reconciling the Cost of Work in Process (Weighted-Average Method)   LO 3–2, 3–3

Ridgecrest Company manufactures plastic storage crates and has the following information available for the month of April:

Work in process, April 1	
(100% complete for materials, 40% for conversion)	31,200 units
Direct materials	$ 48,000
Conversion cost	$ 66,000
Number of units started	94,800 units
April costs	
Direct materials	$135,600
Conversion cost	$201,600
Work in process, April 30	
(100% complete for materials, 20% for conversion)	48,000 units

Required:

Using the weighted-average method of process costing, complete each of the following steps:

1. Reconcile the number of physical units worked on during the period.
2. Calculate the number of equivalent units.
3. Calculate the cost per equivalent unit rounded to five decimal places.
4. Reconcile the total cost of work in process.

E3–10 Calculating Equivalent Units, Cost per Equivalent Unit, Reconciling the Cost of Work in Process (FIFO)   LO 3–S1

Refer to E3-9 for information regarding Ridgecrest Company.

Required:

Complete all requirements for E3-9 using the FIFO method.

E3–11 Calculating Equivalent Units, Cost per Equivalent Unit, Reconciling the Cost of Work in Process (Weighted-Average Method)   LO 3–2, 3–3

Legacy Company manufactures umbrellas and has the following information available for the month of May:

Work in process, May 1	
(100% complete for materials, 90% for conversion)	36,000 units
Direct materials	$ 64,500
Conversion cost	$ 87,500
Number of units started	90,500 units
May costs	
Direct materials	$103,000
Conversion cost	$189,500
Work in process, May 31	
(100% complete for materials, 20% for conversion)	33,500 units

Required:

Using the weighted-average method of process costing, complete each of the following steps:

1. Reconcile the number of physical units worked on during the period.
2. Calculate the number of equivalent units.
3. Calculate the cost per equivalent unit rounded to five decimal places.
4. Reconcile the total cost of work in process.

LO 3–S1   **E3–12 Calculating Equivalent Units, Cost per Equivalent Unit, Reconciling the Cost of Work in Process (FIFO)**

Refer to E3-11 for information regarding Legacy Company.

Required:

Complete all requirements for E3-11 using the FIFO method.

LO 3–2, 3–3   **E3–13 Calculating Equivalent Units, Cost per Equivalent Unit, Reconciling the Cost of Work in Process (Weighted-Average Method)**

Arboles Company manufactures pencils and has the following information available for the month of July:

Work in process, July 1	
(100% complete for materials, 60% for conversion)	75,000 units
Direct materials	$ 5,000
Conversion cost	$17,500
Number of units started	100,000 units
July costs	
Direct materials	$ 6,500
Conversion cost	$24,000
Work in process, July 31	
(100% complete for materials, 10% for conversion)	70,000 units

Required:

Using the weighted-average method of process costing, complete each of the following steps:

1. Reconcile the number of physical units worked on during the period.
2. Calculate the number of equivalent units.
3. Calculate cost per equivalent unit, rounded to five decimal places.
4. Reconcile the total cost of work in process.

LO 3–S1   **E3–14 Calculating Equivalent Units, Cost per Equivalent Unit, Reconciling the Cost of Work in Process (FIFO)**

Refer to E3-13 for information regarding Arboles Company.

Required:

Complete all requirements for E3-13 using the FIFO method of process costing.

LO 3–2, 3–3   **E3–15 Calculating Equivalent Units, Cost per Equivalent Unit, Reconciling the Cost of Work in Process (Weighted-Average Method)**

Mirada Company manufactures handheld calculators and has the following information available for the month of July:

Work in process, July 1	
(100% complete for materials, 25% for conversion)	126,000 units
Direct materials	$240,000
Conversion cost	$394,000
Number of units started	220,000 units
July costs	
Direct materials	$426,000
Conversion cost	$484,000
Work in process, July 31	
(100% complete for materials, 10% for conversion)	144,000 units

Required:

Using the weighted-average method of process costing, complete each of the following steps:

1. Reconcile the number of physical units worked on during the period.

2. Calculate the number of equivalent units.

3. Calculate cost per equivalent unit, rounded to five decimal places.

4. Reconcile the total cost of work in process.

E3–16 Calculating Equivalent Units, Cost per Equivalent Unit, Reconciling the Cost   LO 3–S1
of Work in Process (FIFO)

Refer to E3-15 for information regarding Mirada Company.

Required:

Complete all requirements for E3-15 using the FIFO method of process costing.

E3–17 Calculating Equivalent Units, Unit Costs, and Cost Assigned (Weighted-   LO 3–3
Average Method)

Vista Vacuum Company has the following production information for the month of March. All materials are added at the beginning of the manufacturing process.

Units

- Beginning inventory of 6,000 units that are 100 percent complete for materials and 25 percent complete for conversion.

- 28,000 units started during the period.

- Ending inventory of 9,000 units that are 20 percent complete for conversion.

Manufacturing Costs

- Beginning inventory was $40,000 ($19,400 materials and $20,600 conversion costs).

- Costs added during the month were $58,800 for materials and $113,800 for conversion ($55,000 labor and $58,800 applied overhead).

Required:

1. Calculate the number of equivalent units of production for materials and conversion for March.

2. Calculate the cost per equivalent unit for materials and conversion for March. Round your intermediate calculations to five decimal places.

3. Determine the costs to be assigned to the units transferred out and the units still in process.

E3–18 Calculating Cost per Equivalent Unit (Weighted-Average Method)   LO 3–3

Canyon Company's Assembly Department has the following production and manufacturing information for February:

Units

- 28,000 in beginning inventory that are 100 percent complete for materials and 20 percent for conversion.

- 44,600 units finished and transferred out.

- 17,500 units in ending inventory that are 100 percent complete for materials and 45 percent complete for conversion.

Costs	Materials	Conversion
Beginning	$13,500	$ 47,200
Current	30,000	111,400

Required:

Calculate cost per equivalent unit using the weighted-average method. Round your answer to five decimal places.

LO 3–4   **E3–19 Calculating Physical Units, Equivalent Units and Cost per Equivalent Unit (Weighted-Average Method) for a Subsequent Department**

Stem Games manufactures playing cards. It has three departments: Printing, Cutting & Collating, and Wrapping. Transferred-in costs are considered materials costs. The following information is available for the Wrapping department for the month of October:

	Physical Units
Beginning work in process	280,000
(100% complete for materials, 80% complete for conversion)	
Decks transferred in	3,160,000
Decks completed and transferred to Finished Goods Inventory	3,200,000
Ending Work in Process	?
(100% complete for materials, 45% complete for conversion	

	Costs:
Beginning work in process:	
Direct materials	$ 188,900
Conversion cost	$ 19,840
Costs transferred in	$1,777,500
October costs:	
Direct materials	$ 63,200
Conversion costs	$ 277,880

Required:

Using the weighted-average method of process costing,

1. Reconcile the number of physical decks worked on during the month.
2. Calculate the number of equivalent decks for the Wrapping department.
3. Calculate the cost per equivalent deck.

LO 3–4   **E3–20 Reconcile the Total Cost of Work in Process**

Using the information from E3-19, reconcile the total cost of beginning inventory, transferred in costs, and current period costs to the cost of units transferred out and ending work in process.

LO 3–4   **E3–21 Identifying Steps for Preparing a Process Costing Production Report**

Place the following steps required to prepare a process costing production report into their correct order. List separately any step that should not be included in the process.
1. Reconcile the total cost of work in process inventory.
2. Apply manufacturing overhead to specific jobs.
3. Calculate cost per equivalent unit.
4. Record costs incurred for each job on a separate job cost sheet.
5. Convert physical units into equivalent units.
6. Reconcile the number of physical units.
7. Prepare a production report.

LO 3–4   **E3–22 Computing Missing Information from Production Report**

Fincher Farms uses process costing to account for the production of canned vegetables. Direct materials are added at the beginning of the process and conversion costs are incurred uniformly throughout the process. Beginning work in process is 30 percent complete; ending work in process is 40 percent complete.

The following is an excerpt from the production report for Fincher Farms:

FINCHER FARMS
Process Costing Production Report (Weighted-Average Method)
For the month ended January 31, 2018

	Physical Units		
Units to be accounted for			
Beginning work in process	40,000		
Started into production	a.		
Total units	340,000		

		Equivalent Units	
	Physical Units	Direct Materials	Conversion Cost
Units accounted for			
Completed and transferred	260,000	260,000	c.
Ending work in process	b.	80,000	d.
Total units	340,000	340,000	292,000

Required:

Find the missing amounts for letters a–d. You should do them in the order listed.

E3–23 Complete a Production Report   LO 3–4

Brite Toothbrushes has gathered the following information to complete its Production Report for the month of April.

BRITE TOOTHBRUSHES
Process Costing Production Report (Weighted Average Method)
Assembly Department
For the Month Ended April 30, XXXX

UNITS		Physical Units		
Units to be accounted for:				
Beginning work in process	50% complete as to conversion	2,500		
Started into production		55,000		
Total units		57,500		

			Equivalent Units	
			Direct Materials	Conversion Costs
Units accounted for:				
Completed and transferred out		45,000		
Ending work in process	30% complete as to conversion	?		
Total units		?		

COSTS	Direct Materials	Conversion Costs	Total Cost
Cost of beginning work in process	42,500	7,500	50,000
Current period costs	?	?	?
Total costs	991,875	297,375	1,289,250
Equivalent units	?	?	
Cost per equivalent units	?	?	?

	Direct Materials	Conversion Costs	Total Cost
Costs to be accounted for			
Beginning work in process	?	?	?
Current period costs	?	?	?
Total costs	?	?	?
Costs accounted for:			
Completed and transferred out	?	?	?
Ending work in process	?	?	?
Total costs			

Required:

Using the provided information, complete the report.

LO 3–S2   **E3–24 Recording Manufacturing Costs in Process Costing**

Mesa Company produces wooden rocking chairs. The company has two production departments, Cutting and Assembly. The wood is cut and sanded in Cutting and then transferred to Assembly to be assembled and painted. From Assembly, the chairs are transferred to Finished Goods Inventory and then are sold.

Mesa has compiled the following information for the month of February:

	Cutting Department	Assembly Department
Direct materials (not yet paid)	$150,000	$ 24,000
Direct labor	130,000	198,000
Applied manufacturing overhead	300,000	334,000
Cost of goods completed and transferred out	468,000	506,000

Required:

Prepare the following journal entries for Mesa:

1. Amount of direct materials, direct labor, and manufacturing overhead incurred for the Cutting Department.
2. Transfer of products from Cutting to Assembly.
3. Amount of direct materials, direct labor, and manufacturing overhead incurred by the Assembly Department.
4. Transfer of chairs from Assembly to Finished Goods.

LO 3–S2   **E3–25 Recording Manufacturing Costs in Process Costing**

Sereno Company makes piñatas for children's birthday parties. Information for Sereno's last six months of operation is listed as follows.

Required:

Prepare the journal entries to record each of the following transactions.

(a) Purchased $15,600 of raw materials on credit.
(b) Issued $9,200 of direct materials into production.
(c) Recorded $16,500 in unpaid direct labor.
(d) Applied $24,000 in manufacturing overhead.
(e) Completed pinatas costing $39,500.
(f) Recorded $16,000 in actual manufacturing overhead. Credit miscellaneous accounts.
(g) Sold piñatas for $66,000 that cost $44,000 to produce.

GROUP A PROBLEMS

LO 3–2, 3–3, 3–4   **PA3–1 Preparing a Process Costing Production Report (Weighted-Average Method)**

Sandia Corporation manufactures metal toolboxes. It adds all materials at the beginning of the manufacturing process. The company has provided the following information:

	Units	Costs
Beginning work in process (30% complete)	80,000	
Direct materials		$ 80,000
Conversion cost		190,000
Total cost of beginning work in process		$270,000
Number of units started	152,000	
Number of units completed and transferred to finished goods	?	
Ending work in process (50% complete)	68,000	
Current period costs		
Direct materials		$180,000
Conversion cost		314,000
Total current period costs		$494,000

Required:

1. Using the weighted-average method of process costing, complete each of the following steps:
   a. Reconcile the number of physical units worked on during the period.
   b. Calculate the number of equivalent units.
   c. Calculate the cost per equivalent unit rounded to five decimal points.
   d. Reconcile the total cost of work in process.
2. Summarize the preceding steps in a production report for Sandia Corporation.

PA3–2 Preparing a Process Costing Production Report (FIFO)   LO 3–S1

Refer to the information for Sandia Corporation in PA3-1.

Required:

Complete all requirements for PA3-1 using the FIFO method.

PA3–3 Preparing a Process Costing Production Report (Weighted-Average Method)   LO 3–2, 3–3, 3–4

Saddleback Company makes camping lanterns using a single production process. All direct materials are added at the beginning of the manufacturing process. Information for the month of March follows:

	Units	Costs
Beginning work in process (30% complete)	117,800	
Direct materials		$ 192,000
Conversion cost		344,000
Total cost of beginning work in process		$ 536,000
Number of units started	243,000	
Number of units completed and transferred to finished goods	334,800	
Ending work in process (65% complete)	?	
Current period costs		
Direct materials		$ 507,400
Conversion cost		648,000
Total current period costs		$1,155,400

Required:

1. Using the weighted-average method of process costing, complete each of the following steps:
   a. Reconcile the number of physical units worked on during the period.
   b. Calculate the number of equivalent units.
   c. Calculate the cost per equivalent unit rounded to five decimal places.
   d. Reconcile the total cost of work in process.

2. Summarize the preceding steps in a March production report for Saddleback Company.

LO 3–S1   **PA3–4 Preparing a Process Costing Production Report (FIFO)**

Refer to the information in PA3-3 for Saddleback Company.

Required:

Complete all requirements for PA3-3 using the FIFO method.

LO 3–2, 3–3, 3–4   **PA3–5 Preparing a Process Costing Production Report (Weighted-Average Method)**

Glencove Co. makes one model of radar gun used by law enforcement officers. All direct materials are added at the beginning of the manufacturing process. Information for the month of September follows:

	Units	Costs
Beginning work in process (40% complete)	?	
Direct materials		$1,336,500
Conversion cost		625,800
Total cost of beginning work in process		$1,962,300
Number of units started	36,400	
Number of units completed and transferred to finished goods	34,800	
Ending work in process (75% complete)	21,850	
Current period costs		
Direct materials		$2,402,400
Conversion cost		1,266,500
Total current period costs		$3,668,900

Required:

1. Using the weighted-average method of process costing, complete each of the following steps:
   a. Reconcile the number of physical units worked on during the period.
   b. Calculate the number of equivalent units.
   c. Calculate the cost per equivalent unit rounded to five decimal places.
   d. Reconcile the total cost of work in process.

2. Summarize the preceding steps in a September production report for Glencove Company.

LO 3–S1   **PA3–6 Preparing a Process Costing Production Report (FIFO)**

Refer to the information in PA3-5 for Glencove Company.

Required:

Complete all requirements for PA3-5 using the FIFO method.

GROUP B PROBLEMS

LO 3–2, 3–3, 3–4   **PB3–1 Preparing a Process Costing Production Report (Weighted-Average Method)**

Mallory Inc. produces a popular brand of energy drink. It adds all materials at the beginning of the manufacturing process. The company has provided the following information:

	Units	Costs
Beginning work in process (30% complete)	40,000	
Direct materials		$ 20,000
Conversion cost		92,000
Total cost of beginning work in process		$112,000
Number of units started	104,000	
Number of units completed and transferred to finished goods	?	
Ending work in process (70% complete)	46,000	
Current period costs		
Direct materials		$ 62,000
Conversion cost		164,000
Total current period costs		$226,000

Required:

1. Using the weighted-average method of process costing, complete each of the following steps:
   a. Reconcile the number of physical units worked on during the period.
   b. Calculate the number of equivalent units.
   c. Calculate the cost per equivalent unit rounded to five decimal places.
   d. Reconcile the total cost of work in process.

2. Summarize the preceding steps in a production report for Mallory Inc.

PB3–2 Preparing a Process Costing Production Report (FIFO)   LO 3–S1

Refer to the information about Mallory Inc. in PB3-1.

Required:

Complete all requirements for PB3-1 using the FIFO method.

PB3–3 Preparing a Process Costing Production Report (Weighted-Average Method)   LO 3–2, 3–3, 3–4

Crismon Company makes camping tents in a single production department. All direct materials are added at the beginning of the manufacturing process. Information for the month of July follows:

	Units	Costs
Beginning work in process (30% complete)	46,200	
Direct materials		$ 242,000
Conversion cost		368,000
Total cost of beginning work in process		$ 610,000
Number of units started	125,000	
Number of units completed and transferred to finished goods	154,800	
Ending work in process (35% complete)	?	
Current period costs		
Direct materials		$ 563,400
Conversion cost		772,400
Total current period costs		$1,335,800

Required:

1. Using the weighted-average method of process costing, complete each of the following steps:
   a. Reconcile the number of physical units worked on during the period.
   b. Calculate the number of equivalent units.
   c. Calculate the cost per equivalent unit rounded to five decimal places.
   d. Reconcile the total cost of work in process.

2. Summarize the preceding steps in a July production report for Crismon Company.

LO 3–S1   **PB3–4   Preparing a Process Costing Production Report (FIFO)**

Refer to the information in PB3-3 for Crismon Company.

Required:

Complete all requirements for PB3-3 using the FIFO method.

LO 3–2, 3–3, 3–4   **PB3–5   Preparing a Process Costing Production Report (Weighted-Average Method)**

Ivy Glen Inc. makes one model of lighted baby toy. All direct materials are added at the beginning of the manufacturing process. Information for the month of September follows:

	Units	Costs
Beginning work in process (20% complete)	?	
Direct materials		$151,000
Conversion cost		152,208
Total cost of beginning work in process		$303,208
Number of units started	257,400	
Number of units completed and transferred to finished goods	294,800	
Ending work in process (85% complete)	83,400	
Current period costs		
Direct materials		$321,750
Conversion cost		482,052
Total current period costs		$803,802

Required:

1. Using the weighted-average method of process costing, complete each of the following steps:
    a. Reconcile the number of physical units worked on during the period.
    b. Calculate the number of equivalent units.
    c. Calculate the cost per equivalent unit rounded to five decimal places.
    d. Reconcile the total cost of work in process.

2. Summarize the preceding steps in a September production report for Ivy Glen Inc.

LO 3–S1   **PB3–6   Preparing a Process Costing Production Report (FIFO)**

Refer to the information in PB3-5 for Ivy Glen Inc.

Required:

Complete all requirements for PB3-5 using the FIFO method.

SKILLS DEVELOPMENT CASES

LO 3–1   **S3–1   Video Case Assignment: Identifying Characteristics of Process Costing**

©McGraw-Hill Education

Go to www.YouTube.com and search for **How It's Made**, a television show produced by the Discovery Channel that shows how thousands of products and services are created. Find a product or service for which process costing would be appropriate, such as toothpaste, matches, batteries, potato chips, or coins.

Watch the video and answer the following questions:

- What product or service did you choose? Why is process costing appropriate for this setting?

- Why does the company that makes the product or service need a cost system? Describe two decisions a manager might make based on cost information.

- Prepare a diagram to show the various processes required to make the product or service. Describe the raw materials used in each process and name two costs that would be included in conversion cost for each process.

- How would the company determine the cost of units in process at any given point in time? Why would managers need to know the cost of items in process?

S3–2 Researching Companies That Use Process Costing

Consider the many different products a person might use or consume in a typical day from toothpaste to a slice of pizza.

Required:

Choose three items that you use regularly and whose manufacturer you believe is likely to use process costing. Investigate the manufacturing company of each item and its website for information to support or contradict your belief.

S3–3 Evaluating the Implications of Process Costing in a Service Industry

Overnight package delivery is a multimillion dollar industry that has grown steadily since it began. The four largest package carriers are the U.S. Postal Service (USPS), Federal Express (FedEx), United Parcel Service (UPS), and DHL. Suppose you have a document that must be delivered to each of the cities listed in the following table by the close of business tomorrow. Using each company's website, determine the price to ship your letter and record the information in the following table.

	Carefree, AZ	Happy Valley, TN	Experiment, PA	Opportunity, MT
USPS				
FedEx				
UPS				
DHL				

To answer the following questions, assume that the prices charged by the companies are directly related to the cost of delivery. Remember that process costing averages the total cost across all units (in this case shipments) so that the cost of each unit (shipment) is the same. Job order costing charges different amounts depending on the amount of materials, labor, and overhead needed to fill the order.

Required:

1. Based on their pricing, which of the delivery companies appear(s) to use process costing?
2. For each company that does not appear to use process costing, what factors are likely to impact the cost (and thus pricing) of the overnight delivery service?
3. In this industry, what are the potential advantages and disadvantages of process costing?

4

Activity-Based Costing and Cost Management

CHAPTER FOUR

YOUR LEARNING OBJECTIVES

LO 4–1 Assign indirect costs to products or services using a single volume-based cost driver.

LO 4–2 Classify activities as unit-, batch-, product-, or facility-level activities.

LO 4–3 Assign indirect costs to activity cost pools and select a cost driver for each pool.

LO 4–4 Assign indirect costs to products or services using activity rates.

LO 4–5 Assign indirect costs to products or services using activity proportions.

LO 4–6 Compare the results of a volume-based cost system to activity-based costing.

LO 4–7 Apply activity-based costing to a service industry.

LO 4–8 Describe how managers use activity-based management and other cost management methods.

©Mark Dierker/McGraw-Hill Education

E very year, millions of Americans make a New Year's resolution to lose weight and keep it off, only to give up within a week or two. The reason so many diets fail is because they focus on short-term success (measured by changes in the scale) that are difficult to sustain in the long run.

Business managers face similar pressure to "trim the waste" (not the "waist"), and consultants promising to deliver "lean" results are as plentiful as diet programs promising to help you lose weight. A lean enterprise is one that delivers high value at the lowest possible cost, with very little waste or inefficiency. You can think of the accounting system as a tool that measures cost and other information, much like your bathroom scale is a tool that measures weight. But an accounting system in and of itself cannot make an organization lean any more than an accurate scale can make you lose weight. It is simply a tool to help managers gauge their progress and identify potential opportunities for improvement.

In this chapter, we use Toyota Motor Corporation to illustrate several cost management topics. Our primary focus is on the use of activity-based costing as a tool for measuring the cost of products and services. We then discuss different approaches that managers can use to **manage** or reduce cost, including activity-based management (ABM), just-in-time manufacturing (JIT), total quality management (TQM), and target costing.

Few companies have been as successful at adopting a lean philosophy as Toyota Motor Corporation. However, recent events—including product failures, widespread recalls, and production delays resulting from a natural disaster—have called some of these techniques into question.

To highlight Toyota's focus on lean thinking, let's visit Toyota City, home of Toyota's corporate headquarters and its largest manufacturing facility in Japan. The Tsutsumi plant employs more than 5,000 people and produces almost half a million cars a year, which represents about 10 percent of Toyota's worldwide production capability. Refer to Exhibit 4–1 for a visual representation of Toyota's global operations. In addition to its domestic operations in Japan, Toyota has manufacturing facilities in 26 countries around the globe. To keep things simple, we will limit our example to two of the models produced at the Tsutsumi plant: the Toyota Prius and the Scion tC (touring coupe).

When Toyota first introduced the Prius in 1997, it was the world's first mass-produced hybrid vehicle. Demand for a more environmentally friendly and fuel efficient mode of transportation was huge. By 2011, Toyota had produced more than two million Priuses, more than half of which were sold in the United States.

The Scion brand was introduced in 2004 to appeal to the millennial generation. Scion models generally have a lower price point than the competition and are available in a limited number of trim packages (with standard features), allowing consumers to customize the product to their unique tastes with after-market accessories.

As you will see shortly, differences in how products are designed, manufactured, and sold can impact how costs are assigned under different cost systems, and thus the decisions that managers ultimately make based on that cost information. For simplicity, we will present amounts in U.S. dollars rather than Japanese yen for our numerical examples. The numbers do not represent the true price, cost, or production data for Toyota. This information is proprietary and not publicly available to consumers or Toyota's competitors.

EXHIBIT 4–1	Toyota's Global Operations

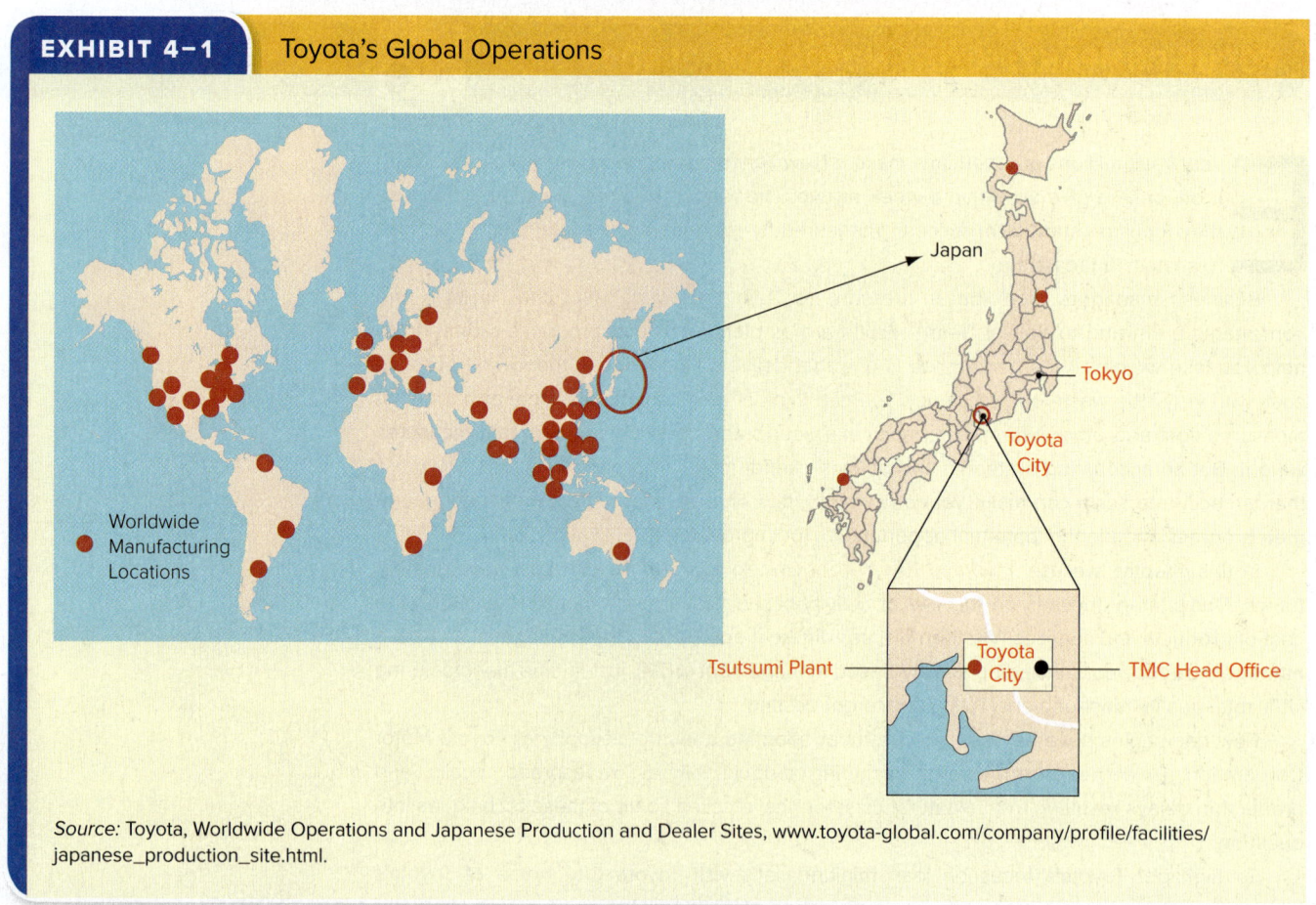

Source: Toyota, Worldwide Operations and Japanese Production and Dealer Sites, www.toyota-global.com/company/profile/facilities/japanese_production_site.html.

Review of volume-based cost systems

- Step 1: Determine the cost driver
- Step 2: Calculate the predetermined overhead rate
- Step 3: Assign indirect costs to individual products or services

Activity-based costing (ABC)

- Step 1: Identify and classify activities
- Step 2: Form activity cost pools and assign indirect costs to each pool
- Step 3: Select a cost driver for each activity cost pool
- Step 4: Assign indirect costs to products or services based on their activity demands
- Activity-based costing in service industries

Cost management methods

- Activity-based management (ABM)
- ABM and Sustainability
- Just-in-time (JIT)
- Total quality management (TQM)
- Target costing and life cycle cost management
- Summary of ABC and ABM

This chapter will illustrate two different methods that can be used to assign **indirect costs** to products and services. Recall from earlier chapters that, unlike direct materials and direct labor costs, which can be directly traced to individual products and services, indirect costs are those that cannot be directly attributed to specific products and services. Indirect costs are also referred to as **overhead costs**. These costs can be related to manufacturing activities (called manufacturing overhead), or to nonmanufacturing activities such as research and development, selling, or administrative functions (called corporate overhead).

Managers need cost information for a variety of purposes, including pricing, resource allocation, and cost control. For companies that incur a lot of indirect costs and that provide a wide range of products or services, the method used to assign indirect costs can have a major impact on the reported cost of those products and services.

In previous chapters, we assigned indirect (overhead) costs to products or services using a single allocation base, or cost driver, such as direct labor hours. This type of cost system is sometimes called a **volume-based cost system** because the cost driver is related to the volume of units produced or customers served. Later in this chapter, we introduce an alternative way to assign indirect costs to products or services called **activity-based costing**. But first, let's review how to assign indirect costs using a single volume-based cost driver.

COACH'S TIP

The previous two chapters described two systems that can be used to track the *total* cost of products and services: job order costing and process costing. This chapter provides more detail about how to assign *indirect* costs to products and services. The methods described here can be used with either job order costing or process costing.

Review of Volume-Based Cost Systems

Recall from earlier chapters that there are three steps to assigning indirect costs in a volume-based cost system:

1. Determine the cost driver (allocation base).
2. Calculate the predetermined overhead rate.
3. Assign indirect costs to individual products or services by multiplying the predetermined overhead rate by the cost driver.

Each of these steps is discussed in more detail as follows.

STEP 1: DETERMINE THE COST DRIVER

Remember that indirect costs are those that cannot be traced to specific products or services, or that are not worth the effort to trace. Instead, they must be allocated based on some observable measure called a cost driver (allocation base).

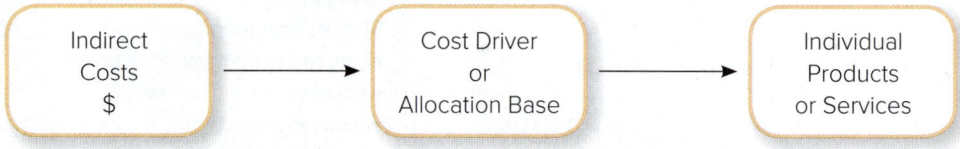

In a volume-based cost system, the cost driver varies in direct relation to volume. Examples of **volume-based cost drivers** include direct labor hours, machine hours, direct materials costs, sales revenue, or any other measure that varies in direct proportion to production or sales volume.

To illustrate how to allocate indirect costs using a volume-based cost driver, assume that the Tsutsumi plant produces only two types of automobiles: the Prius and the Scion tC. For simplicity and ease of calculation, monetary values are expressed in U.S. dollars, while total cost and volume numbers are expressed in thousands. Assume the following hypothetical cost and production information for the Prius and Scion:

ESTIMATED ANNUAL PRODUCTION INFORMATION			
	Prius	**Scion**	**Total**
Units produced	100	300	400
Total direct labor hours	3,500	9,000	12,500
Direct labor hours per unit	35	30	

PER-UNIT COST INFORMATION		
	Prius	**Scion**
Direct materials	$8,000	$5,000
Direct labor	2,800	1,800
Manufacturing overhead	?	?

Notice that the direct materials and direct labor cost of each product have already been determined. These costs are directly traceable to the two products and are not affected by the method used to allocate indirect costs. But how much manufacturing overhead cost should be assigned or allocated to each model? We address this question next.

Assume Toyota estimates that the total manufacturing overhead cost will be $3,000,000 per year, and that the company uses a traditional volume-based cost system in which indirect costs are allocated to products based on direct labor hours.

STEP 2: CALCULATE THE PREDETERMINED OVERHEAD RATE

The next step is to compute the predetermined overhead rate by dividing the estimated total manufacturing overhead cost by the estimated total value of the cost driver, as follows:

$$\text{Predetermined Overhead Rate} = \frac{\text{Estimated Total Manufacturing Overhead Cost}}{\text{Estimated Total Cost Driver}}$$

In our Toyota example, estimated total manufacturing overhead cost of $3,000,000 will be divided by the estimated total direct labor hours (12,500), as follows:

$$\text{Predetermined Overhead Rate} = \frac{\$3,000,000}{12,500} = \$240 \text{ per Direct Labor Hour}$$

STEP 3: ASSIGN INDIRECT COSTS TO INDIVIDUAL PRODUCTS OR SERVICES

To determine how much manufacturing overhead cost to assign to the individual products, we multiply the $240 predetermined overhead rate by the number of direct labor hours required for each product, as shown below:

	Prius	Scion	Total
Total direct labor hours	3,500	9,000	12,500
Predetermined overhead rate	× $ 240	× $ 240	
Total manufacturing overhead	$840,000	$2,160,000	$3,000,000
Number of units produced	÷ 100	÷ 300	
Manufacturing overhead cost per unit	$ 8,400	$ 7,200	

> **COACH'S TIP**
>
> Notice that the total amount of overhead assigned to the Scion is higher than the amount assigned to the Prius. In this hypothetical example, the Scion is the high-volume product. In general, a volume-based cost system will assign more total cost to the highest volume product. But on a per unit basis, the Scion has a lower per unit cost because the total manufacturing overhead is spread over more units.

To compute the **unit manufacturing cost,** we need to add the **manufacturing overhead** cost per unit, which we calculated in Step 3, to the **direct materials** and **direct labor** costs.

PER-UNIT COST INFORMATION		
	Prius	Scion
Direct materials	$ 8,000	$ 5,000
Direct labor	2,800	1,800
Manufacturing overhead	8,400	7,200
Total manufacturing cost per unit	$19,200	$14,000

If we subtract the total manufacturing cost per unit from the unit sales price, we get the gross margin for each unit sold. Remember that gross margin takes into account only the **manufacturing costs** of the product, before nonmanufacturing costs such as distribution fees; advertising; and other selling, general, and administrative expenses have been deducted.

We'll use hypothetical prices (provided as follows) to find the gross margin for the two models:

	Prius	Scion
Unit selling price	$31,000	$15,000
Less: Manufacturing cost per unit	19,200	14,000
Gross profit per unit	$11,800	$ 1,000
Gross profit margin (% of sales)	38.1%	6.7%

The gross margin analysis suggests that the Prius is the more profitable product, with a gross margin percentage of 38.1 percent compared to only 6.7 percent for the Scion. Although these numbers do not necessarily reflect the actual cost or profit of Toyota's products, they show how the cost allocation system can impact the reported cost and profitability of each product.

In the next section, we compute the cost of these products using an alternative costing system, activity-based costing. But first, complete the following Self-Study Practice to make sure you can compute unit manufacturing costs using a volume-based cost system.

💡 How's it going? — Self-Study Practice

KeepSafe Company makes floor and wall safes for storing valuables. The company applies manufacturing overhead to products on the basis of direct labor hours. Estimated cost and production information on the two products follows:

PER-UNIT COST INFORMATION

	Floor Safe	Wall Safe
Direct materials	$20	$15
Direct labor	10	15
Manufacturing overhead	?	?

PRODUCTION INFORMATION

	Floor Safe	Wall Safe
Units produced	35,000	10,000
Direct labor hours per unit	1	1.5
Total direct labor hours	35,000	15,000

Estimated total manufacturing overhead is $600,000.

1. Compute the predetermined overhead rate per direct labor hour.
2. How much of the total manufacturing overhead would be allocated to each product?
3. Compute the total manufacturing cost per unit for each product.

After you have finished, check your answers against the solutions. in the margin.

Activity-Based Costing (ABC)

Activity-based costing (ABC) is a method of assigning indirect costs to products and services based on the **activities** they require. The goal of ABC is to identify the major activities that place demands on a company's resources and then assign indirect costs to the products and services that create those demands. For companies that produce a variety of products or provide different types of services, ABC can supply managers with useful information about the cost of the activities required to produce those products and services. Managers can then use this information to make decisions (e.g., set prices), change the way the company does

---

SOLUTION TO SELF-STUDY PRACTICE

1. PREDETERMINED OVERHEAD RATE = $600,000 ÷ (35,000 + 15,000) = $12 PER DIRECT LABOR HOUR.

2.

	Floor Safe	Wall Safe
Total direct labor hours	35,000	15,000
Manufacturing overhead rate	× $12	× $12
Total manufacturing overhead	$420,000	$180,000

3.

Unit Cost

	Floor Safe	Wall Safe
Direct materials	$20	$15
Direct labor	10	15
Manufacturing overhead (per unit)	($12 × 1) = 12	($12 × 1.5) = 18
Total manufacturing cost (per unit)	$42	$48

business (e.g., eliminate unnecessary activities), and ultimately improve performance (e.g., reduce costs or increase sales).

As you will see, ABC requires companies to collect different types of information than traditional accounting systems. Most companies that implement ABC use sophisticated information systems, such as an **enterprise resource planning (ERP) system.** An ERP system is an integrated management information system that cuts across the entire organization (enterprise), including manufacturing, supplier management, customer relationship management, and accounting. Like an ABC system, an ERP system is designed to provide managers with timely information that they can use to make strategic and operational decisions. However, these systems are extremely costly to implement and maintain, so managers must evaluate whether the benefits of such a system are worth the cost.

While ABC has many advantages, it is not appropriate for every company. If a company makes a single product or produces many products that are similar in nature, a more sophisticated cost system such as ABC may not be worth the cost of implementation and data tracking. A simpler cost system may do just fine. While this may sound a bit like the distinction between job order costing (for companies that provide customized products or services) and process costing (for companies that provide homogenous products or services), the focus of ABC is on assigning *indirect* costs to products or services based on the activities they require.

ABC involves two stages of cost assignment or allocation. In the first stage, indirect costs are assigned to activity cost pools. In the second stage, indirect costs are allocated from the activity cost pools to individual products and services. See Exhibit 4–2 for a diagram of this two-stage process.

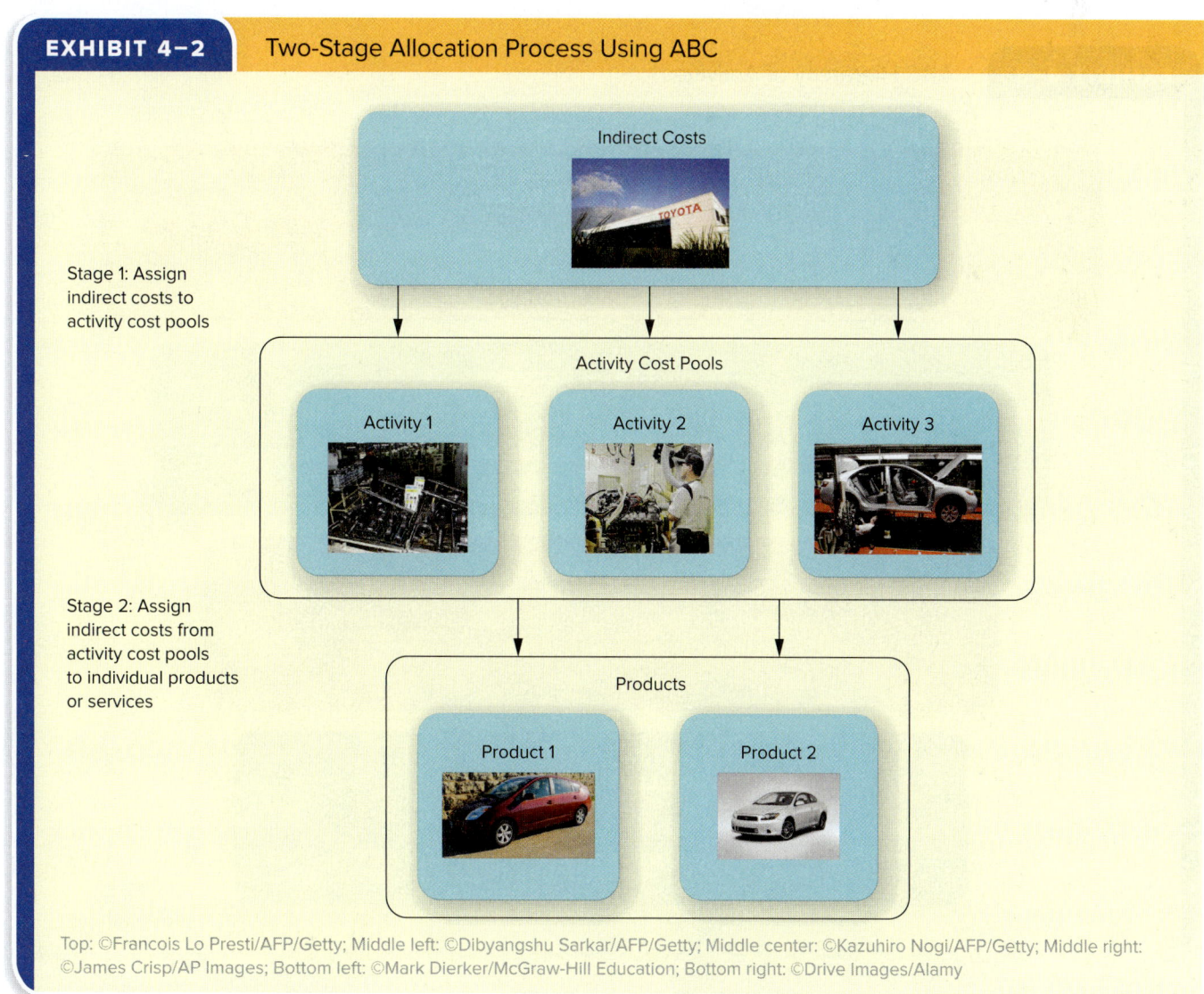

| EXHIBIT 4–2 | Two-Stage Allocation Process Using ABC |

Indirect Costs

Stage 1: Assign indirect costs to activity cost pools

Activity Cost Pools

Activity 1   Activity 2   Activity 3

Stage 2: Assign indirect costs from activity cost pools to individual products or services

Products

Product 1   Product 2

The two stages for allocating indirect costs in an activity-based costing system are broken down into more detailed steps:

Stage 1 Allocations $\left\{ \begin{array}{l} \textbf{1.} \text{ Identify and classify activities.} \\ \textbf{2.} \text{ Form activity cost pools and assign indirect costs to each pool.} \end{array} \right.$

Stage 2 Allocations $\left\{ \begin{array}{l} \textbf{3.} \text{ Select a cost driver for each activity cost pool.} \\ \textbf{4.} \text{ Assign indirect costs to products or services based on their activity demands.} \end{array} \right.$

STEP 1: IDENTIFY AND CLASSIFY ACTIVITIES

Learning Objective 4–2
Classify activities as unit-, batch-, product-, or facility-level activities.

Because activities are the backbone of the ABC system, the first step is to identify the major activities that the organization must perform in order to provide products and/or services to customers. The activities can range from very broad activities that relate to the company as a whole (e.g., a speech given by the CEO to the board of directors) to a very specific activity performed for an individual product or service (e.g., a bank teller processing a transaction for a customer). This hierarchy of activities is shown in Exhibit 4–3.

Facility-level activities are the most general category and are performed to benefit the organization as a whole, as opposed to specific products, customers, units, or batches. The term *facility* applies primarily to manufacturing activities, but all company-wide activities should be included, such as selling, general, and administrative activities, and corporate support

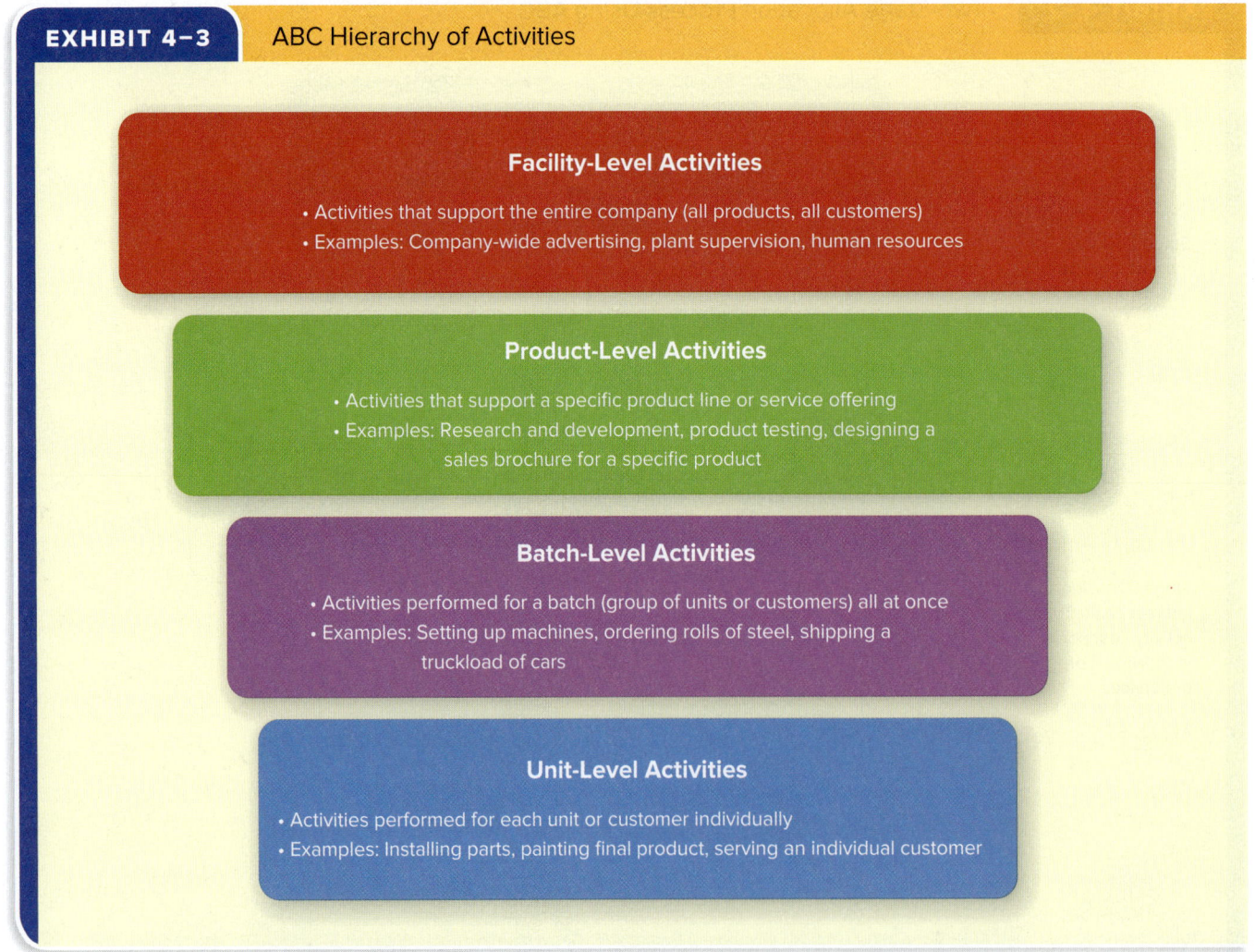

EXHIBIT 4–3 ABC Hierarchy of Activities

Facility-Level Activities

- Activities that support the entire company (all products, all customers)
- Examples: Company-wide advertising, plant supervision, human resources

Product-Level Activities

- Activities that support a specific product line or service offering
- Examples: Research and development, product testing, designing a sales brochure for a specific product

Batch-Level Activities

- Activities performed for a batch (group of units or customers) all at once
- Examples: Setting up machines, ordering rolls of steel, shipping a truckload of cars

Unit-Level Activities

- Activities performed for each unit or customer individually
- Examples: Installing parts, painting final product, serving an individual customer

functions (e.g., accounting, payroll, and legal services). Although generally accepted accounting principles (GAAP) do not allow the costs of nonmanufacturing activities to be included in cost of goods sold or inventory for external reporting purposes, managers may find it useful to assign these costs to individual products and customers for internal decision making.

Product-level activities are performed for a specific product line or type of service offering. After the product-level activities are performed, the company can make numerous units and batches of the product without repeating these activities. Examples include designing a new product, creating and testing prototype models, and creating metal dies and casts that will be used to make the product. In the auto industry, safety crash tests are performed for each product or model, but not for every single unit produced.

Batch-level activities are performed for a group or batch of units all at once. These activities vary with the number of batches produced but are independent of the number of units in each batch. An example is a machine setup that occurs before each production run. At Toyota, batch-level activities would include reprogramming robotics, performing quality control for a batch of units (but not every unit), and ordering and receiving raw materials. These activities must be performed each time a batch or group of units is produced, but do not have to be repeated for each individual unit in the batch.

Unit-level activities are performed for each individual unit or customer. These activities vary in direct proportion to the number of units produced or the number of customers served. Examples of unit-level activities for Toyota include the installation of automobile components such as the frame, body, engine, and tires. Unit-level activities also include any quality testing performed on each individual unit as it passes through the assembly process.

To make sure you understand how to classify activities using the ABC hierarchy, take the following Self-Study Practice.

 How's it going?   Self-Study Practice

1. Which of the following would be classified as a unit-level activity by an ice cream manufacturer such as Ben & Jerry's?
   a. Purchasing the ingredients to make a batch of cookie dough ice cream.
   b. Performing quality checks on each batch produced to make sure the flavor is right.
   c. Conducting research and development on a new flavor of ice cream.
   d. Maintaining the equipment used to produce various flavors of ice cream.
   e. Pouring the ice cream into containers before freezing it.

2. Which of the activities in question 1 (a through e) would be classified as a product-level activity by an ice cream manufacturer?

After you have finished, check your answers against the solutions in the margin.

Solution to Self-Study Practice
1. e
2. c

STEP 2: FORM ACTIVITY COST POOLS AND ASSIGN INDIRECT COSTS TO EACH POOL

After the activities have been identified and classified, the next step is to combine similar activities into activity cost pools. You can imagine that a company as large as Toyota has employees performing hundreds, if not thousands, of activities. To keep the cost system manageable, we must simplify the number of activities by grouping like or similar activities together. One way to combine activities is based on the activity hierarchy presented in Step 1. For example, unit-level activities can be grouped together; batch-level activities can be grouped together, and so on. This does not mean that an ABC system must have an activity cost pool for every level of the hierarchy, but it provides a framework for combining similar

Learning Objective 4–3
Assign indirect costs to activity cost pools and select a cost driver for each pool.

activities together. At a minimum, an ABC system should include at least one activity cost pool that captures non-unit-level activities, such as batch-level, product-level, or facility-level activities.

For simplicity, let's assume that Toyota has grouped its production activities into the following three categories:

- Machining and installation (unit level)
- Machine setup (batch level)
- Engineering and quality control (product level)

Recall that the total manufacturing overhead cost for our hypothetical Toyota example was $3,000,000 per year. In an ABC system, this indirect cost must be assigned to the three activity cost pools.

While some costs are relatively easy to assign to specific activities, others may relate to multiple activities and must be allocated based on some measure, such as time spent on each activity. An example is a production manager who oversees all manufacturing-related activities. The supervisor could keep track of the time spent on each of these activities, and accountants would use the time records to allocate the cost of supervision among the activities. Let's take a closer look at this example.

Assume the production manager makes $120,000 per year and has kept track of the time spent supervising the three major activities. The allocation of the manager's salary across the three activity cost pools appears as follows:

	Supervision Hours	Allocation Percentage	Manager's Salary	Salary Allocation
Machining and Installation	800	$800 \div 2,000 = 40\%$	$\times \$120,000 =$	$ 48,000
Machine Setup	600	$600 \div 2,000 = 30\%$	$\times \$120,000 =$	36,000
Engineering and Quality Control	600	$600 \div 2,000 = 30\%$	$\times \$120,000 =$	36,000
	2,000			$120,000

Because the manager spends 40 percent of his or her time supervising machining and installation activities, $48,000 (40% × $120,000) of his salary should be assigned to that activity cost pool. The allocation to the remaining activity cost pools is determined the same way, by multiplying the allocation percentage by the total cost of the manager's salary.

Similar allocations would be made for all manufacturing overhead costs to assign them to one of the three activity pools. For example, facility costs such as rent, utilities, and janitorial services might be allocated based on the number of square feet each activity requires, while payroll costs might be allocated based on the number of employees involved in each activity.

After the Stage 1 allocations are complete, the $3,000,000 in manufacturing overhead cost is distributed among the three activity cost pools, as shown in Exhibit 4–4. The next step is to identify the cost driver that will be used to assign the indirect cost from each activity cost pool to individual products and services (Stage 2).

STEP 3: SELECT A COST DRIVER FOR EACH ACTIVITY COST POOL

The next step is to select a cost driver for each activity cost pool. Unlike traditional cost systems that assign indirect costs using only volume-based cost drivers, ABC systems include measures that capture factors other than volume, which are called non-volume-based cost drivers. A **non-volume-based cost driver** is an allocation base that is not strictly related to the number of units produced or customers served. Some common examples of volume-based and non-volume-based measures are shown next:

| EXHIBIT 4–4 | Stage 1 Allocation of Indirect Costs to Activity Cost Pools |

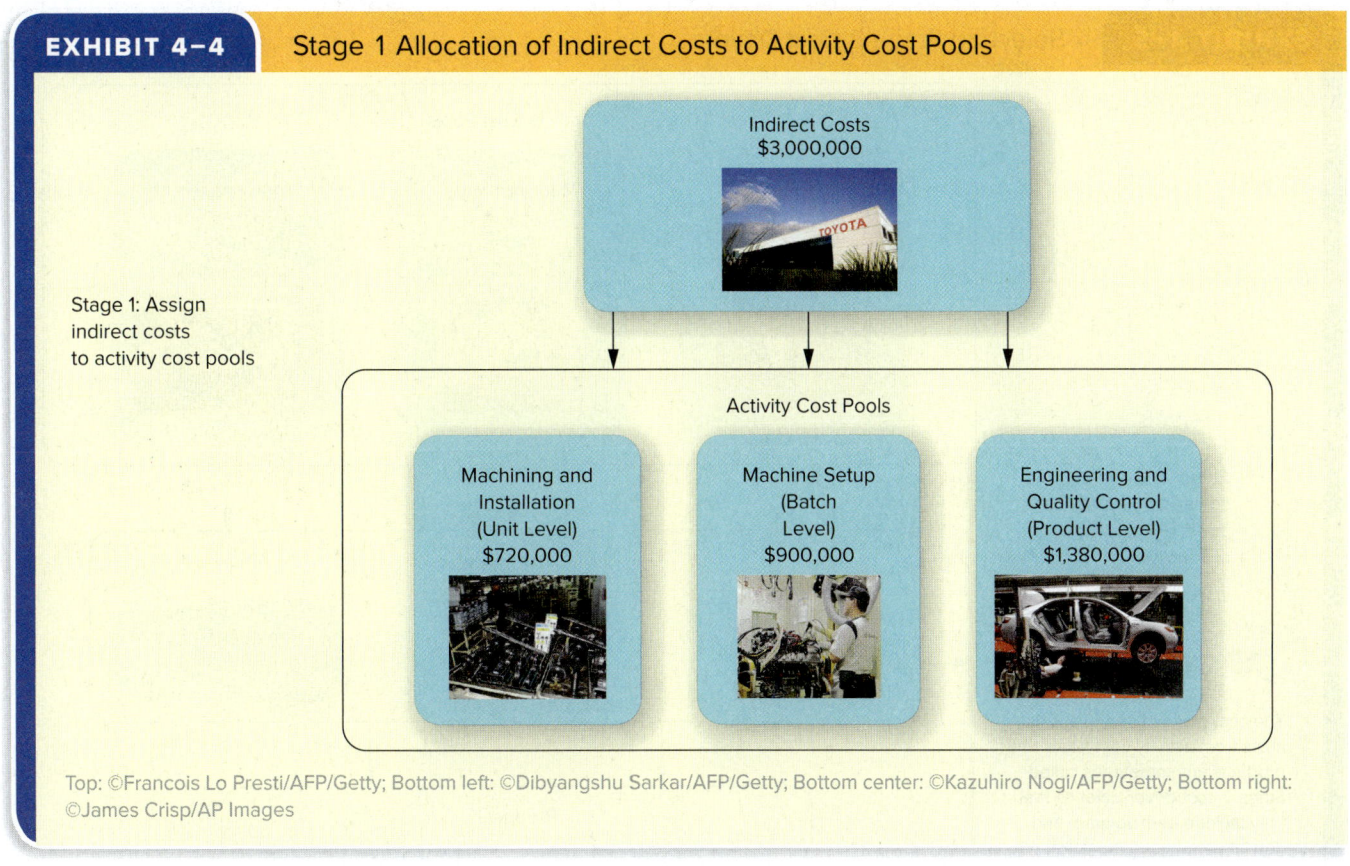

Top: ©Francois Lo Presti/AFP/Getty; Bottom left: ©Dibyangshu Sarkar/AFP/Getty; Bottom center: ©Kazuhiro Nogi/AFP/Getty; Bottom right: ©James Crisp/AP Images

Volume-Based Cost Drivers	Non-Volume-Based Cost Drivers
Number of units produced	Number of batches or setup time
Number of direct labor hours	Processing time per unit
Number of machine hours	Number of quality inspections
Total direct materials cost	Number of design changes

Most ABC systems will include both volume-based **and** non-volume-based cost drivers. If the activity must be performed for each individual unit, a volume-based cost driver, such as the number of units produced, direct labor hours, or machine hours, is appropriate. If the activity is not related to the number of units, a non-volume-based cost driver, such as the number of setups or engineering hours, may be more appropriate. By incorporating cost drivers that capture aspects of the production process other than volume, ABC can assign more indirect cost to products that require more setup time, more complex processing, more design changes, more quality inspections, and the like.

Exhibit 4–5 shows the cost drivers that we will use to assign indirect costs in our Toyota example. Machine hours is the driver for the machining and installation activity. The number of setups is the driver for the machine setup activity. The number of engineering and inspection hours is the driver for engineering and quality control costs. The Stage 2 allocations for each of these cost pools are discussed in the next section.

STEP 4: ASSIGN INDIRECT COSTS TO PRODUCTS OR SERVICES BASED ON THEIR ACTIVITY DEMANDS

The final step in ABC is to assign indirect costs from the activity cost pools to specific products and services based on their activity demands. One of two methods can be used to assign indirect costs to individual products or services: the activity rate method or the activity proportion method. The method used is a matter of preference, but may depend on how the information is presented and whether complete information on all product or service lines is available.

EXHIBIT 4–5   Selecting Stage 2 Cost Drivers

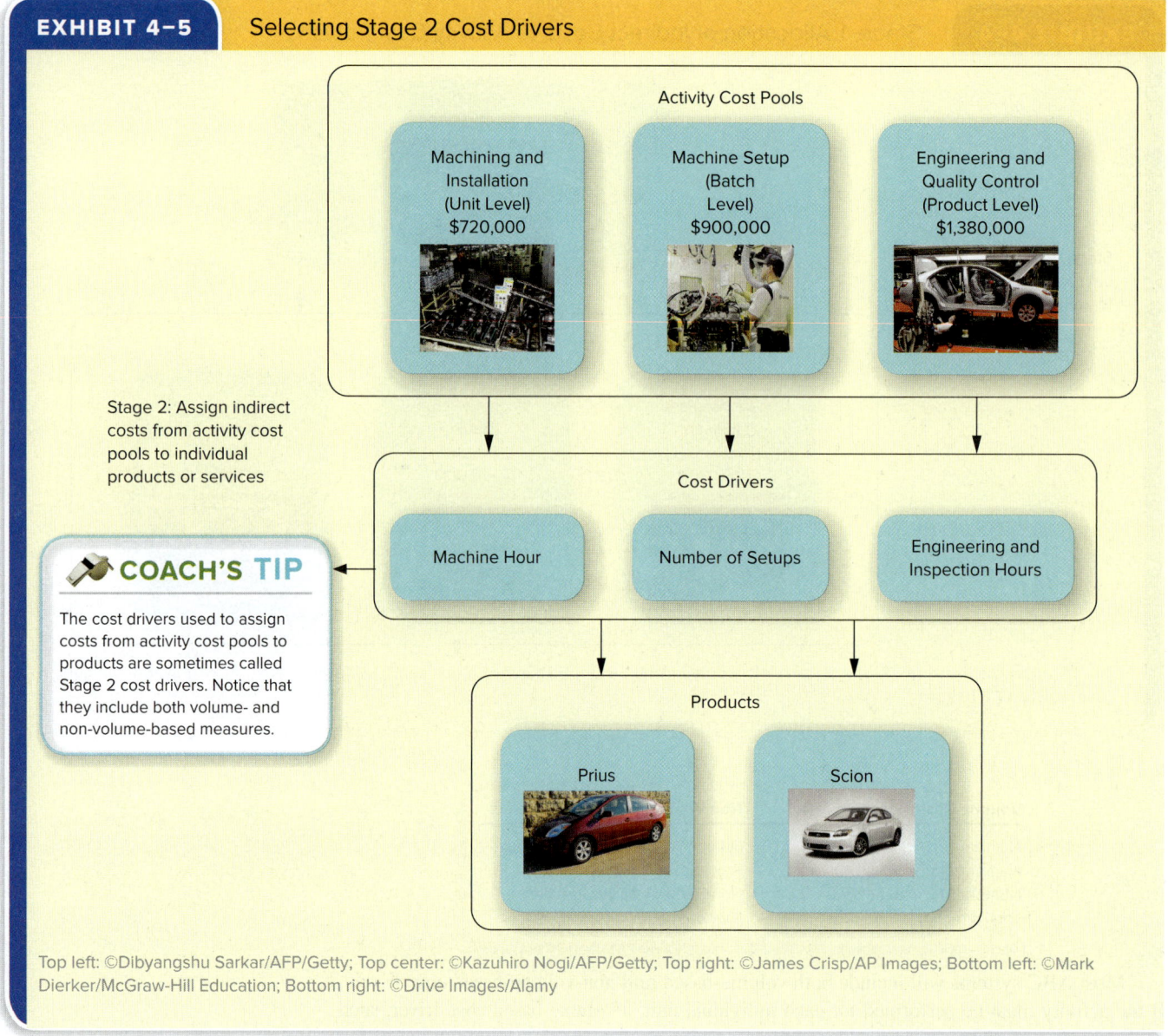

Activity Cost Pools

| Machining and Installation (Unit Level) $720,000 | Machine Setup (Batch Level) $900,000 | Engineering and Quality Control (Product Level) $1,380,000 |

Stage 2: Assign indirect costs from activity cost pools to individual products or services

Cost Drivers

| Machine Hour | Number of Setups | Engineering and Inspection Hours |

COACH'S TIP

The cost drivers used to assign costs from activity cost pools to products are sometimes called Stage 2 cost drivers. Notice that they include both volume- and non-volume-based measures.

Products

Prius   Scion

Top left: ©Dibyangshu Sarkar/AFP/Getty; Top center: ©Kazuhiro Nogi/AFP/Getty; Top right: ©James Crisp/AP Images; Bottom left: ©Mark Dierker/McGraw-Hill Education; Bottom right: ©Drive Images/Alamy

Activity-Rate Method

Learning Objective 4–4
Assign indirect costs to products or services using activity rates.

The first method involves computing an **activity rate** for each activity cost pool. This rate is just like the predetermined overhead rate computed earlier in the chapter, except that we compute a separate rate for each activity cost pool using the following formula:

$$\frac{\text{Activity}}{\text{Rate}} = \frac{\text{Total Activity Cost}}{\text{Total Cost Driver}}$$

To illustrate the activity-rate method, let's assign the cost of the first activity cost pool: machining and installation. The total indirect cost assigned to this activity cost pool from Stage 1 was $720,000. In Stage 2, we assign this cost to the two products on the basis of machine hours using the following information:

| Activity Cost Pool | Total Activity Cost | COST DRIVER: MACHINE HOURS | | |
		Prius	Scion	Total
Machining and Installation	$720,000	2,500	7,500	10,000

Based on this information, the activity rate would be computed as follows:

$$\text{Activity Rate} = \frac{\$720,000}{10,000} = \frac{\$72 \text{ per}}{\text{Machine Hour}}$$

To assign the machining and installation costs to the two products, we simply multiply the $72 activity rate by the number of machine hours required by each product, as shown next:

	Prius	Scion	Total
Machine Hours	2,500	7,500	
Activity Rate	× $72	× $72	
	$180,000	$540,000	$720,000

COACH'S TIP

You can check your work by confirming that the total cost assigned is $720,000 ($180,000 + $540,000 = $720,000).

Activity-Proportion Method

ABC costs can also be allocated to products and services using activity proportions or percentages. We compute the **activity proportion** by dividing the cost driver for each product by the **total** cost driver for all products combined, as follows:

Learning Objective 4–5
Assign indirect costs to products or services using activity proportions.

	ACTIVITY PROPORTIONS BASED ON MACHINE HOURS	
	Prius	Scion
Machine Hours by Product	2,500	7,500
Total Machine Hours	÷ 10,000	÷ 10,000
	25%	75%

These activity proportions tell us that 25 percent of the machine-related activity is related to the Prius, while 75 percent is related to the Scion. To assign the $720,000 in machining and installation costs, we can multiply the total activity cost by the activity proportion for each product, as follows:

	Prius	Scion	Total
Activity Cost	$720,000	$720,000	
Activity Proportion	× 25%	× 75%	
	$180,000	$540,000	$720,000

COACH'S TIP

When working the homework problems, pay careful attention to the instructions for how to round the activity rates and percentages as the rounding errors are magnified when you have to multiply a rounded number in a subsequent calculation.

As you can see, the results of the activity rate and activity proportion methods are mathematically equivalent. The end result will be the same as long as there is no rounding error in the activity rates or percentages. You can use whichever approach makes the most sense to you, assuming all the necessary information is available. For example, you must have cost driver information for all of the product lines in order to compute the activity proportions (%).

Next, we will demonstrate the ABC calculations for the second activity cost pool, machine setup, then ask you to practice the ABC computations for the engineering and quality control activity cost pool on your own.

Machine Setup Activity Cost Pool

Recall that the total manufacturing overhead cost assigned to the machine setup pool in Stage 1 was $900,000. This cost will be assigned based on number of setups, a batch-level cost driver. A setup occurs every time a new batch of units is produced. The number of setups varies inversely with the number of units in each batch. The larger the batch size, the fewer setups required.

For example, if Toyota produces the Prius in batches of 250 units, it would take 400 setups to produce 100,000 units (100,000 ÷ 250 = 400). How many setups are needed to produce 300,000 Scion units if the batch size is 3,000?

Annual Production Information	Prius	Scion	Total
Total number of units produced	100,000	300,000	400,000
Average batch size (units per batch)	250	3,000	
Number of Setups	100,000 ÷ 250 = 400	?	?

Based on this information, the Scion would require 100 setups (300,000 ÷ 3,000) to produce 300,000 units; therefore, a total of 500 setups are required (400 for the Prius and 100 for Scion). We can use this cost driver information to assign the $900,000 in machine setup cost to the two products using either activity rates or activity proportions. The computations for both methods are summarized as follows:

Activity Rate		Activity Proportions	
$\frac{\$900,000}{500} = \$1,800$ per setup		**Prius**	**Scion**
		400 ÷ 500 = 80%	100 ÷ 500 = 20%
Prius	**Scion**		
400 setups	100 setups	$900,000	$900,000
× $1,800	× $1,800	× 80%	× 20%
$720,000	$180,000	$720,000	$180,000

In this hypothetical example, the Prius receives a larger proportion (80 percent) of the total setup-related costs than the Scion, even though the Prius is a lower-volume product. By utilizing a batch-level cost driver, the ABC system assigns more cost to the Prius because it is produced in smaller batches, thus requiring more setup activity.

To make sure you understand how to do ABC calculations using both activity rates and activity proportions, complete the following Self-Study Practice to assign the engineering and quality control costs for our Toyota example.

 How's it going?   *Self-Study Practice*

Assume the following activity costs and drivers for the engineering and quality control activity for Toyota:

Activity Cost Pool	Total Cost	COST DRIVER: ENGINEERING AND INSPECTION HOURS		
		Prius	**Scion**	**Total**
Engineering and Quality Control	$1,380,000	3,000	1,000	4,000

1. Compute an activity rate and assign the engineering and quality control costs to the two products. Verify that the total cost assigned is $1,380,000.

2. Compute activity proportions and assign the engineering and quality control costs to the two products. Verify that the total cost assigned is $1,380,000.

After you have finished, check your answers against the solutions in the margin.

Solution to Self-Study Practice

1. Activity Rate Method

$1,380,000 ÷ 4,000 = $345 per hour

Prius: 3,000 × $345 = $1,035,000
Scion: 1,000 × $345 =   345,000
Total $1,380,000

2. Activity Proportion Method

Prius: 3,000 ÷ 4,000 = 75%
Scion: 1,000 ÷ 4,000 = 25%

Prius: $1,380,000 × 75% = $1,035,000
Scion: $1,380,000 × 25% =   345,000
Total $1,380,000

Compute Total Manufacturing Overhead

After we have completed the Stage 2 allocations (including the engineering and quality control costs from the Self-Study Practice), we can compute the total manufacturing overhead assigned to each product line. The total manufacturing overhead cost should sum to $3,000,000, as shown below:

SUMMARY OF STAGE 2 ABC ALLOCATIONS	Prius	Scion	Total
Machining and installation	$ 180,000	$ 540,000	$ 720,000
Machine setup	720,000	180,000	900,000
Engineering and quality control	1,035,000	345,000	1,380,000
Total manufacturing overhead cost	$1,935,000	$1,065,000	$3,000,000

COACH'S TIP

Notice that more of the total manufacturing overhead cost is assigned to the Prius than the Scion. Even though the Prius is a lower-volume product, it is produced in smaller batches and requires more engineering and quality control activities than the Scion.

Calculate Unit Costs and Gross Margin

To calculate unit costs under ABC, we first need to state the manufacturing overhead costs on a per-unit basis by dividing the total manufacturing overhead assigned to each product by the number of units produced, as shown in the following table:

	Prius	Scion
Total manufacturing overhead cost	$1,935,000	$1,065,000
Number of units produced	÷ 100	÷ 300
Manufacturing overhead cost per unit	$ 19,350	$ 3,550

These numbers represent only the *manufacturing overhead* cost assigned to each product. We still need to add the direct materials and direct labor costs, which were provided on a per-unit basis when we reviewed volume-based cost systems in the first section of this chapter. Remember that the direct materials and direct labor costs remain the same regardless of the method used to assign indirect (overhead) costs.

Per-Unit Cost Information	Prius	Scion
Direct materials	$ 8,000	$ 5,000
Direct labor	2,800	1,800
Manufacturing overhead (using ABC)	19,350	3,550
Total manufacturing cost per unit	$30,150	$10,350

Notice that the Prius now appears to be almost three times more costly to produce than the Scion, largely due to the amount of manufacturing overhead that was assigned to the product under ABC. Subtracting the unit manufacturing costs under ABC from the hypothetical unit sales price provided earlier results in the following gross margin analysis:

	Prius	Scion
Unit selling price	$31,000	$15,000
Less: Manufacturing cost per unit	30,150	10,350
Gross profit per unit	$ 850	$ 4,650
Gross profit margin (% of sales)	2.7%	31.0%

COACH'S TIP

The ABC system now shows that the the Scion is the more profitable product, while the Prius is only marginally profitable. Although this is a hypothetical example, it shows how the cost *measurement* system can impact how indirect costs are assigned to product lines and thus the profitability of those products.

Compare Volume-Based and Activity-Based Cost Systems

Exhibit 4–6 compares the unit manufacturing overhead cost and gross margin percentage of each product under a volume-based cost system to activity-based costing. Remember that the only difference between the two methods is how they assign indirect costs (manufacturing overhead) to each product. The volume-based system used only one measure, direct labor hours, as the cost driver, while the ABC method used multiple activity drivers—machine hours, number of setups, and engineering and inspection hours—to assign manufacturing overhead cost to each product.

The largest difference in cost and gross profit between the two systems occurs with the Prius. The volume-based cost system allocated $8,400 in manufacturing overhead to each unit, while the ABC system allocated $19,350 in manufacturing overhead to each unit. Although the Prius required fewer total direct labor hours than the Scion (because fewer units were produced), it is produced in smaller batches, requiring more setup activity. The Prius also required a disproportionate share of the engineering and quality control activity. The opposite effect occurs with the Scion. While the volume-based cost system allocated $7,200 in manufacturing overhead to each unit of Scion, the ABC method allocated only $3,550.

Although this simplified example is not intended to reflect the realities of Toyota's production process or cost system, it illustrates a major disadvantage of traditional volume-based cost systems. Systems that assign indirect costs based solely on the basis of volume tend to overcost high-volume products and undercost low-volume products. In this example, the volume-based cost system assigned too much indirect cost to the Scion (because it required more total direct labor hours) and not enough cost to the Prius. An ABC system incorporates other important factors that drive costs, such as the complexity of the production process and the additional setup, design, and quality control activities required by newer or more innovative products.

The differences in manufacturing overhead cost affect the reported profitability of each product, as measured by the gross profit percentage. Remember that gross margin is the profit before nonmanufacturing costs such as selling and administrative expenses have been taken into account. In terms of profitability, the traditional system suggests that the Prius is the more profitable product, while the ABC system suggests that the Scion is more profitable. The reality is that we will never know the true profitability of each product because a large portion of the manufacturing cost is shared between the two products. However, ABC provides a more detailed look at the cost of the activities that are required by each product. The result is more "actionable" information that managers can use to make decisions.

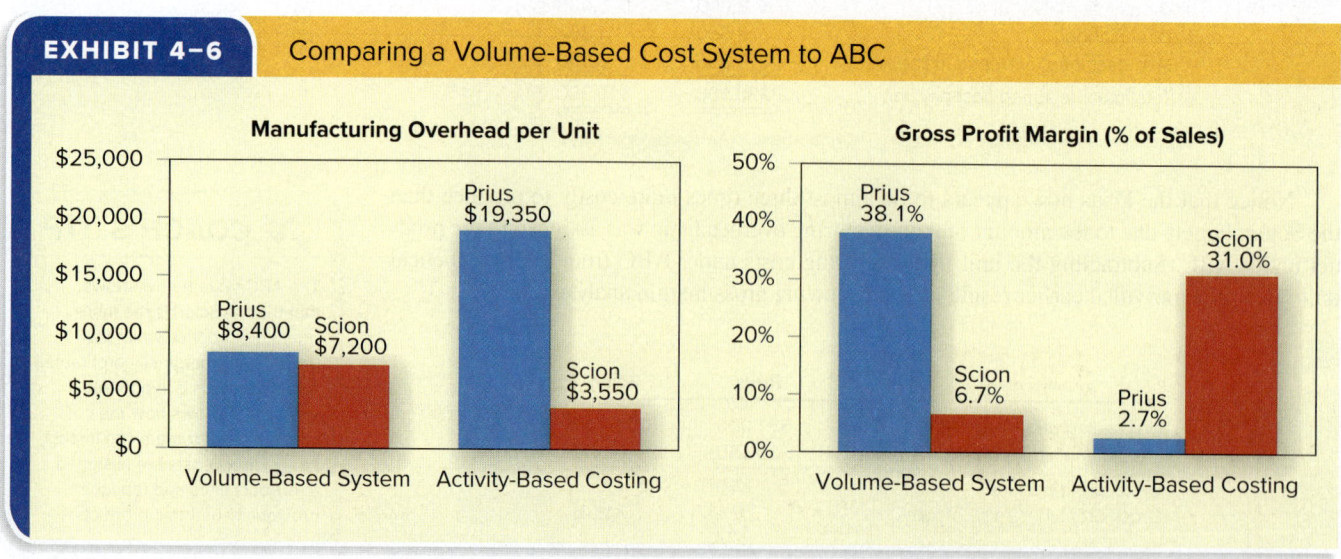

EXHIBIT 4–6   Comparing a Volume-Based Cost System to ABC

If this had been a realistic scenario, what should Toyota managers do with this information? Managers may need to rethink the price of the product, but in this example the price of the Prius would have to increase substantially to cover its manufacturing costs. It is not clear that customers would be willing to pay that much of a price premium, even for such an innovative product. In many industries, market forces such as supply, demand, and competitor prices determine the price of a product, not just its cost. (Later in the chapter, we discuss an approach called target costing, which uses the market price to determine the target cost, rather than using cost information to set the price.)

While an ABC system may sometimes (not always) provide better information about the cost of products and services, more accurate information in and of itself is not a good reason to implement an ABC system. The real benefit of activity-based costing comes from the information it provides to managers to pursue cost management. In a later section, we discuss several approaches that managers can use, in conjunction with ABC, to manage costs and improve profitability. But first, let's take a look at how activity-based costing can be used in service industries.

Activity-Based Costing in Service Industries

The Toyota example illustrates how ABC can be used to assign indirect costs in a manufacturing setting. ABC can also be useful in service industries, particularly when different types of customers require different levels of service. Although service providers do not have **manufacturing overhead** they incur many indirect costs, such as rent, supplies, supervision, advertising, and administrative expenses. How should these indirect costs be assigned to different services and customers? Should they be spread evenly across the number of customers served or assigned based on some other volume- or non-volume-based cost drivers? A volume-based cost system is appropriate as long as every customer or client places a similar demand on the company's resources. In many service industries, however, some customers and clients require more attention and a higher level of service than others.

Consider, for example, two customers who use the same bank. One always uses the ATM for deposits and withdrawals, pays his bills online, and receives his bank statements by e-mail. The other customer comes into the bank once per week to make deposits, pays her bills with checks, and receives her bank statements by regular mail. She also has a safe deposit box at the bank, calls frequently to check on interest rates, and makes an appointment twice per year to speak with the bank's investment advisor. Which customer is more costly to serve? Why?

This example illustrates how different activities can drive cost in a service setting. The goal of an ABC system is to assign indirect costs to customers or services based on the underlying activities they require. The main difference between ABC in manufacturing and non-manufacturing settings is that volume is generally expressed in terms of units of service, or customers, rather than physical units. As with our previous ABC analysis, we begin by identifying and classifying activities using the activity hierarchy. Exhibit 4–7 shows how the activity hierarchy would be applied to several service industries, such as entertainment venues, restaurants, and airlines.

As a more concrete example, think about all of the activities that a university must perform to provide a service (education) to students. For this example, we will assume that the student is the customer. (Just remember that the customer is not always right in this setting!)

Facility- or *university-level activities* include all activities that are performed at the university level that benefit all programs and students, such as providing world-class facilities (classrooms, the library, computer lab, etc.), supporting sports teams, and maintaining campus security. University administration would also be included in this category.

A *product or service-level activity* relates to a product or service the university offers, such as a degree program or a particular course. Developing courses and launching a new degree program are examples of product or service-level activities.

Batch or *group-level activities* are performed for a group of customers (students) all at once. A lecture given to a section of students is an example of a group-level activity, where the batch size is equal to the number of students in the section.

Learning Objective 4–7
Apply activity-based costing to a service industry.

EXHIBIT 4–7   ABC Hierarchy of Activities in Service Industries

	Entertainment Venue	Restaurant	Airline
Facility-Level Activities	Creating the company's Facebook page	Offering a Groupon worth $50 toward any menu item	Developing an airline app for smartphones
Service-Level Activities	Booking a musical that will run for three weeks	Creating a new menu item	Promoting a new route from New York to St. Louis
Group-Level Activities	Hiring security for a concert	Serving a private party	Flying a group of passengers from New York to St. Louis
Customer-Level Activities	Selling a ticket to a customer	Taking a customer's order	Checking a passenger's bag

And finally, a *unit-* or *customer-level activity* is one that is performed for each student individually. These activities will vary in direct proportion to the number of students. Grading exams, advising, and registering students are examples of customer-level activities that are performed for each student.

Let's consider a hypothetical example. Anywhere State University (ASU) serves 20,000 students at a total cost of $5,000,000 per semester. For simplicity, we assume that each student is enrolled in the same number of credit hours per semester. Otherwise we would need to measure volume in terms of student credit hours or full-time equivalent (FTE) students.

In a volume-based cost system, the total indirect cost of $5,000,000 would be spread across the 20,000 students enrolled at the university, resulting in an average cost of $250 per student ($5,000,000 ÷ 20,000 = $250). This average rate implies that that every student places similar demands on university resources. Do you think this is a reasonable assumption?

Now assume that ASU serves two types of students: graduate students and undergraduate students. Although undergraduates make up about 90 percent of the student population, the university offers just as many graduate degree programs as undergraduate degree programs. There are fewer graduate students in each degree program and graduate classes are taught in much smaller sections than undergraduate classes. To better understand the cost of serving these two types of students, accountants at ASU have conducted an ABC analysis and identified the following key activities:

- Providing classrooms and other facilities (university-wide)
- Developing degree programs (service-level)
- Teaching classes (group-level)
- Serving students (customer-level)

The accountants have assigned $5,000,000 to the four activities (Stage 1), selected cost drivers (Stage 2), and computed the following activity rates:

Activity	Cost Driver	Total Cost	Total Activity Cost Driver	Activity Rate
Providing classrooms and other facilities	Square feet	$2,000,000	500,000 sq. ft.	$4 per square foot
Developing degree programs	Number of degree programs	1,500,000	50 programs	$30,000 per degree program
Teaching classes	Number of sections	1,000,000	400 sections	$2,500 per section
Serving students	Number of students	500,000	20,000 students	$25 per student
		$5,000,000		

Cost driver values and activity proportions for the two student populations are summarized below.

Activity	Cost Driver	Total Cost	COST DRIVER BY PRODUCT LINE (ACTIVITY PROPORTION)		
			Undergraduate	Graduate	Total
Providing classrooms and other facilities	Square Feet	$2,000,000	450,000 (90%)	50,000 (10%)	500,000 (100%)
Developing degree programs	Number of degree programs	1,500,000	25 (50%)	25 (50%)	50 (100%)
Teaching classes	Number of sections	1,000,000	240 (60%)	160 (40%)	400 (100%)
Serving students	Number of students	500,000	18,000 (90%)	2,000 (10%)	20,000 (100%)

An ABC system will assign the cost of each activity to the two types of students using either activity rates or activity proportions. For example, undergraduate students will be assigned 90 percent of the cost of providing classrooms and other facilities (90% × $2,000,000 = $1,800,000). Alternatively, we could multiply 450,000 square feet of space devoted to undergraduate students by the activity rate of $4 per square foot (450,000 sq. ft. × $4 = $1,800,000). Graduate students would be assigned the remaining 10 percent, or $200,000 (10% × $2,000,000 = $200,000; or 50,000 sq. ft. × $4 = $200,000). Similar calculations would be made for the other three activity cost pools, resulting in the following ABC allocations:

Activity	ABC COST ALLOCATIONS		
	Undergraduate	Graduate	Total Cost
Providing classrooms and other facilities	$1,800,000	$ 200,000	$2,000,000
Developing degree programs	750,000	750,000	1,500,000
Teaching classes	600,000	400,000	1,000,000
Serving students	450,000	50,000	500,000
Total cost assigned	$3,600,000	$1,400,000	$5,000,000
Number of students	÷ 18,000	÷ 2,000	
Cost per student	$ 200	$ 700	

Notice that the total cost assigned to the two groups is $5,000,000, just as it was in the volume-based cost system. However, using ABC, the total cost assigned to undergraduate students is $3,600,000, or $200 per student. The total cost of serving graduate students is $1,400,000, or $700 per student. As a point of comparison, the average cost per student under the volume-based cost system was $250 per student. Which method do you think produced a more logical result? Most would agree that it is more costly to serve graduate students because the university offers a wide range of graduate degree programs to a relatively small group of students, and graduate classes are taught in much smaller sections than undergraduates. This may explain why most universities charge more for graduate tuition than undergraduate tuition.

This example and the Toyota example presented earlier in the chapter illustrate how ABC can be used to determine the cost of products and services that vary in terms of how they are designed, manufactured, and delivered to the customer. By assigning indirect costs based on the underlying activities that go into making a product or providing a service, ABC should provide a more accurate representation of how much the product or service costs. However, to reap the benefits of ABC, managers must use the information to fundamentally change the way the company does business. The next section describes several cost management tools that managers can use to *manage* or *reduce* costs, as opposed to simply measuring costs in a different way.

Cost Management Methods

In this section, we introduce several techniques that managers can use to manage or reduce costs while still providing value to consumers. It is important to note that the methods described here are management approaches, not accounting methods. As such, we do not go into great depth on these topics. The most important thing for you to understand is how an accounting method such as activity-based costing can be used to complement these approaches to management.

ACTIVITY-BASED MANAGEMENT (ABM)

Activity-based management (ABM) encompasses all of the actions that managers take to improve operations or reduce costs based on ABC data. To reap the benefits of ABC, managers must use it to change the way they do business and identify areas that would benefit from process improvements.

The first step in any improvement program is to target areas that need improvement. Managers should start by asking the following questions:

1. What activities does the company perform?
2. How much does it cost to perform each activity?
3. Does the activity add value to the customer?

The first question focuses managers' attention on activities as the drivers of cost within the organization. Managers who want to manage costs must manage the underlying activities. Reducing or streamlining the number of activities required to perform a task can improve profit by either reducing costs (e.g., reduced workforce) or allowing more work to be performed for the same cost (e.g., increased efficiency).

The second question focuses managers' attention on those activities that have the most potential for improvement. Managers can compare the cost of performing key activities with other firms in the industry or to the best performing firms in other industries, a process called **benchmarking.** Benchmarking can be used to pinpoint areas in which the company is ahead or behind the competition and provide managers incentives to improve their own performance. Alternatively, managers might decide to outsource some activities to an outside firm that can perform them more cost-effectively. The costs and benefits of outsourcing are discussed further in Chapter 7.

The third question relates to one of the most important steps in ABM, which is the identification and elimination of non-value-added activities. A **value-added activity** is one that enhances the perceived value of the product or service to the customer. A **non-value-added activity** is one that, if eliminated, would not reduce the value of the product or service to the customer. To the extent possible, managers should attempt to reduce or eliminate non-value-added activities. Common examples of non-value-added activities in a manufacturing setting include reworking faulty units, storing units in inventory, moving parts or products from one place to another, expediting orders, and scheduling production runs. Non-value-added activities in a service setting like a doctor's office could include the time a patient spends in the exam room waiting for the doctor, the time it takes to manually input patient information into a computer system, and follow-up visits to correct a misdiagnosis. All of these activities create costs, including the opportunity cost of lost revenue. Some activities, such as preparing reports and complying with regulatory requirements, are necessary but do not add value to

the customer. As part of ABM, managers should attempt to streamline these activities to be performed as cost-effectively as possible.

ABM AND SUSTAINABILITY

Although ABC was originally designed to provide managers with detailed information about the **cost** of activities, it can be adapted to provide managers with sustainability-related information. For example, a well-designed ABC system could capture and report information about environmental costs such as greenhouse gas (GHG) emissions. Rather than assigning costs (an economic measure) to activities and then to products and services, the system could trace GHG emissions (an environmental measure) to activities and then to products and services. Such a system would provide actionable information for managers who have been tasked with reducing GHG emissions, just as traditional ABC data provides managers with actionable information for reducing costs.

As an example, Toyota had a stated goal to reduce GHG emissions from its North American operations by 12 percent from 2010 to 2016. As of 2014, the company had achieved a 9 percent reduction and was well on its way to meeting this goal. According to Toyota, managers achieve their environmental goals using the same *kaizen* (continuous improvement) approach the company is famous for—by continuously analyzing their processes to identify ways to make them more cost-efficient as well as energy-efficient. For example, managers at one of Toyota's parts manufacturing divisions eliminated a major step (activity) in the chip melting process, reducing GHG emissions by 336 metric tons per year and saving $55,000 in annual operating costs. (http://www.toyota.com/usa/environmentreport2014/carbon.html)

SPOTLIGHT ON Sustainability

While sustainability is most often associated with environmental initiatives, the triple bottom line should measure performance in three areas: economic (profit), environment (planet), and society (people). The third pillar (people) is often overlooked, but a truly sustainable business strategy should make social issues a priority as well.

Toyota's sustainability strategy also includes measures of social impact, including the well-being of its employees and the surrounding communities in which the company operates. Toyota's people-focused sustainability initiatives include the following goals:

- Ensuring employee safety and well-being, including workplace safety and physical and mental health programs.
- Development of human resources through education, on-the-job-training, and programs to develop and promote local personnel.
- Fostering an environment of diversity and inclusion by increasing opportunities for women in the workforce and programs to help employees achieve an appropriate work/life balance.
- Creating a positive work environment, including programs to increase employee loyalty and a culture of teamwork through communication and friendly competition.

Toyota keeps track of various metrics to gauge performance toward all of these goals, just as they track measures of economic performance and environmental impact. These measures are reported in Toyota's annual corporate social responsibility (CSR) report and on the company website. Refer to Skills Development Case 4–5 for more details on how Toyota measures performance in all areas of sustainability (economic, environmental, and social).

www.toyota-global.com/sustainability/society/employees/#approach03

JUST-IN-TIME (JIT)

Some manufacturing firms use an approach called **just-in-time (JIT)** to eliminate non-value-added activities, reduce costs, and improve quality. Under a JIT system, a company purchases materials and manufactures products at just the right time and in just the right quantity to fill customer orders. JIT is a demand-pull system in which materials and products are **pulled** through the manufacturing system based on customer demand. In traditional manufacturing settings, products are **pushed** through the manufacturing process and often end up sitting in work in process inventory waiting for the next step in the production process or in finished goods waiting for a customer to purchase the product.

There are many costs associated with holding inventory, including handling costs, storage costs, product obsolescence, spoilage, quality problems, and the opportunity cost of having working capital tied up in inventory. In addition to reducing these costs, firms that implement JIT must have a strong commitment to quality and develop close relationships with suppliers and customers. Because it is a demand-pull system, managers must be able to accurately forecast customer demand and share this information with all members of the supply chain. A **supply chain** is the network of organizations and activities required to move goods and services from suppliers to consumers. Adopters of JIT tend to rely on fewer suppliers, but require them to adhere to very strict quality standards. We'll talk more about managing quality in the next section.

The development of close relationships with a few key suppliers can result in reduced costs and improved quality. However, it does carry risks, as Toyota and many other companies learned the hard way in 2011 when a series of natural disasters took out their key suppliers. See the Spotlight on Decision Making feature for a discussion of the lessons that Toyota learned from this tragedy.

A side benefit of JIT is that it simplifies the cost accounting system. Product costing is much easier in a JIT environment because there is no need to worry about how much cost should be reported as inventory (an asset) and how much should be reported as cost of goods sold (on the income statement). This means that managerial accountants can switch roles from being measurement experts to being information providers and partners in managerial decision making.

Because quality plays such an important role in successfully executing a just-in-time strategy, companies like Toyota have implemented total quality management (TQM) systems to ensure quality standards are met.

SPOTLIGHT ON Decision Making

Supply Chain Disruptions and the Implications for JIT and Lean Manufacturing

On March 11, 2011, an earthquake off the coast of Japan triggered a series of catastrophic events that highlighted the interconnected nature of our global economy and the critical role of the supply chain. The 9.0 magnitude quake created a massive tsunami, causing widespread destruction, including power outages, fires, a collapsed dam, and a nuclear crisis at the Fukushima power plant. In addition to almost 20,000 lives lost and the devastating impact on local communities, the disaster set off a chain reaction that affected businesses in many industries around the world.

Although Toyota and other Japanese auto manufacturers suffered only minor damage from the quake and tsunami, many of their key suppliers were located in the worst-hit region of Japan. With the supply of critical components shut down and virtually no inventory of parts on hand, Toyota was forced to scale back production for several months. Toyota estimated that it lost production of approximately 300,000 vehicles in Japan and 100,000 at overseas plants due to the shutdown of suppliers.[1] The parts shortage affected auto manufacturers around the globe, including Ford and General Motors. The electronics industry was also hit hard. Japan supplies about 20 percent of the semiconductors used to produce smart phones, tablets, and computers.

The supply chain disruptions that occurred in Japan and the trickle-down effect on the rest of the world's economy led many to question the value of Toyota's lean manufacturing approach, which includes minimizing inventory and developing relationships with a few key suppliers in an effort to drive down costs. In response, Toyota has changed some of its sourcing and purchasing strategies, including using local suppliers for overseas production and standardizing component design across suppliers so that parts can be more easily substituted in the event of a future supply chain disruption.

---

[1] Makiko Kitamura and Yuki Hagiwara, "Toyota Says Global Production Will Return to Normal by December," *Bloomberg Businessweek*, April 22, 2011.

TOTAL QUALITY MANAGEMENT (TQM)

Total quality management (TQM) is a management approach that aims to improve product quality by reducing and eliminating errors, streamlining activities, and continuously improving production processes. Developed by William Deming and first implemented by Japanese manufacturers, including Toyota, TQM holds all parties involved in the production process accountable for the quality of the product and customer experience.

An important part of TQM is the preparation of a **cost of quality report** that summarizes the costs incurred to prevent, detect, and correct quality problems. This report should include details about the following quality costs:

- **Prevention costs** are incurred to keep quality problems from happening in the first place. Examples include design changes to the product to reduce defects, statistical process control, and quality training. Although prevention activities are costly, most quality experts believe the most effective way to manage quality costs is to avoid problems in the first place.

- **Appraisal or inspection costs** are incurred to identify defective products during the production process, including the cost of the quality control department and employees who test the product. Unfortunately, inspection activities do not address what's causing the defect, which means the defect could continue to occur.

- **Internal failure costs** result from the defects that are caught during the appraisal or inspection process. These costs include scrapped or discarded products, the cost of repairs (rework), and the opportunity cost of downtime created by quality problems. The more effective a company's appraisal (inspection) activities, the better its chance of catching defects internally. Although costly, internal failures are preferred over external failures.

- **External failure costs** occur when a defective product is discovered only after the product has made its way into the customer's hands. These costs include warranty costs, recalls, product replacement, legal fees, and damage to the company's reputation due to poor quality. External failure costs represent the worst-case scenario, and can prove to be extremely costly, as Toyota has learned in recent years.

For decades, Toyota was considered the gold standard for product quality. That reputation took a major hit in late 2009 when the company was forced to recall 8.5 million vehicles due to mechanical failures, including uncontrolled acceleration from "sticky pedals" and improperly placed floor mats. In early 2010, Toyota estimated the total cost of the recall for faulty accelerator pedals at 180 billion yen (about U.S. $2 billion). This external failure cost included 100 billion yen (U.S. $1.1 billion) to fix the faulty accelerators and another 80 billion yen (U.S. $900 million) in lost sales revenue.[2]

Unfortunately, Toyota's quality problems did not stop there. They were forced to recall millions of Priuses for faulty brakes just a few months later. All this came at a time when U.S. auto manufacturers were making great improvements in product quality. In 2011, General Motors overtook Toyota as the largest auto manufacturer in the world.

It is very difficult to assess quantitatively the impact these highly publicized recalls, including a congressional investigation, have had on Toyota's brand equity or reputation. Although auto manufacturers routinely issue product recalls, each recall Toyota has made over the years has further eroded its reputation for quality. It has also led many to question whether Toyota's lean manufacturing approach and commitment to cost cutting, in combination with rapid growth, are to blame for Toyota's quality problems. The debate continues as to whether Toyota can regain its reputation for world-class quality and its position as the number one auto manufacturer in the world.

Next, we discuss another approach to cost management that Toyota and other companies have used to effectively manage costs while making sure that the company can earn an acceptable return for its shareholders.

[2] Kelsey Swanekamp, "Toyota Expects Recall to Cost $2 Billion," *Forbes.com,* February 4, 2010, http://www.forbes.com/2010/02/04/toyota-earnings-recall-markets-equities-prius.html.

TARGET COSTING AND LIFE CYCLE COST MANAGEMENT

Target costing is a proactive approach to cost management that managers can use to determine what costs **should be** for the company to earn an acceptable profit across a product's life cycle.

The **product life cycle** represents the life of the product from its infancy (an idea), through design, development, product introduction, growth, maturity, and eventual decline. It is important for managers to think about costs and profitability across the entire product life cycle because costs tend to be higher in the early stages of the life cycle, while most of the revenues are earned in the growth and maturity stages of the life cycle. In today's digital age, product life cycles are becoming shorter and shorter, so managers must be able to estimate life cycle costs accurately to make good product introduction decisions.

With target costing, managers determine the target price based on factors such as market competition and what managers believe consumers will be willing to pay for the product or service. The desired profit margin is then subtracted from the target price to determine the target cost.

$$\text{Target Price} - \text{Target Profit} = \text{Target Cost}$$

This is in stark contrast to a **cost-plus pricing** approach, in which the company first determines how much a product or service costs, and then adds a markup (profit) to arrive at the sales price. Although cost-plus pricing is common in some industries, such as government contractors and the construction industry, market forces dictate prices in many industries, including the automobile industry.

Target costing was first introduced at Toyota in 1959.[3] At Toyota, target costing is called **cost planning** because it requires managers to think about costs up front so that they can design, manufacture, and deliver products at a cost that will satisfy both customers (through the market price) and shareholders (through a target profit). Although managerial accounting often focuses on manufacturing costs, or the costs incurred while the product is being produced, most of these costs are committed (unchangeable) by the time production starts. The goal of target costing is to determine the target cost of the product **before** manufacturing begins. The target cost should reflect all of the costs that will be incurred across the value chain. The **value chain** is the linked set of activities required to design, develop, produce, market, and deliver the product to customers, as well as aftermarket customer service. The concept of a value chain is related to that of a supply chain, but they are not exactly the same thing. While supply chain typically refers to the flow of products and services from suppliers through to the consumer, the value chain concept begins with the consumer and works backward to ensure that all the activities required to deliver the product to the customer are value-added. To set an appropriate target cost, companies must have a clear understanding of what matters to customers and design their value chain to deliver that to consumers.

Toyota uses target costing extensively to ensure that its products are profitable. As a simplified example, assume that Toyota is planning to introduce a new vehicle with the following estimates:

Market price	$30,000
Annual demand	20,000 units
Life cycle	3 years
Target profit	20% return on sales

The target cost is computed by subtracting the target profit from the market price, as follows:

$$\underset{\$30{,}000}{\underset{\text{Price}}{\text{Target}}} - \underset{\$6{,}000}{(20\% \times \$30{,}000)} = \underset{\$24{,}000}{\underset{\text{Cost}}{\text{Target}}}$$

---

[3] Robin Cooper and Takao Tanaka, "Toyota Motor Corporation: Target Costing System," Harvard Business School Case 9-197-031. Copyright Harvard Business School Publishing, 1997.

The $24,000 target cost is the most the company can spend on one unit of product, on average, and still achieve the 20 percent return on sales (given a target sales price of $30,000). Remember that the target cost must cover all costs incurred across the product's life cycle. While it may be difficult for the company to meet the target cost in the early stages of the product life cycle, the average cost per unit is likely to decrease over time due to learning curves, continuous improvement efforts, and the economies of scale that result from increases in production (spreading constant fixed costs over more units).

Given the target unit cost of $24,000, how much can Toyota spend across the entire product life cycle? To find out, we multiply the target unit cost by the number of units per year over the entire life cycle of the product, as follows:

$$20,000 \text{ units per year} \times 3 \text{ years} \times \$24,000 = \$1,440,000,000$$

The next step is to determine whether it is feasible to design, develop, manufacture, and deliver the product at a total life-cycle cost of $1,440,000,000. If not, managers must find ways to reduce the cost by changing the way the product is designed, produced, delivered, and so forth. To achieve cost reduction goals, managers from all areas (design, development, manufacturing, and accounting) must work together to find creative ways to achieve the target cost without affecting the end value to the consumer. An important part of this process is called **value engineering**, which involves analyzing the functionality of the product to determine which functions add value to the customer and then finding ways to deliver those functions while meeting the target cost.

This process is very time consuming. Toyota's cost planning process begins at least four years before the product launch. This gives managers time to meet the target cost through product redesign, process reengineering, supplier management, or other cost management techniques. Activity-based management plays a key role in target costing by helping managers find ways to achieve the target cost while still providing the value and features consumers are willing to pay for.

SUMMARY OF ABC AND ABM

We began the chapter by comparing managers' efforts to make their business lean to a person's quest to lose weight. In difficult economic times, managers are often asked to do more with fewer resources, or to "trim the fat" without "cutting into the muscle" of the organization.

A volume-based accounting system is a bit like a bathroom scale that measures just one thing (pounds). The scale may be perfectly accurate, but it doesn't really tell a person how to lose (or gain) weight. For that, we need a more sophisticated device that measures the factors that affect weight (calorie intake, number of steps taken, hours of exercise, etc.) and can provide actionable information to help control weight. Similarly, in product costing, managers sometimes need a sophisticated measurement tool like activity-based costing to identify strategies for controlling costs.

To receive the true benefits of ABC, managers must go beyond simply *measuring* costs to find ways to *manage* or reduce them. This is where cost management approaches—such as activity-based management (ABM), just-in-time (JIT), total quality management (TQM), and target costing—come into play. None of these methods are a magic pill, but they are management approaches that successful organizations such as Toyota have used to run a healthy but lean organization, albeit with a few setbacks along the way.

Although ABC and ABM have many potential benefits, those benefits must be weighed against the costs of obtaining more accurate information. Implementing an ABC system is not a trivial task. It requires a great deal of time and effort from many employees across the entire organization (not just accountants), and the support of upper management. Because of the unique nature of the drivers required by ABC, new types of data must be collected and added to the accounting system. Employees must spend time tracking the time spent on various activities, a task that many will consider non-value-added. In short, implementing and maintaining an activity-based costing system can present a formidable challenge, and management must weigh its potential benefits against its costs.

REVIEW THE CHAPTER

DEMONSTRATION CASE

Grapeville Estates produces two types of wine. The first is a standard-variety chardonnay produced in large batches and aged for a relatively short period of time (about four months) in large metal containers (vats). The second wine is a limited-edition cabernet made in very small batches from premium grapes and then aged for more than three years in special French oak barrels to provide a particular taste. The barrels require significant maintenance between batches and can be used only a few times before they lose some of the oak flavor that they transfer to the wine.

The company currently uses a volume-based cost system with total manufacturing overhead cost of $375,000 applied to the two products at a rate of 150 percent of direct labor dollars. Assume the following production and cost information for the most recent year:

	Standard Chardonnay	Vintage Cabernet
Number of bottles produced	200,000	25,000
Unit cost information		
Direct materials (grapes and bottles)	$2.00	$4.00
Direct labor	1.00	2.00
Manufacturing overhead	?	?
Manufacturing cost per unit (bottle)	?	?

The company has conducted an ABC analysis and traced the manufacturing overhead cost to four activity cost pools, with the following costs and drivers:

Activity Cost Pool	Total Cost	Total Amount of Cost Driver		Activity Rate	
Purchasing and receiving	$ 90,000	450,000	Pounds of grapes	?	per pound
Setup for production	100,000	400	Number of batches	?	per batch
Fermenting and aging	80,000	200,000	Number of fermentation days	?	per fermentation day
Quality control	105,000	20,000	Number of inspections	?	per inspection
	$375,000				

The activities required by the two products follow:

	Standard Chardonnay	Vintage Cabernet
Pounds of grapes	400,000	50,000
Number of batches	200	200
Number of fermentation days	30,000	170,000
Number of inspections	2,000	18,000

Required:

1. Compute the manufacturing cost per bottle of the two products using the volume-based cost system.
2. Compute the activity rate for each of the four cost pools under ABC.
3. Compute the total manufacturing overhead cost that would be assigned to each product using ABC. Verify that the total cost sums to $375,000.
4. Compute the unit manufacturing cost of each product using ABC.
5. Compare the unit manufacturing cost under ABC with the volume-based cost system. Which product was overcosted under the volume-based cost system compared to ABC and which was undercosted?
6. Explain why ABC provided different information than the current cost system.

Suggested Solution

1.

	Standard Chardonnay	Vintage Cabernet
Direct materials (grapes and bottles)	$2.00	$4.00
Direct labor	1.00	2.00
Manufacturing overhead (150% of direct labor)	1.00 × 150% = 1.50	$2.00 × 150% = 3.00
Manufacturing cost per bottle	$4.50	$9.00

2.

Purchasing and Receiving	Setup for Production	Fermenting and Aging	Quality Control
$\frac{\$90,000}{450,000} = \$0.20$ per pound	$\frac{\$100,000}{400} = \$250$ per batch	$\frac{\$80,000}{200,000} = \$0.40$ per fermentation day	$\frac{\$105,000}{20,000} = \$5.25$ per inspection

3.

Standard Chardonnay			Vintage Cabernet		
Purchasing and receiving	400,000 pounds × $0.20 =	$ 80,000	Purchasing and receiving	50,000 pounds × $0.20 =	$ 10,000
Setup for production	200 batches × $250 =	50,000	Setup for production	200 batches × $250 =	50,000
Fermenting and aging	30,000 fermentation days × $0.40 =	12,000	Fermenting and aging	170,000 fermentation days × $0.40 =	68,000
Quality control	2,000 inspections × $5.25 =	10,500	Quality control	18,000 inspections × $5.25 =	94,500
		$152,500			$222,500

Total manufacturing overhead cost assigned = $152,500 + $222,500 = $375,000

4.

	Standard Chardonnay	Vintage Cabernet
Manufacturing overhead	$152,500	$222,500
Number of bottles produced	÷ 200,000	÷ 25,000
Manufacturing overhead cost per bottle	$ 0.76	$ 8.90

5.

	Standard Chardonnay	Vintage Cabernet
Direct materials (grapes and bottles)	$2.00	$ 4.00
Direct labor	1.00	2.00
Manufacturing overhead cost per bottle (from ABC)	0.76	8.90
Manufacturing cost per bottle (from ABC)	$3.76	$14.90
Manufacturing cost per bottle (current system; from requirement 1)	$4.50	$ 9.00
Difference between existing system and ABC	$0.74	$ (5.90)

Under the volume-based cost system, the standard chardonnay was overcosted and the vintage cabernet was undercosted.

6. The current cost system captured only the volume of units produced. The ABC system captured other non-volume-based drivers, including the number of setups, fermentation days, and inspections. Even though the vintage cabernet is a low-volume product, it is produced in smaller batches and requires more fermentation days and more stringent quality control than the standard chardonnay.

CHAPTER SUMMARY

LO 4–1   **Assign indirect costs to products or services using a single volume-based cost driver. p. 160**

- A traditional cost system assigns indirect (overhead) costs to products or services using a volume-based measure, such as the number of direct labor hours, machine hours, or units produced. This system, while simple, assumes that all indirect costs are driven by volume and ignores other factors, such as the complexity of the production process and other non-volume drivers of cost.

- Unlike traditional cost systems that rely strictly on volume-based allocation measures, activity-based costing (ABC) systems include measures that capture something other than the sheer volume of units produced or customers served.

LO 4–2   **Classify activities as unit- , batch- , product- , or facility-level activities. p. 164**

- Activity-based costing systems capture the following types of activities:
  - Unit-level activities are performed for each individual unit.
  - Batch-level activities are performed for a group of units all at once.
  - Product-level activities are performed to support a general product or service line rather than specific units or batches.
  - Facility-level activities are performed for the company overall that do not relate to specific products, batches, or units.

LO 4–3   **Assign indirect costs to activity cost pools and select a cost driver for each pool. p. 165**

- The first stage of ABC is to assign indirect costs to activity cost pools. The goal is to create as few activity cost pools as possible while capturing the major activities performed.

- The next step is to identify a cost driver for each of the activity cost pools. The goal is to identify a driver that has a cause-and-effect relationship with the underlying activity that occurs in each activity cost pool.

LO 4–4   **Assign indirect costs to products or services using activity rates. p. 168**

- An activity rate is computed for each cost pool by dividing the total indirect cost assigned to the pool by the total quantity or amount of the cost driver.

- To assign the indirect cost to individual products or services, multiply the activity rate by the cost driver for each product or service.

LO 4–5   **Assign indirect costs to products or services using activity proportions. p. 169**

- To calculate an activity proportion, divide the cost driver of each individual product or service by the total quantity or amount of the cost driver.

- To assign the indirect cost to individual products or services, multiply the activity proportion by the total indirect cost of that activity cost pool.

LO 4–6   **Compare the results of a volume-based cost system to activity-based costing. p. 172**

- The only difference between a volume-based cost system and activity-based costing is how each assigns indirect (overhead) costs to products or services.

- Volume-based cost systems tend to overcost high-volume, simple products and undercost low-volume, customized, or complex products.

- By taking into account both volume and non-volume drivers of costs, ABC should provide a more accurate picture of the cost of producing diverse products or serving customers with diverse needs.

LO 4–7   **Apply activity-based costing to a service industry. p. 173**

- Activity-based costing can be applied to service industries as well as manufacturing industries.

- The main difference between ABC in manufacturing and nonmanufacturing settings is that volume is generally expressed in terms of units of service, or customers, rather than physical units.

- An ABC system is useful for identifying the cost of serving different types of customers who place different demands on organizational resources.

Describe how managers use activity-based management and other cost management methods. p. 176 LO 4–8

- Activity-based management encompasses all actions that managers take to reduce costs or improve processes based on ABC information.
- Other methods managers can use for cost management include
  - Identifying and eliminating non-value-added activities.
  - Managing costs across the entire product life cycle.
  - Managing inventory costs by using just-in-time inventory.
  - Reducing quality costs by engaging in total quality management (TQM).
  - Using target costing to design products and processes to meet customer demands and provide the necessary profit to stakeholders.

KEY TERMS

Activity-Based Costing (ABC) p. 162
Activity-Based Management (ABM) p. 176
Activity Proportion p. 169
Activity Rate p. 168
Appraisal or Inspection Costs p. 179
Batch-Level Activities p. 165
Cost-Plus Pricing p. 180
Cost of Quality Report p. 179
External Failure Costs p. 179

Facility-Level Activities p. 164
Internal Failure Costs p. 179
Just-in-Time (JIT) System p. 177
Manufacturing Costs p. 161
Manufacturing Overhead p. 173
Non-Value-Added Activity p. 176
Non-Volume-Based Cost Driver p. 166
Prevention Costs p. 179
Product-Level Activities p. 165

Product Life Cycle p. 180
Supply Chain p. 178
Target Costing p. 180
Total Quality Management (TQM) p. 179
Unit-Level Activities p. 165
Value-Added Activity p. 176
Value Chain p. 180
Value Engineering p. 181
Volume-Based Cost Drivers p. 160

PRACTICE MATERIAL

QUESTIONS

1. What is the difference between a volume-based cost driver and a non-volume-based cost driver?

2. Explain the statement that traditional costing systems use volume-based allocation measures.

3. What are the potential negative consequences of a traditional volume-based costing system?

4. How does activity-based costing differ from traditional costing systems?

5. What types of business might use activity-based costing?

6. Describe the two stages of activity-based costing.

7. Identify the categories (hierarchy) of activities in an activity-based costing system for a manufacturing company.

8. How do the ABC categories (hierarchy) in a service company differ from those in a manufacturing company?

9. Why must costs be classified into different categories for ABC? What is the basis for these categories?

10. Consider a construction company that builds semicustom homes. Give an example of each of the following activities: facility level, product level, batch level, and unit level.

11. Consider a company that offers drivers' education and defensive driving courses. Give an example of each of the

following activities: customer level, group level, service level, facility level.

12. Explain the difference between the activity-rate method and the activity-proportion method of ABC.

13. Define activity-based management and explain how it is related to activity-based costing.

14. How can ABC be adapted to include sustainability-related metrics? Give an example of an environmental performance measure that could be tracked by an ABC system.

15. What is benchmarking? How does it benefit a company?

16. What is a non-value-added activity? Considering the construction company in question 10, give an example of a value-added and a non-value-added activity.

17. What are the four types of quality costs that comprise total quality management (TQM)?

18. What is target costing? How does activity-based management play a role in target costing?

19. Explain the concept of a just-in-time inventory system. What is its primary benefit?

20. Briefly discuss the advantages and disadvantages of activity-based costing and activity-based management.

MULTIPLE CHOICE

1. Traditional (non-ABC) cost systems assign indirect (overhead) costs on the basis of

    a. Non-volume-based cost drivers.
    b. Unit- or volume-based cost drivers.
    c. Activity-based cost drivers
    d. Facility-level cost drivers.

2. Both traditional and ABC cost systems focus on assigning

    a. Direct costs.   **c.** Manufacturing costs.
    b. Indirect costs.   **d.** Nonmanufacturing costs.

3. Which of the following is a volume-based allocation measure?

    a. Number of units produced.
    b. Number of direct labor hours.
    c. Number of machine hours.
    d. All of the above.

4. Number of setups is an example of a

    a. Unit-level activity.   **c.** Product-level activity.
    b. Batch-level activity.   **d.** Facility-level activity.

5. Which of the following is **not** a customer-level activity at a doctor's office.

    a. Inputting patient data into the computer system.
    b. Checking a patient's vital signs.
    c. Negotiating a new contract with an insurance company.
    d. Performing an outpatient procedure.

Use the following information for questions 6–10:

Hi-Def Video Company makes two types of digital DVD players, economy and deluxe, with the following per-unit cost information:

	Economy (8,000 units)	Deluxe (2,000 units)
Direct materials	$50	$100
Direct labor	25	25
Manufacturing overhead	?	?
Manufacturing cost per unit	?	?

    The company currently applies $1 million in manufacturing overhead to the two products on the basis of direct labor hours. Both products require two hours of direct labor.

6. What rate is currently used to apply manufacturing overhead to the two products?

    a. $100 per unit.
    b. $100 per direct labor hour.
    c. $50 per unit.
    d. $50 per direct labor hour.

7. Using the rate calculated in question 6, what is the full manufacturing cost per unit of the deluxe product?

    a. $50.   **c.** $175.
    b. $100.   **d.** $225.

Assume that High-Def has decided to implement an ABC system and has assigned the $1 million in manufacturing overhead to four activities, which will be assigned to the two products based on the following cost drivers:

Activity Cost Pools	Activity Cost	Cost Driver	Cost Driver for Each Product Line	
			Economy	Deluxe
Materials handling	$ 250,000	Number of parts	40,000	60,000
Quality control	500,000	Number of inspections	8,000	12,000
Finishing	200,000	Number of direct labor hours	16,000	4,000
Packaging	50,000	Number of packages shipped	2,000	2,000
Total	$1,000,000			

8. What is the activity rate for the materials handling activity cost pool?

    a. $ 2.50 per part.   **c.** $ 8.00 per part.
    b. $ 4.00 per part.   **d.** $10.50 per part.

9. Using the activity proportion method, how much of the quality control cost would be assigned to the economy model?

    a. 20% of $500,000 = $100,000.
    b. 40% of $500,000 = $200,000.
    c. 60% of $500,000 = $300,000.
    d. 80% of $500,000 = $400,000.

10. In comparing the results of ABC with the volume-based cost system (based on direct labor hours), which of the following statements is most likely to be true?

    a. The current cost system will overcost the deluxe model compared to ABC.
    b. The current cost system will undercost the economy model compared to ABC.
    c. The current cost system will overcost the economy model compared to ABC.
    d. Both *a* and *b* are true.

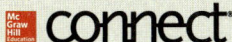 **Find More Learning Solutions on Connect.**

MINI-EXERCISES

M4–1 Comparing Traditional and ABC Systems

LO 4–1, 4–6

Catarina Company is considering a switch from its traditional costing system to an activity-based system. It has compiled the following information regarding its product lines:

	Traditional Costing	ABC
Revenue	$325,000	$325,000
Overhead		
Product X	52,000	71,000
Product Y	50,000	31,000
	$102,000	$102,000

Explain why the overhead costs for each product could be so different between the two costing systems.

M4–2 Identifying Cost Drivers in an ABC System

LO 4–3

Patterson makes electronic components for handheld games and has identified several activities as components of manufacturing overhead: factory rent, factory utilities, quality inspections, materials handling, machine setup, employee training, machine maintenance, inventory security costs, and supervisor salaries. For each activity that Patterson has identified, choose a cost driver to allocate that cost. Explain your reasoning.

M4–3 Identifying Cost Drivers in an ABC System

LO 4–3

For each of the following activities, indicate the appropriate category (unit, batch, product, or facility level) and suggest a possible cost driver for each pool:

1. Factory utilities.
2. Machine setups.
3. Research and development for a new product.
4. Sanding rough edges of the product.
5. Packaging the product for shipment.
6. Developing new packaging for a new product line.
7. Maintenance on equipment.
8. Assembling the product's component parts.
9. Materials handling costs.
10. Quality control testing.

M4–4 Identifying terms in ABC and ABM

LO 4–1, 4–2, 4–3, 4–4, 4–5, 4–6, 4–8

Use the following terms to complete the sentences that follow; terms may be used once, more than once, or not at all.

Activity proportion

Activity rate

Activity-based management (ABM)

Batch-level

Cost driver

Cost-plus pricing

External failure costs

First

Inspection costs

Internal failure costs

Non-value-added

Non-volume-based

Product-level

Second

Target costing

Third

Total costs

Total quality management (TQM)

Unit-level

Value engineering

Value-added

Variable costs

Volume-based

1. _____include(s) product recalls, warranty costs, and legal fees.

2. _____ involves analyzing the functionality of a product to determine which functions add value to the customer and then finding ways to deliver those functions while meeting the target cost.

3. Activities such as expediting an order or scheduling a production run are considered _____.

4. When managers use activity-based costing data to improve operations or reduce costs it is called _____.

5. In a volume-based cost system, the _____ varies in direct relation to volume.

6. _____ activities include research and development and product testing.

7. _____ allocation measures include the number of quality inspections and the number of design changes.

8. This stage of ABC is assigning indirect costs to activity cost pools with the goal to create as few pools as possible: _____

9. Dividing the activity demands of each individual product by the total quantity of the cost driver results in a(n) _____.

10. _____ cost systems tend to undercost low-volume, customized, or complex products.

LO 4–1, 4–2, 4–8   **M4–5 Matching Terminology**

Match each of the terms on the left with the appropriate definition on the right. Not all definitions will be used.

_____ 1. Activity-Based Costing

_____ 2. Appraisal or Inspection Costs

_____ 3. Batch-Level Activities

_____ 4. External Failure Costs

_____ 5. Facility-Level Activities

_____ 6. Just-in-Time System

_____ 7. Prevention Costs

_____ 8. Unit-Level Activities

_____ 9. Value-Added Activity

_____10. Value Chain

A. Activities that are performed to benefit the organization as a whole.

B. Activities that are independent of the of the number of units, but are performed for a group all at once.

C. Activities that vary in direct proportion to the number of units produced or customers served.

D. An activity, which if eliminated, would not change the perceived worth of the product or service.

E. An activity, which if eliminated, would change the perceived worth of the product or service.

F. A demand-pull system.

G. A demand-push system.

H. A report that provides details about internal failure costs.

I. Costs incurred to keep quality problems from happening.

J. Costs incurred to identify defective products before they get to customers.

K. Costs that result from the defects caught during the inspection process.

L. Warranty costs, recalls, and product replacement costs.

M. A linked set of activities required to design, develop, produce, market, deliver the product to customers, and aftermarket service.

N. A process that involves analyzing the feasibility of a product to meet a projected life cycle cost.

O. A method that identifies the major activities that place demands on a company's resources and then assigns indirect costs to the products/services that create those demands.

M4–6 Matching Terminology

Match each of the definitions by inserting the appropriate term letter in the space provided. Not all terms will be used.

_____ 1. An activity, such as machine setups, that occurs before each production run.

_____ 2. A cost driver that captures aspects of the production process that relates to activities other than the volume of production or sales.

_____ 3. Total activity cost divided by total cost driver.

_____ 4. All the actions taken to improve operations or reduce costs based on ABC data.

_____ 5. An activity, which if eliminated, would NOT change the perceived worth of the product or service.

_____ 6. A report that provides details about internal failure costs.

_____ 7. Costs that result from the defects caught during the inspection process.

_____ 8. A process to determine what costs should be in order to earn an acceptable profit across a product life cycle.

_____ 9. A process which uses the cost of the product plus a markup to arrive at the sales price.

_____ 10. A linked set of activities required to design, develop, produce, market, deliver the product to customers, and aftermarket service.

A. Activity-Based Costing (ABC)
B. Activity-Based Management
C. Activity Proportion
D. Activity Rate
E. Appraisal or Inspection Costs
F. Batch-Level Activities
G. Cost-Plus Pricing
H. Cost of Quality Report
I. External Failure Costs
J. Facility-Level Activities
K. Internal Failure Costs
L. Just-in-Time System
M. Non-Value-Added Activity
N. Non-Volume-Based Cost Driver
O. Prevention Costs
P. Product Level Activities
Q. Product Life Cycle
R. Supply Chain
S. Target Costing
T. Total Quality Management
U. Unit-Level Activities
V. Value-Added Activity
W. Value Chain
X. Value Engineering
Y. Volume-Based Cost Driver

M4–7 Calculating Activity Rates

Halsted Corp. has identified three cost pools in its manufacturing process: equipment maintenance, setups, and quality control. Total cost assigned to the three pools is $214,500, $101,400, and $153,000, respectively. Cost driver estimates for the pools are 10,000 machine hours, 150 setups, and 450 quality inspections, respectively. Calculate the activity rate for each of Halsted's cost pools.

M4–8 Assigning Costs Using Activity Rates

Acoma Co. has identified one of its cost pools to be quality control and has assigned $125,000 to that pool. Number of inspections has been chosen as the cost driver for this pool; Acoma performs 25,000 inspections annually. Suppose Acoma manufactures two products that consume 10,000 and 15,000 inspections each. Using activity rates, determine the amount of quality control cost to be assigned to each of Acoma's product lines.

M4–9 Assigning Costs Using Activity Proportions

Refer to the information presented in M4–8. Suppose that Acoma manufacturers only the two products mentioned and they consume 100 percent of the company's quality inspections. Using activity proportions, determine how much quality control cost will be assigned to each of Acoma's product lines.

LO 4–4 | **M4–10 Calculating Activity Rates for ABC System**

Lakeside Inc. manufactures four lines of remote control boats and uses activity-based costing to calculate product cost. Compute the activity rates for each of the following activity cost pools:

Activity Cost Pools	Estimated Total Cost	Estimated Cost Driver
Machining	$366,600	13,000 machine hours
Setup	69,825	350 batches
Quality control	108,800	800 inspections

LO 4–4 | **M4–11 Assigning Costs Using Activity Rates**

Refer to the information presented in M4–10. Suppose the Speedy boat requires 2,500 machine hours, 100 batches, and 300 inspections. Using the activity rates calculated in M4–10, determine the amount of overhead assigned to the Speedy product line.

LO 4–5 | **M4–12 Assigning Costs Using Activity Proportions**

Refer to the information presented in M4–10. Suppose the Luxury boat requires 4,680 machine hours, 70 batches, and 208 inspections. Using activity proportions, determine the amount of overhead assigned to the Luxury product line.

LO 4–4, LO 4–7 | **M4–13 Calculating Activity Rates for a Service Company**

Sunrise Accounting provides basic tax services and "rent-a-controller" accounting services. Sunrise has identified three activity pools, the related costs per pool, the cost driver for each pool, and the expected use for each pool. Compute the activity rate for each of the activity pools.

Activity	Total Activity Cost	Cost Driver	Expected Tax Services Usage	Expected Controller Services Usage
Transportation costs	$50,000	Mileage	5,000 miles	35,000 miles
Electronic processing	$75,000	Processing hours	20,000 hours	30,000 hours
Office support	$20,000	Administrative hours	3,500 hours	1,500 hours

LO 4–4, 4–7 | **M4–14 Assigning Costs Using Activity Rates for a Service Company**

Refer to the information provided in M4–13. Barry Gold, a tax client of Sunrise Accounting, requires 20 miles of transportation, 50 hours of processing time, and 3 hours of office support. Using the activity rates calculated in M4–13, determine the amount of overhead assigned to Barry Gold.

LO 4–5, 4–7 | **M4–15 Assigning Costs Using Activity Proportions for a Service Company**

Refer to the information provided in M4–13. Using activity proportions, determine the amount of overhead assigned to Controller Services.

LO 4–8 | **M4–16 Classifying Activities as Value-Added or Non-Value-Added**

Canterbury Corp. has identified the following activities in its manufacturing process. Indicate whether each activity is value-added or non-value-added.

- Product design research
  - Materials handling
  - Machining
  - Assembly of components
  - Finished goods inventory storage
  - Rework after a quality inspection
  - Painting end product
  - Raw materials inventory storage

LO 4–2 | **M4–17 Classifying Activities According to Level**

Refer to the activities presented in M4–16. Classify each cost as facility, product, batch, or unit level.

M4–18 Cost of Quality   LO 4–8

Wilson's Tax Service is tracking costs of quality. Classify each of the following as Prevention (P),
Appraisal or Inspection (AI), Internal Failure (IF), or External Failure (EF) costs.

_____1. Review of tax return for missing items/errors.

_____2. Training of employees on new tax software.

_____3. Correction of errors found on review of tax returns.

_____4. Reprinting of corrected tax returns.

_____5. Legal costs resulting from lawsuits related to incorrect tax returns.

EXERCISES

**E4–1 Classifying Activities According to Level, Determining Value-Added or
Non-Value-Added**   LO 4–1, 4–3, 4–8

Lindwood Company manufactures coffee cups in several different sizes and has identified the
following activities in its manufacturing process:
- Storing inventory
- Creating molds
- Pouring plaster
- Firing pots in kiln
- Sanding and finishing
- Painting
- Performing quality control
- Ordering materials
- Delivering an order to a large customer such as Home Depot
- Insuring the manufacturing facility
- Reconfiguring machinery between batches

Required:

1. Classify each activity listed as facility, product, batch, or unit level.

2. Identify a cost driver for each activity listed.

3. Indicate whether each activity is value-added or non-value-added.

E4–2 Assigning Costs to Activity Cost Pools, Identifying a Cost Driver   LO 4–2, 4–3

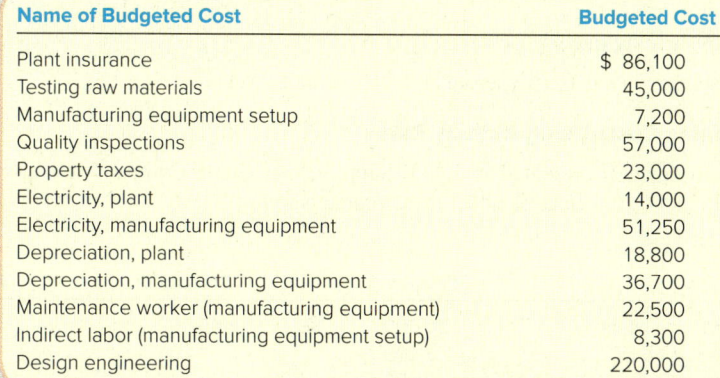

Name of Budgeted Cost	Budgeted Cost
Plant insurance	$ 86,100
Testing raw materials	45,000
Manufacturing equipment setup	7,200
Quality inspections	57,000
Property taxes	23,000
Electricity, plant	14,000
Electricity, manufacturing equipment	51,250
Depreciation, plant	18,800
Depreciation, manufacturing equipment	36,700
Maintenance worker (manufacturing equipment)	22,500
Indirect labor (manufacturing equipment setup)	8,300
Design engineering	220,000

Required:

1. Assign each of the budgeted costs above to one of the following activity cost pools:

   - Engineering
   - Equipment setup
   - Quality control
   - Factory facilities
   - Manufacturing equipment

2. Compute the total cost of each pool.
3. Indicate whether the activities in each pool are unit, batch, product, or facility level.
4. Identify the most likely driver for each cost pool from the following list:

   - Number of inspections/tests
   - Square feet
   - Machine hours
   - Engineering hours
   - Number of setups

Use the following table to organize your answer. The engineering cost pool is done as an example. Other pools may have more than one cost item included.

Activity Cost Pools	1. Costs Included in Pool	2. Total Cost of Pool	3. Unit, Batch, Product, or Facility	4. Cost Driver
Engineering	Design engineering	$220,000	Product	Engineering hours
Equipment setup				
Quality control				
Factory facilities				
Manufacturing equipment				

LO 4–2, 4–4   **E4–3 Calculating Activity Rates, Classifying Activities**

Gable Company uses three activity cost pools. Each pool has a cost driver. Information for Gable Company follows:

Activity Cost Pools	Total Cost of Pool	Cost Driver	Estimated Cost Driver
Machining	$312,000	Number of machine hours	80,000
Designing costs	73,600	Number of design hours	8,000
Setup costs	71,600	Number of batches	500

Required:

1. Compute the activity rate for each activity.
2. Classify each activity as facility, product, batch, or unit level.

LO 4–4   **E4–4 Assigning Costs Using Activity Rates**

Refer to the information presented in E4–3. Suppose that Gable Company manufactures three products, A, B, and C. Information about these products follows:

	Product A	Product B	Product C
Number of machine hours	30,000	40,000	10,000
Number of design hours	3,200	1,800	3,000
Number of batches	50	175	275

Required:

Using the activity rates calculated in E4–3, determine the amount of overhead assigned to each product.

E4–5 Assigning Costs Using Activity Proportions

LO 4–5, 4–6

Refer to the information presented in E4–3. Suppose that Gable Company manufactures three products. Information about its three products follows:

	Product A	Product B	Product C
Number of machine hours	30,000	40,000	10,000
Number of designer hours	3,200	1,800	3,000
Number of batches	50	175	275

Required:

1. Using activity proportions, determine the amount of overhead assigned to each product.
2. Compare these results with those obtained using activity rates in E4–4.

E4–6 Calculating Activity Rates, Assigning Costs

LO 4–3, 4–4

Fellar Corp. has identified the following information:

Activity cost pools	
Materials handling	$60,000
Machine maintenance	51,750
Cost drivers	
Number of material moves	960
Number of machine hours	75,000

Required:

1. Calculate the activity rate for each cost pool.
2. Determine the amount of overhead assigned to Fellar's products if they have the following activity demands:

	Product A	Product B
Number of material moves	600	360
Number of machine hours	42,000	33,000

3. Using activity proportions, determine the amount of overhead assigned to Fellar's products.
4. Compare the results obtained in Steps 2 and 3.

E4–7 Calculating Traditional Overhead Rates, Assigning Costs

LO 4–1

Bluefield Corp. has two product lines, A and B. Bluefield has identified the following information about its overhead and potential cost drivers:

Total overhead	$112,500
Cost drivers	
Number of labor hours	2,500
Number of machine hours	59,800

Required:

1. Suppose Bluefield Corp. uses a traditional costing system with number of labor hours as the cost driver. Determine the amount of overhead assigned to each product line if Product A requires 70 percent of the labor hours and Product B requires 30 percent.
2. Suppose Bluefield uses a traditional costing system with machine hours as the cost driver. Determine the amount of overhead assigned to each product line if Product A consumes 22,100 machine hours and Product B consumes 37,700.

LO 4–3, 4–4   E4–8 Calculating Activity Rates, Assigning Costs

Refer to the information about Bluefield Corp. presented in E4–7. Bluefield has decided to use an ABC costing system and has identified the following detailed information about its cost pools and cost drivers:

Activity cost pools	
Materials handling	$90,000
Machine maintenance	$22,500
Cost drivers	
Number of material moves	500
Number of machine hours	59,800

Required:

1. Calculate Bluefield's activity rate for each cost pool.

2. Determine the amount of overhead assigned to Bluefield's products if each has the following activity demands:

	Product A	Product B
Number of material moves	200	300
Number of machine hours	22,100	37,700

LO 4–1   E4–9 Calculating Traditional Overhead Rates, Assigning Costs

Schell Company manufactures automobile floor mats. It currently has two product lines, the Standard and the Deluxe.

Schell has a total of $39,060 in overhead. It currently uses a traditional cost system with overhead applied to the product on the basis of either labor hours or machine hours. Schell has compiled the following information about possible cost drivers and its two product lines:

Schell Company Total	Quantity/Amount Consumed by Standard Floor Mat Line	Quantity/Amount Consumed by Deluxe Floor Mat Line
600 labor hours	400 labor hours	200 labor hours
7,150 machine hours	4,150 machine hours	3,000 machine hours

Required:

1. Suppose Schell uses a traditional costing system with direct labor hours as the cost driver. Determine the amount of overhead assigned to each product line.

2. Suppose Schell uses a traditional costing system with machine hours as the cost driver. Determine the amount of overhead assigned to each product line.

LO 4–4   E4–10 Assigning Costs Using Activity Rates

Refer to the information given in E4–9 regarding Schell Company. Suppose that Schell has conducted further research into its overhead and potential cost drivers. As a result, the company has compiled the following detailed information, breaking total overhead into three cost pools:

Activity Cost Pools	Cost Driver	Cost Assigned to Pool	Quantity/Amount Consumed by Standard Floor Mat Line	Quantity/Amount Consumed by Deluxe Floor Mat Line
Materials handling	Number of moves	$ 3,750	30 moves	70 moves
Quality control	Number of inspections	$13,860	400 inspections	600 inspections
Machine maintenance	Number of machine hours	$21,450	4,150 machine hours	3,000 machine hours

Required:

1. Calculate the activity rates for each cost pool assuming Schell uses an ABC system.
2. Calculate the amount of overhead that Schell will assign to the Standard floor mat line.
3. Determine the amount of overhead Schell will assign to the Deluxe product line.

E4–11 Comparing Traditional Costing Systems and Activity-Based Costing

LO 4–6

Refer to your solutions obtained in E4–9 and E4–10.

Required:

1. Discuss the costs and benefits to Schell of moving from a traditional costing system to an ABC system.
2. Compare the results of each potential traditional costing system to those obtained in the ABC approach.

E4–12 Assigning Costs Using Traditional System, ABC System

LO 4–1, 4–3, 4–4, 4–5, 4–6

Bunker makes two types of briefcase, fabric and leather. The company is currently using a traditional costing system with labor hours as the cost driver but is considering switching to an activity-based costing system. In preparation for the possible switch, Bunker has identified two activity cost pools: materials handling and setup. Pertinent data follow:

	Fabric Case	Leather Case
Number of labor hours	15,000	9,000
Number of material moves	440	660
Number of setups	40	80

Total estimated overhead costs are $150,000, of which $110,000 is assigned to the materials handling cost pool and $40,000 is assigned to the setup cost pool.

Required:

1. Calculate the overhead assigned to the fabric case using the traditional costing system based on direct labor hours.
2. Calculate the overhead assigned to the fabric case using ABC. (Round activity rates or activity proportions to four decimal places if necessary.)
3. Was the fabric case over- or undercosted by the traditional cost system compared to ABC?

E4–13 Assigning Costs Using Traditional System, ABC System

LO 4–1, 4–3, 4–4, 4–5, 4–6

Refer to E4–12.

Required:

1. Calculate the overhead assigned to the leather case line using the traditional costing system based on direct labor hours.
2. Calculate the overhead assigned to the leather case line using ABC. (Round activity rates or activity proportions to four decimal places if necessary.)
3. Was the leather case over- or undercosted by the traditional cost system compared to ABC?

E4–14 Assigning Costs Using Traditional System, ABC System

LO 4–1, 4–3, 4–4, 4–5

Julio produces two types of calculator, standard and deluxe. The company is currently using a traditional costing system with machine hours as the cost driver but is considering a move to activity-based costing. In preparing for the possible switch, Julio has identified two cost pools: materials handling and setup. The collected data follow:

	Standard Model	Deluxe Model
Number of machine hours	25,000	30,000
Number of material moves	550	850
Number of setups	80	500

Total estimated overhead costs are $303,560, of which $140,000 is assigned to the material handling cost pool and $163,560 is assigned to the setup cost pool.

Required:

1. Calculate the overhead assigned to each product using the traditional cost system. Round the overhead rate to four decimal places if necessary.

2. Calculate the overhead assigned to each product using ABC. Round activity rates to four decimal places if necessary.

LO 4–3, 4–4, 4–5, 4–7   E4–15 Computing Activity Rates, Assigning Costs for a Service Industry

The University of Dental Health (UDH) is a state-run university focusing on the education and training of dentists, dental assistants, dental hygienists, and other dental professionals. The university provides both traditional undergraduate courses to 12,000 students and continuing professional education (CPE) courses to 8,000 practicing professionals. UDH has just hired a new controller who wants to utilize ABC. The controller has identified three key activities performed by the university and the cost of each of these activities:

- UDH has 3 buildings with a total of 200,000 square feet of classroom and facility space. Due to the large space requirements for labs and other training facilities, the undergraduate program utilizes 170,000 square feet. Total cost, $2,300,000.

- UDH offers career placement services for undergraduate students, career counseling for active professionals taking CPE courses, and other student services to both groups. Total cost, $660,000.

- UDH offers 1,200 different instructional courses each year, 800 of which are undergraduate courses. Total cost, $3,360,000.

Required:

1. Select a cost driver and compute an activity rate for each of the three activities identified by the controller.

2. Compute cost driver values and activity proportions for each group of students for each activity.

3. Determine the amount of costs assigned to each group of students and the cost per student to UDH to provide these three key activities.

LO 4–4   E4–16 Calculate Total Manufacturing Costs and Gross Profit,

Rosehut Olive Oil Company makes two grades of olive oil: standard and extra virgin. Rosehut has identified two activity cost pools, the related costs per pool, the cost driver for each pool, and the expected usage for each pool.

Activity	Total Activity Cost	Cost Driver	Standard	Extra Virgin
Washing, Pressing & Filtering (WPF)	$1,537,500	Washing, Pressing, and Filtering hours	45,000 hours	105,000 hours
Bottling	$412,500	Number of bottles	300,000 bottles	75,000 bottles

Additional information about each grade of olive oil is as follows:

Grade	Sales Revenue	Direct Materials Costs	Direct Labor Costs
Standard	$5,100,000	$900,000	$375,000
Extra Virgin	$2,100,000	$600,000	$150,000

Required:

1. Calculate the activity rate for each cost pool.

2. Using the activity rates, determine the total amount of overhead assigned to each product.

3. Determine total manufacturing cost for each product.

4. Calculate the gross profit for each product.

E4–17 Identifying Value-Added and Non-Value-Added Activities   LO 4–8

Corey Hart has just opened an interior design business. Corey is targeting customers in established neighborhoods who want to restore and update their homes. Corey Hart's staff of interior designers performs the following activities on a daily basis:

Activity	Time
Advertising	1 hour
Answering client questions	3 hours
Billing clients	3.5 hours
Cleaning the office	1.5 hours
Client consultations (in-home)	5 hours
Completing paperwork for client file	1 hour
Designing	3 hours
Entertaining prospective clients for lunch	3 hours
On-site supervision of installers	4.5 hours
Staff meeting	2 hours

Required:

Compute the time spent each day on value-added and non-value-added activities.

E4–18 Describing the Benefits of JIT   LO 4–8

A number of manufacturers recently have moved to a JIT inventory system. JIT systems have a number of potential benefits but also can have negative consequences for a company whose suppliers are not dependable.

Required:

1. Discuss the reasons a company might implement a JIT system.
2. What are the potential benefits of a JIT system?
3. What are the potential negative consequences of using a JIT system?
4. Discuss whether you believe the potential benefits outweigh the possible costs.

E4–19 Calculating Target Cost   LO 4–8

Turtle Inc. has developed a new and improved widget. The company plans to sell the product through an existing website. Turtle's marketing department believes the product will sell for $80. Turtle's goal is a 40 percent profit margin on the widget.

Required:

1. If current prototypes cost $49.50 to produce, will Turtle meet its profit goal?
2. Calculate the target cost necessary for Turtle to earn 40 percent profit.
3. Suggest at least three areas that Turtle might investigate to find ways to cut the prototype cost enough to meet the target profit for this product.

E4–20 Calculating Target Cost   LO 4–8

Majesty Company uses target costing to ensure that its products are profitable. Assume Majesty is planning to introduce a new product with the following estimates:

Estimated market price	$1,200
Annual demand	100,000 units
Life cycle	5 years
Target profit	30% return on sales

Required:

1. Compute the target cost of this product.
2. Compute the target cost if Majesty wants a 40 percent return on sales.
3. Compute the target cost if Majesty wants a 15 percent return on sales.

LO 4–8 **E4–21 Explaining the Concept of TQM**

Your co-worker has come to you for help for several things the boss mentioned recently. Specifically, the boss was discussing the company's move to a TQM approach for its manufacturing process and repeatedly mentioned multiple types of quality costs and whether activities are value-added or non-value-added.

Required:

Explain each of these concepts to your co-worker. Include the relationship between these concepts and activity-based management.

LO 4–8 **E4–22 Classifying Costs of Quality**

Classify each of the following as Prevention (P), Appraisal or Inspection (AI), Internal Failure (IF), or External Failure (EF) costs.

_____ **1.** Cost of scrapped product.
_____ **2.** Damage to company's reputation.
_____ **3.** Cost of rework.
_____ **4.** Quality training.
_____ **5.** Costs of the quality control department.
_____ **6.** Cost of downtime created by quality problems.
_____ **7.** Simplifying the product design to reduce defects.
_____ **8.** Product replacement costs.

GROUP A PROBLEMS

LO 4–1, 4–3, 4–4, 4–6 **PA4–1 Assigning Costs Using Traditional System, ABC System**

Hazelnut Corp. manufactures lawn ornaments. It currently has two product lines, the basic and the luxury. Hazelnut has a total of $171,500 in overhead.

The company has identified the following information about its overhead activity cost pools and the two product lines:

Activity Cost Pools	Cost Driver	Cost Assigned to Pool	Quantity/Amount Consumed by Basic	Quantity/Amount Consumed by Luxury
Materials handling	Number of moves	$ 14,000	20 moves	50 moves
Quality control	Number of inspections	$ 37,500	250 inspections	125 inspections
Machine maintenance	Number of machine hours	$120,000	5,000 machine hours	5,000 machine hours

Required:

1. Suppose Hazelnut used a traditional costing system with machine hours as the cost driver. Determine the amount of overhead assigned to each product line.
2. Calculate the activity rates for each cost pool in Hazelnut's ABC system.
3. Calculate the amount of overhead that Hazelnut will assign to the basic line if it uses an ABC system.
4. Determine the amount of overhead Hazelnut will assign to the luxury line if it uses an ABC system.
5. Compare the results for a traditional system with that of an ABC system. Which do you think is more accurate and why?

PA4–2 Assigning Costs Using Traditional System, Assigning Costs Using Activity Proportions

LO 4–1, 4–3, 4–5, 4–6

Carlise has identified the following information about its overhead activity cost pools and the two product lines:

Activity Cost Pools	Cost Driver	Cost Assigned to Pool	Quantity/Amount Consumed by Indoor Line	Quantity/Amount Consumed by Outdoor Line
Materials handling	Number of moves	$20,000	575 moves	425 moves
Quality control	Number of inspections	$82,500	6,000 inspections	4,000 inspections
Machine maintenance	Number of machine hours	$36,900	21,000 machine hours	20,000 machine hours

Required:

1. Suppose Carlise used a traditional costing system with machine hours as the cost driver. Determine the amount of overhead assigned to each product line.
2. Calculate the activity proportions for each cost pool in Carlise's ABC system.
3. Calculate the amount of overhead that Carlise will assign to the Indoor line if it uses an ABC system.
4. Determine the amount of overhead Carlise will assign to the Outdoor line if it uses an ABC system.
5. Compare the results for a traditional system with an ABC system. Which do you think is more accurate and why?

PA4–3 Selecting Cost Drivers, Assigning Costs Using Activity Rates

LO 4–1, 4–3, 4–4, 4–6

Harbour Company makes two models of electronic tablets, the Home and the Work. Basic production information follows:

	Home	Work
Direct materials cost per unit	$ 30	$ 48
Direct labor cost per unit	20	30
Sales price per unit	300	500
Expected production per month	700 units	400 units

Harbour has monthly overhead of $175,200, which is divided into the following cost pools:

Setup costs	$ 68,800
Quality control	58,400
Maintenance	48,000
Total	$175,200

The company has also compiled the following information about the chosen cost drivers:

	Home	Work	Total
Number of setups	42	58	100
Number of inspections	340	390	730
Number of machine hours	1,700	1,300	3,000

Required:

1. Suppose Harbour uses a traditional costing system with machine hours as the cost driver. Determine the amount of overhead assigned to each product line.
2. Calculate the production cost per unit for each of Harbour's products under a traditional costing system.
3. Calculate Harbour's gross margin per unit for each product under the traditional costing system.
4. Select the appropriate cost driver for each cost pool and calculate the activity rates if Harbour wanted to implement an ABC system.
5. Assuming an ABC system, assign overhead costs to each product based on activity demands.
6. Calculate the production cost per unit for each of Harbour's products in an ABC system.
7. Calculate Harbour's gross margin per unit for each product under an ABC system.
8. Compare the gross margin of each product under the traditional system and ABC. Explain the change in profitability for each product.

LO 4–1, 4–3, 4–4, 4–6   **PA4–4 Selecting Cost Drivers, Assigning Costs Using Activity Rates**

Keller Company makes two models of battery-operated boats, the Sandy Beach and the Rocky River. Basic production information follows:

	Sandy Beach	Rocky River
Direct materials cost per unit	$20	$28
Direct labor cost per unit	15	19
Sales price per unit	70	90
Expected production per month	1,200 units	960 units

Keller has monthly overhead of $22,360, which is divided into the following cost pools:

Setup costs	$ 5,200
Quality control	11,000
Maintenance	6,160
Total	$22,360

The company has also compiled the following information about the chosen cost drivers:

	Sandy Beach	Rocky River	Total
Number of setups	14	26	40
Number of inspections	140	300	440
Number of machine hours	1,400	1,400	2,800

Required:

1. Suppose Keller uses a traditional costing system with machine hours as the cost driver. Determine the amount of overhead assigned to each product line.
2. Calculate the production cost per unit for each of Keller's products under a traditional costing system.
3. Calculate Keller's gross margin per unit for each product under the traditional costing system.
4. Select the appropriate cost driver for each cost pool and calculate the activity rates if Keller wanted to implement an ABC system.
5. Assuming an ABC system, assign overhead costs to each product based on activity demands.
6. Calculate the production cost per unit for each of Keller's products with an ABC system.
7. Calculate Keller's gross margin per unit for each product under an ABC system.
8. Compare the gross margin of each product under the traditional system and ABC. Explain the change in profitability for each product.

LO 4–8   **PA4–5 Describing the Impact of ABM and TQM on a Company**

In recent years, the managerial concepts of activity-based management (ABM), activity-based costing (ABC), and total quality management (TQM) have received considerable attention from manufacturing and other companies. The development of a global economy as well as consumers' ability to shop around has led to increased competition in the market and pressure on companies to focus efforts on cost-cutting measures wherever possible.

Required:

1. Conduct online or library research for articles about companies that have successfully implemented ABM, TQM, and/or ABC within their organizations.
2. Read and briefly summarize at least three such articles.
3. Choose one of these companies and write a memo to your classmates outlining the company's implementation. Include their timelines, any problems encountered, and perceived benefits.

GROUP B PROBLEMS

PB4–1 Assigning Costs Using Traditional System, ABC System

LO 4–1, 4–3, 4–4, 4–6

Homerun Corp., which manufactures baseball bats, currently has two product lines, the Traditional and the Acrylic, and $47,125 in total overhead.

The company has identified the following information about its activity cost pools and the two product lines:

Activity Cost Pools	Cost Driver	Cost Assigned to Pool	Quantity/Amount Consumed by Traditional Line	Quantity/Amount Consumed by Acrylic Line
Materials handling	Number of moves	$17,500	100 moves	75 moves
Quality control	Number of inspections	$ 5,625	1,000 inspections	875 inspections
Machine maintenance	Number of machine hours	$24,000	8,000 machine hours	12,000 machine hours

Required:

1. Suppose Homerun used a traditional costing system with machine hours as the cost driver. Determine the amount of overhead assigned to each product line.
2. Calculate the activity rates for each cost pool in Homerun's ABC system.
3. Calculate the amount of overhead that Homerun will assign to the Traditional line if it uses an ABC system.
4. Determine the amount of overhead Homerun will assign to the Acrylic line if it uses an ABC system.
5. Compare the results for the traditional system with those of the ABC system. Which do you think is more accurate and why?

PB4–2 Assigning Costs Using Traditional System, Assigning Costs Using Activity Proportions

LO 4–1, 4–3, 4–5, 4–6

Paradiso Corp. is the manufacturer of food processors. It currently has two product lines, the Basic and the Industrial. Paradiso has $85,170 in total overhead. The company has identified the following information about its overhead activity cost pools and the two product lines:

Activity Cost Pools	Cost Driver	Cost Assigned to Pool	Quantity/Amount Consumed by Basic	Quantity/Amount Consumed by Industrial
Materials handling	Number of moves	$21,420	235 moves	275 moves
Quality control	Number of inspections	$43,350	578 inspections	867 inspections
Machine maintenance	Number of machine hours	$20,400	18,000 machine hours	16,000 machine hours

Required:

1. Suppose Paradiso used a traditional costing system with machine hours as the cost driver. Determine the amount of overhead assigned to each product line.
2. Calculate the activity proportions for each cost pool in Paradiso's ABC system.
3. Calculate the amount of overhead that Paradiso will assign to the Basic product line if it uses an ABC system.
4. Determine the amount of overhead Paradiso will assign to the Industrial product line if it uses an ABC system.
5. Compare the results for a traditional system with those of an ABC system. Which do you think is more accurate and why?

LO 4–1, 4–3, 4–4, 4–6   PB4–3 Selecting Cost Drivers, Assigning Costs Using Activity Rates

Berry Good Company makes two types of energy drinks, cherry and strawberry. Basic production information follows:

	Cherry	Strawberry
Direct materials cost per unit	$0.70	$0.80
Direct labor cost per unit	0.25	0.25
Sales price per unit	2.50	2.50
Expected production per month	140,000 units	190,000 units

Berry Good has monthly overhead of $159,670, which is divided into the following cost pools:

Setup costs	$ 75,000
Quality control	25,000
Maintenance	40,500
Engineering	19,170
Total	$159,670

The company has also compiled the following information about the chosen cost drivers:

	Cherry	Strawberry	Total
Number of setups required	40	60	100
Number of inspections	275	350	625
Number of machine hours	1,500	750	2,250
Number of engineering hours	65	70	135

Required:

1. Suppose Berry Good used a traditional costing system with machine hours as the cost driver. Determine the amount of overhead assigned to each product line.
2. Calculate the production cost per unit for each of Berry Good's products under a traditional costing system.
3. Calculate Berry Good's gross margin per unit for each product under the traditional costing system.
4. Select the appropriate cost driver for each cost pool and calculate the activity rates if Berry Good wanted to implement an ABC system.
5. Assuming an ABC system, assign overhead costs to each product based on activity demands.
6. Calculate the production cost per unit for each of Berry Good's products with an ABC system.
7. Calculate Berry Good's gross margin per unit for each product under an ABC system.
8. Compare the gross margin of each product under the traditional system and ABC. Explain the change in profitability for each product.

LO 4–1, 4–3, 4–4, 4–6   PB4–4 Selecting Cost Drivers, Assigning Costs Using Activity Rates

Summit Company makes two models of snowboards, the Junior and the Expert. Its basic production information follows:

	Junior	Expert
Direct materials cost per unit	$ 92	$115
Direct labor cost per unit	51	75
Sales price per unit	390	615
Expected production per month	4,000 units	9,000 units

Summit has monthly overhead of $484,746, which is divided into the following cost pools:

Setup costs	$136,364
Quality control	163,020
Maintenance	78,840
Engineering	106,522
Total	$484,746

The company has also compiled the following information about the chosen cost drivers:

	Junior	Expert	Total
Number of setups required	60	86	146
Number of inspections	975	675	1,650
Number of machine hours	350	650	1,000
Number of engineering hours	352	612	964

Required:

1. Suppose Summit used a traditional costing system with machine hours as the cost driver. Determine the amount of overhead assigned to each product line.
2. Calculate the production cost per unit for each of Summit's products under a traditional costing system.
3. Calculate Summit's gross margin per unit for each product under the traditional costing system.
4. Select the appropriate cost driver for each cost pool and calculate the activity rates if Summit wanted to implement an ABC system.
5. Assuming an ABC system, assign overhead costs to each product based on activity demands.
6. Calculate the production cost per unit for each of Summit's products with an ABC system.
7. Calculate Summit's gross margin per unit for each product under an ABC system.
8. Compare the gross margin of each product under the traditional system and ABC. Explain the change in profitability for each product.

PB4–5 Defining Concepts of Target Costing, Just-in-Time, and Lean Manufacturing　　LO 4–8

In recent years, the managerial concepts of target costing, just-in-time inventory systems, and lean manufacturing processes have received considerable attention from manufacturing companies. Increased competition in the marketplace and growing pressure have led companies to focus efforts on cost-cutting measures wherever possible while still generating acceptable profits.

Required:

1. Briefly define each of these concepts.
2. Conduct online or library research for articles about companies that have successfully utilized target costing, just-in-time inventory systems, and/or implemented lean manufacturing practices.
3. Read and briefly summarize at least three such articles.
4. Choose one of these companies and write a memo to your classmates outlining the company's utilization or implementation of these concepts. Include their timeline, any problems encountered, and perceived benefits.

SKILLS DEVELOPMENT CASES

LO 4–2, 4–8

S4–1 Video Case Assignment: Identifying Unit-, Batch-, Product-, and Facility-Level Costs

Go to www.YouTube.com and search for **How It's Made,** a television show produced by the Discovery Channel that shows how thousands of products and services are created. Search for a product that provides a form of transportation, such as an automobile, ATV, bus, helicopter, or amphibious vehicle.

Required:

Watch the video and answer the following questions:

1. What product did you choose? Briefly describe how the product is made.
2. Provide an example of the following activities that would be performed by the company that creates this product:
   - Unit-level activity
   - Batch-level activity
   - Product-level activity
   - Facility-level activity
3. Provide an example of the following activities that would be performed by the company that creates this product:
   - Value-added activity
   - Non-value-added activity
4. Would the company that makes this product benefit from ABC? Why or why not?

LO 4–8   S4–2 Researching Companies That Have Implemented Activity-Based Costing

Review recent issues of business publications (e.g., *Bloomberg Businessweek, The Wall Street Journal*) for information about companies that have implemented activity-based costing. Choose one company to research in detail.

Required:

Answer the following questions:

1. Briefly describe the company, its products, and its history.
2. If the company has multiple divisions or segments, has one or more of them implemented activity-based costing (ABC)?
3. If one or more divisions or segments use ABC, what factor(s) prompted the decision to do so?
4. What type of costing system was utilized prior to the conversion to ABC?
5. Were any specific difficulties experienced during the switch?
6. What benefits has the company or one or more of its divisions or segments identified as a result of implementing ABC?
7. Did the move to an ABC system impact other areas of the company and/or result in changes to other aspects of its operation?
8. Does the company view the ABC implementation as successful?

LO 4–1, 4–6, 4–8   S4–3 Implementing ABC and Ethical Dilemmas

Assume you recently accepted a job with a company that designs and builds helicopters for commercial and military use. The company has numerous contracts with the U.S. military that require the use of cost-plus pricing. In other words, the contracted price for each helicopter is calculated at a certain percentage (about 130 percent) of the total cost to produce it. Unlike the cost-plus pricing approach used for military contracts, the prices for civilian helicopters are based on the amount that individuals and corporations are willing to pay for a state-of-the-art helicopter. As your first assignment, the company controller has asked you to reevaluate the costing system currently used to determine the cost of producing helicopters. The company assigns manufacturing overhead based on the number of units produced. The result is that every helicopter is assigned the same amount of overhead regardless of whether it is for military or civilian use. As part of your assignment, you collected the following information about several other potential allocation bases and how they differ for the two types of customers the company serves:

	Military Contracts		Civilian Contracts		
	Units in Allocation Base	Percent of Total	Units in Allocation Base	Percent of Total	Total
Units produced	1,000	50%	1,000	50%	2,000
Labor hours	800,000	40	1,200,000	60	2,000,000
Machine hours	700,000	70	300,000	30	1,000,000
Number of setups	50	25	150	75	200
Engineering hours	3,000	30	7,000	70	10,000
Quality inspections	4,000	20	16,000	80	20,000

When you presented these data to the controller, you recommended that the company move to an ABC system that incorporates both volume-based and non-volume-based cost drivers. He responded that he wanted you to choose the system that would assign the highest percentage of the total overhead cost to the military contracts. His reasoning was that the cost-plus agreement with the U.S. government would result in a higher contract price for military helicopters without affecting the price of civilian helicopters, which are set by the market.

Required:

1. Explain how changing to an ABC system would impact the profitability of the two types of products.
2. Which costing method do you think the company should use to apply manufacturing overhead to the two types of products? Defend your answer.
3. Identify the ethical issues involved in this scenario. What are your potential courses of action for responding to the controller's request? What are the potential personal, professional, and legal implications of the alternative courses of action you considered? How would you ultimately respond to this situation?

S4–4 Classifying and Evaluating Sustainability Metrics   LO 4–3, 4–6, 4–7

Restaurants such as Subway generally offer a limited number of food categories (subs, salads, wraps, etc.) that are similarly priced. On the other hand, a restaurant such as Applebee's will have a broader menu in which each entrée is individually priced. Consider the "behind the scenes" operation of each restaurant.

Required:

1. Assuming that the prices reflect the restaurants' cost, explain why these two restaurants price their products so differently.
2. How might a Subway store's overhead differ from Applebee's? How could these differences impact the restaurants' costing systems?
3. Briefly explain a process that each might use to estimate product costs. Include overhead costs as well as whether or how those might be pooled. For any cost pools, identify an appropriate cost driver.

S4–5 Classifying and Evaluating Sustainability Metrics   LO4–8

Sustainability accounting should include measures of economic, environmental and social impact. Consider the following metrics which were obtained from Toyota's 2017 corporate social responsibility (CSR) report and Sustainability website (http://www.toyota-global.com/sustainability/report/sr/):

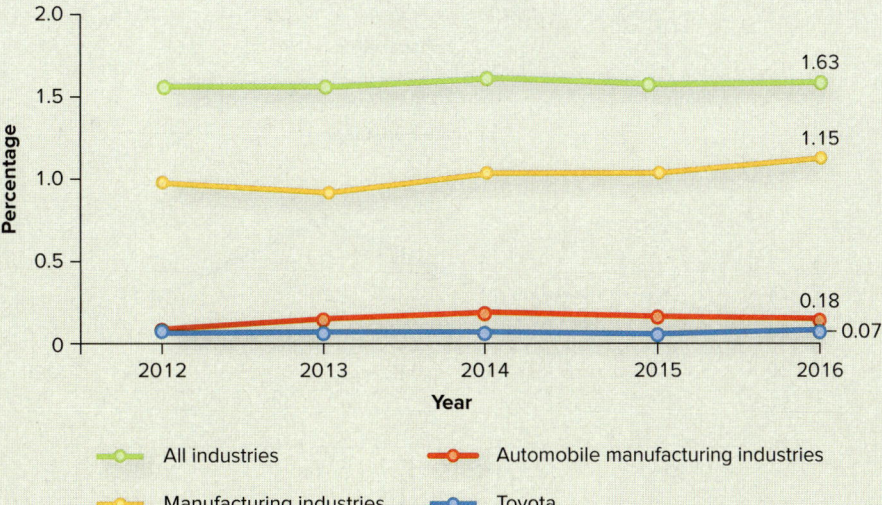

Frequency of Industrial Accidents
(Frequency rate of lost workday cases: TCM)

Percentage of Employees Who Smoke

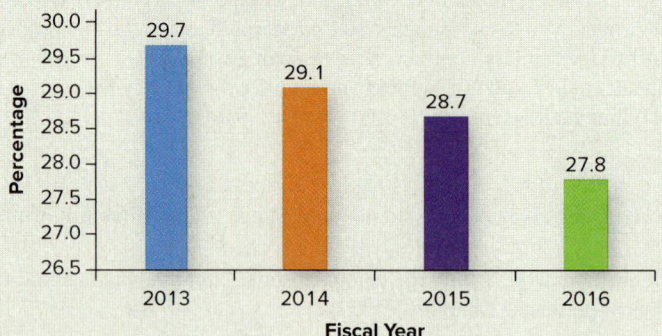

Use of Child Care and Nursing Care Leave (Japan)

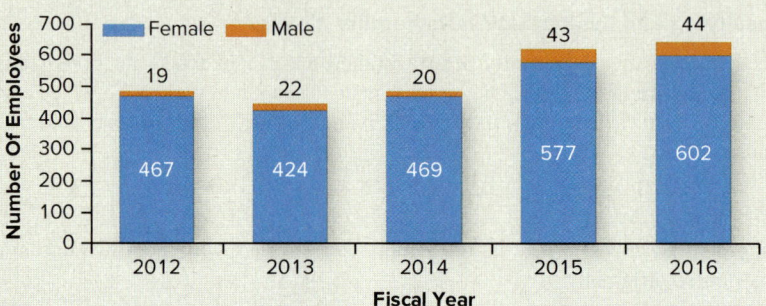

Total Waste Volume and Waste Volume per Unit Produced at TMC

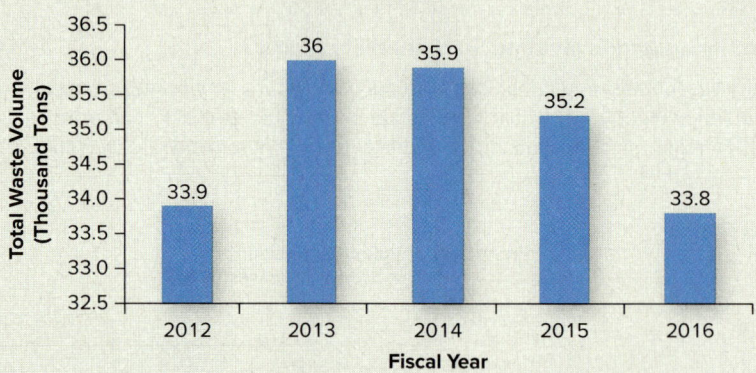

Employee Satisfaction

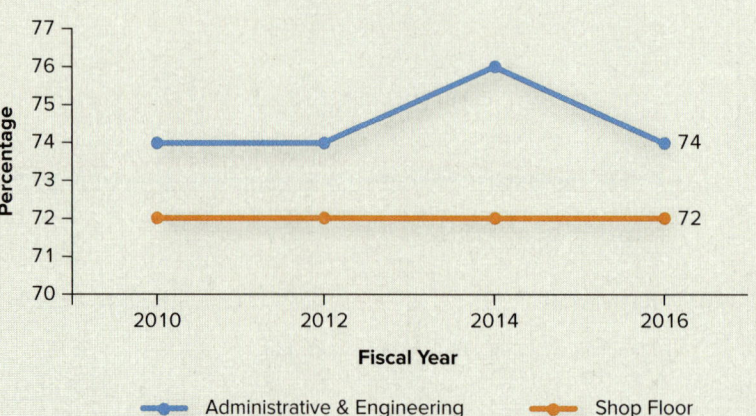

Required:

1. For each measure, indicate whether it is primarily measuring economic, environmental, or social impact.
2. How would you evaluate Toyota's performance in the three areas of sustainability?
3. What actions could managers take to improve performance on each metric?
4. For any measure that you identify as environmental or social, explain whether and how it might ultimately impact economic performance.

5

Cost Behavior

CHAPTER FIVE

YOUR LEARNING OBJECTIVES

LO 5–1 Identify costs as variable, fixed, step, or mixed.

LO 5–2 Prepare a scattergraph to depict the relationship between total cost and activity.

LO 5–3 Use the high-low method to estimate cost behavior.

LO 5–4 Use least-squares regression to estimate cost behavior.

LO 5–5 Prepare and interpret a contribution margin income statement.

LO 5–S1 Compare variable costing to full absorption costing.

©Don Ryan/AP images

As you sit with your friends in your local Starbucks Coffee shop, the conversation quickly turns to spring break and your plans to escape to your favorite destination (beach, mountain, or city) for a few days of relaxation. Assume that the major costs of the trip will be transportation, food, entertainment, and a condo that will sleep six to eight people. In planning the trip, you find yourself asking the following questions:

- How much can I afford to spend on this vacation?
- Should I fly or drive to my destination?
- How many people must go on the trip to keep it affordable yet enjoyable?
- How many nights can I afford to stay and remain within my budget?

Answering these questions requires you to understand cost behavior, the topic of this chapter. Cost behavior refers to the way in which total and per-unit costs change as a result of a change in something else. In the spring break example, costs of transportation, food, entertainment, and lodging will differ depending on whether you fly or drive, the number of people on the trip, and the number of nights stayed. Understanding these cost behavior patterns is the key to helping you decide whether you can afford the trip, whether to drive or fly, how many nights to stay, and how many people to invite along.

In business, managers make a variety of decisions, such as what product or service to offer, what type of equipment to buy, how many workers to hire, how many units to produce, and whether to make or buy components. Managers must understand cost behavior in order to make these decisions. In the next two chapters, we use a hypothetical Starbucks Coffee shop to illustrate the role of cost behavior in managerial decision making. We lay the foundation in this chapter by estimating cost behavior patterns. In the next chapter, we apply the cost behavior concepts to a managerial decision-making technique called cost-volume-profit analysis. As always, we make a number of simplifying assumptions, but using this familiar company should help you understand how to apply the concepts of cost behavior to a real-world business setting.

ORGANIZATION OF THE CHAPTER

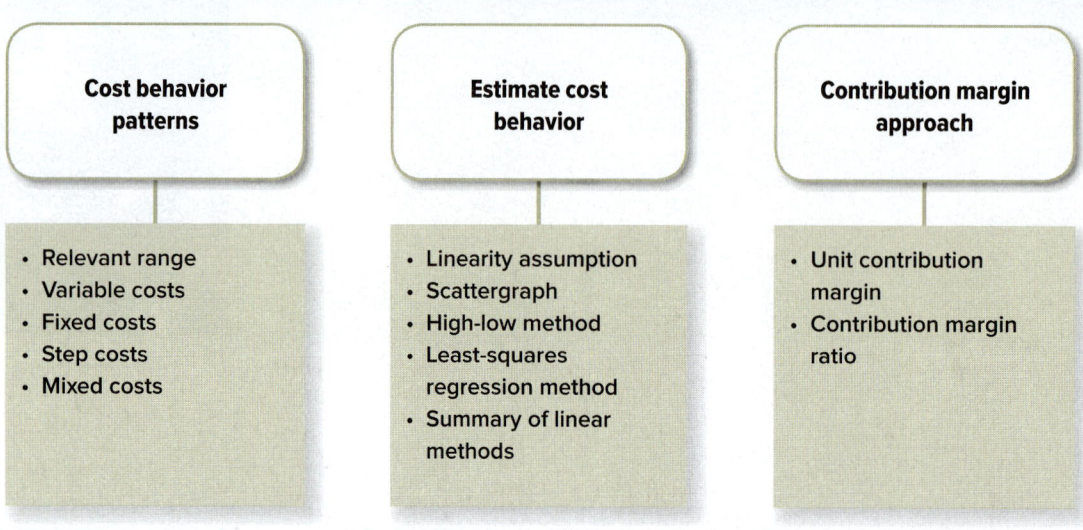

Cost behavior patterns	Estimate cost behavior	Contribution margin approach
• Relevant range • Variable costs • Fixed costs • Step costs • Mixed costs	• Linearity assumption • Scattergraph • High-low method • Least-squares regression method • Summary of linear methods	• Unit contribution margin • Contribution margin ratio

Previous chapters described how to calculate the cost of a physical product such as a California Pizza Kitchen pizza, a bottle of Fetzer wine, or a Toyota automobile. The method used to determine the cost of these products depended on the type of product (we used job order costing for unique products and process costing for homogeneous products) and the need to capture the underlying activities required to make the products (activity-based costing). Although the mechanics of the various costing methods differ, all have the same basic objective: to calculate the full manufacturing cost of each unit produced. This product costing information was used to determine Cost of Goods Sold (on the income statement) and the value of Work in Process Inventory and Finished Goods Inventory (on the balance sheet).

The costing systems described in the previous chapters were all examples of *full absorption costing,* a costing method that assigns **all manufacturing costs** to the product as it is being produced. Although full absorption costing is required for external reporting, this method is not always useful for internal management decision making. For internal purposes, managers often need information that is based on cost behavior. We call the costing system that provides this type of information *variable costing.* The supplement to this chapter provides a detailed discussion of the differences between full absorption and variable costing.

First, let's shift gears from product costing to focus on cost behavior. Instead of classifying costs as either manufacturing (product) or nonmanufacturing (period) costs, we now classify costs based on **how they behave in response to a change in some measure of activity**. A solid understanding of cost behavior is the key to almost all of the managerial decision-making approaches discussed throughout the remainder of this book.

Cost Behavior Patterns

Cost behavior refers to the way total cost behaves, or changes, when some measure of activity changes. Some of the most common activity measures include the number of units produced, customers served, direct labor hours, or machine hours. As you learned in Chapter 4, these are all examples of volume-based cost drivers. Other factors that drive cost, such as the number of setups, orders, and shipments, are examples of non-volume-based cost drivers. In this chapter, we focus on how costs behave or change in response to changes in a volume-based driver, such as the number of units produced or customers served.

RELEVANT RANGE

When we analyze cost behavior, we must limit our analysis to the **relevant range**, or the range of activity over which we expect our assumptions about cost behavior to hold true. For example, we will use a straight line to describe the relationship between total cost and activity. In reality, the relationship between total cost and activity may not be perfectly linear. However, as long as we limit our analysis to a fairly narrow range of activity—that is, the relevant range—we can assume that the relationship is linear and come close to estimating true cost behavior.

The relevant range also applies to fixed costs. When we say that a cost is fixed, this assumption will only hold true over a limited range of activity. For example, each Starbucks location can serve a limited number of customers per hour based on factors such as the number of cash registers or espresso machines it has. Beyond this point, fixed costs will not remain constant because additional equipment would have to be purchased to serve more customers. Later in the chapter, we describe *step costs,* or costs that are fixed over a limited range of activity, and then increase when a capacity limit is reached.

When analyzing cost behavior, we must limit our analysis to the relevant range and be aware that our assumptions and conclusions may not extend beyond that limited range of activity.

> **COACH'S TIP**
>
> You can think of the relevant range as a company's "normal" operating range. If we try to extend our analysis beyond the normal range, our assumptions may not hold true.

VARIABLE COSTS

Variable costs are those that change **in total** in direct proportion to changes in activity. If activity increases by 50 percent, total variable costs should also increase by 50 percent. If activity decreases by 20 percent, total variable costs should also decrease by 20 percent. Examples of variable costs incurred by Starbucks Coffee include coffee beans, milk, sugar, cups, and paper products. All of these costs will increase, in total, as Starbucks sells more coffee drinks.

Although **total** variable costs change with activity, **per unit** variable costs remain constant. For example, the cost of coffee used in each cup should be the same regardless of how many cups are served. This ignores any discount that a company may receive by purchasing ingredients "in bulk," or in large quantities.

See Exhibit 5–1 for charts that show how the total and per-unit cost of coffee beans changes with the number of coffee drinks served. As the graph on the left shows, the total cost of coffee beans increases in direct proportion to increases in the number of coffee drinks served. As the graph on the right shows, however, the **per-unit** cost of coffee beans remains constant, regardless of how many drinks are served.

> **Learning Objective 5–1**
> Identify costs as variable, fixed, step, or mixed.

FIXED COSTS

Fixed costs remain the same **in total** regardless of activity level. For Starbucks Coffee, fixed costs include rent, manager salaries, depreciation on equipment, and insurance. The total cost of these items remains the same regardless of how many coffee drinks are served each month. On a **per-unit** basis, however, fixed costs decrease with increases in activity levels because

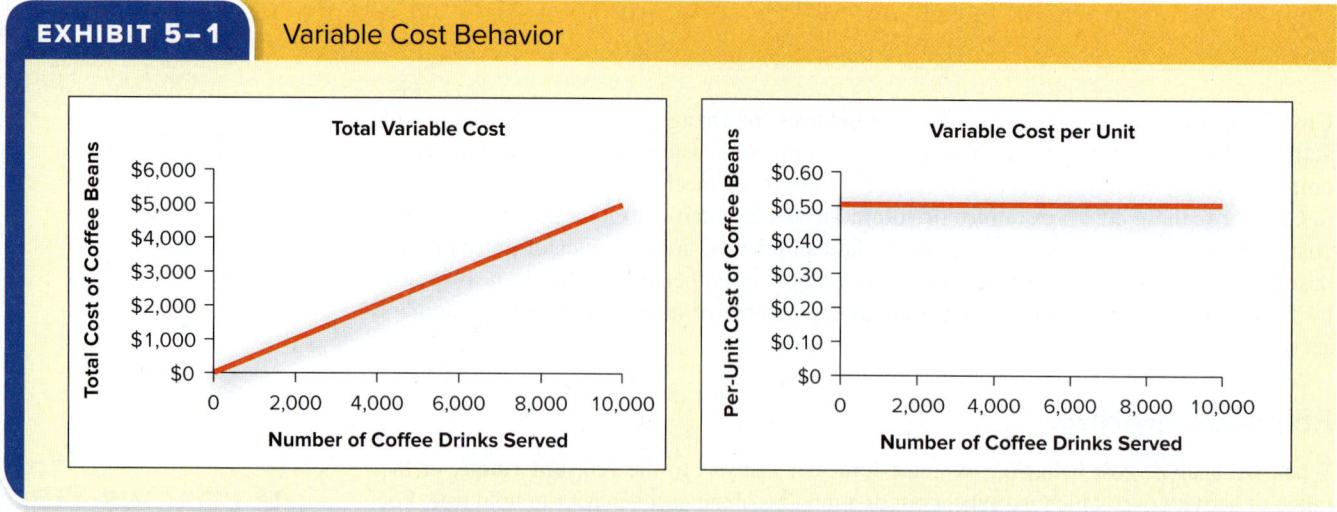

EXHIBIT 5–1   Variable Cost Behavior

the fixed costs are spread over more units. The charts in Exhibit 5–2 show how the total and per-unit cost of monthly rent changes with the number of coffee drinks served.

When we say that a cost is fixed, it does not mean that the cost can never change or that it does not fluctuate over time. It simply means that the total cost is independent of a specific measure of activity, such as the number of units produced or customers served. Fixed costs can be classified as discretionary fixed costs or committed fixed costs. As the name implies, **discretionary fixed costs** are those for which managers have discretion over the level of spending. Because managers can choose how much to spend on these costs, they are relatively easy to change in the short-run. Examples include employee training programs, advertising budgets, and travel expenses. When times get tough and managers are asked to reduce spending, discretionary fixed costs are often one of the first things to go. **Committed fixed costs**, on the other hand, are much more difficult to change because managers are often locked-in to the level of spending due to contractual agreements. Examples include a long-term lease on an office building or depreciation on property, plant, and equipment.

Regardless of whether a fixed costs is discretionary or committed, the total amount does not change based on the level of activity. However, when the total fixed cost is divided by the number of units, the per unit cost decreases as activity increases. This may give managers the impression that they can increase profits simply by producing more units. As an extreme example, imagine what would happen if a Starbucks manager decided to make as many cups of coffee as possible each day regardless of whether there were enough customers to buy

EXHIBIT 5–2   Fixed Cost Behavior

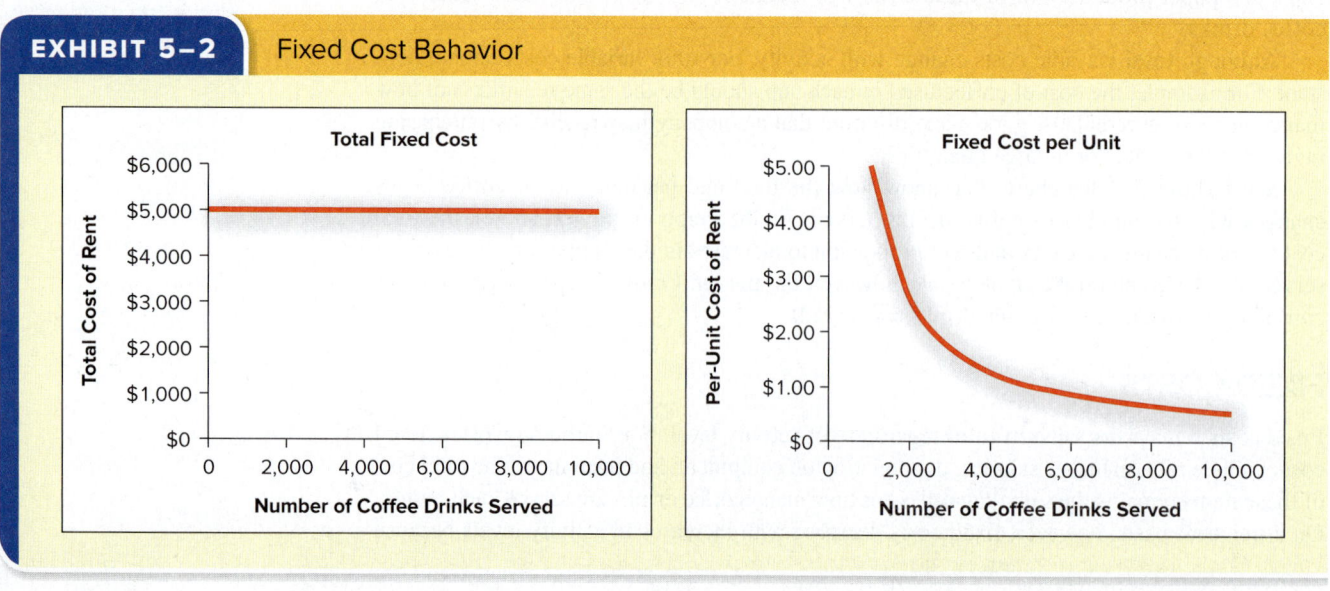

them. Although doing so would drive down the per unit cost of each cup, it would also result in a lot of coffee being thrown away, with no revenue from customers to cover the cost.

Although this example may seem far-fetched, it is not uncommon for managers to believe that they can drive down costs by producing more units than they can sell. The difference is that, in most companies, the unsold units are not thrown away at the end of the day like a cold cup of coffee. Instead, unsold units are stored in a warehouse as inventory—a solution that adds unnecessary costs for insurance, storage, handling, and so on. The bottom line is that, while increasing production lowers the average cost of each unit produced (because the fixed costs are spread over more units), it does not translate into increased profit unless sales increase by more than the variable costs.

STEP COSTS

Step costs are fixed over a range of activity and then increase in a steplike fashion when a capacity limit is reached. Depending on the width of the steps, step costs may be treated as either step-variable or step-fixed costs, as shown in Exhibit 5–3.

As the graph on the left in Exhibit 5–3 shows, **step-variable costs** tend to be fixed over a fairly narrow range of activity and rise in multiple steps across the relevant range. At Starbucks Coffee, a step-variable cost would be the wages paid to servers. Starbucks relies heavily on part-time labor, and managers try to schedule more workers when more customers are expected. Once employees are on the job, however, they must be paid regardless of how many customers they serve. Because the steps are so narrow and the total cost generally increases with the number of coffee drinks served, Starbucks can treat the cost of server wages as a variable cost. Imagine drawing a straight line through the steps that are shown in the graph on the left. We can use a straight line to capture the cost function and be reasonably accurate, even though labor wages are not perfectly variable.

As the graph on the right side of Exhibit 5–3 shows, **step-fixed costs** are fixed over a much wider range of activity than step-variable costs. To allow more customers to be served, for example, Starbucks might hire an additional supervisor or rent additional space or equipment. Because these costs are fixed over a fairly wide range of activity, they are treated as fixed costs. But we need to specify the range of activity over which that assumption will hold true. In this case, the cost of supervision is fixed at $40,000 up to about 6,000 units, but will step up to $80,000 if we go beyond that relevant range of activity.

COACH'S TIP

Think of step costs as "buying" a limited amount of capacity. In the spring break example, renting the condo provides the capacity to sleep up to eight people. If more than eight people come on the trip, it may be necessary to rent another unit, which will add more cost. Thus, the cost of lodging is "fixed" only within a limited range.

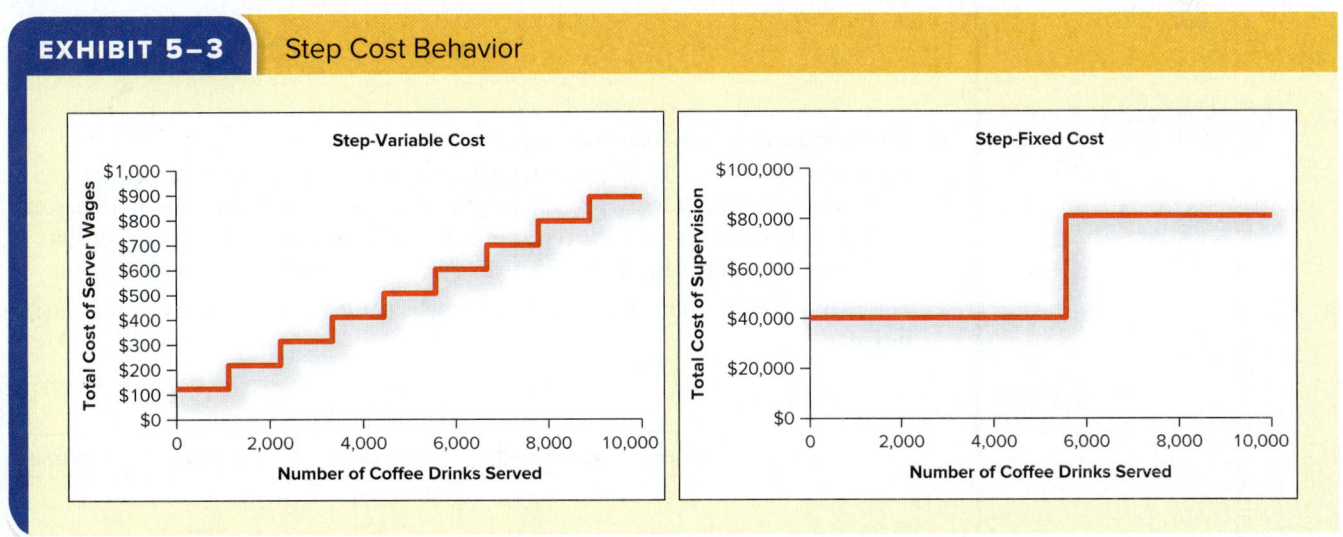

EXHIBIT 5–3 | Step Cost Behavior

MIXED COSTS

Mixed costs, also known as **semivariable costs**, have both a fixed and a variable component. The fixed portion represents the base amount that will be incurred regardless of activity. The variable cost is the amount that will change based on changes in activity or usage. An example

| EXHIBIT 5–4 | Mixed Cost Behavior |

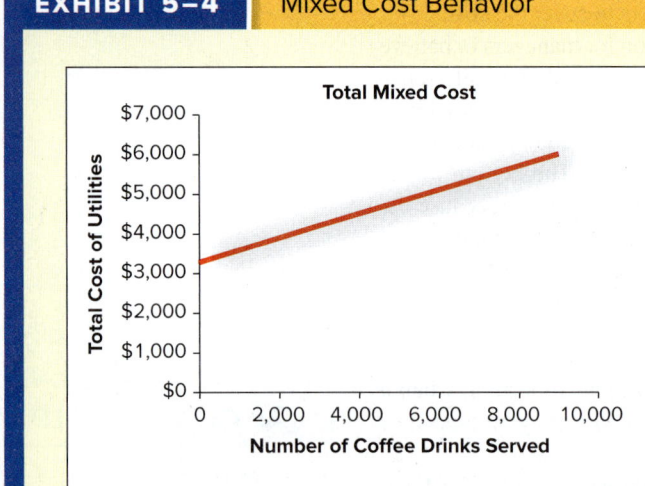

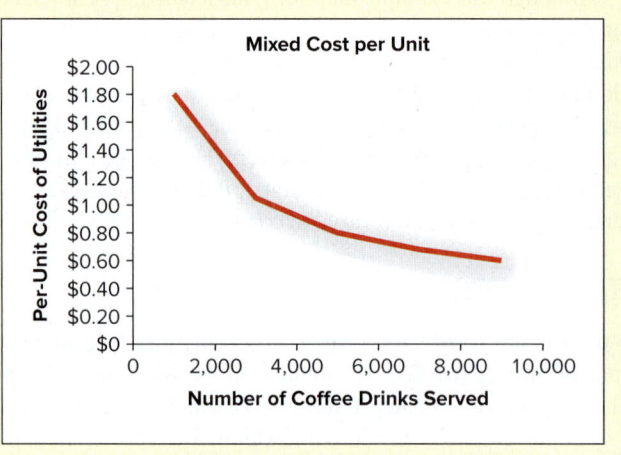

COACH'S TIP

When you see total cost increasing and per-unit cost decreasing with activity level, you can conclude that the cost has both a fixed and a variable component. That is, it is a mixed cost.

of a mixed cost is a cell phone plan that has a fixed charge each month, plus a variable charge for each minute of usage, text message sent, or gigabyte of data used. Many utility expenses behave the same way. Most companies incur a minimum utility charge each month regardless of activity, but the total utility expense increases as activity does.

Mixed costs have both a fixed and a variable component, which means both the total cost and the per-unit cost change with the level of activity (see Exhibit 5–4). Because part of the cost is variable, the total mixed cost rises with increases in activity as in the graph on the left. Because part of the cost is fixed, however, the mixed cost per unit falls with increases in activity as in the graph on the right.

The next section discusses how to separate the fixed and variable components of mixed costs. First take a moment to make sure you understand how variable, fixed, step, and mixed costs differ by completing the following Self-Study Practice.

 How's it going?   Self-Study Practice

1. Which of the following statements is true?
   a. If activity increases by 10 percent, total fixed cost will increase by 10 percent.
   b. If activity increases by 10 percent, per-unit variable cost will decrease by 10 percent.
   c. If activity increases by 10 percent, per-unit fixed cost will increase by 10 percent.
   d. If activity increases by 10 percent, total variable cost will increase by 10 percent.

2. For each row in the following table, indicate whether the cost is variable, fixed, step, or mixed.

	UNITS OF ACTIVITY				
	0 Units	**100 Units**	**200 Units**	**300 Units**	**400 Units**
Total cost of A	$ 0	$200	$400	$600	$800
Total cost of B	500	500	500	750	750
Total cost of C	350	400	450	500	550
Total cost of D	750	750	750	750	750

After you have finished, check your answers against the solutions in the margin.

Estimate Cost Behavior

To make decisions, managers must be able to estimate how costs will change as a result of a specific decision. For example, a Starbucks manager might be considering whether to open an hour earlier or close an hour later every day. To make this decision, the manager needs to estimate how much additional revenue would be generated by serving more customers during those hours, and how much it would cost to do so. What costs would change as a result of this decision? Variable costs such as direct materials and employee wages would increase, while fixed costs such as rent and insurance would be incurred regardless. But what about utilities, employee benefits, and supervision costs? It is difficult to say exactly how these costs would change because they are not strictly variable or strictly fixed.

To determine how total costs will change, the Starbucks manager must first determine how much of the cost is variable and how much of it is fixed. We know from the previous section that variable and fixed costs behave differently, so it is important to separate these two effects for managerial decision making. We'll begin by discussing three methods that can be used to estimate cost behavior: scattergraph, high-low, and least-squares regression. Later in the chapter, we introduce the *contribution margin income statement*. This framework, which classifies costs as either variable or fixed, provides the foundation for analyzing many of the managerial decisions you will encounter in the next few chapters.

LINEAR ASSUMPTION

The three methods we use to estimate cost behavior are based on the **linearity assumption**, or the assumption that the relationship between total cost and activity can be approximated by a straight line, as shown in the following formulas and graphic.

$$y = a + b(x)$$

Total Cost = Total Fixed Cost + (Variable Cost per Unit × Activity)

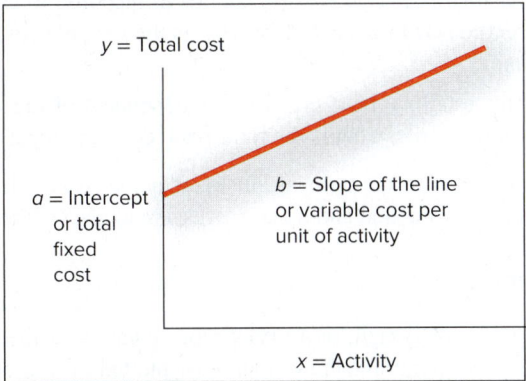

These terms are interpreted as follows.

- *y* is total cost, which is shown on the vertical axis. It is called the **dependent variable** because we assume that *y* is dependent on *x*. The total cost represented by *y* can be any cost we want to analyze, including total manufacturing overhead cost, total labor cost, total utilities cost, and so forth.

- *x* is the activity that causes *y* (total cost) to change. This variable is also called the *cost driver* or the **independent variable**.

- *a* is the amount of cost that will be incurred regardless of activity level (*x*), or the **total fixed cost**. This term is also called the *intercept term* or *constant*.

- *b* indicates how much *y* (total cost) will change as *x* (activity) changes. In other words, *b* is the **variable cost per unit of x** and is represented by the **slope** of the line.

With the linearity assumption as a base, we can use three different methods, usually in combination, to estimate cost behavior:

- **Scattergraph**: A graph that provides a visual representation of the relationship between total cost (y) and activity level (x). Preparing a scattergraph is a useful first step in analyzing cost behavior because it helps determine the nature of the relationship and whether the linearity assumption is valid.

- **High-low method**: A simple approach that uses the two most extreme activity observations to determine the slope of the line (variable cost per unit) and the intercept (total fixed cost).

- **Least-squares regression**: A statistical technique for finding the best fitting line based on historical data. The x coefficient provides an estimate of the variable cost per unit, while the intercept or constant provides an estimate of the total fixed cost.

To illustrate each of these methods, consider the following data for our hypothetical Starbucks location:

Month	Number of Customers Served (x)	Total Overhead Cost (y)
January	9,000	$15,000
February	15,000	15,750
March	12,500	16,000
April	6,000	12,500
May	5,000	13,250
June	10,000	13,000

To estimate the relationship between the number of customers served (x) and total overhead cost (y), we will use the three linear methods to answer the following questions:

1. What does the relationship between total overhead cost (y) and number of customers served (x) look like? Can we use a straight line to approximate the relationship?

2. How much does total overhead cost (y) change in response to changes in the number of customers served (x)? In other words, what is the variable cost per customer served (slope of the line)?

3. How much of the total overhead cost (y) is independent of the number of customers served (x)? In other words, what is the total fixed cost (intercept)?

A scattergraph can answer the first question, as illustrated in the next section. In the sections that follow, we'll use the high-low method and linear regression to answer the last two questions.

SCATTERGRAPH

We begin by preparing a scattergraph, or a visual representation of the relationship between total cost and activity. A scattergraph shows total cost plotted on the vertical (y) axis and a measure of activity, or cost driver, plotted on the horizontal (x) axis. This graph can be created by manually plotting data points on graph paper or by using a computer program such as Excel. Exhibit 5–5 shows the steps for creating a scattergraph for our Starbucks example using Excel.

We can use scattergraphs to get a "feel" for the data and answer preliminary questions, such as whether the linear assumption is reasonable and whether there are unusual patterns or outliers in the data. In this example, the scattergraph shows a slightly positive relationship between total overhead cost (y) and the number of customers served (x). In general, as the number of customers increases, the total overhead cost also increases. Although the points do not fall in a perfect line, we can use a straight line to approximate, or estimate, the relationship.

EXHIBIT 5–5   Creating a Scattergraph in Excel

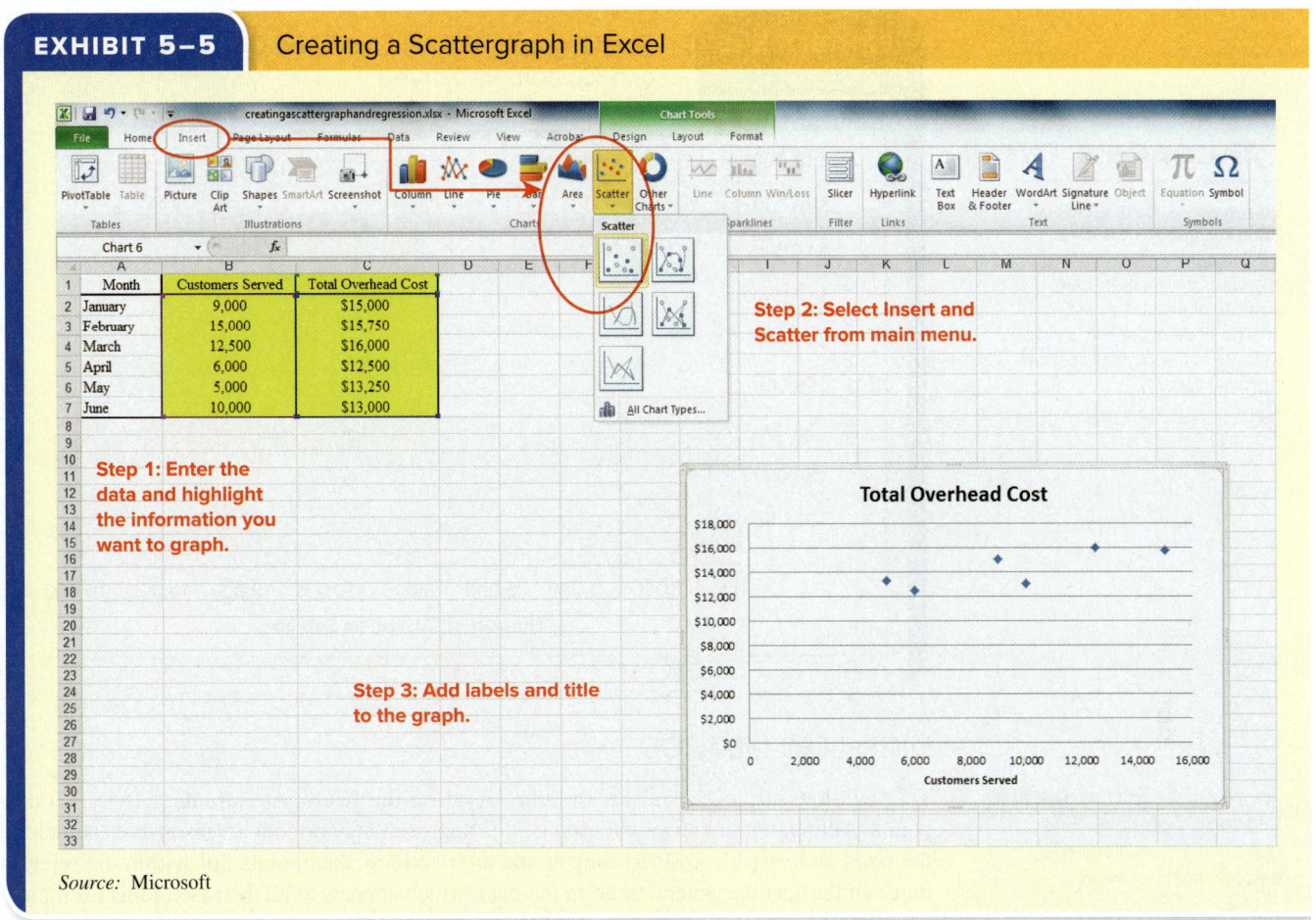

Source: Microsoft

Once a scattergraph has been created and we have confirmed that the relationship between total cost and activity is roughly linear, the next step is to fit a line through the data that will provide an estimate of total fixed cost and variable cost per unit. This is sometimes called the *visual fit method.* To illustrate, try drawing a straight line through the data in Exhibit 5–6 to represent the relationship between total overhead cost (*y*) and the number of customers served (*x*). Where does your line intercept the *y*-axis? Can you determine the slope (variable cost per customer served) of the line?

Depending on how you drew your line, it will probably intercept the *y*-axis somewhere between $10,000 and $14,000. This intercept represents your estimate of total fixed cost, or the total amount of overhead cost that will be incurred regardless of the number of customers served. If your line slopes upward, the total cost increases with the number of customers served, indicating a variable cost. The steeper the slope, the higher the variable cost per customer served, but it is difficult to determine the exact slope of the line simply by looking at the scattergraph.

As you can see, visually fitting a line in a scattergraph is subjective and inexact. The high-low method and least-squares regression will provide more precise estimates of the total fixed cost and variable cost per unit. These two methods use different mathematical formulas to estimate the slope of the line and the intercept, but how we interpret the slope and intercept remains the same regardless of the method used.

| EXHIBIT 5–6 | Scattergraph of Total Overhead Cost and Customers Served |

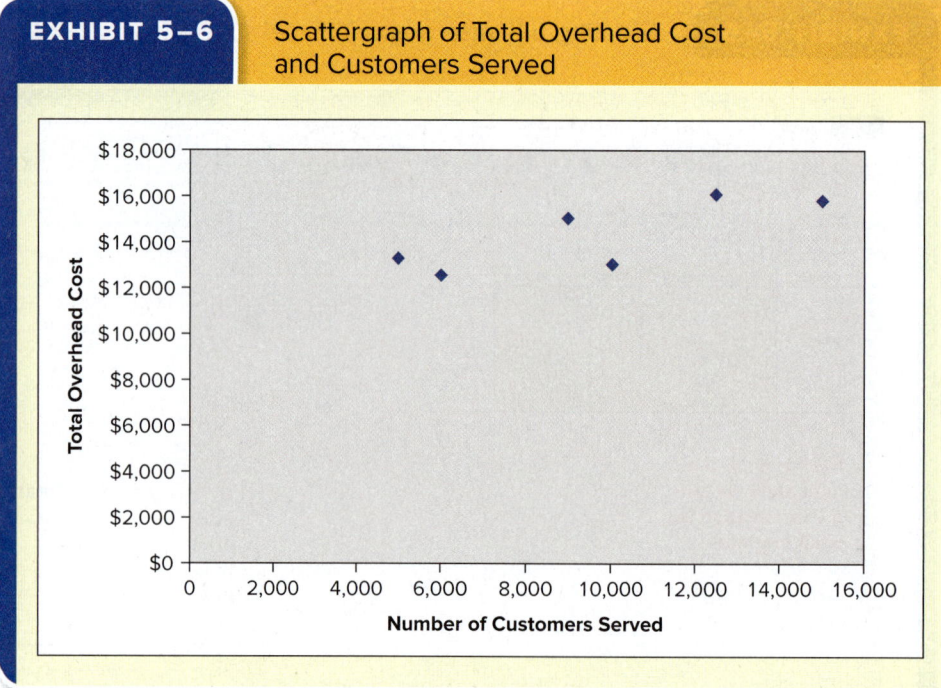

HIGH-LOW METHOD

The high-low method calculates the line based on the two most extreme activity (x) data points. Although it only uses two points, this approach may provide a reasonable estimate of the fixed and variable costs as long as the high and low data points fall within the relevant range and reflect the general trend in the data, which appears to be the case in this example.

The first step in the high-low method is to find the two most extreme activity (x) observations. The data we have been using for our Starbucks example follow:

Month		Number of Customers Served (x)	Total Overhead Cost (y)
January		9,000	$15,000
February	High x	15,000	15,750
March		12,500	16,000
April		6,000	12,500
May	Low x	5,000	13,250
June		10,000	13,000

The high-low method will use the high (February) and low (May) data points to estimate the variable cost per unit and the total fixed cost. It ignores all of the other months.

The second step is to calculate the slope of the line based on the high and low data points. You may recall from your junior high or high school algebra class that the slope of a line is calculated as "rise over run," or the change in y over the change in x. We use the same formula here to calculate how much total cost (y) changes with a corresponding change in activity level (x). The calculation gives us the variable cost per unit as shown in the following equation:

$$\text{Variable Cost per Unit} = \frac{\text{Difference in Total Cost}}{\text{Difference in Activity}} = \frac{(y_1 - y_2)}{(x_1 - x_2)}$$

Applying this formula to the Starbucks data from February and May results in the following:

$$\text{Variable Cost per Unit} = \frac{\$15,750 - \$13,250}{15,000 - 5,000} = \frac{\$2,500}{10,000} = \$0.25 \text{ per Unit}$$

This formula shows that total overhead cost increased by $2,500 when the number of customers served increased by 10,000. Thus, the slope of the line, or variable cost per unit, is $0.25 per customer served.

Now that we know the variable cost per unit (slope), the third step is to solve for total fixed cost (intercept) by plugging the variable cost information back into the linear cost equation and rearranging the equation so that only total fixed cost appears on the left side of the equal sign, as follows:

$$y = a + b \quad x$$

Total Cost = Total Fixed Cost + (Variable Cost per Unit × Activity)

Total Fixed Cost = Total Cost − (Variable Cost per Unit × Activity)

Because we now know that the variable cost is $0.25 per customer served, we can solve for total fixed cost by subtracting total variable cost from total cost at **either** the high **or** the low data point. The high and low data points for our Starbucks example follow:

Month		Number of Customers Served (x)	Total Overhead Cost (y)
February	High x	15,000	$15,750
May	Low x	5,000	13,250

First let's use the data from February to solve for the total fixed cost:

Total Overhead Cost (February) = Total Fixed Cost + Total Variable Cost (February)

$15,750 = Total Fixed Cost + ($0.25 × 15,000)

Total Fixed Cost = $15,750 − ($0.25 × 15,000)

Total Fixed Cost = $12,000

We get exactly the same result if we use May instead:

Total Overhead Cost (May) = Total Fixed Cost + Total Variable Cost (May)

$13,250 = Total Fixed Cost + ($0.25 × 5,000)

Total Fixed Cost = $13,250 − ($0.25 × 5,000)

Total Fixed Cost = $12,000

Regardless of whether we use the high (February) or low (May) data point, we get a total fixed cost of $12,000.

See Exhibit 5–7 for a visual depiction of the results of the high-low method. Notice that the line is drawn so that it goes through the most extreme (high and low) values on the horizontal (x) axis. Notice also that the line intersects the y-axis at $12,000, which is the estimated total fixed cost. Although it is difficult to determine the slope of the line from the graph, we know from the high-low formula that the variable cost (slope) is $0.25 per customer served.

Managers can use the results of the high-low method to predict total overhead cost in the future as long as they have an estimate of the number of customers to be served and assuming that estimate falls within the relevant range of activity. For example, if Starbucks expects to serve 8,000 customers in July, it would budget for $12,000 in fixed overhead cost plus variable overhead of $2,000 ($0.25 × 8,000 customers) for total overhead cost of $14,000.

The high-low method is simple to apply, but it suffers from a major (and sometimes critical) defect. It utilizes only two data points. Generally, two points are not enough to produce reliable results. Additionally, periods in which the activity is unusually low or unusually high may produce inaccurate results. A cost formula that is estimated solely using data from these unusual periods may seriously misrepresent the true cost relationship that holds during

EXHIBIT 5–7   High-Low Method Shown on the Scattergraph

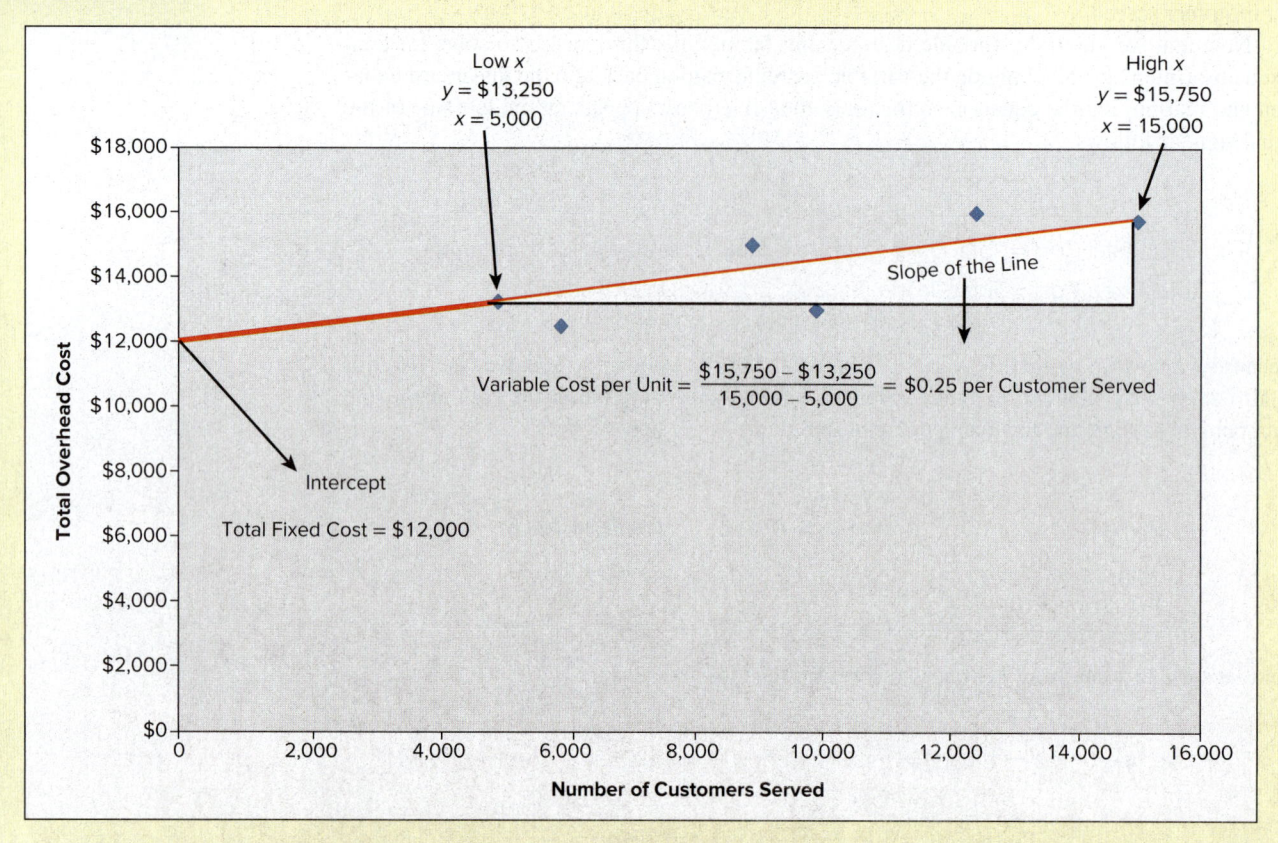

normal periods. For example, a retailer like Walmart should not base its cost analysis on its busiest shopping day of the year (the Friday after Thanksgiving) because it does not represent normal operations. Generally, managers can obtain more accurate information from other methods of cost analysis that utilize a larger number of data points. A manager who chooses to use the high-low method should do so with a full awareness of the method's limitations.

The next section illustrates the least-squares regression method, a linear approach that uses all available data to find the best fitting line. First, complete the following Self-Study Practice to make sure you understand how to estimate fixed and variable costs using the high-low method.

 How's it going?   *Self-Study Practice*

A car rental agency has collected the following information regarding the number of car rentals and the total cost of running the agency for the past four months:

Month	Number of Car Rentals	Total Cost
January	600	$41,000
February	400	32,000
March	860	55,000
April	740	56,000

Using the high-low method, determine the variable cost per rental and the total fixed cost.

After you have finished, check your answers against the solutions in the margin.

Solution to Self-Study Practice

High (March): 860 rentals $55,000
Low (February): 400 rentals $32,000

Variable Cost = ($55,000 − $32,000) ÷ (860 − 400) = $23,000 ÷ 460
= $50 per rental

Total Fixed Cost = $55,000 − ($50 × 860) = $12,000
or $32,000 − ($50 × 400) = $12,000

LEAST-SQUARES REGRESSION METHOD

Least-squares regression is a statistical technique that uses all of the available data to find the best fitting line. The best fitting line is the one that minimizes the sum of the squared errors, where error is the vertical difference between the regression line and the actual data values, as shown in Exhibit 5–8.

> **Learning Objective 5–4**
> Use least-squares regression to estimate cost behavior.

It would be cumbersome to find the regression line manually using formulas, but computer programs and statistical packages make calculating least-squares regression very easy. It takes only a few clicks of the mouse to obtain regression results, but it is critical that you understand what the results mean and how to use them for managerial decision making. One word of caution is that we generally need more than six data points to get reliable regression results. But for simplicity and comparison, we'll use the same data that we used for the high-low method.

Exhibit 5–9 shows how to calculate least-squares regression using Excel. Other computer programs and statistical calculators will produce a similar output. The key to using least-squares regression effectively is to correctly interpret the results.

Exhibit 5–10 presents regression results for our Starbucks example. Although the regression output contains a lot of additional information, we will focus our attention on the interpretation of three values: R square, the intercept (also called the constant), and the x coefficient (also called the slope of the line). Again, be aware that this analysis was based on only 6 data points. In reality we would need at least 20 data points to get reliable regression results. But we will use this data set to illustrate how to interpret the results of regression.

R square is a measure of the "goodness of fit" of the model. In a perfect world, an R square of 1 indicates a perfect fit between the data and the regression line. In reality, there is likely to be some variation around the regression line, as you can see in Exhibit 5–8. The R square value tells us how much of the variability in y (total overhead cost) is explained

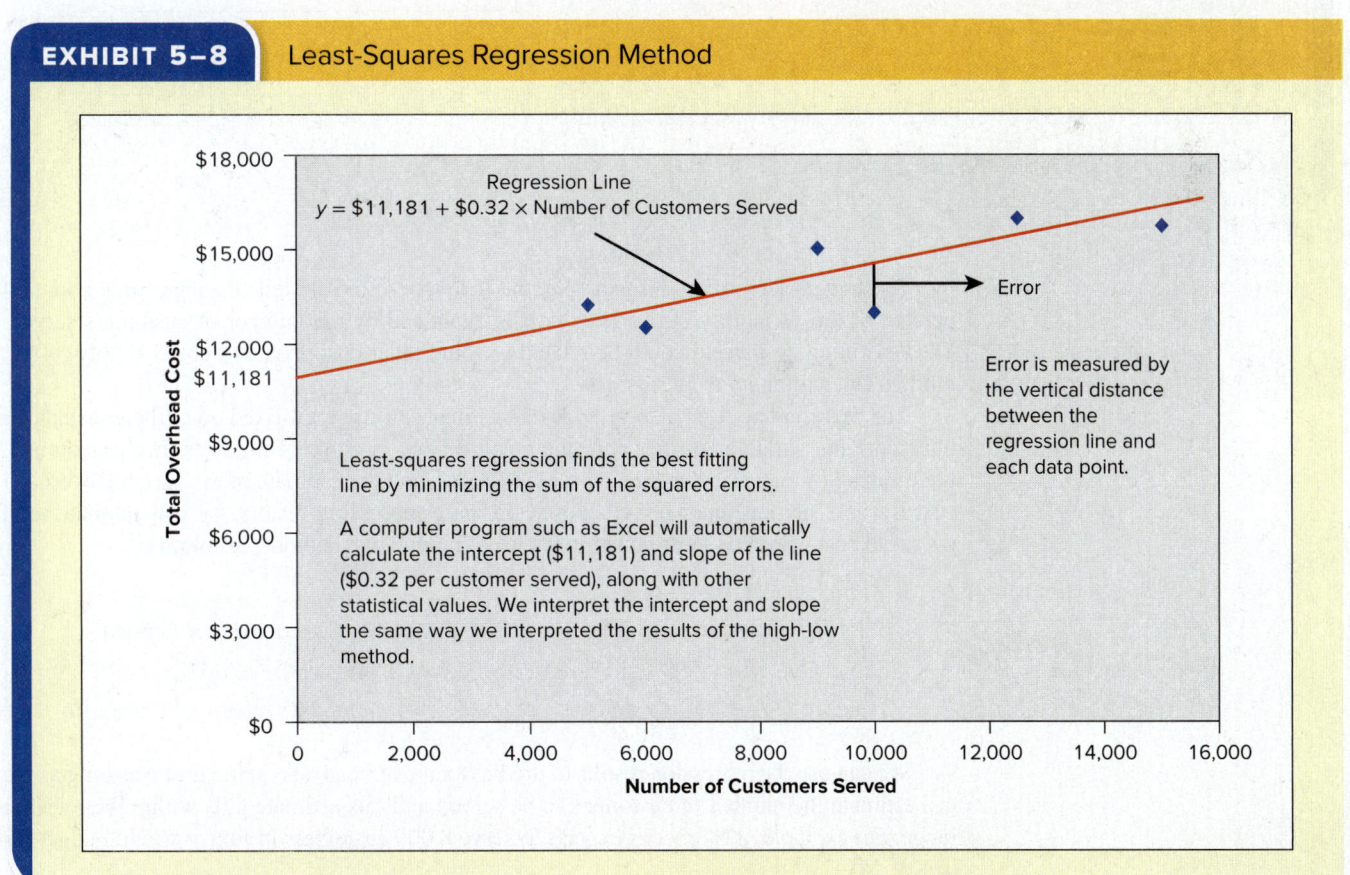

EXHIBIT 5–8   Least-Squares Regression Method

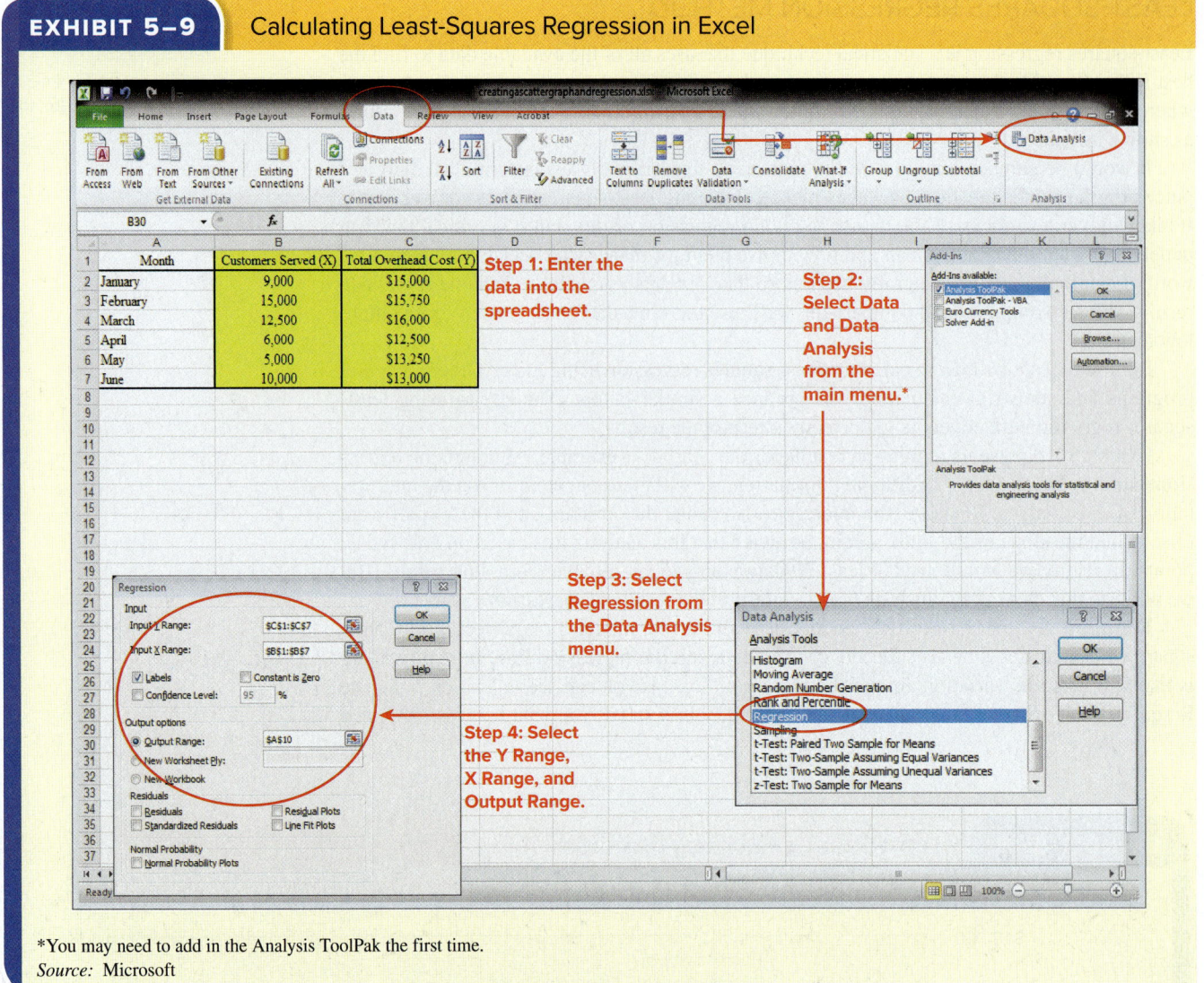

| EXHIBIT 5–9 | Calculating Least-Squares Regression in Excel |

Step 1: Enter the data into the spreadsheet.

	A	B	C
1	Month	Customers Served (X)	Total Overhead Cost (Y)
2	January	9,000	$15,000
3	February	15,000	$15,750
4	March	12,500	$16,000
5	April	6,000	$12,500
6	May	5,000	$13,250
7	June	10,000	$13,000

Step 2: Select Data and Data Analysis from the main menu.*

Step 3: Select Regression from the Data Analysis menu.

Step 4: Select the Y Range, X Range, and Output Range.

*You may need to add in the Analysis ToolPak the first time.

Source: Microsoft

by *x* (customers served). In this example, the R square of 0.6440 tells managers that about 64 percent of the variability in overhead cost is explained by the number of customers served. The remaining 36 percent could be related to some other cost driver, or could simply reflect random fluctuation in overhead costs.

The regression output also provides an estimate of the total fixed cost (the constant, or intercept) and variable cost per unit (the *x* coefficient, or slope of the line). In this example, the estimate of total fixed overhead cost is $11,181, and the estimate of the variable overhead cost is $0.32 per customer served. Based on these regression results, we can estimate total overhead cost using the same equation we used in previous methods, as follows:

> Total Overhead Cost = Total Fixed Cost + (Variable Cost per Unit × Activity)
>
> Total Overhead Cost = $11,181 + ($0.32 × Number of Customers Served)

We can use the regression results to predict total overhead cost in the future as long as we can estimate the number of customers to be served and this estimate falls within the relevant range. For example, if Starbucks expects to serve 8,000 customers in July, it would budget for

EXHIBIT 5–10 Interpreting Regression Output from Excel

R square tells you how much of the variation in *y* (Total Overhead Cost) is explained by *x* (Customers Served).

The intercept of $11,181 is the estimate of total fixed cost. The coefficient of $0.32 is the slope of the regression line, or the estimated variable cost per customer served.

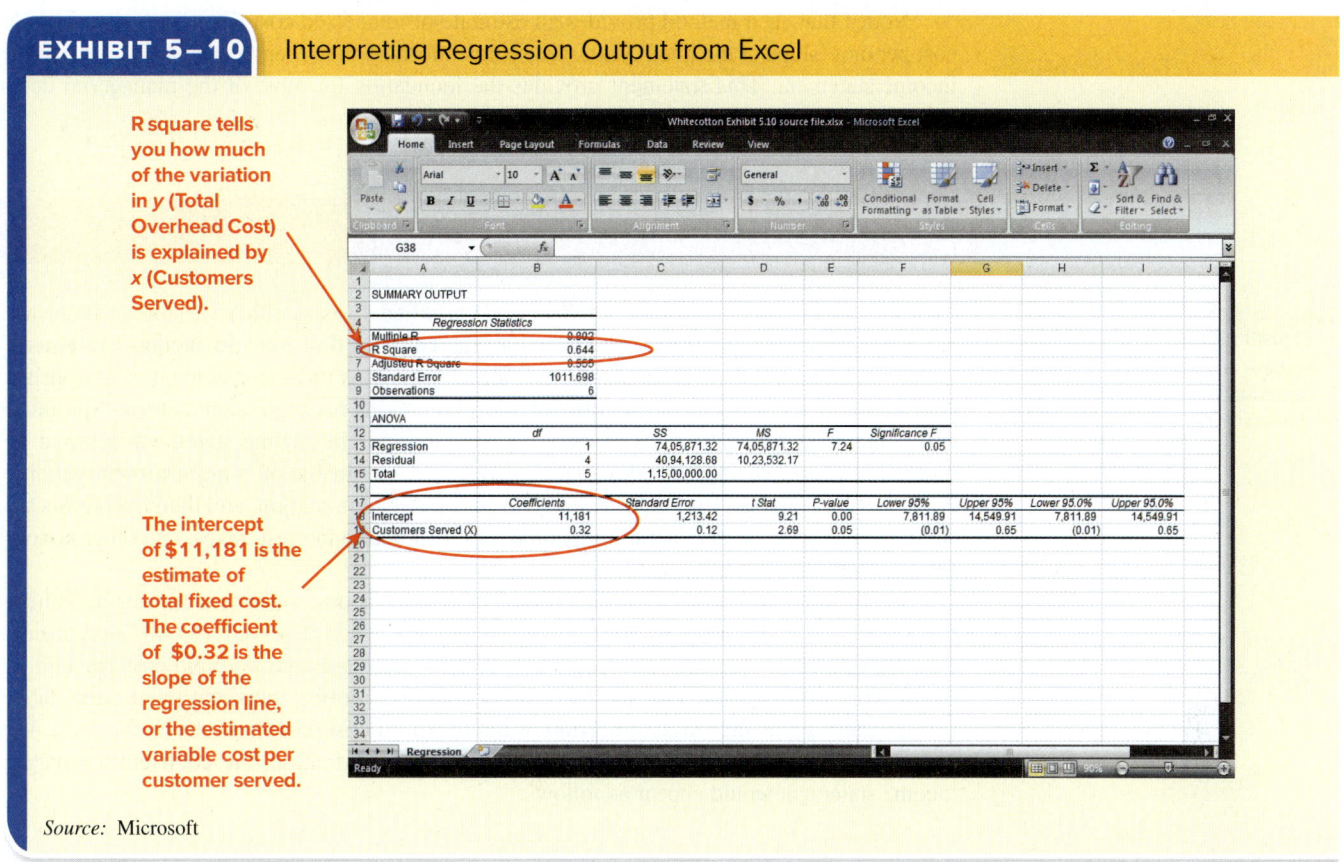

Source: Microsoft

$11,181 in fixed overhead cost plus $2,560 ($0.32 × 8,000 customers) in variable overhead costs, for estimated total overhead cost of $13,741.

SUMMARY OF LINEAR METHODS

The previous sections described three methods for estimating cost behavior. All of the methods relied on a linear approach, which assumes that the relationship between total cost (*y*) and activity (*x*) can be described using a straight line. The following table summarizes the three methods:

Method	Approach	Estimating Variable and Fixed Cost	Advantages	Limitations
Scattergraph	Use a graph to visualize the relationship between total cost (*y*) and activity (*x*)	Total Fixed Cost = Intercept Variable Cost per Unit = Slope of the Line	Simple and intuitive	Subjective and inexact
High-low method	Use the highest and lowest *x* values to fit the line	Variable cost per Unit $= \dfrac{(y_1 - y_2)}{(x_1 - x_2)}$ Total Fixed Cost = Total Cost − Total Variable Cost (based on either high or low *x*)	Simple and intuitive	Uses only two data points, which may not represent the general trend in the data
Least-squares regression	Use a statistical package to find the line that minimizes the sum of squared errors	Total Fixed Cost = Intercept Variable Cost per Unit = *x* Coefficient	Uses all data points Easy to calculate in Excel	Requires more data and assumptions Proper interpretation of results is critical

Notice that each method provides an estimate of total fixed cost (intercept) and variable cost per unit (slope of the line). Next, we use this information to prepare a contribution margin income statement. This statement provides the foundation for most of the managerial decisions we will evaluate in future chapters.

Contribution Margin Approach

Now that we have analyzed cost behavior and classified costs as either variable or fixed, we can prepare a new type of income statement, the **contribution margin income statement**. Unlike an income statement intended for external users, this income statement is appropriate only for internal management use. Instead of differentiating between manufacturing (product) and nonmanufacturing (period) costs, a contribution margin income statement is based on cost behavior, or whether cost is variable or fixed. In a contribution margin format, variable costs are first deducted from sales revenue to get contribution margin, and then fixed costs are subtracted to arrive at net operating income, or profit before interest, taxes, and other nonoperating costs have been deducted.

To illustrate, let's construct a contribution margin income statement for our hypothetical Starbucks Coffee shop for the month of February when it served 15,000 cups of coffee. We assume an average sales price of $2.50 per unit and total variable cost per unit of $1.00. The $1.00 variable cost includes direct materials (coffee, cups, etc.) and direct labor (server wages) plus the variable portion of the overhead cost (supplies, electricity, etc.). We assume that total fixed costs are $12,000. Using this information, the contribution margin income statement would appear as follows:

 **COACH'S TIP**

Notice that fixed costs are stated on a total basis rather than per unit or as a percentage of sales because those measures will change as the sales volume changes. When you see fixed cost stated on a per-unit basis, you should immediately calculate total fixed cost because that is the number that is truly fixed.

STARBUCKS COFFEE
Contribution Margin Income Statement
For the Month of February
15,000 Units Sold

	Total	Per Unit	Percent of Sales
Sales revenue	$37,500	$2.50	100%
Less: Variable costs	15,000	1.00	40
Contribution margin	22,500	$1.50	60%
Less: Fixed costs	12,000		
Net operating income	$10,500		

Contribution margin is the difference between sales revenue and variable costs:

Contribution Margin = Sales Revenue − Variable Costs

The contribution margin represents the amount of profit remaining after only variable costs have been deducated from sales revenue. Note that this is not the same as gross profit margin, which is the profit remaining after all manufacturing costs have been taken into account.

The contribution margin goes first to cover fixed costs, and whatever is left is net operating income. In this example, the total contribution margin earned on 15,000 units sold is $22,500 ($37,500 − $15,000). When fixed costs of $12,000 are subtracted, it leaves net operating income is $10,500.

The contribution margin income statement is not used for external reporting (GAAP). Rather, it provides a tool for managers to use for "what-if" analysis or to analyze what will happen to profit if something changes. To do so, managers focus on either the unit contribution margin or the contribution margin as a percentage of sales.

UNIT CONTRIBUTION MARGIN

The **unit contribution margin** is the difference between the unit sales price ($2.50) and unit variable costs ($1.00). It tells us how much each additional unit sold contributes to profit. Because fixed costs do not change with volume (at least within the relevant range), each additional unit sold contributes $1.50 to profit.

What would happen if Starbucks sold 16,000 cups of coffee instead of 15,000? As long as this is within the relevant range of operations (i.e., fixed costs will not increase), we can quickly determine that an extra 1,000 units will add $1,500 (1,000 × $1.50) in net operating income. We can verify this answer by creating a new contribution margin income statement based on 16,000 units, as follows:

STARBUCKS COFFEE
Contribution Margin Income Statement
For the Month of March
16,000 Units Sold

	Total	Per Unit	Percent of Sales
Sales revenue	$40,000	$2.50	100%
Less: Variable costs	16,000	1.00	40
Contribution margin	24,000	$1.50	60%
Less: Fixed costs	12,000		
Net operating income	$12,000		

> **COACH'S TIP**
>
> Notice that net operating income is $12,000 for 16,000 units, but only $10,500 for 15,000 units, or a difference of $1,500. In this case, the extra 1,000 units generated an additional $1,500 in net operating profit (1,000 extra units × $1.50 = $1,500).

In the next chapter, we use the unit contribution margin in a number of scenarios involving the relationship between cost, volume, and profit.

CONTRIBUTION MARGIN RATIO

The contribution margin can also be stated as a ratio or percentage of sales. The **contribution margin ratio** is calculated as follows:

$$\text{Contribution Margin Ratio} = \frac{\text{Unit Contribution Margin}}{\text{Unit Sales Price}} = \frac{\$1.50}{\$2.50} = 60\%$$

The contribution margin ratio tells managers how much contribution margin is generated by every dollar of sales. In this case, every $1.00 of sales generates $0.60 in contribution margin. Because total fixed costs do not change with changes in sales volume (at least within the relevant range), any change in contribution margin directly impacts profit.

As an example, assume the manager of our Starbucks Coffee shop wants to spend an extra $2,000 each month for local advertising. She believes the additional exposure will increase monthly sales revenue by $5,000. Should she do it?

Because we know that the contribution margin ratio is 60 percent, we can quickly determine that a $5,000 increase in sales revenue will increase contribution margin by $3,000 ($5,000 × 60%). Of course, fixed costs would go up by $2,000 due to the additional advertising expense. The net effect on profit would be a $1,000 increase as follows:

Increased sales		$5,000
Less: Increased variable costs		2,000
Increased contribution margin	($5,000 × 60%)	3,000
Less: Increased fixed costs		2,000
Increased net operating income		$1,000

In the next chapter, we use both the unit contribution margin and contribution margin ratio to evaluate how changes in product prices, sales volume, or costs affect contribution margin and thus profit. Take a moment to complete the following Self-Study Practice to make sure you understand how to prepare a contribution margin income statement.

 How's it going?   Self-Study Practice

In the same month that a company sold 750 units for $80 each, it reported total variable costs of $45,000 and total fixed costs of $10,000.

Calculate the following:

1. Total contribution margin.

2. Contribution margin per unit.

3. Contribution margin ratio.

4. Net operating income (loss).

After you have finished, check your answers against the solutions in the margin.

Solution to Self-Study Practice

1. (750 × $80) − $45,000 = $15,000
2. $15,000 ÷ 750 = $20
3. $20 ÷ $80 = 25%
4. $15,000 − $10,000 = $5,000

SUPPLEMENT 5A   VARIABLE VERSUS FULL ABSORPTION COSTING

This supplement describes the differences between an accounting system designed to meet external reporting requirements (GAAP) versus a system that is designed strictly for internal decision making.

As explained in earlier chapters, GAAP requires that all manufacturing costs be treated as product costs. Product costs are accumulated in various inventory accounts and reported on the balance sheet until the product is sold. When the product is sold, the full cost of manufacturing the product is reported as cost of goods sold. This external reporting approach is sometimes called **full absorption costing** because product costs reflect the full cost of manufacturing. Any nonmanufacturing costs are expensed during the period incurred rather than being assigned to the product. Remember that period expenses are never reported as inventory; instead, they are always reported on the income statement during the period incurred.

Although full absorption costing is required for external reporting, this method is not always the most useful for internal management decision making. For internal purposes, managers often need to know how costs will change as a result of a specific decision, such as introducing a new product, selling more units, or investing in automated equipment. To understand how costs will change, they need to know which costs are fixed and which are variable. This approach to costing is called **variable costing** because the key distinction is whether a particular cost is variable or fixed, not whether it relates to manufacturing or nonmanufacturing activities. The next two chapters will illustrate how managers can use variable costing to determine the number of units needed to break even, analyze how changing prices and costs will affect profitability, and make a variety of other important decisions. It's important to note that variable costing is used only for internal decision making and does not meet GAAP reporting requirements.

Exhibit 5A–1 provides a summary of the key differences between full absorption costing and variable costing. Because the two systems are designed for different purposes, the reports will contain different information, the meaning and interpretation of which will also be different.

When accountants prepare an external income statement using full absorption costing, they focus on gross margin, which is the difference between sales revenue and cost of goods sold. You may recall from a previous chapter that we computed Cost of Goods Sold by taking the beginning balance of Finished Goods Inventory and adding Cost of Goods Manufactured, then subtracting the ending balance of Finished Goods Inventory. In this chapter, we will use the following simple formula for computing Cost of Goods Sold:

$$\text{Cost of Goods Sold} = \text{Full Manufacturing Cost per Unit} \times \text{Units Sold}$$

Two things are important to notice here. First, cost of goods sold is based on the full manufacturing cost per unit. In other words, it must include ALL manufacturing costs, regardless of whether they are variable or fixed. Second, it is based on the number of units sold, not the number of units produced. The full manufacturing cost of units produced but not sold would be included as inventory (an asset) on the balance sheet. Nonmanufacturing (period) expenses are subtracted from gross margin to arrive at net operating income.

EXHIBIT 5A–1 Calculation and Uses of Full Absorption Costing and Variable Costing

	Full Absorption Costing	Variable Costing
Purpose	External financial reporting (GAAP)	Internal decision making
Cost classification	Manufacturing versus nonmanufacturing costs	Variable versus fixed costs
Income statement formulas	Sales	Sales
	Less: Cost of goods sold	Less: Variable costs
	Gross margin	**Contribution margin**
	Less: Nonmanufacturing expenses	Less: Fixed expenses
	Net operating income	Net operating income
Treatment of fixed manufacturing overhead	Divided between cost of goods sold and ending inventory	Expensed during the period incurred

COACH'S TIP

Notice that gross margin and contribution margin are not the same. **Contribution margin** is the difference between sales revenue and variable costs; it is used only for internal reporting. **Gross margin** is the difference between sales revenue and the cost of goods sold; it appears on external financial statements.

When accountants prepare a variable costing income statement for internal decision making, they first compute contribution margin, which is the difference between sales revenue and variable costs. Fixed costs are then deducted from contribution margin to arrive at net operating income. No distinction is made between manufacturing or nonmanufacturing costs.

Because full absorption costing and variable costing use different rules for reporting costs, they can sometimes lead to different bottom line or profit results for companies that create a physical product that can be stored as inventory. Under full absorption costing, all product or manufacturing costs must be distributed between inventory (the balance sheet) and cost of goods sold (the income statement). Changing inventory levels can affect how these manufacturing costs are distributed and thus the bottom line. This is not an issue for service companies because only product or manufacturing costs can be stored as inventory.

The next section illustrates the difference between full absorption costing and variable costing for a manufacturing company and shows how to reconcile the difference in profit between the two methods. It is important for managers to understand why these two methods can produce different results because they are likely to encounter both methods in practice. Even if a manager prefers to use variable costing for internal purposes, GAAP currently requires the use of full absorption costing for external reporting.

Reconciling Variable and Full Absorption Costing

In terms of the effect on profits, variable costing and full absorption costing have one critical difference: the treatment of fixed manufacturing overhead. Under full absorption costing, all manufacturing costs, including fixed manufacturing overhead, are included in Cost of Goods Sold, but only for the units sold. The full manufacturing cost of units not sold would be reported as inventory on the balance. Variable costing deducts all fixed costs, including fixed manufacturing overhead, during the period incurred. The two methods also report variable nonmanufacturing costs such as sales commissions or shipping expenses in different sections of the income statement, but it does not cause a difference in bottom line profit because the same amount is deducted under both methods.

To see how these difference can impact profits, consider a company that produces and sells only one product. Assume this is the company's first month of operation, so it had no inventory on hand at the beginning of the month. Costs and production information follow.

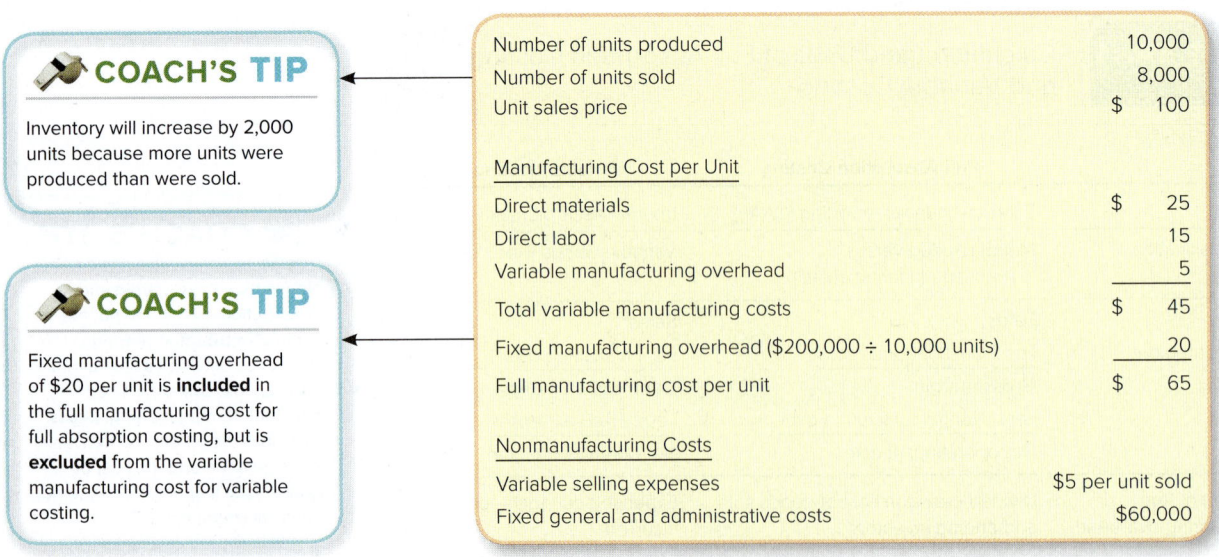

COACH'S TIP

Inventory will increase by 2,000 units because more units were produced than were sold.

COACH'S TIP

Fixed manufacturing overhead of $20 per unit is **included** in the full manufacturing cost for full absorption costing, but is **excluded** from the variable manufacturing cost for variable costing.

Number of units produced	10,000
Number of units sold	8,000
Unit sales price	$ 100
Manufacturing Cost per Unit	
Direct materials	$ 25
Direct labor	15
Variable manufacturing overhead	5
Total variable manufacturing costs	$ 45
Fixed manufacturing overhead ($200,000 ÷ 10,000 units)	20
Full manufacturing cost per unit	$ 65
Nonmanufacturing Costs	
Variable selling expenses	$5 per unit sold
Fixed general and administrative costs	$60,000

The following tables show the computation of net operating income under each method:

FULL ABSORPTION COSTING Income Statement Month 1	
Sales revenue (8,000 units × $100)	$800,000
Less: Cost of goods sold	
Units sold × Full manufacturing cost per unit	
(8,000 units × $65)	520,000
Gross margin	$280,000
Less: Selling expenses (8,000 units × $5)	40,000
Less: General and administrative expenses	60,000
Net operating income	$180,000

VARIABLE COSTING Income Statement Month 1	
Sales revenue (8,000 units × $100)	$800,000
Less: Variable cost of units sold	
Units sold × Variable cost per unit	
8,000 units × ($45 + $5)	400,000
Contribution margin	$400,000
Less: Fixed manufacturing costs	200,000
Less: General and administrative expenses	60,000
Net operating income	$140,000

$40,000 difference in profit

The $40,000 difference in profit is due to the different treatment of fixed manufacturing overhead under the two costing methods. Full absorption costing requires that all manufacturing costs (including fixed manufacturing overhead) be spread over the number of units produced, but only a portion of the total manufacturing cost is reported as cost of goods sold. The remainder is reported as inventory (an asset) on the balance sheet.

In this example, the $200,000 fixed manufacturing overhead cost is spread over the 10,000 units produced for a fixed overhead rate of $20 per unit. This cost is then divided between the 8,000 units sold and the 2,000 units remaining in ending inventory. Because 2,000 units are not yet sold, full absorption costing reports $40,000 of the $200,000 in fixed manufacturing overhead as an asset on the balance sheet rather than as an expense on the income statement. This cost will eventually be expensed, but not until the units are sold.

In contrast, variable costing deducts the entire $200,000 in fixed manufacturing overhead as an expense during the period incurred. The rationale is that the fixed cost will be incurred regardless of how many units are produced and sold. Thus, variable costing assigns $20 less to each of the 2,000 units in ending inventory, or a total of $40,000. This difference in the treatment of fixed manufacturing overhead explains the $40,000 difference in profit between the two methods.

The difference in profit between full absorption costing and variable costing is directly related to the fixed manufacturing overhead cost per unit and the change in inventory as shown in the following formula:

Difference in Variable Costing and Full Absorption Profit	=	Change in Ending Inventory (Units Produced − Units Sold)	×	Fixed Manufacturing Overhead per Unit Produced
$40,000	=	(10,000 − 8,000)	×	$20

As you can see from this formula, it is a change in inventory that creates a difference in full absorption and variable costing profit. If there is no change in inventory, variable costing and full absorption costing will produce the same net operating income. For example, if the company produces 10,000 units and sells 10,000 units in month 2, net operating income under full absorption costing and variable costing would be computed as follows:

FULL ABSORPTION COSTING	
Income Statement	
Month 2	
Sales revenue (10,000 units × $100)	$1,000,000
Less: Cost of goods sold	
(10,000 units × $65)	650,000
Gross margin	$350,000
Less: Selling expenses (10,000 units × $5)	50,000
Less: General and administrative expenses	60,000
Net operating income	$240,000

VARIABLE COSTING	
Income Statement	
Month 2	
Sales revenue (10,000 units × $100)	$1,000,000
Less: Variable cost of units sold	
Units sold × Variable cost per unit	
10,000 units × ($45 + $5)	500,000
Contribution margin	$500,000
Less: Fixed manufacturing costs	200,000
Less: General and administrative expenses	60,000
Net operating income	$240,000

No difference in profit

In this case, both full absorption and variable costing yield net operating income of $240,000. Net operating income is higher in month 2 than it was in month 1 because more units were sold, but there is no difference in operating profit between the two methods.

Finally, consider the case in which production is less than sales, or inventory is reduced. In month 3, assume that 10,000 units were produced and 12,000 units were sold. The additional 2,000 units sold were from the inventory created in month 1. Net operating income under full absorption and variable costing would be computed as follows:

FULL ABSORPTION COSTING	
Income Statement	
Month 3	
Sales revenue (12,000 units × $100)	$1,200,000
Less: Cost of goods sold	
Units sold × Full manufacturing cost per unit	
(12,000 units × $65)	780,000
Gross margin	$420,000
Less: Selling expenses (12,000 units × $5)	60,000
Less: General and administrative expenses	60,000
Net operating income	$300,000

VARIABLE COSTING	
Income Statement	
Month 3	
Sales revenue (12,000 units × $100)	$1,200,000
Less: Variable cost of units sold	
Units sold × Variable cost per unit	
12,000 units × ($45 + $5)	600,000
Contribution margin	$600,000
Less: Fixed manufacturing costs	200,000
Less: General and administrative expenses	60,000
Net operating income	$340,000

$40,000 difference in profit

In this case net operating income is higher with variable costing ($340,000) than with full absorption costing ($300,000). The $40,000 difference in profit is due to the 2,000 unit decrease in inventory. This is simply a reversal of the extra $40,000 that full absorption costing reported in month 1 by deferring a portion of the fixed manufacturing overhead into inventory (an asset). When the inventory is finally sold, it will be reported at a higher cost under full absorption costing than under variable costing due to the extra $20 in fixed manufacturing overhead per unit.

This example illustrates a major limitation of full absorption costing. Full absorption costing sometimes provides managers with an incentive to overproduce, or produce more units than it sells. Although this strategy can boost short-term profit under full absorption costing, the effect will reverse if/when the inventory is finally sold. In addition, the resulting inventory is very costly to maintain in terms of storage, handling, insurance, and obsolescence.

In this hypothetical example, the inventory was built up and then depleted within a three-month period. In reality, managers may be reluctant to drive down inventory because of the negative effect it will have on full absorption (GAAP) profit. If managers continue to build inventory period after period, the inventory costs will continue to rise, further compounding the problem. These issues are avoided under variable costing because profit is a strict function of sales volume rather than production volume.

REVIEW THE CHAPTER

DEMONSTRATION CASE

The manager of a local bakery and café is trying to determine how the store's monthly costs vary with the number of customers served. The manager knows that direct materials and direct labor costs tend to be higher when the bakery has more customers but is not sure about the overhead, or indirect, costs of running the business.

The following table shows the number of customers and total overhead cost for the past 12 months:

Month	Number of Customers (x)	Total Overhead Cost (y)
January	1,200	$10,500
February	1,150	8,225
March	1,550	11,551
April	1,634	11,750
May	1,780	12,225
June	1,000	10,000
July	1,600	9,835
August	1,350	10,555
September	1,825	14,000
October	1,850	11,444
November	2,000	12,000
December	1,725	10,998

Required:

1. Give examples of overhead costs for a bakery café that would behave as a:
   a. Variable cost.
   b. Fixed cost.
   c. Step cost.
   d. Mixed cost.

2. Prepare a scattergraph to illustrate the relationship between total overhead cost (y) and number of customers (x). What does this scattergraph tell you about the relationship between total overhead and the number of customers served?

3. Use the high-low method to calculate the variable overhead cost per customer and total fixed overhead cost. Use the results to estimate total overhead for 1,500 customers.

4. Use least-squares regression to estimate the variable overhead cost per customer and total fixed overhead cost. Round the intercept (total fixed cost) and slope (variable cost per unit) estimates to two decimal places. Use the regression results to estimate the total amount of overhead for 1,500 customers.

5. Compare the estimate of variable overhead cost per unit and total fixed overhead costs between the high-low and regression methods. If the methods provide different estimates, explain why.

Suggested Solution

1. Examples of overhead costs for a bakery and café:

   a. Variable costs: paper supplies, indirect materials, beverages
   b. Fixed costs: rent, insurance, taxes
   c. Step costs: supervisor salaries, baking equipment
   d. Mixed costs: utilities, janitorial service, equipment maintenance

2. The relationship between total overhead cost and number of customers served appears to be positive and fairly linear. Total overhead cost appears to be a mixed cost because it has a fixed component (intercept) and a positive slope (variable cost).

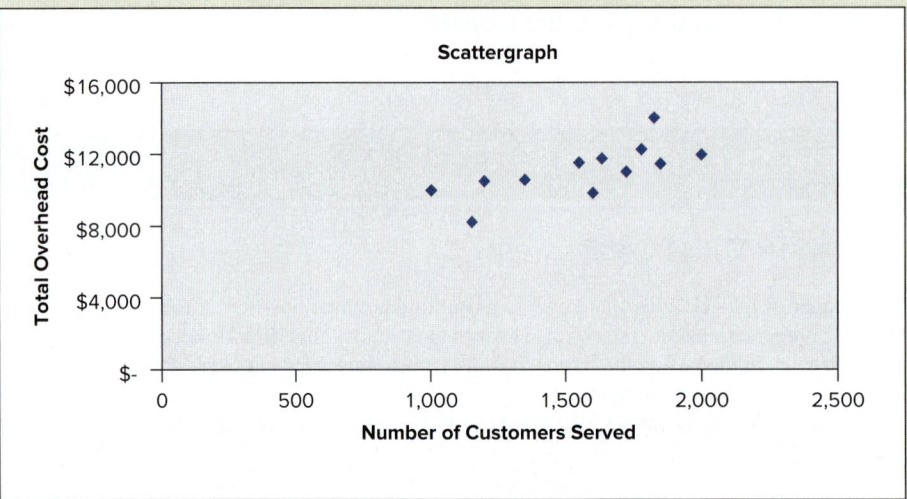

3. The high-low method should be based on the high and low x (number of customers):

Month	Number of Customers (x)	Total Overhead Cost (y)
November (high)	2,000	$12,000
June (low)	1,000	$10,000
Difference	1,000	$ 2,000

   Variable Overhead Cost per Unit = $2,000 ÷ 1,000 = $2 per Customer

   Fixed Overhead Cost (based on June) = $10,000 − (1,000 × $2) = $8,000

   Fixed Overhead Cost (based on November) = $12,000 − (2,000 × $2) = $8,000
   Estimated Total Overhead for 1,500 Customers = $8,000 + ($2 × 1,500) = $11,000

4. Least-squares regression results:

SUMMARY OUTPUT	
Regression Statistics	
Multiple R	0.72331837
R Square	0.523189464
Adjusted R Square	0.475508411
Standard Error	1046.579751
Observations	12
ANOVA	
	df
Regression	1
Residual	10
Total	11
	Coefficients
Intercept	$5,915.80
Number of Customers	$3.33

Estimated Total Overhead for 1,500 Customers = $5,915.80 + ($3.33 × 1,500) = $10,910.80

5. Comparison of high-low and regression:

Method	Variable Overhead Cost per Customer	Total Fixed Overhead Cost
High-low	$2.00	$8,000.00
Regression	$3.33	$5,915.80

   The high-low method provides a higher estimate of total fixed cost (intercept) and a lower estimate of the variable cost per unit (slope of the line) compared to the regression results. The total fixed cost (intercept) is $8,000 for high-low compared to $5,915.80 for regression. The high-low line is also flatter (variable cost = $2.00) than the regression line based on all of the available data (variable cost = $3.33). The two methods provide different results because the high-low method is based on only two data points, while regression uses all of the data points to find the best fitting line.

CHAPTER SUMMARY

Identify costs as variable, fixed, step, or mixed. p. 211   LO 5–1

- Variable costs increase in total in direct proportion to increases in activity level.
- Fixed costs remain constant in total regardless of changes in activity level.
- Step costs increase in a steplike fashion when a capacity constraint is reached.
- Mixed costs contain a fixed component plus a variable component that changes with activity level.

Prepare a scattergraph to depict the relationship between total cost and activity. p. 216   LO 5–2

- A scattergraph provides a visual representation of the relationship between total cost and activity.
- A scattergraph is created by plotting activity level on the horizontal (x) axis and total cost on the vertical (y) axis.
- If the scattergraph suggests that the relationship between total cost and activity is roughly linear, a straight line can be used to approximate that relationship.
- The slope of the line represents the variable cost per unit of activity.
- The intercept of the line represents the total fixed cost.

Use the high-low method to estimate cost behavior. p. 218   LO 5–3

- The high-low method is one of three linear methods that can be used to estimate the relationship between total cost and activity. The high-low method steps are to
  1. Identify the two data points that represent the highest and lowest activity (x) levels.
  2. Calculate the variable cost per unit by dividing the change in total cost across the high and low points by the change in activity level across the high and low points.
  3. Calculate the total fixed cost by subtracting the total variable cost from the total cost at either the high or low point.

Use least-squares regression to estimate cost behavior. p. 221   LO 5–4

- Least-squares regression uses all available data to find the best fitting line.
- The best fitting line is the one that minimizes the sum of squared errors, or the squared vertical distance between the data points and the regression line.
- The regression output provides an estimate of total fixed cost (intercept) and the variable cost per unit (x coefficient or slope of the line).
- Although least-squares regression is easily computed using a computer program such as Excel, properly interpreting the information is critical for managerial use.

LO 5–5   Prepare and interpret a contribution margin income statement. p. 224

- Contribution margin is the difference between sales revenue and variable costs. The contribution margin can be expressed in total, per unit, or as a percentage or ratio of sales.

- The unit contribution margin, which is the difference between a unit's selling price and its variable cost, indicates how profit will change as a result of selling one more or one less unit.

- The contribution margin ratio is computed by dividing the unit contribution margin by the unit selling price or by dividing the total contribution margin by total sales revenue. The contribution margin ratio shows how much a given change in sales revenue will affect the contribution margin and net operating income.

LO 5-S1   Compare variable costing to full absorption costing. p. 226

- Full absorption costing is the accounting method used for external reporting (GAAP). It requires that all manufacturing costs be treated as a product cost and included as inventory until the product is sold. Nonmanufacturing costs are expensed in full during the period incurred.

- Variable costing is used only for internal decision making. This method is based on cost behavior, or whether costs are variable or fixed, rather than whether they are related to manufacturing or nonmanufacturing activities.

- Profit will differ under full absorption costing versus variable costing when inventory levels change. This difference can be explained by the amount of fixed manufacturing overhead that is included in inventory under full absorption costing but expensed in full under variable costing.

- When inventory levels increase, full absorption costing will result in a higher reported profit than variable costing. When inventory levels decrease, variable costing will result in a higher reported profit than full absorption costing. If inventory remains steady, the two methods should provide the same results.

KEY TERMS

Committed Fixed Costs p.212

Contribution Margin p.224

Contribution Margin Income Statement p.224

Contribution Margin Ratio p.226

Cost Behavior p.211

Dependent Variable p.215

Discretionary Fixed Costs p.212

Full Absorption Costing p.227

High-Low Method p.216

Independent Variable p.215

Least-Squares Regression p.216

Linearity Assumption p.215

Mixed Costs p.213

R Square p.221

Relevant Range p.211

Scattergraph p.216

Step Costs p.213

Step-Fixed Cost p.213

Step-Variable Cost p.213

Unit Contribution Margin p.225

Variable Costing p.227

PRACTICE MATERIAL

QUESTIONS

1. Define each of the following terms: variable cost, fixed cost, step cost, and mixed cost. Give an example of each.

2. Explain what happens to the following when activity level decreases:

    a. Total fixed cost.
    b. Total variable cost.
    c. Total mixed cost.
    d. Fixed cost per unit.
    e. Variable cost per unit.
    f. Mixed cost per unit.

3. Explain the difference between discretionary and common fixed costs. Give an example of each.

4. What is the relevant range and why is it important?

5. The formula for estimating cost behavior is $y = a + bx$. Explain what each term represents.

6. Why is a scattergraph useful?

7. Describe the three methods used to estimate cost behavior. What are the strengths and weaknesses of each method? Will these methods always yield exactly the same results?

8. What does the R square value measure?

9. Why is a contribution margin income statement more useful to managerial decision makers than the income statement intended for external users?

10. Explain how to calculate total contribution margin, contribution margin per unit, and contribution margin ratio. What is the meaning of each?

11. When activity level increases, explain what happens to:

   a. Contribution margin per unit.
   b. Contribution margin ratio.
   c. Total contribution margin.
   d. Total fixed cost.
   e. Profit.

12. Explain the difference between absorption costing and variable costing. Why do internal users need variable costing information?

13. What is the critical item that is treated differently in full absorption versus variable costing? Explain how each method treats it.

14. When will variable costing show the same profit as full absorption costing?

15. How does profit change under full absorption costing versus variable costing due to an increase in finished goods inventory? Due to a decrease in finished goods inventory?

MULTIPLE CHOICE

1. Which of the following increases when activity level increases?

   a. Total variable cost.
   b. Total fixed cost.
   c. Total mixed cost.
   d. Both a and c.

2. Which of the following is not a method used to estimate cost behavior?

   a. Regression analysis.
   b. Break-even analysis.
   c. High-low method.
   d. Scattergraph.

3. Which approach to estimating cost behavior is most helpful in identifying data outliers?

   a. Least-squares regression.
   b. High-low method.
   c. Contribution margin income statement.
   d. Scattergraph.

4. Consider the following information for a local concession stand's first four weeks of operation:

Week	Number of Drinks Served	Total Cost
1	1,000	$2,500
2	2,000	3,250
3	1,750	3,000
4	2,250	3,200

Using the high-low method, what is the equation for total operating cost for this concession stand?

   a. Total Cost = $1,750 + ($0.75 × Number of drinks served).
   b. Total Cost = $1,000 + ($1.75 × Number of drinks served).
   c. Total Cost = $1,940 + ($0.56 × Number of drinks served).
   d. Total Cost = $1,750 + ($0.56 × Number of drinks served).

5. Bombay Co. sells handmade rugs. Its variable cost per rug is $30, and each rug sells for $50. What are Bombay's contribution margin per unit and contribution margin ratio?

   a. $20 and 40 percent.
   b. $30 and 60 percent.
   c. $20 and 60 percent.
   d. $30 and 40 percent.

6. Suppose you are given the following results from a least-squares regression performed on a local coffee shop's weekly cost data:

	Coefficients
Intercept	$836.07
x Variable 1 (customers served)	1.69

Which of the following statements is true?

   a. Total weekly variable cost is $836.07.
   b. The coffee shop incurs $1.69 in variable costs for each customer served.
   c. Total weekly fixed costs are $836.07.
   d. Both b and c are true.
   e. None of the above is true.

7. Total contribution margin is

   a. The difference between total variable cost and total fixed cost.
   b. The difference between total sales revenue and total cost of goods sold.
   c. The difference between total sales revenue and total fixed cost.
   d. The difference between total sales revenue and total variable cost.
   e. None of the above is true.

8. Last year, Ritter Company sold 5,000 bird feeders for $20 each. Total fixed costs were $42,000, and Ritter's net operating income was $30,000. What was its total variable cost last year?

   a. $28,000.
   b. $58,000.
   c. $70,000.
   d. Cannot be determined.

9. Which of the following would be subtracted from total sales revenue when calculating contribution margin?

   a. Factory machinery depreciation.
   b. Direct materials used.
   c. Factory supervisor's salary.
   d. Office machinery depreciation.

10. Hathaway Corp. manufactures garden hoses. Last month, its ending inventory level increased. If we compare the company's results under absorption costing versus variable costing,

    a. Both would show the same amount of profit.
    b. Variable costing would show more profit.
    c. Absorption costing would show more profit.
    d. Effect on profit cannot be determined.

 **Find More Learning Solutions on Connect.**

MINI-EXERCISES

LO 5–1   **M5–1 Identifying Cost Behavior**

Heather Oak is trying to prepare a personal budget and has identified the following list of monthly costs. Identify each cost as fixed, variable, or mixed. Indicate a possible cost driver for any variable or mixed cost.

1. Rent.
2. Utilities.
3. Car payment.
4. Cell phone bill.
5. Gasoline.
6. Cable bill.
7. Groceries.
8. Dining out.

LO 5–1   **M5–2 Identifying Cost Behavior**

Shannon's Kettle Corn is a small refreshment stand located near a football stadium. Its fixed expenses total $400 per week and the variable cost per bag of popcorn is $0.50. Complete the table for the various activity levels for one week.

	Number of Bags of Popcorn		
	500	1,000	1,500
Total fixed cost			
Fixed cost per bag of popcorn			
Total variable cost			
Variable cost per bag of popcorn			
Total cost			
Total cost per bag of popcorn			

LO 5–1   **M5–3 Defining Cost Behavior**

Match each of the following costs with its appropriate definition:

____ 1. Fixed cost per unit
____ 2. Fixed costs in total
____ 3. Variable cost per unit
____ 4. Variable costs in total
____ 5. Step costs

A. Vary directly and proportionally with changes in volume.
B. Varies inversely with the activity level.
C. Remains constant in the short run, regardless of changes in activity.
D. Constant over small ranges of output, but increases as levels of activity increase.

LO 5–2   **M5–4 Defining Terms on a Scattergraph**

Complete each of the following sentences with the appropriate term from the list below:

1. The horizontal (x) axis on a scattergraph plots _____.
2. On a scattergraph, the steeper the slope of the line, the higher the _____.
3. On a scattergraph, the point where the line intersects the vertical (y) axis indicates the _____.
4. The vertical (y) axis on a scattergraph plots _____.

A. Total cost
B. Total variable cost
C. Variable cost per unit
D. Activity level
E. Total fixed cost

M5–5 Defining Terms for the High-Low Method   LO 5–3

Indicate whether each of the following statements about the high-low method is true or false:

a. The formula for the high-low method is

$$\frac{(\text{Highest Cost} - \text{Lowest Cost})}{(\text{Highest Activity} - \text{Lowest Activity})}$$

b. The high-low method can be expressed as

$$\frac{\text{Change in Cost}}{\text{Change in Activity}} = \text{Fixed Cost per Unit}$$

c. The high-low method forces a line between the two most extreme activity data points.
d. The high-low method relies on the fact that the slope of a line is calculated as "run over rise."
e. When using the high-low method, the slope of the line is interpreted as the fixed-cost component of a mixed cost.

M5–6 Defining Terms in Least-Squares Regression   LO 5–4

Match each of the following terms associated with the least-squares regression method with its appropriate definition:

_____ **1.** R square

_____ **2.** Error

_____ **3.** Intercept

_____ **4.** Coefficient of the x variable

A. Estimate of total fixed cost.
B. Vertical distance between the prediction line and each data point.
C. Measure of the model's goodness of fit.
D. Direction of the correlation between the variables.
E. Estimate of variable cost.

M5–7 Estimating Cost Behavior   LO 5–2, 5–3

Castle Inc. has the following information:

	Month	Amount	Units
Cost A	January	$20,000	40,000
	February	$40,000	80,000

	Month	Amount	Units
Cost B	January	$50,000	40,000
	February	$70,000	80,000

	Month	Amount	Units
Cost C	January	$25,000	40,000
	February	$25,000	80,000

Indicate whether these costs are variable, fixed, or mixed. Explain your answers.

M5–8 Predicting Cost Behavior   LO 5–2, 5–3

Randy Company produces tennis rackets. If the fixed cost per racket is $15 when 20,000 rackets are produced, what is the fixed cost per racket when 30,000 rackets are produced?

M5–9 Preparing a Scattergraph   LO 5–2

Sherri's Tan-O-Rama is a local tanning salon. The following information reflects its number of appointments and total costs for the first half of the year:

Month	Number of Appointments	Total Cost
January	250	$5,000
February	300	6,000
March	500	6,200
April	225	5,300
May	150	5,450
June	175	5,230

Prepare a scattergraph by plotting Sherri's Tan-O-Rama's data on a graph. Then draw a line that you believe best fits the data points. Using the graph and line you have drawn, estimate the firm's total fixed cost per month.

LO 5-3   **M5-10 Estimating Cost Behavior Using High-Low Method**

Refer to the Tan-O-Rama data in M5-9. Using the high-low method, calculate the total fixed cost per month and the variable cost per tanning appointment. How does the estimate of fixed cost compare to what you estimated in M5-9?

LO 5-4   **M5-11 Estimating Cost Behavior Using Least-Squares Regression**

Refer to the Tan-O-Rama data in M5-9. Suppose Sherri performed a least-squares regression and obtained the following results:

	Coefficients
Intercept	4,768.53
x Variable 1	2.86

Put Sherri's results into a linear equation format ($y = a + bx$) and explain what each component means. Compare the regression results to those obtained in M5-9 and M5-10. Which method is most accurate? Why?

LO 5-5   **M5-12 Calculating Unit Contribution Margin and Contribution Margin Ratio**

Refer to the Tan-O-Rama regression output given in M5-11. Suppose that the company charges $6 per tanning session. Calculate the unit contribution margin and contribution margin ratio as well as the total contribution margin if the shop books 400 tanning sessions this month.

LO 5-2   **M5-13 Preparing a Scattergraph**

Handy's Hats makes the world's best hats. Information for the last eight months follows:

Month	Number of Hats Produced	Total Cost
January	8,000	$7,000
February	4,500	5,000
March	7,000	6,250
April	8,600	7,750
May	3,750	5,000
June	6,000	6,250
July	3,000	4,250
August	5,000	5,750

Prepare a scattergraph by plotting Handy's data on a graph. Then draw a line that you believe best fits the data points. Using the graph and line you have drawn, estimate Handy's total fixed cost per month.

LO 5-3   **M5-14 Estimating Cost Behavior Using High-Low Method**

Refer to the Handy's Hats data in M5-13. Using the high-low method, calculate the total fixed cost per month and the variable cost per hat. How does the estimate of fixed cost compare to what you estimated in M5-13?

LO 5-4   **M5-15 Estimating Cost Behavior Using Least-Squares Regression**

Refer to the Handy's Hats data in M5-13. Suppose Handy performed a least-squares regression and obtained the following results:

	Coefficients
Intercept	2718.59
x Variable 1	0.56

Put Handy's results into a linear equation format ($y = a + bx$) and explain what each component means. Compare the regression results to those obtained in M5–13 and M5–14. Which method is most accurate? Why?

M5–16 Preparing a Contribution Margin Income Statement

LO 5–5

Refer to the data for Handy's Hats in M5–13. Suppose that Handy's expects to sell 4,000 hats during the month of September and that each hat sells for $2.75. Using this information along with the regression results given in M5–15, prepare Handy's contribution margin income statement for the month of September.

M5–17 Estimating Cost Behavior Using High-Low Method

LO 5–3

Baker Company produced 1,500 units in May at a total cost of $10,000 and 4,000 units in June at a total cost of $18,000. Compute the variable cost per unit and the total fixed cost using the high-low method.

M5–18 Preparing a Contribution Margin Income Statement

LO 5–5

Following is relevant information for Snowdon Sandwich Shop, a small business that serves sandwiches:

Total fixed cost per month	$1,500
Variable cost per sandwich	2.50
Sales price per sandwich	5.25

During the month of June, Snowdon sold 600 sandwiches. Using the preceding information, prepare its contribution margin income statement for the month of June.

M5–19 Calculating Unit Contribution Margin and Contribution Margin Ratio

LO 5–5

Red Hawk Enterprises sells handmade clocks. Its variable cost per clock is $8, and each clock sells for $18. Calculate Red Hawk's unit contribution margin and contribution margin ratio. Suppose Red Hawk sells 2,000 clocks this year. Calculate the total contribution margin.

M5–20 Compare Full Absorption Costing to Variable Costing

LO 5–S1

Determine whether each the following statements describes variable costing (VC), full absorption costing (FA), or both (B):

_____ 1. Measures gross margin as the difference between sales revenue and cost of goods sold.

_____ 2. Used primarily for internal decision making.

_____ 3. Has the highest net income when production is greater than sales.

_____ 4. Shows the same profit for a given level of sales, regardless of production.

_____ 5. Has the highest cost of goods sold when sales are greater than production.

_____ 6. Accounts for a portion of fixed manufacturing overhead as an asset.

_____ 7. Required by GAAP for external reporting.

_____ 8. May lead managers to produce more units than the market demands.

_____ 9. When production and sales are equal, results in all of the current period manufacturing overhead being deducted on the income statement.

_____ 10. Measures contribution margin as the difference between sales revenue and variable costs.

EXERCISES

E5–1 Matching Terminology

LO 5–1, 5–5, 5–S1

Match each of the terms on the left by inserting the appropriate definition letter in the space provided. Not all definitions will be used.

_____ 1. Contribution margin

_____ 2. Contribution margin income statement

_____ 3. Contribution margin ratio

_____ 4. Fixed cost

_____ 5. Full absorption costing

_____ 6. Linearity assumption

_____ 7. Mixed cost

_____ 8. Relevant range

_____ 9. Scattergraph

_____ 10. Step-variable cost

_____ 11. Unit contribution margin

_____ 12. Variable cost

_____ 13. Variable costing

A. The way in which total cost behaves or changes, when some measure of activity changes.

B. The range of activity over which assumptions about cost behavior hold true.

C. A cost that changes in total in direct proportion to changes in activity while the per unit cost remains constant.

D. A cost that is fixed over a narrow range of activity and increases multiple times across a relevant range.

E. A cost that remains the same in total regardless of the activity level.

F. Both the total cost and the cost per unit change with the level of activity.

G. A cost that is fixed over a wide range of activity, but increases when a capacity limit is reached.

H. The expression of the relationship between total cost and activity expressed as $y = a + b(x)$.

I. A visual representation of the relationship between total cost and activity level.

J. The use of the two most extreme activity points to determine the variable cost per unit.

K. A measure of how well the data is represented by the formula $y = a + b(x)$.

L. The difference between sales revenue and variable costs.

M. The difference between the unit sales price and the unit variable costs.

N. Unit contribution margin divided by the unit sales price.

O. An external reporting method that reflects both the fixed and variable manufacturing costs in cost of goods sold.

P. A costing method that focuses on cost behavior.

Q. An internal income statement that separates fixed and variable costs.

LO 5–1   **E5–2 Identifying Cost Behavior Patterns**

Steve Silversmith produces unique and exclusive sterling silver rings, pendants, buckles, and chains. Steve pays one supervisor to oversee the work performed by several part-time silversmiths. He pays each silversmith to work 20 hours per week or 40 hours week, depending on production demand. He also hires a jewelry expert to perform quality assurance inspections and pays her based on the weight (per ounce of silver) of each piece inspected. The controller and the sales manager are discussing potential price increases due to the increasing cost of silver and increases in other costs. The following are several costs they are discussing:

a. Depreciation on production equipment.
b. Supervisor salary.
c. Packaging (each piece is packaged in a designer carton).
d. Silver.
e. Part-time labor (silversmith).
f. Production facility utilities.
g. Quality assurance.
h. Mortgage on the production facility.

Required:

Indicate whether each cost is a variable, fixed, step, or mixed cost within Steve's relevant range of activity.

E5–3 Identifying Cost Behavior Graphs   LO 5–1

Match each of the following graphs to the correct cost behavior.

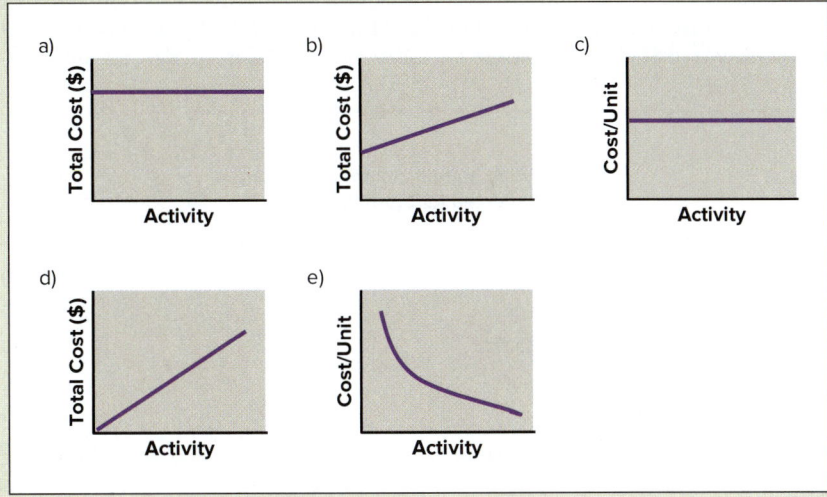

Cost Behavior

——   **1.** Variable cost per unit.

——   **2.** Total variable cost.

——   **3.** Fixed cost per unit.

——   **4.** Total fixed cost.

——   **5.** Total mixed cost.

E5–4 Determining Cost Behavior and Calculating Expected Cost   LO 5–1

Morning Dove Company manufactures one model of birdbath, which is very popular. Morning Dove sells all units it produces each month. The relevant range is 0 to 1,500 units, and monthly production costs for the production of 500 units follow. Morning Dove's utilities and maintenance costs are mixed with the fixed components shown in parentheses.

Production Costs	Total Cost
Direct materials	$1,500
Direct labor	7,500
Utilities ($100 fixed)	650
Supervisor's salary	3,000
Maintenance ($280 fixed)	480
Depreciation	800

Required:

1. Identify each cost as variable, fixed, or mixed, and express each cost as a rate per month or per unit (or combination thereof). State any assumptions you make.
2. Determine the total fixed cost per month and the variable cost per unit for Morning Dove.
3. State Morning Dove's linear cost equation for a production level of 0 to 1,500 units.
4. Calculate Morning Dove's expected total cost if production increased to 1,200 units per month.

**E5–5 Calculating Contribution Margin and Contribution Ratio, Preparing
         Contribution Margin Income Statement**   LO 5–5

Refer to the information for Morning Dove Company in E5–4. Suppose it sells each birdbath for $25.

Required:

1. Calculate the unit contribution margin and contribution margin ratio for each birdbath sold.
2. Prepare a contribution margin income statement assuming that Morning Dove produces and sells 1,400 units.

LO 5–1, 5–5   **E5–6 Explaining Cost Behavior and Implications of Relevant Range**

Refer to the information for Morning Dove Company in E5–4. Morning Dove Company's owner, Sylvester, believes that he can sell 2,000 birdbaths during the month of April and has predicted a net operating income of $6,820 as shown in the following contribution margin statement:

MORNING DOVE COMPANY
Contribution Margin Income Statement
Expected for 2,000 Units

Sales revenue (2,000 × $25.00)	$50,000
Less: Variable costs (2,000 × $19.50)	39,000
Contribution margin (2,000 × $5.50)	$11,000
Less: Fixed costs	4,180
Net operating income	$ 6,820

Required:

Explain to Sylvester why his prediction is incorrect. Be specific about his incorrect assumptions and give him as much detail as possible about what the accurate contribution margin statement would show.

LO 5–3   **E5–7 Estimating Cost Behavior Using High-Low Method**

Mountain Dental Services is a specialized dental practice whose only service is filling cavities. Mountain has recorded the following for the past nine months:

Month	Number of Cavities Filled	Total Cost
January	625	$5,600
February	700	6,000
March	500	4,500
April	425	4,100
May	450	4,500
June	300	3,200
July	375	3,500
August	550	4,900
September	575	5,400

Required:

1. Use the high-low method to estimate total fixed cost and variable cost per cavity filled.
2. Using these estimates, calculate Mountain's total cost for filling 500 cavities.
3. How closely does your estimate match the actual cost for March? If they are different, explain why.

LO 5–2   **E5–8 Estimating Cost Behavior Using Scattergraph Method**

Refer to the information in E5–7 regarding Mountain Dental.

Required:

1. Create a scattergraph using Mountain's activity and cost information and draw a line on the graph that you believe has the best fit.
2. Using this graph and your best fitting line, estimate Mountain Dental's total fixed cost.
3. Does your line differ from the one calculated using the high-low method? If so, why?

E5–9 Estimating Cost Behavior Using Least-Squares Regression Method

LO 5–4

Refer to the information in E5–7 regarding Mountain Dental.

Required:

1. Perform a least-squares regression using Mountain's activity and cost information and state the linear cost equation ($y = a + bx$).
2. Explain what each component of the cost equation represents.
3. Do the regression results differ from those obtained using the high-low and scattergraph methods? If so, why?

E5–10 Preparing Contribution Margin Income Statement

LO 5–5

Consider Mountain Dental's cost equation results obtained in E5–7 using the high-low method.

Required:

1. Determine Mountain Dental's unit contribution margin and contribution margin ratio if it charges $45 for cavity filled.
2. Prepare a contribution margin income statement for October assuming Mountain expects to fill 610 cavities during the month.

E5–11 Preparing Contribution Margin Income Statement

LO 5–5

Consider Mountain Dental's cost equation results obtained in E5–9 using least-squares regression.

Required:

1. Determine Mountain Dental's unit contribution margin and contribution margin ratio if it charges $45 for each cavity filled.
2. Prepare a contribution margin income statement for October assuming Mountain expects to fill 610 cavities during the month.

E5–12 Estimating Cost Behavior Using Scattergraph, High-Low Method, and Least-Squares Regression

LO 5–2, 5–3, 5–4

Odessa, Inc., manufactures one model of computer desk. The following data are available regarding units shipped and total shipping costs:

Month	Number of Units Shipped	Total Shipping Cost
January	75	$3,250
February	60	2,300
March	40	1,700
April	20	1,200
May	70	2,300
June	80	2,700
July	50	2,000

Required:

1. Prepare a scattergraph of Odessa's shipping cost and draw the line you believe best fits the data.
2. Based on this graph, estimate Odessa's total fixed shipping costs per month.
3. Using the high-low method, calculate Odessa's total fixed shipping costs and variable shipping cost per unit.
4. Perform a least-squares regression analysis on Odessa's data.
5. Using the regression output, create a linear equation ($y = a + bx$) for estimating Odessa's shipping costs.

E5–13 Estimating Cost Behavior Using Scattergraph and High-Low Methods

LO 5–2, 5–3

Camp Rainbow offers overnight summer camp programs for children ages 10 to 14 every summer during June and July. Each camp session is one week and can accommodate up to 200 children. The camp is not coed, so boys attend during the odd-numbered weeks and girls attend during the even-numbered weeks. While at the camp, participants make crafts, participate in various sports, help care for the camp's resident animals, have cookouts and hayrides, and help assemble toys for local underprivileged children.

The camp provides all food as well as materials for all craft classes and the toys to be assembled. One cabin can accommodate up to 10 children, and one camp counselor is assigned to each cabin. Three camp managers are on-site regardless of the number of campers enrolled.

Following is the cost information for Camp Rainbow's operations last summer:

Week	Number of Campers	Cost to Run Camp
1	90	$ 8,050
2	118	8,460
3	156	10,900
4	174	11,100
5	188	13,670
6	184	14,300
7	170	12,325
8	156	11,270

Required:

1. For each of the following items, identify whether the cost is variable, fixed, mixed, step-variable, or step-fixed. State any assumptions you make.

   a. Cost of meals for campers.
   b. Cost of camp counselor wages.
   c. Cost of crafting materials.
   d. Depreciation on the cabins.
   e. Feed for the camp animals.
   f. Electricity for the camp.
   g. Camp managers' salaries.
   h. Cost of toys to be assembled by campers.
   i. Housekeeping (e.g., cleaning cabins between sessions, laundering bed linens).

2. Prepare a scattergraph of Camp Rainbow's operating cost and draw the line you believe best fits the data.

3. Based on this graph, estimate Camp Rainbow's total fixed costs per month.

4. Using the high-low method, calculate Camp Rainbow's total fixed operating costs and variable operating cost per child.

5. Using the high-low method results, calculate the camp's expected operating cost if 170 children attend a session.

LO 5–4   **E5–14   Estimating Cost Behavior Using Least-Squares Regression**

Refer to the Camp Rainbow data presented in E5–13.

Required:

1. Perform a least-squares regression analysis on Camp Rainbow's data.

2. Using the regression output, create a cost equation ($y = a + bx$) for estimating Camp Rainbow's operating costs.

3. Using the least-squares regression results, calculate the camp's expected operating cost if 170 children attend a session.

4. Compare this estimated cost to the actual cost incurred during week 7. Explain why these numbers might differ.

LO 5–3, 5–4   **E5–15   Comparing High-Low Method and Least-Squares Regression Results**

Consider Camp Rainbow's cost estimated in E5–13 using the high-low method and in E5–14 using regression. The two methods yielded very different results, especially in their estimates of fixed cost.

Required:

1. Describe the differences in the cost estimates generated by these two methods.

2. Explain why you believe the differences exist.

3. Explain which method is more reliable and why.

E5–16 Preparing Contribution Margin Income Statement

LO 5–5

Consider Camp Rainbow's cost equation results obtained in E5–14 using least-squares regression. Suppose that Rainbow is contemplating staying open one additional week during the summer.

Required:

1. Determine Rainbow's contribution margin per camper if each camper pays $175 to attend the camp for a week.
2. Prepare a contribution margin income statement for week 9 assuming Rainbow expects to have 170 campers that week.
3. Explain whether Rainbow should add a ninth week to its schedule.

E5–17 Determining Cost Behavior, Preparing Contribution Margin Income Statement

LO 5–1, 5–5

Riverside Inc. makes one model of wooden canoe. Partial information for it follows:

	Number of Canoes Produced and Sold		
	540	620	780
Total costs			
Variable costs	$ 67,500	?	?
Fixed costs	150,000	?	?
Total costs	$217,500	?	?
Cost per unit			
Variable cost per unit	?	?	?
Fixed cost per unit	?	?	?
Total cost per unit	?	?	?

Required:

1. Complete the preceding table.
2. Identify three costs that would be classified as fixed costs and three that would be classified as variable costs for Riverside.
3. Suppose Riverside sells its canoes for $500 each. Calculate the contribution margin per canoe and the contribution margin ratio.
4. Next year Riverside expects to sell 700 canoes. Prepare a contribution margin income statement for the company.

E5–18 Predicting How Sustainability Initiatives Will Impact the Contribution Margin Income Statement

LO 5–5

Starcups Coffee Company is launching a new sustainability initiative that would reward customers for purchasing a reusable cup. During the cup promotion, customers would pay an extra $1.00 for the reusable cup and would receive a 25 percent discount each time they return with the cup to buy a cup of coffee.

    Each week Starcups serves 40,000 customers who purchase an average of 2.5 cups of coffee per week (100,000 cups total). Starcups's contribution margin income statement for a typical week is shown as follows:

	Units	Per Unit	Total
Sales Revenue	100,000	$ 4.00	$ 400,000
Variable Costs	100,000	1.50	150,000
Contribution Margin	100,000	$ 2.50	$ 250,000
Fixed Costs			100,000
Net Operating Income			$ 150,000

Assume the new cup promotion is expected to impact sales volume, revenue, fixed, and variable costs as follows:

- Starcups estimates that 25 percent of its current customers (10,000) will participate in the promotion. The remainder of its existing customer base (30,000) will continue to buy an average of 2.5 cups of coffee per week.

- Starcups expected to attract 5,000 new customers to participate in the promotion.

- Customers who participate in the promotion will pay an additional $1.00 for the reusable cup. They will then receive a 25 percent discount on repeat visits when they bring back their reusable cup.

- The additional variable cost of purchasing the reusable cup is $1.50. The variable cost savings of the paper cup is $0.25.

- Starcups expects that customers who participate in the reusable cup promotion will visit an average of 4 times per week, including the first purchase of the reusable cup.

- Starcups will spend a total of $10,000 per week advertising the reusable cup promotion.

Required:

1. Prepare a contribution margin income statement to predict how the reusable cup promotion will impact weekly net operating income. Include a separate contribution margin calculation for current customers who will not participate in the promotion, the first purchase for customers who buy the reusable cup, and the repeat visits for customers who buy the reusable cup.

2. Compute the difference in total revenue, total variable costs, total contribution margin, total fixed costs, and total operating income before and after the promotion.

3. How will this sustainability initiative impact the company's triple bottom line?

LO 5–5   E5–19 Calculating Contribution Margin and Contribution Ratio, Preparing Contribution Margin Income Statement

Refer to the information presented in E5–17 for Riverside. Each of the following scenarios is a variation of Riverside's original data.

Required:

Prepare Riverside's contribution margin income statement for each independent scenario.
1. Riverside raises the sales price to $600 per canoe.
2. Both sales price and variable cost per unit increase by 10 percent.
3. Riverside cuts its fixed cost by 20 percent.

LO 5–3, 5–5   E5–20 Estimating Cost Behavior Using High-Low Method, Preparing Contribution Margin Income Statement

Joyce Murphy runs a courier service in downtown Seattle. She charges clients $0.50 per mile driven. Joyce has determined that if she drives 3,300 miles in a month, her total operating cost is $875. If she drives 4,400 miles in a month, her total operating cost is $1,095.

Required:

1. Using the high-low method, determine Joyce's variable and fixed operating cost components. Show this as a linear formula ($y = a + bx$).

2. Prepare a contribution margin income statement for Joyce's service assuming she drove 3,700 miles last month.

LO 5–3, 5–5   E5–21 Estimating Cost Behavior Using High-Low Method, Preparing Contribution Margin Income Statement

Bethany Link delivers parts for several local auto parts stores. She charges clients $0.75 per mile driven. She has determined that if she drives 2,100 miles in a month, her average operating cost is $0.55 per mile. If Bethany drives 4,200 miles in a month, her average operating cost is $0.40 per mile.

Required:

1. Using the high-low method, determine Bethany's variable and fixed operating cost components. Show this as a linear cost formula ($y = a + bx$).

2. Prepare a contribution margin income statement for the business last month, when Bethany drove 2,400 miles.

E5–22 Explaining the Need for Variable Costing   LO 5–5, 5S–1

Your friend, Manuel Rodriguez, has been working as a staff accountant for Williams Company, a small local manufacturing company. His job responsibilities to date have entailed several aspects of financial accounting: preparing monthly financial statements for the owners/investors and the bank with which Williams maintains a line of credit. Manuel has been offered a promotion to cost accountant. In that capacity, he would be responsible for overseeing Williams's manufacturing facility and tracking all production costs. He would also be expected to generate a contribution margin income statement on a regular basis for company employees to use. Manuel has come to you for help in understanding the difference between the contribution margin statement and the income statements he has prepared in the past.

Required:

Explain to Manuel the differences between these two income statement formats. Include in your explanation the basis for separating costs, targeted users, and information that can be obtained from each one.

E5–23 Comparing Full Absorption Costing and Variable Costing   LO 5–S1

The following information pertains to the first year of operation for Crystal Cold Coolers Inc.:

Number of units produced	3,000
Number of units sold	2,500
Unit sales price	$ 350
Direct materials per unit	80
Direct labor per unit	60
Variable manufacturing overhead per unit	10
Fixed manufacturing overhead per unit ($225,000 ÷ 3,000 units)	75
Total variable selling expenses ($15 per unit sold)	37,500
Total fixed general and administrative expenses	65,000

Required:

Prepare Crystal Cold's full absorption costing income statement and variable costing income statement for the year.

E5–24 Estimating Cost Behavior Using Least-Squares Regression and High-Low Method   LO 5–3, 5–4

Tempe Office Services and Supplies (TOSS) provides various products and services in the Tempe Research Park, home to numerous high-tech and bio-tech companies. Making color copies is one of its most popular and profitable services. The controller performed a regression analysis of data from the Color Copy Department with the following results:

Intercept	238.69
R square	.968
Number of observations	6
x coefficient	.069

The regression output was based on the following data:

Month	Number of Color Copies	Color Copy Department Costs
July	17,000	$1,445
August	21,250	1,658
September	22,950	1,785
October	18,700	1,530
November	20,400	1,615
December	25,500	2,040

Required:

1. What is the variable cost per color copy for TOSS?
2. What is the fixed cost for the Color Copy Department?
3. Based on the regression output obtained by the controller, what cost formula should be used to estimate future total costs for the Color Copy Department?
4. How accurate will the cost formula developed in requirement 3 be at predicting the total cost for the Color Copy Department?
5. Use the high-low method to estimate the variable and fixed costs for the Color Copy Department. What cost formula should be used based on your analysis?
6. If 22,100 copies are made during January, what is the total cost predicted by each method?

GROUP A PROBLEMS

LO 5–2, 5–3, 5–4   **PA5–1 Estimating Cost Behavior Using Scattergraph, High-Low, and Least-Squares Regression Methods**

Garfield Company manufactures a popular brand of dog repellant known as DogGone It, which it sells in gallon-size bottles with a spray attachment. The majority of Garfield's business comes from orders placed by homeowners who are trying to keep neighborhood dogs out of their yards. Garfield's operating information for the first six months of the year follows:

Month	Number of Bottles Sold	Operating Cost
January	800	$11,000
February	1,400	15,740
March	1,750	15,800
April	2,400	19,675
May	3,480	27,245
June	3,800	35,000

Required:

1. Prepare a scattergraph of Garfield's operating cost and draw the line you believe best fits the data.
2. Based on this graph, estimate Garfield's total fixed costs per month.
3. Using the high-low method, calculate Garfield's total fixed operating costs and variable operating cost per bottle.
4. Perform a least-squares regression analysis on Garfield's data.
5. Determine how well this regression analysis explains the data.
6. Using the regression output, create a linear cost equation ($y = a + bx$) for estimating Garfield's operating costs.

PA5–2 Estimating Cost Behavior Using Scattergraph, High-Low, and Least-Squares Regression Methods   LO 5–2, 5–3, 5–4

Leslie Sporting Goods is a locally owned store that specializes in printing team jerseys. The majority of its business comes from orders for various local teams and organizations. While Leslie's prints everything from bowling team jerseys to fraternity/sorority apparel to special event shirts, summer league baseball and softball team jerseys are the company's biggest source of revenue.

A portion of Leslie's operating information for the company's last year follows:

Month	Number of Jerseys Printed	Operating Cost
January	215	$5,500
February	210	5,740
March	380	5,800
April	625	8,675
May	750	9,000
June	630	9,760
July	400	6,200
August	350	6,155
September	300	5,980
October	330	6,010
November	200	4,950
December	150	4,500

Required:

1. Prepare a scattergraph of Leslie's operating cost and draw the line you believe best fits the data.
2. Based on this graph, estimate Leslie's total fixed costs per month.
3. Using the high-low method, calculate the store's total fixed operating costs and variable operating cost per jersey.
4. Using the high-low method results, calculate the store's expected operating cost if it printed 480 jerseys.
5. Perform a least-squares regression analysis on Leslie's data.
6. Using the regression output, create a linear equation $(y = a + bx)$ for estimating Leslie's operating costs.
7. Using the least-squares regression results, calculate the store's expected operating cost if it prints 625 jerseys.

PA5–3 Estimating Cost Behavior Using High-Low and Regression, Preparing and Interpreting Contribution Margin Income Statement   LO 5–3, 5–4, 5–5

Refer to your solutions for Leslie's Sporting Goods in PA5–2.

Required:

1. Consider the pattern of Leslie's activity and costs throughout the year. Would you consider this to be a seasonal business? Explain your answer and how this information could impact the relative proportion of fixed and variable costs for the store's business.
2. Using the cost estimates obtained with the high-low and regression methods, predict the store's operating costs for the upcoming months based on the following expected sales levels:

Month	Expected Number of Jerseys
January	240
February	180
March	300
April	590
May	710
June	660

3. Explain why there are differences between cost predictions based on the high-low method and least-squares regression. Which do you think is more accurate? Why?

4. Using the regression results, prepare contribution margin income statements for January through June. Assume that the average sales price is $18 per jersey.

5. Based on the regression equation, what is Leslie's expected fixed cost per month? What would Leslie expect total annual fixed cost to be?

LO 5–1, 5–5

PA5–4 Predicting Cost Behavior, Calculating Contribution Margin and Contribution Margin Ratio, Calculating Profit

Presidio, Inc., produces one model of mountain bike. Partial information for the company follows:

Cost Data	Number of Bikes Produced and Sold		
	625	800	1,050
Total costs			
Variable costs	$125,000	$?	$?
Fixed costs per year	?	?	?
Total costs	?	?	?
Cost per unit			
Variable cost per unit	?	?	?
Fixed cost per unit	?	?	?
Total cost per unit	?	$543.75	?

Required:

1. Complete Presidio's cost data table.

2. Calculate Presidio's contribution margin ratio and its total contribution margin at each sales level indicated in the cost data table assuming the company sells each bike for $650.

3. Calculate net operating income at each of the sales levels assuming a sales price of $650.

LO 5S-1

PA5–5 Comparing Full Absorption and Variable Costing

Refer to the information for Presidio, Inc., in PA5–4. Additional information for Presidio's most recent year of operations follows:

Number of units produced	2,000
Number of units sold	1,300
Sales price per unit	$ 650.00
Direct materials per unit	60.00
Direct labor per unit	90.00
Variable manufacturing overhead per unit	40.00
Fixed manufacturing overhead per unit ($235,000 ÷ 2,000 units)	117.50
Total variable selling expenses ($10 per unit sold)	13,000.00
Total fixed general and administrative expenses	70,000.00

Required:

1. Without any calculations, explain whether Presidio's profit will be higher with full absorption costing or variable costing.

2. Prepare a full absorption costing income statement and a variable costing income statement for Presidio. Assume there was no beginning inventory.

3. Compute the difference in profit between full absorption costing and variable costing. Reconcile the difference.

PA5–6 Comparing Full Absorption and Variable Costing

Dance Creations manufactures authentic Hawaiian hula skirts that are purchased for traditional Hawaiian celebrations, costume parties, and other functions. During its first year of business, the company incurred the following costs:

Variable Cost per Hula Skirt	
Direct materials	$ 9.60
Direct labor	3.40
Variable manufacturing overhead	1.05
Variable selling and administrative expenses	0.40
Fixed Cost per Month	
Fixed manufacturing overhead	$16,125
Fixed selling and administrative expenses	4,950

Dance Creations charges $30 for each skirt that it sells. During the first month of operation, it made 1,500 skirts and sold 1,375.

Required:

1. Assuming Dance Creations uses variable costing, calculate the variable manufacturing cost per unit for last month.
2. Prepare a variable costing income statement for the last month.
3. Assuming Dance Creations uses full absorption costing, calculate the full manufacturing cost per unit for the last month.
4. Prepare a full absorption costing income statement.
5. Compare the two income statements and explain any differences.
6. Suppose next month Dance Creations expects to produce 1,500 hula skirts and sell 1,600. Without recreating the new income statements, calculate the difference in profit between variable costing and full absorption costing. Which would be higher? Why?

GROUP B PROBLEMS

**PB5–1 Estimating Cost Behavior Using Scattergraph, High-Low, and Least-Squares
Regression Methods**

Odie Company manufactures a popular brand of cat repellant known as Cat-B-Gone, which it sells in gallon-size bottles with a spray attachment. The majority of Odie's business comes from orders placed by homeowners who are trying to keep neighborhood cats out of their yards. Odie's operating information for the first six months of the year follows:

Month	Number of Bottles Sold	Operating Cost
January	1,000	$ 8,000
February	1,100	7,700
March	1,300	9,900
April	2,000	14,000
May	2,400	17,250
June	3,000	20,000

Required:

1. Prepare a scattergraph of Odie's operating cost and draw the line you believe best fits the data.
2. Based on this graph, estimate Odie's total fixed costs per month.
3. Using the high-low method, calculate Odie's total fixed operating costs and variable operating cost per bottle.

4. Perform a least-squares regression analysis on Odie's data.

5. Determine how well this regression analysis explains the data.

6. Using the regression output, create a linear equation ($y = a + bx$) for estimating Odie's operating costs.

LO 5–2, 5–3, 5–4   **PB5–2 Estimating Cost Behavior Using Scattergraph, High-Low, and Least-Squares Regression Methods**

Sigrid's Custom Graphics specializes in creating and painting store window advertisement displays. The majority of its business comes from local retailers and fast-food restaurants.

A portion of Sigrid's operating information for the past year follows:

Month	Number of Window Displays	Operating Cost
January	40	$1,800
February	42	1,720
March	66	2,500
April	75	2,675
May	80	3,250
June	83	3,300
July	81	3,270
August	88	3,220
September	80	2,980
October	58	2,090
November	67	1,950
December	77	2,925

Required:

1. Prepare a scattergraph of Sigrid's operating cost and draw the line you believe best fits the data.

2. Based on this graph, estimate Sigrid's total fixed costs per month.

3. Using the high-low method, calculate Sigrid's total fixed operating costs and variable operating cost per window.

4. Using the high-low method results, calculate the expected operating cost for the business if it paints 96 windows.

5. Perform a least-squares regression analysis on Sigrid's data.

6. Using the regression output, create a linear equation ($y = a + bx$) for estimating Sigrid's operating costs.

7. Using the least-squares regression results, calculate the store's expected operating cost if it paints 96 windows.

LO 5–2, 5–3, 5–4   **PB5–3 Estimating Cost Behavior Using High-Low and Regression, Preparing and Interpreting Contribution Margin Income Statement**

Refer to your solutions for Sigrid's Custom Graphics in PB5–2.

Required:

1. Consider the pattern of the company's activity and costs throughout the year. Would you consider this to be a seasonal business? Explain your answer and how this information could impact the relative proportion of fixed and variable costs for the business.

2. Using your cost estimates obtained with the high-low and regression methods, predict the store's operating costs for the upcoming months based on the following expected sales levels:

Month	Expected Number of Windows
January	44
February	48
March	70
April	76
May	87
June	85

3. Explain why there are differences between cost predictions based on the high-low method and on least-squares regression. Which do you think is more accurate? Why?

4. Using the regression results, prepare contribution margin income statements for January through June. Assume that the business charges $80 per window on average.

5. Based on the regression equation, what is the expected fixed cost per month for the business? What would Sigrid's expect total annual fixed cost to be?

PB5–4 Predicting Cost Behavior, Calculating Contribution Margin and Contribution Margin Ratio, Calculating Profit   LO 5–5

Vestibule produces one model of ski vest. Partial information for the company follows:

Cost Data	Number of Ski Vests Produced and Sold		
	1,650	1,700	2,100
Total costs			
Variable costs	$?	$?	$15,750
Fixed costs per year	?	?	?
Total costs	?	?	?
Cost per unit			
Variable cost per unit	?	?	?
Fixed cost per unit	?	?	?
Total cost per unit	$ 28	?	?

Required:

1. Complete Vestibule's cost data table.

2. Calculate Vestibule's contribution margin ratio and its total contribution margin at each sales level indicated in the cost data table assuming the company sells each vest for $30.

3. Calculate profit at each of the sales levels assuming a sales price of $30.

PB5–5 Comparing Full Absorption and Variable Costing   LO 5S–1

Refer to the information for Vestibule in PB5–4. Additional information for Vestibule's most recent year of operations follows:

Number of units produced	3,000
Number of units sold	2,800
Sales price per unit	$ 30.00
Direct materials per unit	3.00
Direct labor per unit	2.00
Variable manufacturing overhead per unit	1.50
Fixed manufacturing overhead per unit ($15,000 ÷ 3,000 units)	5.00
Total variable selling expenses ($1 per unit sold)	2,800.00
Total fixed general and administrative expenses	20,250.00

Required:

1. Without any calculations, explain whether Vestibule's profit will be higher with full absorption costing or variable costing.

2. Prepare a full absorption costing income statement and a variable costing income statement for Vestibule. Assume there was no beginning inventory.

3. Compute the difference in profit between full absorption costing and variable costing. Reconcile the difference.

LO 5S–1   **PB5–6 Comparing Full Absorption and Variable Costing**

Herb Garden manufactures garden planters for growing fresh herbs to use in cooking. Individuals as well as local restaurants purchase the planters. Recently, the company incurred the following costs:

Variable Cost per Planter	
Direct materials	$ 8.50
Direct labor	2.40
Variable manufacturing overhead	1.50
Variable selling and administrative expenses	0.65
Fixed Cost per Month	
Fixed manufacturing overhead	$12,025
Fixed selling and administrative expenses	8,640

Herb Garden charges $17 for each planter that it sells. During the first month of operation, it made 6,500 planters and sold 6,225.

Required:

1. Assuming Herb Garden uses variable costing, calculate the variable manufacturing cost per unit for last month.
2. Prepare a variable costing income statement for the last month.
3. Assuming Herb Garden uses full absorption costing, calculate the full manufacturing cost per unit for the last month.
4. Prepare a full absorption costing income statement.
5. Compare the two income statements and explain any differences.
6. Suppose next month Herb Garden expects to produce 6,500 planters and sell 6,700 of them. Without recreating the new income statements, calculate the difference in profit between variable costing and full absorption costing. Which would be higher? Why?

SKILLS DEVELOPMENT CASES

LO 5–S1   **S5–1 Case Assignment: Identifying Cost Behavior and Predicting Difference in Variable and Absorption Costing**

Go to www.YouTube.com and search for **How It's Made**, a television show produced by the Discovery Channel that shows how thousands of products and services are created. Find a product that interests you and answer the following questions:

- What product did you choose and how is it made?
- Identify two variable costs of making this product. What makes it a variable cost?
- Identify two fixed costs of making this product. What makes it a fixed cost?
- Identify one step cost of making this product. What makes it a step cost?
- Identify one mixed cost of making this product. What makes it a mixed cost?
- Describe how a company would determine the cost of making this product under full absorption costing. What costs would be included in cost of goods sold and finished goods inventory? What costs would be treated as operating expenses?
- Describe how a company that makes this product would compute gross margin and contribution margin.
- Will gross margin and contribution margin always be the same? Why or why not?
- Describe when and why profit will be different under variable costing versus full absorption costing. Be specific about what would cause the difference in profit and what costs would contribute to the difference.

S5–2 Analyzing Cost Behavior and the Impact on Profit   LO 5–1

Ink Spot Inc. is a new business located in upstate New York. It prints promotional flyers for local businesses and distributes them at public places or area events. The flyers are either placed on the windshield of cars in parking lots or distributed by hand to people.

Ink Spot's owner, Dana Everhart, is facing a difficult decision. She could purchase a commercial printer and produce the flyers in house. However, the machinery, costing approximately $20,000, is quite expensive. The printer has an estimated useful life of four years and would be depreciated using the straight-line method with no salvage value. If Dana purchases the printer, she would also have to buy paper and toner for the machine and pay for maintenance or repairs as needed. She estimates that it would cost $0.02 per page to print the flyers herself.

Alternatively, Dana could pay a local printing company $0.05 per copy to print the flyers. She would incur no printing costs other than the $0.05 per page if she chooses this alternative. However, $0.05 per page is considerably more than Dana would have to pay for paper and toner if she owned a commercial printer.

Dana plans to charge customers $0.08 per page for each flyer Ink Spot distributes.

Required:

1. Why does Dana need to understand cost behavior? How does it impact Dana and her business?
2. Name at least three costs in addition to the cost of producing the flyers that a business such as Ink Spot would incur, and describe the cost behavior of each one.
3. Considering the decision Dana must make, determine the cost behavior of each alternative. For any mixed cost, determine the amount of the variable and fixed components as much as possible.
4. Discuss other factors about Ink Spot's operating environment that Dana should consider when deciding whether to make the flyers or buy them from a local printing company.
5. Discuss factors other than cost that Dana should consider.

6

Cost-Volume-Profit Analysis

CHAPTER SIX

YOUR LEARNING OBJECTIVES

LO 6-1 Use cost-volume-profit analysis to find the break-even point.

LO 6-2 Use cost-volume-profit analysis to determine the sales needed to achieve a target profit.

LO 6-3 Compute the margin of safety.

LO 6-4 Analyze how changes in prices and cost structure affect cost-volume-profit relationships.

LO 6-5 Calculate the degree of operating leverage and use it to predict the effect a change in sales will have on profit.

LO 6-6 Perform multiproduct cost-volume-profit analysis and explain how the product or sales mix affects the analysis.

©Nick Ut/AP Images

FOCUS COMPANY: STARBUCKS COFFEE

You don't have to go far to buy a cup of Starbucks Coffee. Started as a small coffee shop in Seattle's Pike Place Market more than three decades ago, Starbucks Coffee can now be found on street corners, college campuses, and airports across the country and abroad. Consider the following facts about Starbucks:

- Over the past 15 years, Starbucks has opened an average of 3 stores per day.
- In 2015, there were more than 21,000 Starbucks locations in 66 countries. About half of the stores are company-operated and half are licensed to other businesses such as airports, universities, and grocery stores.
- Starbucks spends more on employee health insurance than on coffee beans.
- Starbucks uses 4 billion paper cups per year.
- When Starbucks eliminated the 8-ounce cup from its menu (making the "tall" the new "small"), it increased revenue by 25 cents per cup with only 2 cents of added product cost.[1]

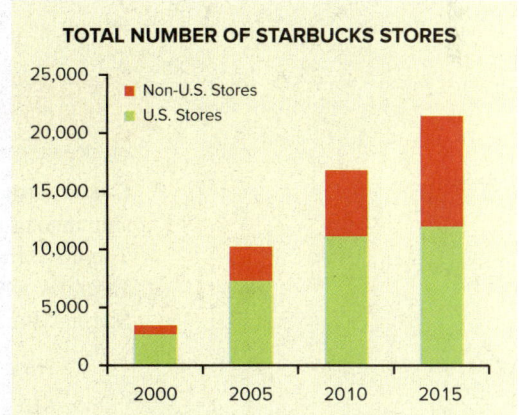

How does Starbucks decide how much to charge for a cup of coffee; how many customers must a particular location serve to be profitable; and how do changes in prices, costs, and product offerings affect the bottom line? This chapter introduces a decision-making approach that can help managers answer these and many other questions. Cost-volume-profit analysis is a decision-making tool that models how changes in prices, costs, volume, or product mix affect the bottom line.

---

[1] Taylor Clark, *Starbucked: A Double Tall Tale of Caffeine, Commerce, and Culture* (New York: Little, Brown and Company, 2007).

Throughout this chapter, we use a hypothetical Starbucks Coffee shop as our focus company. Initially, we limit our analysis to the sale of one type of product: coffee. Later in the chapter, we expand our analysis to show how to incorporate the other products that Starbucks sells, such as Teavana tea, sandwiches, pastries, and coffee mugs. As usual, we use hypothetical numbers for our examples, but they will give you a good idea of how to apply cost-volume-profit analysis in a real-world situation.

ORGANIZATION OF THE CHAPTER

Cost-volume-profit analysis	Apply cost-volume-profit analysis	Multiproduct cost-volume-profit analysis
• Assumptions of cost-volume-profit analysis • CVP graph • Basic CVP analysis • Profit equation method • Unit contribution margin method • Contribution margin ratio method	• Margin of safety • CVP for decision making • Changes in cost structure • Degree of operating leverage	• Weighted-average contribution margin • Weighted-average contribution margin ratio

Cost-Volume-Profit Analysis

Cost-volume-profit (CVP) analysis is a decision-making tool that focuses on the relationship among the volume and mix of units sold, prices, variable costs, fixed costs, and profit. The CVP framework allows managers to evaluate how changing one or more of these key variables will impact profitability, while holding everything else constant. For example, a Starbucks manager might ask the following questions:

- How many customers must I serve each month to break even, or earn zero profit?
- My boss expects the business to earn $18,000 in profit each month. How much total sales revenue is needed to achieve this goal?
- Economic conditions have had a negative impact on customer demand. How much can sales drop before the business is operating at a loss?
- I've been thinking about investing in technology that would speed up service to customers. How many additional customers must we serve each day to justify this investment?
- If I expand our product offering to sell green tea, muffins, and sandwiches, how will it affect the bottom line?

Each of these questions can be addressed using cost-volume-profit analysis, but they require us to make some key assumptions. If the assumptions do not hold true, our conclusions will be flawed as well.

ASSUMPTIONS OF COST-VOLUME-PROFIT ANALYSIS

Cost-volume-profit analysis is based on the following assumptions, most of which were introduced in Chapter 5 when we analyzed cost behavior patterns.

Assumption	Explanation
1. Linear cost and revenue functions	We will use a straight line to approximate the relationship between total cost and sales volume, as well as total revenue and sales volume.
2. All costs can be classified as either fixed or variable	For mixed costs, we must determine the total fixed cost and variable cost per unit. (Refer to Chapter 5 for a review of the methods used to estimate cost behavior.) We assume step costs will remain fixed within the relevant range.
3. Only volume affects total cost and total revenue	We ignore other factors that can affect costs and revenue, such as employee learning curves, productivity gains, and volume discounts for buying in bulk.
4. Production volume is equal to sales volume	This simplifies the analysis because some costs vary with production while others vary with sales volume. Holding inventory constant also eliminates any differences in profit that are due to the costing method used to value inventory for external reporting. (See the supplement to Chapter 5 for further discussion of the effect of changing inventory levels on profit.)
5. Constant product mix	For companies that sell multiple products and services, we assume that the relative proportion of units sold or sales revenue generated by each product or service line remains constant.

To illustrate, let's start with a simple but unrealistic scenario in which Starbucks sells only one type and size of coffee. Assume the price is $2.50 per unit and variable costs are $1.00 per unit. Recall from Chapter 5 that variable costs, such as the cost of coffee beans and supplies, increase in direct proportion to the number of units produced or customers served. Fixed costs are $12,000 per month, including rent, insurance, equipment depreciation, salaries, and other costs that must be paid each month regardless of the number of customers served.

CVP GRAPH

A cost-volume-profit graph, or **CVP graph**, provides a visual representation of the relationship between total revenue, total costs, volume, and profit. Refer to Exhibit 6–1 for a CVP graph based on the hypothetical data in our Starbucks example. The total revenue (blue) line is based on the number of units sold multiplied by the unit sales price ($2.50). A higher unit sales price will result in a steeper total revenue line. The total cost (red) line is the sum of the total fixed and total variable costs. Notice that the total cost line intercepts the y-axis at $12,000. This is the total fixed costs, or the total cost that will be incurred regardless of volume. The variable cost per unit ($1) is represented by the slope of the total cost line, which increases by $1 with each additional unit sold.

The **break-even point** is the point at which the total revenue and total cost lines cross (leaving zero profit). In this example, the break-even point corresponds to 8,000 units, or $20,000 in total sales revenue (8,000 units × $2.50). The difference between the total revenue line and the total cost line is profit, reported as net operating income on the income statement. Anything below 8,000 units results in a loss because total cost is higher than total revenue. Anything above 8,000 units results in a profit. For example, if Starbucks sells 20,000 units, profit will be $18,000 ($50,000 in total revenue − $32,000 in total cost).

EXHIBIT 6–1	Cost-Volume-Profit Graph

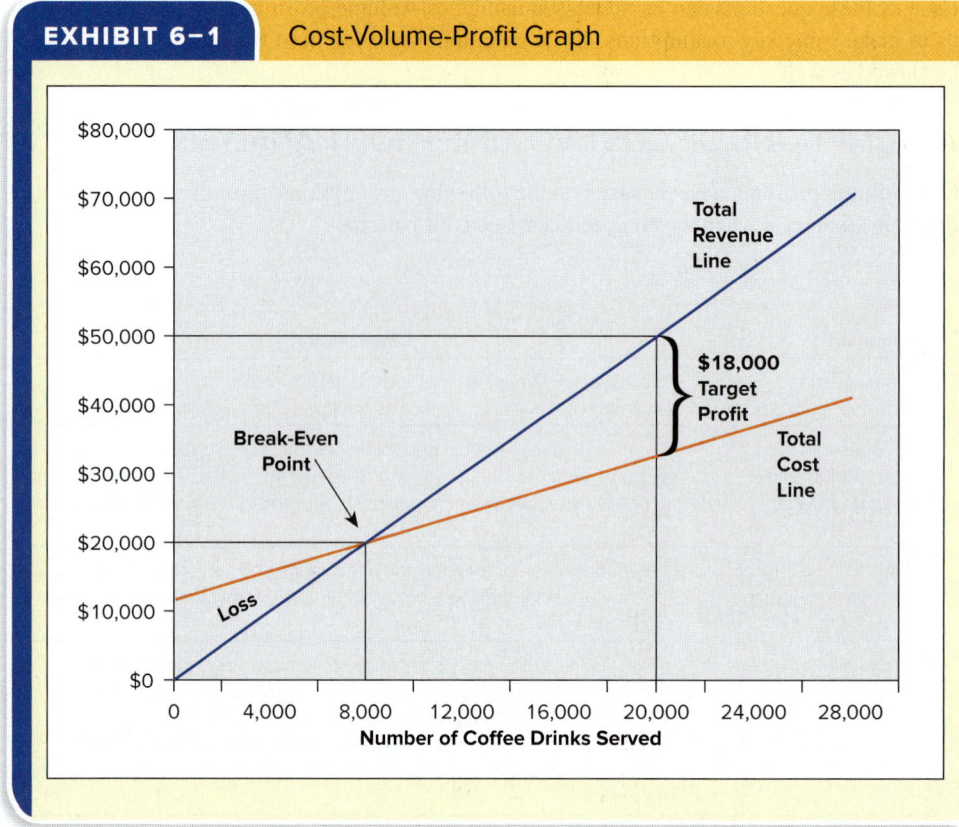

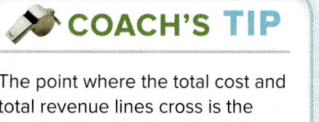

COACH'S TIP

The point where the total cost and total revenue lines cross is the break-even point. At a break-even point of 8,000 units, total revenue and total costs are both equal to $20,000, leaving zero profit.

The CVP graph provides a visual snapshot of the CVP relationships, including the break-even point, but we will use equations and formulas to do the detailed calculations and compute exact numbers.

BASIC CVP ANALYSIS

The cost-volume-profit framework can be used to analyze many different managerial decisions. Two of the simplest types of CVP analysis are break-even analysis (How many units or sales dollars do I need to break even, or earn zero profit?) and target profit analysis (How many units or sales dollars do I need to earn a target profit?).

As you will see shortly, break-even analysis is a special case of target profit analysis, where the target profit is equal to zero. Once you understand the break-even model, it is very easy to extend it to a target profit other than zero.

There are several different approaches or methods we can use to model the relationship between revenues, costs, profit, and volume, including the following:

- Profit Equation Method
- Unit Contribution Margin Method
- Contribution Margin Ratio Method

Each of these methods provides a different way to express the CVP relationships, or a different approach to answering the same basic question. Which method you choose is partly a matter of personal preference, but also depends on how the question is asked and what data you have available to answer it. As long as you have complete information, you can use any of these methods and come to the same final answer.

In the next section, we will illustrate how to use each of these methods to find the break-even point and then extend the example to incorporate a target profit.

PROFIT EQUATION METHOD

The profit equation method uses an equation in which profit is defined as the difference between total sales revenue and total fixed and variable costs as follows:

> Total Sales Revenue − Total Variable Costs − Total Fixed Costs = Profit
>
> (Unit Price × Q) − (Unit Variable Costs × Q) − Total Fixed Costs = Profit

Where Q = Quantity of units sold

Notice that total sales revenue and variable costs are a function of the number of units sold (Q), while total fixed costs are independent of the number of units sold. In CVP analysis, we allow any single factor in the equation to vary while holding everything else constant. We can solve for Q to determine the number of units needed to break even or to earn a target profit. Or if we already know the number of units *(Q)*, we can solve for one of the other unknown variables, such as the sales prices needed to break even or the maximum fixed costs to earn a target profit.

Break-Even Analysis

Break-even analysis is the simplest form of cost-volume-profit analysis. The goal of **break-even analysis** is to determine the level of sales (in either units or total sales dollars) needed to break even, or earn zero profit.

In our hypothetical Starbucks example, the unit price is $2.50, the unit variable cost is $1.00, and the total fixed costs are $12,000. To find the break-even point in units, we simply set the profit equation equal to zero and solve for the quantity of units (Q), as follows:

Learning Objective 6–1
Use cost-volume-profit analysis to find the break-even point.

> (Unit Price × Q) − (Unit Variable Costs × Q) − Total Fixed Costs = Profit
>
> ($2.50 × Q) − ($1.00 × Q) − $12,000 = 0
>
> $1.50 Q = $12,000
>
> Q = $12,000 ÷ $1.50
>
> Q = 8,000

COACH'S TIP

To find the break-even point, set the profit equation equal to zero. If you want to earn a profit, set the equation equal to the target profit.

This analysis shows that Starbucks needs to sell 8,000 units to break even, which translates into $20,000 in total sales revenue (8,000 units × $2.50 = $20,000). Note that these are the same break-even numbers shown in the CVP graph in Exhibit 6–1. Although breaking even is important, most managers want to do more than that. They want to earn a profit. The profit equation approach can be easily extended to include a target profit by setting the profit equation equal to an amount other than zero.

Target Profit Analysis

Target profit analysis is an extension of break-even analysis that allows managers to determine the number of units or total sales revenue needed to earn a target profit. For example, if our hypothetical Starbucks manager wants to earn $18,000 in profit, how many units of coffee must the store sell each month? To answer this question, we can set the profit equation

Learning Objective 6–2
Use cost-volume-profit analysis to determine the sales needed to achieve a target profit.

equal to $18,000 and then determine how many units (Q) must be sold to meet this target, as follows:

$$(\text{Unit Price} \times Q) - (\text{Unit Variable Costs} \times Q) - \text{Total Fixed Costs} = \text{Profit}$$

$$(\$2.50 \times Q) - (\$1.00 \times Q) - \$12,000 = \$18,000$$

$$\$1.50\, Q = \$12,000 + \$18,000$$

$$\$1.50\, Q = \$30,000$$

$$Q = \$30,000 \div \$1.50$$

$$Q = 20,000$$

According to this analysis, Starbucks would need to sell 20,000 units in order to earn $18,000 in target profit. This translates into $50,000 in total sales revenue (20,000 units × $2.50). Again, these results are consistent with the target profit shown on the CVP graph in Exhibit 6–1. The equations simply provide a more precise way to compute the numbers.

UNIT CONTRIBUTION MARGIN METHOD

An alternative tool that can be used to answer most cost-volume-profit questions is the contribution margin income statement. This income statement, which was introduced in Chapter 5, makes a distinction between variable costs and fixed costs. Recall that **contribution margin** is the difference between sales revenue and variable costs, or the amount of profit available to cover fixed costs and profit.

The **unit contribution margin** tells us how much each unit sold contributes toward fixed costs and profit. In our Starbucks example, the unit selling price was $2.50 and the unit variable cost was $1.00, which gives us a unit contribution margin of $1.50. This amount is used first to cover total fixed costs, with the remainder as profit. As with the profit equation approach, we can use the unit contribution margin method for both break-even and target profit analysis.

Break-Even Analysis

To find the break-even point using the unit contribution margin, we need to determine the number of units (Q) that must be sold to cover $12,000 in fixed costs, leaving zero profit.

	Per Unit	Number of Units	Total
Sales revenue	$2.50		
Less: Variable costs	1.00		
Contribution margin	$1.50	$\times\, Q =$	$12,000
Less: Fixed costs			12,000
Net operating income			0

COACH'S TIP

How many units (Q) must be sold to cover the $12,000 in fixed costs, leaving zero profit?

At the break-even point, total contribution margin must equal total fixed costs. To solve for the break-even point in units, divide the total fixed costs ($12,000) by the unit contribution margin ($1.50), as shown in the following break-even formula:

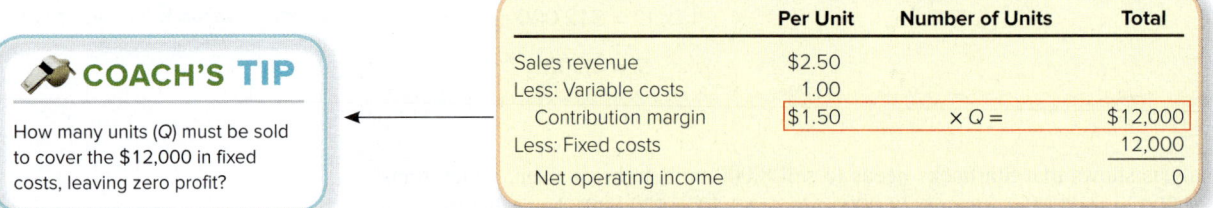

$$\frac{\text{Total Fixed Costs}}{\text{Unit Contribution Margin}} = \text{Break-Even Units } (Q)$$

$$\frac{\$12,000}{\$1.50} = 8,000 \text{ Units}$$

A break-even point of 8,000 units translates to $20,000 in total sales revenue (8,000 × $2.50). This is the same break-even point we calculated using the profit equation method. There is not a single "right" way to solve cost-volume-profit problems. Your best strategy is to use the approach that makes the most sense to you without memorizing specific equations or formulas.

Target Profit Analysis

The unit contribution margin can also be used for target profit analysis. For example, how many units must be sold to earn $18,000 in profit? In this case, the total contribution margin must be enough to cover $12,000 in total fixed costs **plus** $18,000 in target profit, as follows:

	Per Unit	Number of Units (Q)	Total
Sales revenue	$2.50		
Less: Variable costs	1.00		
Contribution margin	$1.50	× Q =	$?
Less: Fixed costs			12,000
Net operating income			$18,000

> **COACH'S TIP**
>
> To determine the number of units needed to earn a target profit, start at the bottom of the income statement and work your way up to Q.

We need to generate $30,000 ($12,000 + $18,000) in total contribution margin to reach the target profit. We can divide the total contribution margin by the unit contribution margin to determine how many units must be sold to reach this target. This logic is summarized in the following target profit formula:

$$\frac{\text{Total Fixed Costs} + \text{Target Profit}}{\text{Unit Contribution Margin}} = \text{Target Units } (Q)$$

$$\frac{\$12,000 + \$18,000}{\$1.50} = 20,000 \text{ Units}$$

Once we know that 20,000 units are needed to reach the target profit, we can multiply that 20,000 by the unit sales price, variable costs, and contribution margin to determine the total dollar values needed to earn $18,000 in target profit, as follows:

	Per Unit	Number of Units (Q)	Total
Sales revenue	$2.50	× 20,000 =	$50,000
Less: Variable costs	1.00	× 20,000 =	20,000
Contribution margin	$1.50	× 20,000 =	$30,000
Less: Fixed costs			12,000
Net operating income			$18,000

In the next section, we introduce a more direct way to determine the total sales revenue needed to earn a target profit. For now, make a mental note that $50,000 in total sales revenue is needed to generate $18,000 in profit.

CONTRIBUTION MARGIN RATIO METHOD

The third way to approach cost-volume-profit problems is based on the contribution margin ratio, or the contribution margin stated as a percentage of sales dollars, as shown below:

	Per Unit	Percent of Sales
Sales price	$2.50	100%
Less: Variable cost	1.00	40%
Contribution margin	$1.50	60% ($1.50 ÷ $2.50)

The contribution margin ratio tells us how much contribution margin is generated as a percentage of sales revenue. In this example, variable costs make up 40 percent of sales revenue, which leaves 60 percent of every sales dollar as contribution margin. Because fixed costs do not change with sales volume, each additional $1.00 in sales revenue will add $0.60 to profit.

We can use the contribution margin ratio to determine the total sales revenue needed to earn a target profit, including a break-even profit of zero. If Starbucks's contribution margin is 60 percent, how much total sales revenue is needed to cover $12,000 in fixed costs, with nothing left over as profit?

Break-Even Analysis

To solve for the break-even point in sales revenue, we simply divide total fixed costs of $12,000 by the 60 percent contribution margin ratio, as follows:

$$\frac{\text{Total Fixed Costs}}{\text{Contribution Margin Ratio (\%)}} = \text{Break-Even Sales (\$)}$$

$$\frac{\$12,000}{60\%} = \$20,000$$

Notice that this formula is almost identical to the formula for break-even units, except the denominator is the contribution margin ratio rather than the unit contribution margin. The contribution margin ratio allows us to solve for total sales revenue in one step rather than first solving for units and then multiplying by the unit sales price. The end result is the same.

	Per Unit	Percent of Sales	Total
Sales revenue	$2.50	100%	$20,000
Less: Variable costs	1.00	40%	8,000
Contribution margin	$1.50	60%	$12,000
Less: Fixed costs			12,000
Net operating income			0

Target Profit Analysis

To find the sales dollars needed to earn a target profit, we simply add the target profit to the total fixed costs in the numerator, and then divide by the contribution margin ratio. For example, the total sales revenue needed to earn $18,000 in target profit would be computed as follows:

$$\frac{\text{Total Fixed Costs} + \text{Target Profit}}{\text{Contribution Margin Ratio (\%)}} = \text{Target Sales (\$)}$$

$$\frac{\$12,000 + \$18,000}{60\%} = \$50,000$$

Notice that $50,000 is the same total sales revenue we found earlier by multiplying 20,000 target units by the unit sales price (20,000 units × $2.50 = $50,000). The contribution margin ratio provides a different way to solve the problem, but results in the same answer.

	Per Unit	Percent of Sales	Total
Sales revenue	$2.50	100%	$50,000
Less: Variable costs	1.00	40%	20,000
Contribution margin	$1.50	60%	$30,000
Less: Fixed costs			12,000
Net operating income			$18,000

At this point, you may be wondering why you need to know more than one way to solve a CVP problem. It is important that you understand the relationships among the various methods and formulas rather than memorizing a single formula or approach to the problem. Doing so will help you on exams if you aren't given all of the information needed to answer the question a certain way.

It will help you in the real world, too. Managers must often deal with missing or incomplete information. For example, managers may not have ready access to the detailed price and quantity information needed to use the profit equation or unit contribution margin methods. In addition, managers are accustomed to dealing with information that is provided on a total dollar basis, particularly when they deal with multiple products or services that have different unit prices, costs, and quantities. Although the unit contribution margin method is very intuitive, the contribution margin ratio method is more practical, particularly as the number of products or services increases.

To make sure you understand how to calculate the break-even point and target profit using the profit equation, unit contribution margin, or contribution margin ratio methods, complete the following Self-Study Practice:

💡 How's it going?   Self-Study Practice

A company sells a product for $60 per unit. Variable costs are $36 per unit, and monthly fixed costs are $120,000. Answer the following questions.

1. What is the break-even point in units and in total sales revenue?
2. What is the contribution margin ratio?
3. What level of total sales would be required to earn a target profit of $60,000?

After you have finished, check your answers against the solutions in the margin.

Solution to Self-Study Practice
1. Break-Even Units = Fixed Costs ÷ Contribution Margin per Unit
   = $120,000 ÷ ($60 − $36) = 5,000 units
   Break-Even Sales Revenue = 5,000 units × $60 price = $300,000
2. Contribution Margin Ratio = $24 ÷ $60 = 40%
3. Target Sales = (Fixed Costs + Target Profit) ÷ Contribution Margin Ratio
   = ($120,000 + $60,000) ÷ 40% = $450,000

Apply Cost-Volume-Profit Analysis

The previous section illustrated the two most common applications of cost-volume-profit analysis: break-even and target profit analysis. In this section, we extend this basic analysis to several other applications of cost-volume-profit analysis.

MARGIN OF SAFETY

The **margin of safety** is the difference between actual or budgeted sales and the break-even point. Think of the margin of safety as a buffer zone that identifies how much sales can drop before the business will suffer a loss. This application of CVP analysis is most relevant to companies that face a significant risk of **not** making a profit, such as start-up businesses or companies that face extreme competition or abrupt changes in demand. The formula for calculating the margin of safety is:

Learning Objective 6–3
Compute the margin of safety.

Actual or Budgeted Sales − Break-Even Sales = Margin of Safety

Existing companies base the margin of safety on the most recent period's sales; new businesses base it on budgeted or expected sales. For example, if you were thinking of opening a new Starbucks location and had developed a business plan based on an anticipated or budgeted sales level, it would be wise to compare that level to the break-even point. Doing so would show you how much cushion you have between making a profit and suffering a loss.

To apply the margin of safety, let's assume that our hypothetical Starbucks location sold 15,000 coffee drinks during the most recent month (February) as shown in the following contribution margin income statement:

STARBUCKS COFFEE HOUSE
Contribution Margin Income Statement
For the Month of February
15,000 Units Sold

	Total	Per Unit
Sales revenue	$37,500	$2.50
Less: Variable costs	15,000	1.00
Contribution margin	$22,500	$1.50
Less: Fixed costs	12,000	
Net operating income	$10,500	

Notice that the company operated above the break-even point during February with sales of $37,500 and a net operating income of $10,500. Recall that the break-even point was 8,000 units, or $20,000 in total sales. Thus, the margin of safety is calculated as follows:

Actual or Budgeted Sales − Break-Even Sales = Margin of Safety

$37,500 − $20,000 = $17,500

Expressing the margin of safety as a percentage of actual or budgeted sales provides a better idea of how large this buffer zone is. To calculate margin of safety as a percentage, divide the margin of safety by the actual or budgeted sales. In this case, the margin of safety as a percentage of February's actual sales is 46.7 percent ($17,500 ÷ $37,500). In other words, Starbucks's monthly sales could drop as much as $17,500 or 46.7 percent before the company would no longer be profitable.

CVP FOR DECISION MAKING

Learning Objective 6–4
Analyze how changes in prices and cost structure affect cost-volume-profit relationships.

Managers can use CVP to make many different decisions, such as whether to change the price of the product, buy materials from a different supplier, pay employees a salary instead of commission, spend more on advertising, or invest in automated equipment. The CVP model allows managers to perform "what if" analysis to see how changing one or more variables will affect the others. In the next section, we use the CVP framework to analyze several different managerial scenarios. We will use the month of February as the base case, or point of comparison for evaluating each of these independent scenarios.

As you can see in the contribution margin income statement above, the company sold 15,000 units in February and reported a net operating income of $10,500.

Scenario 1: Changing Prices

Assume that the manager of our Starbucks store is considering increasing the price of coffee to $4 with no effect on unit variable cost or total fixed costs. However, the manager is unsure how customers will react to the price increase. He wants to know what level of total sales revenue will be required to earn at least the same monthly profit as in February, when the company earned $10,500.

The following table summarizes the effect the proposed price increase would have on the unit contribution margin and contribution margin ratio:

	CURRENT PRICE		PROPOSED PRICE	
	Per Unit	**Percent**	**Per Unit**	**Percent**
Sales price	$2.50	100%	$4.00	100%
Less: Variable cost	1.00	40%	1.00	25%
Contribution margin	$1.50	60%	$3.00	75%

COACH'S TIP

The proposed price increase will double the unit contribution margin ($1.50 to $3.00). This means the company will need to sell one-half as many units to break even.

Notice that both the unit contribution margin and the contribution margin ratio increase with the increase in sales price. As a result, every unit and dollar of sales will generate more contribution margin and thus profit.

To determine the sales level needed to earn a target profit of at least $10,500, we can use the contribution margin ratio formula introduced earlier in the chapter, as follows:

$$\frac{\text{Total Fixed Costs} + \text{Target Profit}}{\text{Contribution Margin Ratio (\%)}} = \text{Target Sales (\$)}$$

$$\frac{\$12,000 + \$10,500}{75\%} = \$30,000$$

This analysis shows that the company needs to generate $30,000 in total sales revenue to earn $10,500 in profit. Because the proposed sales price is $4, this translates into 7,500 units ($30,000 ÷ $4). As we discovered earlier in the chapter, you could get this same number by dividing the total fixed costs plus the target profit by the new unit contribution margin as follows:

$$\frac{\text{Total Fixed Costs} + \text{Target Profit}}{\text{Unit Contribution Margin}} = \text{Target Units (}Q\text{)}$$

$$\frac{\$12,000 + \$10,500}{\$3.00} = 7,500 \text{ Units}$$

Scenario 2: Changing Variable Costs and Volume

Assume the Starbucks manager is trying to find a way to increase profit to $16,800 per month. To achieve this goal, he plans to purchase higher quality coffee beans to improve the taste of the product. This will raise variable costs by $0.25 per unit and is expected to increase sales volume by 20 percent. The manager believes that consumers will be willing to pay a higher price for better tasting coffee, but is not sure what price to charge. What unit sales price would be needed to earn a target profit of $16,800?

In this example, two components in the model are changing at the same time:

- Unit variable costs will increase from $1.00 to $1.25.
- Volume will increase from 15,000 units to 18,000 units (15,000 × 120%).

Total fixed costs are assumed to remain unchanged at $12,000, and the target profit is $16,800. In this case, we cannot use the contribution margin to solve the problem because we don't know the unit sales price. However, we can set up a profit equation with the unit sales price as the unknown variable, as follows:

$$
\text{(Unit Price} \times Q) - \text{(Unit Variable Costs} \times Q) - \text{Total Fixed Costs} = \text{Profit}
$$

$$
\text{(Unit Price} \times 18{,}000) - (\$1.25 \times 18{,}000) - \$12{,}000 = \$16{,}800
$$

$$
\text{(Unit Price} \times 18{,}000) - \$22{,}500 - \$12{,}000 = \$16{,}800
$$

$$
\text{(Unit Price} \times 18{,}000) = \$16{,}800 + \$22{,}500 + \$12{,}000
$$

$$
\text{(Unit Price} \times 18{,}000) = \$51{,}300
$$

$$
\text{Unit Price} = \$51{,}300 \div 18{,}000
$$

$$
\text{Unit Price} = \$2.85
$$

The Starbucks manager would need to raise the unit price to $2.85 to meet the target profit of $16,800, assuming all of the other variables in the CVP model are as expected.

SPOTLIGHT ON Big DATA Analytics

Grinding Coffee (and Data) at Starbucks

Are you one of the millions of people who use the Starbucks app to order and pay for your skinny vanilla latte and blueberry scone? If so, think about how much data you are providing Starbucks every time you click the "pay" button on your phone: what you ordered, what time, where you were, how long it's been since you purchased something . . . and if you allow access to other apps on your phone, no telling what else. Now multiply that by the 90 million or so transactions that Starbucks processes every week. That is the definition of big data!

Gerri Martin-Flickinger, Starbucks's chief technology officer (CTO), recently told shareholders: "We know a lot about what people are buying, where they're buying, how they're buying . . . and if we combine this information with other data, like weather, promotions, inventory, insights into local events, we can actually deliver better personalized service to customers."

Here are just a few examples of how managers at Starbucks use big data analytics:

- Personalizing the customer experience by providing recommendations based on previous buying habits.
- Targeted marketing, such as offering reward points on frequently purchased items for loyal customers and discounts to re-engage customers who have not purchased anything recently.
- Analyzing weather conditions by region to promote different products (e.g., hot or cold drinks).
- Identifying new store locations based on key metrics such as traffic patterns, population density, transportation links, and average income levels.
- Using analytics and data visualization tools to compare key performance metrics (KPIs) across locations.

Sources:
https://www.cio.com/article/3050920/analytics/starbucks-cto-brews-personalized-experiences.html
https://www.intel.ie/content/www/ie/en/it-managers/starbucks-analytics.html

Scenario 3: Changing Fixed Costs and Prices

Assume the Starbucks manager is considering starting a customer appreciation program that would reward customers by giving them their tenth cup of coffee for free. If all customers participated in this program, the average unit selling price would drop from $2.50 to $2.25 per unit [(9 units × $2.50) ÷ 10]. In addition, the company would spend an additional $3,000 per month to advertise the rewards program. The manager wants to know how much sales volume is needed to earn a target profit of $16,800.

In this example, two components in the model are changing at the same time:

- Price will drop from $2.50 to $2.25 per unit.
- Fixed costs will increase from $12,000 to $15,000.

Unit variable costs are assumed to remain the same at $1.00, and the target profit is $16,800. Because the price decreased to $2.25 and variable costs remained at $1.00, the new unit contribution margin is $1.25. We can use the target profit formula from earlier in the chapter to determine the number of units (Q) that must be sold to reach the $16,800 target profit, as follows:

$$\frac{\text{Total Fixed Costs} + \text{Target Profit}}{\text{Unit Contribution Margin}} = \text{Target Units } (Q)$$

$$\frac{\$15,000 + \$16,800}{\$1.25} = 25,440 \text{ units}$$

In this case, the Starbucks manager would need to sell 25,440 units at an average sales price of $2.25 in order meet the target profit of $16,800, assuming all of the other variables in the model remain the same.

Before we continue, complete the following Self-Study Practice to make sure you can compute the margin of safety and understand how changing prices, costs, or volume affects profit.

 How's it going?   Self-Study Practice

Last month's contribution margin income statement for Calico Industries follows:

Contribution Margin Income Statement
10,000 Units Sold

	Per Unit	Total	Percent of Sales
Sales revenue	$4.00	$40,000	100%
Less: Variable costs	1.50	15,000	37.5%
Contribution margin	$2.50	$25,000	62.5%
Less: Fixed costs		10,000	
Net operating income		$15,000	

Break-Even Units = $10,000 ÷ $2.50 = 4,000 units

Break-Even Sales = $10,000 ÷ 62.5% = $16,000

1. Compute Calico's margin of safety in dollars and as a percentage of sales.

2. Assume the sales price increases by 25 percent with no effect on unit variable costs. Compute the new unit contribution margin and contribution margin ratio.

3. Given the price increase described in question 2, how many units must be sold to earn the same profit as last month?

After you have finished, check your answers against the solutions in the margin.

CHANGES IN COST STRUCTURE

Next, we analyze how changes in cost structure affect the cost-volume-profit relationship. **Cost structure** refers to how a company uses variable costs versus fixed costs to perform its operations. Some companies have a relatively high proportion of variable costs such as direct materials and direct labor while others have relatively high fixed costs such as facilities, equipment, and salaries. Managers face many decisions that can affect their cost structure and have implications for cost-volume-profit analysis.

A common example is the decision to automate a process that is currently done manually. Automation typically reduces variable costs (by reducing direct labor) while increasing fixed costs (by increasing equipment depreciation, maintenance, and supervision).

Assume that the Starbucks manager is considering investing in equipment that would allow customers to place their own order using a touch screen at the counter. The store could lease the machine for $14,000 per month (increasing monthly fixed costs from $12,000 to $26,000). The automation would save $0.70 in variable costs per unit (from $1.00 to $0.30). The unit sales price will be $2.50 under either alternative. What level of volume would be needed to justify this expenditure?

One way to solve this problem is to use the profit equation method. Instead of setting a single profit equation equal to zero (to find the break-even point), we set two profit equations equal to each other so that they yield the same profit. Doing so allows us to find the **indifference point,** or the point at which managers should be indifferent about which alternative to choose because they yield the same profit.

Profit Equation (before automation)	=	Profit Equation (after automation)
(Unit Price × Q) − (Unit Variable Cost × Q) − Total fixed costs	=	(Unit Price × Q) − (Unit Variable Cost × Q) − Total fixed costs
$2.50 Q − $1.00 Q − $12,000	=	$2.50 Q − $0.30 Q − $26,000
$1.50 Q − $12,000	=	$2.20 Q − $26,000
−$0.70 Q	=	−$14,000
Q	=	20,000

At a sales volume of 20,000 units, the company will make the same profit with or without automation. To verify that we did the algebra correctly, we can plug $Q = 20,000$ back into the profit equation to make certain the profit is the same:

Profit Equation (before automation)	=	Profit Equation (after automation)
(Unit Price × Q) − (Unit Variable Cost × Q) − Total fixed cost	=	(Unit Price × Q) − (Unit Variable Cost × Q) − Total fixed cost
$2.50 (20,000) − $1.00 (20,000) − $12,000	=	$2.50 (20,000) − $0.30 (20,000) − $26,000
$50,000 − 20,000 − $12,000	=	$50,000 − $6,000 − $26,000
$18,000	=	$18,000

At 20,000 units, profit will be $18,000 under either alternative. If volume is more than 20,000 units, the company will make a higher profit with the automated ordering system. But if volume is less than 20,000 units per month, profit will be higher without automation. See Exhibit 6–2 for a visual depiction of the effect of automation on the cost-volume-profit relationship.

As long as the manager expects demand to exceed 20,000 units per month, the investment in automation should result in increased profit. However, there is a greater risk with automation in the event that demand is not as large as expected. This risk is reflected in a measure called *degree of operating leverage,* which is discussed next.

DEGREE OF OPERATING LEVERAGE

In physics, a lever is a tool that allows a small amount of force to move a heavy object. In business, managers can use fixed costs as a lever to turn relatively small changes in sales revenue into larger changes in profit. Decisions about the use of debt versus equity affect a company's **financial leverage**. Decisions about whether to use fixed or variable costs to run the business affect a company's **operating leverage**. These two types of leverage are highly related, but we will focus on operating leverage here. Financial leverage will be covered in your finance classes.

EXHIBIT 6–2   Effect of Automation on the CVP Relationship

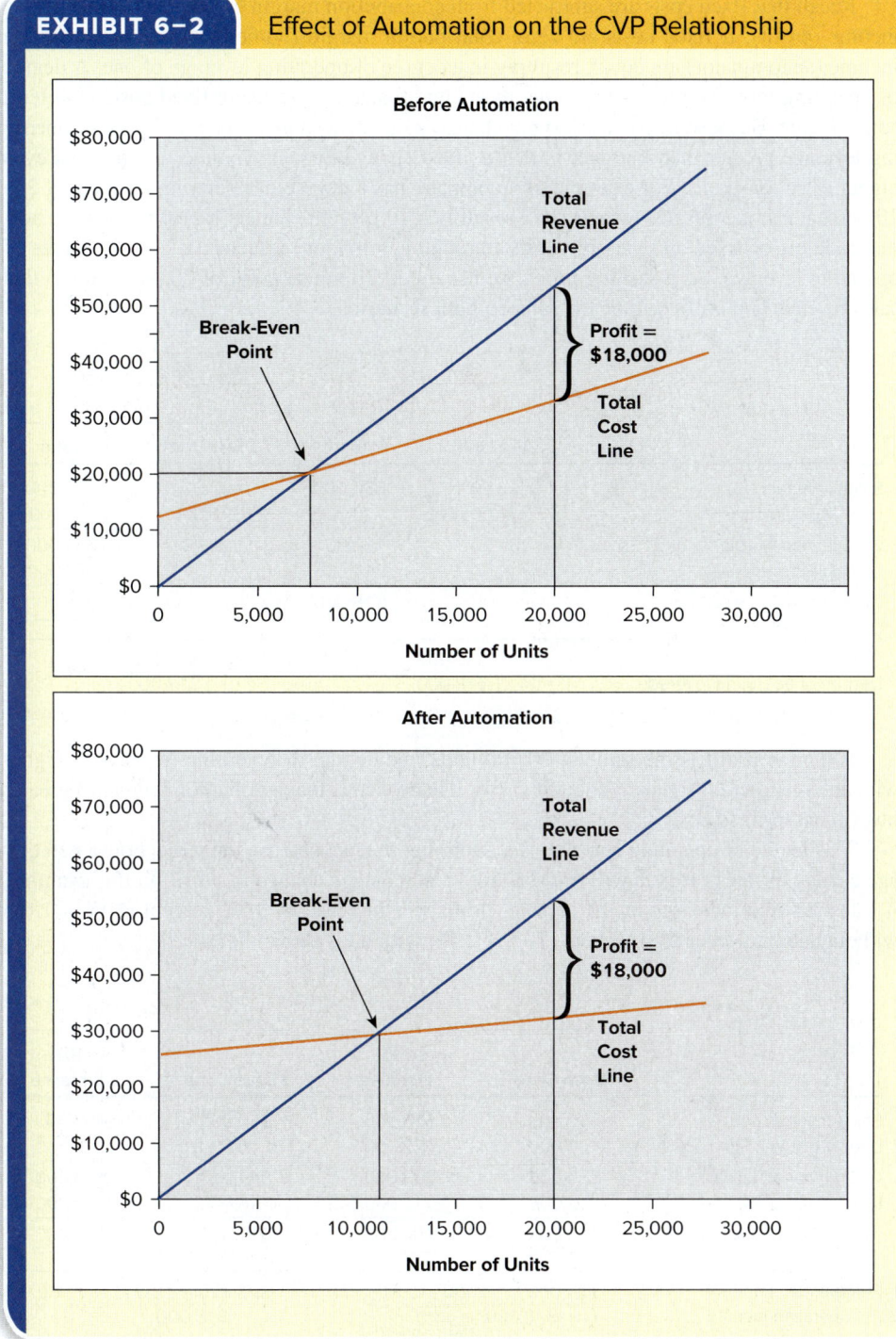

Degree of operating leverage measures the extent to which fixed costs are used to operate the business. In general, higher fixed costs indicate that a company is more highly leveraged. Degree of operating leverage is calculated as follows:

$$\text{Degree of Operating Leverage} = \frac{\text{Contribution Margin}}{\text{Net Operating Income}}$$

Recall that fixed costs are subtracted from contribution margin to calculate net operating income (profit). If fixed costs are zero, contribution margin (numerator) and net operating income (denominator) are equal, resulting in a degree of operating leverage of one. A degree of operating leverage greater than one means that managers are using fixed costs to at least some degree. Because fixed costs do not change with changes in volume, a degree of operating leverage greater than one means that a given change in sales volume will have an even bigger effect on profit. For example, if a company has a degree of operating leverage of 2, a 10 percent change in sales revenue will result in a 20 percent change in profit. Let's see how the trade-off of fixed and variable costs (through automation) affects Starbucks's degree of operating leverage. As a starting point, we use the indifference point of 20,000 units so that sales revenue and profit will be the same in both scenarios.

	20,000 UNITS SOLD (NO AUTOMATION)		20,000 UNITS SOLD (AUTOMATION)	
	Per Unit	Total	Per Unit	Total
Sales revenue	$2.50	$50,000	$2.50	$50,000
Less: Variable costs	1.00	20,000	0.30	6,000
Contribution margin	$1.50	$30,000	$2.20	$44,000
Less: Fixed costs		12,000		26,000
Net operating income		$18,000		$18,000
Degree of operating leverage		$\frac{\$30,000}{\$18,000}=1.67$		$\frac{\$44,000}{\$18,000}=2.44$

Although profit is the same at 20,000 units, the degree of operating leverage is higher with automation (2.44) than without it (1.67). The reason is that automation requires a greater investment in fixed costs.

The degree of operating leverage is a multiplier that we can use to predict how a percentage change in sales revenue will translate into a percentage change in profit. In this example, if sales revenue increases by 10 percent, profit will increase by 16.7 percent (10% × 1.67) without automation or 24.4 percent (10% × 2.44) with it, as shown below.

	NO AUTOMATION		AUTOMATION	
	Base Case	10% Increase	Base Case	10% Increase
Sales revenue	$50,000	$55,000	$50,000	$55,000
Less: Variable costs	20,000	22,000	6,000	6,600
Contribution margin	$30,000	$33,000	$44,000	$48,400
Less: Fixed costs	12,000	12,000	26,000	26,000
Net operating income	$18,000	$21,000	$18,000	$22,400
Percentage change in net operating income		$\frac{\$21,000-18,000}{\$18,000}=16.7\%$		$\frac{\$22,400-18,000}{\$18,000}=24.4\%$

Starting at the same level of profit ($18,000), the company will experience a larger increase in profit with automation than without it.

Keep in mind that operating leverage works in both directions. It magnifies the effect of both increases and decreases in sales revenue. If sales decrease by 10 percent, the company will experience a more dramatic decline in profit with automation than without it. In general, a company with a high degree of operating leverage (high fixed costs) will experience greater swings in profit as a result of changes in sales revenue and is therefore considered riskier than a comparable company with a smaller degree of operating leverage. In making choices about cost structure, managers must consider both the rewards (potential for increased profit) and amount of risk (upside and downside) they are willing to bear.

Complete the following Self-Study Practice to make sure you understand the effect of cost structure on the degree of operating leverage and profit.

 How's it going?   Self-Study Practice

Alpha and Beta Companies make a similar product. Alpha makes the product manually; Beta uses robots to do much of the assembly. Last month, both companies sold 20,000 units and made the same profit as follows:

	Alpha (20,000 units)		Beta (20,000 units)	
	Per Unit	Total	Per Unit	Total
Sales revenue	$100	$200,000	$100	$200,000
Less: Variable costs	60	120,000	20	40,000
Contribution margin	$ 40	80,000	$ 80	$160,000
Less: Fixed costs		20,000		100,000
Net operating income		$ 60,000		$ 60,000

1. Calculate the degree of operating leverage for each company.

2. If sales increase by 10 percent, how much will profit increase for each company?

3. Which company is better positioned to withstand a decrease in demand? Why?

After you have finished, check your answers against the solutions in the margin.

SPOTLIGHT ON **Sustainability**

Social entrepreneurship is a growing area of sustainability that focuses on the economic and social elements of the triple bottom line. A social enterprise is an organization that uses an economic or business model to address an important societal issue such as poverty, hunger, education, health, or disease. An excellent example is TOMS, the company who pioneered the "one-for-one" business model. The company started out by donating a pair of shoes for every pair sold, but has expanded to give "the gift of sight" for each pair of sunglasses sold, "the gift of water" for each bag of coffee sold, and the "gift of kindness" for each backpack sold, to name just a few. The company has now created an electronic marketplace to help other social entrepreneurs launch their own business venture and to encourage consumers to buy goods from companies that are designed to give back.

Although a social enterprise is designed to create a positive social impact, its managers need a firm understanding of the economics of the business to accomplish that goal. Cost-volume-profit analysis is a powerful tool for analyzing the economics of social enterprises. When a social enterprise is first started, the goal may simply be to generate enough revenue to cover its costs (i.e., to break even). For example, the price of a pair of TOMS shoes must be set high enough to cover the variable cost of two pairs of shoes (one to be sold and one to be donated), plus the fixed costs of operating the business. As the social enterprise grows, the model can be expanded to include a target profit. The idea behind social entrepreneurship is to simultaneously earn a profit while making a positive impact on society.

Refer to PA6–7 and PB6–7 to see how cost-volume-profit analysis can be applied to a social enterprise.

Multiproduct Cost-Volume-Profit Analysis

Learning Objective 6–6
Perform multiproduct cost-volume-profit analysis and explain how the product or sales mix affects the analysis.

In the previous examples, we simplified the CVP analysis by assuming that Starbucks sells only one type and size of coffee drink. But we all know that Starbucks, and most other businesses, offer more than one product or service. For example, Starbucks sells coffee, tea, pastries, sandwiches, salads, mugs, T-shirts, and other novelty items. Each of these items is likely to have a different price and unit cost, which makes the CVP analysis more complex.

The key to performing CVP analysis in a multiproduct or service setting is to make an assumption about the relative mix of products or services sold. The mix can be stated in terms of the number of units sold (called the *product mix*) or as a percentage of total sales dollars (called the *sales mix*). The **product mix** is used to compute the weighted-average contribution margin **per unit**, while the **sales mix** is used to compute the weighted-average contribution margin **ratio**, or contribution margin as a percentage of sales. Either of these numbers can be used for multiproduct cost-volume-profit analysis, including break-even or target profit analysis. Which method you use depends on how the information is presented and whether you are trying to solve for the number of units or total sales revenue. As with the single-product scenarios, both methods will yield the same answer as long as you have complete information, including unit sales prices. The only caveat is that the analysis will be valid only for the assumed product or sales mix.

WEIGHTED-AVERAGE CONTRIBUTION MARGIN

Let's start by stating the product mix in units, which will be used to calculate a weighted-average unit contribution margin. The weighted-average unit contribution margin is then used in place of the single product unit contribution margin in the cost-volume-profit analysis. The **weighted-average unit contribution margin** is the average unit contribution margin of multiple products weighted according to the **percentage of units sold.**

To illustrate, let's extend our Starbucks example to incorporate two product offerings: coffee and pastries. While still unrealistic, this simple setting illustrates the concepts and techniques needed to apply CVP to even more product and service offerings. Assume the unit price and variable cost of the two products are as follows:

	Coffee	Pastries
Sales price	$2.50	$4.00
Less: Variable cost	1.00	1.25
Unit contribution margin	$1.50	$2.75

Notice that pastries have a higher unit contribution margin ($2.75) than coffee ($1.50). We can calculate a weighted average of these two numbers, with the weight based on the relative proportion (mix) of units sold.

Assume that 60 percent of units sold are coffee and 40 percent pastries. Based on this product mix, the weighted-average unit contribution margin would be calculated as follows:

	Coffee	Pastries
Unit contribution margin	$1.50	$2.75
Unit mix (weight)	× 60%	× 40%
	$0.90	$1.10
Weighted-average unit contribution margin	$0.90 + $1.10 = $2.00	

The $2 weighted-average unit contribution margin means that Starbucks will make an average of $2 in contribution margin for each unit sold, but **only** if 60 percent of the units are coffee and 40 percent are pastries. This weighted-average contribution margin can be used in place of the single product contribution margin in the CVP analysis.

Break-Even Analysis

As we learned earlier, at the break-even point, total fixed costs must exactly equal the contribution margin. If we divide the total fixed costs by the weighted-average unit contribution margin, we get the total number of units needed to break even. We then use the assumed product mix percentages to determine how many units of each product type must be sold.

Assuming Starbucks's monthly fixed costs are $12,000, the break-even point would be calculated as follows:

$$\frac{\text{Total Fixed Costs}}{\text{Weighted-Average Unit Contribution Margin}} = \text{Break-Even Units } (Q)$$

$$\frac{\$12,000}{\$2} = 6,000 \text{ Units}$$

This shows that 6,000 total units are required to break even. But how many of these units should be coffee and how many pastries? Because the $2 weighted-average unit contribution margin was based on a 60 percent/40 percent product mix, we must use the same mix to determine the number of units of each product, as follows:

$$\text{Coffee Units} = 6,000 \times 60\% = 3,600$$

$$\text{Pastry Units} = 6,000 \times 40\% = 2,400$$

The company will break even if it sells 3,600 units of coffee and 2,400 units of pastries.

What would happen if the company sold 6,000 total units, but 3,000 (50%) were coffee and 3,000 (50%) were pastries? Would the company still break even? It would not because the break-even point was based on the 60/40 product mix. By shifting the product mix toward the pastry product (and away from coffee), the company will earn **more** contribution margin because each pastry unit contributes a higher contribution margin than a unit of coffee. Because fixed costs do not change, the company will earn a slight profit.

The next example shows how shifting the product mix toward coffee would affect the CVP analysis.

Target Profit Analysis

Next, we extend the cost-volume-profit analysis to include a target profit. Assume that Starbucks serves four coffee drinks for every pastry (or a 4:1 ratio). The new product mix is 80 percent (4 out of 5) coffee units and 20 percent (1 out of 5) pastry units. The weighted-average unit contribution margin based on this product mix is calculated as follows:

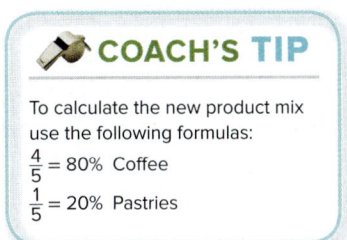

COACH'S TIP

To calculate the new product mix use the following formulas:

$\frac{4}{5} = 80\%$ Coffee

$\frac{1}{5} = 20\%$ Pastries

	Coffee	Pastries
Unit contribution margin	$1.50	$2.75
Unit mix (weight)	× 80%	× 20%
	$1.20	$0.55
Weighted-average unit contribution margin		$1.20 + $0.55 = $1.75

Notice that the new weighted-average unit contribution margin of $1.75 (based on an 80/20 product mix) is lower than the $2.00 unit contribution margin calculated in the previous example (using a 60/40 product mix). Because the coffee product is now weighted more heavily, the weighted-average unit contribution margin is lower.

If the Starbucks manager wants to earn a monthly profit of $9,000 and monthly fixed costs remain at $12,000, how many coffee and pastry units must be sold? To find out, we use the same target profit formula as before but divide by the new weighted-average unit contribution margin, as shown below:

$$\frac{\text{Total Fixed Costs} + \text{Target Profit}}{\text{Weighted-Average Unit Contribution Margin}} = \text{Target Units } (Q)$$

$$\frac{\$12,000 + \$9,000}{\$1.75} = 12,000 \text{ Units}$$

We then multiply 12,000 target units by the new product mix (80/20) to determine how many units of each product must be sold to reach the target profit, as follows:

$$\text{Coffee Units} = 12,000 \times 80\% = 9,600$$

$$\text{Pastry Units} = 12,000 \times 20\% = 2,400$$

The company will earn $9,000 if it sells 9,600 coffee drinks and 2,400 pastries. We can confirm this result by preparing a contribution margin income statement as follows:

STARBUCKS COFFEE
Contribution Margin Income Statement
Based on Target Profit of $9,000

	Coffee (9,600 units)		Pastries (2,400 units)		Overall (12,000 units)
	Per Unit	Total	Per Unit	Total	Total
Sales revenue	$2.50	$24,000	$4.00	$9,600	$33,600
Less: Variable costs	1.00	9,600	1.25	3,000	12,600
Contribution margin	$1.50	$14,400	$2.75	$6,600	$21,000
Less: Fixed costs					12,000
Net operating income					$ 9,000

This statement confirms the results of our target profit analysis. Profit will be $9,000 if the company sells 12,000 units, with 9,600 units of coffee (80 percent) and 2,400 units of pastries (20 percent).

WEIGHTED-AVERAGE CONTRIBUTION MARGIN RATIO

We can also perform multiproduct CVP analysis by using the sales mix (stated in terms of total sales dollars) to compute the **weighted-average contribution margin ratio**. This approach is commonly used in business because managers often have aggregated information about revenue and costs by product line (as opposed to the detailed information about prices, quantities, etc.)

Consider the following contribution margin statement for Starbucks. This is the same income statement we just prepared for a target profit of $9,000, but the numbers have been restated as a percentage of total sales revenue.

STARBUCKS COFFEE
Contribution Margin Income Statement
Based on Target Profit of $9,000

	Coffee		Pastries		Overall	
	Total	**Percent**	**Total**	**Percent**	**Total**	**Percent**
Sales revenue	$24,000	100%	$9,600	100%	$33,600	100%
Less: Variable costs	9,600	40	3,000	31.25	12,600	37.5
Contribution margin	$14,400	60%	$6,600	68.75%	$21,000	62.5%
Less: Fixed costs					12,000	
Net operating income					$ 9,000	

COACH'S TIP

To compute the weighted-average contribution margin ratio, divide total contribution margin by total sales revenue, as follows:

$21,000 ÷ $33,600 = 62.5%

The weighted-average contribution margin ratio tells you how much contribution margin is generated (on average) for each dollar of sales based on the total sales revenue mix. In this case, the company generates $0.625 for every $1.00 of sales.

The **weighted-average contribution margin ratio** reflects the contribution margin ratios of the two products weighted according to the relative percentage of total sales revenue. In this example, the sales mix is approximately 71.43 percent ($24,000 ÷ $33,600) from coffee and 28.57 percent ($9,600 ÷ $33,600) from pastries. The sales mix is based on total sales revenue (dollars) not units.

The 62.5 percent overall or weighted-average contribution margin ratio means that every dollar of sales revenue will generate an average of $0.625 in contribution margin. But this number only holds if the sales mix is 71.43 percent coffee and 28.57 percent pastries.

Managers can use the 62.5 percent weighted-average contribution margin ratio to determine how much total sales revenue is needed to break even or earn a target profit. Assume that the Starbucks manager wants to earn a target profit of $15,000. Given the assumed sales mix, what is the total sales revenue needed to achieve this target profit?

To answer this question, we can use the target sales formula, with the weighted-average contribution margin ratio as the denominator:

$$\frac{\text{Total Fixed Costs} + \text{Target Profit}}{\text{Weighted-Average Contribution Margin Ratio \%}} = \text{Target Sales (\$)}$$

$$\frac{\$12,000 + \$15,000}{62.5\%} = \$43,200$$

To determine how much of the $43,200 in target sales revenue must come from each product line, we multiply by the assumed sales mix, as follows:

$$\text{Coffee Sales Revenue} = \$43,200 \times 71.43\% = \$30,858$$

$$\text{Pastry Sales Revenue} = \$43,200 \times 28.57\% = \$12,342$$

Notice that we used the total sales mix (not the unit sales mix) to determine how much of the total sales revenue must come from coffee and pastries. Remember that the 62.5 percent weighted-average contribution margin ratio was weighted according to the sales mix (percent of sales revenue), not the product mix (percent of units sold).

If the company achieves this target sales revenue, it should earn $15,000 in target profit. We can confirm this result with the following contribution margin income statement:

STARBUCKS COFFEE
Contribution Margin Income Statement
Based on Target Profit of $15,000

	Coffee		Pastries		Overall	
	Total	**Percent**	**Total**	**Percent**	**Total**	**Percent**
Sales revenue	$30,858	100%	$12,342	100%	$43,200	100%
Less: Variable costs	12,343	40	3,857	31.25	16,200	37.5
Contribution margin	$18,515	60%	$ 8,485	68.75%	$27,000	62.5%
Less: Fixed costs					12,000	
Net operating income					$15,000	

The most important thing to remember when performing cost-volume-profit analysis in a multiproduct setting is to assume and maintain a constant product or sales mix. The mix can be stated in terms of the number of units sold or as a percentage of total sales revenue. The only difference between the two is the unit sales price (which is excluded from the product mix but included in the sales mix). Either approach provides the same end result. Most students are more comfortable solving CVP problems in terms of units and then multiplying the result by the price to find total sales revenue. In the real world, however, managers often need to work with aggregated reports that are stated in dollars and percentages. In this sense, the contribution margin ratio approach is more valuable in the real world.

REVIEW THE CHAPTER

DEMONSTRATION CASE A: SINGLE PRODUCT

Cereality is a cereal bar and café designed to appeal to college students and others who love the idea of mixing Cocoa Puffs and Lucky Charms at almost any time of the day.
    Assume the following cost structure for Cereality:

	Cereal
Unit sales price	$3.75
Unit variable cost	0.75
Unit contribution margin	$3.00
Monthly fixed costs	$6,000

Required:

1. How many customers must Cereality serve each month to break even?
2. How much total sales revenue must Cereality earn each month to break even?
3. If the owners want to earn an operating profit of $7,500 per month, how many customers must they serve?
4. If Cereality expects to serve 3,000 customers next month, what is the margin of safety in units? In total sales dollars? As a percentage of expected sales?

Suggested Solution

1. Break-Even Units = Total Fixed Costs ÷ Unit Contribution Margin

   $$= \$6,000 ÷ \$3.00 = 2,000 \text{ Customers}$$

2. Break-Even Sales Revenue = Total Fixed Costs ÷ Contribution Margin Ratio

   $$= \$6,000 ÷ 80\% = \$7,500$$

   Or:

   $$2,000 \text{ customers} \times \$3.75 = \$7,500$$

3. Target Units = (Total Fixed Costs + Target Profit) ÷ Unit Contribution Margin

   $$= (\$6,000 + \$7,500) ÷ \$3.00 = 4,500 \text{ Units}$$

4. Margin of Safety = 3,000 − 2,000 = 1,000 units; 1,000 × \$3.75

   $$= \$3,750; \$3,750 ÷ (3,000 \times \$3.75) = 33.33\%$$

DEMONSTRATION CASE B: MULTIPRODUCT

Cereality is considering adding a yogurt product to its cereal line with the following unit price and cost information:

	Cereal	Yogurt
Unit sales price	$3.75	$3.00
Unit variable cost	0.75	1.50
Unit contribution margin	$3.00	$1.50
Monthly fixed costs	$6,000	

Assume the product mix is four units of cereal for every one unit of yogurt.

Required:

1. Compute the weighted-average unit contribution margin.
2. How many units of each product must be sold to break even?
3. Explain what would happen to the break-even point if the unit sales mix was 1:1.
4. Using the new sales mix of 1:1, how many units of each product must be sold to earn $7,500 per month?

Suggested Solution

1. Weighted-average contribution margin:

	Cereal	Yogurt
Unit contribution margin	$3.00	$1.50
Unit mix (weight)	× 80%	× 20%
	$2.40	$0.30
Weighted-average unit contribution margin	$2.40 + $0.30 = $2.70	

2. Break-Even Units = Total Fixed Costs ÷ Weighted-Average Unit Contribution Margin

   $$= \$6,000 ÷ \$2.70 = 2,222 \text{ Total Units}$$

   Cereal Units = 2,222 × 80% = 1,778 units

   Yogurt Units = 2,222 × 20% = 444 units

3. If the sales mix was 1:1, or 50 percent from each product, the break-even point would increase. The reason is that the unit sales mix would shift toward yogurt, which has a lower unit contribution margin than cereal. This means the company would need to sell more total units to break even.

4. New weighted-average contribution margin:

	Cereal	Yogurt
Unit contribution margin	$3.00	$1.50
Unit mix (weight)	× 50%	× 50%
	$1.50	$0.75
Weighted-average unit contribution margin	$1.50 + $0.75 = $2.25	

$$\text{Target Units} = (\text{Total Fixed Costs} + \text{Target Profit}) \div \text{Weighted-Average Unit Contribution Margin}$$
$$= (\$6,000 + \$7,500) \div \$2.25 = 6,000 \text{ Total Units}$$

Cereal Units = $6,000 \times 50\% = 3,000$ units

Yogurt Units = $6,000 \times 50\% = 3,000$ units

CHAPTER SUMMARY

LO 6–1　Use cost-volume-profit analysis to find the break-even point.

- The break-even point is the point at which the company is making zero profit. The break-even point can be found using the profit equation method, the unit contribution margin method, or the contribution margin ratio method.

- To find the break-even point using the profit equation method, set the profit equation equal to zero and solve for the quantity of units.

- To find the break-even point in units using the unit contribution margin method, divide total fixed costs by the unit contribution margin.

- To find the break-even point in sales revenue using the contribution margin ratio method, divide total fixed costs by the contribution margin ratio.

LO 6–2　Use cost-volume-profit analysis to determine the sales needed to achieve a target profit.

- Target profit analysis is an extension of break-even analysis that allows managers to determine the number of units sold or total sales revenue required to earn a target profit.

- For a business to earn a profit, its total contribution margin must be enough to cover fixed costs plus the desired target profit. Target profit can be analyzed using the profit equation method, the unit contribution margin method, or the contribution margin ratio method.

- To determine the number of units needed to earn a target profit using the profit equation method, set the profit equation equal to the target profit and solve for the number of units (Q).

- To determine the number of units needed to earn a target profit using the unit contribution margin method, divide the target contribution margin (total fixed costs + target profit) by the unit contribution margin.

- To determine the total sales needed to earn a target profit using the contribution margin ratio method, divide the target contribution margin (total fixed costs + target profit) by the contribution margin ratio.

LO 6–3　Compute the margin of safety.

- The margin of safety is the difference between actual or budgeted sales and break-even sales. It indicates how much cushion there is between the current (or expected) level of sales and the break-even point.

LO 6–4　Analyze how changes in prices and cost structure affect cost-volume-profit relationships.

- To analyze how changes in prices or cost structure affect the cost-volume-profit relationships, we allow one or more variables to change while holding everything else constant.

- All else equal, an increase in the selling price will increase the contribution margin and lower the break-even point.

Calculate the degree of operating leverage and use it to predict the effect a change in sales will have on profit.   LO 6–5

• Operating leverage occurs when a company uses fixed costs to leverage a relatively small change in sales revenue into a larger effect on profit.

• Degree of operating leverage is calculated as the ratio of contribution margin to net operating income. This number is the multiplication factor that explains how a percentage change in sales revenue translates into a percentage change in profit.

Perform multiproduct cost-volume-profit analysis and explain how the product or sales mix affects the analysis.   LO 6–6

• The key to multiproduct cost-volume-profit analysis is to assume and maintain a constant product or sales mix.

• The weighted-average unit contribution margin is calculated based on the relative proportion of units sold (product mix). It can be used to solve for the number of units needed to break even or earn a target profit.

• The weighted-average contribution margin ratio is calculated based on the relative proportion of total sales revenue (sales mix). It can be used to solve for the total revenue needed to break even or earn a target profit.

Managerial Analysis Tools	
Name of Measure	**Formula**
Contribution margin per unit	Unit Sales Price − Variable Cost per Unit or $\dfrac{\text{Total Contribution Margin}}{\text{Number of Units Sold}}$
Contribution margin ratio	$\dfrac{\text{Unit Contribution Margin}}{\text{Unit Sales Price}}$ or $\dfrac{\text{Total Contribution Margin}}{\text{Total Sales Revenue}}$
Break-even units	$\dfrac{\text{Total Fixed Costs}}{\text{Unit Contribution Margin}}$
Break-even sales revenue	Break-Even Units × Unit Sales Price or $\dfrac{\text{Total Fixed Costs}}{\text{Contribution Margin Ratio}}$
Target units	$\dfrac{\text{Total Fixed Costs} + \text{Target Profit}}{\text{Unit Contribution Margin}}$
Target sales revenue	Target Units × Unit Sales Price or $\dfrac{\text{Total Fixed Costs} + \text{Target Profit}}{\text{Contribution Margin Ratio}}$
Margin of safety	Actual or Budgeted Sales − Break-Even Sales
Margin of safety percentage	$\dfrac{\text{Actual or Budgeted Sales} - \text{Break-Even Sales}}{\text{Actual or Budgeted Sales}}$
Degree of operating leverage	$\dfrac{\text{Contribution Margin}}{\text{Net Operating Income}}$

KEY TERMS

Break-Even Analysis p. 261
Break-Even Point p. 259
Cost Structure p. 269
Cost-Volume-Profit (CVP) Analysis p. 258

CVP Graph p. 259
Degree of Operating Leverage p. 271
Margin of Safety p. 265
Product Mix p. 273
Sales Mix p. 273

Target Profit Analysis p. 261
Weighted-Average Contribution Margin Ratio p. 276
Weighted-Average Unit Contribution Margin p. 274

PRACTICE MATERIAL

QUESTIONS

1. Identify and briefly describe the assumptions of CVP.

2. Why should managers create a CVP graph?

3. When considering a CVP graph, how is the break-even point shown?

4. Your supervisor has requested that you prepare a CVP graph for your company's product but does not understand its meaning or how changes would affect the graph. Explain to your supervisor how your graph would be affected by

   a. an increase in the selling price.
   b. a decrease in variable cost per unit.
   c. an increase in fixed costs.

5. Why is it important for a company to know its break-even point? What happens to the break-even point if variable cost per unit decreases? If total fixed cost increases?

6. Explain the difference between unit contribution margin and contribution margin ratio.

7. A company's cost structure can have a high proportion of fixed costs or a high proportion of variable costs. Which cost structure is more vulnerable to decreases in demand? Why?

8. Explain the difference between calculating the break-even point in units and in dollars. How can one be used to double-check the other?

9. Apple Company and Baker Company are competitors in the same industry. They have similar variable costs per unit and selling prices, but Baker has more fixed costs. Explain the impact of this on each company's break-even point.

10. Bert Company and Ernie Company are competitors in the same industry. The companies produce a similar product and have the same amount of fixed costs and the same

selling price per unit. However, Bert has higher variable cost per unit. Compare the break-even point of each company.

11. Explain the difference between break-even analysis and target profit analysis.

12. Explain margin of safety. Why is it important for managers to know their margin of safety?

13. Give an example of a company to which margin of safety is particularly important and explain why.

14. Explain how a decision to automate a manufacturing facility would likely impact a company's cost structure and its break-even point.

15. Explain degree of operating leverage and how it relates to fixed cost.

16. How does degree of operating leverage help managers predict changes in profit? In general, would you prefer a higher or lower degree of operating leverage?

17. Why is sales mix important to multiproduct CVP analysis? Explain how sales mix is factored into CVP analysis.

18. How is weighted-average unit contribution margin calculated?

19. What will happen to a company's break-even point if the product mix shifts to favor a product with a lower contribution margin per unit?

20. How do you use the weighted-average contribution margin ratio in cost-volume-profit analysis?

21. Why is the weighted-average contribution margin ratio approach commonly used in practice?

22. What is the difference between the product mix and the sales mix?

MULTIPLE CHOICE

1. Which of the following is **not** an assumption of CVP analysis?

   a. A straight line can be used to approximate the relationship between total cost and activity within the relevant range.
   b. Production and sales are equal.
   c. Sales mix remains constant for any company selling more than one product.
   d. All costs can be accurately described as either fixed, variable, mixed, or step.

2. Contribution margin ratio is represented by

   a. (Sales − Total Fixed Costs) ÷ Sales.
   b. (Sales − Variable Cost) ÷ Sales.
   c. (Total Fixed Costs − Variable Cost) ÷ Sales.
   d. Variable Cost ÷ Sales.

3. When total contribution margin equals total fixed costs, a company has

   a. A net loss.   c. Zero profit.
   b. Net income.   d. Higher variable cost and fixed cost.

4. Baugh Company expects to sell 5,000 chairs for $10 per unit. The contribution margin ratio is 30 percent and Baugh will break even at this sales level. What are Baugh's fixed costs?

   a. $15,000.   **c.** $35,000.
   b. $30,000.   **d.** None of the above.

5. Whistler Co. sells one model of radio. Suppose its cost per radio is $125 and its total fixed costs are $4,130. Each radio sells for $195. How many radios must Whistler sell to break even?

   a. 33.   **c.** 45.
   b. 21.   **d.** 59.

6. Recent information for Shady Co., which makes automobile sunscreens, follows:

Selling price per screen	$ 18
Total fixed cost per month	1,225
Variable cost per screen	7

   If Shady wants to earn $1,250 profit next month, how many screens must it sell?

   a. 109.   **c.** 186.
   b. 136.   **d.** 225.

7. Various information for Happy Camper Co., which makes sleeping bags, follows:

Selling price per bag	$ 30
Total fixed cost per month	2,250
Variable cost per bag	21
Last month's profit	1,260

How many sleeping bags did the company sell last month?

   a. 159.   **c.** 140.
   b. 250.   **d.** 390.

8. Refer to the information in question 7 for Happy Camper. Suppose it decides to lower its selling price to $27. How many sleeping bags must it sell to match last month's profit?

   a. 585.   **c.** 780.
   b. 375.   **d.** 130.

9. Which of the following statements about a CVP graph is true?

   a. Total revenue is a downward-sloping line.
   b. Break-even is the point at which the total revenue and total cost lines intersect.
   c. The dollar value of sales revenue and total cost are plotted on the horizontal x-axis.
   d. The total cost line includes only fixed costs.

10. When performing multiproduct CVP analysis,

   a. Sales mix is assumed to remain constant.
   b. A weighted-average contribution margin is used to determine the break-even point.
   c. Both a and b are true.
   d. The products must be analyzed separately.

connect **Find More Learning Solutions on Connect.**

MINI-EXERCISES

M6-1 Matching Terminology

Match each of the terms by inserting the appropriate definition letter in the space provided. Not all definitions will be used.

____ 1. Break-even point
____ 2. Break-even analysis
____ 3. Cost-volume-profit analysis
____ 4. Degree of operating leverage
____ 5. Margin of safety
____ 6. Sales mix
____ 7. Target profit analysis
____ 8. Weighted-average contribution margin ratio

A. The proportion of products based upon the number of units sold.
B. The proportion of products sold based on total sales revenue.
C. Analysis that focuses on relationships among revenue, volume, mix of units sold, variable and fixed costs.
D. Analysis that focuses on determining the number of units or sales revenue required to generate a desired net income.
E. Analysis that focuses on determining the number of units or sales revenue required to generate a zero profit.
F. Analysis to determine if changing underlying assumptions would affect the decision.
G. Contribution margin = Fixed costs.
H. Analysis that expresses each line of the income statement as a percentage of total sales.

I. Average unit contribution of multiple products weighted by the percentage of units sold.

J. Average contribution margin ratio of multiple products weighted by the percentage of total sales revenue.

K. Actual (or budgeted) sales plus break-even sales.

L. The extent to which fixed costs are used to operate a business.

M. The extent to which variable costs are used to operate a business.

N. Difference between actual or budgeted sales and the break-even point.

LO 6–1, 6–2   **M6–2** **Calculating Contribution Margin, Contribution Margin Ratio**

Determine the missing amounts in the following table:

Unit Sales Price	Unit Variable Costs	Unit Contribution Margin	Contribution Margin Ratio
$22.00	$10.00	$?	?
?	10.00	24.00	?
50.00	?	?	25%

LO 6–1   **M6–3** **Calculating Contribution Margin and Contribution Margin Ratio, Finding Break-Even Point**

Juniper Enterprises sells handmade clocks. Its variable cost per clock is $6, and each clock sells for $24. Calculate Juniper's contribution margin per unit and contribution margin ratio. If the company's fixed costs total $6,660, determine how many clocks Juniper must sell to break even.

LO 6–2   **M6–4** **Determining Sales Needed to Achieve a Target Profit**

Refer to the information presented in **M6–3**. How many units must Juniper sell to earn a profit of at least $5,400?

LO 6–1, 6–4   **M6–5** **Analyzing Changes in Price Structure**

Refer to the information presented in **M6–3**. Suppose that Juniper raises its price by 20 percent, but costs do not change. What is its new break-even point?

LO 6–1, 6–4   **M6–6** **Analyzing Changes in Cost Structure**

Refer to the information presented in **M6–3**. Suppose that Juniper's variable costs decrease by $0.50. What is the new break-even point?

LO 6–1, 6–4   **M6–7** **Analyzing Changes in Cost Structure**

Refer to the information presented in **M6–3**. Suppose that Juniper's fixed costs increase to $7,200. What is the new break-even point?

LO 6–1   **M6–8** **Finding Break-Even Point**

Laguna Print makes advertising hangers that are placed on doorknobs. It charges $0.04 and estimates its variable cost to be $0.01 per hanger. Laguna's total fixed cost is $4,500 per month, which consists primarily of printer depreciation and rent. Calculate the number of advertising hangers that Laguna must sell in order to break even.

LO 6–1, 6–4   **M6–9** **Calculating Break-Even Point After Cost Structure Change**

Refer to the information presented in **M6–8**. Suppose that the cost of paper has increased and Laguna's variable cost per unit increases to $0.015 per hanger. Calculate its new break-even point assuming this increase is **not** passed along to customers.

LO 6–3   **M6–10** **Calculating Margin of Safety**

Jasper Company has sales of $185,000 and a break-even sales point of $120,000. Compute Jasper's margin of safety and its margin of safety ratio.

M6–11 Calculating Target Profit   LO 6–2

Heather Hudson makes stuffed teddy bears. Recent information for her business follows:

Selling price per bear	$ 35.00
Total fixed cost per month	1,500.00
Variable cost per bear	24.00

If Heather wants to earn $1,250 in profit next month, how many bears will she have to sell?

M6–12 Identifying Margin of Safety   LO 6–3

Refer to the information in **M6–11** for Heather Hudson. If she sells 275 bears next month, determine the margin of safety in units, sales dollars, and as a percentage of sales.

M6–13 Calculating Degree of Operating Leverage   LO 6–5

Refer to the information in **M6–11** for Heather Hudson. Determine the degree of operating leverage if she sells 350 bears this month.

M6–14 Predicting Effects on Profit   LO 6–4

Refer to the information in **M6–11** for Heather Hudson. Suppose sales increase by 20 percent next month. Calculate the effect that increase will have on her profit.

M6–15 Analyzing Multiproduct CVP   LO 6–6

Seascape Company has two products: Product A has a contribution margin per unit of $4 and Product B has a contribution margin of $6 per unit. Calculate the weighted-average unit contribution margin if Seascape has a 25/75 product mix. Explain how a shift in the product mix would affect Seascape's weighted-average contribution margin and its break-even point.

M6–16 Analyzing Multiproduct CVP   LO 6–6

Complete the following table:

Product A Unit Contribution Margin	Product B Unit Contribution Margin	Product Mix	Weighted-Average Contribution Margin
$ 9.00	$ 8.00	70/30	?
2.50	4.20	20/80	?
15.75	11.90	60/40	?
45.60	55.50	35/65	?

M6–17 Analyzing Multiproduct CVP   LO 6–6

Edgewater Enterprises manufactures two products. Information follows:

	Product A	Product B
Sales price	$13.50	$16.75
Variable cost per unit	$ 6.15	$ 6.85
Product mix	40%	60%

Calculate Edgewater's weighted-average contribution margin per unit.

M6–18 Analyzing Multiproduct CVP   LO 6–6

Refer to the information presented in **M6–17**. Calculate the break-even point if Edgewater's total fixed costs are $230,000.

M6–19 Analyzing Multiproduct CVP   LO 6–6

Refer to the information presented in **M6–17**. Suppose that each product's sales price increases by 10 percent. Sales mix remains the same and total fixed costs are $230,000. Calculate the new break-even point for Edgewater.

LO 6–6   **M6–20 Analyzing Multiproduct CVP, Calculating Weighted-Average Contribution Margin Ratio**

Information for Pueblo Company follows:

	Product A	Product B
Sales revenue	$40,000	$60,000
Less: Total variable cost	14,000	24,000
Contribution margin	$26,000	$36,000

Determine Pueblo's (overall) weighted-average contribution margin ratio.

LO 6–6   **M6–21 Calculating Break-Even Sales Using Weighted-Average Contribution Margin Ratio**

Refer to the information presented for Pueblo Company in **M6–20**. Determine its break-even sales dollars if total fixed costs are $35,000.

LO 6–6   **M6–22 Calculating Target Sales**

Refer to the information in **M6–20** regarding Pueblo Company. Determine target sales needed to earn a $25,000 target profit if total fixed costs are $35,000.

EXERCISES

LO 6–1   **E6–1 Understanding CVP Relationships**

Suppose your sister works for a small real estate office as a receptionist. Her employer might be forced to lay off several employees. The employer explained that the company was not "breaking even" and that layoffs would start next month unless things change. The boss has also asked all employees to think of ways that the company could hit that magical break-even point and, ultimately, earn a profit. Your sister has come to you for help in understanding the boss's comments and wants suggestions to pass along.

Required:

1. Explain the following concepts and their relationships to your sister: break-even, variable cost, fixed cost, contribution margin, and profit.
2. Help your sister identify five suggestions to offer the boss that would improve the company's performance.
3. Explain why just breaking even will not ensure that your sister keeps her job over the long term.

LO 6–1   **E6–2 Identifying Elements on a CVP Graph**

On the graph presented, match each element to its appropriate description.

Element	Description
_____ Point A	1. Break-even point
_____ Area G	2. Number of units of activity
_____ Area C	3. Loss zone
_____ Line H	4. Total cost
_____ Line I	5. Total revenue
_____ Area B	6. Dollars
_____ Area F	7. Profit
_____ Axis E	8. Fixed costs
_____ Axis D	9. Target profit
	10. Variable costs

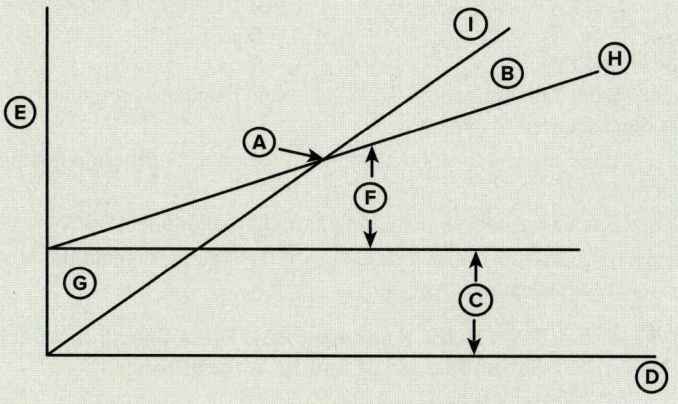

E6–3 Determining Break-Even Point, Target Profit, Margin of Safety

LO 6–1, 6–2, 6–3

Cove's Cakes is a local bakery. Price and cost information follows:

Price per cake	$ 17.00
Variable cost per cake	
Ingredients	2.50
Direct labor	1.40
Overhead (box, etc.)	0.20
Fixed cost per month	$3,850.00

Required:

1. Determine Cove's break-even point in units and sales dollars.
2. Determine the bakery's margin of safety if it currently sells 450 cakes per month.
3. Determine the number of cakes that Cove must sell to generate $2,000 in profit.

E6–4 Analyzing Changes in Price, Cost Structure, Degree of Operating Leverage

LO 6–4, 6–5

Refer to the information for Cove's Cakes in **E6–3**.

Required:

1. Calculate Cove's new break-even point under each of the following independent scenarios:
   a. Sales price increases by $1.00 per cake.
   b. Fixed costs increase by $500 per month.
   c. Variable costs decrease by $0.35 per cake.
   d. Sales price decreases by $0.50 per cake.

2. Refer to the original information presented in **E6–3**. Assume that Cove sold 400 cakes last month. Calculate the company's degree of operating leverage.

3. Using the degree of operating leverage, calculate the change in profit caused by a 10 percent increase in sales revenue.

E6–5 Calculating Contribution Margin and Contribution Margin Ratio; Identifying Break-Even Point, Target Profit

LO 6–1, 6–2

Sandy Bank, Inc., makes one model of wooden canoe. Partial information for it follows:

Number of canoes produced and sold	400	600	750
Total costs			
Variable costs	$ 67,500	?	?
Fixed costs	150,000	?	?
Total costs	$217,500	?	?
Cost per unit			
Variable cost per unit	?	?	?
Fixed cost per unit	?	?	?
Total cost per unit	?	?	?

Required:

1. Complete the preceding table.
2. Suppose Sandy Bank sells its canoes for $550 each. Calculate the contribution margin per canoe and the contribution margin ratio.
3. This year Sandy Bank expects to sell 820 canoes. Prepare a contribution margin income statement for the company.
4. Calculate Sandy Bank's break-even point in units and in sales dollars.
5. Suppose Sandy Bank wants to earn $75,000 profit this year. Calculate the number of canoes that must be sold to achieve this target.

LO 6–1, 6–2, 6–3, 6–4   **E6–6**   **Identifying Break-Even Point, Analyzing How Price Changes Affect Profitability; Calculating Margin of Safety, Target Profit**

Refer to the information in **E6–5** regarding Sandy Bank.

Required:

1. Suppose that Sandy Bank raises its selling price to $675 per canoe. Calculate its new break-even point in units and in sales dollars.
2. If Sandy Bank sells 650 canoes, compute its margin of safety in units and as a percentage of sales. (Use the new sales price of $675.)
3. Calculate the number of canoes that Sandy Bank must sell at $675 each to generate $100,000 profit.

LO 6–1, 6–2, 6–3, 6–4   **E6–7**   **Determining Break-Even Point and Analyzing Changes in Price and Cost Structure**

Izzy Ice Cream has the following price and cost information:

Price per 2-scoop sundae	$ 5.00
Variable cost per sundae:	
Ingredients	1.35
Direct labor	0.45
Overhead	0.20
Fixed cost per month	$3,000

Required:

1. Determine Izzy's break-even point in units and sales dollars.
2. Determine how many sundaes must be sold to generate a profit of $6,000.
3. Calculate Izzy's new break-even point for each of the following independent scenarios:
   a. Sales price decreases by $0.50.
   b. Fixed costs decrease by $300 per month.
   c. Variable costs increase by $0.50 per sundae.
4. Based on the original information, how many sundaes must Izzy sell to generate a profit of $10,000, if sales price increases by $0.50 and variable costs increase by $0.30?

LO 6–2, 6–3, 6–4, 6–5, 6–6   **E6–8**   **Matching Terms to Definitions**

Match the definitions on the left with the most appropriate term on the right. Terms may be used once, more than once, or not at all.

Description	Terms
_____ 1. Buffer zone that identifies how much sales can drop before the business suffers a loss.	A. Weighted-average contribution margin
	B. Margin of safety
_____ 2. An investment in technology that increases total fixed costs while reducing the variable cost per unit.	C. Product mix
	D. Cost structure
	E. Indifference point

Description	Terms
___ 3. $\dfrac{\text{Total Fixed Costs} + \text{Target Profit}}{\text{Contribution Margin Ratio}}$	**F.** Target contribution margin
___ 4. How a company uses variable costs versus fixed costs to perform its operations.	**G.** Target sales revenue
	H. Degree of operating leverage
___ 5. The proportion of units sold from each product or service line.	**I.** Automation
	J. Target units
___ 6. When two profit equations yield the same profit.	
___ 7. Actual or budgeted sales minus break-even sales.	
___ 8. Total fixed costs plus target profit.	
___ 9. $\dfrac{\text{Contribution Margin}}{\text{Net Operating Income}}$	
___ 10. $\dfrac{\text{Total Fixed Costs} + \text{Target Profit}}{\text{Unit Contribution Margin}}$	

E6–9 Analyzing Break-Even Point, Preparing CVP Graph, Calculating Degree of Operating Leverage, Predicting Effect of Price Structure Changes   LO 6–1, 6–4, 6–5

Joyce Murphy runs a courier service in downtown Seattle. She charges clients $0.50 per mile driven. Joyce has determined that if she drives 3,300 miles in a month, her total operating cost is $875. If she drives 4,400 miles in a month, her total operating cost is $1,095. Joyce has used the high-low method (covered in Chapter 5) to determine that her monthly cost equation is total monthly cost = $215 + $0.20 per mile driven.

Required:

1. Determine how many miles Joyce needs to drive to break even.
2. Calculate Joyce's degree of operating leverage if she drives 4,200 miles.
3. Suppose Joyce took a week off and her sales for the month decreased by 25 percent. Using the degree of operating leverage, calculate the effect this will have on her profit for that month.

E6–10 Calculating Contribution Margin, Contribution Margin Ratio, Margin of Safety   LO 6–2, 6–3

Last month, Laredo Company sold 450 units for $25 each. During the month, fixed costs were $2,520 and variable costs were $9 per unit.

Required:

1. Determine the unit contribution margin and contribution margin ratio.
2. Calculate the break-even point in units and sales dollars.
3. Compute Laredo's margin of safety in units and as a percentage of sales.

E6–11 Analyzing Break-Even Point, Preparing CVP Graph   LO 6–1

Dana's Ribbon World makes award rosettes. Following is information about the company:

Variable cost per rosette	$ 1.60
Sales price per rosette	3.00
Total fixed costs per month	889.00

Required:

1. Determine how many rosettes Dana's must sell to break even.
2. Calculate the break-even point in sales dollars.
3. Prepare a CVP graph for Dana's assuming the relevant range is 0 to 1,500 rosettes.

E6–12 Calculating Target Profit, Margin of Safety, Degree of Operating Leverage   LO 6–2, 6–3, 6–4, 6–5

Refer to the information regarding Dana's Ribbon World in **E6–11.**

Required:

1. Suppose Dana's would like to generate a profit of $800. Determine how many rosettes it must sell to achieve this target profit.
2. If Dana's sells 1,100 rosettes, compute its margin of safety in units, in sales dollars, and as a percentage of sales.
3. Calculate Dana's degree of operating leverage if it sells 1,100 rosettes.
4. Using the degree of operating leverage, calculate the change in Dana's profit if unit sales drop to 935 units. Confirm this by preparing a new contribution margin income statement.

LO 6–1, 6–5   **E6–13 Determining Contribution Margin from Degree of Operating Leverage**

Dublin Company and Gary Corp. have degrees of operating leverage of 4.5 and 2.7, respectively. Both companies have net income of $80,000.

Required:

1. Without performing any calculations, discuss what the degrees of operating leverage tell us about the two companies.
2. Determine each company's total contribution margin.
3. Compare the companies' cost structures.

LO 6–1, 6–5   **E6–14 Calculating Break-Even Point, Degree of Operating Leverage**

Lobster Trap Company is considering automating its manufacturing facility. Company information before and after the proposed automation follows:

	Before Automation	After Automation
Sales revenue	$198,000	$198,000
Less: Variable costs	78,000	38,000
Contribution margin	$120,000	$160,000
Less: Fixed costs	15,000	58,000
Net operating income	$105,000	$102,000

Required:

1. Calculate Lobster Trap's break-even sales dollars before and after automation.
2. Compute Lobster Trap's degree of operating leverage before and after automation.
3. Interpret the meaning of your calculations in requirement 2.

LO 6–1, 6–4   **E6–15 Calculating Break-Even Point with Different Cost Structures**

Remo Company and Angelo Inc. are separate companies that operate in the same industry. Following are variable costing income statements for the two companies showing their different cost structures:

	Remo Co.	Angelo Inc.
Sales revenue	$275,000	$275,000
Less: Variable costs	200,000	125,000
Contribution margin	75,000	150,000
Less: Fixed costs	35,000	110,000
Net operating income	$ 40,000	$ 40,000

Required:

1. Briefly describe the similarities and differences between these two companies.
2. Calculate the break-even sales revenue for each company.

LO 6–5   **E6–16 Calculating Degree of Operating Leverage**

Refer to the information in **E6–15** for Remo Company and Angelo Inc.

Required:

1. Calculate each company's degree of operating leverage.
2. Explain why companies with the same total sales and net operating income can have different degrees of operating leverage.
3. Compare these two companies' vulnerability to market fluctuations.

E6–17 Analyzing Break-Even and Target Profit   LO 6–1, 6–2

Tommy's Tile Service is planning on purchasing new tile cleaning equipment that will improve their ability to remove tough stains from ceramic tiles. The company's contribution margin is 30 percent and its current break-even point is $250,000 in sales revenue. Purchasing the new equipment will increase fixed costs by $7,500.

Required:

1. Determine the company's current fixed costs.
2. Determine the company's new break-even point in sales.
3. After the purchase of the equipment, how much revenue does the company need to generate a profit of $100,000?

E6–18 Analyzing Multiproduct CVP   LO 6–6

Biscayne's Rent-A-Ride rents two models of automobiles: the standard and the deluxe. Information follows:

	Standard	Deluxe
Rental price per day	$30.00	$38.00
Variable cost per day	10.50	15.20

Biscayne's total fixed cost is $18,500 per month.

Required:

1. Determine the contribution margin per rental day and contribution margin ratio for each model that Biscayne's offers.
2. Which model would Biscayne's prefer to rent? Explain your answer.
3. Calculate Biscayne's break-even point if the product mix is 50/50.
4. Calculate the break-even point if Biscayne's product mix changes so that the standard model is rented 75 percent of the time and the deluxe model is rented for only 25 percent.
5. Calculate the break-even point if Biscayne's product mix changes so that the standard model is rented 25 percent of the time and the deluxe model is rented for 75 percent.

E6–19 Analyzing Multiproduct CVP   LO 6–6

Refer to the information presented in **E6–18** for Biscayne's Rent-A-Ride.

Required:

1. Determine Biscayne's new break-even point in each of the following **independent** scenarios:
    a. Product mix is 40/60.
    b. Sales price increases on both models by 20 percent. (Assume a product mix of 50/50.)
    c. Fixed costs increase by $5,200. (Assume a product mix of 50/50.)
    d. Variable costs increase by 30 percent. (Assume a product mix of 50/50.)

E6–20 Analyzing Multiproduct CVP   LO 6–6

Tiago makes three models of camera lens. Its product mix and contribution margin per unit follow:

	Percentage of Unit Sales	Contribution Margin per Unit
Lens A	25%	$38
Lens B	40	30
Lens C	35	43

Required:

1. Determine the weighted-average contribution margin per unit.
2. Determine the number of units of each product that Tiago must sell to break even if fixed costs are $187,000.
3. Determine how many units of each product must be sold to generate a profit of $73,000.

LO 6–6   **E6–21   Analyzing Multiproduct CVP**

Refer to the information in **E6–20** for Tiago. Suppose the product mix has shifted to 40/30/30.

Required:

1. Determine the new weighted-average contribution margin per unit.
2. Determine the number of units of each product that Tiago must sell to break even if fixed costs are $187,000.
3. Determine how many units of each product must be sold to generate a profit of $73,000.
4. Explain why these results differ from those calculated in **E6–20**.

LO 6–6   **E6–22   Multiproduct CVP Analysis**

Juniper Corp. makes three models of insulated thermos. Juniper has $400,000 in total revenue and total variable costs of $240,000. Its sales mix is given below:

	Percentage of Total Sales
Thermos A	35%
Thermos B	45
Thermos C	20

Required:

1. Calculate the (overall) weighted-average contribution margin ratio.
2. Determine the total sales revenue Juniper needs to break even if fixed costs are $80,000.
3. Determine the total sales revenue needed to generate a profit of $90,000.
4. Determine the sales revenue from each product needed to generate a profit of $90,000.

LO 6–6   **E6–23   Multiproduct CVP Analysis**

Refer to the information in **E6–22** for Juniper Corp. Suppose Juniper has improved its manufacturing process and expects total variable costs to decrease by 20 percent. The company expects sales revenue to remain stable at $400,000.

Required:

1. Calculate the new weighted-average contribution margin ratio.
2. Determine total sales that Juniper needs to break even if fixed costs after the manufacturing improvements are $62,400.
3. Determine the total sales revenue that Juniper must generate to earn a profit of $90,000.
4. Determine the sales revenue from each product needed to generate a profit of $90,000.

E6–24   Computing Target Profit, Preparing Contribution Margin Income Statement,
LO 6–2, 6–3   **Computing Margin of Safety**

Erin Shelton, Inc., wants to earn a target profit of $800,000 this year. The company's fixed costs are expected to be $1,000,000 and its variable costs are expected to be 60 percent of sales. Erin Shelton, Inc., earned $700,000 in profit last year.

Required:

1. Calculate break-even sales for Erin Shelton, Inc.
2. Prove your answer from requirement 1 using a contribution margin income statement format.
3. Calculate the required sales to meet the target profit of $800,000.
4. Prove your answer from requirement 3 using a contribution margin income statement format.
5. When the company earns $800,000 of net income, what is its margin of safety and margin of safety as a percentage of sales? Interpret your findings.

GROUP A PROBLEMS

PA6–1 Calculating Contribution Margin, Contribution Margin Ratio, Break-Even Point

LO 6–1, 6–2

Hermosa, Inc., produces one model of mountain bike. Partial information for the company follows:

Number of bikes produced and sold	400	800	1,000
Total costs			
Variable costs	$125,000	$?	$?
Fixed costs per year	?	?	?
Total costs	?	?	?
Cost per unit			
Variable cost per unit	?	?	?
Fixed cost per unit	?	?	?
Total cost per unit	?	$543.75	?

Required:

1. Complete the table.
2. Calculate Hermosa's contribution margin ratio and its total contribution margin at each sales level indicated in the table assuming the company sells each bike for $650.
3. Consider the contribution margins just calculated and total fixed costs. Determine whether Hermosa's break-even point will be more or less than 500 units.
4. Calculate Hermosa's break-even point in units and sales revenue.

PA6–2 Analyzing Break-Even Point, Setting Target Profit, Degree of Operating Leverage

LO 6–1, 6–2, 6–5

Russell Preston delivers parts for several local auto parts stores. He charges clients $0.75 per mile driven. Russell has determined that if he drives 3,000 miles in a month, his average operating cost is $0.55 per mile. If he drives 4,000 miles in a month, his average operating cost is $0.50 per mile. Russell has used the high-low method (covered in Chapter 5) to determine that his monthly cost equation is total cost = $600 + $0.35 per mile.

Required:

1. Determine how many miles Russell needs to drive to break even.
2. Assume Russell drove 1,800 miles last month. Without making any additional calculations, determine whether he earned a profit or a loss last month.
3. Determine how many miles Russell must drive to earn $1,000 in profit.
4. Prepare a contribution margin income statement assuming Russell drove 1,800 miles last month. Use this information to calculate Russell's degree of operating leverage.

PA6–3 Calculating Contribution Margin, Contribution Margin Ratio, Break-Even Point, Target Profit

LO 6–1, 6–2

Hawk Homes, Inc., makes one type of birdhouse that it sells for $30 each. Its variable cost is $15 per house, and its fixed costs total $13,840 per year. Hawk currently has the capacity to produce up to 2,000 birdhouses per year, so its relevant range is 0 to 2,000 houses.

Required:

1. Prepare a contribution margin income statement for Hawk assuming it sells 1,100 birdhouses this year.
2. Without any calculations, determine Hawk's total contribution margin if the company breaks even.
3. Calculate Hawk's contribution margin per unit and its contribution margin ratio.
4. Calculate Hawk's break-even point in number of units and in sales revenue.
5. Suppose Hawk wants to earn $20,000 this year. Determine how many birdhouses it must sell to generate this amount of profit. Is this possible?
6. Prepare a CVP graph for Hawk including lines for both total cost and sales revenue. Clearly identify fixed cost and the break-even point on your graph.

LO 6–1, 6–2, 6–5

PA6–4 Analyzing Break-Even Point, Target Profit, Degree of Operating Leverage

Ramada Company produces one golf cart model. A partially complete table of company costs follows:

	600	800	1,000
Number of golf carts produced and sold	600	800	1,000
Total costs			
Variable costs	$?	$400,000	$?
Fixed costs per year	?	250,000	?
Total costs	?	$650,000	?
Cost per unit			
Variable cost per unit	?	?	?
Fixed cost per unit	?	?	?
Total cost per unit	?	?	?

Required:

1. Complete the table.
2. Ramada sells its carts for $1,200 each. Prepare a contribution margin income statement for each of the three production levels given in the table.
3. Based on these three statements (and without any additional calculations), estimate Ramada's break-even point in units.
4. Calculate Ramada's break-even point in number of units and in sales revenue.
5. Assume Ramada sold 400 carts last year. Without performing any calculations, determine whether Ramada earned a profit last year.
6. Calculate the number of carts that Ramada must sell to earn $65,000 profit.
7. Calculate Ramada's degree of operating leverage if it sells 850 carts.
8. Using the degree of operating leverage, calculate the change in Ramada's profit if sales are 10 percent less than expected.

LO 6–3, 6–6

PA6–5 Analyzing Multiproduct CVP, Break-Even Point, Target Profit, Margin of Safety

Lindstrom Company produces two fountain pen models. Information about its products follows:

	Product A	Product B
Sales revenue	$75,000	$125,000
Less: Variable costs	33,000	38,000
Contribution margin	$42,000	$ 87,000
Total units sold	5,000	5,000

Lindstrom's fixed costs total $78,500.

Required:

1. Determine Lindstrom's weighted-average unit contribution margin and weighted-average contribution margin ratio.
2. Calculate Lindstrom's break-even point in units and in sales revenue.
3. Calculate the number of units that Lindstrom must sell to earn a $150,000 profit.
4. Calculate Lindstrom's margin of safety and margin of safety as a percentage of sales if it sells 8,000 total pens.

LO 6–5, 6–6

PA6–6 Multiproduct CVP, Analyzing Break-Even Point, Target Profit, Degree of Operating Leverage

Pin Cushion Company produces two models of sewing basket. Information about Pin Cushion's products is given below:

	Product A	Product B
Sales revenue	$28,000	$43,000
Less: Variable costs	11,400	19,800
Contribution margin	$16,600	$23,200
Total units sold	780	1,820

Pin Cushion's fixed costs total $35,200.

Required:

1. Determine Pin Cushion's weighted-average unit contribution margin and weighted-average contribution margin ratio.
2. Calculate Pin Cushion's break-even units and break-even sales revenue.
3. Calculate the number of units of each product that must be sold to break even.
4. Calculate the total sales necessary for Pin Cushion to earn a profit of $63,200.
5. Calculate the sales revenue generated from each product line if Pin Cushion earns its target profit of $63,200.
6. Using the original information, calculate Pin Cushion's degree of operating leverage.

PA6–7 CVP in Social Enterprises, Multiproduct CVP, Break-Even Point, Target Profit Analysis   LO 6–6

Hoodys for Good manufactures and sells hooded sweatshirts. The company locates its manufacturing facilities in areas with high unemployment rates and provides on-site day care and education for its employees' children. The company recently started a "one for one" program where they donate one sweatshirt for every one sold to an international charity to provide to a child in need. The customer pays the shipping cost for items purchased, but the company pays to ship to the international charities.

Cost information is summarized below:

Variable Costs	
Direct Materials	$3.00 per unit produced
Direct Labor	$2.50 per unit produced
Variable Manufacturing Overhead	$0.50 per unit produced
Shipping	$3.00 per unit donated
Fixed Costs	
Salaries	$20,000 per month
Advertising	$60,000 per month
Production Equipment	$40,000 per month

Required: Answer each of the following independent questions.

1. Assume that the price of each sweatshirt sold is $30.
   a. How much contribution margin is earned on each unit sold to a paying customer?
   b. How much contribution margin is lost on each unit donated to charity?
   c. If one sweatshirt is donated for each one sold, what is the weighted-average contribution margin per unit produced?
   d. How many total units must be produced to break even? How many must be sold and how many donated?
2. If the company expects to sell 5,000 sweatshirts and donate 5,000 sweatshirts per month, what price must be charged to earn a target profit of $20,000 per month?
3. Assume that Hoodys for Good's managers are trying to decide whether to set the price at $40 or $60. If the price is set at $40, they think they can sell 10,000 units (and donate 10,000 units). If the price is set at $60, they only expect to be able to sell (and donate) 6,000 units.
   a. If the company's goal is to maximize economic profit, what price should they charge? Why?
   b. If the company's goal is to do the most social good, what price should they charge? Why?

GROUP B PROBLEMS

LO 6–1, 6–2   **PB6–1 Calculating Contribution Margin, Contribution Margin Ratio, Break-Even Point**

Franklin, Inc., produces one model of seat cover. Partial information for the company follows:

Number of seat covers produced and sold	1,500	1,700	4,200
Total costs			
Variable costs	$?	$?	$15,750
Fixed costs per year	?	?	?
Total costs	?	?	?
Cost per unit			
Variable cost per unit	?	?	?
Fixed cost per unit	?	?	?
Total cost per unit	$31.00	?	?

Required:

1. Complete the table.
2. Calculate Franklin's contribution margin ratio and its total contribution margin at each sales level indicated in the table assuming the company sells each seat cover for $30.
3. Consider the contribution margins just calculated and total fixed costs for the company. Determine whether Franklin's break-even point will be more or less than 1,500 units.
4. Calculate Franklin's break-even point in units and sales revenue.

LO 6–1, 6–2, 6–5   **PB6–2 Preparing Contribution Margin Income Statement, Analyzing Break-Even Point, Setting Target Profit**

Regina Star delivers flowers for several local flower stores. She charges clients $0.85 per mile driven. Regina has determined that if she drives 1,200 miles in a month, her average operating cost is $0.80 per mile. If she drives 2,000 miles in a month, her average operating cost is $0.60 per mile. Regina has used the high-low method (covered in Chapter 5) to determine that her monthly cost equation is total cost = $600 + $0.30 per mile.

Required:

1. Determine how many miles Regina needs to drive to break even.
2. Assume Regina drove 900 miles last month. Without making any additional calculations, determine whether she earned a profit or a loss for the month.
3. If Regina wants to earn $800 a month, determine how many miles she must drive.
4. Prepare a contribution margin income statement assuming Regina drove 1,200 miles last month. Use this information to calculate Regina's degree of operating leverage.

LO 6–1, 6–2   **PB6–3 Calculating Contribution Margin, Contribution Margin Ratio, Break-Even Point, Target Profit**

Ivy Kay, Inc., makes one type of doggie sweater that it sells for $25 each. Its variable cost is $12.50 per sweater and its fixed costs total $8,600 per year. Ivy Kay currently has the capacity to produce up to 1,000 sweaters per year, so its relevant range is 0 to 1,000 sweaters.

Required:

1. Prepare a contribution margin income statement for Ivy Kay assuming it sells 600 sweaters this year.
2. Without any calculations, determine Ivy Kay's total contribution margin if the company breaks even.
3. Calculate Ivy Kay's contribution margin per unit and its contribution margin ratio.
4. Calculate Ivy Kay's break-even point in number of units and in sales revenue.
5. Suppose Ivy Kay wants to earn $3,000 this year. Determine how many sweaters it must sell to generate this amount of profit. Is this possible?
6. Prepare a CVP graph for Ivy Kay including lines for both total cost and sales revenue. Clearly identify fixed cost and the break-even point on your graph.

LO 6–1, 6–2, 6–5   **PB6–4 Analyzing Break-Even Point, Target Profit, Degree of Operating Leverage**

King Peak Company produces one security door model. A partially complete table of its costs follows:

Number of doors produced and sold	400	500	700
Total costs			
Variable costs	$40,000	$?	$?
Fixed costs per year	65,000	?	?
Total costs	105,000	?	?
Cost per unit			
Variable cost per unit	?	?	?
Fixed cost per unit	?	?	?
Total cost per unit	?	?	?

Required:

1. Complete the table.
2. King Peak sells its doors for $200 each. Prepare a contribution margin income statement for each of the three production levels in the table.
3. Based on these three statements (and without any additional calculations), estimate King Peak's break-even point in units.
4. Calculate King Peak's break-even point in number of units and in sales revenue.
5. Assume King Peak sold 600 doors last year. Without performing any calculations, determine whether it earned a profit last year.
6. Calculate the number of doors that King Peak must sell to earn a $10,000 profit.
7. Calculate King Peak's degree of operating leverage if it sells 700 doors.
8. Using the degree of operating leverage, calculate the change in King Peak's profit if sales are 20 percent more than expected. (Assume costs did not change.)

PB6–5 Analyzing Multiproduct CVP, Break-Even Point, Target Profit, Margin of Safety   LO 6–3, 6–6

Joan Company produces two backpack models. Information about its products follows: Joan's fixed costs total $51,700.

	Product A	Product B
Sales revenue	$135,000	$77,000
Less: Variable costs	81,000	38,500
Contribution margin	$ 54,000	$38,500
Total units sold	15,000	5,000

Required:

1. Determine Joan's weighted-average unit contribution margin and weighted-average contribution margin ratio.
2. Calculate Joan's break-even point in units and in sales revenue.
3. Calculate the number of units that Joan must sell to earn a $95,000 profit.
4. Calculate Joan's margin of safety and margin of safety as a percentage of sales if it sells 35,000 total backpacks.

PB6–6 Multiproduct CVP, Analyzing Break-Even Point, Target Profit, Degree of Operating Leverage   LO 6–5, 6–6

Sapphire Company produces two models of electric lawnmower. Information about Sapphire's products is given below:

	Product A	Product B
Sales revenue	$264,400	$396,600
Less: Variable costs	171,400	213,000
Contribution margin	$ 93,000	$183,600
Total units sold	300	500

Sapphire's fixed costs total $104,625.

Required:

1. Determine Sapphire's weighted-average unit contribution margin and weighted-average contribution margin ratio.
2. Calculate Sapphire's break-even units and break-even sales dollars.
3. Calculate the number of units of each product that must be sold to break even.
4. Calculate the total sales necessary for Sapphire to earn a profit of $172,305.
5. Calculate the sales revenue generated from each product line if Sapphire earns its target of $172,305 profit.
6. Using the original information, calculate Sapphire's degree of operating leverage.

LO 6–6   **PB6–7** **CVP in Social Enterprises, Multiproduct CVP, Break-Even Point, Target Profit Analysis**

Backpacks for Good manufactures and sells backpacks for educational and recreational uses. The company locates its manufacturing facilities in areas with high unemployment rates and provides on-site day care and education for its employees' children. The company recently started a "one for one" program where they donate one backpack for every one sold to a local charity to provide to a child in need. The customer pays the shipping cost for items purchased, but the company pays to ship to the local charities.

Cost information is summarized below:

Variable Costs	
Direct Materials	$7.00 per unit produced
Direct Labor	$5.00 per unit produced
Variable Manufacturing Overhead	$2.00 per unit produced
Shipping	$2.00 per unit donated
Fixed Costs	
Salaries	$40,000 per month
Advertising	$75,000 per month
Production Equipment	$25,000 per month

Required: Answer each of the following independent questions.

1. Assume that the price of each backpack sold is $50.
   a. How much contribution margin is earned on each backpack sold to a paying customer?
   b. How much contribution margin is lost on each backpack donated to charity?
   c. If one backpack is donated for each one sold, what is the weighted-average contribution margin per unit produced?
   d. How many total units must be produced to break even? How many must be sold and how many donated?
2. If the company expects to sell 8,000 backpacks and donate 8,000 backpacks per month, what price must be charged to earn a target profit of $60,000 per month?
3. Assume that Backpacks for Good's managers are trying to decide whether to set the price at $80 or $100. If the price is set at $80, they think they can sell 10,000 units (and donate 10,000 units). If the price is set at $100, they only expect to be able to sell (and donate) 8,000 units.
   a. If the company's goal is to maximize economic profit, what price should they charge? Why?
   b. If the company's goal is to do the most social good, what price should they charge? Why?

SKILLS DEVELOPMENT CASES

LO 6–1, 6–2   **S6–1** **Video Case Assignment: Estimating Variable and Fixed Costs and Performing Cost-Volume-Profit Analysis**

Go to www.YouTube.com and search for **How It's Made,** a television show produced by the Discovery Channel that shows how thousands of products and services are created. Find a product that you have purchased in the last year, such as a toothbrush, ball point pen, jeans, headphones, candy bar, etc.

Required:

1. What product did you choose and how is it made?
2. How much did you pay for this product?
3. What are the major variable costs of making this product?
4. Provide your best guess of the variable cost per unit for this product. You do not need to do extensive research to find out the cost of the inputs, but try to come up with a reasonable estimate.
5. Based on your answers, compute the unit contribution margin and contribution margin ratio.
6. Provide a managerial interpretation of the unit contribution margin and contribution margin ratio for this product. How would managers use this information to make decisions?
7. Provide a numerical example showing how to find the break-even point. You will need to make an assumption about total fixed costs as this information is very difficult to estimate.
8. Prepare a contribution margin income statement that shows the break-even point in both units and sales dollars.
9. Provide a numerical example showing how managers could use the contribution margin ratio to determine the total sales revenue needed to earn a target profit. You will need to make an assumption about total fixed costs as this information is very difficult to estimate.
10. Prepare a contribution margin income statement that shows the target profit in terms of both units and total sales dollars.

S6–2 Evaluating the Effect of Decisions on Contribution Margin, Break-Even Point, Margin of Safety   LO 6–1, 6–3, 6–5

Companies must make many decisions regarding day-to-day business activities. For each of the following decision-making situations, discuss its impact on a company's contribution margin, break-even point, margin of safety, and degree of operating leverage.

Required:

1. Whether to pay employees a fixed salary or an hourly wage.
2. Whether to pay commissions to salespeople.
3. Whether to purchase a building or rent space.
4. Whether to purchase component parts or manufacture them.
5. Whether to create its own delivery department (including the purchase and maintenance of delivery vehicles) or contract with a third party, such as FedEx.

S6–3 Researching Cost of Operating Vending Machines, Performing Cost-Volume-Profit Analysis, Multiproduct CVP   LO 6–1, 6–6

Suppose you have decided to start a small business selling snacks from vending machines. You have secured a location for one candy vending machine in a local bookstore. Rental for the space will cost $200 per month.

Vending machines can be purchased at wholesale clubs such as Sam's Club and Costco. You can also purchase the snacks to stock the machines in bulk there.

Required:

1. Either visit a local warehouse club or review its website to determine the initial cost to purchase a snack vending machine.
2. Assume you are initially going to have only one type of snack bar in your machine. What type of snack bar will you choose? If you purchase the bars in bulk, what is your cost per bar?
3. How much will you charge for each bar sold?
4. What is your contribution margin per bar? How many bars must you sell to cover the cost of the vending machine?
5. When you have covered the initial investment, what will the monthly break-even point be in number of bars and in sales dollars?
6. Repeat requirements 2 through 5 assuming you decided to have a drink vending machine instead of a snack machine. Remember to find the price for a beverage vending machine. You may assume rental for the vending machine space is $200 per month regardless of its type.

7. Assume your machine can accommodate more than one product, for example, a snack machine that can dispense both chips and candy bars or a drink machine that offers both soda and water. Repeat requirements 2 through 5 assuming you have decided to offer two products. The products should have different prices, variable costs, and contribution margins. Perform the analyses for three levels of sales mix: 50/50, 30/70, and 70/30.

LO 6–1, 6–2   **S6–4** **Researching a Company Website, Performing Cost-Volume-Profit Analysis**

Pink Jeep Tours offers off-road tours to individuals and groups visiting the Southwestern U.S. hotspots of Sedona, Arizona, and Las Vegas, Nevada. Take a tour of the company's website at www.pinkjeep.com. Suppose you are the manager for the Pink Jeep office in Sedona. From the company website, choose two tours offered there. One tour should last all day, and the other should be a shorter tour of two to four hours.

For the following requirements, assume that each Jeep tour has four adult passengers plus a tour guide.

Required:

1. List the various costs Pink Jeep would incur to offer each tour. Indicate whether each cost identified is variable, fixed, or mixed based on the number of tours offered.

2. Briefly research each cost listed in requirement 1 and estimate its amount. Estimate variable costs on a per-Jeep-tour basis and fixed costs on a monthly basis. Break any mixed cost into variable and fixed components. State any assumptions that you must make when estimating these costs (and be aware that many assumptions must be made).

3. What is Pink Jeep's total variable cost for each tour? Does this cost differ for each type of tour? Explain.

4. Using the current tour prices listed on Pink Jeep's website, determine the contribution margin per Jeep tour for each tour type.

5. Assume Pink Jeep ran **only** the all-day excursion tour in the month of August. In this case, how many tours are needed to break even?

6. Assume Pink Jeep ran **only** the shorter tour during August. In this case, how many tours are needed to earn $30,000 in profit for the month?

7

Incremental Analysis for Short-Term Decision Making

CHAPTER SEVEN

YOUR LEARNING OBJECTIVES

LO 7–1 Describe the five steps in the decision-making process.

LO 7–2 Define and identify relevant costs and benefits.

LO 7–3 Analyze a special-order decision.

LO 7–4 Analyze a make-or-buy decision.

LO 7–5 Analyze a keep-or-drop decision.

LO 7–6 Analyze a sell-or-process-further decision.

LO 7–7 Prioritize products to maximize short-term profit with constrained resources.

©Jeff Pachoud/AFP/Getty Images

FOCUS COMPANY: IKEA

IKEA was started in 1943 by a young Swedish boy named Ingvar Kamprad who lived on the small farm of Elmtaryd in the village of Agunnaryd. Ingvar began his business by selling fish, vegetable seeds, and magazines to local farmers, which he delivered on a bicycle. His entrepreneurial spirit soon led him to expand into other household products, which he sold primarily through mail-order catalogs. IKEA began to specialize in home furnishings in 1953 when Ingvar purchased a small furniture factory and opened a nearby showroom in Älmhult, Sweden.

Even in the early days, IKEA's strategy was built around the design, delivery, and sale of high-quality furniture at an affordable price. IKEA revolutionized the furniture-buying experience for millions of future customers with innovations such as flat packaging (to avoid transporting and storing air), self-assembly (with visual instructions that can be deciphered in any language), and a unique retail experience that includes child care, Swedish meatballs, and a shopping maze full of innovative products and furnishings. While affordability and self-service remain a key part of the IKEA experience, the company also offers services such as home delivery and assembly.

Today, IKEA's vision is to help consumers live a better life at home by offering a wide range of well-designed, functional home products at prices so low that as many people as possible will be able to afford them. The company's core values include function, quality, design, value, and sustainability.

Throughout this chapter, we will use IKEA examples to illustrate how managers can use accounting information to make a variety of short-term decisions, including

- Whether to accept an offer from a large university to supply desks for all of its dormitories.
- Whether to outsource the food served in IKEA restaurants.
- Whether to eliminate one of its least profitable bookcases.

- Whether to add lighting and electronic outlets to an entertainment wall unit.
- Which patio table to manufacture given a limited supply of hardwood.

Although we use fictitious scenarios and numbers, these examples will demonstrate a quantitative approach to managerial decision making called incremental analysis. The goal of incremental analysis is to make decisions that will maximize the company's short-term accounting profit. While this is an important objective for most companies, it is certainly not the only criteria that should be used when making decisions. Thus, we will also discuss other strategic and qualitative factors that managers should factor into their decisions. Finally, we will discuss the role of sustainability reporting in business and illustrate how managers can make decisions that are not only good for profit, but also for people and the planet.

ORGANIZATION OF THE CHAPTER

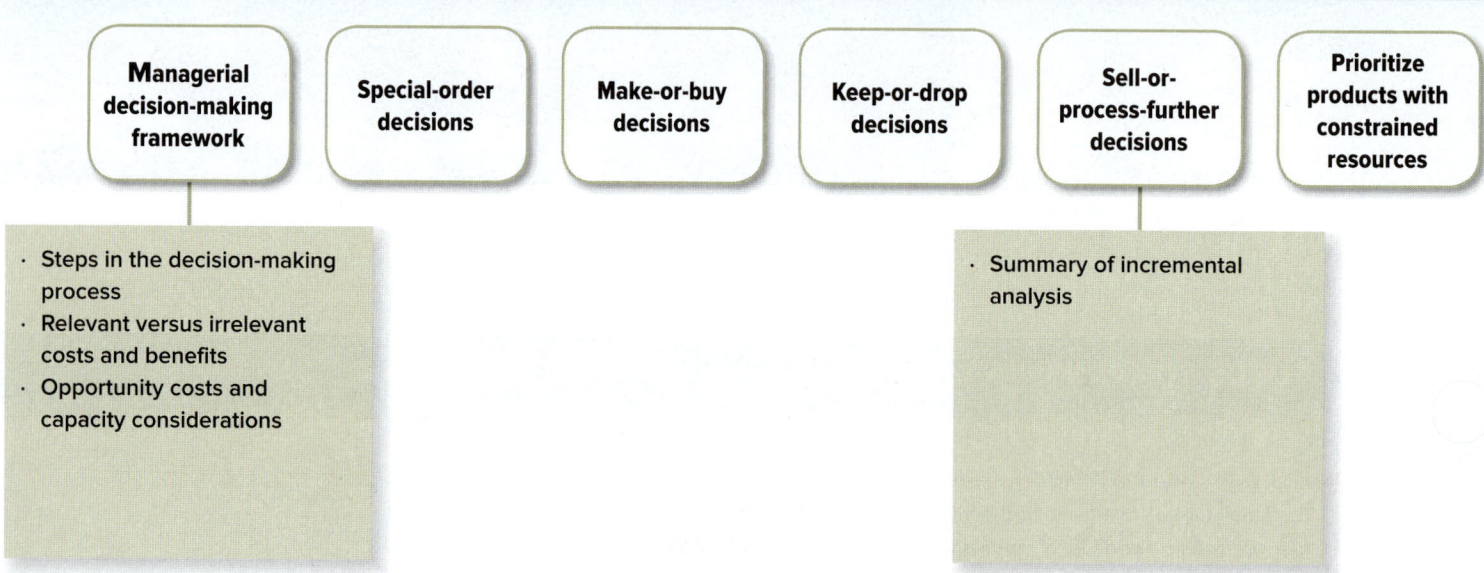

Managerial Decision-Making Framework

Learning Objective 7–1
Describe the five steps in the decision-making process.

In this chapter, we illustrate how managers use cost and other managerial accounting information to make short-term decisions. We will use a decision-making approach called incremental analysis, which involves comparing the relevant costs and benefits of alternative decision choices. Let's start with a description of the decision-making framework and then consider how managers at IKEA would use this approach to make a variety of short-term decisions.

STEPS IN THE DECISION-MAKING PROCESS

The decision-making process involves the five steps shown in the following graphic:

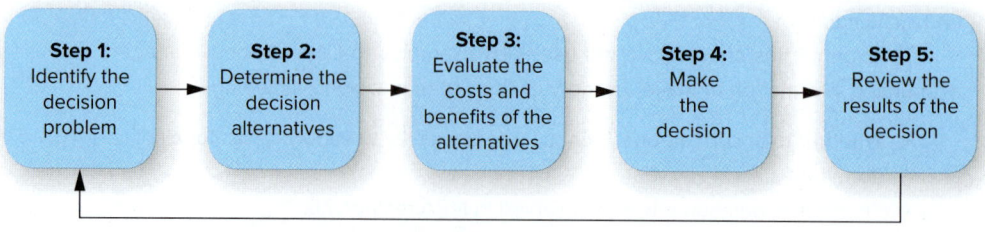

This general framework is adapted from other business disciplines and can be used to analyze a variety of decision problems. We'll explore each step in more detail in the sections that follow.

Step 1: Identify the Decision Problem

The first step in the decision-making process is to identify the decision problem. Each of us makes hundreds of decisions each day, from mundane things like deciding what to eat, what to wear, and what route to drive to school or work, to more important decisions like where to go to school, what car to buy, and whom to marry. Whether conscious or unconscious, we go through the same basic process when making all decisions: identifying the problem, determining our options, weighing the costs and benefits of those options, making the decision, and getting feedback about the wisdom of our decisions.

To illustrate this process, let's apply it to a decision problem that most of us have faced at some point in our lives: deciding where to live.

Step 2: Determine the Decision Alternatives

Once you have identified the problem, the next step is to determine the possible solutions, called **decision alternatives**. This is a critical step because the remainder of the decision process hinges on the decision alternatives identified here. If a potential alternative is not included in this initial stage, it will not be considered in later phases of the analysis. For the decision about where to live, assume you have narrowed it down to two options: lease a house with two roommates or rent a one-bedroom apartment on your own. This rules out other potential alternatives such as living with your parents or buying your own home; thus, these alternatives will not be considered further.

Step 3: Evaluate the Costs and Benefits of the Alternatives

Our main focus will be on Step 3 of the decision-making process, which involves comparing the costs and benefits of the decision alternatives identified in Step 2. The approach we use is called **incremental analysis** or **differential analysis** because it focuses on the factors that will change, or differ, between the decision alternatives. In managerial accounting, this approach is sometimes called **relevant costing** because only those costs that change or differ between the decision alternatives are relevant for decision making. We will discuss relevant costs and benefits in more detail shortly.

Assume that you have determined the following information about the two housing options you are considering:

- Option 1: Rent for a 1-bedroom apartment is $800 per month. Utilities are estimated to be $150 per month. It is close to campus so you can bike to school, which would save you about $75 per month in fuel and parking.

- Option 2: Rent for a 3-bedroom house is $1,800 per month, or $600 per person. Utilities are estimated at $450, or $150 per person. The house has a great backyard and lots of room for socializing, but would require you to drive to campus and would not provide much privacy or quiet study time.

Exhibit 7–1 provides a comparison of the costs and benefits of these decision alternatives. In this example, sharing a 3-bedroom house is expected to cost $125 per month less than renting a 1-bedroom apartment on your own. Notice that your utilities expense is the same under both options. As such, this factor is not relevant to the decision because you will have to pay $150 per month regardless of which option you choose. What really matters is the *difference* in costs and benefits between the two options.

Step 4: Make the Decision

Once you have evaluated the costs and benefits of the decision alternatives, the next step is to use the information to make a decision. Based strictly on the quantitative data, you would decide to share the 3-bedroom house because it is less expensive than renting a 1-bedroom apartment. However, cost is only a subset of the information that is relevant to this decision. You should

EXHIBIT 7-1	Applying the Five-Step Managerial Decision-Making Process to a Personal Decision

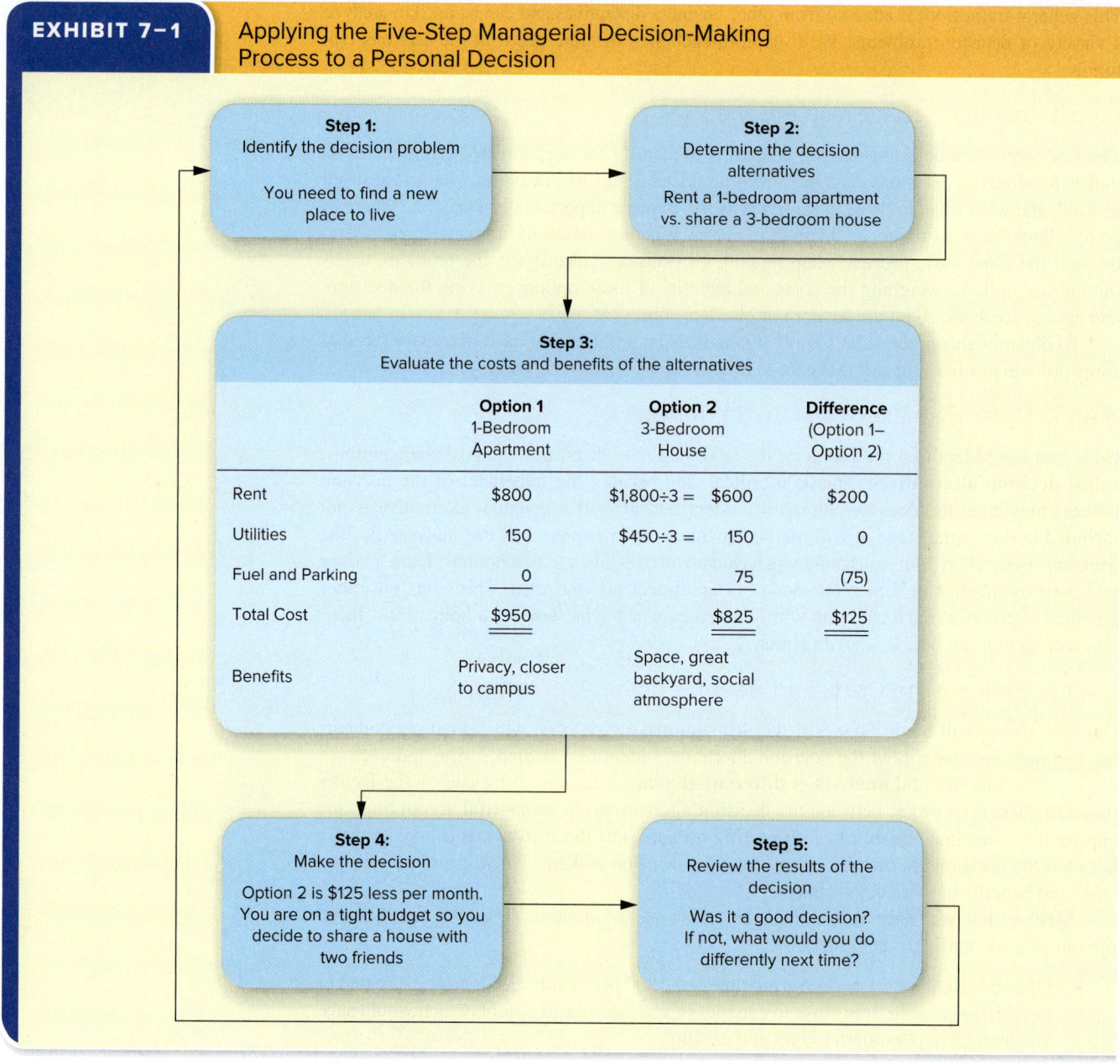

Step 1:
Identify the decision problem

You need to find a new place to live

Step 2:
Determine the decision alternatives

Rent a 1-bedroom apartment vs. share a 3-bedroom house

Step 3:
Evaluate the costs and benefits of the alternatives

	Option 1 1-Bedroom Apartment	Option 2 3-Bedroom House	Difference (Option 1– Option 2)
Rent	$800	$1,800÷3 = $600	$200
Utilities	150	$450÷3 = 150	0
Fuel and Parking	0	75	(75)
Total Cost	$950	$825	$125
Benefits	Privacy, closer to campus	Space, great backyard, social atmosphere	

Step 4:
Make the decision

Option 2 is $125 less per month. You are on a tight budget so you decide to share a house with two friends

Step 5:
Review the results of the decision

Was it a good decision? If not, what would you do differently next time?

also consider other important factors that are difficult to quantify or put a number on—we call these qualitative factors. For example, how much do you value privacy over social activities? How well do you know the people that you would share the house with? Are they trustworthy and reliable? How much do you value their friendship and what happens if it doesn't work out?

In business, managers face similar trade-offs between financial considerations and qualitative factors such as strategic issues, quality considerations, legal and ethical concerns, and the like. For all of the decisions that we analyze throughout this chapter, we first perform a quantitative analysis to determine which alternative is "best" based strictly on the numbers. We then discuss other qualitative factors that might come into play to influence managers' decisions.

Step 5: Review the Results of the Decision

The final step in the decision-making process is to review the results of the decision to determine if you made the right choice or whether you should do something different the next time you are faced with a similar decision. With any decision, there are likely to be unexpected costs and benefits that you did not foresee that will influence how you make decisions in the future.

Managerial accounting provides feedback to managers about the results of previous decisions so that they can take corrective action or make adjustments going forward. The role of managerial accounting information in performance evaluation and control is discussed in more detail in other chapters. For now, we will focus on using managerial accounting information to make future decisions, rather than evaluating past decisions.

RELEVANT VERSUS IRRELEVANT COSTS AND BENEFITS

The rest of this chapter focuses on the third step of the decision-making process, which involves comparing the costs and benefits of the decision alternatives. One of the most important parts of this process is determining which costs (and benefits) are relevant to the decision at hand.

> **Learning Objective 7–2**
> Define and identify relevant costs and benefits.

Relevant Costs

A **relevant cost** has the potential to influence a specific decision and should therefore be considered in the analysis. To be relevant, it must meet both of the following criteria:

- Occurs in the future.
- Differs between decision alternatives.

Costs that differ between decision alternatives are also called **differential costs** or **incremental costs**. In Exhibit 7–1, the difference in monthly rent between the house and the apartment was $200. Only the difference in cost was relevant to the decision of whether to rent the house or the apartment.

Another term for relevant cost is **avoidable cost**—that is, a cost that can be avoided by choosing one decision alternative instead of another. In Exhibit 7–1, the costs of fuel and on-campus parking could be avoided if you lived in an apartment near campus and could ride your bike to class. This cost was relevant to the decision because it differed between the two alternatives.

Irrelevant Costs

Irrelevant costs are those that will not influence a decision, either because they have already been incurred or because they do not differ between the decision alternatives. **Sunk costs**, or costs that were incurred in the past, are not relevant because they will not change based on a future decision. Sunk costs may be used to evaluate the outcome of *previous* decisions (Step 5 of the decision process). However, they are not relevant for *future* decisions, which is the focus of this chapter.

Future costs that remain the same across decision alternatives are also irrelevant. In the housing example, the monthly utility costs were estimated to be $150 regardless of whether you share the rental house or rent the apartment. You can either ignore this cost altogether, or include the same amount in both options so that the net effect is zero.

OPPORTUNITY COSTS AND CAPACITY CONSIDERATIONS

Another type of cost that must be considered in decision making is the **opportunity cost** or the forgone benefit (lost opportunity) of choosing one decision alternative over another. We all face opportunity costs anytime we make a choice about what to do with our limited time or money. Similarly, business managers face opportunity costs when they are forced to choose one alternative over another because of limited resources such as cash, employee time, equipment availability, or space.

Opportunity costs are relevant for decision making, but they only come into play when the capacity of a critical resource is limited. **Capacity** is a measure of the limit placed on a specific resource. It could be the number of people who will fit in a restaurant or an airplane, the number of employees who are available to serve clients, the amount of machine time that is available to make a product, or the amount of shelving space that is available for merchandise.

If a company has **idle** or **excess capacity**, it has more than enough resources to satisfy demand. Because it has not yet reached the limit on its resources, opportunity costs are not relevant. When a company is operating at **full capacity**, the limit on one or more of its resources has been reached, and making the choice to do one thing means giving up the opportunity to do something else. At full capacity, opportunity costs become relevant and should be incorporated into the analysis. In the last section of the chapter, we discuss how to prioritize multiple products based on capacity considerations.

In the next section, we use several IKEA examples to illustrate how to use **incremental analysis** to analyze four common managerial decisions:

- Special-order decisions.
- Make-or-buy decisions.
- Keep-or-drop decisions.
- Sell-or-process-further decisions.

Although each of these decisions is slightly different, we can use a consistent approach, called incremental analysis, to compare the costs and benefits of the decision alternatives. This same basic approach can be applied to many other managerial decisions.

First, make sure that you understand the decision-making process and can correctly identify relevant costs by completing the following Self-Study Practice.

 How's it going?   Self-Study Practice

1. Which of the following steps in the decision-making process are out of sequence?
    a. Identify the decision problem.
    b. Evaluate the costs and benefits of the alternatives.
    c. Determine the decision alternatives.
    d. Make the decision.
    e. Review the results of the decision-making process.

2. Which of the following costs would **not** be relevant to the decision of whether to take the bus or drive your vehicle to school for a semester? Assume that you will continue to own your vehicle under either alternative.
    a. The cost of the fuel you use driving to and from campus.
    b. The cost of on-campus parking.
    c. The wear and tear on your vehicle due to the extra mileage.
    d. The time you could spend studying while traveling on the bus instead of driving to school.
    e. The monthly cost of liability insurance on your vehicle.

After you have finished, check your answers against the solutions in the margin.

Special-Order Decisions

Special-order decisions require managers to decide whether to accept or reject an order that is outside the scope of normal sales. These one-time orders, or special orders, are often offered at a lower price than customers normally pay for the product or service. The decision that managers must make is whether to accept or reject the offer. We can analyze this decision by comparing the incremental costs and benefits of accepting (versus rejecting) the special order.

As an example, assume that a major university has approached IKEA about buying some "sit-or-stand" desks to be installed in university dorm rooms. The university has offered to buy 5,000 of these desks at a price of $200 each. These desks normally sell for $300 in IKEA stores, catalogs, and the company website. Assume the estimated costs of producing the sit-or-stand desk are as follows:

	Unit Cost
Direct materials (wood top, metal legs, lifting mechanism)	$125.00
Direct labor	30.00
Variable manufacturing overhead (50% of direct labor cost)	15.00
Fixed manufacturing overhead (factory rent, supervision, etc.)	50.00
Total manufacturing cost	$220.00

At first glance, it appears that managers should reject the special order because the $200 offer price is less than the $220 that it costs to produce each desk. However, this analysis is not correct. To correctly analyze this decision, managers should ask the following questions:

1. How much will total revenue and total costs change if the special order is accepted?

2. Does the company have the capacity to fill the special order without affecting sales made through its normal channels (e.g., store, phone, or web sales)? If not, opportunity costs will also have to be included in the analysis.

3. Are there other strategic or qualitative factors to consider?

Let's begin by assuming that IKEA has enough capacity to fill the special order without disrupting the production and sale of desks sold through normal channels.

Incremental Analysis (with Excess Capacity)

To determine the impact that the special order will have on profitability, we can compare the increased revenue from the special order to the incremental costs of filling the order, as follows:

Incremental Analysis of the Special Order for 5,000 Sit-or-Stand Desks

	Per Unit	Total
Incremental revenue	$ 200	$1,000,000
Less: Incremental costs		
Direct materials	(125)	(625,000)
Direct labor	(30)	(150,000)
Variable overhead	(15)	(75,000)
Fixed overhead	—	—
Total incremental cost	(170)	(850,000)
Incremental profit	$30	$ 150,000

COACH'S TIP

Fixed costs are excluded from the incremental analysis because they will be incurred regardless of whether or not the company accepts the special order. In the short term, fixed costs will not change, so any price that exceeds the variable costs of filling the order will yield an incremental profit.

This incremental analysis shows that the special order will increase total revenues by $1,000,000 and total costs by $850,000, for a $150,000 net increase in profit. Notice that fixed costs, such as rent, supervision, and insurance, are excluded from the incremental analysis because they will be incurred regardless of whether the special order is accepted or rejected. In other words, fixed costs are not relevant to this decision. The only costs that are relevant to this decision are the variable costs of filling the special order. Since the special-order price of $200 is more than the $170 variable cost per unit, each unit will generate an extra $30 in incremental or extra profit, or $150,000 total.

Qualitative Analysis

Two important cautions should be noted when making this type of short-term analysis. First, this analysis should only be used for one-time or special orders. Managers would not want to use it to make long-term pricing decisions because revenues must cover **all** costs, including fixed costs, if the company is to be profitable in the long run. Managers should also consider whether accepting the special order will impact the price that other customers are willing to pay for sales made through regular channels.

Second, the results of this analysis are valid only if the company has excess, or idle, production capacity. If not, the company would not be able to fill the special order without canceling or deferring sales made through regular channels, resulting in lost sales (an opportunity cost) or unhappy customers (a qualitative factor). The following section illustrates how to analyze special orders when capacity is limited.

SPOTLIGHT ON Service

Turning Unused Capacity into Revenue

Travel providers such as airlines, hotels, and car rental agencies often use special pricing to fill unused capacity. Online travel sites like priceline.com and hotwire.com provide discounted prices to consumers who are willing to travel at off-peak times, stay at any hotel within a certain class, or rent any car that is available. The airline, hotel, or car rental company generates extra revenue from the unused capacity; consumers get a bargain price for travel; and the online travel site generates advertising revenue from related travel services such as dining, entertainment, and tourist attractions.

What is the incremental cost to an airline of one extra passenger on a flight? If there is an empty seat on the plane, it is literally peanuts and a soft drink. The incremental cost of filling an empty hotel room is the cost of cleaning the room and incidental supplies like toiletries. Because fixed costs are going to be incurred anyway, any price that exceeds these variable costs will generate extra profit. But this approach to pricing only works in the short run. To make money in the long run, companies need a solid base of customers who are willing to pay full price for their services.

Incremental Analysis (when Capacity is Limited)

Now assume that IKEA is operating at full production capacity and cannot fill the special order for 5,000 sit-or-stand desks without reducing production and sale of desks sold through normal channels. The desks normally sell in IKEA stores, catalogs, and the company website for $300 each. Should IKEA's managers accept the university's offer to pay $200 per desk?

The limited production capacity creates an opportunity cost because filling the special order would mean passing up the opportunity to sell to normal customers. The opportunity cost can be measured as the contribution margin that would have been earned on sales made through regular channels. Again, we can focus on contribution margin because fixed costs will not change in the short run.

Because the desks normally sell for $300 each and the variable cost is $170 per unit, the contribution margin earned on a normal sale is $130 ($300 − $170) per unit. When capacity is constrained, IKEA will have to give up $130 per unit in contribution margin due to lost sales to regular customers. When the opportunity cost of lost sales is incorporated into the incremental analysis, we see that the incremental revenue from the special order is no longer enough to cover the incremental costs, as follows:

Incremental Analysis of the Special Order for 5,000 Sit-or-Stand Desks (When Capacity is Limited)		
	Per Unit	**Total**
Incremental revenue	$ 200	$1,000,000
Less: Incremental costs		
Direct materials	(125)	(625,000)
Direct labor	(30)	(150,000)
Variable overhead	(15)	(75,000)
Fixed overhead	—	—
Opportunity cost of lost sales ($300 – $170)	(130)	(650,000)
Total incremental cost	(300)	1,500,000
Incremental profit (loss)	$(100)	$ (500,000)

> **COACH'S TIP**
>
> Opportunity costs occur any time capacity is limited and accepting one option means giving up something else. For a special order, it is measured as the lost contribution margin from a regular sale.

The net result of accepting the special order would be a $500,000 decrease in profit. Notice that the incremental cost associated with the special order is $300 when the opportunity cost of lost sales is considered, compared to an offer price of $200. When a company is operating at full capacity, managers should not accept a special order for less than the price they could get through normal channels.

This analysis assumes that capacity cannot be increased in the short run and that it is not possible to back order or defer the sales to a future period. It is also possible that some existing customers would decide to purchase a different type of IKEA desk, which would potentially offset some of the opportunity costs. Finally, there may be other strategic reasons for accepting the special order, such as the opportunity to enter a new market or region, or to increase brand awareness by partnering with a major university. As always, the numerical analysis must be balanced against these qualitative factors.

Complete the following Self-Study Practice to make sure you understand how to analyze special-order decisions.

How's it going? Self-Study Practice

Big Top Tent Company has received a special order for 10,000 units at a discounted price of $100 each. The product, which normally sells for $150, has the following manufacturing costs:

	Cost per Unit
Direct materials	$ 40
Direct labor	20
Variable manufacturing overhead	20
Fixed manufacturing overhead	30
Unit cost	$110

1. Assume Big Top has enough extra capacity to fill the order without affecting the production or sale of its product to regular customers. If Big Top accepts the offer, what effect will the order have on the company's short-term profit?

2. If Big Top is at full capacity, what price would be needed to cover all incremental costs, including opportunity costs?

After you have finished, check your answers against the solutions in the margin.

Solution to Self-Study Practice

1. ($100 price – $80 variable cost) = $20 incremental profit × 10,000 units = $200,000

2. Minimum price = $150 (regular price)

Make-or-Buy Decisions

The next managerial decision we analyze is whether to perform an activity or function in-house or purchase it from an outside supplier. Traditionally, these decisions were called **make-or-buy decisions**, but more recently they have been referred to as **outsourcing decisions**. Almost any business function can be outsourced, including production activities and support functions such as payroll, information technology, distribution, and technical support. The key question is whether the organization wants to perform the activities with its own resources and employees, or hire a third party to perform the activities.

Managers should ask the following questions when analyzing make-or-buy decisions:

1. How much will costs and revenue **change** depending on whether the company makes or buys the product or service?

2. Are there opportunity costs associated with either alternative? For example, what else could the company do with the resources that are currently devoted to an in-house function? Could the resources be deployed to some better use?

3. Are there other qualitative factors to consider, such as corporate strategy, sustainability goals, employee morale, risk, quality, and reliability?

As an example, let's consider the food service provided at IKEA. After wandering the maze of household products, IKEA customers have the opportunity to enjoy some authentic Swedish cuisine in the IKEA cafe or bistro. While food service is an important part of the IKEA shopping experience, is this a function that the company should provide internally, or should they outsource to another company that specializes in food service?

For this hypothetical example, assume IKEA currently provides its own food service and that a typical IKEA store serves an average of 15,000 customers per month, with the following revenue and costs associated with the food service function:

REVENUE AND COSTS OF SERVING FOOD TO 15,000 CUSTOMERS PER MONTH

	Per Customer	Per Month
Food service revenue	$10.00	$150,000
Less: Direct material (cost of food)	$ 2.50	37,500
Direct labor (wages)	1.00	15,000
Variable overhead (condiments and supplies)	0.50	7,500
Fixed overhead (supervisor salary, depreciation, share of building rent)	2.00	30,000
Operating profit	$ 4.00	$ 60,000

Assume IKEA has been negotiating with an outside supplier to provide food service. Under the proposed agreement, IKEA would pay the supplier 50 percent of the revenues generated from food service, or an average of $5 per customer. In exchange, the supplier would be responsible for buying the food, hiring workers to prepare and serve it to customers, and all variable expenses, such as condiments, paper, and cleaning supplies. The supplier would also be required to hire the current IKEA food service supervisor to oversee the food service operation. IKEA would continue to provide facilities, equipment, and utilities, but would use some of the space currently used for food preparation for a new service to provide on-site assembly assistance. Assume the supervisor makes $5,000 per month and the new assembly service would generate $15,000 in contribution margin per month.

Should IKEA continue to provide its own food service or outsource this function? To answer this question, managers should first perform an incremental analysis to determine how revenue and costs are likely to change if they decide to outsource.

Incremental Analysis

If IKEA chooses to outsource, the company will have to pay the supplier 50 percent of the revenue earned on food service, or $75,000 per month (15,000 customers × $10.00 × 50 percent). This assumes that the supplier will continue to serve the same number of customers per month at an average price of $10. From a pure profit perspective, managers will need to eliminate at least $75,000 in costs and/or generate enough revenue from the new service offerings for the outsourcing decision to make economic sense.

How much cost could IKEA eliminate or avoid by outsourcing? All of the variable costs (direct materials, direct labor, and variable overhead) can be eliminated because the supplier will be responsible for these costs. But what about the fixed costs? Only a portion of the fixed costs are avoidable, because IKEA will still be responsible for providing the facilities, equipment, and utilities. Most of the fixed costs are not relevant because they will be incurred regardless of the outsourcing decision. Only the supervisor's salary ($5,000 per month) is avoidable because this cost will now be paid by the supplier.

In addition to the direct cost savings, managers must consider whether there are any opportunity costs associated with outsourcing. Remember that opportunity costs arise any time a critical resource is limited. In this case, IKEA has an alternative use for the space that is currently devoted to food preparation that could be used for a new service line. The opportunity costs are measured by the contribution margin that could be earned on the new service offering. It can be considered a cost (negative) of insourcing or a benefit (positive) of outsourcing. Either way, it will be a $15,000 difference in favor of outsourcing.

The following table summarizes the incremental analysis of this make-or-buy decision. Although the revenues and costs of both options are shown, what really matters is the **difference** between the two options. The costs and revenues of the in-house option have been subtracted from the outsource option, so that a negative number represents a cost of outsourcing, while a positive number represents a benefit of outsourcing.

	Option 1: Keep In-House	Option 2: Outsource	Difference: (Cost) or Benefit of Outsourcing
Food service revenue	$ 150,000	$ 75,000	$(75,000)
Less:			
Direct materials	(37,500)	-	37,500
Direct labor	(15,000)	-	15,000
Variable overhead	(7,500)	-	7,500
Fixed overhead	(30,000)	(25,000)	5,000
Revenue from new service offering	-	15,000	15,000
Operating profit	$ 60,000	$ 65,000	$ 5,000

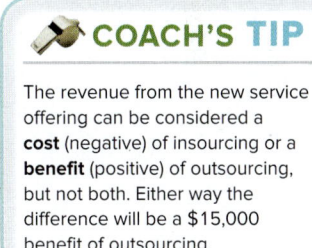

COACH'S TIP

The revenue from the new service offering can be considered a **cost** (negative) of insourcing or a **benefit** (positive) of outsourcing, but not both. Either way the difference will be a $15,000 benefit of outsourcing.

Overall, the incremental analysis shows that IKEA will save $5,000 per month by outsourcing the food service function. As always, the quantitative analysis is only a starting point, and must be weighed against many other considerations.

Qualitative Analysis

Before making a final decision, IKEA's managers would want to consider many other qualitative factors, such as the following:

- Will the quality of the food service be as good, or even better, than IKEA could provide internally? Sometimes quality can be improved by outsourcing because the supplier specializes in that function.

- Is the function a critical part of the company's business strategy? Many companies choose to outsource functions that are less critical to their business success and for which they do not have a strategic advantage or core competency. Since IKEA's core competency is the design of innovative furniture, it may make sense to outsource less critical activities to others.

- Are there any safety or liability issues to consider? For example, what happens if a customer gets sick from eating the food? Even if the supplier is legally responsible, IKEA could bear some of the costs and its reputation and brand could be severely impacted. This happened a few years ago when horse meat was detected in a few batches of Swedish meatballs. IKEA quickly took action to remove the product (donating more than 3.5 million servings to European food banks) and has since implemented new procedures and supplier policies to strengthen the traceability of food in its supply chain.

- How will outsourcing impact employees and other critical stakeholders? What will happen to employees who are let go? Will the supplier hire them? How will it impact the local community?

- How does the decision impact the triple bottom line? The incremental analysis only focuses on the economic aspect of the triple bottom line. Are there environmental or social impacts to consider?

To make sure you understand how to analyze make-or-buy decisions, complete the following Self-Study Practice.

 How's it going?   Self-Study Practice

Which of the following costs would **not** be relevant to the decision of whether to make a part internally or buy it from an outside supplier?

a. Cost of materials needed to make the part internally.

b. Cost of power to run the machines that make the part.

c. Fact that the supplier does not maintain high quality standards.

d. Share of the rent on the factory (where several parts are made).

e. Opportunity cost of the space currently used to produce the part.

After you have finished, check your answers against the solutions in the margin.

Solution to Self-Study Practice

d. The rent on the factory will be incurred regardless and is therefore irrelevant.

Keep-or-Drop Decisions

Learning Objective 7–5
Analyze a keep-or-drop decision.

The next decision we consider is whether to eliminate a particular division or segment of the business. Businesses can be segmented (divided) in a number of ways, such as by product line, service offering, or geographic region. If a particular business segment is not performing as well as expected, managers may decide to eliminate it. These decisions are called **keep-or-drop decisions** or **continue-or-discontinue decisions**. In deciding whether to eliminate a business segment, managers should ask the following questions:

- How much will total revenue and total costs change if the segment is eliminated?

- Will other segments or product lines be affected?

- Are there opportunity costs associated with keeping the segment? For example, could resources be deployed to more profitable uses if the segment were eliminated?

- Are there other qualitative factors to consider, such as the impact on employees and the company's reputation in the community?

Assume that IKEA produces three types of bookshelves: the Billy, the Finnby, and the Borgsjö. IKEA's managers are considering dropping the Finnby model because it generated a $200,000 loss last year.

The following segmented income statement shows the revenue and costs of the three models:

SEGMENT DATA FOR BOOKCASE PRODUCTS				
	Billy Bookcase	Finnby Bookcase	Borgsjö Bookcase	Total
Sales revenue	$5,000,000	$1,500,000	$3,500,000	$10,000,000
Less: Variable costs	2,000,000	1,000,000	1,400,000	4,400,000
Contribution margin	$3,000,000	$ 500,000	$2,100,000	$ 5,600,000
Less: Direct fixed costs	500,000	400,000	300,000	1,200,000
Segment margin	$2,500,000	$ 100,000	$1,800,000	$ 4,400,000
Less: Common fixed costs*	1,000,000	300,000	700,000	2,000,000
Net operating income (loss)	$1,500,000	$ (200,000)	$1,100,000	$ 2,400,000

*Common fixed costs are allocated to the three products as a percentage of total sales revenue.

This segmented income statement is based on the contribution margin approach introduced in Chapter 5. However, it has been expanded to include a new line item called **segment margin**, which is calculated as sales revenue less all costs that are directly attributable to the segment, including variable costs and direct fixed costs. A **direct fixed cost** is a fixed cost that can be attributed to a specific segment of the business. Examples include a machine used to produce only one type of product, a supervisor who is responsible for a specific division, and advertising aimed at a specific region or product line. Even though these costs are fixed, or independent of the number of units produced or sold, they relate to only one segment and could be avoided if the segment were eliminated.

Unlike direct fixed costs that relate to a specific segment, **common fixed costs** are shared by multiple segments and thus will be incurred even if a segment is eliminated. In evaluating segment profitability, managers should focus on the segment margin rather than the bottom-line profit margin. The segment margin tells managers how much incremental profit a segment generates to help cover common fixed costs and contribute to company-wide profit. Although the Finnby bookcase is not profitable in terms of net operating income, it generates $100,000 in segment margin, which helps cover the common fixed costs.

The second question that managers must address is whether the elimination of one product or segment will affect the costs and revenues of other segments. For example, will customers who were planning to buy the Finnby bookcase purchase one of the other models instead? Let's assume that the elimination of the Finnby bookcase will increase sales of the Bojgsjö bookcase by 10 percent, with no effect on the Billy bookcase. Remember that variable costs change in direct proportion to changes in sales, so both the sales revenue and variable costs of the Bojgsjö bookcase would increase by 10 percent. The net effect will be a 10 percent increase in the contribution margin of the Bojgsjö bookcase.

The third question is whether any opportunity costs should be considered. Would the elimination of the Finnby bookcase free resources (people, space, or machines) that could be used in another way? Perhaps another product could be developed that would contribute more to profit than the Finnby bookcase. For the following incremental analysis, we assume that there are no alternative uses for the resources and thus no opportunity costs.

Incremental Analysis

Based on the information given in the previous section, we can prepare an incremental analysis of the decision to eliminate the Finnby bookcase, as follows:

Elimination of the Finnby Bookcase	
Lost sales revenue	$(1,500,000)
Less: Avoidable variable costs	1,000,000
Less: Avoidable direct fixed costs	400,000
Lost segment margin	$ (100,000)
Effect on Borgsjö bookcase (10% increase)	
Increased sales ($3,500,000 × 10%)	$ 350,000
Less: Increased variable cost ($1,400,000 × 10%)	(140,000)
Increased contribution margin ($2,100,000 × 10%)	$ 210,000
Net effect of eliminating the Finnby	$ 110,000

This analysis shows that **IKEA** will lose $100,000 in segment margin from the elimination of the Finnby bookcase but will gain an additional $210,000 in contribution margin from increased sales of the Bojgsjö bookcase. The net effect is an $110,000 increase in profit. All other costs are irrelevant, and no opportunity costs are included in the decision analysis. Based strictly on the incremental profit analysis, managers should choose to eliminate the Finnby bookcase from the product offerings.

An alternative way to analyze this decision is to create a new segmented income statement for the company without the Finnby bookcase, as follows:

COACH'S TIP

You may notice that the format of the incremental analysis changes somewhat from decision to decision, and there is more than one way to work each problem.

Unfortunately, there is no set format for doing incremental analysis. The key is to focus on what is the same in each analysis: the comparison of relevant, or differential, costs and benefits.

	Billy Bookcase	Bojgsjö Bookcase	Total
Sales revenue	$5,000,000	$3,500,000 × 110% = $3,850,000	$8,850,000
Less: Variable costs	2,000,000	1,400,000 × 110% = 1,540,000	3,540,000
Contribution margin	$3,000,000	2,100,000 × 110% = $2,310,000	$5,310,000
Less: Direct fixed costs	500,000	300,000	800,000
Segment margin	$2,500,000	$2,010,000	$4,510,000
Less: Common fixed costs*	1,130,000	870,000	2,000,000
Net operating income	$1,370,000	$1,140,000	$2,510,000

*Common fixed costs were reallocated to the remaining two products as a percentage of total sales revenue.

Net operating income from the remaining two product lines is estimated to be $2,510,000, compared to $2,400,000 with all three product lines. The $110,000 difference is the net effect of eliminating the Finnby bookcase. Based strictly on the incremental analysis, IKEA should discontinue the Finnby bookcase because it will increase profit by $110,000 per year.

Qualitative Analysis

As in the other decision scenarios, the quantitative analysis is only a starting point for making the decision. Managers must always consider other important factors, including the effect of the decision on customer loyalty and employee morale.

Managers must also think about the likely impact of discontinuation on other products and customers. The previous example involved **substitute products** or products that can be used in place of one another. In this example, IKEA customers might choose to buy the Bojgsjö bookcase if the Finnby bookcase is not available. In that scenario, eliminating one product could boost sales of another product line.

But sometimes firms have **complementary products**, or products that are used together. Common examples include **Brother** printers and cartridges, **Apple** iPhones and iTunes, and

SPOTLIGHT ON Decision Making

Is Amazon costing the U.S. Postal Service "massive amounts of money"?

This question made headlines when President Trump took to his Twitter account and claimed Amazon was using the U.S. Postal Service as its "delivery boy" and costing taxpayers "billions of dollars." The Twitter battle was part of an on-going feud between the U.S. president and Amazon founder and CEO Jeff Bezos.

The U.S. Postal Service (USPS) has not posted a profit since 2007—two years after Amazon first offered two-day free shipping—but is the USPS delivery contract with Amazon helping or hurting its bottom line? Here are some additional facts and estimates to consider:

- Approximately 40 percent of Amazon packages are delivered by the USPS. However, Amazon does most of the up-front delivery work, dropping off pallets of presorted packages (arranged by zip code and carrier) to be delivered the "last mile" to the customer.

- Although no one (other than the USPS and Amazon) knows exactly how much Amazon pays for delivery, analysts estimate it at about $2 per package, or roughly one-half of the amount private carriers such as FedEx and UPS charge.

- The USPS already delivers mail Monday–Saturday, making the incremental cost of delivery fairly low. However, the contract with Amazon required the USPS to add Sunday delivery.

- A large percentage of USPS costs are "fixed," including high administrative costs and mandated health care and pension costs.

- Federal law requires postal rates to cover the direct costs of delivery plus a fair portion of the "institutional" or "common" fixed costs. Currently, these costs are allocated at about 5.5 percent of direct delivery costs, but critics argue this rate is far too low and should be raised to 24–28 percent.

- Raising postal rates to reflect the "true" or "full" cost of delivery could result in lost revenue if Amazon gives more of their business to competitors such as UPS or FedEx, who are not constrained by government regulation.

- Package delivery is the USPS's highest growth line of business and accounts for roughly 28 percent of total revenue.

As you can see, determining whether Amazon is helping or hurting the USPS is not as straight-forward as one might think. If you apply the incremental costing approach described in this chapter, the revenue received from Amazon is likely more than enough to cover the incremental costs of delivery and a portion of the common fixed costs as well. From a full-cost perspective, however, the true cost of delivery is likely higher than the discounted price Amazon pays. Yet, those common fixed costs won't go away if Amazon and other high-volume customers take more of their business to FedEx or UPS, so they might be considered irrelevant when evaluating the profitability of the USPS–Amazon contract.

Sources:
https://www.washingtonpost.com/news/wonk/wp/2018/04/04/is-the-post-office-making-or-losing-money-delivering-amazon-packages/?tid=pm_business_pop&noredirect=on

https://www.cbsnews.com/news/post-office-lose-money-amazon-contract-usps-fact-check-trump-tweets-again-today-2018-04-03/

https://ir.citi.com/XlnLvxkr5F%2FJvyPr1NMI%2FPclgrn%2BXqplW8cqbv2lmZxLKrWAiRT%2BcFMjQe6C%2BuQT9n1mvCnznGU%3D

Nintendo game systems and games. In the case of complementary products, eliminating one product can have a negative effect on the related product. When choosing to discontinue products, managers must carefully anticipate the effect on other related product lines.

As previously discussed, managers should also consider more than just the economic impact of their decisions. Incremental analysis is a very short-term oriented approach that only considers one aspect of the triple bottom line. With a keep-or-drop decision, employee jobs are often at risk, which can have a negative impact on the company's environmental and social measures.

Before continuing, complete the following Self-Study Practice to make sure you can analyze decisions to eliminate a business segment.

How's it going?   Self-Study Practice

Big Top Tent Company is trying to decide whether to keep or drop one of its outdoor wedding tents. The company's segmented income statement shows that this product is generating a net loss, as follows:

Sales revenue	$100,000
Less: Variable costs (canvas, ropes, and direct labor)	70,000
Contribution margin	$ 30,000
Less: Direct fixed costs (supervision)	10,000
Segment margin	$ 20,000
Less: Allocated common fixed costs	30,000
Net operating income (loss)	$(10,000)

The company estimates that eliminating this product line will increase the contribution margin on a related product line by $25,000. Based on this information, what impact would dropping the line have on the company's overall profitability?

a. $5,000 increase.

b. $10,000 increase.

c. $20,000 decrease.

d. $35,000 decrease.

After you have finished, check your answers against the solutions in the margin.

Sell-or-Process-Further Decisions

The next managerial decision we consider is whether to sell a product "as is" or add additional features so that it can be sold for a higher price. Once again, we can analyze this decision by comparing the incremental costs and benefits of this decision. If the increased revenue from the added features is enough to offset the incremental cost, the company should process further; otherwise it is better off selling the product as is.

As an example, assume that IKEA is trying to decide whether to add new features to one of its entertainment wall units, including lighted shelves and outlets for charging electronic devices. Based on the existing design (without these added features), managers expect to sell 10,000 units at a price of $150 each. If they add the new features to the design, they believe they can increase the price to $200, but will only be able to sell 8,000 units because of the higher price point. The enhanced product would also have higher manufacturing costs because it would require additional components and take more time to manufacture. The company would also need to spend an additional $10,000 updating the design specifications and assembly instructions for the product. The following table summarizes the expected costs and revenues from selling the product based on the current design versus selling it with the enhanced features:

	Current Design	Enhanced Design
Demand	10,000 units	8,000 units
Unit sales price	$ 150	$ 200
Variable costs per unit:		
Direct materials	$ 30.00	$ 45.00
Direct labor	15.00	17.50
Variable manufacturing overhead	5.00	7.50
Total variable cost per unit	$ 50.00	$ 70,00
Total fixed cost	$100,000	$110,000

Incremental Analysis

We can use incremental analysis to determine whether the company should sell the product as it is currently designed or move forward with the enhanced design. The first step is to compare the incremental revenues and costs of the two alternatives as summarized in the following table.

	Existing Design	Enhanced Design	Difference
Sales revenue	10,000 units × $150 = $1,500,000	8,000 × $200 = $1,600,000	$100,000
Variable costs	10,000 units × $ 50 = 500,000	8,000 × $ 70 = 560,000	(60,000)
Contribution margin	10,000 units × $100 = $1,000,000	8,000 × $130 = $1,040,000	$ 40,000
Fixed costs	100,000	110,000	(10,000)
Operating profit	$ 900,000	$ 930,000	$ 30,000

The incremental analysis shows that total revenue will increase by $100,000 with the new design because the increased sales price is more than enough to offset the reduction in demand. Variable costs are expected to increase by $60,000 due to the higher variable manufacturing costs, for a net increase in contribution margin of $40,000. Fixed costs will also increase by $10,000 due to the redesign of the product, resulting in a net increase in operating profit of $30,000.

Based strictly on the incremental analysis, managers should move forward with the enhanced design because it will increase operating profit by $30,000. Note, however, that the analysis incorporated no opportunity costs. By spending time enhancing this product, IKEA's product designers may be sacrificing time that could be better spent designing new products that could earn even more profit. Whenever possible, managers need to incorporate these opportunity costs and other qualitative factors into the decision-making process.

SUMMARY OF INCREMENTAL ANALYSIS

This chapter applied incremental or relevant cost analysis to a number of short-term decisions. Although the decision problems were different, the same basic approach was used to analyze each decision. In all cases, we focused only on the relevant or incremental costs and benefits of the decision alternatives. Some common rules for analyzing relevant costs and benefits are summarized here:

- Relevant costs and benefits occur in the **future** and **differ** between the decision alternatives.

- Relevant costs are also sometimes called **avoidable** or **differential costs**—costs that will change based on the decision made.

- Variable costs are usually relevant to the decision because they vary with the number of units produced or sold.

- Fixed costs may not be relevant because they do not change with the number of units produced or sold.
- Fixed costs that are directly related to the decision, also called direct fixed costs, may be avoidable and thus relevant.
- Common or allocated fixed costs are shared by multiple products or services and are generally not relevant.
- Opportunity costs are the lost benefit of choosing one alternative over another. These costs are relevant and occur when capacity is reached or resources are constrained. Opportunity costs can be treated either as a benefit of one option, or as a cost of the other, but not both.
- The quantitative analysis provides a starting point for making decisions but must be balanced against other qualitative factors such as quality considerations, customer loyalty, employee morale, sustainability goals, and many other important factors.

SPOTLIGHT ON Sustainability

Reporting and Managerial Decision Making

The incremental analysis presented throughout this chapter focused strictly on the economic impact of managers' decisions. With the increased focus on sustainability, many companies are issuing sustainability reports that provide information on the company's triple bottom line performance. Although these reports are voluntary, companies who report sustainability information to stakeholders are more likely to incorporate environmental and social impacts into their decision making.

The Global Reporting Initiative (GRI) provides the most widely accepted standards for sustainability reporting, including guidelines, definitions, and examples of performance indicators that capture economic, social, and environmental measures of performance. The following represent just a few of the performance indicators that might be included in an organization's sustainability report:

- Total number and rates of new employee hires and employee turnover by age group, gender, and region.
- Proportion of spending on local suppliers at significant locations of operation.
- Percentage of new suppliers that were screened using labor practices criteria.

These metrics are relevant to several of the managerial decisions that we examined in this chapter. For example, both the keep-or-drop and outsourcing decisions were based on the assumption that direct labor costs can be eliminated by reducing the workforce. How would this decision impact the number and rate of employees hired and turnover by age group, gender, and region? If a firm is considering outsourcing and one of its sustainability indicators is the proportion of spending on local suppliers, would that be relevant to the decision?

In make or buy decisions, companies are often looking to save money by outsourcing to countries where direct labor is less expensive. Unfortunately this is often in locations of the world where human rights violations and child labor practices are more prevalent. Companies that are committed to achieving their sustainability goals and that must report their progress toward those goals put numerous policies in place to protect workers throughout the supply chain, including workers hired by suppliers and subsuppliers.

The bottom line is that there is no longer a single bottom line, and managers must incorporate multiple factors into their decisions. While incremental analysis provides a good starting point for understanding the economic implications, managers need other information to capture the social and environmental aspects of sustainability.

Prioritize Products with Constrained Resources

Learning Objective 7–7
Prioritize products to maximize short-term profit with constrained resources.

The final issue we consider in this chapter is how managers should prioritize products when resources are limited or constrained. A **constrained resource** could be anything that is needed to operate the business, such as cash, employees, raw materials, machines, or facilities. When any of these resources are in limited supply and the company is unable to meet customer demand, managers must decide which products to produce or which customers to serve.

In the long term, companies can manage constrained resources by eliminating non-value-added activities, such as rework and waiting, or by increasing the capacity of the constrained resources by hiring more workers, buying bigger or faster machines, or leasing additional space. All of these actions take time, however, and may result in higher costs.

In the short run, managers can maximize profit by prioritizing products or customers based on the amount of contribution margin generated by the most constrained resource, called the **bottleneck**. The bottleneck limits the total number of units that can be produced and therefore determines how much contribution margin can be earned given the limited resource. We focus on contribution margin because fixed costs do not change in the short run and are therefore irrelevant for this type of decision.

If labor is the most constrained resource, managers should focus on maximizing the amount of contribution margin earned per direct labor hour. If a machine is the most constrained resource, they should focus on maximizing the amount of contribution margin earned per machine hour. If raw materials is the limited resource, they should focus on the amount of contribution margin generated for each unit of raw materials used. Prioritizing in this way results in the highest possible short-term profit.

To illustrate, assume that one of IKEA's factories produces three sizes of outdoor patio tables: 2-person (small), 4-person (medium), and 6-person (large). The company has a limited supply of acacia hardwood used to make the tables and managers must determine which products to make to maximize this month's profit. Selling prices, variable costs, raw material requirements, and demand for the three products are summarized as follows:

	Small	Medium	Large
Unit sales price	$140.00	$160.00	$200.00
Unit variable costs	60.00	70.00	100.00
Unit contribution margin	$ 80.00	$ 90.00	$100.00
Raw materials required per unit	20 ft.	30 ft.	40 ft.
Monthly demand (units)	5,000 units	4,000 units	5,000 units
Total raw materials required	100,000 ft.	120,000 ft.	200,000 ft.

> **COACH'S TIP**
>
> The standard unit of measurement for lumber is a "board foot," which is 1 foot square by 1 inch thick. For simplicity, we will call it a foot. In this example, managers would need 420,000 feet of acacia wood to produce all three products.

Assume the company has only 300,000 feet of acacia wood available. Which products should managers produce in order to maximize this month's profit?

To answer this question, we need to determine how much contribution margin is generated *per unit of the constrained resource*. Because raw materials (acacia wood) is the constrained resource, we need to divide the unit contribution margin by the amount of raw materials required to make each unit, as follows:

	Small	Medium	Large
Unit contribution margin	$80.00	$90.00	$100.00
Raw materials required per unit	÷20 ft.	÷30 ft.	÷40 ft.
Contribution margin per foot	$ 4.00	$ 3.00	$ 2.50

Although the small table has the lowest contribution margin per unit ($80), it also requires the least amount of raw materials (20 ft.) to produce. The small table will generate $4.00 in contribution margin for each foot of acacia wood used. The medium table will generate $3.00 in contribution margin per foot of raw materials used. The large table generates only $2.50 in contribution margin for each foot of acacia wood used.

To maximize short-term profit, IKEA's managers should give top priority to the small table. They should produce as many units as they can sell, but not more. Producing more units than the market demands will increase variable costs without an increase in revenue. In addition there are out-of-pocket and opportunity costs associated with storing unsold units in inventory.

When demand for the highest priority product is met, managers should move to the next best product, and produce as many units as they can sell. They continue this process until demand for all of the products is met or they run out of acacia wood.

In this case, the demand for the small table is 5,000 units and each table requires 20 feet of raw materials, or a total of 100,000 feet (5,000 × 20 ft.). This product generates $80 in contribution margin **per unit,** or $4.00 in contribution margin **per foot** of raw materials. Thus, the total contribution margin earned on the small tables is $400,000 (5,000 units × $80 per table, or 100,000 ft. × $4.00 per ft.)

Next, they should produce as many medium tables as they can sell. Demand for the medium tables is 4,000 units and each table requires 30 ft. of acacia wood, or 120,000 total feet. The contribution margin earned on the medium table is $90 per unit or $3.00 per foot. Thus, the total contribution margin earned on the medium table is $360,000 (4,000 units × $90 per table, or 120,000 ft. × $3.00 per ft.)

The company does not have enough acacia wood to meet the demand for all three products, so whatever is left should be used to make as many large tables as possible. So far, we have used a total of 220,000 feet of raw materials (100,000 for the small table + 120,000 for the medium table). A total of 300,000 feet are available, which leaves 80,000 feet (300,000 − 220,000) for the large table. Since the large table requires 40 ft. of acacia wood, we can only produce 2,000 units with the remaining 80,000 feet of raw materials (80,000 ÷ 40 = 2,000), as summarized in the following computation:

COACH'S TIP

You have to work backwards to figure out how many units can be made with the remaining resources. There are only 300,000 feet of raw materials available and the first two products used 220,000. That leaves 80,000 for the third product. How many large tables can they make with 80,000 feet of material if each unit takes 40 feet?

80,000 ÷ 40 feet per unit
= 2,000 units

Producing 2,000 large tables will generate $200,000 in total contribution margin (2,000 units × $100 per unit, or 80,000 feet × $2.50 per foot).

Priority	1 Small	2 Medium	3 Large
Contribution margin per foot	$4.00	$3.00	$2.50
Units produced	5,000 units	4,000 units	2,000 units
Raw materials required per unit	20 board ft.	30 board ft.	40 board ft.
Total raw material requirements	100,000	120,000	80,000 remaining
Total contribution margin generated	$400,000	$360,000	$200,000

To summarize, **IKEA** should produce 5,000 small tables, 4,000 medium tables, and 2,000 large tables. Doing so will generate $960,000 in total contribution margin ($400,000 + $360,000 + $200,000). This is the maximum amount of contribution margin that can be generated with only 300,000 feet of acacia wood. Any other combination of units will either exceed the 300,000 ft. limit on raw materials or will result in less overall contribution margin.

This analysis assumes that total fixed costs will remain the same regardless of how many units of each product are produced and that raw material is the only constrained resource. In reality, other resources may be limited or constrained, such as labor time, machine time, or space. Managers would need more sophisticated decision models to optimize profit given multiple constraints. These methods are covered in supply chain and operations management courses.

REVIEW THE CHAPTER

DEMONSTRATION CASE

Stone River Furniture Company manufactures wood furniture for home offices and living rooms. A segmented income statement for three of its products lines is shown as follows:

	Single Desk	(2,000 Units)	Double Desk	(500 Units)	Entertainment Stand	(1,000 Units)
	Per Unit	Total	Per Unit	Total	Per Unit	Total
Sales revenue	$400	$800,000	$600	$300,000	$900	900,000
Variable costs	200	400,000	400	200,000	400	400,000
Contribution margin	$200	$400,000	$200	$100,000	$500	$500,000
Fixed costs		250,000		125,000		125,000
Operating profit		$150,000		$ (25,000)		$375,000

Perform an incremental analysis for each of the following independent scenarios.

1. The local high school has approached Stone River with an offer to buy 500 single desks at a special order price of $300. In addition to the variable costs of filling the order, it would cost $12,500 to modify the desks to fit the school's classrooms.

   a. If the company has the capacity to fill the special order without affecting normal sales, how much incremental profit (loss) would be made on the special order?

   b. If the company has the idle capacity to produce 200 desks and would be forced to cancel the sale of 300 desks sold through normal channels, how much incremental profit (loss) would be made on the special order?

2. The company is considering outsourcing production of the entertainment unit to another manufacturer who has agreed to supply it for $550 per unit. In addition to the variable cost savings, the company could eliminate $100,000 in fixed costs by outsourcing. What is the incremental profit (loss) of outsourcing?

3. The company is considering dropping the double desk line because it is unprofitable. Only $50,000 of the fixed costs are directly attributable to the double desk product and could be eliminated if the product is dropped. Dropping the double desk line is expected to increase sales of the single desk model by 10 percent. What is the incremental profit (loss) of dropping the double desk line?

4. The company is considering adding lighting and electrical outlets to the entertainment unit. Doing so will increase variable costs by $50 per unit and fixed costs by $25,000. Managers believe they can sell the enhanced model for $1,000, but would only be able to sell 800 units of the higher-priced model. What is the incremental profit (loss) of the enhanced model?

5. The company has a limited supply of the birch wood that is used in all three of its products. The single desk requires 50 feet of birch wood; the double desk requires 80 feet; and the entertainment unit requires 100 feet. If the company has 40,000 feet of birch wood and an unlimited demand for all three products, how many units of each product should they produce and how much contribution margin will the company earn?

Suggested Solution

1.   a.

Analysis of the Special Order:

Incremental revenue	500 units × $300 = $ 150,000
Incremental variable costs	500 units × $200 = $(100,000)
Incremental fixed costs	$ (12,500)
Incremental profit (loss)	$ 37,500

b.

Analysis of the Special Order:

Incremental revenue	500 units × $300 = $ 150,000
Incremental variable costs	500 units × $200 = $(100,000)
Incremental fixed costs	$ (12,500)
Contribution margin on lost sales	300 units × $(200) = $ (60,000)
Incremental profit (loss)	$ (22,500)

2.

Analysis of the Outsourcing Decision

Cost of outsourcing	1,000 units × $550 = $(550,000)
Variable cost savings	1,000 units × $400 = $ 400,000
Fixed cost savings	$ 100,000
Incremental profit (loss)	$ (50,000)

3.

Analysis of the Keep or Drop Decision

Lost contribution margin on double desk	$(100,000)
Fixed costs savings	$ 50,000
Gained contribution margin on single desk	10% × $400,000 = $ 40,000
Incremental profit (loss)	$ (10,000)

4.

Analysis of the Enhanced Design

Contribution margin of existing design	(1,000 units) × ($900 − $400) = $(500,000)
Contribution margin on enhanced design	800 units × ($1,000 − $450) = $ 440,000
Increased fixed costs	$ (25,000)
Incremental profit (loss)	$ (85,000)

5.

	Single Desk	Double Desk	Entertainment Stand
Unit contribution margin	$ 200	$ 200	$ 500
Raw material requirements	÷ 50 ft.	÷ 80 ft.	÷ 100 ft.
Contribution margin per ft.	$4.00	$2.50	$5.00

Managers should prioritize the entertainment stand first because it has the highest contribution margin per foot. Each unit takes 100 feet, so they should be able to produce 400 units with 40,000 feet of direct materials (40,000 ÷ 100 = 400). Total contribution margin will be $200,000 (400 units × $500, or 40,000 ft. × $5.00 per foot).

CHAPTER SUMMARY

LO 7–1 **Describe the five steps in the decision-making process.**

- The managerial decision-making process has five steps:
  - Identify the decision problem.
  - Determine the decision alternatives.
  - Evaluate the costs and benefits of the alternatives.
  - Make the decision.
  - Review the results of the decision.

LO 7–2 **Define and identify relevant costs and benefits.**

- When making decisions, managers should focus only on costs and benefits that are relevant to the decision. To be relevant, a cost or benefit must meet the following criteria:
  - It must occur in the future, not the past. Sunk costs are never relevant.
  - The total amount of the cost or benefit must change depending on which alternative is selected.
- Relevant costs are sometimes called **differential costs, incremental costs,** or **avoidable costs**. Costs that will not change regardless of the alternative selected are irrelevant and should be ignored.

- Opportunity costs are the forgone (lost) benefits of choosing one alternative over another. Opportunity costs occur when resources are limited or when capacity constraints are reached. They are always relevant for decision making.

Analyze a special-order decision.   LO 7–3

- A special order is outside the scope of normal sales. If the incremental revenue exceeds the incremental costs of filling the special order, it will increase short-term profitability.

- If a company has excess capacity, only the variable costs of filling the special order are relevant.

- Fixed costs do not change in the short run and are therefore not included in the incremental analysis.

- If a company is operating at full capacity, the opportunity cost of lost sales is relevant and should be incorporated into the incremental analysis.

- Other qualitative factors such as the effect on routine customers and the opportunity to capture new customers must also be considered.

Analyze a make-or-buy decision.   LO 7–4

- Make-or-buy decisions involve deciding whether to perform a particular function in-house versus buying it from an outside supplier. They are also called insource versus outsource decisions.

- The relevant costs of making a product or providing a service internally include all variable costs plus any incremental fixed costs.

- The opportunity costs of making something internally include alternative uses for the internal resources.

- Many qualitative considerations, including quality, reliability, and environmental concerns, are also important in make-or-buy decisions.

Analyze a keep-or-drop decision.   LO 7–5

- Managers must often decide whether to eliminate a business segment that is not performing as well as expected.

- To decide whether to eliminate a segment, managers should focus on the segment margin, or the amount of profit generated by the segment after variable costs and direct fixed costs have been deducted.

- Common fixed costs would be incurred even if the segment is eliminated and are not relevant to the decision.

- Managers must also consider how elimination of the segment would affect other segments or product lines and whether alternative uses for the resources currently devoted to the business segment exist.

Analyze a sell-or-process-further decision.   LO 7–6

- A sell-or-process-further decision determines whether to sell a product as is or continue to refine it.

- The incremental revenue should be compared to the incremental cost of continuing to enhance the product or service.

Prioritize products to maximize short-term profit with constrained resources.   LO 7–7

- A constrained resource occurs when its capacity is insufficient to meet the demands placed on it.

- The most constrained resource is also called the bottleneck, which limits the system's overall output.

- To maximize short-term profit, managers should prioritize products based on the amount of contribution margin earned per unit of the most constrained (bottleneck) resource.

KEY TERMS

Avoidable Cost p. 307	**Differential Costs** p. 307	**Keep-or-Drop Decisions** p. 314
Bottleneck p. 321	**Direct Fixed Cost** p. 315	**Make-or-Buy Decisions** p. 312
Capacity p. 307	**Excess Capacity** p. 308	**Segment Margin** p. 315
Common Fixed Costs p. 315	**Full Capacity** p. 308	**Special-Order Decisions** p. 308
Complementary Products p. 316	**Idle Capacity** p. 308	**Substitute Products** p. 316
Constrained Resource p. 320	**Incremental Analysis** p. 305	
Differential Analysis p. 305	**Incremental Costs** p. 307	

PRACTICE MATERIAL

QUESTIONS

1. Briefly describe the five steps of the management decision-making process.

2. Suppose you are considering a part-time job to earn some extra spending money. List four factors that could affect that decision and would be included in Step 3 of your decision-making process.

3. Tom Ellis recently bought a plasma television and has since stated that he would not recommend it to others. This indicates that Tom has completed which step of the decision-making process?

4. What are the criteria for a cost to be considered relevant to any decision?

5. How is an avoidable cost related to a relevant cost?

6. Explain opportunity cost and list two opportunity costs of your decision to enroll in classes this semester.

7. Why should opportunity costs be factored into the decision-making process, and why is it often difficult to do so?

8. Explain excess capacity and full capacity. Include the implications that each has for a company's production decisions.

9. How are the concepts of full capacity and opportunity cost interrelated?

10. What is a special-order decision? Why can managers ignore fixed overhead costs when making special-order decisions?

11. How might the acceptance of a special order have negative consequences for a company?

12. How does excess capacity impact a special-order decision?

13. Suppose that you are the manager of a local deli. Give an example of each of the following decisions that you might have to make and identify three factors that would be relevant to each decision:
   a. Special order.
   b. Make or buy.
   c. Keep or drop.

14. Briefly describe three problems that might result from a decision to buy a component part from an external supplier. For each problem, identify one way to avoid or correct it.

15. How do opportunity costs affect make-or-buy decisions? How are opportunity costs shown in a make-or-buy analysis?

16. When a product line is eliminated, why aren't the total fixed costs associated with that line **not** automatically eliminated as well?

17. How might the decision to drop a product line affect a company's remaining products?

18. Briefly explain what happens to total variable costs when a product line is dropped.

19. Identify three opportunity costs that might result from a decision to eliminate a business segment.

20. Explain how a constrained resource impacts management decisions in both the long term and the short term.

21. Why do decisions involving a constrained resource focus on contribution margin instead of profit margin?

MULTIPLE CHOICE

1. The decision-making approach in which a manager considers only costs and benefits that differ for alternatives is called
   a. Incremental analysis.
   b. Outsourcing.
   c. Differential analysis.
   d. Either (a) or (c).

2. Which of the following is not a step of the management decision-making process?
   a. Review results of the decision.
   b. Contact competitors who have made similar decisions.
   c. Evaluate the costs and benefits of the alternatives.
   d. Determine the decision alternatives.

3. Sunk costs are always

   a. Opportunity costs.   c. Relevant.
   b. Avoidable.   d. Irrelevant.

4. When making a one-time special-order decision, a company can ignore fixed overhead because

   a. The cost will be incurred regardless of the decision.
   b. The cost is avoidable.
   c. The cost cannot be determined.
   d. None of the above.

5. When making make-or-buy decisions, managers should consider

   a. Alternate uses for any facility currently being used to make the item.
   b. The costs of direct materials included in making the item.
   c. Qualitative factors such as whether the supplier can deliver the item on time and to the company's quality standards.
   d. All of the above.

6. Which of the following costs is not likely to be completely eliminated by a decision to drop a product line?

   a. The variable overhead traced to that product line.
   b. The cost of direct materials used to make the product.

   c. The common fixed costs allocated to that product line.
   d. All of the above will be completely eliminated.

7. Which of the following causes opportunity costs to become relevant to management decisions?

   a. Sunk cost.
   b. Operating at full capacity.
   c. Operating with idle or excess capacity.
   d. Avoidable costs.

8. Which of the following could be a constrained resource?

   a. Machine hours.   c. Factory space.
   b. Direct materials.   d. All of the above.

9. When resources are constrained, managers should prioritize products in order to maximize

   a. Contribution margin per unit of the constrained resource.
   b. Sales volume.
   c. Opportunity cost.
   d. Fixed cost per unit of the constrained resource.

10. Which of the following is not an important qualitative factor?

   a. Employee morale.
   b. Customer loyalty.
   c. Cost per unit.
   d. Quality considerations.

Mc Graw Hill Education **connect**   **Find More Learning Solutions on Connect.**

MINI-EXERCISES

M7–1 Matching Key Terms and Concepts to Definitions

LO 7–1, 7–2, 7–3, 7–4, 7–5, 7–6, 7–7

A number of terms and concepts from this chapter and a list of descriptions, definitions, and explanations follow. For each term listed on the left, choose at least one corresponding item from the right. Note that a single term may have more than one description and a single description may be used more than once or not at all.

_____ 1. Excess capacity.

_____ 2. Identify the decision problem.

_____ 3. Bottleneck.

_____ 4. Special-order decision.

_____ 5. Differential costs.

_____ 6. Evaluate the costs and benefits of alternatives.

_____ 7. Make-or-buy decision.

_____ 8. Sunk costs.

_____ 9. Opportunity costs.

_____ 10. Keep-or-drop decision.

_____ 11. Full capacity.

_____ 12. Avoidable costs.

A. Short-term management decision made using differential analysis.

B. Management decision in which lost revenue is compared to the reduction of costs to determine the overall effect on profit.

C. Exists when a company has not yet reached the limit on its resources.

D. Costs that have already been incurred.

E. Management decision in which fixed manufacturing overhead is ignored as long as there is enough excess capacity to meet the order.

F. Costs that can be avoided by choosing one option over another.

G. Step 5 of the management decision-making process.

H. Management decision in which relevant costs of making a product internally are compared to the cost of purchasing that product.

I. Costs that are relevant to short-term decision making.

J. Resource that is insufficient to meet the demands placed on it.

K. First step of the management decision-making process.

L. Costs that are always irrelevant to management decisions.

M. Exists when a company has met its limit on one or more resources.

N. Benefits given up when one alternative is chosen over another.

O. Costs that change across decision alternatives.

P. Step 3 of the management decision-making process.

LO 7–1   **M7–2 Identifying Steps in the Decision-Making Process**

Listed below are a number of activities managers may perform. Identify which of these activities are steps in management's decision-making process and place those steps into the order in which they should be executed. Activities listed may be used once, more than once, or not at all.

1. Analyze how changes in cost structure affect CVP relationships.
2. Make the decision.
3. Eliminate the product line.
4. Evaluate the costs and benefits of the alternatives.
5. Prioritize products to maximize short-term profits.
6. Determine the decision alternatives.
7. Process the product further.
8. Review the results of the decision.
9. Use cost-volume-profit analysis to determine sales needed to break even.
10. Identify the decision problem.

LO 7–2   **M7–3 Identifying Relevant and Irrelevant Costs**

Isabella Canton is considering taking a part-time job at a local clothing store. She loves the store and shops there often, but unfortunately, employee discounts are given only to full-time employees. If Isabella takes this job, she would have to withdraw from her Tuesday night basket-weaving class to work. Accepting the job would also mean that Isabella must give up her volunteer work at the local animal sanctuary, an activity that she enjoys a great deal. The new job would pay approximately $125 per week but would cost Isabella $15 per week in gas. Isabella would be able to keep her Saturday afternoon job at the library that pays $40 per week.

A list of factors that Isabella has identified follows. For each one, indicate whether it is relevant or irrelevant to Isabella's decision.

1. The $125 income from the new job.
2. The $40 income from the library.
3. The $50 nonrefundable registration fee Isabella paid for the basket-weaving class.
4. The $15 cost for gas.
5. The $75 per month that Isabella spends for clothing.
6. The time Isabella spends volunteering at the animal sanctuary.

LO 7–2   **M7–4 Identifying Relevant and Irrelevant Costs**

The local summer baseball league wants to buy new uniforms for its teams. The current uniforms are quite old and will require $400 in repairs before they can be handed out to players next week for the upcoming season. The old uniforms will be replaced as soon as new ones can be purchased. League leaders have investigated several possible fundraisers and have narrowed the choice to two options: candy sales and car washes. Each option can generate the $2,500 that the new uniforms would cost.

Option 1:

The candy sales option would require the league to purchase 2,000 candy bars at a cost of $0.75 each. The players and coaches would then sell the bars for $2.00 each. The league estimates that it would take about four weeks to sell the candy and collect all of the money.

Option 2:

The car wash option would require about $200 for buckets, sponges, soap, and towels. A local business has offered to donate the water (estimated at $300 total) and a location. The car washes would be held on Saturdays, and each team would be required to provide workers. Each car wash day is expected to generate $450 in proceeds, so the league expects that it would take six weeks to raise $2,500.

Required:

1. Several factors related to the league's choice follow. Indicate whether each factor is relevant or irrelevant to deciding which project to engage in and briefly explain why.
   (a) Repair costs for the old uniforms, $400.
   (b) Initial outlay to purchase the candy bars, $1,500.
   (c) Initial outlay to purchase car wash supplies, $200.

(d) Cost of water for the car wash option, $300.

(e) Cost of the new uniforms, $2,500.

(f) Additional two weeks that the car wash option would require to raise the money.

2. List three qualitative factors that the league should consider in making its choice.

Questions M7–5 through M7–8 refer to Blowing Sand Company, which produces window fans.

M7–5 Analyzing Special-Order Decision

LO 7–2, 7–3

Blowing Sand Company has just received a one-time offer to purchase 10,000 units of its Gusty model for a price of $22 each. The Gusty model normally sells for $30 and costs $26 to produce ($17 in variable costs and $9 of fixed overhead). Because the offer came during a slow production month, Blowing Sand has enough excess capacity to accept the order.

1. Should Blowing Sand accept the special order?

2. Calculate the increase or decrease in short-term profit from accepting the special order.

M7–6 Considering Impact of Full Capacity on Special-Order Decision

LO 7–3

Explain how the analysis and decision in M7–5 would have been affected if Blowing Sand were operating at full capacity.

M7–7 Analyzing Keep-or-Drop Decision

LO 7–2, 7–5

Suppose that Blowing Sand Company also produces the Drafty model fan, which currently has a net loss of $43,000 as follows:

	Drafty Model
Sales revenue	$150,000
Less: Variable costs	125,000
Contribution margin	$ 25,000
Less: Direct fixed costs	18,000
Segment margin	$ 7,000
Less: Common fixed costs	50,000
Net operating income (loss)	$ (43,000)

Eliminating the Drafty product line would eliminate $18,000 of direct fixed costs. The $50,000 of common fixed costs would be redistributed to Blowing Sand's remaining product lines.

Will Blowing Sand's net operating income increase or decrease if the Drafty model is eliminated? By how much?

M7–8 Analyzing Make-or-Buy Decision

LO 7–2, 7–4

Blowing Sand Company also has the Blast fan model. It is the company's top-selling model with sales of 30,000 units per year. This model has a dual fan as well as a thermostat component that causes the fan to cycle on and off depending on the room temperature. Blowing Sand has always manufactured the thermostat component but is considering buying the part from a supplier.

It costs Blowing Sand $5 to make each thermostat ($2.50 variable and $2.50 fixed). Flurry Co. has offered to sell the component to Blowing Sand for $4. Blowing Sand's decision to purchase the part from Flurry would eliminate all variable costs but none of the fixed costs. Blowing Sand has no other possible uses for the area currently dedicated to the thermostat production.

Should Blowing Sand continue to make the thermostat or purchase the part from Flurry Co.? Justify your answer.

M7–9 Analyzing Sell-or-Process Further Decisions

LO 7–6

More Parts Liquidators specializes in buying excess parts inventories for resale or to incorporate into other products. They recently purchased parts for $100,000 and they have a buyer willing to pay $120,000. The company can also incorporate these parts into a new product at a cost of $75,000 and sell the new product for $190,000. What should More Parts Liquidators do? Support your answer with calculations.

M7–10 Identifying Capacity Impact on Special-Order Decisions

LO 7–2, 7–3, 7–7

Your roommate, Joe Thompson, has taken a summer intern position at a local manufacturing company. Because he is a junior majoring in accounting, the company expects him to have a grasp of managerial accounting basics. However, Joe didn't attend class very often and made only a C− in managerial accounting. On his first day, the company president gave Joe a tour of the production facility and talked extensively about one of the company's direct materials becoming a constrained resource. Because Joe's entire internship is likely going to revolve around this limited resource and its impact on company decisions, he is in a panic to understand the concept.

Explain to Joe the terms *full capacity, excess capacity,* and *constrained resource.* Also briefly explain how a constrained resource could affect special-order and production decisions for his employer.

LO 7–2, 7–7   M7–11 Prioritizing Products with Constrained Resource

Anne Sugar makes large ceramic pots for use in outdoor landscaping. She currently has two models, one square and the other round. Because of the size of Anne's creations, only one pot can be fired in the kiln at a time. Information about each model follows:

	Square	Round
Sales price	$70	$90
Variable cost	$15	$20
Firing time	2.5 hours	3.5 hours

Assume that Anne can sell as many pots as she can create but that she is limited as to the number of hours that the kiln can be run.

Compute the contribution margin per unit and contribution margin per hour of firing time. Which type of pot should Anne produce to maximize her short-term profit?

LO 7–2, 7–7   M7–12 Prioritizing Products with Constrained Resource

Refer to the information presented in M7–11. Suppose that Anne has developed a rectangular, medium-size ceramic pot. It requires four hours of kiln time; however, two medium-size pots can fit in the kiln at once. The medium-size pots would sell for $60 each and have variable cost of $10 per pot.

If Anne has only 40 hours of firing time available per week, what is the maximum amount of contribution margin she can earn per week?

EXERCISES

LO 7–1, 7–2, 7–5, 7–7   E7–1 Matching Terminology

Match each of the terms by inserting the appropriate definition letter in the space provided. Not all definitions will be used.

____ **1.** Capacity

____ **2.** Common fixed costs

____ **3.** Complementary products

____ **4.** Constrained resource

____ **5.** Direct fixed cost

____ **6.** Idle capacity

____ **7.** Incremental analysis

____ **8.** Segment margin

____ **9.** Substitute products

A. Examination of alternatives focusing on costs that change between alternatives.

B. A cost that has the potential to influence a specific decision.

C. A cost that can be avoided by choosing one alternative instead of another.

D. A cost that has already been incurred.

E. A forgone benefit of choosing one alternative over another.

F. A measure of the limit placed on a specific resource.

G. When the limit of resources has not yet been reached.

H. An order that is outside the scope of normal sales.

I. Sales revenue less all costs that are directly attributable to that division.

J. A cost attributable to a specific division that does not change based on volume.

K. A product that can be used in place of another.

L. A cost attributable to a specific division that changes based on volume.

M. The cause of an increase in revenue.

N. A product that can be used in conjunction with another product.

O. A cost shared by multiple divisions that will not change even if one division is eliminated.

P. A limited supply of facilities.

E7–2 Identifying Steps in Decision-Making Process

LO 7–1

Listed below are a number of statements concerning management's decision-making process. Identify whether each statement is correct or incorrect. For all incorrect statements, indicate how to correct the statement.

1. The final step in management's decision-making process is to actually make the decision.
2. In making business decisions, management will ordinarily only consider financial information because it's objectively determined.
3. The first step in management's decision-making process is to determine the decision alternatives.
4. Relevant costing is used for short-term decision making because it focuses only on the costs and benefits that are relevant to the decision at hand.
5. Under incremental analysis, variable costs will change under different courses of action, but fixed costs will never change.
6. Decisions involve a choice among alternative courses of action.
7. When using differential analysis, some costs will change under alternative courses of action, but revenues will not change.

E7–3 Identifying Steps in Decision-Making Process and Relevant Costs

LO 7–1, 7–2

Assume you need to buy a new vehicle. The junker that you paid $5,000 for two years ago has a current value of $1,500. You have narrowed the choice down to a used 2008 Jeep Cherokee with a blue book value of $8,000 and a new Hyundai Elantra with a sticker price of $12,995. You plan to drive either vehicle for at least five more years.

Required:

1. List the five steps in the decision-making process and briefly describe the key factors you would consider at each step.
2. Indicate whether each of the following factors would be relevant or irrelevant to your decision:
   (a) The $5,000 you paid for your junker two years ago.
   (b) The $1,500 your vehicle is worth today.
   (c) The blue book value of the Jeep Cherokee.
   (d) The sticker price of the Hyundai Elantra.
   (e) The difference in fuel economy for the Jeep and the Hyundai.
   (f) The cost of on-campus parking.
   (g) The difference in insurance cost for the Jeep and the Hyundai.
   (h) The difference in resale value five years from now for the Jeep and the Hyundai.
   (i) The fact that the Hyundai comes with a warranty while the Jeep does not.
3. Consider only the costs you classified as irrelevant in requirement 2.
   (a) Would any of these costs be relevant if you were deciding whether to keep your present vehicle or buy a new one?
   (b) Would any of these costs be relevant if you were deciding whether to get rid of your vehicle and ride your bike to work and school?

E7–4 Identifying Relevant Costs and Calculating Differential Costs

LO 7–2

Maria Turner has just graduated from college with a degree in accounting. She had planned to enroll immediately in the master's program at her university but has been offered a lucrative job at a well-known company. The job is exactly what Maria had hoped to find after obtaining her graduate degree.

In anticipation of master's program classes, Maria has already spent $450 to apply for the program. Tuition is $8,000 per year, and the program will take two years to complete. Maria's expected salary after completing the master's program is approximately $60,000. If she pursues the master's degree, Maria would stay in her current home that is near the campus and costs $600 per month in rent. She would also remain at her current job that pays $25,000 per year. Additionally, Maria's immediate family is nearby. She spends considerable time with family and friends, especially during the holidays. This would not be possible if she accepts the job offer because of the distance from her new location.

The job Maria has been offered includes a salary of $50,000. She would have to relocate to another state, but her employer would pay the $5,000 for moving expenses. Maria's rent in the new location would be approximately $800 per month. The new location is a fast-growing, active city that offers a number of cultural activities that Maria would enjoy. The city is also home to Maria's favorite Major League Baseball team, and she would expect to buy season tickets.

Required:

1. Help Maria make her decision by categorizing the factors involved in making her choice. Complete the following chart regarding the factors in Maria's decision. A single factor may have multiple columns checked.

	Relevant	Irrelevant	Sunk Cost	Qualitative
$450 spent on application fee				
$8,000 per year tuition				
$60,000 salary with master's degree				
$600 per month current rent				
$25,000 current salary				
Time spent with family and friends				
$50,000 new salary				
$5,000 moving expenses				
$800 rent per month in new location				
Cultural activities in the new location				
Ability to have MLB season tickets				

2. For each of the following items, identify the differential amount in Maria's alternatives. For example, the incremental cost of tuition is $16,000 if Maria chooses to pursue the master's degree.
   (a) Rent.
   (b) Salary for the next two years.
   (c) Salary after two years.
   (d) Moving expenses.

LO 7–2   **E7–5 Completing Statements Regarding Relevant Costs and Benefits**

The following are a number of statements concerning relevant versus irrelevant costs and benefits. Complete each statement by providing the missing term or phrase.

1. _____ are costs that have already been incurred and are not relevant to future decisions.
2. _____ is a measure of the limit placed on a specific resource.
3. A/an _____ is the forgone benefit of choosing to do one thing instead of another.
4. Monthly utility costs are estimated to be $1,200 regardless of the course of action; in this case the utility costs are considered a/an _____.
5. When a company has not yet reached the limit on its resources, it has _____.
6. A/an _____ has the potential to influence a particular decision and will change depending on the alternative a manager selects.
7. At _____ opportunity costs become relevant and should be incorporated into the analysis.
8. When managers are forced to choose one alternative over another due to limited employee time and equipment availability, the business manager is facing _____ costs.

The following information pertains to E7–6 through E7–10.

Morning Sky, Inc. (MSI), manufactures and sells computer games. The company has several product lines based on the age range of the target market. MSI sells both individual games as well as packaged sets. All games are in CD format, and some utilize accessories such as steering wheels, electronic tablets, and hand controls. To date, MSI has developed and manufactured all the CDs itself as well as the accessories and packaging for all of its products.

The gaming market has traditionally been targeted at teenagers and young adults; however, the increasing affordability of computers and the incorporation of computer activities into junior high and elementary school curriculums has led to a significant increase in sales to younger children. MSI has always included games for younger children but now wants to expand its business to capitalize on changes in the industry. The company currently has excess capacity and is investigating several possible ways to improve profitability.

E7–6 Analyzing Special-Order Decision

MSI has been approached by a fourth-grade teacher from Portland about the possibility of creating a specially designed game that would be customized for her classroom and environment. The teacher would like an educational game to correspond to her classroom coverage of the history of the Pacific Northwest, and the state of Oregon in particular. MSI has not sold its products directly to teachers or school systems in the past, but its Marketing Department identified that possibility during a recent meeting.

The teacher has offered to buy 1,000 copies of the CD at a price of $5 each. MSI could easily modify one of its existing educational programs about U.S. history to accommodate the request. The modifications would cost approximately $500. A summary of the information related to production of MSI's current history program follows:

Direct materials	$ 1.50
Direct labor	0.60
Variable manufacturing overhead	2.25
Fixed manufacturing overhead	2.00
Total cost per unit	$ 6.35
Sales price per unit	$12.00

Required:

1. Compute the incremental profit (or loss) from accepting the special order.
2. Should MSI accept the special order?
3. Suppose that the special order had been to purchase 1,000 copies of the program for $4.50 each. Compute the incremental profit (or loss) from accepting the special order under this scenario.
4. Suppose that MSI is operating at full capacity. To accept the special order, it would have to reduce production of the history program. Compute the special order price at which MSI would be indifferent between accepting or rejecting the special order.
5. Provide two reasons why a company might accept a special order that did not increase profits.

E7–7 Analyzing Make-or-Buy Decision

MSI is considering outsourcing the production of the handheld control module used with some of its products. The company has received a bid from Monte Legend Co. (MLC) to produce 10,000 units of the module per year for $16 each. The following information pertains to MSI's production of the control modules:

Direct materials	$ 9
Direct labor	4
Variable manufacturing overhead	2
Fixed manufacturing overhead	3
Total cost per unit	$18

MSI has determined that it could eliminate all variable costs if the control modules were produced externally, but none of the fixed overhead is avoidable. At this time, MSI has no specific use in mind for the space that is currently dedicated to the control module production.

Required:

1. Compute the difference in cost between making and buying the control module.
2. Should MSI buy the modules from MLC or continue to make them?
3. Suppose that the MSI space currently used for the modules could be utilized by a new product line that would generate $35,000 in annual profit. Recompute the difference in cost between making and buying under this scenario. Does this change your recommendation to MSI? If so, how?

LO 7–2, 7–5   **E7–8 Analyzing Keep-or-Drop Decision**

MSI is considering eliminating a product from its ToddleTown Tours collection. This collection is aimed at children one to three years of age and includes "tours" of a hypothetical town. Two products, The Pet Store Parade and The Grocery Getaway, have impressive sales. However, sales for the third CD in the collection, The Post Office Polka, have lagged the others. Several other CDs are planned for this collection, but none is ready for production.

MSI's information related to the ToddleTown Tours collection follows:

Segmented Income Statement for MSI's ToddleTown Tours Product Lines

	Pet Store Parade	Grocery Getaway	Post Office Polka	Total
Sales revenue	$50,000	$45,000	$15,000	$110,000
Variable costs	23,000	19,000	10,000	52,000
Contribution margin	$27,000	$26,000	$ 5,000	$ 58,000
Less: Direct fixed costs	4,800	3,100	3,500	11,400
Segment margin	$22,200	$22,900	$ 1,500	$ 46,600
Less: Common fixed costs*	14,400	12,960	4,320	31,680
Net operating income (loss)	$ 7,800	$ 9,940	$(2,820)	$ 14,920

*Allocated based on total sales revenue.

MSI has determined that elimination of the Post Office Polka (POP) program would not impact sales of the other two items. The remaining fixed overhead currently allocated to the POP product would be redistributed to the remaining two products.

Required:

1. Will MSI's net operating income increase or decrease if the POP product is eliminated? By how much?
2. Should MSI drop the POP product?
3. Suppose that $3,700 of the common fixed costs could be avoided if the POP product line were eliminated. Would your recommendation to MSI change? Why or why not?

LO 7–2, 7–6   **E7–9 Analyzing Sell-or-Process-Further Decision**

MSI's educational products are currently sold without any supplemental materials. The company is considering the inclusion of instructional materials such as an overhead slide presentation, potential test questions, and classroom bulletin board materials for teachers. A summary of the expected costs and revenues for MSI's two options follows:

	CD Only	CD with Instructional Materials
Estimated demand	50,000 units	50,000 units
Estimated sales price	$20.00	$35.00
Estimated cost per unit		
Direct materials	$ 1.25	$ 1.75
Direct labor	2.50	5.50
Variable manufacturing overhead	2.50	5.75
Fixed manufacturing overhead	2.00	2.00
Unit manufacturing cost	$ 8.25	$15.00
Additional development cost		$65,000

Required:

1. Compute the increase or decrease in profit that would result if instructional materials were added to the CDs.
2. Should MSI add the instructional materials or sell the CDs without them?
3. Suppose that the higher price of the CDs with instructional materials is expected to reduce demand to 32,000 units. Repeat requirements 1 and 2 under this scenario.

E7–10 Identifying Qualitative Factors in Short-Term Decision Making LO 7–2, 7–3, 7–4, 7–5, 7–6

Refer to E7–6 through E7–9.

Required:

Identify at least three qualitative factors that MSI should consider when making each decision.

E7–11 Analyzing Make or Buy Decision LO 7–2, 7–4

Frannie Fans currently manufactures ceiling fans that include remotes to operate them. The current cost to manufacture 10,000 remotes is as follows:

	Cost
Direct materials	$65,000
Direct labor	$55,000
Variable overhead	$30,000
Fixed overhead	$50,000
Total	$200,000

Frannie is approached by Lincoln Company which offers to make the remotes for $18 per unit.

Required:

1. Compute the difference in cost between making and buying the remotes if none of the fixed costs can be avoided. What is the change in net income? Should managers make or buy the remotes?
2. Compute the difference in cost between making and buying the remotes if $20,000 of the fixed costs can be avoided. What is the change in net income? Should managers make or buy the remotes?
3. What is the change in net income if fixed cost of $20,000 can be avoided and Frannie could rent out the factory space no longer in use for $20,000? Should managers make or buy the remotes?

E7–12 Analyzing Keep-or-Drop Decision LO 7–2, 7–5

Anderson Publishing has two divisions: Book Publishing & Magazine Publishing. The Magazine division has been losing money for the last 5 years and Anderson is considering eliminating that division. Anderson's information about the two divisions is as follows:

	Book Division	Magazine Division	Total
Sales Revenue	$7,800,000	$3,300,000	$11,100,000
Cost of Goods sold			
Variable manufacturing costs	2,000,000	997,000	2,997,000
Fixed manufacturing costs	1,077,500	1,200,000	2,277,500
Gross Profit	$4,722,500	$1,103,000	$ 5,825,500
Operating Expenses			
Variable operating expenses	135,000	198,000	333,000
Fixed operating expenses	2,916,000	1,189,000	4,105,000
Net income	1,671,500	(284,000)	$ 1,387,500

Only 20 percent of the fixed manufacturing costs and 60 percent of the fixed operating expenses are directly attributable to each division. The remainder are common or shared between the two divisions.

Required:

1. Present the financial information in the form of a segmented income statement (using the contribution margin approach).
2. What will be the impact on net income if the Magazine Division is eliminated?

LO 7–2, 7–3 **E7–13 Analyzing Special-Order Decision**

Ironwood Company manufactures a variety of sunglasses. Production information for its most popular line, the Clear Vista (CV), follows:

	Per Unit
Sales price	$37.50
Direct materials	6.00
Direct labor	3.00
Variable manufacturing overhead	2.00
Fixed manufacturing overhead	5.00
Total manufacturing cost	$16.00

Suppose that Ironwood has been approached about producing a special order for 2,000 units of custom CV sunglasses for a new semiprofessional volleyball league. All units in the special order would be produced in the league's signature colors with a specially designed logo emblem attached to the side of the glasses. The league has offered to pay $32.00 per unit in the special order. Additional costs for the special order total $2.00 per unit for mixing the special frame color and purchasing the emblem with the league's logo that will be attached to the glasses.

Required:

1. Assume Ironwood has the idle capacity necessary to accommodate the special order. Calculate the additional contribution margin Ironwood would make by accepting the special order.
2. Suppose Ironwood is currently operating its production facility at full capacity and accepting the special order would mean reducing production of its regular CV model. Should Ironwood accept the special order in this case? Why or why not?
3. Calculate the special order price per unit at which Ironwood is indifferent between accepting or rejecting the special order.

LO 7–2, 7–6 **E7–14 Analyzing Sell-or-Process-Further Decision**

Wholesome Dairy processes milk. The cost of the milk processing is $1,250,000. Wholesome is looking to increase its net income and is exploring the possibility of expanding its products to include cream and/or ice cream. It takes 1 gallon of milk to make a half gallon of ice cream

Product	Units Produced	Selling Price	Additional Processing costs
Milk	750,000 gallons	$2.97 per gallon	
Ice Cream	?	$5.99 per half gallon	$0.20 per half gallon

Required:

1. How many half gallons of ice cream can Wholesome make?
2. What are the additional processing costs to convert the milk to ice cream?
3. Should Wholesome sell the milk or process it further and sell ice cream?

E7–15 Making Decisions Involving Constrained Resource   LO 7–2, 7–7

Cordova manufactures three types of stained glass window, cleverly named Products A, B, and C. Information about these products follows:

	Product A	Product B	Product C
Sales price	$35	$45	$75
Variable costs per unit	17	21	32
Fixed costs per unit	5	5	5
Required number of labor hours	1.25	2.00	2.50

Cordova currently is limited to 40,000 labor hours per month.

Required:

Assuming an infinite demand for each of Cordova's products, compute the number of units of each product the company should produce. Justify your answer.

E7–16 Making Decisions Involving Constrained Resource   LO 7–2, 7–7

Refer to the information presented in E7–15. Cordova's marketing department has determined the following demand for its products:

Product A	18,000 units
Product B	12,000 units
Product C	4,000 units

Required:

Given the company's limited resource and expected demand, compute how many units of each product Cordova should produce to maximize its profit.

E7–17 Identifying Relevant and Irrelevant Costs and Benefits   LO 7–2, 7–3, 7–4, 7–5, 7–6

The following is a list of decisions and an associated cost or benefit that may or may not be relevant to the decision. For each situation, state whether the associated cost or benefit is relevant to the related decision. If a cost or benefit is irrelevant, justify your answer by briefly stating why it's irrelevant.

1. Decision: Should you take the bus or drive your car to school for the semester? Cost: $300 repair bill to fix brakes.

2. Decision: Eliminate an unprofitable segment. Cost: Unavoidable fixed overhead.

3. Decision: Make or buy a component used in manufacturing a product. Benefit: Selling price of the final product.

4. Decision: Accept a special order. Cost: Variable overhead.

5. Decision: Sell unassembled and unfinished furniture or sell finished assembled furniture. Cost: The cost of producing an unfinished and unassembled table.

6. Decision: XYZ Tire Company is considering dropping one of its 10 models of tires. Cost: Common fixed costs.

7. Decision: ABC Golf Co. produces custom golf clubs and is considering purchasing the putter from a manufacturer of custom putters. Cost: Direct labor.

8. Decision: A major regional airline has been approached to provide 200 seats at a discounted price to Tampa, Florida, for an executive training session. The airline has excess capacity on the scheduled flight date. Cost: Cost of flight crew.

9. Decision: A major regional airline has been approached to provide 200 seats at a discounted price to Tampa, Florida, for an executive training session. The airline has excess capacity on the scheduled flight date. Cost: In-flight meals.

10. Decision: A major regional airline has been approached to provide 200 seats at a discounted price to Tampa, Florida, for an executive training session. The airline does not have excess capacity on the scheduled flight date. Benefit: Discounted ticket price.

GROUP A PROBLEMS

LO 7–2, 7–3   **PA7–1 Analyzing Special-Order Decision**

Mohave Corp. makes several varieties of beach umbrellas and accessories. It has been approached by a company called Lost Mine Industries about producing a special order for a custom umbrella called the Ultimate Shade (US). The special-order umbrellas with the Lost Mine Company logo would be distributed to participants at an upcoming convention sponsored by Lost Mine.

Lost Mine has offered to buy 1,500 of the US umbrellas at a price of $11 each. Mohave currently has the excess capacity necessary to accept the offer. The following information is related to the production of the US umbrella:

Direct materials	$ 5.00
Direct labor	2.00
Variable manufacturing overhead	3.50
Fixed manufacturing overhead	2.50
Total cost	$13.00
Regular sales price	$ 19.00

Required:

1. Compute the incremental profit (or loss) from accepting the special order.
2. Should Mohave accept the special order?
3. Suppose that the special order had been to purchase 2,000 umbrellas for $9.00 each. Recompute the incremental profit (or loss) from accepting the special order under this scenario.
4. Assume that Mohave is operating at full capacity. Calculate the special-order price per unit at which Mohave would be indifferent between accepting or rejecting the special order.

LO 7–2, 7–4   **PA7–2 Analyzing Make-or-Buy Decision**

Mohave Corp. (see PA7–1) is considering outsourcing production of the umbrella tote bag included with some of its products. The company has received a bid from a supplier in Vietnam to produce 8,000 units per year for $7.50 each. Mohave has the following information about the cost of producing tote bags:

Direct materials	$3
Direct labor	2
Variable manufacturing overhead	1
Fixed manufacturing overhead	2
Total cost per unit	$8

Mohave has determined that all variable costs could be eliminated by outsourcing the tote bags, while 60 percent of the fixed overhead cost is unavoidable. At this time, Mohave has no specific use in mind for the space currently dedicated to producing the tote bags.

Required:

1. Compute the difference in cost between making and buying the umbrella tote bag.
2. Based strictly on the incremental analysis, should Mohave buy the tote bags or continue to make them?
3. Suppose that the space Mohave currently uses to make the bags could be utilized by a new product line that would generate $10,000 in annual profits. Recompute the difference in cost between making and buying the umbrella tote bag. Does this change your recommendation to Mohave? If so, how?
4. Assume Mohave has a sustainability goal to increase the percentage of spending from local suppliers. If Mohave's managers are responsible for improving this metric, how might it impact their sourcing decisions?
5. What other strategic or sustainability-related goals should Mohave consider before making a final decision?

PA7–3 Analyzing Keep-or-Drop Decision

LO 7–2, 7–5

Mohave Corp. (see PA7–1 and PA7–2) is considering eliminating a product from its Sand Trap line of beach umbrellas. This collection is aimed at people who spend time on the beach or have an outdoor patio near the beach. Two products, the Indigo and Verde umbrellas, have impressive sales. However, sales for the Azul model have been dismal.

Mohave's information related to the Sand Trap line is shown as follows:

Segmented Income Statement for Mohave's
Sand Trap Beach Umbrella Products

	Indigo	Verde	Azul	Total
Sales revenue	$60,000	$60,000	$30,000	$150,000
Variable costs	34,000	31,000	26,000	91,000
Contribution margin	$26,000	$29,000	$ 4,000	$ 59,000
Less: Direct fixed costs	1,900	2,500	2,000	6,400
Segment margin	$24,100	$26,500	$ 2,000	$ 52,600
Common fixed costs*	17,840	17,840	8,920	44,600
Net operating income (loss)	$ 6,260	$ 8,660	$(6,920)	$ 8,000

*Allocated based on total sales revenue.

Mohave has determined that eliminating the Azul model would cause sales of the Indigo and Verde models to increase by 10 percent and 15 percent, respectively. Variable costs for these two models would increase proportionately. Although the direct fixed costs could be eliminated, the common fixed costs are unavoidable. The common fixed costs would be redistributed to the remaining two products.

Required:

1. Will Mohave's net operating income increase or decrease if the Azul model is eliminated? By how much?
2. Should Mohave drop the Azul model?
3. Suppose that Mohave had no direct fixed overhead in its production information and the entire $51,000 of fixed cost was common fixed cost. Would your recommendation to Mohave change? Why or why not?

PA7–4 Analyzing Sell-or-Process-Further Decision

LO 7–2, 7–6

The Rosa model of Mohave Corp. (see PA7–1, PA7–2, and PA7–3) is currently manufactured as a very plain umbrella with no decoration. The company is considering changing this product to a much more decorative model by adding a silk-screened design and embellishments. A summary of the expected costs and revenues for Mohave's two options follows:

	Rosa Umbrella	Decorated Umbrella
Estimated demand	10,000 units	10,000 units
Estimated sales price	$8.00	$ 19.00
Estimated manufacturing cost per unit		
Direct materials	$2.50	$ 5.50
Direct labor	1.50	4.00
Variable manufacturing overhead	0.50	2.50
Fixed manufacturing overhead	2.00	2.00
Unit manufacturing cost	$6.50	$ 14.00
Additional development cost		$10,000

Required:

1. Compute the difference in profit between selling the Rosa umbrella with the additional decorations or without.
2. Should Mohave add decorations to the Rosa umbrella?
3. Suppose that the higher price of the decorated umbrella is expected to reduce estimated demand for this product to 8,000 units. Repeat requirements 1 and 2 under this new scenario.

LO 7–2, 7–5   **PA7–5 Analyzing Keep-or-Drop Decision**

Ben Blum recently graduated from Moonshadow University's accounting program. He has been hired as an analyst by Primrose Tire Company and one of his first assigned tasks was to evaluate the North East division of Primrose. This division has been heavily focused on producing a special snow and mud tire. Sales of the special tire have been disappointing and management is now evaluating whether to eliminate the North East division. Ben performed the following analysis and is preparing to address the board of directors of Primrose with his recommendation that the North East division should be eliminated, resulting in an increase to total company profit of $49,000.

	All Other Divisions	North East	Total
Sales revenue	$3,328,400	$200,000	$3,528,400
Cost of goods sold	1,957,040	153,000	2,110,040
Gross profit	$1,371,360	$ 47,000	$1,418,360
Operating expenses	1,055,880	96,000	1,151,880
Net operating income (loss)	$ 315,480	$ (49,000)	$ 266,480

The North East division's cost of goods sold includes $33,000 in fixed costs and operating expenses include $46,000 in fixed costs. None of the fixed costs will be eliminated if the North East division is discontinued.

Required:

Do you agree with Ben's analysis? Use incremental analysis to support your conclusion.

LO 7–2, 7–7   **PA7–6 Making Decisions Involving Constrained Resource**

Blossom, Inc., is a small company that manufactures three versions of patio tables. Unit information for its products follows:

	Table A	Table B	Table C
Sales price	$38	$42	$56
Direct materials	6	7	8
Direct labor	1	3	7
Variable manufacturing overhead	2	2	2
Fixed manufacturing overhead	3	4	5
Required number of labor hours	0.50	0.50	1.00
Required number of machine hours	4.0	2.50	2.0

Blossom has determined that it can sell a limited number of each table in the upcoming year. Expected demand for each model follows:

Table A	50,000 units
Table B	20,000 units
Table C	30,000 units

Required:

1. Suppose that direct labor hours has been identified as the bottleneck resource. Determine how Blossom should prioritize production by rank ordering the products from 1 to 3.
2. If Blossom has only 36,000 direct labor hours available, calculate the number of units of each table that Blossom should produce to maximize its profit.
3. Suppose that the number of machine hours has been identified as the most constrained resource. Determine how Blossom should prioritize production by rank ordering the products from 1 to 3.
4. If Blossom has only 230,000 machine hours available, calculate the number of units of each table that Blossom should produce to maximize its profit.

PA7–7 Analyzing Sell-or-Process-Further Decision

Chino Company manufactures fabric and clothing. Managers can either sell the unfinished fabric to other clothing manufacturers or incur additional conversion costs to create a finished garment. The costs incurred to produce the unfinished fabric are $400,000, which are allocated to the products based on the sales value of the unfinished fabric. Following is information concerning the clothing that can be produced from the fabric:

Product	Number of Units	Selling Price of Unfinished Fabric	Selling Price after Processing Further	Additional Processing Cost
Pants	6,000	$20.00	$30.00	$28,450
Shirts	12,000	23.20	32.40	64,400
Coats	4,000	38.80	43.20	18,300

Required:

1. Which costs are relevant to the decision to sell or process further?
2. Which products should be sold as unfinished fabric and which should be further processed?
3. Assume that the $400,000 in costs is allocated based on the number of units of output. Which products should be sold as unfinished fabric and which should be further processed?

PA7–8 Analyzing Special-Order Decision

Camino Company manufactures designer to-go coffee cups. Each line of coffee cups is endorsed by a high-profile celebrity and designed with special elements selected by the celebrity. During the most recent year, Camino Company had the following operating results while operating at 80 percent (96,000 units) of its capacity:

Sales revenue	$960,000
Cost of goods sold	492,000
Gross profit	$468,000
Operating expenses	36,000
Net operating income	$432,000

Camino's cost of goods sold and operating expenses are 80 percent variable and 20 percent fixed. Camino has received an offer from a professional wrestling association to design a coffee cup endorsed by its biggest star and produce 20,000 cups for $8 each (total $160,000). These cups would be sold at wrestling matches throughout the United States. Acceptance of the order would require a $60,000 endorsement fee to the wrestling star, but no other increases in fixed operating expenses.

Required:

1. Prepare an incremental analysis of the special order.
2. Should Camino accept this special order?
3. If Camino were operating at full capacity, would your answer in requirement 2 change? If so, what price would Camino require for the special order?

PA7–9 Analyzing Make-or-Buy Decision

Old Camp Company manufactures awnings for its own line of tents. The company is currently operating at capacity and has received an offer from one of its suppliers to make the 10,000 awnings it needs for $18 each. Old Camp's costs to make the awning are $7 in direct materials and $5 in direct labor. Variable manufacturing overhead is 80 percent of direct labor. If Old Camp accepts the offer, $32,000 of fixed manufacturing overhead currently being charged to the awnings will have to be absorbed by other product lines.

Required:

1. Prepare an incremental analysis for the decision to make or buy the awnings.
2. Should Old Camp continue to manufacture the awnings or should they purchase the awnings from the supplier?
3. Would your answer to requirement 2 change if the capacity released by purchasing the awnings allowed Old Camp to record a profit of $22,000?

GROUP B PROBLEMS

LO 7–2, 7–3   **PB7–1 Analyzing Special-Order Decision**

Greenview Corp. makes several varieties of wooden furniture. It has been approached about producing a special order for Wilderness rocking chairs. A local senior citizens group would use the special-order chairs in a newly remodeled activity center.

The senior citizens group has offered to buy 80 of the Wilderness chairs at a price of $65 each. Greenview currently has the excess capacity necessary to accept the offer. A summary of the information related to production of Greenview's Wilderness model follows:

Direct materials	$30
Direct labor	22
Variable manufacturing overhead	12
Fixed manufacturing overhead	11
Total cost	$75
Regular sales price	$99

Required:

1. Compute the incremental profit (or loss) from accepting the special order.
2. Should Greenview accept the special order?
3. Suppose that the special order had been to purchase 100 rocking chairs for $60 each. Recompute the incremental profit (or loss) from accepting the special order.
4. Assume Greenview is operating at full capacity. Calculate the special-order price per unit at which Greenview would be indifferent between accepting or rejecting the special order.

LO 7–2, 7–4   **PB7–2 Analyzing Make-or-Buy Decision**

Greenview Corp. (see PB7–1) is considering the possibility of outsourcing the production of the upholstered chair pads included with some of its wooden chairs. The company has received a bid from a company in China to produce 1,000 units per year for $9 each. Greenview has the following information about its own production of the chair pads:

Direct materials	$ 4
Direct labor	1
Variable manufacturing overhead	2
Fixed manufacturing overhead	3
Total cost per unit	$10

Greenview has determined that all variable costs could be eliminated by dropping production of the chair pads, and that 30 percent of the fixed manufacturing overhead is avoidable. At this time, Greenview has no specific use in mind for the space currently dedicated to producing the chair pads.

Required:

1. Compute the difference in cost between making and buying the chair pads.
2. Should Greenview buy the chair pads or continue to make them?
3. Suppose that a new product line that Greenview wants to develop could utilize the space currently used for the chair pads. How much profit must the new product line generate for Greenview to be indifferent between making or buying the chair pads?
4. Assume Greenview has a sustainability goal to increase the percentage of spending from local suppliers. If Greenview's managers are responsible for improving this metric, how might it impact their sourcing decisions?
5. What other strategic or sustainability-related goals should Greenview consider before making a final decision?

PB7–3 Analyzing Keep-or-Drop Decision

Greenview Corp. (see PB7–1 and PB7–2) is considering eliminating a product from its line of outdoor tables. Two products, the Sunrise and Noche tables, have impressive sales. However, sales for the Blanco model have been dismal.

Information related to Greenview's outdoor table line is as follows.

	Sunrise	Noche	Blanco	Total
Segmented Income Statement for Greenview's Outdoor Table Products				
Sales revenue	$110,000	$77,000	$33,000	$220,000
Variable costs	77,000	52,000	25,500	154,500
Contribution margin	$ 33,000	$25,000	$ 7,500	$ 65,500
Less: Direct fixed costs	3,200	2,400	3,000	8,600
Segment margin	$ 29,800	$22,600	$ 4,500	$ 56,900
Common fixed costs*	16,800	11,760	5,040	33,600
Net operating income (loss)	$ 13,000	$10,840	$ (540)	$ 23,300

*Allocated based on total sales revenue.

Greenview has determined that eliminating the Blanco model will cause sales of the Sunrise and Noche tables to increase by 10 percent and 5 percent, respectively. Variable costs for these two models will increase proportionately. Direct fixed costs are avoidable, but common fixed costs will remain unchanged.

Required:

1. Will Greenview's net operating income increase or decrease if the Blanco model is eliminated? By how much?
2. Should Greenview drop the Blanco model?
3. Suppose Greenview had $3,800 of direct fixed overhead that was traceable to the Blanco model. Would your recommendation to Greenview change? Why or why not?

PB7–4 Analyzing Sell-or-Process-Further Decision

Greenview (see PB7–1 to PB7–3) currently manufactures one model of a plain, unfinished oak bookcase. The company is considering changing this product by adding a long-wearing finish and more appealing trim. A summary of the expected costs and revenues for Greenview's two options follows:

	Unfinished Bookcase	Finished Bookcase
Estimated demand	8,000 units	8,000 units
Estimated sales price	$50.00	$80.00
Estimated cost per unit		
Direct materials	$11.00	$15.00
Direct labor	8.00	20.00
Variable manufacturing overhead	0.50	1.50
Fixed manufacturing overhead	5.00	5.00
Unit manufacturing cost	$24.50	$41.50
Additional implementation cost		$75,000

Required:

1. Compute the difference in profit between selling the bookcases finished or unfinished.
2. Should Greenview finish the bookcases?
3. Suppose that choosing to process the bookcases further would reduce the number of units sold to 6,500. Repeat requirements 1 and 2 under this new scenario.

LO 7–2, 7–5 **PB7–5 Analyzing Keep-or-Drop Decision**

Barb Bach recently graduated from Coral College's accounting program. She has been hired as an analyst by Rainier Ski Co. and one of her first assigned tasks was to evaluate the Colorado division of Rainier Ski Co. This division has been heavily focused on producing a special snowboard. Sales of the snowboard have been disappointing and management is now evaluating whether to eliminate the Colorado division. Barb performed the following analysis and is preparing to address the board of directors of Rainier Ski Co. with her recommendation that the Colorado division should be eliminated, resulting in an increase to total company profit of $49,000.

	All Other Divisions	Colorado	Total
Sales revenue	$3,328,400	$ 300,000	$3,628,400
Cost of goods sold	1,957,040	153,000	2,110,040
Gross profit	$1,371,360	$ 147,000	$1,518,360
Operating expenses	1,055,880	196,000	1,251,880
Net operating income (loss)	$ 315,480	$ (49,000)	$ 266,480

The Colorado division's cost of goods sold includes $70,000 in fixed costs and operating expenses include $90,000 in fixed costs. None of the fixed costs will be eliminated if the Colorado division is discontinued.

Required:

Do you agree with Barb's analysis? Use incremental analysis to support your conclusion.

LO 7–2, 7–7 **PB7–6 Making Decisions Involving Constrained Resource**

Prospector Company makes three types of long-burning scented candles. The models vary in terms of size and type of materials (fragrance, decorations, etc.). Unit information for Prospector follows:

	Candle X	Candle Y	Candle Z
Sales price	$18.00	$20.00	$24.00
Direct materials	2.00	1.75	2.25
Direct labor	2.00	4.00	8.00
Variable manufacturing overhead	1.00	1.25	1.25
Fixed manufacturing overhead	2.00	2.00	2.50
Required number of pounds beeswax	1.5	2.0	2.0
Required number of labor hours	5.0	6.0	5.0

Prospector has determined that it can sell a limited number of each candle in the upcoming year. Expected demand for the three models follows:

Candle X	22,000 units
Candle Y	8,000 units
Candle Z	15,000 units

Required:

1. Suppose that disease in the suppliers' hives has severely restricted the production of beeswax. Thus, beeswax has been identified as the bottleneck. Determine how Prospector should prioritize production by rank ordering the products from 1 to 3.
2. If only 50,000 pounds of beeswax is available, calculate the number of units of each candle that Prospector should produce to maximize its profit.

3. Suppose that the number of labor hours has been identified as the most constrained resource. Determine how Prospector should prioritize production by rank ordering the products from 1 to 3.

4. If only 215,000 direct labor hours are available, calculate the number of units of each candle that Prospector should produce to maximize its profit.

PB7–7 Analyzing Sell-or-Process-Further Decision

LO 7–2, 7–6

Golden Trophy Inc. manufactures trophies and other promotional awards. The company uses an extrusion process in which metals and plastic are molded into a metal base of different sizes and shapes. Managers can either sell the unfinished base to other trophy companies, or incur additional conversion costs to convert it into a finished trophy. The cost incurred to produce the metal bases is $360,000, which is allocated to the products based on the sales value of the metal base. Following is information concerning the products that can be produced:

Product	Number of Units	Selling Price of the Metal Vase	Selling Price of the Finished Trophy	Additional Processing Cost
Trophy A	4,500	$105.00	$110.80	$46,200
Trophy B	6,200	92.00	118.50	85,500
Trophy C	980	124.30	146.50	22,450

Required:

1. Which costs are relevant to the decision to sell or process further?
2. Which products should be sold as an unfinished base and which should be further processed?
3. Assume that the $360,000 in costs is allocated based on the number of units of output. Which products should be sold as an unfinished base and which should be further processed?

PB7–8 Analyzing Special-Order Decision

LO 7–2, 7–3

Shasta Co. manufactures designer pillows for college dorm rooms. Each line of pillow is endorsed by a high-profile sports star and designed with special elements selected by the sports star. During the most recent year, Shasta Co. had the following operating results while operating at 80 percent (115,200 units) of its capacity:

Sales revenue	$1,382,400
Cost of goods sold	1,036,800
Gross profit	$ 345,600
Operating expenses	230,400
Net operating income	$ 115,200

Shasta's cost of goods sold and operating expenses are 75 percent variable and 25 percent fixed. Shasta has received an offer from Honeysuckle Community College to design a pillow endorsed by a soccer star who graduated from the college and produce 25,000 pillows for $10 each (total $250,000). These pillows would be sold at the college bookstore. Acceptance of the order would require a $50,000 endorsement fee to the soccer star, but no other increases in fixed operating expenses.

Required:

1. Prepare an incremental analysis of the special order.
2. Should Shasta accept this special order?
3. If Shasta were operating at full capacity, would your answer in requirement 2 change? If so, what price would Shasta require for the special order?

LO 7–2, 7–4   PB7–9 Analyzing Make-or-Buy Decision

Gold Dust Co. manufactures tablet PCs. The company is currently operating at capacity and has received an offer from one of its suppliers to make the 20,000 glass screens it needs for $26 each. Gold Dust's costs to make the glass screen are $10 in direct materials and $8 in direct labor. Variable manufacturing overhead is 75 percent of direct labor. If Gold Dust accepts the offer, $48,000 of fixed manufacturing overhead currently being charged to the glass screens will have to be absorbed by other product lines.

Required:

1. Prepare an incremental analysis for the decision to make or buy the glass screens.
2. Should Gold Dust continue to manufacture the glass screens or should they purchase the screens from the supplier?
3. Would your answer to requirement 2 change if the capacity released by purchasing the glass screens allowed Gold Dust to record a profit of $38,000?

SKILLS DEVELOPMENT CASES

LO 7–2   S7–1 Evaluating Netflix's Decision to Separate Its Lines of Business and Raise Prices

For most products and services, managers know that raising prices will reduce demand, while lowering prices will increase demand. What managers don't always know is how *much* demand will change in response to a change in price. In economics, the sensitivity of demand to changing prices is called the price elasticity of demand (PED). It is computed by dividing the percentage change in demand by the percentage change in price. Although PED will be negative in most cases, indicating an inverse relationship between price and demand, it is usually interpreted as an absolute value. On an absolute value basis, a PED less than one indicates that the demand is relatively inelastic, while a PED greater than one indicates that demand is relatively elastic.

In July 2011, Netflix decided to separate its DVD-by-mail service from its streaming video service. In addition to the hassle of receiving two bills instead of one, Netflix subscribers now had to pay about $16 for both services, when they previously only paid about $10. Many Netflix customers were outraged by this decision, and the company reportedly lost about 1 million of its 25 million subscribers due to this decision.

In response to the uproar from customers and investors, Netflix co-founder and CEO, Reed Hastings, posted a letter of explanation on the company website. He did not apologize for the decision to split the services and raise prices, which he maintained was the right strategic decision given the importance of streaming video to Netflix's future. However, he acknowledged that he should have done a better job of communicating the rationale for the change to customers in advance of making the change.

Consider the following additional information and estimates:

- Prior to the split, Netflix had about 25 million subscribers who were paying an average subscription fee of $10 per month.

- After the split, Netflix estimated the following:

  21 million subscribers would continue with the streaming video service.

  12 million of those subscribers would also continue with the DVD-by-mail service.
  3 million users would subscribe to DVD-by-mail only.

- The new subscription fee for each service is $8 per month.

- Assume that variable costs of the DVD-by-mail service (for shipping, handling, and DVD replacement) are $0.40 per movie exchange and that the average user exchanges 5 movies per month. The variable costs of the streaming video service are negligible.

Required:

1. In general, would you classify the demand for Netflix services as elastic or inelastic? Explain.
2. Determine how much Netflix's monthly profit would increase or decrease with the new pricing and subscription structure.
3. If you were a Netflix customer, how would you react to this change?

4. If you were a Netflix shareholder, how would you react to this change? Optional: This is an opportunity for you to research what actually happened to Netflix's stock price in the days and months after the price change.

5. Do you think Netflix made the change to boost short-term or long-term profit?

6. In your opinion, was Netflix's decision to separate the streaming video from DVD-by-mail a good one?

S7–2 Evaluating Decision to Eliminate Collegiate Sports Programs: Quantitative and Qualitative Considerations

LO 7–5

Due to budget cutbacks, colleges and universities across the country are struggling to cut expenses. Frequent casualties of these money-saving decisions are organized sports teams. Suppose that a fictional college, West Tennessee State (WTS), has identified three teams to eliminate in its effort to cut costs: men's lacrosse, women's softball, and men's diving. A summary of each sport's annual revenue and costs follows:

	Men's Lacrosse	Women's Softball	Men's Diving
Revenue	$ 25,600	$ 37,800	$ 14,900
Less: Expenses			
Scholarships	150,000	130,000	40,000
Coaches salaries	53,000	49,700	62,800
Team travel	21,100	28,500	13,200
Venue maintenance	15,000	20,000	35,000
Equipment	4,300	2,800	800
Team support	16,600	11,200	6,300
Net operating income (loss)	$(234,400)	$(204,400)	$(143,200)

The combined net loss from these three programs is $582,000.

Required:

1. If the three programs were eliminated, do you think WTS would see an immediate improvement in its bottom line? Why or why not?

2. Determine whether each individual line item would be completely eliminated, partially eliminated, or not eliminated. Label the items as avoidable, partially avoidable, or unavoidable, and explain any assumptions you made in determining the classification.

3. Research actual examples of colleges or universities that have eliminated sports programs. List five that have eliminated sports teams in the past three years and identify which teams were eliminated.

4. Major sports such as men's football and basketball are seldom, if ever, eliminated even though they generally have the highest dollar amount of expenses. Why are these sports retained? What other factors could affect which teams are eliminated?

5. Choose one of the institutions identified in requirement 3 to investigate in more detail. For that college or university, discuss the factors that led to its choice(s), the anticipated impact on direct participants (coaches, athletes, etc.), and the total amount of savings expected. Also include reactions from the student body and the local and college communities.

S7–3 Evaluating Walmart's Decision to Raise Hourly Wages and Eliminate Salaried Positions: Quantitative and Qualitative Considerations

LO 7–5

In January 2018, Walmart announced it would raise its starting wage from $9 to $11 and it would be firing 3,500 store co-managers, a salaried person who acts as a lieutenant underneath each store manager.

Required:

1. Explain how the Walmart decision impacts variable costs, fixed costs, and operating leverage.

2. Research the Walmart decisions and write a brief paragraph explaining Walmart's point of view in making the decisions. Include any information you can find about how the decisions will affect profitability of its stores.

3. Describe the "typical" Walmart customer or employee who was most impacted by these decisions.

4. Write a brief paragraph from this typical employee's point of view explaining how Walmart's decision would impact the employee.

5. Identify three possible effects of this decision on Walmart's business. Be specific in terms of both the segment and the possible impact.

LO 7–4 **S7–4 Researching Outsourcing Issues in National and Local Press**

Outsourcing, particularly to overseas companies, is a hot-button topic that has garnered much attention in the academic, national, and local business media.

Required:

1. Conduct an Internet search for articles about outsourcing. What are some of the major reasons that companies decide to outsource? What are the advantages and disadvantages of outsourcing from the perspective of the company and its stockholders, managers, employees, and the local community?

2. Search for a recent article on outsourcing in a national business publication such as *Fortune, BusinessWeek,* or *The Wall Street Journal.* Briefly summarize the article's main points, including any outsourcing trends, companies making outsourcing decisions, or issues related to politics or the U.S. economy.

3. Search the archives of your local or regional newspaper for articles about outsourcing. Try to identify a specific company in your area that has outsourced part of its operations. Describe the part of the business that was outsourced. For example, did it outsource part of its manufacturing operation, or a support function such as information technology or customer support? What likely factors came into play in making the decision? What impact, if any, will this decision have on customers, employees, and the local community?

4. Discuss whether you or someone you know has been personally affected by a company's decision to outsource.

8

Budgetary Planning

YOUR LEARNING OBJECTIVES

LO 8–1 Describe (a) how and why organizations use budgets for planning and control and (b) potential behavioral issues to consider when implementing a budget.

LO 8–2 Describe the major components of the master budget and their interrelationships.

LO 8–3 Prepare the following components of the operating budget:

    a. Sales budget.

    b. Production budget.

    c. Direct materials purchases budget.

    d. Direct labor budget.

    e. Manufacturing overhead budget.

    f. Cost of goods sold budget.

    g. Selling and administrative expense budget.

    h. Budgeted income statement.

LO 8–4 Prepare the cash budget and describe the relationships among the operating budgets, cash budget, and budgeted balance sheet.

LO 8–5 Prepare a merchandise purchases budget for a merchandising firm.

©SumanBhaumik/Shutterstock

FOCUS COMPANY: LEVI STRAUSS & CO.

Have you ever spent time planning a major event, such as a graduation party, bar mitzvah, or wedding? If so, you probably realize the importance of having a budget to help you decide where to hold the event, how many people to invite, and what food to serve. These and many other decisions affect the cost and success of any event.

Business managers use budgets in a similar way. Rather than budgeting for a one-time event, however, managers use budgets to plan their ongoing operations so they will be able to meet the organization's short-term and long-term objectives. Both profit-oriented and nonprofit organizations use budgets. The only difference is whether their short- and long-term objectives are oriented toward earning a profit or reaching some other objective such as providing education, feeding the poor, or improving health care.

In this chapter, we describe the budgeting process using a company that makes a product most everyone is familiar with: Levi blue jeans. Levi Strauss emigrated from Bavaria to New York in 1846. In 1853, he followed the California gold rush to San Francisco, where he started a west coast division of his family's dry goods business. He struck gold in 1872 when one of his customers, a tailor named Jacob Davis, came to him with an idea for making work pants more durable by using rivets or metal fasteners at points of strain, such as the corner pocket or the base of the fly. Levi saw the potential in this novel approach to making clothing and helped Jacob apply for a patent on the idea. The patent was granted to Jacob Davis and Levi Strauss & Company on May 20, 1873, and the quintessential American garment, the blue jean, was born.

In this chapter, we prepare a master budget for a hypothetical division of Levi Strauss & Co. In the next chapter, we determine whether this division achieved its budget by comparing actual to budgeted results. First, let's cover some basic concepts in budgeting.

Role of budgets in organizations

· Planning and control cycle
· Benefits of budgeting
· Behavioral effects of budgets
· Components of the master budget

Prepare the operating budgets

· Sales budget
· Production budget
· Direct materials purchases budget
· Direct labor budget
· Manufacturing overhead budget
· Budgeted cost of goods sold
· Selling and administrative expense budget
· Budgeted income statement

Prepare the cash budget and merchandise purchases budget

· Budgeted cash receipts
· Budgeted cash payments
· Cash budget
· Budgeted balance sheet
· Budgeting in nonmanufacturing firms

Role of Budgets in Organizations

The first chapter of this book described three functions of management: planning, implementing, and controlling. Refer to Exhibit 1–2 for a review of this process. Although these functions were described as three distinct tasks, they are part of an interrelated process that is often referred to as the **planning and control cycle.** In this chapter, we focus on the planning phase of this cycle by creating budgets that reflect what managers expect to happen in the future. In the next chapter, we move into the control phase of the cycle by computing variances that compare actual to budgeted results. Because the topics are interrelated, we will use the same focus company, Levi Strauss & Co., to tie them together. We will start by preparing a master budget for a hypothetical division of that makes a single product: 441 blue jeans. In the next chapter, we will prepare detailed variances for direct materials, direct labor, and manufacturing overhead to see how the actual cost of manufacturing the jeans compared to the budget, using an approach called *standard costing.*

PLANNING AND CONTROL CYCLE

Planning is the future-oriented part of the planning and control cycle, during which managers set objectives or goals for the future. **Implementing** occurs when managers put the plan into action. **Controlling** is the review part of the cycle in which managers look back to determine whether they met the goals set during the planning phase. If the goals have not been met, managers can take corrective action to improve future results. The changes made during the control phase of the process will be reflected in future plans, starting the cycle over again.

The starting point of the planning process is managers' **strategic plan** or vision of what they want the organization to achieve over the long term. The strategic plan is then translated into long-term and short-term objectives, along with the tactics that will be used to achieve those objectives. A **long-term objective** is a specific goal that managers want to achieve over the long term, typically 5 to 10 years. A **short-term objective** is a specific goal that managers need to achieve in the short run, usually no longer than a year, to reach their long-term goals. **Tactics** are specific actions or mechanisms managers use to achieve the objectives. For example, assume a company's long-term objective is to gain a 20 percent share of the market over the next five years. A short-term objective might be to increase sales revenue by 5 percent during the next year. One possible tactic for achieving that goal would be to increase the amount spent on advertising and promotion to generate additional sales.

An important part of the planning process is the creation of a **budget**, a detailed document that translates the company's objectives into financial terms. A budget identifies the resources and expenditures that will be required over a limited planning horizon (typically a year), which can be broken into shorter periods (for example, months or quarters).

Budgets are used in organizations of all types: large and small; for-profit and not-for-profit; manufacturing, merchandising, and service. Although the types of budgets will differ depending on the organization, the basic principles are the same. The next section discusses the benefits of budgets and describes some behavioral issues that managers may encounter when using budgets for planning and control.

BENEFITS OF BUDGETING

Budgeting has several benefits, which are summarized in Exhibit 8–1. **One of the major advantages of budgeting is that it forces managers to look to the future.** In your own life, you or your parents may have prepared a budget to help save for college, a future vacation, or retirement. In business, budgets force managers to look ahead and address potential problems. For example, a budget can help managers plan ahead to ensure they have enough cash on hand to pay the company's bills or enough inventory to avoid running out of merchandise during periods of peak demand.

Budgets also play an important communication role within organizations. They provide a mechanism for managers to share their priorities for the future and communicate those priorities to others throughout the organization. Because budgets span the entire organization, they also require managers from different functional areas to communicate and coordinate in order to achieve the organization's objectives.

Finally, **budgets serve an important role in motivating and rewarding employees.** If a budget is implemented correctly, it should motivate employees to work hard to meet the company's objectives. **Budgets also provide a useful benchmark for evaluating and rewarding employee performance.** We discuss the motivational effects of budgets in the next section; their role in performance evaluation is addressed in the next two chapters.

BEHAVIORAL EFFECTS OF BUDGETS

Although budgets are intended to motivate employees to work hard to achieve the organization's goals, they can sometimes create unintended effects. The way in which managers and employees behave in response to budgets depends, in large part, on how goals and budgets are

EXHIBIT 8–1	Benefits of Budgeting

Thinking ahead	Communication	Motivation
• Forcing managers to look ahead and state their goals for the future • Providing lead time to solve potential problems	• Communicating management's expectations and priorities • Promoting cooperation and coordination between functional areas of the organization	• Providing motivation for employees to work toward organizational objectives • Providing a benchmark for evaluating performance

set. Two considerations are especially critical: the relative difficulty of meeting goals and the degree of employee participation in establishing goals.

In setting budgetary goals, finding the right level of difficulty is key. Research suggests that **budgets that are tight but attainable are more likely to motivate people** than budgets that are either too easy or too difficult to achieve. Think about your own personal goals. If the goal is too easy, you will not have to work very hard to achieve it. If you set your goal too high, however, you may quickly become frustrated and give up. Similarly, managers must try to find the "just-right" level of difficulty in setting budgetary goals so that they have motivating rather than demotivating effects on employee behavior.

Involving employees at all levels of the organization in the budgeting process is also important. **Participative budgeting** allows employees throughout the organization to have input into the budget-setting process. This bottom-up approach to budgeting can be contrasted with a **top-down approach** in which top management sets the budget and imposes it on employees throughout organization. In general, **a participative approach is more likely to motivate people to work toward an organization's goals than a top-down approach.**

One downside to participative budgeting is that employees may try to build a little extra cushion, or **budgetary slack**, into their budgets. They can do so by understating expected sales or overstating budgeted expenses, making it more likely that they will look good by coming in under budget for expenses or over budget for revenues. Budgets can also create a "use-it-or-lose-it" mentality that encourages managers to spend their entire budget to avoid a reduction in resources the next budget period. Many of these dysfunctional behaviors can be minimized by implementing the following budget-setting guidelines:

- **Use different budgets for planning than for performance evaluation.** Although budgetary slack can make planning difficult, it provides a way for managers to hedge against uncertainty, or future events they may not be able to anticipate or control. Some budget slack can be beneficial, particularly in organizations that face major fluctuations in demand or costs that are beyond the manager's control.

- **Use a continuous, or rolling, budget approach.** Under continuous budgeting, the company maintains a rolling budget that always extends a certain period into the future. When one budget period passes, another is automatically added at the end. This approach keeps managers in continuous planning mode, always looking into the future, and helps avoid the budget games that are sometimes played at the end of a budget period.

- **Use a zero-based budgeting approach.** Under zero-based budgeting, the entire budget must be constructed from scratch each period rather than using last period's budget as the starting point. While time-consuming, it makes managers justify their budget each year and can help control unnecessary spending.

As this discussion indicates, managers must take a variety of behavioral factors into account in designing and implementing a budget system. There is not a one-size-fits-all

SPOTLIGHT ON Ethics

Playing Budget Games

Managers who are evaluated and rewarded for meeting budgetary goals may engage in game playing. For example, a sales manager who has reached his or her sales quota for the week may try to defer sales to a future period by telling customers to come back later to make their purchase. Managers may even be tempted to postdate orders so that they **appear** to have been made in a different time period. Alternatively, a salesperson who has not met his or her quota may cut prices at the end of the period to increase sales volume and meet the sales goal.

By engaging in these tactics, managers are putting their own self-interest ahead of the organization's objectives. Although the complete elimination of such budget games is difficult to achieve, organizations must try to design their budgets and control systems to minimize these dysfunctional behaviors.

solution to budgeting. The best approach depends on the nature of the business environment, type of organization, and tasks that managers must perform within the organization.

Before continuing, take a moment to make sure you understand the basic principles of budgeting by completing the following Self-Study Practice.

 How's it going?   Self-Study Practice

Which of the following statements is (are) false? You may select more than one answer.

1. Planning is the forward-looking phase of the planning and control cycle.
2. Controlling is the backward-looking phase of the planning and control cycle.
3. Employees are more likely to be motivated by a top-down approach to budgeting than by a participative approach.
4. The creation of budgetary slack is not a problem for planning purposes, but it may cause problems in evaluating employees' performance.

After you have finished, check your answers against the solutions in the margin.

Solution to Self-Study Practice
Statements 3 and 4 are false.

COMPONENTS OF THE MASTER BUDGET

The **master budget** is a comprehensive set of budgets that covers all phases of an organization's planned activities for a specific period of time. Within the master budget, individual budgets can be classified as either operating budgets or financial budgets. See Exhibit 8–2 for an illustration of the components of the master budget. Note that each part of the budget is either based on or provides input into another part of the budget. Understanding these interrelationships is key to developing a master budget.

Operating budgets cover the organization's planned operating activities for a particular period of time, including expected sales, production, direct materials purchases, direct labor, manufacturing overhead, and selling and administrative expenses. When all of these operating budgets are combined, they form a **budgeted income statement**, which represents management's expectation of net operating income.

Learning Objective 8–2
Describe the major components of the master budget and their interrelationships.

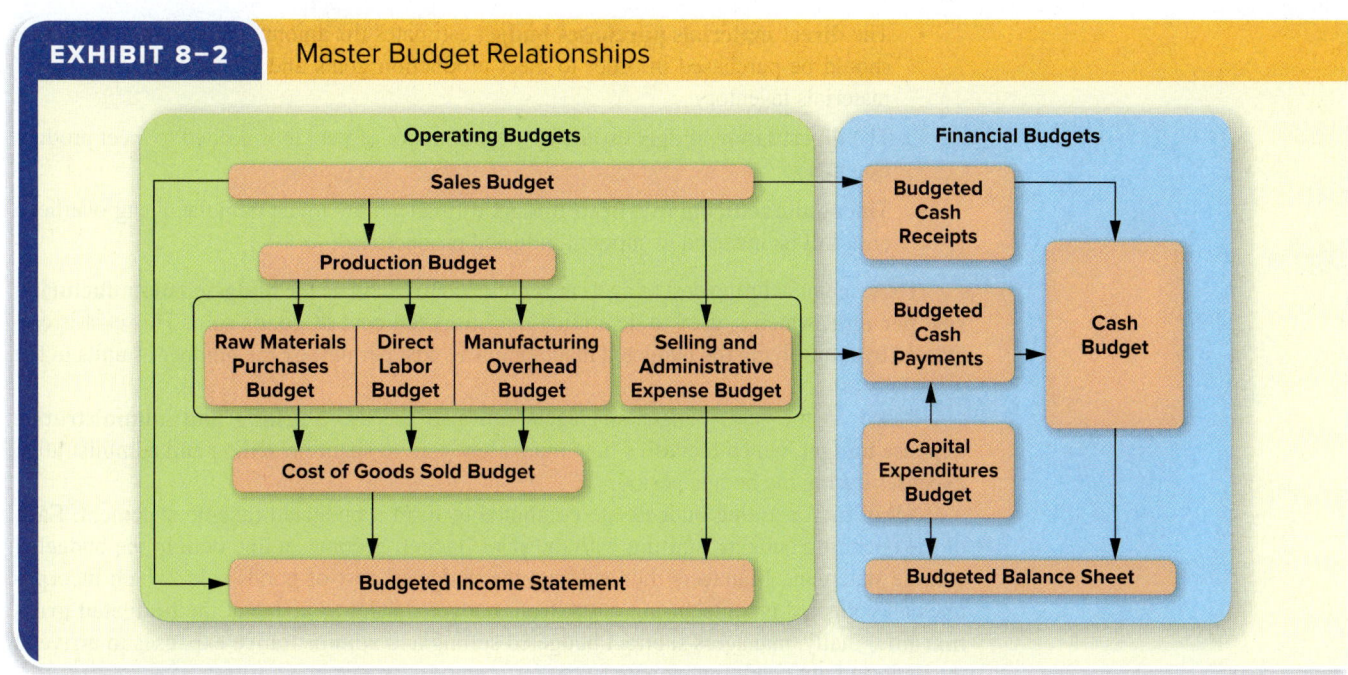

EXHIBIT 8–2   Master Budget Relationships

Financial budgets focus on the financial resources needed to support operations. The primary financial budget that we prepare in this chapter is the **cash budget**, which provides information about budgeted cash receipts, payments, and financing. We focus primarily on the cash budget because it provides critical information for managing daily operations. The capital expenditures budget relates to the purchase of long-term assets, such as buildings and equipment. Capital budgeting is discussed in Chapter 11. Note that both the cash budget and the capital expenditures budget will impact the **budgeted balance sheet**, which shows the expected balance of assets, liabilities, and owners' equity at the end of the budget period.

The starting point for preparing the master budget is the **sales budget** or **sales forecast**. The sales forecast is generally stated in terms of the number of units that are expected to be sold, while the sales budget translates the sales forecast into an estimate of total sales revenue by multiplying the number of units by the budgeted sales price. The sales budget is the most critical part of the master budget because it affects every other budget. Managers use it to determine how many units to produce, how much material to buy, how many people to hire, and the like. If managers do not have a good estimate of future sales, they run the risk of lost revenue or dissatisfied customers (if the sales budget is set too low) or an excess supply of inventory that may become spoiled or obsolete (if the sales forecast is set too high).

Managers use a variety of information to determine the sales forecast including

COACH'S TIP

Notice in Exhibit 8–2 that the sales budget affects almost all other budgets in the master budget. If the sales budget is wrong, the rest of the master budget will be incorrect.

- Actual sales for the preceding period.
- Research on overall industry trends.
- Input from top management about target sales objectives (for example, market share goals).
- Input from research and development about new product introductions, new features of existing products, and so on.
- Planned marketing activities (for example, advertising and sales promotions).

Sales managers use all of these factors to determine their best estimate of future sales, which is reflected in the sales budget.

After the sales budget is set, managers use it to prepare the **production budget**, which shows how many units must be produced each period. The number of units to be produced may differ from the number of units to be sold depending on how much finished goods inventory managers want on hand at the beginning and end of each period.

Based on the production budget, managers can estimate the materials, labor, and manufacturing overhead costs needed to meet those production goals.

- The **direct materials purchases budget** estimates the amount of direct materials that should be purchased in order to meet production goals and planned levels of direct materials inventory.
- The **direct labor budget** estimates the amount of direct labor needed to meet production goals.
- The **manufacturing overhead budget** estimates how much manufacturing overhead cost will be incurred to support budgeted production.

These manufacturing cost budgets are combined to calculate the **budgeted manufacturing cost per unit**, which is used to determine the **budgeted cost of goods sold**. This cost is calculated by multiplying the budgeted manufacturing cost per unit by the number of units in the sales forecast.

Based on the sales budget, managers can also prepare a **selling and administrative expense budget**, which identifies how much they plan to spent on selling and administrative expenses during the budget period.

All of the operating budgets are combined to form a budgeted income statement. Each of the operating budgets, starting with the sales budget, becomes a line item in the budgeted income statement. Managers then subtract the budgeted cost of goods sold, which incorporates all budgeted manufacturing costs, from budgeted sales to arrive at the **budgeted gross margin**. Finally, managers subtract budgeted selling and administrative expenses to arrive at the budgeted net operating income.

Note in Exhibit 8–2 that all operating budgets are connected in some way to one or more financial budgets. In the next section, we illustrate how to prepare the various operating budgets needed to complete a budgeted income statement. We then show how these operating budgets are used to prepare the cash budget and budgeted balance sheet.

SPOTLIGHT ON Big DATA Analytics

Utilizing technology and analytics to improve the customer experience at Levi Strauss.

The budgeting examples used in this chapter are intentionally simplistic so that you, the student, can focus on the basic concepts and computations required to prepare a master budget and easily understand how all of the pieces fit together.

Of course, strategic planning and demand forecasting is extremely complex in a multinational corporation such as Levi Strauss, and managers rely on much more sophisticated tools and analytic techniques to gain actionable insight from a vast array of data.

Here are just a few examples of how Levi Strauss & Co. has collaborated with analytics experts such as Intel and SAS to improve the customer experience, manage inventory, and improve operating efficiency.

- By installing RFID sensors in clothing, Levi Strauss was able to use Intel's cloud-based analytics program to monitor, in real time, the location of each item in inventory. The system allowed salespeople to quickly find misplaced items and put them back on the shelf so that customers would have an improved shopping experience. The system also alerted managers when inventory of a particular size or color was low so that they could replenish the stock from the storeroom or offer to order it for customers.[1]

- Levi Strauss collaborated with SAS to analyze millions of transactions from locations across the globe to improve demand planning and inventory management. The goal was to make sure they have the right product, in the right size, and the right color, delivered to the right location when customers want it. See the following promotional video from SAS describing the complexity of the data and the benefits of an end-to-end solution for providing actionable and intelligent data to managers.[2]

[1] https://www.intel.com/content/dam/www/public/us/en/documents/case-studies/enhancing-in-store-retail-experience-study.pdf
[2] https://www.sas.com/en_us/customers/levi-strauss.html

Prepare the Operating Budgets

In this section, we prepare the operating budgets for a hypothetical division of Levi Strauss & Co. For this example, we will assume this division manufactures and sells one type of blue jeans, called the Levi 441. In reality, Levi Strauss contracts with overseas suppliers (primarily in Asia) to manufacture the clothing that is sold under one of its brand names, such as Levi's, Dockers, or Denizen. But for illustrative purposes, we will prepare the manufacturing budgets *as if* the manufacturing operations were performed by Levi Strauss employees, as they were in the early days of the company's history. Although we make a number of simplifying assumptions and the numbers are not intended to represent the actual cost of producing and selling Levi jeans, the objective of this example is to show the structure of the various operating budgets and how they relate to one another. We prepare the budgets in Excel, as most managers would in practice, and display all budgeted amounts in whole dollars.[3]

[3] Although displaying the values in whole dollars may create the *appearance* of minor rounding errors, there is no true rounding error because Excel maintains the full numeric value and all decimal points in memory. This is a major advantage of using Excel; it prevents rounding errors from compounding when the budget numbers are used in subsequent calculations.

SALES BUDGET

The starting point for the master budget is the sales forecast or sales budget. The sales department typically provides this information based on a variety of sources, including prior sales, industry trends, and planned marketing activities. The budget is generally prepared for an entire year and is broken down into monthly or quarterly periods. In this example, we prepare the sales budget on a quarterly basis.

To create the sales budget you need an estimate of the number of units to be sold each quarter, along with an estimate of the average budgeted sales price. Multiplying budgeted units by the budgeted sales price gives the budgeted sales revenue. Summing the unit and total sales values across all four quarters gives the yearly total in the far right column. See Exhibit 8–3 for the Levi's hypothetical sales budget for 2018.

EXHIBIT 8–3   Sales Budget

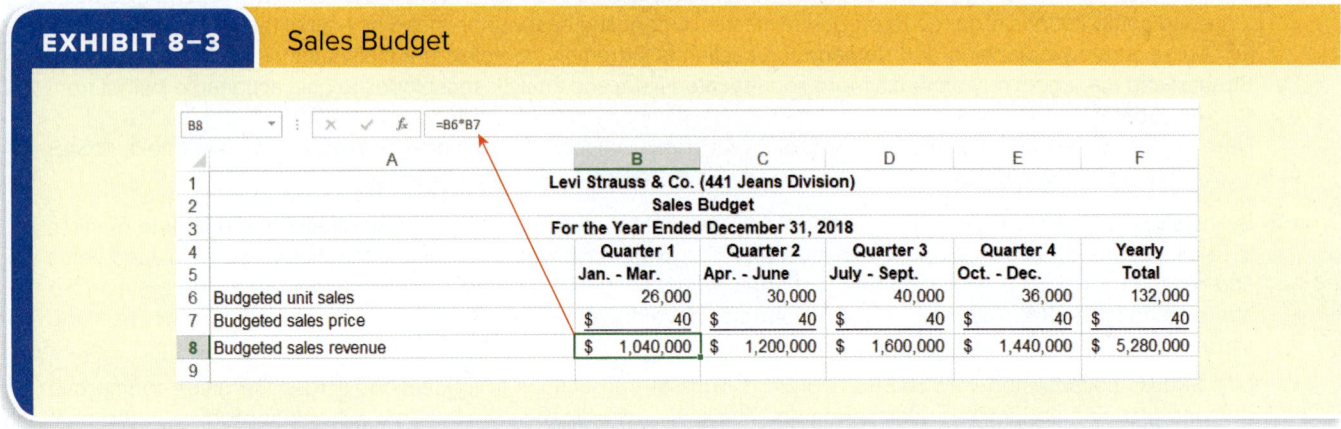

B8	fx =B6*B7				
	A	B	C	D	E	F
1		Levi Strauss & Co. (441 Jeans Division)				
2		Sales Budget				
3		For the Year Ended December 31, 2018				
4		Quarter 1	Quarter 2	Quarter 3	Quarter 4	Yearly
5		Jan. - Mar.	Apr. - June	July - Sept.	Oct. - Dec.	Total
6	Budgeted unit sales	26,000	30,000	40,000	36,000	132,000
7	Budgeted sales price	$ 40	$ 40	$ 40	$ 40	$ 40
8	Budgeted sales revenue	$ 1,040,000	$ 1,200,000	$ 1,600,000	$ 1,440,000	$ 5,280,000
9						

PRODUCTION BUDGET

The production budget is based on the sales budget and the amount of finished goods inventory managers want to have on hand at the beginning and end of the budget period. If managers are planning to build inventory, they need to produce more units than they expect to sell. If they want to reduce inventory, they should produce fewer units than they expect to sell. The relationship between budgeted sales, beginning and ending finished goods inventory, and production is summarized in the following formula:

Budgeted Unit Sales	+	Budgeted Ending Finished Goods Inventory	−	Budgeted Beginning Finished Goods Inventory	=	Budgeted Production Units

In the past, manufacturing companies held substantial inventories of finished goods, which created a marked difference between the sales budget and the production budget. Today, however, companies such as Dell and Nike are moving toward a make-to-order approach in which the product is manufactured to fill a specific customer order. In these companies, the production and sales budget are virtually the same.

Traditional manufacturing companies maintain finished goods inventory as a buffer between budgeted sales and production. For example, assume that Levi Strauss & Co. wants to **maintain an ending finished goods inventory equal to 5 percent of the *next* period's budgeted sales.** Stated another way, beginning finished goods inventory should be equal to 5 percent of the *current* period's budgeted sales. See Exhibit 8–4 for the resulting production budget based on this assumption.

The Excel formula at the top of Exhibit 8–4 shows that the ending finished goods inventory in quarter 1 is computed by multiplying budgeted sales for quarter 2 (cell C6) by 5

EXHIBIT 8-4	Production Budget

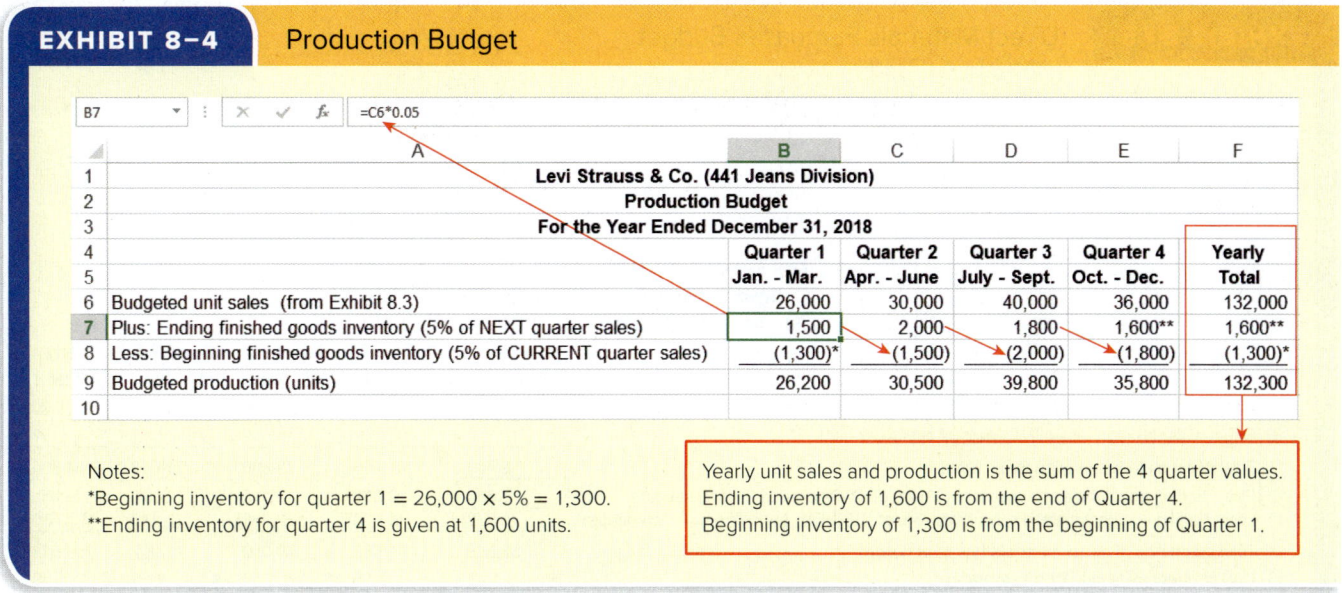

	A	B	C	D	E	F
		Quarter 1	Quarter 2	Quarter 3	Quarter 4	Yearly
1	Levi Strauss & Co. (441 Jeans Division)					
2	Production Budget					
3	For the Year Ended December 31, 2018					
4		Quarter 1	Quarter 2	Quarter 3	Quarter 4	Yearly
5		Jan. - Mar.	Apr. - June	July - Sept.	Oct. - Dec.	Total
6	Budgeted unit sales (from Exhibit 8.3)	26,000	30,000	40,000	36,000	132,000
7	Plus: Ending finished goods inventory (5% of NEXT quarter sales)	1,500	2,000	1,800	1,600**	1,600**
8	Less: Beginning finished goods inventory (5% of CURRENT quarter sales)	(1,300)*	(1,500)	(2,000)	(1,800)	(1,300)*
9	Budgeted production (units)	26,200	30,500	39,800	35,800	132,300
10						

B7 · : × ✓ *fx* =C6*0.05

Notes:
*Beginning inventory for quarter 1 = 26,000 x 5% = 1,300.
**Ending inventory for quarter 4 is given at 1,600 units.

Yearly unit sales and production is the sum of the 4 quarter values.
Ending inventory of 1,600 is from the end of Quarter 4.
Beginning inventory of 1,300 is from the beginning of Quarter 1.

percent. The ending inventory from quarter 1 then becomes the beginning inventory for quarter 2. The beginning inventory for quarter 1 is computed by multiplying quarter 1 unit sales by 5 percent (26,000 x .05 = 1,300). You cannot compute quarter 4 ending inventory without knowing the next year's quarter 1 sales. This number is given at 1,600 units.

Be careful when computing the yearly total column as you can't always sum the values across the four quarters. Total unit sales and total production units are both summed across the four quarters. However, the units in beginning and ending finished goods inventory are at a specific point in time. Beginning finished goods inventory (1,300 units) is from the beginning of quarter 1. Ending finished goods inventory (1,600 units) is from the end of quarter 4.

DIRECT MATERIALS PURCHASES BUDGET

Next, managers prepare a budget to determine how much direct materials to purchase. For this example, we assume that 2 yards of denim are required to produce one pair of 441 jeans, and that the cost of denim is $1.50 per yard. All other materials, such as thread, rivets, and zippers, are considered *indirect materials* and will be included in the manufacturing overhead budget.

The starting point for preparing the direct materials purchases budget is the production budget. We then need to adjust for the amount of direct materials managers want to have on on hand at the beginning and end of each period. The formula for computing direct materials purchases follows:

Learning Objective 8–3c
Prepare the direct materials purchases budget.

$$\begin{matrix} \text{Raw Materials} \\ \text{Needed for} \\ \text{Production} \end{matrix} + \begin{matrix} \text{Budgeted Ending} \\ \text{Raw Materials} \\ \text{Inventory} \end{matrix} - \begin{matrix} \text{Budgeted Beginning} \\ \text{Raw Materials} \\ \text{Inventory} \end{matrix} = \begin{matrix} \text{Budgeted} \\ \text{Raw Materials} \\ \text{Purchases} \end{matrix}$$

Let's apply this formula to the direct materials needed to make a pair of 441 jeans. Assume that Levi Strauss plans its purchase of direct materials so that it has enough denim on hand at the beginning of each quarter to meet 3 percent of that quarter's production needs. In other words, the ending value of direct materials inventory should be equal to 3 percent of the *next* quarter's production needs. Recall that each pair of 441 jeans requires 2 yards of denim and each yard costs $1.50. See Exhibit 8–5 for Levi's direct materials purchases budget based on these assumptions.

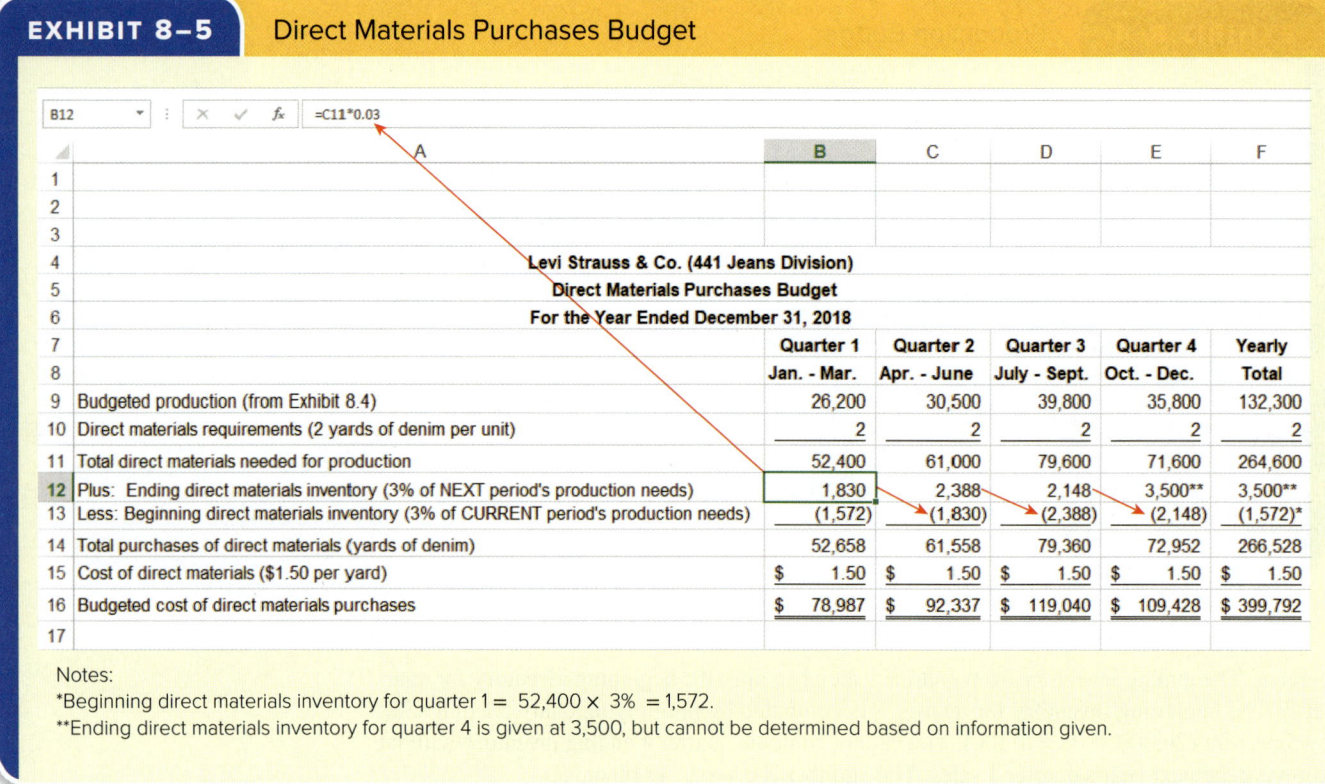

EXHIBIT 8–5   Direct Materials Purchases Budget

B12			fx	=C11*0.03					
	A				B	C	D	E	F
1									
2									
3									
4		Levi Strauss & Co. (441 Jeans Division)							
5		Direct Materials Purchases Budget							
6		For the Year Ended December 31, 2018							
7					Quarter 1	Quarter 2	Quarter 3	Quarter 4	Yearly
8					Jan. - Mar.	Apr. - June	July - Sept.	Oct. - Dec.	Total
9	Budgeted production (from Exhibit 8.4)				26,200	30,500	39,800	35,800	132,300
10	Direct materials requirements (2 yards of denim per unit)				2	2	2	2	2
11	Total direct materials needed for production				52,400	61,000	79,600	71,600	264,600
12	Plus: Ending direct materials inventory (3% of NEXT period's production needs)				1,830	2,388	2,148	3,500**	3,500**
13	Less: Beginning direct materials inventory (3% of CURRENT period's production needs)				(1,572)	(1,830)	(2,388)	(2,148)	(1,572)*
14	Total purchases of direct materials (yards of denim)				52,658	61,558	79,360	72,952	266,528
15	Cost of direct materials ($1.50 per yard)				$ 1.50	$ 1.50	$ 1.50	$ 1.50	$ 1.50
16	Budgeted cost of direct materials purchases				$ 78,987	$ 92,337	$ 119,040	$ 109,428	$ 399,792
17									

Notes:

*Beginning direct materials inventory for quarter 1 = 52,400 × 3% = 1,572.

**Ending direct materials inventory for quarter 4 is given at 3,500, but cannot be determined based on information given.

Notice that the starting point for preparing the direct materials purchases budget is budgeted production (not budgeted sales). We multiply budgeted production by the amount of materials required for each unit (2 yards) to find the total amount of denim needed for production. Then, as shown in the previous formula, we add the budgeted ending direct materials inventory and subtract the beginning direct materials inventory to determine the amount of direct materials that needs to be purchased during the budget period. In this example, the ending inventory is based on 3 percent of next period's production needs, so the first quarter ending inventory equals 3 percent of second quarter production needs. This ending value of inventory becomes the beginning inventory for the next period. Multiplying the total amount of direct materials (yards of denim) purchased by $1.50 gives the budgeted cost of direct materials purchases.

The total yearly values are summed across the four quarters for units produced, total yards of materials purchased and total cost of materials purchased. The beginning value of direct materials inventory is from the beginning of quarter 1. The ending value of direct materials inventory is from the end of quarter 4. The amount of material required per unit (2 yards) and cost per yard ($1.50) remains the same in all columns.

DIRECT LABOR BUDGET

Learning Objective 8–3d
Prepare the direct labor budget.

Next we can prepare a budget to show how much direct labor must be hired to support budgeted production levels. For this example, we assume that each pair of 441 jeans requires 0.25 hours (15 minutes) of direct labor time and that the hourly direct labor rate is $14. See Exhibit 8–6 for the resulting direct labor budget

Notice that the direct labor budget is based on the production budget, multiplied by the amount of labor time required per unit and then multiplied again by the hourly direct labor rate. The direct labor budget is much simpler than the direct materials budget because you do not have to account for beginning and ending inventory, since direct labor cannot be stored the way that direct materials can.

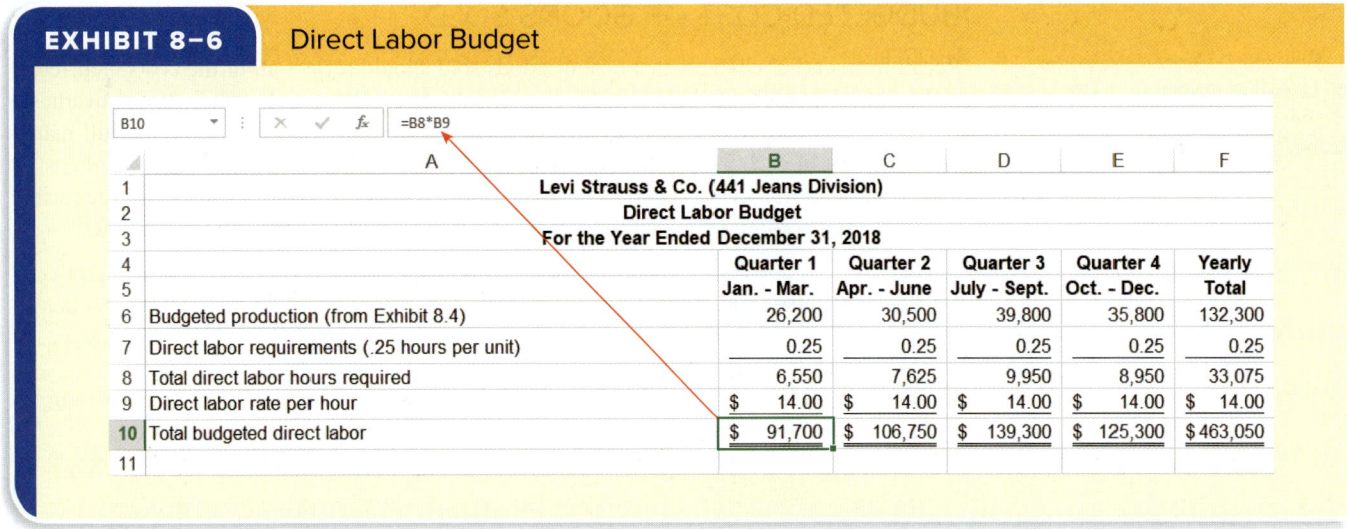

EXHIBIT 8–6 Direct Labor Budget

B10	fx =B8*B9					
	A	B	C	D	E	F
1		Levi Strauss & Co. (441 Jeans Division)				
2		Direct Labor Budget				
3		For the Year Ended December 31, 2018				
4		Quarter 1	Quarter 2	Quarter 3	Quarter 4	Yearly
5		Jan. - Mar.	Apr. - June	July - Sept.	Oct. - Dec.	Total
6	Budgeted production (from Exhibit 8.4)	26,200	30,500	39,800	35,800	132,300
7	Direct labor requirements (.25 hours per unit)	0.25	0.25	0.25	0.25	0.25
8	Total direct labor hours required	6,550	7,625	9,950	8,950	33,075
9	Direct labor rate per hour	$ 14.00	$ 14.00	$ 14.00	$ 14.00	$ 14.00
10	Total budgeted direct labor	$ 91,700	$ 106,750	$ 139,300	$ 125,300	$ 463,050
11						

MANUFACTURING OVERHEAD BUDGET

Next we can prepare the manufacturing overhead budget. Recall from previous chapters that manufacturing overhead includes all costs other than direct materials and direct labor that are incurred during the manufacturing process. This includes costs such as indirect materials, power to run machines, depreciation on machines, rent and insurance on the factory, and any other production-related cost. It does not include selling costs, such as advertising and shipping costs, or administrative costs, legal counsel, accounting services, insurance, and so on. These nonmanufacturing costs are included in the selling and administrative expense budget that will be discussed shortly.

Some manufacturing overhead costs, such as the cost of indirect materials (zippers, thread, rivets) and power to run machines will vary based on the number of units produced or the number of direct labor hours worked. Other costs, such as factory rent, insurance, and depreciation will be incurred regardless of the number of units produced. Since clothing manufacturing is a labor-intensive business, we will assume that variable overhead is applied based on direct labor cost. For our hypothetical example, we use a variable overhead rate equal to 40 percent of direct labor cost. Fixed manufacturing overhead is estimated to be $66,150 per quarter. Refer to Exhibit 8–7 for the resulting manufacturing overhead budget.

EXHIBIT 8–7 Manufacturing Overhead Budget

B10	fx =SUM(B8:B9)					
	A	B	C	D	E	F
1		Levi Strauss & Co. (441 Jeans Division)				
2		Manufacturing Overhead Budget				
3		For the Year Ended December 31, 2018				
4		Quarter 1	Quarter 2	Quarter 3	Quarter 4	Yearly
5		Jan. - Mar.	Apr. - June	July - Sept.	Oct. - Dec.	Total
6	Total budgeted direct labor (from Exhibit 8.6)	$ 91,700	$ 106,750	$ 139,300	$ 125,300	$ 463,050
7	Variable overhead rate (40% of Direct Labor)	40%	40%	40%	40%	40%
8	Budgeted variable manufacturing overhead	$ 36,680	$ 42,700	$ 55,720	$ 50,120	$ 185,220
9	Budgeted fixed manufacturing overhead	66,150	66,150	66,150	66,150	264,600
10	Total budgeted manufacturing overhead	$ 102,830	$ 108,850	$ 121,870	$ 116,270	$ 449,820
11						

BUDGETED COST OF GOODS SOLD

Recall from earlier chapters that cost of goods sold should reflect all of the costs incurred to make a physical product, including direct materials, direct labor, and manufacturing overhead. Before we can prepare a cost of goods sold budget, we must first determine the full manufacturing cost of each unit produced. This unit cost will be used to compute budgeted cost of goods sold and to value the units in ending finished goods inventory for external reporting purposes. The per-unit manufacturing costs of our 441 jeans is summarized as follows:

Budgeted Manufacturing Costs		Per Unit
Direct materials	2 yards of denim per unit × $1.50 per yard	$3.00
Direct labor	0.25 hours per unit × $14 per hour	3.50
Variable manufacturing overhead	40% of direct labor cost	1.40
Fixed manufacturing overhead	$264,600 per year ÷ 132,300 units produced	2.00
Budgeted manufacturing cost per unit		$9.90

Notice that the per-unit costs for direct materials, direct labor, and variable manufacturing overhead are based on the amount of direct materials, labor time, and variable manufacturing overhead required to produce a single pair of jeans. In contrast, budgeted fixed manufacturing overhead per unit is computed by dividing the total budgeted fixed manufacturing overhead cost by budgeted production units for the entire year. Calculating the fixed manufacturing overhead cost on a yearly basis avoids fluctuations in average unit cost due to seasonal changes in production levels. Budgeted cost of goods sold can then be computed on a quarter-by-quarter basis by multiplying budgeted unit sales by the budgeted manufacturing cost per unit as shown in Exhibit 8–8.

Note that budgeted cost of goods sold is based on the sales budget, not the production budget. The budgeted cost of units produced but not sold will appear on the budgeted balance sheet as Finished Goods Inventory. We prepare a budgeted balance sheet in the next section. But first let's complete the operating budgets needed to prepare a budgeted income statement.

EXHIBIT 8–8   Cost of Goods Sold Budget

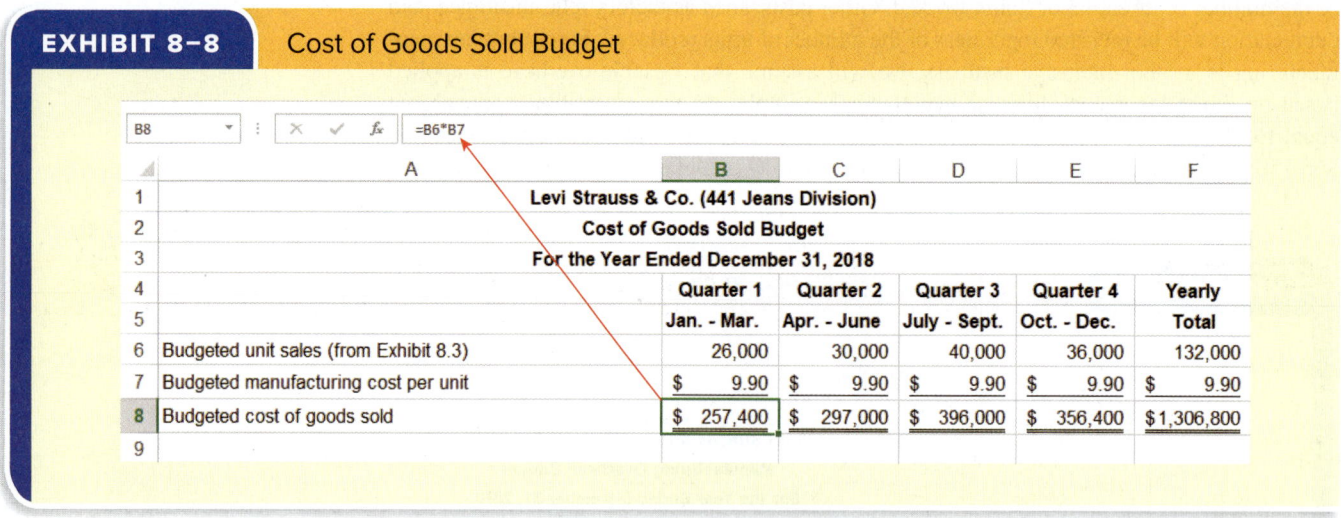

	A	B	C	D	E	F
		B8 ▾ : × ✓ *fx* =B6*B7				
1		Levi Strauss & Co. (441 Jeans Division)				
2		Cost of Goods Sold Budget				
3		For the Year Ended December 31, 2018				
4		Quarter 1	Quarter 2	Quarter 3	Quarter 4	Yearly
5		Jan. - Mar.	Apr. - June	July - Sept.	Oct. - Dec.	Total
6	Budgeted unit sales (from Exhibit 8.3)	26,000	30,000	40,000	36,000	132,000
7	Budgeted manufacturing cost per unit	$ 9.90	$ 9.90	$ 9.90	$ 9.90	$ 9.90
8	Budgeted cost of goods sold	$ 257,400	$ 297,000	$ 396,000	$ 356,400	$1,306,800
9						

SELLING AND ADMINISTRATIVE EXPENSE BUDGET

The last operating budget we need to prepare is the selling and administrative expense budget, which includes all costs related to selling the product (such as advertising, shipping, and sales commissions) and managing the business (such as administrative costs, legal counsel, accounting services, and other corporate functions). We assume that Levi Strauss's selling costs are budgeted at 10 percent of sales revenue. Fixed administrative expenses are estimated to be $200,000 per quarter. The resulting selling and administrative expense budget is shown in Exhibit 8–9.

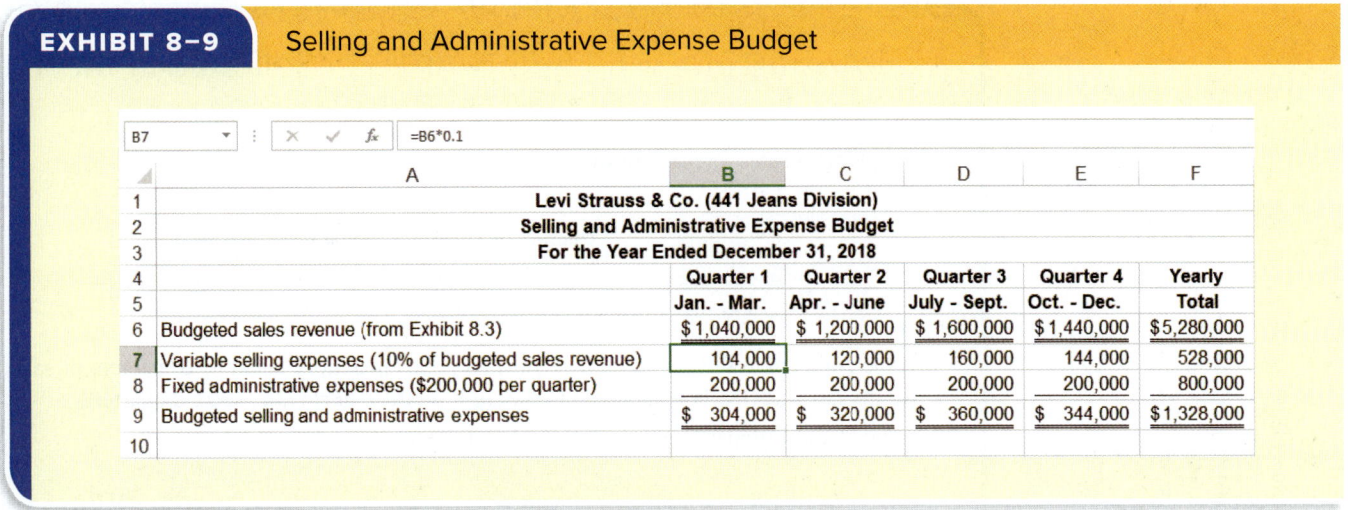

EXHIBIT 8–9   Selling and Administrative Expense Budget

	B7	▼ :	× ✓ *fx*	=B6*0.1			

◢	A	B	C	D	E	F
1		Levi Strauss & Co. (441 Jeans Division)				
2		Selling and Administrative Expense Budget				
3		For the Year Ended December 31, 2018				
4		Quarter 1	Quarter 2	Quarter 3	Quarter 4	Yearly
5		Jan. - Mar.	Apr. - June	July - Sept.	Oct. - Dec.	Total
6	Budgeted sales revenue (from Exhibit 8.3)	$1,040,000	$1,200,000	$1,600,000	$1,440,000	$5,280,000
7	Variable selling expenses (10% of budgeted sales revenue)	104,000	120,000	160,000	144,000	528,000
8	Fixed administrative expenses ($200,000 per quarter)	200,000	200,000	200,000	200,000	800,000
9	Budgeted selling and administrative expenses	$ 304,000	$ 320,000	$ 360,000	$ 344,000	$1,328,000
10						

BUDGETED INCOME STATEMENT

When all of the operating budgets are completed, we can prepare a budgeted income statement, as shown (Exhibit 8–10). We start with budgeted sales revenue and then subtract budgeted cost of goods sold to arrive at budgeted gross margin. Budgeted selling and administrative expenses are then deducted to arrive at budgeted net operating income.

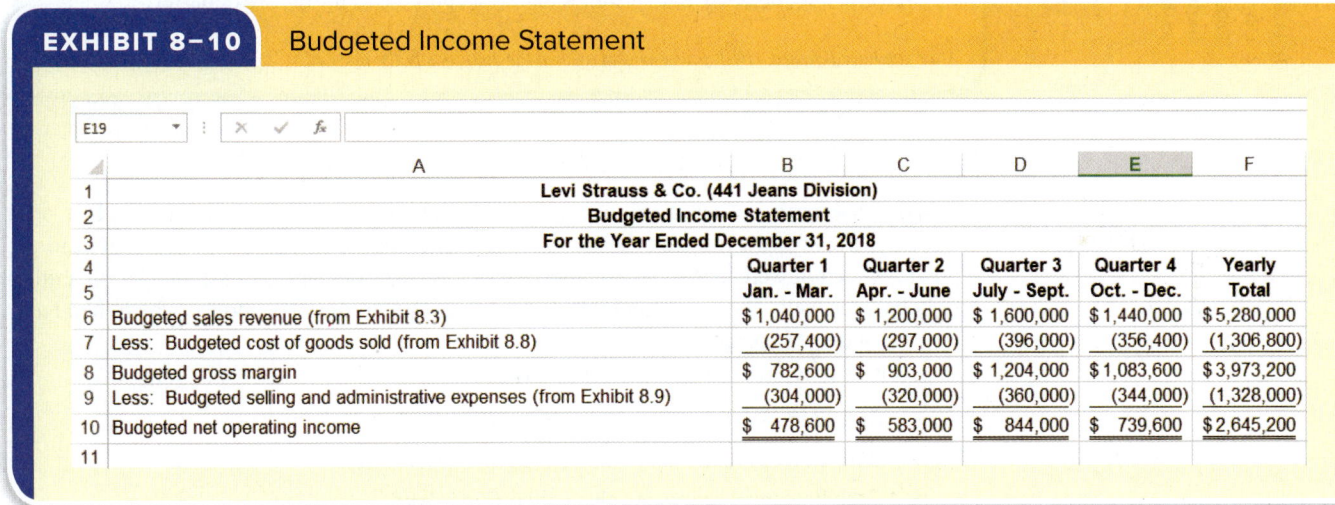

EXHIBIT 8–10   Budgeted Income Statement

	E19	▼ :	× ✓ *fx*				

◢	A	B	C	D	E	F
1		Levi Strauss & Co. (441 Jeans Division)				
2		Budgeted Income Statement				
3		For the Year Ended December 31, 2018				
4		Quarter 1	Quarter 2	Quarter 3	Quarter 4	Yearly
5		Jan. - Mar.	Apr. - June	July - Sept.	Oct. - Dec.	Total
6	Budgeted sales revenue (from Exhibit 8.3)	$1,040,000	$1,200,000	$1,600,000	$1,440,000	$5,280,000
7	Less: Budgeted cost of goods sold (from Exhibit 8.8)	(257,400)	(297,000)	(396,000)	(356,400)	(1,306,800)
8	Budgeted gross margin	$ 782,600	$ 903,000	$1,204,000	$1,083,600	$3,973,200
9	Less: Budgeted selling and administrative expenses (from Exhibit 8.9)	(304,000)	(320,000)	(360,000)	(344,000)	(1,328,000)
10	Budgeted net operating income	$ 478,600	$ 583,000	$ 844,000	$ 739,600	$2,645,200
11						

Before you move on, take a moment to make sure you understand the key relationships among the operating budgets by completing the next Self-Study Practice.

Prepare the Cash Budget and Merchandise Purchases Budget

The cash budget is a future-oriented version of the statement of cash flows that provides managers with critical information needed to manage their daily operations. It helps managers plan ahead to make certain they have enough cash on hand to meet their operating needs, including paying suppliers, employees, landlords, and other stakeholders. If they don't have enough cash on hand, it gives them time to find other ways to finance their operations, for example, by taking out a loan or finding new investors.

💡 How's it going?   Self-Study Practice

1. Toy Town's sales forecast for the next four quarters follows:

	Quarter 1	Quarter 2	Quarter 3	Quarter 4
Sales forecast (units)	12,000	14,000	15,000	18,000

If the company wants to maintain a finished goods inventory equal to 20 percent of sales for the next quarter, how many units should it produce during the second quarter?

2. Calico Coat Company's production budget follows:

	Quarter 1	Quarter 2	Quarter 3	Quarter 4
Budgeted production (units)	15,000	13,000	14,000	12,000

Each unit requires 5 yards of direct materials at a cost of $3 per yard. The company plans its direct materials purchases so that ending direct materials inventory equals 10 percent of the current quarter's production needs. At the beginning of the first quarter, 5,000 yards of direct materials were on hand.

What is the budgeted cost of direct materials purchases for the first quarter?

After you have finished, check your answers against the solutions in the margin.

Because cash is such a critical resource, most managers prepare a cash budget on a monthly, weekly, or even daily basis. However, since the operating budgets prepared in the previous section were stated on a quarterly basis, we will prepare the cash budget on a quarterly basis as well. The operating budgets feed directly into the cash budget, which then feeds into the budgeted balance sheet.

The cash budget consists of three sections:

- Budgeted cash receipts (also called *collections*).
- Budgeted cash payments (also called *disbursements*).
- Cash borrowed or repaid (also called *financing*).

These cash inflows and outflows affect the cash budget as follows:

$$\text{Beginning Cash Balance} + \text{Budgeted Cash Receipts} - \text{Budgeted Cash Payments} \pm \text{Cash Borrowed or Repaid} = \text{Ending Cash Balance}$$

🔨 COACH'S TIP

A cash budget can help you manage your own personal spending. For example, your rent might be due at the first of the month, but you don't get paid for another two weeks. Or perhaps you receive financial aid at the start of the semester, but it needs to last for four months. A cash budget will lay out the timing of these cash inflows and outflows so that you can be sure you have enough cash on hand to pay your bills.

BUDGETED CASH RECEIPTS

The first step in preparing the cash budget is to calculate budgeted cash receipts, which are based on the sales budget. Remember, however, that sales revenue is recognized when revenue is earned, not when cash is received. Sometimes cash is received in advance of the sale, such as when a customer puts down a deposit for a future sale. Other times it is received after the sale, such as when a customer purchases an item on credit and pays for it later.

For our example, assume that 40 percent of Levi Strauss's sales revenue are cash sales. The other 60 percent are credit sales, which are collected as follows:

- 75 percent of credit sales collected in the quarter of sale.
- 25 percent of credit sales collected in the quarter following the sale.

Managers would prepare a schedule of cash receipts that shows when the cash will be collected, as shown in Exhibit 8–11.

EXHIBIT 8–11   Budgeted Cash Receipts

B9	✕ ✓ *fx*	=B6*0.6*0.75				
	A	B	C	D	E	F
1		Levi Strauss & Co. (441 Jeans Division)				
2		Budgeted Cash Receipts				
3		For the Year Ended December 31, 2018				
4		Quarter 1	Quarter 2	Quarter 3	Quarter 4	Yearly
5		Jan. - Mar.	Apr. - June	July - Sept.	Oct. - Dec.	Total
6	Budgeted sales revenue (from Exhibit 8.3)	$ 1,040,000	$ 1,200,000	$ 1,600,000	$ 1,440,000	$ 5,280,000
7	Cash sales (40% of total sales)	$ 416,000	$ 480,000	$ 640,000	$ 576,000	$ 2,112,000
8	Credit sales (60% of total sales):	-	-	-	-	-
9	Collected during the quarter of sale (75% of credit sales)	468,000	540,000	720,000	648,000	2,376,000
10	Collected in the quarter following sale (25% of credit sales)	125,000	156,000	180,000	240,000	701,000
11	Budgeted cash receipts	$ 1,009,000	$ 1,176,000	$ 1,540,000	$ 1,464,000	$ 5,189,000
12						

Notes:
Quarter 1: Cash sales = $1,040,000 × 40% = $416,000
Quarter 1: Cash collected from quarter 1 credit sales = $1,040,000 × 60% × 75% = $468,000
Quarter 1   Cash collected from last year's quarter 4 credit sales assumed to be $125,000.

In this hypothetical example, quarter 1 budgeted sales were $1,040,000, 40 percent of which is collected in cash ($1,040,000 × 40% = $416,000). The remaining 60 percent of sales is on credit, 75 percent of which will be collected in quarter 1. Thus, the portion of quarter 1 credit sales collected during quarter 1 is $468,000 ($1,040,000 × 60% × 75%). Notice that we multiply sales revenue by two percentages. First, we multiply it by 60 percent to determine how much of the quarter 1 sales will be on credit. We then multiply by 75 percent to determine how much of the quarter 1 credit sales will be collected during quarter 1. The remaining 25 percent of quarter 1 credit sales will be collected during quarter 2 ($1,040,000 × 60% × 25% = $156,000). Similar calculations would be made for sales made during quarters 2, 3, and 4. The only value that cannot be computed from the data provided is the cash collected during quarter 1 from last year's fourth quarter credit sales. This value is given at $125,000.

BUDGETED CASH PAYMENTS

The second step in preparing a cash budget is to estimate the cash payments that will be made to suppliers, employees, and other parties. Most of the information for cash payments comes from the operating budgets, including the direct materials purchases budget, the direct labor budget, the manufacturing overhead budget, and the selling and administrative expense budget.

Like the timing differences between sales revenue and cash receipts, cash payments are not always made in the same period the expense is incurred. For example, managers may purchase direct materials on account in one budget period and pay for them in the next. Or they may purchase a piece of equipment in one period, pay for it in the next period, then recognize depreciation expense over several years while the asset is in use.

To continue our Levi Strauss example, assume the following:

- 20 percent of direct materials purchases is paid for in the quarter purchased.
- 80 percent of direct materials purchases is paid for in the quarter following purchase.
- Manufacturing overhead includes $50,000 in depreciation expense (a noncash item).
- All other operating expenses are paid in cash during the quarter incurred.
- Management plans to invest in new sewing equipment during quarter 1 at a total cost of $1,200,000. They will pay 50 percent down ($600,000) in quarter 1 and pay the remaining balance in three $200,000 installments during quarters 2, 3, and 4.

Based on this information, managers would prepare a schedule of budgeted cash payments as shown in Exhibit 8–12.

EXHIBIT 8–12   Budgeted Cash Payments

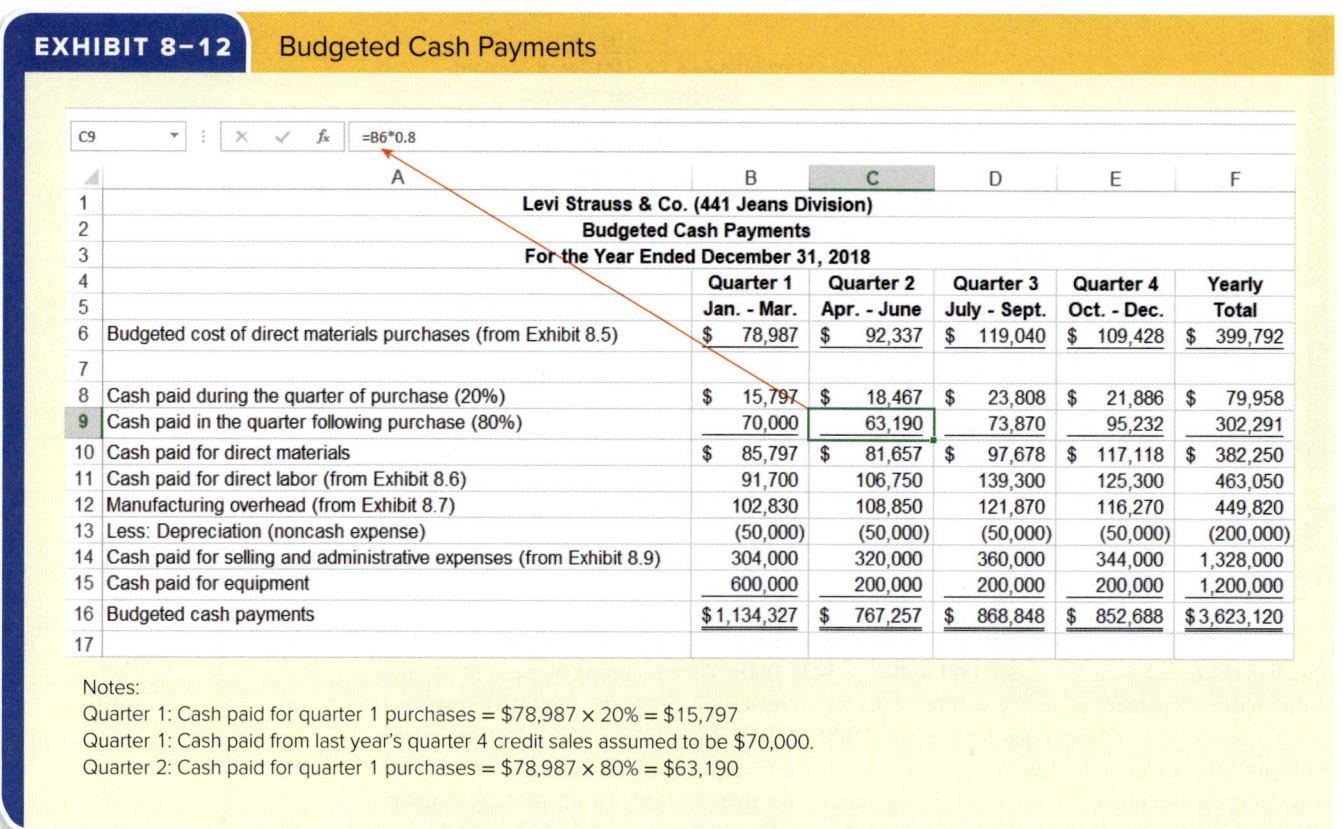

C9 f_x =B6*0.8					
A	B	C	D	E	F
1	Levi Strauss & Co. (441 Jeans Division)				
2	Budgeted Cash Payments				
3	For the Year Ended December 31, 2018				
4		Quarter 1	Quarter 2	Quarter 3	Quarter 4	Yearly
5		Jan. - Mar.	Apr. - June	July - Sept.	Oct. - Dec.	Total
6 Budgeted cost of direct materials purchases (from Exhibit 8.5)	$ 78,987	$ 92,337	$ 119,040	$ 109,428	$ 399,792
7					
8 Cash paid during the quarter of purchase (20%)	$ 15,797	$ 18,467	$ 23,808	$ 21,886	$ 79,958
9 Cash paid in the quarter following purchase (80%)	70,000	63,190	73,870	95,232	302,291
10 Cash paid for direct materials	$ 85,797	$ 81,657	$ 97,678	$ 117,118	$ 382,250
11 Cash paid for direct labor (from Exhibit 8.6)	91,700	106,750	139,300	125,300	463,050
12 Manufacturing overhead (from Exhibit 8.7)	102,830	108,850	121,870	116,270	449,820
13 Less: Depreciation (noncash expense)	(50,000)	(50,000)	(50,000)	(50,000)	(200,000)
14 Cash paid for selling and administrative expenses (from Exhibit 8.9)	304,000	320,000	360,000	344,000	1,328,000
15 Cash paid for equipment	600,000	200,000	200,000	200,000	1,200,000
16 Budgeted cash payments	$1,134,327	$ 767,257	$ 868,848	$ 852,688	$3,623,120
17					

Notes:
Quarter 1: Cash paid for quarter 1 purchases = $78,987 × 20% = $15,797
Quarter 1: Cash paid from last year's quarter 4 credit sales assumed to be $70,000.
Quarter 2: Cash paid for quarter 1 purchases = $78,987 × 80% = $63,190

The direct materials purchases budget indicates that a total of $78,987 in direct materials would be purchased in quarter 1. Only 20 percent of this amount will be paid for during quarter 1 ($78,987 × 20% = $15,797), with the remaining 80 percent paid during quarter 2 ($78,987 × 80% = $63,190). The direct labor expense is assumed to be paid during the month incurred, based on the direct labor budget from Exhibit 8–6.

The manufacturing overhead budget included $50,000 in depreciation expense. Depreciation is a noncash expense, or one that does not involve an actual exchange of cash. The cash flow occurs when the asset is purchased. We need to subtract or back out the depreciation expense from the manufacturing overhead budget to determine the amount of cash paid for manufacturing overhead. Selling and administrative expenses are paid in cash during the period incurred, so no adjustment is needed for these items.

Finally, we include the cash payments for new sewing equipment. This line item would be tied to the capital expenditures budget. Capital budgeting is a more complex topic that will be covered in detail in Chapter 11. In the next section, we will combine the cash receipts and cash payments to form a cash budget. First, take the next Self-Study Practice to make certain you can calculate cash receipts and payments:

How's it going? — Self-Study Practice

Big Ben Clock Company's budget for the first two months of the year included the following:

	January	February
Budgeted sales revenue	$120,000	$140,000
Budgeted raw materials purchases	80,000	70,000
All other expenses	20,000	30,000

Other information follows:

- 60 percent of sales are received in cash. The remaining 40 percent of sales is on credit, collected as follows: 30 percent in the month of sale, 65 percent the following month, and 5 percent never collected.

- 80 percent of direct materials purchases is paid for in the month of purchase and the remainder in the following month.

- All other expenses are paid in cash with the exception of $5,000 in monthly depreciation expense.

Based on this information, calculate Big Ben's budgeted cash receipts and payments for February.

After you have finished, check your answers against the solutions. in the margin.

Solution to Self-Study Practice

Cash Receipts		February
February cash sales	60% × $140,000	$ 84,000
February credit receipts	40% × 30% × $140,000	16,800
January credit receipts	40% × 65% × $120,000	31,200
Total cash receipts		$132,000

Cash Payments		February
February raw materials purchases	80% × $70,000	$56,000
January raw materials purchases	20% × $80,000	16,000
Cash paid for other expenses	30,000 – $5,000	25,000
Total cash payments		$97,000

CASH BUDGET

The final step in preparing the cash budget is to combine the cash receipts and cash payments with the beginning balance of cash to determine whether managers will have enough cash to pay their obligations, or whether they need to borrow money to finance their operations.

Assume the following additional information for our Levi Strauss example:

- Cash on hand at the beginning of quarter 1 was $108,000.

- The company wants to maintain a minimum cash balance of $100,000.

- The company has a floating line of credit with the bank where it can borrow and repay cash in increments of $1,000. No interest is charged if the loan is paid off by the end of the next quarter. The balance on the loan at the beginning of quarter 1 is zero.

Based on this information, managers would prepare a cash budget as shown in Exhibit 8–13.

Cash on hand at the beginning of quarter 1 was $108,000. When you add quarter 1 budgeted cash receipts of $1,009,000 and subtract cash payments of $1,134,327, you get a preliminary cash deficiency (before financing) of $17,327. The minimum cash balance is $100,000, so managers would need to borrow $117,327 to cover the $17,327 deficit and keep a $100,000 balance. Since cash must be borrowed in increments of $1,000, the company will need to borrow $118,000, raising the ending balance in the cash account to $100,673 ($(17,327) + $118,000).

In quarter 2, cash receipts are budgeted at $1,176,000 and cash payments are budgeted at $767,257, leading to a preliminary cash balance (before financing) of $509,416. The cash surplus will be used to pay off the $118,000 bank loan from quarter 1. Since the loan was paid off within 90 days, no interest will accrue. Paying off the $118,000 loan brings the cash balance to $391,416 ($509,416 − $118,000).

EXHIBIT 8–13 Cash Budget

▲	A	B	C	D	E	F
1		Levi Strauss & Co. (441 Jeans Division)				
2		Cash Budget				
3		For the Year Ended December 31, 2018				
4		Quarter 1	Quarter 2	Quarter 3	Quarter 4	Yearly
5		Jan. - Mar.	Apr. - June	July - Sept.	Oct. - Dec.	Total
6	Beginning cash balance	$ 108,000	$ 100,673	$ 391,416	$ 1,062,568	$ 108,000
7	Plus: Budgeted cash receipts (from Exhibit 8.11)	1,009,000	1,176,000	1,540,000	1,464,000	5,189,000
8	Less: Budgeted cash payments (from Exhibit 8.12)	(1,134,327)	(767,257)	(868,848)	(852,688)	(3,623,120)
9	Cash Balance before Financing	$ (17,327)	$ 509,416	$ 1,062,568	$ 1,673,880	$ 1,673,880
10	Cash Borrowed or (Repaid)	118,000	(118,000)	-	-	-
11	Ending Cash Balance	$ 100,673	$ 391,416	$ 1,062,568	$ 1,673,880	$ 1,673,880
12						

Similar calculations are made in quarters 3 and 4. Notice that no financing is needed since the company continues to generate a cash surplus. If the cash balance continues to build, managers may decide to invest some of the excess cash in an interest-bearing certificate of deposit (CD) or other investment. Before they tie up cash in this type of investment, however, managers would look to the cash budget to help them predict or forecast how much cash they will need in the coming months. The cash budget is crucial for helping managers plan their short-term financing and investing needs.

BUDGETED BALANCE SHEET

Based on all of the previous budgets, we can prepare a **budgeted balance sheet.** Just as the operating budgets were combined into a pro forma (forward-looking) income statement, the financial budgets can be combined into a pro forma (forward-looking) balance sheet.

Several of the budgets prepared in the previous sections affect the year-end balance sheet, as described below:

- The $1,673,880 cash balance at the end of quarter 4 (see Exhibit 8–13) would appear as an asset on the balance sheet.

- Any sales revenue not collected by December 31 would be included in Accounts Receivable. Quarter 4 sales were $1,440,000 (see Exhibit 8–3), 60 percent on credit and 25 percent of which is collected in the quarter following the sale. Thus, the uncollected portion of quarter 4 credit sales would be $216,000 ($1,440,000 × 60% × 25%).

- Direct materials on hand at the end of quarter 4 (3,500 yards of denim × $1.50 per yard = $5,250) would appear as Direct Materials Inventory (see Exhibit 8–5).

- The 1,600 units produced (see Exhibit 8–4) but not sold during the year would appear as Finished Goods Inventory and be valued at the full manufacturing cost (see Exhibit 8–8) of $9.90 per unit (1,600 × $9.90 = $15,840).

- The cost of direct materials purchased in quarter 4 but not paid as of December 31 would be included in Accounts Payable in the liabilities section of the balance sheet ($109,428 × 80% = $87,542) (see Exhibit 8–5).

- All other amounts (Property, Plant, and Equipment; Long-Term Liabilities; and Owner's Equity) are given, but would be impacted by the capital expenditures budget that is discussed in Chapter 11.

The budgeted balanced sheet would show the year-end value of all assets, liabilities and stockholders' equity, as shown in Exhibit 8–14:

EXHIBIT 8–14	Budgeted Balance Sheet

	A	B	C	D	E
1		Levi Strauss & Co. (441 Jeans Division)			
2		Budgeted Balance Sheet			
3		As of December 31, 2018			
4					
5	Assets			Liabilities	
6	Cash (Quarter 4 ending cash balance)	$ 1,673,880		Accounts Payable (80% of quarter 4 raw materials purchases)	$ 87,542
7	Accounts Receivable (25% of quarter 4 credit sales)	216,000		Long-Term Liabilities (Assumed)	$ 250,000
8	Direct Materials Inventory (3,500 yards of denim x $1.50 per yard)	5,250		Total Liabilities	$ 337,542
9	Finished Goods Inventory (1,600 units x $9.90 per unit)	15,840			
10	Property, Plant, and Equipment (Assumed)	1,200,000		Stockholders' Equity	2,773,428
11	Total Assets	$ 3,110,970		Total Liabilities and Stockholders' Equity	$ 3,110,970

As you can see from this extended example, all of the individual budgets or schedules within the master budget are interrelated. The operating budgets are used to create a budgeted income statement. These budgets, along with the cash budget and other financial budgets, are then used to create a budgeted balance sheet. Refer to Exhibit 8–15 for an overview of all of the components of the master budget.

BUDGETING IN NONMANUFACTURING FIRMS

As noted at the beginning of this chapter, all organizations can benefit from budgeting, including nonprofit organizations (e.g., universities, hospitals, government agencies), service firms (e.g., hair salons, law firms), merchandisers (e.g., clothing stores and home improvement stores), and manufacturers. The specific budgets prepared will depend on the type of organization, the key sources of revenue, and the major costs of operations.

For example, a service business such as a real estate company, law firm, or hair salon does not manufacture or sell a physical product. As such, service firms do not use a production budget or manufacturing overhead budget. However, they would need to prepare budgets that reflect sales revenue, salaries, sales commissions, rent, utilities, advertising, and other operating expenses, just as a manufacturing company would.

The previous example illustrated the typical budgets for a manufacturing company. As described at the beginning of the chapter, Levi Strauss outsources most of its manufacturing to various suppliers around the world. In reality, their budgeting process would be more similar to that of a merchandising company. Instead of preparing a production and direct materials purchases budget, they would prepare a merchandise purchases budget. This budget is used to determine how much merchandise should be purchased from suppliers to meet sales demand and provide adequate levels of inventory. The formula for the merchandise purchases budget is very similar to the production and direct materials purchases budgets, except the company is purchasing merchandise from a supplier rather than producing it themselves.

> **Learning Objective 8–5**
> Prepare a merchandise purchases budget for a merchandising firm.

$$\text{Budgeted Sales} + \text{Budgeted Ending Merchandise Inventory} - \text{Budgeted Beginning Merchandise Inventory} = \text{Budgeted Merchandise Purchases}$$

As an example, assume that you are a purchasing manager for a Gap retail store and that you are responsible for purchasing denim jeans. The goal is to make sure that you purchase enough jeans to meet the sales budget, but not so much that you wind up with excess inventory that has to be marked down when new merchandise arrives. In your experience, inventory on hand at the beginning of each quarter should equal 20 percent of that quarter's sales, as shown in Exhibit 8–16. In other words, ending inventory should be equal to 20 percent of next quarter's sales.

EXHIBIT 8-15 Summary of the Master Budget

Levi Strauss & Co. (LS&Co. Jeans Division)
Master Budget
For the Year Ended December 31, 2018

	Quarter 1 Jan. - Mar.	Quarter 2 Apr. - June	Quarter 3 July -Sept	Quarter 4 Oct. - Dec.	Yearly Total
Sales Budget					
Budgeted unit sales	26,000	30,000	40,000	36,000	132,000
Budgeted sales price	$ 40.00	$ 40.00	$ 40.00	$ 40.00	$ 40.00
Budgeted sales revenue	$ 1,040,000	$ 1,200,000	$ 1,600,000	$ 1,440,000	$ 5,280,000
Production Budget					
Budgeted unit sales (from Exhibit 8.3)	26,000	30,000	40,000	36,000	132,000
Plus: Ending finished goods inventory (5% of NEXT period sales)	1,500	2,000	1,800	1,600	1,600
Less: Beginning finished goods inventory (5% of CURRENT period sales)	(1,300)	(1,500)	(2,000)	(1,800)	(1,300)
Budgeted production	26,200	30,500	39,800	35,800	132,300
Direct Material Purchases Budget					
Budgeted production (from Exhibit 8.4)	26,200	30,500	39,800	35,800	132,300
Direct material requirements (2 yards of denim per unit)	2	2	2	2	2
Total direct material needed for production	52,400	61,000	79,600	71,600	264,600
Plus: Ending direct material inventory (3% of NEXT period's production needs)	1,830	2,388	2,148	3,500	3,500
Less: Beginning direct material inventory (3% of CURRENT period's production needs)	(1,572)	(1,830)	(2,388)	(2,148)	(1,572)
Total purchases of direct material (yards of denim)	52,658	61,558	79,360	72,952	266,528
Cost of direct material ($1.50 per yard)	$ 1.50	$ 1.50	$ 1.50	$ 1.50	$ 1.50
Budgeted cost of direct material purchases	78,987	92,337	119,040	109,428	399,792
Direct Labor Budget					
Budgeted production (from Exhibit 8.4)	26,200	30,500	39,800	35,800	132,300
Direct labor requirements (.25 hours per unit)	0.25	0.25	0.25	0.25	0.25
Total direct labor hours required	6,550	7,625	9,950	8,950	33,075
Direct labor rate per hour	$ 14.00	$ 14.00	$ 14.00	$ 14.00	$ 14.00
Total budgeted direct labor	$ 91,700	$ 106,750	$ 139,300	$ 125,300	$ 463,050
Manufacturing Overhead Budget					
Total budgeted direct labor (from Exhibit 8.6)	91,700	106,750	139,300	125,300	463,050
Variable overhead rate (40% of Direct Labor)	40%	40%	40%	40%	40%
Budgeted variable manufacturing overhead	$ 36,680	$ 42,700	$ 55,720	$ 50,120	$ 185,220
Budgeted fixed manufacturing overhead	66,150	66,150	66,150	66,150	264,600
Total budgeted manufacturing overhead	$ 102,830	$ 108,850	$ 121,870	$ 116,270	$ 449,820
Cost of Goods Sold Budget					
Budgeted unit sales (from Exhibit 8.3)	26,000	30,000	40,000	36,000	132,000
Budgeted manufacturing cost per unit	$ 9.90	$ 9.90	$ 9.90	$ 9.90	$ 9.90
Budgeted cost of goods sold	$ 257,400	$ 297,000	$ 396,000	$ 356,400	$ 1,306,800
Selling and Administrative Expense Budget					
Budgeted sales revenue (from Exhibit 8.3)	$ 1,040,000	$ 1,200,000	$ 1,600,000	$ 1,440,000	$ 5,280,000
Variable selling expenses (10% of budgeted sales revenue)	104,000	120,000	160,000	144,000	528,000
Fixed administrative expenses ($200,000 per quarter)	200,000	200,000	200,000	200,000	800,000
Budgeted selling and administrative expenses	$ 304,000	$ 320,000	$ 360,000	$ 344,000	$ 1,328,000

	Quarter 1 Jan. - Mar.	Quarter 2 Apr. - June	Quarter 3 July -Sept	Quarter 4 Oct. - Dec.	Yearly Total
Budgeted Income Statement					
Budgeted sales revenue	$ 1,040,000	$ 1,200,000	$ 1,600,000	$ 1,440,000	$ 5,280,000
Less: Budgeted cost of goods sold	(257,400)	(297,000)	(396,000)	(356,400)	(1,306,800)
Budgeted gross margin	$ 782,600	$ 903,000	$ 1,204,000	$ 1,083,600	$ 3,973,200
Less: Budgeted selling and administrative expenses	(304,000)	(320,000)	(360,000)	(344,000)	(1,328,000)
Budgeted income from operations	$ 478,600	$ 583,000	$ 844,000	$ 739,600	$ 2,645,200
Budgeted Cash Receipts					
Budgeted sales revenue (from Exhibit 8.3)	$ 1,040,000	$ 1,200,000	$ 1,600,000	$ 1,440,000	$ 5,280,000
Cash sales (40% of total sales)	$ 416,000	$ 480,000	$ 640,000	$ 576,000	$ 2,112,000
Credit sales (60% of total sales):					
Collected during the quarter of sale (75% of credit sales)	468,000	540,000	720,000	648,000	2,376,000
Collected in the quarter following sale (25% of credit sales)	125,000	156,000	180,000	240,000	701,000
Budgeted cash receipts	$ 1,009,000	$ 1,176,000	$ 1,540,000	$ 1,464,000	$ 5,189,000
Budgeted Cash Payments					
Budgeted cost of direct materials purchases (from Exhibit 8.5)	$ 78,987	$ 92,337	$ 119,040	$ 109,428	$ 399,792
Cash paid during the quarter of purchase (20%)	$ 15,797	$ 18,467	$ 23,808	$ 21,886	$ 79,958
Cash paid in the quarter following purchase (80%)	70,000	63,190	73,870	95,232	302,291
Cash paid for direct materials	$ 85,797	$ 81,657	$ 97,678	$ 117,118	$ 382,250
Cash paid for direct labor (from Exhibit 8.6)	91,700	106,750	139,300	125,300	463,050
Manufacturing overhead (from Exhibit 8.7)	102,830	108,850	121,870	116,270	449,820
Less: Depreciation (noncash expense)	(50,000)	(50,000)	(50,000)	(50,000)	(200,000)
Cash paid for selling and administrative expenses (from Exhibit 8.9)	304,000	320,000	360,000	344,000	1,328,000
Cash paid for equipment	600,000	200,000	200,000	200,000	1,200,000
Budgeted cash payments	$ 1,134,327	$ 767,257	$ 868,846	$ 852,666	$ 3,623,120
Cash Budget					
Beginning cash balance	$ 108,000	$ 100,673	$ 391,416	$ 1,062,568	$ 108,000
Plus: Budgeted cash receipts (from Exhibit 8.11)	1,009,000	1,176,000	1,540,000	1,464,000	5,189,000
Less: Budgeted cash payments (from Exhibit 8.12)	(1,134,327)	(787,257)	(868,848)	(852,688)	(3,623,120)
Cash Balance before Financing	$ (17,327)	$ 509,418	$ 1,062,568	$ 1,673,880	$ 1,673,880
Cash Borrowed or (Repaid)	118,000	(118,000)			
Ending Cash Balance	$ 100,673	$ 391,416	$ 1,062,588	$ 1,673,880	$ 1,673,880

Budgeted Balance Sheet
As of December 31, 2018

Assets		Liabilities	
Cash (Quarter 4 ending cash balance)	$ 1,673,880	Accounts Payable (80% of quarter 4 raw material)	$ 87,542
Accounts Receivable (25% of quarter 4 credit sales)	216,000	Long-Term Liabilities (Assumed)	250,000
Raw Materials Inventory (3,500 yards of denim x $1.50 per yard)	5,250	Total Liabilities	337,542
Finished Goods Inventory (1,600 units x $9.90 per unit)	15,840		
Property, Plant, and Equipment (Assumed)	1,200,000	Stockholders' Equity	2,773,428
Total Assets	$ 3,110,970	Total Liabilities and Stockholders' Equity	$ 3,110,970

EXHIBIT 8–16	Merchandise Purchases Budget

	A	B	C	D	E	F
1		GAP				
2		Merchandise Purchases Budget				
3		For the Year Ended December 31, 2018				
4		Quarter 1	Quarter 2	Quarter 3	Quarter 4	Yearly
5		Jan - Mar.	Apr. - June	July -Sept	Oct - Dec.	Total
6	Budgeted unit sales	30,000	20% 20,000	20% 10,000	20% 40,000	100,000
7	Plus: Planned ending inventory (20% of next quarter's sales)	4,000	2,000	8,000	6,000	6,000
8	Less: Planned beginning inventory (20% of current quarter sales)	(6,000)	(4,000)	(2,000)	(8,000)	(6,000)
9	Budgeted purchases (units)	28,000	18,000	16,000	38,000	100,000
10	Cost of merchandise ($16 per unit)	$ 16.00	$ 16.00	$ 16.00	$ 16.00	$ 16.00
11	Total cost of merchandise purchased	$ 448,000	$ 288,000	$ 256,000	$ 608,000	$ 1,600,000
12						

The quarter 1 ending inventory of 4,000 is based on 20 percent of quarter 2 sales (0.20 × 20,000). Quarter 1 beginning inventory is the same as the previous quarter's ending inventory, which would have been based on 20 percent of quarter 1 sales (30,000 × 20% = 6,000). According to the previous formula, in order to meet quarter 1 unit sales of 30,000 units and still have 4,000 units in ending inventory, managers need to purchase 28,000 units (30,000 + 4,000 − 6,000). Each unit costs $16, for a total cost of merchandise purchased of $448,000 (28,000 units × $16). Managers would make similar calculations to determine how much merchandise to purchase each quarter.

The merchandise purchases budget would then feed into the cost of goods sold budget, budgeted income statement, cash budget, and budgeted balance sheet. All of the other budgets prepared by a merchandising firm would be very similar to those of a manufacturing firm.

REVIEW THE CHAPTER

DEMONSTRATION CASE A: OPERATING BUDGETS

Sky High Parachute Company manufactures and sells parachutes to adventure companies. The company's sales forecast for the coming year follows:

	Quarter 1	Quarter 2	Quarter 3	Quarter 4
Budgeted sales (units)	40,000	35,000	45,000	50,000

Other budgeted information follows:

- The budgeted sales price for each parachute is $1,000.
- The company budgets production so that ending finished goods inventory equals 10 percent of the next quarter's budgeted sales.
- Each parachute requires 20 square yards of a specialty material that costs $15 per square yard.
- The company purchases direct materials so that 10 percent of each quarter's production needs are left over at the end of the quarter to be used as beginning inventory in the next quarter. At the beginning of the first quarter, 70,000 square yards of material were on hand.
- Each parachute requires 15 hours of direct labor at a rate of $12 per hour.
- Manufacturing overhead costs are budgeted at $1 million per quarter plus $50 per unit produced.
- Selling and administrative expenses are budgeted at $500,000 per quarter plus 10 percent of total sales revenue.

Required:

Prepare the following operating budgets for quarters 1 through 3. (You do not have enough information to prepare all of the budgets for quarter 4.)

1. Sales budget.
2. Production budget.
3. Direct materials purchases budget.
4. Direct labor budget.
5. Manufacturing overhead budget.
6. Selling and administrative expense budget.

Suggested Solution

1.

	A	B	C	D	E
2					
3	**Sales Budget**	Quarter 1	Quarter 2	Quarter 3	Quarter 4
4	Budgeted unit sales	40,000	35,000	45,000	50,000
5	Budgeted sales price	$ 1,000	$ 1,000	$ 1,000	
6	Budgeted sales revenue	$ 40,000,000	$ 35,000,000	$ 45,000,000	
7					

2.

	A	B	C	D	E
8	**Production Budget**	Quarter 1	Quarter 2	Quarter 3	Quarter 4
9	Budgeted unit sales	40,000	35,000	45,000	50,000
10	Plus: Planned ending inventory (10% of next quarter sales)	3,500	4,500	5,000	
11	Less: Planned beginning inventory	4,000	3,500	4,500	
12	Budgeted production	39,500	36,000	45,500	
13					

3.

	A	B	C	D	E
13					
14	**Direct Materials Purchases Budget**	Quarter 1	Quarter 2	Quarter 3	Quarter 4
15	Budgeted production	39,500	36,000	45,500	
16	Materials requirements (20 sq. yards per unit)	20	20	20	
17	Total materials needed for production (sq. yards)	790,000	720,000	910,000	
18	Plus: Planned ending inventory	79,000	72,000	91,000	
19	Less: Planned beginning inventory	(70,000)	(79,000)	(72,000)	
20	Total purchases of direct materials (sq. yards)	799,000	713,000	929,000	
21	Cost of direct materials ($15 per square yard)	$ 15	$ 15	$ 15	
22	Budgeted cost of direct materials purchases	$ 11,985,000	$ 10,695,000	$ 13,935,000	
23					

4.

	A	B	C	D	E
23					
24	**Direct Labor Budget**	Quarter 1	Quarter 2	Quarter 3	Quarter 4
25	Budgeted production	39,500	36,000	45,500	
26	Direct labor requirements (15 hours per unit)	15	15	15	
27	Total direct labor hours required	592,500	540,000	682,500	
28	Direct labor cost per hour	$ 12	$ 12	$ 12	
29	Total budgeted direct labor cost	$ 7,110,000	$ 6,480,000	$ 8,190,000	
51					

5.

	A	B	C	D	E
30					
31	**Manufacturing Overhead Budget**	Quarter 1	Quarter 2	Quarter 3	Quarter 4
32	Budgeted production	39,500	36,000	45,500	
33	Variable overhead rate ($50 per unit)	$ 50	$ 50	$ 50	
34	Total variable manufacturing overhead	$ 1,975,000	$ 1,800,000	$ 2,275,000	
35	Fixed manufacturing overhead	1,000,000	1,000,000	1,000,000	
36	Total budgeted manufacturing overhead	$ 2,975,000	$ 2,800,000	$ 3,275,000	
37					

6.

	A	B	C	D	E
38					
39	**Selling and Administrative Expense Budget**	**Quarter 1**	**Quarter 2**	**Quarter 3**	**Quarter 4**
40	Budgeted sales revenue	$ 40,000,000	$ 35,000,000	$ 45,000,000	
41	Variable selling expenses	4,000,000	3,500,000	4,500,000	
42	Fixed administrative expenses	500,000	500,000	500,000	
43	Budgeted selling and admininistrative expenses	$ 4,500,000	$ 4,000,000	$ 5,000,000	
44					

DEMONSTRATION CASE B: CASH BUDGET

Assume that Sky High Parachute Company's budgeted income statement is as follows:

	Quarter 1	Quarter 2	Quarter 3	Quarter 4
Budgeted sales revenue	$40,000,000	$35,000,000	$45,000,000	$50,000,000
Budgeted cost of goods sold	15,600,000	13,650,000	17,550,000	19,500,000
Budgeted gross margin	24,400,000	21,350,000	27,450,000	30,500,000
Budgeted selling and administrative expenses	4,500,000	4,000,000	5,000,000	5,500,000
Budgeted net operating income	$19,900,000	$17,350,000	$22,450,000	$25,000,000

Budgeted sales revenue is collected as follows:

- 60 percent of sales revenue is collected in cash.
- The remainder of sales is on credit and is collected as follows:
  - During the quarter of sale, 35 percent.
  - During the quarter following the sale, 60 percent.
  - Uncollected, 5 percent.

Cost of goods sold (manufacturing costs) consists of the following:

- Materials purchases represent 70 percent of cost of goods sold. The company pays for 40 percent of materials during the quarter of purchase and the remainder the next quarter.
- The remaining 30 percent of cost of goods sold is made up of direct labor and manufacturing overhead including $400,000 in depreciation (a noncash expense). All of the cash payments for direct labor and overhead are paid during the quarter incurred.
- Selling and administrative expenses are paid in the quarter after they are incurred.

Required:

Prepare the following schedules for quarters 2, 3, and 4. (You do not have enough information to prepare the cash budget for quarter 1, so assume its ending cash balance is $500,000.)

1. Cash receipts.
2. Cash payments.
3. Cash budget.

Suggested Solution

1.

	A	B	C	D	E
8					
9	**Budgeted Cash Receipts**	**Quarter 1**	**Quarter 2**	**Quarter 3**	**Quarter 4**
10	Budgeted sales revenue	$ 40,000,000	$ 35,000,000	$ 45,000,000	$ 50,000,000
11	Cash sales (60% of current quarter sales)		$ 21,000,000	$ 27,000,000	$ 30,000,000
12	Credit sales:				
13	Credit sales collected in current quarter (40% of current quarter sales x 35%)		4,900,000	6,300,000	7,000,000
14	Credit sales collected in next quarter (40% of previous quarter sales x 60%)		9,600,000	8,400,000	10,800,000
15	Budgeted cash receipts		$ 35,500,000	$ 41,700,000	$ 47,800,000
32					

2.

	A	B	C	D	E
16					
17	**Budgeted Cash Payments**	**Quarter 1**	**Quarter 2**	**Quarter 3**	**Quarter 4**
18	Budgeted direct materials purchased (70% of Cost of Goods Sold)	$ 10,920,000	$ 9,555,000	$ 12,285,000	$ 13,650,000
19	Cash paid during the quarter of purchase		$ 3,822,000	$ 4,914,000	$ 5,460,000
20	Cash paid in the quarter following purchase		6,552,000	5,733,000	7,371,000
21	Cash paid for direct materials		$ 10,374,000	$ 10,647,000	$ 12,831,000
22	Direct labor and overhead (30% of Cost of Goods Sold)		4,095,000	5,265,000	5,850,000
23	Less: Depreciation		(400,000)	(400,000)	(400,000)
24	Cash paid for selling and administrative expenses		4,500,000	4,000,000	5,000,000
25	Budgeted cash payments		$ 18,569,000	$ 19,512,000	$ 23,281,000
38					

3.

	A	B	C	D	E
26					
27	**Cash Budget**	**Quarter 1**	**Quarter 2**	**Quarter 3**	**Quarter 4**
28	Beginning cash balance		$ 500,000	$ 17,431,000	$ 39,619,000
29	Plus: Budgeted cash receipts		35,500,000	41,700,000	47,800,000
30	Less: Budgeted cash payments		(18,569,000)	(19,512,000)	(23,281,000)
31	Preliminary cash balance		$ 17,431,000	$ 39,619,000	$ 64,138,000
32					

CHAPTER SUMMARY

LO 8–1 **Describe (a) how and why organizations use budgets for planning and control and (b) potential behavioral issues to consider when implementing a budget.**

- Managers use budgets to plan for the future, to communicate organizational goals, to motivate employees to achieve results, and as a benchmark for evaluating performance.

- Budgets can create a number of behavioral effects that should be considered when designing and implementing a budgetary control system.

- Budgets that are tight but attainable are more likely to motivate people to work hard than budgets that are either too easy or too difficult to achieve.

- Participative budgeting allows individuals to provide input into the budget-setting process. However, it may lead to the creation of budgetary slack.

- Using different budgets for planning than for evaluating performance, rolling budgets, and zero-based budgets can mitigate some of the dysfunctional behaviors that may impact the budgeting process.

LO 8–2 **Describe the major components of the master budget and their interrelationships.**

- The master budget is a comprehensive set of budgets that covers all phases of an organization's planned activities for a specific period.

- The master budget contains two types of budgets: operating budgets and financial budgets.

- Operating budgets include all budgets needed to prepare a budgeted income statement including the sales budget, production budget, direct materials purchases budget, direct labor budget, manufacturing overhead budget, and selling and administrative expense budget.

- Financial budgets provide information about financial resources and obligations needed to prepare a budgeted balance sheet. They include the cash budget and the capital expenditures budget.

LO 8–3 **Prepare the following components of the operating budget.**

- **Sales budget.** The starting point of the budgeting process is the development of the sales budget. It is based on a variety of inputs and affects all other components of the master budget.

- **Production budget.** This budget is based on the sales budget and the planned levels of beginning and ending finished goods inventory.
- **Direct materials purchases budget.** This budget is based on the production budget and the planned levels of beginning and ending direct materials inventory.
- **Direct labor budget.** This budget is based on the production budget and shows how much labor is required to produce (or serve) each unit.
- **Manufacturing overhead budget.** This budget is based on the production budget and provides information about expected variable and fixed manufacturing overhead costs.
- **Cost of goods sold budget.** This budget is based on the budgeted manufacturing cost per unit multiplied by budgeted unit sales.
- **Selling and administrative expense budget.** This budget is based on the sales budget and provides information about expected selling and administrative expenses.
- All of the operating budgets can be combined to prepare a **budgeted income statement.**

Prepare the cash budget and describe the relationships among the operating budgets, cash budget, and budgeted balance sheet.   LO 8–4

- The **cash budget** is a future-oriented version of the statement of cash flows. This budget helps managers determine whether they need to borrow money to finance operations or whether they should invest excess cash to earn interest.
- The first step in preparing the cash budget is to prepare a schedule of cash receipts based on the sales budget and an estimate of how and when cash will be received from customers.
- The second step in preparing the cash budget is to prepare a schedule of cash payments for all operating expenses based on when those costs will be paid.
- The final step in preparing the cash budget is to compute the ending balance of the Cash account based on the beginning balance, cash receipts, and cash payments. This helps managers determine whether they need to borrow money to maintain a minimum cash balance.
- The ending balance of cash appears on the **budgeted balance sheet** along with the budgeted balances for all other Asset, Liability, and Equity accounts.

Prepare a merchandise purchases budget for a merchandising firm.   LO 8–5

- Service firms and merchandisers also use budgets to plan and control their operations, though the nature of the budgets will differ.
- The merchandise purchases budget is very similar to the direct materials purchases budget. It is based on the sales budget, plus ending inventory needs, less any beginning inventory.
- All other budgets prepared by a merchandising or services firm are similar to those of a manufacturing firm.

KEY TERMS

Budget p. 353

Budgetary Slack p. 354

Budgeted Balance Sheet p. 356

Budgeted Cost of Goods Sold p. 356

Budgeted Gross Margin p. 356

Budgeted Income Statement p. 355

Budgeted Manufacturing Cost per Unit p. 356

Cash Budget p. 356

Direct Labor Budget p. 356

Direct Materials Purchases Budget p. 356

Financial Budgets p. 356

Long-Term Objective p. 352

Manufacturing Overhead Budget p. 356

Master Budget p. 355

Operating Budgets p. 355

Participative Budgeting p. 354

Production Budget p. 356

Sales Budget p. 356

Sales Forecast p. 356

Selling and Administrative Expense Budget p. 356

Short-Term Objective p. 352

Strategic Plan p. 352

Tactics p. 352

Top-Down Approach p. 354

PRACTICE MATERIAL

QUESTIONS

1. Briefly describe why budgetary planning is important to managers.

2. What role do budgets play in the planning and control cycle?

3. What is a strategic plan and how does it relate to short- and long-term goals?

4. Suppose that your strategic plan is to retire comfortably at the age of 55. List several long-term objectives, short-term objectives, and tactics that would enable you to accomplish this goal.

5. Identify and briefly discuss the benefits of budgeting.

6. Suppose a company chooses not to develop budgets. Describe three potential negative consequences of this decision.

7. What are the advantages and disadvantages of participative budgeting compared to top-down budgeting?

8. What is budgetary slack and why might it be detrimental to a company?

9. Briefly explain how each of the following helps to minimize dysfunctional behaviors caused by budgeting:
   (a) Different budgets for different purposes.
   (b) Continuous budgeting.
   (c) Zero-based budgeting.

10. What is the master budget, and what are its components?

11. Explain why the sales budget is the starting point for a company's budgeting process. Which budgets does the sales budget affect? Which budgets are not affected by the sales budget?

12. What sources does a company utilize to determine its sales forecast? What could happen if one of the sources used is inaccurate?

13. What are the components of the operating budgets?

14. What are the components of the cash budget?

15. How are the operating budgets, cash budget, and the budgeted balance sheet interrelated?

16. Why is the preparation of a cash budget important?

17. In preparing a cash budget, why must an adjustment be made for depreciation expenses?

18. What is the ultimate goal or end result of a company's entire budgeting process?

19. How does the budgeting process differ for a service company compared to a manufacturing company?

20. How is a merchandiser's budgeting process different from that of a manufacturing company?

MULTIPLE CHOICE

1. Budgets help companies
   a. Meet short-term objectives.
   b. Meet long-term objectives.
   c. Both a and b.
   d. None of the above.

2. Which phases of the management process are impacted by budgeting?
   a. Planning.
   b. Directing/leading.
   c. Controlling.
   d. All of the above.

3. Which of the following statements is true?
   a. GAAP requires all companies to prepare budgets.
   b. Only newly formed companies need budgets.
   c. Most service firms prepare production budgets.
   d. Most companies would benefit from budgeting.

4. Shasta Company plans to double its profits in five years. This is an example of a
   a. Long-term objective.   c. Tactic.
   b. Short-term objective.   d. Sales forecast.

5. Which of the following is **not** considered a direct benefit of budgeting?
   a. Better communication.
   b. Motivating employees.
   c. Developing new product lines.
   d. Forcing managers to think ahead.

6. Which of the following budgets would be prepared earliest in a company's budgeting process?
   a. Budgeted income statement.
   b. Budgeted balance sheet.
   c. Direct materials purchases budget.
   d. Production budget.

7. Which of the following budgets is affected by the sales budget?
   a. Direct labor budget.
   b. Cash receipts and payments budget.
   c. Selling and administrative budget.
   d. All of the above.

8. ABC Company expects to sell 100,000 units of its primary product in January. Expected beginning and

ending finished goods inventory for January are 20,000 and 45,000 units, respectively. How many units should ABC produce?

    a. 100,000.   **c.** 75,000.
    b. 125,000.   **d.** 35,000.

9. Which of the following is **not** considered an operating budget?

    a. Cash budget.
    b. Budgeted income statement.
    c. Selling and administrative expense budget.
    d. Direct materials purchases budget.

10. Raya Company is calculating its expected cash receipts for the month of June. This should **not** include

    a. Cash sales made during June.
    b. Credit sales made during May.
    c. Credit sales made during June.
    d. Credit sales made during July.

connect Find More Learning Solutions on Connect.

MINI-EXERCISES

M8–1 Explaining the Role of Managerial Accounting in the Planning and Control Cycle   LO 8–1

Your boss believes that the three management functions of planning, directing/leading, and controlling are unrelated. He also thinks that managerial accounting has no role in any of the functions. Is your boss correct? Explain why or why not.

M8–2 Describing Advantages of Budgetary Planning   LO 8–1

Calypso Cal (CC), which manufactures surfboards, has a "Live today, worry about tomorrow later" motto. In keeping with this philosophy, CC has not set any long-term or short-term objectives or budgets for the company. Describe three potential consequences of CC's philosophy.

M8–3 Matching Terminology   LO 8–1, 8–2, 8–3, 8–4

Match each of the terms by inserting the appropriate definition letter in the space provided. Not all definitions will be used.

_____ **1.** Cash Budget

_____ **2.** Financial Budgets

_____ **3.** Short-Term Objective

_____ **4.** Strategic Plan

_____ **5.** Budgeted Cost of Goods Sold

_____ **6.** Budgeted Balance Sheet

A. A statement that summarizes budgeted sales revenue and expenses for the budget period.

B. A budget showing how many units need to be produced in each budget period.

C. A statement showing the estimated total sales revenue to be generated in each budget period.

D. A statement that shows expected assets, liabilities, and owners' equity at the end of the budget period.

E. A goal that management wants to achieve within one year or less.

F. Budgeted manufacturing cost per unit times the budgeted unit sales.

G. A financial budget providing information about cash receipts and payments.

H. A vision of the organization's achievements over the long term.

I. Budgets that focus on the financial resources needed to support operations.

J. A budget that indicates the quantity of materials, labor, and overhead to be used in production.

M8–4 Classifying Components of Master Budget   LO 8–2

Classify each of the following budgets as an operating (O) or financial (F) budget:

a. Cash budget
b. Sales budget
c. Direct materials purchases budget
d. Selling and administrative expense budget

e. Budgeted balance sheet
f. Manufacturing overhead budget
g. Direct labor budget
h. Budgeted income statement
i. Production budget

LO 8–3a   **M8–5** **Preparing Sales Budget**

Beatrice Company estimates that unit sales of its lawn chairs will be 7,200 in October; 7,400 in November; and 7,100 in December. Prepare Beatrice's sales budget for the fourth quarter assuming each unit sells for $27.50.

LO 8–3c   **M8–6** **Preparing Direct Materials Purchases Budget**

Preston, Inc., manufactures wooden shelving units for collecting and sorting mail. The company expects to produce 480 units in July and 400 units in August. Each unit requires 10 feet of wood at a cost of $1.50 per foot. Preston wants to always have 300 feet of wood on hand in materials inventory. Prepare Preston's direct materials purchases budget for July and August.

LO 8–3d   **M8–7** **Preparing Direct Labor Budget**

Refer to the information in M8–6 for Preston, Inc. Each unit requires 1.75 hours of direct labor, and labor wages average $9 per hour. Prepare Preston's direct labor budget for July and August.

LO 8–3b   **M8–8** **Preparing Production Budget**

Becker Bikes manufactures tricycles. The company expects to sell 350 units in May and 480 units in June. Beginning and ending finished goods for May is expected to be 95 and 60 units, respectively. June's ending finished goods is expected to be 70 units. Prepare Becker's production budget for May and June.

LO 8–3c   **M8–9** **Preparing Direct Materials Purchases Budget**

Refer to the information in M8–8 for Becker Bikes. Each unit requires 3 wheels at a cost of $5 per wheel. Becker requires 20 percent of next month's material production needs on hand each month. July's production units is expected to be 450 units. Prepare Becker's direct materials purchases budget for May and June.

LO 8–3d   **M8–10** **Preparing Direct Labor Budget**

Refer to the information in M8–8 for Becker Bikes. Each unit requires 1.5 direct labor hours and Becker's hourly labor rate is $12 per hour. Prepare Becker's direct labor budget for May and June.

LO 8–3e   **M8–11** **Preparing Manufacturing Overhead Budget**

Refer to the information in M8–8 for Becker Bikes. The company's variable overhead is $2.50 per unit produced and its fixed overhead is $3,000 per month. Prepare Becker's manufacturing overhead budget for May and June.

LO 8–3e   **M8–12** **Preparing Manufacturing Overhead Budget**

Winslow Company expects sales of its financial calculators to be $200,000 in the first quarter and $236,000 in the second quarter. Its variable overhead is approximately 19 percent of sales, and fixed overhead costs are $46,500 per quarter. Prepare Winslow's manufacturing overhead budget for the first two quarters.

LO 8–3g   **M8–13** **Preparing Selling and Administrative Expense Budget**

Fillmore, Inc., expects sales of its housing for electric motors to be $87,000, $81,000, and $92,000 for January, February, and March, respectively. Its variable selling and administrative expenses are 8 percent of sales, and fixed selling and administrative expenses are $11,000 per month. Prepare Fillmore's selling and administrative expense budget for January, February, and March.

LO 8–4   **M8–14** **Preparing Schedule of Cash Receipts**

Getty Company expects sales for the first three months of next year to be $200,000, $235,000, and $298,000, respectively. Getty expects 35 percent of its sales to be cash and the remainder to be credit sales. The credit sales will be collected as follows: 60 percent in the month of the sale and 40 percent in the following month. Prepare a schedule of Getty's cash receipts for the months of February and March.

M8–15 Preparing Cash Payments Budget

LO 8–4

Lindell Company made direct material purchases of $48,000 and $60,000 in September and October, respectively. The company pays 60 percent of its purchases in the month of purchase and 40 percent is paid in the following month. How much cash was paid for purchases in October?

M8–16 Preparing Data for the Cash Budget

LO 8–4

Crew Clothing (CC) sells women's resort casual clothing to high-end department stores and in its own retail boutiques. CC expects sales for January, February, and March to be $450,000, $510,000, and $530,000, respectively. Twenty percent of CC's sales are cash, with the remainder collected evenly over two months. During December, CC's total sales were $760,000. CC is beginning its budget process and has asked for your help in preparing the cash budget. Compute CC's expected cash receipts from customers for each month.

M8–17 Preparing Merchandise Purchases Budget

LO 8–5

Garfield Corp. expects to sell 1,300 units of its pet beds in March and 900 units in April. Each unit sells for $110. Garfield's ending inventory policy is 30 percent of the following month's sales. Garfield pays its supplier $40 per unit. Prepare Garfield's purchases budget for March.

EXERCISES

E8–1 Understanding Behavioral Effects of Budgeting

LO 8–1

Samantha is the production manager for Wentworth Company. Each year, she is involved in the company's budgeting process. Company President Leslie has asked Samantha to submit the facility's budgeted production for the upcoming year. Leslie's typical process is to take the budget that Samantha provides and add 10 percent to it. That amount then becomes Samantha's target production level for the upcoming year. Additionally, Samantha can earn a bonus only if the facility exceeds the budgeted production level.

Required:

1. Explain any incentive Samantha might have to be dishonest with Leslie about the production level she thinks the facility can achieve.

2. Explain the impact Samantha's inaccurate production estimates could have on other company employees.

E8–2 Using Terms to Complete Sentences about Budgets

LO 8–1, 8–2

Use the following terms to complete the sentences that follow. Terms may be used once, more than once, or not at all:

Capital expenditures budget	Rolling budget
Participative	Zero-based budget
Budgetary slack	Directing/leading
Operating budgets	Master budget
Control	Production budget
Planning	Financial budgets
Sales forecast	Cost of goods sold budget
Budgeted income statement	Top-down
Budgeted balance sheet	

1. The _____ is a set of interrelated budgets that constitutes a plan of action for a specific period.

2. The _____ establish goals for the company's sales and production personnel.

3. A(n) _____ approach to budgeting is more likely to motivate people to work toward an organization's goal than a(n) _____ approach.

4. Managers who intentionally understate expected sales or overstate expected expenses are creating _____.

5. Comparing actual results to budgeted plans is an example of management performing its _____ function.

6. The starting point for preparing the master budget is the _____.

7. The _____ provides information about a company's expected revenue, expenses, and profitability for a period of time.

8. Using a(n) _____, when one budget period passes, another is automatically added at the end.

9. The _____ provides information about a company's expected financial position at a specific point in time.

10. Once the _____ has been prepared, the direct materials purchases, the direct labor, and the manufacturing overhead budgets can be prepared.

LO 8–2

E8–3 Classifying, Ordering Components of the Master Budget

Organize the following budgets in order of preparation by placing the number before it. Indicate how each budget would be affected by a sales forecast that is overstated.

_____   Cash budget.

_____   Selling and administrative expense budget.

_____   Manufacturing overhead budget.

_____   Direct materials purchases budget.

_____   Budgeted balance sheet.

_____   Sales budget.

_____   Direct labor budget.

_____   Budgeted income statement.

_____   Budgeted cost of goods sold.

_____   Production budget.

LO 8–3b

E8–4 Calculating Unknowns Based on Production, Sales, Beginning and Ending Inventory Values

Complete the following table:

NUMBER OF UNITS			
Production	Sales	Ending Inventory	Beginning Inventory
?	500	125	75
930	?	90	125
750	710	?	80
900	1,200	85	?
805	?	225	160
845	795	290	?

LO 8–3a, b

E8–5 Calculating Sales and Production Budgets

Shadee Corp. expects to sell 600 sun visors in May and 800 in June. Each visor sells for $18. Shadee's beginning and ending finished goods inventories for May are 75 and 50 units, respectively. Ending finished goods inventory for June will be 60 units.

Required:

1. Prepare Shadee's sales budget for May and June.

2. Prepare Shadee's production budget for May and June.

LO 8–3c, e

E8–6 Preparing Direct Materials Purchases and Manufacturing Overhead Budgets

Refer to the information in E8–5 for Shadee Corp. Each visor requires a total of $4.00 in direct materials that includes an adjustable closure that the company purchases from a supplier at a cost of $1.50 each. Shadee wants to have 30 closures on hand on May 1, 20 closures on May 31, and 25 closures on June 30. Additionally, Shadee's fixed manufacturing overhead is $1,000 per month, and variable manufacturing overhead is $1.25 per unit produced.

Required:

1. Prepare Shadee's May and June direct materials purchases budget for the closures.

2. Prepare Shadee's manufacturing overhead budget for May and June.

E8–7 Preparing Direct Labor Budget

LO 8–3d

Refer to the information in E8–5 for Shadee Corp. Suppose that each visor takes 0.30 direct labor hours to produce and Shadee pays its workers $9 per hour.

Required:

Prepare Shadee's direct labor budget for May and June.

E8–8 Preparing Cost of Goods Sold Budget

LO 8–3f

Refer to E8–5 through E8–7 for Shadee Corp. Use the information and solutions presented to complete the requirements.

Required:

1. Determine Shadee's budgeted manufacturing cost per visor. (**Note:** Assume that fixed overhead per unit is $2.)

2. Prepare Shadee's budgeted cost of goods sold for May and June.

E8–9 Preparing Selling and Administrative Expense Budget

LO 8–3g

In addition to the information in E8–5 through E8–8 regarding Shadee Corp., the following data are available:
- Selling costs are expected to be 6 percent of sales.
- Fixed administrative expenses per month total $1,200.

Required:

Prepare Shadee's selling and administrative expense budget for May and June.

E8–10 Preparing Budgeted Income Statement

LO 8–3h

Use the information and solutions from E8–5 through E8–9 for Shadee Corp.

Required:

Prepare Shadee's budgeted income statement for the months of May and June.

E8–11 Calculating Cash Receipts

LO 8–4

Refer to information in E8–5 for Shadee Corp. It expects the following unit sales for the third quarter:

July	625
August	490
September	450

Sixty percent of Shadee's sales are cash. Of the credit sales, 50 percent is collected in the month of the sale, 45 percent is collected during the following month, and 5 percent is never collected.

Required:

Calculate Shadee's total cash receipts for August and September.

E8–12 Preparing Production, Direct Materials Purchases Budgets

LO 8–3b, c

Croy Inc. has the following projected sales for the next five months:

Month	Sales in Units
April	3,850
May	3,875
June	4,260
July	4,135
August	3,590

Croy's finished goods inventory policy is to have 60 percent of the next month's sales on hand at the end of each month. Direct materials cost $3.10 per pound, and each unit requires 2 pounds. Direct materials inventory policy is to have 50 percent of the next month's production needs on hand at the end of each month. Direct materials on hand at March 31 totaled 3,865 pounds.

Required:

1. Prepare a production budget for April, May, and June.

2. Prepare a direct materials purchases budget for April and May.

LO 8–3d   **E8–13 Preparing Direct Labor Budget**

Alleyway Corp. manufactures two styles of leather bowling bag, the Strike and Turkey. Budgeted production levels for October follow:

	Strike	Turkey
Production	2,500 bags	3,250 bags

Two departments, Cutting and Sewing, produce the bowling bags. Direct labor hours needed for each style are as follows:

	Cutting	Sewing
Strike	0.1 hour per bag	0.3 hour per bag
Turkey	0.2 hour per bag	0.5 hour per bag

Hourly direct labor rates are $15 for the Cutting Department and $12 for Sewing.

Required:

Prepare Alleyway's direct labor budget for October.

LO 8–3g   **E8–14 Preparing Selling and Administrative Expense Budget**

The following information is available for Pioneer Company:
- Sales price per unit is $95.

- November and December, sales were budgeted at 3,100 and 3,600 units, respectively.

- Variable costs are 11 percent of sales (6 percent commission, 2 percent advertising, 3 percent shipping).

- Fixed costs per month are sales salaries, $5,000; office salaries, $2,500; depreciation, $2,500; building rent, $3,500; insurance, $1,500; and utilities, $800.

Required:

Prepare Pioneer's selling and administrative expense budgets for November and December.

LO 8–3h   **E8–15 Preparing Budgeted Income Statement**

Ceder Company has compiled the following data for the upcoming year:
- Sales are expected to be 15,000 units at $41.00 each.

- Each unit requires 2 pounds of direct materials at $2.00 per pound.

- Each unit requires 1.5 hours of direct labor at $15.00 per hour.

- Manufacturing overhead is $3.00 per unit.

- Beginning direct materials inventory is $3,500.00.

- Ending direct materials inventory is $4,100.00.

- Selling and administrative costs totaled $135,870.00.

Required:

1. Prepare Ceder's cost of goods sold budget.

2. Prepare Ceder's budgeted income statement.

E8–16 **Preparing Cash Budget**   LO 8–4

Walter Company has the following information for the month of March:

Cash balance, March 1	$16,320
Collections from customers	36,450
Paid to suppliers	22,300
Manufacturing overhead	6,100
Direct labor	8,250
Selling and administrative expenses	4,200

Walter pays wages and other cash expenses in the month incurred. Manufacturing overhead includes $1,200 for machinery depreciation, but the amount for selling and administrative expenses is exclusive of depreciation. Additionally, Walter also expects to buy a piece of property for $7,000 during March. Walter can borrow in increments of $1,000 and would like to maintain a minimum cash balance of $10,000.

Required:

Prepare Walter's cash budget for the month of March.

E8–17 **Calculating Cash Receipts**   LO 8–4

McFarland Company makes 60 percent of its sales in cash. Credit sales are collected as follows: 60 percent in the month of sale and 40 percent in the month following the sale.
    McFarland's budgeted sales for upcoming months follow:

June	$22,500
July	25,000
August	23,000
September	21,000

Required:

Compute McFarland's expected cash receipts for August.

E8–18 **Preparing Cash Receipts and Cash Payments Budgets**   LO 8–4

Martin Clothing Company is a retail company that sells hiking and other outdoor gear specially made for the desert heat. It sells to individuals as well as local companies that coordinate adventure getaways in the desert for tourists. The following information is available for several months of the current year:

Month	Sales	Purchases	Cash Expenses Paid
May	$120,000	$ 90,000	$24,000
June	115,000	95,000	31,000
July	160,000	150,000	38,250
August	145,000	80,000	34,700

The majority of Martin's sales (70 percent) are cash, but a few of the excursion companies purchase on credit. Of the credit sales, 40 percent are collected in the month of sale and 60 percent are collected in the following month. All of Martin's purchases are on account with 55 percent paid in the month of purchase and 45 percent paid the following month.

Required:

1. Prepare a schedule of cash receipts for July and August.
2. Prepare a schedule of cash payments for July and August.

LO 8–5 **E8–19** **Preparing a Merchandise Purchases Budget**

Shamrock Shades operates in mall kiosks throughout the southwestern United States. Shamrock purchases sunglasses from bulk discounters and sells the sunglasses in the mall kiosks. Shamrock is in the process of budgeting for the coming year and has projected sales of $400,000 for January, $480,000 for February, $640,000 for March, and $680,000 for April. Shamrock's desired ending inventory is 25 percent of the following month's cost of goods sold. Cost of goods sold is expected to be 40 percent of sales.

Required:

Compute the required purchases for each month of the first quarter (January through March).

LO 8–3h, 8–5 **E8–20** **Preparing a Merchandise Purchases Budget and a Budgeted Income Statement**

Citrus Girl Company (CGC) purchases quality citrus produce from local growers and sells the produce via the Internet across the United States. To keep costs down, CGC maintains a warehouse, but no showroom or retail sales outlets. CGC has the following information for the second quarter of the year:

1. Expected monthly sales for April, May, June, and July are $220,000, $190,000, $310,000, and $90,000, respectively.
2. Cost of goods sold is 30 percent of expected sales.
3. CGC's desired ending inventory is 20 percent of the following month's cost of goods sold.
4. Monthly operating expenses are estimated to be:
   - Salaries: $30,000.
   - Delivery expense: 4 percent of monthly sales.
   - Rent expense on the warehouse: $4,500.
   - Utilities: $800.
   - Insurance: $175.
   - Other expenses: $260.

Required:

1. Prepare the merchandise purchases budget for each month in the second quarter.
2. Prepare a budgeted income statement for each month in the second quarter.

LO 8–3b, c **E8–21** **Preparing Production and Direct Materials Purchases Budgets**

Galactic Inc. manufactures flying drone toys. Sales units for January, February, March, April and May were 300, 280, 352, 312, and 380 respectively.

Required:

1. The company's policy for ending finished goods is 25 percent of next month's sales. Prepare a production budget for the first quarter.
2. The drone toy includes 2 LED lights, which cost $15 each. The company requires ending direct materials to be 20 percent of next month's materials requirement. Prepare a direct materials purchases budget for the first quarter.

LO 8–3d, e **E8–22** **Preparing the Direct Labor and Manufacturing Overhead Budgets**

Refer to the information in E8–21 for Galactic Inc. Each unit requires 3 direct labor hours and Galactic's hourly labor rate is $15 per hour. The company's variable overhead is $4.00 per unit produced and its fixed overhead is $5,500 per month.

Required:

1. Prepare Galactic's direct labor budget for the first quarter.
2. Prepare Galactic's manufacturing overhead budget for the first quarter.

LO 8–3f **E8–23** **Cost of Goods Sold Budget**

Refer to the information in E8–21 through E8–22 for Galactic Inc. Use the information and solutions presented to complete the requirements.

Required:

1. Determine Galactic's budgeted manufacturing cost per drone. (**Note:** assume that fixed overhead per unit is $17.75.)

2. Prepare Galactic's budgeted cost of goods sold for January and February.

E8–24 Determining Balances for a Budgeted Balance Sheet   LO 8–4

Paul's Pool Service provides pool cleaning, chemical application, and pool repairs for residential customers. Clients are billed weekly for services provided and usually pay 60 percent of their fees in the month the service is provided. In the month following service, Paul collects 35 percent of service fees. The final 5 percent is collected in the second month following service. Paul purchases his supplies on credit, and pays 50 percent in the month of purchase and the remaining 50 percent in the month following purchase. Of the supplies Paul purchases, 85 percent is used in the month of purchase, and the remainder is used in the month following purchase.

   The following information is available for the months of June, July, and August, which are Paul's busiest months:

- June 1 cash balance $14,600.

- June 1 supplies on hand $3,800.

- June 1 accounts receivable $8,000.

- June 1 accounts payable $3,700.

- Estimated sales for June, July, and August are $24,000, $36,000, and $38,000, respectively.

- Sales during May were $22,000, and sales during April were $16,000.

- Estimated purchases for June, July, and August are $9,000, $17,000, and $12,000, respectively.

- Purchases in May were $5,000.

Required:

1. Prepare budgeted cash receipts and budgeted cash payments for each month.

2. Compute the balances necessary to prepare a budgeted balance sheet for August 31 for each of the following accounts:

- Cash
- Supplies Inventory
- Accounts Receivable
- Accounts Payable

GROUP A PROBLEMS

PA8–1 Preparing Operating Budgets   LO 8–3a, b, c, d, e, f, g

Iguana, Inc., manufactures bamboo picture frames that sell for $25 each. Each frame requires 4 linear feet of bamboo, which costs $2.00 per foot. Each frame takes approximately 30 minutes to build, and the labor rate averages $12.00 per hour. Iguana has the following inventory policies:

   Ending finished goods inventory should be 40 percent of next month's sales.

   Ending direct materials inventory should be 30 percent of next month's production.

Expected unit sales (frames) for the upcoming months follow:

March	275
April	250
May	300
June	400
July	375
August	425

Variable manufacturing overhead is incurred at a rate of $0.30 per unit produced. Annual fixed manufacturing overhead is estimated to be $7,200 ($600 per month) for expected production of 4,000 units for the year. Selling and administrative expenses are estimated at $650 per month plus $0.60 per unit sold.

Required:

Prepare the following for Iguana, Inc., for the second quarter (April, May, and June). Include each month as well as the quarter 2 total for each budget.

1. Sales budget.
2. Production budget.
3. Direct materials purchases budget.
4. Direct labor budget.
5. Manufacturing overhead budget.
6. Budgeted cost of goods sold.
7. Selling and administrative expenses budget.

LO 8–3h   **PA8–2 Preparing Budgeted Income Statement**

Refer to the information in PA8–1.

Required:

Prepare Iguana's budgeted income statement for quarter 2.

LO 8–4   **PA8–3 Preparing Cash Budget**

Refer to the information in PA8–1. Iguana, Inc., had $10,800 cash on hand on April 1. Of its sales, 80 percent is in cash. Of the credit sales, 50 percent is collected during the month of the sale, and 50 percent is collected during the month following the sale.

Of direct materials purchases, 80 percent is paid for during the month purchased and 20 percent is paid in the following month. Direct materials purchases for March 1 totaled $2,000. All other operating costs are paid during the month incurred. Monthly fixed manufacturing overhead includes $150 in depreciation. During April, Iguana plans to pay $3,000 for a piece of equipment.

Required:

Prepare the following for Iguana for quarter 2:

1. Budgeted cash receipts. Include each month (April to June) as well as quarter 2 totals.
2. Budgeted cash payments.
3. Cash budget. Assume the company can borrow in increments of $1,000 to maintain a $10,000 minimum cash balance. No interest is charged if the loan is paid off by the end of the next quarter.

LO 8–3a, b, c, d   **PA8–4 Preparing Operating Budget Components**

Wesley Power Tools manufactures a wide variety of tools and accessories. One of its more popular items is a cordless power handisaw. Each handisaw sells for $44. Wesley expects the following unit sales:

January	2,000
February	2,200
March	2,700
April	2,500
May	1,900

Wesley's ending finished goods inventory policy is 30 percent of the next month's sales.

Suppose each handisaw takes approximately 0.75 hours to manufacture, and Wesley pays an average labor wage of $18 per hour.

Each handisaw requires a plastic housing that Wesley purchases from a supplier at a cost of $7.00 each. The company has an ending direct materials inventory policy of 25 percent of the following month's production requirements. Materials other than the housing unit total $4.50 per handisaw.

Manufacturing overhead for this product includes $72,900 annual fixed overhead (based on production of 27,000 units) and $1.20 per unit variable manufacturing overhead. Wesley's selling expenses are 7 percent of sales dollars, and administrative expenses are fixed at $18,000 per month.

Required:

Prepare the following for the first quarter:

1. Sales budget.
2. Production budget.
3. Direct materials purchases budget for the plastic housings.
4. Direct labor budget.

PA8–5 Preparing Operating Budget Components

LO 8–3f, g, h

Refer to the information presented in PA8–4 regarding Wesley Power Tools.

Required:

Prepare the following for the first quarter:

1. Cost of goods sold budget.
2. Selling and administrative expense budget.
3. Budgeted income statement for the handisaw product.

PA8–6 Preparing Operating Budgets for a Merchandising Firm

LO 8–5

Red Canyon T-shirt Company operates a chain of T-shirt shops in the southwestern United States. The sales manager has provided a sales forecast for the coming year, along with the following information:

	Quarter 1	Quarter 2	Quarter 3	Quarter 4
Budgeted unit sales	40,000	60,000	30,000	60,000

- Each T-shirt is expected to sell for $15.
- The purchasing manager buys the T-shirts for $6 each.
- The company needs to have enough T-shirts on hand at the end of each quarter to fill 25 percent of the next quarter's sales demand.
- Selling and administrative expenses are budgeted at $80,000 per quarter plus 10 percent of total sales revenue.

Required:

Prepare the following operating budgets for quarters 1, 2, and 3. (You do not have enough information to complete quarter 4.)

1. Sales budget.
2. Merchandise purchases budget.
3. Cost of goods sold budget.
4. Selling and administrative expense budget.
5. Budgeted income statement.

GROUP B PROBLEMS

PB8–1 Preparing Operating Budgets

LO 8–3a, b, c, d, e, f, g

Beach Wind Company manufactures kites that sell for $20 each. Each kite requires 2 yards of lightweight canvas, which costs $0.60 per yard. Each kite takes approximately 30 minutes to build, and the labor rate averages $8 per hour. Beach Wind has the following inventory policies:

Ending finished goods inventory should be 30 percent of next month's sales.
Ending direct materials inventory should be 20 percent of next month's production.

Expected kite sales for the upcoming months are:

March	850
April	700
May	650
June	720
July	830
August	760

Variable manufacturing overhead is incurred at a rate of $0.40 per unit produced. Annual fixed manufacturing overhead is estimated to be $9,000 ($750 per month) for expected production of 9,000 units for the year. Selling and administrative expenses are estimated at $820 per month plus $0.75 per unit sold.

Required:

Prepare the following for Beach Wind for the second quarter (April, May, and June). Include each month as well as the quarter 2 total in each budget.

1. Sales budget.
2. Production budget.
3. Direct materials purchases budget.
4. Direct labor budget.
5. Manufacturing overhead budget.
6. Budgeted cost of goods sold.
7. Selling and administrative expenses budget.

LO 8–3h   **PB8–2** **Preparing Budgeted Income Statement**

Refer to the information in PB8–1.

Required:

Prepare Beach Wind's budgeted income statement for quarter 2.

LO 8–4   **PB8–3** **Preparing Cash Budget**

Refer to the information in PB8–1. Beach Wind Company had $12,200 cash on hand on April 1. Of its sales, 60 percent is cash. Of the credit sales, 50 percent is collected during the month of the sale and 50 percent is collected during the month following the sale.

Of direct materials purchases, 60 percent is paid for during the month purchased, and 40 percent is paid in the following month. Direct materials purchases for March totaled $800. All other operating costs are paid during the month incurred. Monthly fixed manufacturing overhead includes $280 in depreciation. Beach Wind plans to spend $15,000 on equipment during April.

Required:

Prepare the following for quarter 2:

1. Budgeted cash receipts. Include each month (April to June) as well as quarter 2 totals.
2. Budgeted cash payments.
3. Cash budget. Assume the company can borrow in increments of $1,000 to maintain a minimum cash balance of $10,000. No interest is charged if the loan is paid off by the end of the next quarter.

LO 8–3a, b, c, d   **PB8–4** **Preparing Operating Budget Components**

Boscoe Power Tools manufactures a wide variety of tools and accessories. One of its more popular craft-related items is the cord free glue gun. Each glue gun sells for $30. Boscoe expects the following unit sales:

January	8,000
February	7,400
March	8,700
April	9,500
May	9,150

Boscoe's ending finished goods inventory policy is 25 percent of the following month's budgeted sales.

Suppose each glue gun takes approximately 0.5 hours to manufacture, and Boscoe pays an average labor wage of $18 per hour.

Each glue gun requires a heating element that Boscoe purchases from a supplier at a cost of $1.25 each. The company has an ending direct materials inventory policy of 30 percent of the following month's production requirements. Materials other than the heating elements total $3.25 per glue gun.

Manufacturing overhead for this product includes $96,900 annual fixed overhead (based on production of 102,000 units) and variable manufacturing overhead of $1.00 per unit. Boscoe's selling expenses are 5 percent of sales dollars, and administrative expenses for this product are fixed at $17,500 per month.

Required:

Prepare the following for the first quarter:

1. Sales budget.
2. Production budget.
3. Direct materials purchases budget for the heating element.
4. Direct labor budget.

PB8–5 Preparing Operating Budgets Components

LO 8–3f, g, h

Refer to the information presented in PB8–4 regarding Boscoe Power Tools.

Required:

Prepare the following for the first quarter:

1. Cost of goods sold budget.
2. Selling and administrative expense budget.
3. Budgeted income statement for the glue gun product.

PB8–6 Preparing Operating Budgets for a Merchandising Firm

LO 8–5

Blue Skies T-shirt Company operates a chain of T-shirt shops in the northeastern United States. The sales manager has provided a sales forecast for the coming year, along with the following information:

	Quarter 1	Quarter 2	Quarter 3	Quarter 4
Budgeted unit sales	50,000	70,000	45,000	65,000

- Each T-shirt is expected to sell for $20.
- The purchasing manager buys the T-shirts for $8 each.
- The company needs to have enough T-shirts on hand at the end of each quarter to fill 30 percent of the next quarter's sales demand.
- Selling and administrative expenses are budgeted at $60,000 per quarter plus 15 percent of total sales revenue.

Required:

Prepare the following operating budgets for quarters 1, 2, and 3. (You do not have enough information to complete quarter 4.)

1. Sales budget.
2. Merchandise purchases budget.
3. Cost of goods sold budget.
4. Selling and administrative expense budget.
5. Budgeted income statement.

SKILLS DEVELOPMENT CASES

LO 8–1   **S8–1   Interviewing, Writing a Real-World Budget Process Report**

Budgets can be used in almost any type of organization including large corporations, small businesses, government organizations, universities, churches, and student clubs.

Required:

Choose any local organization and interview two people who are involved in its budget process. Try to choose one person who actually worked on preparing the budget (e.g., an accountant or the treasurer) and another person who is affected by the budget (e.g., a person in charge of spending the budget, or an employee who is evaluated based on his or her ability to meet budgetary goals).

1. Based on your interviews, write a brief description of the budgeting process within this organization. The description should be a factual account of the steps taken to develop and distribute the budget without any qualitative evaluations of the process. You should identify the type of budgeting (top-down or participative) and the personnel involved in the budgeting process as well as any recent and/or anticipated adjustments to the process and the overall importance management places on budgets.

2. Separately consider each of the people you interviewed. How satisfied does each seem with the organization's budgeting process? What step(s) of the process were they the most and least satisfied with? Did either of your interviewees identify a particular step of the process that has been troublesome?

3. Suppose the organization you investigated has retained you as a consultant. Based on the information compiled from the organization and your knowledge from this course, what recommendations would you make to this organization regarding its budgeting process?

LO 8–1   **S8–2   Researching Online Budget Tools**

Numerous personal financial planning or budgeting tools are available on the Internet, many of them free. Choose at least two different online budgeting sites and input information for a typical person of your age. (**Note:** You may either create a fictitious profile or use your own personal information. If you choose to use your personal data, be sure to read the sites' privacy policies.)

Required:

1. Use each tool to develop a monthly budget.

2. Compare and contrast the two online budgeting tools. Do you prefer aspects of one over the other? Are there things that you dislike? Explain.

3. How helpful do you think such tools are in personal financial management? What are the pros and cons?

9

Standard Costing and Variance Analysis

CHAPTER NINE

YOUR LEARNING OBJECTIVES

LO 9–1 Describe the standard-setting process and explain how standard costs relate to budgets and variances.

LO 9–2 Prepare a flexible budget and show how total costs change with sales volume.

LO 9–3 Calculate and interpret the direct materials price and quantity variances.

LO 9–4 Calculate and interpret the direct labor rate and efficiency variances.

LO 9–5 Calculate and interpret the variable overhead rate and efficiency variances.

LO 9–S1 Calculate and interpret the fixed overhead spending and volume variances.

LO 9–S2 Prepare journal entries to record direct materials and direct labor variances.

©andresr/Getty Images

The previous chapter described the role of budgets in the planning and control cycle. This chapter illustrates the use of variances in the control phase of that process. A **variance** is simply the difference between actual and budgeted results. Variances act as signals to managers that their planned results are (or are not) being achieved.

Think about an air traffic control system. Before takeoff, the pilot must file a flight plan that describes where the plane is going and how it will get there. The flight plan is similar to the role of a budget in business. The budget states where the business is heading and how managers plan to get it there. All of the signals that guide pilots during the flight serve as control mechanisms. Just as the pilot uses the plane's instrument panel to monitor the plane's progress, managers keep a close eye on key indicators, including variances, to determine whether the business is on track to achieve its plan. If it veers too far off course, managers need a signal that they should take corrective action.

In the last chapter, you began the study of the planning and control cycle by preparing a master budget for a hypothetical division of Levi Strauss & Co. In this chapter, we continue this example by calculating cost variances for direct materials, direct labor, and manufacturing overhead. We also discuss how to prepare a different kind of budget, the flexible budget, which serves as a benchmark for evaluating performance. First, you need to become familiar with standard cost systems, the basis for these budgets and variances.

Standard cost systems	Variable cost variances
• Ideal versus attainable standards • Types of standards • Standard cost card • The flexible budget • Variance analysis • Favorable or unfavorable variances	• Direct materials variances • Direct labor variances • Variable manufacturing overhead variances • Summary of variable cost variances

Standard Cost Systems

Learning Objective 9–1
Describe the standard-setting process and explain how standard costs relate to budgets and variances.

In previous chapters, we discussed several different types of cost systems, including job order vs. process costing (Chapters 2 and 3), activity-based costing vs. volume-based costing (Chapter 4), and full absorption vs. variable costing (Chapter 5). These systems differed in terms of the nature of the product or service, how indirect costs were assigned to products/services, and whether the information would be used by internal or external users. In this chapter, we introduce yet another type of cost system called a standard cost system.

There are three types of cost systems that record either actual or standard costs:

- **Actual cost system**: In an actual cost system, all costs are recorded at actual amounts. Although this method is very simple, we often don't know the actual cost until after an expense has been incurred, too late for managers to use the information to make decisions. As a result, actual cost systems are rarely used in practice.

- **Normal cost system**: In a "normal" cost system, direct materials and direct labor are recorded at actual amounts, while manufacturing overhead costs are applied to products or services using one or more predetermined overhead rates. At the end of the period, any difference in actual and applied manufacturing overhead is closed to Cost of Goods Sold (in most cases) to adjust from applied to actual cost. This method was described in detail in Chapter 2.

- **Standard cost system**: In a standard cost system, all costs are applied to products or services based on preset standards. Unlike normal costing, where only manufacturing overhead costs are based on estimated rates, standard costing establishes preset standards for **all** manufacturing costs, including direct materials, direct labor, and manufacturing overhead. The difference in actual and standard cost is called a variance, and serves as an important signal to managers about whether the standards are being met. At the end of the budget period, the variances are typically closed to Cost of Goods Sold to adjust from standard to actual cost.

Standard cost systems are frequently used in practice, particularly in well-established businesses such as Levi Strauss that are able to specify, in advance, what **should** be spent on direct materials, direct labor, and manufacturing overhead. The use of standards helps maintain consistency and quality in the production process. It also helps managers budget and control costs. Fast-food companies such as McDonald's have perfected the use of standard cost systems, which explains why a Big Mac tastes virtually the same at any location around the globe.

In a standard cost system, managers establish standards or benchmarks for every aspect of the production process, including the price that **should** be paid for direct materials, how much material **should** be used to make each unit, how much **should** be paid for direct labor, and how much time it **should** take to make the product. A standard cost system integrates these standards into the managerial accounting system to help managers plan (budget) and control spending.

IDEAL VERSUS ATTAINABLE STANDARDS

Standards can be set at varying levels of difficulty or attainability. The most extreme case is an **ideal standard**, or one that can be achieved under perfect or ideal conditions. An example is the performance standard of a world-class athlete, such as a 4-minute mile. Standards that are almost impossible to achieve are unlikely to motivate most people to try to achieve them. At the other end of the spectrum is an **easily attainable standard**, or one that can be met without much effort. Research suggests that **tight but attainable standards**—the happy medium between these two extremes—are best for motivating individuals to work hard to achieve results.

What these general guidelines mean to a particular business depends on the type of task and the person performing it. Imagine, for example, that you just started training for a 10-kilometer charity run. You can run a 10-minute mile but would like to improve your running time. It would be unrealistic to set a 4-minute mile as your performance standard because most people are not physically capable of achieving that ideal standard. What standard would motivate you to train hard without being so difficult that it would cause you to give up? This type of standard is sometimes called a *stretch goal*—one you must stretch yourself to achieve. Similarly, organizations should set standard costs that are difficult but not impossible to achieve. To foster continuous improvement, the standards should increase in difficulty over time, just as you would decrease your target running time as your strength and training improve.

COACH'S TIP

Managers should set standards that allow a reasonable amount of downtime for preventive maintenance, employee breaks, training, and the like. Failure to build these factors into the standards can reduce performance over the long run because of dissatisfied customers, low employee morale, and high turnover rates.

TYPES OF STANDARDS

Standard cost systems rely on two types of standards, quantity standards and price standards, as illustrated by the following examples:

	Definition	Examples
Quantity standard	The amount of input that should be used in each unit of product or service	Number of ounces of aluminum in a Coca Cola can Number of tons of steel in a Ford F-150 truck Number of yards of denim in a pair of Levi jeans
Price standard	The price that should be paid for a specific quantity of input	Price per ounce of aluminum Price per ton of steel Price per yard of denim

Notice that these direct materials standards are stated in terms of the quantity and price of the **input** (ounces, tons, or yards) that **should** be required to create a single unit of output. Similar quantity and price standards are developed for direct labor and other inputs. The quantity standard for direct labor is the amount of time (in hours, minutes, or seconds) that workers **should** take to produce a single unit of product. The price standard for labor, called the **standard labor rate**, is the expected hourly cost of labor including employee taxes and benefits.

As mentioned previously, we calculate variances by comparing actual costs to budgeted or standard costs. It's not unusual to use the terms *standard* and *budget* interchangeably, but they have slightly different meanings. Standards are expressed at a very detailed level to reflect the cost and quantity of the **inputs** that go into a product or service, such as the amount of flour needed to make a cake. A budget, on the other hand, is the dollar amount we expect to spend to achieve a given level of **output**. In other words, a budget depends not only on the standard amount of input but also on the level of output, such as the number of cakes you plan to make. As you will see shortly, we can develop budgets for different levels of output, but the standards used in the budgets remain the same.

EXHIBIT 9–1	Standard Cost Card for 441 Jeans

Manufacturing Costs	Standard Quantity	Standard Price (Rate)	Standard Unit Cost
Direct materials (denim)	2 yards per unit	$1.50 per yard	$3.00
Direct labor	0.25 hrs. per unit	$14.00 per hr.	3.50
Variable overhead (40% of direct labor cost)	0.25 hrs. per unit	$5.60 per hr.	1.40
Fixed overhead ($30,000 ÷ 15,000 units)			2.00
Standard manufacturing cost per unit			$9.90

COACH'S TIP

Take a careful look at this standard cost card as we will use these numbers throughout the chapter. How much denim should be used in each pair of jeans? How much should a yard of denim cost? How much time should it take to make a pair of jeans? What is the standard labor rate? How is variable manufacturing overhead applied? What about fixed manufacturing overhead?

STANDARD COST CARD

The standard costs are summarized on a **standard cost card**, a form that shows the standard cost of all the inputs required to make the product. The **standard unit cost** is the expected cost to produce one unit based on standard prices and quantities. For variable costs, we calculate the standard unit cost by multiplying the standard price by the standard quantity of each input. Exhibit 9–1 shows a hypothetical standard cost card for Levi Strauss 441 jeans.

According to the standard cost card, it should take 2 yards of denim to make a pair of 441 jeans. The standard price of denim is $1.50 per yard, which results in a standard unit cost for direct materials of $3.00 (2 yards × $1.50 per yard).

The direct labor standard says it should take 0.25 hours (15 minutes) to make a pair of 441 jeans. The standard labor rate (including taxes and benefits) is $14.00 per hour, which makes the standard unit cost for direct labor $3.50 ($14.00 × 0.25 hours).

Variable overhead costs such as indirect materials (thread, rivets, and zippers), indirect labor (supervision), and power to the run machines are applied at a rate equal to 40 percent of direct labor cost. The standard direct labor rate was $14.00 per hour, so the standard variable overhead rate is 40 percent of $14.00, or $5.60 per hour. Because direct labor is the cost driver for variable overhead, the standard quantity is the number of direct labor hours required per unit (0.25 hours). Multiplying the standard variable overhead rate by the standard quantity of labor hours gives a standard unit cost for variable overhead of $1.40 ($5.60 × 0.25).

Budgeted fixed manufacturing overhead of $30,000 is spread over estimated production of 15,000 units per month, resulting in a fixed manufacturing overhead rate of $2.00 per unit. Fixed manufacturing overhead costs are analyzed differently than variable costs in a standard cost system. The detailed variances for fixed manufacturing overhead costs are covered in Supplement 9A.

Adding the standard cost for all of the inputs together, we arrive at a standard unit manufacturing cost of $9.90 ($3.00 + $3.50 + $1.40 + $2.00). According to the standard cost card, this is what it **should cost** to produce one pair of 441 jeans. In the next section, we will compare the standard cost for each of these inputs to the **actual cost**, a process called variance analysis. But first, we need to create a more meaningful benchmark of comparison called the flexible budget.

THE FLEXIBLE BUDGET

Learning Objective 9–2
Prepare a flexible budget and show how total costs change with sales volume.

In the last chapter, we created a master budget for a hypothetical division of Levi Strauss & Co. The starting point for preparing the master budget was the sales forecast, or managers' best estimate of future sales. The sales forecast affected all other components of the master budget, including the production budget, the direct materials purchases budget, the direct labor budget, the manufacturing overhead budget, and the selling and administrative expense budget.

The master budget is an example of a **static budget**—that is, a budget that is based on a single (fixed) estimate of volume. While the master budget is useful for planning purposes, it may not be a good benchmark for evaluating performance after the fact if the sales forecast is incorrect. If the sales forecast is wrong, the entire master budget will be wrong. So we may need to adjust the budget for different levels of volume by preparing a flexible budget.

A **flexible budget** is a revised budget that shows how budgeted costs will change if volume changes. It is still a budget in the sense that it is an *estimate* of spending as opposed to actual cost. In a flexible budget, total variable costs will be adjusted up or down as volume changes. Total fixed costs, however, should remain the same regardless of volume.

For this chapter, assume that the master budget for Levi Strauss was based on producing and selling 15,000 pairs of jeans per month. For simplicity, we assume that production and sales are equal, so there is no change in finished goods inventory. How would the budget change if only 10,000 units were produced? What costs would change if 20,000 units were produced?

Exhibit 9–2 shows the master and flexible budgets for Levi Strauss based on the standard costs card previously developed.

Keep the following key points in mind when preparing a flexible budget:

1. Both the master budget and the flexible budget are based on standard costs. The standard unit costs are multiplied by different numbers of units to show how total cost will change as volume changes.

2. **Total** variable costs will change based on the volume in a flexible budget; however, **total** fixed costs will remain the same.

Managers can use the flexible budget as part of the planning process to predict how the budget will change under various scenarios, such as a "worst case" or "best case" scenario. They can also use the flexible budget as a benchmark for evaluating performance *after the fact,* or

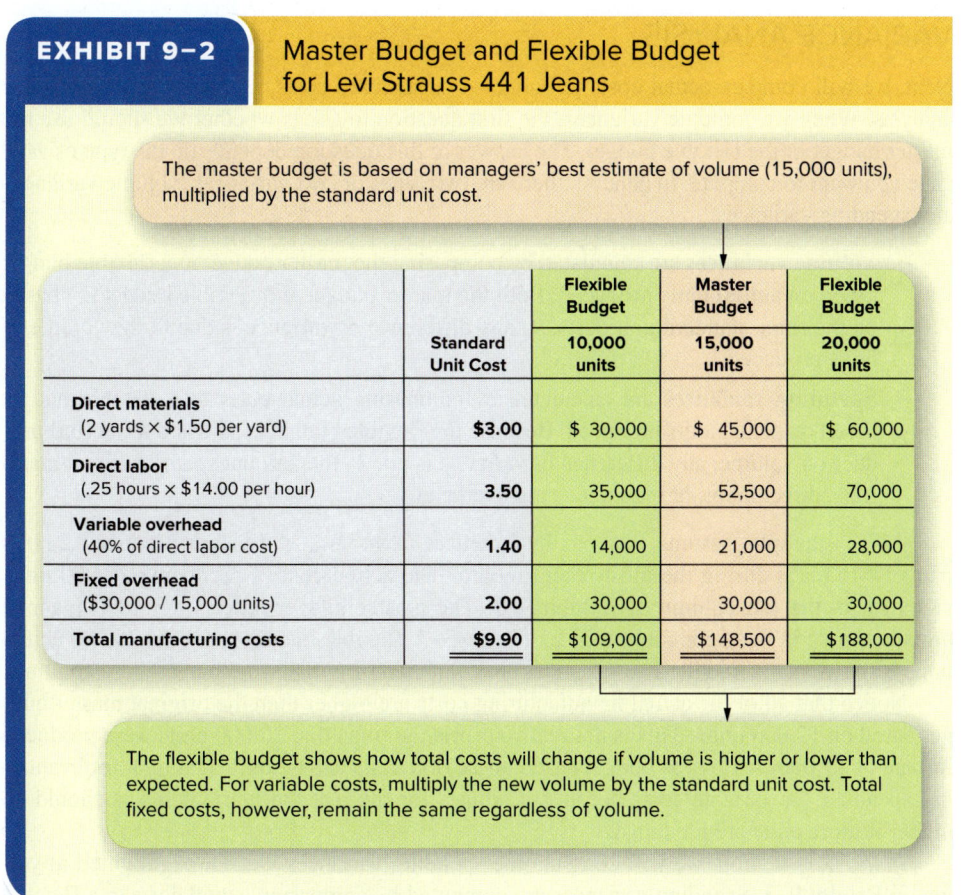

EXHIBIT 9–2 **Master Budget and Flexible Budget for Levi Strauss 441 Jeans**

The master budget is based on managers' best estimate of volume (15,000 units), multiplied by the standard unit cost.

	Standard Unit Cost	Flexible Budget 10,000 units	Master Budget 15,000 units	Flexible Budget 20,000 units
Direct materials (2 yards × $1.50 per yard)	$3.00	$ 30,000	$ 45,000	$ 60,000
Direct labor (.25 hours × $14.00 per hour)	3.50	35,000	52,500	70,000
Variable overhead (40% of direct labor cost)	1.40	14,000	21,000	28,000
Fixed overhead ($30,000 / 15,000 units)	2.00	30,000	30,000	30,000
Total manufacturing costs	$9.90	$109,000	$148,500	$188,000

The flexible budget shows how total costs will change if volume is higher or lower than expected. For variable costs, multiply the new volume by the standard unit cost. Total fixed costs, however, remain the same regardless of volume.

COACH'S TIP

Notice that only total variable costs change in the flexible budget. Total fixed costs remain the same, regardless of volume.

as part of the control process. The remainder of this chapter focuses on the use of flexible budgets as part of the budgetary control process.

Before we continue, complete the following Self-Study Practice to make sure you understand how to prepare a flexible budget.

 How's it going?   Self-Study Practice

Assume that Papa John's standard unit cost and master budget for 20,000 units are as follows:

	Standard Unit Cost	Master Budget (20,000 units)	Flexible Budget (25,000 units)
1. Pizza dough	$0.80	$16,000	
2. Pizza sauce	0.20	4,000	
3. Direct labor	1.00	20,000	
4. Variable manufacturing overhead	0.25	5,000	
5. Fixed manufacturing overhead	0.50	10,000	
	$2.75	$55,000	

Prepare a flexible budget for 25,000 units and enter the amounts in the Flexible Budget column.

After you have finished, check your answers against the solutions in the margin.

VARIANCE ANALYSIS

Next, we will compare actual costs to budgeted or standard costs, a process called variance analysis. When we compute variances, the first question to ask is whether we should use the master budget or the flexible budget. The answer to this question depends on the type of variance you want to compute. In general, there are two types of cost variances: volume variances and spending variances.

- **Volume variances** are calculated by comparing the master budget to a flexible budget based on **actual** units produced. Both the master budget and flexible budget are based on the same standard unit costs, so any difference or variance is due to the volume of units produced.

- **Spending variances** are calculated by comparing actual costs to a flexible budget based on actual units produced. Because the flexible budget is adjusted for **actual** production volume, any difference or variance is due to the amount spent on direct materials, direct labor, or manufacturing overhead.

As an example, assume that our hypothetical Levi Strauss division produced 20,000 pair of 441 jeans during the most recent month. The actual cost of producing 20,000 units is shown in the left column of Exhibit 9–3. The master budget based on 15,000 planned units is shown in the right column of Exhibit 9–3. A flexible budget based on 20,000 actual units is shown in the middle. The variances are computed by comparing each of these columns.

Notice that all of the actual manufacturing costs are higher than the original master budget based on 15,000 units. This is not really surprising given that 20,000 units were produced instead of 15,000. A flexible budget based on 20,000 units is a better benchmark for evaluating spending for variable costs because it adjusts for the fact that variable costs should be higher if more units are produced.

In the next section, we will compute the spending variances that are highlighted in yellow in Exhibit 9–3. Spending variances are computed by comparing actual costs to a flexible

EXHIBIT 9–3	Using the Flexible Budget to Calculate Spending and Volume Variances

	Actual Results 20,000 units	Spending Variances		Flexible Budget 20,000 units	Volume Variances	Master Budget 15,000 units	
Direct Materials (DM)	$70,000	DM Price Variance	DM Quantity Variance	$60,000	X	$45,000	
Direct Labor (DL)	$64,000	DL Rate Variance	DL Efficiency Variance	$70,000	X	$52,500	
Variable Manufacturing Overhead (VOH)	$24,000	VOH Rate Variance	VOH Efficiency Variance	$28,000	X	$21,000	
Fixed Manufacturing Overhead (FOH)	$32,000	FOH* Spending Variance		$30,000	FOH* Volume Variance		FOH* Applied

*Fixed overhead variances are covered in the supplement to this chapter.

budget adjusted for **actual** production volume. Spending variances can be broken down even further into a price or rate variance that reflects how much was paid for the input; or a quantity or efficiency variance that reflects how much of the input was used in production.

Unlike spending variances that compare actual cost to the flexible budget, volume variances are computed by comparing the master budget to the flexible budget. The only volume variance we will compute is the fixed overhead volume variance, which is described in Supplement 9A to this chapter. As you can see in Exhibit 9–3, the variances for fixed manufacturing overhead are computed and interpreted differently than those for variable costs.

FAVORABLE OR UNFAVORABLE VARIANCES

Any variance we compute must be labelled as either *favorable* or *unfavorable,* depending on how it impacts short-term profitability. A **favorable variance** (F) occurs when actual costs are less than budgeted or standard costs. An **unfavorable variance** (U) occurs when actual costs are more than budgeted or standard costs. Common causes of favorable and unfavorable variances include the following:

Causes of Favorable (F) Variances	Causes of Unfavorable (U) Variances
• Paying a lower price than expected for direct materials	• Paying a higher price than expected for direct materials
• Using less direct materials than expected	• Using more direct materials than expected
• Paying a lower rate than expected for direct labor	• Paying a higher rate than expected for direct labor
• Taking less time to produce a unit than expected	• Taking more time than expected to produce a unit
• Paying less than expected for manufacturing overhead costs	• Paying more than expected for manufacturing overhead costs
• Using less of a variable overhead resource than expected	• Using more of a variable overhead resource than expected
• Producing and selling more units than expected.	• Producing and selling fewer units than expected.

COACH'S TIP

The words **favorable** and **unfavorable** do not necessarily mean good and bad performance. They simply reflect a difference between actual and standard costs. Variances that are unfavorable in the short-run could have positive effects in the long run, and vice versa.

In the next section, we calculate detailed variances that illustrate each of these potential causes.

Variable Cost Variances

In this section, we illustrate how to break the spending variances for variable manufacturing costs into two components: a price variance and a quantity variance. The approach we use is very similar to the method we used to separate the volume variance from the spending variance. But we are diving one level deeper to compute variances for direct materials, direct labor, and variable manufacturing overhead. Fixed manufacturing overhead variances are covered in Supplement 9A.

Exhibit 9–4 shows the general framework we will use to compute price and quantity variances for variable manufacturing costs. The color coding of the boxes matches the columns in Exhibit 9–3 when we compared actual costs to the flexible budget and the master budget. For spending variances, we ignore the master budget and focus on the difference between actual results and the flexible budget.

Exhibit 9–4 shows that the total spending variance is computed by comparing actual cost ($AQ \times AP$) to the flexible budget ($SQ \times SP$). It is very important that you remember to use the flexible budget when computing spending variances, so that we hold actual production volume constant. The middle green box in Exhibit 9–4 is $AQ \times SP$, or the actual quantity of input multiplied by the standard price. This number on its own is not particularly meaningful, but will help us decompose the spending variance into two distinct parts: the price variance and the quantity variance.

COACH'S TIP

It is tempting for students to use the master budget when computing cost variances. But when computing spending variances, you should ignore the fact that mangers planned to produce 15,000 units. Use 20,000 actual units to compute the flexible budget.

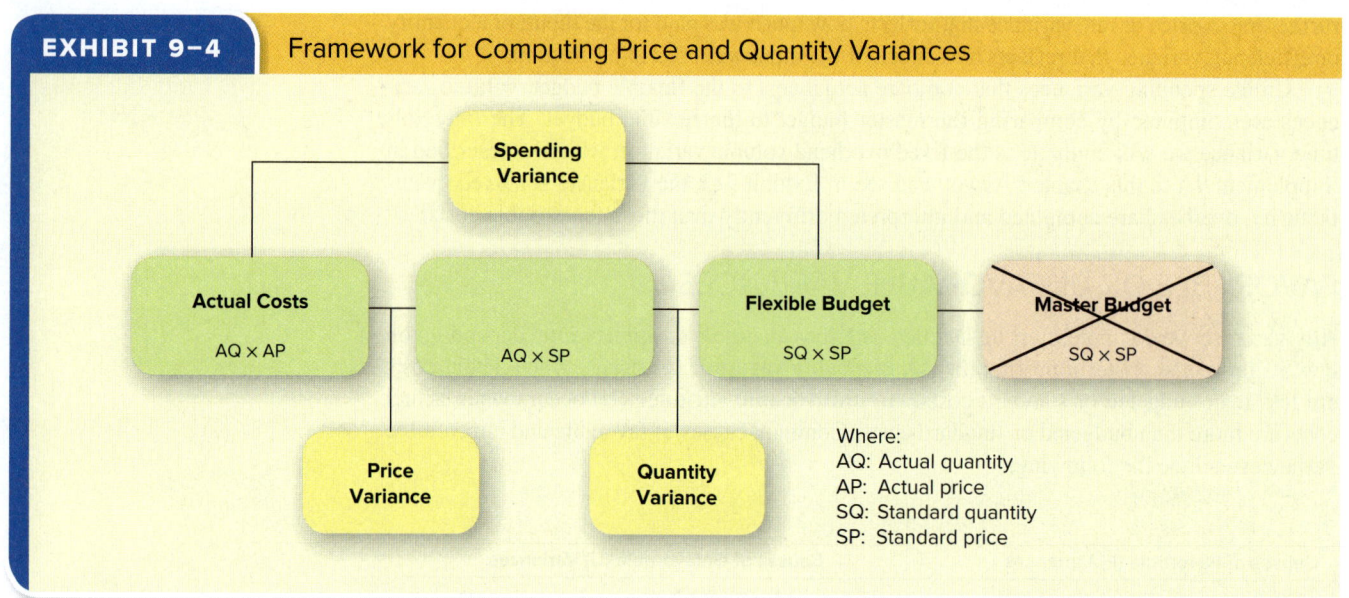

| **EXHIBIT 9–4** | Framework for Computing Price and Quantity Variances |

Where:
AQ: Actual quantity
AP: Actual price
SQ: Standard quantity
SP: Standard price

COACH'S TIP

Pay close attention to the values that are in paraphrases in the variance formula. For the price variance, it will be the difference in actual and standard price. For the quantity variance, it will be a difference in actual and standard quantity. This will tell you both the name of the variance and what is causing the variance.

We compute the **price variance** by comparing actual costs ($AQ \times AP$) to ($AQ \times SP$). Actual quantity is used in both formulas, so any variance must be due to a difference in actual price and standard price. The short-cut formula for computing the price variance follows.

$$Price\ Variance = (AQ \times SP) - (AQ \times AP)$$

$$Price\ Variance = AQ \times (SP - AP)$$

If the actual price is more than the standard price, it will result in an unfavorable price variance. If the actual price is less than the standard price, it will result in a favorable price variance.

We compute the **quantity variance** by comparing the middle green box (AQ × SP) to the flexible budget (SQ × SP). Notice that standard price is the same in both, so any variance is due to the difference in actual and standard quantity. The formula for the quantity variance follows.

$$\text{Quantity Variance} = (SQ \times SP) - (AQ \times SP)$$

$$\text{Quantity Variance} = (SQ - AQ) \times SP$$

The quantity variance compares the actual quantity of input used in manufacturing to the standard quantity, or the amount of input that should have been used to achieve the actual output. Remember to use actual units when computing SQ. While it may seem counterintuitive to use an actual value to compute a standard amount, the flexible budget is always based on actual production volume.

When combined, the price variance and quantity variance make up the total spending variance. If both variances are favorable or both unfavorable, we add them together; if one is favorable and the other unfavorable, we net them against one another. Alternatively, we can compute the total spending variance by comparing actual cost (AQ × AP) to the flexible budget (SQ × SP). Computing the spending variance both ways is a good check to make sure you computed the individual variances correctly.

Next, we will use this general framework to compute the price and quantity variances for direct materials, direct labor, and variable overhead for our hypothetical Levi Strauss example.

DIRECT MATERIALS VARIANCES

Recall that Levi Strauss's direct materials standard was 2 yards of denim at a cost of $1.50 per yard, for a standard unit cost of $3.00. The master budget was based on 15,000 units, but actual production was 20,000 units.

Actual direct materials costs are shown below:

- Purchased 50,000 yards of denim at a total cost of $70,000.
- Used 50,000 yards of denim to make 20,000 pairs of jeans.

Let's start by identifying the terms we will use in our formulas.

Actual price (AP): $70,000 ÷ 50,000 = $1.40 per yard

Actual quantity (AQ): 50,000 yards

Standard price (SP): $1.50 per yard

Standard quantity (SQ): 2 yards × 20,000 units = 40,000 yards.

Exhibit 9–5 shows how these numbers would be used to compute the direct materials price and quantity variances.

The **direct materials price variance** is computed based on 50,000 actual yards of denim multiplied by the difference in the standard price ($1.50) and the actual price ($1.40), as follows:

$$\text{Direct Materials Price Variance} = AQ \times (SP - AP)$$

$$\text{Direct Materials Price Variance} = 500,000 \times (\$1.50 - \$1.40)$$

$$\text{Direct Materials Price Variance} = \$5,000 \text{ F}$$

The direct materials price variance is $5,000 favorable because the actual price paid for denim was 10 cents less than the standard price. **The purchasing manager is responsible for the direct materials price variance**. What are some potential explanations for this favorable price variance? Perhaps the purchasing manager negotiated a reduced price, or the company received a quantity discount that was not factored into the standard price. Alternatively, the

COACH'S TIP

Don't rely on the formula to determine whether a variance is favorable or unfavorable. In most cases, the formula is set up so that a negative number will result in an unfavorable variance and a positive number will result in a favorable variance. But that won't always be the case, so you should use judgment to determine if the variance is favorable or unfavorable.

Learning Objective 9–3
Calculate and interpret the direct materials price and quantity variances.

COACH'S TIP

Remember that SQ is based on the ACTUAL number of units produced (i.e., the flexible budget). SQ is the amount of material we **should have used** to produce 20,000 actual units.

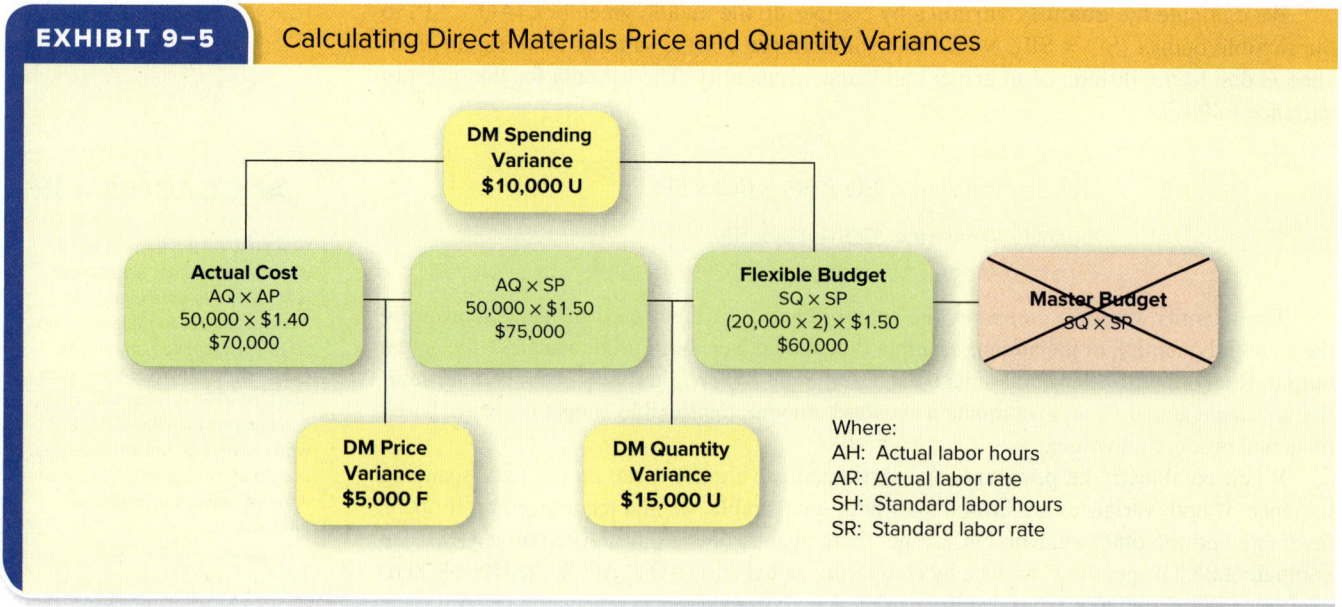

EXHIBIT 9–5 | Calculating Direct Materials Price and Quantity Variances

DM Spending Variance $10,000 U

Actual Cost	AQ × SP	Flexible Budget	Master Budget
AQ × AP	50,000 × $1.50	SQ × SP	SQ × SP
50,000 × $1.40	$75,000	(20,000 × 2) × $1.50	
$70,000		$60,000	

DM Price Variance $5,000 F

DM Quantity Variance $15,000 U

Where:
AH: Actual labor hours
AR: Actual labor rate
SH: Standard labor hours
SR: Standard labor rate

purchasing manager may have purchased lower quality materials. If so, a favorable price variance is not necessarily a good thing. Although it has a positive effect on short-term spending, it could have a negative effect over the long term if customers detect a difference in product quality and decide not to buy Levis anymore.

The **direct materials quantity variance** compares the actual quantity of materials used in production to the standard quantity allowed, while holding the standard price constant. This variance is sometimes called the **direct materials usage variance**. The standard quantity of denim needed to produce 20,000 actual units is 40,000 yards (2 yards × 20,000). However, the company actually used 50,000 yards of denim. To find the quantity variance, we multiply the difference of 10,000 yards by the $1.50 standard price, as follows:

Direct Materials Price Variance = (SQ − AQ) × SP

Direct Materials Price Variance = (40,000 − 50,000) × $1.50

Direct Materials Price Variance = $15,000 U

The direct materials quantity or usage variance is $15,000 unfavorable because managers used more denim than the standard allowed to produce 20,000 units. **The production manager is generally responsible for the direct materials quantity or usage variance**. What are some potential explanations for an unfavorable usage variance? Perhaps there was more "scrap" or wasted material in the process than expected. If so, managers may want to redesign the pattern to utilize the material more efficiently. Or perhaps the product mix has changed and the company is producing larger sizes that require more direct materials. The variance serves as a signal to managers and provides a starting point for investigation.

Combining the $5,000 favorable direct materials price variance with the $15,000 unfavorable direct materials quantity variance results in a $10,000 unfavorable **direct materials spending variance**. Notice that this is the same total spending variance shown in Exhibit 9–3. when we compared actual direct materials cost to the flexible budget. Now, however, we have a better idea of **why** the direct materials cost more than expected.

Before you continue, complete the following Self-Study Practice to see whether you can calculate the direct materials variances for Papa John's Pizza.

How's it going? — Self-Study Practice

Papa John's standard cost card for direct materials includes the following costs.

	Standard Quantity	Standard Price	Standard Unit Cost
Direct materials (ingredients)	20 oz.	$0.10 per oz.	$2.00

Actual results were as follows:

- The number of units produced was 15,000.
- 315,000 ounces of ingredients were purchased and used for a total cost of $28,350.

Calculate the following variances and label them as favorable or unfavorable:

1. Direct materials price variance.
2. Direct materials quantity (usage) variance.
3. Direct materials spending variance.

After you have finished, check your answers against the solutions in the margin.

Solution to Self-Study Practice

1. Actual Price (AP) = $28,350 ÷ 315,000 = $0.09 per oz.
   Direct Materials Price Variance: AQ × (SP − AP) = 315,000 × ($0.10 − $0.09) = $3,150 F
2. Standard Quantity (SQ) = 15,000 units × 20 oz. = 300,000
   Direct Materials Quantity Variance = (SQ − AQ) × SP = (300,000 − 315,000) × $0.10 = $1,500 U
3. Direct Materials Spending Variance = Direct Materials Price Variance + Direct Materials Quantity Variance = $3,150 F + $(1,500) U = $1,650 F

DIRECT LABOR VARIANCES

Next, we break the spending variance for direct labor into a price and a quantity variance. We will use the same general framework, with a few modifications:

- The quantity of direct labor is stated in terms of labor hours (denoted by an H instead of a Q), while the price is stated as an hourly labor rate (denoted by an R instead of a P).
- The price variance for direct labor is called the **direct labor rate variance**.
- The quantity variance for direct labor is called the **direct labor efficiency variance**.

Recall that the direct labor standard for our hypothetical Levi Strauss example was 15 minutes (0.25 hours) per unit at a standard labor rate of $14 per hour.

Assume employees were paid $64,000 for 4,000 actual hours, for an average labor rate of $16 per hour.

Let's start by identifying the following terms:

Actual labor rate (AR): $64,000 ÷ 4,000 hours = $16.00 per hour.

Actual labor hours (AH): 4,000 hours.

Standard labor rate (SR): $14.00 per hour.

Standard labor hours (SH): 0.25 × 20,000 actual units = 5,000 hours.

Exhibit 9–6 shows how this information would be used to compute the direct labor rate and direct labor efficiency variances.

The **direct labor rate variance** compares the actual direct labor rate ($16.00) to the standard direct labor rate ($14.00), multiplied by 4,000 actual direct labor hours, as follows:

Direct Labor Rate Variance = AH × (SR − AR)

Direct Labor Rate Variance = 4,000 × ($14.00 − $16.00)

Direct Labor Rate Variance = $8,000 U

Learning Objective 9–4
Calculate and interpret the direct labor rate and efficiency variances.

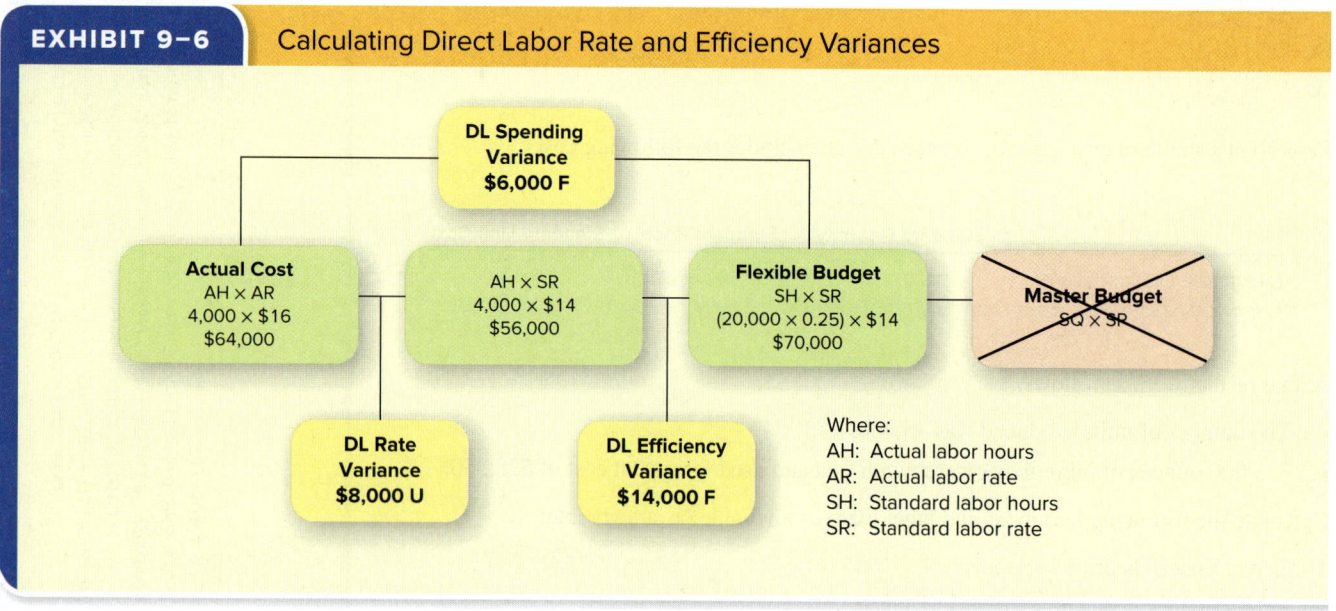

EXHIBIT 9-6 Calculating Direct Labor Rate and Efficiency Variances

The $8,000 unfavorable direct labor rate variance occurred because the company paid an average of $16 per hour when the standard labor rate was $14. **The hiring manager and production manager are responsible for the direct labor rate variance.** Many factors can influence this variance, including labor market conditions, how and when workers were hired and promoted, and turnover rates in the organization. Perhaps the market wage rate has increased, but the standard wage rate has not been adjusted in several years. Although the labor rate variance is unfavorable in this example, it is not necessarily a signal of bad performance if the result is a more skilled work force. However, the direct labor standard should be updated if the labor rate is expected to remain at $16 per hour.

The **direct labor efficiency variance** compares actual direct labor hours (AH) to standard labor hours (SH), while holding the standard labor rate constant. The direct labor quantity standard is 0.25 hours per unit multiplied by 20,000 actual units produced, or 5,000 standard hours. Actual direct labor hours were 4,000. Multiplying the 1,000 difference by the standard labor rate of $14 per hour results in a $14,000 favorable labor efficiency variance, as follows:

$$\text{Direct Labor Efficiency Variance} = (\text{SH} - \text{AH}) \times \text{SR}$$

$$\text{Direct Labor Efficiency Variance} = ((0.25 \times 20,000) - 4,000) \times \$14$$

$$\text{Direct Labor Efficiency Variance} = \$14,000 \text{ F}$$

The direct labor efficiency variance is favorable because employees worked 4,000 hours when the standard allowed for 5,000 hours (0.25 hours per unit × 20,000 units). In other words, it took less than 0.25 hours to make each unit (on average), so the workforce was more efficient than expected. **The production manager is responsible for the direct labor efficiency variance.** A variety of factors can affect this variance, including the skill level of the employees, how long they have been with the company, and how complicated the production process is. As employees learn, they take less time to perform the same task, so the direct labor quantity standard should be reviewed and updated periodically to be sure it is a good benchmark for evaluating employee productivity.

The overall **direct labor spending variance** is the combination of the $8,000 unfavorable direct labor rate variance and the $14,000 favorable direct labor efficiency variances, for a net favorable spending variance of $6,000.

VARIABLE MANUFACTURING OVERHEAD VARIANCES

Variable manufacturing overhead costs include indirect materials such as thread, rivets, and zippers, labor supervision, and power to run machines. Because clothing manufacturing is a labor-intensive industry, we assume that variable manufacturing costs are applied as a percentage of direct labor cost. As you learned in earlier chapters, however, overhead costs can vary with many other factors, including the number of machine hours and non-volume-based cost drivers such as the number of setups, material-handling transactions, and the like. Companies that use activity-based costing would do a separate analysis for each activity cost driver (a task that is beyond the scope of this book).

Learning Objective 9–5
Calculate and interpret the variable overhead rate and efficiency variances.

We will use the same framework we used to analyze the direct labor variances to compute the variable overhead variances, with a few modifications:

- The price for variable manufacturing overhead is the variable overhead rate (denoted by an R). The price variance is called the **variable overhead rate variance**.

- The quantity is stated in terms of direct labor hours (denoted by an H). The quantity variance is called the **variable overhead efficiency variance**.

Let's apply this framework to our Levi Strauss example. Recall that variable manufacturing overhead is applied at 40 percent of direct labor cost. The standard direct labor rate per hour is $14, so the standard variable overhead rate per hour is $5.60 ($14 × 40%). The standard quantity is based on direct labor hours, or 0.25 direct labor hours per unit. Actual results were as follows:

- Actual units produced were 20,000.
- Actual direct labor hours were 4,000.
- Actual variable overhead costs were $24,000.

Let's start by identifying the terms we will use in the variance framework:

Actual VOH rate (AR): $24,000 ÷ 4,000 hours = $6.00 per per hour.

Actual direct labor hours (AH): 4,000 hours.

Standard VOH rate (SR): $5.60 per hour.

Standard direct labor hours (SH): 0.25 × 20,000 units = 5,000 hours.

Exhibit 9–7 shows how these variances would be computed for our Levi Strauss example.

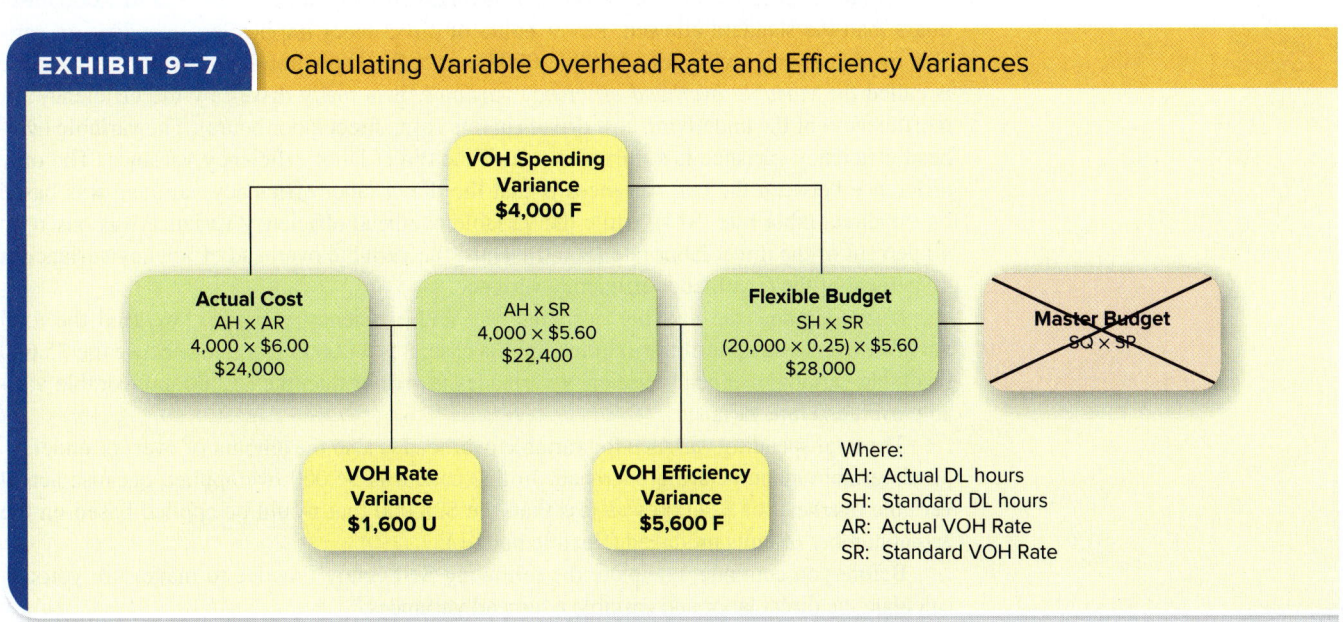

EXHIBIT 9–7 Calculating Variable Overhead Rate and Efficiency Variances

VOH Spending Variance
$4,000 F

Actual Cost
AH × AR
4,000 × $6.00
$24,000

AH × SR
4,000 × $5.60
$22,400

Flexible Budget
SH × SR
(20,000 × 0.25) × $5.60
$28,000

Master Budget
SQ × SR

VOH Rate Variance
$1,600 U

VOH Efficiency Variance
$5,600 F

Where:
AH: Actual DL hours
SH: Standard DL hours
AR: Actual VOH Rate
SR: Standard VOH Rate

The **variable overhead rate variance** provides information about the actual variable overhead rate in comparison to the standard variable overhead rate, holding actual direct labor hours constant. In this example, the standard variable overhead rate was $5.60 while actual variable overhead costs were $6.00 per direct labor hour. When we multiply the $0.40 difference by 4,000 actual direct labor hours, we get an unfavorable variable overhead rate variance of $1,600, as follows:

Variable Overhead Rate Variance = AH × (SR − AR)

Variable Overhead Rate Variance = 4,000 × ($5.60 − $6.00)

Variable Overhead Rate Variance = $1,600 U

The variable overhead rate variance is unfavorable because the actual variable overhead rate was higher than the standard variable overhead rate. What may have caused this variance? Managers may have spent more on variable overhead items such as indirect materials, supervision, or power than expected. Perhaps direct labor cost is not the only driver of variable manufacturing overhead. Even if variable overhead costs are partially driven by direct labor, other factors are likely to influence spending on variable overhead costs.

The **variable overhead efficiency variance** is based on the difference between the actual and standard quantity of the cost driver used to assign variable overhead; in this case, direct labor hours. Actual direct labor hours were 4,000 while the standard direct labor hours allowed for production was 5,000 hours (20,000 units × 0.25 hours per unit). We compute the variable overhead efficiency variance by multiplying the 1,000 hour difference by the standard variable overhead rate, as follows:

Variable Overhead Efficiency Variance = (SH − AH) × SR

Variable Overhead Efficiency Variance = (5,000 − 4,000) × $5.60

Variable Overhead Efficiency Variance = $5,600 F

The variable overhead efficiency variance is favorable because employees worked 1,000 fewer hours than the standard allowed. Fewer hours of direct labor implies less spending on variable overhead, or a savings of $5,600 (1,000 hours × $5.60 per hour). Although this variance is called the *variable overhead efficiency variance,* it is really driven by the efficiency (or inefficiency) of the underlying cost driver (in this case, direct labor hours). The variable overhead efficiency variance is a mirror image of the direct labor efficiency variance. The only difference between the two variances is that the direct labor efficiency variance was based on the direct labor rate ($14), while the variable overhead efficiency variance was based on 40 percent of the direct labor rate ($5.60). Thus, the variable overhead efficiency variance is 40 percent of the direct labor efficiency variance.

If we combine the variable overhead rate and efficiency variances, we find the total **variable overhead spending variance**. In this case, it is $4,000 favorable because the $5,600 favorable variable overhead efficiency variances is greater than the $1,600 unfavorable variable overhead rate variances.

The total spending variance for variable overhead is also the amount of over- or underapplied variable manufacturing overhead. In this case it is $4,000 overapplied because actual variable overhead of $24,000 was less than the $28,000 that would be applied based on the actual number of units produced (flexible budget).

Before you continue, complete the following Self-Study Practice to make sure you can calculate the direct labor and variable overhead variances.

How's it going?   Self-Study Practice

Papa John's uses a standard cost system and applies variable overhead at a rate equal to 25 percent of direct labor cost. The standard cost card for direct labor and variable overhead includes the following costs:

	Standard Quantity	Standard Rate
Direct labor	0.3 hrs.	$10.00 per hr.
Variable overhead	0.3 hrs.	2.50 per hr.

Actual results were as follows:

- The number of units produced and sold was 15,000.
- The direct labor cost was $38,000 for 4,000 hours ($9.50 per hour).
- The variable overhead cost was $12,000 for 4,000 hours ($3.00 per hour).

Calculate the following variances and label them as favorable or unfavorable:

1. Direct labor rate variance.
2. Direct labor efficiency variance.
3. Direct labor spending variance.
4. Variable overhead rate variance.
5. Variable overhead efficiency variance.
6. Variable overhead spending variance.

After you have finished, check your answers against the solutions in the margin.

SUMMARY OF VARIABLE COST VARIANCES

In this chapter, we calculated many different variances. You are probably beginning to suffer from calculation overload. How in the world are you going to remember how to calculate all these variances? Exhibit 9–8 provides a summary of all of the variances calculated in this chapter, along with a definition of the terms used in the formulas.

Of course, calculating the variance is only part of it. Tips for understanding and interpreting the variances follow:

- Variances are always calculated by comparing actual results to budgeted or standard results. Variances provide a signal to managers that they are (or are not) achieving their objectives so they can take corrective action if necessary.

- Companies try to hold specific managers responsible for each variance while removing the effects of factors that are beyond a manager's control.

- The formulas for variances allow only one factor such as price, quantity, or volume to change, while holding everything else constant at actual or standard values (depending on the type of variance). Doing so makes it easier to assign responsibility to the manager who has control over that variance.

- The driving factor for the variance always appears in parentheses in the formula and in the name of the variance. If you forget the name of a particular variance, just look at the terms in parentheses to determine the cause of the variance.

- Try not to memorize rules or rely on formulas to determine whether a variance is favorable or unfavorable; just think about it. Paying a higher price for materials or labor is unfavorable. Using more direct materials or hiring more workers to produce the same number of units is unfavorable. But remember that favorable is not always good and unfavorable is not always bad.

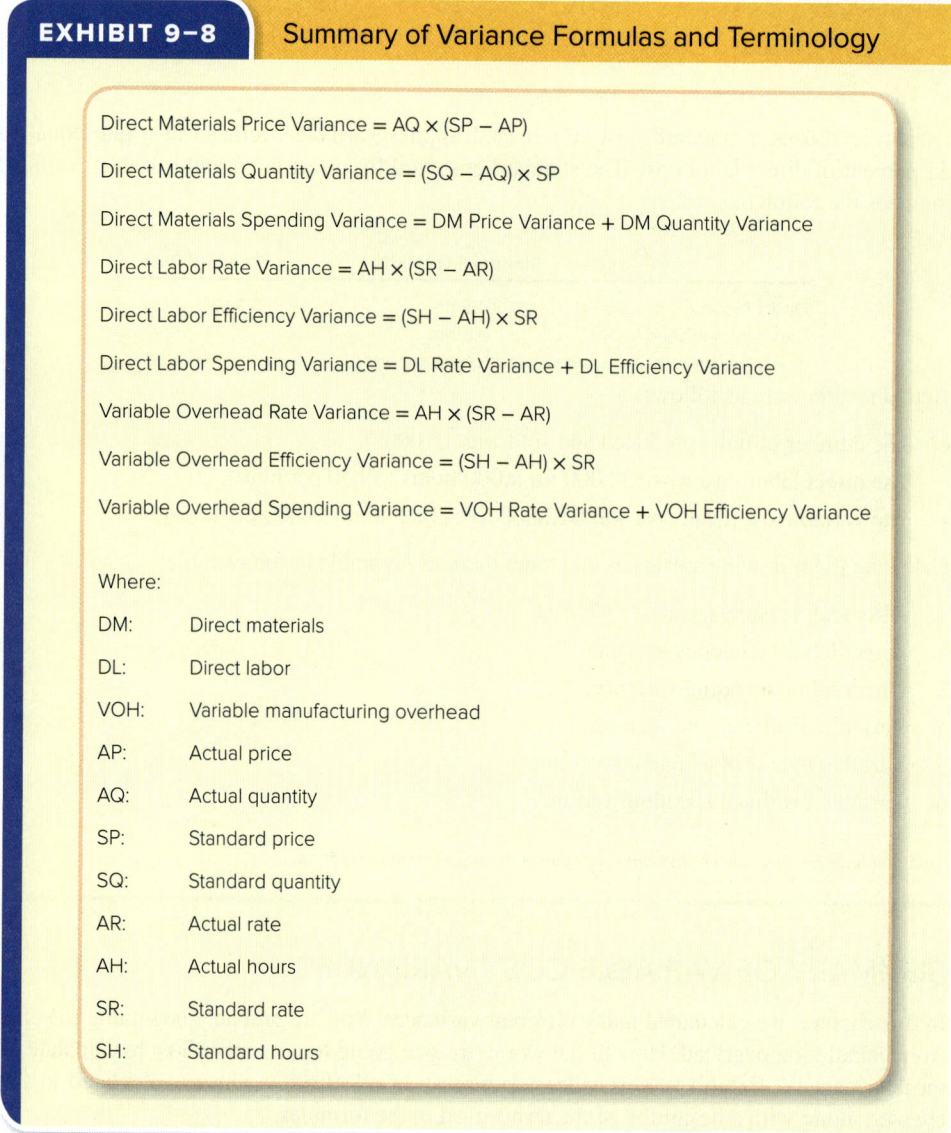

EXHIBIT 9–8 Summary of Variance Formulas and Terminology

Direct Materials Price Variance = AQ × (SP − AP)

Direct Materials Quantity Variance = (SQ − AQ) × SP

Direct Materials Spending Variance = DM Price Variance + DM Quantity Variance

Direct Labor Rate Variance = AH × (SR − AR)

Direct Labor Efficiency Variance = (SH − AH) × SR

Direct Labor Spending Variance = DL Rate Variance + DL Efficiency Variance

Variable Overhead Rate Variance = AH × (SR − AR)

Variable Overhead Efficiency Variance = (SH − AH) × SR

Variable Overhead Spending Variance = VOH Rate Variance + VOH Efficiency Variance

Where:

DM: Direct materials

DL: Direct labor

VOH: Variable manufacturing overhead

AP: Actual price

AQ: Actual quantity

SP: Standard price

SQ: Standard quantity

AR: Actual rate

AH: Actual hours

SR: Standard rate

SH: Standard hours

In the chapter, we calculated variances for variable manufacturing costs, including direct materials, direct labor, and variable manufacturing overhead. In addition to the variable cost variances, the accounting system would also record the fixed manufacturing overhead variances described in Supplement 9A. The detailed journal entries used to record manufacturing costs and variances in a standard cost system are covered in Supplement 9B.

SUPPLEMENT 9A FIXED MANUFACTURING OVERHEAD VARIANCES

Learning Objective 9–S1
Calculate and interpret the fixed overhead spending and volume variances.

This supplement covers the variances for fixed manufacturing overhead. The framework used to analyze fixed overhead variances differs from that used to analyze variable cost variances. Fixed manufacturing overhead costs such as rent, machine depreciation, and factory supervision are incurred to provide the capacity to perform work. However, total fixed costs do not vary with volume in the same way that variable costs do. Even so, managers need to budget for total fixed costs. It's possible that the actual amount spent on fixed costs will be higher or lower than budgeted due to factors other than volume, such as an unexpected change in the cost of insurance or rent.

Exhibit 9A–1 shows the framework for analyzing fixed overhead variances. Although this framework looks a lot like the framework for analyzing variable costs, we calculate and interpret the variances differently.

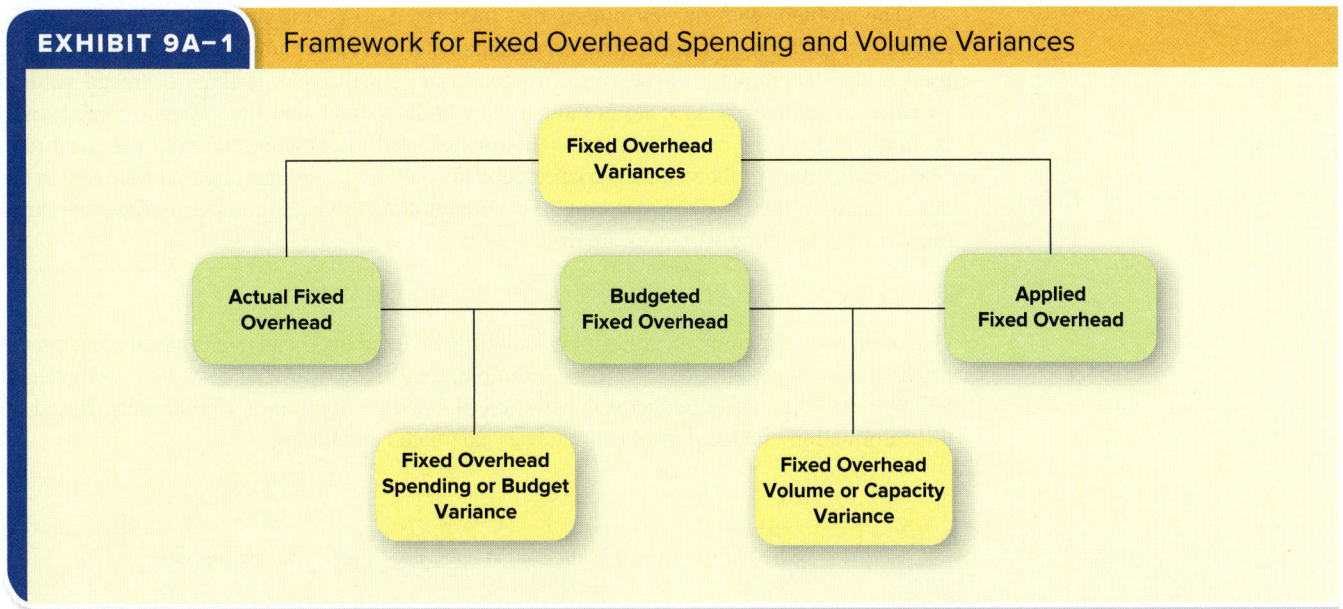

| EXHIBIT 9A–1 | Framework for Fixed Overhead Spending and Volume Variances |

FIXED OVERHEAD SPENDING VARIANCE

The first fixed overhead variance shown in Exhibit 9A–1 is the **fixed overhead spending variance**, also called the **fixed overhead budget variance**. It is calculated by comparing actual fixed overhead costs to budgeted fixed overhead costs. For example, if Levi Strauss budgeted $30,000 for fixed manufacturing overhead but actually spent $32,000, it would report a $2,000 unfavorable fixed overhead spending variance, as follows:

$$\text{Fixed Overhead Spending Variance} = \text{Budgeted Fixed Overhead} - \text{Actual Fixed Overhead}$$

$$\text{Fixed Overhead Spending Variance} = \$30,000 - \$32,000 = \$2,000 \text{ U}$$

The fixed overhead spending variance is unfavorable because actual fixed costs were more than budgeted. Unlike the spending variances for variable costs, the fixed overhead spending variance cannot be decomposed into a price variance and a quantity variance. Instead, we can compute another variance called the *fixed overhead volume variance.*

FIXED OVERHEAD VOLUME VARIANCE

The second fixed overhead variance shown in Exhibit 9A–1 is the **fixed overhead volume variance or capacity variance.** Fixed overhead volume variances relate to the method used to **apply** fixed manufacturing costs to individual products or customers. Even though the total costs are fixed, we still use a fixed overhead rate to apply the cost to products so that they reflect the full manufacturing cost per unit. Depending on how accurately we estimate the fixed overhead rate, the amount of fixed overhead applied is likely to differ from the amount budgeted.

The fixed overhead rate is computed by dividing budgeted total fixed overhead cost by some measure of volume, as follows:

$$\text{Fixed Overhead (FOH) Rate} = \frac{\text{Budgeted Total FOH}}{\text{Volume}}$$

The problem with this formula is that total fixed costs (the numerator) should remain constant regardless of volume (the denominator). If **actual** volume differs from the value used in the denominator of the fixed overhead rate, it will create a fixed overhead volume variance. A volume variance has nothing to do with how much managers spent on fixed costs. It simply reflects the accuracy of the denominator used to compute the fixed overhead rate. The interpretation of the volume variance depends on the type of measure that was used in the denominator of the fixed overhead rate. Two common methods for computing fixed overhead rates and the resulting variances are discussed next.

Fixed Overhead Rate Based on Budgeted Volume

One of the most common methods for calculating the fixed overhead rate is based on budgeted production volume. In our Levi Strauss example, total fixed overhead costs were budgeted at $30,000, and the master budget was based on planned production of 15,000 units. Based on this information, the fixed overhead rate was calculated as follows:

$$\text{Fixed Overhead (FOH) Rate} = \frac{\$30,000}{15,000 \text{ Units}} = \$2.00 \text{ per Unit}$$

Levi Strauss would then apply fixed overhead at a rate of $2.00 for each unit produced. This rate is intended to cover all of the indirect fixed costs of production, such as rent, depreciation, and insurance. The amount of fixed overhead applied will equal $30,000 only if the company actually produces 15,000 units. If the company produces anything other than 15,000 units, the amount of fixed overhead applied will differ from the $30,000 budgeted.

The difference between applied and budgeted fixed overhead is called the **fixed overhead volume variance** and is computed as follows:

$$\text{Fixed Overhead Volume Variance} = \text{Applied Fixed Overhead} - \text{Budgeted Fixed Overhead}$$

$$\text{Fixed Overhead Volume Variance} = (\text{FOH Rate} \times \text{Actual Volume}) - (\text{FOH Rate} \times \text{Budgeted Volume})$$

Notice that the only difference between applied and budgeted fixed overhead is the volume of units produced (actual versus budgeted). The fixed overhead rate is the same in both. Thus, we can also compute the fixed overhead volume variance for our Levi Strauss example as follows:

$$\text{Fixed Overhead Volume Variance} = \text{FOH Rate} \times (\text{Actual Volume} - \text{Budgeted Volume})$$

$$\text{Fixed Overhead Volume Variance} = \$2.00 \times (20,000 \text{ Units} - 15,000 \text{ Units}) = \$10,000 \text{ F}$$

Levi Strauss expected to produce 15,000 units, but actually produced 20,000 units. Multiplying the 5,000 additional units by the $2.00 fixed overhead rate results in a $10,000 favorable volume variance. It is favorable because producing more units than expected drives down the fixed cost per unit (getting more volume from the same total cost). But remember that the total fixed costs do not change with volume. From an overall company perspective, a favorable volume variance results in higher profit only if the increased revenue from the units sold is enough to cover the increased variable costs associated with the increase in volume.

When fixed overhead rates are based on budgeted production volume, total over- or under-applied fixed manufacturing overhead is the sum of the fixed overhead spending variance and the fixed overhead volume variance. The $2,000 unfavorable fixed overhead spending variance combines with the $10,000 favorable fixed overhead volume variance for a total fixed overhead variance of $8,000 favorable. Favorable means that actual fixed overhead was less than applied; that is, fixed overhead was overapplied by $8,000. These variances are summarized in Exhibit 9A–2.

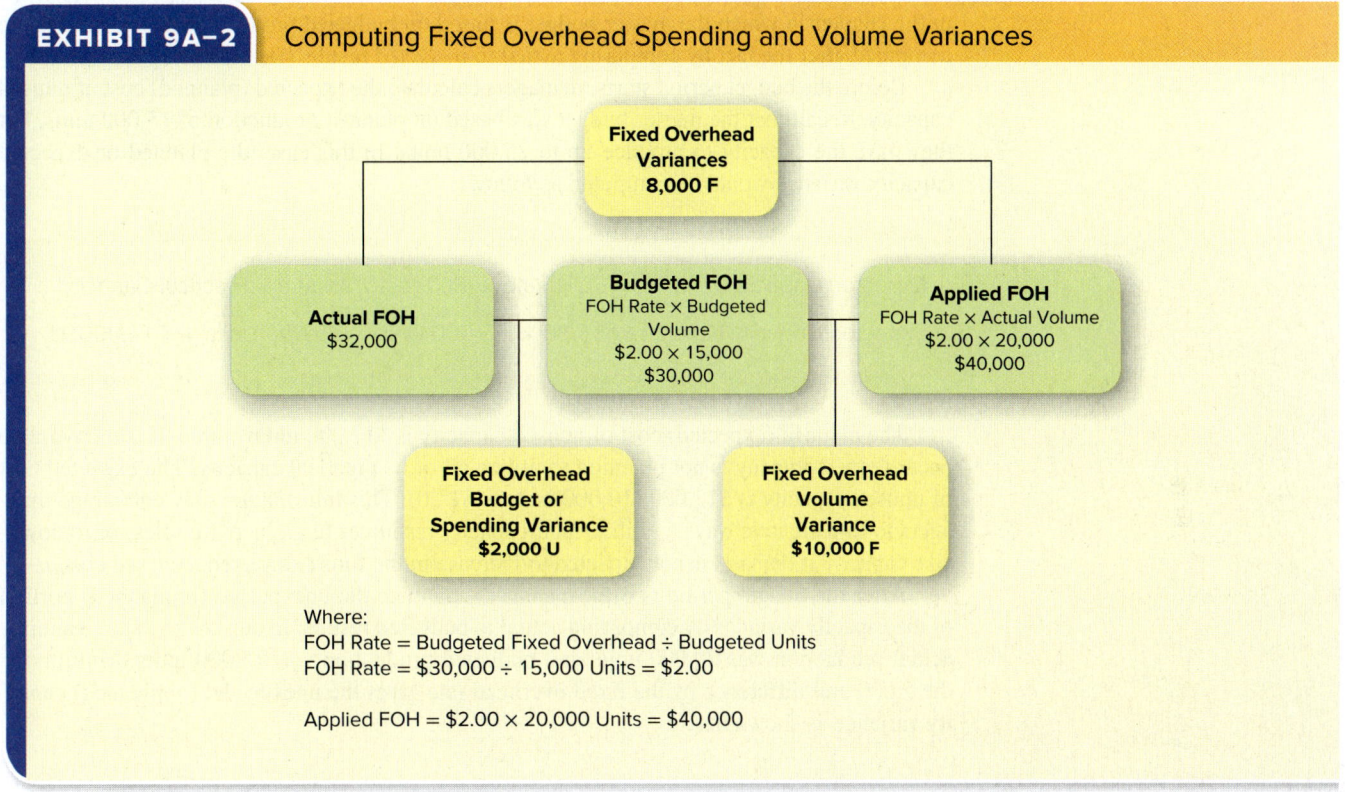

EXHIBIT 9A–2   Computing Fixed Overhead Spending and Volume Variances

Fixed Overhead
Variances
8,000 F

Actual FOH
$32,000

Budgeted FOH
FOH Rate × Budgeted Volume
$2.00 × 15,000
$30,000

Applied FOH
FOH Rate × Actual Volume
$2.00 × 20,000
$40,000

Fixed Overhead
Budget or
Spending Variance
$2,000 U

Fixed Overhead
Volume
Variance
$10,000 F

Where:
FOH Rate = Budgeted Fixed Overhead ÷ Budgeted Units
FOH Rate = $30,000 ÷ 15,000 Units = $2.00

Applied FOH = $2.00 × 20,000 Units = $40,000

Fixed Overhead Rate Based on Practical Capacity

Although fixed overhead rates are often based on budgeted production levels, many experts believe that a better approach is to base fixed overhead rates on practical capacity. **Practical capacity** is the volume that **could be** achieved under normal (not ideal) operating conditions. Practical capacity allows some downtime for necessary activities such as employee training, shift changes, breaks, and preventive maintenance. In practice, practical capacity is often set around 80 percent of the theoretical or maximum capacity of the resource.

For example, if the maximum or theoretical capacity of an airplane is 120 passengers (based on the number of seats), the practical capacity might be set at 96 passengers (80 percent of 120) because not all of the seats will be filled on every flight and some seats may be filled by nonrevenue customers such as frequent fliers, flight crew, and relatives.

Using practical capacity as the denominator in the fixed overhead rate prevents the rate from fluctuating due to changes in demand. Basing fixed overhead rates on capacity also highlights the cost of any unused capacity for management attention (and potential action).

As an example, assume that budgeted fixed overhead of $30,000 provides Levi Strauss the practical capacity to produce up to 25,000 units per month. The fixed overhead rate based on practical capacity would be computed as follows:

COACH'S TIP

Examples of capacity include the number of people who can fill a football stadium, the number of seats on an airplane, the number of pages a copy machine can print per minute, and the number of patients a doctor can see per day.

$$\text{Fixed Overhead (FOH) Rate} = \frac{\$30,000}{25,000 \text{ Units}} = \$1.20 \text{ per Unit}$$

The fixed overhead rate based on practical capacity is $1.20 per unit. Notice that this is less than the $2.00 fixed overhead rate we used throughout the chapter based on expected or budgeted production of 15,000 units. If the company produces anything other than 25,000 units, it will have a **fixed overhead capacity variance**. There are two types of capacity variances: one that is calculated in advance of the budget period (based on the master budget production volume of 15,000 units) and another that is calculated after the budget period (based on actual production of 20,000 units). This is consistent with the general approach described in the chapter in which the master budget is based on budgeted production and variances are computed after the fact by comparing actual to budgeted results (flexible budget).

Before the budget period starts, managers calculate the expected (planned) cost of unused capacity. Recall that the master budget was based on planned production of 15,000 units, but they have the capacity to produce up to 25,000 units. In this case, the planned or expected capacity variance would be computed as follows:

Expected Capacity Variance = FOH Rate × (Budgeted Volume − Practical Capacity)

Expected Capacity Variance = $1.20 × (15,000 Units − 25,000 Units) = $12,000 U

The planned (expected) cost of unused capacity is $12,000 unfavorable. It is unfavorable because the company is not planning to utilize all of its practical capacity. The expected cost of unused capacity is $12,000 (10,000 units × $1.20). This information may encourage managers to find creative ways to utilize their capacity resources (e.g., increase sales) or to downsize capacity if demand is not expected to increase in the future (e.g., reduce fixed costs).

After the budget period is over, managers calculate the unexpected (unplanned) portion of the capacity variance by comparing actual to budgeted results. In our Levi Strauss example, actual production was 20,000 units and budgeted production was 15,000 units. Multiplying the 5,000 unit difference by the fixed overhead rate gives the unexpected (unplanned) capacity variance as shown here:

Unexpected Capacity Variance = FOH Rate × (Actual Volume − Budgeted Volume)

Unexpected Capacity Variance = $1.20 × (20,000 Units − 15,000 Units) = $6,000 F

Notice that the formula for the unexpected capacity variance is the same as the volume variance presented earlier, with a fixed overhead rate based on **practical capacity** rather than budgeted production volume. The unexpected capacity variance is favorable because the company produced more units than expected and thus utilized more of the practical capacity than initially planned.

SUPPLEMENT 9B RECORDING DIRECT MATERIALS AND DIRECT LABOR IN A STANDARD COST SYSTEM

Learning Objective 9–S2
Prepare journal entries to record direct materials and direct labor variances.

This supplement describes the journal entries used to record direct materials and direct labor in a standard cost system. The entries for recording manufacturing overhead costs would be similar but are not described here.

In preparing journal entries for a standard cost system, keep in mind these common rules:

- Standard costs are debited to Direct Materials Inventory, Work in Process, Finished Goods, and eventually Cost of Goods Sold based on standard (not actual) amounts.

- Actual costs are credited to Cash, Accounts Payable, or other appropriate accounts such as accumulated depreciation or prepaid assets.
- The difference between standard cost (debit) and actual cost (credit) is recorded as one or more cost variances.
- Unfavorable variances should appear as debit entries; favorable variances should appear as credit entries.
- At the end of the accounting period, all variances should be closed to Cost of Goods Sold to adjust from standard cost to the actual cost.

We illustrate this process using the variances we calculated for our Levi Strauss example.

Record Standard Direct Materials Costs

Recall that the standard price of denim is $1.50 per yard and the standard quantity is 2 yards per unit. During the period, the purchasing manager bought 50,000 yards of denim on account for $70,000 (an average price of $1.40 per yard). The journal entry to record the purchase of direct materials follows:

	Debit	Credit
Direct Materials Inventory (50,000 × $1.50)............................	75,000	
Direct Materials Price Variance (50,000 × $0.10).............		5,000
Accounts Payable (50,000 × $1.40)		70,000

Notice that the debit to Direct Materials Inventory is based on the standard price per unit of $1.50, but the credit to Accounts Payable is based on the actual price of $1.40 per unit. The difference of $0.10 multiplied by 50,000 actual yards of denim purchased is the direct materials price variance of $5,000. This variance is favorable because the actual price was less than the standard price. Notice that the favorable variance appears as a credit.

Next let's record the journal entry to transfer the cost of denim out of Direct Materials Inventory and into Work in Process Inventory. During the period, Levi Strauss employees used 50,000 yards of denim to produce 20,000 units. The entry to transfer the cost from Direct Materials Inventory to Work in Process Inventory follows:

COACH'S TIP

Notice that the variance is the "plug figure" that makes the debits and credits balance. Here the actual cost (credit) is less than the standard cost (debit), resulting in a favorable (credit) variance.

	Debit	Credit
Work in Process Inventory ((20,000 × 2) × $1.50)	60,000	
Direct Materials Quantity Variance (10,000 × $1.50)...............	15,000	
Direct Materials Inventory (50,000 × $1.5)........................		75,000

Notice that the amount debited to Work in Process Inventory is based on what it **should have cost** the company to produce 20,000 units. Because each unit requires 2 yards of denim, the standard quantity allowed to produce 20,000 units is 40,000 yards of material, multiplied by a standard price of $1.50 per yard. The amount that is transferred out of Direct Materials Inventory, however, is based on the 50,000 yards that were actually used multiplied by the standard price of $1.50. Multiplying the 10,000 yard difference by the standard price of $1.50 results in an unfavorable direct materials quantity variance of $15,000. Notice that this unfavorable variance appears as a debit entry; a favorable variance would appear as a credit entry.

Before you continue, complete the following Self-Study Practice to see whether you can record the direct materials price and quantity variances.

COACH'S TIP

A debit entry reflects an unfavorable variance. The quantity of materials actually taken from Direct Materials Inventory (a credit) was more than the standard quantity that should have been used to make 20,000 units (a debit).

Solution to Self-Study Practice

Purchase of Direct Materials

	Debit	Credit
Direct Materials Inventory (315,000 × $0.10)	31,500	
Direct Materials Price Variance		3,150
Accounts Payable (315,000 × $0.09)		28,350

Transfer to Cost of Goods Sold

	Debit	Credit
Cost of Goods Sold (15,000 × 20 × $0.10)	30,000	
Direct Materials Quantity Variance	1,500	
Direct Materials Inventory		31,500

How's it going?   Self-Study Practice

Papa John's standard cost card for direct materials includes the following costs:

	Standard Quantity	Standard Price	Standard Unit Cost
Direct materials (Ingredients)	20 oz.	$0.10 per oz.	$2.00

Actual results were as follows:

- The number of units produced and sold was 15,000.
- 315,000 ounces of ingredients were purchased and used for a total cost of $28,350.

Prepare the journal entries to record the purchase of direct materials and the transfer of the cost to the Cost of Goods Sold account.

After you have finished, check your answers against the solutions in the margin.

Record Standard Direct Labor Costs

Recall that the standard quantity for labor was 0.25 hour per unit produced and the standard labor rate was $14. The actual cost of direct labor was $64,000 for 4,000 hours, for an average labor rate of $16 per hour. The entry to record direct labor costs and variances is shown below:

	Debit	Credit
Work in Process Inventory [(20,000 × .25) × $14 per hr.)	**70,000**	
Direct Labor Rate Variance [4,000 × ($14 − $16)]	**8,000**	
Direct Labor Efficiency Variance [$14 × (5,000 − 4,000)] ...		**14,000**
Wages Payable or Cash (4,000 hrs. × $16 per hr.)		**64,000**

Again, the amount that is debited to Work in Process Inventory is based on the standard price and standard quantity of labor. However, the amount credited to cash or wages payable is based on the actual amount paid or owed to employees. The difference in actual and standard cost are explained by the two variances. The direct labor rate variance is unfavorable and appears as a debit entry. The direct labor efficiency variance is favorable and appears as a credit entry.

All other manufacturing costs would be recorded in Work in Process Inventory at the standard cost based on the actual number of units produced. When a unit is complete, its total manufacturing cost is transferred out of Work in Process Inventory and into Finished Goods and eventually Cost of Goods Sold. So Cost of Goods Sold will initially be recorded based on the standard cost per unit.

Before financial statements are prepared, accountants must make adjusting entries to eliminate all of the variance accounts. The most common method of disposing of the variances is to increase or decrease Cost of Goods Sold to adjust from standard cost to actual cost. Unfavorable variances would be debited to Cost of Goods Sold (to increase it from standard to actual), while favorable variances would be credited to Cost of Goods Sold (to reduce it from standard to actual). As a manager, you probably won't need to concern yourself too much with these detailed accounting entries. However, it is important for you to understand that ultimately the variances will be reflected in Cost of Goods Sold, which will impact the company's profitability through the Income Statement.

REVIEW THE CHAPTER

DEMONSTRATION CASE

Bunko Beds produces bunk beds for children. It sells the beds through Pottery Barn Kids and other retail outlets. The standard cost card for producing one of Bunko's most popular beds follows:

Manufacturing Costs	Standard Quantity	Standard Price (Rate)	Standard Unit Cost
Direct materials (1 × 12" treated pine)	50 ft.	$ 2.50 per ft.	$125.00
Direct labor	5 hrs.	10.00 per hr.	50.00
Manufacturing overhead costs			
Variable manufacturing overhead (based on direct labor hours)	5 hrs.	5.00 per hr.	25.00
Fixed manufacturing overhead $120,000 ÷ 3,000 units = $40 per unit			40.00
Standard manufacturing cost per unit			$240.00

Bunko's master budget was based on planned production and sales of 3,000 beds. Actual results were as follows:

- Produced 2,500 beds.
- Purchased and used 130,000 feet of direct materials at a total cost of $312,000.
- Total direct labor cost was $123,750 for 11,250 hours.
- Variable overhead cost was $54,000.
- Fixed overhead cost was $115,000.

Required:

Calculate the following variances and label them as favorable (F) or unfavorable (U):

1. Direct materials variances:
   a. Direct materials price variance.
   b. Direct materials quantity variance.
   c. Direct materials spending variance.

2. Direct labor variances:
   a. Direct labor rate variance.
   b. Direct labor efficiency variance.
   c. Direct labor spending variance.

3. Variable manufacturing overhead variances:
   a. Variable overhead rate variance.
   b. Variable overhead efficiency variance.
   c. Variable overhead spending variance.

4. Fixed manufacturing overhead variances:
   a. Fixed overhead spending variance.
   b. Fixed overhead volume variance.

Suggested Solution

1. Direct materials variances:
   AQ = 130,000 ft.
   AP = $312,000 ÷ 130,000 = $2.40 per ft.
   SQ = 50 ft. × 2,500 actual units = 125,000 ft.
   SP = $2.50 per ft.

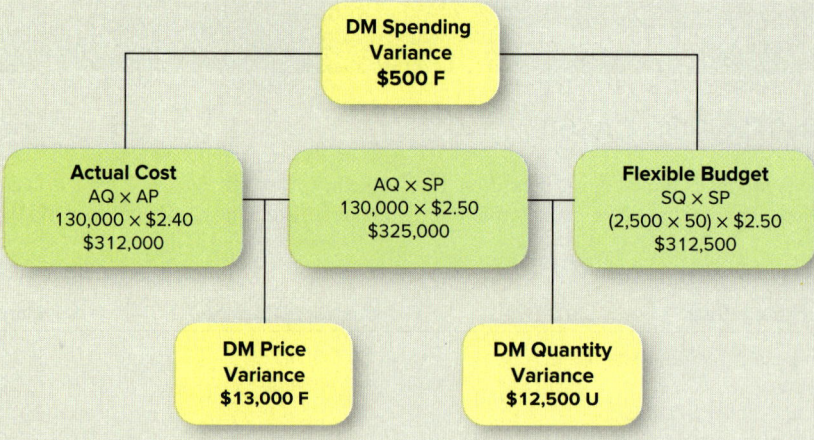

2. Direct labor variances:
   AH = 11,250 hrs.
   AR = $123,750 ÷ 11,250 = $11 per hr.
   SH = 5 hrs. × 2,500 actual units = 12,500 hrs.
   SR = $10 per hr.

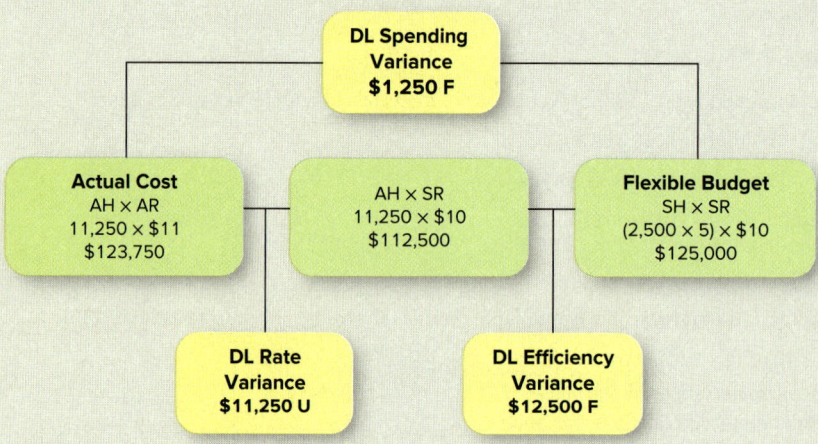

3. Variable manufacturing overhead variances:
   AH = 11,250
   AR = $54,000 ÷ 11,250 = $4.80 per hr.
   SH = 5 hrs. × 2,500 units = 12,500
   SR = $5.00 per hr.

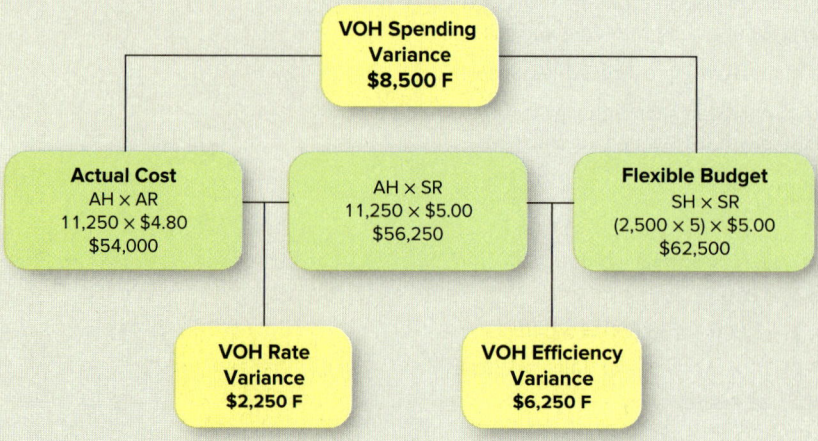

4. Fixed manufacturing overhead spending variance:

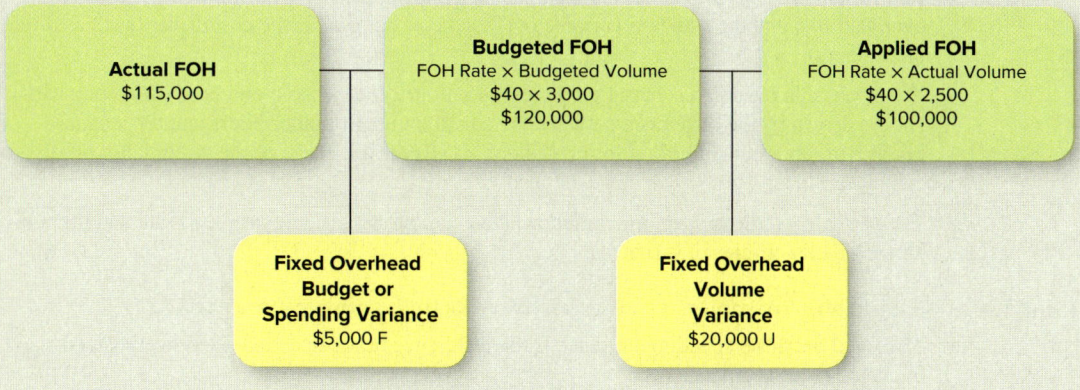

CHAPTER SUMMARY

Describe the standard-setting process and explain how standard costs relate to budgets and variances.

LO 9–1

- Standard costs, which are set at the beginning of the accounting period to reflect what manage-ment believes costs **should be**, should be set so that they are difficult but not impossible to achieve.
- The standard price is the amount that **should** be paid for a particular quantity of input.
- The standard quantity is the amount of input that **should** be used to produce a single unit of output.
- Budgeted costs are based on the standard costs for inputs multiplied by a specific level of output.
- Variances are the difference between actual and budgeted or standard costs.

Prepare a flexible budget and show how total costs change with sales volume.

LO 9–2

- A master budget is a static budget based on estimated or budgeted sales volume.
- A flexible budget shows how total costs are expected to change if actual production or sales are more or less than expected.
- A flexible budget is used to evaluate managerial performance after the fact by separating the effect of spending (that is, cost control) from the effect of volume.
- Spending variances are calculated by comparing actual costs to the flexible budget.
- Volume variances are calculated by comparing the flexible budget to the master budget.

Calculate and interpret the direct materials price and quantity variances.

LO 9–3

- The spending variances for direct materials can be decomposed into a price and a quantity component.
- The direct materials price variance represents the difference between the actual and the standard price paid for direct materials while holding the actual quantity of materials purchased constant.
- The direct materials quantity variance represents the difference between the actual quantity of materials used in production and the standard quantity allowed given the actual units pro-duced, holding the standard price constant.
- The direct materials spending variance is the sum of the direct materials price and direct mate-rials quantity variances.

Calculate and interpret the direct labor rate and efficiency variances.

LO 9–4

- The direct labor rate variance represents the difference between the actual direct labor rate and the standard direct labor rate, with actual labor hours held constant.
- The direct labor efficiency variance represents the difference between the actual number of labor hours and the standard number of labor hours allowed for the actual volume of output, with the standard labor rate held constant.
- The direct labor spending variance is the sum of the direct labor rate and direct labor effi-ciency variances.

LO 9–5   Calculate and interpret the variable overhead rate and efficiency variances.

- The variable overhead rate variance represents the difference between the actual variable overhead cost and the standard variable overhead cost per unit of the cost driver (such as direct labor hours).

- When variable overhead is based on direct labor hours, the variable overhead efficiency variance is driven by the difference between the actual number of labor hours and the standard number of labor hours allowed for production. It is a mirror image of the direct labor efficiency variance.

- The variable overhead spending variance is the sum of the variable overhead rate and the variable overhead efficiency variances.

LO 9–S1   Calculate and interpret the fixed overhead spending and volume variances.

- The fixed overhead spending variance is the difference between actual fixed overhead cost and budgeted fixed overhead cost.

- The fixed overhead volume and capacity variances are represented by the difference between actual and applied fixed overhead costs. These variances relate to the denominator used to apply fixed overhead.

- The fixed overhead volume variance is computed as the difference between actual volume and budgeted volume, multiplied by the fixed overhead rate. The variance is favorable if more units were produced than expected and unfavorable if fewer units were produced than expected.

- Capacity variances can be computed when the fixed overhead rate is based on practical capacity—the volume that could be achieved under normal (not ideal) operating conditions—rather than budgeted volume. The planned capacity variance is computed as the difference between budgeted volume and practical capacity multiplied by the fixed overhead rate. The unplanned capacity variance is computed as the difference between actual volume and budgeted volume, multiplied by the fixed overhead rate.

LO 9–S2   Prepare journal entries to record direct materials and direct labor variances.

- In a standard cost system, manufacturing costs are debited to Direct Materials Inventory, Work in Process, Finished Goods Inventory, and Cost of Goods Sold based on standard costs rather than actual costs.

- Actual costs are recorded with a credit to cash, accounts payable, or other appropriate account.

- The difference between the standard cost (debit) and actual cost (credit) represents the cost variance. Unfavorable variances appear as debit entries, while favorable variances result in credit entries.

- At the end of the accounting period, all variances should be closed to the Cost of Goods Sold account to adjust from standard cost to actual cost.

KEY TERMS

PRACTICE MATERIAL

QUESTIONS

1. Briefly describe the difference between budgetary planning and control.

2. What are standard costs? When are they set?

3. Explain a standard cost system and how a company uses it.

4. What is the difference between ideal and easily attainable standards?

5. What type of standard is best for motivating individuals to work hard?

6. Briefly describe the two types of standards on which a standard cost system relies.

7. What is a standard cost card, and why is it important?

8. How do the terms standard and budget relate to one another and how do they differ?

9. Explain what the terms favorable variance and unfavorable variance mean.

10. How do the master budget, flexible budget, and static budget differ from one another?

11. What type of variance is created by comparing the master budget to the flexible budget?

12. What type of variance is calculated by comparing actual costs to the flexible budget?

13. The spending variance can be separated into two components. Name and briefly describe them.

14. What are the two direct materials variances? What factors can affect each variance and who is generally responsible for the variance?

15. Explain how a manager might make a trade-off between the direct materials price and the direct materials quantity variances.

16. What are the two direct labor variances? What factors can affect each variance and who is generally responsible for the variance?

17. Explain how a manager might make a trade-off between the direct labor rate and the direct labor efficiency variances.

18. What is the key difference between a normal cost system and a standard cost system?

19. What are the two variable overhead variances? What factors can affect each variance and who is generally responsible for the variance?

20. What is the fixed overhead spending variance? What factors can affect the variance and who is generally responsible for the variance?

21. Suppose you have computed a favorable fixed overhead volume variance of $1,000. How would you interpret that variance?

22. What does the term practical capacity mean? How does it differ from budgeted?

23. What happens to all of the variances that have been recorded during a period?

MULTIPLE CHOICE

1. In general, variances tell managers

   a. Nothing.
   b. Whom to promote and whom to fire.
   c. Whether budgeted goals are being achieved.
   d. Which departments are running at full capacity.

2. In distinguishing between budgets and standards, which of the following is true?

   a. The terms mean exactly the same thing.
   b. Standards are used to develop budgets.
   c. Budgets are used to develop standards.
   d. Budgets and standards are unrelated.

3. Variances are always noted as favorable or unfavorable. What do these terms indicate?

   a. Whether actual results are more or less than standard or budgeted amounts.
   b. Whether the manager in a particular department is doing a good job.
   c. Whether a company is performing as well as its competitors.
   d. All of the above.

4. What type of budget is an integrated set of operating and financial budgets that reflects managements' expectations for a given sales level, and what type shows how budgeted costs and revenues will change across different levels of sales volume?

   a. Flexible budget, master budget.
   b. Standard budget, flexible budget.
   c. Master budget, static budget.
   d. Master budget, flexible budget.

5. When computing spending variances, actual results are compared to

   a. The flexible budget.
   b. The master budget.
   c. The variances.
   d. Last year's actual results.

6. Spending variances may be separated into

   a. Price and quantity variances.
   b. Price and volume variances.
   c. Volume and quantity variances.
   d. Quantity and quality variances.

7. Temecula Company has calculated its direct materials price variance to be $1,000 favorable and its direct materials quantity variance to be $3,000 unfavorable. Which of the following could explain both of these variances?

   a. The production manager has recently hired more skilled laborers.
   b. The purchases manager bought less expensive raw materials but they were of lower quality.
   c. A machine in the factory malfunctioned resulting in considerable wasted direct materials.
   d. The purchases manager bought higher quality materials.

8. In producing its product, Ranger Company used 1,500 hours of direct labor at an actual cost of $15 per hour. The standard for Ranger's production level is 1,400 hours at $14 per hour. What is Ranger's direct labor rate variance?

   a. $1,500 favorable.
   b. $1,400 favorable.
   c. $1,500 unfavorable.
   d. $1,400 unfavorable.

9. Refer to the preceding question about Ranger Company. In producing its product, Ranger Company used 1,500 pounds of direct materials at an actual cost of $1.50 per pound. The standard for Ranger's production level was 1,400 pounds at $1.40 per pound. What is Ranger's direct materials quantity variance?

   a. $150 favorable.
   b. $140 favorable.
   c. $150 unfavorable.
   d. $140 unfavorable.

10. An unfavorable fixed overhead volume or capacity variance indicates that a company

    a. Manufactured fewer units than it expected.
    b. Manufactured more units than it expected.
    c. Underestimated its total fixed overhead cost.
    d. Overestimated its total fixed overhead cost.

 **Find More Learning Solutions on Connect.**

MINI-EXERCISES

LO 9–1, 9–2, 9–3, 9–4, 9–5, 9–S1, 9–S2

M9–1 Using Variance Terminology

Use the following terms to complete the sentences that follow; terms may be used once, more than once, or not at all:

Static	Purchasing manager
Flexible	Favorable
Volume	Unfavorable
Spending	Debit
Production manager	Credit
Variable overhead rate	Fixed overhead budget
Variable overhead efficiency	Fixed overhead volume
Fixed overhead spending	

1. A _____ budget is based on a fixed estimate of sales volume.
2. A _____ variance represents the difference between actual and expected levels of activity.
3. The _____ is typically responsible for the direct materials quantity variance.
4. The variable overhead rate variance is _____ when the actual variable overhead rate is less than the standard variable overhead rate.
5. Unfavorable variances appear as _____ entries; favorable variances appear as _____ entries.
6. The _____ variance is the difference between the number of actual direct labor hours used and the number of standard direct labor hours multiplied by the standard variable overhead rate.
7. Using less direct materials than expected results in a _____ variance.
8. The _____ is typically responsible for the direct labor efficiency variance.
9. The _____ variance is sometimes also called the *denominator variance*.
10. When recording journal entries, the actual cost is a _____ and the standard cost is a _____.

LO 9–1, 9–2, 9–3, 9–4

M9–2 Matching Terminology

Match each of the terms by inserting the appropriate definition letter in the space provided. Not all definitions will be used.

_____ **1.** Actual Accounting System

_____ **2.** Direct Labor Efficiency Variance

_____ **3.** Direct Labor Rate Variance

_____ **4.** Direct Materials Price Variance

_____ **5.** Direct Materials Spending Variance

_____ **6.** Ideal Standard

_____ **7.** Normal Cost System

_____ **8.** Standard Cost System

_____ **9.** Unfavorable Variance

_____ **10.** Variance

A. The difference between actual price and standard price times the actual quantity of materials purchased.

B. Difference between actual and planned results.

C. The difference between actual labor hours and standard labor hours multiplied by the standard labor rate.

D. The difference between actual price and standard price times the actual quantity of materials used.

E. The difference between actual cost and the flexible budget for materials.

F. The difference between actual labor hours and standard labor hours multiplied by the actual labor rate.

G. Standards that can be achieved only under perfect conditions.

H. When actual costs are greater than planned costs.

I. When actual sales are greater than planned sales.

J. Standards that are tight but are used to motivate individuals to work hard and achieve results.

K. The difference between the actual rate and the standard rate multiplied by the actual labor hours used.

L. An accounting system that records all costs based on estimated amounts.

M. The difference between the actual rate and the standard rate multiplied by the standard labor hours allowed.

N. An accounting system that records all actual amounts after the expense has occurred.

O. An accounting system that records all direct materials and direct labor at actual amounts, while assigning manufacturing overhead costs using predetermined overhead rates.

M9–3 Creating Grading Scale Based on Ideal, Tight but Attainable, Easily Attainable Standards   LO 9–1

Consider the grading scale for a university class that has 500 possible points. The possible course grades are A, B, C, D, and F. Create a grading scale for the class that would fall into each of the following categories: an ideal standard, an easily attainable standard, and a tight but attainable standard. What are the implications for student motivation?

M9–4 Explaining Costs That Change with Flexible Budget Activity   LO 9–2

When preparing a company's flexible budget, which manufacturing cost(s) will change as the volume increases or decreases? Which manufacturing cost(s) will not change as the volume changes?

LO 9–2 **M9–5 Preparing a Flexible Budget**

Evanson Company expects to produce 500,000 units of their product during the year. Monthly production is expected to range from 40,000 to 80,000 units. The company has budgeted manufacturing costs per unit to be as follows:

Direct materials	$4
Direct labor	5
Variable manufacturing overhead	6
Fixed manufacturing overhead	3

Prepare a flexible manufacturing budget using 20,000 unit increments.

LO 9–1 **M9–6 Describing How to Set Standards in Standard Cost System**

Dabney Company manufactures widgets and would like to use a standard cost system. Explain how Dabney will determine the standards for direct materials and direct labor to use in its costing system.

LO 9–4 **M9–7 Calculating Unknown Values for Direct Labor Variances**

For each of the following independent cases, fill in the missing amounts in the table:

Case	Direct Labor Rate Variance	Direct Labor Efficiency Variance	Direct Labor Spending Variance
A	$ 750 U	$1,200 F	$?
B	2,000 F	?	3,500 U
C	1,000 F	?	1,800 F
D	?	500 U	2,500 U
E	?	1,100 F	1,950 U
F	650 U	1,150 U	?

LO 9–3 **M9–8 Interpreting Direct Materials Cost Variances**

Kelton Corp. has calculated its direct materials price and quantity variances to be $500 favorable and $800 unfavorable, respectively. Kelton's production manager believes that these variances indicate that the purchasing department is doing a good job but production is doing a poor job. Explain whether the production manager's conclusions are correct.

LO 9–3 **M9–9 Calculating Direct Materials Cost Variances**

Acoma, Inc., has determined a standard direct materials cost per unit of $8 (2 feet × $4 per foot). Last month, Acoma purchased and used 4,200 feet of direct materials for which it paid $15,750. The company produced and sold 2,000 units during the month. Calculate the direct materials price, quantity, and spending variances.

LO 9–4 **M9–10 Calculating Direct Labor Cost Variances**

Paradise Corp. has determined a standard labor cost per unit of $12 (0.5 hour × $24 per hour). Last month, Paradise incurred 950 direct labor hours for which it paid $22,325. The company produced and sold 1,950 units during the month. Calculate the direct labor rate, efficiency, and spending variances.

LO 9–5 **M9–11 Calculating Variable Manufacturing Overhead Variances**

Beverly Company has determined a standard variable overhead rate of $2.50 per direct labor hour and expects to incur 0.5 labor hour per unit produced. Last month, Beverly incurred 950 actual direct labor hours in the production of 2,000 units. The company has also determined that its actual variable overhead rate is $2.40 per direct labor hour. Calculate the variable overhead rate and efficiency variances as well as the total amount of over- or underapplied variable overhead.

LO 9–S1 **M9–12 Calculating Fixed Manufacturing Overhead Spending Variance**

Cholla Company's standard fixed overhead rate is based on budgeted fixed manufacturing overhead of $10,200 and budgeted production of 30,000 units. Actual results for the month of October reveal that Cholla produced 28,000 units and spent $9,900 on fixed manufacturing overhead costs. Calculate Cholla's fixed overhead spending variance.

M9–13 Calculating Fixed Manufacturing Overhead Volume Variance
LO 9–S1

Refer to **M9–12** for Cholla Company. Calculate Cholla's fixed overhead rate and the fixed overhead volume variance.

M9–14 Preparing Journal Entries to Record Direct Material Costs Variances
LO 9–S2

During May, Camino Corp. purchased direct materials for 4,400 units at a total cost of $63,800. Camino's standard direct materials cost is $14 per unit. Prepare the journal entry to record this transaction.

M9–15 Preparing Journal Entries to Record Direct Labor Costs Variances
LO 9–S2

Andora Company reported the following information for the month of November. The standard cost of labor for the month was $38,000, but actual wages paid were $37,300. Andora has calculated its direct labor rate and efficiency variances to be $1,500 favorable and $800 unfavorable, respectively. Prepare the necessary journal entry to record Andora's direct labor cost for the month, assuming that standard labor costs are recorded directly to Cost of Good Sold.

EXERCISES

E9–1 Calculating Unknown Values for Direct Materials, Direct Labor Variances
LO 9–3, 9–4

Ironwood Company manufactures cast-iron barbeque cookware. During a recent windstorm, it lost some of its cost accounting records. Ironwood has managed to reconstruct portions of its standard cost system database but is still missing a few pieces of information.

	Direct Materials	Direct Labor
Standard amount per pan produced	2.5 lb.	1.10 hr.
Standard price	$4.20 per lb.	$16.00 per hr.
Actual amount used per pan produced	2.4 lb.	1.20 hr.
Actual price	$4.10 per lb.	$15.50 per hr.
Actual number of pans produced and sold	2,500 pans	2,500 pans
Direct materials price variance	?	
Direct materials quantity variance	?	
Direct materials spending variance	?	
Direct labor rate variance		?
Direct labor efficiency variance		?
Direct labor spending variance		?

Required:

Use the information in the table to determine the unknown amounts. You may assume that Ironwood does not keep any raw materials on hand.

E9–2 Preparing Flexible Budget for Manufacturing Costs
LO 9–2

Olive Company makes silver belt buckles. The company's master budget appears in the first column of the table.

	Master Budget (5,000 units)	Flexible Budget (4,000 units)	Flexible Budget (6,000 units)	Flexible Budget (7,000 units)
Direct materials	$15,000			
Direct labor	30,000			
Variable manufacturing overhead	8,000			
Fixed manufacturing overhead	18,000			
Total manufacturing cost	$71,000			

Required:

Complete the table by preparing Olive's flexible budget for 4,000, 6,000, and 7,000 units.

LO 9–2   **E9–3 Preparing a Flexible Budget Performance Report**

Gleason Guitars produces acoustic guitars. The table below contains budget and actual information for the month of June:

	Actual Costs (225 units)	Spending Variance	Flexible Budget (225 units)	Volume Variance	Master Budget (200 units)
Direct materials	$15,500				$14,000
Direct labor	26,200				22,000
Variable overhead	8,250				8,000
Fixed overhead	11,500				11,000
Total manufacturing costs					

Required:

Complete the table.

LO 9–3   **E9–4 Interpreting Direct Materials Price, Quantity Variances**

Perfect Pet Collar Company makes custom leather pet collars. The company expects each collar to require 1.5 feet of leather and predicts leather will cost $2.50 per foot. Suppose Perfect Pet made 60 collars during February. For these 60 collars, the company actually averaged 1.75 feet of leather per collar and paid $2.00 per foot.

Required:

1. Compute the standard direct materials cost per unit.
2. Without performing any calculations, determine whether the direct materials price variance will be favorable or unfavorable.
3. Without performing any calculations, determine whether the direct materials quantity variance will be favorable or unfavorable.
4. Give a potential explanation for this pattern of variances.
5. Where would you begin to investigate the variances?
6. Calculate the direct materials price and quantity variances.

LO 9–3, 9–4   **E9–5 Calculating Direct Materials and Direct Labor Variances**

Suds & Cuts is a local pet grooming shop owned by Collin Bark. Collin has prepared the following standard cost card for each dog bath given:

	Standard Quantity	Standard Rate	Standard Unit Cost
Shampoo	2 oz.	$0.10 per oz.	$0.20
Water	20 gal.	$0.05 per gal.	1.00
Direct labor	0.75 hr.	$9.00 per hr.	6.75

During the month of July, Collin's employees gave 360 baths. The actual results were 725 ounces of shampoo used (cost of $116), 6,500 gallons of water used (cost of $455), and labor costs for 230 hours (cost of $2,300).

Required:

1. Calculate Suds & Cuts direct materials variances for both shampoo and water for the month of July.
2. Calculate Suds & Cuts direct labor variances for the month of July.
3. Identify a possible cause of each variance.

E9–6 Calculating Direct Materials and Direct Labor Variances   LO 9–3, 9–4

Crystal Charm Company makes handcrafted silver charms that attach to jewelry such as a necklace or bracelet. Each charm is adorned with two crystals of various colors. Standard costs follow:

	Standard Quantity	Standard Price (Rate)	Standard Unit Cost
Silver	0.25 oz.	$20.00 per oz.	$ 5.00
Crystals	2	$0.25 crystal	0.50
Direct labor	1.5 hrs.	$15.00 per hr.	22.50

During the month of January, Crystal Charm made 1,800 charms. The company used 420 ounces of silver (total cost of $9,240) and 3,650 crystals (total cost of $803), and paid for 2,880 actual direct labor hours (cost of $42,480).

Required:

1. Calculate Crystal Charm's direct materials variances for silver and crystals for the month of January.
2. Calculate Crystal Charm's direct labor variances for the month of January.
3. Identify a possible cause of each variance.

E9–7 Calculating Direct Material and Labor Variances   LO 9–3, 9–4

Betty's Bakery has the following standard cost sheet for one unit of its most popular cake:

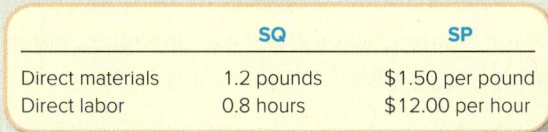

	SQ	SP
Direct materials	1.2 pounds	$1.50 per pound
Direct labor	0.8 hours	$12.00 per hour

During the month of May, the company made 600 cakes and incurred the following actual costs:
    Direct materials purchased and used (900 pounds), $1,170
    Direct labor (660 hours), $7,590

Required:

1. Calculate the direct materials price variance.
2. Calculate the direct materials quantity variance.
3. Calculate the direct materials spending variance.
4. Calculate the direct labor rate variance.
5. Calculate the direct labor efficiency variance.
6. Calculate the direct labor spending variance.

E9–8 Calculating Direct Materials Variances   LO 9–3

Parker Plastic, Inc., manufactures plastic mats to use with rolling office chairs. Its standard cost information for last year follows:

	Standard Quantity	Standard Price (Rate)	Standard Unit Cost
Direct materials (plastic)	12 sq ft.	$ 0.72 per sq. ft.	$8.64
Direct labor	0.25 hr.	$12.20 per hr.	3.05
Variable manufacturing overhead (based on direct labor hours)	0.25 hr.	$ 1.20 per hr.	0.30
Fixed manufacturing overhead ($378,000 ÷ 900,000 units)			0.42

Parker Plastic had the following actual results for the past year:

Number of units produced and sold	1,000,000
Number of square feet of plastic used	11,800,000
Cost of plastic purchased and used	$ 8,260,000
Number of labor hours worked	245,000
Direct labor cost	$ 2,891,000
Variable overhead cost	$ 318,500
Fixed overhead cost	$ 355,000

Required:

Calculate Parker Plastic's direct materials price and quantity variances.

LO 9–4   **E9–9 Calculating Direct Labor Variances**

Refer to the information presented in **E9–8** for Parker Plastic.

Required:

Calculate Parker Plastic's direct labor rate and efficiency variances.

LO 9–5   **E9–10 Calculating Variable Overhead Variances**

Refer to the information presented in **E9–8** for Parker Plastic.

Required:

Calculate Parker Plastic's variable overhead rate and efficiency variances and its over- or underapplied variable overhead.

LO 9–S1   **E9–11 Calculating Fixed Manufacturing Overhead Spending, Volume Variances**

Refer to the information presented in **E9–8** for Parker Plastic.

Required:

Calculate Parker Plastic's fixed overhead spending and volume variances and its over- or underapplied fixed overhead.

LO 9–S2   **E9–12 Preparing Journal Entries to Record Direct Materials, Direct Labor, Variable Overhead Costs, and Variances**

Refer to the information presented in **E9–8** for Parker Plastic.

Required:

Prepare the journal entry to record the following for Parker Plastic:

1. Direct materials costs and related variances. Assume the company purchases raw materials as needed and does not maintain any ending inventories.
2. Direct labor and related variances.
3. Variable overhead costs and related variances.
4. Fixed overhead transactions assuming overhead is applied based on budgeted production.

LO 9–5   **E9–13 Calculating Variable Manufacturing Overhead Variances**

Lamp Light Limited (LLL) manufactures lampshades. It applies variable overhead on the basis of direct labor hours. Information from LLL's standard cost card follows:

	Standard Quantity	Standard Rate	Standard Unit Cost
Variable manufacturing overhead	0.6	$0.80	$0.48

During August, LLL had the following actual results:

Units produced and sold	25,000
Actual variable overhead	$9,490
Actual direct labor hours	16,000

Required:

Compute LLL's variable overhead rate variance, variable overhead efficiency variance, and over- or underapplied variable overhead.

E9–14 Calculating Fixed Manufacturing Overhead Spending, Volume Variances   LO 9–S1

Lamp Light Limited (LLL) in **E9–13** calculates a fixed overhead rate based on budgeted fixed overhead of $32,400 and budgeted production of 24,000 units. Actual results were as follows:

Number of units produced and sold	25,000
Actual fixed overhead	$32,000

Required:

Calculate the following for LLL:

1. Fixed overhead rate based on budgeted production.
2. Fixed overhead spending variance.
3. Fixed overhead volume variance.
4. Over- or underapplied fixed overhead.

E9–15 Determining Actual Costs, Standard Costs, and Variances   LO 9–3, 9–4

Amber Company produces iron table and chair sets. During October, Amber's costs were as follows:

Actual purchase price	$ 2.30 per lb.
Actual direct labor rate	$ 7.50 per hour
Standard purchase price	$ 2.10 per lb.
Standard quantity for sets produced	970,000 lbs.
Standard direct labor hours allowed	11,000
Actual quantity purchased in October	1,115,000 lbs.
Actual direct labor hours	10,000
Actual quantity used in October	1,000,000 lbs.
Direct labor rate variance	$5,500 F

Required:

1. Calculate the total cost of purchases for October.
2. Compute the direct materials price variance based on quantity purchased.
3. Calculate the direct materials quantity variance based on quantity used.
4. Compute the standard direct labor rate for October.
5. Compute the direct labor efficiency variance for October.

E9–16 Calculating Fixed Manufacturing Overhead Capacity Variances   LO 9–S1

Haines Manufacturing Company (HMC) bases its fixed overhead rate on practical capacity of 30,000 units per year. Budgeted and actual results for the most recent year follow:

	Budgeted	Actual
Fixed manufacturing overhead	$600,000	$560,000
Number of units produced	20,000	22,000

Required:

Calculate the following for HMC:

1. Fixed overhead rate based on practical capacity.
2. Fixed overhead spending variance.
3. Expected (planned) capacity variance.
4. Unexpected (unplanned) capacity variance.
5. Total over- or underapplied fixed manufacturing overhead.

LO 9–5   E9–17 Calculating Variable Manufacturing Overhead Variances

See Clear Company manufactures clear plastic CD cases. It applies variable overhead based on the number of machine hours used. Information regarding See Clear's overhead for the month of December follows:

	Standard Quantity	Standard Rate	Standard Unit Cost
Variable manufacturing overhead	0.1 machine hours per case	$0.60 per machine hour	$0.06

During December, See Clear had the following actual results:

Number of units produced and sold	628,000
Actual variable overhead cost	$30,240
Actual machine hours	63,000

Required:

Compute See Clear's variable overhead rate variance, variable overhead efficiency variance, and over- or underapplied variable overhead.

LO 9–S1   E9–18 Calculating Fixed Manufacturing Overhead Volume Variances

See Clear Company calculates a fixed overhead rate based on budgeted fixed overhead of $192,000 and budgeted production of 600,000 units. Actual results were as follows:

Number of units produced and sold	628,000
Actual fixed overhead	$195,000

Required:

Calculate the following for See Clear:

1. Fixed overhead rate based on budgeted production.
2. Fixed overhead spending variance.
3. Fixed overhead volume variance.
4. Over- or underapplied fixed overhead.

LO 9–S1   E9–19 Calculating Fixed Manufacturing Overhead Capacity Variances

Haives Manufacturing Company (HMC) bases its fixed overhead rate on practical capacity of 80,000 units per year. Budgeted and actual results for the most recent year follow:

	Budgeted	Actual
Fixed manufacturing overhead	$540,000	$520,000
Number of units produced	70,000	75,000

Required:

Calculate the following for HMC:

1. Fixed overhead rate based on practical capacity.
2. Fixed overhead spending variance.
3. Expected (planned) capacity variance.
4. Unexpected (unplanned) capacity variance.

E9–20 Determining Actual, Standard Costs, and Variances   9–4

For each of the following independent cases, fill in the missing amounts:

	Casey Co.	Kevin, Inc.	Jess Co.	Valerie, Inc.
Units produced	2,000	?	120	1,500
Standard hours per unit	3.5	0.9	?	?
Standard hours	?	900	300	?
Standard rate per hour	$14.50	$?	$10.50	$7
Actual hours worked	6,800	975	?	4,900
Actual labor cost	$?	$?	$3,090	$31,850
Direct labor rate variance	$1,700 F	$975 F	$ 150 U	$?
Direct labor efficiency variance	$?	$765 U	$?	$ 2,800 U

GROUP A PROBLEMS

PA9–1 Calculating Direct Material, Direct Labor, Variable Overhead Variances   LO 9–3, 9–4, 9–5

Barley Hopp, Inc., manufactures custom-ordered commemorative beer steins. Its standard cost information follows:

	Standard Quantity	Standard Price (Rate)	Standard Unit Cost
Direct materials (clay)	1.5 lbs.	$ 1.60 per lb.	$ 2.40
Direct labor	1.5 hrs.	$12.00 per hr.	18.00
Variable manufacturing overhead (based on direct labor hours)	1.5 hrs.	$ 1.20 per hr.	1.80
Fixed manufacturing overhead ($250,000 ÷ 100,000 units)			2.50

Barley Hopp had the following actual results last year:

Number of units produced and sold	110,000
Number of pounds of clay used	178,200
Cost of clay	$ 267,300
Number of labor hours worked	150,000
Direct labor cost	$2,025,000
Variable overhead cost	$ 200,000
Fixed overhead cost	$ 270,000

Required:

Calculate the following for Barley Hopp:

1. Direct materials price, quantity, and spending variances.
2. Direct labor rate, efficiency, and spending variances.
3. Variable overhead rate, efficiency, and spending variances.

PA9–2 Calculating Fixed Manufacturing Overhead Spending, Volume Variances   LO 9–S1

Refer to the information for Barley Hopp in **PA9–1**.

Required:

Compute the following for Barley Hopp:

1. Fixed overhead spending variance.
2. Fixed overhead volume variance.
3. Total over- or underapplied fixed manufacturing overhead.

LO 9–S2   **PA9–3** **Preparing Journal Entries to Record Direct Materials, Direct Labor, Variable Manufacturing Overhead Variances**

Refer to the information in **PA9–1** for Barley Hopp.

Required:

Prepare the journal entry to record the following for Barley Hopp:

1. Direct materials costs and related variances. Assume the company purchases direct materials as needed and does not maintain any ending inventories.
2. Direct labor and related variances

LO 9–3, 9–4, 9–5   **PA9–4** **Calculating Direct Materials, Direct Labor, Variable Manufacturing Overhead Variances**

Bullseye Company manufactures dartboards. Its standard cost information follows:

	Standard Quantity	Standard Price (Rate)	Standard Unit Cost
Direct materials (cork board)	2.5 sq. ft.	$ 2.00 per sq. ft.	$ 5.00
Direct labor	1 hr.	$14.00 per hr.	14.00
Variable manufacturing overhead (based on direct labor hours)	1 hr.	$ 0.50 per hr.	0.50
Fixed manufacturing overhead ($40,000 ÷ 160,000 units)			0.25

Bullseye has the following actual results for the month of September:

Number of units produced and sold	140,000
Number of square feet of corkboard used	360,000
Cost of corkboard used	$ 756,000
Number of labor hours worked	148,000
Direct labor cost	$1,938,800
Variable overhead cost	$ 72,000
Fixed overhead cost	$ 50,000

Required:

Calculate the following for Bullseye:

1. Direct materials price, quantity, and spending variances.
2. Direct labor rate, efficiency, and spending variances.
3. Variable overhead rate, efficiency, and spending variances.

LO 9–S1   **PA9–5** **Calculating Fixed Manufacturing Overhead Spending, Volume Variances**

Refer to the information in **PA9–4.**

Required:

Calculate the following for Bullseye:

1. Fixed overhead spending variance.
2. Fixed overhead volume variance.
3. Total over- or underapplied fixed manufacturing overhead.

PA9–6 Preparing Journal Entries to Record Direct Materials, Direct Labor, Variable Manufacturing Overhead Variances

LO 9–S2

Refer to the information in **PA9–4** for Bullseye Company.

Required:

Prepare the journal entries to record the following for Bullseye:

1. Direct materials costs and related variances. Assume the company purchases direct materials as needed and does not maintain any ending inventories.
2. Direct labor and related variances.

PA9–7 Calculating Direct Materials, Direct Labor, Variable Manufacturing Overhead, Fixed Manufacturing Overhead Variances

LO 9–3, 9–4, 9–5, 9–S1

Rip Tide Company manufactures surfboards. Its standard cost information follows:

	Standard Quantity	Standard Price (Rate)	Standard Unit Cost
Direct materials (fiberglass)	15 sq. ft.	$ 5 per sq. ft.	$ 75.00
Direct labor	10 hrs.	$15 per hr.	150.00
Variable manufacturing overhead (based on direct labor hours)	10 hrs.	$ 6 per hr.	60.00
Fixed manufacturing overhead ($24,000 ÷ 300 units)			80.00

Rip Tide has the following actual results for the month of June:

Number of units produced and sold	312
Number of square feet of fiberglass used	4,920
Cost of fiberglass used	$27,552
Number of labor hours worked	3,060
Direct labor cost	$47,736
Variable overhead cost	$14,790
Fixed overhead cost	$24,600

Required:

Calculate the following for Rip Tide:

1. Direct materials price, quantity, and spending variances.
2. Direct labor rate, efficiency, and spending variances.
3. Variable overhead rate, efficiency, and spending variances.
4. Fixed overhead spending (budget) and volume variances.

PA9–8 Preparing Journal Entries to Record Direct Materials and Direct Labor Variances

LO 9–S2

Refer to the information in **PA9–7** for Rip Tide.

Required:

Prepare the journal entries to record the following for Rip Tide:

1. Direct materials costs and related variances.
2. Direct labor and related variances.

GROUP B PROBLEMS

LO 9–3, 9–4, 9–5 **PB9–1 Calculating Direct Materials, Direct Labor, Variable Manufacturing Overhead Variances**

Sweetly Sent, Inc., manufactures scented pillar candles. Its standard cost information for the month of February follows:

	Standard Quantity	Standard Price (Rate)	Standard Unit Cost
Direct materials (wax)	15 oz.	$ 0.05 per oz.	$0.75
Direct labor	0.25 hr.	$14.00 per hr.	3.50
Variable manufacturing overhead (based on direct labor hours)	0.25 hr.	$ 0.40 per hr.	0.10
Fixed manufacturing overhead ($10,000 ÷ 40,000 units)			0.25

Sweetly Sent has the following actual results for the month of February:

Number of units produced and sold	38,500
Number of ounces of wax purchased and used	583,000
Cost of wax used	$ 37,895
Number of labor hours worked	9,900
Direct labor cost	$136,620
Variable overhead cost	$ 3,630
Fixed overhead cost	$ 9,900

Required:

Calculate the following for Sweetly Sent:

1. Direct materials price, quantity, and spending variances.
2. Direct labor rate, efficiency, and spending variances.
3. Variable overhead rate, efficiency, and spending variances.

LO 9–S1 **PB9–2 Calculating Fixed Manufacturing Overhead Spending and Volume Variances**

Refer to the information for Sweetly Sent in **PB9–1**.

Required:

Compute the following for Sweetly Sent:

1. Fixed overhead spending variance.
2. Fixed overhead volume variance.
3. Total over- or underapplied fixed manufacturing overhead.

LO 9–S2 **PB9–3 Preparing Journal Entries to Record Direct Materials, Direct Labor, Variable Manufacturing Overhead Variances**

Refer to the information in **PB9–1** for Sweetly Sent.

Required:

Prepare the journal entry to record the following for Sweetly Sent:

1. Direct materials costs and related variances. Assume the company purchases direct materials as needed and does not maintain any ending inventories.
2. Direct labor and related variances.

PB9–4 Calculating Direct Materials, Direct Labor, Variable Manufacturing Overhead   LO 9–3, 9–4, 9–5
Variances

Dolles Clay, Inc., manufactures basic terra cotta planters. Its standard cost information for the past year follows:

	Standard Quantity	Standard Price (Rate)	Standard Unit Cost
Direct materials (clay)	2 lbs.	$ 0.80 per lb.	$1.60
Direct labor	0.5 hr.	$12.00 per hr.	6.00
Variable manufacturing overhead (based on direct labor hours)	0.5 hr.	$ 0.40 per hr.	0.20
Fixed manufacturing overhead ($480,000 ÷ 800,000 units)			0.60

Dolles Clay has the following actual results for the past year:

Number of units produced and sold	675,000
Number of pounds of clay used	1,305,000
Cost of clay purchased and used	$ 991,800
Number of labor hours worked	337,500
Direct labor cost	$3,712,500
Variable overhead cost	$ 157,500
Fixed overhead cost	$ 505,000

Required:

Calculate the following for Dolles Clay:

1. Direct materials price, quantity, and spending variances.
2. Direct labor rate, efficiency, and spending variances.
3. Variable overhead rate, efficiency, and spending variances.

PB9–5 Calculating Fixed Manufacturing Overhead Spending, Volume Variances   LO 9–S1

Refer to the information for Dolles Clay in **PB9–4.**

Required:

Compute the following for Dolles Clay:

1. Fixed overhead spending variance
2. Fixed overhead volume variance.
3. Over- or underapplied fixed manufacturing overhead.

PB9–6 Preparing Journal Entries to Record Direct Materials, Direct Labor, Variable   LO 9–S2
Manufacturing Overhead Variances

Refer to the information in **PB9–4** for Dolles Clay.

Required:

Prepare the journal entries to record the following for Dolles Clay:

1. Direct materials costs and related variances. Assume the company purchases direct materials as needed and does not maintain any ending inventories.
2. Direct labor and related variances.

LO 9–3, 9–4, 9–5, 9–S1   **PB9–7 Calculating Direct Materials, Direct Labor, Variable Manufacturing Overhead, Fixed Manufacturing Overhead Variances**

First Trax Company manufactures snowboards. Its standard cost information follows.

	Standard Quantity	Standard Price (Rate)	Standard Unit Cost
Direct materials (fiberglass)	12 sq. ft.	$ 6 per sq. ft.	$ 72.00
Direct labor	5 hr.	$16 per hr.	80.00
Variable manufacturing overhead (25% of direct labor cost)	5 hr	$ 4 per hr	20.00
Fixed manufacturing overhead ($60,000 ÷ 500 units)			120.00

First Trax has the following actual results for the month of June:

Number of units produced and sold	600
Number of square feet of fiberglass purchased and used	7,800
Cost of fiberglass purchased and used	$42,900
Number of labor hours worked	2,700
Direct labor cost	$40,500
Variable overhead cost	$12,600
Fixed overhead cost	$62,000

Required:

Calculate the following for First Trax:

1. Direct materials price, quantity, and spending variances.
2. Direct labor rate, efficiency, and spending variances.
3. Variable overhead rate, efficiency, and spending variances.
4. Fixed overhead spending (budget) and volume variances.

LO 9–S2   **PB9–8 Preparing Journal Entries to Record Variable and Fixed Manufacturing Overhead Variances**

Refer to the information in **PB9–7** for First Trax.

Required:

Prepare the journal entries to record the following for First Trax:

1. Direct materials costs and related variances.
2. Direct labor and related variances.

SKILLS DEVELOPMENT CASES

LO 9–1, 9–2, 9–3, 9–4, 9–5, 9–S1   **S9–1 Video Case Assignment: Explaining Variance for a Manufacturing Firm**

Go to www.YouTube.com and search for **How It's Made**, a television show produced by the Discovery Channel that shows how thousands of products and services are created. Find any product that interests you. Assume the company that makes this product uses a standard cost system, answer the following questions:

- How would the company go about setting standards for this product? What types of standards would be included?

- How would managers of the company use the standard costs?

- Assume the company reported the following variances in the most recent period. Can you think of a scenario that would explain each combination of variances?
  - Unfavorable direct materials price variance, favorable direct materials usage variance, and unfavorable direct materials spending variance.
  - Favorable direct labor rate variance, unfavorable direct labor efficiency variance, and unfavorable direct labor spending variance.
  - Unfavorable direct labor efficiency variance and unfavorable variable overhead efficiency variance.
  - Favorable fixed overhead spending variance and favorable fixed overhead volume variance.

S9–2 Evaluating Managerial Performance by Comparing Actual to Budgeted Results   LO 9–1, 9–2

Suppose Acore Pharmaceuticals has four sales representatives assigned to the state of Arizona. These sales reps are responsible for visiting physicians in their assigned area, introducing the company's current or upcoming products, providing samples, getting feedback about the products, and generating sales. Each sales rep is given an expense budget that includes samples of Acore's products, travel expenses related to the company vehicle that Acore provides, and entertainment expenses such as buying meals or hosting small "meet and greet" receptions.

The following table includes both budgeted and actual amounts for each sales rep for the first half of the current year. As you can see, each was allotted the same amount of resources and expected to generate the same amount of sales for the six-month period.

Sales Rep	Samples Budget	Samples Actual	Travel Budget	Travel Actual	Entertainment Budget	Entertainment Actual	Sales Budget	Sales Actual
Terry	$7,200	$ 4,200	$18,000	$28,000	$4,800	$1,900	$90,000	$ 78,000
Maria	7,200	15,500	18,000	12,000	4,800	9,900	90,000	130,000
Samantha	7,200	2,900	18,000	18,000	4,800	4,600	90,000	43,000
Abraham	7,200	5,300	18,000	16,200	4,800	4,500	90,000	92,000

Required:

1. Calculate the expense and sales variances for each rep. Evaluate each of them and rank them in order of performance. Explain your rationale for these rankings. Suppose $100,000 in bonuses is available to be split among these sales reps. How would you allocate the money to them?
2. Now suppose that you find additional information about the territories to which Acore's Arizona reps are assigned. (If you're not familiar with Arizona, you can find a map at www.mapofarizona.net.)
   - Terry has the northern Arizona territory that includes everything north of Phoenix between the California and New Mexico borders. This territory encompasses a large amount of Native American reservation land as well as the Grand Canyon National Park. Flagstaff is the largest city in the territory.
   - Maria has the Phoenix area that includes the Phoenix metropolitan area and all suburbs (Glendale, Scottsdale, Mesa, and Sun City).
   - Samantha's Southwestern Arizona territory includes all areas south and west of Phoenix. Yuma is the largest city in this region.
   - Abraham's southeastern Arizona area includes everything south and east of Phoenix. Tucson is included in this territory.

   Does this new information change your evaluation of Acore's Arizona sales reps? If so, how? Does your allocation of the bonus money change as a result of the additional information? If so, explain how.
3. Do you need any other information to evaluate these employees' performances for the first half of the year?
4. What, if any, adjustments would you make to the budgets for the remainder of the year?
5. Do you think that Acore's policy of allocating the same amount of expenses and expected sales to the four sales reps is adequate? What factors would you use in setting budgets for next year?

LO 9–1 **S9–3 Developing Standard Costs Using Time Studies, Incentives to Distort Standard**

To be able to use a standard costing system, a company must develop standards that will serve as the guide for the amount of a resource (e.g., direct materials, direct labor) that should be consumed in the production of a unit. One way to accomplish this is to conduct a time or process study that examines the work of one individual whose results are then used as the standard. This standard serves as a base against which actual results will be compared and ultimately affects performance evaluations.

Suppose you work for an ice packaging service company and your job is to fill each plastic bag with 7 pounds of crushed ice and close the bag with a metal fastener. These bags are then delivered to local grocery and convenience stores for sale. Assume also you were chosen as the subject for a time or process study. Because some amount of spillage is normal, the study will measure the amount of ice each bag has. Your time to fill and fasten each bag will also be measured. These numbers will then serve as company standards for everyone within the company doing your job.

Required:

1. Is there any motivation for you to intentionally spill some ice or to purposefully take longer than normal to fill and/or fasten the bag?
2. How might these standards affect employees (including you) later?
3. How might the company mitigate this problem?

10

Decentralized Performance Evaluation

CHAPTER TEN

YOUR LEARNING OBJECTIVES

LO 10–1 List and explain the advantages and disadvantages of decentralization.

LO 10–2 Describe the different types of responsibility centers and explain how managers of each type are evaluated.

LO 10–3 Describe the four dimensions of the balanced scorecard and explain how they are used to evaluate managerial performance.

LO 10–4 Compute and interpret return on investment, investment turnover, and profit margin.

LO 10–5 Compute and interpret residual income.

LO 10–6 Explain how transfer prices are set in decentralized organizations.

©GaudiLab/Shutterstock

FOCUS COMPANY: APPLE INC.

Apple Computers Inc. began in 1976 when two guys named Steve started building circuit boards in a garage to sell to fellow computer geeks at the Homebrew Computer Club. Steve Wozniak was the technical wizard who built the computers, while Steve Jobs was an ambitious entrepreneur looking to start his own company. When they got their first big order for 50 computers, their biggest problem was figuring out how to pay for the components when they had little cash and no assets to use as collateral for a loan. But Steve Jobs somehow convinced a local supplier to let them buy the parts on 30-day credit terms. As Steve Wozniak tells it, "Steve is very persuasive. We'd get the parts and then stuff them into the circuit boards, have them soldered, get them back in the garage and test them. And we could turn the whole cycle around in ten days and get paid. It worked really great because we had only one level of management."[1]

When companies are small, the owners can make all of the decisions about how to build, market, distribute, and price their products and services. But as a company grows, takes on outside investors, expands into new regions, introduces new products, and hires employees to manage various parts of the business, it is no longer possible for the owners to be directly involved in every aspect of the company's operations. Instead, owners must delegate responsibility to employees and managers to make decisions on their behalf. The delegation of responsibility and decision-making authority throughout an organization is called *decentralization.*

Today, Apple Inc. is a multibillion dollar company that designs and markets some of the world's most popular consumer electronics, including the iPhone, iPad, and Apple watch, as

---

[1] Stephen Wozniak, "Homebrew and How the Apple Came to Be," n.d., http://www.atariarchives.org/deli/homebrew_and_how_the_apple.php

well as innovative services such as iTunes, iCloud, and Apple pay. The company employs more than 50,000 people and has operations around the globe.

As you read this chapter, put yourself in the shoes of a stakeholder at Apple and consider the following questions:

- As an Apple customer, how would you evaluate the company's performance?
- If you were a sales manager in an Apple retail store, how would your boss evaluate your performance?
- If you were a distribution manager responsible for shipping Apple products to Best Buy and Costco, how would your boss evaluate your performance?
- If you were a development engineer responsible for designing a new model of iPhone, how would your boss evaluate your performance?
- If you owned stock in Apple, how would you measure the company's performance?

As you can see, performance can be measured in different ways depending on what and who is being evaluated. Throughout this chapter, we use Apple to illustrate several methods for evaluating managerial performance in a decentralized organization. Although some of the numbers we use in our examples are hypothetical, they are intended to illustrate the techniques that Apple and other companies use to evaluate the performance of their managers and business units.

ORGANIZATION OF THE CHAPTER

Decentralization of responsibility	Designing a performance evaluation system	Transfer pricing
· Advantages and disadvantages of decentralization · Types of responsibility centers	· Balanced scorecard · Financial performance measures · Limitations of financial performance measures	· Market-price method · Cost-based method · Negotiation

Decentralization of Responsibility

As children, most of us couldn't wait to grow up and do everything our parents told us we were too young to do—drive a car, stay out late, date, or get a job. It didn't take long, though, to realize that all that freedom comes with a great deal of responsibility. With responsibility comes the authority to make decisions for ourselves, to take action on behalf of others, and, ultimately, to be held accountable for our decisions and actions.

In business, employees are given the responsibility and authority to make decisions on behalf of their employer. How do organizations make sure that employees act responsibly or make decisions that are in the organization's best interest? The methods they use are not very different from the ones parents use to monitor and control their children, including setting clear rules and guidelines for conduct, directly observing behavior, and measuring and evaluating the outcome of their decisions. The approach an organization uses depends, in part, on how decision-making authority is delegated throughout the organization.

ADVANTAGES AND DISADVANTAGES OF DECENTRALIZATION

In a **decentralized organization**, decision-making authority is spread throughout the organization, and lower-level managers are given the authority and responsibility of managing their individual units. In a **centralized organization**, decision-making authority is kept at the very top of the organization. High-level executives make all the strategic and operational decisions and charge lower-level managers with implementing those decisions.

> **Learning Objective 10–1**
> List and explain the advantages and disadvantages of decentralization.

In most organizations, the distinction between centralized and decentralized operations is not an either-or matter but a question of **how much** decision-making authority to delegate. The advantages and disadvantages of decentralization are summarized as follows:

Advantages of Decentralization	Disadvantages of Decentralization
• Recognizes that lower-level managers may have more knowledge about their area of responsibility and can make quicker and more informed decisions. • Fosters the development of managerial expertise. • Allows top management to focus on strategic issues without worrying about the day-to-day details.	• Sometimes results in the duplication of resources when managers in multiple areas perform the same function. • Gives managers the opportunity to make decisions that benefit themselves, but are not necessarily in the best interest of the organization.

The primary advantage of decentralization is that lower-level managers are "closer to the action" and thus have better information about their area of the business. They can make more informed and faster decisions, allowing upper management to focus on strategic issues rather than operational details. Decentralization also allows employees to develop their managerial skills so that they can move into more senior positions within the organization.

On the flip-side, decentralization may result in duplication of resources when people in different parts of the business are performing the same function. To minimize this issue, many companies choose to centralize key support functions that cut across the organization, such as human resources, accounting, information technology, and purchasing.

Another major disadvantage of decentralization is that it gives managers the opportunity to make decisions that are in their own self-interest, but may not be in the best interest of the company and its owners. The performance evaluation system provides a way to monitor and motivate managers to make decisions that are in the best interest of the company. Ideally, the company's incentive and reward system should be designed so that the manager's goals are aligned with the organization's goals and objectives. Unfortunately, that is much easier said than done, and companies find it difficult to achieve in practice.

In the next section, we use Apple to illustrate a variety of methods for measuring and evaluating managerial performance. To do so, we need to understand how Apple is organized and what managers in the various business units are responsible for. Refer to Exhibit 10–1 for an illustration of Apple's organizational structure, based on information provided in the company's 2017 annual report.

| EXHIBIT 10–1 | Organizational Chart for Apple |

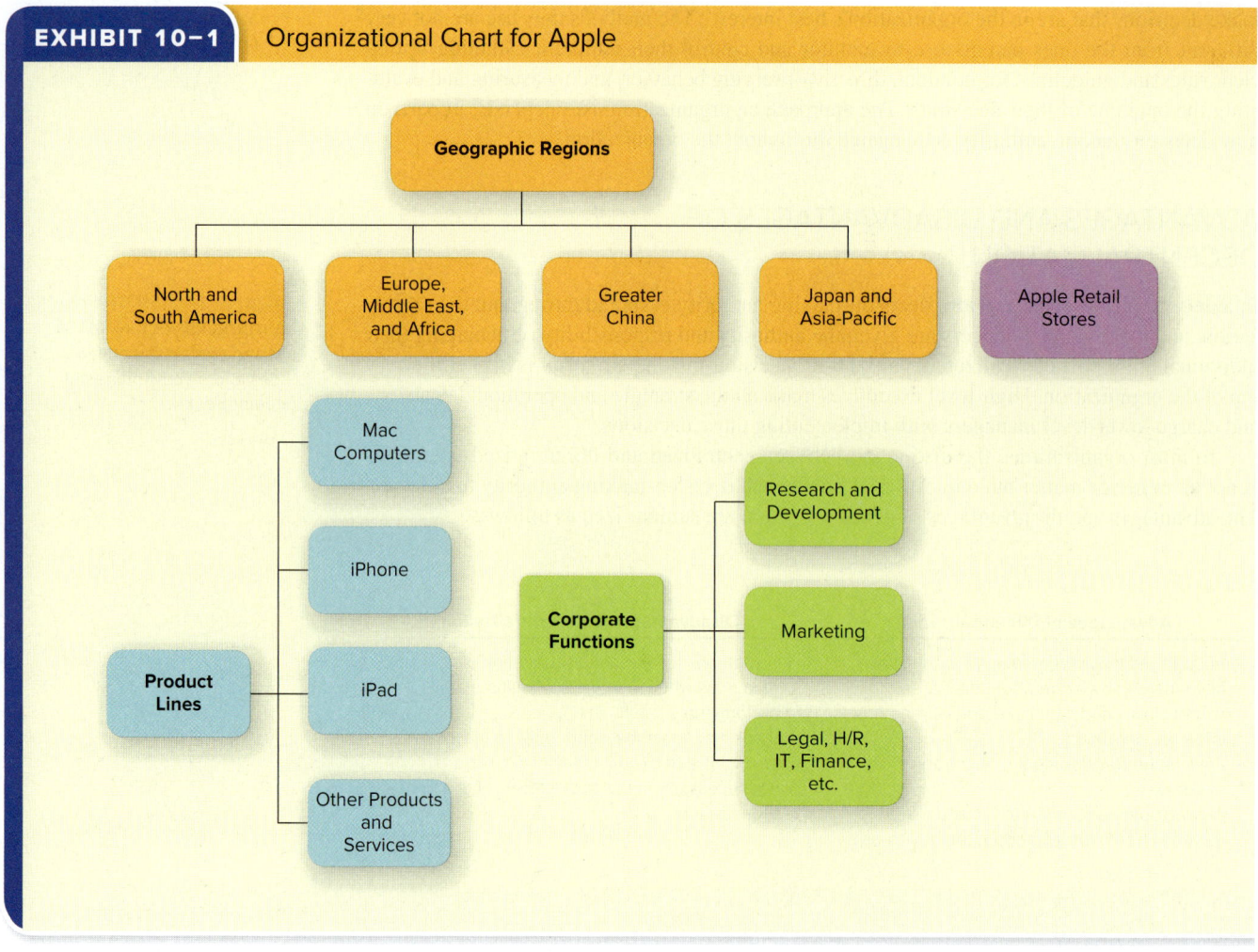

Apple manages its business primarily on a geographic basis, with operations divided into North/South America, Europe/Middle East/Africa, Greater China, and Japan/Asia-Pacific. Apple retail stores are operated as a separate business unit from these geographic segments. In addition to these geographic divisions, Apple is organized by major product lines and service offerings. Exhibit 10–2 shows the relative size of Apple's major operating units expressed as a percentage of the company's net sales revenue for 2017.

As you can see, Apple's largest geographic region is North and South America, which made up about 42 percent of total sales revenue in 2017. The iPhone was by far the largest source of revenue, representing 62 percent of 2017 net revenues. "Other products and services" includes newer products such as the Apple watch, Apple TV, and services like iTunes, iCloud, and Apple Pay. This category has grown in recent years while older products such as Mac computers, iPads, and iPods have decreased as a percentage of total sales revenue. In addition to these revenue-generating units, Apple has many support functions that operate out of its corporate headquarters in Cupertino, California, including research and development, supply chain management, finance, information technology, and human resources.

Like many large corporations, Apple uses a matrix reporting structure, where managerial responsibility cuts across geographic region, product type, and support function. For example, Apple might have a manager who is responsible for supply and demand planning (function) for the iPad (product line) for the northeastern United States (region). This manager would report to and be evaluated by multiple supervisors, including a supply chain supervisor, product supervisor, and regional supervisor.

EXHIBIT 10–2 Revenue Percentages for Apple's Operating Units

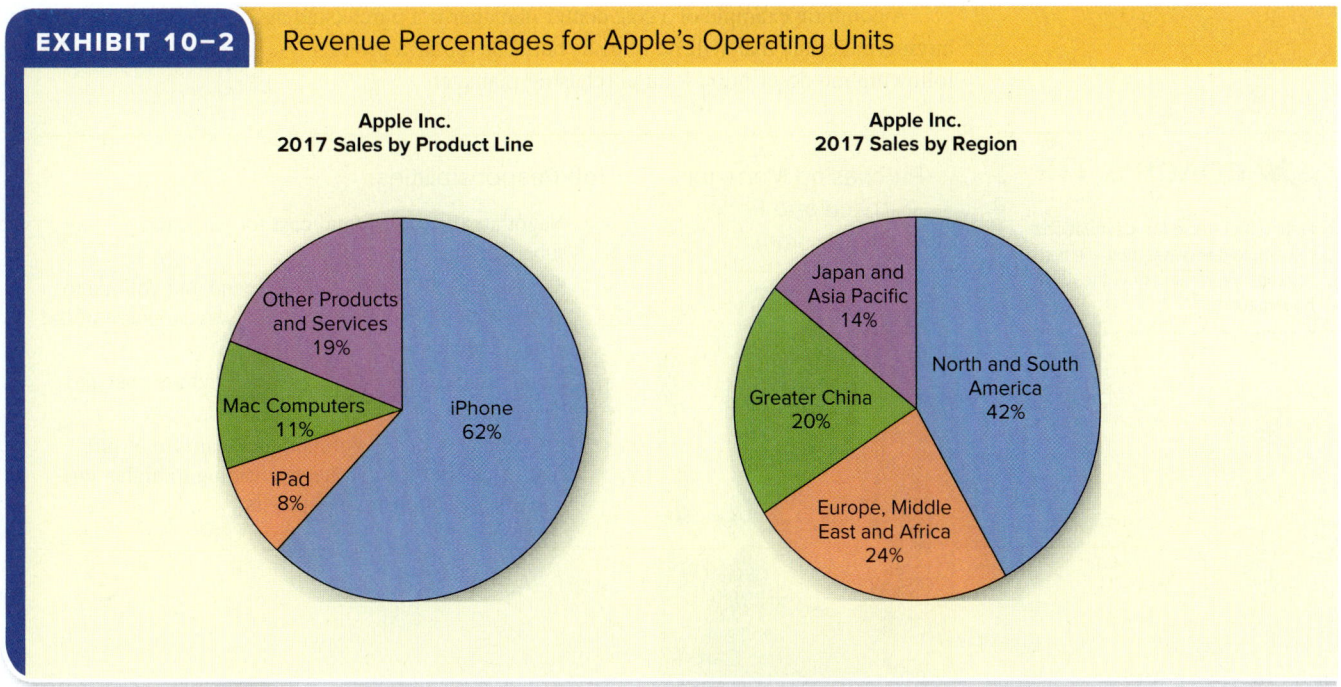

TYPES OF RESPONSIBILITY CENTERS

In **responsibility accounting**, managers are given responsibility for a particular part of the business and are then evaluated based on performance in that area. The area of business that managers are responsible for is referred to as a **responsibility center**. As described in the previous section, responsibility centers can be based on geographic regions, product lines, functional characteristics, or some combination of the three.

> **Learning Objective 10–2**
> Describe the different types of responsibility centers and explain how managers in each type are evaluated.

One of the most important concepts in responsibility accounting is the **controllability principle**, which states that managers should only be evaluated based on things that are within their control. In general, there are four types of responsibility centers that vary according to what the manager can control and, thus, what he/she should be held responsible for:

- The manager of a **cost center** is responsible for controlling **cost**.
- The manager of a **revenue center** is responsible for generating **revenue**.
- The manager of a **profit center** is responsible for generating **profit** (revenue minus cost).
- The manager of an **investment center** is responsible for **profit** (revenue minus cost) and the **investment of assets**.

Next, we provide examples to illustrate how managers in each of these responsibility centers might be evaluated. Although we focus primarily on managers' responsibility for financial performance, it is important to note that managers are responsible for nonfinancial performance as well. We will discuss a mechanism for measuring performance on nonfinancial dimensions in a later section.

Cost Centers

Cost center managers have the authority to incur costs to support their areas of responsibility. All of Apple's corporate support functions would be treated as cost centers, including advertising, human resources, purchasing, supply chain management, information technology, legal services, and accounting. Notice that these cost centers do not generate revenue directly from the customer, although they may have an impact on revenue through other measures, such as customer satisfaction and service quality.

A common example of a cost center manager is a purchasing agent who is responsible for buying materials that will be used to build or repair a product. As an example, consider the following job description for a purchasing manager.

Purchasing Manager (Service and Repair Division)

©Mash/Getty Images

Job Responsibilities:

- Negotiate the lowest total **cost** for parts and subassemblies.
- Seek opportunities to leverage spend and volume to mitigate **cost** increases late in the service phase of the product life cycle.
- Ensure that the database contains accurate **cost** and lead time for all active part numbers.
- Collaborate with cross-functional teams to ensure **cost**-effective repair strategies leading to higher customer satisfaction at lowest **costs**.

As you can see from this job description, cost center managers are evaluated based primarily on their ability to manage or control cost. One of the tools that organizations use to measure the performance of cost center managers is the budgetary planning and control system described in previous chapters. For example, a purchasing manager is responsible for the direct materials price variance, which indicates whether the price paid for materials was more or less than budgeted. But the purchasing manager should not be held responsible for the direct materials quantity or usage variance because he or she has no control over how the materials are actually used in production. In addition to controlling costs, cost center managers should be held responsible for the quality of service provided to other units within the organization.

Revenue Centers

Revenue center managers are responsible for generating revenues for their segment of the business. Companies often give revenue center managers sales targets or quotas and then evaluate and reward them based on whether they meet those targets.

Consider the following job description for a revenue center manager:

Account Manager Online Sales Team

©Fuse/Getty Images

Job Responsibilities:

- The Account Manager is responsible for meeting all **revenue** and unit goals by selling products, systems, and services **within an assigned sales territory**.
- The ideal candidate should possess a track record of **sales success** and proven ability to **exceed all sales goals**.
- The Account Manager will have responsibility for accounts within an assigned territory while acquiring new accounts to meet individual and strategic team goals.

As you can see, revenue center managers are evaluated primarily on their ability to meet revenue or sales goals. Later in the chapter, we consider other measures for evaluating revenue center managers, including customer satisfaction, customer retention, and customer turnover.

Profit Centers

Profit center managers are responsible for generating profits for their area of the business. Unlike cost center managers who are only responsible for cost, and revenue center managers who are only responsible for revenue, profit center managers are responsible for both. Consider the following job description for a product manager responsible for the overall profitability of the iPhone.

Product Manager (iPhone)

©Monkey Business Images Ltd/ Getty Images

Job Responsibilities:

- Responsible for driving strategic initiatives related to the success of the iPhone in the Apple Retail Stores.
- Ownership and development of all iPhone metrics including **sales, profitability, and customer experience**.
- Lead all contract negotiations between Apple Retail and carriers.
- Work closely with key internal partners including: Marketing, Finance, Training, Operations, Information Systems, Legal, Fulfillment, and Logistics.

The most common method of evaluating a profit center manager is based on the **segmented income statement**, or an income statement that is broken down by product line, region, or other business segment. This type of income statement was introduced in a previous chapter as a way of evaluating whether a business segment should be continued or discontinued based on its **segment margin**. The segment margin is also useful for evaluating the manager of a profit center because it separates those costs that are within the segment manager's control from those costs that are outside it. **Remember that managers should be held accountable only for the costs and revenues that are within their control**.

Segment margin is calculated as sales revenue less all costs that are directly attributable to a particular business segment, including variable costs and direct fixed costs. A **direct fixed cost** is one that is incurred by the business segment and is therefore within the control of the segment manager. Even though these costs are fixed, or independent of the number of units produced or sold, direct fixed costs are incurred to support that specific business segment and are therefore considered within the segment manager's control. In contrast, **common fixed costs** are typically incurred at a higher level of the organization and are considered outside of the segment manager's control. In evaluating a profit center manager, we should focus on the segment margin rather than the bottom-line profit margin, which includes costs that are not controllable by the manager.

As you can see, a profit center manager has more responsibility than cost and revenue center managers. Because they are responsible for both revenues and costs, profit center managers often supervise revenue and cost center managers, who have direct responsibility for these key metrics that affect profitability.

Investment Centers

Investment center managers have the authority to make decisions about how and where to invest the company's assets to drive long-term profitability. They have more responsibility than cost center, revenue center, and profit center managers because they are also responsible for investing the company's assets. Consider the following job description for a real estate manager at Apple:

Real Estate Manager	Job Responsibilities:
	• Set and implement strategy for retail real estate, including **identifying new locations,** closing real estate transactions, and managing all real estate negotiations.
	• Develop and execute real estate and **capital expenditure plan.**
	• Create initial store business model and **pro forma financial statements.**
	• Present locations for approval. Negotiate and close real estate deals.
	• Partner with internal teams for successful store development. Work with senior executives, store operations, design, development, and analysis teams to create and implement company-wide initiatives.

©Jill Braaten/McGraw-Hill Education

In addition to being responsible for profitability, investment center managers have to make decisions about how to invest the company's assets. As such, the metrics used to evaluate investment center managers must take into account both profitability and the amount of investment used to generate that profitability. Later in this chapter, we discuss some common measures that are used to evaluate investment center performance. The next chapter describes several tools that managers can use to make sound capital investment decisions.

For now, complete the following Self-Study Practice to make sure that you understand the differences between the four types of responsibility centers.

 How's it going?   Self-Study Practice

Which of the following statements about responsibility centers is (are) true? You may select more than one answer.

1. Cost center managers are responsible for generating sales in their area of the business.
2. Revenue center managers are responsible for controlling costs and generating revenue in their area of the business.
3. Profit center managers are responsible for controlling costs and generating revenue but not for investing assets.
4. Investment center managers are responsible for investing assets but not for controlling costs or generating revenue.
5. None of these statements are true.

After you have finished, check your answers against the solutions in the margin.

Designing a Performance Evaluation System

A major advantage of decentralization is that it allows top-level managers to focus on the strategic objectives of the organization, while lower-level managers are given authority to make decisions about how to run their particular part of the business. The goal of a performance evaluation system is to ensure that managers make decisions that are consistent with the company's strategic objectives as opposed to other factors, such as their own self-interest.

The performance evaluation system should reflect the company's business strategy. For example, a company such as Apple that competes on the basis of innovation and product differentiation is likely to have a very different strategy than a company that sells commodity-type products in a well-established industry. In a recent annual report, Apple stated its business strategy as follows:

> *The Company's business strategy leverages its unique ability to . . . provide its customers products and solutions with innovative design, superior ease-of-use and seamless integration. The Company believes a high-quality buying experience with knowledgeable salespersons who can convey the value of the Company's products and services greatly enhances its ability to attract and retain customers. Therefore, the Company's strategy also includes building and expanding its own retail and online stores and its third-party distribution network to effectively reach more customers and provide them with a high-quality sales and post-sales support experience. The Company believes ongoing investment in research and development ("R&D"), marketing and advertising is critical to the development and sale of innovative products, services and technologies.* (Apple, 2017 Form 10K)

Apple's performance evaluation system should reflect this business strategy and include measures that provide feedback to managers about how they are contributing to the company's success. In other words, it should help managers understand how the decisions they make on a daily basis will help the company achieve its strategic objectives. This is important because not all employees will see the immediate effect of their actions on the company's financial results. For example, a manager in a retail store can see the relationship between his efforts (customer service) and financial results (sales revenue), but a manager who works in research and development may not see the results of her efforts for years. The next section discusses the balanced scorecard, a performance measurement system designed to align managers' goals with the organization's strategic vision by focusing on a broad set of performance metrics that are linked to the company's strategy.

BALANCED SCORECARD

The **balanced scorecard** is a comprehensive performance measurement system that translates an organization's strategic vision into a set of operational performance metrics. The balanced scorecard measures performance along several dimensions and includes measures that reflect past performance (called *lagging indicators*) as well as future performance (called *leading indicators*).

The basic idea of the balanced scorecard is that organizational performance should be measured in four key areas:

- Financial perspective.
- Customer perspective.
- Internal business processes perspective.
- Learning and growth perspective.

> **Learning Objective 10–3**
> Describe the four dimensions of the balanced scorecard and explain how they are used to evaluate managerial performance.

Exhibit 10–3 illustrates these dimensions.

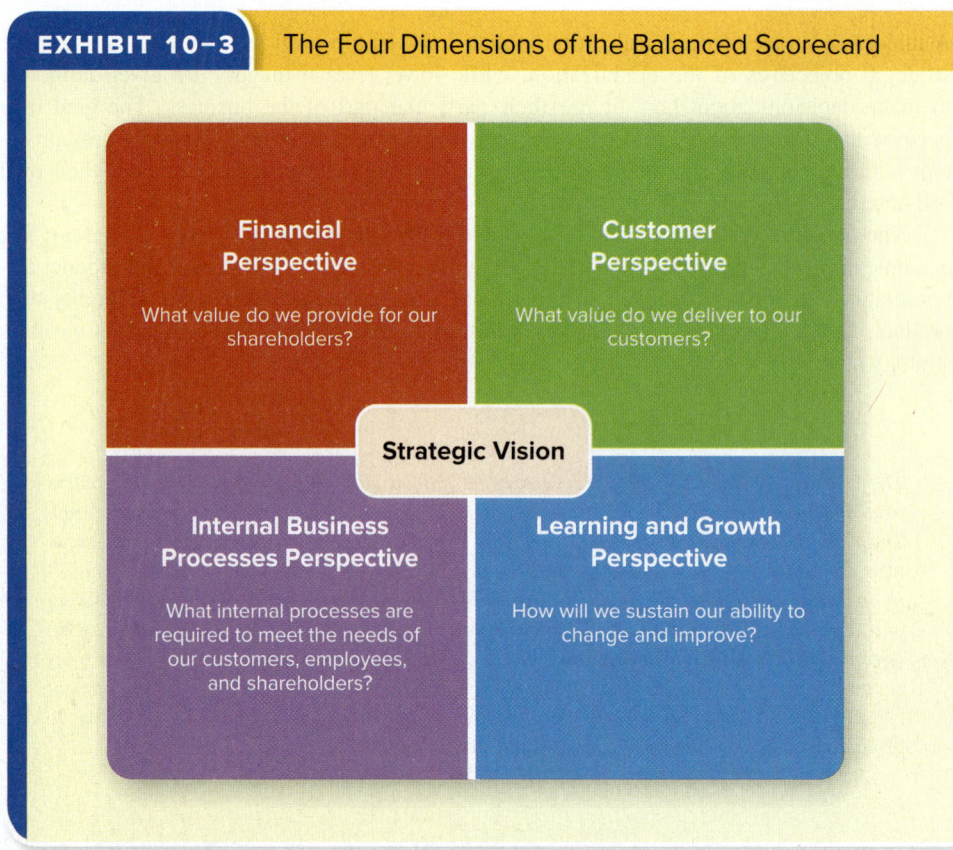

EXHIBIT 10–3 The Four Dimensions of the Balanced Scorecard

Financial Perspective

What value do we provide for our shareholders?

Customer Perspective

What value do we deliver to our customers?

Strategic Vision

Internal Business Processes Perspective

What internal processes are required to meet the needs of our customers, employees, and shareholders?

Learning and Growth Perspective

How will we sustain our ability to change and improve?

Each area of the balanced scorecard should include specific objectives and measures that tell managers what they need to do to contribute to the company's overall success. The measures provide feedback to managers about how they are performing and what they need to improve upon.

For the balanced scorecard to be effective, the objectives and measures included in each category should have a cause and effect relationship so that performance on one dimension of the scorecard will eventually lead to performance in another area. For example, the learning and growth perspective typically contains leading indicators, or measures that predict *future* performance. These leading indicators should result in improved business processes and customer satisfaction, which will ultimately contribute to financial performance. As an example, consider the simplified balanced scorecard linkages for Apple shown in Exhibit 10–4.

Notice that each dimension of the balanced scorecard includes objectives (goals) and specific measures (metrics) that are used to evaluate performance in each area. In this hypothetical example, Apple's objectives are stated fairly generically. In reality, the balanced scorecard would include more specific goals or targets for each metric that indicate whether managers are on track to achieve the stated objectives.

Apple's objective for learning and growth is to foster an environment of creativity and innovation by hiring the most passionate and talented employees and investing heavily in research and development. Some specific metrics that Apple could use to measure success on this dimension include the dollars spent on research and development (R&D), the number of new patent applications, and employee satisfaction, which could be measured by the employee turnover rate. Although most of this data is proprietary and housed in Apple's internal accounting system, the total amount invested in research and development is reported in Apple's external financial statements, and summarized below:

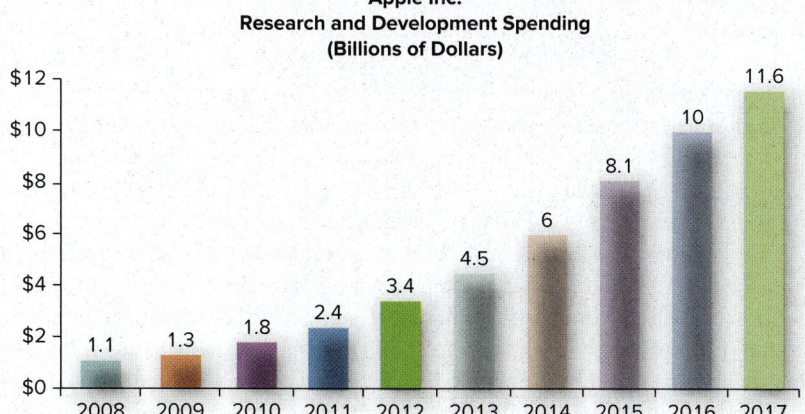

**Apple Inc.
Research and Development Spending
(Billions of Dollars)**

Year	Spending
2008	1.1
2009	1.3
2010	1.8
2011	2.4
2012	3.4
2013	4.5
2014	6
2015	8.1
2016	10
2017	11.6

EXHIBIT 10–4	Applying the Balanced Scorecard to Apple Inc.

Financial

- Objective: Generate superior returns for shareholders.
- Measures: Sales growth, profitability, return on investment, residual income, economic value added.

Customer

- Objective: Delight customers by providing them with new products and services with innovative design, superior ease of use, and exceptional post-sales support.
- Measures: Percentage of sales from new products, customer satisfaction, percentage of repeat customers, market share.

Internal Business Processes

- Objective: Design, manufacture, and deliver new products to market that exceed customer expectations in terms of quality, performance, and design.
- Measures: Percentage of new products launched, average days to market, manufacturing cycle time, inventory stockouts, number of defects.

Learning and Growth

- Objective: Foster an environment of creativity and innovation by hiring the most passionate and talented employees and investing heavily in research and development.
- Measures: Research and development spending, number of new patent applications, employee satisfaction.

🏀 **COACH'S TIP**

Start at the bottom with the leading indicators and work your way up to the lagging measures of financial performance.

As you can see, Apple has increased its R&D expenditures from $1.1 billion in 2008 to $11.6 billion in 2017. R&D is a great example of a leading indicator, or a predictor of *future* performance. If the R&D efforts are successful, it will eventually translate into increased financial performance through other metrics, such as the number of new patents awarded; the number of new products introduced; customer satisfaction; and, eventually, sales revenue. We know that Apple's investment in research and development has paid off over the past decade as Apple products continue to dominate the marketplace and you can't go anywhere without seeing someone texting on an iPhone or checking messages on an Apple watch.

Internal business processes include all of the activities that are required to get products from the idea stage into the hands of customers. Some metrics that Apple might use to measure performance on this dimension include the number of new products introduced, the number of days from product launch to store shelf, supplier reliability ratings, the number of inventory stock-outs, and the number of defects. It is worth noting that Apple outsources most of its manufacturing activities to companies in China. For a company that manufactures its own products, metrics such as average manufacturing cost and manufacturing cycle time would also be included in the internal business processes perspective of the balanced scorecard.

SPOTLIGHT ON Sustainability

Sustainability and the Balanced Scorecard

There is an old saying in business that "you can't manage what you can't measure." The flip side to this statement is that "what gets measured is what gets managed." These statements are still true today and are relevant for managers as they integrate sustainability practices into their business strategy. Without measuring sustainability performance, managers are essentially flying blind and have no way of knowing whether they are achieving their sustainability goals and what they need to do to improve.

The balanced scorecard provides a useful tool for organizations to incorporate sustainability goals and metrics into the performance evaluation system. The goal of the balanced scorecard is to include a broad set of financial and nonfinancial performance indicators that are linked to the company's long-term strategy. This approach aligns well with sustainability, which requires a long-term view that focuses managers' attention on more than just economic or financial results. While traditional accounting methods are effective for measuring economic or financial results, the balanced scorecard can be expanded to include measures that capture the environmental and societal aspects of the triple bottom line.

There are three ways that organizations can use the balanced scorecard to integrate sustainability metrics into the performance evaluation system:

1. Add one or more categories to the existing scorecard to capture sustainability goals and measures. For example, a company might add a fifth category to capture all sustainability measures. Alternatively, they could add two categories, one for environmental and another for societal metrics.

2. Create a separate sustainability balanced scorecard (SBSC) that focuses exclusively on sustainability goals and metrics. The scorecard could still include the traditional balanced scorecard categories, but it could also be expanded to include other categories such as society or community.

3. Integrate sustainability objectives and measures into the existing categories of the balanced scorecard. For example, environmental measures often align well with internal business processes, while social measures align well with the customer perspective (for customer-focused initiatives) or the learning and growth perspective (for employee-focused initiatives). Some companies also add a fifth category to capture community or social initiatives that don't fall into one of the other categories.

Although the first approach is simplest and the second signals the importance of sustainability to internal and external stakeholders, most experts agree that the best approach is to integrate sustainability measurements into the existing performance evaluation system. This is particularly important for companies that view sustainability as an integral part of their daily operations and core business strategy, as opposed to an add-on or afterthought.

Refer to Problems PA10–6 and PB10–6 for a demonstration of how the sustainability measures identified by the Global Reporting Initiative (GRI) and other sources could be incorporated into the balanced scorecard.

The customer perspective provides the link between internal business processes and financial results. Potential metrics include the percentage of sales from new products, customer satisfaction, percentage of repeat customers, and market share. Performance on these metrics should translate into financial performance.

Apple's financial objective is to generate superior returns for its shareholders, including Apple employees who own a sizeable portion of the company's stock. The company stock price is one measure of financial success, although it is influenced to some extent by factors that are outside of the company's control. Other financial performance measures include sales growth, profitability, return on investment, residual income, and economic value added. Some of these financial measures will be discussed in more detail in the next section of this chapter.

To summarize, the balanced scorecard is an integrated performance measurement system that links a company's strategy to performance in four areas: learning and growth, internal business processes, customer perspective, and financial results. It is useful for communicating the company's strategic objectives to managers and employees throughout the organization so that everyone knows how their actions contribute to the company's overall success. Although the balanced scorecard is a useful tool for linking a company's strategic vision to operational metrics, it can be very time-consuming to implement and requires the involvement of employees at all levels of the organization. In addition, while the intent of the balanced scorecard is to focus managers' attention on the company's long-term strategy, managers are often rewarded based on short-term financial results. Unless the company's incentive and reward system is redesigned to align with the measures captured by the balanced scorecard, it may not serve its intended purpose.

Next, we discuss three common measures for evaluating financial performance, return on investment, residual income and economic value added.

FINANCIAL PERFORMANCE MEASURES

This section discusses several methods for evaluating financial performance. We will start by looking at the overall financial performance of the company (based on the external financial statements) and then drill down to measures that evaluate the performance of investment center managers and the division they are responsible for.

Return on Investment

One of the most common ways to measure financial performance is **return on investment (ROI)**. In general, ROI is computed by dividing some measure of profitability, such as net operating income, by some measure of investment, such as average invested assets. There are many variations of ROI, including return on assets (ROA), return on capital employed (ROCE), and return on equity (ROE). The difference is the value used to measure investment in the denominator of the ROI formula. We will use a commonly accepted definition of ROI, which calculates the return on average invested assets, as follows:

$$\text{Return on Investment (ROI)} = \frac{\text{Net Operating Income}}{\text{Average Invested Assets}}$$

COACH'S TIP

Giving employees an ownership interest in the company (e.g., stock or stock options) is another mechanism for aligning the goals of employees and owners.

Learning Objective 10–4
Compute and interpret return on investment, investment turnover, and profit margin.

A company's overall ROI can be computed from information provided in its external financial statements. Consider the following data reported in Apple's 2017 annual report.

APPLE INC.
Consolidated Income Statements
(in millions)

	For the Year Ended September 30, 2017	For the Year Ended September 24, 2016
Net sales	$229,234	$215,639
Cost of sales	141,048	131,376
Gross margin	88,186	84,263
Operating expenses:		
Research and development	11,581	10,045
Selling, general, and administrative	15,261	14,194
Total operating expenses	26,843	24,239
Net operating income	$ 61,344	$ 60,024

APPLE INC.
Consolidated Balance Sheets
(in millions)

	September 30, 2017	September 24, 2016
ASSETS:		
Total current assets	$128,645	$106,869
Long-term marketable securities	194,714	170,430
Property, plant, and equipment, net	33,783	27,010
Goodwill	5,717	5,414
Acquired intangible assets, net	2,298	3,206
Other assets	10,162	8,757
Total assets	$375,319	$321,686
LIABILITIES AND SHAREHOLDERS' EQUITY:		
Total liabilities	241,272	193,437
Total shareholders' equity	134,047	128,249
Total liabilities and shareholders' equity	$375,319	$321,686

The numerator in the ROI calculation is net operating income. This is a line item on the income statement that represents net income from normal operating activities, before "other" income, interest, and taxes. Apple's net operating income for fiscal year 2017 was $61,344 million (or $61.3 billion).

The denominator in the ROI calculation is average invested assets. Because ROI is computed over a period of time, such as a quarter or year, we need to average the value of invested assets at the beginning and end of that period. We would compute Apple's **average** investment in assets (in millions) for fiscal year 2017 based on total assets from the 2016 balance sheet ($321,686) and the 2017 balance sheet ($375,319):

$$\text{Average Invested Assets} = \frac{\text{Beginning Total Assets} + \text{Ending Total Assets}}{2}$$

$$\text{Average Invested Assets} = \frac{\$321,686 + \$375,319}{2} = \$348,503$$

Based on these numbers, Apple's ROI for 2017 would be computed as follows:

$$\text{Return on Investment} = \frac{\text{Net Operating Income}}{\text{Average Invested Assets}} = \frac{\$61,344}{\$348,503} = 17.6\%$$

This analysis shows that Apple generated a return on average invested assets of 17.6 percent during 2017. As a point of comparison, Microsoft's ROI for the same fiscal year was 10.9 percent, while Samsung's ROI for was just over 19 percent. Thus, while Apple outperformed Microsoft in terms of ROI, it did not perform quite as well as Samsung. Overall, this financial metric suggests that Apple provides a high return on investment for its shareholders. But we need a bit more detail to evaluate the different divisions that contributed to this overall measure of performance.

Return on investment can also be used to evaluate the performance of investment center managers, who are responsible for profitability and investing in assets for a particular segment of the business. Unfortunately, the data needed to analyze managerial performance at the division level is not publicly available. To demonstrate how ROI can be used to evaluate investment center managers, consider the following hypothetical data for two Apple divisions: retail stores and online stores.

	Retail Store	Online Store
Sales revenue	$ 3,000,000	$ 6,000,000
Less: Operating expenses	(2,880,000)	(5,400,000)
Net operating income	$ 120,000	$ 600,000
Average invested assets	$ 2,000,000	$ 2,000,000
Return on investment	$\frac{\$120,000}{\$2,000,000} = 6\%$	$\frac{\$600,000}{\$2,000,000} = 30\%$

Notice that both divisions have the same level of investment ($2,000,000 in average invested assets). Yet the Apple retail division had an ROI of 6 percent, compared to 30 percent for the online Apple store. To gain a better understanding of the factors contributing to ROI, it is useful to break it into two separate components: **investment turnover** and **profit margin**.

$$\begin{array}{ccccc} \text{Return on} & = & \text{Investment} & \times & \text{Profit} \\ \text{Investment (ROI)} & & \text{Turnover} & & \text{Margin} \end{array}$$

$$\frac{\text{Net Operating Income}}{\text{Average Invested Assets}} = \frac{\text{Sales Revenue}}{\text{Average Invested Assets}} \times \frac{\text{Net Operating Income}}{\text{Sales Revenue}}$$

Developed by executives at DuPont in the early 1900s, this method is often referred to as the **DuPont method**. **Investment turnover** is the ratio of sales revenue to average invested assets. **Profit margin** is the ratio of net operating income to sales revenue. Notice that sales revenue is included in both ratios and when cancelled out, leaves you with the original ROI formula.

The DuPont formula shows that there are two ways to increase ROI:

1. Increase investment turnover by generating more sales revenue per dollar of invested assets

2. Increase profit margin by reducing costs without a corresponding decrease in revenues.

Applying the DuPont method to Apple's two hypothetical divisions provides the following results:

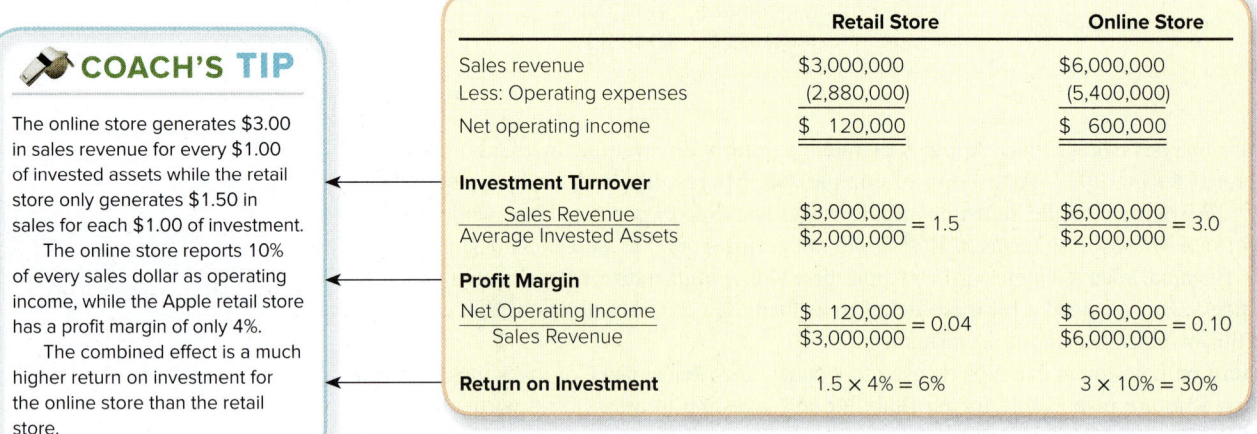

	Retail Store	Online Store
Sales revenue	$3,000,000	$6,000,000
Less: Operating expenses	(2,880,000)	(5,400,000)
Net operating income	$ 120,000	$ 600,000
Investment Turnover		
$\dfrac{\text{Sales Revenue}}{\text{Average Invested Assets}}$	$\dfrac{\$3,000,000}{\$2,000,000} = 1.5$	$\dfrac{\$6,000,000}{\$2,000,000} = 3.0$
Profit Margin		
$\dfrac{\text{Net Operating Income}}{\text{Sales Revenue}}$	$\dfrac{\$120,000}{\$3,000,000} = 0.04$	$\dfrac{\$600,000}{\$6,000,000} = 0.10$
Return on Investment	1.5 × 4% = 6%	3 × 10% = 30%

The relationship between investment turnover, profit margin, and return on investment is shown graphically in Exhibit 10–5.

This analysis shows that two factors are driving the difference in ROI for Apple's two divisions. The first factor is the amount of sales revenue generated per dollar invested in assets. The investment turnover ratio indicates how efficiently the division uses assets to generate sales revenue. Apple's retail division generates sales equal to 1.5 times its investment base; Apple's online store generates twice that amount—3 times its investment base—from the same level of investment.

EXHIBIT 10–5   Investment Turnover, Profit Margin, and Return on Investment

Apple Retail Store

| Investment $2,000,000 | 1.5× investment turnover | Sales revenue $3,000,000 | 4% profit margin | Operating profit $120,000 |

6% Return on investment

Apple Online Store

| Investment $2,000,000 | 3× investment turnover | Sales revenue $6,000,000 | 10% profit margin | Operating profit $600,000 |

30% Return on investment

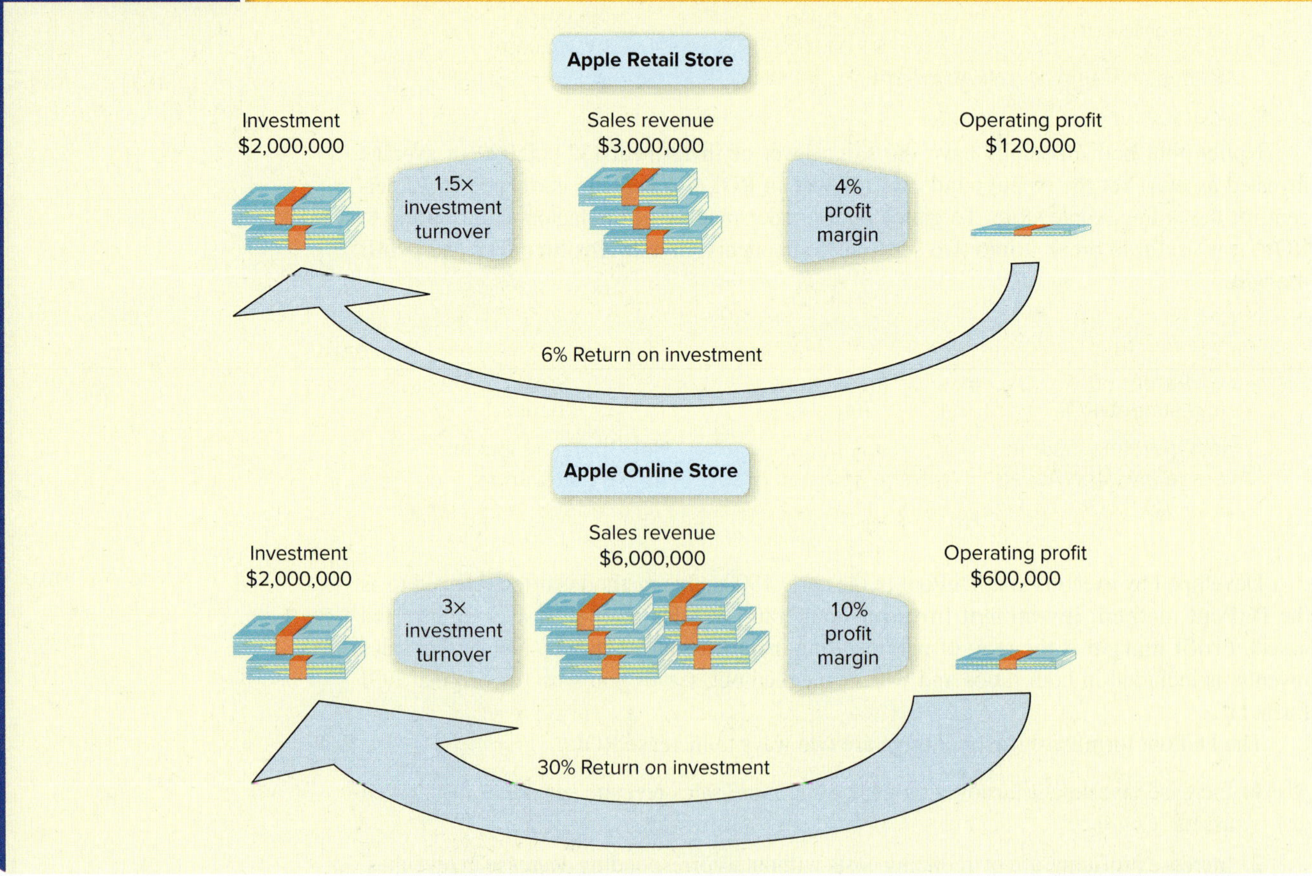

The second factor that drives the difference in ROI is profit margin. The profit margin shows how much of a segment's sales revenue remains as operating income after operating costs have been deducted. Apple's online store generates $0.10 in operating profit for every dollar of sales; Apple's retail division generates only $0.04 for every dollar of sales. This difference in profit margin is rooted in the different cost structures of the two segments. Apple's brick and mortar stores tend to have relatively high fixed costs (for rental space, utilities, and other overhead costs) compared to the online store. In sum, Apple's online store generates more sales revenue from the same level of investment **and** keeps a higher percentage of that sales revenue as operating income. The end result is that the ROI for Apple's online store (30%) is much higher than that for Apple's retail division (6%).

Next, we will discuss an alternative method of evaluating financial performance, residual income. First, to make sure you understand how to calculate ROI, profit margin, and investment turnover, complete the following Self-Study Practice.

 How's it going?   Self-Study Practice

Consider the following sample data for Apple's North and South America region:

Sales revenue	$1,000,000
Operating expenses	900,000
Net operating income	100,000
Beginning total assets	300,000
Ending total assets	500,000

1. Compute the region's ROI, profit margin, and investment turnover.
2. Show how the ROI is related to profit margin and investment turnover.

After you have finished, check your answers against the solutions in the margin.

Solution to Self-Study Practice

1. ROI = $100,000 ÷ (($300,000 + $500,000)/2)= 25%
   Profit margin = $100,000 ÷ $1,000,000 = 10%
   Investment turnover = $1,000,000 ÷
   (($300,000 + $500,000)/2) = 2.5
2. ROI = Profit Margin × Investment Turnover
   = 10% × 2.5 = 25%

Residual Income

An alternative measure of financial performance compares net operating income to the minimum acceptable profit based on the **required rate of return**. The required rate of return is also called the **hurdle rate**. Managers set the hurdle rate to reflect the lowest possible return they are willing to accept on a given investment. The hurdle rate will depend on a number of factors, including the risk of the investment, the cost of financing it, and the return that could be earned on other investments (e.g., opportunity cost).

Residual income is the amount of net operating income earned over and above the minimum amount needed to meet the required rate of return, and is computed as follows:

> **Learning Objective 10–5**
> Compute and interpret residual income.

Residual Income = Net Operating Income − Minimum Acceptable Profit

Residual Income = Net Operating Income − (Average Invested Assets
× Hurdle Rate)

A positive residual income means that the investment generated more than the minimum acceptable operating profit. A negative residual income means that the investment did not meet the minimum acceptable profit based on the required rate of return, or hurdle rate.

To continue our previous example, assume that Apple's hurdle rate is 10 percent. In our previous example, both divisions had an average investment in assets of $2,000,000. Thus, the minimum acceptable profit would be $200,000 ($2,000,000 × 10%). Comparing each division's net operating income to this minimum requirement results in the following residual income analysis:

	Retail Store	Online Store
Net operating income	$ 120,000	$ 600,000
Less: Minimum acceptable profit ($2,000,000 × 10% hurdle rate)	(200,000)	(200,000)
Residual income	$ (80,000)	$ 400,000

Notice that the Apple retail store has a negative residual income of $80,000. A negative residual income occurs because the division's net operating income of $120,000 is less than the minimum required income of $200,000. The online store's residual income is $400,000. This is "extra" profit, over and above the minimum requirement of $200,000.

Residual income can also be computed by comparing each division's ROI to the hurdle rate and then multiplying the difference by the average investment in assets, as follows:

	Retail Store	Online Store
Return on investment	6%	30%
Less: Hurdle rate	(10%)	(10%)
Residual return	(4%)	20%
Average invested assets	× $2,000,000	× $2,000,000
Residual income	$ (80,000)	$ 400,000

The retail store's ROI of 6 percent is less than the 10 percent hurdle rate. Multiplying the 4 percent shortfall in ROI by average invested assets of $2,000,000 results in a negative residual income of $80,000. The online store's ROI was 30 percent, or 20 percent above the hurdle rate, resulting in residual income of $400,000 (20% × $2,000,000).

Before you continue, complete the following Self-Study Practice to make sure you understand how to calculate residual income and its relationship to ROI.

 How's it going?   Self-Study Practice

Consider the following hypothetical data for Apple's North and South America region:

Net operating income	$100,000
Average invested assets	$400,000
Return on investment	25%

1. Using a hurdle rate of 10 percent, compute the division's residual income.
2. Explain how residual income is related to the 25 percent ROI.

After you have finished, check your answers against the solutions in the margin.

Return on Investment versus Residual Income

Although ROI and residual income are directly related, ROI suffers from one major disadvantage that residual income does not. Managers may sometimes reject an investment simply because it would lower the division's ROI, even though it might benefit the company as a whole.

To illustrate, assume that the manager of Apple's online store has an opportunity to develop a new technology that would require an up-front investment of $1,000,000. The technology would save the company $150,000 a year in operating costs. Thus, the project's expected ROI is 15 percent ($150,000 ÷ $1,000,000). Recall from the previous example that the online store has an ROI of 30 percent, and Apple's minimum required rate of return (hurdle rate) is 10 percent. Will the manager of the online store want to invest in the project? The answer to this question depends on whether the manager is evaluated based on ROI or residual income. The proposed project would generate a positive residual income because its expected return (15%) is more than the required 10 percent hurdle rate. However, the project would reduce the online division's ROI because the 15 percent return is less than the current ROI of 30 percent. If the manager invests in this project, the division's ROI will drop from 30 percent to 25 percent, as shown in the following table:

	Status Quo (without project)	Effect of Proposed Project	If Project Is Accepted
Return on Investment Analysis			
Net operating income	$600,000	150,000	$750,000
Average invested assets	÷ $2,000,000	÷ $1,000,000	÷ $3,000,000
Return on investment	30%	15%	25%
Residual Income Analysis			
Net operating income	$600,000	$150,000	$750,000
Less: Minimum acceptable profit			
(10% of average invested assets)	(200,000)	(100,000)	(300,000)
Residual income	$400,000	$ 50,000	$450,000

COACH'S TIP

Notice that the project would have a negative effect on the online store's ROI because its rate of return is less than the current ROI of 30%.

The project would generate a positive residual income, however, because its return is higher than the company's required rate of return of 10%.

This example shows how a performance evaluation system can create **goal incongruence**, or a conflict of interest between what is best for the manager and what is best for the organization and its owners. A manager who is evaluated and rewarded based on ROI may not want to invest in a project that is in the best interest of the company if doing so will have a negative impact on the manager's own performance evaluation. The residual income method helps to align the manager's goals with the organization's objective of earning a minimum ROI of 10 percent. Regardless of the division's current ROI, its residual income will increase as long as the manager invests only in projects that exceed the company's minimum required return.

Economic Value Added

Economic value added (EVA™) is a metric developed by Stern, Stewart and Co. to measure the economic wealth that is created when a company's after-tax net operating income exceeds its **cost of capital**. From a conceptual perspective, EVA is very similar to residual income. However, EVA makes a number of important adjustments, which are summarized as follows:

- Measures profitability based on **after-tax net operating income** rather than pretax net operating income. Many managerial decisions have important tax ramifications and so performance should be measured on an after-tax basis.

- Uses the **cost of capital** as the hurdle rate. Conceptually, the cost of capital represents the after-tax cost of financing the company's operations through some combination of debt and equity. The cost of capital is described in more detail in the next chapter.

- Uses **total capital employed** as the measure of investment rather than average invested assets. For external financial statements, accounting rules (GAAP) allow only certain types of investments to be capitalized or treated as assets. Using total capital employed allows companies like Apple to capitalize other important investments, such as research and development, brand equity, and a highly trained or creative workforce (human capital).

EVA measures whether the company is generating sufficient after-tax income to cover the cost of capital. While the detailed calculations of EVA are beyond the scope of this text, you should understand how it relates to residual income and what it tells managers about the company's financial performance. If EVA is positive, the company is creating economic wealth by generating profits in excess of its cost of capital. If EVA is negative, the company is not generating enough after-tax profit to cover its cost of capital, which reduces the company's overall economic value.

LIMITATIONS OF FINANCIAL PERFORMANCE MEASURES

In this section, we discussed several measures that can be used to measure financial performance, including return on investment (ROI), residual income, and economic value added (EVA). While each method provides a different view of the company's financial performance, it is important to note that they are all lagging measures of performance. In other words, they tell you how a particular part of the business did in the past, but not necessarily how it will do in the future. As previously discussed, a performance evaluation system should be designed to focus manager's attention on more than just the bottom line. If managers are evaluated and rewarded based entirely on financial results, they may not make decisions that are in the best interest of the organization in the long-run.

As we have seen, performance evaluation systems that encourage alignment between managers' goals and the organization's goals create an environment in which managers are more likely to make decisions that are consistent with the organization's objectives rather than their own self-interest. A performance evaluation system can also impact managers' willingness to cooperate with other divisions to achieve the larger company's objectives, as we will see in the next section on transfer pricing.

Transfer Pricing

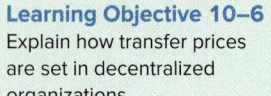

Learning Objective 10-6
Explain how transfer prices are set in decentralized organizations.

The final issue we consider in this chapter is how decentralized organizations deal with the transfer or sale of goods and services between divisions. A **transfer price** is the amount that one division charges when it sells goods or services to another division of the same company. Internal transfers or exchanges happen quite often in today's business environment because many large corporations are composed of relatively independent business units that are owned by the same parent company. Business transactions between units or divisions of the same company are called **related-party transactions**.

You can think about transfer prices in terms of the deal you might get when you buy something from a relative. Maybe you want to buy a car from your brother-in-law, a meal at your cousin's restaurant, or a cut and style at your sister's hair salon. How much would you expect to pay for a product or service when buying from a relative?

At a minimum, you should be willing to pay for any variable costs that your relative incurs. For example, if your brother, an auto mechanic, agrees to repair your car, you should at least be willing to pay for the parts. The minimum transfer price is called the *floor*.

The maximum amount you should be willing to pay (the *ceiling*) is the market price. In other words, you should not have to pay more for the product or service than you would if you bought it from a complete stranger.

Exhibit 10–6 illustrates the range of potential transfer prices for this type of related-party transaction.

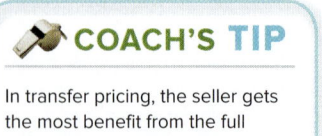

COACH'S TIP

In transfer pricing, the seller gets the most benefit from the full market price, while the buyer would prefer to pay only variable costs. Managers often negotiate to a "fair" price somewhere in between.

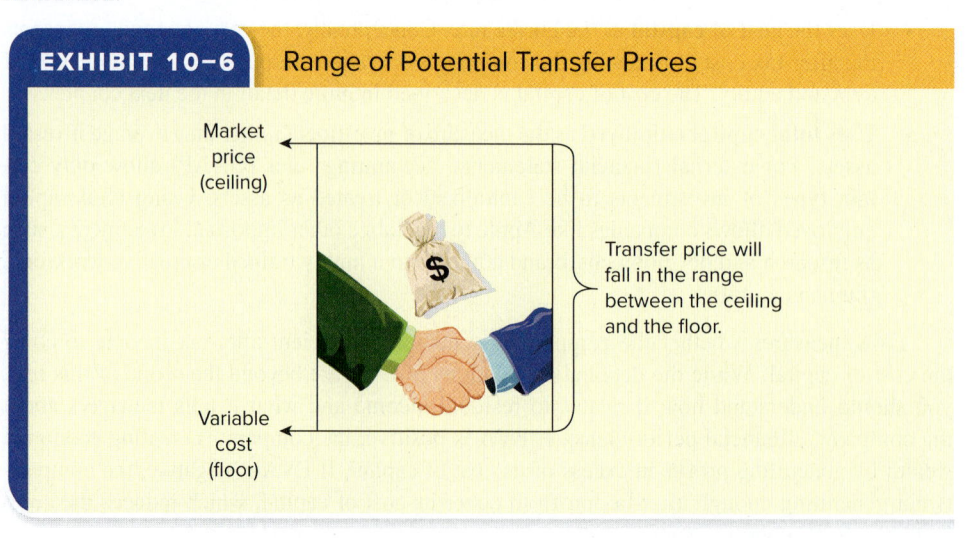

EXHIBIT 10–6   Range of Potential Transfer Prices

Market price (ceiling)

Variable cost (floor)

Transfer price will fall in the range between the ceiling and the floor.

The same rules apply to transfer prices in decentralized organizations. The only difference is that the managers of decentralized business units are not necessarily friendly relatives, even if they have the same parent company. If business managers are evaluated based on their ability to control costs and/or generate revenue, their goals may be in conflict. Although the transfer price does not really matter from the overall company's perspective,[2] it can impact each manager's performance evaluation.

Consider the following estimated cost and price information for an Apple watch. According to iSupply, a company that breaks down popular consumer products to determine their cost, the direct cost of a first generation Apple watch is only about $84.00, including $81.50 for all of the components plus $2.50 for assembly. This ignores all of the indirect costs of designing, producing, and selling Apple products, including manufacturing overhead, distribution costs, marketing expenses, administrative overhead, and lots of R&D. Although most of these indirect costs are fixed, assume that the additional variable costs of producing and distributing each Apple watch is $5.00, bringing the total variable cost to $89.00 per unit.

Assume that the retail price of the Apple Sport Watch is $349.00 and that external retailers such as Best Buy and Walmart pay a wholesale price of $299.00. These costs and prices are summarized in Exhibit 10–7.

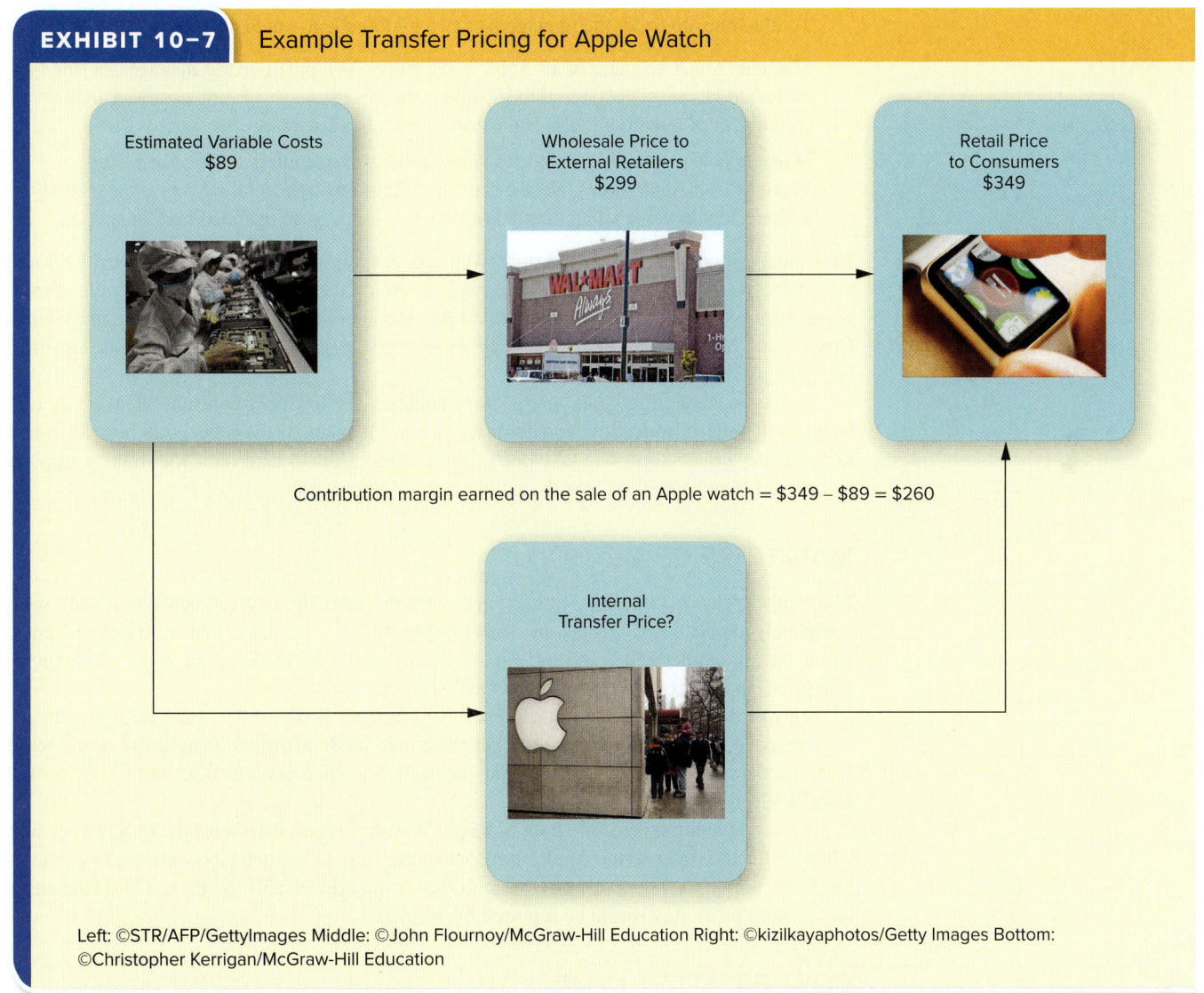

EXHIBIT 10–7 Example Transfer Pricing for Apple Watch

Estimated Variable Costs $89

Wholesale Price to External Retailers $299

Retail Price to Consumers $349

Contribution margin earned on the sale of an Apple watch = $349 − $89 = $260

Internal Transfer Price?

Left: ©STR/AFP/GettyImages Middle: ©John Flournoy/McGraw-Hill Education Right: ©kizilkayaphotos/Getty Images Bottom: ©Christopher Kerrigan/McGraw-Hill Education

---

[2] Transfer prices **can** have a major impact on multinational companies due to variations in tax rates from one country to the next. The tax implications of transfer prices are extremely complex and must be considered as part of the tax planning process.

The difference between the retail price of $349 and the variable costs of $89 is a contribution margin of $260 per unit. Since all other costs are fixed, this is the amount of incremental profit generated from the sale of each watch. So how does this incremental profit get distributed among the various parties involved in the sale of an Apple watch?

If the device is sold through an independent retailer such as Walmart, the incremental profit reported by each company is determined by the wholesale price, or the amount that Apple charges Walmart for the merchandise. The wholesale price is revenue for Apple, but would be reported as Cost of Goods Sold for Walmart. Given a wholesale price of $299, Apple's share of the incremental profit would be $210 per unit ($299 wholesale price − $89 variable cost). When Walmart sells the device to consumers for $349, it would report incremental profit of $50 per unit ($349 retail price − $299 wholesale cost). Again, this ignores fixed costs as they won't change in the short-run and within the relevant range.

But what if the watch is sold through Apple.com or an Apple store? By selling the device directly to consumers, Apple can keep the entire $260 in incremental profit. But how does this profit get reported within various divisions within Apple? The internal transfer price is similar to the wholesale price for external retailers. It determines how much one division will charge another for the transfer of goods or services, and therefore how much incremental profit each division will report.

To illustrate, consider the managers of two hypothetical Apple divisions:

> Manager A is a manager of an Apple retail store. As a profit center manager, he/she is evaluated based on net operating income (sales revenue − operating costs). A major component of operating costs is the cost of merchandise sold.

> Manager B is responsible for sale of Apple products to retailers such as Best Buy, Walmart, and Apple stores. He/she is evaluated based on the total sales revenue earned within a territory, including internal sales to the Apple store operated by Manager A.

How much should the Apple retail store (Manager A) have to pay for the Apple watch? Should it be the same price that Walmart would pay? Or should the Apple store get a discount since it is part of the same company? Keep in mind that the internal transfer price will be reported as Cost of Goods Sold on Manager A's performance report, but will be reported as sales revenue on Manager B's performance report.

As you can see, the goals of the two managers are in direct conflict. Manager A (the buyer) will benefit from a low transfer price, while Manager B (the seller) will benefit from a high transfer price. Apple can take one of three approaches to determine the internal transfer price: market-price method, cost-based method, or negotiation.

MARKET-PRICE METHOD

The market-price method for setting transfer prices treats the two segments as if they were completely independent businesses. The market price is the price that an unrelated party would pay for similar goods and services. In this example, the market price is the $299 wholesale price paid by external retailers such as Walmart.

This scenario provides the most benefit to Manager B (the seller) because it maximizes sales revenue for his division. The market price method does little to benefit the Apple retail store manager because he or she is paying the same price that external competitors pay for the same product.

Under the market-price method, Manager B would report sales revenue of $299 per unit when it sells the watch to the Apple store. When the Apple store sells the watch to a consumer for $349, Manager A would report a contribution margin of $50 ($349 − $299), the same incremental profit that would be reported by Walmart.

COST-BASED METHOD

Instead of looking to the market to see what outside parties would pay for the product or service, the cost-based method looks internally to determine how much it costs to produce the product or provide the service. The transfer price could be based on variable cost, full cost, or cost plus some percentage markup.

In this example, the minimum transfer price is the variable cost of the device ($89). The minimum transfer price provides the most benefit to the buyer (Manager A) because it gives all of the incremental profit to the retail store. The Apple store would report incremental profit of $260 per unit ($349 − $89). The seller would report sales revenue of $89, just enough to cover the variable cost of the device itself, leaving zero incremental profit.

Many companies have a cost-plus transfer pricing policy. For example, Apple could have a policy that dictates that all internal transfers will be recorded at full cost plus 25 percent. If so, we would need to compute the full cost of the Apple watch by assigning the indirect fixed manufacturing costs to the product as well. As you have seen throughout this book, there are many different methods for assigning indirect costs to products or services. Companies that use cost-based transfer pricing must set very clear standards and rules about how costs should be computed for internal transfers.

NEGOTIATION

A final option is to let division managers negotiate the appropriate transfer price. In this method, the negotiated price should fall somewhere between the $89 variable cost (floor) and the market price of $299 (ceiling). As with any negotiation, the final price will depend on the relative power of the buyer and seller, their negotiation skills, and how much inside information each party has about the other division's cost, capacity, and demand.

In this particular example, the manager of the Apple retail store may not have a lot of power to negotiate because it is a "captive customer." The store only sells Apple products, which means the manager is not able to negotiate based on the price of competing products. As such, the negotiated transfer price may be close to the market price of $299.

Another issue that affects negotiation is the capacity of the selling division. If the selling division has excess capacity (extra units available for sale), the sales manager should be willing to accept any price above variable cost because it will generate incremental profit. However, if the selling division has limited capacity, the manager will be not be willing to sell for less than the market price because doing so would result in lost sales to external parties (an opportunity cost).

Because the parent company (Apple) earns more profit when its products are sold through Apple channels rather than a third party, the company must carefully design its performance evaluation system to encourage managers to work together to achieve company goals.

Remember that the internal transfer price determines how revenues and costs are reported between divisions. This is only important if the managers of the divisions are evaluated based on their ability to control cost, generate revenue, or create profit. If they are evaluated based on other measures, such as customer satisfaction or total firm value (e.g., economic value added), the internal transfer price is less important.

To make sure you understand the different ways to set transfer prices in decentralized organizations, complete the following Self-Study Practice.

 How's it going?　　　　　　　Self-Study Practice

Kraft Foods owns both Tombstone Pizza and Kraft Cheese. Assume that Tombstone Pizza (the buyer) has approached Kraft Cheese (the seller) to ask for a special deal on the cheese used to produce Tombstone's frozen pizza.

Which of the following statements is true?

1. The minimum price the seller should accept is the variable cost of producing and selling the cheese.
2. The maximum price the buyer should pay is the market price.
3. Both statements above are true.
4. None of these statements is true.

After you have finished, check your answers against the solutions in the margin.

Solution to Self-Study Practice
Statements 1, 2, and 3 are true.

REVIEW THE CHAPTER

DEMONSTRATION CASE

Consider the following data for two divisions of Peter Piper Pizza:

	Northwest Region	Southwest Region
Average invested assets	$ 6,000,000	$ 6,000,000
Sales revenue	$ 18,000,000	$ 9,000,000
Less: Operating expenses	(17,460,000)	(8,100,000)
Net operating income	$ 540,000	$ 900,000

Required:

1. Compute the investment turnover, profit margin, return on investment, and residual income for each division. Assume a 10 percent hurdle rate.
2. Explain the relationship between each division's residual income and its return on investment.
3. The manager of the Southwest Region has the opportunity to invest an additional $2,000,000 in a project expected to generate additional operating income of $220,000 per year. Calculate Southwest's new return on investment and residual income if the manager accepts the project.
4. Would Southwest's manager, who is evaluated based on the region's ROI, want to invest in the project? What if the manager were evaluated based on residual income? Why or why not?

Suggested Solution

1.

	Northwest Region	Southwest Region
$\text{Investment Turnover} = \dfrac{\text{Sales Revenue}}{\text{Average Invested Assets}}$	$\dfrac{\$18{,}000{,}000}{\$6{,}000{,}000} = 3$	$\dfrac{\$9{,}000{,}000}{\$6{,}000{,}000} = 1.50$
$\text{Profit Margin} = \dfrac{\text{Net Operating Income}}{\text{Sales Revenue}}$	$\dfrac{\$540{,}000}{\$18{,}000{,}000} = 3\%$	$\dfrac{\$900{,}000}{\$9{,}000{,}000} = 10\%$
$\text{Return on Investment} = \dfrac{\text{Net Operating Income}}{\text{Average Invested Assets}}$	$\dfrac{\$540{,}000}{\$6{,}000{,}000} = 9\%$	$\dfrac{\$900{,}000}{\$6{,}000{,}000} = 15\%$
Net operating income	$ 540,000	$ 900,000
Minimum acceptable profit (10% × average invested assets)	(600,000)	(600,000)
Residual income	$ (60,000)	$ 300,000

2. The Northwest Region has a negative residual income because its return on investment, which is 9 percent, is less than the 10 percent hurdle rate [1 percent of $6,000,000 = $(60,000)].

The Southwest Region has a positive residual income because its return on investment, which is 15 percent, is higher than the 10 percent hurdle rate (5 percent of $6,000,000 = $300,000).

3.

	Southwest Region (before project)	Proposed Project	Southwest Region (if project is accepted)
Return on Investment Analysis			
$\dfrac{\text{Net Operating Income}}{\text{Average Invested Assets}} = \text{Return on Investment}$	$\dfrac{\$900{,}000}{\$6{,}000{,}000} = 15\%$	$\dfrac{\$220{,}000}{\$2{,}000{,}000} = 11\%$	$\dfrac{\$1{,}120{,}000}{\$8{,}000{,}000} = 14\%$
Residual Income Analysis			
Net operating income	$ 900,000	$ 220,000	$1,120,000
Minimum acceptable profit (10% of average invested assets)	(600,000)	(200,000)	(800,000)
Residual income	$ 300,000	$ 20,000	$ 320,000

4. If the manager's evaluation is based on return on investment (ROI), Southwest's regional manager probably would **not** want to invest in the project because it would lower the division's ROI. The project's expected ROI of 11 percent is less than the division's current ROI of 15 percent. Thus, investing the extra $2,000,000 would lower the region's ROI to 14 percent.

However, if the manager's evaluation is based on the region's residual income, the manager **would** want to invest in the project because it would increase the region's residual income. Residual income will increase as long as the project's return (11 percent) is higher than the minimum required rate of return (10 percent).

CHAPTER SUMMARY

List and explain the advantages and disadvantages of decentralization. p. 441   LO 10–1

- Decentralization means delegating decision-making authority to managers at all levels of the organization.

- The advantages of decentralization include the ability to make decisions more quickly based on local information, the development of managerial expertise, and the increased opportunity for upper management to focus on strategic issues.

- The disadvantages of decentralization include the potential for duplicating resources and for making suboptimal decisions (those that are not made in the best interests of the organization as a whole).

Describe the different types of responsibility centers and explain how managers in each type are evaluated. p. 443   LO 10–2

- **Cost center:** Managers are responsible for controlling costs within their area of responsibility, such as distribution, advertising, accounting, or human resources. Cost center managers are evaluated based on their ability to control costs while providing the necessary support to the organization.

- **Revenue center:** Managers are responsible for generating sales revenue within their area of responsibility, such as a store, a district, or a region. They are evaluated based on their ability to meet sales quotas and other measures of success like customer retention.

- **Profit center:** Managers are responsible for earning a profit within their area of responsibility through both revenue generation and cost control. They are typically evaluated based on a profitability measure such as segment margin, which includes only those costs that are within the segment manager's direct control.

- **Investment center:** Managers are responsible for both profit and the investment of assets. They are evaluated based on measures that include both profit and investment, such as return on investment, residual income, or economic value added.

Describe the four dimensions of the balanced scorecard and explain how they are used to evaluate managerial performance. p. 447   LO 10–3

- The balanced scorecard is a comprehensive performance measurement system that translates the organization's vision and strategy into a set of operational performance measures.

- The balanced scorecard measures operational performance on four key dimensions: customer perspective, learning and growth perspective, internal business processes perspective, and financial perspective.

- The customer perspective focuses on customers' perception of the company through measures such as customer retention, customer satisfaction, and market share.

- The learning and growth perspective focuses on the organization's ability to change and improve through measures such as the amount of money spent on research and development and employee education and training.

- The internal business processes perspective focuses on the internal processes required to meet customer needs through measures such as on-time-delivery, quality, inventory stock-outs, and process efficiency.

- The financial perspective focuses on traditional financial measures of performance, such as return on investment, residual income, and economic value added.

LO 10–4 **Compute and interpret return on investment, investment turnover, and profit margin. p. 451**

- Return on investment (ROI) is the most common measure for evaluating financial performance.
- ROI is computed by dividing net operating income by average invested assets.
- The DuPont formula shows that ROI equals the profit margin multiplied by the investment turnover ratio.
- Profit margin is the amount of profit generated for every dollar of sales revenue.
- Investment turnover is the amount of sales revenue generated for every dollar of invested assets.
- Companies can increase ROI either by increasing the profit margin (reducing costs without reducing sales) or by increasing the asset turnover rate (increasing sales without increasing assets).

LO 10–5 **Compute and interpret residual income. p. 455**

- Residual income equals the difference between an investment center's net operating income and the minimum profit it must make to cover its hurdle rate (that is, the minimum rate of return on its assets).
- Managers can earn residual income by investing in projects that earn more than the required rate of return (or hurdle rate).
- Economic value added is similar to residual income, but focuses on how much economic wealth the company generates over and above its cost of capital.

LO 10–6 **Explain how transfer prices are set in decentralized organizations. p. 458**

- A transfer price is the price charged when one unit or division of a company sells goods or services to another unit or division of the same company.
- The maximum transfer price (*ceiling*) is the external market price, or the amount that would be charged to an unrelated party.
- The minimum transfer price (*floor*) is the variable cost (to the seller) of producing the product.
- The market-price method is based on the price that an unrelated party would pay for the product or service.
- Cost-based transfer prices can be set based on variable cost, full cost, or cost plus some percentage markup.
- Transfer prices can also be set through negotiation between the buying and selling divisions.

KEY TERMS

Balanced Scorecard p.447	Goal Incongruence p.457	Required Rate of Return p.455
Centralized Organization p.441	Hurdle Rate p.455	Residual Income p.455
Controllability Principle p.443	Investment Center p.443	Responsibility Accounting p.443
Cost Center p.443	Investment Turnover p.453	Responsibility Center p.443
Decentralized Organization p.441	Profit Center p.443	Return on Investment p.450
DuPont Method p.453	Profit Margin p.453	Revenue Center p.443
Economic Value Added p.457	Related-Party Transactions p.458	Transfer Price p.458

PRACTICE MATERIAL

QUESTIONS

1. Explain how centralized and decentralized companies differ. What are the advantages and disadvantages of each?

2. Why does decentralization create the need for responsibility accounting in an organization?

3. What is the controllability principle and why is it crucial to responsibility accounting?

4. Name the four types of responsibility centers and describe the managers' responsibilities and authority in each.

5. Briefly explain the difference between segment margin and net operating income.

6. Why are profit center managers evaluated on segment margin instead of net operating income?

7. How do investment center managers differ from profit center managers?

8. What role do return on investment and residual income play in responsibility accounting?

9. Return on investment may be separated into two components. Name them and describe what each can tell you.

10. Explain how relying on return on investment for performance evaluation of investment center managers could lead to goal incongruence.

11. How is residual income calculated?

12. What benefit does residual income offer in comparison to return on investment when evaluating performance?

13. How does EVA differ from residual income?

14. What are the primary limitations of financial measures of performance?

15. Other than the one(s) mentioned in the text, give an example of an action that management might take to improve financial performance in the short run that could prove detrimental in the long run.

16. Explain the balanced scorecard approach to performance evaluation. What advantages does this approach have over using only financial measurements?

17. What are the four dimensions of a balanced scorecard? What does each dimension represent?

18. Why must a company consider its incentive and reward system when implementing a balanced scorecard approach?

19. Why are incentive systems that emphasize long-term performance more consistent with a balanced scorecard approach?

20. What is a transfer price?

21. Explain why two managers employed by the same company may be diametrically opposed to each other when considering a transfer price.

22. Explain the meaning of minimum and maximum transfer prices and identify who (the buyer or the seller) would determine each.

23. What is the market-price method of transfer pricing?

24. How does excess capacity affect a transfer price?

25. Describe the cost-based method of transfer pricing.

26. What are negotiated transfer prices? Explain two possible disadvantages of allowing managers to negotiate a transfer price.

MULTIPLE CHOICE

1. Sally Thorne is a profit center manager for ABC Company's Phoenix district. Last year, her performance evaluation was based on the operating performance of ABC's entire Southwest region. This is a violation of

   a. The hurdle rate principle.
   b. The controllability principle.
   c. The balanced scorecard approach.
   d. Negotiated transfer pricing rules.

2. Responsibility centers include

   a. Cost centers.
   b. Profit centers.
   c. Investment centers.
   d. All of these.

3. Which of the following statements is true?

   a. A profit center manager is responsible for investing company assets.
   b. A cost center manager should be evaluated based on sales revenue.

   c. A profit center manager should be evaluated based on return on investment.
   d. An investment center manager is responsible for costs, revenue, and the investment of assets.

4. Which of the following is most likely to be classified as a cost center manager?

   a. Accounting manager.
   b. Sales manager.
   c. Regional manager.
   d. All of these are cost center managers.

5. Return on investment and residual income are useful for evaluating

   a. Cost center managers.
   b. Revenue center managers.
   c. Profit center managers.
   d. Investment center managers.

6. EVA is a variation of

   a. Residual income.
   c. The DuPont method.
   b. Return on investment.
   d. All of the above.

7. Raymond Calvin is an investment center manager for XYZ Corp. and is evaluated solely on the return on investment for his division. Which of the following will improve Raymond's evaluation?

   a. Increasing the amount invested in assets while keeping operating income the same.
   b. Increasing the amount of operating income while keeping invested assets the same.
   c. Decreasing the amount invested in assets while keeping operating income the same.
   d. Either b or c.

8. Which of the following statements is true?

   a. Return on investment considers a company's hurdle rate for investments.

   b. Residual income considers a company's hurdle rate for investments.
   c. Projects may be rejected based on return on investment even though they produce positive residual income.
   d. Both b and c.

9. Which of the following is not a component of the balanced scorecard method of measuring performance?

   a. Customer perspective.
   b. Management perspective.
   c. Learning and growth perspective.
   d. Internal business processes perspective.

10. Transfer price could be based on

   a. Variable costs.
   b. Full cost.
   c. Market price.
   d. Any of the above.

 **Find More Learning Solutions on Connect.**

MINI-EXERCISES

LO 10–1, 10–2, 10–3, 10–4, 10–5, 10–6

M10–1 Using Terms to Complete Sentences about Decentralized Performance Evaluation

Use the following terms to complete the sentences that follow; terms may be used once, more than once, or not at all:

Congruence	Increase
Controllability principle	Internal business
Customer	Investment
Decentralization	Learning and growth
Decrease	Profit
Economic value added (EVA)	Residual income (RI)
External market price	Responsibility accounting
Financial	Return on investment (ROI)
Full cost	Sales revenue
Incongruence	Transfer pricing

  1. Managers of a(n) _____ center are evaluated based on measures such as ROI and residual income.

  2. Suboptimal decisions and duplication of resources are considered disadvantages of _____.

  3. A positive _____ results when managers invest in projects that earn more than the hurdle rate.

  4. The _____ perspective focuses on processes required to meet customer needs through measures such as on-time delivery and quality.

  5. The _____ states that managers should be held responsible only for what they can control.

  6. _____ measures the economic wealth that is created when a company's after-tax operating income exceeds its cost of capital.

  7. The _____ perspective typically contains leading indicators, which are measures that reflect future performance.

  8. A change in the investment turnover ratio from 1.5 to 3.2 will _____ the division's ROI.

  9. The maximum transfer price is the _____.

  10. Goal _____ results when there is conflict between a manager and the organization as a whole.

M10–2 Describing Difference in Centralized and Decentralized Organizations   LO 10–1

Lupe Bornes recently graduated from college and received job offers in management from two different companies. The positions are similar in terms of title, salary, and benefits, but the companies vary in organizational structure. Alpha Company is centralized while Beta Company is decentralized. Explain to Lupe what he can infer about each company and how it is likely to affect his position within each one.

M10–3 Describing Structure of Real-World Organizations Responsibility Centers   LO 10–2

Responsibility centers can be created in a variety of ways. Give a real-world example of a company whose responsibility centers would likely be created on the basis of each of the following: functional area, product line, and geographic area.

M10–4 Classifying Responsibility Centers   LO 10–2

In each of the following situations, identify which type of responsibility center is appropriate based on the decision-making authority the manager would possess:

1. The manager of the accounting department in Ford's corporate office.
2. The sales manager of a Ford dealership.
3. The general manager of a Ford dealership.
4. The manager of Ford's corporate division.
5. The production manager in a Ford plant.

M10–5 Applying Balanced Scorecard to Real-World Company   LO 10–3

Consider the manager of your local Applebee's restaurant. Using a balanced scorecard approach, identify three measures for each of the four dimensions of the balanced scorecard.

M10–6 Applying Balanced Scorecard to Online Company   LO 10–3

Choose a company that has an online sales segment; it can be a company that operates entirely online or a brick-and-mortar store with an online site. Assuming a balanced scorecard approach, identify five specific measures that the company could use to measure performance from the customer perspective. For each measure identified, indicate how that information would be obtained.

M10–7 Calculating Return on Investment, Residual Income   LO 10–4, 10–5

Violet Company has sales of $520,000, net operating income of $310,000, average invested assets of $940,000, and a hurdle rate of 10 percent. Calculate Violet's return on investment and its residual income.

M10–8 Calculating Return on Investment, Residual Income   LO 10–4, 10–5

Myrtle Company has sales of $140,000, cost of goods sold of $70,000, operating expenses of $20,000, average invested assets of $400,000, and a hurdle rate of 6 percent. Calculate Myrtle's return on investment and its residual income.

M10–9 Calculating Return on Investment, Residual Income   LO 10–4, 10–5

Augusta Corp's Golf Division has sales of $200,000, cost of goods sold of $105,000, operating expenses of $35,000, average invested assets of $900,000, and a hurdle rate of 12 percent. Calculate the Golf Division's return on investment and its residual income.

M10–10 Impact of New Investment on ROI, Residual Income   LO 10–4, 10–5

The Western Division of Claremont Company had net operating income of $135,000 and average invested assets of $560,000. Claremont has a required rate of return of 15 percent. Western has an opportunity to increase operating income by $12,000 with a $108,000 investment in assets. Compute Western Division's return on investment and residual income currently and if it undertakes the project.

M10–11 Describing Transfer Pricing Implications   LO 10–2, 10–6

Assume that your cousin Matilda Flores manages a local glass shop that was recently bought by a company that produces custom picture frames. As a result, Matilda will soon be providing glass to the Frame Division. She has heard upper management mention a transfer price but does not understand what this term means or how it might affect her division. Briefly explain transfer pricing to Matilda and how it will impact her division's performance in the future.

LO 10–6   **M10–12 Identifying Minimum, Maximum Transfer Prices**

Peppertree Company has two divisions, East and West. Division East manufactures a component that Division West uses. The variable cost to produce this component is $2.00 per unit; full cost is $2.75. The component sells on the open market for $3.10. Assuming Division East has excess capacity, what is the lowest price Division East will accept for the component? What is the highest price that Division West will pay for it?

LO 10–6   **M10–13 Calculating Cost-Plus Transfer Price**

Medlock Company has two divisions, Wheel and Chassis. The Wheel Division manufactures a wheel assembly that the Chassis Division uses. The variable cost to produce this assembly is $4.00 per unit; full cost is $5.00. The component sells on the open market for $9.00. What will the transfer price be if Medlock uses a pricing rule of variable cost plus 60 percent?

LO 10–6   **M10–14 Negotiating Transfer Prices**

Tuckey Company is considering allowing the managers of its two divisions to negotiate a transfer price for the component that Division A manufactures and sells to Division B. Identify the range of possible transfer prices that could result from the negotiation. Briefly describe benefits and possible negative consequences of allowing the managers to negotiate a transfer price.

EXERCISES

LO 10–1, 10–2, 10–3, 10–4, 10–5   **E10–1 Matching Terminology**

Match each of the terms by inserting the appropriate definition letter in the space provided. Not all definitions will be used.

_____ 1. Balanced Scorecard
_____ 2. Centralized Organization
_____ 3. DuPont Method
_____ 4. Hurdle Rate
_____ 5. Investment Center
_____ 6. Profit Center
_____ 7. Cost Center
_____ 8. Revenue Center
_____ 9. Profit margin
_____ 10. Return on Investment (ROI)

A. An organization in which high-level executives make most of the decisions and charge others with implementing those decisions.

B. A performance measurement system that focuses on return on investment.

C. The ratio of net operating income to sales revenue.

D. A center where the manager has the responsibility to generate revenues.

E. An organization that delegates decision making to managers throughout the organization.

F. The minimum required rate of return for a project.

G. A performance method that looks at investment turnover and profit margin to gain a better understanding of the contributing factors.

H. A center where the manager has the responsibility to control both revenue and costs.

I. A performance measurement system that includes both lagging and leading indicators.

J. Net operating income divided by average invested assets.

K. A center where the manager has the responsibility to control revenue, costs, and manage assets.

L. When the present value of the capital expenditure equals the present value of the expected net annual cash flows.

M. A center where the manager is only responsible to control costs.

E10–2 Explaining Relationships among Decentralization, Responsibility Accounting, Controllability, Balanced Scorecard   LO 10–1, 10–2, 10–3

Assume you are the vice president of operations for a local company. Your company is in the process of converting from a small, centralized organization in which its president makes all decisions to a larger, geographically dispersed one with decentralized decision-making authority.

Required:

Write a brief memo to other company managers explaining how decentralization, responsibility accounting, controllability, and the balanced scorecard method of performance evaluation are all related. Include the most obvious changes the managers are likely to see as this transition takes place and how it will impact their performance evaluations in the future.

E10–3 Identifying Responsibility Center Types   LO 10–2

Match the most likely type of responsibility center classification to each of the following positions. You may use a classification once, more than once, or not at all.

Employment Positions	Possible Responsibility Center Classification
_____ Sales manager	a. Cost center
_____ Regional manager	b. Revenue center
_____ Company president	c. Profit center
_____ Purchasing manager	d. Investment center
_____ Human resources manager	
_____ Chief financial officer	
_____ Production facility manager	

E10–4 Finding Unknowns Using Return on Investment, Profit Margin, Investment Turnover   LO 10–4

Fleetwood Company recently had a computer malfunction and lost a portion of its accounting records. The company has reconstructed some of its financial performance measurements, including components of the return on investment calculations.

Required:

Help Fleetwood rebuild its information database by completing the following table:

Return on Investment	Profit Margin	Investment Turnover
?	5%	1.9
18%	?	2.0
3%	5%	?
23%	?	1.5

E10–5 Finding Unknowns Using Return on Investment, Profit Margin, Investment Turnover   LO 10–4

Krall Company recently had a computer malfunction and lost a portion of its accounting records. The company has reconstructed some of its financial performance measurements including components of the return on investment calculations.

Required:

Help Krall rebuild its information database by completing the following table:

Return on Investment	Profit Margin	Investment Turnover	Operating Income	Sales Revenue	Average Invested Assets
?	?	?	$ 70,000	$ 700,000	$1,400,000
?	8%	0.50	100,000	?	2,500,000
?	12%	1.25	?	1,400,000	?
10%	?	2.00	?	600,000	?

LO 10–4, 10–5   **E10–6 Calculating Return on Investment, Residual Income, Determining Effect of Changes in Sales, Expenses, Invested Assets, Hurdle Rate on Each**

Solano Company has sales of $500,000, cost of goods sold of $370,000, other operating expenses of $50,000, average invested assets of $1,600,000, and a hurdle rate of 6 percent.

Required:

1. Determine Solano's return on investment (ROI), investment turnover, profit margin, and residual income.

2. Several possible changes that Solano could face in the upcoming year follow. Determine each scenario's impact on Solano's ROI and residual income. (**Note:** Treat each scenario independently.)

   a. Company sales and cost of goods sold increase by 30 percent.
   b. Operating expenses decrease by $10,000.
   c. Operating expenses increase by 20 percent.
   d. Average invested assets increase by $300,000.
   e. Solano changes its hurdle rate to 12 percent.

LO 10–4, 10–5   **E10–7 Calculating Return on Investment, Residual Income, Determining Effect of Changes in Sales, Expenses, Invested Assets, Hurdle Rate on Each**

Kaler Company has sales of $1,210,000, cost of goods sold of $735,000, other operating expenses of $148,000, average invested assets of $3,400,000, and a hurdle rate of 12 percent.

Required:

1. Determine Kaler's return on investment (ROI), investment turnover, profit margin, and residual income.

2. Several possible changes that Kaler could face in the upcoming year follow. Determine each scenario's impact on Kaler's ROI and residual income. (**Note:** Treat each scenario independently.)

   a. Company sales and cost of goods sold increase by 15 percent.
   b. Operating expenses increase by $73,000.
   c. Operating expenses decrease by 10 percent.
   d. Average invested assets decrease by $285,000.
   e. Kaler changes its hurdle rate to 9 percent.

LO 10–4, 10–5   **E10–8 Evaluating Managerial Performance Using Return on Investment, Residual Income**

Orange Corp. has two divisions: Fruit and Flower. The following information for the past year is available for each division:

	Fruit Division	Flower Division
Sales revenue	$ 600,000	$ 900,000
Cost of goods sold and operating expenses	450,000	600,000
Net operating income	$ 150,000	$ 300,000
Average invested assets	$1,200,000	$1,600,000

Orange has established a hurdle rate of 12 percent.

Required:

1. Compute each division's return on investment (ROI) and residual income for last year. Determine which manager seems to be performing better.

2. Suppose Orange is investing in new technology that will increase each division's operating income by $144,000. The total investment required is $1,600,000, which will be split evenly between the two divisions. Calculate the ROI and return on investment for each division after the investment is made.

3. Determine whether both managers will support the investment. Explain how their support will differ depending on which performance measure (ROI or residual investment) is used.

E10–9 Evaluating Managerial Performance Using Return on Investment, Residual Income   LO 10–4, 10–5

Luke Company has three divisions: Peak, View, and Grand. The company has a hurdle rate of 6 percent. Selected operating data for the three divisions follow:

	Peak	View	Grand
Sales revenue	$ 325,000	$220,000	$ 298,000
Cost of goods sold	216,000	123,000	202,000
Miscellaneous operating expenses	45,000	36,000	39,000
Average invested assets	1,100,000	990,000	1,000,000

Required:

1. Compute the return on investment for each division.

2. Compute the residual income for each division.

E10–10 Developing Balanced Scorecard   LO 10–3

Choose a company with which you regularly do business. Assume you have been hired as a consultant to help overhaul its performance evaluation system.

Required:

1. Briefly outline a balanced scorecard approach that could be used to evaluate the performance of the company's managers.

2. For each of the four perspectives, identify three metrics that could be part of the balanced scorecard.
3. Explain the reasoning behind each metric that you chose.

E10–11 Determining the Impact of Various Transactions on Investment Turnover, ROI, Residual Income, and Profit Margin   LO 10–4, 10–5

Poseidon Corporation manufactures a variety of gear for water sports. Poseidon has three divisions: Lake, River, and Ocean. Each division is managed as an investment center. During the current year, the Ocean division experienced the following transactions:

a. A special order was accepted at a selling price significantly less than the ordinary selling price. The sale will not impact other sales because this was a one-time order and Ocean has excess capacity. The selling price was in excess of total variable costs.
b. One of three production managers in the Ocean Division submitted his resignation. The position will not be filled due to current efficiencies experienced in the production department.
c. Due to the popularity of open-ocean swimming during the Olympics, the company experienced a surge in sales during the summer months. Sales returned to their normal level for the remainder of the year.
d. Equipment costing $500,000 was purchased to replace fully depreciated, obsolete equipment.
e. The company's after-tax cost of capital increased from 8 percent to 10 percent, with no effect on the minimum required rate of return.
f. The company's effective tax rate decreased from 35 percent to 30 percent.

Required:

For each transaction listed in this exercise, determine the impact on investment turnover, return on investment, residual income, and economic value added. Use the following table to organize your answers. Use (I) for increase, (D) for decrease, (N) for no effect, or a question mark (?) if you're unable to determine the impact of the transaction. Each transaction should be treated independently.

Transaction	Return on Investment	Residual Income	Economic Value Added
a.			
b.			
c.			
d.			
e.			
f.			

LO 10–3   E10–12 Describing Balanced Scorecard Objectives and Perspectives

Your brother-in-law, Fred Miles, has just taken a new position as the plant manager of a local production facility. He has been told that the company uses a balanced scorecard approach to evaluate its managers. Fred is not familiar with this approach because his previous experience as a production manager focused only on whether the plant met the company's budgeted production.

Required:

1. Briefly explain to Fred how performance evaluations at his new company will differ from those at his previous company.

2. Give Fred five possible objectives that the new company will use, in addition to production level, to evaluate his performance. For each objective that you identify, be sure to indicate a plausible metric for measuring it.

LO 10–6   E10–13 Understanding Transfer Price Importance

Refer to E10–12. Suppose Fred's plant manufactures a component used by another division of the organization. He has approached you for help in understanding why everyone seems to be making such a big deal about the transfer price that he plans to charge for the component. Fred's comment was, "Transfer prices do not impact the amount of profit earned by the company as a whole, so they don't affect me. I don't care what transfer price is used."

Required:

1. Explain whether Fred is correct or incorrect.

2. Explain how the transfer price could affect Fred or someone he works with.

LO 10–2   E10–14 Determining Different Types of Responsibility Centers

The University of Dental Health (UDH) is a state-run university focusing on the education and training of dentists, dental assistants, dental hygienists, and other dental professionals. UDH has just hired a new controller who wants to organize UDH by responsibility centers so that responsibility accounting can be implemented. The controller has asked for your assistance in identifying each of the following UDH functions as either a cost center (C) or a profit center (P).

UDH Center	Cost or Profit
Accounting	
Bookstore	
Cafeterias	
Career services	
Community workshops (providing continuing professional education necessary for state licensure)	
Custodial services	
Financial aid	
Human resources	
Information technology	
Residence halls	
Student parking lots (fee based)	
University newspaper/radio station	

LO 10–6   E10–15 Determining Transfer Price

The Molding Division of Cotwold Company manufactures a plastic casing used by the Assembly Division. This casing is also sold to external customers for $25 per unit. Variable costs for the casing are $12 per unit and fixed cost is $3 per unit. Cotwold executives would like for the Molding Division to transfer 8,000 units to the Assembly Division at a price of $18 per unit.

Required:

1. Assume the Molding Division is operating at full capacity. Explain whether it should accept the transfer price proposed by management.

2. Identify the minimum transfer price that the Molding Division will accept and explain why.

E10–16 Determining Transfer Price

Refer to the information presented in E10–15. Assume that the Molding Division has enough excess capacity to accommodate the request.

Required:

1. Explain whether the Molding Division should accept the $18 transfer price proposed by management.
2. Calculate the effect on the Molding Division's net income if it accepts the $18 transfer price.

E10–17 Determining Transfer Price

Refer to the information presented in E10–15. Assume that the Molding Division has excess capacity, but the Assembly Division requires the casing to be made from a specific blend of plastics. This would raise the variable cost per unit to $20.

Required:

1. Explain whether the Molding Division should accept the $18 transfer price proposed by management.
2. Determine the minimum transfer price that it will accept.
3. Determine the mutually beneficial transfer price so that the two divisions equally split the profits from the transfer.

E10–18 Matching Measures of Performance with the Correct Balanced Scorecard Perspective

The following is a list of various metrics used to measure performance. For each metric, identify the correct balanced scorecard perspective with which the metric is associated. For Learning and Growth, use LG; for Customer, use C; for Financial, use F; and for Internal Business, use IB. Each perspective may be used once, more than once, or not at all.

Metric	Balanced Scorecard Perspective
Average stock price	
Economic value added	
Employee turnover rates	
Manufacturing cycle time	
Market share	
Number of days from product launch to shelf	
Number of defects	
Number of new patent applications	
Percentage of repeat customers	
Percentage decrease in operating costs	
Percentage of sales generated by new products	
Research and development spending as a percentage of net revenues	

E10–19 Determining Minimum, Maximum, Negotiated Transfer Prices

Shaw is a lumber company that also manufactures custom cabinetry. It is made up of two divisions: Lumber and Cabinetry. The Lumber Division is responsible for harvesting and preparing lumber for use; the Cabinetry Division produces custom-ordered cabinetry. The lumber produced by the Lumber Division has a variable cost of $2.00 per linear foot and full cost of $3.00. Comparable quality wood sells on the open market for $6.00 per linear foot.

Required:

1. Assume you are the manager of the Cabinetry Division. Determine the maximum amount you would pay for lumber.
2. Assume you are the manager of the Lumber Division. Determine the minimum amount you would charge for the lumber if you have excess capacity. Repeat assuming you have no excess capacity.

3. Assume you are the president of Shaw. Determine a mutually beneficial transfer price assuming there is excess capacity.

4. Explain the possible consequences of simply letting the two division managers negotiate a price.

LO 10–6   **E10–20 Identifying Minimum, Maximum Transfer Prices, Determining Effect on Each Division's Profit**

Tulip Company is made up of two divisions: A and B. Division A produces a widget that Division B uses in the production of its product. Variable cost per widget is $0.75; full cost is $1.00. Comparable widgets sell on the open market for $1.50 each. Division A can produce up to 2 million widgets per year but is currently operating at only 50 percent capacity. Division B expects to use 100,000 widgets in the current year.

Required:

1. Determine the minimum and maximum transfer prices.

2. Calculate Tulip Company's total benefit of having the widgets transferred between these divisions.

3. If the transfer price is set at $0.75 per unit, determine how much profit Division A will make on the transfer. Determine how much Division B will save by not purchasing the widgets on the open market.

4. If the transfer price is set at $1.50 per unit, determine how much profit Division A will make on the transfer. Determine how much Division B will save by not purchasing the widgets on the open market.

5. What transfer price would you recommend to split the difference?

LO 10–3   **E10–21 Identifying Balanced Scorecard Perspectives**

Identify which perspective(s) of the balanced scorecard each of the following critical success factors relates to by placing an X in the appropriate cell. Each success factor could relate to more than one category.

	BALANCED SCORECARD PERSPECTIVES			
Critical Success Factor	**Financial**	**Customer**	**Internal Business**	**Learning and Growth**
Contribution margin by product				
Quality				
Employee empowerment				
Information systems capabilities				
New markets				
Product innovation				
Productivity				

GROUP A PROBLEMS

LO 10–4, 10–5   **PA10–1 Calculating Return on Investment, Residual Income, Determining Effect of Changes in Sales, Expenses, Invested Assets, Hurdle Rate on Each**

Coolbrook Company has the following information available for the past year:

	River Division	Stream Division
Sales revenue	$1,200,000	$1,800,000
Cost of goods sold and operating expenses	900,000	1,300,000
Net operating income	$ 300,000	$ 500,000
Average invested assets	$1,200,000	$1,800,000

The company's hurdle rate is 6 percent.

Required:

1. Calculate return on investment (ROI) and residual income for each division for last year.

2. Recalculate ROI and residual income for each division for each independent situation that follows:

    a. Operating income increases by 10 percent.

    b. Operating income decreases by 10 percent.

    c. The company invests $250,000 in each division, an amount that generates $100,000 additional income per division.

    d. Coolbrook changes its hurdle rate to 10 percent.

PA10–2 Calculating Unknowns, Predicting Relationship among Return on Investment, Residual Income, Hurdle Rates

LO 10–4, 10–5

The following is partial information for Charleston Company's most recent year of operation. It manufactures lawn mowers and categorizes its operations into two divisions: Bermuda and Midiron.

	Bermuda Division	Midiron Division
Sales revenue	?	$600,000
Average invested assets	$2,500,000	?
Net operating income	$ 160,000	$150,000
Profit margin	20%	?
Investment turnover	?	0.16
Return on investment	?	?
Residual income	$ 40,000	$ (30,000)

Required:

1. Without making any calculations, determine whether each division's return on investment is above or below Charleston's hurdle rate. How can you tell?

2. Determine the missing amounts in the preceding table.

3. What is Charleston's hurdle rate?

4. Suppose Charleston has the opportunity to invest additional assets to help expand the company's market share. The expansion would require an average investment of $2,800,000 and would generate $140,000 in additional income. From Charleston's perspective, is this a viable investment? Why or why not?

5. Suppose the two divisions would equally share the investment and profits from the expansion project. If return on investment is used to evaluate performance, what will each division manager think about the proposed project?

6. In requirement 5, will either manager's preference change if residual income is used to measure division performance? Explain your answer.

PA10–3 Evaluating Managerial Performance, Proposed Project Impact on Return on Investment, Residual Income

LO 10–4, 10–5

Wescott Company has three divisions: A, B, and C. The company has a hurdle rate of 8 percent. Selected operating data for the three divisions are as follows:

	Division A	Division B	Division C
Sales revenue	$1,255,000	$ 920,000	$ 898,000
Cost of goods sold	776,000	675,000	652,000
Miscellaneous operating expenses	64,000	52,000	53,100
Interest and taxes	48,000	41,000	41,500
Average invested assets	8,300,000	1,930,000	3,215,000

Wescott is considering an expansion project in the upcoming year that will cost $5 million and return $450,000 per year. The project would be implemented by only one of the three divisions.

Required:

1. Compute the ROI for each division.

2. Compute the residual income for each division.

3. Rank the divisions according to the ROI and residual income of each.

4. Compute the return on the proposed expansion project. Is this an acceptable project?

5. Without any additional calculations, state whether the proposed project would increase or decrease each division's ROI.

6. Compute the new ROI and residual income for each division if the project was implemented within that division.

LO 10–6   **PA10–4**   **Identifying Minimum, Maximum, Mutually Beneficial Transfer Prices**

Grover Corp. is a manufacturing company that produces golf clubs. Birdie is a division of Grover that manufactures putters. Birdie's putters are used in Grover's golf club sets and are sold to other golf wholesalers. Cost information per putter follows:

Variable cost	$25.00
Full cost	28.00
Market price	42.00

In addition, its capacity data follow:

Capacity per year	40,000 putters
Current production level	30,000 putters

Required:

1. Assuming Grover produces 3,000 putters per year, determine the overall benefit of using putters from Birdie instead of purchasing them externally.

2. Determine the maximum price that the production facility would be willing to pay to purchase the putters from Birdie. How is the overall benefit divided between the two divisions if this transfer price is used?

3. Determine the minimum that Birdie will accept as a transfer price. How is the overall benefit divided between the two divisions if this transfer price is used?

4. Determine the mutually beneficial transfer price for the putters.

5. How would your answer change if Birdie were currently operating at capacity?

LO 10–6   **PA10–5**   **Identifying Minimum, Maximum, Mutually Beneficial Transfer Prices**

Going Places, Inc., manufactures a variety of luggage for airline passengers. The company has several luggage production divisions, including the Suitable Cases Division, as well as a wholly owned subsidiary, It's Mine, that manufactures small identification tags used on luggage. Each piece of luggage that Suitable Cases produces has two identification tags for which it previously paid the going market price of $2 each. Financial information for Suitable Cases and It's Mine follows:

	Suitable Cases Division	It's Mine
Sales		
4,500 bags × $150.00 each	$675,000	
200,000 tags × $2.00 each		$400,000
Variable expenses		
4,500 bags × $85.00 each	382,500	
200,000 tags × $0.50 each		100,000

It's Mine has a production capacity of 250,000 tags.

Required:

1. Determine how much Going Places will save on each tag if the Suitable Cases Division obtains them from It's Mine instead of an external supplier.

2. Determine the maximum and minimum transfer prices for the tags. Who sets these?

3. Suppose Going Places has set a transfer price policy of variable cost plus 60 percent for all related-party transactions. Determine how much each party will benefit from the internal transfer.

4. Determine the mutually beneficial transfer price.

PA10–6 Categorizing Sustainability Metrics based on the Triple Bottom Line and the Balanced Scorecard LO 10–3

The following table lists several metrics from the Global Reporting Initiatives' (GRI) sustainability reporting standards and other industry sources.

For each metric, classify it based on its impact on the triple bottom line (People, Profit, or Planet) and indicate which balanced scorecard perspective it is most likely to fall within (Financial, Customer, Internal Business, Learning and Growth, or Society/Community). You can use more than one category when appropriate. The first metric is shown as an example.

Sustainability Metric	Triple bottom line impact: People, Profit, or Planet?	Balanced Scorecard Perspective: Financial, Customer, Internal Business, Learning/Growth, or Society/Community
Gallons of water consumed	Planet	Internal Business
Hours of R&D devoted to environmentally friendly products		
Average hours of training per employee by gender		
Number of substantiated complaints related to product health hazards		
Dollars invested in area of high poverty		
Number of formal grievances about environmental impacts		
Tons of nonrenewable materials used in manufacturing		
Total hours of employee training on human rights policies		
Total cost of work-related injuries, diseases, and fatalities		
Total greenhouse gas (GHG) emissions		
Total utilities cost		

GROUP B PROBLEMS

PB10–1 Calculating Return on Investment, Residual Income, Determining Effect of Changes in Sales, Expenses, Invested Assets, Hurdle Rate on Each LO 10–4, 10–5

Escuda Company has the following information available for the past year:

	Fence Division	Brick Division
Segment sales	$2,200,000	$1,300,000
Segment cost of goods sold and operating expenses	1,700,000	1,000,000
Segment income	$ 500,000	$ 300,000
Average invested assets	$4,100,000	$3,000,000

The company's hurdle rate is 12 percent.

1. Determine Escuda's return on investment (ROI) and residual income for each division for last year.
2. Recalculate Escuda's ROI and residual income for both divisions for each independent situation that follows:
   a. Net operating income increases by 10 percent.
   b. Net operating income decreases by 10 percent.
   c. The company invests $400,000 in each division, an amount that generates $80,000 additional income per division.
   d. Escuda changes its hurdle rate to 9 percent.

LO 10–4, 10–5 **PB10–2 Calculating Unknowns, Predicting Relationship among Return on Investment, Residual Income, Hurdle Rates**

The following is partial information for Tonopah Company's most recent year of operation. Tonopah manufactures children's shoes and categorizes its operations into two divisions: Girls and Boys.

	Girls Division	Boys Division
Sales revenue	$2,000,000	?
Average invested assets	?	$1,250,000
Net operating income	$ 500,000	$ 300,000
Profit margin	?	15%
Investment turnover	0.8	?
Return on investment	?	?
Residual income	$ 260,000	$ 180,000

Required:

1. Without making any calculations, determine whether each division's return on investment is above or below Tonopah's hurdle rate. How can you tell?
2. Determine the missing amounts in the preceding table.
3. What is Tonopah's hurdle rate?
4. Suppose Tonopah has the opportunity to invest additional assets to help expand the company's market share. The expansion would require an investment of $6,200,000 and would generate $800,000 in additional income. From Tonopah's perspective, is this a viable investment? Why or why not?
5. Suppose the two divisions would equally share the investment and profits from the expansion project. If return on investment is used to evaluate performance, what will each division think about the proposed project?
6. In requirement 5, will either manager's preference change if residual income is used to measure division performance? Explain your answer.

LO 10–4, 10–5 **PB10–3 Evaluating Managerial Performance, Impact of Proposed Project on Return on Investment, Residual Income**

Yummy Company has three divisions: Chips, Cookies, and Crackers. The company has a hurdle rate of 7 percent. Selected operating data for the three divisions follow:

	Chips Division	Cookies Division	Crackers Division
Sales revenue	$ 458,000	$ 560,000	$ 486,000
Cost of goods sold	316,000	313,925	233,600
Miscellaneous operating expenses	58,000	72,000	42,000
Interest and taxes	29,000	39,000	35,500
Average invested assets	1,600,000	1,450,000	2,630,000

Yummy is considering an expansion project in the upcoming year that will cost $5,250,000 and return $525,000 per year. The project would be implemented by only one of the three divisions.

Required:

1. Compute the ROI for each division.
2. Compute the residual income for each division.
3. Rank the divisions according to the ROI and residual income of each.
4. Compute the return on the proposed expansion project. Is this an acceptable project to Yummy?
5. Without any additional calculations, state whether the proposed project would increase or decrease each division's ROI.
6. Compute the new ROI and residual income for each division if the project was implemented within that division.

PB10–4 Identifying Minimum, Maximum, Mutually Beneficial Transfer Prices   LO 10–6

Quail Company produces outdoor gear. Salter is a division of Quail that manufactures unbreakable zippers used in Quail's gear and sold to other manufacturers. Cost information per zipper follows:

Variable cost	$1.60
Full cost	2.20
Market price	5.00

In addition, Salter's capacity data follow:

Capacity per year	2,000,000 zippers
Current production level	1,500,000 zippers

Required:

1. Assuming Quail produces 300,000 sleeping bags per year, what is the overall benefit of using zippers from Salter instead of purchasing them externally?
2. Determine the maximum price that the sleeping bag production facility would be willing to pay to purchase the zippers from Salter. How is the overall benefit divided between the two divisions if this transfer price is used?
3. Determine the minimum that Salter will accept as a transfer price. How is the overall benefit divided between the two divisions if this transfer price is used?
4. Determine the mutually beneficial transfer price for the zippers.
5. How would your answer change if Salter were currently operating at capacity?

PB10–5 Identifying Minimum, Maximum, Mutually Beneficial Transfer Prices   LO 10–6

Monona produces bottled water. The company recently purchased Cabot Co., a manufacturer of plastic bottles. In the past, Monona has purchased plastic bottles on the open market at $0.20 each. Financial information for the past year for Monona and Cabot follows:

	Monona	Cabot
Sales		
500,000 units × $2.00 each	$1,000,000	
1,200,000 units × $0.20 each		$240,000
Variable expenses		
500,000 units × $0.25 each	125,000	
1,200,000 units × $0.04 each		48,000

Cabot has a production capacity of 2 million units.

Required:

1. Determine how much Monona will save on each bottle if it obtains them from Cabot instead of an external supplier.
2. Determine the maximum and minimum transfer prices for the plastic bottles. Who sets these?
3. Suppose Monona has determined a transfer price rule of variable cost plus 50 percent for all related-party transactions. Determine how much each party will benefit from the internal transfer.
4. Determine the mutually beneficial transfer price.

PB10–6 Categorizing Sustainability Metrics based on the Triple Bottom Line and the Balanced Scorecard   LO 10–3

The following table lists several metrics from the Global Reporting Initiatives' (GRI) sustainability reporting standards and other industry sources.

For each metric, classify it based on its impact on the triple bottom line (People, Profit, or Planet) and indicate which balanced scorecard perspective it is most likely to fall within (Financial, Customer, Internal Business, Learning and Growth, or Society/Community). You can use more than one category when appropriate. The first metric is shown as an example.

Sustainability Metric	Triple bottom line impact: People, Profit, or Planet?	Balanced Scorecard Perspective: Financial, Customer, Internal Business, Learning/Growth, or Society/Community
Total fuel consumption from nonrenewable sources	Planet	Internal Business
Number of new patents for environmentally friendly technology		
Ratio of salary and other pay (e.g., bonuses) of females to males by employee category		
Total number of grievances about unfair labor practices filed through formal grievance mechanisms		
Revenues generated from environmentally friendly products		
Total employee work hours devoted to volunteer or community service		
Percentage of new suppliers that were screened using human rights criteria		
Total number and cost of hazardous waste spills		
Total number of breaches of customer privacy and loss of customer data		
Percentage of recycled materials used in production		
Total employee wage and benefits expense		

SKILLS DEVELOPMENT CASES

LO 10–3   **S10–1 Researching Use of Balanced Scorecard in Business**

This chapter discussed the use of the balanced scorecard for evaluating managerial and organizational performance. Many companies have adopted this performance measurement in recent years.

Required:

Research or visit a company that has implemented the balanced scorecard and write a brief report of its experience. You should include information such as when the company implemented the balanced scorecard, what performance measurement approach it had used previously, any difficulties it experienced with the implementation, and the benefits received from the new method.

LO 10–1   **S10–2 Explaining Impact of Organizational Structure, Budgetary Processes on Employee Morale**

In the last several chapters, you have learned about many aspects of organizational structure, budgeting, and performance evaluation. None of these company characteristics operates in isolation. They all interrelate to form an organization's culture and influence employee morale. The following table has several combinations of organizational structure and budgeting preparation style:

Organizational Structure	Budget Creation Process
Centralized	Top Down
Decentralized	Participative
Centralized	Participative
Decentralized	Top Down

Required:

For each combination in the table, write a brief paragraph summarizing both the potential advantages and disadvantages for a company using the combination. Consider the impact on managers and other employees as well as the potential impact on outside parties such as customers or other organizational stakeholders.

11

Capital Budgeting

CHAPTER ELEVEN

YOUR LEARNING OBJECTIVES

LO 11–1 Calculate the accounting rate of return and describe its major weaknesses.

LO 11–2 Calculate the payback period and describe its major weaknesses.

LO 11–3 Calculate net present value and describe why it is superior to the other capital budgeting techniques.

LO 11–4 Predict the internal rate of return and describe its relationship to net present value.

LO 11–5 Use the net present value method to analyze mutually exclusive capital investments.

LO 11–6 Use the profitability index to prioritize independent capital investment projects.

LO 11–S1 Use present value and future value tables to incorporate the time value of money.

©Christof Stache/AFP/Getty Images

Assume you just graduated from college and landed your first professional job. Your old Honda Civic has over 200,000 miles and you need a reliable car to drive to work. You currently live 30 miles from your new office, but you hope to move closer once you've saved a little money. You also like to mountain bike on the weekend and need a car or small SUV to haul your bike to some of the out-of-the-way trails you enjoy.

After test driving several cars, you've narrowed your choice down to the Toyota Rav4 or Chevy Malibu. Both vehicles come with the option of a hybrid engine, which you think is a wise choice not only to save money on gas, but also to limit your impact on the environment.

You came across an article on Edmunds.com that estimated the price premium for hybrid engines by comparing the sticker prices of similarly-featured gasoline-powered versus hybrid-powered vehicles. They also estimated the annual fuel savings of the hybrid engine based on the reported fuel economy (MPG) of each model, assuming annual mileage of 15,000 and a gasoline price of $2.50 per gallon. They then divided the price premium by the annual fuel savings to estimate how long it would take to recoup the extra cost of the hybrid engine.

This analysis suggested that consumers would recover the price premium on a Toyota RAV4 hybrid in just over 2 years; but it would take 6 years to recover the hybrid premium on a Chevy Malibu.

If you decide to buy a Toyota Rav4, does it make economic sense to invest the additional money in a hybrid engine? What about the Chevy Malibu? Do you see any flaws in the analysis? What other factors would influence your decision about which car to purchase?

Managers face similar decisions in business called **capital investment decisions**. A capital investment involves a major up-front investment that is expected to pay off in the future in the form of either increased revenue or cost savings. Some common capital budgeting decisions include:

- Whether to expand operations by opening a new location.
- Whether to lease or buy a piece of equipment.
- Whether to invest in new technology that would save on labor costs.

- How to prioritize research and development projects when investment funds are limited.
- Which sustainability initiatives to invest in to achieve economic, environmental, and societal benefits.

To illustrate how managers would make these decisions, we continue the Apple example that we started in the previous chapter by considering several of methods or tools that managers can use to help them make capital investment decisions.

ORGANIZATION OF THE CHAPTER

Capital budgeting process	Discounted cash flow methods	Applying NPV and Sensitivity Analysis
• Capital investment decisions • Accounting rate of return • Net cash flow versus net income • Payback period	• Time value of money • Net present value • Internal rate of return • Profitability index • Summary of capital budgeting methods	• Evaluating mutually exclusive projects • Prioritizing independent projects

Capital Budgeting Process

Capital budgeting is a decision-making process that managers use to determine how to invest the company's funds in major capital assets, such as new facilities, equipment, new products, and research and development projects.[1]

Apple Inc. spent almost **15 billion** dollars on capital expenditures in 2017, including new and remodeled retail stores, manufacturing facilities and equipment, data centers, corporate office buildings, and infrastructure. The company also invests billions of dollars in sustainability-enhancing projects, which are described in Apple's annual impact or corporate social responsibility (CSR) report. For example, 100 percent of Apple facilities worldwide are now powered by renewable energy sources such as wind, solar, and biogas. The company recently invested in a new recycling robot named "Daisy" that can quickly disassemble used iPhones to extract valuable materials such as tungsten and aluminum alloy that would otherwise have to be extracted from the earth. Although these sustainability investments are more costly than traditional alternatives in the short-run, they will yield economic, societal, and environmental benefits over the long run.

How do managers at Apple decide whether investments of this magnitude are worth it? Throughout this chapter, we describe several capital budgeting tools that managers can use to assess the economic or financial impact of capital investments. As with all of the other managerial decisions we have considered throughout this book, the economic analysis provides a

---

[1] We use the term **capital assets** in a much broader sense than in financial accounting. For example, human capital is developed through education and on-the-job training. It is valuable capital, even though it is not counted as an asset on the balance sheet. Similarly, financial accounting rules (GAAP) do not allow companies to capitalize research and development expenses even though they require a major capital investment. For capital budgeting purposes, we treat these types of expenditures as capital investments.

starting point that must be integrated with other strategic considerations, including the impact of the decision on employees, the environment, and society.

CAPITAL INVESTMENT DECISIONS

In general, managers make two types of capital investment decisions:

- **Screening decisions** require managers to determine whether a proposed project meets some minimum criteria. Screening decisions are often used to narrow down a set of projects for further consideration.

- **Preference decisions** require managers to evaluate and compare more than one capital investment alternative. Because companies typically have limited funds to invest in capital projects, managers must prioritize and select from the available options.

We will start by applying several capital budgeting techniques to a single project to illustrate how managers would decide whether it is acceptable or unacceptable (a screening decision). Later in the chapter, we demonstrate how managers would choose between multiple projects (a preference decision). Those projects can be either independent or mutually exclusive:

- **Independent projects** are unrelated to one another, so that investing in one project does not preclude investment in other projects. For example, if Apple chooses to open a new retail store in Manhattan, that decision does not preclude it from opening a retail store in Los Angeles. Each project can be evaluated on its own merit.

- **Mutually exclusive projects** are competing alternatives, where managers would invest in one alternative or another, but not both. For example, an Apple manager might be faced with the decision of whether to lease or buy the fixtures for a retail store. Choosing one option automatically eliminates the other option from consideration.

Exhibit 11–1 shows five different methods that managers can use to evaluate capital investments. Both the accounting rate of return and the payback period are called **non-discounting**

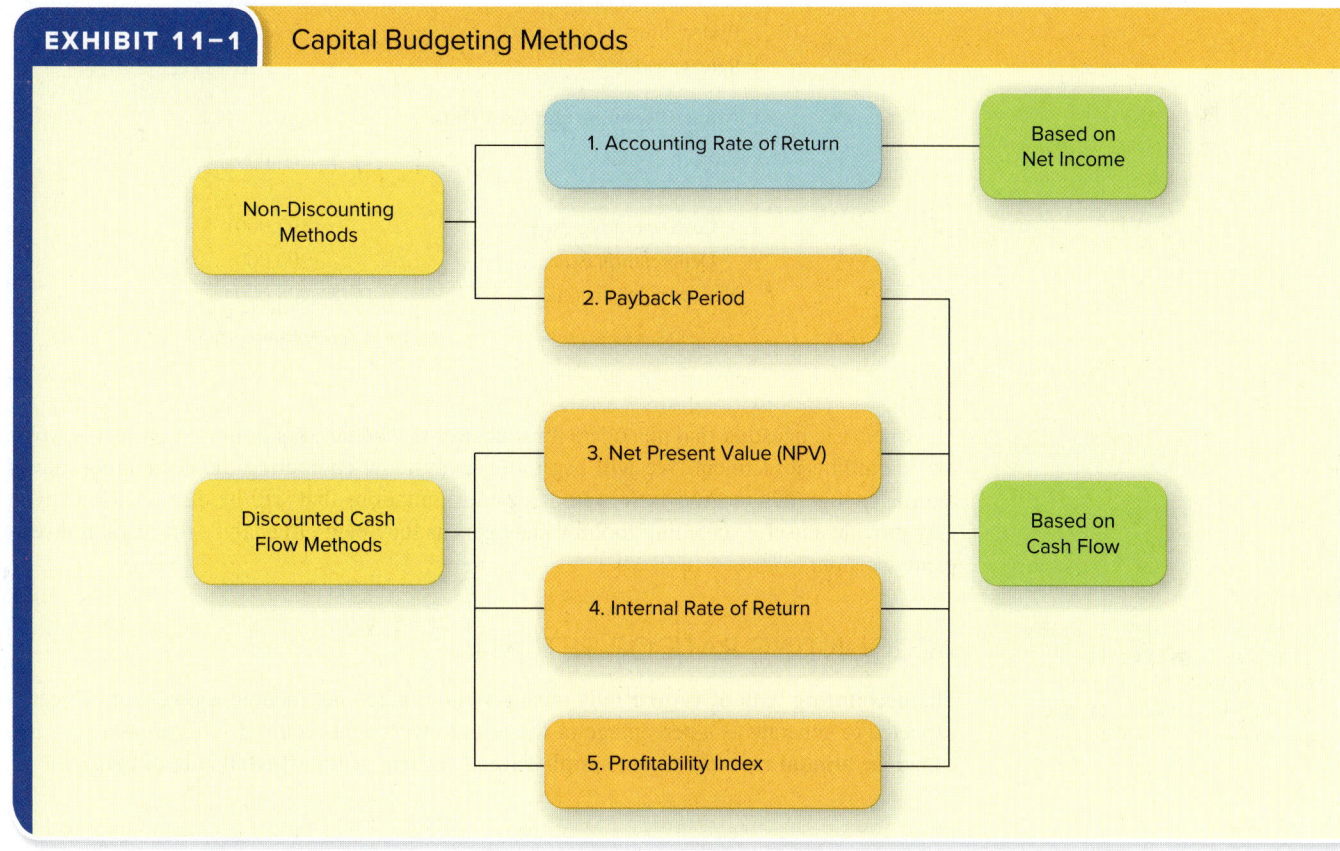

EXHIBIT 11–1   Capital Budgeting Methods

methods because they ignore the time value of money. The **time value of money** is the principle that money is more valuable today than it will be in the future. The other three methods, net present value, internal rate of return, and profitability index are referred to as **discounted cash flow methods**. These methods are generally superior to non-discounting methods because they incorporate the time value of money. (We discuss time value of money in more depth in the supplement to this chapter.)

Most of the capital budgeting methods we consider use cash flow to measure the expected costs and benefits of capital projects. The focus is on how much cash must be invested and when that cash will be returned. Only the accounting rate of return is based on net income (an accounting measure) rather than cash flow. As you learned in your financial accounting course, accountants use **accrual-based accounting** that recognizes revenue when it is earned and expenses when they are incurred, regardless of when cash is received or paid. As a result, net cash flow and net income will often differ. Both measures provide useful information to managers, but they measure different things. We'll discuss the ramifications of using one measure over the other later in the chapter.

To illustrate how the five capital budgeting methods work, assume that Apple managers are evaluating a proposal to develop a new iPad that would be marketed to children and their parents. The new device, called the iKids Touch, would be designed to appeal to children, with durable components, "kid friendly" controls, and bright colors. It would also restrict the types of content that can be downloaded onto the device to age-appropriate music, books, and educational games. Managers are evaluating the iKids Touch as an independent project, or one that would not preclude Apple from investing in alternative projects. Below are some estimates for this hypothetical project:

**DATA PROJECTIONS
FOR iKIDS TOUCH**

Initial investment	$1,000,000
Project life	5 years
Salvage value	$ 0

Annual Revenue and Cost Data

Projected sales	$ 700,000
Less:	
Cash operating expenses	(392,000)
Depreciation expense	(200,000)
Net operating income	$ 108,000

The basic question that managers must answer is whether this proposed project is worth the $1 million investment. We will begin our analysis by computing the accounting rate of return. Though this method suffers from several limitations that will be discussed shortly, it may provide a useful screening tool for managers as they begin to analyze this capital investment decision.

ACCOUNTING RATE OF RETURN

The **accounting rate of return** tells managers how much net income a potential project is expected to generate as a percentage of the initial investment required. This approach is also called the **annual rate of return**, **simple rate of return**, or **unadjusted rate of return**.

We calculate the accounting rate of return by dividing net operating income by the original investment in assets. In this example, the iKids Touch project's accounting rate of return would be computed as follows:

$$\frac{\text{Net Operating Income}}{\text{Initial Investment}} = \text{Accounting Rate of Return}$$

$$\frac{\$108,000}{\$1,000,000} = 10.8\%$$

> **COACH'S TIP**
>
> This formula is very similar to the return on investment formula presented in the previous chapter. However, it uses the **initial** investment as the denominator rather than average invested assets.

To determine whether the project is acceptable, managers would compare the 10.8 percent accounting rate of return to the minimum required rate of return, also called the *hurdle rate*. Managers set the hurdle rate to reflect the minimum acceptable rate of return for a project, given its risk and other factors like prevailing interest rates and the company's capital structure. If Apple has a minimum required rate of return of less than 10.8 percent, this project would be acceptable. If the minimum required rate of return is higher than 10.8 percent, the project would be unacceptable.

The accounting rate of return is a simple and intuitive approach that is often used as a preliminary screening tool to evaluate capital investments. However, it suffers from two major limitations. First, it does not incorporate the time value of money. Second, it is based on accounting income rather than cash flow. For years, accounting and finance experts have debated the relative usefulness of net income versus cash flow for evaluating capital projects. While research suggests that **both** are useful, the bottom line is that cash is king. Cash is more objective than net income, is not as easily manipulated, and is not influenced by accounting choices such as the method used to depreciate the capital assets.

The capital budgeting techniques we consider throughout the remainder of this chapter are based on cash flow rather than net income.

NET CASH FLOW VERSUS NET INCOME

In this chapter, we assume that the only difference between net income and net cash flow is depreciation expense. Other differences between net income and net cash flow are discussed in more detail in Chapter 12. To keep things simple, we also ignore the effect of income taxes, which are based on another set of accounting rules set by the Internal Revenue Service.[2]

In our hypothetical Apple example, the original cost of the investment is $1 million. There is no salvage value, so the assets will be fully depreciated over five years at a rate of $200,000 per year. The depreciation is subtracted as an expense on the income statement, as follows:

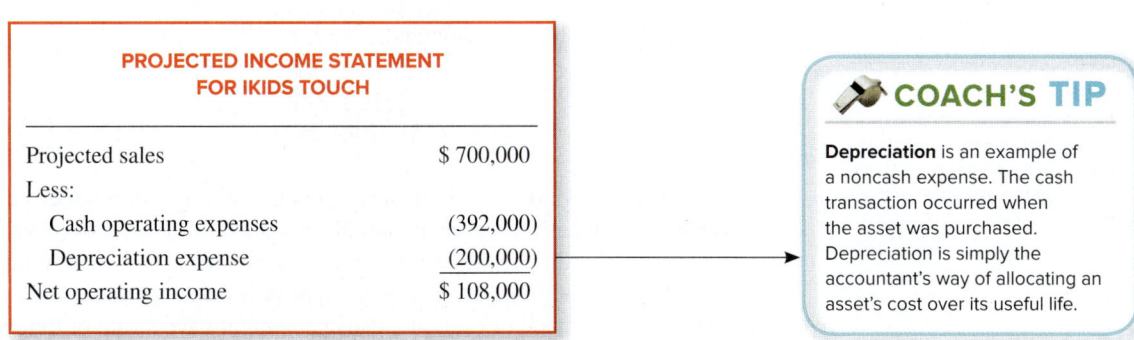

PROJECTED INCOME STATEMENT FOR IKIDS TOUCH

Projected sales	$ 700,000
Less:	
Cash operating expenses	(392,000)
Depreciation expense	(200,000)
Net operating income	$ 108,000

> **COACH'S TIP**
>
> **Depreciation** is an example of a noncash expense. The cash transaction occurred when the asset was purchased. Depreciation is simply the accountant's way of allocating an asset's cost over its useful life.

---

[2] When taxes are taken into account, depreciation expense has an indirect effect on cash flow by reducing a company's tax burden. The benefit of depreciation expense on cash flow, also called the *depreciation tax shield*, is discussed in more advanced accounting and finance texts.

Notice that the net income figure of $108,000 is **after** the depreciation expense of $200,000 has been deducted. But the company doesn't actually pay $200,000 in cash for depreciation. The $1,000,000 was paid up-front and is simply **allocated** across the 5-year life of the project.

To convert from net income to net cash flow, we must **add** back the depreciation that was deducted in the computation of net income, as follows:

$$\underset{\$108{,}000}{\text{Net Income}} + \underset{\$200{,}000}{\text{Depreciation}} = \underset{\$308{,}000}{\text{Net Cash Flow}}$$

Alternatively, we could have started with sales revenue and subtracted only the cash operating expenses, as follows:

$$\underset{\$700{,}000}{\text{Sales Revenue}} - \underset{\$392{,}000}{\text{Cash Expenses}} = \underset{\$308{,}000}{\text{Net Cash Flow}}$$

Regardless of whether we compute net cash flow by starting with net income and adding back depreciation (called the indirect method), or by starting with sales revenue and subtracting only the cash expenses (the direct method), the result is net cash flow of $308,000. The capital budgeting techniques illustrated throughout the remainder of this chapter use annual net cash flow of $308,000 to evaluate the capital investment rather than $108,000 in net income.

PAYBACK PERIOD

Learning Objective 11-2
Calculate the payback period and describe its major weaknesses.

The **payback period** is the amount of time it takes for a capital investment to "pay for itself." In the simplest case, in which cash flows are equal each year, the payback period is calculated by dividing the initial investment in the project by its annual cash flow.

In our hypothetical Apple example, the original investment is $1 million, and the cash inflow from the project is estimated at $308,000 per year. Thus, the payback period is calculated as follows:

$$\frac{\text{Initial Investment}}{\text{Annual Cash Flow}} = \text{Payback Period}$$
$$\frac{\$1{,}000{,}000}{\$308{,}000} = 3.25 \text{ years}$$

A payback period of 3.25 tells managers that the project is expected to pay for itself, or generate enough cash to cover the initial investment, in a little over three years. In general, projects with shorter payback periods are preferred over those with longer payback periods. The payback method is a very intuitive approach that is often used as a screening tool for potential investments. For example, managers might have a rule of thumb that projects must be able to recoup the original investment within at least four years before they are considered further. In this case, a project with a 3.25 year payback would be acceptable.

Irregular cash flows make the payback method a bit more cumbersome to compute. If cash flows are not the same every year, the payback period must be computed on a year-by-year basis until the project generates enough cash to cover the initial investment. For example, if Apple expects the cash flows for the iKids Touch project to be $250,000, $300,000, $340,000, $375,000, and $300,000 in years 1 to 5, respectively, the payback period would be calculated as follows:

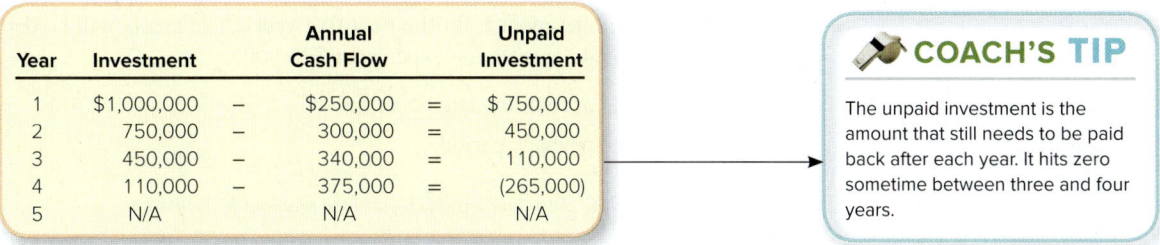

Year	Investment		Annual Cash Flow		Unpaid Investment
1	$1,000,000	–	$250,000	=	$ 750,000
2	750,000	–	300,000	=	450,000
3	450,000	–	340,000	=	110,000
4	110,000	–	375,000	=	(265,000)
5	N/A		N/A		N/A

COACH'S TIP

The unpaid investment is the amount that still needs to be paid back after each year. It hits zero sometime between three and four years.

This analysis shows that the payback period is somewhere between three and four years. If we assume that cash flow is uniform during the fourth year, the payback period would be estimated as follows:

$$\text{Payback} = 3 \text{ years} + (\$110{,}000 \div \$375{,}000) = 3.293 \text{ years}$$

The payback method is relatively simple and is commonly used to determine how long it will take for a project to recoup its initial investment. However, as with the accounting rate of return method, it does not incorporate the time value of money. In addition, this method does not take into account anything that happens after the payback period. It ignores any benefits (and costs) that occur after the project has paid for itself. The next three methods we discuss are superior to the accounting rate of return and payback methods because they incorporate the time value of money and consider all of the cash flows that occur throughout the entire life of the project.

Before we move on, take the next Self-Study Practice to make sure you understand the accounting rate of return and payback methods.

SPOTLIGHT ON Decision Making

One of the most common applications of the payback method relates to the decision to refinance a home loan. When homeowners refinance their mortgage to get a lower interest rate, they must pay up-front costs (referred to as *closing costs*) to have their home appraised and to cover other transaction costs. They may also pay a small percentage of the new loan amount (referred to as *points*) to get a lower interest rate. In general, the more points paid up front, the lower the interest rate and the greater the savings down the road.

To decide whether or not to refinance or pay additional points, homeowners can compute the payback period by dividing the up-front cost of refinancing by the monthly savings on their mortgage payment. For example, if Jim and Sarah are considering paying $2,400 to refinance a loan and reduce their mortgage payment by $150 per month, the payback period would be 16 months ($2,400 ÷ $150 = 16). Unless the couple plans to stay in the home (and not refinance again) for at least 16 months, they should stay with their existing mortgage.

Notice that this simple analysis ignores anything that happens after the 16-month payback period. For example, what if Jim and Sarah refinanced to a mortgage that had a very low interest rate for two years, but, after those two years, the interest rate would increase dramatically? Or what if the loan had a low monthly payment with a large balloon payment at the end? Should these factors be considered in their decision to refinance? The answer is yes, but the payback method does not consider anything that happens beyond the payback period.

How's it going?   Self-Study Practice

Timberland Company is considering investing $1,000,000 in a project that is expected to generate $175,000 in net income for the next five years. The assets will be depreciated over five years for an annual depreciation expense of $200,000.

1. Calculate the accounting rate of return.
2. Calculate the payback period.

After you have finished, check your answers against the solutions in the margin.

Discounted Cash Flow Methods

Although the accounting rate of return and the payback method are simple and intuitive methods for screening capital investments, neither takes into account the time value of money. This is a major weakness because capital investments generally span multiple years; and **time is money**.

TIME VALUE OF MONEY

You have probably already had some exposure to time value of money concepts in other business classes. On a personal level, you encounter it any time you must take out a loan to buy a car or house, to pay for tuition, or when you invest money in a savings account or certificate of deposit (CD). Because the time value of money is so important to capital budgeting decisions, this section provides a brief review of the concept. The detailed calculations are described in the supplement to this chapter.

The **time value of money** is the simple idea that the value of a dollar changes over time because it can be invested to earn interest. Given a choice between receiving $1,000 today or $1,000 a year from now, which would you prefer? You should have answered today because you could invest the money and have even more than $1,000 in the future.

For example, if you invest $1,000 today at 10 percent interest, you would have $1,100 [$1,000 × (1 + 10%)] a year from now. If you reinvest the $1,100 at the same 10 percent rate, you will earn even more interest in the following year due to a force called **compounding**, where interest is earned on top of interest. At the end of three years, you would have $1,331, as shown in the following diagram:

COACH'S TIP

To compute the future value of $1,000 in three years, we multiply each year's accumulating value by (1 + Interest Rate) as follows:

$1,000 × (1 + 10%) = $1,100
$1,100 × (1 + 10%) = $1,210
$1,210 × (1 + 10%) = $1,331

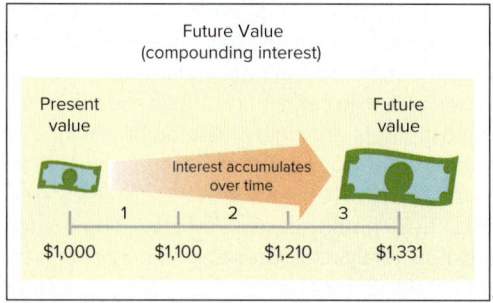

This is an example of a **future value** problem. We know how much money we have today ($1,000), but need to know how much it will be worth at some point in the future.

The capital budgeting techniques presented in this chapter involve **present value** calculations. In a present value problem, we know how much money will be received or paid at some point in the future, but we need to know how much it is worth today. Instead of compounding (adding interest on top of interest), present value problems involve **discounting** future cash flows back to their equivalent value in today's (present value) dollars. For example, if the interest rate is 10 percent, receiving $1,000 in three years is equivalent to receiving $751 today, as shown below:

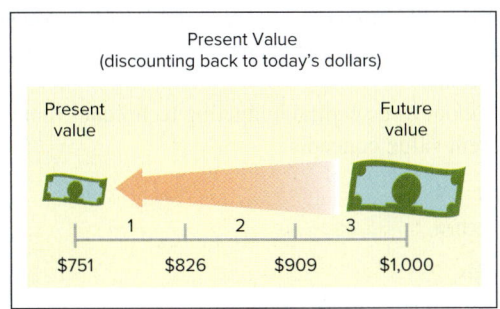

Present Value
(discounting back to today's dollars)

Present value ← Future value

| 1 | 2 | 3 |

$751 $826 $909 $1,000

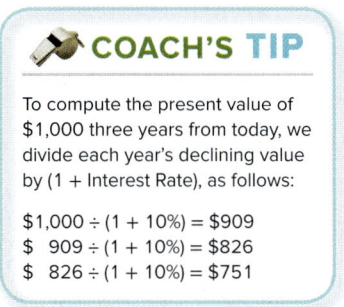

COACH'S TIP

To compute the present value of $1,000 three years from today, we divide each year's declining value by (1 + Interest Rate), as follows:

$1,000 ÷ (1 + 10%) = $909
$ 909 ÷ (1 + 10%) = $826
$ 826 ÷ (1 + 10%) = $751

As you can see, discounting is exactly the opposite of compounding. Just as interest builds up over time through compounding, discounting involves backing out the interest to find the equivalent value in today's present value dollars. To compute the future value, we multiply each year's accumulating balance by 110 percent (1 + interest rate). To compute the present value, we divide each year's declining balance by 110 percent (1 + interest rate). Notice that dividing by 110 percent is the same as multiplying by .909 (1 ÷ 1.10 = .909). To discount for two years, we would need to multiply the future value by .826 (.909 × .909 = .826). To discount for three years, we would need to multiply by .751 (.909 × .909 × .909 = .751). This logic explains where the discount factors shown in Table 11–2A come from. We can use this table to convert a future cash flow to its present value. We just need to know how far into the future the cash flow will occur, and what the appropriate discount rate is.

The capital budgeting methods described in the remainder of the chapter will require you to solve two types of present value problems. The first involves calculating the present value of a single cash flow that will happen at some point in the future, similar to the example above. The second involves computing the present value of an **annuity**, or a stream of cash

---

SPOTLIGHT ON Decision Making

The Power of Compounding

Compound interest is a remarkably powerful economic force. In fact, the ability to earn interest on interest is the key to building economic wealth. If you save $1,000 per year for the first 10 years of your career, you will have more money when you retire than if you saved $15,000 per year for the last 10 years of your career. This surprising outcome occurs because the money you save early in your career will earn more interest than the money you save at the end of your career. If you start saving money now, the majority of your wealth will not be the money you saved but the interest your money was able to earn over time.

The accompanying chart illustrates the power of compounding over a brief 10-year period. If you deposit $1 each year in an account earning 10 percent interest, at the end of just 10 years, only 63 percent of your balance will be made up of money you have saved. The rest will be interest you have earned. After 20 years, only 35 percent of your balance will be from saved money. The lesson associated with compound interest is that even though saving money is difficult, you should start now.

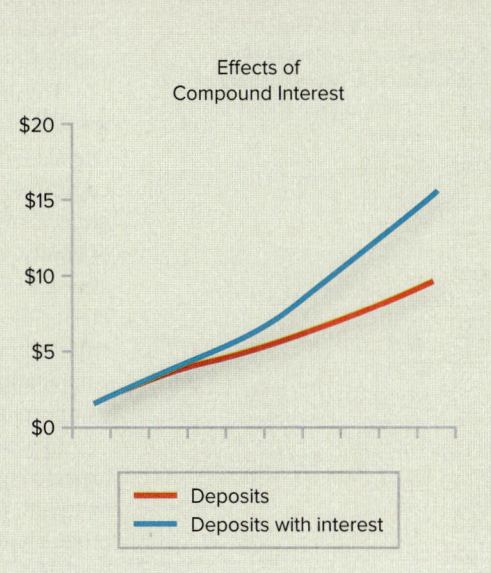

Effects of Compound Interest

$20
$15
$10
$5
$0

—— Deposits
—— Deposits with interest

flows that occur uniformly across time. For example, rather than receiving a single cash flow of $1,000 in three years, what if we received $1,000 at the end of **each** of the next three years? Rather than making a separate calculation for each year, we could use the PV of an annuity table (Table 11–4A in the supplement to this chapter), which aggregates the present value factors across multiple years so that we only have to make one calculation. In this example, we would multiply $1,000 by 2.4869 for a present value of $2,487. If you need a refresher on how to use these tables, you should review the chapter supplement, paying particular attention to the present value calculations.

Next, we will learn about three capital budgeting techniques that rely heavily on the time value of money and present value concepts:

- Net present value.
- Internal rate of return.
- Profitability index.

All three are **discounted cash flow methods**, which means they incorporate the time value of money by stating future cash in terms of their present value. As with any quantitative analysis, we must make some assumptions to use these methods. These assumptions are summarized as follows:

- All future cash flows happen at the end of the year. In reality, companies receive and pay cash throughout the year. But for simplicity, we assume that all cash flows happen at the end of the year.
- Cash inflows are immediately reinvested in another project. The net present value method assumes that cash inflows are reinvested at the minimum or required rate of return. The internal rate of return method assumes that cash flows are reinvested at the project's internal rate of return. This difference in assumption will be discussed later in the chapter when comparing the two methods.
- All future cash flows can be projected with 100 percent certainty. In general, the further a cash flow extends into the future, the more uncertain it is. But we assume that all cash flows are known with certainty.

Managers must be aware of these assumptions and understand how they affect the analysis and conclusions. Later in the chapter, we illustrate how managers can use sensitivity analysis, sometimes called *what if* analysis, to evaluate how changing the underlying assumptions will affect the analysis and conclusions.

NET PRESENT VALUE

Learning Objective 11–3
Calculate net present value and describe why it is superior to the other capital budgeting techniques.

The **net present value (NPV) method** compares the present value (PV) of a project's future cash inflows to the PV of its cash outflows. The difference between the present value of the cash inflows and outflows is called the **net present value**.

To compute net present value, we need to know the appropriate **discount rate**, or the rate we will use to discount future cash flows to reflect the time value of money. The discount rate should reflect the company's **cost of capital**, also called the **weighted-average cost of capital**. Conceptually, the cost of capital is how much it costs the company to fund capital projects. Mathematically, it is computed by averaging the after-tax cost of debt and the cost of equity, weighted according to the relative mix of these two sources of capital funding. The after-tax cost of debt is the interest rate paid on bonds and other forms of debt, after adjusting for the tax benefit of the interest expense. The cost of equity is the return that investors require in exchange for the risk of investing in the company's stock. Although the detailed computation of the cost of capital is beyond the scope of this textbook, you should understand it conceptually and how it is used for evaluating capital investment alternatives.

In general terms, if a project has a positive net present value, it means that the project is expected to generate enough future cash to cover the cost of capital, creating economic value or wealth for the company and its shareholders. A negative net present value means that the project will not generate enough future cash flows to cover the cost of capital and will reduce the firm's economic value.

Let's apply the NPV method to Apple's hypothetical investment in the iKids Touch project. First, we show how to compute NPV manually using the present value tables in the supplement to this chapter. Then, we will illustrate how to compute NPV using Excel. Most managers in today's business world use the latter method, but computing NPV manually first will help you understand **how** the NPV function in Excel works.

For our iKids Touch example, we will begin with the simple scenario in which cash flows are the same each year. Recall that the project requires an initial investment of $1,000,000 and will generate $308,000 in cash flow for each of the next five years. Assume that Apple's cost of capital is 12 percent.

Because the cash flows are the same each year, we can use the present value of annuity table shown in Table 11–4A. This table shows that the present value of a five-year annuity discounted at a 12 percent interest rate is 3.6048. To compute the present value of the this five-year annuity, we multiply 3.6048 by the annual cash flow of $308,000. We then subtract the $1,000,000 cash outflow that happens at the start of the project (time zero), as follows:

Year	Annual Cash Flow		PV of an Annuity (12%)	Present Value
1–5	$308,000	×	3.6048	$ 1,110,278
	Less: Initial investment			(1,000,000)
			NPV	$ 110,278

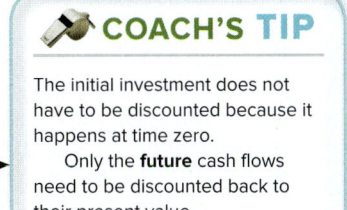

COACH'S TIP

The initial investment does not have to be discounted because it happens at time zero.
   Only the **future** cash flows need to be discounted back to their present value.

The net present value of this project is $110,278. We will discuss what this NPV means to a manager shortly, but first, let's consider a case in which the cash flows are unequal from year to year.

If the cash flows from the project are not equal each year, we cannot use the PV of an annuity table. Instead, we must use the present value of $1 table (Table 11–2A). This table provides the present value factors on a year-by-year basis, rather than aggregating the values across all five years as the annuity table does.

To illustrate, assume that the expected cash flows for the iKids Touch project for years 1 to 5 are $250,000, $300,000, $340,000, $375,000, and $300,000, respectively. The project requires an investment of $1,000,000 and the cost of capital is still 12 percent.

To compute the present value of an uneven stream of cash flows, we multiply the cash flow for each year by the present value of $1 factor discounted at a rate of 12 percent, as shown in Table 11–2A. We then sum the present value of the future cash flows, and, finally, subtract the cash outflow for the original investment to determine the net present value, as shown:

COACH'S TIP

If you sum the PV of $1 factors for years 1–5, you get the PV of an annuity factor of 3.6048 that we used when cash flows were even every year.

Year	PV of $1 (12%)
1	0.8929
2	0.7972
3	0.7118
4	0.6355
5	0.5674
	3.6048

Notice that the PV factor decreases over time to reflect the time value of money. A dollar received 5 years from now is only worth about 57 cents in today's dollars.

Year	Annual Cash Flow		PV of $1 (12%)	Present Value
1	$250,000	×	0.8929	$ 223,225.00
2	300,000	×	0.7972	239,160.00
3	340,000	×	0.7118	242,012.00
4	375,000	×	0.6355	238,312.50
5	300,000	×	0.5674	170,220.00
	Present value of future cash flows			$ 1,112,929.50
	Less: Initial investment			(1,000,000.00)
			NPV	$ 112,929.50

Measured in today's dollars, this $1,000,000 investment will generate $1,112,929.50 in future benefits, for a net benefit or NPV of $112,929.50.

In the real world, managers will probably use excel or another tool to compute NPV rather than relying on tables and PV factors. However, using the tables first will help you understand how the excel function works.

Exhibit 11–2 shows how to use Excel to calculate the NPV for the iKids Touch.

EXHIBIT 11–2   Computing NPV in Excel

Step 1:   Input future cash flows (years 1-*n*) in spreadsheet.

Step 2:   Use the NPV function to compute the PV of the future cash flows.

Step 3:   Subtract the initial investment to get the NPV of the project.

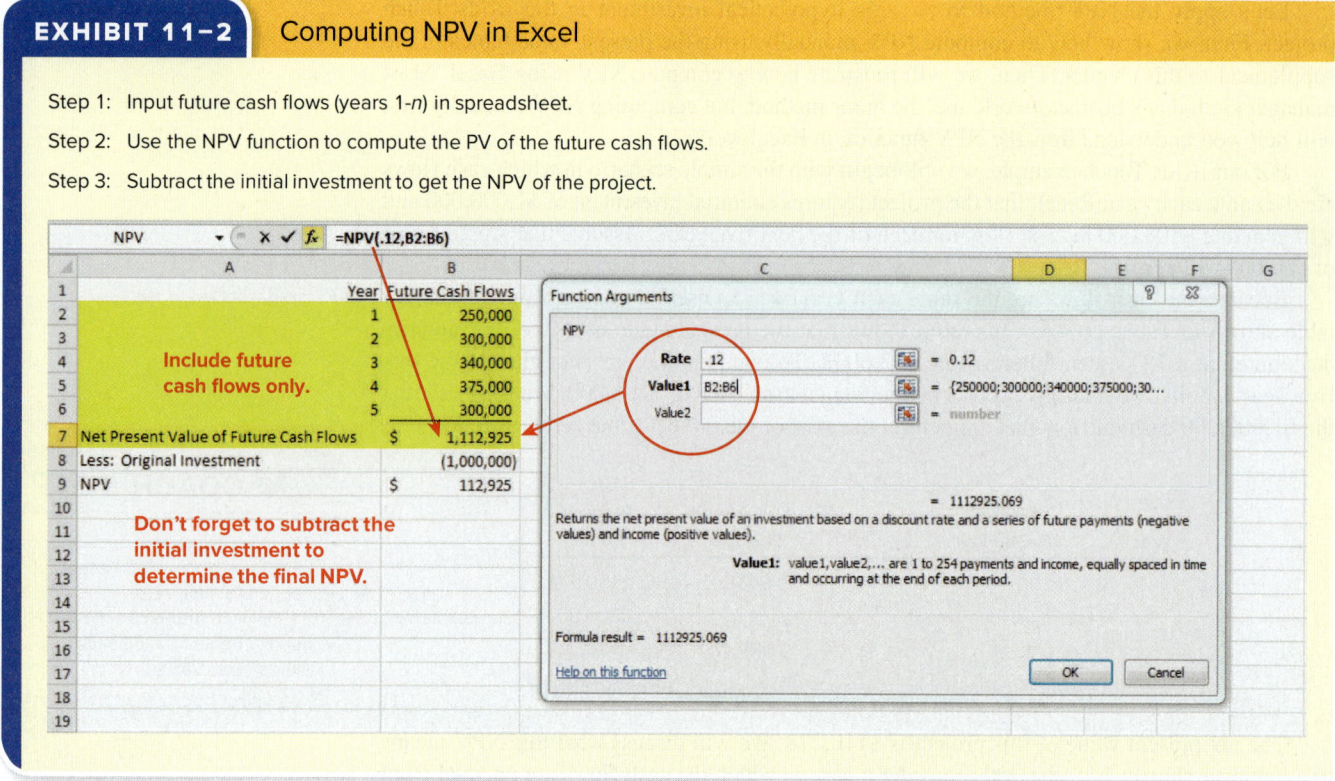

The NPV function in Excel returned a value of $1,112,925 for the cash inflows in years 1 through 5. However, the original investment at time zero was excluded from the NPV formula because the investment happens at the start of the project (time zero) and therefore does not need to be discounted. When we subtract the $1,000,000 investment from the present value of the future cash flows, we get an NPV of $112,925. This is within $5 of the NPV we computed using the present value tables. The difference is due to rounding in the present value tables. Computing NPV in Excel is more exact because the program does not round the factors to four decimal places.

We have described several different ways to compute NPV, but how does it help managers make capital investment decisions? When used to make a screening decision, a positive NPV indicates that the project should be accepted because it will yield a return in excess of the company's cost of capital (12 percent for our Apple example). A negative NPV indicates that the project will yield a return less than the company's cost of capital and thus managers should reject the project.

Based strictly on the economic analysis, the iKids Touch project should be accepted because it generates a positive net present value. The future cash flows associated with the project are more than enough to cover the cost of the capital. Investing in projects that exceed the cost of capital will add to the company's economic wealth.

Would the project have been acceptable if the cost of capital was 14 percent? What about 16 percent? As the cost of capital increases, the future cash flows must be discounted at a higher rate to compensate for the time value of money, yielding a lower net present value. For example, raising the discount rate to 14 percent will yield an NPV of $57,470. Exhibit 11–3 shows how the NPV will change when the discount rate, or cost of capital, changes. Can you predict from this graph the rate at which the NPV will be zero?

The discount rate that yields a zero NPV is called the **internal rate of return**. In this example, the internal rate of return appears to be a little less than 16.5 percent, based on the visual depiction in Exhibit 11–3. We'll discuss the internal rate of return in more depth in the next section.

 **COACH'S TIP**

Try computing the NPV of the project using a 14% discount rate.

If you do it in Excel, you just have to change one cell. If you use the tables, you will need to recompute the whole thing.

Either way, you should get an NPV of about $57,470.

EXHIBIT 11–3	Relationship Between NPV and the Discount Rate

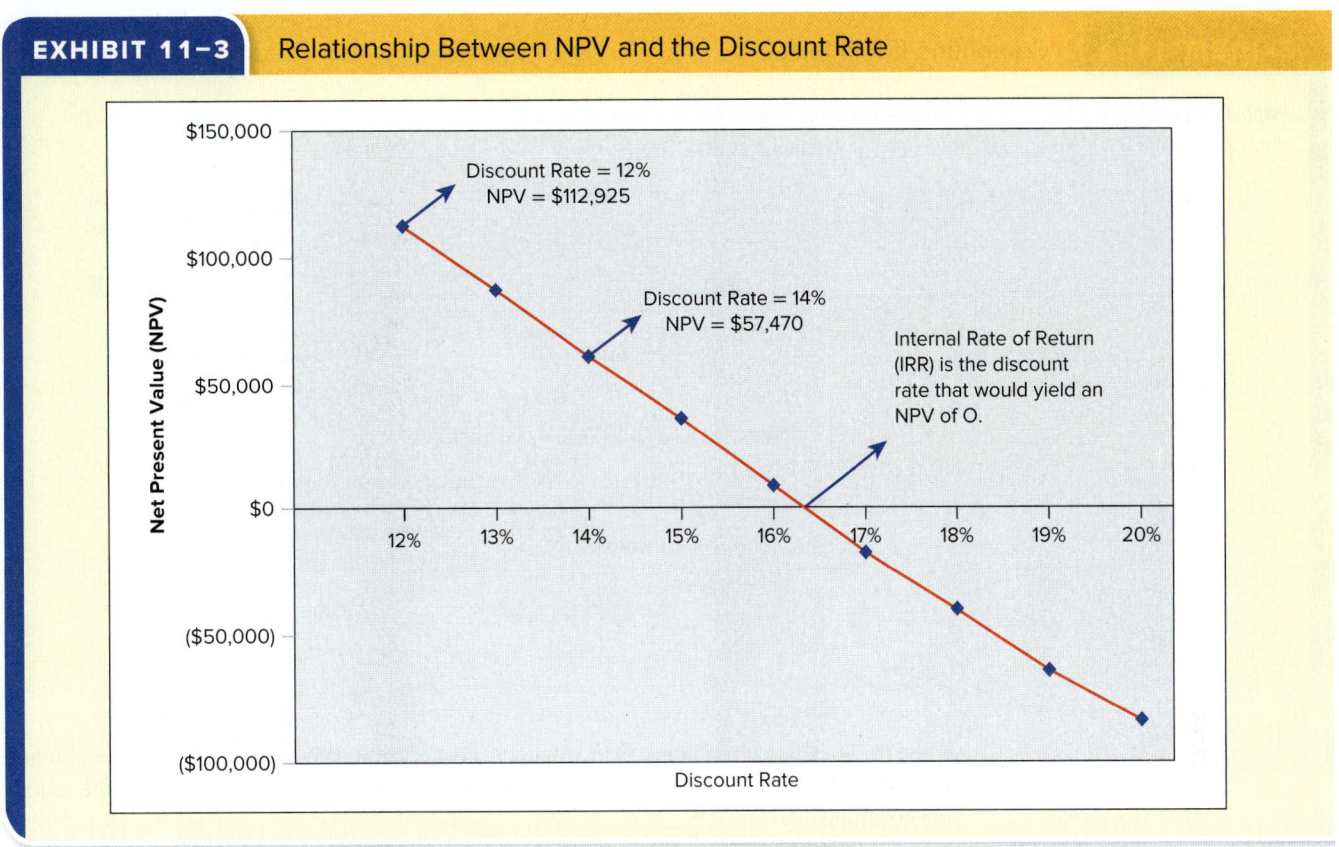

INTERNAL RATE OF RETURN

The **internal rate of return** (IRR) is the rate of return that yields a zero net present value. Mathematically, it can be computed by setting the present value of the future cash inflows equal to original investment, then solving for the discount rate. Solving for the internal rate of return mathematically is time-consuming, but we can get pretty close using a trial-and-error approach. As Exhibit 11–3 shows, the NPV is positive using a discount rate of 16 percent, but negative using a discount rate of 17 percent. So the internal rate of return must be between 16 percent and 17 percent.

> **Learning Objective 11–4**
> Predict the internal rate of return and describe its relationship to net present value.

In practice, most managers would use Excel or a financial calculator to solve for the internal rate of return. Exhibit 11–4 illustrates the steps to compute the IRR in Excel. One important note about the IRR function is that you must **include** the original investment in the calculation of IRR. Otherwise it is impossible to find the rate at which the present value of the cash inflows equals the present value of the cash outflows. In contrast, the NPV function in Excel **excludes** the original investment because it happens at time zero and does not need to be discounted.

Following the steps outlined in Exhibit 11–4 results in an internal rate of return of 16.25 percent. Notice that this falls within the 16 to 17 percent range we estimated using trial and error. But how would managers use this information to decide whether they should invest $1 million in the iKids Touch project?

To determine whether this is an acceptable investment, managers would compare the internal rate of return to the cost of capital. If the internal rate of return is greater than the cost of capital, the project is acceptable. If the internal rate of return in less than the cost of capital, the project is unacceptable.

As you can see, the IRR is closely related to the NPV method. A positive NPV occurs when the internal rate of return is greater than the cost of capital. A negative NPV occurs

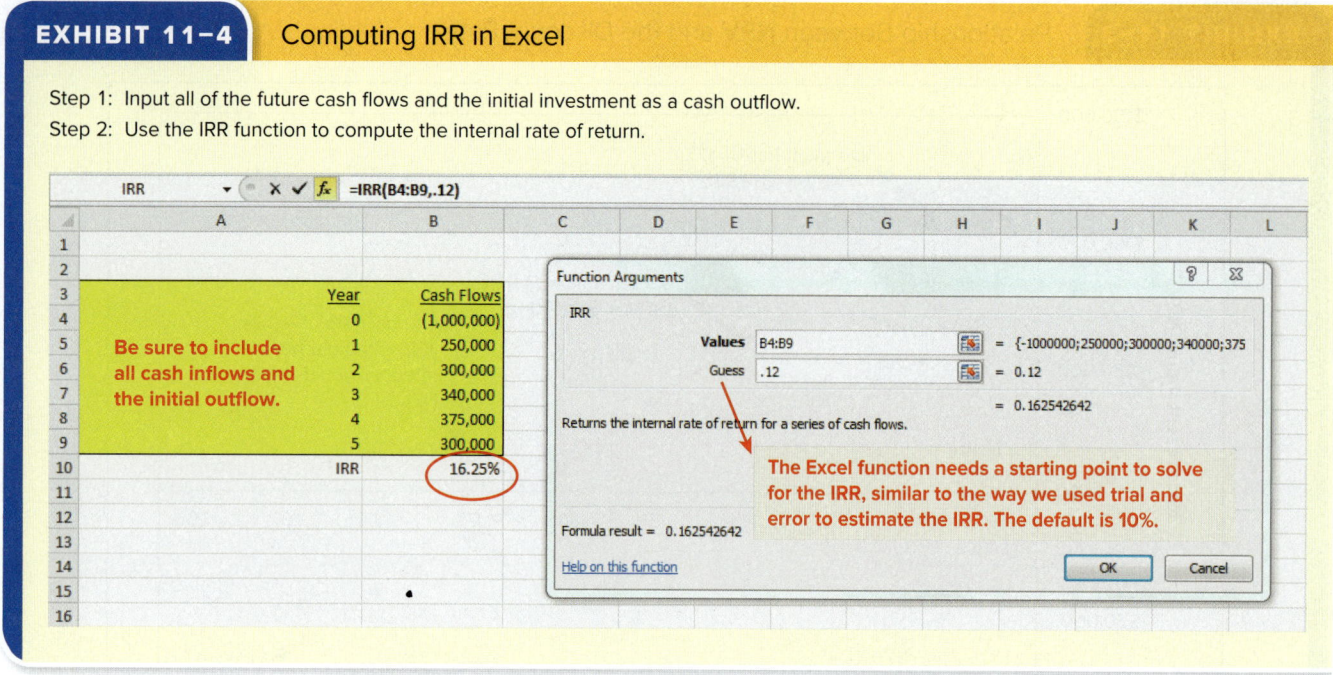

EXHIBIT 11–4   Computing IRR in Excel

Step 1: Input all of the future cash flows and the initial investment as a cash outflow.

Step 2: Use the IRR function to compute the internal rate of return.

when the internal rate of return is less than the cost of capital. When the internal rate of return is equal to the cost of capital, NPV is zero. These relationships are summarized in the following equations:

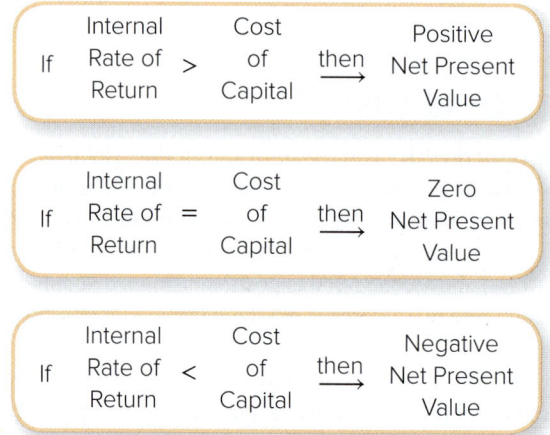

As you can see, the internal rate of return and NPV method are highly related and will provide consistent information for managers when deciding whether a single project is acceptable or unacceptable (screening decisions). However, the NPV method is preferred over IRR when managers must choose between competing alternatives (preference decisions). NPV is preferred for these decisions because of a key assumption about how the future cash flows are reinvested into other projects. The NPV method assumes that cash flows are reinvested at the cost of capital rate, while the IRR method assumes that the cash flows are reinvested in projects with the same internal rate of return. In general, assuming that funds will be reinvested at the cost of capital is more realistic and conservative, particularly if the IRR of the project is very high. Managers may not be able to reinvest the cash flows in an equally attractive project.[3] The NPV method ensures that managers invest in projects that meet or exceed the cost of capital.

---

[3] There is a modified internal rate of return (called MIRR in Excel) that allows managers to specify the reinvestment rate. This topic can be found in many corporate finance textbooks.

One advantage of IRR compared to NPV is that it is stated on a relative or percentage basis. It is easier for managers to interpret a relative measure (such as a 20 percent internal rate of return) than it is an absolute dollar value, particularly if they don't have anything to compare it to. For example, a project that earns a $100,000 NPV might be great for a small start-up company, but not so impressive for a large company like Apple. The next capital budgeting technique we discuss overcomes this disadvantage by translating the NPV into a relative measure that can be used to compare projects of varying size.

PROFITABILITY INDEX

The **profitability index** is the ratio of a project's benefits (measured by the present value of the future cash flows) to its costs (or required investment). It is a derivative of the NPV method, but it provides a relative measure of the project's performance rather than an absolute dollar amount. When we computed NPV, we first calculated the present value of the *future* cash inflows, and then subtracted the original investment, or cash outflow. The profitability index is stated as a ratio of these two items instead. For example, in our Apple scenario, the NPV of the cash flows from years 1 to 5 was $1,112,925 and the original investment (at time zero) was $1,000,000. The profitability index would be computed as follows:

$$\frac{\text{Present Value of Future Case Flows}}{\text{Initial Investment}} = \text{Profitability Index}$$

$$\frac{\$1,112,925}{\$1,000,000} = 1.11$$

What does a profitability index of 1.11 mean? A profitability index greater than one indicates that the present value of the future cash flows (numerator) is greater than the initial investment (denominator), meaning that the project is acceptable. Any project with a positive NPV will generate a profitability index greater than one. A profitability index of 1 occurs when the present value of the future cash flow are equal to the initial investment, or an NPV of zero. A profitability index of less than one occurs when the NPV of the project is negative, or the present value of the future cash flows is less than the required investment in the project. A profitability index less than one (negative NPV) suggests that the project will not generate enough future cash flow to cover the cost of capital and therefore the project should be rejected. In this case, the profitability index is greater than one, indicating that Apple should move ahead with the iKids Touch project.

Notice that the NPV, IRR, and profitability index methods all suggest that the iPod Touch project is acceptable. The three methods will always result in the same conclusion when deciding whether a project is acceptable (a screening decision). It will not necessarily be true when choosing between competing projects (preference decisions). We will evaluate these types of decisions in the next section of this chapter. First, let's recap the capital budgeting methods.

SUMMARY OF CAPITAL BUDGETING METHODS

Exhibit 11–5 provides a summary of the five capital budgeting methods we discussed in this chapter.

Any of these methods can be used for screening decisions or to evaluate a single project to determine whether it is acceptable. The discounted cash flow methods (NPV, IRR, and profitability index) are superior to the accounting rate of return and payback methods because they incorporate the time value of money. The NPV method is best for evaluating mutually exclusive projects, or deciding between two competing alternatives. The profitability index is best for prioritizing independent projects when limited investment funds are available.

Each of these methods provides a starting point for analysis but other important factors must also be taken into account. As you learned in Chapter 7, quantitative analysis is only part

EXHIBIT 11–5	Comparing Capital Budgeting Methods		
Method	**Formula**	**Advantages**	**Limitations**
Accounting rate of return	$\dfrac{\text{Net Income}}{\text{Initial Investment}}$	• Simple and intuitive. • May be used as a screening tool.	• Does not incorporate the time value of money. • Some would argue that cash flow is a better measure of performance than net income for capital budgeting.
Payback period	$\dfrac{\text{Initial Investment}}{\text{Annual Cash Flow}}$	• Simple and intuitive. • May be used as a screening tool.	• Does not incorporate the time value of money. • Ignores cash flows after the payback period.
Net present value	Present Value of Future Cash Flows – Initial Investment	• Incorporates the time value of money. • Encourages managers to invest in projects that exceed the company's cost of capital. • Preferred method for evaluating mutually exclusive capital investments.	• May be difficult to determine the discount rate. • Is not useful for comparing projects of varying size.
Internal rate of return	Discount Rate That Yields 0 NPV	• Incorporates the time value of money. • Provides a relative measure of performance.	• Assumes that funds will be reinvested in projects to earn the same internal rate of return, which may be unrealistic.
Profitability index	$\dfrac{\text{Present Value of Future Cash Flows}}{\text{Initial Investment}}$	• Incorporates the time value of money. • Provides a relative measure of performance. • Allows managers to compare projects of varying size. • Preferred method for prioritizing independent projects when limited investment funds are available.	• May be difficult to determine the discount rate. • Isn't as useful for evaluating mutually exclusive projects as NPV.

of the decision-making process. In order to make good decisions, managers must combine quantitative information with other important considerations, such as the strategic direction of the business and what is in the best interest of key stakeholders like employees, customers, and the local community.

The same capital budgeting methods can also be used to evaluate the outcome of previous capital budgeting decisions. Similar to the control process described in Chapter 9 (where actual results are compared to expected or budgeted results), companies may conduct a **postaudit**, using the same technique they used to make the original capital investment decision, to determine whether managers are investing in the "right" projects, or projects that contribute to the firm's economic value. The postaudit should be based on the **actual** cash flows rather than the estimates that were used to make the original decision. It serves as a monitoring mechanism to prevent managers from using inflated estimates to rationalize capital expenditures. The postaudit is an important part of the feedback loop aimed at improving future managerial decisions.

In the next section, we illustrate how to use the NPV method and the profitability index to make preference decisions that require managers to compare and select among competing alternatives. But first, complete the following Self-Study Practice to make sure you understand the various capital budgeting methods.

💡 How's it going?   Self-Study Practice

1. Which of the following statements regarding the five capital budgeting methods is true? You may select more than one answer.

   a. Both the accounting rate of return and the payback period consider the time value of money.
   b. Both the accounting rate of return and the payback period are based on accounting measures rather than on cash flow.
   c. Both the NPV method and the IRR ignore the time value of money.
   d. The accounting rate of return is based on net income; the other four methods are based on cash flow.

2. Jackson Company's cost of capital is 10 percent. The NPV of a project using the 10 percent discount rate is $(15,333). Which of the following statements is true? You may select more than one answer.

   a. The present value of the project's future cash flows is more than the original cost of the investment.
   b. The present value of the project's future cash flows is less than the original cost of the investment.
   c. The profitability index is less than one.
   d. The IRR on this project is more than 10 percent.

After you have finished, check your answers against the solutions in the margin.

Solution to Self-Study Practice

1. d
2. b and c

Applying NPV and Sensitivity Analysis

The final section of this chapter illustrates how managers can use the capital budgeting methods to make preference decisions by evaluating more than one investment alternative. First, we analyze **mutually exclusive projects**, or projects that require managers to select one option or another, but not both. We will then illustrate how managers can prioritize **independent projects** when resources are limited.

EVALUATING MUTUALLY EXCLUSIVE PROJECTS

Recall that mutually exclusive projects involve an either/or choice, such as whether to lease or buy equipment. Managers will do one or the other, but not both. To make these decisions, managers should compare the costs and benefits of the various alternatives. This decision-making approach is very similar to the method used in Chapter 7 to analyze make-or-buy decisions, special-order decisions, and keep-or-drop decisions. We can apply the same general framework to capital budgeting decisions, but to do so, we must use an approach, like NPV or profitability index, that incorporates the time value of money.

> **Learning Objective 11–5**
> Use the net present value method to analyze mutually exclusive capital investments.

Case 1: Lease or Buy Equipment

A common investment decision is whether to purchase or lease a capital asset such as a building or piece of equipment. In your personal life, you may have faced a similar dilemma when deciding whether to lease or buy a home or a car.

To illustrate, assume that an office manager at Apple plans to replace an office copy machine with a new model. The manager is trying to decide whether to buy the machine outright or lease it from an office supply company. She has gathered the following information about the two options:

Purchase Option		Lease Option	
Purchase price	$20,000	Annual lease payment	$6,000
Useful life	4 years	(includes all supplies	
Salvage value after 4 years	$ 4,000	and maintenance)	
Depreciation expense	$ 4,000	Contract length	4 years
Annual cash operating costs	$ 1,000		

If Apple's cost of capital (discount rate) is 10 percent, should the company lease or buy the copier? We can answer this question by comparing the cost of the two decision options, after taking into account the time value of money. As we learned in Chapter 7, the first step is to identify the costs that are relevant to this specific decision, as summarized below:

- The purchase price of $20,000 is relevant because Apple will pay that amount if it buys the copier, but not if it leases the copier.

- The salvage value is relevant because Apple will own the copier if it buys the copier and can sell it at the end of four years.

- The depreciation expense is not relevant because it is a noncash expense. There is no cash flow associated with depreciation (ignoring the effect of taxes).

- The cash operating costs of $1,000 are relevant because they will be incurred only if Apple buys the copier.

- The annual lease payments of $6,000 are relevant because they will be incurred only if Apple leases the copier.

To analyze this decision, we can use the NPV method to compare the relevant costs (in present dollar values) of each option. The annual cash operating costs and lease payments are the same amount in each of the four years, so we can use the PV of annuity table (Table 11–4A) to determine the present value of these cash payments. For the purchase option, there is an additional cash flow from the sale of the copier for its salvage value at the end of four years. Because this is a one-time cash flow, we will need to use the PV of $1 table (Table 11–2A) to discount the amount. These calculations are shown in the following table:

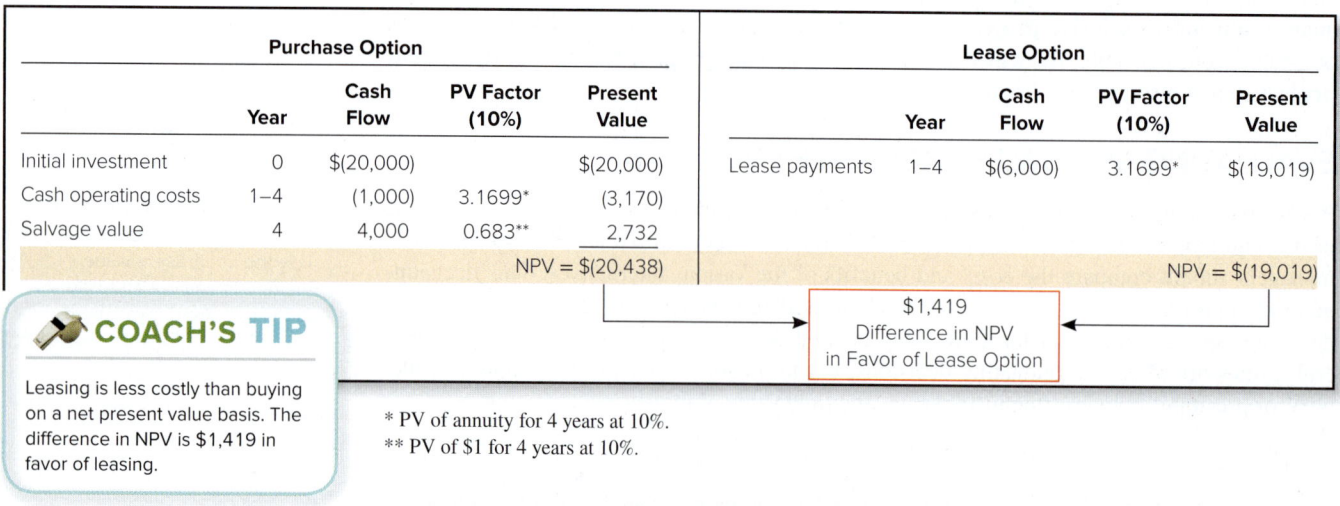

Purchase Option				
	Year	Cash Flow	PV Factor (10%)	Present Value
Initial investment	0	$(20,000)		$(20,000)
Cash operating costs	1–4	(1,000)	3.1699*	(3,170)
Salvage value	4	4,000	0.683**	2,732
			NPV =	$(20,438)

Lease Option				
	Year	Cash Flow	PV Factor (10%)	Present Value
Lease payments	1–4	$(6,000)	3.1699*	$(19,019)
			NPV =	$(19,019)

$1,419
Difference in NPV
in Favor of Lease Option

* PV of annuity for 4 years at 10%.
** PV of $1 for 4 years at 10%.

The NPV analysis shows that it is less costly to lease the copier than to purchase it. The lease option will save the company about $1,419, measured in today's (present value) dollars. Of course, this analysis is contingent on a number of assumptions, including the

10 percent discount rate, a four-year decision horizon, and $4,000 estimated salvage value. A change in any of these assumptions could reverse the decision. For example, if the machine were estimated to be worth more than $4,000 at the end of four years, the purchase option would be less costly. When analyzing capital investment decisions, managers should perform **sensitivity analysis**, or "what if" analysis, to see whether changing the underlying assumptions would affect the decision. What would happen if the discount rate increased to 12 percent? What if it decreased to 8 percent? Building a spreadsheet in Excel makes it much easier to perform this type of sensitivity analysis.

Note that we ignored the tax implications of owning versus leasing the copier. These issues are covered in advanced managerial accounting and corporate finance textbooks.

Case 2: Investing In Automation

The next mutually exclusive decision we consider is whether or not to invest in automation. Examples of possible investments include

- Investing in robots to reduce direct labor costs.
- Investing in bar code or radio frequency identification (RFID) technology to reduce inventory costs and improve the flow of material through production.
- Investing in computerized accounting systems to save on record-keeping costs.

Each of these investments requires a major up-front investment that is expected to save money in the long run. We can use the NPV method to compare the future cost savings (on a present-value basis) to the initial investment.

As an example, assume that Apple is thinking of renovating one of the facilities where its final products are packaged and prepared for shipment to customers. The renovation would include the installation of robots to assemble the various items that must be included in each package (e.g., phone, charger, instruction manual, earphones), pack them into larger boxes, and prepare them for shipping.

The renovation would require a $10 million investment that would have the following benefits:

- Automation will increase the capacity of the plant and allow it to boost production and sales by 20 percent. The company is currently producing 100,000 units per year.
- The company will be able to reduce direct labor cost per unit by 30 percent.
- Factory supervision costs will increase by $500,000 per year.
- The estimated useful life of the equipment is six years, at which point it will have a residual or salvage value of $1,000,000. Straight-line depreciation of the assets will be $1,500,000 per year [($10,000,000 − $1,000,000) ÷ 6 years = $1,500,000].
- All other price and cost data are expected to remain the same and are summarized in the income statement below.

EFFECT OF AUTOMATION ON NET INCOME					
	CURRENT (NO AUTOMATION)		PROPOSED (AUTOMATION)		DIFFERENCE
Production and sales volume	100,000 units		120,000 units		20,000 units
	Per Unit	**Total**	**Per Unit**	**Total**	**Total**
Sales revenue	$150	$15,000,000	$150	$18,000,000	$ 3,000,000
Variable costs					
Direct materials	$ 25		$ 25		
Direct labor	50		35		
Variable manufacturing overhead	10		10		
Total variable manufacturing costs	85	8,500,000	70	8,400,000	100,000
Contribution margin	$ 65	6,500,000	$ 80	9,600,000	3,100,000
Fixed manufacturing costs		2,500,000		4,500,000	(2,000,000)
Net operating income		$ 4,000,000		$ 5,100,000	$ 1,100,000

The shaded portion of the table highlights the variables that are expected to change as a result of automation. Production and sales volume are expected to increase by 20 percent, from 100,000 to 120,000 units. Direct labor costs are expected to decrease by 30 percent, from $50 to $35 per unit ($50 × 70%). Fixed costs are expected to increase by $2,000,000, including $500,000 for factory supervision and $1,500,000 for depreciation. The net effect of these changes is that automation is expected to increase annual net income by $1,100,000.

Let's calculate the NPV of this investment using a 12 percent discount rate. Remember that the net present value method is based on cash flow rather than net income. Thus, we need to add back the depreciation (a noncash expense) to the change in net income to get net cash flow ($1,100,000 + $1,500,000 = $2,600,000). Alternatively, we could have left the depreciation out of the fixed manufacturing overhead costs and simply reported net cash flow rather than net income. We also need to incorporate the initial investment (at time zero) and the salvage value of the machinery at the end of six years. This analysis is summarized in the following table:

Year	Investment/ Salvage Value	Net Income	Add Back Depreciation	Net Cash Flow	PV of $1 (12%)	Present Value
0	$(10,000,000)	—	—	$(10,000,000)	1.0000	$(10,000,000)
1		$1,100,000	$1,500,000	2,600,000	0.8929	2,321,540
2		1,100,000	1,500,000	2,600,000	0.7972	2,072,720
3		1,100,000	1,500,000	2,600,000	0.7118	1,850,680
4		1,100,000	1,500,000	2,600,000	0.6355	1,652,300
5		1,100,000	1,500,000	2,600,000	0.5674	1,475,240
6	1,000,000	1,100,000	1,500,000	3,600,000	0.5066	1,823,760
					NPV	$ 1,196,240

The positive NPV of $1,196,240 means that the proposed investment in automation will generate a return in excess of the 12 percent cost of capital. Any return in excess of the cost of capital is acceptable and will create economic wealth for the firm. Once again, however, this analysis is contingent on a number of assumptions and ignores the effect of taxes.

PRIORITIZING INDEPENDENT PROJECTS

Learning Objective 11–6
Use the profitability index to prioritize independent capital investment projects.

The previous decision scenarios involved mutually exclusive capital investment decisions. For example, choosing to lease the copy machine eliminates the option of purchasing. Similarly, choosing to automate the production facility means not staying with the status quo.

Other investment decisions involve choosing among independent projects, where accepting one does not necessarily preclude accepting another unrelated project. However, managers typically have limited funds to invest and therefore must prioritize their investment resources.

When resources are limited, managers should prioritize projects based on the **profitability index**. Recall that the profitability index is computed by dividing the present value of the future cash flows by the initial investment. Because it is stated as a ratio rather than a dollar value, the profitability index allows managers to easily compare projects that vary in size. Specifically, the profitability index tells managers how much future benefit (measured in terms of present value) each project will generate per dollar of investment.

Case 3: Evaluating Research and Development Projects

To illustrate, assume Apple's managers is are trying to decide how to prioritize their limited research and development budget. They are considering the following independent projects:

	Project A	Project B	Project C
Present value of future cash flows	$600,000	$810,000	$1,200,000
Initial investment	300,000	450,000	800,000
Net present value	$300,000	$360,000	$ 400,000
Profitability index	$\frac{\$600,000}{\$300,000} = 2.0$	$\frac{\$810,000}{\$450,000} = 1.8$	$\frac{\$1,200,000}{\$ 800,000} = 1.5$

How should Apple prioritize these three projects? If they base the decision strictly on NPV, project C would be given highest priority because it has the highest NPV. However, project C also requires the largest investment. The profitability index, on the other hand, considers both the present value of the future cash flows (benefits) and the initial investment (cost).

Project A generates the most net present value on a "per-dollar of investment" basis. It generates $2.00 in present value for every $1.00 invested, while project B generates $1.80 per dollar invested, and project C generates $1.50 per dollar invested. When investment funds are limited, the profitability index allows managers to prioritize projects based on how much benefit (measured in terms of present value) is generated per dollar of investment.

You may notice that the profitability index is conceptually similar to the method used to prioritize constrained or bottleneck resources in Chapter 7. In a capital budgeting context, the limited resource is cash. The profitability index measures the amount of economic value (represented by the present value of future cash flows) that is generated per unit of the scarce resource (in this case, cash for investments).

Case 4: Evaluating Sustainability Projects

The final decision scenario we illustrate is the evaluation of sustainability initiatives. Most sustainability projects require a significant upfront investment of resources, the benefits of which are sometimes hard to quantify and which usually occur over a very long time horizon. By definition, sustainability initiatives require a long-term view and involve more than just economic benefits. Even so, it is important to try to quantify the costs and benefits of these initiatives. In addition, the environmental and societal benefits should be highlighted and quantified when possible so that managers can make informed decisions and be able to justify those decisions to others.

To illustrate, assume Apple has set aside up to $1,000,000 to invest in sustainability-enhancing initiatives. The director of sustainability has solicited proposals from the various divisions and has narrowed it down to the following three proposals:

- Project A would redesign the packaging of all future iPhone models to reduce the amount of cardboard and plastic used in packaging and shipping. The project is expected to reduce the cost of materials by 10 percent and the cost of packing and shipping by 20 percent. In addition, it will reduce the company's greenhouse gas emissions by 2 percent.

- Project B would install solar panels and other energy-saving features in one of the corporate office buildings in Cupertino, California. The project is expected to reduce the operating cost of the building by 10 percent and reduce the company's carbon footprint by 1 percent.

- Project C would create a new employee wellness center that would include a classroom for employee training, an employee fitness room, and on-site child care. The project is expected make it easier to attract and retain highly qualified employees, reduce turnover and retraining costs, and improve employee morale and productivity.

The first step in analyzing this decision is to quantify the economic costs and benefits of these projects. The capital budgeting tools that you learned throughout this chapter provide an excellent framework for this analysis. Because the projects span multiple years, the costs and benefits should be stated in terms of their present values. In this case, managers might apply a different discount rate (cost of capital) to the various projects to reflect the perceived risk of each project. In general, projects with a longer time horizon and more uncertainty about the future cash flows will be perceived as riskier than those with a shorter life cycle. The discount rate that is used to compute NPV can be adjusted to reflect these differences in risk. However, the projects cannot be evaluated based strictly on these economic outcomes. The decision framework should also highlight the potential benefit to the other elements of the triple bottom line, such as the impact on the environment (planet) and society (people).

The following table summarizes the economic costs and benefits of these three hypothetical projects.

	Project A (Repackaging iPhone)	Project B (Solar Panels)	Project C (Employee Wellness Center)
Required Investment	$ (800,000)	$(1,000,000)	$(1,000,000)
Present Value of Future Cash Flows	$1,000,000	$ 1,220,000	$ 800,000
Net Present Value	$ 200,000	$ 220,000	$ (200,000)
Profitability Index	1.25	1.22	0.80
Cost of Capital	6%	6%	8%
Internal Rate of Return	8%	7.5%	7%
Payback Period	4 years	5 years	10 years

Which project should managers invest in? In this case, the economic analysis suggests that projects A and B are the most economically viable, as they both have a positive NPV, a profitability index greater than one, and an internal rate of return that exceeds the cost of capital. They also have relatively short payback periods. Project B generates a higher NPV than Project A, but it requires a higher level of investment. Project A generates more present value per dollar of investment than Project B. It also has a slightly higher internal rate of return. Managers could reasonably argue in favor of either Project A or Project B, based strictly on the economic measures, and most likely would base their decision on other qualitative factors.

Project C, on the other hand, has a negative NPV and only generates $0.80 in present value per dollar of investment. This project does not generate a high enough internal return to compensate for the cost of capital. Note also that this project has a longer payback period and was assigned a higher cost of capital than the other two projects, which reflects a longer life cycle and greater uncertainty about future cash flows. In general, the benefits of this project are harder to quantify than the other two projects and therefore more difficult to justify on an economic basis. Even so, managers may choose to invest in this project for reasons other than the immediate economic benefit.

As you can see, there is not always a clear-cut answer in capital budgeting decisions, particularly when they involve projects that have nonfinancial goals and benefits, as in the case of sustainability initiatives. But the tools presented throughout this chapter provide a framework for analyzing the economic costs and benefits of capital projects and provide a starting point for making the decision. As always, the economic analysis must be weighed against other considerations and strategic priorities.

SUPPLEMENT 11A TIME VALUE OF MONEY

Learning Objective 11–S1
Use present value and future value tables to incorporate the time value of money.

This supplement provides additional details about how to use present value and future value tables to incorporate the time value of money. Although you can use a calculator or computer to do the computations, you need to understand where the numbers come from. In some business situations, you will know the dollar amount of a cash flow that occurs in the future and will need to determine its value now. This type of situation is known as a **present value** problem. The opposite occurs when you know the dollar amount of a cash flow that occurs today and need to determine its value at some point in the future, which requires solving a **future value** problem. The following table illustrates the basic difference between present value and future value problems:

	Now	Future
Present value	?	$1,000
Future value	$1,000	?

Present and future value problems may involve two types of cash flow: a single payment or an annuity (a fancy word for a series of equal cash payments). Thus, you need to learn how to deal with four different situations related to the time value of money:

1. Future value of a single payment.
2. Present value of a single payment.
3. Future value of an annuity.
4. Present value of an annuity.

Computing Future and Present Values of a Single Amount

Future Value of a Single Amount   In problems involving the future value of a single amount, you will be asked to calculate how much money you will have in the future as the result of investing a certain amount right now. If you were to receive a gift of $10,000, for instance, you might decide to put it in a savings account and use the money as a down payment on a house after you graduate. The future value computation would tell you how much money you will have from this gift when you graduate. To solve a future value problem, you need to know three things:

1. Amount to be invested.
2. Interest rate (i) the amount will earn.
3. Number of periods (n) in which the amount will earn interest.

The future value concept is based on compound interest, which simply means that interest is calculated on top of interest. Thus, the amount of interest for each period is calculated using the principal plus any interest earned in prior periods. Graphically, the calculation of the future value of $1 for three periods at an interest rate of 10 percent may be represented as follows:

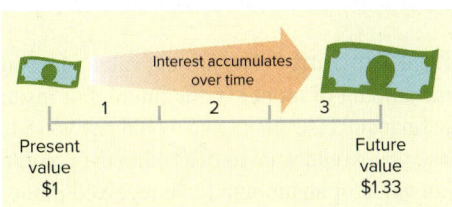

Assume that on January 1, 2018, you deposit $1,000 in a savings account that has annual interest rate of 10 percent compounded annually. At the end of three years, the $1,000 will have increased to $1,331 as follows:

Year	Amount at Start of Year	+	Interest during the Year	=	Amount at End of Year
1	$1,000	+	$1,000 × 10% = $100	=	$1,100
2	1,100	+	1,100 × 10% = 110	=	1,210
3	1,210	+	1,210 × 10% = 121	=	1,331

Using Table 11–1A, you can quickly determine how much money you will have after 3 years if you invest $1,000 today, as follows:

TABLE 11-1A	Future Value of $1

Periods	2%	3%	3.75%	4%	4.25%	5%	6%	7%	8%
0	1.0000	1.0000	1.0000	1.0000	1.0000	1.0000	1.0000	1.0000	1.0000
1	1.0200	1.0300	1.0375	1.0400	1.0425	1.0500	1.0600	1.0700	1.0800
2	1.0404	1.0609	1.0764	1.0816	1.0868	1.1025	1.1236	1.1449	1.1664
3	1.0612	1.0927	1.1168	1.1249	1.1330	1.1576	1.1910	1.2250	1.2597
4	1.0824	1.1255	1.1587	1.1699	1.1811	1.2155	1.2625	1.3108	1.3605
5	1.1041	1.1593	1.2021	1.2167	1.2313	1.2763	1.3382	1.4026	1.4693
6	1.1262	1.1941	1.2472	1.2653	1.2837	1.3401	1.4185	1.5007	1.5869
7	1.1487	1.2299	1.2939	1.3159	1.3382	1.4071	1.5036	1.6058	1.7138
8	1.1717	1.2668	1.3425	1.3686	1.3951	1.4775	1.5938	1.7182	1.8509
9	1.1951	1.3048	1.3928	1.4233	1.4544	1.5513	1.6895	1.8385	1.9990
10	1.2190	1.3439	1.4450	1.4802	1.5162	1.6289	1.7906	1.9672	2.1589
20	1.4859	1.8061	2.0882	2.1911	2.2989	2.6533	3.2071	3.8697	4.6610

Periods	9%	10%	11%	12%	13%	14%	15%	20%	25%
0	1.0000	1.0000	1.0000	1.0000	1.0000	1.0000	1.0000	1.0000	1.0000
1	1.0900	1.1000	1.1100	1.1200	1.1300	1.1400	1.1500	1.2000	1.2500
2	1.1881	1.2100	1.2321	1.2544	1.2769	1.2996	1.3225	1.4400	1.5625
3	1.2950	1.3310	1.3676	1.4049	1.4429	1.4815	1.5209	1.7280	1.9531
4	1.4116	1.4641	1.5181	1.5735	1.6305	1.6890	1.7490	2.0736	2.4414
5	1.5386	1.6105	1.6851	1.7623	1.8424	1.9254	2.0114	2.4883	3.0518
6	1.6771	1.7716	1.8704	1.9738	2.0820	2.1950	2.3131	2.9860	3.8147
7	1.8280	1.9487	2.0762	2.2107	2.3526	2.5023	2.6600	3.5832	4.7684
8	1.9926	2.1436	2.3045	2.4760	2.6584	2.8526	3.0590	4.2998	5.9605
9	2.1719	2.3579	2.5580	2.7731	3.0040	3.2519	3.5179	5.1598	7.4506
10	2.3674	2.5937	2.8394	3.1058	3.3946	3.7072	4.0456	6.1917	9.3132
20	5.6044	6.7275	8.0623	9.6463	11.5231	13.7435	16.3665	38.3376	86.7362

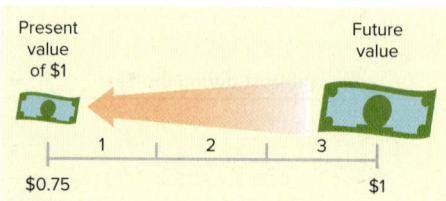

$1,000 × 1.3310 = $1,331

COACH'S TIP

Future value of $1 at 10% interest for 3 years = **1.3310**.

Note that the increase of $331 is due to the time value of money.

Present Value of a Single Amount   The present value of a single amount is the value to you today of receiving some amount of money in the future. For instance, you might be offered an opportunity to invest in a financial instrument that would pay you $1,000 in three years. Before you decide whether to invest, you would want to determine the present value of the instrument.

To compute the present value of an amount to be received in the future, we must discount (a procedure that is the opposite of compounding) at i interest rate for n periods. In discounting, the interest is subtracted rather than added as it is in compounding. Graphically, the present value of $1 due at the end of the third period with an interest rate of 10 percent can be represented as follows:

Present value of $1

Future value

1   2   3

$0.75 $1

Assume that today is January 1, 2018, and you have the opportunity to receive $1,000 cash on December 31, 2021 (three years from today). At an interest rate of 10 percent per year, how much is the $1,000 payment worth to you on January 1, 2018 (today)? You could discount the amount year by year, but it is easier to use Table 11–2A, Present Value of $1.

To determine how much $1,000 to be received in three years is worth in today's dollars, we simply multiply by the PV of $1 factor for $n = 3$ and $i = 10$ percent, as follows:

TABLE 11–2A		Present Value of $1							

Periods	2%	3%	3.75%	4%	4.25%	5%	6%	7%	8%
1	0.9804	0.9709	0.9639	0.9615	0.9592	0.9524	0.9434	0.9346	0.9259
2	0.9612	0.9426	0.9290	0.9246	0.9201	0.9070	0.8900	0.8734	0.8573
3	0.9423	0.9151	0.8954	0.8890	0.8826	0.8638	0.8396	0.8163	0.7938
4	0.9238	0.8885	0.8631	0.8548	0.8466	0.8227	0.7921	0.7629	0.7350
5	0.9057	0.8626	0.8319	0.8219	0.8121	0.7835	0.7473	0.7130	0.6806
6	0.8880	0.8375	0.8018	0.7903	0.7790	0.7462	0.7050	0.6663	0.6302
7	0.8706	0.8131	0.7728	0.7599	0.7473	0.7107	0.6651	0.6227	0.5835
8	0.8535	0.7894	0.7449	0.7307	0.7168	0.6768	0.6274	0.5820	0.5403
9	0.8368	0.7664	0.7180	0.7026	0.6876	0.6446	0.5919	0.5439	0.5002
10	0.8203	0.7441	0.6920	0.6756	0.6595	0.6139	0.5584	0.5083	0.4632
20	0.6730	0.5537	0.4789	0.4564	0.4350	0.3769	0.3118	0.2584	0.2145

Periods	9%	10%	11%	12%	13%	14%	15%	20%	25%
1	0.9174	0.9091	0.9009	0.8929	0.8850	0.8772	0.8696	0.8333	0.8000
2	0.8417	0.8264	0.8116	0.7972	0.7831	0.7695	0.7561	0.6944	0.6400
3	0.7722	0.7513	0.7312	0.7118	0.6931	0.6750	0.6575	0.5787	0.5120
4	0.7084	0.6830	0.6587	0.6355	0.6133	0.5921	0.5718	0.4823	0.4096
5	0.6499	0.6209	0.5935	0.5674	0.5428	0.5194	0.4972	0.4019	0.3277
6	0.5963	0.5645	0.5346	0.5066	0.4803	0.4556	0.4323	0.3349	0.2621
7	0.5470	0.5132	0.4817	0.4523	0.4251	0.3996	0.3759	0.2791	0.2097
8	0.5019	0.4665	0.4339	0.4039	0.3762	0.3506	0.3269	0.2326	0.1678
9	0.4604	0.4241	0.3909	0.3606	0.3329	0.3075	0.2843	0.1938	0.1342
10	0.4224	0.3855	0.3522	0.3220	0.2946	0.2697	0.2472	0.1615	0.1074
20	0.1784	0.1486	0.1240	0.1037	0.0868	0.0728	0.0611	0.0261	0.0115

$$\$1,000 \times 0.7513 = \$751.30$$

COACH'S TIP

Present value of $1 discounted at 10% interest for 3 years = **0.7513**.

What does a PV of $751.30 mean? It is the amount you would pay now to have the right to receive $1,000 at the end of three years, assuming an interest rate of 10 percent. Conceptually, you should be indifferent between having $751.30 today and receiving $1,000 in three years. If you had $751.30 today but wanted $1,000 in three years, you could simply deposit the money in a savings account that pays 10 percent interest, and it would grow to $1,000 in three years.

What if you could earn only 6 percent instead of 10 percent interest? Would the present value increase or decrease? To answer this, we would take the same approach using Table 11–2A except that the interest rate would change to $i = 6$ percent. Referring to Table 11–2A, we see the present value factor for $i = 6$ percent, $n = 3$, is 0.8396. Thus, the present value of $1,000 to be received at the end of three years, assuming a 6 percent interest rate, would be $839.60 ($1,000 × 0.8396). Notice that when we assume a 6 percent interest rate, the present value is higher than when we assumed a 10 percent interest rate. To reach $1,000 three years from now, you would need to deposit more money in a savings account that earns only 6 percent interest than you would in one that earns 10 percent interest.

Before we move on, take a moment to complete the following Self-Study Practice to make sure you can compute the present value and future value of a single amount.

How's it going? Self-Study Practice

1. If the interest rate in a present value problem increases from 8 percent to 10 percent, will the present value increase or decrease?

2. What is the present value of $10,000 to be received 10 years from now if the interest rate is 5 percent, compounded annually?

3. If $10,000 is deposited now in a savings account that earns 5 percent interest, compounded annually, how much will it be worth 10 years from now?

After you have finished, check your answers against the solutions in the margin.

Computing Future and Present Values of an Annuity

Instead of a single payment, many business problems involve multiple cash payments over a number of periods. An **annuity** is a series of consecutive payments characterized by

 1. An equal dollar amount each interest period.

 2. Interest periods of equal length (year, half a year, quarter, or month).

 3. An equal interest rate each interest period.

Examples of annuities include monthly payments on a car or house, yearly contributions to a savings account, and monthly pension benefits.

Future Value of an Annuity   If you are saving money for some purpose, such as remodeling your home or taking a vacation, you might decide to deposit a fixed amount of money in a savings account each month. The future value of an annuity tells you how much money will be in your savings account at some point in the future.

The future value of an annuity includes compound interest on each payment from the date of payment to the end of the term of the annuity. Each new payment accumulates less interest than prior payments because the number of periods in which to accumulate interest decreases. The future value of an annuity of $1 for three periods at 10 percent may be represented graphically as:

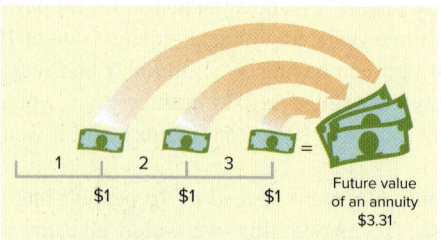

Assume that each year for three years, you deposit $1,000 cash into a savings account that earns 10 percent interest per year. You make the first $1,000 deposit on December 31, 2018, the second one on December 31, 2019, and the last one on December 31, 2020. The first $1,000 deposit earns compound interest for two years (for total principal and interest of $1,210); the second deposit earns interest for one year (for total principal and interest of

$1,100). The third deposit earns no interest because it was made on the day that the balance is computed. Thus, the total amount in the savings account at the end of three years is $3,310 ($1,210 + $1,100 + $1,000).

To calculate the future value of this annuity, we could compute the interest on each deposit. However, a faster way is to multiply the $1,000 by the future value of an annuity factor from Table 11–3A, as follows:

| TABLE 11–3A | Future Value of an Annuity of $1 | | | | | | | | |

Periods*	2%	3%	3.75%	4%	4.25%	5%	6%	7%	8%
1	1.0000	1.0000	1.0000	1.0000	1.0000	1.0000	1.0000	1.0000	1.0000
2	2.0200	2.0300	2.0375	2.0400	2.0425	2.0500	2.0600	2.0700	2.0800
3	3.0604	3.0909	3.1139	3.1216	3.1293	3.1525	3.1836	3.2149	3.2464
4	4.1216	4.1836	4.2307	4.2465	4.2623	4.3101	4.3746	4.4399	4.5061
5	5.2040	5.3091	5.3893	5.4163	5.4434	5.5256	5.6371	5.7507	5.8666
6	6.3061	6.4684	6.5914	6.6330	6.6748	6.8019	6.9753	7.1533	7.3359
7	7.4343	7.6625	7.8386	7.8983	7.9585	8.1420	8.3938	8.6540	8.9228
8	8.5830	8.8923	9.1326	9.2142	9.2967	9.5491	9.8975	10.2598	10.6366
9	9.7546	10.1591	10.4750	10.5828	10.6918	11.0266	11.4913	11.9780	12.4876
10	10.9497	11.4639	11.8678	12.0061	12.1462	12.5779	13.1808	13.8164	14.4866
20	24.2974	26.8704	29.0174	29.7781	30.5625	33.0660	36.7856	40.9955	45.7620

Periods*	9%	10%	11%	12%	13%	14%	15%	20%	25%
1	1.0000	1.0000	1.0000	1.0000	1.0000	1.0000	1.0000	1.0000	1.0000
2	2.0900	2.1000	2.1100	2.1200	2.1300	2.1400	2.1500	2.2000	2.2500
3	3.2781	3.3100	3.3421	3.3744	3.4069	3.4396	3.4725	3.6400	3.8125
4	4.5731	4.6410	4.7097	4.7793	4.8498	4.9211	4.9934	5.3680	5.7656
5	5.9847	6.1051	6.2278	6.3528	6.4803	6.6101	6.7424	7.4416	8.2070
6	7.5233	7.7156	7.9129	8.1152	8.3227	8.5355	8.7537	9.9299	11.2588
7	9.2004	9.4872	9.7833	10.0890	10.4047	10.7305	11.0668	12.9159	15.0735
8	11.0285	11.4359	11.8594	12.2997	12.7573	13.2328	13.7266	16.4991	19.8419
9	13.0210	13.5975	14.1640	14.7757	15.4157	16.0853	16.7856	20.7989	25.8023
10	15.1929	15.9374	16.7220	17.5487	18.4197	19.3373	20.3037	25.9587	33.2529
20	51.1601	57.2750	64.2028	72.0524	80.9468	91.0249	102.4436	186.6880	342.9447

*There is one payment each period.

$1,000 × 3.3100 = $3,310

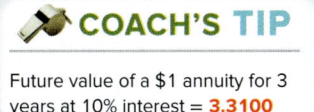

Present Value of an Annuity   The present value of an annuity is the value now of a series of equal amounts to be received (or paid out) for some specified number of periods in the future. A good example is a retirement program that offers employees a monthly income after retirement. The present value of an annuity of $1 for three periods at 10 percent can be represented graphically as:

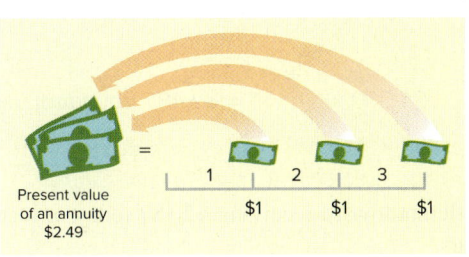

Present value of an annuity $2.49

Assume you are to receive $1,000 cash on each December 31 for three years: 2018, 2019, and 2020. How much would the sum of these three $1,000 future amounts be worth on January 1, 2018, assuming an interest rate of 10 percent per year? One way to determine this is to use Table 11–2A to calculate the present value of each single amount as follows:

			FACTOR FROM TABLE 11.2A		
Year	Amount		*i* = 10%		Present Value
1	$1,000	×	0.9091 (*n* = 1)	=	$ 909.10
2	$1,000	×	0.8264 (*n* = 2)	=	826.40
3	$1,000	×	0.7513 (*n* = 3)	=	751.30
			Total present value	=	$2,486.80

Alternatively, we can compute the present value of this annuity more easily by using Table 11–4A as follows:

TABLE 11–4A	Present Value of Annuity of $1

Periods*	2%	3%	3.75%	4%	4.25%	5%	6%	7%	8%
1	0.9804	0.9709	0.9639	0.9615	0.9592	0.9524	0.9434	0.9346	0.9259
2	1.9416	1.9135	1.8929	1.8861	1.8794	1.8594	1.8334	1.8080	1.7833
3	2.8839	2.8286	2.7883	2.7751	2.7620	2.7232	2.6730	2.6243	2.5771
4	3.8077	3.7171	3.6514	3.6299	3.6086	3.5460	3.4651	3.3872	3.3121
5	4.7135	4.5797	4.4833	4.4518	4.4207	4.3295	4.2124	4.1002	3.9927
6	5.6014	5.4172	5.2851	5.2421	5.1997	5.0757	4.9173	4.7665	4.6229
7	6.4720	6.2303	6.0579	6.0021	5.9470	5.7864	5.5824	5.3893	5.2064
8	7.3255	7.0197	6.8028	6.7327	6.6638	6.4632	6.2098	5.9713	5.7466
9	8.1622	7.7861	7.5208	7.4353	7.3513	7.1078	6.8017	6.5152	6.2469
10	8.9826	8.5302	8.2128	8.1109	8.0109	7.7217	7.3601	7.0236	6.7101
20	16.3514	14.8775	13.8962	13.5903	13.2944	12.4622	11.4699	10.5940	9.8181

Periods*	9%	10%	11%	12%	13%	14%	15%	20%	25%
1	0.9174	0.9091	0.9009	0.8929	0.8550	0.8772	0.8696	0.8333	0.8000
2	1.7591	1.7355	1.7125	1.6901	1.6681	1.6467	1.6257	1.5278	1.4400
3	2.5313	2.4869	2.4437	2.4018	2.3612	2.3216	2.2832	2.1065	1.9520
4	3.2397	3.1699	3.1024	3.0373	2.9745	2.9137	2.8550	2.5887	2.3616
5	3.8897	3.7908	3.6959	3.6048	3.5172	3.4331	3.3522	2.9906	2.6893
6	4.4859	4.3553	4.2305	4.1114	3.9975	3.8887	3.7845	3.3255	2.9514
7	5.0330	4.8684	4.7122	4.5638	4.4226	4.2883	4.1604	3.6046	3.1611
8	5.5348	5.3349	5.1461	4.9676	4.7988	4.6389	4.4873	3.8372	3.3289
9	5.9952	5.7590	5.5370	5.3282	5.1317	4.9464	4.7716	4.0310	3.4631
10	6.4177	6.1446	5.8892	5.6502	5.4262	5.2161	5.0188	4.1925	3.5705
20	9.1285	8.5136	7.9633	7.4694	7.0248	6.6231	6.2593	4.8696	3.9539

*There is one payment each period.

$1,000 × 2.4869 = $2,487 (rounded)

COACH'S TIP

Present value of $1 annuity at 10% for 3 years = **2.4869**.

You should be indifferent toward receiving $2,487 today or receiving $1,000 at the end of each of the next 3 years.

REVIEW THE CHAPTER

DEMONSTRATION CASE

Maddox Company is considering investing $800,000 in a new project. Projected annual revenues, expenses, and profit for the next four years follow:

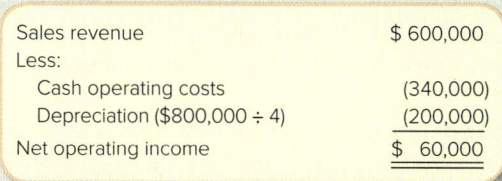

Sales revenue	$ 600,000
Less:	
Cash operating costs	(340,000)
Depreciation ($800,000 ÷ 4)	(200,000)
Net operating income	$ 60,000

The project's assets are expected to have no salvage value at the end of four years. The company's required rate of return is 12 percent.

Required:

1. Compute the accounting rate of return.
2. Compute the payback period.
3. Compute the four-year NPV using a 12 percent discount rate.
4. Without computing the exact IRR, explain whether it would be higher or lower than the 12 percent required rate of return.
5. Compute the exact IRR using Excel.

Suggested Solution

1. Accounting rate of return = $60,000 ÷ $800,000 = 7.5%
2. Payback period = $800,000 ÷ ($60,000 + $200,000) = 3.08 years
3.

Year	Annual Cash Flow		PV of an Annuity		Present Value
0	$(800,000)		—		$(800,000)
1–4	$60,000 + $200,000 = $260,000	×	3.0373*		789,698
			NPV	=	$ (10,302)

* PV of annuity of $1 for $n = 4$, $i = 12\%$.

4. Because the NPV is negative at a discount rate of 12 percent, the IRR must be less than 12 percent.
5. The exact IRR is 11.3879 percent.

CHAPTER SUMMARY

Calculate the accounting rate of return and describe its major weaknesses. p. 486   LO 11–1

- The accounting rate of return is calculated as net income divided by the initial investment.
- The major weakness of the accounting rate of return is that it does not incorporate the time value of money. It is also the only capital budgeting method that uses net income rather than cash flow to measure the benefits of a potential investment.

Calculate the payback period and describe its major weaknesses. p. 488   LO 11–2

- The payback method computes the amount of time it will take for a capital investment to "pay for itself," or earn back enough cash to cover the original investment.
- The major weakness of the payback method is that it does not incorporate the time value of money. It also ignores all cash flows that occur after the payback period is over.

LO 11–3   Calculate net present value and describe why it is superior to the other capital budgeting techniques. p. 492

- The net present value method compares the present value of future cash flows to the original investment.

- Future cash flows are converted to a present value basis to reflect the discount rate or cost of capital.

- The net present value method is preferred over the accounting rate of return and payback period methods because it incorporates the time value of money.

- The net present value method is preferred over the internal rate of return method because it assumes that cash flows are reinvested at the cost of capital rather than the internal rate of return.

LO 11–4   Predict the internal rate of return and describe its relationship to net present value. p. 495

- The internal rate of return is the return that will yield a zero net present value.

- If the internal rate of return is higher than the required rate of return, the net present value will be positive, indicating that the project is acceptable.

- If the internal rate of return is less than the required rate of return, the net present value will be negative, indicating that the project is unacceptable.

LO 11–5   Use the net present value method to analyze mutually exclusive capital investments. p. 499

- The net present value method can be used to compare and make a choice between mutually exclusive capital investment projects.

- An example of a mutually exclusive choice is the decision to lease or buy an asset. The option with the lowest net present value is preferred from a pure cost perspective.

- The net present value method can also be used to analyze the decision to invest in automation. In this case, the future cost savings from automation (on a net present value basis) are compared to the cost of the investment. A positive net present value suggests that the investment in the project is acceptable; otherwise it is unacceptable.

LO 11–6   Use the profitability index to prioritize independent capital investment projects. p. 502

- The profitability index should be used to prioritize investment in independent projects when investment funds are limited.

- The profitability index is computed by dividing the present value of future cash flows by the initial investment.

- A profitability index greater than 1 means that a project has a positive net present value. A profitability index less than 1 means that a project has a negative net present value.

- The profitability index tells you how much benefit (measured as the present value of future cash flows) is generated for each dollar of investment.

LO 11–S1   Use present value and future value tables to incorporate the time value of money. p. 504

- In a present value problem, you know the dollar amount of a cash flow that occurs in the future and you want to know its value now.

- The present value of a single payment is computed by multiplying the amount by the PV of $1 factor that reflects the interest rate (i) and number of periods (n).

- The present value of an annuity is computed by multiplying the annual cash flow by the PV of annuity factor that reflects the interest rate (i) and number of periods (n).

- In a future value problem, you know the dollar amount of a cash flow that occurs today and need to determine its value at some point in the future.

- The future value of a single payment is computed by multiplying the amount by the FV of $1 factor that reflects the interest rate (i) and number of periods (n).

- The future value of an annuity is computed by multiplying the annual cash flow by the FV of annuity factor that reflects the interest rate (i) and number of periods (n).

KEY TERMS

Accounting Rate of Return p. 486
Annuity p. 491
Capital Budgeting p. 484
Compounding p. 490
Cost of Capital p. 492
Discounted Cash Flow Methods p. 492
Discounting p. 491
Discount Rate p. 492

Future Value p. 490
Independent Projects p. 485
Internal Rate of Return p. 495
Mutually Exclusive Projects p. 485
Net Present Value Method p. 492
Payback Period p. 488
Preference Decisions p. 485
Present Value p. 490

Profitability Index p. 497
Screening Decisions p. 485
Sensitivity Analysis p. 501
Simple Rate of Return p. 486
Time Value of Money p. 490
Unadjusted Rate of Return p. 486

PRACTICE MATERIAL

QUESTIONS

1. Explain the difference between screening decisions and preference decisions.

2. What is the difference between independent projects and mutually exclusive projects? Give an example of each from your own experiences.

3. Briefly explain what the time value of money means.

4. Which capital budgeting methods incorporate the time value of money and which do not? Which are considered superior and why?

5. What is a company's hurdle rate? How is it relevant to capital budgeting?

6. How do cash flow and net income differ? Explain why this difference is important to capital budgeting.

7. In everyday terms, explain what information the payback period provides about an investment.

8. What do a positive NPV and a negative NPV indicate about an investment?

9. When would you use an annuity factor in a net present value calculation instead of a present value factor for a single cash flow?

10. Explain how the internal rate of return and net present value are related. If a project has an NPV of $50,000 using a 10 percent discount factor, what does this imply about that project's IRR?

11. Why is the net present value method generally preferred over the internal rate of return method?

12. Briefly explain how the profitability index is calculated and interpreted.

13. Explain the basic difference between future value and present value.

14. If you deposited $10,000 in a savings account that earns 10 percent, how much would you have at the end of 10 years?

15. If you hold a valid contract that will pay you $8,000 cash 10 years from now and the going rate of interest is 10 percent, what is its present value?

16. When would you use the PV of annuity table instead of the PV of $1 table?

17. Use Tables 11.1A to 11.4A to complete the following schedule:

	Table Values		
	$i = 5\%$ $n = 4$	$i = 10\%$ $n = 7$	$i = 14\%$ $n = 10$
FV of $1			
PV of $1			
FV of annuity of $1			
PV of annuity of $1			

MULTIPLE CHOICE

1. Which of the following requires managers to determine whether a proposed capital investment meets some minimum criterion?

   a. Preference decision.
   b. Screening decision.
   c. Cash payback period.
   d. None of the above.

2. ABC Company is considering a $500,000 investment to automate its production process. The new equipment will allow ABC to save $75,000 each year in labor costs. What is this project's payback period?

   a. 4.00 years.
   b. 5.67 years.
   c. 6.67 years.
   d. 8.00 years.

3. What is the accounting rate of return for a project that requires an investment of $725,000 and yields total net income of $320,000 over four years?

   a. 11 percent.
   b. 12.5 percent.
   c. 19.75 percent.
   d. 44 percent.

4. When choosing among several independent projects that are **not** mutually exclusive, managers should

   a. Rely primarily on the accounting rate of return.
   b. Compare their net present values regardless of the projects' sizes.
   c. Calculate the profitability index of each project for comparison.
   d. Rely solely on the internal rates of return for comparison.

5. When deciding whether to lease or buy a long-term asset, managers should

   a. Flip a coin.
   b. Compare the net present value of the two options.
   c. Consider only the cash outflows.
   d. Always choose to buy a long-term asset.

6. Which of the following methods ignore the time value of money?

   a. Payback method and accounting rate of return.
   b. Payback method and internal rate of return.
   c. Accounting rate of return and net present value.
   d. Net present value and profitability index.

7. Discounted cash flow methods are considered superior to nondiscounting methods because

   a. Discounted cash flow methods recognize the time value of money.
   b. Discounted cash flow methods are simpler to calculate.
   c. Discounted cash flow methods are always based on accounting measurements of net income and investment.
   d. Both (*a*) and (*c*) are correct.

8. Jennings Company has evaluated a project and found that its internal rate of return is approximately 13.5 percent. Suppose Jennings's cost of capital is 12 percent. What, if anything, can you infer about the net present value (NPV) of this project?

   a. The NPV is less than zero.
   b. The NPV is more than zero.
   c. The NPV is exactly zero.
   d. Nothing can be determined about the project's NPV.

9. Which of the following is a characteristic of an annuity?

   a. An equal dollar amount each interest period.
   b. Interest periods of equal length.
   c. An equal interest rate each interest period.
   d. All of the above.

10. Which of the following statements is true?

   a. When the interest rate increases, the present value of a single amount decreases.
   b. When the number of interest periods increases; the present value of a single amount increases.
   c. When the interest rate increases, the present value of an annuity increases.
   d. None of the above.

 **Find More Learning Solutions on Connect.**

MINI-EXERCISES

LO 11–1, 11–2, 11–3, 11–4, 11–5, 11–6

M11–1 Matching Key Terms and Concepts to Definitions

A number of terms and concepts from this chapter and a list of descriptions, definitions, and explanations appear as follows. For each term listed (1 through 9), choose at least one corresponding item (a through k). Note that a single term may have more than one description and a single description may be used more than once or not at all.

____ **1.** Time value of money	**A.** Discounted cash flow method of capital budgeting.
____ **2.** Profitability index	**B.** Estimate of the average annual return on investment that a project will generate.
____ **3.** Payback period	**C.** Capital budgeting method that identifies the discount rate that generates a zero net present value.
____ **4.** Net present value method	
____ **5.** Future value	**D.** Decision that requires managers to evaluate potential capital investments to determine whether they meet a minimum criterion.
____ **6.** Preference decision	
____ **7.** Internal rate of return method	**E.** Only capital budgeting method based on net income instead of cash flow.
____ **8.** Screening decision	
____ **9.** Accounting rate of return	**F.** Ratio of the present value of future cash flows to the initial investment.

G. Value that a cash flow that happens today will be worth at some point in the future.

H. Concept recognizing that cash received today is more valuable than cash received in the future.

I. Decision that requires a manager to choose from a set of alternatives.

J. How long it will take for a particular capital investment to pay for itself.

K. Capital budgeting technique that compares the present value of the future cash flows for a project to its original investment.

M11–2 Matching Terminology   LO 11–1, 11–3, 11–5

_____ 1. Compounding
_____ 2. Discounted cash flow methods
_____ 3. Discounting
_____ 4. Discount rate
_____ 5. Sensitivity analysis
_____ 6. Simple rate of return

A. How changing underlying assumptions affect decisions.

B. The rate at which the current value of future cash flows is determined.

C. The rate at which the current value of current cash flows is determined.

D. Another term for the accounting rate of return.

E. How much it costs the company to fund its projects.

F. Methods that calculate the time it takes for a capital investment to pay for itself.

G. Methods that incorporate the time value of money.

H. Earning interest on principal.

I. Finding the future value of cash flows.

J. Finding the present value of future cash flows.

K. Earning interest on interest.

M11–3 Calculating Accounting Rate of Return   LO 11–1

What is the accounting rate of return for a project that is estimated to yield total income of $390,000 over three years and costs $920,000?

M11–4 Calculating Payback Period   LO 11–2

A project has estimated annual net cash flows of $80,000 and is estimated to cost $340,000. What is the payback period?

M11–5 Calculating Accounting Rate of Return, Payback Period   LO 11–1, 11–2

Blue Marlin Company is considering the purchase of new equipment for its factory. It will cost $250,000 and have a $50,000 salvage value in five years. The annual net income from the equipment is expected to be $25,000, and depreciation is $40,000 per year. Calculate and evaluate Blue Marlin's annual rate of return and payback period for the equipment.

M11–6 Calculating Net Present Value   LO 11–3

Citrus Company is considering a project that has estimated annual net cash flows of $32,000 for six years and is estimated to cost $150,000. Citrus's cost of capital is 8 percent. Calculate the net present value of the project and whether it is acceptable to Citrus.

M11–7 Determining Internal Rate of Return   LO 11–4

Olive Company is considering a project that is estimated to cost $286,500 and provide annual net cash flows of $57,523 for the next five years. What is the internal rate of return for this project?

LO 11–3, 11–4   **M11–8 Calculating Net Present Value, Predicting Internal Rate of Return**

Vaughn Company has the following information about a potential capital investment:

Initial investment	$ 400,000
Annual cash inflow	$ 70,000
Expected life	10 years
Cost of capital	11%

1. Calculate and evaluate the net present value of this project.
2. Without any calculations, explain whether the internal rate of return on this project is more or less than 11 percent.

LO 11–6   **M11–9 Calculating Profitability Index**

Cullumber Corp. is considering three projects. Project A has a present value of $265,000 and an initial investment of $110,000. Project B has a present value of $400,000 and an initial investment of $220,000. Project C has a present value of $115,000 and an initial investment of $112,000. Using the profitability index, determine how Cullumber should prioritize these projects.

LO 11–S1   **M11–10 Computing Present Value of Complex Contract**

As a result of a slowdown in operations, Tradewind Stores is offering employees who have been terminated a severance package of $100,000 cash paid today; $50,000 to be paid in one year; and an annuity of $20,000 to be paid each year for 20 years. What is the present value of the package assuming an interest rate of 6 percent?

LO 11–S1   **M11–11 Computing Future Value of Complex Contract**

You plan to retire in 20 years. Calculate whether it is better for you to save $30,000 a year for the last 10 years before retirement or $15,000 for each of the next 20 years. Assume you are able to earn 8 percent interest on your investments.

LO 11–5   **M11–12 Using NPV to Evaluate Mutually Exclusive Projects**

Tremaine Company is considering two mutually exclusive long-term investment projects. Project ABC would require an investment of $240,000, have a useful life of 4 years, and annual cash flows of $78,000. Project XYZ would require an investment of $230,000, have a useful life of 5 years, and annual cash flows of $66,000. Using the NPV method and a 12 percent cost of capital, which project do you recommend Tremaine Company accept?

LO 11–6   **M11–13 Using Profitability Index to Prioritize Independent Projects**

An investment manager is currently evaluating three projects:

1. Project 1 requires an initial investment of $10,000, will provide future cash flows of $26,000, and the PV of the future cash flows is $17,000.
2. Project 2 requires an initial investment of $20,000, will provide future cash flows of $60,000, and the PV of the future cash flows is $31,000.
3. Project 3 requires an initial investment of $30,000, will provide future cash flows of $100,000, and the PV of the future cash flows is $56,700.

Rank the projects from most to least desirable using the profitability index.

EXERCISES

LO 11–1, 11–2   **E11–1 Calculating Accounting Rate of Return, Payback Period**

Harwell Printing Co. is considering the purchase of new electronic printing equipment. It would allow Harwell to increase its net income by $45,000 per year. Other information about this proposed project follows:

Initial investment	$300,000
Useful life	5 years
Salvage value	$100,000

Required:

Calculate and evaluate the following for Harwell:

1. Accounting rate of return.
2. Payback period.

E11–2 Calculating Accounting Rate of Return, Payback Period

LO 11–1, 11–2

Bartlett Car Wash Co. is considering the purchase of a new facility. It would allow Bartlett to increase its net income by $53,000 per year. Other information about this proposed project follows:

Initial investment	$510,000
Useful life	8 years
Salvage value	$ 50,000

Required:

Calculate and evaluate the following for Bartlett:

1. Accounting rate of return.
2. Payback period.

E11–3 Calculating Net Present Value, Internal Rate of Return

LO 11–3, 11–4

Merrill Corp. has the following information available about a potential capital investment:

Initial investment	$1,600,000
Annual net income	$ 250,000
Expected life	8 years
Salvage value	$ 350,000
Merrill's cost of capital	10%

Required:

1. Calculate the project's net present value.
2. Without making any calculations, determine whether the internal rate of return (IRR) is more or less than 10 percent.
3. Calculate the net present value using a 20 percent discount rate.
4. Estimate the project's IRR.

E11–4 Calculating Accounting Rate of Return, Payback Period, Net Present Value, Estimating Internal Rate of Return

LO 11–1, 11–2, 11–3, 11–4

Linda's Luxury Travel (LLT) is considering the purchase of two Hummer limousines. Various information about the proposed investment follows:

Initial investment (2 limos)	$600,000
Useful life	8 years
Salvage value	$100,000
Annual net income generated	$ 48,000
LLT's cost of capital	12%

Required:

Help LLT evaluate this project by calculating each of the following:

1. Accounting rate of return.
2. Payback period.
3. Net present value.
4. Based on your calculation of net present value, what would you estimate the project's internal rate of return to be?

LO 11–3, 11–4

E11–5 Analyzing Relationship between Net Present Value and Internal Rate of Return

Consider the relationship between a project's net present value (NPV), its internal rate of return (IRR), and a company's cost of capital. For each scenario that follows, indicate the relative value of the unknown. If cost of capital is unknown, indicate whether it would be higher or lower than the stated IRR. If NPV is unknown, indicate whether it would be higher or lower than zero. Project 1 is shown as an example.

	Net Present Value	Cost of Capital	Internal Rate of Return
Project 1	<0	13%	<13%
Project 2	<0	?	10
Project 3	?	12	14
Project 4	>0	8	?
Project 5	<0	9	?
Project 6	?	10	9

LO 11–S1

E11–6 Comparing Options Using Present Value Concepts

After hearing a knock at your front door, you are surprised to see the Prize Patrol from a large, well-known magazine subscription company. It has arrived with the good news that you are the big winner, having won $20 million. You have three options:

a. Receive $1 million per year for the next 20 years.
b. Have $8 million today.
c. Have $2 million today and receive $700,000 for each of the next 20 years.

Your financial adviser tells you that it is reasonable to expect to earn 12 percent on investments.

Required:

1. Calculate the present value of each option.

2. Determine which option you prefer and explain your reasoning.

LO 11–3, 11–5

E11–7 Deciding to Lease or Buy

Your friend Harold is trying to decide whether to buy or lease his next vehicle. He has gathered information about each option but is not sure how to compare the alternatives. Purchasing a new vehicle will cost $26,500, and Harold expects to spend about $500 per year in maintenance costs. He would keep the vehicle for five years and estimates that the salvage value will be $10,500. Alternatively, Harold could lease the same vehicle for five years at a cost of $3,480 per year, including maintenance. Assume a discount rate of 10 percent.

Required:

1. Calculate the net present value of Harold's options.

2. Advise Harold about which option he should choose and explain your reasoning.

LO 11–6

E11–8 Comparing Projects Using Profitability Index

Shaylee Corp has $2 million to invest in new projects. The company's managers have presented a number of possible options that the board must prioritize. Information about the projects follows:

	Project A	Project B	Project C	Project D
Initial investment	$415,000	$230,000	$ 720,000	$ 945,000
Present value of future cash flows	765,000	415,000	1,200,000	1,560,000

Required:

1. Is Shaylee able to invest in all of these projects simultaneously? Explain.

2. Calculate the profitability index for each project and prioritize them for Shaylee.

E11–9 Computing Growth in Savings Account: Single Amount

On January 1, 2018, you deposited $8,000 in a savings account. The account will earn 8 percent annual compound interest, which will be added to the fund balance at the end of each year.

Required (round to the nearest dollar):

1. What will be the balance in the savings account at the end of 10 years?
2. What is the total interest for the 10 years?
3. How much interest revenue did the fund earn in 2018 and in 2019?

E11–10 Computing Future Value of Annual Deposits

You are saving for a Porsche Carrera Cabriolet, which currently sells for nearly half a million dollars. Your plan is to deposit $15,000 at the end of each year for the next 10 years. You expect to earn 8 percent each year.

Required:

1. Determine how much you will have saved after 10 years.
2. Determine the amount saved if you were able to deposit $17,500 each year.
3. Determine the amount saved if you deposit $15,000 each year, but with 10 percent interest.

E11–11 Using NPV to Evaluate Mutually Exclusive Projects

Tulsa Company is considering investing in new bottling equipment and has two options: Option A has a lower initial cost but would require a significant expenditure to rebuild the machine after four years; Option B has higher maintenance costs, but also has a higher salvage value at the end of its useful life. Tulsa's cost of capital is 11 percent. The following estimates of the cash flows were developed by Tulsa's controller:

	Option A	Option B
Initial investment	$320,000	$454,000
Annual cash inflows	150,000	160,000
Annual cash outflows	70,000	75,000
Costs to rebuild	120,000	0
Salvage value	0	24,000
Estimated useful life	8 years	8 years

Required:

Using the NPV method, determine which option Tulsa should select.

E11–12 Ranking Capital Investment Projects Using Different Criteria

Jill Harrington, a manager at Jennings Company, is considering several potential capital investment projects. Data on these projects follow:

	Project X	Project Y	Project Z
Initial investment	$40,000	$20,000	$50,000
Annual cash inflows	25,000	10,000	25,400
PV of cash inflows	45,000	33,000	70,000

Required:

1. Compute the payback period for each project and rank order them based on this criterion.
2. Compute the NPV of each project and rank order them based on this criterion.
3. Compute the profitability index of each project and rank order them based on this criterion.
4. If Jennings has limited funds to invest, which ranking should Jill recommend?

LO 11–2, 11–3

E11–13 Using Payback Period and NPV to Evaluate a Project

Traditionally, Granite Company has accepted a proposal only if the payback period is less than 50 percent of the asset's useful life. Peggy Casteel is the new accounting manager. She suggested to management that capital budgeting decisions should not be made based solely on the payback period. Granite Company is currently considering purchasing a new machine for the factory that would cost $112,000 and would be sold after 8 years for $50,000. The new machine will generate annual cash flows of $30,000 in its first year of use, $24,000 in its second year of use, $20,000 in the third year, and $14,800 each year thereafter. The company's cost of capital is 12 percent.

Required:

1. Would Granite Company accept this project based solely on the payback period? Why or why not?
2. Would Granite Company accept this project if the NPV method is used to evaluate the machine? Why or why not?
3. What is the likely cause of the difference between your answers for requirement 1 and requirement 2? What type of advice would you provide to management regarding this difference?
4. Without making any computations, if the company's cost of capital was 10 percent, how would this impact the NPV analysis?

LO 11–1, 11–2, 11–3

E11–14 Calculating ARR, Payback Period and NPV

Robertson Resorts is considering whether to expand their Pagosa Springs Lodge. The expansion will create 24 additional rooms for rent. The following estimates are available:

Cost of expansion	$5,000,000
Discount rate	8%
Useful life	20
Annual rental income	$1,250,000
Annual operating expenses	$ 800,000

Robertson uses straight-line depreciation and the lodge expansion will have a residual value $2,000,000.

Required:

1. Calculate the annual net operating income from the expansion.
2. Calculate the annual net cash inflow from the expansion.
3. Calculate the ARR.
4. Calculate the payback period.
5. Calculate the NPV.

LO 11–1, 11–2, 11–3, 11–4, 11–6

E11–15 Comparing Capital Budgeting Methods

The following table contains information about four potential investment projects that Castle Corporation is considering.

Project	Required Investment	Project Life	Acctg ROR	Payback Period	NPV	Profitability Index
A	$ 500,000	5	9%	3.2	$ 62,250	1.13
B	$ 750,000	4	16%	2.8	$ 63,562	1.08
C	$1,000,000	4	12.5%	2.5	$214,920	1.21
D	$1,500,000	5	7.2%	3.1	$244,258	1.16

Required:

1. Rank the four projects in order of preference by using:
   a. Accounting rate of return.
   b. Payback period.
   c. Net present value.
   d. Project profitability index.
2. Which method is the best for evaluating the investments? Why?

GROUP A PROBLEMS

PA11-1 Calculating Accounting Rate of Return, Payback Period, Net Present Value, Estimating Internal Rate of Return

LO 11-1, 11-2, 11-3, 11-4

Balloons By Sunset (BBS) is considering the purchase of two new hot air balloons so that it can expand its desert sunset tours. Various information about the proposed investment follows:

Initial investment (for two hot air balloons)	$ 420,000
Useful life	10 years
Salvage value	$ 50,000
Annual net income generated	$ 37,800
BBS's cost of capital	11%

Required:

Help BBS evaluate this project by calculating each of the following:

1. Accounting rate of return.
2. Payback period.
3. Net present value (NPV).
4. Recalculate the NPV assuming BBS's cost of capital is 15 percent.
5. Based on your calculation of NPV, what would you estimate the project's internal rate of return to be?

PA11-2 Making Automation Decision

LO 11-1, 11-2, 11-3, 11-5

Beacon Company is considering automating its production facility. The initial investment in automation would be $15 million, and the equipment has a useful life of 10 years with a residual value of $500,000. The company will use straight-line depreciation. Beacon could expect a production increase of 40,000 units per year and a reduction of 20 percent in the labor cost per unit.

	Current (no automation)		Proposed (automation)	
Production and sales volume	80,000 units		120,000 units	
	Per Unit	**Total**	**Per Unit**	**Total**
Sales revenue	$90	$?	$90	$?
Variable costs				
Direct materials	$18		$18	
Direct labor	25		?	
Variable manufacturing overhead	10		10	
Total variable manufacturing costs	53		?	
Contribution margin	$37	?	$42	?
Fixed manufacturing costs		1,250,000		2,350,000
Net operating income		?		?

Required:

1. Complete the preceding table showing the totals and summarize the difference in the alternatives.
2. Determine the project's accounting rate of return.
3. Determine the project's payback period.
4. Using a discount rate of 15 percent, calculate the net present value (NPV) of the proposed investment.
5. Recalculate the NPV using a 10 percent discount rate.
6. Would you advise Beacon to invest in the automation?

PA11-3 Comparing, Prioritizing Multiple Projects

LO 11-1, 11-2, 11-3, 11-6

Hearne Company has a number of potential capital investments. Because these projects vary in nature, initial investment, and time horizon, management is finding it difficult to compare them.

Project 1: Retooling Manufacturing Facility

This project would require an initial investment of $4,850,000. It would generate $865,000 in additional net cash flow each year. The new machinery has a useful life of eight years and a salvage value of $1,000,000.

Project 2: Purchase Patent for New Product

The patent would cost $3,400,000, which would be fully amortized over five years. Production of this product would generate $425,000 additional annual net income for Hearne.

Project 3: Purchase a New Fleet of Delivery Trucks

Hearne could purchase 25 new delivery trucks at a cost of $115,000 each. The fleet would have a useful life of 10 years, and each truck would have a salvage value of $5,000. Purchasing the fleet would allow Hearne to expand its customer territory resulting in $200,000 of additional net income per year.

Required:

1. Determine each project's accounting rate of return.
2. Determine each project's payback period.
3. Using a discount rate of 10 percent, calculate the net present value of each project.
4. Determine the profitability index of each project and prioritize the projects for Hearne.

LO 11–1, 11–2, 11–3, 11–4   **PA11–4 Calculating Accounting Rate of Return, Payback Period, Net Present Value, Estimating Internal Rate of Return**

Falcon Crest Aces (FCA), Inc., is considering the purchase of a small plane to use in its wing-walking demonstrations and aerial tour business. Various information about the proposed investment follows:

Initial investment	$ 110,000
Useful life	10 years
Salvage value	$ 10,000
Annual net income generated	$ 4,200
FCA's cost of capital	10%

Required:

Help FCA evaluate this project by calculating each of the following:

1. Accounting rate of return.
2. Payback period.
3. Net present value (NPV).
4. Recalculate FCA's NPV assuming the cost of capital is 6 percent.
5. Based on your calculations of NPV, what would you estimate the project's internal rate of return to be?

LO 11–S1   **PA11–5 Comparing Options Using Present Value Concepts**

After completing a long and successful career as senior vice president for a large bank, you are preparing for retirement. After visiting the human resources office, you have found that you have several retirement options to choose from:

a. An immediate cash payment of $1 million.
b. Payment of $92,000 per year for life.
c. Payment of $82,000 per year for 10 years and then $95,000 per year for life (this option is intended to give you some protection against inflation).

You believe you can earn 8 percent on your investments and your remaining life expectancy is 20 years.

Required:

1. Calculate the present value of each option.
2. Explain which option you prefer and why.

PA11–6 Evaluating Sustainability Projects

Citco Company is considering investing up to $500,000 in a sustainability-enhancing project. Its managers have narrowed their choices to three potential projects.

- Project A would redesign the production process to recycle raw materials waste back into the production cycle, saving on direct materials costs and reducing the amount of waste sent to the landfill.

- Project B would remodel an office building, utilizing solar panels and natural materials to create a more energy-efficient and healthy work environment.

- Project C would build a new training center in an underserved community, providing jobs and economic security for the local community.

The following table summarizes the costs and benefits of these three hypothetical projects:

	Project A (Redesign production process)	Project B (Remodel office building)	Project C (New training facility)
Required Investment	$(500,000)	$(420,000)	$(320,000)
Annual Cost Savings	$ 100,000	60,000	80,000
Project Life	8 years	10 years	6 years
Salvage Value	$ 80,000	$ 75,000	$ 30,000
Payback Period			
NPV			
Profitability Index			
Internal Rate of Return			

Required:

1. Assuming the cost of capital is 12 percent, complete the preceeding table by computing the payback period, NPV, profitability index, and internal rate of return.
2. Based strictly on the economic analysis, in which project should they invest?
3. What other factors should managers consider before reaching a final decision?
4. Repeat requirement 1 using a cost of capital of 14 percent. Which of the capital budgeting indicators changed and which remained the same? Why?

GROUP B PROBLEMS

PB11–1 Calculating Accounting Rate of Return, Payback Period, Net Present Value, Estimating Internal Rate of Return

The Best Cab Company (TBCC) is considering the purchase of four new taxicabs. Various information about the proposed investment follows:

Initial investment (for 4 vehicles)	$200,000
Useful life	5 years
Salvage value	$ 12,000
Annual net income generated	$ 20,000
TBCC's cost of capital	9%

Required:

Help TBCC evaluate this project by calculating each of the following:

1. Accounting rate of return.
2. Payback period.
3. Net present value.
4. Recalculate the NPV assuming the cost of capital is 15 percent.
5. Based on your calculations of NPV, what would you estimate the project's internal rate of return to be?

LO 11–1, 11–2, 11–3, 11–5 **PB11–2 Making Automation Decision**

Gondola Company is considering automating its production facility. The initial investment in automation would be $5,800,000 and the equipment has a useful life of eight years with a residual value of $400,000. The company will use straight-line depreciation. Gondola could expect a production increase of 20,000 units per year and a reduction of 40 percent in the labor cost per unit.

	Current (no automation)		Proposed (automation)	
Production and sales volume	60,000 units		80,000 units	
	Per Unit	**Total**	**Per Unit**	**Total**
Sales revenue	$70	$?	$70	$?
Variable costs				
Direct materials	$15		$15	
Direct labor	20		?	
Variable manufacturing overhead	7		7	
Total variable manufacturing costs	42		?	
Contribution margin	$28	?	$36	?
Fixed manufacturing costs		800,000		1,612,500
Net operating income		?		?

Required:

1. Complete the preceding table showing the totals and summarize the difference in the alternatives.
2. Determine the project's accounting rate of return.
3. Determine the project's payback period.
4. Using a discount rate of 15 percent, calculate the NPV of the proposed investment.
5. Recalculate the NPV using a discount rate of 10 percent.
6. Would you advise Gondola to invest in the automation?

LO 11–1, 11–2, 11–3, 11–6 **PB11–3 Comparing, Prioritizing Multiple Projects**

Harmony Company has a number of potential capital investments. Because these projects vary in nature, initial investment, and time horizon, Harmony's management is finding it difficult to compare them.

Project 1: Retooling Manufacturing Facility

This project would require an initial investment of $2,700,000. It would generate $975,000 in additional cash flow each year. The new machinery has a useful life of seven years and a salvage value of $600,000.

Project 2: Purchase Patent for New Product

The patent would cost $8,200,000, which would be fully amortized over 10 years. Production of this product would generate $1,650,000 additional annual net income for Harmony.

Project 3: Purchase a New Fleet of Delivery Vans

Harmony could purchase 10 new delivery vans at a cost of $25,000 each. The fleet would have a useful life of 10 years, and each van would have a salvage value of $2,500. Purchasing the fleet would allow Harmony to expand its delivery area resulting in $30,000 of additional net income per year.

Required:

1. Determine each project's accounting rate of return and compare the projects.
2. Determine each project's payback period and compare the projects.
3. Using a discount rate of 10 percent, calculate the net present value of each project.
4. Determine the profitability index of each project and prioritize the projects for Harmony.

PB11–4 Calculating Accounting Rate of Return, Payback Period, Net Present Value, Estimating Internal Rate of Return

LO 11–1, 11–2, 11–3, 11–4

Montego Production Co. is considering an investment in new machinery for its factory. Various information about the proposed investment follows:

Initial investment	$860,000
Useful life	6 years
Salvage value	$ 20,000
Annual net income generated	$ 66,000
Montego's cost of capital	11%

Required:

Help Montego evaluate this project by calculating each of the following:

1. Accounting rate of return.
2. Payback period.
3. Net present value.
4. Recalculate Montego's NPV assuming its cost of capital is 12 percent.
5. Based on your calculations of NPV, what would you estimate the project's internal rate of return to be?

PB11–5 Comparing Options Using Present Value Concepts

LO 11–S1

After incurring a serious injury caused by a manufacturing defect, your friend has sued the manufacturer for damages. The manufacturer made your friend three offers to settle the lawsuit:

a. Receive an immediate cash payment of $100,000.
b. Receive $10,000 per year for life.
c. Receive $7,000 per year for 10 years and then $10,000 per year for life (this option is intended to compensate your friend for increased aggravation of the injury over time).

Your friend can earn 8 percent interest and your friend's remaining life expectancy is 20 years.

Required:

1. Calculate the present value of each option.
2. Explain which option your friend should prefer and why.

PB11–6 Evaluating Sustainability Projects

LO 11–2, 11–3, 11–4, 11–6

Citco Company is considering investing up to $500,000 in a sustainability-enhancing project. Its managers have narrowed their choices to three potential projects.

- Project A would redesign the production process to recycle raw materials waste back into the production cycle, saving on direct materials costs and reducing the amount of waste sent to the landfill.

- Project B would remodel an office building, utilizing solar panels and natural materials to create a more energy-efficient and healthy work environment.

- Project C would build a new training center in an underserved community, providing jobs and economic security for the local community.

The following table summarizes the costs and benefits of these three hypothetical projects:

	Project A (Redesign production process)	Project B (Remodel office building)	Project C (New training facility)
Required Investment	$(450,000)	$(300,000)	$(400,000)
Annual Cost Savings	$ 100,000	60,000	80,000
Project Life	8 years	10 years	6 years
Salvage Value	$ 40,000	$ 75,000	$ 80,000
Payback Period			
NPV			
Profitability Index			
Internal Rate of Return			

Required:

1. Assuming the cost of capital is 14 percent, complete the preceeding table by computing the payback period, NPV, profitability index, and internal rate of return.
2. Based strictly on the economic analysis, in which project should they invest?
3. What other factors should managers consider before reaching a final decision?
4. Repeat requirements 1 and 2 using a cost of capital of 12 percent. Which of the capital budgeting indicators changes and which remains the same? Why?

SKILLS DEVELOPMENT CASES

S11–1   Evaluating the Purchase of Alternative Fuel Vehicles

In this activity, you will be evaluating whether to purchase a 2018 Chevrolet Bolt EV (electric vehicle) LT or a 2018 Ford Fusion S Hybrid. Assume you plan on keeping your car for 10 years and at the end of 10 years, the resale value for the Bolt and Fusion will be $10,000 and $2,000 respectively.

Required:

1. Go to Kelley Blue Book's website at https://www.kbb.com and research the price of a 2018 Chevrolet Bolt EV LT and a 2018 Ford Fusion S Hybrid.
2. Go to the Department of Energy's fuel economy website at https://www.fueleconomy.gov/feg/Find.do?action=sbsSelect and do a comparison of the 2018 Chevrolet Bolt EV and 2018 Ford Fusion Hybrid.
   a. What is the estimated fuel economy for the Bolt in MPGe (miles per gallon of gasoline equivalent) and the Fusion in MPG (miles per gallon)?
   b. How far can each car drive on a single charge or full tank?
   c. What is the estimated annual fuel cost of each vehicle based on annual mileage of 15,000 miles?
3. Estimate the number of miles you drive your car each year. Update the annual fuel cost based on your estimated mileage. How much would you expect to save each year if you purchase the Bolt instead of the Fusion?
4. Calculate the total cost of ownership (NPV) of the Bolt based on the current market price, the estimated annual fuel costs for 10 years and the estimated resale value at the end of 10 years. Assume a required rate of return of 10 percent.
5. Calculate the total cost of ownership (NPV) of the Fusion based on the current market price, the estimated annual fuel costs for 10 years and the estimated resale value at the end of 10 years. Assume a required rate of return of 10 percent.
6. Compute the difference in NPV between the Bolt and the Fusion. Which vehicle has a lower total cost of ownership (NPV)?
7. From a purely economic perspective, which car should you purchase?
8. What qualitative factors might affect your decision about which model to purchase?
9. How would the economic analysis change if the following estimates or assumptions were changed? Which vehicle would benefit the most from these changing assumptions?
   a. Required rate of return of 4 percent instead of 10 percent.
   b. Estimated annual mileage doubles.
   c. Estimated salvage value of the Chevy Bolt increases by $6,000.

12

Statement of Cash Flows

CHAPTER TWELVE

YOUR LEARNING OBJECTIVES

LO 12–1 Identify cash flows arising from operating, investing, and financing activities.

LO 12–2 Report cash flows from operating activities, using the indirect method.

LO 12–3 Report cash flows from investing activities.

LO 12–4 Report cash flows from financing activities.

LO 12–5 Interpret cash flows from operating, investing, and financing activities.

LO 12–6 Report and interpret cash flows from operating activities, using the direct method.

LO 12–S1 Report cash flows from PPE disposals using the indirect method.

LO 12–S2 Use the T-account approach for preparing an indirect method statement of cash flows.

©Leonard Zhukovsky/Shutterstock

FOCUS COMPANY: UNDER ARMOUR, INC.

Have you ever studied your bank statements to see how much money you bring in and pay out during a typical month? You don't have to be a financial genius to know that if you spend more than you earn, your savings will quickly disappear, and you will need to get a loan or some other source of financing to see you through.

Most businesses face the same issues as you. During the first nine months of 2016, for example, Under Armour, Inc., paid more cash for its day-to-day operating activities than it brought in from selling its frictionless sportswear. But it was able to generate much-needed financing by borrowing cash from lenders. Also, the company rallied in the fourth quarter and generated an inflow of more than $300 million in operating cash flows. This turnaround in cash flows arose largely as a result of managers doing a better job of collecting from customers on account.

Just like Under Armour's managers, the company's investors and creditors also monitor cash inflows and outflows. Investors want to know whether Under Armour is likely to pay dividends, and creditors want to know whether Under Armour is likely to pay them the amounts they are owed. They find information for making such predictions in the statement of cash flows. Similar to your personal bank statement, the statement of cash flows reports changes in a company's cash situation.

Understand the business	Study the accounting methods	Evaluate the results	Supplement 12A	Supplement 12B
• Business activities and cash flows • Classifying cash flows	• Relationship to other financial statements • Preparing the statement of cash flows	• Evaluating cash flows • Operating cash flows revisited (direct method)	• Reporting disposals of property, plant, and equipment (indirect method)	• T-account approach (indirect method)

Understand the Business

BUSINESS ACTIVITIES AND CASH FLOWS

Accountants measure profitability based on net income, or the difference between revenue and expenses. Under the accrual method of accounting, revenue is always recognized when earned, and expenses are matched against the revenue they help create, regardless of when cash is actually received or paid. Although net income is an extremely useful measure of a company's profitability, managers are often more concerned about cash flow than accounting net income. Even a profitable business can fail if managers do not have enough cash on hand to pay the bills. If a business is not generating sufficient cash from operations, managers may need to generate funds from other sources, such as selling off assets, borrowing money, or issuing stock.

Despite its importance, net income is not what companies use when they pay wages, dividends, or loans. These activities require cash, so financial statement users need information about the company's cash and changes in its cash. Neither the balance sheet nor the income statement provides this information. The balance sheet shows a company's cash balance at a point in time, but it doesn't explain the activities that caused changes in its cash. Cash may have been generated by the company's day-to-day operations, by the sale of the company's buildings, or by the negotiation of new loans. The income statement doesn't explain changes in cash because it focuses on just the operating results of the business, excluding cash that is received or paid when taking out or paying down loans, issuing or acquiring the company's own stock, and selling or investing in long-lived assets. Also, the timing of cash receipts and payments may differ from the accrual-based income statement, which reports revenues when goods or services are provided and expenses when they are incurred. Under Armour, for example, reported positive net income in every quarter in 2016, yet its operating cash flows were negative in three of its four quarterly reports. Such differences between net income and cash flows are the reason GAAP requires every company to report a statement of cash flows.

The statement of cash flows shows the major types of business activity that caused a company's cash to increase or decrease during the accounting period. For purposes of this statement, cash is defined to include cash and cash equivalents. Cash equivalents are short-term, highly liquid investments purchased within three months of maturity. They are considered equivalent to cash because they are both (1) readily convertible to known amounts of cash and (2) so near to maturity their value is unlikely to change.

SPOTLIGHT ON Ethics

Cash Isn't Estimated

Critics of accrual-based net income claim it can be manipulated because it relies on many estimates (of bad debts, inventory market values, assets' useful lives), but cash flows do not involve estimates so they are not easily manipulated. A cash balance changes only when cash has been received or paid. One particularly dramatic illustration of the subjectivity of net income, but not cash, involved the bankruptcy of a department store chain operated by the W. T. Grant Company. Through biased estimates, the company reported net income for nine consecutive years but then shocked everyone when it declared bankruptcy and shut down after the following year. At the time, a statement of cash flows wasn't required. Had it been required, the company would have reported negative operating cash flows in seven of the ten years.

Source: James A. Largay III and Clyde P. Stickney, "Cash Flows, Ratio Analysis and the W. T. Grant Company Bankruptcy," *Financial Analysts Journal* 36, no. 4: 51–54, July/August 1980.

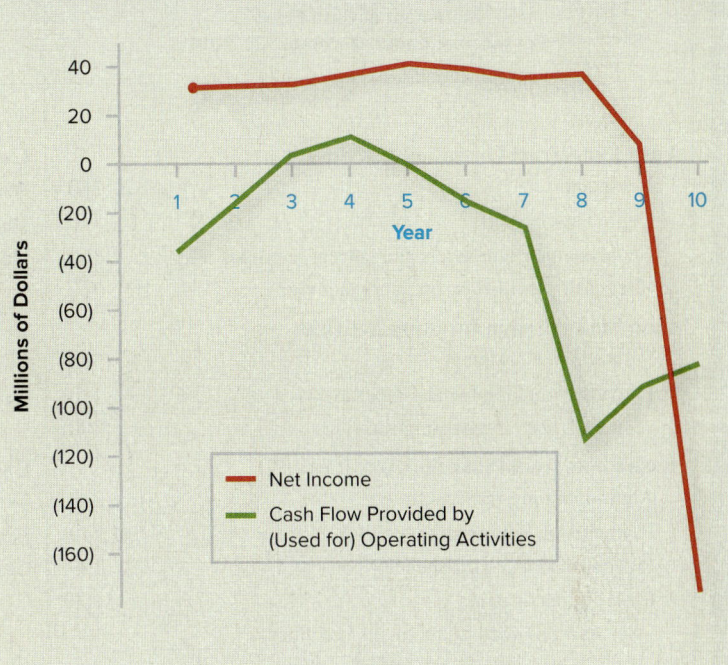

CLASSIFYING CASH FLOWS

The statement of cash flows requires all cash inflows and outflows to be classified as relating to the company's operating, investing, or financing activities. This classification of cash flows is useful because most companies experience different cash flow patterns as they develop and mature. When businesses are just getting started, the cash needed to operate the business generally comes from **financing** activities, such as an owner who puts his/her own money into the business (equity) or who borrows money from the bank. This start-up cash is used to **invest** in assets, such as fixtures and equipment and to pay for **operating** expenses, such as utilities and payroll. For an established business, operating activities often are the focus. Financial statement users are interested in a company's ability to generate operating cash flows that will allow it to continue investing in additional assets and repay the financing it originally obtained. Creditors and investors will tolerate poor operating cash flows for only so long before they stop lending to or investing in the company. For any company to survive in the long run, the amount of cash generated through daily operating activities has to exceed the amount spent on them.

A condensed (and somewhat simplified) version of Under Armour's statement of cash flows is presented in Exhibit 12–1. Don't worry about the details in the three cash flow categories yet. For now, focus on the categories' totals. Notice that each category can result in net cash inflows (represented by a positive number) or net cash outflows (represented by a negative number by using parentheses). The sum of these three categories ($310 − $380 + $190 = $120) represents the overall change in cash on the balance sheet between the beginning and end of the period ($120 + $130 = $250).

Under Armour's cash flows in Exhibit 12–1 suggest the company is financially healthy. The company generated $310 million cash from its day-to-day operations. This money, combined with a little additional cash from financing activities, allowed Under Armour to invest $380 million in additional long-term assets. To learn the specific causes of these cash flows, you would consider the details of each category, as we will do now.

EXHIBIT 12–1	Under Armour's Condensed Statement of Cash Flows

UNDER ARMOUR, INC.
Statement of Cash Flows
For the Year Ended December 31, 2016

		Explanation
(in millions)		
Cash Flows from Operating Activities		**Cash flows related to day-to-day activities**
Net income	$ 260	Assume net income (NI) generates cash inflow
Depreciation	110	Depreciation decreased NI but didn't decrease cash
Changes in current assets and current liabilities	(60)	Differences in the timing of net income and cash flows
Net cash provided by operating activities	310	Indicates overall cash impact of operating activities
Cash Flows Used in Investing Activities		**Cash flows related to long-term assets**
Purchase of equipment	(370)	Cash was used to purchase equipment
Purchase of intangible and other assets	(10)	Cash was used to purchase intangibles
Net cash used in investing activities	(380)	Indicates overall cash impact of investing activities
Cash Flows from Financing Activities		**Cash flows from transactions with lenders, investors**
Additional long-term notes	1,330	Cash received from borrowing
Payments on long-term notes	(1,270)	Cash used to repay amounts previously borrowed
Proceeds from stock issuance	190	Cash received from issuing stock
Cash dividends paid	(60)	Cash used to pay dividends
Net cash provided by financing activities	190	Indicates overall cash impact of financing activities
Net Change in Cash and Cash Equivalents	**120**	$310 + $(380) + $190 = $120
Cash and cash equivalents, beginning of year	130	Cash balance at beginning of the period
Cash and cash equivalents, end of year	$ 250	Cash balance at end of the period (**on balance sheet**)

Operating Activities

Cash flows from operating activities (or **cash flows from operations**) are the cash inflows and outflows related directly to the revenues and expenses reported on the income statement. Operating activities involve day-to-day business activities with customers, suppliers, employees, landlords, and others. Typical cash flows from operating activities include the following:

Inflows	Outflows
Cash provided by	**Cash used for**
Collecting from customers	Purchasing services (electricity, etc.) and goods for resale
Receiving dividends	Paying salaries and wages
Receiving interest	Paying income taxes
	Paying interest

The difference between these cash inflows and outflows is reported on the statement of cash flows as a subtotal, Net Cash Provided by (Used for) Operating Activities.

Investing Activities

Cash flows from investing activities are the cash inflows and outflows related to the purchase and disposal of investments and long-lived assets. Typical cash flows from investing activities include the following:

Inflows	Outflows
Cash provided by	**Cash used for**
Sale or disposal of equipment	Purchase of equipment
Sale or maturity of investments in securities	Purchase of investments in securities

The difference between these cash inflows and outflows is reported on the statement of cash flows as a subtotal, Net Cash Provided by (Used in) Investing Activities.

Financing Activities

Cash flows from financing activities include exchanges of cash with stockholders and cash exchanges with lenders (for principal on loans). Common cash flows from financing activities include the following:

Inflows	Outflows
Cash provided by	**Cash used for**
Borrowing from lenders through formal debt contracts	Repaying principal to lenders
Issuing stock to owners	Repurchasing stock from owners
	Paying cash dividends to owners

The difference between these cash inflows and outflows is reported on the statement of cash flows as a subtotal, Net Cash Provided by (Used in) Financing Activities.

One way to classify cash flows into operating, investing, and financing categories is to think about the balance sheet accounts to which the cash flows relate. **Although exceptions exist, a general rule is that operating cash flows cause changes in current assets and current liabilities, investing cash flows affect noncurrent assets, and financing cash flows affect noncurrent liabilities or stockholders' equity accounts.**[1] Exhibit 12–2 shows how this general rule relates the three sections of the statement of cash flows (SCF) to each of the main sections of a classified balance sheet.

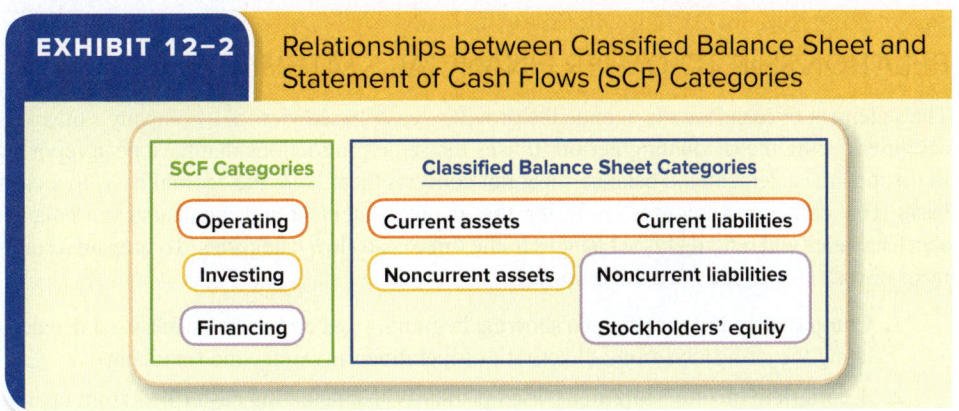

EXHIBIT 12–2 Relationships between Classified Balance Sheet and Statement of Cash Flows (SCF) Categories

SCF Categories	Classified Balance Sheet Categories	
Operating	Current assets	Current liabilities
Investing	Noncurrent assets	Noncurrent liabilities
Financing		Stockholders' equity

💡 **How's it going?**   Self-Study Practice

Brunswick Corporation produces the Life Fitness line of gym equipment. A listing of some of its cash flows follows. Indicate whether each item is disclosed in the operating activities (O), investing activities (I), or financing activities (F) section of the statement of cash flows.

☐ *a.* Stock issued to stockholders.   ☐ *d.* Purchase of equipment.

☐ *b.* Collections from customers.   ☐ *e.* Purchase of investment securities.

☐ *c.* Interest paid on debt.   ☐ *f.* Cash dividends paid.

After you have finished, check your answers against the solutions in the margin.

---

[1] Intermediate accounting courses discuss in detail exceptions to this general rule. Exceptions include investing activities that affect current assets (for example, short-term investments) and financing activities that affect current liabilities (for example, dividends payable and short-term notes payable).

SPOTLIGHT ON The World

Classification Choices under IFRS

To create consistency across companies, GAAP restricts interest and dividend classifications to a single category. IFRS, on the other hand, allows managers to choose between categories, as follows:

	COMPANY PAYS		COMPANY RECEIVES	
	Dividends	Interest	Dividends	Interest
GAAP	F	O	O	O
IFRS	O, F	O, F	O, I	O, I

GAAP classifies dividends paid as financing (F) because they are transactions with stockholders. IFRS allows dividends paid to also be classified as operating (O) to assist users in determining the company's ability to pay dividends out of operating cash flows. GAAP requires the other three items to be classified as operating because they enter into the determination of net income. IFRS allows interest paid to also be classified as financing because it is a cost of obtaining financial resources. IFRS allows interest and dividends received to also be classified as investing (I) because they are returns on investments.

Study the Accounting Methods

RELATIONSHIP TO OTHER FINANCIAL STATEMENTS

The statement of cash flows is intended to provide a cash-based view of a company's business activities during the accounting period. It uses the same transactions that have been reported in the income statement and balance sheet but converts them from the accrual basis to a cash basis. This conversion involves analyzing the income statement and the changes in balance sheet accounts and relating these changes to the three cash flow categories. To prepare a statement of cash flows, you need the following:

1. **Comparative balance sheets**, showing beginning and ending balances, used in calculating the cash flows from all activities (operating, investing, and financing).

2. **A complete income statement**, used primarily in calculating cash flows from operating activities.

3. **Additional data** concerning selected accounts that increase and decrease as a result of investing and/or financing activities.

The approach to preparing the cash flow statement focuses on changes in the balance sheet accounts. It relies on a simple rearrangement of the balance sheet equation:

$$\text{Assets} = \text{Liabilities} + \text{Stockholders' Equity}$$

First, assets can be split into cash and all other assets, which we'll call **noncash assets:**

$$\text{Cash} + \text{Noncash Assets} = \text{Liabilities} + \text{Stockholders' Equity}$$

If we move the noncash assets to the right side of the equation, we get

$$\text{Cash} = \text{Liabilities} + \text{Stockholders' Equity} - \text{Noncash Assets}$$

Given this relationship, the **changes** in cash between the beginning and end of the period must equal the **changes** in the amounts on the right side of the equation between the beginning and end of the period:

> Change in Cash = Change in (Liabilities + Stockholders' Equity − Noncash Assets)

This equation says **changes in cash must be accompanied by and can be accounted for by the changes in liabilities, stockholders' equity, and noncash assets**.

PREPARING THE STATEMENT OF CASH FLOWS

Based on the idea that the change in cash equals the sum of the changes in all other balance sheet accounts, we use the following steps to prepare the statement of cash flows:

1. **Determine the change in each balance sheet account**. From this year's ending balance, subtract this year's beginning balance (i.e., last year's ending balance).

2. **Identify the cash flow category or categories to which each account relates**. Use Exhibit 12–2 as a guide, but be aware that some accounts may include two categories of cash flows. Retained Earnings, for example, can include both financing cash flows (paying dividends) and operating cash flows (generating net income). Similarly, Accumulated Depreciation can be affected by operating activities (depreciation for using equipment in daily operations) as well as investing activities (disposing of equipment).

3. **Create schedules that summarize operating, investing, and financing cash flows**. Let's start with operating cash flows.

Direct and Indirect Reporting of Operating Cash Flows

Two alternative methods may be used when presenting the operating activities section of the statement of cash flows:

1. The **direct method** reports the total cash inflow or outflow from each main type of transaction (that is, transactions with customers, suppliers, employees, etc.). The difference between these cash inflows and outflows equals the Net Cash Provided by (Used in) Operating Activities.

2. The **indirect method** starts with net income from the income statement and adjusts it by eliminating the effects of items that do not involve cash (for example, depreciation) and including items that do have cash effects. Adjusting net income for these items yields the Net Cash Provided by (Used in) Operating Activities.

Direct Method		Indirect Method	
Cash collected from customers	$4,730	Net income	$260
Cash paid to suppliers of inventory	(2,520)	Depreciation	110
Cash paid to employees and suppliers of services	(1,740)		
Cash paid for interest	(30)	Changes in current assets and current liabilities	(60)
Cash paid for income tax	(130)		
Net cash provided by (used in) operating activities	$ 310	Net cash provided by (used in) operating activities	$310

The point to remember about the direct and indirect methods is that they are simply different ways to arrive at the same number. **Net cash flows provided by (used in) operating activities is always the same under the direct and indirect methods**. Also, the choice between the two methods affects only the operating activities section of the statement of cash flows, not the investing and financing sections.

We focus on the indirect method in the following section because it is currently used by about 99 percent of large companies in the United States. The direct method is presented in the last section of this chapter.

Determining Operating Cash Flows Using the Indirect Method

When using the indirect method, operating cash flows are calculated as follows. We explain each of these items below and then we demonstrate how to use Under Armour's financial information to create such a schedule.

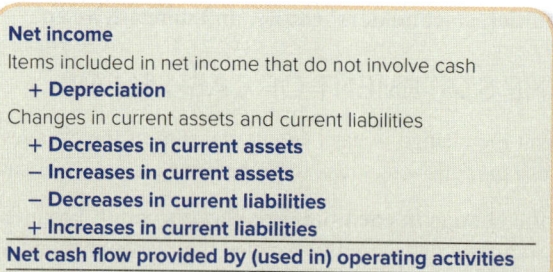

Net income
Items included in net income that do not involve cash
  + Depreciation
Changes in current assets and current liabilities
  + Decreases in current assets
  − Increases in current assets
  − Decreases in current liabilities
  + Increases in current liabilities
Net cash flow provided by (used in) operating activities

Net income. When determining operating cash flows using the indirect method, start with net income as reported on the last line of the company's income statement. By starting with net income, it's as if we are assuming all revenues resulted in cash inflows and all expenses resulted in cash outflows. But we know this is not true, so we add and subtract various amounts to convert that net income number into cash flows from operating activities. The additions and subtractions are explained below.

+ Depreciation. When initially recording depreciation in the accounting system, we increase Depreciation Expense (with a debit) and increase Accumulated Depreciation (with a credit). Notice that this entry for depreciation does not involve cash. To **eliminate** the effect of having deducted Depreciation Expense from Net Income in the income statement, we add it back in the statement of cash flows.

+ Decreases in current assets. Adding decreases in current assets serves two purposes. First, it **eliminates** the effects of some transactions that decreased net income but did not affect cash in the current period. For example, when Supplies are used, net income decreases but cash is not affected. To eliminate these noncash effects from our cash flow computations, we must add back decreases in Supplies and other current assets. Second, adding decreases in current assets allows us to **include** the cash effects of other transactions that did not affect net income in the current period but did increase cash. For example, Cash increases when Accounts Receivable are collected. These cash inflows are captured by adding the amount by which this current asset had decreased.

− Increases in current assets. Subtracting increases in current assets similarly serves two purposes. First, it **eliminates** the effects of transactions that increased net income but did not affect cash in the current period. For example, net income increases when a company provides services on account, but cash is not affected. We eliminate these noncash effects by subtracting increases in current assets. Second, subtracting increases in current assets allows us to **include** the cash effects of other transactions that did not affect net income in the current period but did decrease cash. For example, Cash decreases when a company prepays its insurance or rent, but net income isn't affected until these assets are used up. The cash outflows can be captured by subtracting the increase in these current assets.

− Decreases in current liabilities. Subtracting decreases in current liabilities serves two purposes. First, it **eliminates** the effects of transactions that increased net income but did not affect cash. For example, a company decreases Deferred Revenue and increases net income in the current period it fulfills prior obligations to provide services, but cash is not affected. To eliminate these noncash effects, we subtract decreases in current liabilities. Second, subtracting decreases in current liabilities allows us to **include** the cash effects of other transactions that did not affect net income in the current period but

EXHIBIT 12–3	Information for Preparing a Statement of Cash Flows

UNDER ARMOUR, INC.
Balance Sheet*

(in millions)	December 31, 2016	December 31, 2015		Step 1 Change	Step 2 Related Cash Flow Section
Assets					
Current Assets:					
Cash and Cash Equivalents	$ 250	$ 130		+120	Cash
Accounts Receivable	620	520		+100	O
Inventory	920	780		+140	O
Prepaid Expenses	170	150		+20	O
Total Current Assets	1,960	1,580			
Equipment	1,200	830		+370	I (see notes 1 and 3 below)
Accumulated Depreciation—Equipment	(400)	(290)		−110	O (see notes 2 and 3 below)
Intangible and Other Assets	890	880		+10	I (see notes 1 and 3 below)
Total Assets	$3,650	$3,000			
Liabilities and Stockholders' Equity					
Current Liabilities:					
Accounts Payable	$ 410	$ 200		+210	O
Accrued Liabilities	270	280		−10	O
Total Current Liabilities	680	480			
Notes Payable (long-term)	940	880		+60	F (see note 4 below)
Total Liabilities	1,620	1,360			
Stockholders' Equity:					
Common Stock	830	640		+190	F (see note 5 below)
Retained Earnings	1,200	1,000		+200	O, F (see note 6 below)
Total Stockholders' Equity	2,030	1,640			
Total Liabilities and Stockholders' Equity	$3,650	$3,000			

UNDER ARMOUR, INC.
Income Statement*
For the Year Ended December 31, 2016

(in millions)	
Net Sales	$4,830
Cost of Goods Sold	2,590
Gross Profit	2,240
Operating Expenses:	
Selling, General, and Administrative Expenses	1,710
Depreciation Expense	110
Total Operating Expenses	1,820
Income from Operations	420
Interest Expense	30
Net Income before Income Tax Expense	390
Income Tax Expense	130
Net Income	$ 260

Additional data

1. Equipment costing $370 million and Intangibles and Other Assets costing $10 million were purchased with cash.
2. Accumulated Depreciation increased by $110 for depreciation.
3. No disposals or impairments of equipment or intangibles occurred.
4. Notes payable of $1,270 million were paid and $1,330 million in new notes were borrowed.
5. Shares of common stock were issued for $190 million.
6. Retained Earnings increased by $260 million of net income and decreased by $60 million of cash dividends paid.

*Certain items have been eliminated from this statement to simplify presentation; these items (gains/losses on asset disposals) are discussed in Supplement 12A.

did decrease cash. For example, Cash decreases when a company pays wages that were incurred and expensed in a previous period. These cash outflows are captured by subtracting decreases in current liabilities.

+ Increases in current liabilities. Adding increases in current liabilities serves two purposes. First, it **eliminates** the effects of transactions that decreased net income but did not affect cash. For example, when interest is accrued on a bank loan, a company decreases net income, but its cash is not affected. To eliminate these noncash effects, we add back increases in current liabilities. Second, adding increases in current liabilities allows us to **include** the cash effects of other transactions that did not affect net income in the current period but did increase cash. For example, Cash and Deferred Revenue increase when the company receives cash in advance of providing services. Adding the increase in current liabilities captures these cash inflows.

Under Armour's Operating Cash Flows—Indirect Method

The preceding approach to preparing an operating cash flow schedule can be applied to Under Armour's information in Exhibit 12–3. We start by calculating the changes in all balance sheet accounts (Step 1 as shown to the right of the balances). Then, using the additional data provided below, classify whether the changes involve operating (**O**), investing (**I**), and/or financing (**F**) activities (in Step 2). Cash is not classified as O, I, or F because the change in Cash is reported at the bottom of the statement of cash flows rather than within its three sections.

Next, we use the amount of the change in each account marked by an O in Exhibit 12–3 to complete Step 3, which involves preparing the operating cash flow schedule in Exhibit 12–4. Have a quick look at Exhibit 12–4 right now and then take your time reading the following explanations and make sure you understand the reasons for each item.

EXHIBIT 12–4	**Under Armour's Schedule of Operating Cash Flows**

Step 3 Items	Amount (in millions)	Explanations
Net income	**$260**	Starting point, from the income statement
Items included in net income that do not involve cash		
+ Depreciation	**110**	Depreciation is a noncash expense
Changes in current assets and current liabilities		
– Increase in Accounts Receivable	**(100)**	Cash collections less than sales on account
– Increase in Inventory	**(140)**	Purchases more than cost of goods sold
– Increase in Prepaid Expenses	**(20)**	Prepayments greater than related expenses
+ Increase in Accounts Payable	**210**	Purchases greater than payments to suppliers
– Decrease in Accrued Liabilities	**(10)**	Cash payments more than accrued expenses
Net cash flow provided by (used in) operating activities	**$310**	Overall increase in cash from operations

COACH'S TIP

The depreciation addback is not intended to suggest depreciation creates an increase in cash. Rather, it's just showing that depreciation does not cause a decrease in cash. This is a subtle, but very important, difference in interpretation.

Net Income + Depreciation   Net income and depreciation are the first two lines to appear in a statement of cash flows prepared using the indirect method. They begin the process of converting net income to operating cash flows. They also begin the process of explaining the change in Cash by accounting for changes in the other balance sheet accounts. In the case of Under Armour, the $260 million of net income accounts for the increase in Retained Earnings (the decrease caused by dividends are reported later, in the financing cash flows section). The $110 million of depreciation accounts for the change in Accumulated Depreciation (assuming the company had no disposals).[2]

---

[2] Amortization and impairment losses would be handled in the same way as depreciation. Gains and losses on fixed asset disposals also would be dealt with in a similar manner, as discussed in Chapter Supplement 12A.

Increase in Accounts Receivable   Accounts Receivable increases when sales are made on account and it decreases when cash is collected from customers. An overall increase in this account, then, implies cash collections were less than sales on account. To convert from the higher sales number that is included in net income to the lower cash collected from customers, we subtract the difference ($100 million).

Another way to remember whether to add or subtract the difference is to think about whether the overall change in the account balance is explained by a debit or credit. If the change in the account is explained by a credit, the adjustment in the cash flow schedule is reported like a corresponding debit to cash (added). In Under Armour's case, the increase in Accounts Receivable is explained by a debit, so the adjustment in the cash flow schedule is reported like a credit to cash (a decrease), as follows:

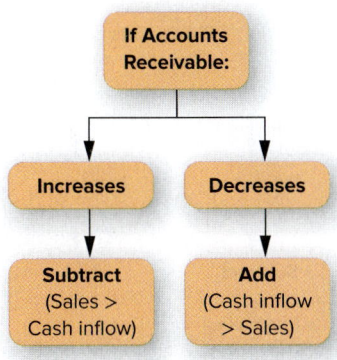

CASH FLOWS FROM OPERATING ACTIVITIES	
Net income	260
– Accounts receivable increase	(100)
. . .	. . .
Net cash inflow	___

Accounts Receivable (A)		
Beg. bal.	520	
Increase	100	
End. bal.	620	

Increase in Inventory   The income statement reports the cost of goods sold during the period, but cash flow from operating activities must report cash purchases of inventory. As shown in the T-account on the left, purchases of goods increase the balance in inventory, and recording the cost of goods sold decreases the balance in inventory.

Inventories (A)	
Beg. bal.	
Purchases	Cost of goods sold
End. bal.	

Inventories (A)		
Beg. bal.	780	
Increase	140	
End. bal.	920	

The above T-account on the right shows a $140 million inventory increase, which means that the cash outflow for inventory purchases is more than the cost of goods sold deducted on the income statement. The extra cash outflow must be subtracted to convert net income to cash flow from operating activities in Exhibit 12–4. (A decrease would be added.)

Increase in Prepaid Expenses   The income statement reports expenses of the period, but cash flow from operating activities must reflect the cash payments. Cash prepayments increase the balance in prepaid expenses, and recording of expenses decreases the balance in prepaid expenses.

Prepaid Expenses (A)	
Beg. bal.	
Cash prepayments	Used-up/expensed
End. bal.	

Prepaid Expenses (A)		
Beg. bal.	150	
Increase	20	
End. bal.	170	

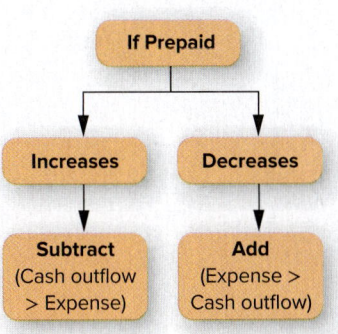

Under Armour's $20 million increase in Prepaid Expenses means cash prepayments this period were more than expenses. These extra cash prepayments must be subtracted in Exhibit 12–4. (A decrease would be added.)

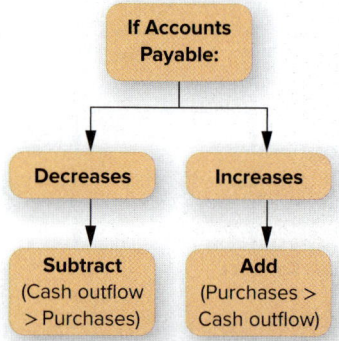

If Accounts Payable:

Decreases → Subtract (Cash outflow > Purchases)

Increases → Add (Purchases > Cash outflow)

Increase in Accounts Payable Cash flow from operations must reflect cash purchases, but not all purchases are for cash. Purchases on account increase Accounts Payable and cash paid to suppliers decreases Accounts Payable.

Accounts Payable (L)		
	Beg. bal.	
Cash payments	Purchases on account	
	End. bal.	

Accounts Payable (L)		
	Beg. bal.	200
	Increase	210
	End. bal.	410

Accounts Payable increased by $210 million, which means that purchases on account were greater than cash payments to suppliers. Thus, to show the lower cash outflow, the increase in Accounts Payable must be added back in Exhibit 12–4. (A decrease would be subtracted.)

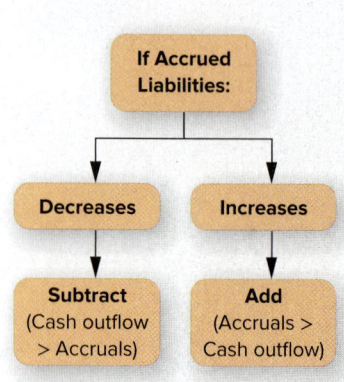

If Accrued Liabilities:

Decreases → Subtract (Cash outflow > Accruals)

Increases → Add (Accruals > Cash outflow)

Decrease in Accrued Liabilities The income statement reports all accrued expenses, but the cash flow statement must reflect only the actual cash payments for expenses. Recording accrued expenses increases the balance in Accrued Liabilities and cash payments for the expenses decreases Accrued Liabilities.

Accrued Liabilities (L)		
	Beg. bal.	
Cash payments	Accrued expenses	
	End. bal.	

Accrued Liabilities (L)		
	Beg. bal.	280
Decrease	10	
	End. bal.	270

Under Armour's Accrued Liabilities decreased by $10 million, which indicates that more expenses were paid than accrued. Consequently, this difference (representing more cash paid) must be subtracted in Exhibit 12–4. (An increase would be added.)

By scanning Exhibit 12–3 you can see that you have now considered the changes in all balance sheet accounts that relate to operating activities (marked by the letter O). The last step in determining the net cash flow provided by (used in) operating activities is to calculate a total. As shown in Exhibit 12–4, the combined effects of all operating cash flows is a net inflow of $310 million.

Now that you have seen how to compute operating cash flows using the indirect method, take a moment to complete the following Self-Study Practice.

💡 **How's it going?**   Self-Study Practice

Indicate whether the following items taken from Brunswick Corporation's cash flow statement would be added (+), subtracted (−), or not included (0) in the reconciliation of net income to cash flow from operations.

☐ *a.* Decrease in inventory.   ☐ *d.* Increase in accounts receivable.

☐ *b.* Increase in accounts payable.   ☐ *e.* Increase in accrued liabilities.

☐ *c.* Depreciation expense.   ☐ *f.* Increase in prepaid expenses.

After you have finished, check your answers against the solutions in the margin.

Under Armour's Investing Cash Flow Calculations

Learning Objective 12–3
Report cash flows from investing activities.

To prepare the investing section of the statement of cash flows, you must analyze accounts related to long-lived tangible and intangible assets. Unlike the analysis of operating activities, where you were concerned only with the *net* change in selected balance sheet accounts, an analysis of investing (and financing) activities requires that you identify and separately report the causes of *both* increases and decreases in account balances. The following relationships are the ones you will encounter most:

Related Balance Sheet Accounts	Investing Activity	Cash Flow Effect
Equipment	Purchase of equipment for cash	Outflow
	Sale of equipment for cash	Inflow
Intangible Assets	Purchase of intangible assets	Outflow
	Sale of intangible assets	Inflow

   Under Armour's balance sheet (Exhibit 12–3) shows two investing assets (noted with an I) that changed during the year: Equipment and Intangible and Other Assets.

Equipment   To determine the cause of the change in the Equipment account, accountants would examine the detailed accounting records for equipment. Purchases of equipment increase the account and disposals of equipment decrease it. The additional data in Exhibit 12–3 indicate Under Armour purchased equipment for $370 million cash. This purchase is a cash outflow, which we subtract in the schedule of investing activities in Exhibit 12–5. In our example, this purchase fully accounts for the change in the Equipment balance, as shown in the Equipment T-account. Note 3 of the additional data in Exhibit 12–3 confirms there were no equipment disposals or impairments during the year. Chapter Supplement 12A explains how equipment disposals affect the statement of cash flows.

	Equipment (A)		
Beg. bal.	830		
Purchases	370	Disposals	0
End. bal.	1,200		

EXHIBIT 12–5	Under Armour's Schedule of Investing Cash Flows

Items	Amount (in millions)	Explanations
Purchase of equipment	$(370)	Payment of cash for equipment
Purchase of intangible and other assets	(10)	Payment of cash for intangibles
Net cash provided by (used in) investing activities	(380)	Subtotal for the statement of cash flows

Intangible and Other Assets   A similar approach is used to determine cash flows associated with intangible assets. For our example, analysis of Under Armour's detailed records indicates the company did not have any reductions in its intangible assets as a result of disposals, impairments, or amortization during the year. However, Under Armour did purchase intangible assets for $10 million cash, as noted in the additional data in Exhibit 12–3. This cash outflow is subtracted in the schedule of investing activities in Exhibit 12–5.

Under Armour's Financing Cash Flow Calculations

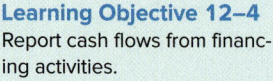

Learning Objective 12–4
Report cash flows from financing activities.

This section of the cash flow statement includes changes in liabilities owed to owners (Dividends Payable) and financial institutions (Notes Payable and other types of debt), as well as changes in stockholders' equity accounts. Interest is considered an operating activity so it is excluded from financing cash flows. The following relationships are the ones you will encounter most often:

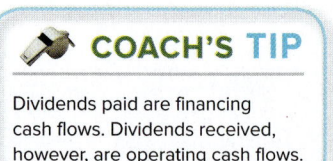

COACH'S TIP

Dividends paid are financing cash flows. Dividends received, however, are operating cash flows.

Related Balance Sheet Accounts	Financing Activity	Cash Flow Effect
Notes Payable	Borrowing cash from banks or other financial institutions	Inflow
	Repayment of loan principal	Outflow
Bonds Payable	Issuance of bonds for cash	Inflow
	Repayment of bond face value	Outflow
Common Stock	Issuance of stock for cash	Inflow
Treasury Stock	Repurchase of stock with cash	Outflow
Retained Earnings	Payment of cash dividends	Outflow

To compute cash flows from financing activities, you should review changes in all debt and stockholders' equity accounts. Increases and decreases must be identified and reported separately. Under Armour's balance sheet in Exhibit 12–3 indicates that Notes Payable, Common Stock, and Retained Earnings changed during the period as a result of financing cash flows (noted with an F).

Notes Payable   The additional data in Exhibit 12–3 indicate Notes Payable (long-term) was affected by both cash inflows and outflows, as shown in the T-account below. These cash flows are reported separately in the schedule of financing activities shown in Exhibit 12–6.

Notes Payable (long-term) (L)			
		Beg. bal.	880
Repayments	1,270	Borrowings	1,330
		End. bal.	940

Common Stock   Under Armour did not repurchase stock during the year, but it did issue stock for $190 million cash. This stock issuance fully accounts for the change in Common Stock, as shown in the following T-account. This cash inflow is listed in the schedule of financing activities in Exhibit 12–6.

Common Stock (SE)	
Beg. bal.	640
Stock issued	190
End. bal.	830

EXHIBIT 12–6 Under Armour's Schedule of Financing Cash Flows

Items	Amount (in millions)	Explanations
Additional long-term notes	$1,330	Cash received when new notes signed
Payments on long-term notes	(1,270)	Cash paid on principal of notes
Proceeds from stock issuance	190	Cash received from stockholders for new stock
Cash dividends paid	(60)	Cash paid to stockholders
Net cash provided by financing activities	190	Subtotal for the statement of cash flows

---

Retained Earnings   Net income increases Retained Earnings and any declared dividends decrease Retained Earnings. Net income has already been accounted for as an operating cash flow. The declared dividends were $60 million (see the additional data in Exhibit 12–3), which decreased Retained Earnings as shown in the following T-account. Because the balance sheet does not report Dividends Payable, we assume all of these declared dividends were paid in cash. This cash outflow is reported in the financing section of the statement of cash flows, as summarized in Exhibit 12–6.

Retained Earnings (SE)			
		Beg. bal.	1,000
Dividends	60	Net income	260
		End. bal.	1,200

Under Armour's Statement of Cash Flows

Now that you have determined the cash flows for the three main types of business activities in Exhibits 12–4, 12–5, and 12–6, you can prepare the statement of cash flows in a proper format. Exhibit 12–7 shows the statement of cash flows for Under Armour using the indirect method. Notice that the $120 million subtotal for Net increase (decrease) in cash and cash equivalents combines cash flows from operating, investing, and financing activities to produce an overall net change in cash. This net change is added to the beginning cash balance to arrive at the ending cash balance, which is the same cash balance as reported on the balance sheet.

Noncash Transactions and Other Supplemental Disclosures   In addition to cash flows, all companies are required to report material investing and financing transactions that did not have cash flow effects (called **noncash investing and financing activities**). For example, the purchase of a $10,000 piece of equipment with a $10,000 note payable to the equipment supplier does not cause either an inflow or an outflow of cash. As a result, these activities are not listed in the three main sections of the statement of cash flows. This important information is normally presented for users in a supplementary schedule to the statement of cash flows or in the financial statement notes. Companies using the indirect method also must disclose the amount of cash paid for interest and for income taxes. Examples of these supplemental disclosures are shown at the bottom of Exhibit 12–7.

 **COACH'S TIP**

When doing homework problems, assume all changes in noncurrent account balances are caused by cash transactions (unless the problem also describes changes caused by noncash investing and financing activities).

| EXHIBIT 12–7 | Under Armour's Statement of Cash Flows (Indirect Method) |

UNDER ARMOUR, INC.
Statement of Cash Flows*
For the Year Ended December 31, 2016

(in millions)

Cash Flows from Operating Activities	
Net income	$ 260
Adjustments to reconcile net income to net cash provided by operating activities:	
Depreciation	110
Changes in current assets and current liabilities:	
Accounts Receivable	(100)
Inventory	(140)
Prepaid Expenses	(20)
Accounts Payable	210
Accrued Liabilities	(10)
Net cash provided by (used in) operating activities	310
Cash Flows from Investing Activities	
Purchase of equipment	(370)
Purchase of intangible and other assets	(10)
Net cash provided by (used in) investing activities	(380)
Cash Flows from Financing Activities	
Additional long-term notes	1,330
Payments on long-term notes	(1,270)
Proceeds from stock issuance	190
Cash dividends paid	(60)
Net cash provided by (used in) financing activities	190
Net increase (decrease) in cash and cash equivalents	120
Cash and cash equivalents at beginning of period	130
Cash and cash equivalents at end of period	$ 250
Supplemental Disclosures	
Cash paid for interest	$ 30
Cash paid for income tax	130

Note: These supplemental disclosures also could include significant noncash transactions (e.g., issued a promissory note to purchase $x of equipment).

*Certain amounts have been adjusted to simplify the presentation.

Evaluate the Results

Unlike the income statement, which summarizes its detailed information in one number (net income), the statement of cash flows does not provide a summary measure of cash flow performance. Instead, it must be evaluated in terms of the cash flow pattern suggested by the subtotals of each of the three main sections. As we discussed at the beginning of this chapter, expect different patterns of cash flows from operating, investing, and financing activities depending on how well established a company is. An established, healthy company will show positive cash flows from operations, which are sufficiently large to fund investing outflows of cash to replace property, plant, and equipment and to fund financing outflows of cash for dividends to stockholders. Any additional cash (called **free cash flow**) can be used in the future to (*a*) expand the business through additional investing activities, (*b*) repay existing financing, or (*c*) simply build up the company's cash balance. After considering where the company stands in relation to this big picture, you should then look at the details within each of the three sections.

EVALUATING CASH FLOWS

Cash Flows from Operating Activities

The operating activities section indicates how well a company is able to generate cash internally through its operations and management of current assets and current liabilities. Most analysts believe this is the most important section of the statement because, in the long run, operations are the only continuing source of cash. Investors will not invest in a company if they believe cash generated from operations is inadequate to pay dividends or expand the company. Similarly, creditors will not lend money or extend credit if they believe cash generated from operations is insufficient to repay them.

When evaluating the operating activities section of the statement of cash flows, consider the absolute amount of cash flow (is it positive or negative?), keeping in mind that operating cash flows have to be positive over the long run for a company to be successful. Also, look at the relationship between operating cash flows and net income.

All other things being equal, when net income and operating cash flows are similar, there is a high likelihood that revenues are realized in cash and that expenses are associated with cash outflows. Any major deviations should be investigated. In some cases, a deviation may be nothing to worry about, but in others, it could be the first sign of big problems to come. Four potential causes of deviations to consider include the following:

1. **Seasonality**. As in Under Armour's case, seasonal variations in sales and inventory levels can cause the relationship between net income and cash flow from operations to fluctuate from one quarter to the next. Usually, this isn't cause for alarm.

2. **The corporate life cycle (growth in sales)**. New companies often experience rapid sales growth. When sales are increasing, accounts receivable and inventory normally increase faster than the cash flows being collected from sales. This often causes operating cash flows to be lower than the related net income. This isn't a big deal, provided the company can obtain cash from financing activities until operating activities begin to generate more positive cash flows.

3. **Changes in revenue and expense recognition**. Most cases of fraudulent financial reporting involve aggressive revenue recognition (recording revenues before performance obligations are fulfilled) or delayed expense recognition (failing to report expenses when they are incurred). Both of these tactics cause net income to increase in the current period, making it seem as though the company has improved its performance. Neither of these tactics, though, affects cash flows from operating activities. As a result, if revenue and expense recognition policies are changed to boost net income, cash flow from operations will be significantly lower than net income, providing one of the first clues the financial statements might contain errors or fraud.

4. **Changes in working capital management**. Working capital is a measure of the amount by which current assets exceed current liabilities. If a company's current assets (such as accounts receivable and inventory) are allowed to grow out of control, its operating cash flows will decrease. More efficient management will have the opposite effect. To investigate this potential cause more closely, managers could compute other ratios such as the inventory and accounts receivable turnover ratios. These ratios are covered in the next chapter.

Cash Flows from Investing Activities

Although it might seem counterintuitive at first, healthy companies tend to show negative cash flows in the investing section of the statement of cash flows. A negative total for this section means the company is spending more to acquire new long-term assets than it is taking in from

Lehman Brothers's Operating Cash Flows and the Financial Crisis

Lehman Brothers Holdings, Inc., was one of the largest and most profitable financial services companies in the world. But cash flow and working capital management problems led to the company's bankruptcy and started a domino effect leading to the stock market crash of 2008. The following comparison of Lehman's net income and net operating cash flows reveals the company's problems:

selling its existing long-term assets. That's normal for any healthy, growing company. In fact, if you see a positive total cash flow in the investing activities section, you should be concerned because it could mean the company is selling off its long-term assets just to generate cash inflows. If a company sells off too many long-term assets, it may not have a sufficient base to continue running its business effectively, which would likely lead to further decline in the future.

Cash Flows from Financing Activities

Unlike the operating and investing activities sections, where a healthy company typically shows positive and negative cash flows, respectively, the financing activities section does not have an obvious expected direction for cash flows. For example, a healthy company that is growing rapidly could need financing cash inflows to fund its expansion. In this case, the company could take out new loans or issue new shares, both of which would result in positive net cash flows from financing activities. Alternatively, a healthy company could use its cash resources to repay existing loans, pay dividends, or repurchase shares, all of which would result in negative net cash flows from financing activities. Thus, it's not possible to evaluate the company's financing cash flows by simply determining whether they are positive or negative on an overall basis. Rather, you will need to consider detailed line items within this section to assess the company's overall financing strategy (is the company moving toward greater reliance on risky debt financing?).

Overall Patterns of Cash Flows

Just as most products go through a series of developmental phases, most companies have life cycles as well. The corporate life cycle phases include an **introductory phase** when the company is being established, a **growth phase** when the company's presence expands, a **maturity phase** when the company stabilizes, and finally a **decline phase** in the event the company loses its way. During each of these phases, a company is likely to show different patterns of net cash flows from operating, investing, and financing activities. Exhibit 12–8 illustrates the cash flow patterns that suggest the life cycle phase being experienced by a company. Although exceptions to these patterns can exist, they can help you to better understand and evaluate a company's cash flows.

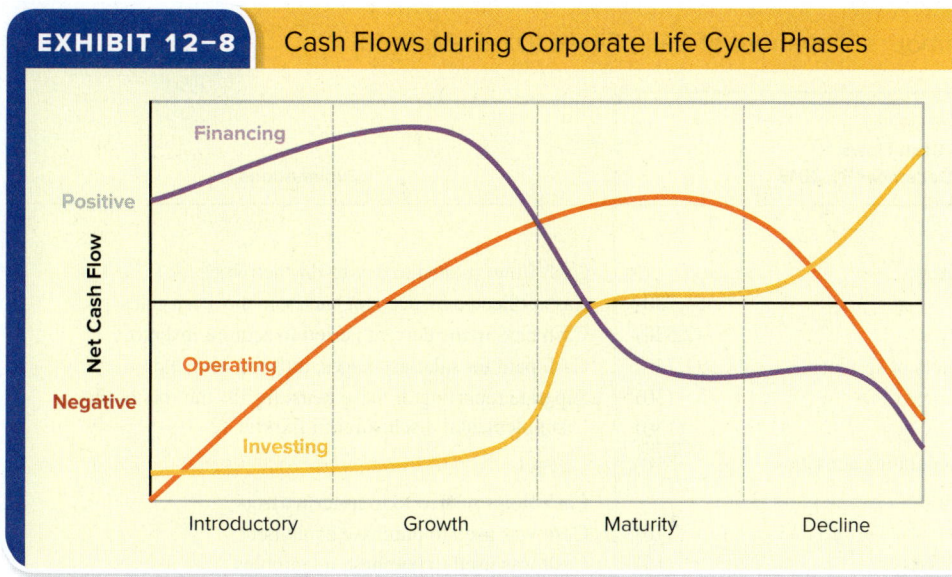

EXHIBIT 12–8 Cash Flows during Corporate Life Cycle Phases

As Exhibit 12–8 suggests, most companies in the introductory (start-up) phase experience negative net operating cash flows. Negative cash flows arise during this phase because companies pay cash out to employees and suppliers but haven't established a large enough customer base to generate sizable cash inflows from customers. Also during the introductory phase, these companies are spending significant amounts of cash on long-term assets (e.g., equipment and buildings), resulting in negative investing cash flows. To fund these negative investing and operating cash flows, companies in the introductory phase rely heavily on cash obtained through financing activities (e.g., borrowing from lenders and obtaining contributions from shareholders). If a company survives the introductory phase, it will enter a growth phase, which is similar to the introductory phase except that operating cash flows turn positive because the company has improved its cash inflows from customers. In the maturity phase, the company continues to enjoy positive operating cash flows but no longer has opportunities for expanding the business, so it stops spending cash on investing activities and instead uses its cash for financing activities such as repaying lenders and returning excess cash to shareholders. Finally, during the decline phase, a company's operating cash flows again become negative, prompting lenders to demand repayment of loans (i.e., negative financing cash flows). To fund these repayments, the company sells off its long-term assets, resulting in significantly positive investing cash flows.

OPERATING CASH FLOWS REVISITED (DIRECT METHOD)

In this section, we demonstrate how to determine operating cash flows using the direct method of presentation. You might ask whether it's worth learning how to use this approach when fewer than 1 percent of public companies report with it. That's a fair question. But you also should ask why *aren't* more companies using it when the FASB recommends it over the indirect method. Some argue companies do not use the direct method of presentation because it reveals too much about their operations. As we show below, useful insights can be gained about a company by analyzing its operating cash flows using the direct method of presentation.

Exhibit 12–9 presents Under Armour's statement of cash flows using the direct method. Because this method lists each operating cash flow component, it allows more detailed analyses of operating cash flows. For example, the direct method would allow Under Armour's managers to determine that a 10 percent increase in product costs would have required an additional cash outflow to inventory suppliers of $252 million (= 10% × $2,520 million). To cover these additional cash outflows, Under Armour could raise prices by 5.3 percent, which could increase cash inflow from customer collections by $250.7 million (= 5.3% × $4,730 million).

The direct method also provides financial statement users with more information to identify potential relationships between cash inflows and outflows. An increase in some activities, such as sales, generally leads to an increase in cash inflows from customers and cash outflows

Learning Objective 12–6
Report and interpret cash flows from operating activities, using the direct method.

EXHIBIT 12-9	Under Armour's Statement of Cash Flows (Direct Method)

UNDER ARMOUR, INC.
Statement of Cash Flows
For the Year Ended December 31, 2016

(in millions)

		Explanations
Cash Flows from Operating Activities		Cash flows related to day-to-day activities
Cash collected from customers	$4,730	Cash collected on account and from any cash sales
Cash paid to suppliers of inventory	(2,520)	Cash paid in the current period to acquire inventory
Cash paid to employees and suppliers of services	(1,740)	Cash paid for salaries, wages, utilities, rent, etc.
Cash paid for interest	(30)	Separate reporting of these items fulfills the role of the
Cash paid for income tax	(130)	supplemental disclosures in Exhibit 12–7
Net cash provided by (used in) operating activities	310	Indicates overall cash impact of operating activities
Cash Flows from Investing Activities		Cash flows related to long-term assets
Purchase of equipment	(370)	Cash was used to purchase equipment
Purchase of intangible and other assets	(10)	Cash was used to purchase intangibles
Net cash provided by (used in) investing activities	(380)	Indicates overall cash impact of investing activities
Cash Flows from Financing Activities		Cash flows from transactions with lenders, investors
Additional long-term notes	1,330	Cash received from borrowing
Payments on long-term notes	(1,270)	Cash used to repay amounts previously borrowed
Proceeds from stock issuance	190	Cash received from issuing stock
Cash dividends paid	(60)	Cash used to pay dividends
Net cash provided by (used in) financing activities	190	Indicates overall cash impact of financing activities
Net Change in Cash and Cash Equivalents	**120**	$310 + $(380) + $190 = $120
Cash and cash equivalents, beginning of year	130	Cash balance at beginning of the period
Cash and cash equivalents, end of year	250	Cash balance at end of the period (on balance sheet)

to inventory suppliers. However, an increase in sales activity only loosely affects other cash outflows, such as interest paid on loans. Knowing the detailed components of operating cash flows allows analysts to more reliably predict a company's future cash flows.[3]

In the remainder of this section, we describe how to prepare the statement of cash flows using the direct method. We focus on preparing just the operating activities section. Instructions on preparing the investing and financing activities sections, which are identical under both the direct and indirect methods, were presented earlier in this chapter.

Reporting Operating Cash Flows with the Direct Method

The direct method presents a summary of all operating transactions that result in either a debit or a credit to cash. It is prepared by adjusting each revenue and expense on the income statement from the accrual basis to the cash basis. We will complete this process for all of the revenues and expenses reported in the Under Armour income statement in Exhibit 12–3 to show the calculations underlying the operating cash flows in Exhibit 12–9. Notice that, with the direct method, we work directly with each revenue and expense listed on the income statement and ignore any totals or subtotals (such as net income).

Converting Sales Revenues to Cash Inflows When sales are recorded, Accounts Receivable increases, and when cash is collected, Accounts Receivable decreases. This means that if Accounts Receivable increases by $100 million, then cash collections were $100 million less than sales on account. To convert sales revenue to the cash collected, we need to subtract $100 million from Sales Revenue. The following flowchart shows this visually:

---

[3] Steven F. Orpurt and Yoonseok Zang, "Do Direct Cash Flow Disclosures Help Predict Future Operating Cash Flows and Earnings?" *The Accounting Review* 84, no. 3, 893–936 (May 2009).

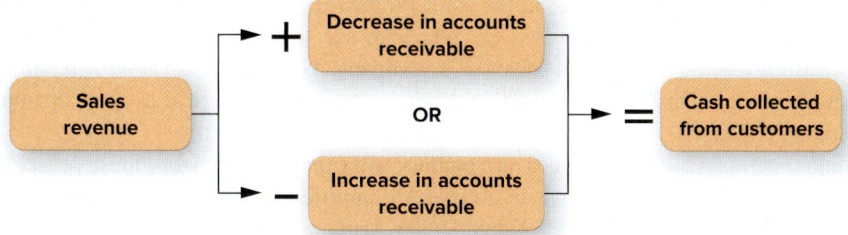

Using information from Under Armour's income statement and balance sheet presented in Exhibit 12–3, we compute cash collected from customers as follows:

		Accounts Receivable (A)	
Net Sales	$4,830	Beg. bal.	520
– Increase in Accounts Receivable	(100)	Increase	100
Cash collected from customers	$4,730	End. bal.	620

Converting Cost of Goods Sold to Cash Paid to Suppliers Cost of Goods Sold represents the cost of merchandise sold during the accounting period, which may be more or less than the amount of cash paid to suppliers during the period. In Under Armour's case, Inventory increased during the year, implying the company bought more merchandise than it sold. If the company paid cash to suppliers of inventory, it would have paid more cash to suppliers than the amount of Cost of Goods Sold. So, the increase in Inventory must be added to Cost of Goods Sold to compute cash paid to suppliers.

Typically, companies buy inventory on account from suppliers (as indicated by an Accounts Payable balance on the balance sheet). Consequently, we need to consider more than just the change in Inventory to convert Cost of Goods Sold to cash paid to suppliers. The credit purchases and payments that are recorded in Accounts Payable also must be considered. Credit purchases increase Accounts Payable and cash payments decrease it. The overall increase in Accounts Payable reported by Under Armour in Exhibit 12–3 indicates that cash payments were less than credit purchases, so the difference must be subtracted in the computation of total cash payments to suppliers.

In summary, to fully convert Cost of Goods Sold to a cash basis, you must consider changes in both Inventory and Accounts Payable as follows:

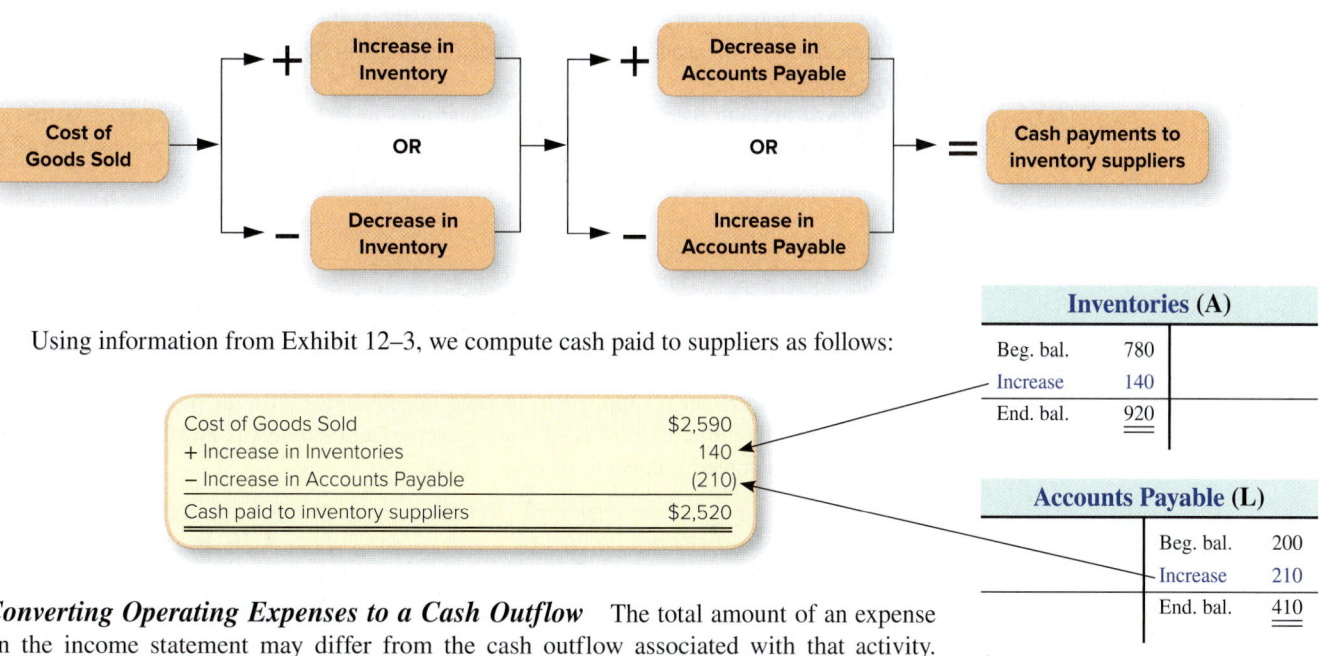

Using information from Exhibit 12–3, we compute cash paid to suppliers as follows:

		Inventories (A)	
		Beg. bal.	780
Cost of Goods Sold	$2,590	Increase	140
+ Increase in Inventories	140	End. bal.	920
– Increase in Accounts Payable	(210)		
Cash paid to inventory suppliers	$2,520	**Accounts Payable (L)**	
		Beg. bal.	200
		Increase	210
		End. bal.	410

Converting Operating Expenses to a Cash Outflow The total amount of an expense on the income statement may differ from the cash outflow associated with that activity. Some amounts, like prepaid rent, are paid before they are recognized as expenses. When prepayments are made, the balance in the asset Prepaid Expenses increases. When expenses are recorded, Prepaid Expenses decreases. When we see Under Armour's prepaids increase by $20 million during the year, it means the company paid more cash than it recorded as operating expenses. This amount must be added in computing cash paid to service suppliers for operating expenses.

Some other expenses, like wages, are paid for after they are incurred. In this case, when expenses are recorded, the balance in Accrued Liabilities increases. When payments are made, Accrued Liabilities decreases. When Under Armour's Accrued Liabilities decrease by $10 million, it means the company paid that much more cash than it recorded as operating expenses. This amount must be added when computing cash paid to employees and service suppliers for operating expenses.

Generally, operating expenses such as Selling, General, and Administrative Expenses can be converted from the accrual basis to the cash basis in the following manner:

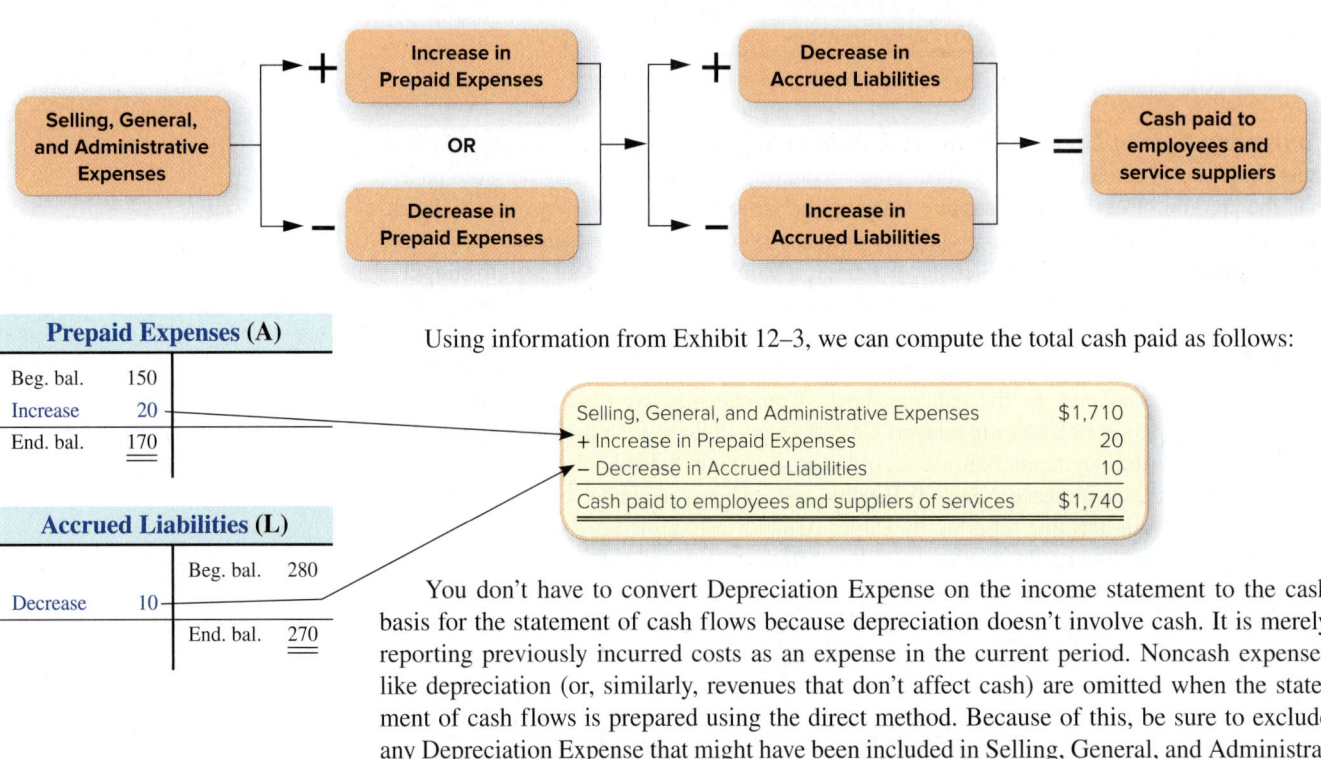

Prepaid Expenses (A)	
Beg. bal.	150
Increase	20
End. bal.	170

Accrued Liabilities (L)	
	Beg. bal. 280
Decrease 10	
	End. bal. 270

Using information from Exhibit 12–3, we can compute the total cash paid as follows:

Selling, General, and Administrative Expenses	$1,710
+ Increase in Prepaid Expenses	20
− Decrease in Accrued Liabilities	10
Cash paid to employees and suppliers of services	$1,740

You don't have to convert Depreciation Expense on the income statement to the cash basis for the statement of cash flows because depreciation doesn't involve cash. It is merely reporting previously incurred costs as an expense in the current period. Noncash expenses like depreciation (or, similarly, revenues that don't affect cash) are omitted when the statement of cash flows is prepared using the direct method. Because of this, be sure to exclude any Depreciation Expense that might have been included in Selling, General, and Administrative Expenses.

The next account listed on the income statement in Exhibit 12–3 is Interest Expense of $30 million. Because the balance sheet does not report Interest Payable, we will assume all of the interest was paid in cash. Thus, interest expense equals interest paid.

Interest Expense	$30
No change in Interest Payable	0
Cash paid for interest	$30

The same logic can be applied to income taxes. Under Armour presents Income Tax Expense of $130 million. Exhibit 12–3 does not report an Income Tax Payable balance, so we assume income tax paid is equal to income tax expense.

Income Tax Expense	$130
No change in Income Tax Payable	0
Cash paid for income tax	$130

You have now seen, in this section, how to determine each amount reported in the operating activities section of the statement of cash flows in Exhibit 12–9 prepared using the direct method. For a quick check on your understanding of this material, complete the following Self-Study Practice.

💡 How's it going?   Self-Study Practice

Indicate whether the following items taken from a cash flow statement would be added (+), subtracted (−), or not included (0) when calculating cash flow from operations using the direct method.

- [ ] *a.* Cash paid to suppliers.
- [ ] *b.* Payment of dividends to stockholders.
- [ ] *c.* Cash collections from customers.
- [ ] *d.* Purchase of equipment for cash.
- [ ] *e.* Payments of interest to lenders.
- [ ] *f.* Payment of taxes to the government.

After you have finished, check your answers against the solutions in the margin.

SUPPLEMENT 12A	**REPORTING DISPOSALS OF PROPERTY, PLANT, AND EQUIPMENT (INDIRECT METHOD)**

Whenever a company sells property, plant, and equipment (PPE), it records three things: (1) decreases in the PPE accounts for the assets sold, (2) an increase in the Cash account for the cash received on disposal, and (3) a gain if the cash received is more than the book value of the assets sold (or a loss if the cash received is less than the book value of the assets sold). The only part of this transaction that qualifies for the statement of cash flows is the cash received on disposal. This cash inflow is classified as an investing activity, just like the original equipment purchase.

Okay, that seems straightforward, so why do we have a separate chapter supplement for this kind of transaction? Well, there is one complicating factor. Gains and losses on disposal are included in the computation of net income, which is the starting point for the operating activities section when prepared using the indirect method. So, just as we had to add back the depreciation subtracted on the income statement, we also have to add back losses reported on disposals of PPE. As the following example shows, the flip side is true for gains on disposal (they are subtracted).

To illustrate, assume Under Armour sold a piece of equipment for $7 million. The equipment originally cost $15 million and had $10 million of accumulated depreciation at the time of disposal. The disposal would have been analyzed and recorded as follows (in millions):

1 Analyze

Assets		=	Liabilities	+	Stockholders' Equity	
Cash	+7				Gain on Disposal (+R)	+2
Accumulated Depreciation (−xA)	+10					
Equipment	−15					

2 Record

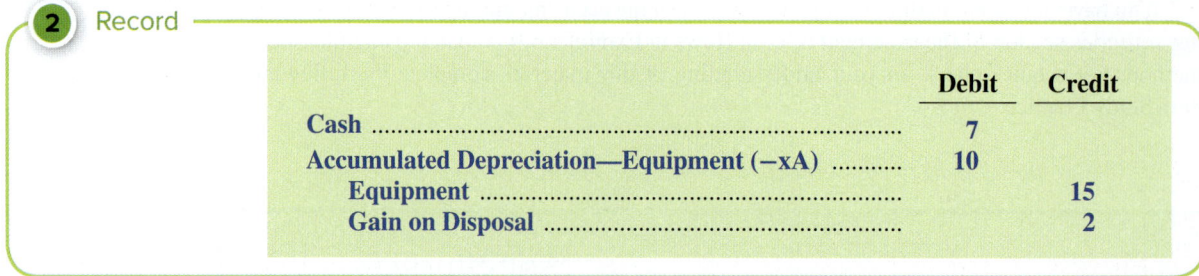

	Debit	Credit
Cash	7	
Accumulated Depreciation—Equipment (−xA)	10	
Equipment		15
Gain on Disposal		2

The $7 million inflow of cash would be reported as an investing activity. The $10 million and $15 million are taken into account when considering changes in the Accumulated Depreciation and Equipment account balances. Lastly, the $2 million Gain on Disposal was included in net income, so we must remove (subtract) it in the operating activities section of the statement. Thus, the disposal would affect two parts of the statement of cash flows:

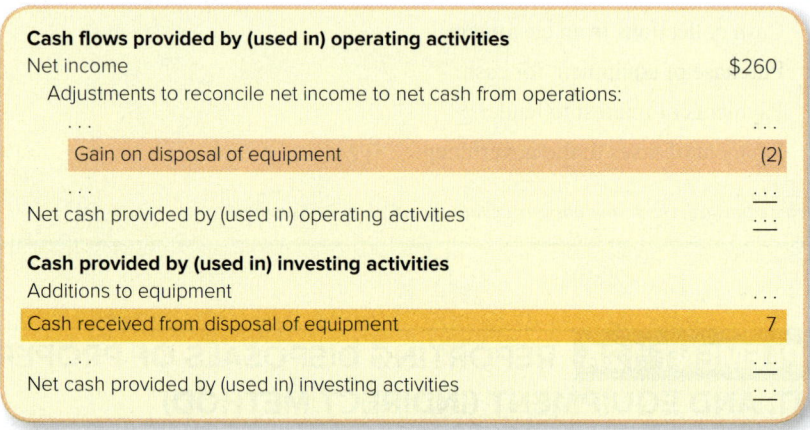

Cash flows provided by (used in) operating activities
Net income	$260
Adjustments to reconcile net income to net cash from operations:	
. . .	. . .
Gain on disposal of equipment	(2)
. . .	. . .
Net cash provided by (used in) operating activities	. . .
Cash provided by (used in) investing activities	
Additions to equipment	. . .
Cash received from disposal of equipment	7
. . .	. . .
Net cash provided by (used in) investing activities	. . .

SUPPLEMENT 12B **T-ACCOUNT APPROACH (INDIRECT METHOD)**

When we began our discussion of preparing the statement of cash flows, we noted that changes in cash must equal the sum of the changes in all other balance sheet accounts. Based on this idea, we used the following three steps to prepare the statement of cash flows:

1. Determine the change in each balance sheet account. From this year's ending balance, subtract this year's beginning balance (i.e., last year's ending balance).

2. Identify the cash flow category or categories to which each account relates. Use Exhibit 12–2 as a guide, but be aware that some accounts may include two categories of cash flows. Retained Earnings, for example, can include both financing cash flows (paying dividends) and operating cash flows (generating net income). Similarly, Accumulated Depreciation can be affected by operating activities (depreciation for using equipment in daily operations) as well as investing activities (disposing of equipment).

3. Create schedules that summarize operating, investing, and financing cash flows.

Instead of creating separate schedules for each section of the statement, many accountants prefer to prepare a single large T-account to represent the changes that have taken place in cash subdivided into the three sections of the cash flow statement. Such an account is presented in Panel A of Exhibit 12B–1. The cash account in Panel A shows increases in cash as debits and decreases in cash as credits. Note how each section matches the three schedules we prepared for Under Armour's cash flows presented in Exhibits 12–4, 12–5, and 12–6. Panel B includes the same T-accounts for the noncash balance sheet accounts we used in our discussion of each cash flow statement section in the body of the chapter. Note how each change in the noncash balance sheet accounts has a number referencing the change in the cash account that it accompanies. You can use the information in the cash flow T-account in Exhibit 12B–1 to prepare the statement of cash flows in proper format, as shown in Exhibit 12–7.

EXHIBIT 12B–1	T-Account Approach to Preparing the Statement of Cash Flows (Indirect Method)

Panel A: Changes in Cash Account

Cash (A)				
Operating				
(1) Net Income	260	100	(3) Accounts Receivable	
(2) Depreciation Expense	110	140	(4) Inventories	
(6) Accounts Payable	210	20	(5) Prepaid Expenses	
		10	(7) Accrued Liabilities	
Net cash flow provided by operating activities	310			
Investing				
		370	(8) Purchased Equipment	
		10	(9) Purchased Intangibles	
		380	Net cash used in investing activities	
Financing				
(10) Additional long-term notes	1,330	1,270	(11) Payment of long-term notes	
(12) Proceeds from stock issuance	190	60	(12) Payment of cash dividends	
Net cash provided by financing activities	190			
Net increase in cash	120			
Beg. bal.	130			
End. bal.	250			

Panel B: Changes in Noncash Accounts

Accounts Receivable (A)			
Beg. bal.	520		
(3) Increase	100		
End. bal.	620		

Inventory (A)			
Beg. bal.	780		
(4) Increase	140		
End. bal.	920		

Prepaid Expenses (A)			
Beg. bal.	150		
(5) Increase	20		
End. bal.	170		

Equipment (A)			
Beg. bal.	830		
(8) Purchases	370	Disposals	0
End. bal.	1,200		

Accumulated Depreciation—Equipment (xA)			
		Beg. bal.	290
Disposals	0	(2) Depreciation	110
		End. bal.	400

Intangible and Other Assets (A)			
Beg. bal.	880		
(9) Purchases	10	Disposals	0
End. bal.	890		

Accounts Payable (A)			
		Beg. bal.	200
		(6) Increase	210
		End. bal.	410

Accrued Liabilities (L)			
		Beg. bal.	280
(7) Decrease	10		
		End. bal.	270

Notes Payable (long-term) (L)			
		Beg. bal.	880
(11) Payments	1,270	(10) Borrowings	1,330
		End. bal.	940

Common Stock (SE)			
		Beg. bal.	640
Stock repurchased	0	(12) Stock issued	190
		End. bal.	830

Retained Earnings (SE)			
		Beg. bal.	1,000
(12) Dividends	60	(1) Net income	260
		End. bal.	1,200

REVIEW THE CHAPTER

DEMONSTRATION CASE A: INDIRECT METHOD

During a recent year (ended April 30), Best Beverage Corp. reported net income of $25,000. The company also reported the following activities:

a. Purchased equipment for $6,000 in cash.
b. Issued common stock for $1,000 in cash.
c. Depreciation of equipment was $9,000 for the year.

Its comparative balance sheet is presented below.

BEST BEVERAGE CORP.
Balance Sheet
Year Ended April 30

	Current Year	Prior Year
Assets		
Current assets:		
Cash and cash equivalents	$ 84,000	$ 48,700
Accounts receivable	53,600	50,000
Inventory	39,600	39,000
Prepaid expenses	5,500	15,000
Equipment	206,000	200,000
Accumulated Depreciation	(126,700)	(117,700)
Total assets	$ 262,000	$ 235,000
Liabilities and Stockholders' Equity		
Current liabilities:		
Accounts payable	$ 48,000	$ 49,000
Accrued liabilities	44,000	42,000
Total current liabilities	92,000	91,000
Stockholders' equity:		
Common Stock	10,000	9,000
Retained earnings	160,000	135,000
Total stockholders' equity	170,000	144,000
Total liabilities and stockholders' equity	$ 262,000	$ 235,000

Required:

Based on this information, prepare the cash flow statement using the indirect method. Evaluate cash flows reported in the statement.

Suggested Solution

BEST BEVERAGE CORP. Balance Sheet At April 30			STEP 1 CHANGE	STEP 2 SCF SECTION
	Current Year	**Prior Year**		
Assets				
Cash and Cash Equivalents	$ 84,000	$ 48,700	+35,300	Cash
Accounts Receivable	53,600	50,000	+3,600	O
Inventory	39,600	39,000	+600	O
Prepaid Expenses	5,500	15,000	−9,500	O
Equipment	206,000	200,000	+6,000	I
Accum. Depreciation	(126,700)	(117,700)	−9,000	O
Total Assets	$ 262,000	$ 235,000		
Liabilities and Stockholders' Equity				
Accounts Payable	$ 48,000	$ 49,000	−1,000	O
Accrued Liabilities	44,000	42,000	+2,000	O
Common Stock	10,000	9,000	+1,000	F
Retained Earnings	160,000	135,000	+25,000	O
Total Liabilities and Stockholders' Equity	$ 262,000	$ 235,000		

BEST BEVERAGE CORP.
Statement of Cash Flows
For the Year Ended April 30

Cash Flows from Operating Activities	
Net income	$ 25,000
Adjustments to reconcile net income to net cash provided by operating activities:	
Depreciation	9,000
Changes in current assets and current liabilities:	
Accounts Receivable	(3,600)
Inventory	(600)
Prepaid Expenses	9,500
Accounts Payable	(1,000)
Accrued Liabilities	2,000
Net cash provided by operating activities	40,300
Cash Flows from Investing Activities	
Purchases of equipment	(6,000)
Net cash used in investing activities	(6,000)
Cash Flows from Financing Activities	
Proceeds from issuance of common stock	1,000
Net cash provided by financing activities	1,000
Net Increase in Cash and Cash Equivalents	35,300
Cash and Cash Equivalents at beginning of year	48,700
Cash and Cash Equivalents at end of year	$ 84,000

Best Beverage reported positive profits but even higher cash flows from operations for the year. The difference between the two is caused primarily by depreciation and decreases in prepaid expenses. That operating cash flows are higher than net income suggests Best Beverage is carefully managing its current assets and current liabilities so that it has sufficient cash to cover the costs of purchases of additional equipment without the need to borrow additional funds. This increase in cash can be used for future expansion or to pay future dividends to stockholders.

DEMONSTRATION CASE B: DIRECT METHOD

The managers at Best Beverage Corp. would like to know the impact on cash flows of a 10 percent increase in product costs.

Required:

Based on the information given in Demonstration Case A and the following income statement, prepare a statement of cash flows using the direct method. By what amount would cash outflows have increased if product costs were 10 percent higher? By what percentage would Best Beverage have to increase its prices to cover a 10 percent increase in cash outflows for product costs? (Assume a price increase will not adversely affect sales volume.)

Given Information

BEST BEVERAGE CORP.
Income Statement
For the Year Ended April 30

Sales Revenue	$636,000
Cost of Goods Sold	240,000
Gross Profit	396,000
Office Expenses	242,000
Depreciation Expense	9,000
Income from Operations	145,000
Interest Expense	0
Income before Income Taxes	145,000
Income Tax Expense	120,000
Net Income	$ 25,000

Suggested Solution

BEST BEVERAGE CORP.
Statement of Cash Flows
For the Year Ended April 30

Cash Flows from Operating Activities	
Cash collected from customers	$ 632,400
Cash paid to suppliers of inventory	(241,600)
Cash paid to employees and suppliers of services	(230,500)
Cash paid for income taxes	(120,000)
Net cash provided by operating activities	40,300
Cash Flows from Investing Activities	
Purchase of equipment	(6,000)
Net cash used in investing activities	(6,000)
Cash Flows from Financing Activities	
Proceeds from issuance of common stock	1,000
Net cash provided by financing activities	1,000
Net Increase in Cash and Cash Equivalents	35,300
Cash and Cash Equivalents at beginning of year	48,700
Cash and Cash Equivalents at end of year	$ 84,000

Cash collected from customers = Sales Revenue − Increase in Accounts Receivable = $636,000 − 3,600
= $632,400
Cash paid for inventory = Cost of Goods Sold + Increase in Inventories + Decrease in Accounts
Payable
= $240,000 + 600 + 1,000 = $241,600
Cash paid to employees, etc. = Office Expenses − Decrease in Prepaids − Increase in Accrued Liabilities
= $242,000 − 9,500 − 2,000 = $230,500

If product costs were 10 percent higher, total cash paid to inventory suppliers would have
increased by $24,160 ($241,600 × 10%). To cover these additional cash outflows, Best Beverage
could increase prices by $24,160, which compared to current collections from customers is 3.8 per-
cent ($24,160 ÷ $632,400).

CHAPTER SUMMARY

Identify cash flows arising from operating, investing, and financing activities. p. 530

LO 12–1

- The statement has three main sections: Cash flows from operating activities, which are related to earning income from normal operations; Cash flows from investing activities, which are related to the acquisition and sale of productive assets; and Cash flows from financing activities, which are related to external financing of the enterprise.
- The net cash inflow or outflow for the period is the same amount as the increase or decrease in cash and cash equivalents for the period on the balance sheet. Cash equivalents are highly liquid investments purchased within three months of maturity.

Report cash flows from operating activities, using the indirect method. p. 536

LO 12–2

- The indirect method for reporting cash flows from operating activities reports a conversion of net income to net cash flow from operating activities.
- The conversion involves additions and subtractions for (1) noncash expenses (such as depreciation expense) and revenues that do not affect current assets or current liabilities and (2) changes in each of the individual current assets (other than cash) and current liabilities (other than debt to financial institutions, which relates to financing).

Report cash flows from investing activities. p. 541

LO 12–3

- Investing activities reported on the cash flow statement include cash payments to acquire fixed assets and investments and cash proceeds from the sale of fixed assets and investments.

Report cash flows from financing activities. p. 542

LO 12–4

- Cash inflows from financing activities include cash proceeds from issuance of debt and common stock. Cash outflows include principal payments on debt, cash paid for the repurchase of the company's stock, and cash dividend payments. Cash payments associated with interest are a cash flow from operating activities.

Interpret cash flows from operating, investing, and financing activities. p. 544

LO 12–5

- A healthy company will generate positive cash flows from operations, some of which will be used to pay for purchases of equipment. Any additional cash (called free cash flow) can be used to further expand the business, pay down some of the company's debt, or simply build up the cash balance. A company is in trouble if it is unable to generate positive cash flows from operations in the long-run because eventually creditors will stop lending to the company and stockholders will stop investing in it.

Report and interpret cash flows from operating activities, using the direct method. p. 547

LO 12–6

- The direct method for reporting cash flows from operating activities accumulates all of the operating transactions that result in either a debit or a credit to cash into categories. The most common inflows are cash received from customers and dividends and interest on investments. The most common outflows are cash paid for purchase of services and goods for resale, salaries and wages, income taxes, and interest on liabilities. It is prepared by adjusting each item on the income statement from an accrual basis to a cash basis.

KEY TERMS

Cash Flows from Financing Activities p.5 33

Cash Flows from Investing Activities p. 532

Cash Flows from Operating Activities (Cash Flows from Operations) p. 532

Direct Method p. 535

Indirect Method p. 535

PRACTICE MATERIAL

QUESTIONS

1. Compare the purposes of the income statement, the balance sheet, and the statement of cash flows.

2. What information does the statement of cash flows report that is not reported on the other required financial statements?

3. What are cash equivalents? How are they reported on the statement of cash flows?

4. What are the major categories of business activities reported on the statement of cash flows? Define each of these activities.

5. What are the typical cash inflows from operating activities? What are the typical cash outflows from operating activities?

6. Describe the types of items used to compute cash flows from operating activities under the two alternative methods of reporting.

7. Under the indirect method, depreciation expense is added to net income to report cash flows from operating activities. Does depreciation cause an inflow of cash?

8. Explain why cash outflows during the period for purchases and salaries are not specifically reported on a statement of cash flows prepared using the indirect method.

9. Explain why a $50,000 increase in inventory during the year must be included in computing cash flows from operating activities under both the direct and indirect methods.

10. Loan covenants require that E-Gadget Corporation (EGC) generate $200,000 cash from operating activities each year. Without intervening during the last month of the current year, EGC will generate only $180,000 cash from operations. What are the pros and cons of each of the following possible interventions: (a) pressuring customers to pay overdue accounts, (b) delaying payment of amounts owing to suppliers, and (c) purchasing additional equipment to increase depreciation?

11. As a junior analyst, you are evaluating the financial performance of Digilog Corporation. Impressed by this year's growth in sales (20 percent increase), receivables (40 percent increase), and inventories (50 percent increase), you plan to report a favorable evaluation of the company. Your supervisor cautions you that those increases may signal difficulties rather than successes. When you ask what she means, she just says you should look at the company's statement of cash flows. What do you think you will find there? What are the cash flow effects when the balances in a company's receivables and inventory increase faster than its sales?

12. What are the typical cash inflows from investing activities? What are the typical cash outflows from investing activities?

13. What are the typical cash inflows from financing activities? What are the typical cash outflows from financing activities?

14. What are noncash investing and financing activities? Give one example. How are noncash investing and financing activities reported on the statement of cash flows?

15. (Supplement 12A) How is the sale of equipment reported on the statement of cash flows using the indirect method?

MULTIPLE CHOICE

1. Where is the overall change in cash shown in the statement of cash flows?

   a. In the top part, before the operating activities section.
   b. In one of the operating, investing, or financing activities sections.
   c. In the bottom part, following the financing activities section.
   d. None of the above.

2. In what order do the three sections of the statement of cash flows appear when reading from top to bottom?

   a. Financing, investing, operating.
   b. Investing, operating, financing.
   c. Operating, financing, investing.
   d. Operating, investing, financing.

3. Total cash inflow in the operating section of the statement of cash flows should include which of the following?

   a. Cash received from customers at the point of sale.
   b. Cash collections from customer accounts receivable.

   c. Cash received in advance of revenue recognition (deferred revenue).
   d. All of the above.

4. If the balance in Prepaid Expenses increased during the year, what action should be taken on the statement of cash flows when following the indirect method, *and why?*

   a. The change in the account balance should be subtracted from net income because the net increase in Prepaid Expenses did not impact net income but did reduce the cash balance.
   b. The change in the account balance should be added to net income because the net increase in Prepaid Expenses did not impact net income but did increase the cash balance.
   c. The net change in Prepaid Expenses should be subtracted from net income to eliminate the effect of adding it in the income statement.
   d. The net change in Prepaid Expenses should be added to net income to eliminate the effect of subtracting it in the income statement.

5. Which of the following would not appear in the investing section of the statement of cash flows?

   a. Purchase of inventory.
   b. Sale of investments.
   c. Purchase of land.
   d. All of the above would appear in the investing section of the statement of cash flows.

6. Which of the following items would not appear in the financing section of the statement of cash flows?

   a. The issuance of the company's own stock.
   b. The repayment of debt.
   c. The payment of dividends.
   d. All of the above would appear in the financing section of the statement of cash flows.

7. Which of the following is not added when computing cash flows from operations using the indirect method?

   a. The net increase in accounts payable.
   b. The net decrease in accounts receivable.
   c. The net decrease in inventory.
   d. All of the above should be added.

8. If a company engages in a material noncash transaction, which of the following is required?

   a. The company must include an explanatory narrative or schedule accompanying the statement of cash flows.
   b. No disclosure is necessary.

c. The company must include an explanatory narrative or schedule accompanying the balance sheet.
d. It must be reported in the investing and financing sections of the statement of cash flows.

9. The *total* change in cash shown on the statement of cash flows for the year should agree with which of the following?

   a. The difference in Retained Earnings when reviewing the comparative balance sheet.
   b. Net income or net loss as found on the income statement.
   c. The difference in cash when reviewing the comparative balance sheet.
   d. None of the above.

10. If a company's current assets (such as accounts receivable and inventories) are allowed to grow out of control, which of the following would occur?

    a. Cash flows from investing activities would be reduced.
    b. Cash flows from operating activities would be reduced.
    c. Cash flows from financing activities would increase.
    d. None of the above.

 **Find More Learning Solutions on Connect.**

MINI-EXERCISES

M12–1 Identifying Companies from Cash Flow Patterns   LO 12–1, 12–5

Based on the cash flows shown, classify each of the following cases as a growing start-up company (S), a healthy established company (E), or an established company facing financial difficulties (F).

	Case 1	Case 2	Case 3
Cash provided by (used for) operating activities	$ 3,000	$(120,000)	$ 80,000
Cash provided by (used for) investing activities	(70,000)	10,000	(40,000)
Cash provided by (used for) financing activities	75,000	75,000	(30,000)
Net change in cash	8,000	(35,000)	10,000
Cash position at beginning of year	2,000	40,000	30,000
Cash position at end of year includes all balance sheet accounts related to operating activities.	$ 10,000	$ 5,000	$ 40,000

M12–2 Matching Items Reported to Cash Flow Statement Categories (Indirect Method)   LO 12–1, 12–2

The Buckle, Inc., included the following in its statement of cash flows presented using the indirect method. Indicate whether each item is disclosed in the operating activities (O), investing activities (I), or financing activities (F) section of the statement or use (NA) if the item does not appear on the statement.

_____ 1. Purchase of investments.
_____ 2. Proceeds from issuance of stock.
_____ 3. Purchase of equipment.

_____ 4. Depreciation.
_____ 5. Accounts payable (decrease).
_____ 6. Inventory (increase).

LO 12–2

M12–3 Determining the Effects of Account Changes on Cash Flows from Operating Activities (Indirect Method)

Indicate whether each item would be added (+) or subtracted (−) in the computation of cash flows from operating activities using the indirect method.

_____ **1.** Depreciation.

_____ **2.** Inventory decrease.

_____ **3.** Accounts payable decrease.

_____ **4.** Accounts receivable increase.

_____ **5.** Accrued liabilities increase.

LO 12–2

M12–4 Computing Cash Flows from Operating Activities (Indirect Method)

For each of the following independent cases, compute cash flows from operating activities. Assume the list below includes all balance sheet accounts related to operating activities.

	Case A	Case B	Case C
Net income	$310,000	$ 15,000	$420,000
Depreciation expense	40,000	150,000	80,000
Accounts receivable increase (decrease)	100,000	(200,000)	(20,000)
Inventory increase (decrease)	(50,000)	35,000	50,000
Accounts payable increase (decrease)	(50,000)	120,000	70,000
Accrued liabilities increase (decrease)	60,000	(220,000)	(40,000)

LO 12–2

M12–5 Computing Cash Flows from Operating Activities (Indirect Method)

For the following two independent cases, show the cash flows from operating activities section of the statement of cash flows for year 2 using the indirect method.

	Case A		Case B	
	Year 2	Year 1	Year 2	Year 1
Sales Revenue	$11,000	$9,000	$21,000	$18,000
Cost of Goods Sold	6,000	5,500	12,000	11,000
Gross Profit	5,000	3,500	9,000	7,000
Depreciation Expense	1,000	1,000	1,500	1,500
Salaries and Wages Expense	2,500	2,000	5,000	5,000
Net Income	1,500	500	2,500	500
Accounts Receivable	300	400	750	600
Inventory	750	500	730	800
Accounts Payable	800	700	800	850
Salaries and Wages Payable	1,000	1,200	200	250

LO 12–3

M12–6 Computing Cash Flows from Investing Activities

Based on the following information, compute cash flows from investing activities under GAAP.

Cash collections from customers	$800
Purchase of used equipment	200
Depreciation expense	200
Sale of investments	450
Dividends received	100
Interest received	200

LO 12–4

M12–7 Computing Cash Flows from Financing Activities

Based on the following information, compute cash flows from financing activities under GAAP.

Purchase of investments	$ 250
Dividends paid	1,200
Interest paid	400
Additional borrowing from bank	2,800

M12–8 Computing Cash Flows Under IFRS   LO 12–1

Using the data from M12–6, calculate the maximum investing cash inflows that could be reported under IFRS. Using data from M12–7, calculate the maximum financing cash flows that could be reported under IFRS.

M12–9 Reporting Noncash Investing and Financing Activities   LO 12–3, 12–4

Which of the following transactions would be considered noncash investing and financing activities?

_____ 1. Additional borrowing from bank.

_____ 2. Purchase of equipment with investments.

_____ 3. Dividends paid in cash.

_____ 4. Purchase of a building with a promissory note.

M12–10 Interpreting Cash Flows from Operating, Investing, and Financing Activities   LO 12–5

Quantum Dots, Inc., is a nanotechnology company that manufactures "quantum dots," which are tiny pieces of silicon consisting of 100 or more molecules. Quantum dots can be used to illuminate very small objects, enabling scientists to see the blood vessels beneath a mouse's skin ripple with each heartbeat, at the rate of 100 times per second. Evaluate this research-intensive company's cash flows, assuming the following was reported in its statement of cash flows.

	Current Year	Previous Year
Cash Flows from Operating Activities		
Net cash provided by (used for) operating activities	$ (50,790)	$ (46,730)
Cash Flows from Investing Activities		
Purchases of research equipment	(250,770)	(480,145)
Proceeds from selling all short-term investments	35,000	—
Net cash provided by (used for) investing activities	(215,770)	(480,145)
Cash Flows from Financing Activities		
Additional long-term debt borrowed	100,000	200,000
Proceeds from stock issuance	140,000	200,000
Cash dividends paid	—	(10,000)
Net cash provided by (used for) financing activities	240,000	390,000
Net increase (decrease) in cash	(26,560)	(136,875)
Cash at beginning of period	29,025	165,900
Cash at end of period	$ 2,465	$ 29,025

M12–11 Matching Items Reported to Cash Flow Statement Categories (Direct Method)   LO 12–1, 12–6

Prestige Manufacturing Corporation reports the following items in its statement of cash flows presented using the direct method. Indicate whether each item is disclosed in the operating activities (O), investing activities (I), or financing activities (F) section of the statement under GAAP or use (NA) if the item does not appear on the statement.

_____ 1. Payment for equipment purchase.

_____ 2. Repayments of bank loan.

_____ 3. Dividends paid.

_____ 4. Proceeds from issuance of stock.

_____ 5. Interest paid.

_____ 6. Receipts from customers.

M12–12 Computing Cash Flows from Operating Activities (Direct Method)   LO 12–6

For each of the following independent cases, compute cash flows from operating activities using the direct method. Assume the list below includes all items relevant to operating activities.

	Case A	Case B	Case C
Sales revenue	$65,000	$55,000	$96,000
Cost of goods sold	35,000	26,000	65,000
Depreciation expense	10,000	2,000	26,000
Salaries and wages expense	5,000	13,000	8,000
Net income (loss)	15,000	14,000	(3,000)
Accounts receivable increase (decrease)	(1,000)	4,000	3,000
Inventory increase (decrease)	2,000	0	(3,000)
Accounts payable increase (decrease)	0	2,500	(1,000)
Salaries and wages payable increase (decrease)	1,500	(2,000)	1,000

LO 12–6   **M12–13 Computing Cash Flows from Operating Activities (Direct Method)**

Refer to the two cases presented in M12–5, and for each case show the cash flow from operating activities section of the Year 2 statement of cash flows using the direct method.

EXERCISES

LO 12–1, 12–2   **E12–1 Matching Items Reported to Cash Flow Statement Categories (Indirect Method)**

NIKE, Inc., is the best-known sports shoe, apparel, and equipment company in the world because of its association with athletes such as LeBron James, Roger Federer, and Madison Keys. Some of the items included in its recent statement of cash flows presented using the indirect method are listed here.

Indicate whether each item is disclosed in the operating activities (O), investing activities (I), or financing activities (F) section of the statement or use (NA) if the item does not appear on the statement.

_____ **1.** Additions to long-term debt.

_____ **2.** Depreciation.

_____ **3.** Additions to equipment.

_____ **4.** Increase (decrease) in notes payable. (The amount is owed to financial institutions.)

_____ **5.** (Increase) decrease in other current assets.

_____ **6.** Cash received from disposal of equipment.

_____ **7.** Reductions in long-term debt.

_____ **8.** Issuance of stock.

_____ **9.** (Increase) decrease in inventory.

_____ **10.** Net income.

LO 12–2   **E12–2 Understanding the Computation of Cash Flows from Operating Activities (Indirect Method)**

Suppose your company sells services of $180 in exchange for $110 cash and $70 on account.

Required:

1. Show the journal entry to record this transaction.

2. Identify the amount that should be reported as net cash flow from operating activities.

3. Identify the amount that would be included in net income.

4. Show how the indirect method would convert net income (requirement 3) to net cash flow from operating activities (requirement 2).

5. What general rule about converting net income to operating cash flows is revealed by your answer to requirement 4?

LO 12–2   **E12–3 Understanding the Computation of Cash Flows from Operating Activities (Indirect Method)**

Suppose your company sells services for $325 cash this month. Your company also pays $100 in salaries and wages, which includes $15 that was payable at the end of the previous month and $85 for salaries and wages of this month.

Required:

1. Show the journal entries to record these transactions.

2. Calculate the amount that should be reported as net cash flow from operating activities.

3. Calculate the amount that should be reported as net income.

4. Show how the indirect method would convert net income (requirement 3) to net cash flow from operating activities (requirement 2).

5. What general rule about converting net income to operating cash flows is revealed by your answer to requirement 4?

E12–4 Understanding the Computation of Cash Flows from Operating Activities (Indirect Method)   LO 12–2

Suppose your company sells services of $150 in exchange for $120 cash and $30 on account. Depreciation of $50 relating to equipment also is recorded.

Required:

1. Show the journal entries to record these transactions.

2. Calculate the amount that should be reported as net cash flow from operating activities.

3. Calculate the amount that should be reported as net income.

4. Show how the indirect method would convert net income (requirement 3) to net cash flow from operating activities (requirement 2).

5. What general rule about converting net income to operating cash flows is revealed by your answer to requirement 4?

E12–5 Understanding the Computation of Cash Flows from Operating Activities (Indirect Method)   LO 12–2

Suppose your company sells goods for $300, of which $200 is received in cash and $100 is on account. The goods cost your company $125 and were paid for in a previous period. Your company also recorded salaries and wages of $70, of which only $30 has been paid in cash.

Required:

1. Show the journal entries to record these transactions.

2. Calculate the amount that should be reported as net cash flow from operating activities.

3. Calculate the amount that should be reported as net income.

4. Show how the indirect method would convert net income (requirement 3) to net cash flow from operating activities (requirement 2).

5. What general rule about converting net income to operating cash flows is revealed by your answer to requirement 4?

E12–6 Preparing and Evaluating a Simple Statement of Cash Flows (Indirect Method)   LO 12–2, 12–5

Suppose your company reports $160 of net income and $40 of cash dividends paid, and its comparative balance sheet indicates the following.

	Beginning	Ending
Cash	$ 35	$205
Accounts Receivable	75	175
Inventory	245	135
Total	355	$515
Salaries and Wages Payable	$ 10	$ 50
Common Stock	100	100
Retained Earnings	245	365
Total	$355	$515

Required:

1. Prepare the operating activities section of the statement of cash flows, using the indirect method.

2. Identify the most important cause of the difference between the company's net income and net cash flow from operating activities.

LO 12–1, 12–2, 12–5   E12–7 Preparing and Evaluating a Simple Statement of Cash Flows (Indirect Method)

Suppose the income statement for Goggle Company reports $95 of net income, after deducting depreciation of $35. The company bought equipment costing $60 and obtained a long-term bank loan for $70. The company's comparative balance sheet, at December 31, is presented here.

	Previous Year	Current Year	Change
Cash	$ 35	$ 240	
Accounts Receivable	75	175	
Inventory	260	135	
Equipment	500	560	
Accumulated Depreciation—Equipment	(45)	(80)	
Total	$825	$1,030	
Salaries and Wages Payable	$ 10	$ 50	
Notes Payable (long-term)	445	515	
Common Stock	10	10	
Retained Earnings	360	455	
Total	$825	$1,030	

Required:

1. Calculate the change in each balance sheet account and indicate whether each account relates to operating, investing, and/or financing activities.

2. Prepare a statement of cash flows using the indirect method.

3. In one sentence, explain why an increase in accounts receivable is subtracted.

4. In one sentence, explain why a decrease in inventory is added.

5. In one sentence, explain why an increase in salaries and wages payable is added.

6. Are the cash flows typical of a start-up, healthy, or troubled company? Explain.

LO 12–2   E12–8 Reporting Cash Flows from Operating Activities (Indirect Method)

The following information pertains to Guy's Gear Company:

Sales		$80,000
Expenses:		
Cost of Goods Sold	$50,000	
Depreciation Expense	6,000	
Salaries and Wages Expense	12,000	68,000
Net Income		$12,000
Accounts Receivable decrease	$ 4,000	
Inventory increase	8,000	
Salaries and Wages Payable increase	750	

Required:

Present the operating activities section of the statement of cash flows for Guy's Gear Company using the indirect method.

E12–9 **Reporting and Interpreting Cash Flows from Operating Activities from an Analyst's Perspective (Indirect Method)**

LO 12–2, 12–5

New Vision Company completed its income statement and balance sheet and provided the following information:

Service Revenue		$66,000
Expenses:		
Salaries and Wages	$42,000	
Depreciation	7,300	
Utilities	6,000	
Office	1,700	57,000
Net Income		$ 9,000
Decrease in Accounts Receivable	$12,000	
Paid cash for equipment	5,000	
Increase in Salaries and Wages Payable	9,000	
Decrease in Accounts Payable	4,250	

Required:

1. Present the operating activities section of the statement of cash flows for New Vision Company using the indirect method.

2. Of the potential causes of differences between cash flow from operations and net income, which are the most important to financial analysts?

E12–10 **Reporting and Interpreting Cash Flows from Operating Activities from an Analyst's Perspective (Indirect Method)**

LO 12–2, 12–5

Pizza International, Inc., reported the following information (in thousands):

Operating Activities				
Net Income	$ 100	Decrease in accounts payable	$ 8,720
Depreciation	33,305	Increase in accrued liabilities	719
Increase in receivables	170	Decrease in income taxes payable	2,721
Decrease in inventory	643	Payments on notes payable	12,691
Increase in prepaid expenses	664	Cash paid for equipment	29,073

Required:

1. Based on this information, compute cash flow from operating activities using the indirect method.

2. What was the primary reason that Pizza International was able to report large positive cash flow from operations despite nearly having a net loss?

E12–11 **Inferring Balance Sheet Changes from the Cash Flow Statement (Indirect Method)**

LO 12–2

Colgate-Palmolive was founded in 1806. Its statement of cash flows reported the following information (in millions) for the nine months ended September 30, 2016:

Operating Activities	
Net Income	$1,960
Depreciation	330
Cash effect of changes in:	
Accounts Receivable	(125)
Inventory	5
Accounts Payable	100
Other	50
Net Cash Provided by Operations	$2,320

Required:

Based on the information reported in the operating activities section of the statement of cash flows for Colgate-Palmolive, indicate whether the following accounts increased (I) or decreased (D) during the period: (*a*) Accounts Receivable, (*b*) Inventories, and (*c*) Accounts Payable.

LO 12–2   E12–12 Inferring Balance Sheet Changes from the Cash Flow Statement (Indirect Method)

A statement of cash flows contained the following information:

Operating Activities	
Net Income	$14,013
Depreciation	1,027
Changes in current assets and current liabilities	
Accounts Receivable	(2,142)
Inventory	596
Accounts Payable	6,307
Accrued Liabilities	(1,217)
Net Cash Provided by Operations	$18,584

Required:

Determine whether the following account balances increased (I) or decreased (D) during the period: (*a*) Accounts Receivable, (*b*) Inventories, (*c*) Accounts Payable, and (*d*) Accrued Liabilities.

LO 12–1, 12–2, 12–3, 12–4, 12–5   E12–13 Preparing and Evaluating a Statement of Cash Flows (Indirect Method) from Comparative Balance Sheets and Income Statements

Consultex, Inc., was founded in 2015 as a small financial consulting business. The company had done reasonably well in 2015–2017 but started noticing its cash dwindle early in 2018. In January 2018, Consultex had paid $16,000 to purchase land and repaid $2,000 principal on an existing promissory note. In March, the company paid $2,000 cash for dividends and $1,000 to repurchase and eliminate Consultex stock that had previously been issued for $1,000. To improve its cash position, Consultex borrowed $5,000 by signing a new promissory note in May and also issued stock to a new private investor for $12,000 cash. Year-end comparative balance sheets and income statements are presented below.

CONSULTEX, INC.
Balance Sheet
October 31

	2018	2017
Assets		
Cash	$11,000	$14,000
Accounts Receivable	14,000	12,000
Prepaid Rent	2,000	3,000
Land	26,000	10,000
Total Assets	$53,000	$39,000
Liabilities and Stockholders' Equity		
Salaries and Wages Payable	$ 2,000	$ 3,000
Income Taxes Payable	1,000	1,000
Notes Payable (long-term)	15,000	12,000
Common Stock	20,000	9,000
Retained Earnings	15,000	14,000
Total Liabilities and Stockholders' Equity	$53,000	$39,000

CONSULTEX, INC.
Income Statement
For the Year Ended October 31

	2018	2017
Sales Revenue	$158,000	$161,000
Salaries and Wages Expense	98,000	97,000
Rent Expense	36,000	30,000
Utilities Expenses	19,700	20,000
Income before Income Tax Expense	4,300	14,000
Income Tax Expense	1,300	4,200
Net Income	$ 3,000	$ 9,800

Requirements:

1. Prepare a properly formatted Statement of Cash Flows for Consultex, Inc., for the year ended October 31, 2018 (using the indirect method).

2. What one thing can Consultex reasonably change in 2019 to avoid depleting its cash?

E12–14   Calculating and Understanding Operating Cash Flows Relating to Inventory Purchases (Indirect Method)

LO 12–2

The following information was reported by three companies. When completing the requirements, assume that any and all purchases on account are for inventory.

	Aztec Corporation	Bikes Unlimited	Campus Cycles
Cost of goods sold	$175	$175	$350
Inventory purchases from suppliers made using cash	200	0	200
Inventory purchases from suppliers made on account	0	200	200
Cash payments to suppliers on account	0	160	160
Beginning inventory	100	100	200
Ending inventory	125	125	250
Beginning accounts payable	0	80	80
Ending accounts payable	0	120	120

Required:

1. What amount did each company deduct on the income statement related to inventory?

2. What total amount did each company pay out in cash during the period related to inventory purchased with cash and on account?

3. By what amount do your answers in requirements 1 and 2 differ for each company?

4. By what amount did each company's inventory increase (decrease)? By what amount did each company's accounts payable increase (decrease)?

5. Using the indirect method of presentation, what amount(s) must each company add (deduct) from net income to convert from accrual to cash basis?

6. Describe any similarities between your answers to requirements 3 and 5. Are these answers the same? Why or why not?

LO 12–3, 12–4
E12–15 Reporting Cash Flows from Investing and Financing Activities

Rowe Furniture Corporation is a Virginia-based manufacturer of furniture. In a recent quarter, it reported the following activities:

Net income	$ 4,135	Payments to reduce notes payable (long-term)	$ 46
Purchase of equipment	871	Sale of investments	134
Borrowings under line of credit (bank)	1,417	Proceeds from sale of equipment	6,594
Proceeds from issuance of common stock	11	Dividends paid	277
Cash received from customers	29,164	Interest paid	90

Required:

Based on this information, present the cash flows from investing and financing activities sections of the cash flow statement.

LO 12–3, 12–4
E12–16 Reporting and Interpreting Cash Flows from Investing and Financing Activities with Discussion of Management Strategy

Gibraltar Industries, Inc., is a manufacturer of steel products for customers such as Home Depot, Lowe's, Chrysler, Ford, and General Motors. In the year ended December 31, 2016, it reported the following activities:

Net income	$ (33,675)	Depreciation	$24,000
Purchase of equipment	10,800	Proceeds from sale of equipment	950
Payments on notes payable to bank	400	Decrease in accounts receivable	40,000
Net proceeds from stock issuance	3,340	Payments to acquire treasury stock	1,540

Required:

Based on this information, present the cash flows from the investing and financing activities sections of the cash flow statement.

LO 12–2, 12–5
E12–17 Interpreting the Cash Flow Statement

The Walt Disney Company reported the following in its 2016 annual report (in millions):

	2016	2015	2014
Net income	$ 9,400	$ 8,400	$ 7,500
Net cash provided by operating activities	13,200	10,900	9,780
Purchase of parks, resorts, and equipment	(4,800)	(4,300)	(3,300)

Required:

1. Note that in all three years, net cash provided by operating activities is greater than net income. Given the above information and what you know about the Walt Disney Company from your own personal observations, provide one reason that could explain the sizable difference between net income and net cash provided by operating activities.

2. Based solely on the results reported above for the three years, did Walt Disney Company need external financing to purchase parks, resorts, and equipment during these years?

LO 12–2, 12–6
E12–18 Comparing the Direct and Indirect Methods

To compare statement of cash flows reporting under the direct and indirect methods, enter check marks to indicate which line items are reported on the statement of cash flows with each method.

Cash Flows (and Related Changes)	Statement of Cash Flows Method	
	Direct	Indirect
1. Net income		
2. Receipts from customers		
3. Accounts receivable increase or decrease		
4. Payments to suppliers		
5. Inventory increase or decrease		
6. Accounts payable increase or decrease		
7. Payments to employees		
8. Salaries and wages payable, increase or decrease		
9. Depreciation expense		
10. Cash flows from operating activities		
11. Cash flows from investing activities		
12. Cash flows from financing activities		
13. Net increase or decrease in cash during the period		

E12–19 Reporting and Interpreting Cash Flows from Operating Activities from an Analyst's Perspective (Direct Method)   LO 12–5, 12–6

Refer to the information for New Vision Company in E12–9.

Required:

1. Present the operating activities section of the statement of cash flows for New Vision Company using the direct method. Assume that Accounts Payable relate to Utilities and Office Expenses on the income statement.

2. If payments for salaries and wages were to increase by 10 percent throughout the year, by what dollar amount and in what direction would operating cash flows change?

E12–20 Reporting and Interpreting Cash Flows from Operating Activities from an Analyst's Perspective (Direct Method)   LO 12–5, 12–6

Refer back to the information given for E12–10, plus the following summarized income statement for Pizza International, Inc. (in millions):

Revenues	$143,551
Cost of Sales	45,500
Gross Profit	98,051
Salary and Wages Expense	56,835
Depreciation	33,305
Office Expenses	7,781
Net Income before Income Tax Expense	130
Income Tax Expense	30
Net Income	$ 100

Required:

1. Based on this information, compute cash flow from operating activities using the direct method. Assume Prepaid Expenses and Accrued Liabilities relate to office expenses.

2. What was the primary reason that Pizza International was able to report large positive cash flow from operations despite nearly having a net loss?

LO 12–S1   **E12–21 (Supplement 12A) Determining Cash Flows from the Sale of Equipment**

Cedar Fair operates amusement parks in the United States and Canada. During a recent year, it reported the following (in millions):

From the income statement	
Loss (gain) on sale of equipment	$ (9)
Depreciation expense	126
From the balance sheet	
Equipment, beginning	1,450
Equipment, ending	1,500
Accumulated depreciation, beginning	1,160
Accumulated depreciation, ending	1,250

Equipment costing $120 was purchased during the year.

Required:

For the equipment that was disposed of during the year, compute the following: (a) its original cost, (b) its accumulated depreciation, and (c) cash received from the disposal.

LO 12–S1   **E12–22 (Supplement 12A) Determining Cash Flows from the Sale of Equipment**

During the period, Teen's Trends sold some excess equipment at a loss. The following information was collected from the company's accounting records:

From the income statement	
Depreciation expense	$ 500
Loss on sale of equipment	4,000
From the balance sheet	
Beginning equipment	12,500
Ending equipment	6,500
Beginning accumulated depreciation	2,000
Ending accumulated depreciation	2,200

No new equipment was bought during the period.

Required:

For the equipment that was sold, determine (a) its original cost, (b) its accumulated depreciation, and (c) the cash received from the sale.

LO 12–S2   **E12–23 (Supplement 12B) Preparing a Statement of Cash Flows, Indirect Method: T-Account Approach**

Golf Universe is a regional and online golf equipment retailer. The company reported the following for the current year:

- Purchased a long-term investment for cash, $15,000.
- Paid cash dividend, $12,000.
- Sold equipment for $6,000 cash (cost, $21,000; accumulated depreciation, $15,000).

- Issued shares of no-par stock, 500 shares at $12 cash per share.
- Net income was $20,200.
- Depreciation expense was $3,000.

Its comparative balance sheet is presented below.

	Ending Balances	Beginning Balances
Cash...	$ 19,200	$ 20,500
Accounts receivable	22,000	22,000
Inventory	75,000	68,000
Investments	15,000	0
Equipment	93,500	114,500
Accumulated Depreciation—Equipment	(20,000)	(32,000)
Total	$204,700	$193,000
Accounts payable	$ 14,000	$ 17,000
Salaries and Wages Payable	1,500	2,500
Income taxes payable	4,500	3,000
Notes Payable (long-term)	54,000	54,000
Common Stock	106,000	100,000
Retained earnings	24,700	16,500
Total	$204,700	$193,000

Required:

1. Following Supplement 12B, complete a T-account worksheet to be used to prepare the statement of cash flows for the current year.

2. Based on the T-account worksheet, prepare the statement of cash flows for the current year in proper format.

GROUP A PROBLEMS

PA12–1 Determining Cash Flow Statement Effects of Transactions

LO 12–1

Motif Furniture is an Austin-based furniture company. For each of the following first-quarter transactions, indicate whether operating (O), investing (I), or financing activities (F) are affected and whether the effect is a cash inflow (+) or outflow (−). Use (NE) if the transaction has no effect on cash.

_____   1. Bought used equipment for cash.

_____   2. Paid cash to purchase new equipment.

_____   3. Declared and paid cash dividends to stockholders.

_____   4. Collected payments on account from customers.

_____   5. Recorded and paid interest on debt to creditors.

_____   6. Repaid principal on loan from bank.

_____   7. Prepaid rent for the following period.

_____   8. Made payment to suppliers on account.

PA12–2 Computing Cash Flows from Operating Activities (Indirect Method)

LO 12–2

The income statement and selected balance sheet information for Direct Products Company for the year ended December 31 are presented below.

Income Statement	
Sales Revenue	$48,600
Expenses:	
Cost of Goods Sold	21,000
Depreciation Expense	2,000
Salaries and Wages Expense	9,000
Rent Expense	4,500
Insurance Expense	1,900
Interest Expense	1,800
Utilities Expense	1,400
Net Income	$ 7,000

Selected Balance Sheet Accounts	Ending Balances	Beginning Balances
Accounts Receivable	$560	$580
Inventory	990	770
Accounts Payable	420	460
Prepaid Rent	25	20
Prepaid Insurance	25	28
Salaries and Wages Payable	100	60
Utilities Payable	20	15

Required:

Prepare the cash flows from operating activities section of the statement of cash flows using the indirect method.

LO 12–2, 12–3, 12–4, 12–5   **PA12–3**   **Preparing a Statement of Cash Flows (Indirect Method)**

XS Supply Company is developing its annual financial statements at December 31. The statements are complete except for the statement of cash flows. The completed comparative balance sheets and income statement are summarized:

	Current Year	Previous Year
Balance Sheet at December 31		
Cash	$ 34,000	$ 29,000
Accounts Receivable	35,000	28,000
Inventory	41,000	38,000
Equipment	121,000	100,000
Accumulated Depreciation—Equipment	(30,000)	(25,000)
Total Assets	$201,000	$170,000
Accounts Payable	$ 36,000	$ 27,000
Salaries and Wages Payable	1,200	1,400
Note Payable (long-term)	38,000	44,000
Common Stock	88,600	72,600
Retained Earnings	37,200	25,000
Total Liabilities and Stockholders' Equity	$201,000	$170,000
Income Statement		
Sales Revenue	$120,000	
Cost of Goods Sold	70,000	
Other Expenses	37,800	
Net Income	$ 12,200	

Additional Data:

a. Bought equipment for cash, $21,000.
b. Paid $6,000 on the long-term note payable.
c. Issued new shares of stock for $16,000 cash.
d. No dividends were declared or paid.
e. Other expenses included depreciation, $5,000; salaries and wages, $20,000; taxes, $6,000; utilities, $6,800.
f. Accounts Payable includes only inventory purchases made on credit. Because there are no liability accounts relating to taxes or other expenses, assume that these expenses were fully paid in cash.

Required:

1. Prepare the statement of cash flows for the current year ended December 31 using the indirect method.
2. Evaluate the statement of cash flows.

PA12–4 Preparing and Interpreting a Statement of Cash Flows (Indirect Method)   **LO 12–2, 12–3, 12–4, 12–5**

Heads Up Company was started several years ago by two hockey instructors. The company's comparative balance sheets and income statement follow, along with additional information.

	Current Year	Previous Year
Balance Sheet at December 31		
Cash	$ 6,300	$4,000
Accounts Receivable	900	1,750
Equipment	5,500	5,000
Accumulated Depreciation—Equipment	(1,500)	(1,250)
Total Assets	$11,200	$9,500
Accounts Payable	$ 500	$1,000
Salaries and Wages Payable	500	750
Note Payable (long-term)	1,700	500
Common Stock	5,000	5,000
Retained Earnings	3,500	2,250
Total Liabilities and Stockholders' Equity	$11,200	$9,500
Income Statement		
Service Revenue	$37,500	
Salaries and Wages Expense	35,000	
Depreciation Expense	250	
Income Tax Expense	1,000	
Net Income	$ 1,250	

Additional Data:

a. Bought new hockey equipment for cash, $500.
b. Borrowed $1,200 cash from the bank during the year.
c. Accounts Payable includes only purchases of services made on credit for operating purposes. Because there are no liability accounts relating to income tax, assume that this expense was fully paid in cash.

Required:

1. Prepare the statement of cash flows for the current year ended December 31 using the indirect method.
2. Use the statement of cash flows to evaluate the company's cash flows.

PA12–5 Computing Cash Flows from Operating Activities (Direct Method)   **LO 12–6**

Refer to the information in PA12–2.

Required:

Prepare the cash flows from operating activities section of the statement of cash flows using the direct method.

PA12–6 Preparing and Interpreting a Statement of Cash Flows (Direct Method)   **LO 12–3, 12–4, 12–5, 12–6**

Refer to PA12–4.

Required:

Complete requirements 1 and 2 using the direct method.

LO 12–S1

PA12–7 (Supplement 12A) Preparing and Interpreting a Statement of Cash Flows with Loss on Disposal (Indirect Method)

Assume the same facts as PA12–4, except for the income statement and additional data item (*a*). The new income statement is shown below. Instead of item (*a*) from PA12–4, assume that the company bought new equipment for $1,800 cash and sold existing equipment for $500 cash. The equipment that was sold had cost $1,300 and had Accumulated Depreciation of $250 at the time of sale.

Income Statement	
Service Revenue	$37,500
Salaries and Wages Expense	35,000
Depreciation Expense	500
Loss on Disposal of Equipment	550
Income Tax Expense	200
Net Income	$ 1,250

Required:

1. Prepare the statement of cash flows for the year ended December 31 using the indirect method.
2. Use the statement of cash flows to evaluate the company's cash flows.

GROUP B PROBLEMS

LO 12–1

PB12–1 Determining Cash Flow Statement Effects of Transactions

For each of the following transactions, indicate whether operating (O), investing (I), or financing activities (F) are affected and whether the effect is a cash inflow (+) or outflow (−). Use (NE) if the transaction has no effect on cash.

_____ 1. Received deposits from customers for products to be delivered the following period.
_____ 2. Principal repayments on loan.
_____ 3. Paid cash to purchase new equipment.
_____ 4. Received proceeds from loan.
_____ 5. Collected payments on account from customers.
_____ 6. Recorded and paid salaries and wages to employees.
_____ 7. Paid cash for building construction.
_____ 8. Recorded and paid interest to debt holders.

LO 12–2

PB12–2 Computing Cash Flows from Operating Activities (Indirect Method)

The income statement and selected balance sheet information for Calendars Incorporated for the year ended December 31 are presented below.

Income Statement			Selected Balance Sheet Accounts	Ending Balances	Beginning Balances
Sales Revenue	$78,000				
Expenses:			Inventory	$ 430	$ 490
Cost of Goods Sold	36,000		Accounts Receivable	1,800	1,500
Depreciation Expense	16,000		Accounts Payable	1,200	1,300
Salaries and Wages Expense	10,000		Salaries and Wages Payable	450	250
Rent Expense	2,500		Utilities Payable	100	0
Insurance Expense	1,300		Prepaid Rent	80	100
Interest Expense	1,200		Prepaid Insurance	70	90
Utilities Expense	1,000				
Net Income	$10,000				

Required:

Prepare the cash flows from operating activities section of the statement of cash flows using the indirect method.

PB12–3 Preparing a Statement of Cash Flows (Indirect Method) LO 12–2, 12–3, 12–4, 12–5

Audio City, Inc., is developing its annual financial statements at December 31. The statements are complete except for the statement of cash flows. The completed comparative balance sheets and income statement are summarized below:

	Current Year	Previous Year
Balance Sheet at December 31		
Cash	$ 60,000	$ 65,000
Accounts Receivable	15,000	20,000
Inventory	22,000	20,000
Equipment	223,000	150,000
Accumulated Depreciation—Equipment	(60,000)	(45,000)
Total Assets	$260,000	$210,000
Accounts Payable	$ 8,000	$ 19,000
Salaries and Wages Payable	2,000	1,000
Note Payable (long-term)	60,000	75,000
Common Stock	100,000	70,000
Retained Earnings	90,000	45,000
Total Liabilities and Stockholders' Equity	$260,000	$210,000
Income Statement		
Sales Revenue	$200,000	
Cost of Goods Sold	90,000	
Other Expenses	60,000	
Net Income	$ 50,000	

Additional Data:

a. Bought equipment for cash, $73,000.
b. Paid $15,000 on the long-term note payable.
c. Issued new shares of stock for $30,000 cash.
d. Dividends of $5,000 were paid in cash.
e. Other expenses included depreciation, $15,000; salaries and wages, $20,000; taxes, $25,000.
f. Accounts Payable includes only inventory purchases made on credit. Because a liability relating to taxes does not exist, assume that they were fully paid in cash.

Required:

1. Prepare the statement of cash flows for the current year ended December 31 using the indirect method.
2. Evaluate the statement of cash flows.

PB12–4 Preparing and Interpreting a Statement of Cash Flows (Indirect Method) LO 12–2, 12–3, 12–4, 12–5

Dive In Company was started several years ago by two diving instructors. The company's comparative balance sheets and income statement, as well as additional information, are presented below.

	Current Year	Previous Year
Balance Sheet at December 31		
Cash	$ 3,200	$4,000
Accounts Receivable	1,000	500
Prepaid Rent	100	50
Total Assets	$ 4,300	$4,550
Salaries and Wages Payable	$ 350	$1,100
Common Stock	1,200	1,000
Retained Earnings	2,750	2,450
Total Liabilities and Stockholders' Equity	$ 4,300	$4,550
Income Statement		
Service Revenue	$33,950	
Salaries and Wages Expense	30,000	
Rent and Office Expenses	3,650	
Net Income	$ 300	

Additional Data:

a. Rent is paid in advance each month, and Office Expenses are paid in cash as incurred.

b. An owner contributed capital by paying $200 cash in exchange for the company's stock.

Required:

1. Prepare the statement of cash flows for the current year ended December 31 using the indirect method.

2. Use the statement of cash flows to evaluate the company's cash flows.

LO 12–6   **PB12–5 Computing Cash Flows from Operating Activities (Direct Method)**

Refer to the information in PB12–2.

Required:

Prepare the cash flows from operating activities section of the statement of cash flows using the direct method.

LO 12–3, 12–4, 12–5, 12–6   **PB12–6 Preparing and Interpreting a Statement of Cash Flows (Direct Method)**

Refer to PB12–4.

Required:

Complete requirements 1 and 2 using the direct method.

SKILLS DEVELOPMENT CASES

LO 12–1, 12–5   **S12–1 Finding Financial Information**

Go to the Home Depot investor relations website (http://ir.homedepot.com) and download the 2016 annual report. Note: Fiscal 2016 for The Home Depot runs from February 1, 2016, to January 29, 2017.

Required:

1. Which of the two basic reporting approaches for the cash flows from operating activities did The Home Depot use?

   a. Direct

   b. Indirect

2. What amount of income tax payments did The Home Depot make during the year ended January 29, 2017?

   a. $639 million

   b. $4,623 million

   c. $3,082 million

   d. $12 million

3. In the fiscal year ended January 29, 2017, The Home Depot generated $9,783 million from operating activities. Indicate where this cash was spent by listing the two largest cash outflows.

   a. Share Repurchase ($7,000 million) and Cash Dividends ($3,404 million)

   b. Share Repurchase ($6,880 million) and Capital Expenditures ($1,621 million)

   c. Long-Term Debt Repayments ($3,045 million) and Share Repurchase ($6,880 million)

   d. Cash Dividends ($3,404 million) and Share Repurchase ($6,880 million)

LO 12–1, 12–5   **S12–2 Comparing Financial Information**

Go to the Home Depot investor relations website (http://ir.homedepot.com) and download the 2016 annual report. Note: Fiscal 2016 for The Home Depot runs from February 1, 2016, to January 29, 2017.

Required:

1. Which of the two basic reporting approaches for the cash flows from operating activities did Lowe's use? Is this the same as what The Home Depot used?

2. What amount of cash did Lowe's receive from issuing long-term debt during the year ended February 3, 2017? How much cash did Lowe's use to repay long-term debt during the same year? What is the net difference between these inflows and outflows? Compare this net inflow or outflow of cash for long-term debt at Lowe's to The Home Depot for Fiscal 2016.

3. In the fiscal year ended February 3, 2017, Lowe's generated $5,617 million from operating activities. Indicate where Lowe's spent much of this money by listing the two largest cash outflows reported in the investing or financing activities sections. Was the reason for Lowe's largest cash outflow similar to or different from The Home Depot's for the same period?

S12–3 Internet-Based Team Research: Examining an Annual Report

LO 12–5

As a team, select an industry to analyze. Using your web browser, each team member should access the annual report or 10-K for one publicly traded company in the industry, with each member selecting a different company.

Required:

1. On an individual basis, each team member should write a short report that incorporates the following:
   a. Has the company generated positive or negative operating cash flows during the past three years?
   b. Has the company been expanding over the period? If so, what appears to have been the source of financing for this expansion (operating cash flows, additional borrowing, issuance of stock)?
   c. Compare and analyze the difference between net income and operating cash flows over the past three years.

2. Then, as a team, write a short report comparing and contrasting your companies using these attributes. Discuss any patterns across the companies that you as a team observe. Provide potential explanations for any differences discovered.

S12–4 Ethical Decision Making: A Real-Life Example

LO 12–1, 12–5

This case is based on a cash flow reporting fraud at Enron. The case is available online in the Connect eBook. To complete this case, you will evaluate the statement of cash flow effects of misclassifying a loan as a sale.

S12–5 Ethical Decision Making: A Mini-Case

LO 12–1, 12–5

This case is available online in the Connect eBook. To complete this case, you will evaluate two alternatives for increasing a sports club's reported operating cash flows.

S12–6 Critical Thinking: Interpreting Adjustments Reported on the Statement of Cash Flows from a Management Perspective (Indirect Method)

LO 12–2

QuickServe, a chain of convenience stores, was experiencing some serious cash flow difficulties because of rapid growth. The company did not generate sufficient cash from operating activities to finance its new stores, and creditors were not willing to lend money because the company had not produced any income for the previous three years. The new controller for QuickServe proposed a reduction in the estimated life of store equipment to increase depreciation expense; thus, "we can improve cash flows from operating activities because depreciation expense is added back on the statement of cash flows." Other executives were not sure that this was a good idea because the increase in depreciation would make it more difficult to report positive earnings: "Without income, the bank will never lend us money."

Required:

What action would you recommend for QuickServe? Why?

S12–7 Using a Spreadsheet that Calculates Cash Flows from Operating Activities (Indirect Method)

LO 12–2

You've recently been hired by B2B Consultants to provide financial advisory services to small business managers. B2B's clients often need advice on how to improve their operating cash flows and, given your accounting background, you're frequently called upon to show them how operating cash flows would change if they were to speed up their sales of inventory and their collections of accounts receivable or delay their payment of accounts payable. Each time you're asked to show the effects of these business decisions on the cash flows from operating activities, you get the uneasy feeling that you might inadvertently miscalculate their effects. To deal with this once and for all, you e-mail your friend Owen and ask him to prepare a template that automatically calculates the net operating cash flows from a simple comparative balance sheet. You received his reply today.

From: Owentheaccountant@yahoo.com
To: Helpme@hotmail.com
Cc:
Subject: Excel Help

Hey pal. I like your idea of working smarter, not harder. Too bad it involved me doing the thinking. Anyhow, I've created a spreadsheet file that contains four worksheets. The first two tabs (labeled BS and IS) are the input sheets where you would enter the numbers from each client's comparative balance sheets and income statement. Your clients are small, so this template allows for only the usual accounts. Also, I've assumed that depreciation is the only reason for a change in accumulated depreciation. If your clients' business activities differ from these, you'll need to contact me for more complex templates. The third worksheet calculates the operating cash flows using the indirect method and the fourth does this calculation using the direct method. I'll attach the screenshots of each of the worksheets so you can create your own. To answer "what if" questions, all you'll need to do is change selected amounts in the balance sheet and income statement.

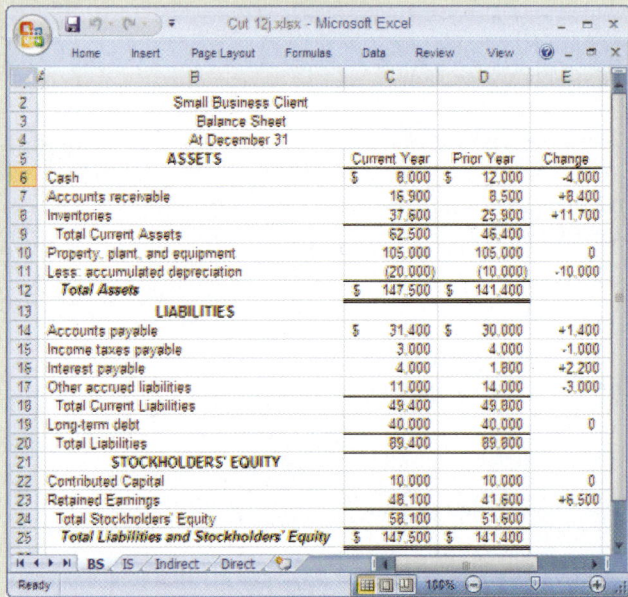

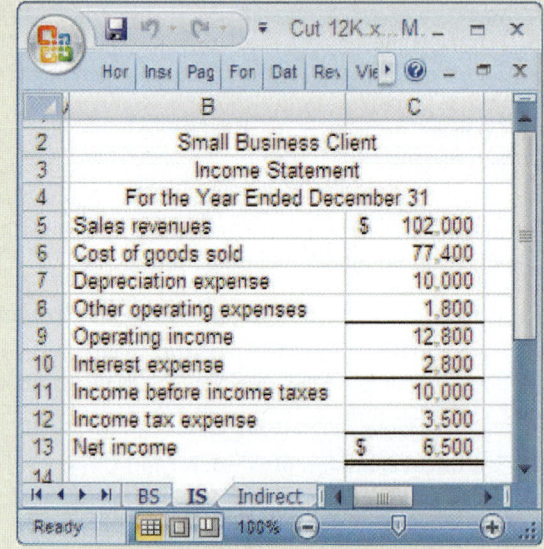

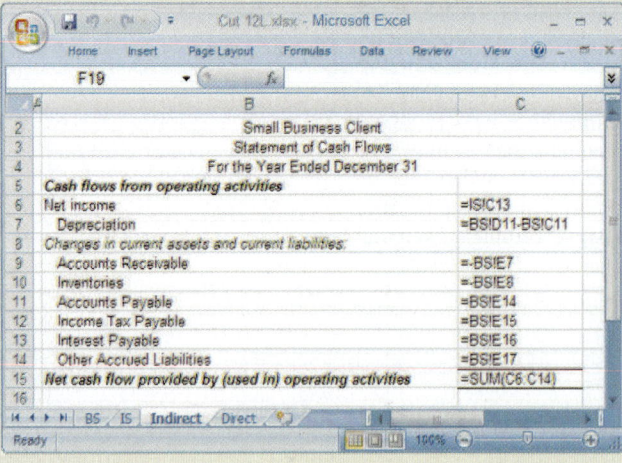

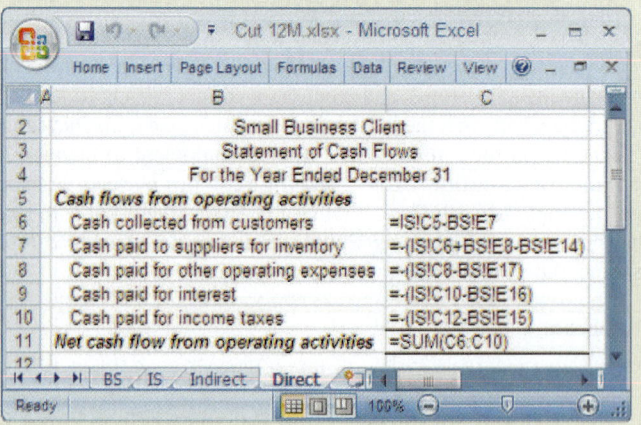

Required:

Copy the account balances from the worksheets for the balance sheet and income statement into a spreadsheet file. Enter formulas into the balance sheet worksheet to compute the change in each account balance, and then enter the formulas for the statement of cash flows (indirect method only) into a third worksheet. From this third worksheet, report the net cash flow provided by (used in) operating activities.

S12–8 Using a Spreadsheet that Calculates Cash Flows from Operating Activities (Direct Method)

LO 12–6

Refer to the information presented in S12–7.

Required:

Complete the same requirements, except use the direct method only.

S12–9 Using a Spreadsheet to Answer "What If" Management Decisions (Indirect or Direct Method)

LO 12–5

Change the amounts for selected balance sheet accounts in the spreadsheets created for either S12–7 or S12–8 to calculate the net cash flows from operating activities if, just before the current year-end, the company's management took the actions listed in the following requirements. Consider each question independently, unless indicated otherwise.

Required:

1. What if the company collected $10,000 of the accounts receivable?
2. What if the company had paid down its interest payable by an extra $2,000?
3. What if the company waited an additional month before paying $6,000 of its accounts payable?
4. What if the company had reported $5,000 more depreciation expense?
5. What if all four of the above events had taken place at the same time?

13

Measuring and Evaluating Financial Performance

CHAPTER THIRTEEN

YOUR LEARNING OBJECTIVES

LO13–1 Describe the purposes and uses of horizontal, vertical, and ratio analyses.

LO13–2 Use horizontal (trend) analyses to recognize financial changes that unfold over time.

LO13–3 Use vertical (common size) analyses to understand important relationships within financial statements.

LO13–4 Calculate financial ratios to assess profitability, liquidity, and solvency.

LO13–5 Interpret the results of financial analyses.

©Kevork Djansezian/Getty Images

FOCUS COMPANY: LOWE'S

Measuring and evaluating financial performance is like judging gymnastics or figure skating at the Olympics. You have to know three things: (1) the general categories to evaluate for each event, (2) the particular elements to consider within each category, and (3) how to measure performance for each element. When assessing financial performance, managers and analysts follow the same process. They evaluate general categories such as profitability, liquidity, and solvency, which are separated into particular elements such as gross profit margin and net profit margin. For each of these elements, managers and analysts measure performance by computing various percentages and ratios, which themselves are based on information reported in the financial statements.

In this chapter, we focus on Lowe's, the second largest home improvement retailer in the world. Lowe's is a giant with more than 2,000 stores and 290,000 employees. The company's success depends on increasing sales in existing markets and successfully entering new markets. At the same time, Lowe's must control costs while maintaining a high level of customer service in its stores. Finally, Lowe's management must anticipate the actions of its larger rival, The Home Depot, and address changes in overall demand for building products over which it has little control.

How do managers, analysts, investors, and creditors assess Lowe's success in meeting these challenges? This chapter will demonstrate how to use horizontal, vertical, and ratio analyses to develop a better understanding of how a company has performed.

Understand the business	Study the accounting methods	Evaluate the results
• Horizontal, vertical, and ratio analyses	• Horizontal (trend) computations • Vertical (common size) computations • Ratio computations	• Interpreting horizontal and vertical analyses • Interpreting ratio analyses

Understand the Business

Learning Objective 13–1
Describe the purposes and uses of horizontal, vertical, and ratio analyses.

As you first learned in Chapter 1, the goal of accounting is to provide relevant and timely information to managers and other users so that they can make more informed business decisions. In this chapter, we explore how financial statements are used in a variety of decisions. Managers analyze financial statements to evaluate past financial performance and make future decisions. Creditors use financial statements to assess compliance with loan covenants. And, of course, analysts use financial statements to generate advice for investors and others. You have learned that no single number fully captures the results of all business activities nor predicts a company's success or failure. Instead, to understand and evaluate the results of business activities, you need to look at a business from many different angles. An understanding of whether a business is successful will emerge only after you have learned to combine all of your evaluations into a complete picture or story that depicts the company's performance. Our goal for this chapter is to demonstrate how you can do this, relying on horizontal, vertical, and ratio analyses to develop the "story" of how well a company has performed.

HORIZONTAL, VERTICAL, AND RATIO ANALYSES

Most good stories have a plot, which the reader comes to understand as it unfolds over time or as one event relates to another. This is the same way financial analyses work. **Horizontal (trend) analyses are conducted to help financial statement users recognize important financial changes that unfold over time.** Horizontal analyses compare individual financial statement line items horizontally (from one period to the next), with the general goal of identifying significant sustained changes (trends). These changes are typically described in terms of dollar amounts and year-over-year percentages. For example, trend analyses could be used to determine the dollar amount and percentage by which Cost of Goods Sold increased this year, relative to prior years. **Vertical analyses focus on important relationships between items on the same financial statement.** These items are compared vertically (one account balance versus another) and are typically expressed as percentages to reveal the relative contributions made by each financial statement item. For example, vertical analyses could show that operating expenses consume one quarter of a company's net sales revenue. **Ratio analyses are conducted to understand relationships among various items reported in one or more of the financial statements.** Ratio analyses allow you to evaluate how well a company has performed given the level of other company resources. For example, while vertical analyses can show that Cost of Goods Sold consumes 65 percent of Net Sales and horizontal analyses can show that this percentage has increased over time, ratio analyses can relate these amounts to inventory levels to evaluate inventory management decisions.

Before we show you how to calculate horizontal, vertical, and ratio analyses (in the next section), we must emphasize that **no analysis is complete unless it leads to an interpretation that helps financial statement users understand and evaluate a company's financial results.** Without interpretation, these computations can appear as nothing more than a list of disconnected numbers.

Study the Accounting Methods

HORIZONTAL (TREND) COMPUTATIONS

Horizontal (trend) analyses help financial statement users recognize financial changes that unfold over time. This approach compares individual financial statement items from year to year with the general goal of identifying significant changes. Because this type of analysis compares results over a series of periods, it is sometimes called **time-series analysis.**

Regardless of the name, trend analyses are usually calculated in terms of year-to-year dollar and percentage changes. A year-to-year percentage change expresses the current year's dollar change as a percentage of the prior year's total by using the following calculation:

> **Learning Objective 13–2**
> Use horizontal (trend) analyses to recognize financial changes that unfold over time.

$$\text{Year-to-Year Change (\%)} = \frac{\text{Change This Year}}{\text{Prior Year's Total}} = \frac{(\text{Current Year's Total} - \text{Prior Year's Total})}{\text{Prior Year's Total}}$$

To demonstrate how to calculate a trend, we analyze Lowe's financial statements. Summaries of Lowe's balance sheets and income statements from two recent years appear in Exhibits 13–1 and 13–2. Dollar and percentage changes from fiscal year 2015 to 2016[1] are shown to the right of the balance sheet and income statement. The dollar changes were calculated by subtracting the fiscal 2015 balances from the fiscal 2016 balances. The percentage changes were calculated by dividing those differences by the fiscal 2015 balances. For example, according to Exhibit 13–1, Cash increased by $153 (= $558 − $405) in fiscal 2016 relative to fiscal 2015 (all numbers in millions). That dollar amount represented an increase of 0.378, or 37.8% (= $153 ÷ $405).

In a later section, we will explain and evaluate the underlying causes of significant changes in account balances. But before we leave this topic, we must note that not all large percentage changes will be significant. For example, the 126.1 percent increase in Other Current Assets is the largest percentage change on the balance sheet (Exhibit 13–1), but the $493 increase is relatively small when compared to other changes, such as the $1,000 increase in Inventories. To avoid focusing on unimportant changes, use the percentage changes to identify potentially significant changes, but then check the dollar change to make sure that it too is significant.

VERTICAL (COMMON SIZE) COMPUTATIONS

A second type of analysis, **vertical (common size) analysis**, focuses on important relationships within a financial statement. When a company is growing or shrinking overall, it is difficult to tell from the dollar amounts whether the proportions within each statement category are changing. Common size financial statements provide this information by expressing each financial statement amount as a percentage of another amount on that statement. The usefulness of common size statements is illustrated by the fact that Lowe's actually presents its balance sheet and income statements in the common size format, illustrated in Exhibits 13–3 and 13–4.

> **Learning Objective 13–3**
> Use vertical (common size) analyses to understand important relationships within financial statements.

---

[1] Like many retail companies, Lowe's 2016 fiscal year ends in early 2017 (on February 3).

EXHIBIT 13–1 | Horizontal (Trend) Analysis of Lowe's Summarized Balance Sheets

LOWE'S
Balance Sheet
(in millions)

	February 3, 2017 (Fiscal 2016)	January 29, 2016 (Fiscal 2015)	Increase (Decrease) Amount	Percent*
Assets				
Current Assets				
Cash	$ 558	$ 405	$ 153	37.8
Short-Term Investments	100	307	(207)	(67.4)
Accounts Receivable	—	—	—	—
Inventories	10,458	9,458	1,000	10.6
Other Current Assets	884	391	493	126.1
Total Current Assets	12,000	10,561	1,439	13.6
Property and Equipment, Net	19,949	19,577	372	1.9
Other Assets	2,459	1,128	1,331	118.0
Total Assets	$34,408	$31,266	$3,142	10.0
Liabilities and Stockholders' Equity				
Current Liabilities	$11,974	$10,492	$1,482	14.1
Long-Term Liabilities	16,000	13,120	2,880	22.0
Total Liabilities	27,974	23,612	4,362	18.5
Stockholders' Equity	6,434	7,654	(1,220)	(15.9)
Total Liabilities and Stockholders' Equity	$34,408	$31,266	$3,142	10.0

*Amount of Increase (Decrease) ÷ Fiscal 2015

EXHIBIT 13–2 | Horizontal (Trend) Analysis of Lowe's Summarized Income Statements

LOWE'S
Income Statements
(in millions)

Year Ended:	February 3, 2017 (Fiscal 2016)	January 29, 2016 (Fiscal 2015)	Increase (Decrease) Amount	Percent*
Net Sales Revenue	$65,017	$59,074	$5,943	10.1
Cost of Sales	42,553	38,504	4,049	10.5
Gross Profit	22,464	20,570	1,894	9.2
Operating and Other Expenses	16,618	15,599	1,019	6.5
Interest Expense	645	552	93	16.8
Income Tax Expense	2,108	1,873	235	12.5
Net Income	$ 3,093	$ 2,546	$ 547	21.5
Earnings per Share	$ 3.48	$ 2.73	$ 0.75	27.5

*Amount of Increase (Decrease) ÷ Fiscal 2015

In a common size balance sheet, each asset appears as a percent of total assets, and each liability or stockholders' equity item appears as a percent of total liabilities and stockholders' equity. For example, in Exhibit 13–3, which presents Lowe's common size balance sheets, Cash was 1.6 percent of total assets ($558 ÷ $34,408 = 0.016) at the end of fiscal 2016.

The common size income statement reports each income statement item as a percentage of sales. For example, in Exhibit 13–4, Cost of Sales was equal to 65.4 percent of Net Sales Revenue in fiscal 2016 ($42,553 ÷ $65,017 = 0.654).

EXHIBIT 13–3 | Vertical (Common Size) Analysis of Lowe's Summarized Balance Sheets

LOWE'S
Balance Sheet
(in millions)

	Fiscal 2016		Fiscal 2015	
	Amount	Percent	Amount	Percent
Assets				
Current Assets				
Cash	$ 558	1.6%	$ 405	1.3%
Short-Term Investments	100	0.3	307	1.0
Inventories	10,458	30.4	9,458	30.3
Other Current Assets	884	2.6	391	1.2
Property and Equipment, Net	19,949	58.0	19,577	62.6
Other Assets	2,459	7.1	1,128	3.6
Total Assets	$34,408	100.0%	$31,266	100.0%
Liabilities and Stockholders' Equity				
Current Liabilities	$11,974	34.8%	$10,492	33.5%
Long-Term Liabilities	16,000	46.5	13,120	42.0
Total Liabilities	27,974	81.3	23,612	75.5
Stockholders' Equity	6,434	18.7	7,654	24.5
Total Liabilities and Stockholders' Equity	$34,408	100.0%	$31,266	100.0%

EXHIBIT 13–4 | Vertical (Common Size) Analysis of Lowe's Summarized Income Statements

LOWE'S
Income Statements
(in millions)

	Fiscal 2016		Fiscal 2015	
	Amount	Percent	Amount	Percent
Net Sales Revenue	$65,017	100.0%	$59,074	100.0%
Cost of Sales	42,553	65.4	38,504	65.2
Gross Profit	22,464	34.6	20,570	34.8
Operating and Other Expenses	16,618	25.6	15,599	26.4
Interest Expense	645	1.0	552	0.9
Income Tax Expense	2,108	3.2	1,873	3.2
Net Income	$ 3,093	4.8%	$ 2,546	4.3%

Learning Objective 13–4
Calculate financial ratios to assess profitability, liquidity, and solvency.

RATIO COMPUTATIONS

Ratio analyses help financial statement users understand relationships among various items reported in the financial statements. These analyses compare the amounts for one or more line items to the amounts for other line items in the same year. Ratio analyses are useful because they consider differences in the size of the amounts being compared, similar to common size statements. In fact, some of the most popular ratios, such as net profit margin and the debt-to-assets ratio, are taken directly from the common size statements. Ratios allow users to evaluate how well a company has performed given the level of its other resources.

Most analysts classify ratios into three categories:

1. **Profitability** ratios, which relate to the company's performance in the current period—in particular, the company's ability to generate income.

2. **Liquidity** ratios, which relate to the company's short-term survival—in particular, the company's ability to use current assets to repay liabilities as they become due.

3. **Solvency** ratios, which relate to the company's long-run survival—in particular, the company's ability to repay lenders when debt matures and to make required interest payments prior to the date of maturity.

Exhibit 13–5 organizes the ratios according to these three categories and demonstrates their calculations for Lowe's in fiscal 2016 using data from Exhibits 13–1 and 13–2.

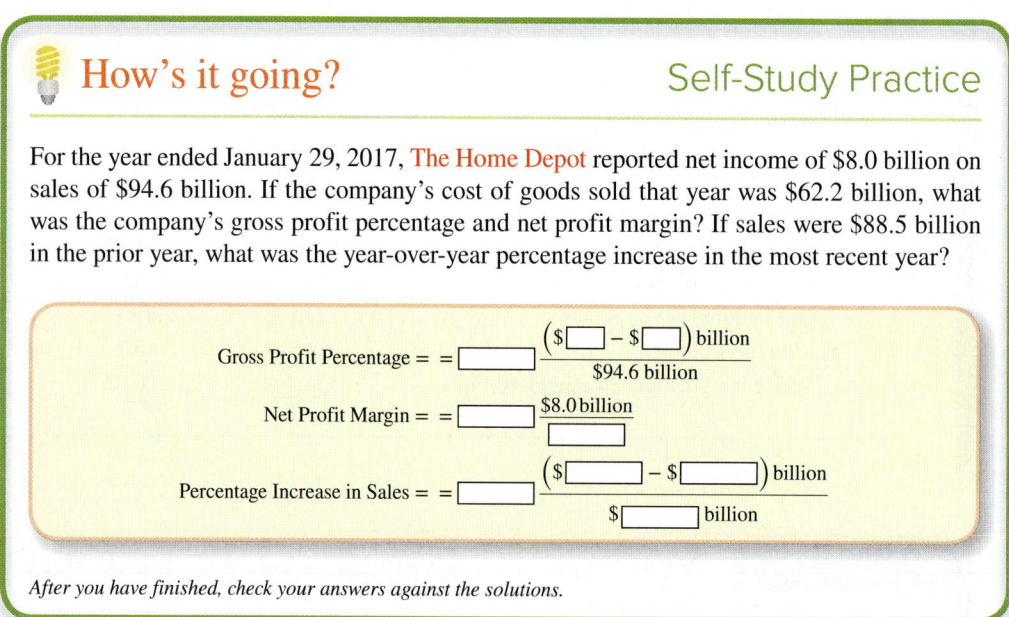

How's it going?   Self-Study Practice

For the year ended January 29, 2017, The Home Depot reported net income of $8.0 billion on sales of $94.6 billion. If the company's cost of goods sold that year was $62.2 billion, what was the company's gross profit percentage and net profit margin? If sales were $88.5 billion in the prior year, what was the year-over-year percentage increase in the most recent year?

$$\text{Gross Profit Percentage} = \boxed{} = \boxed{} \frac{(\$\boxed{} - \$\boxed{}) \text{ billion}}{\$94.6 \text{ billion}}$$

$$\text{Net Profit Margin} = \boxed{} = \boxed{} \frac{\$8.0 \text{ billion}}{\boxed{}}$$

$$\text{Percentage Increase in Sales} = \boxed{} = \boxed{} \frac{(\$\boxed{} - \$\boxed{}) \text{ billion}}{\$\boxed{} \text{ billion}}$$

After you have finished, check your answers against the solutions.

Solution to Self-Study Practice

Gross Profit Percentage $= [(\$94.6 - \$62.2)/\$94.6] \times 100$
$= 34.2\%$

Net Profit Margin $= (\$8.0/\$94.6) \times 100 = 8.5\%$

Percentage Increase in Sales $= [(\$94.6 - \$88.5)/\$88.5] \times 100$
$= 6.9\%$

Evaluate the Results

Learning Objective 13–5
Interpret the results of financial analyses.

INTERPRETING HORIZONTAL AND VERTICAL ANALYSES

As noted in the previous section, financial statement analyses are not complete unless they lead to interpretations that help users understand and evaluate a company's financial results. When interpreting analyses, your goals should be to understand what each analysis is telling you and then combine your findings into a coherent "story" that explains the results of the company's business activities. We demonstrate how to do this, beginning with interpretations of each set of analyses shown in Exhibits 13–1–13–5 and later concluding with an overall summary of Lowe's results.

EXHIBIT 13–5	Common Ratios Used in Financial Statement Analysis

Profitability Ratios

Fiscal 2016 Calculations

(1) Net Profit Margin = $\dfrac{\text{Net Income}}{\text{Revenues}}$

$\dfrac{\$3,093}{\$65,017} = 4.8\%$

(2) Gross Profit Percentage = $\dfrac{\text{Net Sales} - \text{Cost of Goods Sold}}{\text{Net Sales}}$

$\dfrac{\$65,017 - \$42,553}{\$65,017} = 34.6\%$

(3) Fixed Asset Turnover = $\dfrac{\text{Net Revenue}}{\text{Average Net Fixed Assets}}$

$\dfrac{\$65,017}{(\$19,949 + \$19,577)/2} = 3.29$

(4) Return on Equity (ROE) = $\dfrac{\text{Net Income} - \text{Preferred Dividends}^*}{\text{Average Common Stockholders' Equity}}$

$\dfrac{\$3,093 - \$29}{(\$6,434 + \$7,654)/2} = 43.5\%$

(5) Earnings per Share (EPS) = $\dfrac{\text{Net Income} - \text{Preferred Dividends}^*}{\text{Average Number of Common Shares Outstanding}}$

$\dfrac{\$3,093 - \$29}{880} = \$3.48$

(6) Price/Earnings Ratio = $\dfrac{\text{Stock Price (per share)}^\dagger}{\text{Earnings per Share (annual)}}$

$\dfrac{\$81.45}{\$3.48} = 23.4$

Liquidity Ratios

(7) Receivables Turnover = $\dfrac{\text{Net Sales Revenue}}{\text{Average Net Receivables}}$

n/a

Days to Collect = $\dfrac{365}{\text{Receivables Turnover Ratio}}$

n/a

(8) Inventory Turnover = $\dfrac{\text{Cost of Goods Sold}}{\text{Average Inventory}}$

$\dfrac{\$42,553}{(\$10,458 + \$9,458)/2} = 4.3$

Days to Sell = $\dfrac{365}{\text{Inventory Turnover Ratio}}$

$\dfrac{365}{4.3} = 84.9$

(9) Current Ratio = $\dfrac{\text{Current Assets}}{\text{Current Liabilities}}$

$\dfrac{\$12,000}{\$11,974} = 1.00$

Solvency Ratios

(10) Debt-to-Assets = $\dfrac{\text{Total Liabilities}}{\text{Total Assets}}$

$\dfrac{\$27,974}{\$34,408} = 0.81$

(11) Times Interest Earned = $\dfrac{\text{Net Income} + \text{Interest Expense} + \text{Income Tax Expense}}{\text{Interest Expense}}$

$\dfrac{\$3,093 + \$645 + \$2,108}{\$645} = 9.1$

* Note 13 of Lowe's financial statements indicated the company committed to paying a $29 million dividend to its "participating" and other securities, similar to a preferred dividend.
† Stock price is the closing price on the day the company first reports its annual earnings in a press release.

Trends Revealed in Horizontal Analyses

Horizontal (trend) analysis of Lowe's balance sheet in Exhibit 13–1 shows the company grew a fair bit in fiscal 2016. Overall, total assets increased 10 percent. The financing for this growth came from debt. In fact, during 2016, Lowe's total liabilities increased by 18.5 percent (whereas stockholders' equity *decreased* by 15.9 percent). The notes to Lowe's financial statements explain that Lowe's issued about $3 billion of new bonds (and the company also repurchased about $3.5 billion of its common shares that were immediately retired and returned to authorized and unissued status).

COACH'S TIP

Industry averages are reported in the Annual Statement Studies, which are published by the Risk Management Association. You can obtain industry averages also from csimarket.com or google.com/finance, both of which were available free of charge at the time this book was written.

Horizontal analysis of Lowe's income statement in Exhibit 13–2 shows a 10.1 percent increase in Net Sales Revenue and a 10.5 percent increase in Cost of Sales, as a result of more customer transactions. The company explains in the Management's Discussion and Analysis (MD&A) section of its annual report that fiscal 2016 saw 67 million more sales transactions than fiscal 2015, attributable to a longer fiscal year (53 rather than 52 weeks), the acquisition of a Canadian home improvement company (RONA), and the addition of 27 new Lowe's stores in the United States. Because the increase in Net Sales Revenue (10.1 percent) was smaller than the increase in Cost of Goods Sold (10.5 percent), Lowe's saw a decrease in its 2016 gross profit percentage. Although its operating expenses increased by $1 billion from 2015 to 2016, this year-over-year increase was only 6.5 percent. This increase was less than the 10.1 percent increase in Net Sales because the larger scale of Lowe's operations led to greater operating efficiency. The final changes in Lowe's fiscal 2016 expenses related to interest and income tax expenses, which increased as a direct result of carrying more debt and earning more income.

Relationships Noted in Vertical Analyses

Vertical (common size) analysis of Lowe's balance sheet in Exhibit 13–3 highlights key elements of the company. Its most significant assets have always been Inventories and Property and Equipment, with these assets representing 30.4 and 58.0 percent of Lowe's total assets, respectively. Financing for these assets comes from debt and equity. As a result of the bond issuance and stock repurchases in 2016, debt became a significantly greater source of financing (81.3 percent) than equity (18.7 percent) at the end of fiscal 2016.

Vertical analysis of Lowe's income statement in Exhibit 13–4 indicates that Cost of Sales and Operating Expenses are the most important determinants of the company's profitability. Cost of Sales consumed 65.4 percent of Sales in fiscal 2016 and Operating Expenses consumed an additional 25.6 percent. Much of the increase in the company's Net Income (from 4.3 percent of Sales in fiscal 2015 to 4.8 in fiscal 2016) is explained by greater control of Operating Expenses, as was noted earlier in the horizontal analyses.

These findings from the vertical analyses serve to underscore findings from the horizontal analyses. The emerging story is that Lowe's success depends on its ability to use significant investments in Inventories and Property and Equipment to generate sales. By increasing the number of Lowe's stores through domestic expansion and the acquisition of RONA in Canada, Lowe's was able to gain efficiency that improved its net income in an economy benefiting from increased consumer spending.

INTERPRETING RATIO ANALYSES

As shown in other chapters in this book, benchmarks help when interpreting a company's results. These benchmarks can include the company's prior year results, as well as the results of close competitors or the average for the industry. In a competitive economy, companies strive to outperform one another, so comparisons against industry competitors can provide clues about who is likely to survive and thrive in the long run.

In the following analyses, we compare Lowe's financial ratios to the prior year and in some cases to those for The Home Depot and the home improvement industry as a whole.

Fiscal 2016

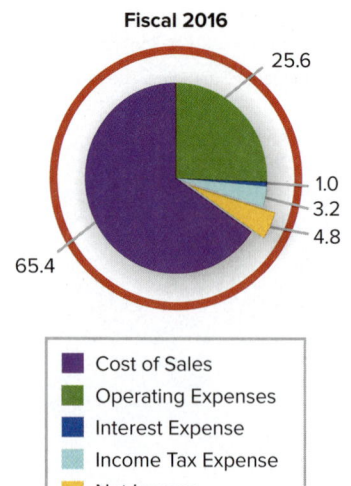

25.6
1.0
3.2
4.8
65.4

■ Cost of Sales
■ Operating Expenses
■ Interest Expense
■ Income Tax Expense
■ Net Income

Profitability Ratios

The analyses in this section focus on the level of profits the company generated during the period. We will analyze ratios (1) through (6) from Exhibit 13–5. The first two profitability ratios come right from the common size income statement in Exhibit 13–4.

(1) Net Profit Margin Net profit margin represents the percentage of revenue that ultimately makes it into net income, after deducting expenses. Using the equation in Exhibit 13–5, the calculation of Lowe's net profit margin for each of the last two years yields

Fiscal Year	2016	2015
Net profit margin = $\dfrac{\text{Net Income}}{\text{Revenues}}$	4.8%	4.3%

As discussed in the previous sections, store expansion and greater operating efficiency boosted Lowe's profits in 2016. Lowe's net profit margin increased from 4.3 percent in 2015 to 4.8 percent in 2016. The Home Depot's net profit margin saw a similar increase over this period, rising from 7.9 to 8.4 percent.

(2) Gross Profit Percentage The horizontal analysis indicated that Lowe's gross profit increased from 2015 to 2016 in terms of total dollars, as a result of a greater number of sales transactions. However, it did not indicate whether that increase was caused solely by greater total sales volume or also by more profit per sale. The gross profit percentage addresses these possibilities by indicating how much profit was made, on average, on each dollar of sales after deducting the cost of goods sold. Lowe's gross profit percentage for the last two years was

Fiscal Year	2016	2015
Gross Profit Percentage = $\dfrac{\text{Net Sales} - \text{Cost of Goods Sold}}{\text{Net Sales}}$	34.6%	34.8%

This analysis shows that in 2016, after deducting the cost of merchandise sold, 34.6 cents of each sales dollar were left to cover other costs, such as employee wages, advertising, and utilities, and to provide profits to the stockholders. The decrease in the gross profit percentage from 2015 to 2016 (34.8% − 34.6%) means that Lowe's made 0.2¢ less gross profit on each dollar of sales in 2016 than in 2015. Thus, the increase in dollars of gross profit is explained only by an increase in total sales volume. Financial statement users also would want to know which of two potential explanations accounts for the decrease in gross profit percentage: (1) Lowe's reduced its selling prices and (2) Lowe's had to pay higher unit costs to initially acquire merchandise. The MD&A section of Lowe's annual report suggests the decrease in gross profit percentage largely resulted from the first of these two reasons (i.e., lower selling prices) by attributing the change to "targeted promotional activity."

(3) Fixed Asset Turnover The fixed asset turnover ratio indicates how much revenue the company generates for each dollar invested in fixed assets, such as store buildings and the property they sit on. Lowe's fixed asset turnover ratios for the two years were

Fiscal Year	2016	2015
Fixed Asset Turnover = $\dfrac{\text{Net Revenue}}{\text{Average Net Fixed Assets}}$	3.29	2.84

This analysis shows Lowe's had $3.29 of sales in 2016 for each dollar invested in fixed assets. Looking at the components of this ratio, we see the increase in 2016 sales was the main factor contributing to the ratio's increase in 2016 (net fixed assets were virtually unchanged between fiscal 2016 and 2015). As discussed in the horizontal analysis, the increased sales resulted from 67 million more sales transactions in fiscal 2016 than in fiscal 2015.

Although Lowe's fixed asset turnover ratio improved in 2016, it is low compared to that of its main competitor, The Home Depot, whose fixed asset turnover ratio was 4.29 in 2016. In terms of using fixed assets to generate sales revenue, The Home Depot has a competitive advantage over Lowe's.

(4) Return on Equity (ROE) The return on equity ratio compares the amount of net income earned for common stockholders to the average amount of common stockholders' equity. (The amount of net income earned for common stockholders is net income minus any dividends on preferred or "participating" stock.) Like the interest rate on your bank account, ROE reports the net amount earned during the period as a percentage of each dollar contributed by common stockholders and retained in the business. Lowe's ROE ratios for the past two years were

Fiscal Year		2016	2015
Return on Equity (ROE) = $\dfrac{\text{Net Income} - \text{Preferred Dividends}}{\text{Average Common Stockholders' Equity}}$		43.5%	30.6%

Lowe's ROE increase from 30.6 to 43.5 percent was inevitable, given our previous analyses. Specifically, horizontal analysis indicated the company decreased its common stockholders' equity through a stock repurchase and it increased its 2016 net income through more profitable operations. Taken together, these results imply net income as a percentage of average common stockholders' equity was sure to rise in 2016. Despite this good news, Lowe's 43.5 percent ROE lagged behind The Home Depot's fiscal 2016 ROE of 149.4 percent. The Home Depot's massive ROE arose from earning $8 billion in net income while also decreasing stockholders' equity by repurchasing $7 billion of common stock and paying more than $3.4 billions in dividends.

(5) Earnings per Share (EPS)   Earnings per share (EPS) indicates the amount of earnings generated for each share of outstanding common stock. Consistent with the increase in ROE, the EPS ratio increased from 2.73 in 2015 to 3.48 in 2016, as shown below. This represents an increase of $0.75 per share ($3.48 − $2.73).

Fiscal Year		2016	2015
Earnings per Share (EPS) = $\dfrac{\text{Net Income} - \text{Preferred Dividends}}{\text{Average Number of Common Shares Outstanding}}$		$3.48	$2.73

(6) Price/Earnings (P/E) Ratio   The P/E ratio relates the company's stock price to its EPS, as follows:

Fiscal Year		2016	2015
Price/Earnings Ratio = $\dfrac{\text{Stock Price (per share)}}{\text{Earnings per Share (annual)}}$		23.4	25.1

Using the stock price immediately after Lowe's announced its fiscal 2016 and 2015 earnings (on March 1, 2017, and February 24, 2016), the P/E ratio was 23.4 and 25.1, respectively. This means investors were willing to pay 23.4 times earnings to buy a share of Lowe's stock in early 2017 (versus 25.1 times earnings a year earlier). The decrease from the prior year suggests investors were less optimistic about the company's future than they were the year before. Although the housing industry had enjoyed a good year in 2016, investment analysts were forecasting a modest slowdown in home improvement sales in 2017. The Home Depot's P/E ratio also fell during this same period, dropping from 22.8 to 22.4.

Let's pause to summarize what we've learned so far. Lowe's enjoyed improvement in 2016. Additional customer traffic resulted in increased sales, which contributed to increased operating efficiency and a higher net profit margin. Greater sales revenue in 2016, combined with virtually no change in net fixed assets, boosted fixed asset turnover in 2016. These improved results were magnified in the ROE and EPS ratios because Lowe's reduced its stockholders' equity and the number of outstanding common shares in 2016 through stock repurchases. Investors were impressed by these improvements in Lowe's 2016 results but cautious about future economic conditions, as suggested by a decrease in its P/E ratio after the fiscal 2016 results were reported.

Liquidity Ratios

The analyses in this section focus on the company's ability to survive in the short term, by converting assets to cash that can be used to pay current liabilities as they come due. We interpret ratios (7) through (9) from Exhibit 13–5.

(7) Receivables Turnover   Most home improvement retailers have low levels of accounts receivable relative to sales revenue because they either collect the majority of their sales immediately in cash or sell credit card receivables to finance companies (as Lowe's does, as explained in the "Credit Programs" section of its financial statement Note 1). Consequently, the receivables turnover ratio is not terribly meaningful for Lowe's or The Home Depot. The formula is presented in Exhibit 13–5 simply to remind you of how it is calculated.

(8) Inventory Turnover   The inventory turnover ratio indicates how frequently inventory is bought and sold during the year. The measure "days to sell" converts the inventory turnover ratio into the average number of days needed to sell inventory.

Fiscal Year	2016	2015
Inventory Turnover $= \dfrac{\text{Cost of Goods Sold}}{\text{Average Inventory}}$	4.3	4.2
Days to Sell $= \dfrac{365}{\text{Inventory Turnover Ratio}}$	84.9	86.9

The housing industry improved in 2016, which led homeowners to invest more in home renovation projects. As a result, Lowe's inventory turned over slightly faster in 2016 than in 2015. On average, its inventory took 2 fewer days to sell (86.9 − 84.9). These results are a positive sign because almost every retailer's success depends on its ability to offer customers the right product when they need it at a price that beats the competition. Despite its improvement, Lowe's inventory turnover still trails that of The Home Depot (where inventory takes an average of 71.4 days to sell), but The Home Depot has always had a faster inventory turnover because it carries fewer big-ticket items than Lowe's. According to their fiscal 2016 annual reports, the average ticket price was $68.82 at Lowe's and $60.35 at The Home Depot.

Turnover ratios vary significantly from one industry to the next. Companies in the food industry (restaurants and grocery stores) have high inventory turnover ratios because their inventory is subject to spoilage. Companies that sell expensive merchandise (automobiles and high-fashion clothes) have much slower turnover because sales of those items are infrequent, but these companies tend to carry lots of inventory so that customers have a wide selection to choose from when they do buy.

(9) Current Ratio   The current ratio compares current assets to current liabilities, as follows:

Fiscal Year	2016	2015
Current Ratio $= \dfrac{\text{Current Assets}}{\text{Current Liabilities}}$	1.00	1.01

The current ratio measures the company's ability to pay its current liabilities. Lowe's ratio was virtually unchanged between 2015 and 2016, ending fiscal 2016 with a ratio of 1.00. In some instances, a current ratio of only 1.0 is a cause for concern. But in this industry, a current ratio of 1.0 is deemed acceptable because it arises from entering into financing arrangements that benefit the company and its suppliers, as explained in the following Spotlight.

Solvency Ratios

The analyses in this section focus on Lowe's ability to survive over the long term—that is, its ability to repay debt at maturity and pay interest prior to that time. We interpret ratios (10) and (11) from Exhibit 13–5.

SPOTLIGHT ON Business Decisions

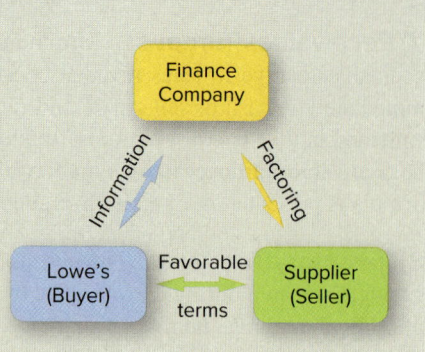

Lowe's Helps Suppliers Collect on Account

Lowe's has a low current ratio because it carries a large balance in Accounts Payable. The large Accounts Payable balance arises because suppliers give Lowe's favorable payment terms, including a longer period to pay its Accounts Payable. Why would suppliers be willing to allow this? The reason is that Lowe's participates in supply chain financing, or what some call "reverse factoring." The way this works is Lowe's tells a finance company what it owes to particular suppliers. The finance company then contacts the suppliers and offers to take over the collection of Lowe's account balance. Just like a normal factoring arrangement, the finance company pays the supplier right away. The finance company charges the supplier a smaller-than-normal factoring fee because it knows Lowe's balance will be easily collected because Lowe's has openly told the finance company how much it owes. The supplier appreciates collecting right away and being charged a smaller factoring fee, so it gives Lowe's more favorable payment terms. Lowe's fiscal 2016 annual report indicates it has made this supply chain financing possible for 15 percent of its suppliers.

COACH'S TIP

Instead of the debt-to-assets ratio, analysts might use a debt-to-equity ratio, which gives the same basic information as debt-to-assets. Debt-to-equity typically is calculated as total liabilities ÷ total stockholders' equity. As with debt-to-assets, the higher the debt-to-equity ratio, the more the company relies on debt (rather than equity) financing.

(10) Debt-to-Assets   The debt-to-assets ratio indicates the proportion of total assets that creditors finance. Remember that creditors must be paid regardless of how difficult a year the company may have had. The higher this ratio, the riskier is the company's financing strategy. Lowe's ratios at the end of fiscal 2016 and 2015 follow.

Fiscal Year	2016	2015
$\text{Debt-to-Assets} = \dfrac{\text{Total Liabilities}}{\text{Total Assets}}$	0.81	0.76

Lowe's ratio of 0.81 in 2016 indicates that creditors contributed 81 percent of the company's financing, implying that it was the company's main source of financing. The debt-to-assets ratio increased from 2015 to 2016 as a result of issuing new bonds (and reducing equity financing by repurchasing its common stock). Although this increase suggests greater financing risk, it is not out of line with others in the home improvement industry. The Home Depot, which had a debt-to-assets ratio of 90 percent at the end of fiscal 2016, relies even more on debt financing.

COACH'S TIP

If a company reports a net loss, rather than net income, include the loss as a negative number in the times interest earned formula. A negative ratio indicates operating results (before the costs of financing and taxes) are insufficient to cover interest costs.

(11) Times Interest Earned   The times interest earned ratio indicates how many times the company's interest expense was covered by its operating results. This ratio is calculated using accrual-based interest expense and net income before interest and income taxes, as follows:

Fiscal Year	2016	2015
$\text{Times Interest Earned} = \dfrac{\text{Net Income} + \text{Interest Expense} + \text{Income Tax Expense}}{\text{Interest Expense}}$	9.1	9.0

A times interest earned ratio above 1.0 indicates that net income (before the costs of financing and taxes) is sufficient to cover the company's interest expense. Lowe's ratio of 9.1 indicates the company is generating more than enough profit to cover its interest expense.

How's it going? Self-Study Practice

Show the computations for the following two ratios for Lowe's for the prior year (fiscal 2015). Use the information in Exhibits 13–1 and 13–2.

a. Times interest earned ratio

b. Current ratio

After you have finished, check your answers against the solutions.

Solution to Self-Study Practice

a. ($2,546 + $552 + $1,873)/$552 = 9.0
b. $10,561 ÷ $10,492 = 1.01

REVIEW THE CHAPTER

DEMONSTRATION CASE

The following information was reported in The Home Depot's annual report.

(in millions of dollars)	January 29, 2017 (Fiscal 2016)	January 31, 2016 (Fiscal 2015)
Net Sales Revenue	$ 94,595	
Cost of Goods Sold	62,282	
Other Expenses	24,356	
Net Income	7,957	
Inventories	$12,549	$11,809
Current Assets	17,724	16,484
Property and Equipment, Net	21,914	22,191
Total Assets	42,966	41,973
Current Liabilities	14,133	12,524
Total Liabilities	38,633	35,657
Total Stockholders' Equity	4,333	6,316

Required:

1. Conduct a horizontal analysis of Inventories and a vertical analysis of the income statement.
2. Compute the following ratios for The Home Depot for the year ended January 29, 2017.

Fixed Asset Turnover	Inventory Turnover	Current Ratio
Return on Equity	Days to Sell	Debt-to-Assets
Gross Profit Percentage		

3. Interpret the meaning of the ratios you calculated in requirement 2.

Suggested Solution

1. Horizontal Analysis	January 29, 2017	January 31, 2016	Increase
Inventories	$12,549	$11,809	$740 6.3%

Vertical Analysis		
Net Sales Revenue	$94,595	100.0%
Cost of Goods Sold	62,282	65.8
Other Expenses	24,356	25.8*
Net Income	$ 7,957	8.4%

* Rounded up so that total sums to 100%.

2. Calculating ratios:

Fixed Asset Turnover	= Net Sales Revenue/Average Net Fixed Assets
	= $94,595 ÷ [($21,914 + $22,191) ÷ 2]
	= 4.29
Return on Equity	= Net Income/Average Common Stockholders' Equity
	= $7,957 ÷ [($4,333 + $6,316) ÷ 2]
	= 1.494 or 149.4%
Gross Profit Percentage	= (Net Sales − Cost of Goods Sold)/Net Sales
	= ($94,595 − $62,282) ÷ $94,595
	= 0.342 or 34.2%
Inventory Turnover	= Cost of Goods Sold/Average Inventory
	= $62,282 ÷ [($12,549 + $11,809) ÷ 2]
	= 5.11
Days to Sell	= 365 ÷ Inventory Turnover Ratio
	= 365 ÷ 5.11
	= 71.4 days
Current Ratio	= Current Assets/Current Liabilities
	= $17,724 ÷ $14,133
	= 1.25
Debt-to-Assets	= Total Liabilities/Total Assets
	= $38,633 ÷ $42,966
	= 0.90

3. Interpreting ratios

- The fixed asset turnover ratio of 4.29 means that, on average, The Home Depot generated $4.29 of sales for each dollar of fixed assets.

- The return on equity of 149.4 percent means that The Home Depot's net income for the year was 149.4 percent of the amount investors contributed to and left in the company.

- The gross profit percentage of 34.2 means each dollar of sales generated 34.2 cents of profit, before considering other expenses related to administration, interest, and income taxes.

- The inventory turnover ratio of 5.11 means that The Home Depot turned over (bought and sold) the equivalent of its entire inventory an average of 5.11 times during the year.

- The days to sell ratio of 71.4 means that, on average, 71.4 days elapsed between the time The Home Depot acquired the inventory and the time the company sold it.

- The current ratio of 1.25 means that at year-end, The Home Depot had $1.25 of current assets for each dollar of current liabilities.

- The debt-to-assets ratio of 0.90 means that The Home Depot relied on current and long-term liabilities to finance 90 percent of its assets, implying that stockholders' equity financed 10 percent (= 100 − 90) of its total assets.

CHAPTER SUMMARY

LO 13–1   Describe the purposes and uses of horizontal, vertical, and ratio analyses.

- Horizontal analyses (also called trend analyses) compare financial statement items to comparable amounts in prior periods with the goal of identifying sustained changes, or trends.

- Vertical analyses create common size financial statements that express each line of the income statement (or balance sheet) as a percentage of total sales (or total assets).

- Ratio analyses compare one or more financial statement items to an amount for other items for the same year. Ratios take into account differences in the size of amounts to allow for evaluations of performance given existing levels of other company resources.

Use horizontal (trend) analyses to recognize financial changes that unfold over time.   **LO 13–2**

- Trend analyses involve computing the dollar amount by which each account changes from one period to the next and expressing that change as a percentage of the balance for the prior period.

Use vertical (common size) analyses to understand important relationships within financial statements.   **LO 13–3**

- Vertical (common size) analyses indicate the proportions within each financial statement category.

Calculate financial ratios to assess profitability, liquidity, and solvency.   **LO 13–4**

- Financial ratios are commonly classified with relation to profitability, liquidity, or solvency. Exhibit 13–5 lists common ratios in these three categories and shows how to compute them.
- Profitability ratios focus on measuring the adequacy of a company's income by comparing it to other items reported on the financial statements.
- Liquidity ratios measure a company's ability to meet its current debt obligations.
- Solvency ratios measure a company's ability to meet its long-term debt obligations.

Interpret the results of financial analyses.   **LO 13–5**

- Financial analyses are not complete unless they lead to an interpretation that helps financial statement users understand and evaluate a company's financial results.
- An understanding of whether a business is successful emerges only after you have learned to combine analyses into a complete picture or story that depicts the company's performance.
- To assist in developing this picture or story, most analysts compare to benchmarks such as the company's performance in prior years or to competitors' performance in the current year.

KEY TERMS

Horizontal (Trend) Analyses p. 583
Liquidity p. 586

Profitability p. 586
Solvency p. 586

Vertical (Common Size) Analysis p. 583

PRACTICE MATERIAL

QUESTIONS

1. What is the general goal of trend analysis?
2. How is a year-over-year percentage calculated?
3. What is ratio analysis? Why is it useful?
4. What benchmarks are commonly used for interpreting ratios?
5. Into what three categories of performance are most financial ratios reported? To what in particular does each of these categories relate?
6. Why are some analyses called *horizontal* and others called *vertical*?
7. Slow Cellar's current ratio increased from 1.2 to 1.5. What is one favorable interpretation of this change? What is one unfavorable interpretation of this change?
8. From last year to this year, Colossal Company's current ratio increased and its inventory turnover decreased. Does this imply a higher, or lower, risk of obsolete inventory?
9. From last year to this year, Berry Barn reported that its Net Sales increased from $300,000 to $400,000 and its Gross Profit increased from $90,000 to $130,000. Was the Gross Profit increase caused by (a) an increase in sales volume only, (b) an increase in gross profit per sale only, or (c) a combination of both? Explain your answer.
10. Explain whether the following situations, taken independently, would be favorable or unfavorable: (a) increase in gross profit percentage, (b) decrease in inventory turnover ratio, (c) increase in earnings per share, (d) decrease in days to collect, and (e) increase in net profit margin.

MULTIPLE CHOICE

1. Which of the following ratios is *not* used to analyze profitability?

a. Net profit margin ratio.   c. Current ratio.
b. Gross profit percentage.   d. Return on equity.

2. Which of the following would *not* directly change the receivables turnover ratio for a company?

a. Selling your inventory on credit at higher prices.
b. A change in your credit policy.
c. Increases in the cost you incur to purchase inventory.
d. All of the above would directly change the receivables turnover ratio.

3. Which of the following ratios is used to analyze liquidity?

a. Earnings per share.   c. Current ratio.
b. Debt-to-assets.   d. Both *b* and *c*.

4. Analysts use ratios to

a. Compare different companies in the same industry.
b. Track a company's performance over time.
c. Compare a company's performance to industry averages.
d. All of the above describe ways that analysts use ratios.

5. Which of the following ratios incorporates stock market data?

a. Inventory turnover.   c. Price/earnings ratio.
b. Earnings per share.   d. All of the above.

6. Given the following ratios for four companies, which company is least likely to experience problems paying its current liabilities promptly?

	Current Ratio	Receivables Turnover Ratio
a.	1.2	7.0
b.	1.2	6.0
c.	1.0	6.0
d.	0.5	7.0

7. A decrease in Selling and Administrative Expenses would directly impact what ratio?

a. Fixed asset turnover ratio.
b. Times interest earned.
c. Current ratio.
d. Gross profit percentage.

8. A bank is least likely to use which of the following ratios when analyzing the likelihood that a borrower will pay interest and principal on its loans?

a. Current ratio.
b. Debt-to-assets ratio.
c. Times interest earned ratio.
d. Price/earnings ratio.

 **Find More Learning Solutions on Connect.**

MINI-EXERCISES

LO 13–2   **M13–1 Calculations for Horizontal Analyses**

Using the following income statements, perform the calculations needed for horizontal analyses. Round percentages to one decimal place.

LOCKEY FENCING CORPORATION
Income Statements
For the Years Ended December 31

	Current	Previous
Net Sales	$100,000	$75,000
Cost of Goods Sold	58,000	45,000
Gross Profit	42,000	30,000
Selling, General, and Administrative Expenses	9,000	4,500
Income from Operations	33,000	25,500
Interest Expense	3,000	3,750
Income before Income Tax	30,000	21,750
Income Tax Expense	9,000	6,525
Net Income	$ 21,000	$15,225

M13–2 Calculations for Vertical Analyses   LO 13–3

Refer to M13–1. Perform the calculations needed for vertical analyses. Round percentages to one decimal place.

M13–3 Interpreting Horizontal Analyses   LO 13–5

Refer to the calculations from M13–1. What are the two most significant year-over-year changes in terms of dollars and in terms of percentages? Give one potential cause of each of these changes.

M13–4 Interpreting Vertical Analyses   LO 13–5

Refer to the calculations from M13–2. Which of the ratios from Exhibit 13–5 have been included in these calculations? Have these two ratios improved or deteriorated in the current year compared to the previous year?

M13–5 Inferring Financial Information Using Gross Profit Percentage   LO 13–4

Your campus computer store reported Sales Revenue of $168,000. The company's gross profit percentage was 60.0 percent. What amount of Cost of Goods Sold did the company report?

M13–6 Inferring Financial Information Using Gross Profit Percentage and Year-over-Year Comparisons   LO 13–2, 13–4

A consumer products company reported a 25 percent increase in sales from last year to this year. Sales last year were $200,000. This year, the company reported Cost of Goods Sold in the amount of $150,000. What was the gross profit percentage this year? Round to one decimal place.

M13–7 Computing the Return on Equity Ratio   LO 13–4

Given the following data, compute the return on equity ratio for the current year (expressed as a percentage with one decimal place).

	Current	Previous
Net income	$ 1,850	$ 1,600
Stockholders' equity	10,000	13,125
Total assets	24,000	26,000
Interest expense	400	300

M13–8 Analyzing the Inventory Turnover Ratio   LO 13–4, 13–5

A manufacturer reported an inventory turnover ratio of 8.6 last year. During the current year, management introduced a new inventory control system that was expected to reduce average inventory levels by 25 percent without affecting sales volume. Given these circumstances, would you expect the inventory turnover ratio to increase or decrease during the current year? Explain.

M13–9 Inferring Financial Information Using the Current Ratio   LO 13–4

Mystic Laboratories reported total assets of $11,200,000 and noncurrent assets of $1,480,000. The company also reported a current ratio of 1.5. What amount of current liabilities did the company report?

M13–10 Inferring Financial Information Using the P/E Ratio   LO 13–4

Last year, Big W Company reported earnings per share of $2.50 when its stock was selling for $50.00. If its earnings this year increase by 10 percent and the P/E ratio remains constant, what will be the price of its stock? Explain.

M13–11 Identifying Relevant Ratios   LO 13–4, 13–5

Identify the ratio that is relevant to answering each of the following questions.

a. How much net income does the company earn from each dollar of sales?
b. Is the company financed primarily by debt or equity?
c. How many dollars of sales were generated for each dollar invested in fixed assets?
d. How many days, on average, does it take the company to collect on credit sales made to customers?
e. How much net income does the company earn for each dollar owners have invested in it?
f. Does the company have sufficient assets to convert into cash for paying liabilities as they come due in the upcoming year?

LO 13–4, 13–5   **M13–12 Interpreting Ratios**

Generally speaking, do the following indicate good news or bad news?

a. Increase in times interest earned ratio.
b. Decrease in days to sell.
c. Increase in gross profit percentage.
d. Decrease in EPS.
e. Increase in fixed asset turnover ratio.

EXERCISES

LO 13–2, 13–3, 13–5   **E13–1 Preparing and Interpreting a Schedule for Horizontal and Vertical Analyses**

The average price of a gallon of gas in 2015 dropped $0.94 (28 percent) from $3.34 in 2014 (to $2.40 in 2015). Let's see whether these changes are reflected in the income statement of Chevron Corporation for the year ended December 31, 2015 (amounts in billions).

	2015	2014
Revenues	$140	$210
Costs of Purchased Crude Oil and Products	70	120
Other Operating Costs	65	60
Income before Income Tax Expense	5	30
Income Tax Expense	—	10
Net Income	$ 5	$ 20

Required:

1. Conduct a horizontal analysis by calculating the year-over-year changes in each line item, expressed in dollars and in percentages (rounded to one decimal place). How did the change in gas prices compare to the changes in Chevron's total revenues and costs of crude oil and products?

2. Conduct a vertical analysis by expressing each line as a percentage of total revenues (round to one decimal place). Excluding income tax and other operating costs, did Chevron earn more profit per dollar of revenue in 2015 compared to 2014?

LO 13–4, 13–5   **E13–2 Computing and Interpreting Profitability Ratios**

Use the information for Chevron Corporation in E13–1 to complete the following requirements.

Required:

1. Compute the gross profit percentage for each year (rounded to one decimal place). Assuming that the change from 2014 to 2015 is the beginning of a sustained trend, is Chevron likely to earn more or less gross profit from each dollar of sales in 2016?

2. Compute the net profit margin for each year (expressed as a percentage with one decimal place). Given your calculations here and in requirement 1, explain whether Chevron did a better or worse job of controlling expenses other than the costs of crude oil and products in 2015 relative to 2014.

3. Chevron reported average net fixed assets of $185 billion in 2015 and $174 billion in 2014. Compute the fixed asset turnover ratios for both years (round to two decimal places). Did the company better utilize its investment in fixed assets to generate revenues in 2015 or 2014?

4. Chevron reported average stockholders' equity of $155 billion in 2015 and $153 billion in 2014. The company has not issued preferred stock. Compute the return on equity ratios for both years (expressed as a percentage with one decimal place). Did the company generate greater returns for stockholders in 2015 or 2014?

LO 13–2, 13–3, 13–5   **E13–3 Preparing and Interpreting a Schedule for Horizontal and Vertical Analyses**

According to the producer price index database maintained by the Bureau of Labor Statistics, the average cost of computer equipment fell 3.8 percent between January and December 2016. Let's see whether these changes are reflected in the income statement of Computer Tycoon Inc. for the year ended December 31, 2016.

	2016	2015
Sales Revenue	$100,000	$120,000
Cost of Goods Sold	60,000	71,500
Gross Profit	40,000	48,500
Selling, General, and Administrative Expenses	36,000	37,000
Interest Expense	500	475
Income before Income Tax Expense	3,500	11,025
Income Tax Expense	1,000	5,000
Net Income	$ 2,500	$ 6,025

Required:

1. Conduct a horizontal analysis by calculating the year-over-year changes in each line item, expressed in dollars and in percentages (rounded to one decimal place). How did the change in computer prices compare to the changes in Computer Tycoon's sales revenues?

2. Conduct a vertical analysis by expressing each line as a percentage of total revenues (round to one decimal place). Excluding income tax, interest, and operating expenses, did Computer Tycoon earn more profit per dollar of sales in 2016 compared to 2015?

E13–4 Computing Profitability Ratios

LO 13–4, 13–5

Use the information in E13–3 to complete the following requirements.

Required:

1. Compute the gross profit percentage for each year (rounded to one decimal place). Assuming that the change from 2015 to 2016 is the beginning of a sustained trend, is Computer Tycoon likely to earn more or less gross profit from each dollar of sales in 2017?

2. Compute the net profit margin for each year (expressed as a percentage with one decimal place). Given your calculations here and in requirement 1, explain whether Computer Tycoon did a better or worse job of controlling operating expenses in 2016 relative to 2015.

3. Computer Tycoon reported average net fixed assets of $54,200 in 2016 and $45,100 in 2015. Compute the fixed asset turnover ratios for both years (round to two decimal places). Did the company better utilize its investment in fixed assets to generate revenues in 2016 or 2015?

4. Computer Tycoon reported average stockholders' equity of $54,000 in 2016 and $40,800 in 2015. The company has not issued preferred stock. Compute the return on equity ratios for both years (expressed as a percentage with one decimal place). Did the company generate greater returns for stockholders in 2016 than in 2015?

E13–5 Computing a Commonly Used Solvency Ratio

LO 13–4, 13–5

Use the information in E13–3 to complete the following requirement.

Required:

Compute the times interest earned ratios for 2016 and 2015. In your opinion, does Computer Tycoon generate sufficient net income (before taxes and interest) to cover the cost of debt financing?

E13–6 Matching Each Ratio with Its Computational Formula

LO 13–4

Match each ratio or percentage with its formula by entering the appropriate letter for each numbered item.

Ratios or Percentages	Formula
_____ 1. Current ratio	**A.** Net income ÷ Total revenue
_____ 2. Net profit margin	**B.** (Net sales revenue − Cost of goods sold) ÷ Net sales revenue
_____ 3. Inventory turnover ratio	
_____ 4. Gross profit percentage	**C.** Current assets ÷ Current liabilities
_____ 5. Fixed asset turnover	**D.** Cost of goods sold ÷ Average inventory

——— **6.** Return on equity

——— **7.** Times interest earned

——— **8.** Debt-to-assets ratio

——— **9.** Price/earnings ratio

——— **10.** Receivables turnover ratio

——— **11.** Earnings per share

E. Net credit sales revenue ÷ Average net receivables

F. (Net income − Preferred dividends) ÷ Average number of common shares outstanding

G. Total liabilities ÷ Total assets

H. (Net income + Interest expense + Income tax expense) ÷ Interest expense

I. Current market price per share ÷ Earnings per share

J. (Net income − Preferred dividends) ÷ Average common stockholders' equity

K. Total revenue ÷ Average net fixed assets

LO 13–4, 13–5 | **E13–7 Computing and Interpreting Selected Liquidity Ratios**

Double West Suppliers (DWS) reported sales for the year of $300,000, all on credit. The average gross profit percentage was 40 percent on sales. Account balances follow:

	Beginning	Ending
Accounts receivable (net)	$45,000	$55,000
Inventory	60,000	40,000

Required:

1. Compute the turnover ratios for accounts receivable and inventory (round to one decimal place).

2. By dividing 365 by your ratios from requirement 1, calculate the average days to collect receivables and the average days to sell inventory (round to one decimal place).

3. Explain what each of these ratios and measures means for DWS.

LO 13–4, 13–5 | **E13–8 Computing and Interpreting Liquidity Ratios**

Cintas Corporation is the largest uniform supplier in North America. Selected information from its annual report follows. For the 2016 fiscal year, the company reported sales revenue of $4.9 billion and Cost of Goods Sold of $2.1 billion.

Fiscal Year	2016	2015
Balance Sheet (amounts in millions)		
Cash and Cash Equivalents	$210	$435
Accounts Receivable, Net	560	500
Inventory	250	230
Prepaid Rent and Other Current Assets	570	570
Accounts Payable	115	110
Salaries and Wages Payable	100	90
Notes Payable (short-term)	250	0
Other Current Liabilities	350	310

Required:

Assuming that all sales are on credit, compute the current ratio (two decimal places), inventory turnover ratio (one decimal place), and accounts receivable turnover ratio (one decimal place) for 2016. Explain what each ratio means for Cintas.

LO 13–4, 13–5 | **E13–9 Computing the Accounts Receivable and Inventory Turnover Ratios**

Procter & Gamble (P&G) manufactures and markets many products you use every day. In 2016, sales for the company were $65,300 (all amounts in millions). The annual report did not report the amount of credit sales, so we will assume that all sales were on credit. The average gross profit percentage was 49.6 percent. Account balances for the year follow:

	Beginning	Ending
Accounts receivable (net)	$4,400	$4,600
Inventory	4,700	5,000

Required:

1. Rounded to one decimal place, compute the turnover ratios for accounts receivable and inventory.

2. By dividing 365 by your ratios from requirement 1, calculate the average days to collect receivables and the average days to sell inventory.

3. Interpret what these ratios and measures mean for P&G.

E13–10 Inferring Financial Information from Profitability and Liquidity Ratios   LO 13–4, 13–5

Dollar General Corporation operates general merchandise stores that feature quality merchandise at low prices to meet the needs of middle-, low-, and fixed-income families in southern, eastern, and midwestern states. For the year ended January 29, 2016, the company reported average inventories of $2,900 (in millions) and an inventory turnover of 4.83. Average total fixed assets were $2,190 (million) and the fixed asset turnover ratio was 9.32.

Required:

1. Calculate Dollar General's gross profit percentage (expressed as a percentage with one decimal place). What does this imply about the amount of gross profit made from each dollar of sales?

   TIP: Work backward from the fixed asset turnover and inventory turnover ratios to compute the amounts needed for the gross profit percentage.

2. Is this an improvement from the gross profit percentage of 30.7 percent earned during the previous year?

E13–11 Analyzing the Impact of Selected Transactions on the Current Ratio   LO 13–4, 13–5

In its most recent annual report, Appalachian Beverages reported current assets of $54,000 and a current ratio of 1.80. Assume that the following transactions were completed: (1) purchased merchandise for $6,000 on account and (2) purchased a delivery truck for $10,000, paying $1,000 cash and signing a two-year promissory note for the balance.

Required:

Compute the updated current ratio, rounded to two decimal places, after each transaction.

E13–12 Analyzing the Impact of Selected Transactions on the Current Ratio   LO 13–4, 13–5

In its most recent annual report, Sunrise Enterprises reported current assets of $1,090,000 and current liabilities of $602,000.

Required:

Determine for each of the following transactions whether the current ratio, and each of its two components, for Sunrise will increase, decrease, or have no change: (1) sold long-term assets for cash, (2) accrued severance pay for terminated employees, (3) wrote down the carrying value of certain inventory items that were deemed to be obsolete, and (4) acquired new inventory by signing an 18-month promissory note (the supplier was not willing to provide normal credit terms).

E13–13 Analyzing the Impact of Selected Transactions on the Current Ratio   LO 13–4, 13–5

Good Sports, Inc., is a private full-line sporting goods retailer. Assume one of the Good Sports stores reported current assets of $88,000 and its current ratio was 1.75, and then completed the following transactions: (1) paid $6,000 on accounts payable, (2) purchased a delivery truck for $10,000 cash, (3) wrote off a bad account receivable for $2,000, and (4) paid previously declared dividends in the amount of $25,000.

Required:

Compute the updated current ratio, rounded to two decimal places, after each transaction.

LO 13–4, 13–5   **E13–14 Analyzing the Impact of Selected Transactions on the Current Ratio**

A company has current assets that total $500,000, has a current ratio of 2.00, and uses the perpetual inventory method. Assume that the following transactions are then completed: (1) sold $12,000 in merchandise on short-term credit for $15,000, (2) declared but did not pay dividends of $50,000, (3) paid prepaid rent in the amount of $12,000, (4) paid previously declared dividends in the amount of $50,000, (5) collected an account receivable in the amount of $12,000, and (6) reclassified $40,000 of long-term debt as a current liability.

Required:

Compute the updated current ratio, rounded to two decimal places, after each transaction.

GROUP A PROBLEMS

LO 13–2, 13–5   **PA13–1 Analyzing Financial Statements Using Horizontal Analyses**

Pinnacle Plus declared and paid a cash dividend of $6,600 in the current year. Its comparative financial statements, prepared at December 31, reported the following summarized information:

	Current	Previous	Increase (Decrease) in Current (versus Previous) Amount	Percentage
Income Statement				
Sales Revenue	$110,000	$ 99,000		
Cost of Goods Sold	52,000	48,000		
Gross Profit	58,000	51,000		
Operating Expenses	36,000	33,000		
Interest Expense	4,000	4,000		
Income before Income Tax Expense	18,000	14,000		
Income Tax Expense (30%)	5,400	4,200		
Net Income	$ 12,600	$ 9,800		
Balance Sheet				
Cash	$ 69,500	$ 38,000		
Accounts Receivable, Net	17,000	12,000		
Inventory	25,000	38,000		
Property and Equipment, Net	95,000	105,000		
Total Assets	$206,500	$193,000		
Accounts Payable	$ 42,000	$ 35,000		
Income Tax Payable	1,000	500		
Note Payable (long-term)	40,000	40,000		
Total Liabilities	83,000	75,500		
Common Stock (par $10)	90,000	90,000		
Retained Earnings	33,500	27,500		
Total Liabilities and Stockholders' Equity	$206,500	$193,000		

Required:

1. Complete the two final columns shown beside each item in Pinnacle Plus's comparative financial statements. Round the percentages to one decimal place.

2. Which account increased by the largest dollar amount? Which account increased by the largest percentage?

LO 13–4, 13–5   **PA13–2 Analyzing Comparative Financial Statements Using Selected Ratios**

Use the data given in PA13–1 for Pinnacle Plus.

Required:

1. Compute the gross profit percentage in the current and previous years. Round the percentages to one decimal place. Are the current year results better, or worse, than those for the previous year?

2. Compute the net profit margin for the current and previous years. Round the percentages to one decimal place. Are the current year results better, or worse, than those for the previous year?

3. Compute the earnings per share for the current and previous years. Are the current year results better, or worse, than those for the previous year?

4. Stockholders' equity totaled $100,000 at the beginning of the previous year. Compute the return on equity (ROE) ratios for the current and previous years. Express the ROE as percentages rounded to one decimal place. Are the current year results better, or worse, than those for the previous year?

5. Net property and equipment totaled $110,000 at the beginning of the previous year. Compute the fixed asset turnover ratios for the current and previous years. Round the ratios to two decimal places. Are the current year results better, or worse, than those for the previous year?

6. Compute the debt-to-assets ratios for the current and previous years. Round the ratios to two decimal places. Is debt providing financing for a larger or smaller proportion of the company's asset growth?

7. Compute the times interest earned ratios for the current and previous years. Round the ratios to one decimal place. Are the current year results better, or worse, than those for the previous year?

8. After Pinnacle Plus released its current year's financial statements, the company's stock was trading at $18. After the release of its previous year's financial statements, the company's stock price was $15 per share. Compute the P/E ratios for both years, rounded to one decimal place. Does it appear that investors have become more (or less) optimistic about Pinnacle's future success?

PA13–3 Vertical Analysis of a Balance Sheet   LO 13–3, 13–5

A condensed balance sheet for Simultech Corporation and a partially completed vertical analysis are presented below.

SIMULTECH CORPORATION					
Balance Sheet (summarized)					
January 31					
(in millions of U.S. dollars)					
Cash	$ 433	29%	Current Liabilities	$ 409	27%
Accounts Receivable	294	19	Long-Term Liabilities	495	33
Inventory	206	14	Total Liabilities	904	b
Other Current Assets	109	a	Common Stock	118	c
Property and Equipment	27	2	Retained Earnings	492	32
Other Assets	445	29	Total Stockholders' Equity	610	d
Total Assets	$1,514	100%	Total Liabilities & Stockholders' Equity	$1,514	100%

Required:

1. Complete the vertical analysis by computing each line item (a)–(d) as a percentage of total assets. Round to the nearest whole percentage.

2. What percentages of Simultech's assets relate to inventory versus property and equipment? Which of these two asset groups is more significant to Simultech's business?

3. What percentage of Simultech's assets is financed by total stockholders' equity? By total liabilities?

LO 13–3, 13–5   **PA13–4 Vertical Analysis of an Income Statement**

A condensed income statement for Simultech Corporation and a partially completed vertical analysis are presented below.

SIMULTECH CORPORATION
Income Statement (summarized)
(in millions of U.S. dollars)

	Current Year		Previous Year	
Sales Revenues	$2,062	100%	$2,200	100%
Cost of Goods Sold	1,637	79	1,721	d
Selling, General, and Administrative Expenses	333	a	346	16
Other Operating Expenses	53	3	12	1
Interest Expense	22	b	26	1
Income before Income Tax Expense	17	1	95	e
Income Tax Expense	6	0	33	1
Net Income	$ 11	c%	$ 62	f%

Required:

1. Complete the vertical analysis by computing each line item (a)–(f) as a percentage of sales revenues. Round to the nearest whole percentage.
2. Does Simultech's Cost of Goods Sold for the current year, as a percentage of revenues, represent better or worse performance as compared to that for the previous year?
3. Has Simultech's net profit margin increased, or decreased, over the two years?

LO 13–4, 13–5   **PA13–5 Interpreting Profitability, Liquidity, Solvency, and P/E Ratios**

Coke and Pepsi are well-known international brands. Coca-Cola Co. sells more than $42 billion each year while annual sales of PepsiCo products exceed $62 billion. Compare the two companies as a potential investment based on the following ratios as reported by csimarket.com for the twelve months ended September 30, 2016:

Ratio	Coca-Cola	PepsiCo
Gross profit percentage	60.6%	55.1%
Net profit margin	17.1%	10.2%
EPS	$1.67	$4.39
Inventory turnover ratio	5.8	9.0
Current ratio	1.24	1.35
Debt-to-assets	0.72	0.85
P/E ratio	25.2	25.1

Required:

1. Which company appears more profitable? Describe the ratio(s) that you used to reach this decision.
2. Which company appears more liquid? Describe the ratio(s) that you used to reach this decision.
3. Which company appears more solvent? Describe the ratio(s) that you used to reach this decision.
4. Are the conclusions from your analyses in requirements 1–3 consistent with the value of the two companies, as suggested by their P/E ratios? If not, offer one explanation for any apparent inconsistency.

LO 13–4, 13–5   **PA13–6 Using Ratios to Compare Loan Requests from Two Companies**

The financial statements for Royale and Cavalier companies are summarized here:

	Royale Company	Cavalier Company
Balance Sheet		
Cash	$ 25,000	$ 45,000
Accounts Receivable, Net	55,000	16,000
Inventory	110,000	25,000
Equipment, Net	550,000	160,000
Other Assets	140,000	46,000
Total Assets	$880,000	$292,000
Current Liabilities	$120,000	$ 15,000
Note Payable (long-term)	190,000	55,000
Capital Stock (par $20)	480,000	210,000
Additional Paid-in Capital	50,000	4,000
Retained Earnings	40,000	8,000
Total Liabilities and Stockholders' Equity	$880,000	$292,000
Income Statement		
Sales Revenue	$800,000	$280,000
Cost of Goods Sold	480,000	150,000
Other Expenses	240,000	95,000
Net Income	$ 80,000	$ 35,000
Other Data		
Per share price at end of year	$ 14.00	$ 11.00
Selected Data from Previous Year		
Accounts Receivable, Net	$ 47,000	$ 14,000
Note Payable (long-term)	190,000	55,000
Equipment, Net	550,000	160,000
Inventory	95,000	38,000
Total Stockholders' Equity	570,000	202,000

These two companies are in the same business and state but different cities. Each company has been in operation for about 10 years. Both companies received an unqualified audit opinion on the financial statements. Royale Company wants to borrow $75,000 cash and Cavalier Company is asking for $30,000. The loans will be for a two-year period. Both companies estimate bad debts based on an aging analysis, but Cavalier has estimated slightly higher uncollectible rates than Royale. Neither company issued stock in the current year. Assume the end-of-year total assets and net equipment balances approximate the year's average and all sales are on account.

Required:

1. Calculate the ratios in Exhibit 13–5 for which sufficient information is available. Round all calculations to two decimal places.

2. Assume that you work in the loan department of a local bank. You have been asked to analyze the situation and recommend which loan is preferable. Based on the data given, your analysis prepared in requirement 1, and any other information (e.g., accounting policies and decisions), give your choice and the supporting explanation.

PA13–7 Analyzing an Investment by Comparing Selected Ratios   LO 13–5

You have the opportunity to invest $10,000 in one of two companies from a single industry. The only information you have is shown here. The word *high* refers to the top third of the industry; *average* is the middle third; *low* is the bottom third.

Ratio	Company A	Company B
Current	Low	High
Inventory turnover	High	Low
Debt-to-assets	Low	Average
Times interest earned	High	Average
Price/earnings	High	Average

Required:

Which company should you select? Write a brief explanation for your recommendation.

GROUP B PROBLEMS

LO 13–2, 13–4, 13–5   **PB13–1 Analyzing Financial Statements Using Horizontal and Ratio Analyses**

Tiger Audio declared and paid a cash dividend of $5,525 in the current year. Its comparative financial statements, prepared at December 31, reported the following summarized information:

	Current	Previous	Increase (Decrease) in Current (versus Previous) Amount	Percentage
Income Statement				
Sales Revenue	$222,000	$185,000		
Cost of Goods Sold	127,650	111,000		
Gross Profit	94,350	74,000		
Operating Expenses	39,600	33,730		
Interest Expense	4,000	3,270		
Income before Income Tax Expense	50,750	37,000		
Income Tax Expense (30%)	15,225	11,100		
Net Income	$ 35,525	$ 25,900		
Balance Sheet				
Cash	$ 40,000	$ 38,000		
Accounts Receivable, Net	18,500	16,000		
Inventory	25,000	22,000		
Property and Equipment, Net	127,000	119,000		
Total Assets	$210,500	$195,000		
Accounts Payable	$ 27,000	$ 25,000		
Income Tax Payable	3,000	2,800		
Note Payable (long-term)	75,500	92,200		
Total Liabilities	105,500	120,000		
Common Stock (par $1)	25,000	25,000		
Retained Earnings	80,000	50,000		
Total Liabilities and Stockholders' Equity	$210,500	$195,000		

Required:

1. Complete the two final columns shown beside each item in Tiger Audio's comparative financial statements. Round the percentages to one decimal place.
2. Which account increased by the largest dollar amount? Which account increased by the largest percentage?

LO 13–4, 13–5   **PB13–2 Analyzing Comparative Financial Statements Using Selected Ratios**

Use the data given in PB13–1 for Tiger Audio.

Required:

1. Compute the gross profit percentage in the current and previous years. Are the current year results better, or worse, than those for the previous year?
2. Compute the net profit margin for the current and previous years. Are the current year results better, or worse, than those for the previous year?
3. Compute the earnings per share for the current and previous years. Are the current year results better, or worse, than those for the previous year?
4. Stockholders' equity totaled $65,000 at the beginning of the previous year. Compute the return on equity ratios for the current and previous years. Are the current year results better, or worse, than those for the previous year?
5. Net property and equipment totaled $115,000 at the beginning of the previous year. Compute the fixed asset turnover ratios for the current and previous years. Are the current year results better, or worse, than those for the previous year?
6. Compute the debt-to-assets ratios for the current and previous years. Is debt providing financing for a larger or smaller proportion of the company's asset growth?
7. Compute the times interest earned ratios for the current and previous years. Are the current year results better, or worse, than those for the previous year?

8. After Tiger released its current year financial statements, the company's stock was trading at $17. After the release of its previous year financial statements, the company's stock price was $12 per share. Compute the P/E ratios for both years. Round to one decimal place. Does it appear that investors have become more (or less) optimistic about Tiger's future success?

PB13–3 Vertical Analysis of a Balance Sheet   LO 13–3, 13–5

A condensed balance sheet for Southwest Airlines and a partially completed vertical analysis are presented below.

SOUTHWEST AIRLINES
Balance Sheet (summarized)
December 31, 2016
(in millions of U.S. dollars)

Cash	$ 1,680	a%	Current Liabilities	$ 6,844	30%
Accounts Receivable	546	2	Long-Term Liabilities	8,001	34
Inventory of Parts and Supplies	337	2	Total Liabilities	14,845	64
Other Current Assets	1,935	b	Common Stock	2,218	9
Property and Equipment, Net	17,044	c	Retained Earnings	6,223	27
Other Assets	1,744	8	Total Stockholders' Equity	8,441	36
Total Assets	$23,286	100%	Total Liabilities & Stockholders' Equity	$23,286	100%

Required:

1. Complete the vertical analysis by computing each line item (a)–(c) as a percentage of total assets. Round to the nearest whole percentage.
2. What percentages of Southwest's assets relate to inventory of parts and supplies versus property and equipment? Which of these two asset groups is more significant to Southwest's business?
3. What percentage of Southwest's assets is financed by total stockholders' equity? By total liabilities?

PB13–4 Vertical Analysis of an Income Statement   LO 13–3, 13–5

A condensed income statement for Southwest Airlines and a partially completed vertical analysis follow.

SOUTHWEST AIRLINES
Income Statement (summarized)
For the Year Ended December 31
(in millions of U.S. dollars)

	2016		2015	
Sales Revenues	$20,425	100%	$19,820	100%
Salaries and Wages Expense	6,798	34	6,383	d
Fuel, Oil, Repairs, and Maintenance	4,692	a	4,621	e
Other Operating Expenses	5,175	b	4,700	24
Other Expenses (Revenues)	213	1	637	3
Income before Income Tax Expense	3,547	17	3,479	18
Income Tax Expense	1,303	6	1,298	7
Net Income	$ 2,244	c%	$ 2,181	f%

Required:

1. Complete the vertical analysis by computing each line item (a)–(f) as a percentage of sales revenues. Round to the nearest whole percentage.
2. Does the percentage that you calculated in 1(a) and (e) suggest that fuel costs, as a percentage of sales, decreased, increased, or stayed the same in 2016 compared to 2015?
3. Refer to the percentages that you calculated in 1(c) and (f). Is Southwest's net profit margin improving, declining, or staying the same?

LO 13–4, 13–5   **PB13–5 Interpreting Profitability, Liquidity, Solvency, and P/E Ratios**

Mattel and Hasbro are the two biggest makers of games and toys in the world. Mattel sells over $5.6 billion of products each year while annual sales of Hasbro products exceed $5 billion. Compare the two companies as a potential investment based on the following ratios reported by csimarket.com for twelve months ending in 2016:

Ratio	Mattel	Hasbro
Gross profit percentage	48.0%	62.0%
Net profit margin	6.4%	10.6%
Return on equity	14.6%	31.3%
EPS	$1.05	$4.38
Receivables turnover ratio	5.3	4.8
Inventory turnover ratio	3.8	3.8
Current ratio	1.87	2.41
Debt-to-assets	0.64	0.63
P/E ratio	24.7	22.7

Required:

1. Which company appears more profitable? Describe the ratio(s) that you used to reach this decision.
2. Which company appears more liquid? Describe the ratio(s) that you used to reach this decision.
3. Which company appears more solvent? Describe the ratio(s) that you used to reach this decision.
4. Are the conclusions from your analyses in requirements 1–3 consistent with the value of the two companies, as suggested by their P/E ratios? If not, offer one explanation for any apparent inconsistency.

LO 13–4, 13–5   **PB13–6 Using Ratios to Compare Loan Requests from Two Companies**

The financial statements for Thor and Gunnar companies are summarized here:

	Thor Company	Gunnar Company
Balance Sheet		
Cash	$ 35,000	$ 32,000
Accounts Receivable, Net	77,000	28,000
Inventory	154,000	30,000
Equipment, Net	770,000	192,000
Other Assets	196,000	68,400
Total Assets	$1,232,000	$350,400
Current Liabilities	$ 168,000	$ 18,000
Note Payable (long-term) (12% interest rate)	266,000	66,000
Common Stock (par $20)	672,000	252,000
Additional Paid-In Capital	70,000	4,800
Retained Earnings	56,000	9,600
Total Liabilities and Stockholders' Equity	$1,232,000	$350,400
Income Statement		
Sales Revenue	$1,120,000	$336,000
Cost of Goods Sold	672,000	180,000
Other Expenses	336,000	114,000
Net Income	$ 112,000	$ 42,000
Other Data		
Per share price at end of year	$ 13.20	$ 19.60
Selected Data from Previous Year		
Accounts Receivable, Net	$ 65,800	$ 27,200
Inventory	133,000	45,600
Equipment, Net	770,000	192,000
Note Payable (long-term) (12% interest rate)	266,000	66,000
Total Stockholders' Equity	798,000	266,400

These two companies are in the same business and state but different cities. Each company has been in operation for about 10 years. Both companies received an unqualified audit opinion on the financial statements. Thor Company wants to borrow $105,000 and Gunnar Company is asking for $36,000. The loans will be for a two-year period. Neither company issued stock in the current year. Assume the end-of-year total assets and net equipment balances approximate the year's average and all sales are on account.

Required:

1. Calculate the ratios in Exhibit 13–5 for which sufficient information is available. Round all calculations to two decimal places.

2. Assume that you work in the loan department of a local bank. You have been asked to analyze the situation and recommend which loan is preferable. Based on the data given, your analysis prepared in requirement 1, and any other information, give your choice and the supporting explanation.

PB13–7 Analyzing an Investment by Comparing Selected Ratios   LO 13–5

You have the opportunity to invest $10,000 in one of two companies from a single industry. The only information you have is shown here. The word *high* refers to the top third of the industry; *average* is the middle third; *low* is the bottom third.

Ratio	Company A	Company B
EPS	High	High
Return on equity	High	Average
Debt-to-assets	High	Low
Current	Low	Average
Price/earnings	Low	High

Required:

Which company should you select? Write a brief explanation for your recommendation.

SKILLS DEVELOPMENT CASES

S13–1 Computing Ratios   LO 13–4

Compute the following three ratios for The Home Depot's year ended January 29, 2017: (i) fixed asset turnover, (ii) days to sell, and (iii) debt-to-assets. To calculate the ratios, use the Fiscal 2016 financial statements of The Home Depot in Appendix A at the end of this book. (Note: Fiscal 2016 for The Home Depot runs from February 1, 2016, to January 29, 2017. See S1-1 for further explanation.)

a. 2.37; 71.4; 0.90
b. 2.37; 47.0; 0.52
c. 4.29; 47.0; 0.90
d. 4.29; 71.4; 0.90

S13–2 Evaluating Financial Information   LO 13–5

Lumber Liquidators, Inc., competes with Lowe's in product lines such as hardwood flooring, moldings, and noise-reducing underlay. The two companies reported the following financial results in fiscal 2016:

	Lumber Liquidators	Lowe's
Gross profit percentage	31.6%	34.6%
Net profit margin	(7.1)%	4.8%
Current ratio	1.93	1.00
Earnings per share	$(2.51)	$3.48

Required:

1. Calculate the difference in gross profit percentage between Lumber Liquidators and Lowe's. What does this indicate about the extent to which the companies mark up their selling prices over cost?

2. Calculate the difference in net profit margin between Lumber Liquidators and Lowe's. Use this analysis along with your calculation in requirement 1 to identify the company that best controls operating expenses other than cost of goods sold.

LO 13–1, 13–2, 13–3, 13–4, 13–5   **S13–3 Internet-Based Team Research: Examining an Annual Report**

As a team, select an industry to analyze. Using your web browser, each team member should access the annual report or 10-K for one publicly traded company in the industry, with each member selecting a different company.

Required:

1. On an individual basis, each team member should write a short report that incorporates horizontal and vertical analyses and as many of the ratios from the chapter as are applicable given the nature of the selected company.

2. Then, as a team, write a short report comparing and contrasting your companies using these attributes. Discuss any patterns across the companies that you as a team observe. Provide potential explanations for any differences discovered. Consider the impact of differences in accounting policies.

LO 13–4, 13–5   **S13–4 Ethical Decision Making: A Mini-Case**

Capital Investments Corporation (CIC) requested a sizable loan from First Federal Bank to acquire a large piece of land for future expansion. CIC reported current assets of $1,900,000 (including $430,000 in cash) and current liabilities of $1,075,000. First Federal denied the loan request for a number of reasons, including the fact that the current ratio was below 2:1. When CIC was informed of the loan denial, the controller of the company immediately paid $420,000 that was owed to several trade creditors. The controller then asked First Federal to reconsider the loan application. Based on these abbreviated facts, would you recommend that First Federal approve the loan request? Why? Are the controller's actions ethical?

LO 13–4, 13–5   **S13–5 Critical Thinking: Analyzing the Impact of Alternative Depreciation Methods on Ratio Analysis**

Speedy Company uses the double-declining-balance method to depreciate its property, plant, and equipment and Turtle Company uses the straight-line method. The two companies are exactly alike except for the difference in depreciation methods.

Required:

1. Identify the financial ratios discussed in this chapter that are likely to be affected by the difference in depreciation methods.

2. Which company will report the higher amount for each ratio that you have identified in response to requirement 1? If you cannot be certain, explain why.

LO 13–2, 13–3   **S13–6 Using a Spreadsheet to Calculate Financial Statement Ratios**

Enter the account names and dollar amounts from the comparative balance sheets in Exhibit 13–1 into a worksheet in a spreadsheet file. Create a second copy of the worksheet in the same spreadsheet file.

Required:

1. To the right of the comparative numbers in the first worksheet, enter the necessary formulas to compute the amount and percent change as shown in Exhibit 13–1.

2. To the right of each column in the second worksheet, enter the necessary formulas to create common size statements similar to those shown in Exhibit 13–3.

3 Ps: People, Profit, and Planet Phrase used in sustainability accounting to represent the three factors in the triple bottom line: people, profit, and planet.

A

Accounting Rate of Return Annual net income as a percentage of the original investment in assets.

Activity-Based Costing (ABC) Method of assigning indirect costs to products or services based on the activities they require.

Activity-Based Management (ABM) All actions that managers take to improve operations or reduce costs based on ABC data.

Activity Proportion A percentage used to assign indirect costs to products and services in activity-based costing. Computed by dividing the activity cost driver for each product or service by the total activity cost driver.

Activity Rate A rate used to assign indirect costs to products and services in activity-based costing. Computed by dividing total activity cost by total activity driver.

Actual Cost System Cost system in which all costs are recorded at actual amounts.

Actual Manufacturing Overhead Actual amount of indirect manufacturing costs incurred during the period.

Allocation Base Measurable item used to apply indirect (overhead) costs to products or services.

Annuity Stream of equal cash flows that occurs uniformly across time.

Applied Manufacturing Overhead Indirect manufacturing costs that are assigned to specific units or jobs using a predetermined overhead rate and the actual value of the cost driver.

Appraisal or Inspection Costs Costs incurred to identify defective products before shipping them to customers.

Avoidable Cost Cost that can be avoided by choosing one decision option instead of another.

B

Balanced Scorecard Comprehensive performance measurement system that translates an organization's vision and strategy into a set of operational performance metrics.

Batch-Level Activities Activities performed for a group of units all at once.

Bottleneck Most constrained resource or the process that limits a system's output.

Break-Even Analysis A form of cost-volume-profit analysis that determines the level of sales (in units or dollars) needed to break even, or earn zero profit.

Break-Even Point Point at which total revenue equals total cost, resulting in zero profit; the point at which fixed costs exactly equal the contribution margin.

Budget Quantification of the resources and expenditures that will be required during a given period of time to achieve a plan.

Budgetary Slack Cushion that managers may try to build into their budget by understating expected sales or overstating budgeting expenses so that they are more likely to come in under budget for expenses and over budget for revenues.

Budgeted Balance Sheet Forward-looking balance sheet that shows expected balance of assets, liabilities, and owners' equity at the end of the budget period.

Budgeted Cost of Goods Sold Budgeted manufacturing cost per unit multiplied by budgeted unit sales.

Budgeted Gross Margin Budgeted sales less budgeted cost of goods sold.

Budgeted Income Statement Forward-looking income statement that summarizes budgeted sales revenues and expenses for the budget period.

Budgeted Manufacturing Cost per Unit The sum of budgeted direct materials, direct labor, and manufacturing overhead stated on a per-unit basis.

C

Capacity Measure of the limited capability of a resource.

Capital Budgeting A decision making process that managers use to determine how to invest the company's funds in major capital assets.

Cash Budget Financial budget that provides information about budgeted cash receipts and payments.

Cash Flows from Financing Activities Cash inflows and outflows related to financing sources external to the company (owners and lenders).

Cash Flows from Investing Activities Cash inflows and outflows related to the purchase or sale of investments and long-lived assets.

Cash Flows from Operating Activities (Cash Flows from Operations) Cash inflows and outflows related to components of net income.

Centralized Organization Organization in which decision-making authority is kept at the top level of the organization.

Committed Fixed Costs Fixed costs that are difficult to change in the short-run because managers have committed to the level of spending through contractual agreements.

Common Fixed Costs Costs shared by multiple segments that may be incurred even if a section is eliminated.

Complementary Products Products that are used together such as a printer and ink cartridge.

Compounding Process of interest being earned on top of interest.

Constrained Resource Resource that is unable to meet the demand placed on it.

Contribution Margin Difference between sales revenue and variable costs.

Contribution Margin Income Statement Type of income statement that separates costs into variable or fixed costs; used to address many managerial problems.

Contribution Margin Ratio Ratio that tells managers how much contribution margin is generated by each dollar of sales revenue. Computed as contribution margin divided by sales revenue.

Controllability Principle Concept that managers should be held responsible for only those things that they can control.

Controlling The stage in the Plan-Implement-Control cycle that involves monitoring actual results to see whether the objectives set in the planning state are being met.

Conversion Costs Sum of direct labor and manufacturing overhead; total cost incurred to convert direct materials into a finished product.

Corporate Social Responsibility (CSR) Report that provides information about a company's sustainability initiatives and outcomes, including social and environmental impact.

Cost Behavior Description of how total costs change when some measure of activity changes.

Cost Center Responsibility center in which the manager has authority over and responsibility for cost.

Cost Driver A measure that has a cause-and-effect relationship with cost and is used to allocate or assign indirect costs to products.

Cost Object Any item for which one wants to determine cost.

Cost of Capital A rate that reflects the cost of funds used to finance a company's operations. Computed as the weighted-average cost of debt and equity.

Cost of Goods Completed Total production cost assigned to goods that were manufactured or completed during an accounting period.

Cost of Goods Manufactured See *cost of goods completed.*

Cost of Goods Sold (COGS) Total manufacturing cost of jobs or units sold during the period.

Cost of Quality Report A report that summarizes the costs incurred to prevent, detect, and correct quality problems generated by companies using a total quality management approach.

Cost-Plus Pricing Pricing approach in which the company first determines how much a product or service costs and then adds a markup percentage (profit) to arrive at the sales price.

Cost Structure The extent to which a company uses variable costs versus fixed costs to perform its operations.

Cost-Volume-Profit (CVP) Analysis Analysis that focuses on relationships among revenue, volume and mix of units sold, variable and fixed costs, and profit.

CVP Graph Graph that shows the relationship among unit sales volume, total revenue, total cost, and profit.

D

Decentralized Organization Organization in which decision-making authority is spread throughout, and managers are responsible for deciding how to manage their particular area of responsibility.

Degree of Operating Leverage The extent to which fixed costs are used to operate the business. If fixed costs are used to a larger degree than variable costs, the company is more highly leveraged.

Dependent Variable Variable that changes in response to some other variable.

Differential Analysis See *Incremental Analysis.*

Differential Costs Costs that differ between decision alternatives.

Direct Costs Costs that can be directly and conveniently traced to a specific cost object.

Direct Fixed Cost Fixed cost that can be attributed to a specific business segment.

Direct Labor Cost of labor that can be directly and conveniently traced to the product.

Direct Labor Budget Budget indicating the amount of direct labor needed to meet expected production.

Direct Labor Efficiency Variance Difference between the actual number of labor hours used and the standard number of labor hours multiplied by the standard labor rate.

Direct Labor Rate Variance Difference between the actual labor rate and the standard labor rate multiplied by the actual number of labor hours used.

Direct Labor Spending Variance Difference between actual direct labor cost and the flexible budget. It is made up of the direct labor rate variance and the direct labor efficiency variances.

Direct Labor Time Ticket Source document used to track how much time a worker spent on various jobs in a job order cost system.

Direct Materials Major material inputs that can be directly and conveniently traced to the product.

Direct Materials Price Variance Difference between the actual price and the standard price paid for direct materials multiplied by the actual quantity of direct materials purchased.

Direct Materials Purchases Budget Budget that indicates the quantity of direct materials that must be purchased to meet production and direct materials inventory needs.

Direct Materials Quantity Variance Difference between the actual quantity and the standard quantity of direct materials used multiplied by the standard price.

Direct Materials Spending Variance Difference between actual direct materials cost and the flexible budget. It is made up of the direct materials price variance and the direct materials quantity variances.

Direct Materials Usage Variance See *Direct Materials Quantity Variance.*

Direct Method Method of presenting the Operating Activities section of the cash flow statement to report the components of cash flows from operating activities as gross receipts and gross payments.

Discount Rate Rate used to discount future cash flows back to their equivalent present value to reflect the time value of money.

Discounted Cash Flow Methods Capital budgeting methods that incorporate the time value of money.

Discounting Process of calculating the cash-equivalent present value of future payments by removing the interest component that is built into future payments.

Discretionary Fixed Costs Fixed costs for which managers have some discretion over the level of spending, such as employee training programs or advertising.

DuPont Method Formula developed by executives at DuPont in the early 1900s; shows that the return on investment is a function of profit margin and investment turnover.

E

Easily Attainable Standard Standard that can be met with relative ease.

Economic Value Added Measures the economic wealth that is created when a company's after-tax operating income exceeds its cost of capital.

Equivalent Unit Measure used to convert partially completed units into the equivalent of a full unit.

Ethics Standards of conduct for judging right from wrong, honest from dishonest, and fair from unfair.

Excess Capacity Occurs when a company has more than enough resources to satisfy demand.

External Failure Costs Costs that occur when a defective product makes its way into the customer's hands.

F

Facility-Level Activities Activities performed to benefit the organization as a whole.

Favorable Variance Variance indicating that actual costs were less than budgeted or standard costs.

Financial Accounting Accounting area focused on providing financial information to external users such as investors, creditors, and regulators.

Financial Budgets Budgets that focus on the financial resources needed to support operations.

Finished Goods Inventory Cost of all units completed and ready for sale at any given point in time.

First-In, First-Out (FIFO) Method Method used to prepare a production report in process costing. Assumes that the units in process at the beginning of the period are completed first, before the units started during the current period.

Fixed Costs Costs that remain the same, in total, regardless of activity level.

Fixed Overhead Budget Variance See *Fixed Overhead Spending Variance.*

Fixed Overhead Capacity Variance Variance that is due to the difference between the amount of capacity available and the amount of capacity used.

Fixed Overhead Spending Variance Variance that represents the difference in actual and budgeted fixed overhead costs.

Fixed Overhead Volume Variance Variance resulting from the difference between actual and budgeted production volume, multiplied by the fixed overhead rate.

Flexible Budget Budget showing how budgeted costs and revenues will change for different levels of production or sales volume.

Full Absorption Costing Costing method required for external reporting (GAAP) in which product costs reflect the full cost of manufacturing.

Full Capacity Occurs when a company is operating its resources to the limit of its capacity. No additional units can be produced or customers served without increasing capacity or incurring opportunity costs.

Future Value Value of cash received in the future.

G

General and Administrative Expenses Costs incurred in running the overall organization.

Goal Incongruence Conflict of interest between a manager and the organization that may cause managers to make decisions that are not in the best interest of the overall organization.

H

High-Low Method Method of estimating cost behavior using the two most extreme activity levels (x values) to estimate fixed and variable costs.

Horizontal (Trend) Analyses Comparing results across time, often expressing changes in account balances as a percentage of prior year balances.

Hurdle Rate Minimum required rate of return for a project.

I

Ideal Standard Standard that can be achieved only under perfect or ideal conditions.

Idle Capacity See *Excess Capacity.*

Implementing The stage in the Plan-Implement-Control cycle that involves putting the plan into action.

Incremental Analysis Decision-making approach that focuses on the differential costs and benefits of alternate decision choices.

Incremental Costs See *Differential Costs.*

Independent Projects Projects unrelated to one another, so that investing in one does not preclude investing in another.

Independent Variable Variable that causes some other variable to change.

Indirect Costs Costs that cannot be traced to a specific cost object or are not worth the effort to trace.

Indirect Materials Materials that cannot be directly or conveniently traced to a specific unit and are therefore treated as manufacturing overhead.

Indirect Method Method that starts with net income from the income statement and then adjusts it by removing items that do not involve cash but were included in net income and adding items that involved cash but were not yet included in net income.

Internal Failure Costs Costs from defects caught during the inspection process.

Internal Rate of Return Discount rate at which the present value of cash inflows exactly equals the present value of the cash outflows.

Inventoriable Costs Costs that are counted as inventory on the balance sheet until the product is sold; another term for product costs.

Investment Center Responsibility center in which the manager has authority over and responsibility for profit (revenue minus cost) and the investment of assets.

Investment Turnover Ratio of sales revenue to the average invested assets.

Irrelevant Cost Cost that is not relevant to a specific decision because it will not change, regardless of a manager's decision.

J

Job Cost Sheet Document used to record all of the costs of producing a particular job or servicing a specific customer.

Job Order Costing Costing system used by companies that make unique products or provide specialty services.

Just-in-Time (JIT) Demand-pull system in which materials are purchased and units manufactured as needed to satisfy demand.

K

Keep-or-Drop Decisions Application of incremental analysis that requires managers to decide whether to retain or eliminate a business segment or product.

L

Least-Squares Regression Statistical method used to estimate cost behavior. It defines the best fitting line as the one that minimizes the sum of squared error.

Linearity Assumption Assumption that the relationship between two variables (x and y) can be approximated by a straight line.

Liquidity The extent to which a company is able to pay its currently maturing obligations.

Long-Term Objective Specific goal that management wants to achieve over a long-term horizon, typically 5 to 10 years.

M

Make-or-Buy Decisions Application of incremental analysis that requires managers to decide whether to perform a particular activity or function in-house or to purchase it from an outside supplier.

Managerial Accounting Accounting area focused on providing information to assist business owners and managers in making business decisions.

Manufacturing Costs Costs incurred to produce a physical product; generally classified as direct materials, direct labor, or manufacturing overhead.

Manufacturing Firms Companies that purchase raw materials and use them to make a finished product to sell to wholesalers, retailers, or customers.

Manufacturing Overhead All costs other than direct materials and direct labor that are incurred to manufacture a physical product.

Manufacturing Overhead Budget Budget that estimates the manufacturing overhead costs needed to support budgeted production.

Margin of Safety Difference between actual or budgeted sales and the break-even point. Identifies how much sales can drop before the business will suffer a loss.

Marketing or Selling Expenses Costs incurred to market and sell a product or service to a customer.

Master Budget Comprehensive set of budgets that covers all phases of an organization's planned activities for a specific period.

Materials Requisition Form Document used to authorize the issuance of materials into production; details the cost and quantities of all materials needed to complete specific jobs.

Merchandising Companies Companies that purchase goods (merchandise) from suppliers and sell them to other businesses or consumers.

Mixed Costs Costs that have both a fixed component and a variable component; also known as *semivariable costs*.

Mutually Exclusive Projects Projects that involve a choice among competing alternatives. Managers choose one or the other, but not both.

N

Net Present Value (NPV) Method Method used to evaluate capital investment decisions. Compares the present value of the future cash inflows to the present value of the cash outflows.

Non-Value-Added Activity Activity that, if eliminated, would not reduce the perceived value of the product or service to the customer.

Non-Volume-Based Cost Driver Allocation base that is not directly related to the number of units produced or customers served.

Nonmanufacturing Costs Costs associated with running a business or selling a product as opposed to manufacturing a product; generally classified as selling, general, and administrative expenses.

Normal Cost System Cost system in which direct materials and direct labor are recorded at actual amounts, while manufacturing overhead is applied to products or services using one or more predetermined overhead rates.

O

Operating Budgets Budgets that cover the organization's planned operating activities for a particular period of time.

Opportunity Cost Forgone benefit or lost opportunity of choosing one alternative instead of another.

Out-of-Pocket Costs Costs that involve an outlay of cash.

Overapplied Overhead Difference between actual and applied overhead when applied overhead is greater than actual.

P

Participative Budgeting Method that allows employees throughout the organization to have input into the budget-setting process.

Payback Period Amount of time it takes a project to generate enough cash to pay for its initial investment.

Period Costs Costs that are related to nonmanufacturing activities and are expensed as soon as they are incurred.

Planning Future-oriented phase of the Plan-Implement-Control cycle that involves setting long-term goals and objectives and short-term tactics necessary to achieve those goals.

Practical Capacity A measure that could be achieved under normal (not ideal) operating conditions.

Predetermined Overhead Rate Rate estimated before the accounting period begins and used throughout the period to assign overhead costs to products or services based on an allocation base or cost driver.

Preference Decisions Decisions that require managers to choose from among a set of alternative capital investment opportunities.

Present Value Value of future cash flows expressed in today's equivalent dollars.

Prevention Costs Costs incurred to prevent quality problems from occurring.

Prime Costs Sum of direct materials and direct labor; represent the costs that can be directly traced to the product.

Process Costing Costing system used by companies that make homogeneous products or services.

Product Costs Costs that are assigned to the product as it is being manufactured and included in inventory until the product is sold. Also called inventoriable costs.

Product-Level Activities Activities performed to support a specific product line.

Product Life Cycle Represents the life of the product from its infancy (an idea) through design, development, product introduction, growth, maturity, and eventual decline.

Product Mix The relative mix or proportion of products that is based on the number of units sold. Used to compute the weighted-average contribution margin per unit.

Production Budget Budget that shows how many units need to be produced in each budget period.

Production Report Process costing report that provides information about the number of units and manufacturing costs that flow through a production process during an accounting period.

Profit Center Responsibility center in which the manager has authority over and responsibility for profit (revenue minus cost).

Profit Margin Ratio of operating profit to sales revenue.

Profitability The extent to which a company generates income.

Profitability Index Factor used to prioritize capital investments; computed as the present value of future cash flows divided by the initial investment.

R

R Square Goodness of fit measure from a regression model that tells managers how much of the variability in the dependent (y) variable is explained by the independent (x) variable.

Raw Materials Inventory Cost of materials purchased from suppliers that have not yet been used in production.

Related-Party Transactions Business transactions between units or divisions of the same company.

Relevant Cost A cost that occurs in the future and differs between decision alternatives.

Relevant Range Range of activity over which assumptions about cost behavior are expected to hold true.

Required Rate of Return Lowest acceptable rate of return. Also called minimum rate of return or hurdle rate.

Residual Income Difference between operating income and minimum profit needed to cover the required rate of return or hurdle rate.

Responsibility Accounting Area of accounting in which managers are given authority over and responsibility for a particular area of the organization and are then evaluated based on the results of that area of responsibility.

Responsibility Center Area over which managers are given responsibility for specific operations of an organization.

Return on Investment (ROI) Common method of evaluating investment center performance; calculated as net operating income divided by average invested assets.

Revenue Center Responsibility center in which the manager has authority over and responsibility for generating revenue.

S

Sales Budget Estimate of the total sales revenue to be generated in each budget period.

Sales Forecast Number of units expected to be sold each budget period. Serves as the starting point for all other components of the master budget.

Sales Mix The relative mix or proportion of products or services sold based on total sales revenue. Used to compute the weighted-average contribution margin ratio.

Sarbanes-Oxley (SOX) Act of 2002 Act passed by Congress to restore investor confidence in and improve the quality of financial reporting by publicly traded companies in the United States.

Scattergraph Graph of the relationship between two variables, such as total cost (y) and activity level (x).

Screening Decisions Decisions made when managers evaluate a proposed capital investment to determine whether it meets some minimum criteria.

Segment Margin Calculated as revenue minus all costs that are directly traceable to a particular business segment.

Selling and Administrative Expense Budget Budget of selling and administration expenses required for the planned level of sales.

Sensitivity Analysis Performing "what if" analysis to determine whether changing any underlying assumptions would affect the analysis and decision.

Service Companies Companies that provide services to other businesses or consumers.

Short-Term Objective Specific goal that management wants to achieve in the short run; usually no longer than one year.

Simple Rate of Return See *Accounting Rate of Return.*

Solvency The ability to survive long enough to repay lenders when debt matures.

Source Document A document that provides the detailed information needed to keep track of the cost of products, projects, or services.

Special-Order Decisions Application of incremental analysis that requires managers to decide whether to accept or reject an order that is outside the scope of normal sales.

Spending Variances Variances calculated by comparing actual costs to the flexible budget.

Standard Cost Card Form that summarizes the standard cost of all the inputs required to make a single unit of product.

Standard Cost System Cost system that records manufacturing costs at standard rather than actual amounts.

Standard Unit Cost Expected cost to produce one unit based on standard prices and quantities.

Static Budget Budget based on a single estimate of sales volume.

Step Costs Costs that are fixed over some range of activity and then increase in a step-like fashion when a capacity limit is reached.

Step-Fixed Cost Step cost with relatively wide steps; typically treated as fixed within a relevant range.

Step-Variable Cost Step cost that is fixed over a narrow range of activity; typically treated as a variable cost because multiple steps are encountered across the relevant range.

Strategic Plan Managers' vision of what they want the organization to achieve over a long-term horizon.

Substitute Products Products where one good can be used instead of another. Examples include butter and margarine, or sugar and artificial sweeteners.

Sunk Costs Costs incurred in the past that are not relevant to future decisions.

Supply Chain The network of organizations and activities required to move goods and services from suppliers to consumers.

Sustainability The ability to meet the needs of today without sacrificing the ability of future generations to meet their own needs.

Sustainability accounting An emerging area of accounting that is aimed at providing managers with a broader set of information to meet the needs of multiple stakeholders, with the goal of ensuring the company's long-term survival in an uncertain and resource-constrained world.

T

Tactics Specific actions or mechanisms that management uses to achieve objectives.

Target Costing Cost management approach that determines what target cost is required to meet the market price and provide a profit for a company's shareholders.

Target Profit Analysis Type of cost-volume-profit analysis that determines the number of units or sales revenue necessary to earn a target profit.

Tight but Attainable Standard A standard that is difficult, but not impossible, to achieve.

Time Value of Money The idea that the value of a dollar changes over time because it can be invested to earn interest.

Top-Down Approach Budgeting method in which top management sets a budget and imposes it on lower levels of the organization.

Total Quality Management (TQM) A management approach that aims to improve product quality by reducing and eliminating errors, streamlining activities, and continuously improving production processes.

Transfer Price Amount charged when one division sells goods or services to another division of the same company.

Transferred-In Cost Manufacturing cost that is transferred from one production process to another in process costing.

Triple Bottom Line A tool used in sustainability accounting that measures performance in three areas: economic, societal, and environmental. Also sometimes called the 3Ps: people, profit, and planet.

U

Unadjusted Rate of Return See *Accounting Rate of Return.*

Underapplied Overhead Difference between actual and applied overhead when actual overhead is greater than the amount applied.

Unfavorable Variance Variance indicating that actual costs were more than budgeted or standard costs.

Unit Contribution Margin Difference between sales price and variable cost per unit; indicates how much each additional unit sold will contribute to fixed costs and profit.

Unit-Level Activities Activities performed for each individual unit or customer.

V

Value-Added Activity Activity that enhances the perceived value of the product or service to the customer.

Value Chain The linked set of activities required to design, develop, produce, market, and deliver a product to customers; includes aftermarket customer service.

Value Engineering A process for determining how much value consumers receive from a product or service based on its features and functionality.

Variable Costing Costing method used for internal reporting that classifies costs as either variable or fixed. Can be used to analyze many managerial decisions.

Variable Costs Costs that change, in total, in direct proportion to changes in activity levels.

Variable Overhead (VOH) Rate Variance Variance driven by the difference in actual and standard variable overhead rates.

Variable Overhead Efficiency Variance Variance driven by the difference in actual amounts and standard amounts of a cost driver (e.g., direct labor hours) multiplied by the standard variable overhead rate.

Variable Overhead Spending Variance Difference in actual variable overhead cost and the flexible budget. It is made up of the variable overhead rate variance and the variable overhead efficiency variance.

Variance Difference between actual and planned results.

Vertical (Common Size) Analysis Expressing each financial statement amount as a percentage of another amount on the same financial statement.

Volume-Based Cost Driver Allocation base that is directly related to number of units produced or customers served.

Volume Variance Variance driven by the difference in actual and budgeted production or sales volume.

W

Weighted-Average Contribution Margin Ratio Average contribution margin ratio of multiple products weighted according to the percentage of total sales revenue.

Weighted-Average Method Method used to prepare a production report in process costing. It averages the cost of the units in beginning inventory with the cost of the units started during the period.

Weighted-Average Unit Contribution Margin Average unit contribution of multiple products weighted according to the percentage of units sold.

Work in Process Inventory Cost of units or jobs that are in process (incomplete) at any given point in time.

Chapter 1

PA1–4

(2)

    a. Direct Material = $4,200

    b. Direct Labor = $37,500

    c. Manufacturing Overhead = $11,500

    d. Prime Cost = $41,700

    e. Conversion Cost = $49,000

    f. Total Product Cost = $53,200

    g. Total Period Cost = $10,200

    h. Total Variable Cost = $44,700

    i. Total Fixed Cost = $18,700

Chapter 2

PA2–1

(3) $44,850 overapplied

(5) Net operating income = $83,850

PA2–3

(1) $7.00 per machine hour

(3) $33,200

(5) $4,000 overapplied

PA2-4

(1) Cost of Job 102 = $53,600

(2) Cost of Job 101 = $55,000

PA2-5

(1)

    Raw Materials Inventory = $6,000

    Work in Process Inventory = $22,000

    Finished Goods Inventory = $59,000

    Cost of Goods Sold = $70,000

    Manufacturing Overhead = $22,900 overapplied

    Selling and Administrative Expenses = $51,300

    Sales Revenue = $91,000

(4) Adjusted Gross Profit = $43,900

PA2–6

    Direct Materials Used In Production = $93,850

    Direct Labor = $100,000

    Total Current Manufacturing Costs = $318,850

    Ending Work in Process Inventory = $9,600

    Cost of Goods Manufactured = $321,250

    Ending Finished Goods Inventory = $31,250

    Unadjusted Cost of Goods Sold = $315,000

    Adjusted Cost of Goods Sold = $325,000

PA2–7

(1)

    a. $36.00 per direct labor hour

    b. $648,000

    c. $7,000 Underapplied

(3)

    a. $79.20 per machine hour

    b. $673,200

    c. $18,200 Overapplied

PA2–8

(1) 140% of Direct labor cost

(3) $12,000 Overapplied

(5) Net operating income = $59,000

Chapter 3

PA3–1

(1)

    a. Ending units = 68,000

    b. Materials = 232,000 e.u.

       Conversion = 198,000 e.u.

    c. Materials = $1.12069

       Conversion = $2.54545

    d. Completed = $601,248

       Ending WIP = $162,752

PA3–2

(1)

    b. Units completed = 164,000

    b. Materials = 152,000 e.u.

       Conversion = 174,000 e.u.

    c. Materials = $1.18421

       Conversion = $1.80460

    d. Started & Completed = $251,060

       Ending WIP = $141,883

PA3–3

(1)

    a. Ending units = 26,000

    c. Materials = $1.93847

       Conversion = $2.82059

PA3–4

(1)

    b. Direct Materials = 243,000 e.u.

       Conversion = 316,360 e.u.

    d. Started & Completed = $897,591

       Ending WIP = $88,906

PA3–5

(1)

    b. Materials = 56,650 e.u.

       Conversion = 51,187.50 e.u.

    d. Units completed = $3,583,287

       Ending WIP = $2,047,913

PA3–6

(1)

    b. Materials = 36,400 e.u.

       Conversion = 43,088 e.u.

    d. Started & Completed = $1,387,978

       Ending WIP = $1,923,789

Chapter 4

PA4–1

(1) Basic Model $85,750

    Luxury Model $85,750

(3) Basic Model $89,000

(4) Luxury Model $82,500

PA4–2

(1) Indoor Model $71,400
   Outdoor Model $68,000
(3) Indoor Model $79,900.18
(4) Outdoor Model $59,499.82

PA 4-3

(2) Home $191.83
   Work $267.80
(4) $688 per setup
   $80 per inspection
   $16 per machine hour
(6) Home $168.99
   Work $307.76

PA4–4

(1) Sandy Beach $11,180
   Rocky River $11,180
(3) Sandy Beach $25.68
   Rocky River $31.35
(5) Sandy Beach $8,400
   Rocky River $13,960
(7) Sandy Beach $28.00
   Rocky River $28.46

Chapter 5

PA5–1

(3) Total Cost = $4,600 + $8.00 (# Bottles)
(6) Total Cost = $4,285 + $7.244 (# Bottles)

PA5–2

(3) Total Cost = $3,375 + $7.50 (# Jerseys)
(4) $6,975
(6) Total Cost = $3,414.06 + $8.22 (# of Jerseys)
(7) $8,551.56

PA5–3

(2) January: $5,175; $5,386.86
   March: $5,625; $5,880.06
   May: $8,700; $9,250.26
(4) Feb Income $(1,653.66)
   April Income $2,356.14
   June Income $3,040.74
(5) $3,414.06 per month

PA5–4

(2) For 800 units: $360,000; 69.23%

PA5–5

(2) Absorption Costing Income $362,250
   Variable Costing Income $280,000

PA5–6

(1) $14.05
(3) $24.80
(5) Difference = $1,343.75

Chapter 6

PA6-1

(4) 548 bikes

PA6-2

(1) 1,500 miles
(3) 4,000 miles
(4) DOL = 6.0

PA6–3

(1) Income $2,660
(3) $15 per unit; 50%
(5) 2,256 units

PA6–4

(2) For 1,000 units, Income = $450,000
(4) 357 carts
(6) 450 units
(8) 17.246% decrease

PA6–5

(1) $12.90 per unit; 64.5%
(4) Margin of Safety = 1,915 units; 23.94%

PA6-6

(1) 56.05%
(3) Product A = 690 units
(5) Product B = $106,317.65
(6) 8.65

PA6-7

(1) b. ($9.00)
(2) $43 per unit
(3) a. $60

Chapter 7

PA7–1

(1) Incremental Profit $750
(4) $19.00

PA7–2

(1) $5,600 in favor of making
(3) $4,400 less expensive to buy

PA7–3

(1) Incremental Profit: $4,950

PA7–4

(1) Incremental profit: $25,000

PA7–5

   Incremental profit: $(30,000)

PA7–6

(2) Product B 20,000 units
   Product A 50,000 units
   Product C 1,000 units
(4) Product C 30,000 units
   Product B 20,000 units
   Product A 30,000 units

PA7–7

(2) Incremental profit:
   $31,550 for pants
   $46,000 for shirts
   $(700) for coats

PA7–8

(1) Incremental profit:
      $12,000

PA7–9

(2) Incremental profit:
      $(20,000)

Chapter 8

PA8–1

(1) May $7,500
(2) April 270 units
(3) June $3,132
(4) 2nd Quarter $6,000
(5) May $702
(6) June $6,440
(7) 2nd Quarter $2,520

PA8–2

      April $1,425

PA8–3

(1) May $7,375
      2nd Quarter $23,438
(2) April $8,213.40
      June $6,870.60
(3) June 30 balance = $12,993.90

PA8–4

(1) March $118,800
(3) February $16,954
      1st Quarter $49,805

PA8–5

(1) March $78,030
(2) 1st Quarter $75,252

PA8–6

      Quarter 3 Net Income:
      $145,000

Chapter 9

PA9–1

(1) DM Price Var = $17,820 F
      DM Quantity Var = $21,120 U
(3) VOH Rate Var = $20,000 U
      VOH Efficiency Var = $18,000 F

PA9–2

(2) FOH Volume Var = $25,000 F

PA9-3

(1) DM Quantity Variance = $21,120 U
(2) DL Efficiency Variance = $180,000 F

PA9-4

(3) Variable Overhead Rate Variance = $2,000 F
      Variable Overhead Efficiency Variance = $4,000 U

PA9-5

(2) FOH Volume Var = $5,000 U

PA9–6

(1) DM Price Var = $36,000 U
      DM Quantity Var = $20,000 U

PA9–7

(2) DL Rate Var = $1,836 U
      DL Efficiency Var = $900 F

Chapter 10

PA10–1

(1) River Division ROI = 25%
      Stream Division Residual Income = $392,000
(2)
      a. River Division ROI = 27.5%
          Stream Division Residual Income = $442,000

PA10–2

(3) 4.8%

PA10–3

(1) ROI Division B = 10%
(2) Residual Income Division C = $(64,300)
(4) 9%
(6) ROI Division A = 6.5%
      Residual Income Division C = $(14,300)

PA10–4

(1) $51,000
(4) $33.50

PA10–5

(1) $1.50 per tag
(4) $1.25

Chapter 11

PA11–1

(1) 9%
(3) $38,122
(4) $(32,234)

PA11–2

(1) Current Income $1,710,000
(3) 6.17 years
(5) $ 124,128

PA11–3

(1) Project 1 = 7.91%
      Project 2 = 12.5%
      Project 3 = 6.96%
(3) Project 1 = $231,188.50
      Project 2 = $788,834.00
      Project 3 = $91,872.50
(4) Project 1 = 1.0477
      Project 2 = 1.2320
      Project 3 = 1.0320

PA11–4

(2) 7.75 years
(3) $(18,892)

PA11–5

(1)   Option 1 = $1,000,000
Option 2 = $903,265
Option 3 = $845,488

PA11-6

(1)   Project A Payback Period = 5 years
Project A NPV = $29,072
Project A PI = 1.058
Project A IRR = 13.55%
Project B Payback Period = 7 years
Project B NPV = $(56,838)
Project B PI = 0.865
Project B IRR = 8.84%
Project C Payback Period = 4 years
Project C NPV = $24,110
Project C PI = 1.075
Project C IRR = 14.52%

(4)   Project A Payback Period = 5 years
Project A NPV = $(8,062)
Project A PI = 0.98
Project A IRR = 13.55%
Project B Payback Period = 7 years
Project B NPV = $(86,807)
Project B PI = 0.793
Project B IRR = 8.84%
Project C Payback Period = 4 years
Project C NPV = $4,764
Project C PI = 1.015
Project C IRR = 14.52%

Chapter 12

PA12-1

(1)   Activity = "I", Cash Flow = "–"

PA12-2

Net cash provided by operating activities = $8,803

PA12-3

(1)   Net cash provided by operating activities = $16,000

PA12-4

(1)   Net cash provided by financing activities = $1,200

PA12-5

Net cash provided by operating activities = $8,803

PA12-6

(1)   Net cash used for investing activities = $(500)

PA12-7

Net cash provided by operating activities = $2,400

Chapter 13

PA13-1

(1)   Change in cash = $31,500, 82.9% increase

PA13-2

(1)   CY Gross profit percentage = 52.7%
(6)   CY Debt-to-assets ratio = 0.40

PA13-3

(3)   Simultech's assets are financed more by liabilities (60%)
than by equity (40%)

PA13-4

(1)   (e) 4%

PA13-5

(2)   Pepsi appears more liquid

PA13-6

(1)   (7) Receivables turnover: Royale = 15.69, Cavalier = 18.67

PA13-7

Company A appears to be a better choice

Chapter 1
1. c 2. d 3. b 4. c 5. b 6. c 7. a 8. d 9. b 10. c

Chapter 2
1. b 2. b 3. e 4. b 5. d 6. d 7. c 8. e 9. f 10. a

Chapter 3
1. b 2. d 3. c 4. a 5. d 6. b 7. d 8. a 9. d 10. b

Chapter 4
1. b 2. b 3. d 4. b 5. c 6. d 7. d 8. a 9. b 10. c

Chapter 5
1. d 2. b 3. d 4. c 5. a 6. d 7. d 8. a 9. b 10. c

Chapter 6
1. d 2. b 3. c 4. a 5. d 6. d 7. d 8. a 9. b 10. c

Chapter 7
1. d 2. b 3. d 4. a 5. d 6. c 7. b 8. d 9. a 10. c

Chapter 8
1. c 2. d 3. d 4. a 5. c 6. d 7. d 8. b 9. a 10. d

Chapter 9
1. c 2. b 3. a 4. d 5. a 6. a 7. b 8. c 9. d 10. a

Chapter 10
1. b 2. d 3. d 4. a 5. d 6. a 7. d 8. d 9. b 10. d

Chapter 11
1. b 2. c 3. a 4. c 5. b 6. a 7. a 8. b 9. d 10. a

Chapter 12
1. c 2. d 3. d 4. a 5. a 6. d 7. d 8. a 9. c 10. b

Chapter 13
1. c 2. c 3. c 4. d 5. c 6. a 7. b 8. d

S